ORGANIZATIONAL BEHAVIOR

MANAGING PEOPLE AND ORGANIZATIONS

THIRD EDITION

GREGORY MOORHEAD
Arizona State University

RICKY W. GRIFFIN
Texas A & M University

HOUGHTON MIFFLIN COMPANY BOSTON TORONTO
Dallas Geneva, Illinois Palo Alto Princeton, New Jersey

For my family: Linda, Alex, and Lindsay. G.M.
For my daughter Ashley, a sweet and shining star. R.W.G.

Senior Sponsoring Editor: Patrick F. Boles
Development Editor: Susan Kahn
Project Editor: Donna Vierra/Linda Hamilton
Assistant Design Manager: Patricia Mahtani
Production Coordinator: Renée Le Verrier
Manufacturing Coordinator: Marie Barnes
Marketing Manager: Diane McOscar/Mary Jo Conrad

Cover Art

Robert Delaunay, *Fenêtre sur la Ville,* 1914. Stadtische Galerie in Lenbachhaus, Munich.

Part Opener Art

Part I: Richard Diebenkorn. *Untitled Work on Paper, 1974.* Acrylic and charcoal on paper. 23¾ × 18¾″. Courtesy Houston Fine Art Press. **Part II:** Mark Rothko. *Light, Earth & Blue.* Oil on canvas. 1954. 76 × 67″. © 1992 Kate Rothko-Prizel and Christopher Rothko/A.R.S., N.Y. **Part III:** Frantisek Kupka. *Disks of Newton (Study for Fugue in Two Colors).* Oil on canvas. 1912. 39⅜ × 29″. Philadelphia Museum of Art: The Louise & Walter Arensberg Collection. **Part IV:** Mark Rothko. *Number 18.* Oil on canvas. 1951. 81¾ × 67″. Munson-Williams-Proctor Institute, Museum of Art, Utica, New York. **Part V:** Richard Diebenkorn. *Ocean Park No. 24.* Oil on canvas. 1969. 93 × 97″. Collection of Laila and Thurston Twigg-Smith. Promised gift to Yale University Art Gallery. **Part VI:** Robert Delaunay. *Simultaneous Windows on the City.* Oil on canvas. 1912. 18 × 15¾″. Hamburger Kunsthalle.

Photo Credits

Chapter 1: p. 7 J.B. Pictures/ © Scott Thode. p. 11 © Karen Kasmauski/Woodfin Camp Associates. p. 18 © Paul Chesley, Photographers/Aspen. p. 21 Cover provided by *Financial World* Magazine, 1328 Broadway, New York, NY 10001, April 3, 1990. Copyright 1990. All rights reserved. **Chapter 2:** p. 40 Courtesy of Walgreen Co. *continued on p. 789.*

Printed in the U.S.A.

Library of Congress Catalog Card Number: 91-71971

ISBN: 0-395-47282-2

ABCDEFGHIJ-D-9987654321

Brief Contents

PART I	**Introduction to Organizational Behavior**	**2**
1	An Overview of Organizational Behavior	4
2	Managing People and Organizations	32
PART II	**Individual Processes in Organizations**	**58**
3	Learning, Perception, and Attribution	60
4	Individual Differences	94
5	Basic Concepts of Motivation	124
6	Advanced Concepts of Motivation	152
PART III	**Interpersonal Processes in Organizations**	**182**
7	Group Dynamics	184
8	Intergroup Dynamics	218
9	Leadership in Organizations	250
10	Power, Politics, and Conflict	284
11	Interpersonal Communication	316
PART IV	**Enhancing Individual and Interpersonal Processes**	**352**
12	Goal Setting and Rewards	354
13	Job Design and Employee Participation	384
14	Performance Appraisal	418
15	Managing Stress	450
16	Decision Making and Creativity	478
PART V	**Organizational Processes and Characteristics**	**520**
17	Dimensions of Organization Structure	522
18	Managing Innovation and Technology in Changing Environments	552
19	Organization Design	584
20	Organization Culture	622
PART VI	**Integrating Individuals, Groups, and Organizations**	**654**
21	Organization Change and Development	656
22	International Aspects of Organizations	698
23	Career Dynamics	728
APPENDIX	Research Methods in Organizational Behavior	763
	Glossary	773
	Name Index	790
	Subject Index	797

CONTENTS

PREFACE xix

PART I INTRODUCTION TO ORGANIZATIONAL BEHAVIOR 2

1 AN OVERVIEW OF ORGANIZATIONAL BEHAVIOR 4

What Is Organizational Behavior? 7
The Historical Roots of Organizational Behavior 9
■ Management in Action ■ Scientific Management
Classical Organization Theory

The Emergence of Organizational Behavior 13
Precursors of Organizational Behavior The Hawthorne Studies
Human Relations Movement Toward Organizational Behavior

Contemporary Organizational Behavior 17
Characteristics of the Field ■ The Ethical Dilemma ■
Basic Concepts of the Field The Importance of Organizational Behavior

Emerging Perspectives on Organizational Behavior 22
The Systems Approach The Contingency Perspective Interactionalism
■ International Perspective ■ Popular Press Perspectives

■ **CASE 1.1** Herman Miller, Inc. Believes People Are Key to Success 28
■ **CASE 1.2** Difficult Transitions 29
■ **EXPERIENTIAL EXERCISE** 30

2 MANAGING PEOPLE AND ORGANIZATIONS 32

A Managerial Perspective on Organizational Behavior 35
The Manager's Job 36
Managerial Functions Managerial Roles ■ A Look at Research ■ The Human Context of Management

Managerial Challenges 41
Work Force Demographics Workplace Issues and Challenges

Organizational Challenges 44
Enhancing Productivity Improving Quality Managing Technology Monitoring Ethics and Social Responsibility

Global Challenges 48
Managing in a Global Environment ■ International Perspective ■ Managing Cultural Diversity

Managing for Effectiveness 50
Individual-Level Outcomes ■ Developing Management Skills ■ Group-Level Outcomes Organizational-Level Outcomes

■ **CASE 2.1** Sam Walton Uses People as Catalyst 54
■ **CASE 2.2** Humanized Robots? 55
■ **EXPERIENTIAL EXERCISE** 57

PART II INDIVIDUAL PROCESSES IN ORGANIZATIONS 58

3 LEARNING, PERCEPTION, AND ATTRIBUTION 60

The Nature of Learning 63
A Definition of Learning The Traditional View: Classical Conditioning The Contemporary View: Learning as a Cognitive Process Learning in Organizations

Reinforcement Theory and Learning 67
Types of Reinforcement in Organizations Schedules of Reinforcement in Organizations

Related Aspects of Learning in Organizations 72
Stimulus Generalization in Organizations Stimulus Discrimination in Organizations Vicarious Learning in Organizations Punishment in Organizations ■ Management in Action ■

Other Managerial Implications of Learning 76

Learning and Motivations *Learning and Training*
■ *International Perspective* ■
Learning and Performance Evaluation/Rewards

The Nature of Perception 79

A Definition of Perception *Perceptual Processes in Organizations*
■ *The Ethical Dilemma* ■

The Nature of Attributions 85

Managerial Implications of Perception and Attribution 88

Perception, Attribution, and Motivation
Perception, Attribution, and Hiring
Perception, Attribution, and Performance Evaluation

■ **CASE 3.1** Tommy Lasorda and Reinforcement Theory 90

■ **CASE 3.2** Differing Perceptions at Clarkston Industries 92

■ **EXPERIENTIAL EXERCISE** 93

4 INDIVIDUAL DIFFERENCES 94

The Nature of Individual Differences 97

People are Unique *People and Situations*

An Overview of Personality 98

The Nature of Personality *Personality Structures*

Personality and Work 104

Locus of Control ■ *Developing Management Skills* ■ *Authoritarianism*
Machiavellianism *Other Traits*

Attitudes and Attitude Formation 107

■ *The Ethical Dilemma* ■ *The Dispositional View of Attitudes*
The Situational View of Attitudes *Cognitive Dissonance* *Attitude Change*

Job-Related Attitudes 112

Job Satisfaction *Other Kinds of Satisfaction*
Commitment and Involvement

Attitudes and Behaviors 117

Managerial Implications of Individual Differences 117

■ *A Look at the Research* ■

■ **CASE 4.1** Attitudes at Eastern Spell Trouble 120

■ **CASE 4.2** Back to the Old Saw 121

■ **EXPERIENTIAL EXERCISE** 123

5 Basic Concepts of Motivation 124

The Nature of Motivation in Organizations 127

The Importance of Motivation *The Motivational Framework*

Historical Perspectives on Motivation 128

Early Views of Motivation *The Scientific Management Approach*
The Human Relations Approach

Need Theories of Motivation 132

Maslow's Hierarchy of Needs ■ *International Perspective* ■
Murray's Manifest Needs ■ *Management in Action* ■
Alderfer's ERG Theory

Herzberg's Two-Factor Theory 139

Development of the Theory *Evaluation of the Theory*

Other Important Needs 142

The Need for Achievement ■ *Developing Management Skills* ■
The Need for Affiliation *The Need for Power*

Integrating the Need Perspectives 145

■ **CASE 5.1** The Big Brown Team 148
■ **CASE 5.2** More Than a Paycheck 149
■ **EXPERIENTIAL EXERCISE** 151

6 Advanced Concepts of Motivation 152

The Equity Theory of Motivation 155

Forming Equity Perceptions *Responses to Perceptions of Equity/Inequity*
Evaluation of Equity Theory ■ *A Look at the Research* ■
Management Implications of Equity Theory

The Expectancy Theory of Motivation 160

The Basic Expectancy Model ■ *The Ethical Dilemma* ■
The Porter-Lawler Extension *Evaluation of Expectancy Theory*
Managerial Implications of Expectancy Theory

Organizational Behavior Modification 166

Behavior Modification in the Workplace *Results of O.B. Mod. Programs*

Participative Management and Motivation 169

Historical Perspectives on Participation *Areas of Participation*
Quality Circles and Participation ■ *Management in Action* ■

Attribution Theory and Motivation 172

The Consequences of Motivation 173
Performance and Productivity *Absenteeism and Turnover*

Concluding Perspectives on Motivation 175

■ **CASE 6.1** Motivation at A. O. Smith Corp. 177
■ **CASE 6.2** Equity in Academia 179
■ **EXPERIENTIAL EXERCISE** 181

PART III Interpersonal Processes in Organizations 182

7 Group Dynamics 184

Overview of Groups and Group Dynamics 187
Definition of Group *The Importance of Studying Groups*

Types of Groups 189
Formal Groups *Informal Groups* ■ *Management in Action* ■

Reasons for Group Formation 192
Internal Sources of Need Satisfaction *External Sources of Need Satisfaction*
Implications of Group Formation

Stages of Group Development 197
Mutual Acceptance *Communication and Decision Making*
Motivation and Productivity *Control and Organization*

Group Performance Factors 200
Composition ■ *A Look at the Research* ■ *Size*
■ *International Perspective* ■ *Norms* *Cohesiveness*

Role Dynamics in Organizations 210
Role Ambiguity *Role Conflict*

Managing Groups in Organizations 211

■ **CASE 7.1** Increasing Steel Exports for Chaparral Steel 214
■ **CASE 7.2** A Difficult Task Force 215
■ **EXPERIENTIAL EXERCISE** 216

8 Intergroup Dynamics 218

Intergroup Interactions 221
Avoidance *Accommodation* *Competition* *Collaboration* *Compromise*

A Model of Intergroup Dynamics 226
■ *A Look at the Research* ■

Factors That Influence Intergroup Behavior 229
Location *Resources* *Time and Goal Interdependence* *Task Uncertainty*
Task Interdependence ■ *Management in Action* ■

Managing Intergroup Behavior in Organizations 235
Location-Based Strategies *Resource-Based Strategies*
Goal-Based Strategies *People- and Group-Based Strategies*
Organization-Based Strategies ■ *International Perspective* ■

■ **CASE 8.1** A Special Type of Intergroup Relations at U-haul 245
■ **CASE 8.2** Seeing Where the Other Half Works 247
■ **EXPERIENTIAL EXERCISE** 248

9 LEADERSHIP IN ORGANIZATIONS 250

The Nature of Leadership 253
A Definition of Leadership *A Framework of Leadership Perspectives*

Early Approaches to Leadership 255
Trait Approaches to Leadership ■ *International Perspective* ■
Behavioral Approaches to Leadership

The Contingency Theory of Leadership 260
Basic Premises *Situational Favorableness* *Scientific Evidence*
■ *Management in Action* ■

The Path-Goal Theory of Leadership 265
Basic Premises *Scientific Evidence*

The Vroom-Yetton-Jago Model of Leadership 268
Basic Premises ■ *Developing Management Skills* ■ *Scientific Evidence*

Other Contemporary Approaches to Leadership 272
The Verticial-Dyad Linkage Model *The Life Cycle Theory*
Leadership Substitutes *Transformational Leadership*
Charismatic Leadership *Leadership as Symbolic Action*
Attributional Perspectives

■ **CASE 9.1** Donald Petersen: A Leader for All Seasons 280
■ **CASE 9.2** Right Boss, Wrong Company 281
■ **EXPERIENTIAL EXERCISE** 283

10 Power, Politics, and Conflict 284

The Nature of Power in Organizations 287
A Definition of Power   The Pervasiveness of Power

Types of Power 288
Bases of Power   ■ The Ethical Dilemma ■
Position Power Versus Person Power

The Uses of Power 292
Using Referent Power   Using Expert Power   Using Legitimate Power
Using Reward Power   Using Coercive Power

Politics and Political Behavior 297
The Pervasiveness of Political Behavior   ■ Management in Action ■
Managing Political Behavior

Conflict in Organizations 307
■ A Look at the Research ■   The Nature of Conflict   Managing Conflict

■ **CASE 10.1** Power and Conflict at CBS 312
■ **CASE 10.2** The Struggle for Power at Ramsey Electronics 313
■ **EXPERIENTIAL EXERCISE** 315

11 Interpersonal Communication 316

Communication in Organizations 319
Purposes of Communication in Organizations
■ A Look at the Research ■   Uncertainty and the Role of Information

Methods of Communication 322
Written Communication   Oral Communication
Nonverbal Communication   ■ Management in Action ■

The Basic Communication Process 325
Source   Encoding   Transmission   Decoding   Receiver/Responder
Feedback   Noise

Communication Networks 329
Small-Group Networks   Organizational Communication Networks

Managing Organizational Communication 336
Improving the Communication Process   ■ International Perspective ■
Improving Organizational Factors in Communication

Electronic Information Processing and Telecommunications 343

■ **CASE 11.1** Exxon's Communication Problems 347
■ **CASE 11.2** Heading Off a Permanent Misunderstanding 348
■ **EXPERIENTIAL EXERCISE** 350

PART IV ENHANCING INDIVIDUAL AND INTERPERSONAL PROCESSES 352

12 GOAL SETTING AND REWARDS 354

Goal Setting in Organizations 356
Motivation and Control *The Role of Goal Setting*

Goal Setting and Motivation 359
The Basic Approach *A Broader Perspective of Goals and Motivation*
Research Evidence

Management by Objectives 363
The MBO Process *MBO in Management Practice*

Reward Systems in Organizations 365
■ *Developing Management Skills* ■ *A Transaction Process*
The Roles, Purposes, and Meanings of Rewards

Types of Rewards 369
Money *Incentive Systems* *Benefits* ■ *Management in Action* ■
Perquisites *Awards*

Managing Reward Systems 375
A Look at the Research ■ *Pay Secrecy* *Participative Pay Systems*
Flexible Reward Systems

■ **CASE 12.1** Apple's New Goals and Strategies Cause Lots of Other Changes 380
■ **CASE 12.2** No More Dawdling over Dishes 381
■ **EXPERIENTIAL EXERCISE** 382

13 JOB DESIGN AND EMPLOYEE PARTICIPATION 384

Historical Approaches to Job Design 387
The Evolution of Job Design *Job Specialization*
Early Alternatives to Job Specialization *Job Enrichment*

The Job Characteristics Approach 395

Job Characteristics   Individual Differences   The Job Characteristics Theory
Evaluation and Implications

Designing Jobs for Groups 401
■ *A Look at the Research* ■ *Group Tasks*
Autonomous Work Groups and Work Teams   Other Group Applications

Social Information and Job Design 404
■ *International Perspective* ■

Emerging Perspectives on Job Design 407
Work Schedules ■ *The Ethical Dilemma* ■ *Automation and Robotics*
Worker Flexibility

Employee Participation 411
■ **CASE 13.1** Job Changes at Corning 413
■ **CASE 13.2** Enriching Jobs at Standard Decoy 415
■ **EXPERIENTIAL EXERCISE** 416

14 PERFORMANCE APPRAISAL 418

Performance Appraisal Systems 421
Purposes of Performance Appraisal ■ *Developing Management Skills* ■

Common Questions about Performance Appraisal 424
Who Does the Appraisal? ■ *Management in Action* ■
How Often Should Employees be Evaluated?
How Is the Appraisal Information to Be Used?

Performance Appraisal Basics 428
Commitment to Objectives   Job Analysis   Measurement of Performance
■ *A Look at the Research* ■

Performance Appraisal Techniques 436
Individual Evaluation   Comparative Evaluation
Multiple-Rater Comparative Evaluation

■ **CASE 14.1** Performance Appraisal in the U.S. Air Force 445
■ **CASE 14.2** The Principal's Dilemma 446
■ **EXPERIENTIAL EXERCISE** 448

15 MANAGING STRESS 450

The Nature of Stress 453
Stress Defined   Stress and the Individual ■ *International Perspective* ■

Common Causes of Stress 457
Organizational Stressors Life Stressors

Type A and Type B Personality Profiles 463
Consequences of Stress 464
■ *Developing Management Skills* ■ *Individual Consequences*
Organizational Consequences Burnout

Managing Stress in the Workplace 468
Individual Coping Strategies ■ *Management in Action* ■
Organizational Coping Strategies

■ **CASE 15.1** Cutback Induces Stress at Citicorp 473
■ **CASE 15.2** Stress Takes Its Toll 475
■ **EXPERIENTIAL EXERCISE** 476

16 DECISION MAKING AND CREATIVITY 478

Decision Making in Organizations 481
Types of Decisions Information Required for Decision Making
■ *The Ethical Dilemma* ■

The Decision-Making Process 487
The Rational Approach The Behavioral Approach
The Practical Approach The Personal Approach

Escalation of Commitment 498
Individual versus Group Decision Making 499
■ *International Perspective* ■

Decision Making in Groups 501
Basic Factors Group Polarization Groupthink
Participation in Decision Making

Group Problem Solving 507
Brainstorming The Nominal Group Technique The Delphi Technique

Creativity in Decision Making 510
Preparation ■ *Management in Action* ■ *Incubation Insight*
Verification

■ **CASE 16.1** Making Tough Decisions at Burroughs Wellcome 515
■ **CASE 16.2** A Big Step for Peak Electronics 516
■ **EXPERIENTIAL EXERCISE** 518

PART V ORGANIZATIONAL PROCESSES AND CHARACTERISTICS 521

17 DIMENSIONS OF ORGANIZATION STRUCTURE 523

Overview of Organization Structure 524
Organization Defined *Organization Structure*

Structural Configuration 527
Division of Labor *Coordinating the Divided Tasks*
■ *Management in Action* ■

Structure and Operations 538
Centralization *Formalization* ■ *A Look at the Research* ■

Responsibility and Authority 542
Responsibility *Authority* *An Alternative View of Authority*
■ *International Perspective* ■

■ **CASE 17.1** The Big Dilemma at Goodyear 547
■ **CASE 17.2** Changing the Rules at Cosmo Plastics 549
■ **EXPERIENTIAL EXERCISE** 550

18 MANAGING INNOVATION AND TECHNOLOGY IN CHANGING ENVIRONMENTS 552

Innovation in Organizations 555
■ *International Perspective* ■ *Innovation* *New Ventures*
Corporate Research

Technology in Organizations 558
Five Perspectives of Technology *Technology in Practice*
■ *Management in Action* ■

Organizational Environments 565
Environmental Components ■ *The Ethical Dilemma* ■
Environmental Uncertainty

Organizational Responses 572
Structural Contingency Perspective *Resource Dependence Perspective*
Population Ecology Perspective

■ **CASE 18.1** Environmental Protection: Problems or Opportunities? 579

■ **CASE 18.2** Technological Shakeup at Smith, Burns, & Graulik 580
■ **EXPERIENTIAL EXERCISE** 582

19 ORGANIZATION DESIGN 584

Universal Approaches to Organization Design 588
The Ideal Bureaucracy ■ *Management in Action* ■
The Classic Principles of Organizing *The Human Organization*

Contingency Approaches to Organization Design 595
Sociotechnical Systems Theory *Structural Imperatives*
Strategy and Strategic Choice

The Mintzberg Framework 605
■ *International Perspective* ■ *Simple Structure* *Machine Bureaucracy*
Professional Bureaucracy *Divisionalized Form* *Adhocracy*

Matrix Organization Design 610
Contemporary Organization Design 612
■ *A Look at the Research* ■

■ **CASE 19.1** Cincinnati Milacron 617
■ **CASE 19.2** A Structural Straitjacket at Wild Wear 618
■ **EXPERIENTIAL EXERCISE** 620

20 ORGANIZATION CULTURE 622

The Nature of Organization Culture 625
What Is Organization Culture? ■ *Management in Action* ■
Historical Foundations

Three Basic Approaches to Describing Organization Culture 634
The Parsons AGIL Model *The Ouchi Framework*
The Peters and Waterman Approach ■ *International Perspective* ■

Managing Organization Culture 642
Taking Advantage of the Existing Culture
Teaching the Organization Culture: Socialization
Changing the Organization Culture ■ *The Ethical Dilemma* ■

■ **CASE 20.1** Tandem's Most Successful Export: Its Culture 649
■ **CASE 20.2** Surviving Plant World's Hard Times 651
■ **EXPERIENTIAL EXERCISE** 652

PART VI Integrating Individuals, Groups, and Organizations 654

21 Organization Change and Development 656

Forces for Change 659
People Technology Information Processing and Communication Competition ■ Management in Action ■

Resistance to Change 662
Organizational Sources of Resistance Individual Sources of Resistance Managing Resistance

Processes for Planned Organization Change 669
Process Methods ■ International Perspective ■ Transition Management Integrated Process of Organization Change

Organization Development 676
Definition of Organization Development System-Wide Organization Development Task-Technological Change Group and Individual Change ■ Developing Management Skills ■

Managing Organization Development 688
Major Problems in Organization Development Efforts Keys to Successful Organization Development

■ **CASE 21.1** Burger King Pulls One Out with Vacuum Management 694
■ **CASE 21.2** Spooked by Computers 695
■ **EXPERIENTIAL EXERCISE** 696

22 International Aspects of Organizations 698

The Emergence of International Management 701
The Growth of International Business Trends in International Business Cross-Cultural Differences and Similarities

Individual Behavior in an International Context 705
Individual Differences across Cultures Managerial Behavior across Cultures ■ The Ethical Dilemma ■ Motivation across Cultures

Interpersonal Processes in an International Context 709
Group Dynamics across Cultures Leadership across Cultures

Power and Conflict across Cultures *Communication across Cultures*
■ *Management in Action* ■

Enhancing Individual and Interpersonal Processes 713
Rewards across Cultures *Job Design across Cultures*
Performance Evaluation across Cultures *Stress across Cultures*
Decision Making across Cultures

Organizational Characteristics in an International Context 717
Environment and Technology across Cultures
Organization Structure and Design across Cultures

Integrating Individuals, Groups, and Organizations 720
Organization Change in an International Context *Careers across Cultures*
■ *A Look at the Research* ■

■ **CASE 22.1** British Airways Bounces Back 724
■ **CASE 22.2** Culture Shock 726
■ **EXPERIENTIAL EXERCISE** 727

23 CAREER DYNAMICS 728

Individual and Organizational Perspectives on Careers 731
Career Choices 733
Choice of Occupation ■ *Developing Management Skills* ■
Choice of Organization *Changing Careers* ■ *International Perspective* ■

Career Stages 741
Entry *Socialization* *Advancement* *Maintenance* *Withdrawal* *Mentoring*

Organizational Career Planning 748
Purposes of Career Planning *Types of Career Programs* *Career Management*
■ *A Look at the Research* ■ *Results of Career Planning*

■ **CASE 23.1** Careers Are Changing as Fast as the Times 757
■ **CASE 23.2** Tom Wayland's Choice 759
■ **EXPERIENTIAL EXERCISE** 760

APPENDIX: RESEARCH METHODS IN ORGANIZATIONAL BEHAVIOR 763

GLOSSARY 773

NAME INDEX 790

SUBJECT INDEX 797

PREFACE

The field of organizational behavior, still in its infancy as a science, remains full of competing and conflicting models and theories. There are few laws or absolute principles that dictate proper conduct for organizational members or predict with certainty their behaviors. The role of human resources in the long-term viability of any business or not-for-profit enterprise is nevertheless recognized as enormously significant. Other resources—financial, informational, and material—are also essential, but only human resources are virtually boundless in their potential impact (positive or negative) on the organization.

The primary objectives of the previous editions of *Organizational Behavior* were to provide some of the tools and insights necessary to understand and analyze the characteristics of human beings and organizational situations in order to contribute to the long-run survival of an enterprise. We hope that the earlier editions also initiated in readers some degree of excitement and enthusiasm for the field of organizational behavior. Responses from many instructors, students, and other readers have indicated that the previous editions did indeed accomplish these objectives.

In this third edition we have tried to build on this solid foundation in several ways. First, we have updated the research on all of the topics discussed in the book. We have also utilized current examples from real organizations to illustrate how research and new developments in the field apply to the everyday situations of typical organizations. We introduce several new theories and approaches that improve and add to the understanding of people and situations in organizations. We have expanded the coverage on the organizational environment, the impact of technology on the organization, organization cultures, and international dimensions and have added new material on ethics. We have also added an entirely new chapter, "Managing People and Organizations" (Chapter 2), that more explicitly links organizational behavior and management. In addition, we have carefully edited and rewritten major portions of the book in an effort to augment its readability and interest level. Finally, in response to feedback from students and instructors, some topics and several chapters have been reorganized.

We hope that our enthusiasm for the field of organizational behavior is contagious and will promote motivation to learn more about the dynamic nature of the behavior of people in organizations.

Organization of the Book

The content of *Organizational Behavior*, Third Edition, is divided into one introductory part and five more general parts that emanate from the characteristics of the field: individual processes, interpersonal processes, enhancing individual and interpersonal processes, organizational process and characteristics, and the integration of individuals, groups, and organizations. Chapter 1 in Part I discusses basic concepts of the field, the importance of the study of organizational behavior, and a brief history of the field. As noted earlier, Chapter 2 develops a managerial perspective on the field of organizational behavior. The four chapters in Part II focus on key aspects of individual processes in organizations: learning and perception, individual differences, basic elements of motivation, and more advanced elements of motivation. Important interpersonal processes—group dynamics, intergroup dynamics, leadership, power, politics, conflict, and interpersonal communication—are discussed in five chapters in Part III. Part IV, also consisting of five chapters, deals with how managers and organizations can enhance individual and interpersonal processes. The major topics covered here are goal setting and rewards, job design and employee participation, performance appraisal, stress, and decision making and creativity. Processes and characteristics of organizations are presented in four chapters in Part V—basic organization structure, environment, technology, innovation, organization design, and organization culture. Part VI includes three chapters that address how individual, group, and organizational characteristics and processes are integrated. The chapters in this part cover organization change and development, international aspects of organizations, and career dynamics. An appendix at the end of the text discusses research methods in organizational behavior.

New to the Third Edition

There are several areas in which the third edition of *Organizational Behavior* has been fine tuned. Beginning with a comprehensive list of topics in the field, both classic and new, we made an extensive review of what coverage users wanted to see in a current text. The result of this survey is the revised organization of this edition. The most apparent change is the addition of a new chapter providing a managerial perspective on the field of organizational behavior. To make room for this chapter we combined our coverage of organization change and organization development into a single chapter. We also changed the sequence of several chapters to improve the logical flow of the text and to group topics into more related categories. Several other minor changes were made. For example, we moved the coverage of role dynamics to Chapter 7 and expanded our coverage of participation in Chapter 13. New examples are incorporated throughout the book—a concerted effort has been made to show how theories and concepts are applied in real organizations. We also added two new types of boxed inserts to this edition. One deals with ethical dilemmas managers face, while the other helps to enhance managerial skills.

Features of the Book

Readability and Ease of Use

We believe that readers will find the style of the third edition to be engaging and accessible. Without sacrificing the level of sophistication with which the content is treated, the language of the text is aimed at the student. In addition to the writing style, the handsome design of this edition contributes to the ease of use for instructors and students alike. The functional use of color in the design highlights the organization and structure of the chapters. Photographs and content-oriented captions add even more visual appeal to the text and serve to further highlight the applicability of the content of the text to the real world of organizations.

Contemporary Focus

The theory and research on each topic in this text represent current, state-of-the-art thinking. Examples are included to illustrate the current use of these ideas and concepts. New developments in the field have been included throughout the book, such as discussions of the revised Vroom-Yetton-Jago model of decision making, escalation of commitment in decision making, the population ecology approach to environmental analysis, and worker participation. Many chapters feature a specially selected topic of current research that is included in a boxed insert entitled "A Look at the Research."

Applications

Throughout the book the companies cited in examples, cases, and boxed items represent a blend of large, well-known and smaller, less well-known firms, in order to show the applicability of the material in all types of organizations. Each chapter opens with a brief critical incident, which provides a concrete example of an issue in organizational behavior, and closes with two cases, one of which is from a real organization and the other of which is hypothetical. Virtually all of the real world cases in this edition are new. In addition, many chapters contain a boxed insert entitled "Management in Action," the subject of which has been carefully chosen to show the application of a concept discussed in the chapter. Some chapters have a boxed insert called "The Ethical Dilemma" that relates the content of the chapter to a situation where ethical issues are particularly important. Still other boxed inserts called "Developing Management Skills" help students learn or practice a critical skill that might help them later in their careers.

International Emphasis

In the third edition of *Organizational Behavior* we have endeavored to show the international nature of organizational behavior. This has been accomplished in three ways. First, we include an entire chapter, "International Aspects of Organizations" (Chapter 22), on international aspects of organizations. Second, many chapters include a boxed insert entitled "International Perspective" that describes how a topic or concept is applied internationally. Finally, we have tried to include as many international examples as possible throughout the text.

Pedagogical Aids

The learning process is facilitated by several features of this book. Each chapter opens with a list of chapter objectives and closes with a section entitled "Summary of Key Points." At the end of each chapter are several discussion questions, designed to stimulate discussion among students. The end-of-chapter cases are designed to help students make the transition from textbook learning to real-world application. In addition, an experiential exercise is included at the end of each chapter to assist in this transition.

Supplemental Materials

Two other books are available to assist students in mastering the textbook material. The first, the *Study Guide,* Third Edition, contains a pretest, chapter synopsis, chapter objectives, chapter outline, list of key terms, and sample test questions (including answers) for each chapter. Second, an activities manual—*OB in Action: Cases and Exercises*, Third Edition—contains additional cases and exercises to help students bridge the gap between theory and practice. There is also a complete package of instructional materials available to help instructors plan and teach this course.

Acknowledgments

Although this book bears the names of two authors, numerous people have contributed to it. Through the years we have had the good fortune to work with many fine professionals who helped us sharpen our thinking about this complex field and to develop new and more effective ways of discussing it. Several reviewers were also important to the development of the third edition. Their contributions were essential to helping us identify areas in need of reworking or minor fine tuning. Any and all errors of omission, interpretation, and emphasis remain the responsibility of the authors. We would like to express a special thanks to the following reviewers for taking the time to provide us with their valuable assistance.

Brendan Bannister
Northeastern University

Mary-Beth Beres
Mercer University Atlanta

Allen Bluedorn
University of Missouri Columbia

John Bunch
Kansas State University

Richaurd R. Camp
Eastern Michigan University

Dan R. Dalton
Indiana University Bloomington

T. K. Das
Baruch College

Thomas W. Dougherty
University of Missouri Columbia

Stanley W. Elsea
Kansas State University

Joseph Forest
Georgia State University

Eliezer Geisler
Northeastern Illinois University

John R. Hollenbeck
Michigan State University

Bruce H. Johnson
Gustavus Adolphus College

Robert T. Keller
University of Houston

Peter Lorenzi
Marquette University

Patricia Manninen
Northshore Community College

Edward K. Marlow
Eastern Illinois University

C. W. Millard
University of Puget Sound

Alan N. Miller
University of Nevada Las Vegas

Herff L. Moore
University of Central Arkansas

Stephan J. Motowidlo
Pennsylvania State University

Richard T. Mowday
University of Oregon

Margaret A. Neale
Northwestern University

Mary Lippitt Nichols
University of Minnesota Minneapolis

Robert J. Paul
Kansas State University

James C. Quick
University of Texas at Arlington

Carol S. Saunders
Texas Christian University

Randall S. Schuler
New York University

Bobby C. Vaught
Southwest Missouri State University

Jack W. Waldrip
American Graduate School of International Management

The third edition could never have been completed without the support of Arizona State University and Texas A&M University. Elmer R. Gooding, Interim Provost; Luis Gomez-Mejia, Acting Chair of the Management Department; Larry Penley, Dean of the College of Business at Arizona State University; Felice Cavallini of IAL; Al Ringleb, Director of the Institute for International Business Studies in Italy; and Don Hellriegel, Head of the Management Department and A. Benton Cocanougher, Dean of the College of Business Administration at Texas A&M University facilitated our work by providing the environment that encourages scholarly activities and contributions to the field.

Several secretaries and graduate assistants were also involved in the development of the third edition. We extend our appreciation to Chris Neck, Phyllis Washburn, Argie Butler, Kerm Harrington, Jon Beard, and Diane Phillips for their help.

We would also like to acknowledge the outstanding team of professionals at Houghton Mifflin Company who helped us prepare this book. Patrick Boles, Senior Sponsoring Editor, has contributed to the success of our work in more ways than anyone can know. Patrick is much more than our editor—he is our friend. Nancy Doherty-Schmitt, Editorial Production Manager, has also been incredibly helpful and supportive throughout our association with Houghton Mifflin. During the actual development of the text itself, Susan Kahn, Senior Development Editor, Donna Vierra, Project Editor, and Linda Hamilton, Project Editor, each made important contributions as they sharpened our thinking, paid attention to details, and tried to keep us on schedule.

Finally, we would like to acknowledge the daily reminders that we get from our families of the importance of our work. They equip us with perspective. When we work too much they drag us away to play. When we play too much they remind us of work that we must do. Mixed in among swim team practices, baseball games, school functions, battles over who is next on the computer, monopoly games, doctor appointments, soccer games, and gymnastics practices, we devoted the time to prepare this revision! Without the support and love of our families we could not survive. It is with all of our love that we dedicate this book to them.

G. M.
R. W. G.

ORGANIZATIONAL BEHAVIOR

MANAGING PEOPLE AND ORGANIZATIONS

PART I

Introduction to Organizational Behavior

CONTENTS

Chapter 1 An Overview of Organizational Behavior

Chapter 2 Managing People and Organizations

CHAPTER OUTLINE

- What Is Organizational Behavior?
- The Historical Roots of Organizational Behavior
  - *Scientific Management*
  - *Classical Organization Theory*
- The Emergence of Organizational Behavior
  - *Precursors of Organizational Behavior*
  - *The Hawthorne Studies*
  - *Human Relations Movement*
  - *Toward Organizational Behavior*
- Contemporary Organizational Behavior
  - *Characteristics of the Field*
  - *Basic Concepts of the Field*
  - *The Importance of Organizational Behavior*
- Emerging Perspectives on Organizational Behavior
  - *The Systems Approach*
  - *The Contingency Perspective*
  - *Interactionalism*
  - *Popular-Press Perspectives*

1

AN OVERVIEW OF ORGANIZATIONAL BEHAVIOR

CHAPTER OBJECTIVES

After studying this chapter, you should be able to:

Define organizational behavior.

Trace the historical roots of organizational behavior.

Discuss the emergence of contemporary organizational behavior, including its precursors, the Hawthorne studies, and human relations.

Describe contemporary organizational behavior—its characteristics, concepts, and importance.

Identify and discuss emerging perspectives in organizational behavior.

Jack Welch, CEO of General Electric, is considered one of the most visionary executives in America. When Welch became CEO in 1981, General Electric was a bloated, slow-moving, bureaucratic corporation with eight volumes of rules, regulations, and procedures. GE provided its employees with a comfortable, secure work environment but offered little opportunity for personal growth.

During the 1980s, Welch virtually remade General Electric. He sold $9 billion worth of GE companies and bought others for $16 billion. All told, he streamlined the corporation from 100 smaller businesses to 14 dominant companies. He eliminated over 100,000 jobs through layoffs, attrition, and sales of businesses. He threw out the rule books and breathed new life into a stale and lethargic corporation. As a result, General Electric changed from a large but inefficient organization to one that balances size and effectiveness with remarkable agility.

Although Welch agonized over his decision to lay off thousands of employees, he is moving full speed ahead to maximize the human capital that remains. In particular, Welch sees an organization in which profitability is but one measure of bottom-line performance. Opportunities for personal fulfillment, achievement, and growth are also important. Indeed, Welch wants General Electric employees to believe they are receiving both intrinsic and financial rewards for their work.[1]

Jack Welch has had to make many difficult decisions in his managerial career. He cares deeply about the people who work for General Electric; he knows that people are essential to any organization's success. This perspective underscores the behavioral context of many managerial activities: A manager's decisions can have profound effects on others, and no manager can succeed without the assistance of others. Thus, any manager—whether responsible for an industrial giant like General Electric, IBM, or Mobil, the Boston Celtics basketball team, the Mayo Clinic, or a local Pizza Hut restaurant—must understand the people who work in the organization.

This book is about those people. It is also about the organization itself and the managers who operate it. The study of organizations and of the collection of people within them together comprise the field of organizational behavior. In this introductory chapter, we begin with a comprehensive definition of organizational behavior and a framework for its study. Then we trace the field's historical roots and its emergence as an independent field. Next, we discuss

1. "'CEO of the Year' Will Focus on Soft Stuff," *USA Today,* July 15, 1991, pp. 1B, 2B; Frank Rose, "A New Age for Business?" *Fortune,* October 8, 1990, pp. 156–164; "Big Changes Are Galvanizing General Electric," *Business Week,* December 18, 1989, pp. 100–102.

New York City hospitals and the Big Apple Circus have recognized the importance of human behavior and behavioral processes in their organizations. Together they have created the Clown Care Unit to fill the need for emotional support shared by both patients and staff. Realizing that laughter and love, as well as more typical treatments, are essential for young patients and their families, the clowns serve to humor while the hospitals set the rules.

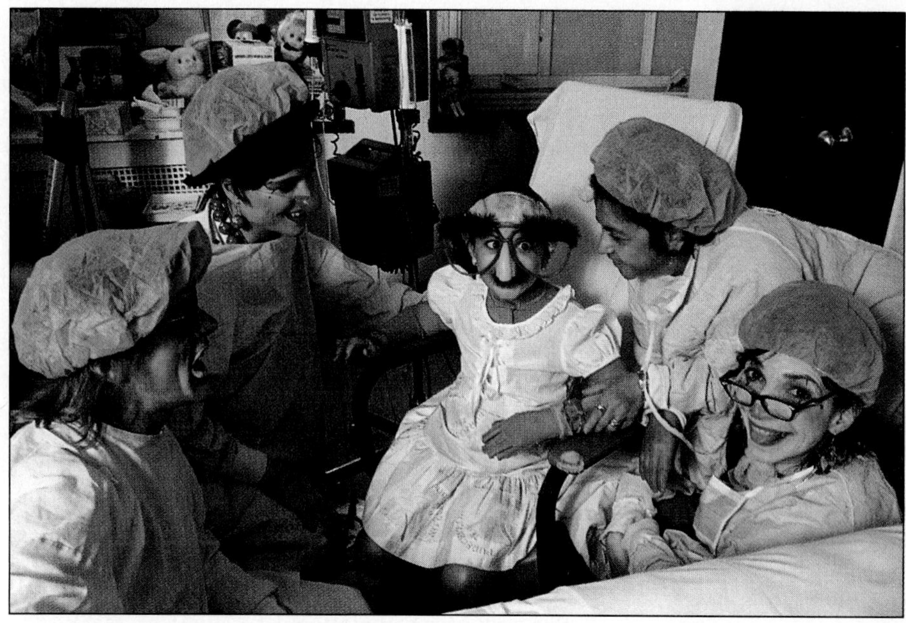

contemporary organizational behavior and present an overview of the rest of this book. Finally, we examine several emerging perspectives that are of special interest to the field.

What Is Organizational Behavior?

■ **Organizational behavior (OB)** is the study of human behavior in organizational settings, the human behavior–organization interface, and the organization itself.

Organizational behavior (OB) is the study of human behavior in organizational settings, the interface between human behavior and the organization, and the organization itself.[2] Although we can focus on any one of these three areas, we must remember that all three are ultimately relevant to a comprehensive understanding of organizational behavior. For example, we can study individual behavior (such as the behavior of Jack Welch) without explicitly considering the organization. But because the organization influences and is influenced by the individual, we cannot fully understand the individual's behavior without learning something about the organization. Similarly, we can study organizations (such as General Electric) without focusing specifically on the people within them. But again, we are looking at only a portion of the puzzle. Eventually we must consider the other pieces, as well as the whole.

2. For a discussion of the meaning of organizational behavior, see Larry Cummings, "Toward Organizational Behavior," *Academy of Management Review,* January 1978, pp. 90–98. For recent updates, see the annual series *Research in Organizational Behavior* (Greenwich, Conn.: JAI Press), edited by Larry Cummings and Barry Staw.

Figure 1.1 illustrates this view of organizational behavior. It shows the linkages among human behavior in organizational settings, the individual-organization interface, the organization, and the environment surrounding the organization. Each individual brings to an organization a unique set of personal characteristics, experiences from other organizations, and personal background. In considering the people who work in organizations, therefore, organizational behavior must look at the unique perspective that each individual brings to the work setting. For example, suppose Texas Instruments hires a consultant to investigate employee turnover. As a starting point, the consultant might analyze the types of people the firm usually hires. The goal of this analysis would be to learn as much as possible about the nature of the company's work force as individuals—their expectations, personal goals, and so forth.

But individuals do not work in isolation. They come in contact with other individuals and with the organization in a variety of ways. Points of contact include managers, coworkers, the formal policies and procedures of the organization, and various changes implemented by the organization. Over time, the individual too changes as a function both of personal experiences and maturity and of work experiences and the organization. The organization, in turn, is affected by the presence and eventual absence of the individual. Clearly, then, the study of organizational behavior must consider the ways in which the individual and the organization interact. Thus, the consultant studying turnover at Texas Instruments might next look at the orientation procedures for newcomers to the organization. The goal of this phase of the study would be to understand some of the dynamics of how incoming individuals interact with the broader organizational context.

An organization, of course, exists before a particular person joins it and continues to exist after he or she has left. Thus, the organization itself represents a crucial third perspective from which to view organizational behavior. For instance, the consultant studying turnover would also need to study the structure

FIGURE 1.1
The Nature of Organizational Behavior

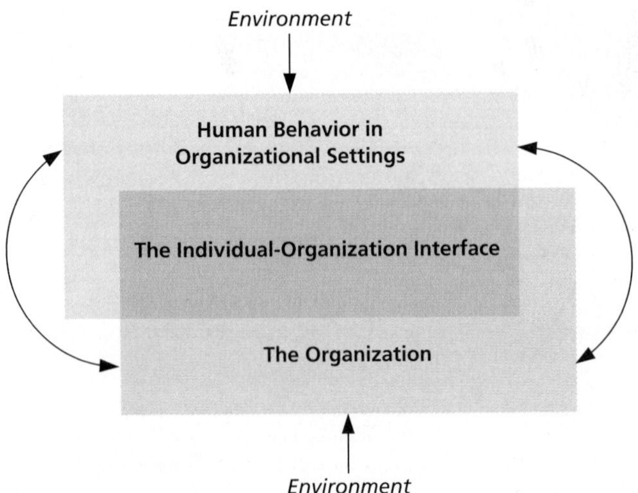

of Texas Instruments. An understanding of factors like the performance evaluation and reward systems, the decision-making and communication patterns, and the design of the firm itself can provide added insight into why some people choose to leave a company and others elect to stay.

Thus, the field of organizational behavior is both exciting and complex. Myriad variables and concepts accompany the interactions just described, and together these factors greatly complicate the manager's ability to understand, appreciate, and manage others in the organization. They also provide unique opportunities to enhance personal and organizational effectiveness. The key, of course, is understanding. To provide a groundwork for this understanding, we look first at the historical roots of the field.

The Historical Roots of Organizational Behavior

- Management is a relatively new field of study, having emerged only within the last 100 years.

Many disciplines, such as physics and chemistry, are literally thousands of years old. Management has also been around in one form or another for centuries. For example, the writings of Aristotle and Plato abound with references and examples of management concepts and practices. But because serious interest in the study of management did not emerge until around the turn of the twentieth century, organizational behavior is only a few decades old.[3]

One reason for the relatively late development of management as a scientific field is that few large business organizations existed until around a hundred years ago. Although management is just as important to a small organization as it is to a large one, large firms were needed to provide both a stimulus and a laboratory for management research. Second, many people assumed that management and other business issues are part of economics. Economists, in turn, assumed that management practices are by nature efficient and effective; therefore, they concentrated on higher levels of analysis such as national economic policy and industrial structures. Finally, management was recognized as a social science rather than a natural science. Thus, its variables and concepts were more difficult to identify, define, measure, and predict than those associated with physical phenomena.

Still, many managers and organizations have come to appreciate the value of history. For example, managers have gleaned significant insights from Homer's *Iliad,* Machiavelli's *The Prince,* and Chaucer's *The Canterbury Tales.* And some organizations, such as Polaroid and Wells Fargo, have even designated corporate historians! *Management in Action* provides more details about how Wells Fargo uses history to remain effective today.

3. Daniel A. Wren, *The Evolution of Management Thought,* 3rd ed. (New York: Wiley, 1987), Chapter 1. See also Stephen J. Carroll and Dennis A. Gillen, "Are the Classical Management Functions Useful in Describing Managerial Work?", *Academy of Management Review,* January 1987, pp. 38–51, and Daniel A. Wren, "Management History: Issues and Ideas for Teaching and Research," *Journal of Management,* Summer 1987, pp. 339–350.

MANAGEMENT IN ACTION

Wells Fargo Relies on History

Wells Fargo & Company was founded in San Francisco in 1852. It originally had two businesses: banking and express services. The Wells Fargo wagon was a familiar fixture in the Old West and appeared in most Western movies; there is even a song about it in *The Music Man.* In 1905, the firm relocated its express services operations to New York but kept its banking business on the West Coast.

The U.S. government nationalized most of this country's express services businesses during World War I. Wells Fargo managers decided they really wanted to concentrate on banking anyway. So when control of its express services business was returned after the war, Wells Fargo sold it and invested the proceeds of the sale into its banking business.

Today Wells Fargo is one of the largest banking services companies in the United States. But the firm has not forgotten its past. To the contrary, Wells Fargo employs a corporate historian with the title of vice president. His job is to maintain the firm's archives and help today's managers understand the lessons to be learned from the past.

Recently Wells Fargo experienced a very real reminder of the value of history. A rival sued the firm for $480 million for allegedly pirating an idea about credit card operations. The corporate historian, however, was able to produce documents from several years earlier that clearly demonstrated that Wells Fargo had actually originated the idea.

SOURCES: "Wells Fargo Heads for the Wild, Wild East," *Business Week,* August 21, 1989, p. 82; "Best in the West," *The Banker,* February 1988, pp. 53–55; "In Wake of Cost Cuts, Many Firms Sweep Their History Out the Door," *The Wall Street Journal,* December 21, 1987, p. 21; John W. Mulligan, "The Return of Wells Fargo," *Institutional Investor,* August 1987, pp. 88–94.

Scientific Management

- **Scientific management,** popular during the early twentieth century, was one of the first approaches to management. It focused on the efficiency of individual workers.
- Key contributors to scientific management included Frederick W. Taylor, Frank and Lillian Gilbreth, Henry Gantt, and Harrington Emerson.
- Taylor identified a phenomenon he called *soldiering*—the practice of working considerably slower than one can.

One of the first approaches to the study of management, popularized during the early 1900s, was **scientific management.** Several individuals helped develop scientific management, including Frank and Lillian Gilbreth (whose lives were portrayed in a book and a subsequent movie, *Cheaper by the Dozen*), Henry Gantt, and Harrington Emerson. But Frederick W. Taylor is most closely identified with this approach.[4] Early in his life, Taylor developed an interest in efficiency and productivity. While working as a foreman at Midvale Steel Company in Philadelphia from 1878 to 1890, he became aware of a phenomenon he called *soldiering*: the practice of working considerably slower than one can. Because managers had never systematically studied jobs in the plant—and, in fact, had little idea how to gauge worker productivity—they were completely unaware of this practice.

To counteract the effects of soldiering, Taylor developed several innovative techniques. He studied all the jobs in the Midvale plant and developed a standardized method for performing each one. He also installed a piece-rate pay system in which each worker was paid for the amount of work he or she

4. Frederick W. Taylor, *Principles of Scientific Management* (New York: Harper, 1911). See also Wren, *The Evolution of Management Thought,* Chapter 6.

completed during the workday rather than for the time spent on the job. These changes boosted productivity markedly.

After leaving Midvale, Taylor spent several years working as a management consultant for industrial firms. At Bethlehem Steel Company, he developed several efficient techniques for loading and unloading rail cars. At Simonds Rolling Machine Company, he redesigned jobs, introduced rest breaks to combat fatigue, and implemented a piece-rate pay system. In every case, Taylor claimed his ideas and methods greatly improved worker output. His book *Principles of Scientific Management,* published in 1911, was greeted with enthusiasm by practicing managers and quickly became a standard reference.

Figure 1.2 summarizes the basic principles of scientific management. An additional aspect of Taylor's approach, not shown in the figure but reflected in his enthusiasm for piece-rate pay systems, was his belief that all employees are economically motivated; that is, Taylor assumed that monetary rewards are the primary incentive managers can use to motivate workers to achieve higher levels of output.

Scientific management quickly became a mainstay of American business thinking. It facilitated job specialization and mass production, thus profoundly influencing the American business system. Taylor had his critics, however. Labor opposed scientific management because of its explicit goal of getting more output from workers. Congress investigated Taylor's methods and ideas because some argued that his incentive system would dehumanize the workplace and reduce workers to little more than robots. Later theorists recognized that Taylor's views of employee motivation were inadequate and narrow. And recently there have

This fish processing plant in Obama, Japan, used the principles of scientific management to set up its assembly line. The work stations are designed to fit a maximum number of women on the line, and the workers have been trained to perform their tasks with a high level of efficiency.

FIGURE 1.2
Basic Concepts of Scientific Management

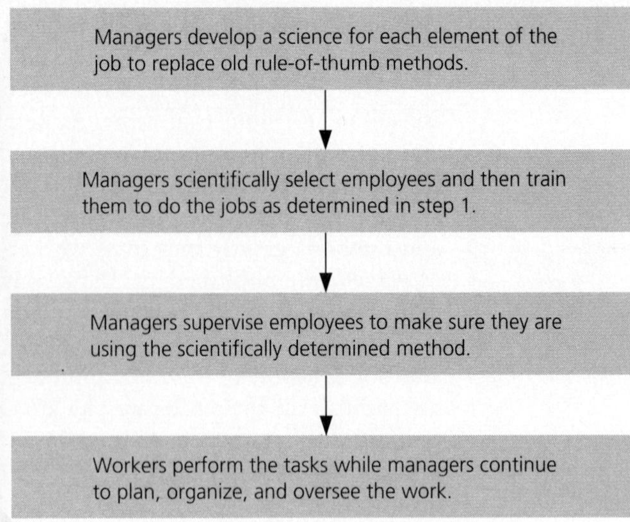

Managers develop a science for each element of the job to replace old rule-of-thumb methods.
Managers scientifically select employees and then train them to do the jobs as determined in step 1.
Managers supervise employees to make sure they are using the scientifically determined method.
Workers perform the tasks while managers continue to plan, organize, and oversee the work.

been allegations that Taylor falsified some of his research findings and paid someone to do his writing for him. Nevertheless, scientific management remains a cornerstone of contemporary management thought.[5]

Classical Organization Theory

- **Classical organization theory,** another early approach to management, focused on how organizations can be structured most effectively.
- Key contributors to classical organization theory included Henri Fayol, Lyndall Urwick, and Max Weber.
- The concept of bureaucracy, as described by Weber, was an early universal approach to organization structure. A bureaucracy is a logical, rational, and efficient model of organizations.

Scientific management dealt almost exclusively with the interaction between a person and his or her job. During the period of scientific management's popularity, another school of management thought emerged. Generally referred to as **classical organization theory,** it was concerned with structuring organizations effectively. Whereas scientific management studied how individual workers could be made more efficient, classical organization theory focused on how a large number of workers and managers could be most effectively organized into an overall structure.

Major contributors to classical organization theory included Henri Fayol, Lyndall Urwick, and Max Weber. Weber, the most prominent of the three, proposed a "bureaucratic" form of structure that he believed would work for all organizations.[6] Although today the term *bureaucracy* generally connotes paperwork, red tape, and inflexibility, Weber's model of bureaucracy embraced

5. For critical analyses, see Charles D. Wrege and Amedeo G. Perroni, "Taylor's Pig-Tale: A Historical Analysis of Frederick W. Taylor's Pig-Iron Experiment," *Academy of Management Journal,* March 1974, pp. 6–27, and Charles D. Wrege and Ann Marie Stoka, "Cooke Creates a Classic: The Story Behind Taylor's Principles of Scientific Management," *Academy of Management Review,* October 1978, pp. 736–749. For a more favorable review, see Edwin A. Locke, "The Ideas of Frederick W. Taylor: An Evaluation," *Academy of Management Review,* January 1982, pp. 14–24.

6. Max Weber, *Theory of Social and Economic Organization,* trans. A. M. Henderson and T. Parsons (London: Oxford University Press, 1921). See also Wren, *The Evolution of Management Thought,* Chapter 10.

TABLE 1.1
Elements of Weber's Ideal Bureaucracy

Elements	Comments
1. Rules and Procedures	A consistent set of abstract rules and procedures should exist to ensure uniform performance.
2. Distinct Division of Labor	Each position should be filled by an expert.
3. Hierarchy of Authority	The chain of command should be clearly established.
4. Technical Competence	Employment and advancement should be based on merit.
5. Segregation of Ownership	Professional managers, rather than owners, should run the organization.
6. Rights and Properties of the Position	These should be associated with the organization, not the person who holds the office.
7. Documentation	A record of actions should be kept regarding administrative decisions, rules, and procedures.

logic, rationality, and efficiency. Weber assumed that the bureaucratic structure would always be the most efficient approach. (Such a blanket prescription represents what is now called a *universal approach.*) Table 1.1 summarizes the elements of Weber's ideal bureaucracy.

In contrast to Weber's views, contemporary organization theorists recognize that different organization structures may be appropriate in different situations. However, Weber's ideas and the concepts associated with his bureaucratic structure are still interesting and relevant today. (Chapters 17 through 20 discuss contemporary organization theory.)

The Emergence of Organizational Behavior

The central themes of both scientific management and classical organization theory were rationality, efficiency, and standardization. The roles of individuals and groups in organizations were either ignored altogether or given only minimal attention. A few writers and managers, however, recognized the importance of individual and social processes in organizations.

Precursors of Organizational Behavior

- Robert Owen, Hugo Munsterberg, and Mary Parker Follett were among the first to recognize the importance of individual behavior to organizations.

In the early nineteenth century, Robert Owen, a British industrialist, attempted to improve the condition of industrial workers. He improved working conditions, raised minimum ages for hiring children, introduced meals for employees, and shortened working hours. In the early twentieth century, the noted German psychologist Hugo Munsterberg argued that the field of psychology could provide important insights into areas such as motivation and the hiring of new employees.

Another writer in the early 1900s, Mary Parker Follett, believed that management should become more democratic in its dealings with employees. An expert in vocational guidance, Follett argued that organizations should strive harder to accommodate their employees' human needs.[7]

The views of Owen, Munsterberg, and Follett, however, were not widely shared by practicing managers. Not until the 1930s did significant change occur in management's perception of the relationship between the individual and the workplace. At that time, a series of now classic research studies led to the emergence of organizational behavior as a field of study.

The Hawthorne Studies

■ The **Hawthorne studies,** conducted between 1927 and 1932, led to some of the first discoveries of the importance of human behavior in organizations.

The **Hawthorne studies** were conducted between 1927 and 1932 at Western Electric's Hawthorne plant near Chicago. (General Electric initially sponsored the research but withdrew its support after the first study was finished.) Several researchers were involved, the best known being Elton Mayo and Fritz Roethlisberger, Harvard faculty members and consultants, and William Dickson, chief of Hawthorne's Employee Relations Research Department.[8]

The first major experiment at Hawthorne studied the effects of different levels of lighting on productivity. The researchers systematically manipulated the lighting of the area in which a group of women worked. The group's productivity was measured and compared with that of another group (the control group) whose lighting was left unchanged. As lighting was increased for the experimental group, productivity went up—but, surprisingly, so did the productivity of the control group. Even when lighting was subsequently reduced, the productivity of both groups continued to increase. Not until the lighting had become almost as dim as moonlight did productivity start to decline. This led the researchers to conclude that lighting had no relationship with productivity—and it was at this point that General Electric withdrew its sponsorship of the project!

In another major experiment, a piecework incentive system was established for a nine-man group that assembled terminal banks for telephone exchanges. Proponents of scientific management would have expected each man to work as hard as he could to maximize his personal income. But the Hawthorne researchers found instead that the group as a whole established an acceptable level of output for its members. Individuals who failed to meet this level were dubbed "chiselers," and those who exceeded it by too much were branded "rate busters." A worker who wanted to be accepted by the group could not produce at too high or too low a level. Thus, as a worker approached the accepted level each day, he slowed down to avoid overproducing.

---

7. Hugo Munsterberg, *Psychology and Industrial Efficiency* (Boston: Houghton Mifflin, 1913). See also Wren, *The Evolution of Management Thought,* Chapter 9.

8. Elton Mayo, *The Human Problems of Industrial Civilization* (New York: Macmillan, 1933); Fritz J. Roethlisberger and William J. Dickson, *Management and the Worker* (Cambridge, Mass.: Harvard University Press, 1939).

After a follow-up interview program with several thousand workers, the Hawthorne researchers concluded that the human element in the workplace was considerably more important than previously believed. The lighting experiment, for example, suggested that productivity might increase simply because workers were singled out for special treatment and thus perhaps felt more valued. In the incentive system experiment, being accepted as a part of the group evidently meant more to the workers than earning extra money. Several other studies supported the overall conclusion that individual and social processes are too important to ignore.

Like the work of Taylor, the Hawthorne studies recently have been called into question. Critics cite deficiencies in research methods and alternative explanations of the findings. Again, however, these studies played a major role in the advancement of the field and are still among its most frequently cited works.[9]

Human Relations Movement

■ Following the Hawthorne studies, the **human relations movement** emerged. Human relationists believed that employee satisfaction is a key determinant of performance.

■ One prominent human relations writer, Douglas McGregor, developed the concepts of Theory X and Theory Y. Theory X takes a negative and pessimistic view of workers, whereas Theory Y takes a more positive and optimistic approach. McGregor advocated the adoption of Theory Y.

The Hawthorne studies created quite a stir among managers and management researchers, providing the foundation for an entirely new school of management thought that came to be known as the **human relations movement.** The basic premises underlying the human relations movement were that people respond primarily to their social environment, that motivation depends more on social needs than on economic needs, and that satisfied employees work harder than unsatisfied employees. This perspective represented a fundamental shift away from the philosophy and values of scientific management and classical organization theory.

The values of the human relationists are exemplified in the work of Douglas McGregor and Abraham Maslow.[10] McGregor is best known for his classic book *The Human Side of Enterprise,* in which he identified two opposing perspectives that he believed typified managerial views of employees. Some managers, McGregor said, subscribed to what he labeled *Theory X,* whose characteristics are summarized in Table 1.2. Theory X takes a generally negative and pessimistic view of human nature and employee behavior. In many ways, it is consistent with the tenets of scientific management. A much more optimistic and positive view of employees is found in *Theory Y,* also summarized in Table 1.2. Theory Y, which is generally representative of the human relations perspective, was the approach McGregor himself advocated.

---

9. Alex Carey, "The Hawthorne Studies: A Radical Criticism," *American Sociological Review,* June 1967, pp. 403–416; Lyle Yorks and David A. Whitsett, "Hawthorne, Topeka, and the Issue of Science versus Advocacy in Organizational Behavior," *Academy of Management Review,* January 1985, pp. 21–30. See also Wren, *The Evolution of Management Thought,* Chapter 13.

10. Douglas McGregor, *The Human Side of Enterprise* (New York: McGraw-Hill, 1960); Abraham Maslow, "A Theory of Human Motivation," *Psychological Review,* July 1943, pp. 370–396. See also Paul H. Lawrence, "Historical Development of Organizational Behavior," in Jay W. Lorsch, ed., *Handbook of Organizational Behavior* (Englewood Cliffs, N.J.: Prentice-Hall, 1987), pp. 1–9.

TABLE 1.2
Theory X and Theory Y

Theory X Assumptions	Theory Y Assumptions
1. People do not like work and try to avoid it. 2. People do not like work, so managers have to control, direct, coerce, and threaten employees to get them to work toward organizational goals. 3. People prefer to be directed, to avoid responsibility, to want security; they have little ambition.	1. People do not naturally dislike work; work is a natural part of their lives. 2. People are internally motivated to reach objectives to which they are committed. 3. People are committed to goals to the degree that they receive personal rewards when they reach their objectives. 4. People will seek and accept responsibility under favorable conditions. 5. People have the capacity to be innovative in solving organizational problems. 6. People are bright, but under most organizational conditions their potentials are underutilized.

SOURCE: Douglas McGregor, *The Human Side of Enterprise* (New York: McGraw-Hill, 1960), pp. 33–34, 47–48. Used with permission of publisher.

■ Abraham Maslow, another pioneer in the human relations movement, developed the well-known hierarchy of human needs.

In 1943, Abraham Maslow published a pioneering theory of employee motivation that became well known and widely accepted among managers. Maslow's theory, which we describe in detail in Chapter 5, assumes that motivation arises from a hierarchical series of needs. As the needs at each level are satisfied, the individual progresses to the next higher level.

The Hawthorne studies and the human relations movement played major roles in developing the foundations for the field of organizational behavior. Some of the early theorists' basic premises and assumptions were incorrect, however. For example, most human relationists believed that employee attitudes such as job satisfaction are the major causes of employee behaviors such as job performance. As we explain in Chapter 6, however, this usually is not the case at all. Also, many of the human relationists' views were unnecessarily limited and situation specific. There was still plenty of room for refinement and development in the emerging field of human behavior in organizations.

Toward Organizational Behavior

■ Organizational behavior began to emerge as a mature field of study in the late 1950s and early 1960s.

Most scholars would agree that organizational behavior began to emerge as a mature field of study in the late 1950s and early 1960s.[11] That period saw the field's evolution from the simple assumptions and behavioral models of the

11. See "Conversation with Lyman W. Porter," *Organizational Dynamics,* Winter 1990, pp. 69–79.

human relationists to the concepts and methodologies of a scientific discipline. Since that time, organizational behavior as a scientific field of inquiry has made considerable strides, although there have been occasional steps backward as well. Many of the ideas discussed in this book have emerged over the past two decades. We turn now to contemporary organizational behavior.[12]

Contemporary Organizational Behavior

Contemporary organizational behavior has two basic characteristics that we need to understand before proceeding further. It also consists of a generally accepted set of concepts that define its domain.

Characteristics of the Field

■ Contemporary organizational behavior has an interdisciplinary focus, drawing from fields such as psychology, sociology, and other related areas.

Contemporary organizational behavior has an interdisciplinary focus and a descriptive nature; that is, it draws from a variety of other fields and attempts to describe behavior (as opposed to prescribing how behavior can be changed in consistent and predictable ways).

An Interdisciplinary Focus In many ways, organizational behavior synthesizes several other fields of study. Psychology, especially industrial or organizational psychology, is perhaps the greatest contributor to the field of organizational behavior. Psychologists study behavior, whereas industrial or organizational psychologists deal specifically with the behavior of people in organizational settings. Many of the concepts that interest psychologists, such as learning and motivation, are also central to students of organizational behavior.

Sociology also has had a major impact on the field of organizational behavior. Sociologists study social systems such as a family, an occupational class, a mob, or an organization. Because a major concern of organizational behavior is the study of organization structures, the field clearly overlaps with areas of sociology that focus on the organization as a social system.

Anthropology is concerned with the interactions between people and their environments, especially their cultural environment. Culture is a major influence on the structure of organizations as well as on the behavior of people within organizations.

Political science also interests organizational behaviorists. We usually think of political science as the study of political systems such as governments. But themes of interest to political scientists include how and why people acquire power, political behavior, decision making, conflict, the behavior of interest

12. See Lorsch, *Handbook of Organizational Behavior*, for an overview of the current state of the field.

groups, and coalition formation. These are also major areas of interest in organizational behavior.

Economists study the production, distribution, and consumption of goods and services. Students of organizational behavior share the economist's interest in areas such as labor market dynamics, productivity, human resource planning and forecasting, and cost-benefit analysis.

Engineering has also influenced the field of organizational behavior. Industrial engineering in particular has long been concerned with work measurement, productivity measurement, work flow analysis and design, job design, and labor relations. Obviously these areas are also relevant to organizational behavior.

Most recently, medicine has come into play in connection with the study of human behavior at work, specifically in the area of stress. Increasingly, research is showing that controlling the causes and consequences of stress in and out of organizational settings is important for the well-being of the individual as well as that of the organization.

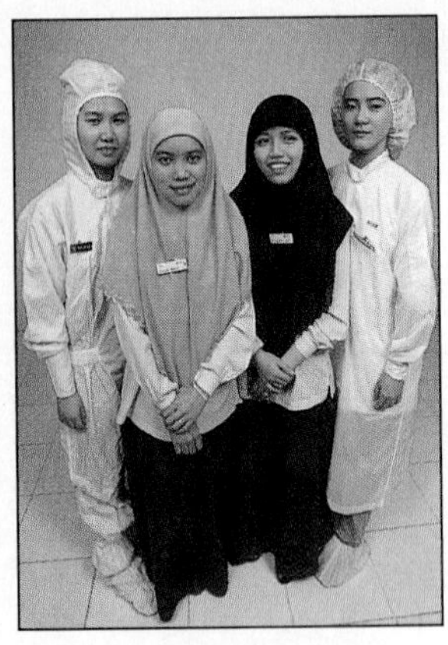

The countries of the Pacific Rim are growing economically and technologically, providing tremendous opportunities for foreign investment. These opportunities come with challenges, one of which is managing an ethnically diverse work force. The Chinese and Malay women shown here work for Hewlett-Packard. For help in understanding how their different cultures may affect their behavior, their managers can look to the field of anthropology for its contributions to organizational behavior.

- Organizational behavior attempts to describe relationships between two or more behavioral variables.

A Descriptive Nature The primary goal of organizational behavior is to describe, rather than prescribe, relationships between two or more behavioral variables. The theories and concepts of the field, for example, cannot predict with certainty that changing a specific set of workplace variables will improve employee performance by a certain amount. At best, the field can suggest that certain general concepts or variables tend to be related to one another in particular settings. For instance, research might indicate that in one organization, employee satisfaction and individual perceptions of working conditions correlate positively. However, we do not know if better working conditions lead to more satisfaction, if more satisfied people see their jobs differently from dissatisfied people, or if both satisfaction and perceptions of working conditions are actually related through other variables. Also, the observed relationship between satisfaction and perceptions of working conditions may be considerably stronger, weaker, or even nonexistent in other settings.

Organizational behavior is descriptive for several reasons: the immaturity of the field, the complexities inherent in studying human behavior, and the lack of valid, reliable, and accepted definitions and measures. Whether the field will ever be able to make definitive predictions and prescriptions is still an open question. But the value of studying organizational behavior nonetheless is firmly established. Because behavioral processes pervade most managerial functions and roles, and because the work of organizations is done primarily by people, the knowledge and understanding gained from the field can help managers significantly in many ways.[13] *The Ethical Dilemma* shows how behavioral concepts can help explain the Exxon oil spill incident in a descriptive fashion.

---

13. Joseph W. McGuire, "Retreat to the Academy," *Business Horizons,* July-August 1982, pp. 31–37; Kenneth Thomas and Walter G. Tymon, "Necessary Properties of Relevant Research: Lessons from Recent Criticisms of the Organizational Sciences," *Academy of Management Review,* July 1982, pp. 345–353. See also Jeffrey Pfeffer, "The Theory Practice Gap: Myth or Reality?", *Academy of Management Executive,* February 1987, pp. 31–32.

THE ETHICAL DILEMMA

Behavioral Processes Affect Exxon

By now just about everyone knows the story: In March 1989, the Exxon oil tanker *Valdez* ran aground off the coast of Alaska and spilled millions of gallons of oil. The environmental cleanup activities and lawsuits continue to this day. It is still not clear how and why the crisis occurred, who is to blame, and how effectively Exxon has handled the situation. Consider, for example, the following "facts" and their "explanations":

1. Exxon fired the ship's captain because of reports that he was intoxicated during the crisis. The captain, however, maintains that his skills were in no way hampered. All agree that stress on the job may have been a factor in the spill.
2. The public criticized Exxon CEO Lawrence Rawl for not issuing public statements about the spill for over a week after it happened. Rawl argues that he was gathering facts and trying to be methodical. All agree that the issue is one of leadership.
3. The public thinks Exxon has not done enough to clean up the spill. Exxon argues it has done all it can do and still represent the best interests of its stockholders. All agree that the issue is one of social responsibility.
4. Exxon recently designated one of its top executives as an environmental watchdog. The company claims it is trying to be socially responsible, whereas critics write off the action as public relations. All agree that it's a matter of different perceptions.
5. Some Exxon customers have stuck with the company, whereas others have changed brands in protest. All agree that attitudes have played a part in their response.

SOURCES: "Firm Finds Valdez Oil Fouls Image," *USA Today,* April 26, 1990, pp. B1, B2; "Exxon Corp. Picks Watchdog of Environment," *The Wall Street Journal,* January 11, 1990, p. B8; "'One Way to End a Career,'" *Newsweek,* May 29, 1989, p. 52; "Public Angry at Slow Action on Oil Spill," *USA Today,* April 21, 1989, pp. B1, B2; "Critics Fault Chief Executive of Exxon on Handling of Recent Alaskan Oil Spill," *The Wall Street Journal,* March 31, 1989, p. B1.

Basic Concepts of the Field

- Basic concepts of organizational behavior can be divided into five basic categories: individual processes; interpersonal processes; enhancing individual and interpersonal processes; organizational processes and characteristics; and integrating individuals, groups, and organizations.

The concepts of primary interest to organizational behavior can be grouped into five basic categories: (1) individual processes; (2) interpersonal processes; (3) methods for enhancing individual and interpersonal processes; (4) organizational processes and characteristics; and (5) approaches to integrating individuals, groups, and organizations. As Figure 1.3 shows, we use these categories as the basic framework for this book.

Chapter 2 develops a managerial perspective on organizational behavior. The four chapters of Part II cover individual processes in organizations. Chapter 3 explores learning, perception, and attribution. Individual differences are the subject of Chapter 4. Chapters 5 and 6 provide in-depth coverage of an especially important topic, motivation in organizations.

Interpersonal processes in organizations is the focus of Part III. Chapter 7 examines group dynamics. Chapter 8 extends this area to intergroup dynamics. Leadership and influence processes are the subject of Chapter 9. Chapter 10

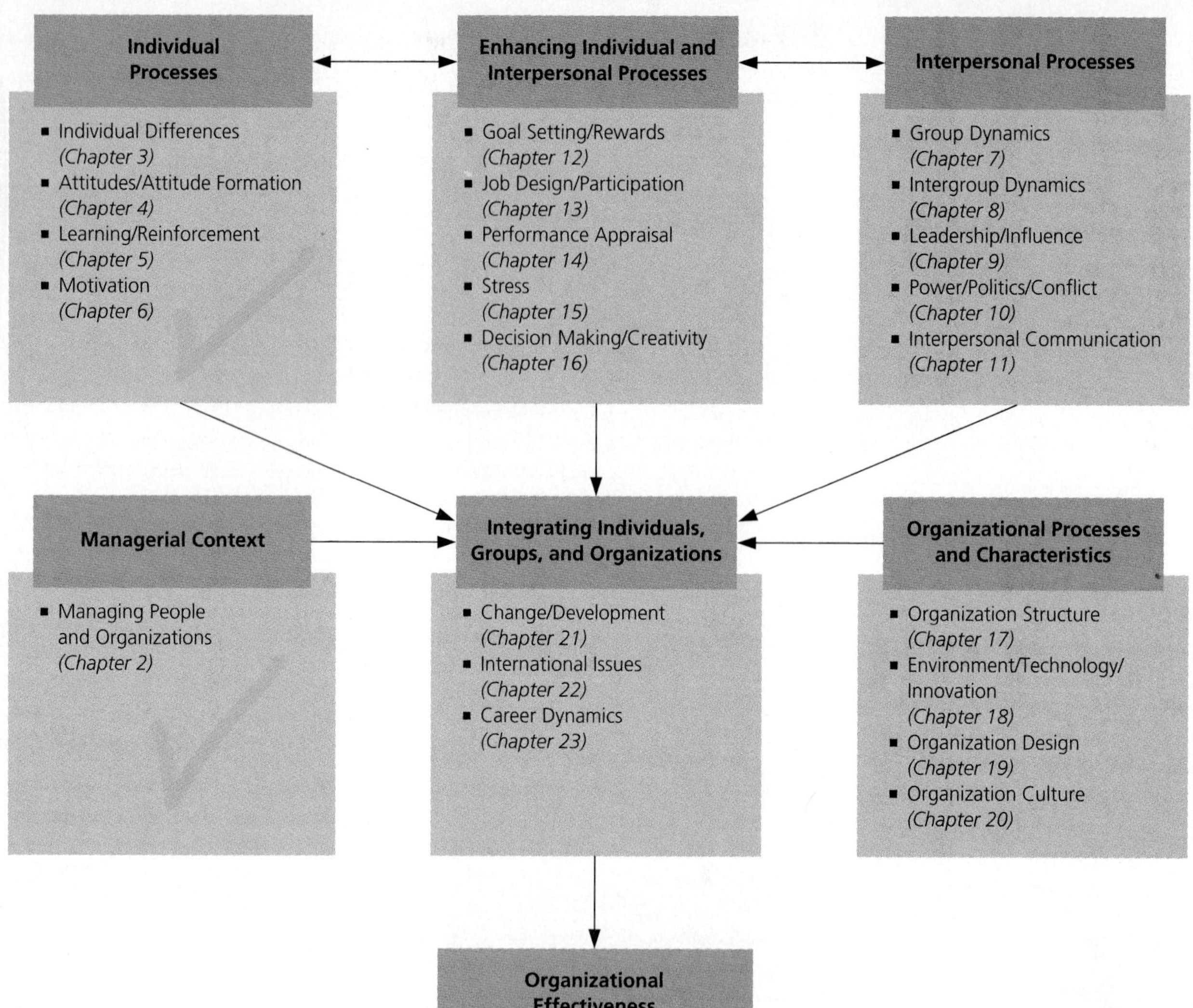

FIGURE 1.3
The Basic Framework for Understanding Organizational Behavior

deals with power, politics, and conflict. Interpersonal communication, the topic of Chapter 11, concludes this part.

Part IV is devoted to enhancing individual and interpersonal processes. Chapter 12 describes goal setting and rewards. Job design and employee participation are the focus of Chapter 13. Chapter 14 discusses performance appraisal. Chapter 15 deals with stress, and Chapter 16 discusses decision making and creativity.

Organizational processes and characteristics are the subject of Part V. Chapter 17 describes organization structure. Three important contextual variables, environment, technology, and innovation, are the subject of Chapter 18. Chapter 19 presents an in-depth treatment of organization design. Finally, organization culture is the topic of Chapter 20.

Part VI concludes the book with a discussion of several approaches to integrating individuals, groups, and organizations. Organization change and development are the focus of Chapter 21. Chapter 22 turns to the increasingly important area of international aspects of organizational behavior. Chapter 23 examines career dynamics. The final topic of discussion, research methods in organizational behavior, is presented in the Appendix.

The Importance of Organizational Behavior

Most people are born and educated in organizations, acquire most of their material possessions from organizations, and die as members of organizations. Many of our activities are regulated by organizations called governments. And most adults spend the better part of their lives working in organizations. Because organizations influence our lives so powerfully, we have every reason to be concerned about how and why those organizations function.

In our relationships with organizations, we may adopt any one of several roles or identities. For example, we can be consumers, employees, or adversaries (such as Ralph Nader in his famous 1960s crusade against unsafe automobile design at General Motors). Since most readers of this book are present or future managers, we will take a managerial viewpoint here. Organizational behavior can greatly clarify the factors that affect how managers manage. It is the field's job to describe the complex human context in which managers work and to define the problems associated with that realm. The value of organizational

Jack Welch is CEO of General Electric. When he assumed that position in 1981 he was given some sage advice by one of his mentors, Walter Wriston. During his own tenure as CEO of Citicorp, Wriston reshaped the entire banking industry and made the firm one of the world's largest financial institutions. The advice he gave Welch underscores the importance of understanding the behavior of people in organizations.

behavior is that it isolates important aspects of the manager's job and offers specific perspectives on the human side of management: people as organizations, people as resources, and people as people.

Emerging Perspectives on Organizational Behavior

Three contemporary perspectives have increasingly influenced organizational behavior: the systems approach, the contingency perspective, and the interactional view. Many of the concepts and theories discussed in the chapters that follow reflect these perspectives; they represent basic points of view that influence much of our contemporary thinking about behavior in organizations.

The Systems Approach

- **Systems theory** views organizations as a set of interrelated elements functioning as a whole.
- Organizational systems use four categories of inputs: material, human, financial, and informational.

Systems theory, or the theory of systems, was first developed in the physical sciences, but it has been extended to other areas, such as management.[14] A *system* is an interrelated set of elements that function as a whole. Figure 1.4 shows a general framework for viewing organizations as systems.

An organizational system receives four kinds of inputs from its environment: material, human, financial, and informational. The organization then combines and transforms the inputs and returns them to the environment in the form of products or services, profits or losses, employee behaviors, and additional information. Finally, the system receives feedback from the environment regarding these outputs.

As an example, we can apply systems theory to Shell Oil Company. Material inputs include pipelines, crude oil, and the machinery used to refine petroleum. Financial inputs take the form of money received from oil and gas sales, stockholder investment, and so forth. Human inputs are oil field workers, refinery workers, office staff, and other people employed by the company. Finally, the company receives information inputs from forecasts about future oil supplies, geological surveys on potential drilling sites, sales projections, and similar analyses.

Through complex refining and other processes, these inputs are combined and transformed to create products such as gasoline and motor oil. As outputs, these products are sold to the consuming public. Profits from operations are fed back into the environment through taxes, investments, and dividends; losses, when they occur, hit the environment by reducing stockholders' incomes. In addition to having on-the-job contacts with customers and suppliers, employees live in the community and participate in a variety of activities away from the workplace. In varying degrees, at least some part of this behavior is influenced

14. Fremont Kast and James Rosenzweig, "General Systems Theory: Applications for Organization and Management," *Academy of Management Journal,* December 1972, pp. 447–465.

FIGURE 1.4
The Systems Approach to Organizations

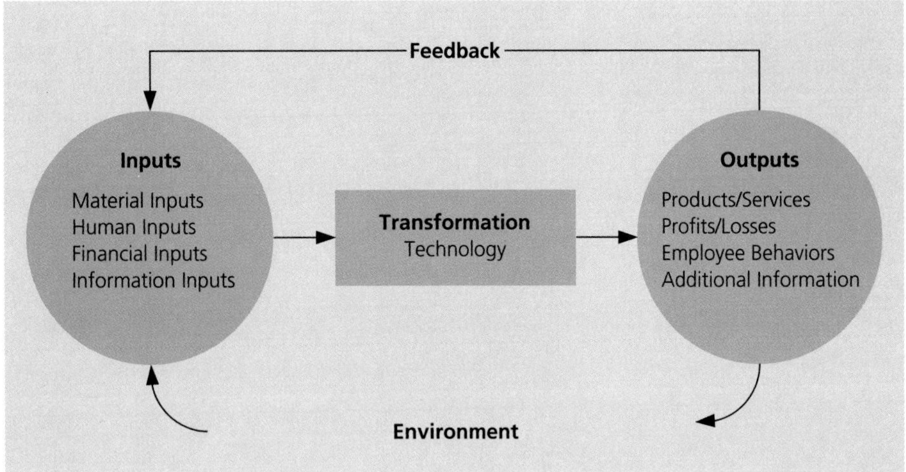

by their experiences as Shell workers. Finally, information about the company and its operations is also released into the environment. The environment, in turn, responds to these outputs and influences future inputs. For example, consumers may buy more or less gasoline depending on the quality and price of Shell's product, and banks may be more or less willing to lend Shell money based on financial information released about the company.

The Contingency Perspective

■ The **contingency perspective** suggests that in most organizations situations and outcomes are contingent on, or influenced by, other variables.

Another useful viewpoint for understanding behavior in organizations comes from **contingency perspective.** In the earlier days of management studies, both researchers and practicing managers searched for universal answers to organizational questions. They sought prescriptions that could be applied to any organization under any conditions. For example, early leadership researchers tried to discover forms of leadership behavior that would always lead employees to be more satisfied and to work harder. Eventually, however, researchers realized that the complexities of human behavior and organizational settings make universal conclusions virtually impossible. They discovered that in organizations most situations and outcomes are *contingent*; that is, the relationship between any two variables is likely to be influenced by other variables.[15]

Figure 1.5 distinguishes universal and contingency perspectives. The universal model, shown at the top of the figure, presumes a direct cause-and-effect linkage between variables. For example, it suggests that whenever a manager encounters a certain problem or situation (such as motivating employees to work harder), there exists a universal approach that will lead to the desired outcome

15. See Fremont Kast and James Rosenzweig, eds., *Contingency Views of Organization and Management* (Chicago: SRA, 1973), for a classic overview and introduction.

FIGURE 1.5
Universal versus Contingency Approaches

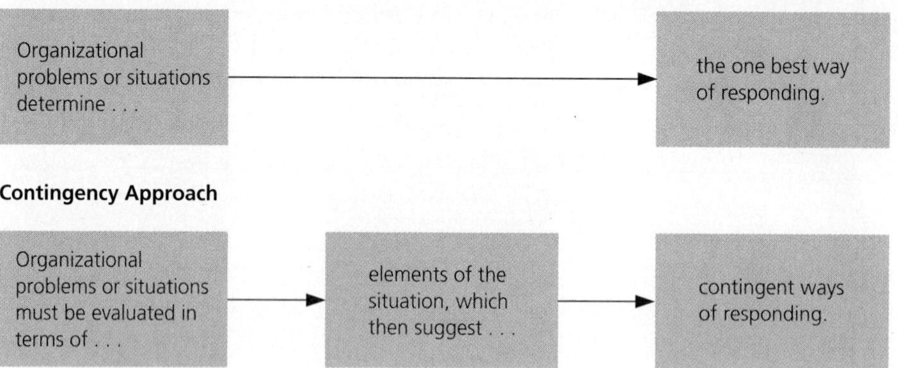

(such as raising pay or increasing autonomy). The contingency perspective, on the other hand, acknowledges several other variables that alter the direct relationship. In other words, appropriate managerial action or behavior in any given situation depends on elements of that situation.

The field of organizational behavior gradually has shifted from a universal approach in the 1950s and early 1960s to a contingency perspective. The contingency perspective is especially strong in the areas of motivation (Chapter 6), job design (Chapter 13), leadership (Chapter 9), and organization design (Chapter 19), but it is becoming increasingly important throughout the field.

When Jim Treybig founded Tandem Computers, he used an open, laid-back management style. His office was always accessible, and he paid little attention to what others were doing. Tandem grew rapidly, but eventually problems set in. Profits started to drop, and a financial scandal occurred. Treybig soon realized that his relaxed approach would not work in a larger, more formal organization. Consequently, he developed a more formalized control process and adopted a clearer hierarchy. As a result, Tandem regained its lost effectiveness. Treybig learned the hard way that what works in one situation (for example, a new, small company) will not necessarily work in another (a larger, more established firm). *International Perspective* describes how McDonald's Corp. has come to better appreciate the contingent nature of management as it expands into foreign markets. Doing business in the United States can be quite different from doing business in Japan or the Soviet Union!

Interactionalism

- **Interactionalism** suggests that individuals and situations interact continuously to determine individuals' behavior.

The interactional view is a relatively new approach to understanding behavior in organizational settings. First presented in terms of interactional psychology, this view assumes that individual behavior results from a continuous and multidirectional interaction between characteristics of the person and characteristics of the situation. More specifically, **interactionalism** attempts to explain how

INTERNATIONAL PERSPECTIVE

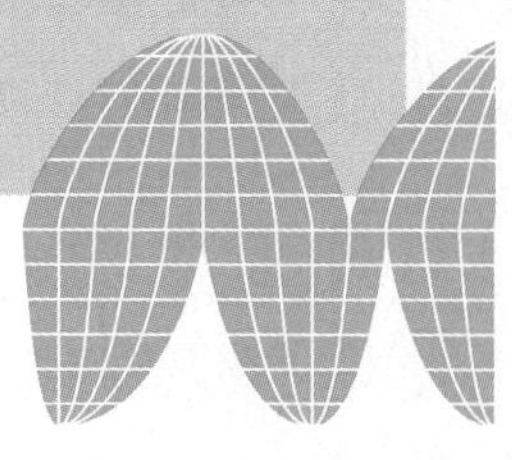

Big Mac Adjusts to Different Cultures

The golden arches of McDonald's are a ubiquitous part of the American landscape. Increasingly, however, the hamburger giant is spreading its message to foreign shores. Along the way, the company is finding that it has to make adjustments and accommodations in its standard operating procedures. Indeed, cultural differences have had an enormous impact on McDonald's.

For example, when the firm decided to open its first restaurant in Japan, it had a big battle over where to open it. McDonald's strategy had always been to open restaurants in the suburbs. Den Fujita, the businessman who received the first McDonald's franchise in Japan, argued that it should be opened in a downtown location. Fujita eventually won, and it turns out he was right. A year after opening, his first McDonald's set a company record for one-day sales. Back in the United States, McDonald's learned from Fujita and now opens restaurants in urban locations in this country as well.

McDonald's has also had some revealing experiences with its Russian restaurants. In the United States, most McDonald's employees are young and see their job as temporary. In the Soviet Union, however, many McDonald's employees have vowed to work there forever. They are extremely enthusiastic and welcome the security their jobs offer. Now company officials are trying to figure out how to bring some of that enthusiasm and excitement back home!

SOURCES: "U.S. Ideas Creep into Soviet Union," *USA Today,* May 11, 1990, pp. B1, B2; "Inside the Golden Arches," *Newsweek,* December 18, 1989, pp. 46–47; "McDonald's Stoops to Conquer," *Business Week,* October 20, 1989, pp. 120–124; Frederick Hiroshi Katayama, "Japan's Big Mac," *Fortune,* September 15, 1986, pp. 114–120.

people select, interpret, and change various situations.[16] Figure 1.6 illustrates this perspective. Note that the individual and the situation are presumed to interact continuously. This interaction is what determines the individual's behavior.

The interactional view implies that simple cause-and-effect descriptions of organizational phenomena are not enough. For example, one set of research studies may suggest that job changes will lead to improved employee attitudes. Another set of studies may propose that attitudes influence how people perceive their jobs in the first place. Both positions probably are incomplete: Employee attitudes may influence job perceptions, but these perceptions may in turn influence future attitudes.

Because interactionalism is a fairly recent contribution to the field, it is less prominent in the chapters that follow than the systems and contingency theories. Nonetheless, the interactional view appears to offer many promising ideas for future development in the field.

16. James Terborg, "Interactional Psychology and Research on Human Behavior in Organizations," *Academy of Management Review,* October 1981, pp. 569–576; Benjamin Schneider, "Interactional Psychology and Organizational Behavior," in Larry Cummings and Barry Staw, eds., *Research in Organizational Behavior,* vol. 5 (Greenwich, Conn.: JAI Press, 1983), pp. 1–32. See also Arnon E. Reichers, "An Interactionist Perspective on Newcomer Socialization Rates," *Academy of Management Review,* April 1987, pp. 278–287.

FIGURE 1.6
The Interactional View of Behavior

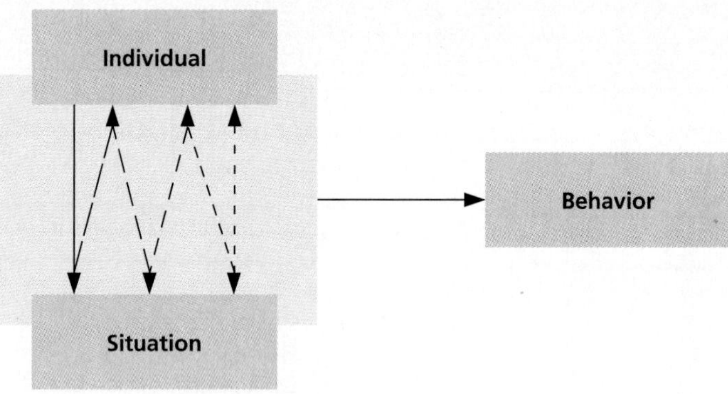

Popular-Press Perspectives

Finally, the popular press also has provided numerous new insights into the field of organizational behavior. Popular books such as *Theory Z, In Search of Excellence,* and *Corporate Cultures* all spent time on the *New York Times* best-seller list. Biographies of successful and less than successful executives like Lee Iacocca and Donald Trump also received widespread attention. These books highlight the management practices—many of them directly linked with concepts from organizational behavior—of successful firms like Kodak, IBM, and others.

Of course, much of what these authors had to say was based on anecdotal evidence subject to different interpretations. Nevertheless, they have helped focus popular attention on many of the important issues and problems confronting business today. As a result, managers entering the 1990s better appreciate both their problems and their prospects in working toward more effective organizational practices in the years to come.

Summary of Key Points

- Organizational behavior (OB) is the study of human behavior in organizational settings, the interface between human behavior and the organization, and the organization itself.
- Serious interest in the study of management first developed around the beginning of this century. Two of the earliest approaches were scientific management (best represented by the work of Taylor) and classical organization theory (exemplified by the work of Weber).
- Organizational behavior began to emerge as a scientific discipline as a result of the Hawthorne studies. McGregor and Maslow led the human relations movement that grew from those studies.
- Contemporary organizational behavior attempts to describe, rather than prescribe, behavioral forces in organizations. Ties to psychology, sociology,

anthropology, political science, economics, engineering, and medicine give organizational behavior an interdisciplinary focus.

- Basic concepts of the field are divided into five categories: individual processes, interpersonal processes, enhancing individual and interpersonal processes, organizational processes and characteristics, and integrating individuals, groups, and organizations. Those categories form the framework for the organization of this book. The study of organizational behavior is important because of the powerful influences organizations exert over our lives.
- Three important emerging perspectives on the field of organizational behavior are the systems view, the contingency perspective, and the interactional view. The popular press also has helped shape organizational behavior into the 1990s.

Discussion Questions

1. Some people have suggested that understanding human behavior is the single most important ingredient for organizational success. Do you agree or disagree with this statement? Why?
2. Is organizational behavior comparable to functional areas such as finance, marketing, and production? Why or why not? Is it similar to statistics in any way?
3. Identify some managerial jobs that are highly affected by human behavior and others that are less so. Which would you prefer? Why?
4. Besides those cited in the text, what reasons can you think of for the importance of organizational behavior?
5. Suppose you have to hire a new manager. One candidate has outstanding technical skills but poor interpersonal skills. The other has exactly the opposite mix of skills. Which would you hire? Why?
6. Some people believe that individuals working in an organization have a basic human right to satisfaction with their work and to the opportunity to grow and develop. How would you defend this position? How would you argue against it?
7. Many universities offer a course in industrial or organizational psychology. The content of those courses is quite similar to this one. Do you think that behavioral material is best taught in a business or psychology program, or is it best to teach it in both?
8. Do you believe the field of organizational behavior has the potential to become prescriptive as opposed to descriptive? Why or why not?
9. Are the notions of systems, contingency, and interactionalism independent of one another? If not, describe ways in which they are related.
10. Get a recent issue of a popular business magazine like *Business Week* or *Fortune* and scan its major articles. Do any of them reflect concepts from organizational behavior? Describe.

11. Interview a local manager or business owner. Ask if he or she has any "universal principles" on which they rely.

CASE 1.1

Herman Miller, Inc. Believes People Are Key to Success

Herman Miller, Inc. is a very unusual corporation in many respects. For one thing, it is named after a man who never worked for the company. In the mid-1920s, young D. J. De Pree borrowed some money from his father-in-law, Herman Miller, to buy Star Furniture Company. To show his gratitude, De Pree renamed the company after his benefactor.

In his early days as a manager and owner, De Pree ran his business pretty much like everyone else did at that time. For example, he viewed his workers as faceless and nameless robots; each was expendable and could easily be replaced with another.

One day in the mid-1930s, one of De Pree's employees, a millwright, died unexpectedly while on the job. The millwright was only 42 years old. Because the death had occurred on the job, De Pree felt obligated to call on the millwright's widow. During his visit, she asked to read him some poetry. He was struck by its beauty and grace and asked for the poet's name. De Pree was shocked to discover that the deceased millwright had written the poems himself.

This event had a significant effect on De Pree. He realized for the first time that his employees were not workhorses but real people with emotions, sensitivity, and talents. He decided on the spot that he needed to change his whole philosophy and approach to management. Specifically, he vowed to acknowledge each of his employee's human dignity, potential, and talent. He also proclaimed that management is not a special class of people in an organization; rather, it is a vital function to which everyone must contribute.

As a result, Herman Miller became one of the first companies in the world to provide profit sharing for its employees and use employee incentive programs. It promoted employee participation before it was faddish to do so. And the firm has worked hard to maintain open channels of communication throughout the organization.

The elder De Pree passed the mantle of leadership first to his older son, Hugh, and then to his younger son, Max. Each has maintained and even enhanced Herman Miller's commitment to and appreciation for its employees. In the early 1960s, the firm sold several of its less profitable furniture lines to concentrate on the market for business and office furniture. Today Herman Miller is the number two company in its industry (behind Steelcase).

But regardless of how big Herman Miller gets, people will always be at the heart of the business. For example, new employees are hired based more on their character and ability to work with others than on their technical skills and experience. The head of the firm's human resources function carries the title "Vice President for People."

Herman Miller is not a democracy, however. Everyone gets a voice in how things are done, but managers retain the final say-so in most areas. However, managers are able to walk the fine line between authoritativeness and autocracy:

They can be open and encourage participation but can also make the tough decisions when necessary.

For example, a line worker recently walked into De Pree's office and claimed that two production managers had been unjustly fired. De Pree listened to her story and then went to investigate. He concluded that indeed an injustice had been committed. He not only offered the production managers their jobs back; he also asked for the resignation of the executive who had fired them.

Because much of its business is tied to the computer industry, Herman Miller went through a sales slump in the 1980s when the computer business bottomed out. But employees never lost their allegiance to the firm. And management responded by maintaining the culture that embraced human values and potential. Coming out of the slump in the early 1990s, Herman Miller looks stronger than ever.

Case Questions

1. How does an understanding of history help managers at Herman Miller today?
2. Why don't more firms use the philosophy and methods that have worked so well for Herman Miller?
3. Can a firm go too far in trying to tap the human potential of its employees?

SOURCES: Brian Dumaine, "Creating a New Company Culture," *Fortune,* January 15, 1990, pp. 127–131; Kenneth Labich, "Hot Company, Warm Culture," *Fortune,* February 27, 1989, pp. 74–78; "A Comeback in Cubicles," *Forbes,* March 21, 1988, pp. 55–56; Beverly Geber, "Herman Miller—Where Profits and Participation Meet," *Training,* November 1987, pp. 62–66.

CASE 1.2 Difficult Transitions

Tony Stark just finished his first week at Reece Enterprises and decided to drive upstate to a small lakefront lodge for some fishing and relaxation. Tony had worked for the past ten years for the O'Grady Company. O'Grady had suffered through some hard times of late, however, and recently shut down several of its operating groups, including Tony's, to cut costs. Fortunately, Tony's experience and recommendations had made finding another position fairly easy. As he drove the interstate, he reflected on the past ten years and the apparent situation at Reece.

At O'Grady, things had been great. Tony had been part of the team from day one. The job had met his personal goals and expectations perfectly, and Tony believed he had grown greatly as a person. His work was appreciated and recognized; he had received three promotions and many more pay increases.

Tony had also liked the company itself. The firm was decentralized, allowing its managers considerable autonomy and freedom. The corporate culture was easygoing. Communication was open. It seemed that everyone knew what was going on at all times, and if you didn't know about something, it was easy to find out.

The people had been another plus. Tony and three other managers went to lunch often and played golf every Saturday. They got along well both personally and professionally and truly worked together as a team. Their boss had been very supportive, giving them the help they needed but also staying out of the way and letting them work.

When word about the shutdown came down, Tony was devastated. He was sure that nothing could replace O'Grady. After the final closing was announced, he spent only a few weeks looking around before he found a comparable position at Reece Enterprises.

As Tony drove, he reflected that *comparable* probably was the wrong word. Indeed, Reece and O'Grady were about as different as you could get. Top managers at Reece apparently didn't worry too much about who did a good job and who didn't. They seemed to promote and reward people based on how long they had been there and how well they played the never-ending political games.

Maybe this stemmed from the organization itself, Tony pondered. Reece was a bigger organization than O'Grady and was structured much more bureaucratically. It seemed that no one was allowed to make any sort of decision without getting three signatures from higher up. Those signatures, though, were hard to get. All the top managers usually were too busy to see anyone, and interoffice memos apparently had very low priority.

Tony also had had some problems fitting in. His peers treated him with polite indifference. He sensed that a couple of them resented that he, an outsider, had been brought right in at their level after they had had to work themselves up the ladder. On Tuesday he had asked two colleagues about playing golf. They had politely declined, saying that they did not play often. But later in the week, he had overheard them making arrangements to play that very Saturday.

That was when Tony decided to go fishing. As he steered his car off the interstate to get gas, he wondered if perhaps he had made a mistake in accepting the Reece offer without finding out more about what he was getting into.

Case Questions

1. Identify several concepts and characteristics from the field of organizational behavior this case illustrates.
2. What advice can you give Tony? How is this advice supported or tempered by behavioral concepts and processes?
3. Is it possible to find an "ideal" place to work? Explain.

EXPERIENTIAL EXERCISE

Purpose: This exercise will help you develop an appreciation for the importance and pervasiveness of organizational behavior concepts and processes in both contemporary organizational settings and popular culture.

Format: Your instructor will divide the class into groups of from three to five members. Each group will be assigned a specific television program to watch before the next class meeting.

Procedure: Arrange to watch the program as a group. Each person should have a pad of paper and a pencil handy. As you watch the show, jot down examples of individual behavior, interpersonal dynamics, organizational characteristics, and other concepts and processes relevant to organizational behavior. After the show, spend a few minutes comparing notes. Compile one list for the entire group. (It is advisable to turn off the television set during this discussion!)

During the next class meeting, have someone in the group summarize the plot of the show and list the concepts it illustrated. The following television shows are especially good for illustrating behavioral concepts in organizational settings:

Network Shows	*Syndicated Shows*
Cheers	M*A*S*H
L.A. Law	Barney Miller
The Simpsons	WKRP in Cincinnati
Dear John	Star Trek
Roseanne	Taxi
Night Court	Trapper John, M.D.

Follow-up Questions

1. What does this exercise illustrate about the pervasiveness of organizations in our contemporary society?
2. What recent and/or classic movies might provide similar kinds of examples?
3. Do you think non-U.S. television would provide more or fewer examples set in organizations?

CHAPTER OUTLINE

- A Managerial Perspective on Organizational Behavior
- The Manager's Job
  - *Managerial Functions*
  - *Managerial Roles*
  - *The Human Context of Management*
- Managerial Challenges
  - *Work Force Demographics*
  - *Workplace Issues and Challenges*
- Organizational Challenges
  - *Enhancing Productivity*
  - *Improving Quality*
  - *Managing Technology*
  - *Monitoring Ethics and Social Responsibility*
- Global Challenges
  - *Managing in a Global Environment*
  - *Managing Cultural Diversity*
- Managing for Effectiveness
  - *Individual-Level Outcomes*
  - *Group-Level Outcomes*
  - *Organization-Level Outcomes*

2

Managing People and Organizations

Chapter Objectives

After studying this chapter, you should be able to:

Develop a managerial perspective on organizational behavior.

Describe the manager's job and relate it to organizational behavior.

Identify major managerial challenges and relate them to organizational behavior.

Identify major organizational challenges and relate them to organizational behavior.

Identify major global challenges and relate them to organizational behavior.

Discuss how to manage for effectiveness from the perspective of organizational behavior.

Robert Lutz is Chrysler Corp.'s top operations executive. He is the individual who is ultimately responsible for ensuring that the firm manufactures ten thousand cars and trucks every day. Even though his business is cars, however, he spends most of his time working with people. Here is how Lutz spends a "typical" day.

He starts at 8:04 A.M. in a meeting with engineers, designers, and parts specialists to discuss a new Chrysler model, the Viper. Two hours later, when the meeting breaks up, he rushes to another Chrysler facility for a meeting with Tom Gale, the firm's vice president responsible for design.

After this meeting ends, Lutz drives to Chrysler's headquarters building for a lunch meeting with the heads of various Chrysler divisions. Following lunch, he heads to his office for a meeting with executives from the firm's international division. This meeting runs a little long, so Lutz is late for his next meeting with the project review committee.

When the project review committee meeting breaks up at 4:30, Lutz remains for a private meeting with one member of the committee. When he returns to his own office at 5:00, there is another manager waiting to see him. Finally, at 5:25 P.M., this meeting ends and Lutz turns to the mound of paperwork on his desk.[1]

While there is really no such thing as a truly "typical" day in the life of a top manager, there is one common thread that permeates virtually all managerial activity: interacting with other people. Indeed, the "typical" day for Robert Lutz at Chrysler is almost entirely devoted to interacting with others. Thus, the management process and the behavior of people in organizations are undeniably intertwined.

This chapter relates the general field of management to the more specific area of organizational behavior. We start by developing a managerial perspective on organizational behavior. Then we characterize the manager's job. Next, we identify and discuss managerial, organizational, and global challenges and relate them to organizational behavior. Finally, we discuss how to manage for effectiveness in the context of organizational behavior.

---

1. Erik Calonius, "How Top Managers Manage Their Time," *Fortune,* June 4, 1990, pp. 250–262; Alex Taylor III, "How a Top Boss Manages His Day," *Fortune,* June 19, 1989, pp. 95–100; "Day in the Life of Tomorrow's Manager," *The Wall Street Journal,* March 20, 1989, p. B1; Ford S. Worthy, "How CEOs Manage Their Time," *Fortune,* January 18, 1988, pp. 88–97.

A Managerial Perspective on Organizational Behavior

- Organizational behavior is not an organizational function or area; rather, it is a perspective that all managers can use to perform their jobs more effectively.
- Managers can use organizational behavior to better understand themselves, their subordinates, their peers and colleagues, and their superiors.

Virtually all organizations have managers with titles like *marketing manager, vice president for human resources, plant manager,* and so forth. But probably no organization has a position called *organizational behavior manager.* The reason for this is simple: Organizational behavior is not an organizational function or area. Instead, it is best described of as a perspective or set of tools that all managers can use to carry out their jobs more effectively.[2]

By understanding organizational behavior concepts, managers can better understand and appreciate the behavior of those around them. For example, managers in an organization are directly responsible for the behaviors of a set of other people—their immediate subordinates, for example. Typical managerial activities in this regard include motivating employees to work harder, ensuring that their jobs are properly designed, dealing with various differences among them, resolving conflicts, evaluating their performance, helping them set goals to achieve rewards, and so forth. The field of organizational behavior abounds with theory and research regarding each of these functions.[3]

Unless they happen to be CEOs, managers also report to others in the organization (and even the CEO reports to the board of directors). In dealing with these individuals, understanding basic issues associated with leadership, power and political behavior, decision making, organization structure and design, and organization culture can also be extremely beneficial. Again, the field of organizational behavior provides many valuable insights into these processes.

Managers can also use their knowledge from the field of organizational behavior with regard to their own behaviors and feelings. For example, understanding one's own needs and motives, how individuals can improve their decision-making capabilities, how individuals respond to and control stress, how one can better communicate with others, and how career dynamics unfold can all be of enormous benefit to individual managers. Organizational behavior once again provides many useful insights into these concepts and processes.

Managers must also interact with a variety of colleagues and peers inside the organization. An understanding of attitudinal processes, group dynamics, intergroup dynamics, organization culture, and political behavior can help managers handle such interactions more effectively. Many useful ideas from the field of organizational behavior have provided greater insight into these processes.

Finally, managers also interact with various individuals from outside the organization, including suppliers, customers, competitors, government officials, representatives of citizens' groups, union officials, and potential partners. Virtually all of the behavioral processes already noted can be relevant. In addition, special understanding of the environment, technology, and, increasingly, inter-

2. Rosabeth Moss Kanter, "The New Managerial Work," *Harvard Business Review,* November-December 1989, pp. 85–92.
3. See Frank Rose, "A New Age for Business?", *Fortune,* October 8, 1990, pp. 156–164.

national issues is also of value. Here again, the field of organizational behavior offers managers an abundance of insight into how and why things happen.

Thus, management and organizational behavior are interrelated in many ways. It is essentially impossible to understand and practice management without considering the numerous areas from the field of organizational behavior. And organizational behavior itself can provide a useful set of tools and perspectives for managing more effectively. We now turn to the nature of the manager's job in more detail.

The Manager's Job

There are many different ways to conceptualize the job of a manager. The most common approaches are in terms of managerial functions and managerial roles.

Managerial Functions

- The manager's job involves four basic functions: planning, organizing, leading, and controlling.

As Figure 2.1 shows, the four basic managerial functions are planning, organizing, leading, and controlling. By applying these functions to the various organizational resources—human, financial, physical, and information—the organization achieves different levels of effectiveness and efficiency.

FIGURE 2.1
Basic Managerial Functions

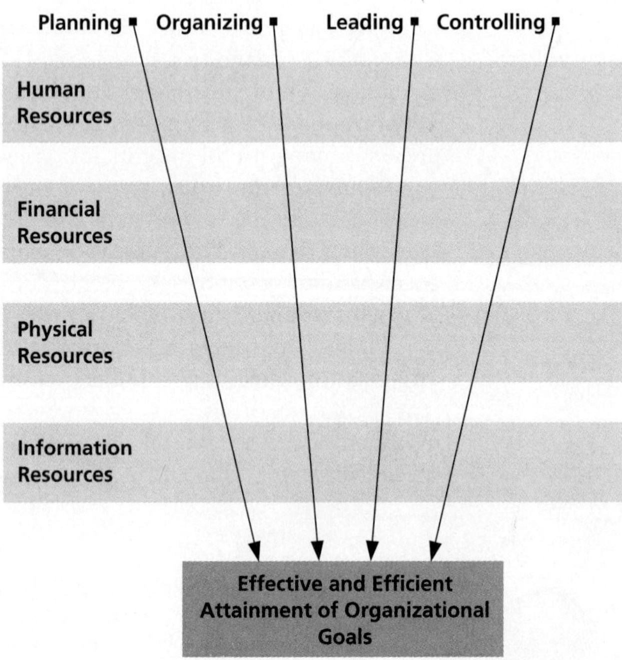

■ **Planning** is the process of determining the organization's desired future position and the best means to get there.

Planning **Planning,** the first managerial function, is the process of determining the organization's desired future position and deciding how best to get there. The planning process at Sears, Roebuck, for example, includes scanning the environment, deciding on appropriate goals, outlining strategies for achieving those goals, and developing tactics to assist in executing the strategies. Behavioral processes and characteristics pervade each of these activities. Perception, for instance, plays a major role in environmental scanning, and creativity and motivation influence how managers set goals, strategies, and tactics.

■ **Organizing** is the process of designing jobs, grouping jobs into units, and establishing patterns of authority between jobs and units.

Organizing The second managerial function is **organizing**—the process of designing jobs, grouping jobs into manageable units, and establishing patterns of authority among jobs and groups of jobs. This process designs the basic structure of the organization. For large organizations like Sears, that structure can be extensive and complicated. As noted earlier, the processes and characteristics of the organization itself are a major theme of organizational behavior.

■ **Leading** is the process of getting the organization's members to work together toward the organization's goals.

Leading **Leading,** the third managerial function, is the process of getting members of the organization to work together toward the organization's goals. A Sears manager, for example, must hire and motivate people, train them, and so forth. Major components of leading include motivating employees, managing group dynamics, and leadership per se, all of which are closely related to major areas of organizational behavior.

■ **Controlling** is the process of monitoring and correcting the actions of the organization and its members to keep them directed toward their goals.

Controlling The fourth managerial function, **controlling,** is the process of monitoring and correcting the actions of the organization and its people to keep them headed toward their goals. A Sears manager has to control costs, inventory, and so on. Again, behavioral processes and characteristics are a key part of this function. Performance evaluation, reward systems, and motivation, for example, all apply to control.

Managerial Roles

■ Managers play ten basic roles in their jobs.

In an organization, as in a play or a movie, a *role* is the part a person plays in a given situation. Managers play a number of different roles. Much of our knowledge about managerial roles comes from the work of Henry Mintzberg.[4] Mintzberg identified ten basic managerial roles in three general categories; these are listed in Table 2.1.

■ Three important interpersonal roles are the **figurehead,** the **leader,** and the **liaison.**

Interpersonal Roles Mintzberg's *interpersonal roles* are primarily social in nature; that is, they are roles in which the manager's main task is to relate to other people in certain ways. The manager sometimes may serve as a **figurehead** for

4. Henry Mintzberg, "The Manager's Job: Folklore and Fact," *Harvard Business Review,* July-August 1975, pp. 49–61.

TABLE 2.1
Important Managerial Roles

Category	Role	Example
Interpersonal	Figurehead	Attend employee retirement ceremony
	Leader	Encourage workers to increase productivity
	Liaison	Coordinate activities of two committees
Informational	Monitor	Scan *Business Week* for information about competition
	Disseminator	Send out memos outlining new policies
	Spokesperson	Hold press conference to announce new plant
Decision-making	Entrepreneur	Develop idea for new product and convince others of its merits
	Disturbance Handler	Resolve dispute
	Resource Allocator	Allocate budget requests
	Negotiator	Settle new labor contract

the organization. Taking visitors to dinner and attending ribbon-cutting ceremonies are part of the figurehead role. In the role of **leader,** the manager works to hire, train, and motivate employees. Finally, the **liaison** role consists of relating to others outside the group or organization. For example, a manager at Intel might be responsible for handling all price negotiations with a key supplier of electronic circuit boards. Obviously, each of these interpersonal roles involves behavioral processes.

- Three key informational roles are the **monitor,** the **disseminator,** and the **spokesperson.**

Informational Roles Mintzberg's three *informational roles* involve some aspect of information processing. The **monitor** actively seeks information that might be of value to the organization in general or to specific managers. The manager who transmits this information to others is carrying out the role of **disseminator.** The **spokesperson** speaks for the organization to outsiders. For example, the manager chosen by Pillsbury to appear at a press conference announcing a merger or other major deal, such as the recent decision to sell its Godfather's Pizza chain, would be serving in this role. Again, behavioral processes are part of each of these roles, because information is almost always exchanged between people.

- Four basic decision-making roles are the **entrepreneur,** the **disturbance handler,** the **resource allocator,** and the negotiator.

Decision-Making Roles Finally, Mintzberg identified four *decision-making roles.* The **entrepreneur** voluntarily initiates change, such as innovations or new strategies, in the organization. The **disturbance handler** helps settle disputes between various parties, such as other managers and their subordinates. The **resource allocator** decides who will get what—how resources in the organization will be

A LOOK AT THE
RESEARCH

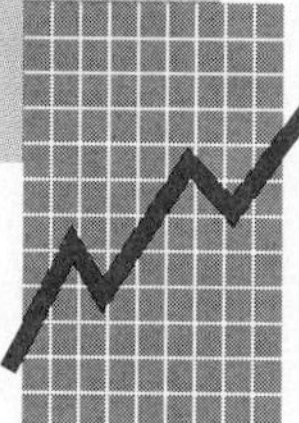

What Do Managers Do?

What do managers do? This apparently simple question actually is quite difficult to answer. No two managers do the same thing. Further, no single manager ever does exactly the same thing two days in a row. There are, however, a few things we do know about managerial work. A starting point in any discussion of managerial work is the research of Henry Mintzberg.

Mintzberg studied a group of CEOs in the mid-1970s. He closely observed their day-to-day activities and learned a good deal about the nature of their jobs. He found, for example, that the CEOs spent an average of 59 percent of their time in scheduled meetings, 22 percent at their desks, 10 percent in unscheduled meetings, 6 percent on the telephone, and 3 percent walking around the company.

Overall, their work was characterized by many different activities, frequent interruptions, and a frantic pace. Breaks were few and far between, and the workweek grew longer and longer. As you can see, much of their work was interacting with other people. The only activity just noted that does not directly involve interaction with others is desk time, and much of that work involves reading or writing correspondence. Clearly, then, managers need to have a keen understanding of human behavior.

Managers interact with subordinates, superiors, and peers. Thus, they must be able to relate well to others in a variety of settings and contexts. By understanding the behavioral processes and interactions that permeate their jobs, managers can perform more effectively.

SOURCES: Henry Mintzberg, "The Manager's Job: Folklore and Fact," *Harvard Business Review,* July-August 1975, pp. 49–61. Excerpt from *The Nature of Managerial Work* by Henry Mintzberg. Copyright © 1973 by Henry Mintzberg. Reprinted by permission of HarperCollins Publishers.

distributed among various individuals and groups. The **negotiator** represents the organization in reaching agreements with other organizations, such as contracts between management and labor unions. Again, behavioral processes clearly are crucial in each of these decisional roles.[5]

Mintzberg's research also provided much insight into how managers allocate their time in performing these roles, especially senior managers at the top of an organization. *A Look at the Research* summarizes his findings.

The Human Context of Management

In addition to understanding the ongoing behavioral processes inherent in their own jobs, managers must understand the basic human element of their work. Organizational behavior offers three major perspectives for understanding this context: people as organizations, people as resources, and people as people.

Above all, organizations are people, and without people there would be no organizations. Consider a neighborhood grocery store owned and operated by a

5. See also William Whitely, "Managerial Work Behavior: An Integration of Results from Two Major Approaches," *Academy of Management Journal,* June 1985, pp. 344–362.

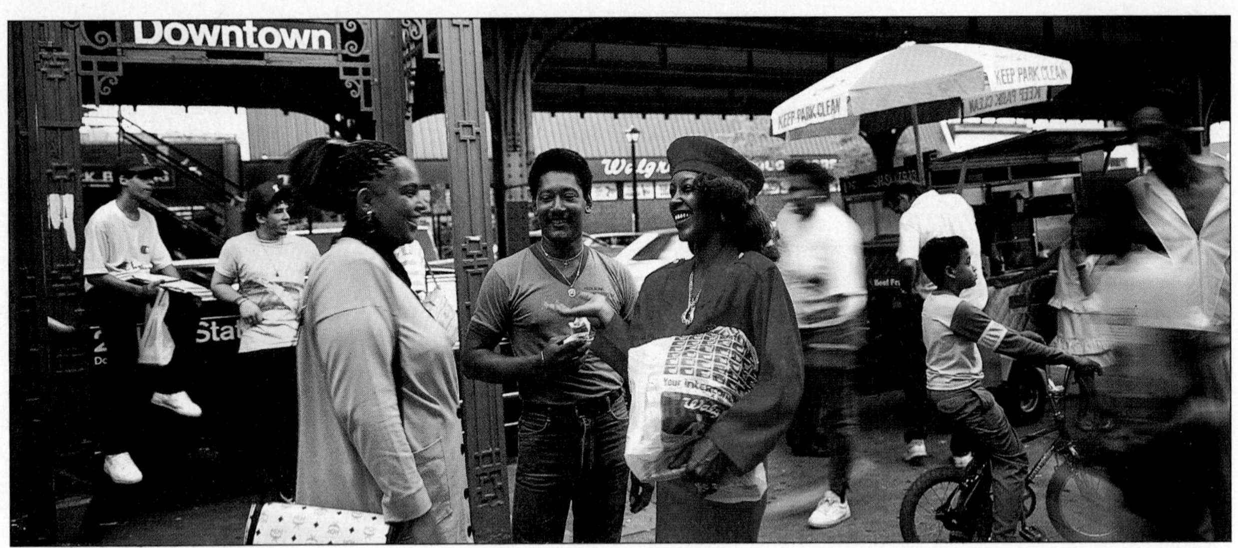

This Bronx neighborhood is made up of people who are extremely diverse, from older residents who have lived there all their lives to newer arrivals speaking a variety of languages. To operate successfully, the Walgreens store here must adapt to this environment of people, fitting the rhythms and needs of its employees and customers.

husband-and-wife team; Exxon, one of the world's largest industrial corporations; the Smithsonian Institution in Washington, D.C.; a neighborhood street gang; the Mayo Clinic, one of this country's finest health care facilities; and your college or university. All of these are organizations, and although they differ dramatically in size, purpose, and structure, they have one thing in common: people. Thus, if managers are to understand the organizations in which they work, they must first understand the people who make up the organizations.

As resources, people are one of an organization's most valuable assets. People create the organization, guide and direct its course, and vitalize and revitalize it. People make its decisions, solve its problems, and answer its questions. In recent years, many Americans have been alarmed about the slowdown in productivity growth in the United States relative to that of other industrial countries, including Japan, West Germany, and France. People are at the core of many of the possible contributors to this trend. To reverse declining productivity, many organizations have taken steps to boost the contribution from their human resources. Some companies have encouraged management and labor to cooperate better; others have increased employee participation in decision making and problem solving. At Westinghouse, for example, groups of employees meet regularly to study major problems faced by the company and to recommend solutions. As managers increasingly recognize the value of potential contributions by their employees, it will become more and more important for managers and employees to grasp the complexities of organizational behavior.

Finally, there is people as people, an argument derived from the simple notion of humanistic management. People spend a large part of their lives in organizational settings, mostly as employees. They have a right to expect something in return beyond wages and employee benefits. Employees seek satisfaction, and many want the opportunity to grow and develop and to learn new skills. An understanding of organizational behavior can help managers better appreciate these needs and expectations.

Of course, human life in organizations can have a negative side. People who are unhappy with their jobs are more likely to be absent frequently and to look for work elsewhere than people who are happy. In recent years increasing attention has been given to the causes and consequences of employee stress at work. Knowledge of organizational behavior can help managers recognize the problems of the workplace and improve the quality of individuals' work experiences.

Managerial Challenges

Beyond its inherent pervasiveness in managerial work, organizational behavior has several implications for various managerial, organizational, and global challenges. From the managerial perspective, any number of critical issues might be discussed, but we will focus on two in particular: work force demographics and workplace issues and challenges.

Work Force Demographics

■ Work force demographic variables such as age, gender, and ethnic composition are all changing.

From a wide variety of perspectives, work force demographics are changing. These changes, in turn, are associated with age, gender, and ethnic composition. Figure 2.2 presents some changing work force demographics.

FIGURE 2.2
Changing Demographics in the American Work Force

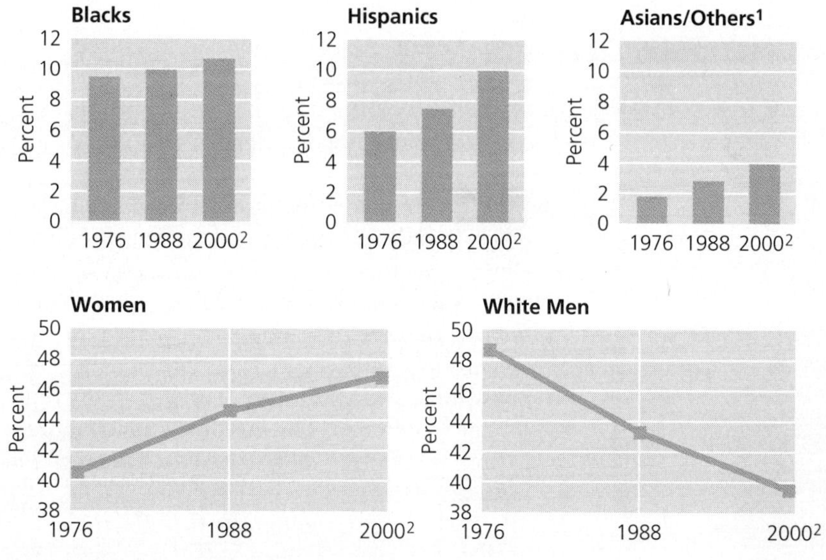

1. Including Native Americans, Alaskan natives, and Pacific Islanders
2. Projected

SOURCE: *The Wall Street Journal,* September 12, 1990, p. B1. Reprinted by permission of *THE WALL STREET JOURNAL,* © 1990 Dow Jones & Company, Inc. All Rights Reserved Worldwide.

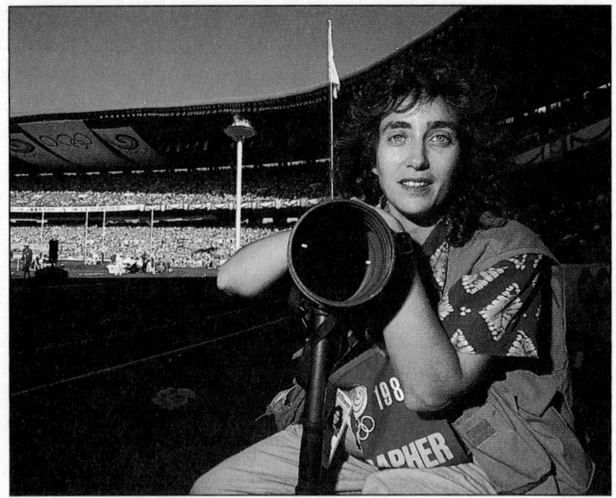

Pauline Lubens, a photographer for the Detroit Free Press, worked at the 1988 Olympic Games in Seoul. As a woman in a field long dominated by men, she is part of a trend of changing demographics. Her newspaper, its parent company Knight-Ridder, and the sports teams she covers have learned to accept her on the basis of her qualifications as a professional.

Age The average age of the American worker is gradually increasing. This is partly because of declining birthrates and partly because people are living and working longer. How is this relevant to managers? For one thing, workers of different ages may want quite different things from their work. Older workers may be more interested in job security and personal growth and development, for instance, whereas younger workers may be more concerned with pay, promotion opportunities, and/or leisure time.[6]

Many organizations are finding retirees to be excellent part-time and/or temporary employees. McDonald's has hired hundreds of elderly workers in recent years. Apple Computer has used many retired workers for temporary assignments and projects. By hiring retirees, the organization gets the expertise of skilled workers and the individuals get extra income and an opportunity to continue to use their skills in a productive way.

Gender An increasing number of women have entered the American work force. In 1950, only 34 percent of American women worked outside their homes; today almost two-thirds work part time or full time outside the home. Many occupations traditionally dominated by women—nurses, teachers, secretaries, and so forth—continue to be popular provinces for females. But women have also moved increasingly into occupations previously dominated by males, such as lawyers, physicians, and executives. Further, many blue-collar jobs are being increasingly sought by women. On the other hand, more and more men are entering occupations previously dominated by women. For example, there are more male secretaries today than ever before.

Such diversity enhances the effectiveness of most organizations, but it also provides special challenges for managers. For example, an executive walking into an unfamiliar office and seeing a male and female conversing can no longer

6. Alan Deutschman, "What 25-Year-Olds Want," *Fortune,* August 27, 1990, pp. 42–50.

assume that the female is the secretary and the male is her boss. Women with little experience supervising others are having to adjust to new supervisory roles. Men who always reported to other men are having to adapt to new working relationships as well.

Ethnic Composition The ethnic composition of the workplace also is changing. One obvious change has been the increasing number of blacks and Hispanics entering the workplace. Further, many of these individuals now hold executive positions. In addition, there has been a dramatic influx of immigrant workers in the last few years. Refugees from Central America and Southeast Asia have entered the American work force in record numbers. These workers, in turn, have posed special problems for the organizations that have hired them. Vast differences in work ethics and values, work norms, and so forth have had to be addressed repeatedly.

Workplace Issues and Challenges

■ Employee privacy, employee rights, and unionization trends are important workplace challenges.

Another set of workplace issues and challenges has behavioral overtones. Three special areas are employee privacy, employee rights, and unionization trends.

Employee Privacy Employee privacy has become a significant issue in many organizations in recent years. For example, some organizations have started to implement random drug tests. Background checks on prospective employees have become more comprehensive. And some firms have implemented extraordinary performance assessment devices, including random checks of telephone calls and frequency counts of keyboard strokes for word processing operators. Some people, however, believe that these and related activities are too intrusive and encroach too much into private lives. Thus, a manager in an organization that is following this trend needs to be sensitive to the resentment these practices may create.[7]

Employee Rights A related concern is employee rights. This issue actually spans a wide range of controversies. For example, issues have surfaced regarding the individual's right to smoke in the workplace. As more and more organizations limit or ban smoking, this issue will continue to be somewhat controversial. Broader controversies involve issues associated with job ownership and individual rights while at work. A popular (albeit not entirely correct) assumption about Japanese organizations is that their employees have lifetime job security. To the extent that U.S. firms adopt this practice, the question becomes one of due process and the right to appeal in instances of dismissal or reassignment.

Unionization Trends A final managerial challenge is the general trend regarding union membership. For the past several years, union membership in the United States has steadily declined. While most managers are likely to applaud this

---

7. "Is Your Boss Spying on You?", *Business Week,* January 5, 1990, pp. 74–75.

trend, organizations will carry the added burden of providing services to their employees that unions previously supplied. A strong balance between organizations and unions tends to free each from charges of exploitation. Without union representation, however, organizations will need to take extra precautions to ensure that workers are treated fairly. If not, union membership may well start to climb again. At the same time, unionism is emerging in unusual areas, ranging from professional to technical to white-collar fields.[8]

Organizational Challenges

- Important organizational challenges for managers include enhancing productivity, improving quality, managing technology, and monitoring ethics and social responsibility.

Managers also face numerous challenges at an organizational level. The four issues most relevant to the domain of organizational behavior concern productivity, quality, technology, and ethics/social responsibility.

Enhancing Productivity

- **Productivity** is an indicator of how much an organization is creating relative to its inputs.

Productivity became a major issue for many organizations during the 1980s. In a general sense, **productivity** is an indicator of how much an organization is creating relative to its inputs. For example, if Honda can produce a car for $6,000 while General Motors needs $8,000 to produce a comparable car, Honda is clearly more productive.[9]

Productivity is important for a variety of reasons. For one thing, it clearly affects an organization's ability to compete effectively. For another, it shapes the overall economic prosperity of the organization's host country. In other words, productively created goods and services not only contribute to the home country's economic health but allow organizations to generate more revenues in the global economy.

While U.S. workers are the most productive in the world, productivity in other industrial countries, especially Japan and Germany, has grown much more rapidly than it has in the United States for the past several years. Figure 2.3 shows productivity trends in recent years. As you can see, the productivity advantage long enjoyed by U.S. firms is rapidly being eroded.

To counter this trend, experts have suggested numerous techniques and strategies. Many of these center around increased cooperation and participation on the part of workers. Ultimately, then, managers and workers will need to work in greater harmony and unity of purpose. The implications for organizational behavior are obvious: The more closely people will work together, the more important it will be to understand behavioral processes and concepts.

---

8. "Unions May Be Poised to End Long Decline, Recover Some Clout," *The Wall Street Journal,* August 28, 1987, pp. 1, 7.

9. John W. Kendrick, *Understanding Productivity: An Introduction to the Dynamics of Productivity Change* (Baltimore: Johns Hopkins, 1977).

FIGURE 2.3
Productivity Trends

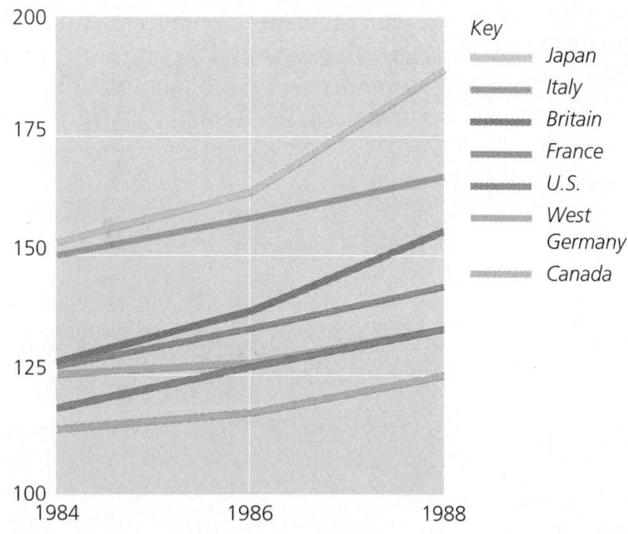

Change in hourly output in manufacturing index: 1977 = 100

SOURCE: Brian O'Reilly, "America's Place in World Competition," *Fortune,* November 6, 1989, p. 84.

Improving Quality

■ **Quality** is the total set of features and characteristics of a product or service that determine its ability to satisfy stated or implied needs.

A related organizational challenge that has attracted much attention is quality. **Quality** is the total set of features and characteristics of a product or service that define its ability to satisfy stated or implied needs.[10] For years, U.S. managers believed that productivity and quality are inversely related: Increasing quality will lower productivity. Learning from the Japanese, however, we have come to realize that improving quality actually *boosts* productivity.

Quality is an important issue for several reasons. First, more and more organizations are using quality as a basis for competition. Ford, Chrysler, and Buick have launched major promotional campaigns in recent years stressing their products' improved quality, especially relative to Japanese competitors such as Honda and Toyota. Second, improving quality tends to increase productivity because making higher-quality products generally results in less waste and rework. Third, enhancing quality lowers costs. Whistler Corporation recently found that it was using 100 of its 250 employees to repair defective radar detectors that were built incorrectly the first time.[11]

As with productivity, many of the things organizations can do to enhance the quality of their products and services depend on the people who work for

10. Ross Johnson and William O. Winchell, *Management and Quality* (Milwaukee: American Society for Quality Control, 1989).

11. Joel Dreyfuss, "Victories in the Quality Crusade," *Fortune,* October 10, 1988, pp. 80–88.

them. Motivating employees to get involved in quality improvement efforts, increasing the level of participation throughout the organization, and rewarding people on the basis of contributions to quality are common suggestions—and all of them rely on human behavior.[12]

Managing Technology

A third significant organizational challenge confronting managers today is the set of issues involving the management of technology. *Technology,* explored more fully in Chapter 18, is the mechanical and intellectual processes the organization uses to transform inputs (raw materials, parts, cash, facilities, people) into products or services (computers, cars, pizza, stock transactions).[13] Historically, managing technology was essentially a reactive process. Whenever a supplier came up with a new piece of equipment to replace an old one, the organization bought it and trained its workers in how to use it.

In recent years, however, this pattern has changed. Computer-assisted manufacturing techniques, automation, and robotics have all transformed the workplace into a truly competitive arena. Firms that proactively manage their technology in creative and innovative ways gain significant competitive advantages over those that do not.

One reason for this trend is the newfound flexibility that recent technology has provided. For example, it used to be costly and time consuming to change an assembly from producing one product to producing another. Increasingly, however, organizations are learning to make such changes more routinely. And some automakers, like Ford, can actually produce different models of automobiles on the same line at the same time.

Again, however, the Japanese continue to set the pace in this area. For example, a division of Matsushita Electric Industrial Co. has developed technology to custom-make bicycles for individual customers. A customer goes into a retail store and is measured for size on a special frame, chooses colors and options, and so forth. Specifications are faxed to the plant, custom blueprints are prepared (by computer), and the bicycle is put into production. The firm can employ 11,231,862 variations on 18 models in 199 color patterns to accommodate any size person and deliver it in less than two weeks! (Actually, managers say they can do it in just a few days—the two-week delay is to heighten customer anticipation.)[14]

Computerized and automated technology like Matsushita's dramatically alters the relationship between people and the work they do. Thus, organizations need to be sensitive to these changes and work to ensure that those most directly affected by a new technology play a meaningful role in developing it.

---

12. See "King Customer," *Business Week,* March 12, 1990, pp. 88–94.

13. Paul D. Collins, Jerald Hage, and Frank M. Hull, "Organizational and Technological Predictors of Change in Automaticity," *Academy of Management Journal,* September 1988, pp. 512–543.

14. Susan Moffat, "Japan's New Personalized Production," *Fortune,* October 22, 1990, pp. 132–135.

Dow Chemical Company has a number of programs that promote social responsibility—a major challenge faced by all organizations. In King's Lynn, England, (shown here) and several other locations around the world the firm helps local residents safely dispose of their hazardous household waste by sponsoring community collection days.

Monitoring Ethics and Social Responsibility

■ Individual **ethics** are personal beliefs about what is right and wrong or good and bad. **Social responsibility** is the organization's obligation to protect and/or contribute to the social environment in which it functions.

A final organizational challenge that has taken on renewed importance relates to ethics and social responsibility. An individual's **ethics** are his or her beliefs about what is right and wrong or good and bad.[15] **Social responsibility** is the organization's obligation to protect and/or contribute to the social environment in which it functions. Thus, while the two concepts are related, they are also distinct from each other.

Both ethics and social responsibility have taken on new significance in recent years. Scandals in organizations ranging from Drexel Burnham Lambert Inc. (stock market fraud) to Beech-Nut (advertising baby apple juice as being 100 percent pure when it was really chemically extended) to the Japanese firm Recruit (bribery of government officials) have made headlines around the world. From the social responsibility angle, increasing attention has been focused on pollution and business's obligation to help clean up our environment, business contributions to social causes, and so forth.[16]

Leadership, organization culture, and group norms—all important organizational behavior concepts—are relevant in managing these processes. For example, a recent brokerage scandal at Dean Witter grew because individual brokers felt pressure from their colleagues to participate. The scandal at Beech-Nut was perpetuated because it had started at the very top of the organization. In contrast, during the Tylenol poisoning crisis in 1982, everyone at Johnson & Johnson knew exactly how to respond. Products were immediately recalled from drugstore shelves, advertising was stopped, and informational briefings were scheduled—all without executive direction. And all because employees knew the organizational culture so well that they knew how they would be expected to respond.[17]

15. Thomas M. Garrett and Richard J. Klonoski, *Business Ethics,* 2nd ed. (Englewood Cliffs, N.J.: Prentice-Hall, 1986).

16. Jerry W. Anderson, Jr., "Social Responsibility and the Corporation," *Business Horizons,* July-August 1986, pp. 22–27.

17. "At Johnson & Johnson, a Mistake Can Be a Badge of Honor," *Business Week,* September 26, 1988, pp. 126–128.

Global Challenges

Another set of important challenges facing managers today are more global in nature. Some of these issues relate to the global environment of business; others involve the challenges of managing cultural diversity.[18]

Managing in a Global Environment

■ Managers face a variety of global challenges brought about by the global nature of business and the need to manage cultural diversity.

It is no secret that the world economy is becoming increasingly global in character. But often people do not realize the true magnitude of this globalization trend or the complexities it creates for managers. Consider, for example, the impact of international business operations on our daily lives. We wake to the sound of Panasonic alarm clocks made in Japan. For breakfast we drink milk from Carnation—a subsidiary of Nestlé, a Swiss firm—and coffee ground from Colombian beans. We dress in clothes sewn in Taiwan and drive to work or school in a Japanese automobile. Along the way, we stop and buy gas imported from the Middle East by Shell, a Dutch company.

Of course, Americans are not alone in experiencing the effects of globalization. Indeed, people in other countries eat at McDonald's restaurants and snack on Mars candy bars and Coca-Cola soft drinks. They drive Fords, use IBM computers, and wear Levi jeans. They use Kodak film and fly on Boeing airplanes.

The globalization trend started in the immediate post–World War II years. The U.S. economy emerged strong and intact. U.S. businesses were the dominant worldwide suppliers in virtually all major industries. But war-torn Europe and the Far East rebuilt. Businesses there were forced to build new plants and other facilities, and their citizens turned to their work as a viable source of economic security. As a result, these economies grew in strength and each developed competitive advantages. And today those advantages are being exploited to their fullest.

The situation is further confounded by the rapid change that has characterized the international arena. When the 1980s began, the Eastern bloc countries (including East Germany) were going nowhere economically, the Japanese and German economies were dominant, many observers were writing off the United States, and countries like South Korea and Taiwan played only minor roles. As the 1990s began, however, much of the Eastern bloc had embraced capitalism and opened their markets, Japan was slowing down, the United States was coming back, Germany had unified, and South Korea and Taiwan had become powerhouses.

Managing in a global economy poses many different challenges and opportunities. For example, at a macro level, property ownership arrangements vary widely. So does the availability of natural resources and components of the infrastructure, as well as the role of government in business. But for our purposes,

18. See Arvind Phatak, *International Dimensions of Management*, 2nd ed. (Boston: Kent, 1989).

INTERNATIONAL PERSPECTIVE

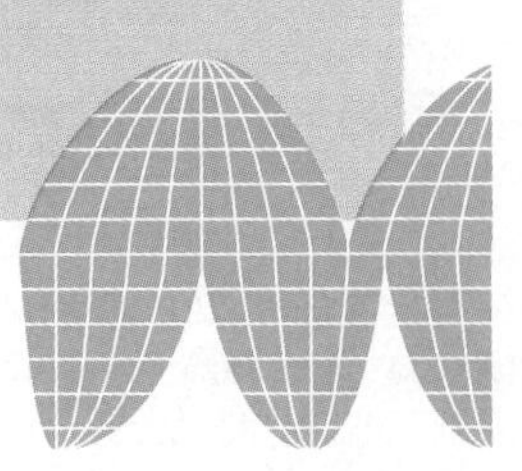

Japanese and American Managers: A Breed Apart or Cut from the Same Cloth?

Much has been made of apparent differences in management style between Japanese and American executives. T. Fujisawa, cofounder of Honda Motor Co., once said, "Japanese and American managers are 95 percent the same, and differ in all important respects." This statement may indeed be an accurate representation of the basic differences between managers in the two cultures.

Regardless of whether an executive works in Tokyo or New York, he or she must deal with issues of strategy, organization design, and organizational control, and strive to see that others in the organization do their best. The CEOs of Ford and Honda, of American and JAL, and of Caterpillar and Komatsu confront the same basic challenges and opportunities. Thus, managerial jobs across cultures clearly are similar in many substantive ways.

But they also differ dramatically in some critical areas. In a Japanese firm, for example, the CEO is a true representative of what the organization stands for. After a recent scandal at Toshiba, the firm's top two managers resigned when there was no objective reason to do so. CEOs of Japanese firms make only a fraction of what their American counterparts earn. And Japanese workers all work together for the good of the organization, shunning individual recognition in favor of group accomplishment. Fujisawa may have known exactly what he was talking about.

SOURCES: Robert H. Doktor, "Asian and American CEOs: A Comparative Study," *Organizational Dynamics,* Winter 1990, pp. 46–56; Graef S. Crystal, "The Great CEO Pay Sweepstakes," *Fortune,* June 18, 1990, pp. 94–102; James R. Lincoln, "Employee Work Attitudes and Management Practice in the U.S. and Japan: Evidence from a Large Comparative Survey," *California Management Review,* Fall 1989, pp. 89–106.

---

a very important consideration is how behavioral processes vary widely across cultural and national boundaries.

For example, values, symbols, and beliefs differ sharply among cultures. Different work norms and the role work plays in a person's life, for example, influence patterns of both work-related behavior and attitudes toward work. They also affect the nature of supervisory relationships, decision-making styles and processes, and organizational configurations. Group and intergroup processes, responses to stress, and the nature of political behaviors also differ from culture to culture. *International Perspective* provides some additional insights into management's role in the global economy. We will return to these and other issues in more detail in Chapter 22.

Managing Cultural Diversity

Earlier we noted that organizational demographics are changing. And as we pointed out previously, globalization also is changing the face of organizational landscapes. Taken together, these trends are serving to increase the cultural diversity of virtually all organizations. This diversity carries additional challenges for both organizations and the managers who work within them. A manager responsible for coordinating the work of a group of white males, all age 30 to

40 and all born and raised in the United States, has a simple task compared to the manager of a group composed of a Native American, two Japanese, a black, two Southeast Asians, and four Hispanics, half of whom are also female.

As organizations expand their reach and become increasingly global, the problems and challenges identified earlier are dramatically accentuated. The simple example just cited, for instance, involves a single manager in a single facility. Consider how much greater the challenge for the CEO of a global firm that has facilities scattered across 50 countries and employs people from 100 different cultural backgrounds! To help managers cope with this increased diversity, many organizations are taking steps to help their managers learn to better deal with cultural differences. For example, some companies provide formal training programs. Others are working to achieve a more effective blend of diversity.[19] Regardless of the steps taken, however, organizations have to remember that cultural diversity is increasing and they must be better prepared to manage it.

Managing for Effectiveness

- Managing for effectiveness involves balancing several individual-level, group-level, and organization-level outcomes.

A final set of issues to be addressed in this chapter relates to the consequences of management. More specifically, what are the outcomes of different types of and approaches to management? As Figure 2.4 illustrates, there are three basic levels of outcomes that determine organizational effectiveness: individual-, group-, and organization-level outcomes. *Developing Management Skills* provides some additional perspectives on the importance of these outcomes.

Individual-Level Outcomes

Several different outcomes at the individual level are important to managers. Given the focus of the field of organizational behavior, it should not be surprising that most of these outcomes are directly or indirectly addressed by various theories and models.

Individual Behaviors First, several individual behaviors result from a person's participation in an organization. One important behavior is productivity. *Productivity,* as defined in terms of an individual, is an indicator of an employee's efficiency and is measured in terms of the products and/or services created per unit of input. For example, if Bill makes 100 units of a product in a day and Sara makes only 90 units in a day, then, assuming the units are of the same quality and Bill and Sara make the same wages, Bill is more productive than Sara.

19. "Learning to Accept Cultural Diversity," *The Wall Street Journal,* September 12, 1990, pp. B1, B9.

Performance, another important individual-level outcome variable, is a somewhat broader concept. It is made up of all work-related behaviors. For example, even though Bill is highly productive, it may also be the case that he refuses to work overtime, expresses negative opinions about the organization at every opportunity, and will do nothing unless it falls precisely within the boundaries of his job. Sara, on the other hand, may always be willing to work overtime, is a positive representative of the organization, and goes out of her way to make as many contributions to the organization as possible. Based on the full array of behaviors, then, we might conclude that Sara actually is the better performer.

Two other important individual-level behaviors are absenteeism and turnover. *Absenteeism* is a measure of attendance. While virtually everyone misses work occasionally, some people miss far more than others. Some look for excuses to miss work and call in sick regularly just for some time off; others miss work only when absolutely necessary. *Turnover* occurs when a person leaves the organization. If the individual who leaves is a good performer and/or if the organization has invested heavily in training the person, turnover can be a costly proposition.

Individual Attitudes Another set of individual-level outcomes influenced by managers consists of individual attitudes. (We discuss attitudes more fully in Chapter 4.) Levels of job satisfaction or dissatisfaction, organizational commitment, and organizational involvement all play an important role in organizational behavior.

Stress Stress, discussed more fully in Chapter 15, is another important individual-level outcome variable. Given its costs, both personal and organizational, it should not be surprising that stress is becoming an increasingly important topic for both researchers in organizational behavior and practicing managers.

FIGURE 2.4
Managing for Effectiveness

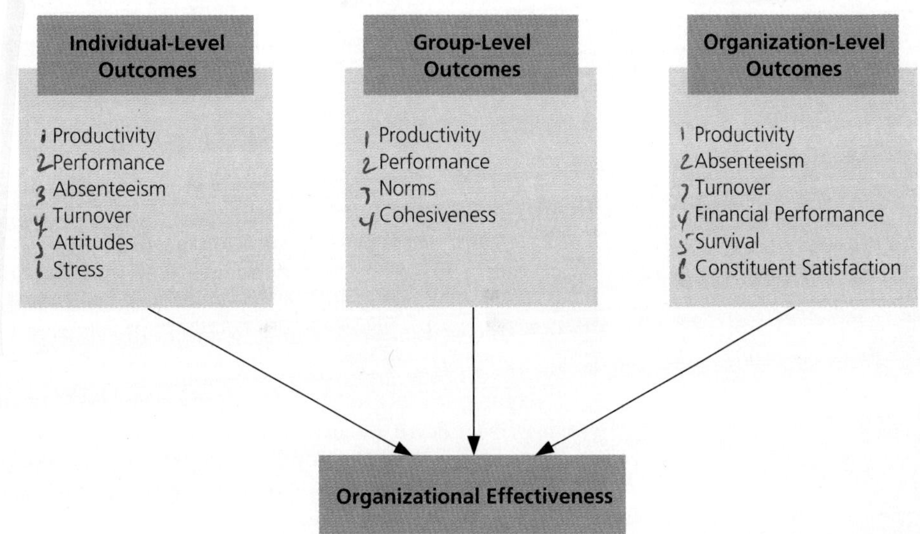

DEVELOPING MANAGEMENT SKILLS

Balancing Outcomes

Assume you are the general manager of a medium-size manufacturing firm. When you took over a few years ago, employees were paid slightly more than the industry average. At the same time, the firm was so deeply in debt that it was bordering on bankruptcy.

You vowed to eliminate debt and restore the organization's financial health. In the years since, you have poured every available dollar into reducing debt. As part of your debt reduction program, you also gradually cut back on wage increases for your workers. These additional funds have allowed you to cut debt even more than you originally expected. At the same time, however, average wages for your employees have gradually slid to the industry average and now hover below that average by around 5 percent.

Today the firm is about one year away from being debt free. All of your extra funds are committed to paying off remaining debt. Unfortunately, your workers are threatening to go out on strike unless they get an immediate pay increase. You face several difficult choices. The two most obvious alternatives are to borrow money to finance a wage increase or to call your workers' bluff and encourage them to be patient. Which would you do, and why?

Group-Level Outcomes

Another set of outcomes exists at the group level. In general, some of these outcomes parallel the individual-level outcomes just discussed. For example, if tasks in an organization are structured at the group rather than the individual level, productivity and performance are likewise important outcome variables. On the other hand, even if all the people in a group have the same or similar attitudes toward their jobs, the attitudes themselves are individual-level phenomena. Individuals, not groups, have attitudes.

But groups can also have unique outcomes that individuals do not share. For example, as we will discuss in Chapter 7, groups develop norms that govern the behavior of individual group members. Groups also develop different levels of cohesiveness. Thus, there are both common and unique outcomes that managers need to assess when considering the individual and group levels.

Organization-Level Outcomes

Finally, a set of outcome variables exists at the organization level. As before, some of these outcomes parallel those at the individual and/or group level, but others are unique. For example, we can measure and compare organizational productivity. We can also develop organization-level indicators of absenteeism and turnover. But profitability is generally assessed only at the organizational level.

Organizations are also commonly assessed in terms of financial performance: stock price, return on investment, growth rates, and so on. They are also evaluated in terms of their ability to survive and of the extent to which they satisfy important constituents like investors, government regulators, employees, unions, and so forth.

The CEO of Hallmark Cards felt there was too much tension between the artists and writers who create the firm's cards and the managers who actually run the business. To help bridge the gap and enhance the firm's effectiveness, Hallmark hired Gordon MacKenzie and gave him the title Creative Paradox. His basic function is to help these two groups understand each other better, thus relieving anxiety and conflict.

Clearly, then, the manager must balance different outcomes across all three levels of analysis. In many cases, these outcomes appear to contradict one another. For example, as illustrated earlier in *Developing Management Skills*, paying workers high salaries can enhance satisfaction and reduce turnover, but it also may detract from bottom-line performance. Thus, the manager must look at the full array of outcomes and attempt to balance them in an optimal fashion. His or her ability to do this will be a major determinant of the organization's success.

Summary of Key Points

- By its very nature, management requires an understanding and appreciation of human behavior. Such an understanding and appreciation can help managers better understand those above and below them in the organization, those at the same level, those in other organizations, and themselves.
- The manager's job can be characterized in terms of four functions and ten roles. The basic managerial functions are planning, organizing, leading, and controlling. The roles consist of three interpersonal roles, three informational roles, and four decision-making roles.
- Several managerial challenges confront managers. Work force demographics include changes in the age, gender, and ethnic composition in the organization. Other workplace challenges pertain to employee privacy, employee rights, and unionization trends.
- There are also several important organizational challenges to consider. These include the need to enhance productivity, improve quality, manage technology, and monitor ethics and social responsibility.
- Global challenges are evolving from a rapid globalization of the business environment. The need to manage cultural diversity is also becoming increasingly important.
- Managing for effectiveness involves the need to balance a variety of individual-level, group-level, and organization-level outcome variables.

Discussion Questions

1. Is it possible for a manager to worry too much about the behavior of her or his subordinates?
2. The text identifies four basic managerial functions. Based on your own experiences or observations, provide examples of each function.
3. Can a manager play more than one role at the same time? Give an example to support your answer.
4. The text argues that we cannot understand organizations without understanding the behavior of the people within them. Do you agree or disagree with this assertion? Why?
5. Interview a local manager or business owner to find out his or her views on

the importance of individual behavior to the success of the organization. Report your findings to the class.

6. What advice would you give a manager to help her or him be better prepared to cope with changes in work force demographics?
7. What limits, if any, should there be regarding an employee's rights to privacy at work?
8. Do you think unions will continue to decline in importance or bounce back and start regaining lost membership? Why?
9. Of the four organizational challenges noted in the text, which do you think is most important? Which is least important? Give reasons for your answers.
10. Are there any businesses that have *not* been affected by globalization? Explain.
11. What individual-, group-, or organization-level outcome variables of consequence can you identify beyond those noted in the text?

CASE 2.1

Sam Walton Uses People as Catalyst

Several years ago, young Sam Walton approached the company he worked for—Ben Franklin, a small five-and-dime chain—with a new idea: Start opening discount stores in small towns. K Mart, the pioneer of discount retailing, had set the standard of concentrating primarily on large, urban areas. At the time, conventional wisdom suggested that a population base of at least 50,000 was necessary to make such a store successful. So managers at Ben Franklin said no.

Walton left Ben Franklin to pursue his idea on his own. Eventually he obtained the financing he needed and opened the first Wal-Mart in tiny Rogers, Arkansas. Shortly afterward, a second store opened in nearby Harrison. Walton then began opening new stores on a regular basis, and Wal-Mart grew into a major regional retailer.

In the late 1960s, a significant turning point occurred in the company's history. Walton's infant empire consisted of 20 Wal-Marts, with more on the drawing boards, when a union tried to organize two of his Missouri stores. Walton consulted with a labor lawyer, who gave him some profound advice. The attorney pointed out that Walton had an important choice to make. On the one hand, he could fight his employees and cultivate an us-versus-them mentality. On the other, he could work to convince his employees that they were all on the same team.

Walton chose the latter approach and held a meeting with his employees. He explained to them that he was willing to work together, to allow them to have input into how the company was run, and to let them share in the rewards if the company's success continued. The employees believed him and abandoned their plans to unionize.

One of the first things Walton did was largely symbolic: He changed the job title of all his employees to *associate.* He also instilled into the company's culture the referents *we, us,* and *our* to illustrate teamwork and a shared commitment. In addition, he decreed that operating employees were to get regular reports on costs, profit margins, and so forth. Whenever a store exceeded its profit goals, all employees in the store were to share in the additional profits. In short, everyone at Wal-Mart was to have a voice and everyone was to benefit from the firm's success.

At this point, Wal-Mart began to grow dramatically. Walton opened between 100 and 200 stores a year. By the end of 1990, Wal-Mart had become the largest retailer in North America. And Wal-Mart has stores in only thirty-five states!

Today Wal-Mart has annual sales of over $20 billion and is a large company by any measure. Nevertheless, the firm has managed to maintain the feel of a small retailer. Employees are still called *associates,* and everyone is encouraged to speak out and participate. For example, an associate recently suggested that the firm hire elderly "people greeters" to welcome customers when they entered a store. The idea worked its way up to Walton, who thought it was marvelous. Consequently, every Wal-Mart store now has official people greeters.

Every Saturday morning, 300 top managers converge in Bentonville, Arkansas (Wal-Mart's headquarters). There they get the latest information about how Wal-Mart and its competitors are doing. They process issues that require decisions and plot strategy for the following week. Walton no longer participates in the day-to-day operations of the firm, but he still comes to these meetings.

At these meetings, messages from company officials are transmitted via satellite to associates at all Wal-Mart stores. On those occasions when Walton himself appears, it reminds long-time associates of the old days. Even though Walton is on television and speaking to almost a quarter of a million people, it seems like he's in the room with them, talking to a handful of people he knows by name.

Case Questions

1. What role has individual behavior played in Wal-Mart's success?
2. Visit a Wal-Mart store (if there is one in your community), and also visit another national retailer. Notice the behavior and expressions of employees in the two stores. Do they differ? If so, how?
3. How might a firm like Wal-Mart most effectively respond to the managerial, organizational, and global challenges noted in the chapter?

SOURCES: "Wal-Mart's Store of the Future Blends Discount Prices, Department Store Feel," *The Wall Street Journal,* May 17, 1991, p. B1. "Mr. Sam Stuns Goliath," *Time,* February 25, 1991, pp. 62–63; "Leaders of the Most Admired," *Fortune,* January 29, 1990, pp. 40–54; Bill Saporito, "Retailing's Winners & Losers," *Fortune,* December 18, 1989, pp. 69–80; John Huey, "Wal-Mart—Will It Take Over the World?", *Fortune,* January 30, 1989, pp. 52–61.

CASE 2.2

Humanized Robots?

Helen Bowers was stumped. Sitting in her office at the plant, she pondered the same questions she had been facing for months: how to get her company's employees to work harder and produce more. No matter what she did, it didn't seem to help much.

Helen had inherited the business three years ago when her father, Jake Bowers, passed away unexpectedly. Bowers Machine Parts, Inc., was founded four decades ago by Jake and had grown into a moderate-size corporation. Bowers makes replacement parts for large-scale manufacturing machines such as lathes and mills. The firm is headquartered in Kansas City and has three plants scattered throughout Missouri.

Although Helen grew up in the family business, she never understood her father's approach. Jake had treated his employees like part of his family. In Helen's view, however, he paid them more than he had to, asked their advice far more often than he should have, and spent too much time listening to their ideas and complaints. When Helen took over, she vowed to change how things were done and bring the firm into the twentieth century. In particular, she resolved to stop handling employees with kid gloves and to treat them like what they were: the hired help.

In addition to changing the way employees were treated, Helen had another goal for Bowers. She wanted to meet the challenge of international competition. Japanese firms had moved aggressively into the market for heavy industrial equipment. She saw this as both a threat and an opportunity. On the one hand, if she could get a toehold as a parts supplier to these firms, Bowers could grow rapidly. On the other, the lucrative parts market was also sure to attract more Japanese competitors. Helen had to make sure that Bowers could compete effectively with highly productive and profitable Japanese firms.

From the day Helen took over, she practiced an altogether different philosophy to achieve her goals. For one thing, she increased production quotas by 20 percent. She instructed her first-line supervisors to crack down on employees and eliminate all idle time. She also decided to shut down the company softball field her father had built. She thought the employees really didn't use it much, and she wanted the space for future expansion.

Helen also announced that future contributions to the firm's profit-sharing plan would be phased out. Employees were paid enough, she believed, and all profits were the rightful property of the owner—her. She had private plans to cut future pay increases to bring average wages down to where she thought they belonged. Finally, Helen also changed a number of operational procedures. In particular, she stopped asking other people for their advice. She reasoned that she was the boss and knew what was best. If she asked for advice and then didn't take it, it would only stir up resentment.

All in all, Helen thought, things should be going much better. Output should be up, and costs should be way down. This combination therefore should be resulting in much higher levels of productivity and profits.

But that's not what was happening. Whenever Helen walked through one of the plants, she sensed that people weren't doing their best. Performance reports indicated that output was only marginally higher than before but scrap rates had soared. Payroll costs indeed were lower, but other personnel costs were up. It seemed that turnover had increased substantially and training costs had gone up as a result.

In desperation, Helen finally had hired a consultant. After carefully researching the history of the organization and Helen's recent changes, the consultant made some remarkable suggestions. The bottom line, Helen felt, was that the consultant thought she should go back to that "humanistic nonsense" her father had used. No matter how she turned it, though, she just couldn't see the wisdom in this. People worked to make a buck and didn't want all that participation stuff.

Suddenly, Helen knew just what to do: She would announce that all employees who failed to increase their productivity by 10 percent would suffer an equal pay cut. She sighed in relief, feeling confident that she had finally figured out the answer.

Case Questions

1. How successful do you think Helen Bowers' new plan will be?
2. What challenges does Helen confront?
3. If you were Helen's consultant, what would you advise her to do?

EXPERIENTIAL EXERCISE

Purpose: This exercise is intended to help you develop a deeper appreciation for the complexities of managing individual behavior.

Format: You will develop a scenario regarding a behavioral problem, along with a recommended course of action. You will then exchange scenarios with a classmate and compare recommendations.

Procedure: Select any of the managerial, organizational, or global challenges noted in this chapter. Working alone (perhaps as an outside-of-class assignment), write a brief scenario describing a hypothetical organization facing that challenge. On a separate page, recommend a course of action that a manager might take to address that challenge. For example, your challenge might be to cope with a new form of technology or a need to enhance quality. Your recommended action might be to form employee advisory groups to help implement the technology or to establish a new employee reward system to improve quality. Try to make the scenario you describe and the course of action you recommend as logically connected and as obviously linked as you possibly can.

Next, exchange scenarios with one of your classmates. Without discussing it, read the other individual's scenario and develop a recommended course of action. After you have finished, verbally summarize your recommendation(s) for your colleague and listen to his or her summary of recommendations for your scenario. Then exchange the written recommendations you prepared for your own scenarios and read them. Discuss similarities and differences between the two sets of recommendations. Explain your logic behind the recommendations you originally set forward, and listen carefully to the logic your colleague used to develop his or her own recommendations.

Follow-up Questions

1. Were the two sets of recommendations basically the same or basically different? Did the discussion alter your view of what should be done?
2. The contingency view, discussed in Chapter 1, would suggest that different courses of action might be equally effective. How likely is it that each of the two sets of recommendations you and your colleague developed might work?

PART II

INDIVIDUAL PROCESSES IN ORGANIZATIONS

CONTENTS

Chapter 3 Learning, Perception, and Attribution

Chapter 4 Individual Differences

Chapter 5 Basic Concepts of Motivation

Chapter 6 Advanced Concepts of Motivation

CHAPTER OUTLINE

The Nature of Learning

A Definition of Learning

The Traditional View: Classical Conditioning

The Contemporary View: Learning as a Cognitive Process

Learning in Organizations

Reinforcement Theory and Learning

Types of Reinforcement in Organizations

Schedules of Reinforcement in Organizations

Related Aspects of Learning in Organizations

Stimulus Generalization in Organizations

Stimulus Discrimination in Organizations

Vicarious Learning in Organizations

Punishment in Organizations

Other Managerial Implications of Learning

Learning and Motivation

Learning and Training

Learning and Performance Evaluation/Rewards

The Nature of Perception

A Definition of Perception

Perceptual Processes in Organizations

The Nature of Attributions

Managerial Implications of Perception and Attribution

Perception, Attribution, and Motivation

Perception, Attribution, and Hiring

Perception, Attribution, and Performance Evaluation

3

LEARNING, PERCEPTION, AND ATTRIBUTION

CHAPTER OBJECTIVES

After studying this chapter, you should be able to:

Define learning, *summarize classical conditioning, discuss learning as a cognitive process, and describe learning in an organizational context.*

Discuss reinforcement theory, including types of reinforcement and schedules of reinforcement.

Describe related aspects of learning such as stimulus generalization, stimulus discrimination, vicarious learning, and punishment.

Identify key managerial implications of learning.

Define perception *and describe basic perceptual processes.*

Discuss the attribution process and describe internal and external attributions.

Identify key managerial implications of perception and attribution.

Most American executives would agree that people should be rewarded at a level commensurate with their contributions to the organization. In other words, more valuable employees should receive greater rewards than less valuable employees. But when it comes to applying this logic to their own compensation, they see things in a much different light!

Indeed, there is considerable controversy regarding the compensation for American executives in general and CEOs in particular. One recent survey of 200 large U.S. corporations revealed that CEOs' average pay was almost $3 million per year. And some made far more—for example, Disney's Michael Eisner earned more than $35 million. Of course, not all of this compensation was salary; part of it included stock options, bonuses, housing allowances, and so forth.

But how well do compensation levels tie in with the performance of the organization? In some cases, there is a direct relationship between long-term performance and profitability and CEO compensation. In others, however, there seems to be no relationship at all. For example, John Gutfreund, CEO of Salomon Brothers, earned more than $5 million even though the brokerage firm had been struggling financially for several years.

How do others assess CEO compensation? As might be expected, it depends on whom you ask. Stockholders at Disney, for example, have little problem with Eisner's pay, because he has led Disney stock prices to new highs. But others believe that pay for CEOs is excessive and should be more directly linked with the organization's performance.[1]

What logic suggests that pay should be tied to performance? And why does compensation for American CEOs seem to defy that logic? The answers to each of these questions are found in two very important aspects of individual behavior in organizations: learning and perception.

These aspects of behavior are the topic of this chapter, the first of four devoted to individual behavior in organizations. First, we examine the role of learning in organizations. Then we describe an important model of learning, reinforcement theory. Next, we discuss perception and the attribution processes

1. Janice Castro, "CEOs: No Pain, Just Gain," *Time,* April 15, 1991, pp. 40–41; Joani Nelson-Horchler, "Paying CEOs: How Much Is a Boss Worth?", *Current,* December 1990, pp. 12–14; Graef S. Crystal, "The Great CEO Pay Sweepstakes," *Fortune,* June 18, 1990, pp. 94–102; "Pay Stubs of the Rich and Corporate," *Business Week,* May 7, 1990, pp. 56–64; "Those Fat Bonuses Don't Seem to Boost Performance," *Business Week,* January 8, 1990, p. 26.

that often follow perception. Subsequent chapters in this part deal with other individual differences and employee motivation.

The Nature of Learning

Most people have a general sense of what *learning* means. However, there are also many misconceptions about this basic human process. In this section we will define learning, summarize traditional and contemporary views of learning, and briefly examine learning in organizations.

A Definition of Learning

■ **Learning** is a relatively permanent change in behavior or potential behavior based on direct or indirect experience.

Learning can be defined as a relatively permanent change in behavior or potential behavior that results from direct or indirect experience.[2] Given the complexities of human learning, however, we also need to examine each component of this definition in more detail.

First, learning involves change. After we have learned, we are somehow different from what we were before—for better or worse. Employees at Ford, for example, learn new job skills and new ideas; unfortunately, other employees in some organizations may also learn to steal and to avoid work.

Second, the change brought about by learning tends to be long lasting. Thus, a student who memorizes material for an exam and promptly forgets it after the test has not really learned anything. Likewise, Ford workers who get less done at the end of the day than in the morning have not learned to work more slowly; they are simply tired.

Third, learning affects behavior or potential behavior. Because we cannot read minds, we must depend on observation to see how much learning has occurred. If a word processing operator who keyboarded 70 words a minute before taking a new training course can now keyboard 85 words a minute, we can infer that learning has occurred. Other kinds of learning are harder to discern. Suppose an employee who has always arrived at work on time sees the boss scold some workers who came in late. The punctual worker now has an added incentive to be on time every day. Even though actual behavior has not been altered, learning has taken place because potential behavior—the likelihood of being tardy—has been reduced.

Finally, the changes brought about by learning result from direct or indirect experience. The word processing operator probably sat and practiced at a real keyboard during the training session (an example of direct experience). But the punctual employee learned about punishment for tardiness only by observing

2. S. H. Hulse, J. Deese, and H. Egeth, *The Psychology of Learning,* 5th ed. (New York: McGraw-Hill, 1980). See also Gib Akins, "Varieties of Organizational Learning," *Organizational Dynamics,* Autumn 1987, pp. 36–48.

Sometimes organizations have to go to extraordinary lengths to help people learn the skills they need to carry out their jobs. These NASA astronauts are aboard a special airplane dubbed the "Vomit Comet" that is able to create brief periods of weightlessness. These experiences help astronauts learn to exist without gravity, preparing them for actual missions aboard space shuttles.

what the boss said to coworkers; nothing was done or said to him or her directly. This is learning through indirect experience, also called *vicarious learning*. We should also distinguish between experience and simple physical maturation. An adult can lift a 20-pound sack of potatoes and a five-year-old cannot. This is so not because of experience and resultant learning but because physical maturation has made the adult stronger.

The Traditional View: Classical Conditioning

■ **Classical conditioning** is a simple form of learning that links a conditioned response with an unconditioned stimulus.

To understand contemporary thinking on learning, we first need to be aware of its historical roots. By far the most influential historical approach to learning is classical conditioning as described by Ivan Pavlov.[3] **Classical conditioning** is a simple form of learning in which a conditioned response is linked with an unconditioned stimulus. Figure 3.1 illustrates the concept of classical conditioning.

Pavlov's theory was based on a famous series of experiments with dogs. Pavlov knew that if he gave meat to the dogs, they would salivate. The meat was an unconditioned, or natural, stimulus, and the salivation an unconditioned, or reflexive, response. This link is shown as step 1 in Figure 3.1. Next, Pavlov began to ring a bell at the same time he presented meat. Prior to that, the dogs did not associate the ringing of the bell with eating, so the bell alone brought

3. Ivan P. Pavlov, *Conditional Reflexes* (New York: Oxford University Press, 1927).

FIGURE 3.1
Classical Conditioning

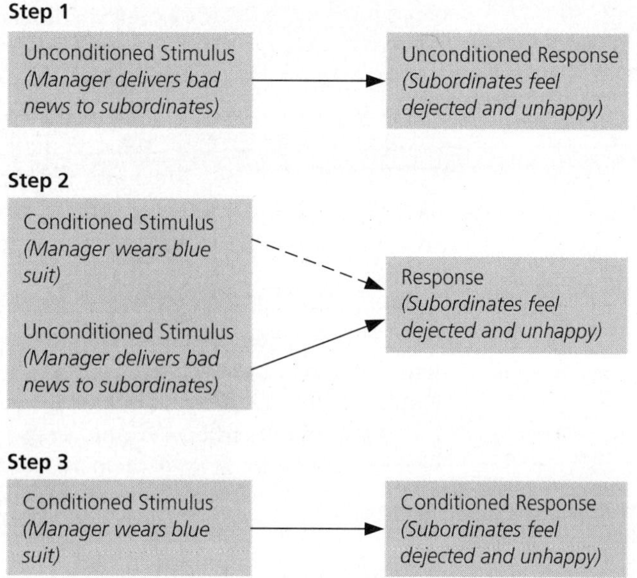

no response. But by ringing the bell while presenting the meat, Pavlov established a relationship between the two stimuli in the minds of the dogs. Step 2 in the figure shows this linkage. Eventually, the dogs associated eating with the sound of the bell so completely that they would salivate whenever the bell was rung, even if no meat was forthcoming (step 3). The bell had become a conditioned stimulus able to call up the newly conditioned, or learned, response.

Figure 3.1 presents an organizational example of classical conditioning. In reality, however, simple forms of this conditioning seldom occur among human beings. Learning theorists soon recognized that although classical conditioning offered some interesting insights into the learning process, it explained human learning inadequately. For one thing, classical conditioning relies on simple cause-and-effect relationships between one stimulus and one response; it cannot deal with more complex forms of learned behavior that typify human beings. For another, classical conditioning ignores the concept of choice; it assumes that behavior is reflexive, or involuntary. Therefore, this perspective cannot explain situations in which people consciously and rationally choose one course of action among many. Because of these shortcomings of classical conditioning, theorists eventually moved on to other approaches that seemed more useful in explaining the processes associated with complex learning.

The Contemporary View: Learning as a Cognitive Process

- Learning is a cognitive process that involves conscious and active behavior.

Although it is not tied to a single theory or model, contemporary learning theory generally views learning as a **cognitive process**; that is, it assumes people are conscious, active participants in how they learn.[4] Figure 3.2 illustrates some underpinnings of the cognitive view of learning.[5]

First, in the cognitive view, people draw on their experiences and use past learning as a basis for present behavior. These experiences represent presumed knowledge, or *cognitions*. For example, an employee faced with a choice of job assignments will use previous experiences in deciding which one to accept. Second, people make choices about their behavior. The employee recognizes her two alternatives and chooses one. Third, people recognize the consequences of their choices. Thus, when the employee finds the job assignment rewarding and fulfilling, she will recognize that the choice was a good one and will understand why. Finally, people evaluate those consequences and add them to prior learning, which affects future choices. Faced with the same job choices next year, the employee very likely will choose the same one.

As implied earlier, several perspectives on learning take a cognitive view. Perhaps foremost among them is *reinforcement theory*. In any event, this approach is most relevant to understanding human learning processes in organizational settings. Before discussing reinforcement theory, however, let's put learning in an organizational context.

Learning in Organizations

Most people associate learning with formal education and with school in particular. While this association is quite logical, we should also note the pervasive extent to which learning also occurs in organizations. From a simple orientation perspective, for example, newcomers to an organization learn when to come to work, how to dress, whom to ask for assistance, where to park, how to apply for annual leave, when to expect a paycheck, how to file an insurance claim, and so forth. From a performance perspective, employees learn how to do their jobs more effectively, what is expected of them in the way of performance outcomes, and what it takes to get rewarded. From a social perspective, employees learn how to get along with their colleagues, which behaviors are acceptable and which are unacceptable, the norms of the group, and so on. From a political perspective, employees learn how to get along with their bosses, whom to avoid, whom to trust, and so forth. And from a career perspective, employees learn how to get ahead, how to get promotions, which job assignments to seek and which to avoid, and the like. Clearly, then, much of organizational life and the behavior of individuals within organizations are influenced by learning and learning processes.

---

4. Hulse, Deese, and Egeth, *The Psychology of Learning*. For recent perspectives, see also Douglas F. Cellar and Gerald V. Barrett, "Script Processing and Intrinsic Motivation: The Cognitive Sets Underlying Cognitive Labels," *Organizational Behavior and Human Decision Processes*, August 1987, pp. 115–135, and Max H. Bazerman and John S. Carroll, "Negotiator Cognition," in L. L. Cummings and Barry M. Staw, eds., *Research in Organizational Behavior*, vol. 9 (Greenwich, Conn.: JAI Press, 1987), pp. 247–288.

5. See Robert Wood and Albert Bandura, "Social Cognitive Theory of Organizational Management," *Academy of Management Review*, July 1989, pp. 361–384.

FIGURE 3.2
Learning as a Cognitive Process

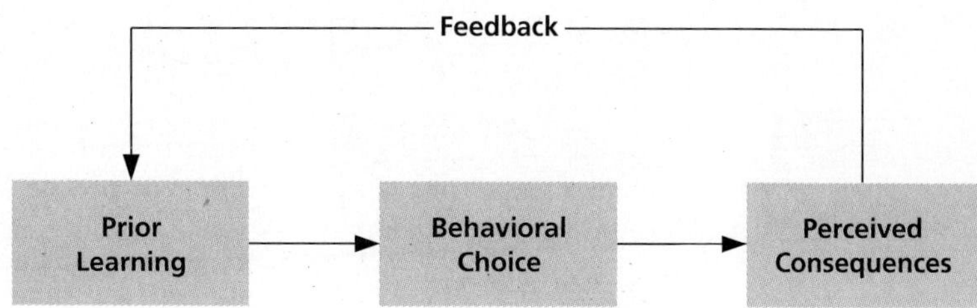

Reinforcement Theory and Learning

■ **Reinforcement theory,** or **operant conditioning,** is based on the idea that behavior is a function of its consequences.

Reinforcement theory, also called **operant conditioning,** is generally associated with the work of B. F. Skinner.[6] In its simplest form, reinforcement theory suggests that behavior is a function of its consequences.[7] Thus, behavior that results in pleasant consequences is more likely to be repeated, and behavior that results in unpleasant consequences is less likely to be repeated.

Reinforcement theory further suggests that in any given situation, people will explore a variety of possible behaviors. Future behavioral choices are affected by the consequences of earlier behaviors. Cognitions, as already noted, also play an important role. Thus, rather than assuming a mechanical stimulus-response linkage suggested by the traditional classical view of learning, contemporary theorists believe that people consciously explore different behaviors and systematically choose those that result in the most desirable outcomes.

Suppose a new employee at General Dynamics in St. Louis wants to learn the best way to get along with his boss. At first, the employee is very friendly and informal, but the boss responds by acting aloof and, at times, annoyed. Because the boss does not react positively, the employee is unlikely to continue this behavior. In fact, the employee starts acting more formal and professional and finds the boss much more receptive to this posture. In all likelihood, the employee will continue this new set of behaviors because they result in positive consequences.

Types of Reinforcement in Organizations

■ **Reinforcement** is the consequences of behavior.

The consequences of behavior are called **reinforcement**. Managers can use various kinds of reinforcement to affect employee behavior. There are four basic forms of reinforcement: positive reinforcement, avoidance, extinction, and punishment.

6. B. F. Skinner, *Science and Human Behavior* (New York: Macmillan, 1953), and *Beyond Freedom and Dignity* (New York: Knopf, 1972).

7. Fred Luthans and Robert Kreitner, *Organizational Behavior Modification and Beyond* (Glenview, Ill.: Scott, Foresman, 1985).

Which form a manager should use depends on the situation. Figure 3.3 summarizes the concepts underlying the four basic kinds of reinforcement.

■ **Positive reinforcement** is a reward or other desirable consequence that a person achieves after exhibiting behavior.

Positive Reinforcement Positive reinforcement perhaps is the part of reinforcement theory that is most familiar to people outside the fields of psychology and organizational behavior. **Positive reinforcement** is a reward or other desirable consequence that follows behavior. A compliment from the boss after completing a difficult job and a salary increase following a period of high performance are examples of positive reinforcement. In general, CEO compensation should be positive reinforcement for effectively managing the organization.

FIGURE 3.3
Kinds of Reinforcement

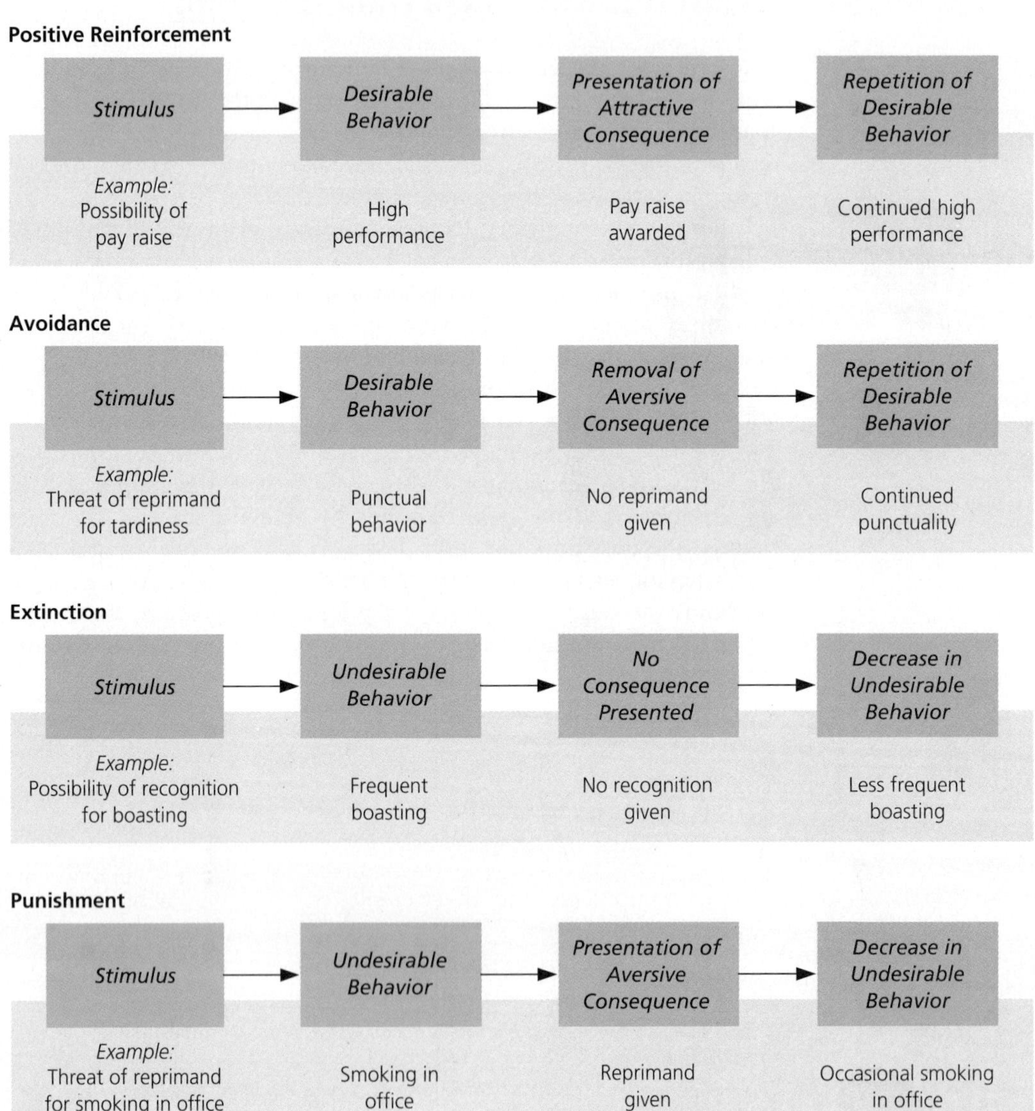

The general effect of providing positive reinforcement after behavior is to maintain or increase the frequency of that behavior.[8] Managers might define "desirable" employee behavior as hard work, punctuality, conscientiousness, and loyalty and commitment to the organization. When employees exhibit these behaviors, the manager may reward them with pay increases, praise, some kind of formal recognition, promotions, and the like. In terms of reinforcement theory, the rewards are intended to ensure the same type of behavior in the future. Of course, different people work for different reasons. Therefore, to be useful as positive reinforcement, rewards should be tailored to the needs of the individual. In addition, a reward should be directly linked with the desirable behavior, and the individual should have ample opportunity to achieve the reinforcement. For example, a person who gets a raise in salary following a period of high performance should be made aware explicitly that the raise was given *because* of the performance. Likewise, the level of performance needed to get the raise should not be set so high as to be impossible to reach.

■ **Avoidance,** or **negative reinforcement,** is the opportunity to avoid or escape from an unpleasant circumstance after exhibiting behavior.

Avoidance **Avoidance,** also known as **negative reinforcement,** is another means of increasing the frequency of desirable behavior. Rather than receiving a reward following a desirable behavior, the person is given the opportunity to avoid an unpleasant consequence. For example, an employee's boss may habitually criticize individuals who dress casually. To avoid criticism, the employee may routinely dress to suit the supervisor's tastes. The employee is engaging in desirable behavior (at least from the supervisor's viewpoint) to avoid an unpleasant, or aversive, consequence.

■ **Extinction** decreases the frequency of behavior by eliminating a reward or desirable consequence that follows that behavior.

Extinction Whereas positive reinforcement and avoidance increase the frequency of desirable behavior, **extinction** decreases the frequency of undesirable behavior, especially behavior that was previously rewarded. In other words, if rewards are withdrawn for behaviors that were previously reinforced, the behaviors probably will become less frequent and eventually die out. For example, a manager with a small staff may encourage frequent visits from subordinates as a way to keep in touch with what is going on. Positive reinforcement might include cordial conversation, attention to subordinates' concerns, and encouragement to come in again soon. As the staff grows, however, the manager may find that such unstructured conversations now make it difficult to get her own job done. She then might brush off casual conversation and reward only to-the-point "business" conversations. Withdrawing the rewards for casual chatting probably will extinguish that behavior. We should also note, of course, that if managers, inadvertently or otherwise, cease to reward valuable behaviors such as good performance and punctuality, those behaviors too may become extinct.[9]

■ **Punishment** is an unpleasant, or aversive, consequence that results from behavior.

Punishment Punishment, like extinction, also tends to decrease the frequency of undesirable behaviors. **Punishment** is presented as an unpleasant, or aversive, consequence of undesirable behavior. In the workplace, undesirable behavior

8. Ibid.
9. Ibid.

might include slacking off, being late, stealing, or arguing unnecessarily with the boss. Examples of punishment are verbal or written reprimands, pay cuts, loss of privileges, layoffs, and termination. Punishment is by nature controversial, and therefore we discuss arguments for and against it in a separate section later in the chapter.

Schedules of Reinforcement in Organizations

- **Schedules of reinforcement** indicate when or how often managers should reinforce certain behaviors.
- With **continuous reinforcement,** behavior is rewarded every time it occurs.

Should the manager try to reinforce every instance of desirable behavior, or is it better to apply reinforcement according to some plan or schedule? Generally, that depends on the situation. Table 3.1 summarizes five basic **schedules of reinforcement** that managers can use.[10]

Continuous Reinforcement **Continuous reinforcement** rewards behavior every time it occurs. Continuous reinforcement is very effective in increasing the frequency of a desirable behavior, especially in the early stages of learning. When reinforcement is withdrawn, however, extinction sets in very quickly. The schedule poses serious practical difficulties as well: The manager must monitor every behavior of an employee and provide effective reinforcement. This schedule, then, is seldom worth much to managers. Offering partial reinforcement according to one of the other four schedules is much more typical.

- **Fixed-interval reinforcement** provides reinforcement on a fixed time schedule.

Fixed-Interval Reinforcement **Fixed-interval reinforcement** means providing reinforcement on a predetermined, constant schedule. The Friday afternoon paycheck is a good example of a fixed-interval reinforcement. Unfortunately, in many situations the fixed-interval schedule will not necessarily maintain high performance levels. If employees know the boss will drop by to check on them every day at 1:00 P.M., they are likely to be working hard at that time, hoping to gain praise and recognition or to avoid the boss's wrath. But at other times of the day, the employees probably will not work as hard because they have learned that reinforcement is unlikely except during the daily visit.

- **Variable-interval reinforcement** varies the amount of time between reinforcement.

Variable-Interval Reinforcement **Variable-interval reinforcement** also uses time as the basis for applying reinforcement, but it varies the interval between reinforcements. This schedule is inappropriate for paying wages, but it can work well for other types of positive reinforcement, such as praise and recognition, and for avoidance. Consider again the group of employees just described. Suppose that instead of coming by at exactly 1:00 P.M. every day, the boss visits at a different time each day: 9:30 A.M. on Monday, 2:00 P.M. on Tuesday, 11:00 A.M. on Wednesday, and so on. The following week, the times change. Because the employees do not know just when to expect the boss, they probably will work fairly hard until her visit. Afterward, they may drop back to lower levels because they have learned that she will not be back until the next day.

---

10. Ibid.

TABLE 3.1
Schedules of Reinforcement

Schedule of Reinforcement	Nature of Reinforcement
Continuous	Behavior is reinforced every time it occurs.
Fixed-Interval	Behavior is reinforced according to some predetermined, constant schedule based on time.
Variable-Interval	Behavior is reinforced after periods of time, but the time span varies from one time to the next.
Fixed-Ratio	Behavior is reinforced according to the number of behaviors exhibited, with the number of behaviors needed to gain reinforcement held constant.
Variable-Ratio	Behavior is reinforced according to the number of behaviors exhibited, but the number of behaviors needed to gain reinforcement varies from one time to the next.

- **Fixed-ratio reinforcement** provides reinforcement after a fixed number of behaviors.

Fixed-Ratio Reinforcement The fixed- and variable-ratio schedules gear reinforcement to the number of desirable or undesirable behaviors rather than to blocks of time. With **fixed-ratio reinforcement**, the number of behaviors needed to obtain reinforcement is constant. Assume a work group enters its cumulative performance totals into the office computer every hour. The manager of the group uses the computer to monitor its activities. He might adopt a practice of dropping by to praise the group every time it reaches a performance level of 500 units. Thus, if the group does this three times on Monday, he stops by each time; if it reaches the mark only once on Tuesday, he stops by only once. The fixed-ratio schedule can be fairly effective in maintaining desirable behavior. Employees tend to develop a feel for what it takes to be reinforced and work hard to keep up their performance.

- **Variable-ratio reinforcement** varies the number of behaviors between reinforcement.

Variable-Ratio Reinforcement With **variable-ratio reinforcement**, the number of behaviors required for reinforcement varies over time. An employee performing under a variable-ratio schedule is motivated to work hard because each successful behavior increases the probability that the next one will result in reinforcement. With this schedule, the exact number of behaviors needed to obtain reinforcement is not crucial; what is important is that the intervals between reinforcement not be so long that the worker gets discouraged and stops trying. The supervisor in the fixed-ratio example could reinforce his work group after it reaches performance levels of 325, 525, 450, 600, and so on. A variable-ratio schedule can be quite effective, but it is difficult and cumbersome to use when formal organizational rewards, such as pay increases and promotions, are the reinforcers. A fixed-interval system is the best way to administer these rewards.

To sum up, relying on any given schedule for all rewards is difficult or impractical. Instead, the manager should use the schedule best suited to the kind of reinforcement being used and try to link outcomes with behaviors according to the needs of the organization and its employees.

Related Aspects of Learning in Organizations

Several additional aspects of learning bear on individual behavior in organizations. Among them are stimulus generalization, stimulus discrimination, vicarious learning, and the arguments for and against punishment.

Stimulus Generalization in Organizations

- **Stimulus generalization** is the process of recognizing the same or similar stimuli in different settings.

Stimulus generalization refers to how people recognize the same or similar stimuli in different settings.[11] In other words, it is the process by which they can generalize a contingent reinforcement from one setting to another. Figure 3.4 illustrates a simple example of the process. Following an initial stimulus-response-consequence sequence, a person learns the behaviors likely to produce some kind of reinforcement. Later, when presented with a similar stimulus in different surroundings, he or she knows that the same response is likely to elicit a similar consequence.

Consider a plant manager for General Electric who has a history of effective troubleshooting. Over the years he has been assigned to several plants, each with a serious operating problem. After successfully dealing with the difficulties, he has always received an extended vacation, a bonus, and a boost in his base salary. He has learned the basic contingencies, or requirements, of reinforcement for his job: The stimulus is the assignment, the response is correcting problems, and the consequences are several positive reinforcers. When the manager gets his next assignment, he probably will generalize from his past experiences. Even though he will be in a different plant with different problems and employees, he will know what is expected of him and understand what it takes to be rewarded.

Stimulus Discrimination in Organizations

- **Stimulus discrimination** is the process of recognizing differences among stimuli.

Stimulus discrimination is the ability to recognize differences among stimuli.[12] This process is also shown in Figure 3.4. As in stimulus generalization, the person learns the basic stimulus-response-consequence sequence for one stimulus. When confronted with a new stimulus, however, he or she can discriminate between the two stimuli and respond differently.

---

11. W. R. Nord, "Beyond the Teaching Machine: The Neglected Area of Operant Conditioning in the Theory and Practice of Management," *Organizational Behavior and Human Performance,* vol. 4, 1969, pp. 375–401.

12. Ibid.

FIGURE 3.4
Stimulus Generalization and Discrimination

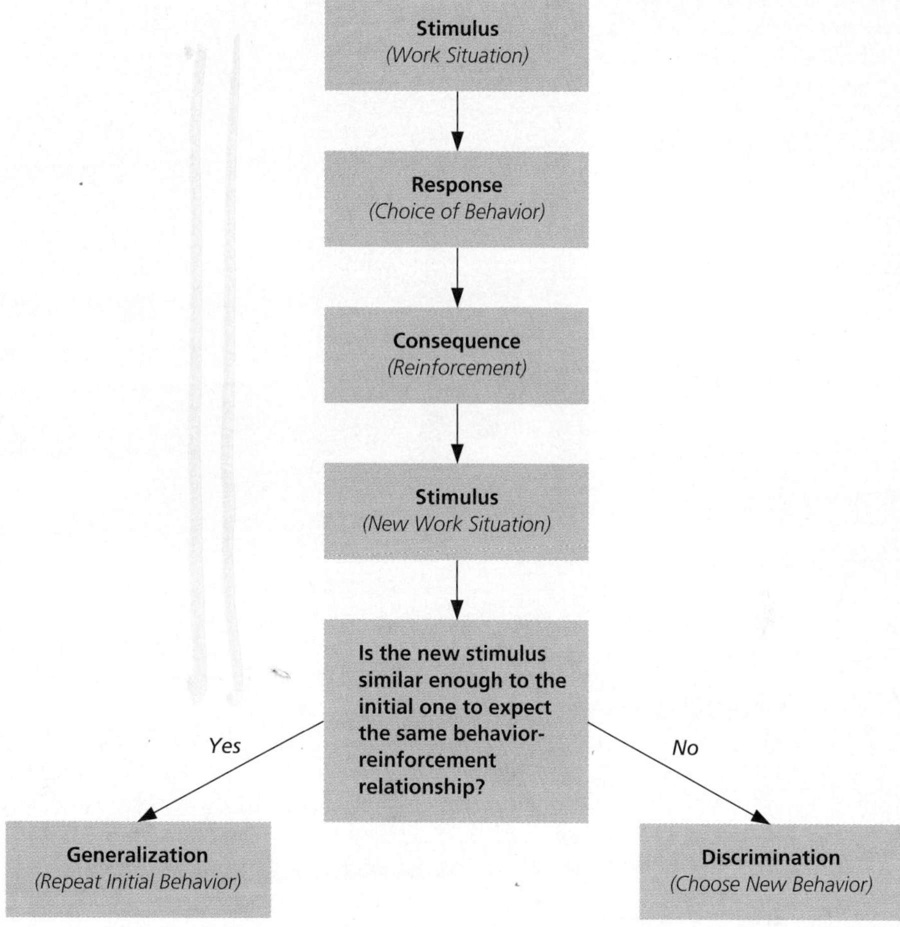

Suppose the troubleshooting plant manager is assigned to a plant that is running smoothly. His routine response to new situations has always been to identify and solve problems, but he now must discriminate between his new situation and his earlier ones. He then will also recognize that he will need a different set of behaviors, or responses, to meet performance expectations and receive positive reinforcement.

Vicarious Learning in Organizations

- **Vicarious learning,** or **modeling,** is the process of learning through the experiences of others.

Vicarious learning, or **modeling**, is learning through the experiences of others.[13] For example, a person can learn to do a new job by observing others or by

13. H. M. Weiss, "Subordinate Imitation of Supervisory Behavior: The Role of Modeling in Organizational Socialization," *Organizational Behavior and Human Performance*, vol. 19, 1977, pp. 89–105.

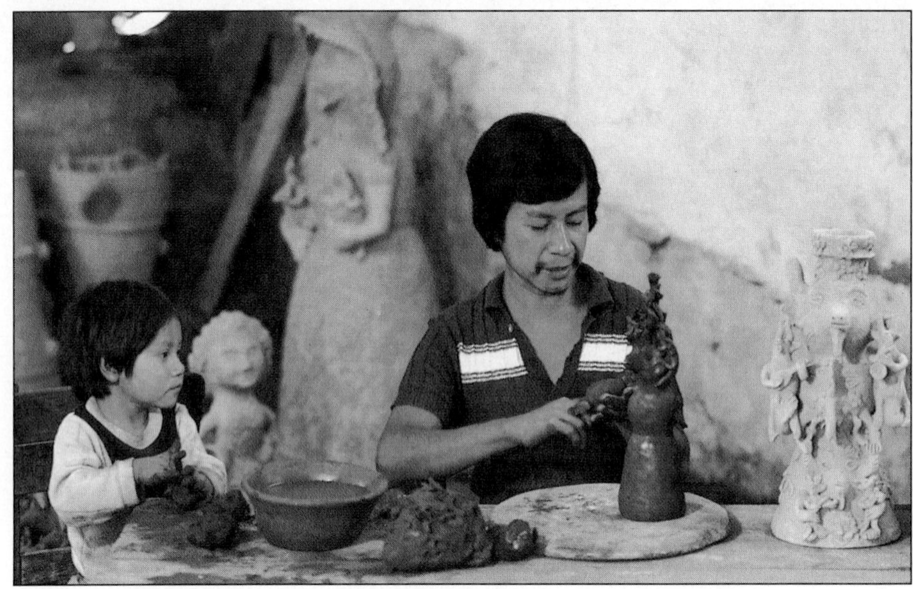

Atzompa Luis Garcia Blanca, a potter from Oaxaca, Mexico, wants to pass his craft to his son just as his father passed it to him. His young son is already beginning to learn the craft by watching his father at work. By combining this vicarious learning with some basic hands-on practice, the child will no doubt become just as skillful as his father.

watching videotapes. And recall the earlier example in which an employee learned to avoid being late by seeing the boss chew out fellow workers.

Several conditions must be met to produce vicarious learning. First, the behavior being modeled must be relatively simple. Although we can learn by watching someone else how to push three or four buttons to set specifications on a machine, we probably cannot learn a complicated sequence of operations without also practicing the various steps ourselves. Second, the behavior being modeled usually must be concrete, not intellectual. We can learn by watching others how to respond to the different behaviors of a particular manager or how to assemble a few components into a final assembly. But we probably cannot learn through simple observation how to write a computer program or to conceptualize or think abstractly. Finally, to learn a job vicariously, we must possess the physical ability needed to do the job. Most of us can watch televised baseball games or tennis matches every weekend but still cannot hit a curveball like José Canseco or execute a backhand like Martina Navratilova.

- **Social learning** is a form of vicarious learning in which people learn behaviors and attitudes in response to what others expect of them.

In recent years, considerable attention has been devoted to a specific type of vicarious learning called **social learning**. Social learning theory suggests that behavior is determined by a person's cognitions and social environment.[14] More specifically, people are presumed to learn behaviors and attitudes at least partly in response to what others expect of them.

Suppose a new employee joins an existing work group. She already has some basis for knowing how to behave (i.e., education and previous experience). However, the group provides a set of very specific cues that help the employee

14. Albert Bandura, *Principles of Behavior Modification* (New York: Holt, 1969). See also Henry P. Sims, Jr., and Dennis Gioia, *The Thinking Organization* (San Francisco: Jossey-Bass, 1986).

see how she needs to tailor her behavior to fit the specific situation she is now in. The group may indicate how the organization expects its members to dress, how people are "supposed" to feel about the boss, and so forth. Hence, the employee learns how to behave in the new situation partly in response to what she already knows and partly in response to what others suggest and demonstrate.

Punishment in Organizations

■ Whereas punishment is an unpleasant, or aversive, consequence that results from behavior, **discipline** is punishment that is officially sanctioned by the organization.

Earlier we defined punishment as the presentation of an unpleasant, or aversive, consequence after an individual engages in undesirable behavior.[15] Thus, any unpleasant consequence that follows behavior can be called *punishment*. A punishment that is structured, official, and organizationally sanctioned is called **discipline.** When a boss yells at an employee who has dropped a bottle of solvent, punishment has taken place. If the boss formally reprimands the worker and puts a written account of the reprimand in the employee's personnel folder, this action represents an attempt at discipline. To be effective, discipline must be perceived as punishing, but in fact it may not always be seen as such. For example, a subordinate planning to quit in the near future might find the supervisor's written reprimand amusing.

Although punishment is common in organizations, many managers and researchers question its practical value for influencing employee behavior. They argue that punishment cannot be effective unless employee behavior is continually observed. Punishment is likely to only suppress behavior temporarily rather than permanently extinguish it, and the side effects of punishment, such as hostility and anger, may outweigh any potential benefits. Furthermore, undesirable behavior often can be changed through extinction or environmental engineering. For example, if two employees who frequently must interact are constantly arguing with each other, it may be possible to stop the bickering without punishing. The manager might alter their environment by having them deal with each other through a neutral third party.

In some situations, however, punishment may be an appropriate tool for altering behavior. Many of life's unpleasantries teach us what to do by means of punishment. Falling off a bike, drinking too much, or going out in the rain without an umbrella all lead to punishing consequences (getting bruised, suffering a hangover, and getting wet), and we often learn to change our behavior as a result. Furthermore, certain types of undesirable behavior may have far-reaching negative effects if they go unpunished. For instance, an employee who sexually harasses a coworker, a clerk who steals money from the petty-cash account, and an executive who engages in illegal stock transactions all deserve punishment.

When punishment is needed, how is it most effectively meted out and how can its negative consequences be reduced? First, punishment should be applied

---

15. See Richard Arvey and John M. Ivancevich, "Punishment in Organizations: A Review, Propositions, and Research Suggestions," *Academy of Management Review,* April 1980, pp. 123–132, for a recent discussion of punishment.

MANAGEMENT IN ACTION

To Punish or Not to Punish?

Regardless of how well managed they are, virtually all organizations occasionally must resort to discipline or punishment. For example, if workers are habitually late, break company rules about smoking, or goof off, punishment may be the only alternative. If this is the case, how should managers proceed? Recent examples suggest that managers should rely on three basic guidelines.

First, managers should use progressive discipline. This means that each instance of undesirable behavior results in a somewhat stronger disciplinary action than the one before. Thus, the first infraction might be followed by a verbal reprimand, the second by a written reprimand, the third by a suspension, and the fourth by dismissal. Honda, Johnsonville Foods, and Herman Miller all use this approach.

Second, many organizations are finding that allowing teams to handle their own discipline works well. Federal Express and Westinghouse are using teams extensively. Each team is responsible for scheduling its own work, hiring its own members, and so forth. Why, then, should it not also discipline its own members? While this approach should be used with caution, it has met with success in many different situations.

Finally, managers need to walk a thin line between being equitable and recognizing situational differences. If two employees break the same rule, the discipline they receive should be comparable. At the same time, a twenty-year veteran employee who comes in 10 minutes late for the first time ever and a new employee who comes in 30 minutes late on the first day almost certainly should be handled in very different ways.

SOURCES: Walter Kiechel III, "How to Discipline in the Modern Age," *Fortune,* May 7, 1990, pp. 179–180; Fred Luthans and Robert Kreitner, *Organizational Behavior Modification and Beyond* (Glenview, Ill.: Scott, Foresman, 1985); Richard Arvey and John M. Ivancevich, "Punishment in Organizations: A Review, Propositions, and Research Suggestions," *Academy of Management Review,* April 1980, pp. 123–132.

---

before the undesirable behavior has been strongly reinforced. Thus, punishment should work better the second time an employee is late rather than the tenth time. Second, the punishment should immediately follow the undesirable behavior to emphasize the connection between the behavior and the consequence in the person's mind. Third, punishment should focus on the behavior, not on the person; thus, it should be impersonal, consistent across time, and impartial. Finally, the punishment should have as much informational value as possible. The employee should know exactly what he or she did to warrant the punishment, the reason why punishment follows such an action, and the consequences of repeating the behavior. *Management in Action* provides some additional insights into current views of punishment in organizations.

Other Managerial Implications of Learning

- Learning is closely related to motivation, performance evaluation and rewards, and employee training.

Beyond the day-to-day implications of learning already noted are others that relate to more general managerial practice. These implications tie in most closely with the areas of motivation, performance evaluation and rewards, and employee training.

Many organizations routinely provide training for their employees. Edward Lowe, a former entrepreneur who invented Kitty Litter, has established a unique training program for would-be entrepreneurs. Students spend ten weeks living in boxcars on Lowe's farm and learn about everything from advertising to writing a business plan. Lowe does some of the teaching himself, but also relies on a team of other successful entrepreneurs.

Learning and Motivation

Motivation is related to learning in several ways. The extent to which valued rewards follow high performance, for example, will affect an employee's willingness to work hard in the future, and the cause-and-effect linkage needs to be clear. In other words, employees should recognize that certain behaviors (such as hard work) cause certain outcomes (desired rewards). Similarly, if rewards do not follow performance, an employee may be less inclined to work hard in the future. Much research on the learning process in organizations has been done recently. These studies have led to the development of a motivational perspective called *organizational behavior modification*.[16] We discuss this view in Chapter 6.

Learning and Training

Learning is the major goal of employee training.[17] Many organizations devote vast resources to training and development to expand the skills and abilities of their employees. Andrew Grove, president of Intel Corporation, heartily believes in the importance of employee training. Intel's employees spend from 2 to 4 percent of their time in the classroom. Much of this training, handled by Intel's own managers, focuses on how employees can benefit the organization while enhancing their own rewards.[18] *International Perspective* describes how one highly successful Japanese company, Honda, approached the training of American workers in plants the company opened in the United States.

---

16. Luthans and Kreitner, *Organizational Behavior Modification and Beyond.*

17. See Kenneth N. Wexley, "Personnel Training," *Annual Review of Psychology,* 1984, pp. 519–553, for a review.

18. Andrew S. Grove, "Why Training Is the Boss's Job," *Fortune,* January 23, 1984, pp. 93–96.

INTERNATIONAL PERSPECTIVE

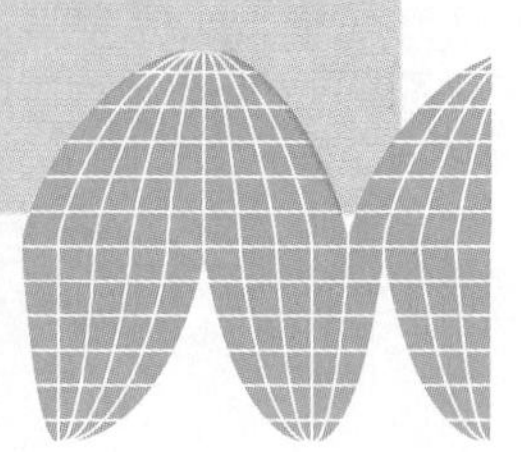

Honda's Approach to Employee Training

Almost everyone is familiar with the facts and many of the myths about Japanese automakers. We hear of their fanatical concern for quality, their participative management styles, and their highly motivated and committed work forces. Companies like Nissan, Toyota, and Honda have become major forces in the American automobile industry in a fairly short time and in recent years have begun to manufacture cars on American soil. Indeed, recent forecasts suggest that by the middle of this decade, one in three new autos sold in the United States may be a Japanese product.

No company exemplifies the push by Japanese firms into the American marketplace more than Honda. Honda's Marysville, Ohio, plant builds about one-third of the cars the company sells in the United States, and Honda recently became the first foreign manufacturer to produce all of its cars' major components in this country. The new Honda Accord wagon, expected to be a major success, was designed in California by Americans and is being produced solely in U.S. plants.

A question long asked by many has been the extent to which American workers can demonstrate the same level of commitment as their Japanese counterparts. To help build this commitment, Honda has gone to extreme lengths to train its American workers in how things need to be done. For example, when a new model of the popular Accord was being introduced, the company flew two hundred American workers representing all parts of the factory to Japan, where the new model already was in production. Working in small groups, the Americans stayed from two weeks to three months observing and learning from their Japanese counterparts. Back in Marysville, these employees are given a great deal of responsibility and are expected to help train others.

SOURCES: Alex Taylor III, "Japan's New U.S. Car Strategy," *Fortune,* September 10, 1990, pp. 65–80; Louis Kraar, "Japan's Gung-Ho U.S. Car Plants," *Fortune,* January 30, 1989, pp. 98–108; "Honda Is Turning Red, White, and Blue," *Business Week,* October 5, 1987, p. 38; "Honda: Made in the U.S.A.," *Newsweek,* January 19, 1987, p. 42.

Learning and Performance Evaluation/Rewards

Learning also ties in with organizational practices in the performance evaluation and reward system. *Performance evaluation* refers to how managers assess the work behavior of individuals and groups; *rewards* are the positive reinforcements (salary, promotion, public recognition) companies give for desirable behavior.[19] We discuss performance evaluation in Chapter 14 and rewards in Chapter 12.

In addition to motivation, performance evaluation and rewards, and training, still other implications can be drawn from learning theory. First, learning theory can explain certain forms of managerial behavior toward subordinates. Suppose a manager always delivers bad news to subordinates in a certain way. If the

19. See Gary P. Latham, "Job Performance and Appraisal," in Cary Cooper and Ivan Robertson, eds., *International Review of Industrial and Organizational Psychology,* vol. 1 (London: Wiley, 1986), pp. 117–156, for a recent review.

subordinates receive the news graciously and constructively, they are giving the manager positive reinforcement. Thus, the manager probably will use the same mode of delivery in the future. Second, many aspects of the learning process underscore the manager's role as a teacher and the subordinate's role as a learner. Finally, learning processes clearly influence the day-to-day interactions, both official and casual, among people in organizations. Almost everything we do in responding to others, for example, has reinforcing consequences for them.

The Nature of Perception

Another very important facet of individual behavior in organizations is *perception*. The vignette about CEO compensation that opens this chapter clearly demonstrates the importance and complexity of perception. The CEOs themselves and some supporters generally perceive their compensation as equitable, whereas others see it as excessive. If everyone perceived everything the same way, things would be a lot simpler (and a lot less exciting!). Of course, just the opposite is true: People perceive the same things in very different ways. In the remainder of this chapter, we focus on perception and attribution.

A Definition of Perception

- **Perception** is the set of processes by which a person becomes aware of and interprets information about his or her environment.

Perception is the set of processes by which an individual becomes aware of and interprets information about the environment. A general discussion of behavioral concepts and processes might identify perception as a single process, but perception actually consists of several distinct processes. Moreover, in perceiving we receive information in many guises, from spoken words or visual images to

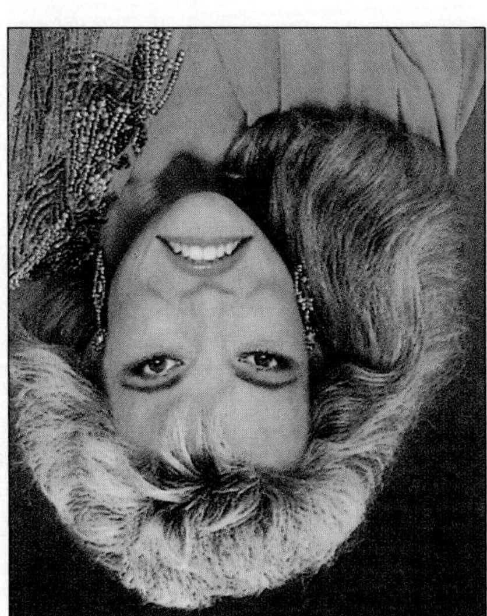

Perceptual processes can greatly distort how we see reality. Here are two photographs of Vanna White. At first glance the photos look very similar. If you turn the page upside down, however, you will see that one photo actually looks hideous. Why the distortion? When looking at the images as printed, you perceptually adjust Vanna's eyes and mouth to make them fit how you think they should look. The context in which the features appear leads to errors in how you see the images.

movements and forms. Through the perceptual processes, the receiver assimilates the varied types of incoming information for the purpose of interpreting it.

People often assume that reality is objective, that we all perceive the same things in the same way. To test this idea, we could ask students at the Universities of Oklahoma and Nebraska to describe the most recent football game between their schools. We probably would hear two quite conflicting stories. These differences would arise primarily because of perception. The fans "saw" the same things but interpreted them in sharply contrasting ways. Factors underlying these differences are perhaps best explained by the perceptual framework shown in Figure 3.5.[20] An object—another person, an event, an activity—is the focal point for perception. A stimulus makes the individual aware of the object. Next, the object is recognized for what it is. The meaning of the object then must be interpreted. Finally, interpretation triggers a response. Responses may include overt behavior, changes in attitudes, or both.

Perceptual Processes in Organizations

The framework described in Figure 3.5 is useful in a general introduction to perception. It is also useful, however, to understand more specific characteristics and processes that affect perception. As Figure 3.6 indicates, perception is influenced by characteristics of the object (what is being perceived), characteristics of the person (the perceiver), and situational processes.[21]

- Perception can be influenced by a variety of characteristics associated with the object being perceived. Key characteristics are contrast, intensity, movement, repetition, and novelty.

Characteristics of the Object Perception is influenced by characteristics of the object that set it apart from its surroundings or cause the perceiver to be more or less aware of the object than would otherwise be the case. Such characteristics include contrast, intensity, movement, repetition, and novelty.

If an object *contrasts* with its surroundings in some way, it is more noticeable. A manager who interviews twenty women and one man for a job will tend to remember the man first simply because he posed such a contrast. Similarly, if one person in an office is dressed very casually and everyone else is dressed formally, we will be most likely to notice the person in casual attire.

Objects may also vary in their *intensity*—in features such as brightness, color, depth, or sound. For instance, we tend to listen carefully to someone who is yelling (or whispering) because the intensity of the sound is unusual.

---

20. See Sheldon S. Zalkind and Timothy W. Costello, "Perception: Some Recent Research and Implications for Administration," *Administrative Science Quarterly*, September 1962, pp. 218–235, for a classic review. For a more recent review, see Robert G. Lord, "An Information Processing Approach to Social Perceptions, Leadership and Behavioral Measurement in Organizations," in L. L. Cummings and B. M. Staw, eds., *Research in Organizational Behavior*, vol. 7 (Greenwich, Conn.: JAI Press, 1985), pp. 87–128.

21. M. W. Levine and J. M. Shefner, *Fundamentals of Sensation and Perception* (Reading, Mass.: Addison-Wesley, 1981). For recent applications and research, see Georgia T. Chao and Steve W. J. Kozlowski, "Employee Perceptions on the Implementation of Robotic Manufacturing Technology," *Journal of Applied Psychology*, vol. 71, no. 1, 1986, pp. 70–76; Steven F. Cronshaw and Robert G. Lord, "Effects of Categorization, Attribution, and Encoding Processes on Leadership Perceptions," *Journal of Applied Psychology*, vol. 72, no. 1, 1987, pp. 97–106.

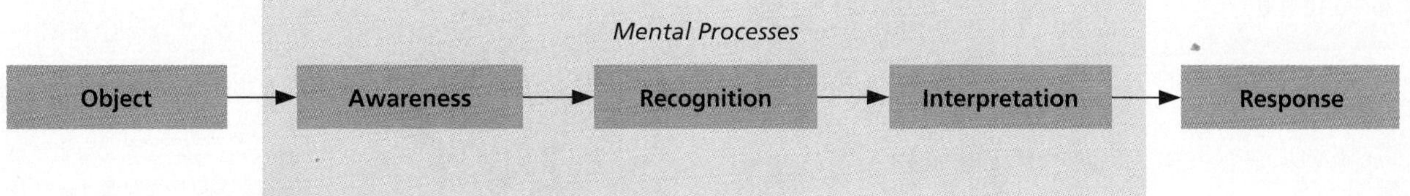

FIGURE 3.5
The Basic Perceptual Framework

We also tend to focus our attention first on objects that are moving or changing. *Movement* stimulates our awareness of an object before we become aware of its surroundings. We notice a flashing neon sign on a dark street, a person walking through a group of standing people, or a single car moving along next to two lanes of stalled traffic.

Repetition also can increase our awareness of objects. Most people can recall the most recent advertising slogans for McDonald's and Coca-Cola because they are repeated over and over on television and radio. Likewise, if a subordinate repeats a request for additional budget support over and over again, the manager is more likely to remember the request than if it had been made only once.

An object's *novelty* also can stimulate our perception of the object. People wearing unusual clothing, books with attention-grabbing covers, and athletic teams with peculiar names all tend to attract our attention. Similarly, we are likely to remember people whose behavior or appearance differs from what we have come to expect. Hence, a manager who has always worn gray suits to work will be noticed by everyone the day he or she wears a brown one. Even though the brown suit is not unusual by itself, it is novel for that manager.

For various reasons, managers invest considerable time and energy in shaping how people perceive their organizations, products, and services. For example, most people think of Phillips Petroleum Co. as simply a petroleum refiner. The company recently undertook a series of commercials to increase people's awareness of other products it has introduced.

- Perception can also be influenced by a variety of characteristics associated with the individual. Key characteristics are salience, disposition, attitudes, self-concept, and personality.

Characteristics of the Person An individual's personal characteristics also affect how he or she perceives and interprets things. The most important characteristics are salience, disposition, attitudes, self-concept, and personality.[22]

Salience is the individual's feeling about the object's importance. The more salient the object is to you, the more attention you are likely to pay to it. If this morning's newspaper contained an article about a dramatic tuition increase at a specific university, students at that university probably would read it carefully. Someone not affiliated with the school, however, might skim right past the article without a second glance. The reason is simple: The information the article contains would be far more salient to the students than to the other person. Thus, a marketing manager for IBM would eagerly read an article about a new advertising campaign by Hewlett-Packard but probably would show significantly less interest in a new stock offering by Sears.

22. Levine and Shefner, *Fundamentals of Sensation and Perception.*

FIGURE 3.6
Characteristics and Processes that Affect Perception

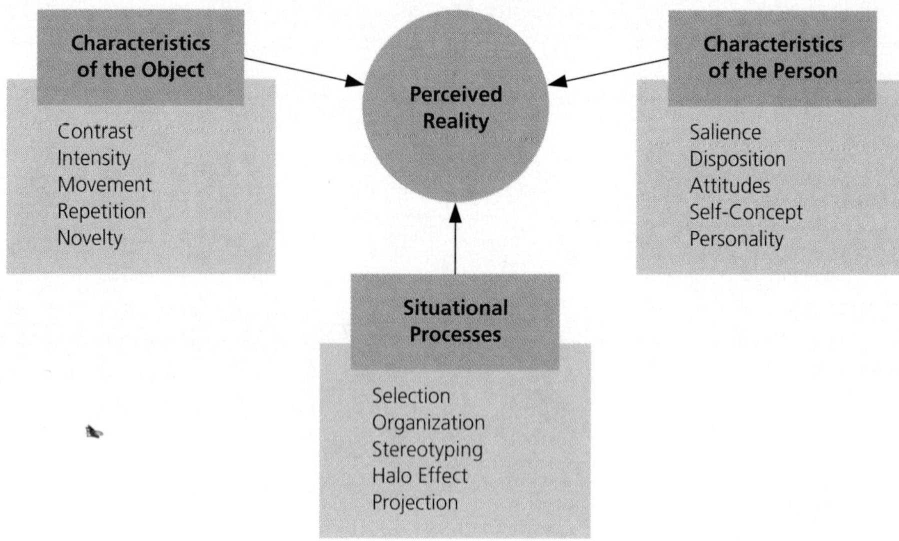

An individual's disposition also affects how he or she perceives things. *Disposition* is a short-term emotional response triggered by various environmental stimuli. Suppose a manager has just been told that she will receive no pay raise next year because of low performance in her work group. Back in her office, no doubt in a lousy mood, she discovers that one of her subordinates has made an error in calculating unit costs. She promptly berates the subordinate for what she perceives as slipshod work. The manager's disposition has made her not only more aware of the subordinate's error but less tolerant of it.

Whereas one's disposition tends to be a short-term mood or emotional response, one's *attitudes* are longer-lasting feelings about things. Attitudes can affect perceptions in dramatic ways. When President Reagan was riding a wave of popularity in 1986, *Newsweek* magazine called him "one of the strongest leaders of the 20th Century." People had positive attitudes about Reagan and therefore saw him in a favorable light. A scant sixteen months later, by which time his popularity had eroded, the same publication noted that "the nation calls for leadership and there is no one home" in the White House.[23] Because people's attitudes had changed, so had their perceptions. We discuss attitudes in more detail in Chapter 4.

Self-concept also can affect perception. *Self-concept* is a person's perception of himself or herself. A person who has a good self-concept tends to see things in a positive and enriching light. A negative self-concept, on the other hand, can give a person's perceptions an unfavorable or limiting cast.

A final characteristic that influences perception is an individual's personality. One's *personality* is the set of distinctive traits and features that make one unique. Different personality traits can cause differences in the ways individuals recognize

23. "Has Reagan Changed?", *Newsweek,* November 23, 1987, p. 20.

and interpret their surroundings. An extrovert may eagerly join in conversation. An introvert, in contrast, may be less interested in what others are talking about. In Chapter 4, we examine personality in more detail.

■ Situational processes also affect perception by serving as filters. Important situational processes are selection, organization, stereotyping, the halo effect, and projection.

Situational Processes In a sense, situational processes act as filters; that is, objective information from the environment is interpreted and shaped as the individual perceives it. The individual's cognitions of the environment are influenced, as we described earlier, by characteristics of both the object and the individual. Subtle interactions that are unique to particular situations may also occur between person and object. This means that the same object may be perceived differently by the same person in different situations. The major situational processes are selection, organization, stereotyping, the halo effect, and projection.[24]

Through the process of *selection,* we pay attention to objects we are comfortable with and filter out those that cause us discomfort. A classic study by DeWitt Dearborn and Herbert Simon clearly demonstrated the effects of selection on managerial behavior.[25] Twenty-three executives were asked to read a case describing various problems faced by a company. Afterward, each executive was instructed to identify the case's single most important problem. Almost without exception, the executives' choices reflected their own functional specialties. Five out of six marketing executives saw sales as the major problem, and four of five production managers identified production problems. The researchers concluded that the managers' selection process filtered in the problems they were most comfortable with because of their functional expertise and filtered out the problems they were less familiar with. *The Ethical Dilemma* provides a more recent example of how selective perception allowed a manager to perform miracles—until he got caught!

When used to describe an element of perception, the term *organization* refers to people's tendency to order their perceptions so that they fit logical, consistent systems of meaning. As with selection, as we organize we often filter out stimuli that do not conform to our view of reality. Consider a manager who believes a particular subordinate is hard working, conscientious, and loyal. One day the manager notices the worker goofing off. Because this perception does not fit the manager's image of the worker, he may "choose" to see the behavior as a well-earned rest after hard work.

Organization also causes us to group and label objects. Almost unconsciously employees develop attitudes about many individual features of the workplace, such as pay, benefits, supervisors, coworkers, working conditions, promotion opportunities, and organizational practices. But when asked to describe how they feel about their jobs, employees tend to collapse these attitudes into an overall impression such as "I can't stand it" or "It couldn't be better."

---

24. James P. Walsh, "Selectivity and Selective Perception: An Investigation of Managers' Belief Structures and Information Processing," *Academy of Management Journal,* December 1988, pp. 873–896.

25. DeWitt C. Dearborn and Herbert A. Simon, "Selective Perception: A Note on the Departmental Identification of Executives," *Sociometry,* vol. 21, 1958, pp. 140–144.

THE ETHICAL DILEMMA

Reality versus Perception

How far can a manager get by altering the perceptions of his or her business? In the case of Don Sheelen, former CEO of Regina Co., perceptions apparently can go a long way.

Sheelen took over Regina in 1984. At the time, Regina was a small vacuum cleaner manufacturer. By 1988, Sheelen had more than tripled sales and reported record-breaking profits. Wall Street was convinced that Sheelen was a genius and that Regina was one of the hottest investments around. At each stockholders' meeting, Sheelen put on a better show than the year before, lavishly extolling the firm's potential. By 1988, the firm's stock price had risen from slightly more than $5.00 a share to $27.50 a share. As a result, Sheelen's own stake in the company skyrocketed to almost $100 million.

Then things started to decline. One of Regina's major new products, the Housekeeper vacuum cleaner, was beset by major quality problems. Thousands of vacuum cleaners were returned because they didn't work properly. Then Sheelen ordered one of his executives to alter the firm's financial reports to understate the number of Housekeepers being returned.

Sheelen started altering other financial reports as well, overstating sales and overprojecting profits. He even attempted to demonstrate the superiority of the Housekeeper over a competing Hoover model for a group of analysts, but he didn't tell them that the model being demonstrated was "souped up" and was not available for sale to the public. Things still looked rosy for Regina.

Eventually, Regina's house of cards started to tumble. A member of the board of directors became troubled when Sheelen stopped reporting financial information at their meetings. After considerable pushing, Sheelen finally relented. The directors were astonished at what they saw. After the news was announced, Regina's stock price fell sharply and Sheelen himself was sent to jail. The final curtain came in the summer of 1990 when Regina was bought by Electrolux.

SOURCES: Amar Bhide and Howard H. Stevenson, "Why Be Honest If Honesty Doesn't Pay." *Harvard Business Review,* September-October 1990, pp. 121–129; Terence R. Mitchell and William G. Scott, "America's Problems and Needed Reforms: Confronting the Ethic of Personal Advantage," *Academy of Management Executive,* August 1990, pp. 23–35; "How Don Sheelen Made a Mess That Regina Couldn't Clean Up," *Business Week,* February 12, 1990, pp. 46–50.

Stereotyping is the process of categorizing people into groups on the basis of certain presumed traits or qualities. Suppose you walk into the reception area of an executive suite. There you notice a man and a woman talking beside a secretary's desk. A typical reaction, owing to a firmly entrenched stereotype, is to assume the woman is the secretary and the man is the executive. Stereotyping consists of three steps. First, we identify categories by which we will sort people (race, region, sex). Next, we associate attributes with those categories (athletic ability, speech patterns, occupations). Finally, we infer that all people in certain categories take on the attributes we have decided on (all blacks are athletic; all people from Boston talk funny; all secretaries are women; all people pursuing an MBA are aggressive and career driven). Needless to say, stereotypes are almost always inaccurate.

In recent years, many researchers have studied stereotyping. Much of the research has focused on either sex role or age stereotyping. One study found that publishing company recruiters clearly assumed that female job applicants were suited for positions such as supervisor of other female employees and editorial assistant whereas male applicants were better suited for jobs such as supervisor of other male workers and editor.[26] Another study found that business students tended to stereotype older workers as less creative, more resistant to change, and less interested in learning new skills.[27]

Still another situational process is the halo effect. The *halo effect* influences our perceptions when we let a single characteristic override our assessment of an individual's other characteristics. For example, if we consider a person friendly and outgoing, we may also assume the person is diligent, loyal, and punctual even if we have evidence to the contrary. In a classic study conducted in the 1940s, two groups of people were given a list of personality traits and asked to describe the individual portrayed. The two lists were the same except that one contained the word *warm* and the other the word *cold*. This one-word difference led to significantly different descriptions. People working with the list containing the word *warm* said the individual must be humorous, intelligent, and popular. The other group said the person was serious and aloof and had few friends.[28]

Finally, perception may be influenced by the process of projection. *Projection* occurs when we see ourselves in others. If we are aggressive, power hungry, and status conscious, we may rationalize these traits by telling ourselves that everyone else is the same and that to get ahead we must take care of ourselves. We focus on examples of behavior by others that reinforce this view. When a colleague asks for another assistant, we see this request as yet another attempt to build a power base. In reality, of course, power may be the furthest thing from our colleague's mind. The request may even indicate that she is so inefficient that she cannot get her job done by herself. Projection, then, can cause misunderstandings or worse.

The Nature of Attributions

Attribution theory, a relatively new addition to the field of organizational behavior, has links to perception, motivation, and leadership.[29] Here we discuss

---

26. S. L. Cohen and K. A. Binker, "Subtle Effects of Sex Role Stereotypes on Recruiters' Hiring Decisions," *Journal of Applied Psychology,* vol. 60, 1975, pp. 566–572.

27. B. Rosen and T. H. Jerdee, "The Influence of Age Stereotypes on Managerial Decisions," *Journal of Applied Psychology,* vol. 61, 1976, pp. 428–432.

28. S. Asch, "Forming Impressions of Personality," *Journal of Abnormal and Social Psychology,* vol. 41, 1946, pp. 258–290.

29. Cronshaw and Lord, "Effects of Categorization, Attribution, and Encoding Processes"; Mark J. Martinko and William L. Gardner, "The Leader/Member Attribution Process," *Academy of Management Review,* April 1987, pp. 235–249; Jeffrey D. Ford, "The Effects of Causal Attributions on Decision Makers' Responses to Performance Downturns," *Academy of Management Review,* October 1985, pp. 770–786.

FIGURE 3.7
The Attribution Process

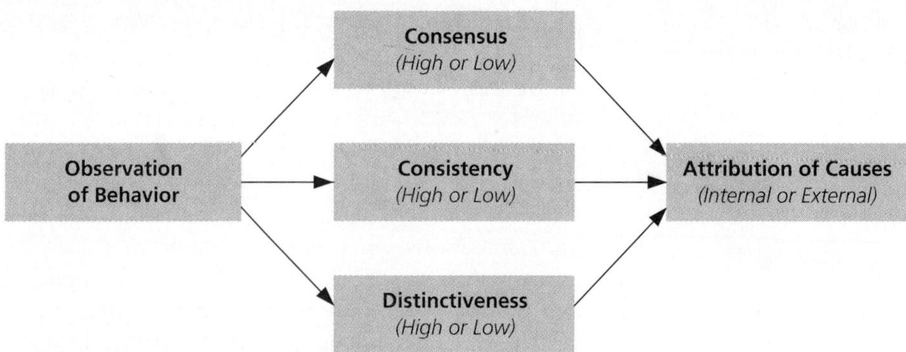

only its implications for perception. For attribution theory's relationship to motivation and to leadership, see Chapters 6 and 9, respectively.

- **Attribution theory** is based on the idea that people observe behavior and then attribute causes to it.

Fritz Heider and H. H. Kelley are the best-known contributors to attribution theory.[30] **Attribution theory** suggests that we observe behavior and then attribute causes to it; that is, we attempt to explain why people behave as they do. The process of attribution is based on perceptions of reality, and these perceptions may vary widely among individuals.

Figure 3.7 illustrates the basic attribution theory framework. To start the process, we observe behavior, either our own or someone else's. We then evaluate the behavior in terms of its degrees of consensus, consistency, and distinctiveness. *Consensus* is the extent to which other people in the same situation behave in the same way. *Consistency* is the degree to which the same person behaves in the same way at different times. *Distinctiveness* is the extent to which the same person behaves in the same way in other situations. As a result of various combinations of consensus, consistency, and distinctiveness, we form impressions or attributions as to the causes of behavior. We may believe the behavior is caused internally (by forces within the person) or externally (by forces in the person's environment).

For example, suppose you observe that one of your subordinates is being rowdy, disrupting others' work and generally making a nuisance of himself. If you can understand the causes of this behavior, you may be able to change it. If the employee is the only one engaging in the disruptive behavior (low consensus), if he behaves like this several times each week (high consistency), and if you have seen him behave like this in other settings (low distinctiveness), a logical conclusion would be that internal factors are causing his behavior.

Suppose, however, that you observe a different pattern: Everyone in the person's work group is rowdy (high consensus), and although the particular employee often is rowdy at work (high consistency), you have never seen him behave this way in other settings (high distinctiveness). This pattern indicates

30. Fritz Heider, *The Psychology of Interpersonal Relations* (New York: Wiley, 1958); H. H. Kelley, *Attribution in Social Interaction* (Morristown, N.J.: General Learning Press, 1971).

TABLE 3.2
Possible Alternative Responses to Different Attributions

Attributions about Success

Attribution	*Possible Responses*
Internal "Sam is successful because he works hard and has lots of ability."	Give Sam positive reinforcement, promote him, hold him up as an example to others.
External "Sam is successful because he has an easy job and a strong work group."	Give Sam more work to do, promote some of his work group.

Attributions about Failure

Attribution	*Possible Responses*
Internal "Sally is doing a poor job because she lacks ability and motivation."	Send Sally to a training program or change the incentive structure.
External "Sally is doing a poor job because she lacks the proper resources and has a weak work group."	Increase Sally's resources and strengthen her work group.

that something in the situation is causing the behavior, that is, that the causes of the behavior are external.

Attributions of behavior have important implications for managers. If we attribute poor performance to internal factors, such as ability or motivation, we will develop certain strategies to improve these factors. On the other hand, if we attribute poor performance to external factors, such as resource constraints or a poorly designed job, we will take different steps to enhance performance. Table 3.2 shows examples of different alternatives.

We also make attributions regarding ourselves. If we attribute a pay raise to our hard work, we may continue to work hard. On the other hand, if we think we were given the raise because the boss liked us, we may put more effort into cementing that friendship.

Attribution theory currently is getting a great deal of attention from organizational behavior researchers in the areas of leadership, motivation, performance appraisal, communication, reward systems, and a variety of other fields.[31] It holds considerable promise for increasing our understanding of behavior in organizational settings.

31. For current examples, see Brendan D. Bannister, "Performance Outcome Feedback and Attributional Feedback: Interactive Effects on Recipient Responses," *Journal of Applied Psychology,* vol. 71, no. 2, 1987, pp. 203–210, and Dennis A. Gioia and Henry P. Sims, Jr., "Cognition-Behavior Connections: Attribution and Verbal Behavior in Leader-Subordinate Interactions," *Organizational Behavior and Human Decision Processes,* vol. 37, 1986, pp. 197–229.

Managerial Implications of Perception and Attribution

■ Perception and attribution processes are particularly important with regard to motivation, hiring, and performance appraisal.

Perception and attribution have many implications for managers in organizations, particularly in motivation, hiring, and performance appraisal.

Perception, Attribution, and Motivation

As we discuss in Chapters 5 and 6, perceptions of the workplace play a major role in motivation. Suppose an employee is experiencing some unexpected money trouble. Because of her disposition (she is worried) and the salience of money (it is unusually important to her at the moment), she will be especially sensitive to issues of compensation. Through projection, she may assume everyone in the organization also cares mainly about money. A large pay raise given to another employee will frustrate her and will intensify her efforts to get a pay raise of her own. She will focus even more attention on her own pay, others' pay, and how they compare to one another. Obviously, as suggested earlier, attribution is also relevant to motivation. A person who believes his pay raise is attributable to effort (internal) rather than to his being the boss's nephew (external) will choose to continue to work hard.

Perception, Attribution, and Hiring

Perception can also affect the hiring of new employees. Contrast or novelty in the job applicant can affect his or her chances of getting the job. The person doing the hiring may stereotype applicants on the basis of race or sex or may allow the halo effect to distort an overall perception of an applicant. An interviewer's disposition during an interview or attitudes toward certain of the applicant's attributes can also affect the interviewer's perceptions of the applicant. For example, a manager with a toothache who believes people should dress professionally for a job interview is likely to be unimpressed by an applicant who shows up wearing sunglasses and a flowered sport coat. Consensus, consistency, and distinctiveness each can also play a role in how a manager formulates a hiring decision.

Perception, Attribution, and Performance Evaluation

Performance evaluation, the topic of Chapter 14, is the assessment of an employee's performance to correct shortcomings, identify strengths, and provide a basis for giving rewards. Several areas of performance evaluation are especially susceptible to perceptual distortion.[32] The contrast between two employees can affect the evaluation. Suppose a manager prepares several performance evaluations of her subordinates in one afternoon, one right after the other. The first two employees receive extremely good evaluations. The next person, however, is only a marginal performer. If the manager is influenced by the high evaluations given to the first two people, the third employee may suffer in comparison; that is, his evaluation may be lower than it would be if the first two employees were unsatisfactory workers.

Selection also may affect performance evaluation. A manager who has a particularly favorable impression of an employee may ignore instances of poor performance. The halo effect and stereotyping also come into play, as do the evaluator's characteristics, such as salience, disposition, and attitudes. In this way, a manager who emphasizes punctuality may weight it heavily as a standard of performance. Another manager may consider punctuality relatively unimportant and barely mention it in a performance evaluation.

Finally, internal versus external attributions as to the causes of performance will also play a significant role in how a manager evaluates a subordinate's performance. Consensus, consistency, and distinctiveness of observed performance will likewise be considered by a manager during performance evaluation.

Summary of Key Points

- Learning is a relatively permanent change in behavior or potential behavior that results from direct or indirect experience. Learning is a cognitive process involving experiences and choices about behavior. Learning typifies a wide variety of organizational activities.
- Reinforcement theory is the learning perspective most relevent for organizations. The basic types of reinforcement are positive reinforcement, avoidance, extinction, and punishment. Schedules of reinforcement include continuous, fixed-interval, variable-interval, fixed-ratio, and variable-ratio.
- Important related aspects of learning are stimulus generalization, stimulus discrimination, vicarious learning, and punishment. Key implications that can be drawn from learning theory bear importantly on motivation, training, and performance evaluation and rewards.
- Perception is the set of processes by which individuals become aware of information about their environment. Basic steps involving perception are awareness, recognition, interpretation, and response.
- Basic perceptual processes are associated with characteristics of the object being perceived, the person perceiving it, and the situational processes. Characteristics of the object are contrast, intensity, movement, repetition,

32. Kenneth N. Wexley and Elaine D. Pulakos, "The Effects of Perceptual Congruence and Sex on Subordinates' Performance Appraisals of Their Managers," *Academy of Management Journal*, December 1983, pp. 666–676.

and novelty. Characteristics of the person include salience, disposition, attitudes, self-concept, and personality. Situational processes are selection, organization, stereotyping, the halo effect, and projection.

- Attribution theory involves the processes by which we perceive and then attribute meaning to the behavior of others. We evaluate such behavior in terms of its consensus, consistency, and distinctiveness and then attribute internal or external causes to it.
- Important managerial implications of perception and attribution bear on motivation, hiring, and performance evaluation.

Discussion Questions

1. Describe some instances of when you were classically conditioned in some way.
2. How might an instructor use reinforcement theory to get students to come to class on time, turn in assignments on time, and take proper notes?
3. Think of a local business with which you have some familiarity, and imagine you are its manager. How might you use positive reinforcement, avoidance, extinction, and punishment to influence your employees' behavior?
4. In the context of your role as a student, identify examples of each schedule of reinforcement that influence your behavior. Which works best? Why?
5. Think of a situation in which you learned something vicariously. What did you learn? In what situations have you used stimulus generalization or discrimination?
6. What is your opinion about the merits of punishment?
7. Use the perceptual framework from the chapter to describe how you recently perceived something important.
8. Recall and describe recent situations in which your perceptions were influenced by salience, disposition, and attitudes.
9. In what ways do selection, organization, and stereotyping differ? In what ways are they similar?
10. Recall a recent instance in which you made attributions about someone else's behavior. How can you use attribution theory to explain those attributions?
11. How do learning and perception affect each other?

CASE 3.1

Tommy Lasorda and Reinforcement Theory

Tommy Lasorda is responsible for the performance of a group of highly skilled, individualistic, and somewhat temperamental employees. Many of them earn more money than he does, and most of them are better known than he is. He has to keep them focused on performance during a period of many distractions, heavy travel schedules, and public scrutiny. What does Lasorda do? He is a baseball manager.

In particular, Lasorda is the manager of the Los Angeles Dodgers professional baseball team, which plays in the National League. The team is one of the best known professional sports franchises and also one of the most successful. The Dodgers usually are among the league leaders in home attendance and have lucrative television contracts as well. The Dodgers won the World Series in 1988, when they stunned the Oakland A's. Lasorda believes that running the Dodgers is highly similar to running any business and that his job is similar to the job of any other manager.

One of the key elements of Lasorda's job is to motivate his players to perform at their best while on the baseball field. He relies heavily on several learning concepts as well as reinforcement theory in his attempts to do this. In particular, Lasorda says he learned early in life that people need to be rewarded for what they do and should enjoy their work. He gives a lot of credit to his father for teaching him the virtues of hard work and for showing him the power of rewards and punishment.

Lasorda uses a number of rewards to get his players to do their best. One major reward, of course, is playing time. Because a major league baseball team has 24 players but only 9 can play at any one time, performing well enough to be in the starting lineup is a major incentive for most players.

Lasorda also uses other forms of reinforcement. He hugs his players when they do well. He also pats them on the back, claps for them, and shouts encouragement at them. He also relies on punishment if he has to. He benches a starter who isn't doing well. He fines a player who breaks the rules. He may even send a player down to the minor leagues if necessary. And on a day-to-day basis, he reprimands players, makes them take extra batting practice, and so forth.

But Lasorda is smart enough to recognize that he can't treat all of his players the same way. Some players respond well to criticism, and some don't. Some players like the enthusiastic hugs, and some don't. Thus, Lasorda works hard to assess the makeup of each of his players and then tailors his behavior to that player.

Another key to Lasorda's success is the image he presents to his players. He believes that if he shows up at the clubhouse in a dejected, depressed, or grumpy mood, his players will adopt the same mindset. But if he appears enthusiastic, self-confident, and proud, his players will respond in kind.

Can other teams learn from Lasorda and the Dodgers? It appears that many are trying. For example, when Walter Haas (owner of jeans maker Levi Strauss) bought the Oakland A's in 1980, the organization was in shambles. Haas soon realized that the A's stadium was an unpleasant place to be and that playing for the A's was a negative experience for the players.

Accordingly, Haas first set out to alter public opinion. He spiffed up the stadium with new paint, an organist, and a playground for children. He hired marketing specialists to help promote the team and put a new emphasis on rewarding people for a job well done. He started paying top players more and hired an astute new manager to run the show.

How well has it worked? In 1980, around 300,000 fans paid to see the A's. In 1990, over 3 million fans came to the same park to see the team.

Case Questions

1. What implications can you draw from reinforcement theory about running a baseball team?
2. What implications can you draw from perception about running a baseball team?
3. Would you want Tommy Lasorda running a business you owned? Why or why not?

SOURCES: "Is Money Talking Too Loud in Dodgertown?" *Business Week,* April 1, 1991, p. 42; "The Baseball Owners Get Beaned," *Business Week,* October 15, 1990, p. 122; Brenton R. Schlender, "Take Me Out to the Gold Mine," *Fortune,* August 13, 1990, pp. 93–100; "Business Secrets of Tommy Lasorda," *Fortune,* July 3, 1989, pp. 130–135.

CASE 3.2 Differing Perceptions at Clarkston Industries

Bill Harrington continued to drum his fingers on his desk. He had a real problem and wasn't sure what to do next. He had a lot of confidence in Jack Reed, but he suspected he was about the last person in the office who did. Perhaps if he ran through the entire story again in his mind he would see the solution.

Bill had been distribution manager for Clarkston Industries for almost twenty years. An early brush with the law and a short stay in prison had made him realize the importance of honesty and hard work. Henry Clarkston had given him a chance despite his record, and Bill had made the most of it. He now was one of the most respected managers in the company. Few people knew his background.

Bill had hired Jack Reed fresh out of prison six months ago. Bill understood how Jack felt when Jack tried to explain his past and asked for another chance. Bill decided to give him that chance just as Henry Clarkston had given him his. Jack eagerly accepted a job on the loading docks and soon was able to load a truck as fast as anyone else in the crew.

Things had gone well at first. Everyone seemed to like Jack, and he made several new friends. Bill had been vaguely disturbed about two months ago, however, when another dock worker reported her wallet missing. He confronted Jack about this and was reassured when Jack understood his concern and earnestly but calmly asserted his innocence. Bill was especially relieved when the wallet was found a few days later.

Events of last week, however, had brewed serious trouble. First, a new personnel clerk came across records about Jack's past while updating employee files. Assuming the information was common knowledge, the clerk mentioned to several employees what a good thing it was to give ex-convicts like Jack a chance. The next day, someone in bookkeeping discovered some money missing from petty cash. Another worker claimed to have seen Jack in the area around the office strongbox, which was open during working hours, earlier that same day.

Most people assumed Jack was the thief. The worker whose wallet had been misplaced suggested that perhaps Jack indeed had stolen it but then returned it when questioned. Several employees had approached Bill and requested that Jack be fired. Meanwhile, when Bill had discussed the problem with Jack, Jack had been defensive and sullen and said little about the petty-cash situation other than to deny stealing the money.

To his dismay, Bill found that rethinking the story did little to solve his problem. Should he fire Jack? The evidence, of course, was purely circumstantial, yet everybody else seemed to see things quite clearly. Bill feared that if he did not fire Jack, he would lose everyone's trust and that some people might even begin to question his own motives.

Case Questions

1. Explain the events in this case in terms of perceptual processes. Identify as many characteristics of the person, the object, and the situation as possible.
2. What should Bill do? Should he fire Jack, or give him another chance?

EXPERIENTIAL EXERCISE

Purpose: This exercise will give you insights into the problems and mechanisms of providing reinforcement to people.

Format: Your instructor will divide the class into groups of three. Each group will develop a reinforcement system that the instructor might use to reinforce student behavior in the classroom.

Procedure: First, develop a list of desirable and undesirable behaviors that students might exhibit in the classroom. For example, responding to questions might be a desirable behavior, whereas whispering to one's neighbor might be an undesirable behavior.

Next, identify various kinds of reinforcement your instructor might use to increase the frequency of the desirable behaviors and decrease the occurrence of the undesirable behaviors. Most of these should be rewards (i.e., positive reinforcement), but a few might also rely on avoidance, punishment, or extinction.

Next, develop appropriate schedules for the various kinds of reinforcement. Make sure to include at least one illustration for each schedule. Your instructor will then select a few groups at random to present their systems to the rest of the class. (A variation might have a member from a group role-play the instructor using the reinforcement system developed by his or her group.)

Follow-up Questions

1. How useful do you think your system would actually be if your instructor used it?
2. How much easier or more difficult would it be to do the same exercise in a work setting?

CHAPTER OUTLINE

The Nature of Individual Differences

People Are Unique

People and Situations

An Overview of Personality

The Nature of Personality

Personality Structures

Personality and Work

Locus of Control

Authoritarianism

Machiavellianism

Other Traits

Attitudes and Attitude Formation

The Dispositional View of Attitudes

The Situational View of Attitudes

Cognitive Dissonance

Attitude Change

Job-Related Attitudes

Job Satisfaction

Other Kinds of Satisfaction

Commitment and Involvement

Attitudes and Behaviors

Managerial Implications of Individual Differences

4

INDIVIDUAL DIFFERENCES

CHAPTER OBJECTIVES

After studying this chapter, you should be able to:

Describe the nature of individual differences.

Discuss personality and individual differences.

Describe personality traits that affect organizations.

Discuss attitudes and attitude formation.

Identify and describe job-related attitudes.

Relate attitudes to behaviors.

Summarize the managerial implications of individual differences.

Herb Kelleher and Robert Crandall are as different as night and day. Nevertheless, each functions very effectively as CEO of a major Dallas-based airline. Kelleher heads Southwest Airlines, and Crandall runs American.

Kelleher is widely known for his zaniness. He wears bizarre costumes on Southwest flights. New Southwest employees view a training tape set to a rap-music video. Kelleher encourages employees to call him "Herbie" or "Uncle Herb." He also hates meetings, preferring to just walk around and talk to people. But behind his zaniness, Kelleher is an astute manager. Southwest has grown to become the ninth largest airline in the United States, has the lowest costs in the industry, and continues to grow rapidly.

Crandall, on the other hand, is a rational, calm, and very conservative executive. He always wears a tie, prefers to be called "Mr. Crandall," and maintains a professionally distant posture with his employees. He seems to be at his best in meetings, which he uses extensively to discuss strategy and his competition. Moreover, his interest in and concern for detail are almost a legend within the company—indeed, his employees fear being unable to answer one of his questions. American has prospered under Crandall's leadership and recently became the largest airline in the United States.[1]

Herb Kelleher and Robert Crandall perform essentially the same job in the same industry. They are even headquartered in the same city. Yet, they differ markedly in several ways. And if we compared them with other successful (and less successful) airline industry executives, we would find that they too differ from one another. These differences add richness and complexity to the texture of organizational life.

This chapter is about differences among individuals. In many ways, the topics of Chapter 3—learning, perception, and attribution—represent individual differences. At a more basic level, there are other systematic differences among individuals that warrant additional exploration. These differences—key dimensions that distinguish people from one another—are the subject of this chapter.

First, we further characterize the nature of individual differences. Then we describe the role of personality and personality variables in individual differences. Next, we address the nature of attitudes and their effect on individuals and follow up with a discussion of several important job-related attitudes. Finally,

1. Kenneth Labich, "American Takes on the World," *Fortune,* September 24, 1990, pp. 40–48; Wilton Woods, "Revolution in the Air," *Fortune,* January 1, 1990, pp. 58–59; "Southwest Airlines: Flying High with 'Uncle Herb,'" *Business Week,* July 3, 1989, pp. 53–55.

we relate attitudes to behaviors and summarize several important managerial implications of individual differences.

The Nature of Individual Differences

Each person is much like everyone else in many important ways. Our biological systems, for example, are quite similar, as is our basic appearance. But each person is also very different from everyone else. The ways we think, the ways we interpret our environment, and the ways we respond to that environment are unique. We call this set of factors *individual differences*.

■ Individual differences are characteristics that set each person apart from other people.

People Are Unique

People are like jigsaw puzzles. Just as a puzzle is a picture assembled by putting various pieces together in a certain way, a person is composed of various attributes fitted together in a particular manner. And just as puzzles have pieces that fit together to form a whole, each of us has a unique set of attributes, or characteristics, that together represent the essence of who we are. Furthermore, although a person may resemble some people more than others, no two persons are exactly alike. Herb Kelleher and Robert Crandall are alike in some ways but very different in others.

Figure 4.1 shows several of the most common attributes that differentiate people from one another. Some differences are physical, and others are psychological. As previously noted, our focus here is on two critical psychological variables: personality and attitudes.

No two people are the same. Like the people in this Los Angeles park, organizations are made up of individuals of different ages, gender, ethnic origin, and religion. Thus, managers need to have a keen understanding of the dynamics of individual differences and cultural diversity if they are to be successful.

FIGURE 4.1
The Uniqueness of People

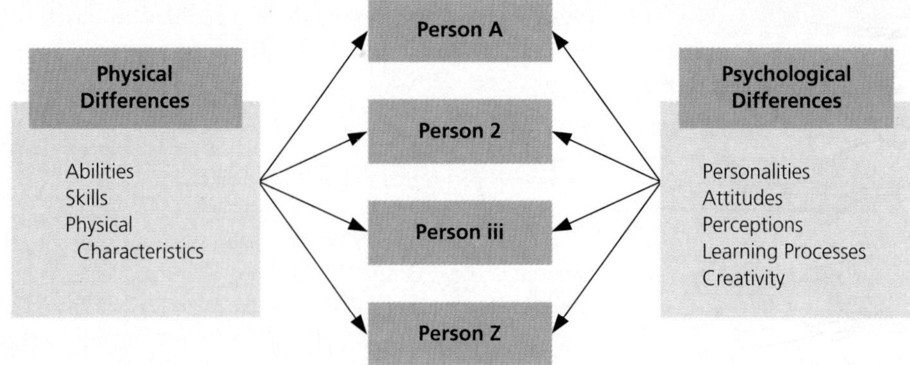

People and Situations

- People are unique in their own right. Situations accent this uniqueness.

People do not function independently of their environment or the situations in which they find themselves. Situational differences can affect how people respond in a variety of ways. Consider a typical manager working for a large company. His attitudes and behaviors have always been essentially positive, and he has been effective on the job. One day, however, his life takes a major change in direction. He gets a big promotion, he gets terminated because of a major cutback, or he and his wife decide to divorce. Any of these changes will place him in a quite different situation, and as a result his attitudes and behaviors may change. He may become happier, more upbeat, and work even harder than in the past, or he may become moody, depressed, and withdrawn. Our individuality is partly shaped by our environment. Groups of people in one situation behave differently than similar groups in other situations. Likewise, an individual whose situation changes also will respond differently to the new situation than he or she did to the old one.[2]

An Overview of Personality

- **Personality** is the set of distinctive traits and dimensions that can be used to characterize people.

One critical component of individual differences is the individual's personality. **Personality** is the set of distinctive traits and dimensions that can be used to characterize individuals.[3] In the next few pages, we take a close look at the determinants of an individual's personality; then we relate personality to the workplace.

---

2. Lawrence A. Pervin, "Persons, Situations, Interactions: The History of a Controversy and a Discussion of Theoretical Models," *Academy of Management Review,* July 1989, pp. 350–360.

3. See Walter Mischel, *Introduction to Personality* (New York: Holt, 1971), for a classic treatment. For a recent view, see Robert C. Carson, "Personality," in Mark Rosenzweig and Lyman Porter, eds., *Annual Review of Psychology,* vol. 40 (Palo Alto, Calif.: Annual Reviews, 1989), pp. 227–248.

The Nature of Personality

The word *personality* is one of the most misused terms in our language. When we describe someone as having "no personality," we actually mean that this person has a particular kind of personality: one that is bland and colorless. Likewise, when we describe a friend as having a "good personality," we mean that she or he is warm, friendly, and outgoing.

Why is the concept of personality important to managers? Many researchers agree that personality plays a major role in how a person perceives his or her work environment, evaluates it, and responds to it. The concept of interactional psychology that we introduced in Chapter 1 relates directly to this assertion.[4] Interactional psychology suggests that individual behavior is a function of continuous interaction between the person and the situation. Characteristics of the person—each a manifestation of personality—influence and are influenced by various factors in the workplace. For example, a person with a strong desire for status will analyze her work setting in terms of its opportunities to gain more status. She will view the situation as either facilitating or hindering the acquisition of status. And, depending on the level of status achieved, this employee may want even more status in the future, leave the situation in frustration, or be at least temporarily satisfied.

Personality Structures

- Personality structure consists of three elements: determinants, stages, and traits.

Comparing individual differences to a jigsaw puzzle leaves an important question unanswered: What is the source of the pieces and their interrelationships? In other words, how are personalities structured? Although we do not have all the answers, the prevailing theories, as Figure 4.2 shows, suggest that personality structure can be understood from the standpoint of three elements: determinants, stages, and traits.[5]

- Personality determinants are biological, social, and cultural factors that may play a role in shaping a person's personality.

Determinants *Determinants* of personality are factors that presumably play a role in shaping a person's personality. The most widely studied determinants are biological, social, and cultural factors.

One biological factor is the extent to which personality traits are genetic, that is, inherited from one's parents. Research suggests that genetics indeed may influence the formation and development of human personality. Biological factors can also affect personality indirectly. For example, physical characteristics such as height and build influence how we feel about ourselves. These feelings, in turn, affect our personality. A person who is teased because she is considerably shorter than her friends may feel defensive about her height and choose activities

---

4. James Terborg, "Interactional Psychology and Research on Human Behavior in Organizations," *Academy of Management Review,* October 1981, pp. 569–576.

5. Mischel, *Introduction to Personality.* See also Robert G. L. Pryor, "Differences among Differences: In Search of General Work Preference Dimensions," *Journal of Applied Psychology,* August 1987, pp. 426–433.

FIGURE 4.2
Personality Structure

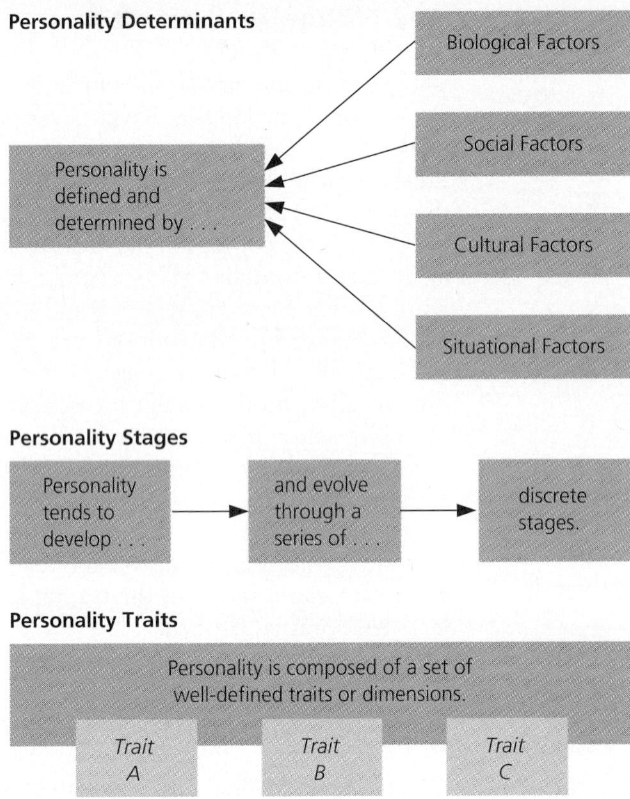

particularly suited to short people, such as gymnastics rather than basketball. But biological determinants have their limits. Scientists today discount an early theory that suggested that personality is directly correlated with a person's overall body shape.[6]

Social factors also are a determinant of personality. Our early experiences with our parents vastly influence our later lives. For example, children who suffer major traumas such as the death of a parent may experience emotional repercussions throughout their lives. As children grow, they tend to develop friendship groups at school and in their neighborhoods. The kinds of people they interact with may influence their own behavior. For instance, a child whose own family is not religious but who develops close friendships with children whose families are religious may develop strong religious beliefs. The influence of social factors does not stop when a person reaches adulthood. Indeed, an increasing body of literature on socialization suggests that social forces in the workplace affect people's personalities, perceptions, and behaviors.[7]

---

6. William H. Sheldon, *Atlas to Men: A Guide for Somatotyping the Adult Male at All Ages* (New York: Harper, 1954).

7. For a thorough review of the socialization literature, see John P. Wanous, Arnon E. Reichers, and S. D. Malik, "Organizational Socialization and Group Development: Toward an Integrative Perspective," *Academy of Management Review*, October 1984, pp. 670–683.

Cultural factors are characteristics of the broader, sociocultural environment that influences personality. Psychologists only recently have begun to investigate these factors, but it is clear that motives, acceptable behaviors, and respect for authority vary from one country to another. Cultural factors also influence social dynamics. The English and Germans, for example, stand farther apart when talking than do Americans, whereas Arabs, Japanese, and Mexicans stand closer together. Finally, culture instills values. A strong sense of competitiveness may characterize people from some cultures, whereas those from other cultures may be more comfortable with cooperation.[8]

In addition to the biological, social, and cultural determinants of personality, situational factors affect personality, often in unpredictable or little understood ways. These factors may shape personality or bring out hidden characteristics. A good example of situational influences appears in the research of Stanley Milgram.[9] Milgram asked subjects to administer what they believed was an electric shock to a person in another room. As the shocks became stronger, the other person began to scream in pain and beg the subject to stop. The experimenter, however, ordered the subject to continue. More than half the subjects were willing, when ordered, to administer a shock clearly labeled as dangerous and possibly life threatening.

The results of this and follow-up studies indicate that people have personality characteristics that are revealed only in specific situations. Real-life examples range from people who spontaneously perform heroic acts without thinking of their personal welfare to those who engage in unethical or illegal behavior when under extreme pressure. As with culture, research into the situational determinants of personality is still in its infancy.

- Personality stages are phases of development through which an individual's personality is presumed to pass.

Stages A second major approach to personality structure suggests that personalities develop in *stages*. The major proponents of stage approaches are Sigmund Freud, Erik Erikson, and Jean Piaget.

Freud, the pioneer of psychoanalytic theory, argued that behavior is caused primarily by unconscious motives.[10] These motives are shaped by a variety of stages of personality development, each of which has sexual undertones. According to Freud, the four stages of personality development are dependent, compulsive, oedipal, and mature. These stages, however, are not generally accepted by contemporary theorists.

Erik Erikson accepted the Freudian concept of personality stages but rejected Freud's stages as being too heavily slanted toward biological and sexual factors.[11] Instead, Erikson focused on the social adaptations people must make as they grow older. He argued that we progress through eight basic stages of development, including mouth and senses (stage 1), latency (stage 4), early adulthood

8. Nancy J. Adler, *International Dimensions of Organizational Behavior* (Boston: Kent, 1986).

9. Stanley Milgram, "Some Conditions of Obedience and Disobedience to Authority," *Human Relations,* February 1965, pp. 57–76.

10. Sigmund Freud, "Lecture XXXIII," *New Introductory Lectures on Psychoanalysis* (New York: Norton, 1933), pp. 153–186. For recent perspectives on Freud's work, see "Re-Examining Freud," *Psychology Today,* September 1989, pp. 48–52.

11. Erik Erikson, *Childhood and Society,* 2nd ed. (New York: Norton, 1963).

These Japanese women grew up in a culture that believed women should stay home and raise a family. As values and customs have changed, so too have women like these. No longer content with the traditional female Japanese career as an "office lady," they have aggressively pursued professional career opportunities in Nissan Motor Co.'s design department. And they are responsible for two of the firm's most recent design triumphs.

(stage 6), and mature adulthood (stage 8). The progression from one stage to the next is marked by a crisis. Healthy personality development is said to depend on the effectiveness with which the individual copes with each crisis. In organizational settings, parallels to Erikson's stages may appear in the form of the crises a person passes through while moving from newcomer status to being a mature and then a senior member of the organization.

Like Freud, Jean Piaget suggested that we pass through stages of personality development.[12] However, Piaget believed that the stages and the progressions between them are conscious activities. The precise stages Piaget suggested are not specifically relevant to organizational settings. His more important contribution, for our purposes, is the argument that the conscious elements of personality formation are at least as significant as the unconscious elements. Of the three stage approaches, the work of Piaget is perhaps best supported by empirical research.[13]

In terms of organizational behavior, the main thing to be learned from these perspectives is the notion of development. People change with the passage of time, and in ways that are at least somewhat predictable rather than purely random and unstable. Furthermore, change generally is healthy and desirable for both the person and the social system in which he or she functions. More than likely, both conscious and unconscious stages, all marked with various crises of transition, typify most employees as they enter, participate in, and eventually leave organizations.

- Personality traits are presumed to be a configuration of dimensions that comprise personality.

Traits *Trait* approaches to personality formation try to identify a configuration of traits that best reflect personality. The most widely known of the trait theorists are Gordon Allport and Raymond Cattell.

Gordon Allport, a noted psychologist, suggested that everyone has a common set of personality traits, but individuals also have and can be differentiated

12. Jean Piaget, "The General Problems of the Psychological Development of the Child," in J. M. Tanner and B. Inhelder, eds., *Discussions on Child Development* (New York: International Universities Press, 1960), pp. 3–27.

13. Mischel, *Introduction to Personality.*

TABLE 4.1
The Immaturity-Maturity Model

Immature Characteristics		Mature Characteristics
Passive	→	Active
Dependent	→	Independent
Few Behaviors	→	Many Behaviors
Shallow Interests	→	Deep Interests
Short-Term Perspective	→	Long-Term Perspective
Subordinate Position	→	Superordinate Position
Little Self-Awareness	→	More Self-Awareness and Control

SOURCE: Adapted from page 50 in *Personality and Organization: The Conflict between the System and the Individual* by Chris Argyris. Copyright © 1957 by Harper & Row, Publishers, Inc. Copyright renewed 1990 by Chris Argyris. Reprinted by permission of HarperCollins Publishers.

by a set of unique traits, called *personal dispositions*.[14] Allport's common traits include social, political, religious, and esthetic propensities. By definition, personal dispositions vary from one person to the next. For instance, one person may be very outgoing and friendly but uninterested in politics. A second person, on the other hand, may be withdrawn but fascinated by politics.

Raymond Cattell, another pioneering psychologist, also advocated a trait framework for understanding personality.[15] In this view, all people can be described and characterized along two specific sets of personality traits, or dimensions. Surface traits reflect people's observable and consistent behaviors (honest or dishonest, warm or cold). Source traits (trusting or suspicious, mature or immature, dominant or submissive) are more difficult to discern because people often keep them hidden.

- The immaturity-maturity model suggests that personality in organizations evolves along seven dimensions.

The Immaturity-Maturity Model In addition to the various theories and models of personality formation developed by psychologists, there is a model of personality formation developed specifically for the context of organizational behavior. Chris Argyris has proposed a model of the workplace personality that combines the stage and trait approaches.[16] His model, summarized in Table 4.1, focuses almost exclusively on people in organizational settings. According to Argyris, an individual's personality develops from immature to mature along seven basic dimensions. Argyris suggests that as people gain experience and self-confidence in their jobs, they tend to move from the immature end to the mature end of each dimension. Thus, they move from passive to active, from having short-term perspectives to developing long-term perspectives, and so forth. Unfortunately, Argyris contends, organizations typically are designed to foster and reward

14. Gordon Allport, *Pattern and Growth in Personality* (New York: Holt, 1961).
15. Raymond Cattell, *The Scientific Analysis of Personality* (Chicago: Aldine, 1965).
16. Chris Argyris, *Personality and Organization: The Conflict between the System and the Individual* (New York: Harper & Row, 1957).

immaturity and stifle and punish maturity. If he is correct, a basic conflict exists between people and the organizations in which they work.

Personality and Work

The historical theory and research on personality we just discussed are important in that they highlight the complexities involved in understanding individual differences as well as various approaches for understanding how they occur. The most direct applications of personality theory for the field of organizational behavior, however, have been through the identification and description of traits that have direct relevance for organizations. Three of these traits are locus of control, authoritarianism, and Machiavellianism.

Locus of Control

■ **Locus of control** is an individual's beliefs about whether or not his or her behavior has a direct effect on the consequences of that behavior.

Locus of control is the extent to which a person believes that his or her behavior has a direct impact on the consequences of that behavior.[17] Some people believe they can control what happens to them—that if they work hard, for instance, they will be successful. These people, called *internals,* have what is termed an *internal locus of control. Externals,* or people with an *external locus of control,* tend to think that what happens to them is determined by fate or luck. They see little or no connection between their behavior and subsequent events. Like attribution theory concepts, locus of control concepts focus on people's interpretations of what happens to them.

Locus of control concepts have some significant managerial implications. Internals are likely to want a voice in how they perform their jobs because they believe that what happens to them will depend on how well they control their environment. Externals, in contrast, may be less inclined to participate in decision making. A good example of an internal in business is Harry Gray, former chief executive officer of United Technologies Corp. In his years at UTC, Gray consistently sought to control his environment through techniques such as grooming potential successors and then driving them off with pressure tactics, dictating corporate policy from the executive suite, and going to unusual lengths to ensure that things would always be done his way.[18] Of course, not all internals are so extreme; many simply want a voice in determining what happens to them. *Developing Management Skills* highlights some of the complexities associated with locus of control.

---

17. J. B. Rotter, "Generalized Expectancies for Internal vs. External Control of Reinforcement," *Psychological Monographs,* vol. 80, 1966, pp. 1–28. See also Paul Spector, "Behavior in Organizations as a Function of Employees' Locus of Control," *Psychological Bulletin,* vol. 91, no. 3, 1982, pp. 482–497; Marilyn E. Gist, "Self-Efficacy: Implications for Organizational Behavior and Human Resource Management," *Academy of Management Review,* July 1987, pp. 472–485.

18. Geoffrey Colvin, "Why Harry Gray Can't Let Go at United Technologies," *Fortune,* November 12, 1984, pp. 16–19; "Coming Attractions," *Fortune,* February 15, 1988, pp. 119–120.

DEVELOPING MANAGEMENT SKILLS

Assessing Locus of Control

Read each pair of statements below and indicate whether you agree more with statement A or with statement B. There are no right or wrong answers. In some cases, you may agree somewhat with both statements; choose the one with which you agree more.

1. _____
   A. Making a lot of money is largely a matter of getting the right breaks.
   B. Promotions are earned through hard work and persistence.
2. _____
   A. There is usually a direct correlation between how hard I study and the grades I get.
   B. Many times the reactions of teachers seem haphazard to me.
3. _____
   A. The number of divorces suggests that more and more people are not trying to make their marriages work.
   B. Marriage is primarily a gamble.
4. _____
   A. It is silly to think you can really change another person's basic attitudes.
   B. When I am right, I can generally convince others.
5. _____
   A. Getting promoted is really a matter of being a little luckier than the next person.
   B. In our society, a person's future earning power is dependent upon her or his ability.
6. _____
   A. If one knows how to deal with people, they are really quite easily led.
   B. I have little influence over the way other people behave.
7. _____
   A. The grades I make are the result of my own efforts; luck has little or nothing to do with it.
   B. Sometimes I feel that I have little to do with the grades I get.
8. _____
   A. People like me can change the course of world affairs if we make ourselves heard.
   B. It is only wishful thinking to believe that one can readily influence what happens in our society at large.
9. _____
   A. A great deal that happens to me probably is a matter of chance.
   B. I am the master of my life.
10. _____
    A. Getting along with people is a skill that must be practiced.
    B. It is almost impossible to figure out how to please some people.

Give yourself 1 point each if you chose the following answers: 1B, 2A, 3A, 4B, 5B, 6A, 7A, 8A, 9B, 10A.
Sum your scores and interpret them as follows:

8–10 = high internal locus of control
6–7 = moderate locus of control
5 = mixed internal/external locus of control
3–4 = moderate external locus of control
1–2 = high external locus of control

(Note: This is an abbreviated version of a longer instrument. The scores obtained here are only an approximation of what your score might be on the complete instrument.)

SOURCE: Adapted from J. B. Rotter, "External Control and Internal Control," *Psychology Today,* June 1971, p. 42.

Authoritarianism

- **Authoritarianism** is the extent to which a person believes that power and status differences in an organization are legitimate.

Authoritarianism is the extent to which a person believes that power and status differences should exist within a social system like an organization.[19] The stronger the belief, the more authoritarian the individual is said to be. The literature on authoritarianism holds several helpful implications for managers. Subordinates who are highly authoritarian may be more willing to accept a directive style of supervision; they are also less likely to argue with a manager's suggestions. Researchers have also found some interesting tie-ins between the authoritarian personality and the Milgram studies summarized earlier. In particular, highly authoritarian people are more likely to obey orders from someone with authority without raising any serious objections, even if they recognize potential dangers or pitfalls.[20]

Machiavellianism

- **Machiavellianism** is a person's motivation to gain power and control the behavior of others.

Machiavellianism is another important personality trait. This concept is named after Niccolo Machiavelli, a sixteenth-century author. In his book *The Prince,* Machiavelli explained how the nobility could more easily gain and use power. The term **Machiavellianism** is now used to describe behavior directed at gaining power and controlling the behavior of others. Research suggests that Machiavellianism is a personality trait that varies from person to person.

Individuals who are high on Machiavellianism tend to be rational and nonemotional, may be willing to lie to attain their personal goals, put little weight on loyalty and friendship, and enjoy manipulating others' behavior. Individuals who are low on Machiavellianism are more emotional, are less willing to lie to succeed, value loyalty and friendship highly, and get little personal pleasure from manipulating others.

Other Traits

- Self-monitoring, self-esteem, Type A and Type B profiles, willingness to take risks, mood tendencies, and an individual's values and ethics are additional personality traits that are relevant to organizational behavior.

In addition to the three key traits just described, several other traits may apply to organizational behavior. *Self-monitoring,* a fairly new concept, is the extent to which people emulate the behavior of others.[21] A person who is a high self-monitor tends to pay close attention to others' behavior and to model his or her own behavior after that of the people observed. A person who is low on the self-monitoring dimension pays considerably less attention to the behavior of others. Such a person tends to react to situations without looking to others for behavioral cues.

---

19. T. W. Adorno, E. Frenkel-Brunswik, D. J. Levinson, and R. N. Sanford, *The Authoritarian Personality* (New York: Harper & Row, 1950).

20. "Who Becomes an Authoritarian?", *Psychology Today,* March 1989, pp. 66–70.

21. Mark Snyder and Nancy Cantor, "Thinking about Ourselves and Others: Self-Monitoring and Social Knowledge," *Journal of Personality and Social Psychology,* vol. 39, no. 2, 1980, pp. 222–234.

Johnathan Rodgers has risen through the ranks at CBS and was recently promoted to the position of President of the CBS Television Stations Division. Managers who achieve successes like this are likely to have high self-esteem and an internal locus of control. People who have an internal locus of control believe that if they work hard they can be successful.

Self-esteem, also recognized as an important personality trait in recent years, is the extent to which a person believes that he or she is a worthwhile and deserving individual. Recent studies have linked self-esteem to job performance, job satisfaction, and the job search process. For example, a person with high self-esteem may be likely to seek a higher-status job, whereas a person with low self-esteem may be satisfied with the status quo.[22] Likewise, higher levels of self-esteem might lead to higher levels of performance and satisfaction from having attained that performance level.

Another important personality trait is the distinction between *Type A* and *Type B* profiles. This concept is related to stress, and we cover it in Chapter 15. *Willingness to take risks, mood tendencies,* and *introversion/extroversion tendencies* are also important. Finally, there is the individual's *values* and *ethics. The Ethical Dilemma* discusses these concepts in more detail.

Attitudes and Attitude Formation

Another individual difference important to managers is employee attitudes. We sometimes speak of "attitude problems" or say that someone has a "bad attitude." Some bars advertise "attitude adjustment specials."

But what is an attitude? How is one formed? What is a "bad attitude" or an "attitude problem"? In this section, we attempt to provide some insight into these questions. After summarizing the dispositional and situational perspectives on attitudes, we address the processes involved in attitude formation. We conclude by explaining the concepts of cognitive dissonance and attitude change.

22. Phyllis Tharenou and Phillip Harker, "Moderating Influences of Self-Esteem on Relationships between Job Complexity, Performance, and Satisfaction," *Journal of Applied Psychology,* November 1984, pp. 623–632; Rebecca A. Ellis and M. Susan Taylor, "Role of Self-Esteem within the Job Search Process," *Journal of Applied Psychology,* November 1983, pp. 632–640.

THE ETHICAL DILEMMA

Values and Ethics as Individual Differences

Are some people inherently honest and ethical and others inherently dishonest and unethical? It really depends on how you define individual differences. In general, most people agree that ethics and values are learned and shaped as a person grows up. By the time people reach adulthood, they usually have a basic personal framework for distinguishing right from wrong and good from bad.

As a result, most people have a personal "code of conduct" that prescribes their own behavior and how they assess the behavior of others. Within this personal code, there are likely to be four sets of alternatives: behavior that is clearly right and ethical (returning money that dropped from someone's pocket), behavior that is clearly wrong and unethical (stealing money from an unattended wallet), behavior that is ambiguous with regard to ethics (what to do with money found on the street with no apparent owner), and unanticipated behaviors that must be evaluated within their situational context (how to intervene if you see your boss find money on the floor).

From another vantage point, the importance of ethical behavior also varies from person to person. Some individuals are very concerned about what others think of them and will go to great lengths to abide by ethical standards that others will appreciate regardless of their own beliefs. Other people have no concern whatsoever about what others think but will fervently adhere to their own personal standards. Still others have no regard at all for ethics or values, putting their own preferences first in all instances. Ethical standards also vary in their rigidity. Some people adhere to their ethical principles religiously, whereas others violate or bend them on a regular basis.

Thus, values and ethics indeed are individual differences. People differ in how they form their values and ethics, the importance they place on adhering to them, and the values and ethics themselves.

SOURCES: Agnes Heller, *General Ethics* (London: Basil Blackwell, 1988); "The Business Ethics Debate," *Newsweek,* May 25, 1987, p. 36; F. Neil Brady, "Aesthetic Components of Management Ethics," *Academy of Management Review,* April 1986, pp. 337–344.

The Dispositional View of Attitudes

- The dispositional view of attitudes holds that attitudes are stable dispositions toward an object.
- According to the dispositional view, attitudes have three basic components: affect, cognition, and intention.

Historically, attitudes were viewed as stable dispositions to behave toward objects in a certain way as a result of experience.[23] For any number of reasons, a person might decide that he or she did not like a particular political figure or a certain restaurant (a disposition). That person would then be expected to express consistently negative opinions of the candidate or restaurant and to maintain the consistent and predictable intention of not voting for the political candidate or patronizing the restaurant. In the traditional dispositional view of attitudes, illustrated in Figure 4.3, attitudes contain three components: affect, cognition, and intention.

23. Gordon W. Allport, "Attitudes," in C. Murchison, ed., *Handbook of Social Psychology* (Worcester, Mass.: Clark University Press, 1935), pp. 798–844. See also Barry Gerhart, "How Important Are Dispositional Factors as Determinants of Job Satisfaction? Implications for Job Design and Other Personnel Programs," *Journal of Applied Psychology,* August 1987, pp. 366–373.

FIGURE 4.3
The Dispositional View of Attitudes

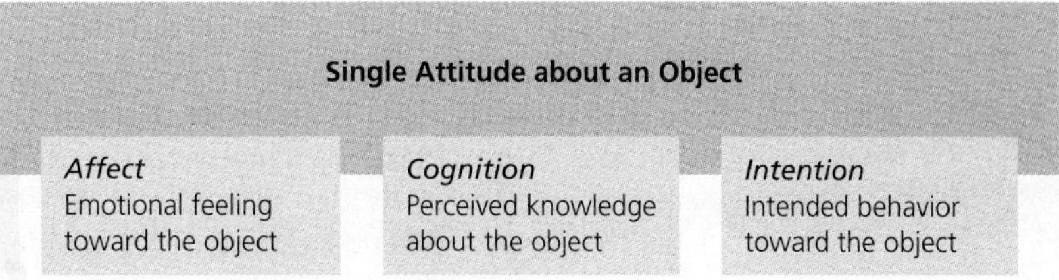

Affect *Affect* refers to the individual's feelings toward something. In many ways, affect is similar to emotion: It is something over which we have little or no conscious control. For example, most people react to words such as *love, hate, sex,* and *war* in a manner that reflects their feelings about what those words convey. Similarly, you may like one of your classes, dislike another, and be indifferent toward a third. If the class you dislike is an elective, you may not be particularly concerned. But if it is the first course in your chosen major, your affective reaction may cause you considerable anxiety.

Cognition *Cognition* is the knowledge a person presumes to have about something. You may believe you like a class because the textbook is excellent, the class meets at your favorite time, the instructor is outstanding, and the workload is light. This "knowledge" may be true, partially true, or totally false. For example, you may intend to vote for a particular candidate because you think you know where the candidate stands on several issues. In reality, depending on the candidate's honesty and your understanding of his or her statements, the candidate's thinking on the issues may be exactly the same as yours, partly the same, or totally different. Cognitions are based on perceptions of truth and reality, and, as we note in Chapter 3, perceptions agree with reality to varying degrees.

Intention *Intention* guides a person's behavior toward something. If you like your instructor, you may intend to take another class from him or her next semester. Intentions are not always translated into actual behavior, however. If the instructor's course next semester is scheduled for 8:00 A.M., you may decide that another instructor is just as good. Some attitudes, and their corresponding intentions, are much more central and significant to an individual than others. You may intend to do one thing (take a particular class) but later alter your intentions because of a more significant and central attitude (fondness for sleeping late).[24]

---

24. Bobby J. Calder and Paul H. Schurr, "Attitudinal Processes in Organizations," in Larry L. Cummings and Barry M. Staw, eds., *Research in Organizational Behavior,* vol. 3 (Greenwich, Conn.: JAI Press, 1981), pp. 283–302.

The Situational View of Attitudes

- The situational view of attitudes contends that attitudes evolve from socially constructed realities.

The dispositional view of attitudes recently has been challenged by Gerald Salancik and Jeffrey Pfeffer.[25] These authors contend that research has not clearly demonstrated that attitudes are stable dispositions composed of precise components that are consistently reflected in individual responses. Instead, they argue, attitudes evolve from socially constructed realities. Figure 4.4 illustrates the situational view.

Salancik and Pfeffer believe the social context delivers information that shapes the individual's attitudes. By means of cues and guides, social information provides a specific prescription for socially acceptable attitudes and behaviors. Such information focuses attention on specific attributes of the setting (for example, the workplace), thus making behaviors and attitudes that dominate in that setting more salient (important to the individual).

Suppose a new employee joins a work group that has existed for some time. Very likely, the members of the group will quickly communicate to the newcomer how they feel about the boss and the reward system and how much effort the group thinks members should put out to perform a given task. As a result, the newcomer tends to adopt an attitude toward the boss and the reward system that is consistent with what she has been told to expect. She is also likely to perform at a level of effort acceptable to the group. The new employee's attitudes and behaviors, then, have been partly shaped by social information and its effects on the individual's perception of reality.

The situational view of attitudes is comparatively new, but it has proved interesting to researchers and managers alike.[26] In general, most research provides at least partial support for this model, but the emerging opinion appears to be that attitudes are shaped by both objective attributes of the workplace and social information. We discuss this perspective from another viewpoint in Chapter 13.

Cognitive Dissonance

- **Cognitive dissonance** is the anxiety a person experiences when two sets of knowledge or perceptions are contradictory or incongruent.

Cognitive dissonance is the anxiety a person experiences when two sets of knowledge or perceptions are contradictory or incongruent. Cognitive dissonance also occurs when a person behaves in a fashion that is inconsistent with her or his attitudes.[27] For example, a person may realize that smoking and overeating are dangerous yet continue to do both. Because the attitudes and behaviors are

25. Gerald Salancik and Jeffrey Pfeffer, "An Examination of Need-Satisfaction Models of Job Attitudes," *Administrative Science Quarterly,* vol. 22, 1977, pp. 427–456; Gerald Salancik and Jeffrey Pfeffer, "A Social Information Processing Approach to Job Attitudes and Task Design," *Administrative Science Quarterly,* vol. 23, 1978, pp. 224–253.

26. Ricky W. Griffin, "Toward an Integrated Theory of Task Design," in Larry L. Cummings and Barry M. Staw, eds., *Research in Organizational Behavior,* vol. 9 (Greenwich, Conn.: JAI Press, 1987), pp. 79–120.

27. Leon Festinger, *A Theory of Cognitive Dissonance* (Palo Alto, Calif.: Stanford University Press, 1957).

FIGURE 4.4
The Situational View of Attitudes

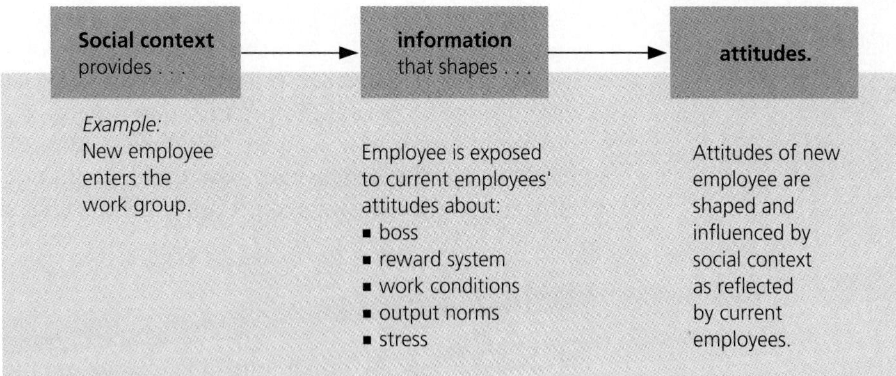

not consistent with each other, the person probably will experience a certain amount of tension and discomfort and may engage in *dissonance reduction*, seeking ways to reduce the dissonance and the tension it causes. The dissonance associated with smoking might be resolved by rationalizing, "Just a pack a day won't affect my health," or "I can quit when I have to." With regard to overeating, the person may decide to go on a diet "next week." In general, then, the person attempts to change the attitude, alter the behavior, or perceptually distort the circumstances to reduce tension and discomfort.

A classic study by Barry M. Staw provides a very insightful example of the processes of dissonance reduction.[28] Staw's subjects were male college students who joined the Reserve Officers Training Corps (ROTC) between 1969 and 1971. During that turbulent period, many male students joined the ROTC to avoid being drafted and sent to serve in the Vietnam War. The legally binding commitment to the ROTC involved on-campus military training while in college and a commission in the reserve forces after graduation. Just after this period, the Selective Service Administration instituted an annual lottery to determine who would be drafted. Each lottery number corresponded to a birthday: the lower the lottery number, the higher the odds of being drafted.

Staw reasoned that ROTC students whose lottery numbers were high enough to keep them out of the draft would begin to experience cognitive dissonance; that is, they had made a commitment that turned out to be unnecessary. He predicted that those who received low numbers would experience less dissonance because their commitment continued to serve its intended purpose: to spare them active duty in the military. Staw asked a group of ROTC students to fill out questionnaires designed to measure their satisfaction with the ROTC program. As predicted, students with high lottery numbers—those who now had the least to gain by being in the program—indicated the most satisfaction. They apparently used satisfaction as a reason to justify their ROTC commitment given that it no longer served its original purpose.

28. Barry M. Staw, "Attitudinal and Behavioral Consequences of Changing a Major Organizational Reward: A Natural Field Experiment," *Journal of Personality and Social Psychology,* vol. 9, 1974, pp. 742–751.

Cognitive dissonance affects people in a variety of ways. We frequently encounter situations in which our attitudes conflict with our behaviors or with one another. Dissonance reduction is the way we deal with these feelings of discomfort and tension. In organizational settings, people contemplating leaving the organization may wonder why they continue to stay and work hard. As a result of this dissonance, they may conclude that the company is not so bad after all, that they have no immediate options elsewhere, or that they will leave "soon."

Attitude Change

How can managers initiate attitude change among employees? For example, if employees are greatly dissatisfied with their pay, it may be necessary to change this attitude to prevent a mass exodus of valuable employees. One approach would be to inform employees that the organization is paying all it can now but hopes to increase wages in the near future. Another would be to demonstrate that no other organization pays more. A third would be to actually increase wages, thus eliminating the cause of the attitude. Employee attitude change is the goal of many organizational change and development techniques, which we discuss in Chapter 21.

Job-Related Attitudes

Attitudes are an important consideration for managers. Employee attitudes may be related to behaviors critical to the organization: Dissatisfied employees, for instance, are more likely to be absent from work or to leave for better opportunities elsewhere. Negative attitudes toward the organization can also spur employees to consider forming or joining a labor union. Theory and research on attitudes can help managers understand employee attitudes toward the workplace. In general, employees develop consistent and identifiable sets of attitudes toward job attributes such as pay, working conditions, and the job's tasks.

Job Satisfaction

- **Job satisfaction** or **dissatisfaction** is an individual's attitude toward her or his job.

Job satisfaction or **dissatisfaction**—an individual's attitude toward his or her job—undoubtedly is one of the most widely studied variables in the field of organizational behavior. When this attitude is positive, employees are said to be satisfied. Dissatisfaction exists when the attitude is negative. Thousands of studies that deal with some aspect of job satisfaction have been published.[29] Obviously,

29. See, for example, Edwin A. Locke, "The Nature and Causes of Job Satisfaction," in Marvin Dunnette, ed., *Handbook of Industrial and Organizational Psychology* (Chicago: Rand-McNally, 1976), pp. 1297–1350; Ricky W. Griffin and Thomas S. Bateman, "Job Satisfaction and Organizational Commitment," in Cary L. Cooper and Ivan T. Robertson, eds., *International Review of Industrial and Organizational Psychology* (New York: Wiley, 1986), pp. 157–188.

all managers should be concerned about the satisfaction or dissatisfaction of their employees.

Figure 4.5 summarizes the primary causes and consequences of job satisfaction and dissatisfaction. The key causes can be grouped into three categories: organizational factors, group factors, and personal factors. The two primary consequences of satisfaction or dissatisfaction relate to absenteeism and turnover.

- Pay, opportunities for promotion, the nature of the job itself, the organization's policies and procedures, and working conditions usually determine job satisfaction or dissatisfaction.

Causes of Satisfaction and Dissatisfaction There are five major organizational factors toward which employees form attitudes: pay, opportunities for promotion, the nature of the work itself, policies and procedures of the organization, and working conditions. Clearly, a person may experience different levels of satisfaction toward each factor. For example, an employee may believe he is underpaid (dissatisfied with pay) but simultaneously feel very positive about the other organizational factors.

The job satisfaction of individuals within a work group also may be influenced by both their coworkers and their supervisor or manager. The supervisor could be regarded as an organizational factor, but because the position is described and defined by the organization, it is often his or her individual characteristics (warmth, understanding, integrity) that most strongly influence employee attitudes.

A person's needs and aspirations also can affect satisfaction. If an employee wants to be in a high-status position, gaining such a position probably will enhance that person's level of job satisfaction. Also important are the instru-

FIGURE 4.5
Causes and Consequences of Job Satisfaction and Dissatisfaction

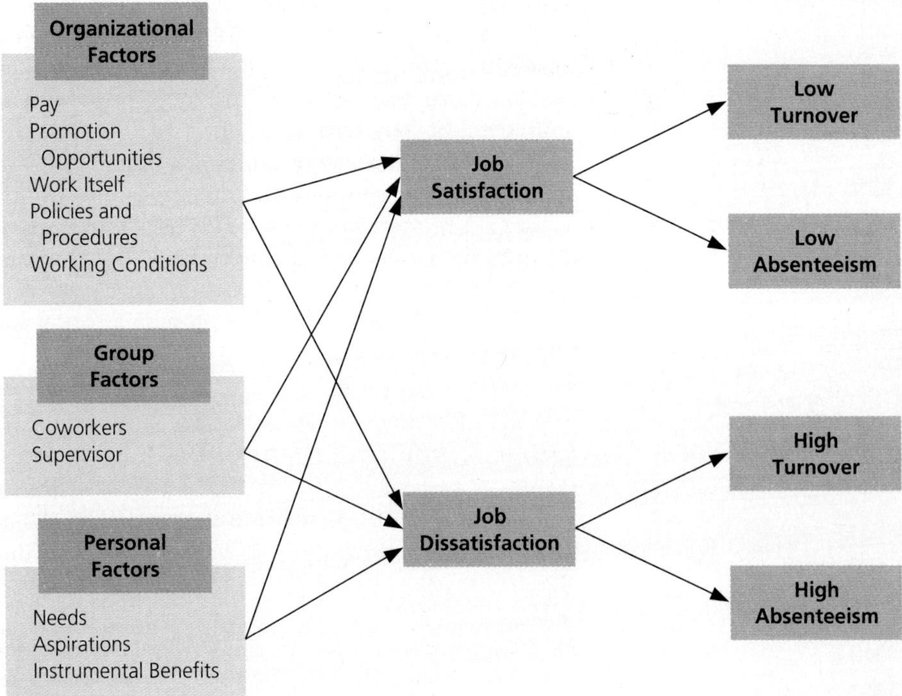

mental benefits of the job, or the extent to which the job enables the employee to achieve other ends. A person finishing her college degree might take a particular job on a temporary basis because it allows flexible scheduling while paying enough to cover her tuition. She may be quite satisfied with the job as long as she is in school but be considerably less satisfied with it on a permanent basis.

- Job satisfaction or dissatisfaction directly affects employee turnover and absenteeism.

Consequences of Satisfaction and Dissatisfaction As Figure 4.5 shows, employee satisfaction affects turnover and absenteeism. When people are dissatisfied with their jobs, they are more likely to call in sick when they really feel fine and may even leave the organization for more attractive jobs elsewhere. Conversely, when employees are satisfied, they come to work more regularly and are less likely to seek other employment.

- Job satisfaction typically is measured with a questionnaire.

Measuring Satisfaction How do managers measure job satisfaction? Several techniques have been developed, including interviews and critical incidents, but by far the most popular device has been questionnaires, often called *attitude* or *opinion surveys*. Basically, attitude questionnaires ask how the person feels about various aspects of his or her job. Table 4.2 presents questions from one popular measure.

Job satisfaction measures can give both managers and researchers a great deal of information about worker attitudes. But the picture such instruments provide may not be entirely accurate. Because instruments measure perceptions of the workplace rather than actual circumstances, the results may be influenced by the wording of questions and the choice of topics covered by the survey. Moreover, the results may be contaminated by individual attitudes toward other dimensions of the workplace that are only tangentially related to the job. For example, a person might indicate low job satisfaction because of having to fight rush-hour traffic every day. Short-term feelings, such as anxiety about a looming deadline, also may distort a person's responses, thereby giving an inaccurate impression of long-term attitudes.

Still, attitude surveys can be a valuable tool for managers. Normative data are available for certain questionnaires, indicating the distribution of responses in a representative population. By using such surveys, a manager can compare the attitudes of his or her employees with those of employees in similar organizations. Surveys can also point to major employee concerns, which can then be remedied. At the least, they can provide a forum for constructive feedback from employees to managers.

Other Kinds of Satisfaction

Many kinds of attitudes exist in the workplace. Some, of course, matter far more to people than others do.[30] A worker who feels underpaid is fairly likely to do

30. Thomas S. Bateman and Dennis W. Organ, "Job Satisfaction and the Good Soldier: The Relationship between Affect and Employee 'Citizenship,'" *Academy of Management Journal*, December 1983, pp. 587–595.

TABLE 4.2
Sample Items from the Minnesota Satisfaction Questionnaire

Ask yourself: How satisfied am I with this aspect of my job?

VS means I am very satisfied with this aspect of my job.

S means I am satisfied with this aspect of my job.

N means I can't decide whether I am satisfied or not with this aspect of my job.

DS means I am dissatisfied with this aspect of my job.

VDS means I am very dissatisfied with this aspect of my job.

On my present job, this is how I feel about:	**VDS**	**DS**	**N**	**S**	**VS**
1. Being able to keep busy all the time	☐	☐	☐	☐	☐
2. The chance to work alone on the job	☐	☐	☐	☐	☐
3. The chance to do different things from time to time	☐	☐	☐	☐	☐
4. The chance to be "somebody" in the community	☐	☐	☐	☐	☐
5. The way my boss handles his employees	☐	☐	☐	☐	☐
6. The competence of my supervisor in making decisions	☐	☐	☐	☐	☐
7. Being able to do things that don't go against my conscience	☐	☐	☐	☐	☐
8. The way my job provides for steady employment	☐	☐	☐	☐	☐
9. The chance to do things for other people	☐	☐	☐	☐	☐
10. The chance to tell people what to do	☐	☐	☐	☐	☐
11. The chance to do something that makes use of my abilities	☐	☐	☐	☐	☐
12. The way company policies are put into practice	☐	☐	☐	☐	☐
13. My pay and the amount of work I do	☐	☐	☐	☐	☐
14. The chances for advancement on this job	☐	☐	☐	☐	☐
15. The freedom to use my own judgment	☐	☐	☐	☐	☐
16. The chance to try my own methods of doing the job	☐	☐	☐	☐	☐
17. The working conditions	☐	☐	☐	☐	☐
18. The way my co-workers get along with each other	☐	☐	☐	☐	☐
19. The praise I get for doing a good job	☐	☐	☐	☐	☐
20. The feeling of accomplishment I get from the job	☐	☐	☐	☐	☐

SOURCE: *Manual for the Minnesota Satisfaction Questionnaire.* Used by permission of the Industrial Relations Center and Vocational Psychology Research, University of Minnesota.

something about it, such as quit or ask for a pay raise. But although employees form attitudes about virtually everything, very few will take drastic action simply because they believe prices in the employee cafeteria are too high or they dislike the color of the company softball team's uniforms. Such dissatisfactions are not likely to be very significant to anyone.

Most research and theory on workplace attitudes have been limited to job satisfaction and typically have addressed satisfaction with other facets of organizational life as a subpart or determinant of job satisfaction. It is important to recognize, however, that reactions to the workplace may come from a variety of sources beyond the job itself.[31] And beyond the routine examples noted earlier, the effects can be quite serious. For example, a worker who has been highly satisfied with his job may become very dissatisfied after being turned down for a promotion or receiving only a small increase in salary when he expected a larger one.

31. Griffin and Bateman, "Job Satisfaction and Organizational Commitment."

Melanie Wells (left) and Jane Ruark are contributing their time and talent to a rehabilitation center for animals, one that prepares injured and orphaned birds such as this great blue heron for their return to the wild. Although many employees exhibit positive job-related attitudes, volunteers are especially likely to be committed and involved. Since they do not receive pay or promotions, the intrinsic rewards they experience from these activities must be quite strong.

Commitment and Involvement

■ Two other important work-related attitudes are **commitment** and **involvement.**

Like job satisfaction, commitment and involvement, two closely related employee attitudes, influence important behaviors such as turnover and absenteeism.[32] **Commitment** can be defined as the individual's feelings of identification with and dedication to the organization. **Involvement** refers to a person's willingness as an organizational "citizen" to go beyond the standard demands of the job.

Several factors have been found to lead to commitment and involvement. Richard M. Steers has suggested that commitment and involvement are enhanced both by personal factors such as age and years of tenure in the organization and by organizational characteristics such as the degree of participation allowed in decision making and the level of security employees perceive.[33] Thus, managers can encourage commitment and involvement by allowing worker participation whenever possible and providing reasonable levels of job security for employees.

Commitment and involvement can lead to several positive outcomes. Committed and involved employees come to work more regularly, are more likely to stay with the organization, and work harder. Thus, managers clearly should nurture and sustain these qualities.

---

32. Richard T. Mowday, Lyman W. Porter, and Richard M. Steers, *Employee-Organization Linkages—The Psychology of Commitment, Absenteeism, and Turnover* (New York: Academic Press, 1982).

33. Richard M. Steers, "Antecedents and Outcomes of Organizational Commitment," *Administrative Science Quarterly,* vol. 22, 1977, pp. 46–56. See also Barbara S. Romzek, "Personal Consequences of Employee Commitment," *Academy of Management Journal,* September 1989, pp. 649–661.

FIGURE 4.6
Attitude-Behavior Relationships

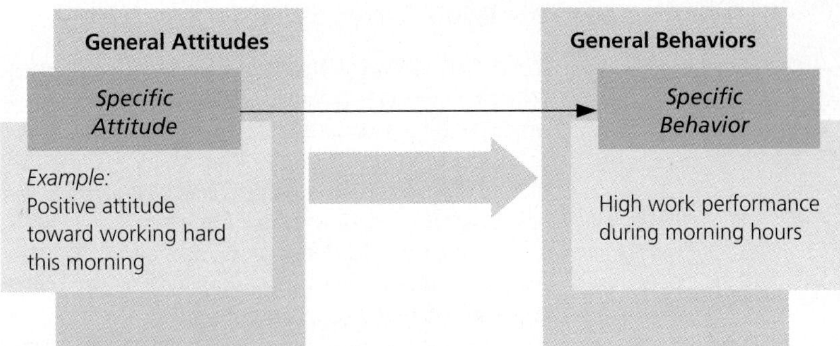

Attitudes and Behaviors

■ Whereas general attitudes may affect general behaviors and specific attitudes may affect specific behaviors, general attitudes such as job satisfaction usually are unrelated to specific behaviors such as employee productivity.

Currently there is considerable disagreement over the relationship between attitudes such as job satisfaction and behaviors like performance, turnover, and absenteeism. However, carefully constructed analyses yield promising insights into these relationships.[34]

In particular, it can be argued that it is inappropriate to investigate relationships between a general attitude such as job satisfaction and specific behaviors such as productivity. A more logical focus, as Figure 4.6 shows, might be on overall job satisfaction and its relationship to a broad view of job performance that encompasses a variety of work-related behaviors. Alternatively, logical relationships might exist between a specific attitude, such as an employee's attitude toward working hard on a given day, and the actual behavior reflected by work produced on that day. In other words, specific attitudes toward certain behaviors are more likely to be associated with those behaviors, whereas more general attitudes toward a set of behaviors are more likely to be associated with the entire set of behaviors rather than with individual ones. Hence, it is important to keep the attitude and behavior properly focused in terms of their relative specificity.[35] *A Look at the Research* provides additional insights into how a recently defined set of employee behaviors is affected by attitudes such as job satisfaction.

Managerial Implications of Individual Differences

While managers can draw many implications from the research and theories on individual differences, one especially important message emerges: We should

34. Cynthia D. Fisher, "On the Dubious Wisdom of Expecting Job Satisfaction to Correlate with Performance," *Academy of Management Review,* vol. 5, 1980, pp. 607–612.

35. M. M. Petty, Gail W. McGee, and Jerry W. Cavender, "A Meta-Analysis of the Relationships between Individual Job Satisfaction and Individual Performance," *Academy of Management Review,* October 1984, pp. 712–721.

A LOOK AT THE **RESEARCH**

The Good Citizen Syndrome

Most of us can recall being graded on "citizenship" in elementary school. Dennis Organ and his associates recently developed and refined a form of citizenship that applies to the workplace. They called this construct *organizational citizen behavior,* or *OCB,* and define it as discretionary contributions to the organization above and beyond what is required. Volunteering to stay after work and help train a new employee would be an example of OCB.

The full array of OCB includes behaviors such as constructive statements about the organization, expressing interest in others' work suggestions for improvements, care of organizational property, "housekeeping" behaviors, punctuality, and other variables. It also includes refraining from negative behaviors such as finding fault with others, expressing displeasure, starting arguments, and complaining about nonsignificant things. In short, then, employees who portray OCB are not, strictly speaking, higher performers. Instead, they provide overall positive contributions to the organization in a wide variety of minor ways.

What determines OCB? Preliminary research suggests that certain personality traits, such as pleasant mood state and conscientiousness, may be contributors. General satisfaction with the workplace also helps shape OCB. While satisfaction with individual facets of the workplace—working conditions or pay, for example—may be unrelated to general behavior, the subjective overall "sum" of those satisfactions helps determine OCB.

Our understanding of OCB is still in its infancy. However, it makes a lot of sense, has a sound theoretical basis, and generally has been supported by scientific research. Thus, both managers and researchers should become more aware of what OCB is and how it contributes to organizational effectiveness.

SOURCES: Dennis W. Organ, "The Motivational Basis of Organizational Citizenship Behavior," in Larry L. Cummings and Barry M. Staw, eds., *Research in Organizational Behavior,* vol. 12 (Greenwich, Conn.: JAI Press, 1990), pp. 43–72; Dennis W. Organ and Mary A. Konovsky, "Cognitive versus Affective Determinants of Organizational Citizenship Behavior," *Journal of Applied Psychology,* February 1989, pp. 157–164; Dennis W. Organ, *Organizational Citizenship Behavior: The Good Soldier Syndrome* (Lexington, Mass.: Lexington Books, 1988); Thomas S. Bateman and Dennis W. Organ, "Job Satisfaction and the Good Soldier: The Relationship between Affect and Employee 'Citizenship,'" *Academy of Management Journal,* December 1983, pp. 587–595.

always remember that people are in fact different. For example, a manager may have one worker who is determined to advance her career with the company. That worker will be very motivated by the opportunity to work on a special project that enhances her chances for promotion. Another worker, however, may be working for the organization only until he can find an opening in another city. Thus, he will be indifferent to the same special project.

Similarly, the things that make one employee extremely satisfied may irritate another. Suppose two workers call in sick on the same day. Their boss decides to call each of them at home. One employee may genuinely appreciate the boss's concern, whereas the other may resent being checked up on. And, of course, either one may be right!

Thus, it is important for a manager to first recognize that such differences exist and then act accordingly. In general, managers should make as few assumptions about people as possible. Instead, they should treat and understand people as the individuals they are.

Summary of Key Points

- Individual differences are a set of unique factors that differentiate people from one another. In addition, the same person may act or feel differently in different situations.
- One important individual difference is personality. Personality structure can be viewed from the standpoint of determinants, stages, and traits. The immaturity-maturity model is sometimes used to characterize workplace personalities.
- Personality traits that are especially relevant to the workplace are locus of control, authoritarianism, and Machiavellianism.
- Another important individual difference is a person's attitude. The dispositional view of attitude formation includes affect, cognition, and intention. The situational view considers a person's social context. Cognitive dissonance occurs when one's attitudes conflict with one's behaviors or with one another. Dissonance reduction is used to resolve the inner conflict that results. Attitude change generally is undertaken via organizational change and development activities.
- Job satisfaction is perhaps the most important work-related attitude and has multiple causes and consequences. Satisfaction can be measured (albeit imperfectly) with questionnaires. Other workplace attitudes include other kinds of satisfaction and commitment and involvement.
- The relationships between attitudes and behaviors are quite complex. Managers need to recognize that people differ in their behavior and in their attitudes.

Discussion Questions

1. Identify biological, social, cultural, and/or situational factors that may have shaped your personality. How much, if any part, of your personality do you think was inherited?
2. Do you believe that stage approaches or trait approaches better explain personality? Why? Are these approaches mutually exclusive?
3. Argyris's immaturity-maturity model applies to the workplace personality. Does it also apply to your experiences as a student? Why or why not?
4. In terms of locus of control, are you primarily an internal or an external person? How can you tell? Cite some examples.
5. Have you ever known anyone who clearly was Machiavellian? Was this person successful or less successful in life? How did others feel about this individual?
6. Prepare a brief personality profile of yourself. Include each major personality trait discussed in the chapter—locus of control, authoritarianism, and Machiavellianism.
7. Debate the relative merits of the dispositional and situational perspectives on attitudes.

8. Recall an instance in which you experienced cognitive dissonance. How did you resolve it?
9. Do you think most workers in the United States are relatively satisfied or relatively dissatisfied with their jobs? Why?
10. In what ways might personality and attitudes be related?

CASE 4.1 Attitudes at Eastern Spell Trouble

Some words—*hate, love,* and *sex,* for example—spark emotional responses from everyone who hears them. And some names—Adolf Hitler, George Bush, Saddam Hussein—have the same effect. For many employees of Eastern Air Lines, the name of Frank Lorenzo could be added to the list.

One of Lorenzo's lifelong dreams was to own an airline. He grew up in New York City in the shadows of LaGuardia Airport and vowed that one day he would be a giant in the industry. His dream stayed with him during his education at Harvard Business School.

Lorenzo finally got his toehold in the airline industry in 1969, when he and a friend invested $25,000 each to start an airline consulting firm called Jet Capital. They took control of Texas International, a small, regional carrier, in 1971. Lorenzo's big break came in 1981, when he succeeded in taking over Continental Airlines. He positioned Continental within an umbrella corporation that he named Texas Air.

After detailed and systematic study, Lorenzo decided that Continental had excessive overhead expenses, much of it attributable to high labor costs. At the time, labor costs for U.S.–based airlines were between 15 and 20 percent higher than those for major international competitors. If Continental was to succeed, Lorenzo reasoned, labor costs had to come down.

Lorenzo initially met with labor leaders and asked to negotiate lower wage rates. They refused, so he withdrew to consider other options. Lorenzo finally decided that labor costs had to be reduced no matter what. In 1983, he made a bold move by taking the airline into bankruptcy to break existing labor contracts and start over with nonunionized employees.

While Continental generally continued to lose money, most observers agree that Lorenzo's move worked. With substantially lower labor costs, Continental was able to reduce fares and increase market share rapidly. At the same time, however, Lorenzo made an enemy of organized labor. Labor leaders viewed his moves at Continental with a mix of uneasiness for their own future and outright hatred for Lorenzo himself.

In 1986, Lorenzo made a series of moves that dramatically increased the size of Texas Air. In short order, he bought People Express and Frontier Airlines. Then he bought Eastern, one of the largest airlines in the country. At the time, his acquisition of Eastern promised to make Texas Air a dominant player in the airline industry. As it turned out, however, Eastern was Lorenzo's downfall.

At the time of the acquisition, Eastern already was having problems with its labor unions. Airline industry unions had a strong presence in Eastern and had chosen the company as its ultimate battleground. As a result, they feared that anything lost at Eastern eventually would be lost everywhere else, but anything gained at Eastern could also be gained elsewhere.

Lorenzo's presence at the helm of Eastern was like a lightning rod. Virtually every concession he requested from labor was denied. When he met with employees, protestors shouted obscenities at him. Picketing workers left over from the battles at Continental reappeared at ticket counters.

In 1989, the confrontation came to a head. The unions went on strike. Lorenzo took Eastern into bankruptcy, hoping to repeat the success of his Continental experience. But the unions this time were too strong. Eventually, a bankruptcy judge took away Lorenzo's control of Eastern and placed it with a trustee.

Although labor problems subsided, Eastern never was able to regain its footing. In 1990, Lorenzo finally threw in the towel. He relinquished his ownership of Texas Air to Scandinavian Airlines System and stepped down as CEO. Labor officials celebrated with party hats and streamers. In January 1991, Eastern was shut down once and for all.

Case Questions

1. What role might individual differences have played in Lorenzo's downfall?
2. What personality traits of Lorenzo may have contributed to his problems?
3. How did attitudes affect Lorenzo and the unions at Eastern?

SOURCES: Agis Salpukas, "Eastern Airlines Brought Down by a Strike So Bitter It Became a Crusade," *The New York Times,* January 20, 1991, p. 22; "Frank Lorenzo: The Final Days," *Business Week,* August 27, 1990, pp. 32–33; "Lorenzo May Land a Little Short of the Runway," *Business Week,* February 5, 1990, pp. 46–47; Peter Nulty, "America's Toughest Bosses," *Fortune,* February 27, 1989, pp. 40–54.

CASE 4.2

Back to the Old Saw

The employees at Henderson Manufacturing Co. were unhappy. When they met outside the building, away from the noise of the big saws, they would exchange gripes and talk about looking for different work. Management found that workers were punching in later in the morning. Several times the vice president himself, Jack Macnam, had to go across the street to the pizza parlor to get employees back to work after their lunch break.

Oddly enough, the trouble started on a banner day for Henderson: the day the company began using its new high-tech saws. The company's principal product is cedar shingles used for roofing and siding, and for twenty years the heart of its manufacturing process had been its huge circular saws. No one was ever allowed to tour the plant, because management was afraid that visitors would be unnerved when they saw the workers' hands moving like lightning around the deadly gleaming steel. Although major accidents were rare, few employees who worked by the saws had a complete set of fingers, and the company's owners lived in fear that a worker would cut off an arm, or worse.

So when a new generation of virtually foolproof saws came out, the company took a big step and invested in three.

The first sign of trouble was some minor grumbling on the factory floor. But management had expected that. The workers had not been told about the new saws and were likely to resist any change. Then, during the second week with the new machines, two saw operators had close calls, and both had to be taken to the hospital for stitches. The saw's advanced safety brake spared both arms, but the next day some workers began talking about a jinx. Management brought the saw manufacturer's representatives in for a lecture about safe use of the new machines, but by the end of the week the saws led to a total of twenty more stitches.

Over the weekend, management got an anonymous tip that drugs may have been involved in the accidents. On Monday, the company began a new policy of unannounced spot tests for drugs. The grumblings on the shop floor grew into outright hostility. Some employees refused to take the tests, and when one worker who'd never had an accident was fired for testing positive, the entire work force walked off the job.

Frustrated, Jack Macnam called in Bruce Ballenge, a senior employee, to discuss the problems. Both were tense; used to the constant scream of the saws, they felt uneasy in the silence. "Bruce," Macnam said, "You've been working here thirty years, and I know you're good at what you do and don't want to lose your job. What's gone wrong down there?"

"I don't know if those employees are using drugs," Ballenge replied, "but that's not the problem. The problem is those new saws."

Macnam nearly fell off his stool. "But we spent $5,000 each on those saws. They're the best money can buy! They're so safe a child could run them."

"I know that," Ballenge replied, "but that's your problem, not ours. Working with those old things, you know they'll just as easily cut your wrist as a stick of cedar, so you're on your toes all the time, you don't mess with them. But with those new saws, you can just about do it one-handed. You don't pay attention all the time, you get careless."

Macnam was astonished, but he had faith in Ballenge's experience. Now that he knew what the problem was and could deal with it directly, he suspected that it might not be too difficult to solve. He called a meeting with the plant manager to discuss the issue and shortly afterward was able to tell the workers that only those who had proved their carefulness over the years would be allowed to work with the saws. In addition, drug testing would stop and the fired worker would be rehired.

The grumbling did not stop right away, but soon you again couldn't hear yourself think on the shop floor of Henderson Manufacturing.

Case Questions

1. What mistakes did Henderson Manufacturing make that led to the walkout?
2. Jack Macnam seems to have solved the problem of the new saws. Is there anything else he should do to improve worker morale?

EXPERIENTIAL EXERCISE

Purpose: This exercise should help you develop an appreciation for the complexities involved in applying personality theory to organizational settings.

Format: Your instructor will divide the class into groups of three or four members. Each group will be the human resources department of a large, regional department store chain. In recent months, the company has decided that it has done a poor job of hiring both department and stockroom managers. The existing job descriptions for the two positions are as follows:

> *Department Manager:* The department manager has full responsibility for keeping merchandise shelves stocked in the department, managing the inventory, and supervising and developing the departmental sales staff. The department manager must take an active role in identifying weaknesses in each member of the sales staff and then helping each individual overcome her or his weaknesses. In addition, the department manager spends approximately half the time on the sales floor working with customers.
>
> *Stockroom Manager:* The stockroom manager has full responsibility for receiving incoming shipments of merchandise, properly storing merchandise in the stockroom, and delivering merchandise to the sales floor as requested by department managers. The stockroom manager must work with delivery personnel to ensure an orderly and systematic delivery system. In addition, the stockroom manager must work with sales personnel to facilitate a smooth system of merchandise stocking.

Your task is to determine how these positions might be more effectively filled in the future.

Procedure: First, develop a personality profile for the person needed for each position. This profile should specify the key personality traits likely to lead to success in the job. Next, draft a set of questions for job applicants that will show how well their personalities match the desired profile.

Follow-up Questions

1. How effective do you think managers can be in developing optimal personality profiles for different kinds of jobs? Explain.
2. How accurately do you think managers can measure personality traits? Explain.
3. Do you think it would be easier to measure attitudes than to measure personalities? Why or why not?

CHAPTER OUTLINE

- The Nature of Motivation in Organizations
  - *The Importance of Motivation*
  - *The Motivational Framework*
- Historical Perspectives on Motivation
  - *Early Views of Motivation*
  - *The Scientific Management Approach*
  - *The Human Relations Approach*
- Need Theories of Motivation
  - *Maslow's Hierarchy of Needs*
  - *Murray's Manifest Needs*
  - *Alderfer's ERG Theory*
- Herzberg's Two-Factor Theory
  - *Development of the Theory*
  - *Evaluation of the Theory*
- Other Important Needs
  - *The Need for Achievement*
  - *The Need for Affiliation*
  - *The Need for Power*
- Integrating the Need Perspectives

5

Basic Concepts of Motivation

CHAPTER OBJECTIVES

After studying this chapter, you should be able to:

Define the concept of needs and describe the basic motivational process.

Describe several historical perspectives on motivation.

Discuss three important need theories of motivation.

Discuss Herzberg's two-factor theory of motivation.

Identify and summarize three other important individual needs.

Describe parallels among the need theories.

In the mid-1980s, AT&T laid off almost seventy thousand workers. IBM enticed eight thousand employees to accept early retirement. All told, Apple Computer, General Motors, Texaco, Ford, A&P, Chrysler, CBS, Safeway, Texas Instruments, and other large American companies eliminated hundreds of thousands of workers from their payrolls during that turbulent decade. Once again, job security had emerged as a critical issue for millions of workers.

During the Great Depression of the 1920s, jobs were scarce and security nonexistent. For workers who experienced this chaotic period, job security remained a basic concern for the remainder of their careers. For many of their children, however, job security diminished in importance. The boom years following World War II meant plentiful jobs and reasonable security for virtually anyone willing to work. Thus, the need for security gradually faded, until the boom ended in the late 1970s. During that era, American businesses in particular realized they had grown too big, taken on excessive overhead, and inflated their payrolls.

To regain their competitive edge, the largest firms in virtually every industry were forced to go through a period of cutbacks and retrenchment. Payrolls were trimmed, facilities closed, and workers left without jobs. As a consequence, job security has once again become a major concern for many workers.[1]

Job security is an important issue for both organizations and people. People are motivated not only by tangible things such as money and benefits but also by intangibles like job security. When people have security, they may take it for granted and look for other incentives to work hard. But if taken away, job security quickly becomes an extremely important need for many workers. The driving force behind this process is motivation.

As we will see in this chapter, motivation is vital to all organizations and, hence, to their managers. Often the difference between highly effective organizations and less effective ones lies in the motivational profiles of their members. Thus, managers need to understand the nature of individual motivation, especially as it applies to work situations.

This is the first of two chapters dealing with employee motivation. Here we examine basic concepts and theories of motivation. In the next chapter, we explore advanced concepts and applications.

---

1. Jaclyn Fierman, "Shaking the Blue-Collar Blues," *Fortune,* April 22, 1991, pp. 209–218; "How Safe Is Your Job?" *Newsweek,* November 5, 1990, pp. 44–47; Alan Deutschman, "What 25-Year-Olds Want," *Fortune,* August 27, 1990, pp. 42–50.

The Nature of Motivation in Organizations

■ **Motivation** is the set of forces that lead people to behave in particular ways.

Motivation is the set of forces that cause people to behave in certain ways.[2] The student who stays up all night to ensure that his or her term paper is the best it can be, the salesperson who works on Saturdays to get ahead, and the doctor who makes follow-up phone calls to patients to check on their conditions are all motivated people. Of course, the student who avoids the term paper by spending the day at the beach, the salesperson who goes home early to escape a tedious sales call, and the doctor who skips follow-up calls to have more time for golf are also motivated. In both examples, these individuals are simply motivated to achieve different types of things. From the manager's viewpoint, the objective is to motivate people to behave in ways that are in the organization's best interest.

The Importance of Motivation

■ Motivation is important in organizations because in conjunction with ability and environment it determines performance.

One of the manager's primary tasks is to motivate people in the organization to perform at high levels. This means getting them to work hard, come to work regularly, and make positive contributions to the organization's mission. But job performance depends on ability and environment as well as on motivation. The relationship can be stated as follows:

$$P = f(M, A, \text{and } E),$$

where P = performance, M = motivation, A = ability, and E = environment. To reach high levels of performance, an employee must want to do the job (motivation), be able to do the job (ability), and have the materials and equipment needed to do the job (environment). A deficiency in any one of these areas will hurt performance. A manager thus should strive to ensure that all three conditions are met.[3]

The Motivational Framework

Current thinking on motivation rests on the concepts of need deficiencies and goal-directed behaviors. Figure 5.1 shows the basic motivational framework we will use to organize our discussion.[4]

---

2. Richard M. Steers and Lyman W. Porter, *Motivation and Work Behavior*, 5th ed. (New York: McGraw-Hill, 1991), pp. 5–6. See also Frank J. Landy and Wendy S. Becker, "Motivation Theory Reconsidered," in Larry L. Cummings and Barry M. Staw, eds., *Research in Organizational Behavior*, vol. 9 (Greenwich, Conn.: JAI Press, 1987), pp. 1–38.

3. Victor H. Vroom, *Work and Motivation* (New York: Wiley, 1964). See also Benjamin Schneider, "The People Make the Place," *Personnel Psychology*, Autumn 1987, pp. 437–454.

4. See Jack W. Brehm and Elizabeth A. Self, "The Intensity of Motivation," in Mark R. Rosenzweig and Lyman W. Porter, eds., *Annual Review of Psychology*, vol. 40 (Palo Alto: Annual Reviews, Inc., 1989), pp. 109–132.

FIGURE 5.1
The Motivational Framework

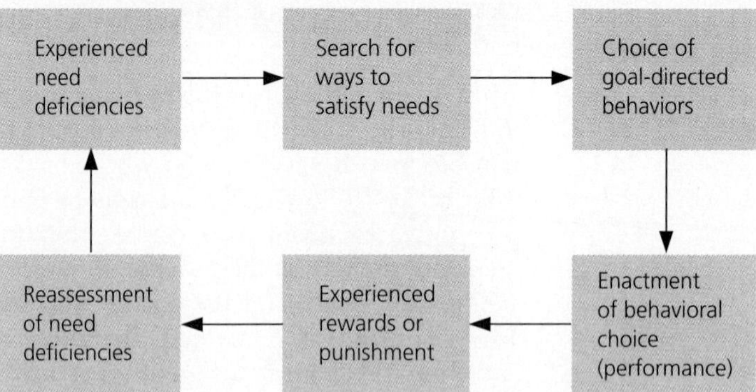

- A **need** is a deficiency that the individual experiences.

The starting point in the motivational process is a need. A **need** is a deficiency experienced by an individual. For example, a person might feel her salary and position are deficient because they do not reflect the importance to the organization of the work she does.

A need triggers a search for ways to satisfy it. The person just described might consider three such options: to simply ask for a raise and a promotion, to work harder in the hope of earning a raise and a promotion, or to look for a new job with a higher salary and a more prestigious title.

Next comes a choice of goal-directed behaviors. While a person actually might pursue more than one option at the same time, most effort will likely be directed at only one option.

In the next phase, the person actually carries out the behavior chosen to satisfy the need. The person in our example may decide to work harder. At this point, she will likely put in longer hours, work harder, and so forth.

Rewards or punishment will follow the performance. In this instance the person will most likely get the raise and promotion because of the higher performance.

Finally, the person assesses the extent to which the need has been satisfied. Suppose the person wanted a 10 percent raise and a promotion to vice president. If she got both, she should be satisfied. On the other hand, if she only got a 7 percent raise and a promotion to assistant vice president, she will have to decide whether to keep trying, accept what she got, or choose one of the other options considered earlier. (Sometimes, of course, a need may go unsatisfied altogether despite the person's efforts.)

Historical Perspectives on Motivation

Historical views on motivation, even though not always accurate, are of interest for several reasons. For one thing, they provide a foundation for contemporary thinking about motivation. For another, because they generally were based on

Managers must be constantly vigilant for ways to motivate employees. John Allegretti was feeling frustrated with his opportunities for promotion at Hyatt and was preparing to quit. Because the firm did not want to lose him, Hyatt executives decided to launch a new business to recycle waste and trash from Hyatt hotels, putting Allegretti (shown here flanked by two Hyatt executives) in charge. The new venture has been so profitable that the Hyatt executives have created similar enterprises for six other promising young managers.

common sense and intuition, an appreciation of their strengths and weaknesses can help managers gain useful insights into employee motivation in the workplace.

Early Views of Motivation

■ One early view of motivation was based on the concept of **hedonism**: the notion that people seek pleasure and comfort and avoid pain and discomfort.

The earliest views on human motivation were dominated by the concept of **hedonism**: the idea that people seek pleasure and comfort and try to avoid pain and discomfort.[5] Although this view seems reasonable as far as it goes, there are many kinds of behavior that it cannot explain. For example, why do recreational athletes exert themselves willingly and regularly, whereas a hedonist prefers to relax? Why do people occasionally risk their lives for others in times of crisis? Why do volunteers give tirelessly of their own time to collect money for charitable causes?

It was the recognition that hedonism is an extremely limited—and often incorrect—view of human behavior that prompted the emergence of other perspectives. William James, for one, argued that instinctive behavior and unconscious motivation are also important in human behavior.[6] Although many of

5. Craig Pinder, *Work Motivation* (Glenview, Ill.: Scott, Foresman, 1984).

6. Ernest R. Hilgard and Richard C. Atkinson, *Introduction to Psychology*, 4th ed. (New York: Harcourt, Brace and World, 1967).

James's ideas eventually were supplanted by other views, they helped reshape contemporary motivation theory.

The Scientific Management Approach

■ Scientific management assumed that employee motivation is economically induced.

As we noted in Chapter 1, Frederick W. Taylor, the chief proponent of scientific management, assumed that employees are economically motivated and work so as to earn as much money as they can.[7] Taylor once used the case of a pig-iron handler named Schmidt to illustrate the concepts of scientific management. Schmidt's job consisted of moving heavy pieces of iron from one pile to another. He appeared to be doing an adequate job and regularly met the standard of 12.5 tons per day. Taylor, however, believed Schmidt was strong enough to do much more. To test his ideas, Taylor designed a piece-rate pay system that would award Schmidt a fixed sum of money for each ton of iron he loaded. Then he had the following conversation with Schmidt and observed his work:

> "Schmidt, are you a high-priced man?"
>
> "Well, I don't know what you mean." [Several minutes of conversation ensue.]
>
> "Well, if you are a high-priced man, you will do exactly as this man tells you tomorrow, from morning until night. When he tells you to pick up a pig and walk, you pick it up and walk, and when he tells you to sit down and rest, you sit down and rest. You do that right straight through the day. And what's more, no back talk. Do you understand that?"
>
> Schmidt started to work, and all day long, and at regular intervals, was told by the man who stood over him with a watch, "Now pick up a pig and walk. Now sit down and rest. Now walk, now rest. . . . " He worked when he was told to work, and rested when he was told to rest and at half-past five in the afternoon, had his 47.5 tons loaded on the car. And he practically never failed to work at this pace and do the task that was set him during the three years the writer was at Bethlehem.[8]

Recent evidence suggests that Taylor may have fabricated the conversation just related; Schmidt himself may have been an invention.[9] If so, this willingness to fabricate shows just how strongly Taylor believed in his economic view of human motivation and in the need to spread the doctrine. But soon researchers

7. Frederick W. Taylor, *Principles of Scientific Management* (New York: Harper, 1911).

8. Ibid., pp. 46–47.

9. See Charles D. Wrege and Amedeo G. Perroni, "Taylor's Pig-Tale: A Historical Analysis of Frederick W. Taylor's Pig-Iron Experiment," *Academy of Management Journal,* March 1974, pp. 6–27.

Davidson College has taken the human relations view of motivation in assuming that environment shapes performance. Focusing on the learning environment of students, the college created Love of Learning. The program brings average students with special potential from a nearby school district to campus for special classes and tutoring. By involving students and parents and creating a nurturing and supportive environment, the program has significantly improved student performance.

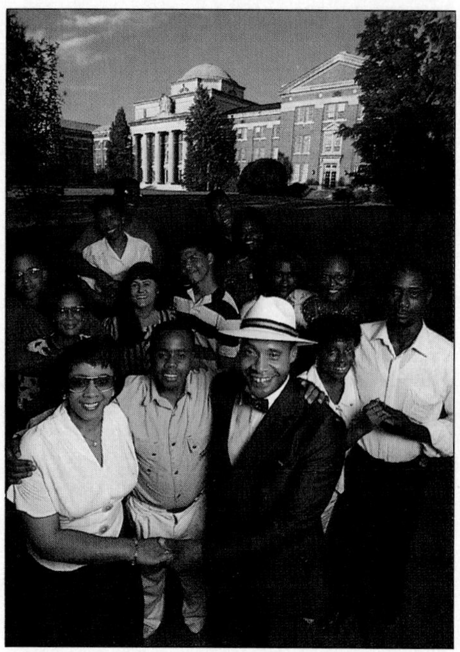

recognized that scientific management theorists' assumptions about motivation could not explain complex human behavior. The next perspective on motivation to emerge in the management literature was the human relations movement.

The Human Relations Approach

- The human relations approach to motivation suggested that favorable employee attitudes result in motivation to work hard.

The human relations view, which we also discussed in Chapter 1, arose from the Hawthorne studies.[10] This perspective suggested that people are motivated by things other than money—in particular that employees, as social beings, are motivated by and respond to the social environment at work. Favorable employee attitudes, such as job satisfaction, were presumed to result in increased employee performance. In Chapter 6, we explore this relationship in more detail. Here it is sufficient to say, as we did in Chapter 1, that the human relations viewpoint left most questions about human behavior unanswered.[11] However, one of the primary theorists associated with this movement, Abraham Maslow, helped develop an important need theory of motivation.

---

10. Pinder, *Work Motivation.* See also Daniel Wren, *The Evolution of Management Thought,* 3rd ed. (New York: Wiley, 1987).

11. Wren, *The Evolution of Management Thought.*

All people have an important need for security, including shelter and food. Even though few Inuit live in igloos today, they must still make long trips in search of fish and game. This Inuit is on such a trip and is shown here making an ice shelter where he will spend the night.

Need Theories of Motivation

■ Need theories of motivation assume that need deficiencies cause behavior.

Need theories represent the starting point for most contemporary thought on motivation,[12] although these theories too attracted critics.[13] The basic premise of need theories is that human motivation is caused primarily by deficiencies in one or more important needs or need categories. Need theorists have attempted to identify and categorize the most salient needs, that is, those that are most important to people. *International Perspective* summarizes some of what we know about the needs of Japanese workers. The best-known need theories are Maslow's hierarchy of needs, Murray's manifest needs, and Alderfer's ERG theory.

Maslow's Hierarchy of Needs

■ Maslow's **hierarchy of needs** theory assumes that human needs are arranged in a hierarchy of importance.

Psychologist Abraham Maslow first presented his **hierarchy of needs** theory in the 1940s.[14] Influenced by the human relations school of thought, Maslow argued that human beings are "wanting" animals: They have innate desires to satisfy a

12. Steers and Porter, *Motivation and Work Behavior.*

13. Gerald R. Salancik and Jeffrey Pfeffer, "An Examination of Need-Satisfaction Models of Job Attitudes," *Administrative Science Quarterly,* September 1977, pp. 427–456.

14. Abraham H. Maslow, "A Theory of Human Motivation," *Psychological Review,* vol. 50, 1943, pp. 370–396; Abraham H. Maslow, *Motivation and Personality* (New York: Harper & Row, 1954).

INTERNATIONAL PERSPECTIVE

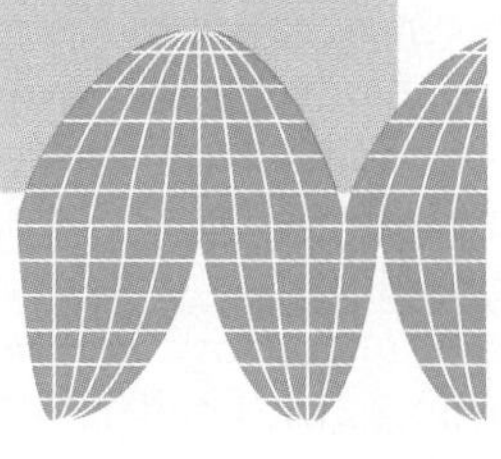

Needs of Many Japanese Workers May Be Changing

Most Americans hold two basic stereotypes about Japanese workers. The first is that they are workaholics, preferring to spend all their time at work. The second is that they all want and enjoy the job security lifetime employment supposedly provides. In reality, both of these pictures are changing.

Consider Akiko Hara. Akiko spent two years working for a Japanese brokerage firm. She soon tired of working fifty-five hours each week, however, and decided to quit. She gave up bonuses, paid vacations, and job security in exchange for a part-time job paying half as much. Why? Because she wanted more out of life than just work.

This pattern is emerging all across Japan. More and more Japanese workers are opting out of their equivalent of the rat race for a different lifestyle. Some seek part-time jobs only. Others work temporary jobs and take a break between assignments. Indeed, over 12 percent of the Japanese work force now falls into one of these two categories.

Japanese businesses, long accustomed to having a full complement of dedicated, full-time employees, are also having to adjust to this new trend. Nissan and Toyota, for example, use many part-time workers. Fuji Bank has 1,500 part-time workers. Asahi Breweries uses 2,000 part-time sales representatives in addition to its 700-person regular staff. Clearly, then, Western stereotypes of Japanese workers are at least partly inaccurate. Indeed, Japanese workers may be at the vanguard of a new, worldwide movement away from permanent, full-time work.

SOURCES: "Japanese Workers Aren't All Workaholics," *The Wall Street Journal,* May 8, 1989, p. A10; "Born in the U.S.A., Sold in Japan," *Time,* November 30, 1987, p. 66; "Most U.S. Companies Are Innocents Abroad," *Business Week,* November 16, 1987, pp. 168–169.

given set of needs. Furthermore, Maslow believed these needs are arranged in a hierarchy of importance, with the most basic needs at the bottom of the hierarchy. Figure 5.2 depicts Maslow's hierarchy of needs.

- In Maslow's theory, the categories of **deficiency needs** are **physiological, security,** and **belongingness needs.**
- Maslow also identified two sets of **growth needs: esteem** and **self-actualization needs.**

The three sets of needs at the bottom of the hierarchy are called **deficiency needs**, because they must be satisfied for the individual to be fundamentally comfortable. The top two sets of needs are termed **growth needs**, because they focus on personal growth and development.

The most basic needs in the hierarchy are **physiological needs.** They include the needs for food, sex, and air. Next in the hierarchy are **security needs**: things that offer safety and security, such as adequate housing and clothing and freedom from worry and anxiety. The vignette that opens this chapter introduced the importance of security needs. **Belongingness needs,** the third level in the hierarchy, are primarily social. Examples include the need for love and affection and the need to be accepted by peers. The fourth level, **esteem needs,** actually encompasses two slightly different kinds of needs: the need for a positive self-image and self-respect and the need to be respected by others. At the top of the hierarchy are what Maslow termed **self-actualization needs.** These involve realizing our full potential and becoming all that we can be.

Beginning at the bottom of the hierarchy, according to Maslow, each need level must be satisfied before the level above it becomes important. Thus, once physiological needs have been satisfied their importance diminishes, and security needs emerge as the primary sources of motivation. This escalation up the hierarchy continues until the self-actualization needs become the primary motivators. However, whenever a previously satisfied lower-level set of needs becomes deficient again, the individual returns to that level. For example, a person who loses his or her job is likely to stop worrying about self-actualization and begin to concentrate on finding another job to satisfy now deficient security needs.

In most organizational settings, physiological needs probably are the easiest to meet. Adequate wages, restrooms, ventilation, and comfortable temperatures are examples of things that can satisfy this most basic level of needs.

Security needs in organizational settings can be satisfied by job continuity (no layoffs), a grievance system (to protect against arbitrary supervisory actions), and an adequate insurance and retirement system (to guard against financial loss from illness and to ensure retirement income).

Most employees' belongingness needs are satisfied by family ties and group relationships inside and outside the organization. In the workplace, for example, people usually develop friendships that provide a basis for social interaction and can play a major role in satisfying social needs. Managers can enhance satisfaction of these needs by fostering a sense of group identity and interaction among employees. At the same time, managers can be sensitive to the probable effects (such as low performance and absenteeism) on employees of family problems or lack of acceptance by coworkers.

Esteem needs in the workplace are met by job titles, choice offices, merit pay increases, awards, and other forms of recognition. Of course, to be sources of long-term motivation, tangible rewards like these must be distributed equitably and be based on performance.

Self-actualization needs perhaps are the hardest to understand and the most difficult to satisfy. Clearly, few people ever become all they could become. In

FIGURE 5.2
Maslow's Hierarchy of Needs

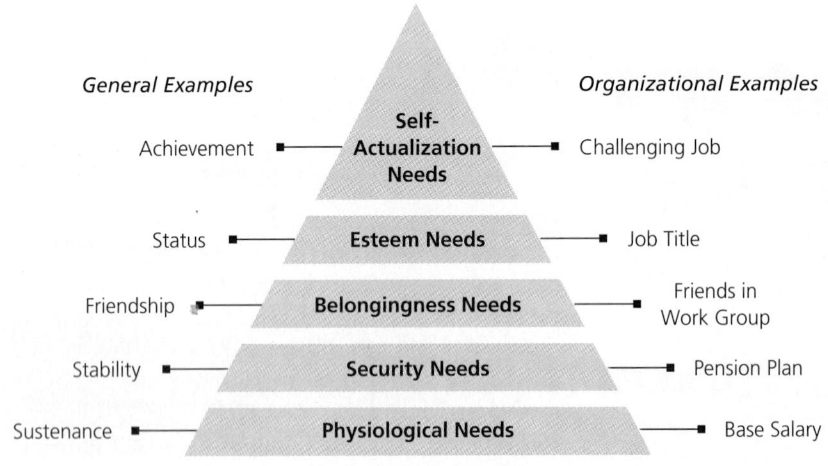

SOURCE: Adapted from Abraham H. Maslow, "A Theory of Human Motivation," *Psychological Review,* vol. 50, 1943, pp. 374–396. Copyright 1943 by the American Psychological Association. Used with permission.

most cases, a person who is doing well on Maslow's hierarchy will have satisfied his or her esteem needs and will be moving toward self-actualization.

Maslow's needs hierarchy makes a certain amount of intuitive sense. Because it was the first motivation theory to be popularized, it is also one of the best known in management circles. Yet research has revealed a number of deficiencies in the theory: Five levels of needs are not always present; the actual hierarchy of needs does not always conform to Maslow's model; and need structures are more unstable and variable than the theory would lead us to believe.[15] Thus, the theory's primary contribution seems to lie in providing a general framework for categorizing needs.[16]

Murray's Manifest Needs

■ Murray's **manifest needs** theory includes a wide variety of fundamental human needs.

Another interesting need construct is H. A. Murray's *manifest needs* theory. First presented by Murray in 1938,[17] the theory identified this set of needs, but only at an abstract level. Its present conceptualization owes much to the work of J. W. Atkinson, who translated Murray's ideas into a more concrete, operational framework.[18]

Like Maslow's needs hierarchy concept, the **manifest needs** theory assumes that people have a set of needs that motivates behavior. The mechanisms by which needs operate, however, are somewhat more complex in this view. Murray suggests that several categories of needs are important to most people and that any number of needs may operate in varying degrees at the same time. In other words, multiple needs motivate behavior simultaneously rather than in some preset order. Table 5.1 summarizes several of the needs that Murray perceived as most powerful.

Unlike Maslow, Murray did not arrange the needs he identified in any particular order of importance. (It is interesting to note that all of the manifest needs are learned needs. In other words, we are not born with any of them; we learn them as we grow.[19]) In addition, Murray believed that each need has two components: direction and intensity. *Direction* refers to the person or object that is expected to satisfy the need. If you are hungry, getting to a local eating establishment may represent the direction of the need. *Intensity* represents the importance of the need. If you are very hungry, the need to get to a restaurant may be very great; if you are only moderately hungry, the intensity may be lower.

---

15. Mahmond A. Wahba and Lawrence G. Bridwell, "Maslow Reconsidered: A Review of Research on the Need Hierarchy Theory," *Organizational Behavior and Human Performance,* April 1976, pp. 212–240.

16. Howard S. Schwartz, "Maslow and Hierarchical Enactment of Organizational Reality," *Human Relations,* vol. 36, no. 10, 1983, pp. 933–956.

17. H. A. Murray, *Explorations in Personality* (New York: Oxford University Press, 1938).

18. J. W. Atkinson, *An Introduction to Motivation* (Princeton, N.J.: Van Nostrand, 1964).

19. Ibid.

TABLE 5.1
Murray's Manifest Needs

Need	Characteristics
Achievement	Individual aspires to accomplish difficult tasks; maintains high standards and is willing to work toward distant goals; responds positively to competition; willing to put forth effort to attain excellence.
Affiliation	Enjoys being with friends and people in general; accepts people readily; makes efforts to win friendships and maintain associations with people.
Aggression	Enjoys combat and argument; easily annoyed; sometimes willing to hurt people to get his or her way; may seek to "get even" with people perceived as having harmed him or her.
Autonomy	Tries to break away from restraints, confinement, or restrictions of any kind; enjoys being unattached, free, not tied to people, places, or obligations; may be rebellious when faced with restraints.
Exhibition	Wants to be the center of attention; enjoys having an audience; engages in behavior that wins the notice of others; may enjoy being dramatic or witty.
Impulsivity	Tends to act on the "spur of the moment" and without deliberation; gives vent readily to feelings and wishes; speaks freely; may be volatile in emotional expression.
Nurturance	Gives sympathy and comfort; assists others whenever possible, interested in caring for children, the disabled, or the infirm; offers a "helping hand" to those in need; readily performs favors for others.
Order	Concerned with keeping personal effects and surroundings neat and organized; dislikes clutter, confusion, lack of organization; interested in developing methods for keeping materials methodically organized.
Power	Attempts to control the environment and to influence or direct other people; expresses opinions forcefully; enjoys the role of leader and may assume it spontaneously.
Understanding	Wants to understand many areas of knowledge; values synthesis of ideas, verifiable generalization, logical thought, particularly when directed or satisfying intellectual curiosity.

SOURCE: Adapted from the *Personality Research Form Manual,* published by Research Psychologists Press, Inc., P.O. Box 984, Port Huron, Michigan 48060. Copyright © 1967, 1974, 1984, by Douglas N. Jackson. Used by permission.

Appropriate environmental conditions are necessary for a need to become manifest. For example, if someone with a high need for power works in a job setting in which power is irrelevant, the need may remain latent—not yet influencing the person's behavior. But if conditions that increase the importance of power arise, the need for power may then manifest itself, and the employee will begin to work toward increasing his or her power.

Little research has been done to evaluate Murray's theory. However, some of the specific needs defined by Murray have been the subject of much research, as we discuss later in this chapter. *Management in Action* summarizes how workers of different ages present different need profiles.

MANAGEMENT IN ACTION

Changing Needs of American Workers

As different age groups enter the workplace, each exhibits needs different from those of the group before. The common stereotype of many American workers is that of the so-called "yuppie": greedy, hard working, and status conscious. Indeed, many workers now entering middle management positions seem to fit that image.

The baby boomers (ages 25 to 44) make up almost 55 percent of the U.S. work force. While they obviously are motivated by a wide array of needs, several needs seem to be especially dominant. Dominant needs among this group appear to be career progression, increasing income, and social mobility. In turn, these individuals exhibit high concern for shared responsibility, communication, and fairness in the workplace. They often work sixty hours or more a week and juggle busy schedules to maintain a full and active lifestyle. Nevertheless, they view their work lives in terms of fun, stimulation, and creativity.

In contrast, younger workers just entering the workplace exhibit a different makeup altogether. They are far more willing to turn down a promotion or a transfer, even if doing so means a career setback. They are more prone to drop out of the corporate scene and pursue other interests. Younger workers are also less willing to put in the long workweeks of their predecessors. They appear more individualistic and less willing to conform to corporate norms.

What will motivate future managers reading this book? Of course, only the readers themselves can say. But whatever the motivation, it is likely to differ from those of people who have entered the work force in the last ten years.

SOURCES: Alan Deutschman, "What 25-Year-Olds Want," *Fortune*, August 27, 1990, pp. 42–50; Louis S. Richman, "The New Middle Class: How It Lives," *Fortune*, August 13, 1990, pp. 104–113; Ronald Henkoff, "Is Greed Dead?", *Fortune*, August 14, 1989, pp. 40–49; Walter Kiechel III, "The Workaholic Generation," *Fortune*, April 10, 1989, pp. 50–62.

Alderfer's ERG Theory

- Alderfer's **ERG theory** represents an extension and refinement of Maslow's need hierarchy theory.
- The ERG theory describes **existence, relatedness,** and **growth needs.**

A third important need theory of motivation is Clayton Alderfer's ERG theory.[20] In many respects, **ERG theory** extends and refines Maslow's needs hierarchy concept, although there are several important differences between the two. The *E*, *R*, and *G* stand for Alderfer's three basic need categories: existence, relatedness, and growth. **Existence needs,** perceived as necessary for basic human existence, roughly correspond to the physiological and security needs of Maslow's hierarchy. **Relatedness needs,** involving the need to relate to others, are similar to Maslow's belongingness and esteem needs. Finally, **growth needs** are analogous to Maslow's needs for self-esteem and self-actualization.

Like Murray, Alderfer suggested that more than one kind of need, for example, relatedness and growth needs, may motivate a person at the same time.

20. Clayton P. Alderfer, *Existence, Relatedness, and Growth* (New York: Free Press, 1972).

FIGURE 5.3
Alderfer's ERG Theory

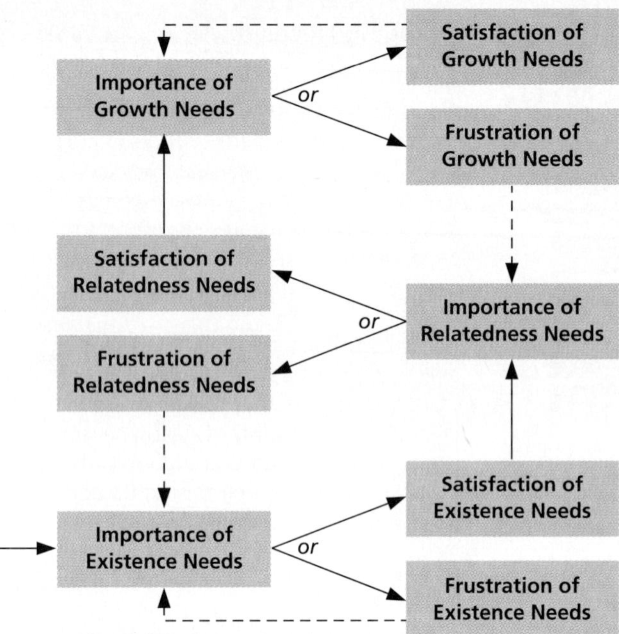

- The ERG theory suggests that if people become frustrated trying to satisfy one set of needs, they will regress back to the previously satisfied set of needs.

A more important difference from Maslow's hierarchy is that ERG theory includes a frustration-regression component and a satisfaction-progression component (see Figure 5.3). The satisfaction-progression process suggests that after satisfying one category of needs, a person progresses to the next level. On this point, Maslow's and Alderfer's theories agree. Maslow, however, assumed the individual will remain at the next level until the needs at that level are satisfied. In contrast, Alderfer argued that a person who is frustrated in trying to satisfy a higher level of needs eventually will regress to the preceding level.[21]

Suppose a manager has satisfied her basic needs at the relatedness level and now is trying to satisfy her growth needs. For a variety of reasons, such as organizational constraints (i.e., few challenging jobs) and the absence of opportunities to advance, she is unable to satisfy those needs. According to Alderfer, frustration of her growth needs will cause the manager's relatedness needs to once again dominate as motivators.

Because Alderfer's theory is a fairly new addition to motivation literature, it has not been studied much. Preliminary evidence suggests, however, that ERG theory may be a more economical and powerful explanation of human motivation than either Maslow's or Murray's need theories.[22]

---

21. Ibid.

22. Clayton P. Alderfer, "An Empirical Test of a New Theory of Human Needs," *Organizational Behavior and Human Performance,* vol. 4, 1969, pp. 142–175.

Herzberg's Two-Factor Theory

Another important foundational theory of motivation is Herzberg's two-factor theory, which in many ways is similar to the need theories just discussed. Herzberg's theory has played a major role in managerial thinking about motivation.

Development of the Theory

■ Herzberg's **two-factor theory** identifies motivation factors, which affect satisfaction, and hygiene factors, which determine dissatisfaction.

Frederick Herzberg and his associates developed the **two-factor theory** in the late 1950s and early 1960s.[23] Herzberg began by interviewing approximately two hundred accountants and engineers in Pittsburgh. He asked them to recall times when they felt especially satisfied and motivated by their jobs and times when they felt particularly dissatisfied and unmotivated. He then asked them to describe what caused the good and bad feelings. The responses to the questions were recorded by the interviewers and later subjected to content analysis. (In a content analysis, the words, phrases, and sentences used by respondents are analyzed and categorized according to their meanings.)

To his surprise, Herzberg found that entirely different sets of factors were associated with the two kinds of feelings about work. For example, a person who indicated "low pay" as a cause of dissatisfaction would not necessarily identify "high pay" as a cause of satisfaction and motivation. Instead, respondents associated entirely different causes, such as recognition or achievement, with satisfaction and motivation.

The findings led Herzberg to conclude that the traditional model of satisfaction and motivation was incorrect. As Figure 5.4 shows, job satisfaction had up until then been viewed as one-dimensional, ranging from satisfaction to dissatisfaction. If this were the case, Herzberg reasoned, a single set of factors should influence movement back and forth along the continuum. But because his research had identified influences from two different sets of factors, Herzberg argued that two different dimensions must be involved.

Figure 5.4 also illustrates Herzberg's inference that there is one dimension ranging from satisfaction to no satisfaction and another ranging from dissatisfaction to no dissatisfaction. Presumably the two dimensions must be associated with the two sets of factors identified in the initial interviews. Thus, Herzberg proposed, employees might be either satisfied or not satisfied and, at the same time, dissatisfied or not dissatisfied.[24]

■ **Motivation factors** are intrinsic to the work itself and include factors such as achievement and recognition.

In addition, Figure 5.4 lists the primary factors identified in Herzberg's interviews. **Motivation factors,** such as achievement and recognition, were often cited by people in the original study as primary causes of satisfaction and

23. Frederick Herzberg, Bernard Mausner, and Barbara Snyderman, *The Motivation to Work* (New York: Wiley, 1959); Frederick Herzberg, "One More Time: How Do You Motivate Employees?", *Harvard Business Review,* January-February 1968, pp. 53–62.

24. Herzberg, Mausner, and Synderman, *The Motivation to Work.*

FIGURE 5.4
Herzberg's Two-Factor Theory

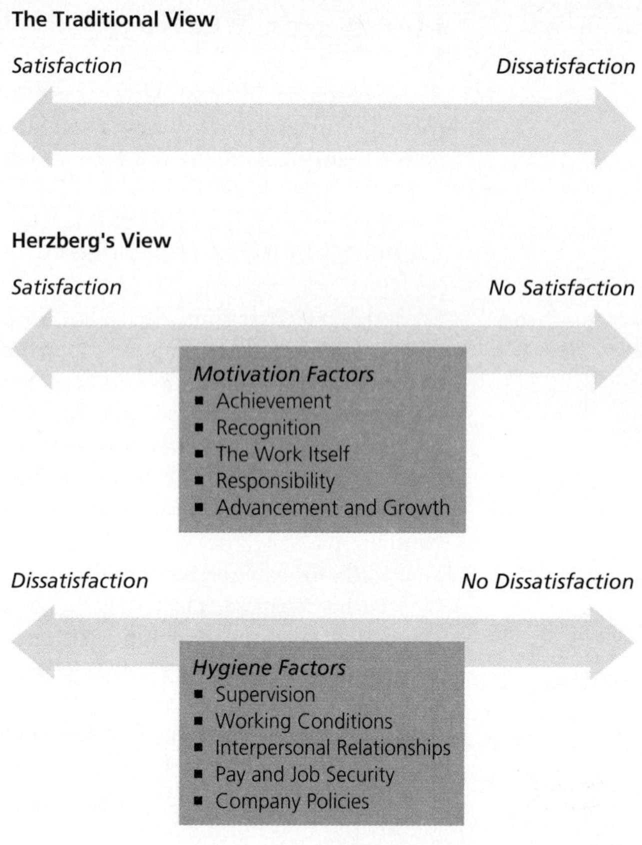

motivation. When present in a job, these factors apparently could cause satisfaction and motivation; when they were absent, the result was feelings of no satisfaction as opposed to dissatisfaction.

- **Hygiene factors** are extrinsic to the work itself and include factors like pay and job security.

The other set of factors, **hygiene factors,** came out in response to the question about dissatisfaction and lack of motivation. The respondents suggested that pay, job security, supervisors, and working conditions, if seen as inadequate, could lead to feelings of dissatisfaction. When these factors were considered acceptable, however, the person still was not necessarily satisfied; rather, she or he was simply not dissatisfied.[25]

To use the two-factor theory in the workplace, Herzberg recommended a two-stage process. First, the manager should try to eliminate situations that cause dissatisfaction, which Herzberg assumed to be the more basic of the two dimensions. To reach this goal—achieving a state of no dissatisfaction—the manager presumably needs to attend to hygiene factors, such as ensuring that pay and job security are adequate, working conditions are reasonable, and so forth.

25. Ibid.

According to Herzberg, once a state of no dissatisfaction exists, trying to further improve motivation through the hygiene factors is a waste of time. At that point, the motivation factors enter the picture. By increasing opportunities for achievement, recognition, responsibility, advancement, and growth, the manager can help subordinates feel satisfied and motivated.

Unlike many other theorists, Herzberg described quite explicitly how managers could apply his theory. He advocated a technique called *job enrichment* for structuring employee tasks.[26] (We discuss job enrichment in Chapter 13.) Herzberg tailored this technique to his key motivation factors. This unusual attention to application may explain the widespread popularity of Herzberg's theory among practicing managers.

Evaluation of the Theory

Because it gained popularity so quickly, Herzberg's theory has been scientifically scrutinized more often than most other theories in the field of organizational behavior.[27] The results have been contradictory to say the least.

The initial study by Herzberg and his associates supported the basic premises of the theory, as did a few follow-up studies.[28] In general, studies that use the same methodology as Herzberg did (content analysis of recalled incidents) tend to support the theory.[29] However, this methodology has itself come under attack. Studies that use other methods for measuring satisfaction and dissatisfaction frequently find results quite different from Herzberg's.[30] If the theory is "method bound," as it appears to be, its validity is at best questionable.

Several other criticisms have been directed against the theory. Critics say the original sample of accountants and engineers may not represent the general working population. Furthermore, they maintain that the theory fails to account for individual differences. Also, subsequent research has found that a factor such as pay may bear on satisfaction in one sample and dissatisfaction in another, and research has found that the effect of a given factor depends on the individual's

26. Herzberg, "One More Time;" Ricky W. Griffin, *Task Design: An Integrative Approach* (Glenview, Ill.: Scott, Foresman, 1982).

27. Pinder, *Work Motivation.*

28. Frederick Herzberg, *Work and the Nature of Man* (Cleveland: World, 1966); Valerie M. Bookman, "The Herzberg Controversy," *Personnel Psychology,* Summer 1971, pp. 155–189; Benedict Grigaliunas and Frederick Herzberg, "Relevance in the Test of Motivation-Hygiene Theory," *Journal of Applied Psychology,* February 1971, pp. 73–79.

29. Pinder, *Work Motivation.*

30. Marvin Dunnette, John Campbell, and Milton Hakel, "Factors Contributing to Job Satisfaction and Job Dissatisfaction in Six Occupational Groups," *Organizational Behavior and Human Performance,* May 1967, pp. 143–174; Charles L. Hulin and Patricia Smith, "An Empirical Investigation of Two Implications of the Two-Factor Theory of Job Satisfaction," *Journal of Applied Psychology,* October 1967, pp. 396–402.

age and organizational level. Finally, say its critics, the theory does not define the relationship between satisfaction and motivation.[31]

It is not surprising, then, that Herzberg's theory is no longer held in high esteem by organizational behavior researchers.[32] Indeed, the field has since adopted far more complex and valid conceptualizations of motivation, most of which we discuss in Chapter 6. But because of its initial popularity and its specific guidance for application, the two-factor theory merits a special place in the history of motivation research.

Other Important Needs

- The **need for achievement** is the desire to accomplish a task or goal more effectively than in the past.

Each theory discussed thus far describes interrelated sets of important individual needs. Several other key needs have been identified. As noted earlier, J. W. Atkinson recently incorporated several of them into Murray's manifest needs framework. However, these needs have been studied most often as needs independent from these theories. The three most frequently cited are the needs for achievement, affiliation, and power.[33]

The Need for Achievement

- People with a high need for achievement tend to set moderately difficult goals, make moderately risky decisions, want immediate feedback, become preoccupied with their task, and assume personal responsibility.

The **need for achievement** is most frequently associated with the work of David McClelland.[34] This need arises from an individual's desire to accomplish a goal or task more effectively than in the past. Need for achievement has been studied at both the individual and societal levels. At the individual level, the primary aim of research has been to pinpoint characteristics of high need achievers, the outcomes associated with high need achievement, and methods for increasing the need for achievement.

Characteristics of High Need Achievers High need achievers tend to set moderately difficult goals and to make moderately risky decisions. For example, when people playing ring toss are allowed to stand anywhere they want to, players with a low need for achievement tend to stand either so close to the target that there is no challenge or so far away that they have little chance of hitting the mark. High need achievers stand at a distance that offers challenge but also allows frequent success.

---

31. Nathan King, "A Clarification and Evaluation of the Two-Factor Theory of Job Satisfaction," *Psychological Bulletin,* July 1970, pp. 18–31. See also Dunnette, Campbell, and Hakel, "Factors Contributing to Job Satisfaction," and R. J. House and L. Wigdor, "Herzberg's Dual-Factor Theory of Job Satisfaction and Motivation: A Review of the Evidence and a Criticism," *Personnel Psychology,* Summer 1967, pp. 369–389.

32. Pinder, *Work Motivation.*

33. Ibid.

34. David McClelland, *The Achieving Society* (Princeton, N.J.: Van Nostrand, 1961).

Highly creative people like Garry Trudeau are likely to have a high need for achievement. The characters in *Doonesbury* are his vehicle for communicating his beliefs about our society and important people within it. To be successful, he must exercise considerable self-discipline to maintain his daily schedule of writing and drawing.

High need achievers also want immediate and specific feedback on their performance. They want to know how well they did something as quickly after finishing it as possible. For this reason, high need achievers frequently take jobs in sales, where they get almost immediate feedback from customers, and avoid jobs in areas such as research and development, where tangible progress is slower and feedback comes at longer intervals.

Preoccupation with their work is another characteristic of high need achievers. They think about it on their way to work, during lunch, and at home. They find putting their work aside difficult, and they become frustrated when they must stop working on a partly completed project.

Finally, high need achievers tend to assume personal responsibility for getting things done. They often volunteer for extra duties and find it difficult to delegate part of a job to someone else. Accordingly, they obtain a feeling of accomplishment when they have done more work than their peers without the assistance of others. *Developing Management Skills* provides some insights into the complexities of managing people with a high need for achievement.

Consequences of Achievement Although high need achievers tend to be successful, they often do not achieve top management posts. The most common explanation is that high need for achievement helps people advance quickly through the ranks, but the traits associated with the need often conflict with the requirements of high-level management positions. Because of the amount of work they are expected to do, top executives must be able to delegate tasks to others; they seldom receive immediate feedback; and they often must make decisions that are either more or less risky than a high need achiever would be comfortable with.[35]

Learning Achievement McClelland estimated that only around 10 percent of the American population has a high need for achievement. Nevertheless, he argued that proper training could greatly boost an individual's need for achievement.[36] The training program developed by McClelland and his associates tries to teach trainees to think like high need achievers, increase personal feedback to trainees about themselves, and develop a group esprit de corps that supports high effort and success. In sum, the trainers work to create a group feeling that will reinforce the characteristics of high need achievers.

High need achievers tend to do well as individual entrepreneurs with little or no group reinforcement. Steven Jobs, the cofounder of Apple Computer, and Nolan Bushnell, a pioneer in electronic video games and founder of Atari, are both recognized as high need achievers, and each has done quite well for himself.

35. Michael J. Stahl, "Achievement, Power, and Managerial Motivation: Selecting Managerial Talent with the Job Choice Exercise," *Personnel Psychology,* Winter 1983, pp. 775–790.

36. David McClelland, "Achievement Motivation Can Be Learned," *Harvard Business Review,* November-December 1965, pp. 6–24. See also Robert L. Helmreich, Linda L. Sawin, and Alan L. Carsrud, "The Honeymoon Effect in Job Performance: Temporal Increases in the Predictive Power of Achievement Motivation," *Journal of Applied Psychology,* May 1986, pp. 185–188.

DEVELOPING
MANAGEMENT
SKILLS

Managing High Need Achievers

Assume you are the manager of a group of five sales representatives. Your firm makes portable fax machines, and sales representatives are paid on commission. Each of the five sales representatives clearly has a high need for achievement. Describe how you should go about managing the group to capitalize on this motivational profile.

Now envision yourself in exactly the same position. This time, however, each of your sales representatives clearly has a low need for achievement. What will you do differently?

Finally, assume that some of the sales representatives have a high need for achievement and others have a low need for achievement. How should you manage the group now? Remember that you have to be fair and avoid discriminating in any way.

Write down your approaches to each of the three situations, and exchange descriptions with a classmate. Discuss with this individual how you agree and disagree.

Achievement and Economic Development McClelland also conducted research on the need for achievement at the societal level. He believed that a nation's level of economic prosperity correlates with its citizens' need for achievement.[37] The higher the percentage of a country's population that has a high need for achievement, the stronger and more prosperous that nation's economy; conversely, the lower the percentage, the weaker the economy. The reason for this correlation is that high need achievers tend toward entrepreneurial success. Hence, one would expect a country with many high need achievers to have a high level of business activity and economic stimulation.

The Need for Affiliation

■ The **need for affiliation** is the need for human companionship.

Individuals also experience the **need for affiliation,** that is, the need for human companionship.[38] Little research has been done on the need for affiliation, but researchers recognize several ways in which people with a high need for affiliation differ from those with a lower need. Individuals with a high need tend to want reassurance and approval from others and usually are genuinely concerned about others' feelings. They are likely to act and think as they believe others want them to, especially those with whom they strongly identify and desire friendship. As we might expect, people with a strong need for affiliation most often work in jobs with a lot of interpersonal contact, such as sales and teaching positions.

37. McClelland, *The Achieving Society.*

38. Stanley Schachter, *The Psychology of Affiliation* (Stanford, Calif.: Stanford University Press, 1959).

The Need for Power

■ The **need for power** is the desire to control the resources in one's environment.

A third major individual need is the **need for power,** that is, the desire to control one's environment, including financial, material, information, and human resources.[39] People vary greatly along this dimension. Some spend time and energy seeking power; others avoid power if at all possible. People with a high need for power can be successful managers if three conditions are met. First, they must seek power for the betterment of the organization rather than for their own interests. Second, they must have a fairly low need for affiliation (fulfilling a personal need for power may well alienate others in the workplace). Third, they need plenty of self-control so that they can curb their desire for power when it threatens to interfere with effective organizational or interpersonal relationships.[40]

Integrating the Need Perspectives

■ While each of the various need-based approaches to motivation is unique, all can be integrated across several common areas.

In this chapter we examined several views of individual motives and needs. Despite their differences, the theories intersect at several points. Both Maslow and Alderfer, for instance, determined a hierarchy of needs, whereas Herzberg proposed two discrete continua for two need categories. The individual needs identified by each of the three theories are strikingly similar. Figure 5.5 illustrates the major likenesses among them.

The hygiene factors described by Herzberg correspond highly with the lower three levels of Maslow's hierarchy. In particular, pay and working conditions correspond to Maslow's physiological needs, job security and company policies correspond to his security needs, and supervision and interpersonal relations correspond to belongingness needs. Herzberg's motivation factors parallel the top two levels of Maslow's hierarchy. Recognition, for example, is equivalent to esteem; achievement, the work itself, responsibility, and advancement and growth might all be categorized as part of the self-actualization process.

There are also clear similarities between Maslow's hierarchy and Alderfer's ERG theory. The existence needs in the ERG theory correspond to the physiological and physical security needs in the hierarchy perspective. The relatedness needs overlap with the interpersonal security needs, the belongingness needs, and the need for respect from others in Maslow's theory. Finally, the growth needs correspond to Maslow's self-esteem and self-actualization needs.

The independent individual needs we discussed can also be correlated with the need theories. The need for affiliation clearly is analogous to relatedness

---

39. David McClelland and David H. Burnham, "Power Is the Great Motivator," *Harvard Business Review,* March-April 1976, pp. 100–110.

40. Pinder, *Work Motivation*; McClelland and Burnham, "Power Is the Great Motivator."

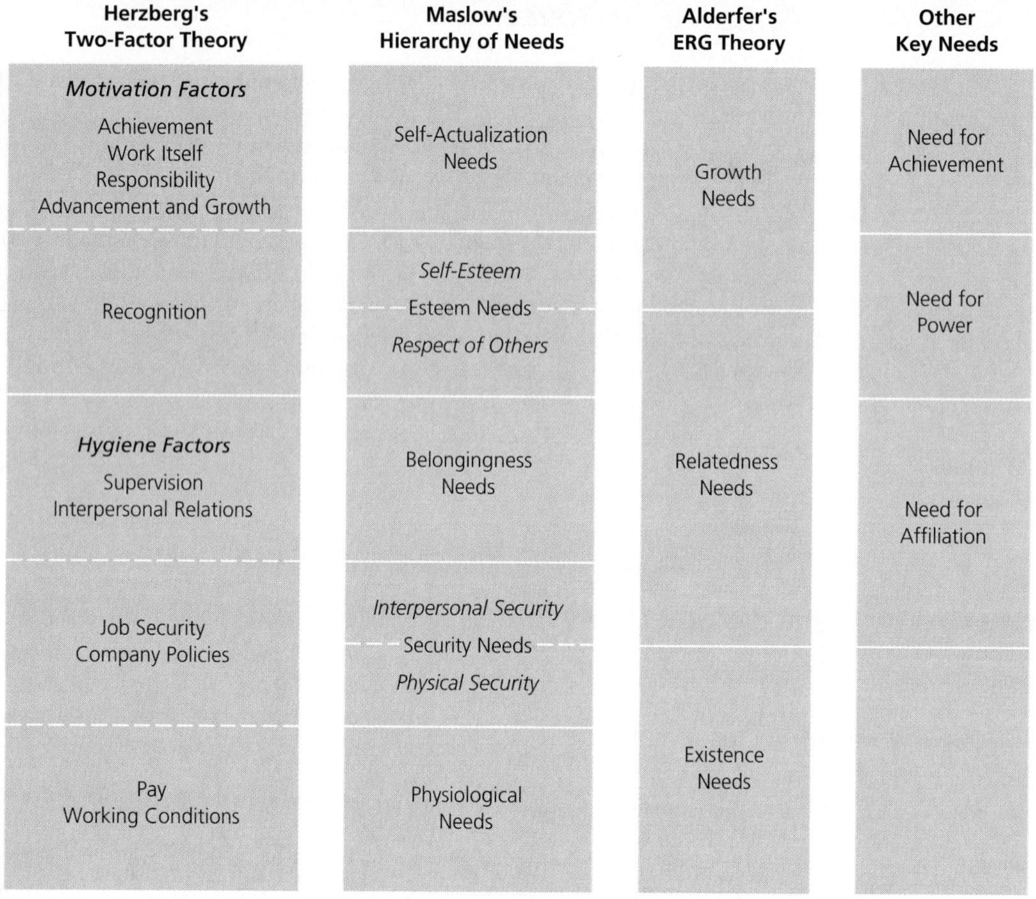

Herzberg's Two-Factor Theory	Maslow's Hierarchy of Needs	Alderfer's ERG Theory	Other Key Needs
Motivation Factors Achievement Work Itself Responsibility Advancement and Growth	Self-Actualization Needs	Growth Needs	Need for Achievement
Recognition	*Self-Esteem* Esteem Needs *Respect of Others*		Need for Power
Hygiene Factors Supervision Interpersonal Relations	Belongingness Needs	Relatedness Needs	Need for Affiliation
Job Security Company Policies	*Interpersonal Security* Security Needs *Physical Security*		
Pay Working Conditions	Physiological Needs	Existence Needs	

FIGURE 5.5
Parallels among the Need Perspectives

needs in the ERG theory, belongingness needs in Maslow's hierarchy, and interpersonal relations in Herzberg's theory. The need for power overlaps with Alderfer's relatedness and growth needs; the need for achievement parallels Alderfer's growth needs and Maslow's self-actualization needs.

Despite the many conceptual similarities among the need theories that have emerged over the years, the theories share an inherent weakness.[41] They do an adequate job of describing the factors that motivate behavior, but they tell us very little about the actual processes of motivation.[42] Even if two people are obviously motivated by interpersonal needs, they may pursue quite different paths to satisfy those needs. In Chapter 6, we describe several theories that try to solve that piece of the motivation puzzle.

---

41. Salancik and Pfeffer, "An Examination of Need-Satisfaction Models of Job Attitudes."
42. Pinder, *Work Motivation*.

Summary of Key Points

- Motivation is the set of forces that cause people to behave in various ways. Motivation starts with a need. People search for ways to satisfy their needs and then behave accordingly. Their performance of this behavior results in rewards or punishment. To varying degrees, a favorable outcome may satisfy the original need.
- The earliest view of motivation was based on the concept of hedonism, the idea that people seek pleasure and comfort and seek to avoid pain and discomfort. Scientific management extended this view by asserting that money is the primary human motivator in the workplace. The human relations view suggested that social factors are primary motivators.
- According to Abraham Maslow, human needs are arranged in a hierarchy of importance, from physiological to security to belongingness to esteem and, finally, to self-actualization. Murray's manifest needs include many work-related needs that may operate simultaneously. Alderfer's ERG theory is a refinement of Maslow's original hierarchy that also includes the frustration-regression component.
- In Herzberg's two-factor theory, satisfaction and dissatisfaction are two distinct dimensions instead of opposite ends of the same dimension. Motivation factors are presumed to affect satisfaction and hygiene factors to affect dissatisfaction. Herzberg's theory is well known among managers but has several deficiencies.
- Other important individual needs include the needs for achievement, affiliation, and power. These needs are part of Murray's theory but have been more widely studied in isolation.

Discussion Questions

1. Is it possible for someone to be unmotivated, or is all behavior motivated?
2. Is it useful to characterize motivation in terms of a deficiency? Why or why not? Is it possible to characterize motivation in terms of excess? If so, how?
3. When has your level of performance been directly affected by motivation? By your ability? By the environment?
4. What are the similarities between the views of human motivation taken by the scientific management theorists and those taken by the human relations theorists? How do they differ?
5. Identify examples from your own experience that support, and others that refute, Maslow's hierarchy of needs theory.
6. Do you think Maslow's hierarchy of needs theory, Murray's manifest needs theory, or Alderfer's ERG model has the greatest value? Explain.
7. Do you agree or disagree with the basic assumptions of Herzberg's two-factor theory? Why?

8. Which of the need theories discussed in the chapter has the most practical value for managers? Which one has the least practical value?
9. How do you evaluate yourself in terms of your needs for achievement, affiliation, and power?
10. Do you agree or disagree with the assertion that the need for achievement can be learned? Do you think it might be easier to learn it as a young child or as an adult?
11. What other important needs might emerge as topics for managerial consideration in the future?

CASE 5.1

The Big Brown Team

To many workers, the scene is all too familiar. Everywhere package deliverer Clay Bois goes, a supervisor follows with a stopwatch, calculating the time it takes him to walk to a customer's door (is he keeping to the standard three-feet-per-second pace?) and noting whether he knocks immediately, as he is supposed to, or wastes precious seconds searching for the doorbell. To get the packages to drivers like Bois for delivery, sorters must handle 1,124 parcels an hour and can make no more than one mistake every two hours; loaders are expected to fill the delivery vans at a rate of at least 500 packages per hour. What keeps these people going?

That is the secret of United Parcel Service, the nation's largest and most profitable transportation company. Of course, supervisors only occasionally ride with drivers, but they have been known to goad slow drivers by asking them if they'd like a sleeping bag. The entire company is run on stopwatches, an approach that began in the 1920s when the company's founder, James E. Casey, turned to time study engineers to help make his business 30 percent more efficient. But rather than creating burnout and high turnover, UPS's approach has earned the company a consistently favorable corporate reputation and an employee turnover rate of only 4 percent.

Much of the company's success with its workers can be attributed to what one UPS board member calls "managerial socialism." In return for their three-feet-per-second pace, UPS workers earn substantial pieces of a company that turns $700 million in profits per year. Attracted to UPS by its high wages, many workers stay because they like being an integral part of a team that's working hard and doing a superb job. Because the company seldom hires outside executives, drivers often can work their way up to supervisory and management levels, and many retire as millionaires.

Drivers start off earning over $16 an hour, about $1 more than they could expect from other trucking companies. After ten years in the company, a middle-level manager may earn $54,000, augmented by a $7,500 dividend and $14,000 in stock. Founder Casey declared that he wanted the company to be "owned by its managers and managed by its owners." In fact, most of the stock is held by 15,000 managers and supervisors, who must sell their stock to the company when they leave or retire. Thus, people who work for the company for any length of time feel driven not by a faceless, impersonal organization but by themselves. As in any good team, everyone's success depends on everyone else.

The lack of status symbols at UPS promotes workers' feelings of being an equal part of an important group. Top executives battle everyone else for parking spaces, stand in the same cafeteria lines, and do their own photocopying. Not even the chairman has his own secretary. Office workers' standards are as strict as those for drivers and loaders: No one is allowed to drink beverages at a desk, and everyone must follow tough grooming standards, including a rule against beards and long mustaches.

Rather than seeing themselves as the drudge workers, UPS's drivers often believe they are the company's heroes. The company, in turn, recognizes them as small-business people, creating their own opportunities by doing their jobs well. Workers' identification with the company is so strong that as much as 80 percent of the work force attends voluntary workshops after hours.

The Teamsters Union, which represents over 100,000 UPS workers, often gripes about the stopwatches and the constant pressure to move things even faster. Indeed, UPS barely averted a nationwide strike in 1990. UPS is in the midst of moving into high-technology package-tracking equipment—in part to compete with Federal Express in the airmail package market—and in the future, it may find it more profitable to improve efficiency through pushing machines rather than people. But at the moment, the company stands as a fine example of how to improve workers' productivity by filling their needs.

Case Questions

1. Explain the behavior of UPS employees in terms of needs.
2. Could the methods used by UPS be adopted by other organizations? Why or why not?
3. What employee needs are UPS's approach most and least likely to satisfy?

SOURCES: "Can UPS Deliver the Goods in a New World?", *Business Week,* June 4, 1990, pp. 80–82; "UPS Isn't about to Be Left Holding the Parcel," *Business Week,* February 13, 1989, p. 69; Kenneth Labich, "Big Changes at Big Brown," *Fortune,* January 18, 1988, pp. 56–64; "Up to Speed: United Parcel Service Gets Deliveries Done by Driving Its Workers," *The Wall Street Journal,* April 22, 1986, p. 1.

CASE 5.2

More Than a Paycheck

Lemuel Greene was a trainer for National Home Manufacturers, a large builder of prefabricated homes. National Home had hired Greene fresh from graduate school with a master's degree in English. At first, the company put him to work writing and revising company brochures and helping with the most important correspondence at the senior level. But soon both Greene and senior management officials began to notice how well he worked with executives on their writing, how he made them feel more confident about it, and how, after working with an executive on a report, that executive often was much more eager to take on the next writing task.

So National Home moved Greene into its prestigious training department. The company's trainers worked with thousands of supervisors, managers, and executives, helping them learn everything from a new computer language to time management skills to how to get the most out of the workers on the plant floor, many of whom were unmotivated high school dropouts. Soon Greene was spending all his time giving short seminars on executive writing as well as coaching his students to perfect their memos and letters.

Greene's move into training meant a big increase in salary, and when he started working exclusively with the company's top brass, it seemed he got a bonus every month. Greene's supervisor, Mirela Albert, knew he was making more than many executives who had been with the company three times as long, and probably twice as much as any of his graduate school classmates who concentrated in English. Yet in her biweekly meetings with him, she could tell that Greene wasn't happy.

When Albert asked him about it, Greene replied that he was in a bit of a rut, he had to keep saying the same things over and over in his seminars, and business memos weren't as interesting as the literature he had been trained on. But then, after trailing off for a moment, he blurted out, "They don't need me!" The fact that the memos filtering down through the company were now flawlessly polished, or that the annual report was 20 percent shorter yet said everything it needed to, didn't fulfill Greene's desire to be needed.

The next week, Greene came to Albert with a proposal: What if he started holding classes for some of the floor workers, many of whom had no future within or outside the company because many could write nothing but their own names? Albert took the idea to her superiors. They told her that they wouldn't oppose it, but Greene couldn't possibly keep drawing such a high salary if he worked with people whose contribution to the company was compensated at $4 an hour.

Greene agreed to a reduced salary and began offering English classes on the factory floor, billed by management (who hoped to avoid a wage hike that year) as an added benefit of the job. At first only two or three workers showed up—and they, Greene believed, only wanted an excuse to get away from the nailing guns for awhile. But gradually word got around that Greene was serious about what he was doing and didn't treat the workers like kids in a remedial class.

At the end of the year, Greene got a bonus from a new source: the vice president in charge of production. Although Greene's course took workers off the job for a couple of hours a week, productivity actually had improved since his course began, employee turnover had dropped, and, for the first time in over a year, some of the floor workers had begun to apply for supervisory positions. Greene was pleased with the bonus, but when Albert saw him grinning as he walked around the building, she knew he wasn't thinking about his bank account.

Case Questions

1. What need theories would explain Lemuel Greene's unhappiness despite his high income level?
2. Greene seems to have drifted into being a teacher. Given his needs and motivations, do you think teaching is an appropriate profession for him?

EXPERIENTIAL EXERCISE

Purpose: This exercise asks you to apply the theories discussed in the chapter to your own needs and motives.

Format: First, you will develop a list of things you want from life. Then you will categorize them according to one of the theories in the chapter. Next, you will discuss your results with a small group of classmates.

Procedure: Prepare a list of approximately fifteen things you want from life. These can be very specific (such as a new car) or very general (such as a feeling of accomplishment in school). Try to include some things you want right now and other things you want later in life. Next, choose the one motivational theory discussed in the chapter that best fits your set of needs. Classify each item from your "wish list" in terms of the need or needs it might satisfy.

Your instructor will then divide the class into groups of three. Spend a few minutes in the group discussing each person's list and its classification according to needs.

After the small-group discussions, your instructor will reconvene the entire class. Discussion should center on the extent to which each theory can serve as a useful framework for classifying individual needs. Students who found that their needs could be neatly categorized or those who found little correlation between their needs and the theories are especially encouraged to share their results.

Follow-up Questions

1. As a result of this exercise, do you now place more or less trust in the need theories as viable management tools?
2. Could a manager use some form of this exercise in an organizational setting to enhance employee motivation?

CHAPTER OUTLINE

- The Equity Theory of Motivation
  - *Forming Equity Perceptions*
  - *Responses to Perceptions of Equity/Inequity*
  - *Evaluation of Equity Theory*
  - *Managerial Implications of Equity Theory*
- The Expectancy Theory of Motivation
  - *The Basic Expectancy Model*
  - *The Porter-Lawler Extension*
  - *Evaluation of Expectancy Theory*
  - *Managerial Implications of Expectancy Theory*
- Organizational Behavior Modification
  - *Behavior Modification in the Workplace*
  - *Results of OB Mod. Programs*
- Participative Management and Motivation
  - *Historical Perspectives on Participation*
  - *Areas of Participation*
  - *Quality Circles and Participation*
- Attribution Theory and Motivation
- The Consequences of Motivation
  - *Performance and Productivity*
  - *Absenteeism and Turnover*
- Concluding Perspectives on Motivation

6

ADVANCED CONCEPTS OF MOTIVATION

CHAPTER OBJECTIVES

After studying this chapter, you should be able to:

Describe equity theory.

Describe expectancy theory.

Discuss organizational behavior modification.

Describe participative management.

Relate attribution theory to motivation.

Identify and describe the consequences of motivation.

American Express Travel Related Services is a division of American Express Corporation. The division is responsible for a wide variety of services related to the travel industry, including travel assistance, joint promotions with airlines and hotels, and travel insurance.

Bonnie Stedt is an executive vice president with the division. She heads up the firm's human resources division. Stedt enjoys her work a great deal—and it shows in the hours she puts in. She routinely works twelve hours every business day. In addition, she works every Saturday morning and most Sunday evenings. Why does she do it? What is she after?

Stedt works as hard as she does for one simple reason: She chooses to. No one forces her to put in those long hours, and she does not expect her subordinates to follow her example. Instead, her viewpoint is quite realistic: "I have one of the best jobs in the company, with total freedom to do my job."

Stedt is as ambitious as most executives, but not to the point of excess. No doubt she would enjoy being CEO someday. At the same time, however, her dedication stems from the enjoyment and satisfaction she gets from her job.[1]

Bonnie Stedt represents what is good—and some say what is bad—about many organizations today. Stedt is highly motivated to work hard and to do a good job. At the same time, some argue that people like Stedt are obsessed with their work and lack balance in their lives. From either perspective, however, Stedt works hard because she is motivated to do so.

In Chapter 5, we introduced a number of basic motivational concepts and theories. For a motivational framework to have value, however, it must capture the full range of complexity that typifies human behavior. Basic need theories are limited in this respect; thus, the field of organizational behavior has turned to more sophisticated conceptualizations of motivation to understand its causes in work settings.

- The need theories of motivation take a content approach by attempting to specify what motivates behavior.

The general distinction between the basic approaches introduced in Chapter 5 and the more advanced theories discussed in this chapter rests on the difference between content and process. The need theories reflect a content perspective in that they attempt to describe what factor or factors motivate behavior; that is, they try to list specific things that motivate behavior. The more sophisticated

1. Brian O'Reilly, "Is Your Company Asking Too Much?" *Fortune,* March 12, 1990, pp. 38–46; Thomas A. Stewart, "Do You Push Your People Too Hard?" *Fortune,* October 22, 1990, pp. 121–128; "Business First, Family Second," *The Wall Street Journal,* May 12, 1989, p. B1.

- The process theories of motivation focus on how motivated behavior occurs in an effort to satisfy needs.

process theories focus on the ways in which motivated behavior occurs;[2] in other words, they explain how people go about satisfying their needs. Process theories also describe how people choose among behavioral alternatives.

First, we discuss the equity theory of motivation. Then we turn to perhaps the most complete motivational framework of all, the expectancy theory. Next, we discuss organizational behavior modification, participative management, attribution theory, and the consequences of motivation. Finally, we present some concluding perspectives on motivation in organizations.

The Equity Theory of Motivation

- **Equity theory** focuses on people's desire to perceive equity and avoid inequity.

First articulated by J. Stacey Adams, **equity theory** is based on the simple premise that people want to be treated fairly.[3] The theory defines *equity* as the belief that we are being treated fairly in relation to others and *inequity* as the belief that we are being treated unfairly in relation to others.

Equity theory is just one of several theoretical formulations derived from social comparison processes.[4] Social comparisons involve evaluating our own situation in the context of others' situations. In this chapter, we focus mainly on equity theory because it is the most highly developed of the social comparison conceptualizations and the one that applies most directly to motivation.

Forming Equity Perceptions

- People form perceptions of equity or inequity by comparing what they give to the organization relative to what they get back and how this ratio compares with those of others.

Figure 6.1 illustrates the four-step process by which people form equity perceptions. Putting this in an organizational setting, the individual first evaluates how she or he is being treated by the organization. Next, the individual develops an evaluation of how a "comparison-other" is being treated. The comparison-other might be a person in the same work group, someone in another part of the organization, or even a composite of several people scattered throughout the organization. After evaluating the treatment of self and other, the individual compares his or her own situation with that of the other. As a consequence of

2. John P. Campbell, Marvin D. Dunnette, Edward E. Lawler, and Karl E. Weick, *Managerial Behavior, Performance, and Effectiveness* (New York: McGraw-Hill, 1970).

3. J. Stacey Adams, "Toward an Understanding of Inequity," *Journal of Abnormal and Social Psychology,* November 1963, pp. 422–436. See also Richard T. Mowday, "Equity Theory Predictions of Behavior in Organizations," in Richard M. Steers and Lyman W. Porter, eds., *Motivation and Work Behavior,* 4th ed. (New York: McGraw-Hill, 1987), pp. 89–110, and Richard C. Huseman, John D. Hatfield, and Edward W. Miles, "A New Perspective on Equity Theory: The Equity Sensitivity Construct," *Academy of Management Review,* October 1987, pp. 222–234.

4. Paul S. Goodman, "Social Comparison Processes in Organizations," in Barry M. Staw and Gerald R. Salancik, eds., *New Directions in Organizational Behavior* (Chicago: St. Clair, 1977), pp. 97–131.

FIGURE 6.1
The Formation of Equity Perceptions

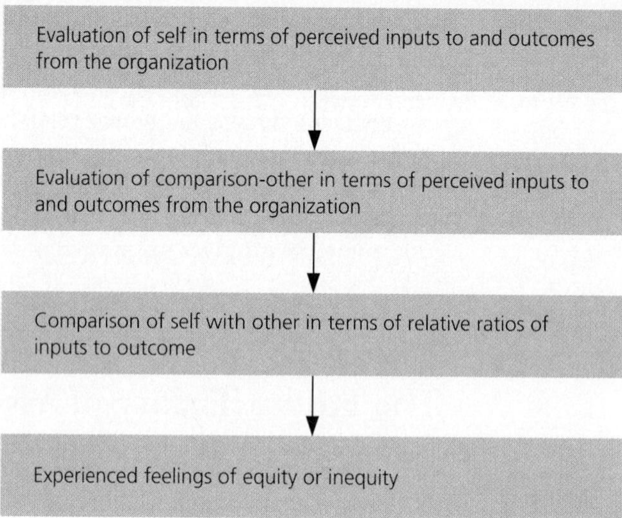

this comparison, the individual tends to perceive either equity or inequity. Depending on the strength of this perception, the person may choose to pursue one of the alternatives discussed in the next section.

Adams describes the equity comparison process in terms of input/outcome ratios. *Inputs* are an individual's contributions to the organization, such as education, experience, effort, and loyalty. *Outcomes* are what he or she receives in return, such as pay, recognition, social relationships, and intrinsic rewards.[5] A person's assessment of inputs and outcomes for both self and other are based partly on objective data (for example, the person's own salary) and partly on perceptions (such as the comparison-other's level of recognition). The equity comparison thus takes the following form:

$$\frac{\text{Outcomes (self)}}{\text{Inputs (self)}} \text{ compared to } \frac{\text{Outcomes (other)}}{\text{Inputs (other)}}$$

The person compares his or her own input-to-outcome ratio with the corresponding ratio of the comparison-other.

A perception of equity does not require that the perceived outcomes and inputs be equal; rather, only their ratios must be the same. A person may believe that his comparison-other deserves to make more money because she works harder; then her higher outcome/input ratio is acceptable. Only if the other's outcomes seem disproportionate to her inputs will the comparison provoke a perception of inequity.

5. Jerald Greenberg and Suzyn Ornstein, "High Job Status as Compensation for Underpayment: A Test of Equity Theory," *Journal of Applied Psychology,* May 1983, pp. 285–297.

These women left secure jobs to start Artemis Capital Group, a municipal bond investment firm. One factor in their decision was that they wanted faster advancement than their employers were offering. For example, some of the women worked for Goldman Sachs where only 1 of 128 partners is a woman. As equity theory suggests, people are motivated by a desire to be treated fairly. While the women denied experiencing discrimination, comparisons with their male colleagues no doubt played a role in their decision to leave.

Responses to Perceptions of Equity/Inequity

■ As a result of perceptions of equity or inequity, people can choose a variety of responses in an effort to maintain equity or reduce perceived inequity.

Figure 6.2 summarizes the results of an equity comparison. A perception of equity motivates the person to maintain the status quo. She or he will continue to provide the same level of input to the organization, at least as long as her or his outcomes do not change and the inputs and outcomes of the comparison-other also do not change. A person who perceives inequity, however, is motivated to reduce it: the greater the inequity, the stronger the level of motivation.

Adams has suggested six common methods people use to reduce inequity.[6] First, we may change our own inputs. Thus, a person may put more or less effort into the job, depending on which way the inequity lies, as a way of altering her own ratio. If she believes she is being underrewarded, she may decrease her effort, and vice versa.

Second, we may change our own outcomes. This might include demanding a pay raise, seeking additional avenues for growth and development, or even stealing.

A third, more complex response is to alter our perceptions of ourselves. After perceiving an inequity, for example, a person may change the original self-assessment and thus decide that he is really contributing less but receiving more than he originally believed.

---

6. J. Stacey Adams, "Inequity in Social Exchange," in L. Berkowitz, ed., *Advances in Experimental Social Psychology,* vol. 2 (New York: Academic Press, 1965), pp. 267–299.

FIGURE 6.2
Responses to Perceptions of Equity and Inequity

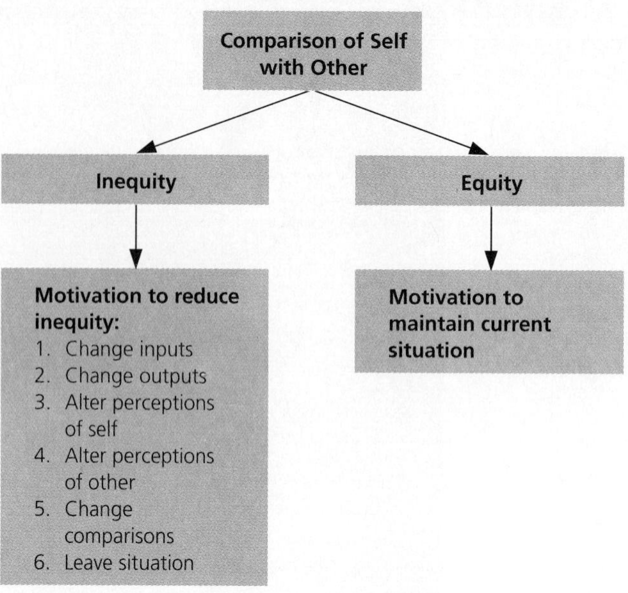

Fourth, we may alter our perception of the other's inputs and/or outcomes. For example, a person who feels underrewarded may conclude that his comparison-other must actually be working more hours than it originally appeared.

Fifth, we may change the object of comparison. A person may conclude, for instance, that the current comparison-other is the boss's personal favorite, is unusually lucky, or has special skills and abilities. Another person thus would provide a more valid basis for comparison.

As a last resort, we may simply leave the situation. Transferring to another department or quitting altogether may seem to be the only way to reduce inequity.

Evaluation of Equity Theory

Equity theory has been the subject of much research. However, most studies have been somewhat narrowly focused,[7] dealing with only one ratio—pay (hourly and piece-rate) versus the quality and/or quantity of worker output given overpayment and underpayment.[8] Findings support the predictions of equity theory quite consistently, especially under conditions of underpayment. When people experience inequity while paid on a piece-rate basis, they tend to reduce their inputs by decreasing quality and to increase their outcomes by producing more units of work. When a person experiences inequity while paid by the hour, the theory predicts an increase in quality and quantity if the person feels overpaid

7. Goodman, "Social Comparison Processes in Organizations," and Mowday, "Equity Theory Predictions of Behavior in Organizations."

8. Craig Pinder, *Work Motivation* (Glenview, Ill.: Scott, Foresman, 1984).

A LOOK AT THE
RESEARCH

The Equity Sensitivity Construct

Equity theory suggests that people want to be treated fairly. It goes on to suggest that individuals base their assessments of equity on comparisons of their inputs and outcomes relative to those of others. The theory also proposes that people will be motivated to reduce or eliminate perceptions of inequity.

Professors Richard C. Huseman and John D. Hatfield of the University of Georgia and Professor Edward W. Miles of Georgia State University recently developed a concept they call *equity sensitivity.* They suggest that not everyone will respond to perceptions of equity or inequity with the same level of intensity. Instead, responses will be influenced by the individual's preferences for different outcome/input ratios.

Their research findings have led them to suggest three equity sensitivity types. First are the "Benevolents," those who are inclined to work hard for relatively less money. In other words, they are willing to give a lot to their organizations and will be less sensitive to any minor inequities that exist.

The second type, "Entitleds," are just the opposite. Entitleds believe the organization owes them a great deal and they should not have to do much in return. Thus, for them to experience equity, things really must be inequitable in their favor!

Finally, "Equity Sensitives" most typically fit the equity theory model; that is, they generally experience equity or inequity in accordance with the basic predictions of the theory. More research is needed to help us fully understand equity sensitivity. However, it makes intuitive sense and has received tentative support from preliminary studies.

SOURCES: Edward W. Miles, John D. Hatfield, and Richard C. Huseman, "The Equity Sensitivity Construct: Potential Implications for Worker Performance," *Journal of Management,* December 1989, pp. 581–588; Reprinted with permission of Richard C. Huseman, John D. Hatfield, and Edward W. Miles, "A New Perspective on Equity Theory: The Equity Sensitivity Construct," *Academy of Management Review,* April 1987, pp. 222–234.

---

and a decrease in quality and quantity if the person feels underpaid. Research evidence provides stronger support for responses to underpayment than for responses to overpayment, but overall, most studies appear to uphold the basic premises of the theory.[9] One interesting new twist on equity theory, explored more fully in *A Look at the Research,* suggests that some people are more sensitive than others to perceptions of inequity.[10]

Managerial Implications of Equity Theory

For managers, the most important implication of equity theory relates to organizational rewards and reward systems. Because "formal" organizational rewards (pay, task assignments) are more easily observable than "informal" rewards

9. Richard A. Cosier and Dan R. Dalton, "Equity Theory and Time: A Reformulation," *Academy of Management Review,* April 1983, pp. 311–319.

10. See Jerald Greenberg, "Cognitive Reevaluation of Outcomes in Response to Underpayment Inequity," *Academy of Management Journal,* March 1989, pp. 174–184.

(intrinsic satisfaction, feelings of accomplishment), they often are at the center of a person's equity perceptions. Social comparisons clearly are a powerful factor in the workplace.

Equity theory offers managers three messages. First, everyone in the organization needs to understand the basis for rewards. If people are to be rewarded more for high-quality work than for quantity of work, that fact needs to be clearly communicated to everyone. Second, people tend to take a multifaceted view of their rewards; they perceive and experience a variety of rewards, some tangible and others intangible. Finally, people base their actions on their perceptions of reality. If two people make exactly the same salary but each thinks the other makes more, each will base his or her experience of equity on the perception rather than on reality. Hence, even if a manager believes two employees are being fairly rewarded, the employees themselves may not necessarily agree.

The Expectancy Theory of Motivation

- **Expectancy theory** suggests that people are motivated by how much they want something and how likely they think they are to get it.

Expectancy theory is a complex, more encompassing model of motivation than equity theory. Over the years since its original formulation, the theory's scope and complexity have continued to grow.

The Basic Expectancy Model

The basic expectancy theory model emerged from the work of Edward Tolman and Kurt Lewin.[11] Victor Vroom, however, is generally credited with first applying the theory to motivation in the workplace.[12] The theory attempts to determine how individuals choose among alternative behaviors. Its premise is that motivation depends on how much we want something and how likely we think we are to get it. The following simple example illustrates this premise.

Suppose a recent college graduate is looking for her first managerial job. While scanning the want ads, she sees that Exxon is seeking a new executive vice president to oversee its foreign operations. The starting salary is $300,000. The student would love the job, but she does not bother to apply because she recognizes that she has no chance of getting it. Continuing on, she sees a position that involves scraping bubble gum from underneath desks in college classroom buildings. The starting salary is $3.50 an hour, and no experience is necessary. Again, however, the student is unlikely to apply; even though she thinks she could get the job, she does not want it. Then she comes across an advertisement for a management training position with a large company. No experience is necessary, the primary requirement is a college degree, and the starting salary is

11. Edward C. Tolman, *Purposive Behavior in Animals* (New York: Appleton-Century-Crofts, 1932); Kurt Lewin, *The Conceptual Representation and the Measurement of Psychological Forces* (Durham, N.C.: Duke University Press, 1938).

12. Victor Vroom, *Work and Motivation* (New York: Wiley, 1964).

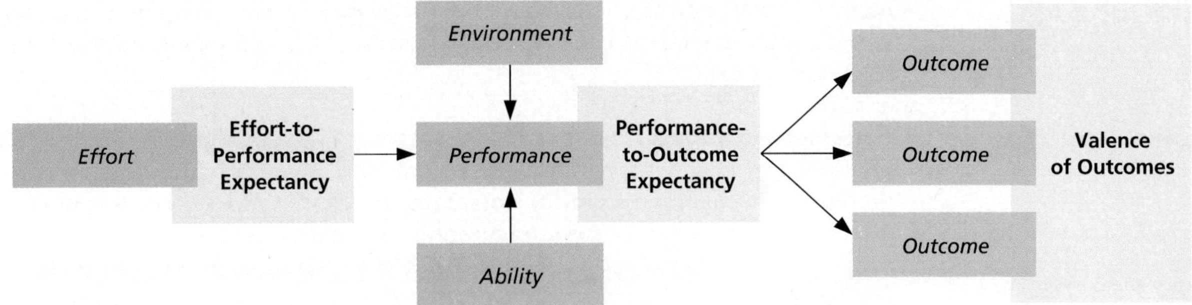

FIGURE 6.3
The Expectancy Theory of Motivation

$25,000. She will probably apply for this position (1) because she wants it and (2) because she thinks she has a reasonable chance of getting it.[13]

Figure 6.3 summarizes the basic expectancy model. The model's general components are effort (the result of motivation), performance, and outcomes. (Note that performance is considered a joint function of effort, environment, and ability; this is consistent with our discussions in Chapter 5.) Expectancy theory emphasizes the linkages among these elements, which are described as *expectancies* and *valences.*

- The **effort-to-performance expectancy** is the individual's perception of the probability that effort will lead to performance.

Effort-to-Performance Expectancy The **effort-to-performance expectancy** is the perceived probability that effort will lead to performance. In a person who believes his or her effort will lead to higher performance, this expectancy is very strong—perhaps approaching 1.0, where 1.0 equals absolute certainty that the outcome will occur. In a person who believes his or her performance will be the same no matter how much effort is made, the expectancy is very low—close to 0, where 0 equals absolutely no chance that the outcome will occur. The person who thinks there is a moderate relationship between effort and performance has an expectancy somewhere between 1.0 and 0.

- The **performance-to-outcome expectancy** is the individual's perception of the probability that performance will lead to certain outcomes.

Performance-to-Outcome Expectancy The **performance-to-outcome expectancy** is a person's perception of the probability that performance will lead to certain other outcomes. If a person thinks a high performer is certain to get a pay raise, this expectancy is close to 1.0. At the other extreme, a person who believes raises are entirely independent of performance has an expectancy close to 0. Finally, if a person thinks performance has some bearing on the prospects for a pay raise, his or her expectancy is somewhere between 1.0 and 0. In a work setting, several

13. This simple example understates the true complexity of most choices. Job-seeking students may have strong geographic preferences, have other job opportunities, and also be considering graduate school. Most decisions, in fact, are quite complex. See Michael J. Stahl and Adrian M. Harrell, "Using Decision Modeling to Measure Second Level Valences in Expectancy Theory," *Organizational Behavior and Human Performance,* August 1983, pp. 23–34; John Wanous, Thomas L. Keon, and Janina C. Latack, "Expectancy Theory and Occupational/Organizational Choices: A Review and Test," *Organizational Behavior and Human Performance,* August 1983, pp. 66–86; Adrian Harrell and Michael Stahl, "Additive Information Processing and the Relationship between Expectancy of Success and Motivational Force," *Academy of Management Journal,* June 1986, pp. 424–433.

performance-to-outcome expectancies are relevant because, as Figure 6.3 shows, several outcomes might logically result from performance. Each outcome will have its own expectancy.

- An **outcome** is anything that might result from performance.
- The **valence** of an outcome refers to how attractive or unattractive an outcome is to a particular individual.

Outcomes and Valences An **outcome** is anything that might possibly result from performance. High-level performance conceivably might produce a pay raise, a promotion, recognition from the boss, fatigue, stress, and less time to rest. The **valence** of an outcome is the attractiveness or unattractiveness of that outcome to the person. Pay raises, promotions, and recognition might all have positive valences, whereas fatigue, stress, and less time to rest might all have negative valences. People vary in the strength of their outcome valences. Stress may be a significant negative factor for one person but only a slight annoyance for another. Similarly, a pay increase may have a strong positive valence for someone desperately in need of money, a slight positive valence for someone interested mostly in getting a promotion, and even a negative valence for someone in an unfavorable tax position!

The basic expectancy framework suggests that three conditions must be met before motivated behavior will occur. First, the effort-to-performance expectancy must be well above zero. The individual must have a reasonable expectation that an exertion of effort will produce high levels of performance. Second, the performance-to-outcome expectancies also must be well above zero. The person must believe that performance may realistically result in valued outcomes. Third, the sum of all the valences for the potential outcomes relevant to the person must be positive. One or more valences may be negative so long as the positives outweigh the negatives. For example, stress and fatigue may have moderately negative valences, but if pay, promotion, and recognition have very high positive valences, the overall valence of the set of outcomes associated with performance will still be positive.

Conceptually, the valences of all relevant outcomes and the corresponding pattern of expectancies are assumed to interact in an almost mathematical fashion to determine the level of motivation. Most people do assess likelihoods of and preferences for various consequences of behavior, but they seldom approach

During the Persian Gulf War in 1991 reporters had a strong desire to get timely and accurate news reports to send back home. They felt that the only way to get these reports was to be on the front lines during combat. Thus, they went to unprecedented lengths to be a part of the action. As predicted by expectancy theory, they were highly motivated to get to the front lines.

THE ETHICAL DILEMMA

Calculated Behavior at Drexel Burnham Lambert

In the mid-1980s, Michael Milken and his employer, the brokerage firm of Drexel Burnham Lambert, were at the top of the financial community. Milken was the most influential individual financier since J. P. Morgan. He pioneered a new and powerful financial tool—junk bonds—which played a major role in the takeover, acquisition, and LBO climate that swept the business world during the 1980s.

What Milken had earned for his efforts so far was clear: a great deal of money and a lot of power. But apparently he wanted far more of both than he could expect from his present position.

So Milken decided to change his methods of operation. Working in concert with a colleague named Dennis Levine and arbitrageur Ivan Boesky, Milken developed an elaborate network of financial dealings that allegedly involved insider trading, stock manipulation, fraud, and numerous other violations of Securities and Exchange Commission regulations.

Using his hidden empire, Milken quickly amassed a fortune of $1.5 billion. But then the roof caved in. First Levine and then Boesky were brought to trial. The information prosecutors gleaned from them led to disclosure of Milken's entire empire. After months of testimony, a plea bargain agreement was reached. Milken pled guilty to six felony counts and agreed to pay $600 million in fines and restitution. He was also barred from the securities industry. In return, the government agreed to drop several dozen other charges.

SOURCES: "'Guilty, Your Honor,'" *Business Week,* May 7, 1990, pp. 32–37; "This Many May Have Mike Milken's Number," *Business Week,* April 28, 1990, p. 56; "How Michael Milken Was Forced to Accept the Prospect of Guilt," *The Wall Street Journal,* April 23, 1990, pp. A1, A6.

---

them in such a calculating manner. *The Ethical Dilemma* describes one interesting—and significant—exception.

The Porter-Lawler Extension

Vroom's original presentation of expectancy theory placed it in the mainstream of contemporary motivation theory. Since then, the model has been refined and extended. Most modifications have focused on the identification and measurement of outcomes and expectancies.[14] An exception is the version of expectancy theory presented by Lyman W. Porter and Edward E. Lawler, which takes a novel view of the relationship between employee satisfaction and performance.[15] Although the conventional wisdom was that satisfaction leads to performance, Porter and Lawler argued the reverse: If rewards are adequate, high levels of performance may lead to satisfaction.

---

14. See Carlla S. Smith and Michael T. Brannick, "A Role and Expectancy Model of Participative Decision-Making: A Replication and Theoretical Extension," *Journal of Organizational Behavior,* March 1990, pp. 91–104.

15. Lyman W. Porter and Edward E. Lawler, *Managerial Attitudes and Performance* (Homewood, Ill.: Dorsey Press, 1968).

■ The **Porter-Lawler extension** of expectancy theory suggests that a high performance level, if followed by equitable rewards, may lead to increased satisfaction.

The **Porter-Lawler extension** appears in Figure 6.4. Some of its features are quite different from the original formulation of expectancy theory. For example, the extended model includes abilities, traits, and role perceptions (how well the individual understands his or her job—see Chapter 7). At the beginning of the motivational cycle, effort is a function of the value of the potential reward for the employee (its valence) and the perceived effort-reward probability (an expectancy). Effort then combines with abilities, traits, and role perceptions to determine performance.

Performance results in two kinds of rewards. *Intrinsic rewards* are intangible—a feeling of accomplishment, a sense of achievement, and so forth. *Extrinsic rewards* are tangible outcomes such as pay and promotion. The individual judges the value of his or her performance to the organization and uses social comparison processes to form an impression of the equity of the rewards received. If the rewards are regarded as equitable, the employee feels satisfied. In subsequent cycles, satisfaction with rewards influences the value of the rewards anticipated, and actual performance following effort influences future perceived effort-reward probabilities.

Evaluation of Expectancy Theory

Expectancy theory has repeatedly been tested by organizational behavior researchers.[16] As noted earlier, the complexity of the theory has been both a blessing and a curse.[17] Nowhere is this double-edged quality more apparent than in the research undertaken to evaluate the theory.

Several studies have supported various parts of the theory. Both kinds of expectancy and valence have been found to be associated with effort and performance.[18] Research has also confirmed expectancy theory's claims that people will not engage in motivated behavior unless they (1) value the expected rewards, (2) believe their efforts will lead to performance, and (3) believe their performance will result in the desired rewards.[19]

However, expectancy theory is so complicated that researchers have found it quite difficult to test.[20] In particular, the measures of various parts of the model may lack validity, and the procedures for investigating relationships among the variables often have been less scientific than researchers would like. Moreover, people are seldom as rational and objective in choosing behaviors as expectancy theory implies. Still, the logic of the model, combined with the

---

16. Terence R. Mitchell, "Expectancy Models of Job Satisfaction, Occupational Preference, and Effort: A Theoretical, Methodological, and Empirical Appraisal," *Psychological Bulletin,* vol. 81, 1974, pp. 1096–1112; John P. Campbell and Robert D. Pritchard, "Motivation Theory in Industrial and Organizational Psychology," in Marvin D. Dunnette, ed., *Handbook of Industrial and Organizational Psychology* (Chicago: Rand McNally, 1976), pp. 63–130.

17. Wanous, Keon, and Latack, "Expectancy Theory and Occupational/Organizational Choices;" Pinder, *Work Motivation.*

18. Pinder, *Work Motivation.*

19. Campbell and Pritchard, "Motivation Theory in Industrial and Organizational Psychology."

20. Pinder, *Work Motivation.*

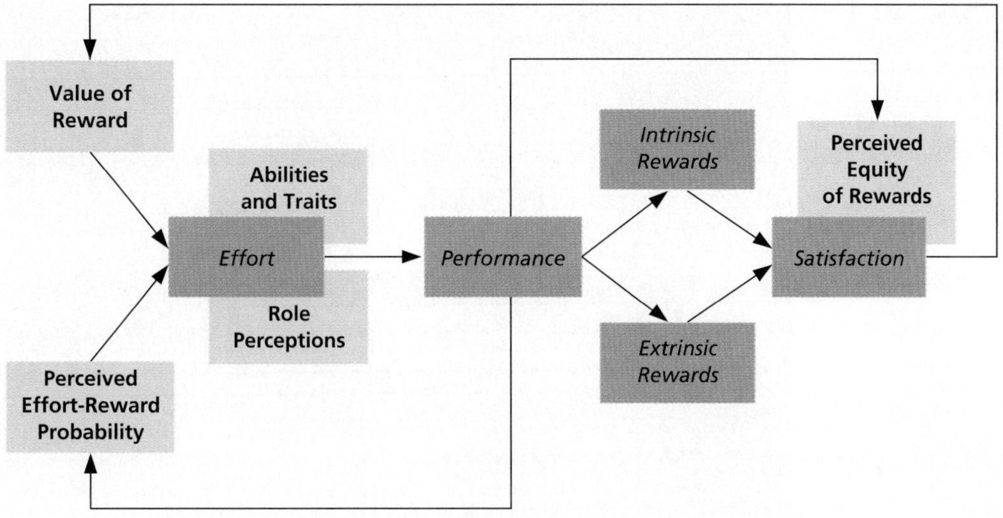

SOURCE: From Lyman W. Porter and Edward E. Lawler: *Managerial Attitudes and Performance.* © Richard D. Irwin, Inc., 1968. Reprinted by permission.

FIGURE 6.4
The Porter-Lawler Extension of Expectancy Theory

consistent, albeit modest, research support for it, suggests that the theory has much to offer.[21]

Managerial Implications of Expectancy Theory

Because expectancy theory is so complex, it is difficult to apply directly in the workplace. A manager would need to figure out what rewards each employee wants and how valuable those rewards are to each individual, measure the various expectancies, and finally adjust the relationships to create motivation. Nevertheless, expectancy theory offers several important and relevant guidelines for the practicing manager. Nadler and Lawler recently summarized these guidelines:

1. Determine the primary outcomes each employee wants.
2. Decide what levels and kinds of performance are needed to meet organizational goals.
3. Make sure the desired levels of performance are possible.
4. Link desired outcomes and desired performance.
5. Analyze the situation for conflicting expectancies.
6. Make sure the rewards are large enough.
7. Make sure the overall system is equitable for everyone.[22]

21. Ibid.

22. David A. Nadler and Edward E. Lawler, "Motivation: A Diagnostic Approach," in J. Richard Hackman, Edward E. Lawler, and Lyman W. Porter, eds., *Perspectives on Behavior in Organizations,* 2nd ed. (New York: McGraw-Hill, 1983), pp. 67–78.

For decades soldiers in Mandalay gave alms to Buddhist monks because of the belief that such giving would help them in a future life. After a recent political clash between soldiers and monks, monks stopped accepting the soldiers' gifts and instead beg for food from farmers such as this one. As a result of the monks' behavior, many of the soldiers have experienced a crisis of conscience and are questioning their devotion to the military. The soldiers may eventually modify their behavior to attain new forms of reinforcement.

Organizational Behavior Modification

Recall from Chapter 3 that we said we would treat the managerial implications of learning theory, especially as they relate to motivation, in this chapter. The major organizational application of learning theory is *organizational behavior modification.*

Behavior Modification in the Workplace

- **Organizational behavior modification (OB Mod.)** is an approach to applying learning theory to organizational settings.

OB Mod. is the application of reinforcement theory to people in organizational settings.[23] As we saw in Chapter 3, reinforcement theory says that we can increase the frequency of desirable behaviors by linking those behaviors with positive consequences and decrease undesirable behaviors by linking them with negative consequences. OB Mod. characteristically uses positive reinforcement to encourage desirable behaviors in employees. Figure 6.5 illustrates the basic steps in OB Mod.

The first step is to identify *performance-related behavioral events*; that is, desirable and undesirable behaviors. For example, a manager of an electronics

23. Fred Luthans and Robert Kreitner, *Organizational Behavior Modification* (Glenview, Ill.: Scott, Foresman, 1975); Fred Luthans and Robert Kreitner, *Organizational Behavior Modification and Beyond* (Glenview, Ill.: Scott, Foresman, 1985).

FIGURE 6.5
The Steps in OB Mod.

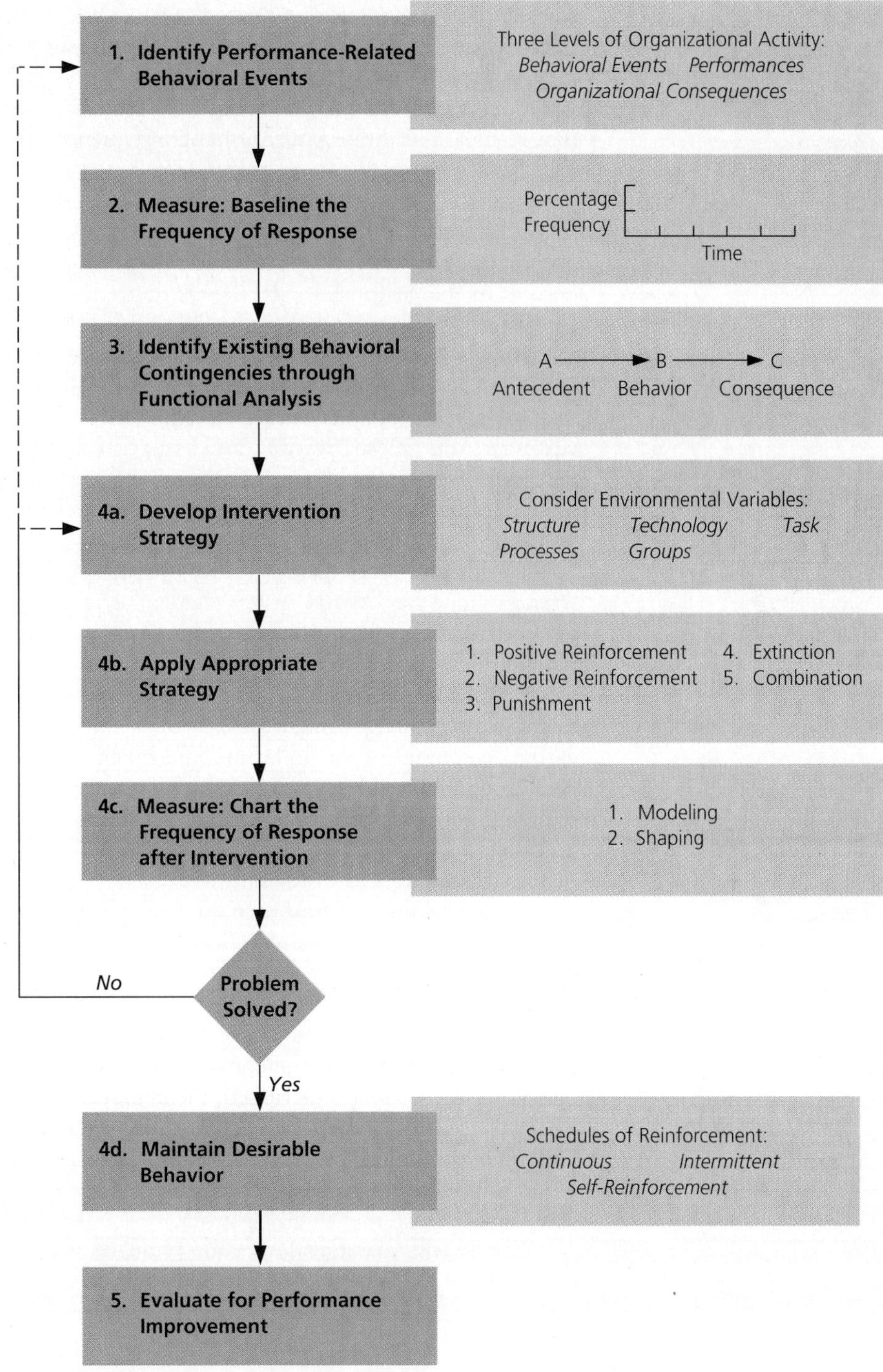

SOURCE: Reprinted, by permission of the publisher, from *Personnel,* July–August 1974.

store might decide that the most important behavior for salespeople working on commission is to greet customers warmly and show them the exact merchandise they came in to see. Note in Figure 6.5 that three kinds of organizational activity are associated with this behavior: the behavioral event itself, the performance that results, and the organizational consequences that befall the individual.

Next, the manager measures *baseline performance*—the existing level of performance for each individual. This usually is stated in terms of a percentage frequency across different time intervals. For example, the electronics store manager may observe that a particular salesperson presently is greeting around 40 percent of the customers each day as desired.

The third step is to identify the existing *behavioral contingencies,* or consequences, of performance; that is, what happens now to employees who perform at various levels? If an employee works hard, does he or she get a reward or just get tired? For example, the electronics store manager may observe that when customers are greeted warmly and assisted competently, they buy something 40 percent of the time, whereas customers who are not properly greeted and assisted make a purchase only 20 percent of the time. Thus, the salesperson earns both gratification from the sales and higher commissions.

At this point, the manager develops and applies an appropriate *intervention strategy.* In other words, some element of the performance-reward linkage—structure, process, technology, groups, or the task—is changed with the goal of making high-level performance more rewarding. Various kinds of positive reinforcement are used to guide employee behavior in desired directions. The electronics store manager might offer a sales commission plan whereby salespeople earn a percentage of the dollar amount taken in by each sale. The manager might also compliment salespeople who give appropriate greetings and ignore those who do not. The reinforcement helps shape the behavior of salespeople. In addition, an individual salesperson who does not get reinforced may model the behavior of more successful salespersons.

After the intervention step, the manager again measures performance to determine whether the desired effect has been achieved. If not, the manager must redesign the intervention strategy or repeat the entire process. For instance, if the salespeople in the electronics store are still not greeting customers properly, the manager may need to look for other forms of positive reinforcement—perhaps a higher-percentage commission.

If performance has increased, the manager must try to maintain the desirable behavior through some schedule of positive reinforcement. For example, higher commissions might be granted for every other sale, for sales over a certain dollar amount, and so forth. (As we saw in Chapter 3, a schedule defines the interval at which reinforcement will be given.)

Finally, the manager looks for improvements in individual employees' behavior. Here the emphasis is on offering significant longer-term rewards, such as promotions and salary adjustments, to sustain ongoing efforts to improve performance.[24]

---

24. Luthans and Kreitner, *Organizational Behavior Modification and Beyond.*

Results of OB Mod. Programs

Unlike the expectancy theory, the OB Mod. approach is relatively simple. As a result, it has been used by many types of organizations, with varying levels of success.[25] A program at Emery Air Freight prompted much of the initial enthusiasm for OB Mod., and other success stories also have caught the attention of practicing managers.[26] For example, B. F. Goodrich increased productivity over 300 percent and Weyerhaeuser increased productivity by at least 8 percent in three different work groups.[27] These results suggest that OB Mod. is a valuable method for improving employee motivation in many situations.

OB Mod. also has certain drawbacks. Not all applications have worked. For example, a program at Standard Oil of Ohio was discontinued because it failed to meet its objectives; another program at Michigan Bell was only modestly successful. Further, managers frequently have only limited means for providing meaningful reinforcement for their employees. In addition, some have argued that OB Mod. is manipulative because it tries to suppress individual freedom of behavioral choice. Much of the research testing OB Mod. has gone on in laboratories and thus is hard to generalize to the real world. And even if OB Mod. works for awhile, the impact of the positive reinforcement may wane once the novelty has worn off, and employees may come to view it as a routine part of the compensation system.[28]

Participative Management and Motivation

- **Participative management,** which focuses on the organization's human resources, is increasingly being seen as a way to enhance employee motivation.

Participative management, another applied approach to employee motivation, focuses on the human resources of an organization. A historical perspective is necessary to fully explain participative management.

Historical Perspectives on Participation

The human relations movement in vogue from the 1930s through the 1950s (see Chapter 1) assumed that employees who are happy and satisfied will work harder.[29] The movement stimulated general interest in worker participation in

25. W. Clay Hamner and Ellen P. Hamner, "Organizational Behavior Modification on the Bottom Line," *Organizational Dynamics,* Spring 1976, pp. 3–21.

26. "At Emery Air Freight: Positive Reinforcement Boosts Performance," *Organizational Dynamics,* Winter 1973, pp. 41–50; Hamner and Hamner, "Organizational Behavior Modification on the Bottom Line."

27. Hamner and Hamner, "Organizational Behavior Modification on the Bottom Line."

28. Edwin Locke, "The Myths of Behavior Mod in Organizations," *Academy of Management Review,* vol. 2, 1977, pp. 543–553.

29. Daniel Wren, *The Evolution of Management Thought,* 2nd ed. (New York: Wiley, 1979).

Ford Motor Company has started involving employees in a wide variety of activities. Through increased participation workers' motivation has been enhanced, leading to major improvements in the quality of the firm's products. For example, Ford incorporated more than 2,600 quality-related improvements made by employees into its 1990 Lincoln Town Car.

various organizational activities. The hope was that if employees were given the opportunity to participate in decision making concerning their work environment, they would be satisfied, and satisfaction supposedly would result in improved performance. But managers tended to see employee participation merely as a way to increase satisfaction, not as a source of potentially valuable input. Eventually, managers began to recognize that employee input was useful in itself, apart from its presumed effect on satisfaction. They came to see employees as valued human resources that can contribute to organizational effectiveness.[30]

The role of participation in motivation can be expressed in terms of both the need theories discussed in Chapter 5 and expectancy theory. Employees who participate in decision making may be more committed to executing decisions properly. Furthermore, the successful process of making a decision, executing it, and then seeing the positive consequences can help satisfy one's need for achievement, provide recognition and responsibility, and enhance self-esteem. Simply being asked to participate in organizational decision making also may enhance an employee's self-esteem. In addition, participation should help clarify expectancies; that is, by participating in decision making, employees may better understand the linkage between their performance and the rewards they want most.

Areas of Participation

At one level, employees can participate in addressing questions and making decisions about their own jobs. Instead of just telling them how to do their jobs, for example, managers can ask employees to make their own decisions about how to do them. Based on their own expertise and experience with their tasks, workers might be able to improve their own productivity. In many situations,

30. Raymond E. Miles, "Conflicting Elements in Managerial Ideologies," *Industrial Relations,* October 1964, pp. 77–91.

they might also be well qualified to make decisions about what materials to use, what tools to use, and so forth.

It might also be helpful to let workers make decisions about administrative matters, such as work schedules. If jobs are relatively independent of one another, employees might decide when to change shifts, take breaks, go to lunch, and so forth. A work group might also be able to schedule vacations and days off for all of its members. Furthermore, employees are getting increasing opportunities to participate in broader issues of product quality. Such participation has become a hallmark of successful Japanese firms, and American companies have followed suit. We discuss participation from another perspective in Chapter 13.

Quality Circles and Participation

- **Quality circles (QCs)** are groups of volunteer employees who meet regularly to identify and propose solutions to quality and related problems in the organization.

Quality circles (QCs) usually are defined as small groups of volunteers who meet regularly to identify, analyze, and solve quality and related problems that pertain to their work.[31] Quality circles became popular in the United States in the early 1980s. Widely used in Japan, they were presumed to have played a role in that country's rapid economic and technological growth.

Several steps are involved in creating successful quality circles. The first step is to seek volunteers. Recruitment usually stresses the circle's potential to help the organization and influence its future. It is crucial, of course, that the participants be true volunteers; participation through coercion probably will have more negative than positive consequences. QCs usually have eight to ten members drawn from the same work area or related areas so that they have a common frame of reference. A circle's membership ordinarily is fixed, although people may be added or dropped as appropriate. The circle usually receives some form of problem-solving training to help it deal with work problems. Training may be provided only at the outset or as an ongoing process.

Quality circle meetings are almost always held on company premises and on company time. One meeting a week is standard, with each meeting lasting about one hour, but variation exists from company to company. During meetings the circle identifies, analyzes, and solves quality problems in its areas of responsibility. Problems may range from eliminating vandalism to reducing defects in a particular production process. Since American firms learned of the success of quality circles in Japan, many have adopted them, including Westinghouse, Hewlett-Packard, Texas Instruments, Eastman Kodak, and Procter & Gamble. Many firms report positive results from quality circles, although little research has been done to assess their effectiveness. One recent study found the disappointing result that while quality circles were effective for awhile, their contributions eventually began to diminish.[32] *Management in Action* reports another problem with quality circles.

31. G. Munchus, "Employer-Employee Based Quality Circles in Japan: Human Resource Implications for American Firms," *Academy of Management Review,* April, 1983, pp. 255–261.

32. Ricky W. Griffin, "A Longitudinal Assessment of the Consequences of Quality Circles in an Industrial Setting," *Academy of Management Journal,* June 1988, pp. 338–358.

MANAGEMENT IN ACTION

Quality Circles: Participation or Exploitation?

Quality circles have been hailed as the potential alchemist's stone for turning employee participation into gold. Advocates claim that QCs provide a focused and manageable intervention strategy that can immediately enhance participation. Moreover, QCs are seen as a way to facilitate a transition to a more fully participative culture throughout an organization.

However, QCs have their critics. One frequent source of concern is organized labor. Some labor leaders are against the notion of participation to begin with. Given this position, it is not surprising that they are opposed to organizations' use of QCs to increase participation.

Unions have gained a new weapon in their fight against QCs. For example, Du Pont recently formed a QC in one of its plants. A local union of chemical workers filed suit against the firm on the basis of unfair labor practices (the union claimed that the QC's agenda encroached on union rights). The union won, and the QC was disbanded.

Of course, the issue is irrelevant when unions and management agree ahead of time to use QCs. Indeed, this is more typically the case. It is only when union opposition occurs that legal problems arise. But even then things can get complicated. For example, at the time of this writing, a major battle is brewing within the U.S. Postal Service. Management and two unions want to adopt the QC concept, but another very powerful union does not. Only time—and litigation—will determine how this one comes out.

SOURCES: "Quality Circles Are Vulnerable to Union Tests," *The Wall Street Journal,* May 28, 1990, pp. B1, B3; "UAW Hotly Debates Whether It Is Too Cozy with Car Companies," *The Wall Street Journal,* June 15, 1989, pp. A1, A8; David D. Van Fleet and Ricky W. Griffin, "Quality Circles: A Review and Suggested Future Directions," in C. L. Cooper and I. Robertson, eds., *International Review of Industrial and Organizational Psychology 1989* (London: Wiley, 1989), pp. 213–234.

Attribution Theory and Motivation

■ **Attribution theory** suggests that employees observe their own behavior, attribute external or internal interpretations to it, and shape future motivated behavior accordingly.

In Chapter 3, we discussed the role of attribution in perception. Here we explore the motivational implications of **attribution theory.**[33] According to the attributional view of employee motivation, a person observes his or her behavior through the processes of self-perception. On the basis of these perceptions, the individual decides whether his or her behavior is a response primarily to external or to internal factors.[34]

Through this attribution of causes, the individual decides whether he or she is basically extrinsically or intrinsically motivated and develops a preferred pattern of future incentives. A person who believes he is extrinsically motivated will seek extrinsic rewards, such as pay or status symbols, as future incentives. One who feels she is intrinsically motivated will look more for intrinsic incentives in the future.

33. H. H. Kelley, *Attribution in Social Interaction* (Morristown, N.J.: General Learning Press, 1971).

34. Craig A. Anderson, "Motivational and Performance Deficits in Interpersonal Settings: The Effect of Attributional Style," *Journal of Personality and Social Psychology,* November 1983, pp. 1136–1147.

Although relatively little work has been done on attribution theory's applications to motivation, there have been some intriguing findings. For example, E. L. Deci reasoned that paying an intrinsically motivated person on an incentive basis (that is, providing extrinsic rewards) would make him or her become more extrinsically motivated and less intrinsically motivated. Deci's research has indicated that if people are paid to do something they already like to do (are intrinsically motivated), their level of "liking" diminishes. Furthermore, if the pay is later withheld, their level of effort also diminishes. Thus, attributional processes appear to play a meaningful role in employee motivation in the workplace.[35]

The Consequences of Motivation

■ A variety of work-related behaviors occur as a result of motivation.

In Chapter 5, we note that all behavior is motivated. The manager's job, then, is to channel the motivation of her or his employees such that their behaviors will enhance the effectiveness of the overall organization. In this section, we take a brief look at the behaviors that are key to organizational effectiveness.

Performance and Productivity

Since the early 1960s in the United States business, government, and the academic community have been concerned about performance and productivity. Much of this concern has been prompted by decreases in American productivity growth compared to other industrial countries, most notably Japan.[36] Although the gap narrowed slightly in the 1980s, the issue still deserves attention.

■ **Productivity** is a measure of how many goods and services an organization creates from its resources.

Productivity refers to the amount of goods and services an organization creates from its resources. If one worker produces 100 units, 3 of which are defective, he or she is more productive than a worker who produces 90 units with 5 defects and less productive than a worker who produces 105 units with no defects. Similarly, a bank that can process an average of 75 customers an hour with 3 teller stations is more productive than a bank that can process only 70 customers an hour with the same number of teller stations. Productivity is the level of outputs relative to inputs. It can be assessed at the level of the individual, the work group, or the organization itself.

■ **Performance** encompasses a broad range of work-related behaviors in addition to productivity.

Performance is a broader concept and can be defined as the total set of job-related behaviors in which employees engage. Thus, in many ways overall performance is quite similar to organizational citizenship behavior as discussed in

---

35. See E. L. Deci, "Effects of Externally Mediated Rewards on Intrinsic Motivation," *Journal of Applied Psychology,* vol. 18, 1971, pp. 105–115. See also Paul C. Jordan, "Effects of an Extrinsic Reward on Intrinsic Motivation: A Field Experiment," *Academy of Management Journal,* June 1986, pp. 405–412.

36. W. Bruce Chew, "No-Nonsense Guide to Productivity," *Harvard Business Review,* January-February 1988, pp. 110–119.

The Special Olympics, an international sports and recreation program for special-needs individuals, relies heavily on the relationship between motivation and performance. The program involves both highly motivated athletes and dedicated volunteers. The encouragement that the volunteers provide helps the athletes improve their performance.

Chapter 4. If worker A can produce 20 units an hour and worker B can produce only 18 units, worker A is more productive than worker B.

But suppose worker B is always willing to work late, assists in training new employees, looks for opportunities to help the organization, always comes to work on time, and has not missed a day of work in three years. Worker A insists on leaving promptly at 5:00 P.M. every day, ignores new employees, never shows initiative, is often several minutes late for work, and misses an average of one day of work per month. Although worker A is more productive, it might be argued that worker B is the better performer across a wider array of activities. Of course, it is up to the manager and the organization to determine exactly what the appropriate job-related behaviors are and how they should be weighted in determining performance. The point is that performance goes beyond the level of outputs. We discuss performance appraisal in detail in Chapter 14.

Absenteeism and Turnover

- **Absenteeism** occurs when an employee is absent from work for any reason.
- **Turnover** occurs when an employee permanently quits working for an organization.

Two intimately related employee behaviors of great interest to managers and researchers are absenteeism and turnover. Both are forms of withdrawal from the workplace. **Absenteeism** occurs when employees are absent from work, for whatever reason. **Turnover** occurs when employees quit working for an organization permanently. Absenteeism is an important dimension of performance, for an absent employee's responsibilities fall on others in the organization. Turnover is also critical, because organizations usually spend considerable time and money recruiting, hiring, and training new employees to replace those who leave.

Figure 6.6 shows a simplified model of employee absenteeism. Based on the work of Richard Steers and Susan Rhodes, the model suggests that job satisfaction and pressures to attend work interact to determine attendance motivation. Actual attendance depends on both motivation and ability to attend.[37]

37. Richard M. Steers and Susan R. Rhodes, "Major Influences on Employee Attendance: A Process Model," *Journal of Applied Psychology,* vol. 63, 1978, pp. 391–407.

FIGURE 6.6
A Model of Employee Absenteeism

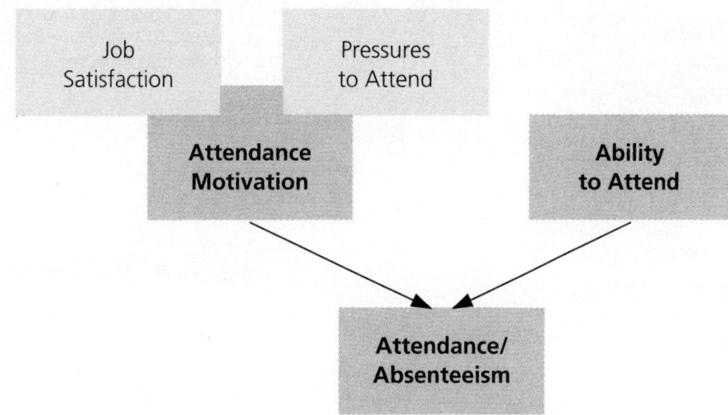

Working with Richard Mowday, Steers also formulated an integrated model of employee turnover.[38] Figure 6.7 presents a simplified form of this model. Individual characteristics interact with information about the job and the organization to determine job expectations and values and with economic and market conditions to determine alternative job opportunities. Expectations, job performance, and organizational characteristics and experiences then determine job satisfaction.

Satisfaction interacts with nonwork factors that support staying or leaving, such as job transfer for a spouse, to influence the employee's desire to stay or leave. A person seeking another job may end the search if offered some kind of accommodation. For example, if the boss learns that a valued employee is thinking about leaving to take a new job with a higher salary, a pay raise may persuade the employee to stay. But if no such accommodation is offered, the employee will continue to ponder the choice of leaving or remaining.

Although the complete model has not been tested, it summarizes a considerable amount of research on employee turnover and can serve as a useful framework for understanding this important phenomenon.

Concluding Perspectives on Motivation

Many of the most important managerial implications of motivation are self-evident. Like the content theories we discussed in Chapter 5, each of the process theories presented in this chapter has potential uses in the workplace. Equity theory provides useful guidelines for managing reward systems. Expectancy theory partially explains why people put different levels of effort into their jobs.

---

38. Richard M. Steers and Richard Mowday, "A Model of Voluntary Employee Turnover," in Larry L. Cummings and Barry M. Staw, eds., *Research in Organizational Behavior,* vol. 3 (Greenwich, Conn.: JAI Press, 1981).

FIGURE 6.7
A Model of Employee Turnover

OB Mod. and participative management provide practical guidelines for implementing motivational strategies. Finally, attribution theory is a promising recent perspective on motivation.

But each of these theories offers only a piece or two of the motivation puzzle. Managers should recognize that no single theory explains or predicts employee motivation completely. The primary message is to understand the value of each viewpoint while remaining alert to its shortcomings.

Summary of Key Points

- The equity theory of motivation assumes people want to be treated fairly. It hypothesizes that people compare their own input-to-outcome ratio in the organization to the ratio of a comparison-other. If they feel their treatment has been relatively inequitable, they take steps to reduce the inequity.
- Expectancy theory, a somewhat more complicated model, follows from the assumption that people are motivated to work toward a goal if they want it and think they have a reasonable chance of achieving it. The effort-to-performance expectancy is the belief that effort will lead to performance. The performance-to-outcome expectancy is the belief that performance will lead to certain outcomes. Valence is the desirability to the individual of the various possible outcomes of performance.
- The Porter-Lawler extension of expectancy theory provides useful insights into the relationship between satisfaction and performance. This model suggests that performance may lead to a variety of intrinsic and extrinsic rewards. When perceived as equitable, these rewards lead to satisfaction.
- Organizational behavior modification is the application of reinforcement principles and concepts to organizational settings. Using a variety of rein-

forcers and reinforcement contingencies, several organizations have achieved impressive motivational improvements through OB Mod.

- Participative management can help improve employee motivation in many business settings. Quality circles have received much attention in recent years as a potentially useful way to increase employee participation.
- Attribution theory also has been applied to employee motivation. The theory suggests that employees perceive their behavior as stemming from either external or internal causes and are motivated by rewards that correspond to the causes of their behavior.
- From a managerial standpoint, motivation theory is primarily intended to channel employee behavior toward high performance, high productivity, low absenteeism, and low turnover.

Discussion Questions

1. Besides the content-process distinction, are there any basic differences between the motivation theories discussed in Chapters 5 and 6?
2. Apply equity theory to a classroom setting. Specify your inputs and potential outcomes. Choose a likely comparison-other, and determine whether you should feel equity or inequity.
3. What might be some managerial implications of equity theory beyond those discussed in the chapter?
4. Do you think expectancy theory is too complex for direct use in organizational settings? Why or why not?
5. Do you agree or disagree with the relationships between performance and satisfaction suggested by Porter and Lawler? Cite examples that both support and refute the model.
6. The OB Mod. theory of motivation seems more application based than the equity or expectancy theories. It is also rather narrow in scope. What are the advantages and disadvantages of a theory that has these characteristics?
7. What are some ways your instructor might use OB Mod. in the classroom to shape your behavior? Are there ways you can shape his or her behavior with some of the same techniques?
8. What are the motivational consequences of participative management—specifically, quality circles—from the frame of reference of another theory or theories?
9. What motivational problems might result from an organization's attempt to set up quality circles?
10. Cite personal examples of attributional processes and motivation.

CASE 6.1

Motivation at A. O. Smith Corp.

A. O. Smith Corp. is a large manufacturing concern. One of Smith's biggest and most profitable businesses has long been its automotive works operation in Milwaukee, Smith's Automotive Products Company. The company makes a number of different subassemblies—automobile and truck frames, engines, transmissions, and so forth—for General Motors, Ford, and Chrysler.

In the early 1980s, however, the company seemed to be headed nowhere fast. For one thing, product quality was atrocious. For example, one of Smith's biggest contracts was making frames for Ford Ranger pickup trucks. Over 20 percent of the frames were coming off the assembly line with defects that had to be repaired before being shipped. In addition, management and labor were in constant conflict over work rules. Employees repeated highly specialized tasks every twenty seconds. Also, partly because they were paid on a piece-rate basis, workers were much more concerned with the quantity of what they produced than with its quality.

In 1981, Smith's situation began to deteriorate even further. Prompted by the invasion of high-quality Japanese imports like Toyota and Nissan, American auto firms realized that they had to start taking quality more seriously themselves. One of their first initiatives was to demand higher quality from suppliers like A. O. Smith.

As a first step, management at Smith unilaterally initiated a quality circle program. Unfortunately, because the union had not been consulted and participation in the program was being mandated, the strategy didn't work particularly well. Quality did improve somewhat, but not nearly as much as expected. Enthusiasm for the program eventually faded.

In 1984, Smith took another big blow. Its biggest customer, General Motors, started cutting back on its orders. The automaker was making fewer and fewer big cars—for which Smith was primarily geared—and more and more smaller cars—an area where Smith was weak. As a result, Smith realized it had to tackle its quality problems all over again.

This time, in collaboration with the unions, participation was systematically implemented throughout the plant. Smith and its unions created problem-solving committees on the shop floor, advisory committees with union representation at the plant level, and an upper-level planning committee with union and management executives.

Surprisingly, this effort too failed to meet expectations. Quality did improve, and long-standing hostilities between management and labor began to wane. Nevertheless, the gains were disappointing. The piece-rate pay system was still leading to poor-quality work, and worker absenteeism was actually increasing—on some days, as much as 20 percent of Smith's workers were not coming in.

In 1986, it looked like "strike three and you're out." Ford, GM, and Chrysler started demanding still higher quality accompanied by parallel demands for lower prices. Smith had to lay off 1,300 workers, and the end seemed near. But this time the initiative for change came from labor itself. The unions suggested giving more control to the rank-and-file workers.

First, Smith agreed to eliminate the piece-rate pay system in exchange for a three-year wage freeze. Then it went to a flexible work system to eliminate the boredom and drudgery that plagued the assembly line. Under the new arrangement, groups of five to seven workers decide for themselves how to divide up the day's work. They schedule production, order maintenance work, allocate overtime among themselves, and stop the line whenever necessary to correct problems.

How well has the new system worked? Quality has risen dramatically; defects have been cut from 20 percent to only 3 percent. Also, productivity has increased and absenteeism is way down. Although it's too soon to know the full story, it looks like A. O. Smith has weathered the storm.

Case Questions

1. What motivation theories are reflected in the experience of A. O. Smith?
2. Put yourself in the role of an employee at A. O. Smith. Explain your likely feelings—and the reasons for those feelings—at each stage of Smith's evolution.
3. What motivational problems might A. O. Smith expect to encounter in the future? Can the firm do something today to head them off?

SOURCES: "The Cultural Revolution at A. O. Smith," *Business Week,* May 29, 1989, pp. 66–68; Marsha E. Hass and Jane Hass Philbrick, "The New Management: Is It Legal?" *Academy of Management Executive,* November 1988, pp. 325–329; Ralph P. Hummel, "Behind Quality Management," *Organizational Dynamics,* Summer 1987, pp. 71–78.

CASE 6.2

Equity in Academia

When the last student left Melinda Wilkerson's office at 5:30 P.M., the young English professor just sat, too exhausted to move. Her desk was piled high with student papers, journals, and recommendation forms. "There goes my weekend," she thought to herself, knowing that reading and commenting on the thirty journals alone would take up all of Saturday. She liked reading the journals, getting a glimpse of how her students were reacting to the novels and poems she had them read, watching them grow and change. But recently, as she picked up another journal from the bottomless pile or greeted another student with a smile, she often wondered whether it was all worth it.

Wilkerson had had such a moment about an hour earlier, when Ron Agua, whose office was across the hall, had waved to her as he walked past her door. "I'm off to the Rat," he announced. "Come join us if you ever get free." For a moment Wilkerson had stared blankly at the student before her, pondering the scene at the Rathskeller, the university's most popular restaurant and meeting place. Agua would be there with four or five of the department's senior members, including Alice Bordy, the department chair. All would be glad to have her join them . . . if only she didn't have so much work.

At the start of her first year as an assistant professor, Wilkerson had accepted her overwhelming workload as part of the territory. Her paycheck was smaller and her hours longer than she had expected, but Agua and the other two new faculty members seemed to be suffering under the same burdens.

But now, in her second semester, Wilkerson was beginning to feel that things weren't right. While the stream of students knocking on her door persisted, she noticed that Agua was spending less time talking and more time at his word processor than he had first semester. When asked, Agua told her he had reduced his course load because of his extra work on the department's hiring and library committees. He seemed surprised when Wilkerson admitted that she didn't know there was such a thing as a course reduction.

As the semester progressed, Wilkerson realized there was a lot she didn't know about the way the department functioned. Agua would disappear once a week or so to give talks to groups around the state and then would turn those talks into papers for scholarly journals—something Wilkerson didn't dream of having time to do. She and Agua were still good friends, but she began to see differences in their approaches. "I cut down my office hours this semester," he told her one day. "With all those students around all the time, I just never had a chance to get my work done."

Wilkerson had pondered that statement for a few weeks. She thought that dealing with students was "getting work done." But when salaries for the following year were announced, she realized what Agua meant. He would be making almost $1,000 more than she; the human resources committee viewed his committee work as a valuable asset to the department, his talks around the state already had earned him notoriety, and his three upcoming publications clearly put him ahead of the other first-year professors.

Wilkerson was confused. Agua hadn't done anything sneaky or immoral—in fact, everything he did was admirable, things she would have liked to do. His trips to the Rat gave him the inside scoop on what to do and whom to talk to, but she couldn't blame him for that either. She could have done exactly the same thing. They worked equally hard, she thought. Yet Agua already was the highly paid star, whereas she was just another overworked instructor.

As she began piling all the books, papers, and journals into her bag, Wilkerson thought about what she could do. She could quit and go somewhere else where she might be more appreciated, but jobs were hard to find and she suspected that the same thing might happen there. She could charge sex discrimination and demand to be paid as much as Agua, but that would be unfair to him and she didn't really feel discriminated against for being a woman. The university simply didn't value what she did with her time as highly as they valued what Agua did with his.

Putting on her coat, Wilkerson spotted a piece of paper that had dropped out of one of the journals. She picked it up and saw it was a note from Wendy Martin, one of her freshman students. "Professor Wilkerson," it read, "I just wanted to thank you for taking the time to talk to me last week. I really needed to talk to someone experienced about it, and all my other professors are men, and I just couldn't have talked to them. You helped me a whole lot."

Sighing, Wilkerson folded the note, put it in her bag, and closed her office door. Suddenly the pile of journals and the $1,000 didn't seem so important.

Case Questions

1. What do you think Melinda Wilkerson will do? Is she satisfied with the way she is being treated?
2. Explain the behaviors of Wilkerson and Agua using the motivation theories in this chapter.

EXPERIENTIAL EXERCISE

Purpose: This exercise will help you recognize both the potential value and the complexity of expectancy theory.

Format: Working alone, you will be asked to identify the various aspects of expectancy theory that are pertinent to your class. You will then share your thoughts and results with some of your classmates.

Procedure: Considering your class as a workplace and your effort in the class as a surrogate for a job, do the following:

1. Identify six or seven things that might happen as a result of good performance in your class (for example, a good grade or a recommendation from your instructor). Your list must include at least one undesirable outcome (for example, a loss of free time).
2. Using a value of 10 for "extremely desirable," −10 for "extremely undesirable," and 0 for "complete neutrality," assign a valence to each outcome. In other words, the valence you assign to each outcome should be somewhere between 10 and −10, inclusive.
3. Assume you are a high performer. On that basis, estimate the probability of each potential outcome. Express this probability as a percentage.
4. Multiply each valence by its associated probability, and sum the results. This total is your overall valence for high performance.
5. Assess the probability that if you exert effort, you will be a high performer. Express the probability as a percentage.
6. Multiply this probability by the overall valence for high performance calculated in step 4. This score reflects your motivational force, that is, your motivation to exert high effort.

Now form groups of three or four. Compare your scores on motivational force. Discuss why some scores differ widely. Also, note whether any group members had similar force scores but different combinations of factors leading to those scores.

Follow-up Questions

1. What does the exercise tell you about the strengths and limitations of expectancy theory?
2. Would this exercise be useful for a manager to run with a group of subordinates? Why or why not?

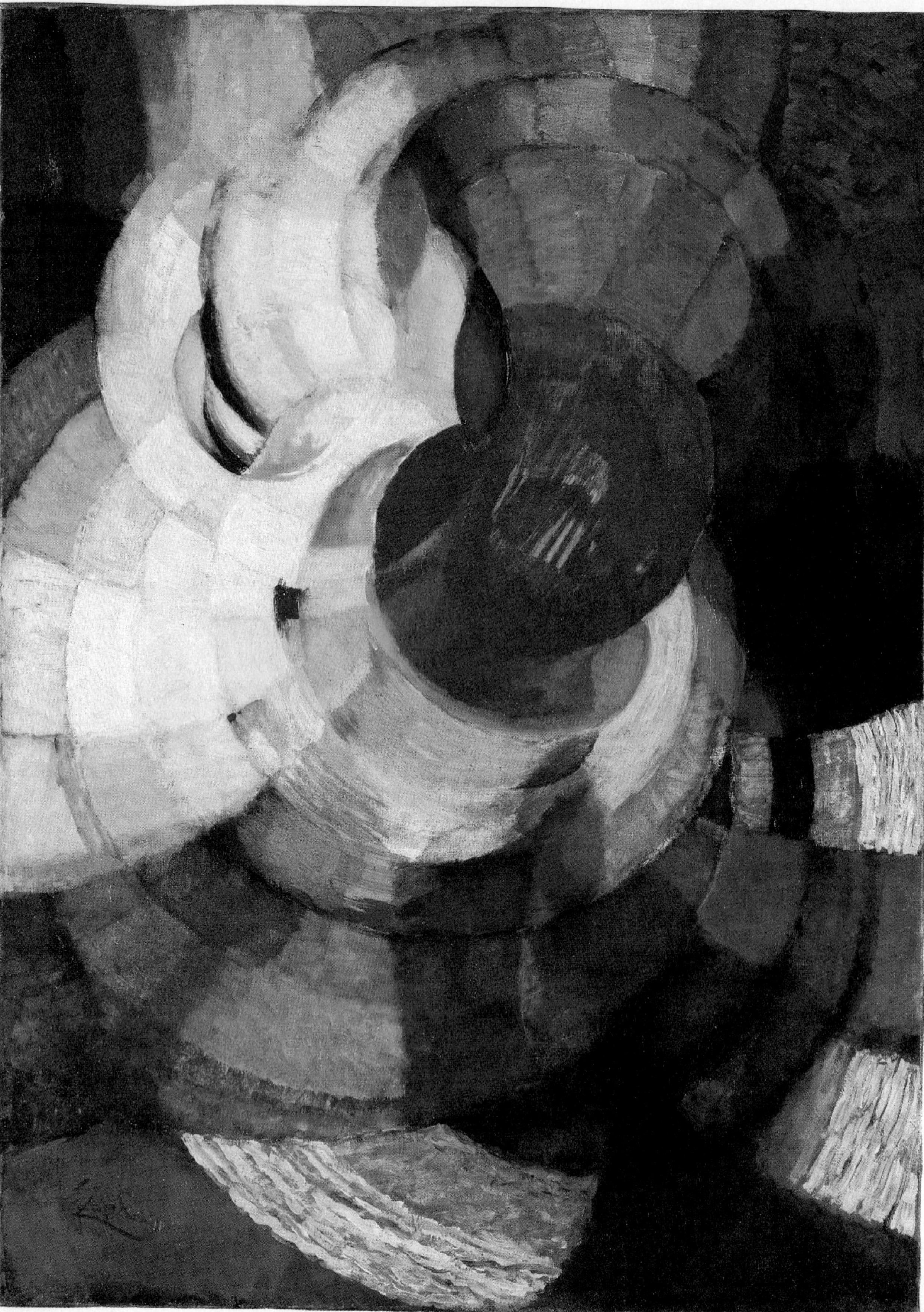

PART III

Interpersonal Processes in Organizations

CONTENTS

Chapter 7 Group Dynamics

Chapter 8 Intergroup Dynamics

Chapter 9 Leadership in Organizations

Chapter 10 Power, Politics, and Conflict

Chapter 11 Interpersonal Communication

CHAPTER OUTLINE

- Overview of Groups and Group Dynamics
  - *Definition of Group*
  - *The Importance of Studying Groups*
- Types of Groups
  - *Formal Groups*
  - *Informal Groups*
- Reasons for Group Formation
  - *Internal Sources of Need Satisfaction*
  - *External Sources of Need Satisfaction*
  - *Implications of Group Formation*
- Stages of Group Development
  - *Mutual Acceptance*
  - *Communication and Decision Making*
  - *Motivation and Productivity*
  - *Control and Organization*
- Group Performance Factors
  - *Composition*
  - *Size*
  - *Norms*
  - *Cohesiveness*
- Role Dynamics in Organizations
  - *Role Ambiguity*
  - *Role Conflict*
- Managing Groups in Organizations

7

Group Dynamics

CHAPTER OBJECTIVES

After studying this chapter, you should be able to:

Define the term group *and discuss why the study of groups is important in managing organizations.*

Describe the differences between formal and informal groups in organizations.

Discuss the reasons for group formation and their impact on managing groups.

Trace the stages of development of groups from initial introduction to a mature stage of productivity and control.

Summarize the key factors affecting group performance.

Describe the impact of role dynamics on behavior in organizations.

Discuss the factors that managers must consider in managing groups in organizations.

Bringing a new packaged food product to market normally takes from five to seven years. With its ready-to-eat dessert, Jello Pudding Snacks, General Foods did it in three years. A team of nine people were given the task of developing the idea for a ready-to-eat dessert from the basic concept, to building a new plant to manufacture the product, to delivery of the product to grocery store shelves. The team performed as a group of entrepreneurs might if they were starting their own company. The quick development and start-up propelled the new dessert to dominance in the market, which now translates into more than $100 million in annual sales.

Since the success of that first high-performance team, General Foods has expanded the use of teams throughout the company. In its plants, employee productivity teams have improved working conditions and reduced costs. The teams have fostered increased motivation, commitment, innovation, and performance through the "family" relationships that developed within the groups. The sense of belonging and energy among team members has resulted in greater enthusiasm and improved productivity.[1]

This chapter is about work groups in organizations—groups such as the new-product development team at General Foods, a football team, an engineering work group, and a group of nurses working the night shift at a local hospital. First, we define *group* and summarize the importance of groups in organizations. Then we describe different types of groups and discuss the stages groups go through as they develop from newly formed groups to mature, high-performing units. Next, we identify four key factors in group performance. Then we briefly review the importance of role ambiguity and role conflict in group dynamics. Finally, we summarize the important elements in managing groups within organizations.

Figure 7.1 presents a three-phase model of group dynamics. The first phase includes the type of group and the reasons for group formation. The second phase encompasses a four-step process of group development and the four primary group performance factors. The final phase includes a mature group that is productive and adaptive. This model serves as the framework for our discussion of groups in this chapter.

---

1. Reprinted with permission from Psychology Today Magazine. Copyright © 1989 (Sussex Publishers, Inc.)

FIGURE 7.1
A General Model of Group Dynamics

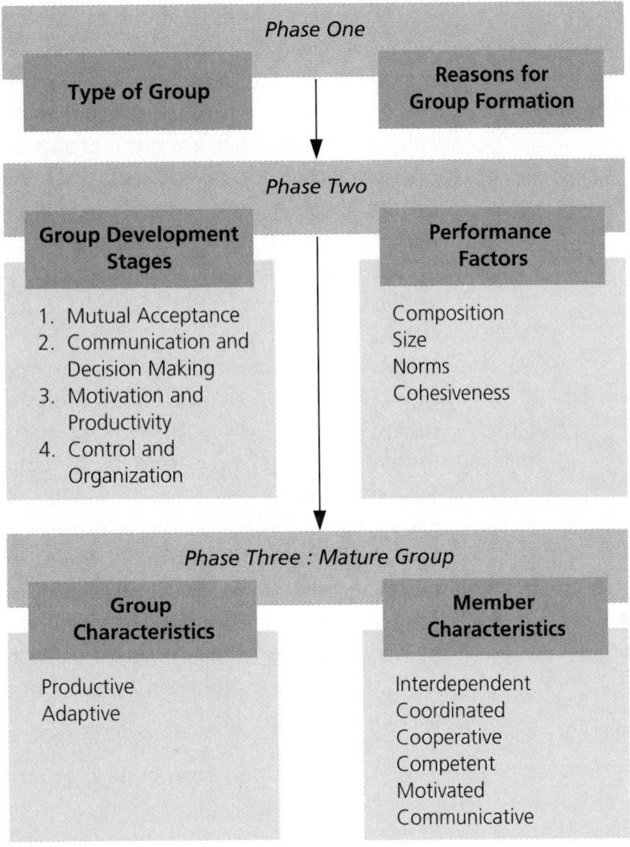

Overview of Groups and Group Dynamics

Work groups consist of people who are trying to make a living for themselves and their families. The work group often is the primary source of social identity for employees and can affect their performance at work as well as their relationships outside the organization.[2] A group in an organization often takes on a life of its own that transcends the individual members. Let us see what we mean by the term *group*.

Definition of Group

Definitions of *group* are as abundant as the research on groups. Groups can be defined in terms of perceptions, motivation, organization, interdependencies, and

2. Blake E. Ashforth and Fred Mael, "Social Identity Theory and the Organization," *Academy of Management Review,* January 1989, pp. 20–39.

interactions.[3] A simple and comprehensive definition has been offered by Marvin Shaw: A **group** is two or more persons who interact with one another in such a manner that each person influences and is influenced by each other person.[4] The concept of *interaction* is essential to this definition. Two people who are physically near each other are not a group unless they interact and have some influence on each other. Coworkers may work side by side on related tasks, but if they do not interact they are not a group. The presence of others may influence the performance of a group: An audience may stimulate the performance of actors, or an evaluator may inhibit the employee's behavior.[5] However, neither the audience nor the evaluator can be considered part of the group unless interaction occurs.

■ A **group** is two or more people who interact with one another such that each person influences and is influenced by each other person.

Note that our definition makes no mention of a group goal or the motivations of group members. This omission implies that members of a group may identify little or not at all with the group's goal. Consider a team in an essentially individual sport, such as a high school golf or tennis team. A star performer who joins the school team to attract scholarship offers may care little about the group goal of winning the regional championship. In fact, the entire team may be composed of individuals whose motives are personal and who give no thought to the group purpose. Nevertheless, the team members will interact with and influence one another and thus can be considered a group. Of course, the quality of the interactions and the group's performance may be affected by the members' lack of interest in the group goal. But a goal does exist even if it is secondary to certain group members.

Our definition of *group* also suggests a limit on group size. A collection of people so large that its members cannot interact with and influence one another does not meet this definition. And in reality, the dynamics of large assemblies of people usually differ significantly from those of small groups. Our focus in this chapter is on small groups in which the members interact with and influence one another.

The Importance of Studying Groups

We cannot study behavior in organizations without attempting to understand the behavior of people in group settings. Groups are everywhere in our society. Most people belong to several groups—a family, bowling team, church group, fraternity or sorority, work group at the office.[6] Some groups are formally

---

3. Marvin E. Shaw, *Group Dynamics: The Psychology of Small Group Behavior,* 3rd ed. (New York: McGraw-Hill, 1981).

4. Ibid., p. 11.

5. Gerald R. Ferris and Kendrith M. Rowland, "Social Facilitation Effects on Behavioral and Perceptual Task Performance Measures: Implications for Work Behavior," *Group & Organization Studies,* December 1983, pp. 421–438; Jeff Meer, "Loafing Through a Tough Job," *Psychology Today,* January 1985, p. 72.

6. J. Paul Sorrels and Bettye Myers, "Comparison of Group and Family Dynamics," *Human Relations,* May 1983, pp. 477–490.

established in a work or social organization; others are more loosely knit associations of people.

To understand the behavior of people in organizations, we must understand the forces that affect individuals as well as the ways individuals affect the organization. The behavior of individuals both affects and is affected by the group.

The accomplishments of groups are strongly influenced by the behavior of their individual members. For example, the addition of one key all-star player to a basketball team may be the difference between a bad season and a league championship. At the same time, a group has a profound effect on the behaviors of its members.[7] In the 1987 strike involving NFL football players, some players crossed the picket line but others who needed the money did not because they feared reprisal.[8] Thus, the behavior of many individuals was affected by factors within the group. We discuss this further in the section on group norms.

From a managerial perspective, the work group is the primary means by which managers coordinate individuals' behavior to achieve organizational goals. Managers direct the activities of individuals, but they also direct and coordinate interactions within groups. For example, the manager's efforts to boost salespersons' performance has been shown to have both individual and group effects.[9] Therefore, the manager must pay attention to both the individual and the group in trying to increase employee performance. Because the behavior of individuals is key to the group's success or failure, the manager must be aware of individual needs and interpersonal dynamics to manage groups effectively and efficiently.

Professional beach volleyball teams compete in tournaments across the country, vying for over $2 million in prize money. While they are not traditional formal groups of the type we might find inside a large organization, they nevertheless have clear boundaries and relatively constant membership.

Types of Groups

Our first task in understanding group processes is to develop a typology of groups that provides insight into their dynamics. Groups may be loosely categorized according to their degrees of formalization (formal or informal) and permanence (relatively permanent or relatively temporary). Table 7.1 shows this classification scheme.

Formal Groups

- A **formal group** is formed by the organization to do its work and usually is included in the organization chart.
- A **command group** is a relatively permanent, formal group with functional reporting relationships.

Formal groups are established by the organization to do its work and usually are included in the organization chart. Formal groups include the **command** (or

7. Alfred W. Clark and Robert J. Powell, "Changing Drivers' Attitudes Through Peer Group Decision," *Human Relations,* February 1984, pp. 155–162.

8. See Bill Saporito, "The Life of a Scab," *Fortune,* October 26, 1987, pp. 91–94; Jill Lieber, "A Test of Loyalty," *Sports Illustrated,* October 5, 1987, pp. 41–43.

9. Francis J. Yammarino and Alan J. Dubinsky, "Salesperson Performance and Managerially Controllable Factors: An Investigation of Individual and Work Group Effects," *Journal of Management,* vol. 16, 1990, pp. 87–106.

TABLE 7.1
Classification Scheme for Types of Groups

	Relatively Permanent	Relatively Temporary
Formal	Command Groups *Quality Assurance Department* *Cost Accounting Group*	Task Groups *Pope's Special Council on Finances* *Task Force on New-Product Quality*
Informal	Friendship Groups *Friends who do many activities together (attend the theater, play games, travel)*	Interest Groups *Bowling Group* *Women's Network*

- A **task group** is a relatively temporary, formal group established to do a specific task.

functional) **group,** which is relatively permanent and characterized by functional reporting relationships, and the **task group,** which is created to perform a specific task and is relatively temporary. In business organizations, most employees work in command groups, typically specified on an official organization chart. Figure 7.2 shows a simple organization chart with two command groups highlighted. The size, shape, and organization of a company's command groups can vary considerably.

Typical command groups in organizations include the quality assurance department, the industrial engineering department, the cost accounting department, and the personnel department. Other types of command groups include work teams organized as in the Japanese style of management, in which subsections of manufacturing and assembly processes are assigned to a team of workers to complete. The team members decide among themselves who will do each task. *Management in Action* describes how Federal Express organized its clerical workers into teams that manage themselves.

Teams are becoming widespread in automobile manufacturing. General Motors is organizing its highly automated assembly lines into work teams of between five and twenty workers.[10] Command groups, whether entire departments or sophisticated work teams, are the dominant type of work group in organizations.

Task, or special-project, groups are usually temporary. Task groups often are established to solve a particular problem. Once such a group solves the problem or makes recommendations, it is usually dissolved. While serving in a task group, people typically remain members of their command groups, or functional departments, and continue to carry out the normal duties of their jobs. If the task group requires a great deal of time and effort, the members' command group duties may be temporarily reduced.

Task groups exist in organizations around the world. For example, in 1981 the Pope established a special task force of cardinals to study the financial condition of the Vatican and develop new ways to raise money.[11]

10. "Detroit vs. the UAW: At Odds over Teamwork," *Business Week,* August 24, 1987, pp. 54–55.
11. Shawn Tully, "The Vatican's Finances," *Fortune,* December 21, 1987, pp. 28–40.

FIGURE 7.2
Command Groups on an Organization Chart

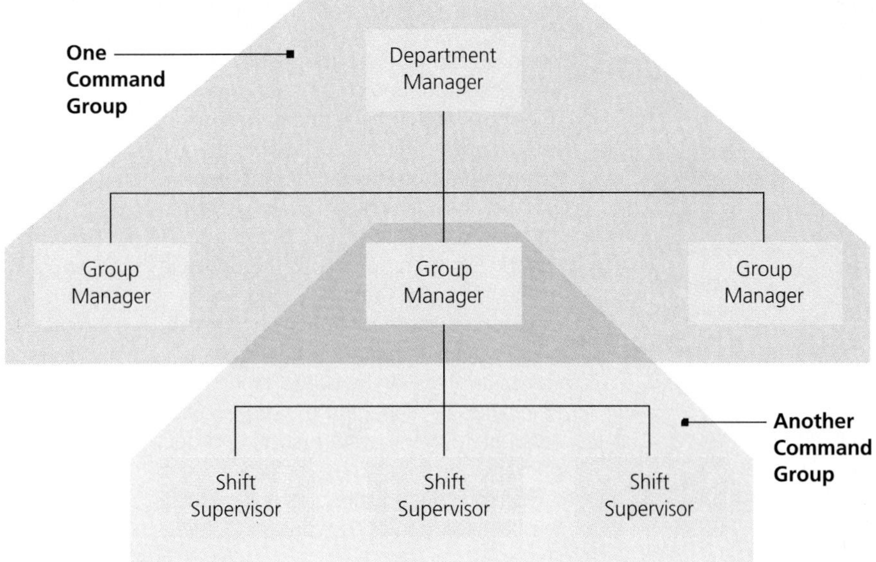

Informal Groups

- An **informal group** is established by its members.
- A **friendship group** is relatively permanent and informal and draws its benefits from the social relationships among its members.
- An **interest group** is relatively temporary and informal and is organized around a common activity or interest of its members.

Whereas formal groups are established by an organization, **informal groups** are formed by their members. They consist of the friendship group, which is relatively permanent, and the interest group, which may be shorter lived. **Friendship groups** arise from friendly relationships among members and the enjoyment they get from being together. **Interest groups** are organized around a common activity or interest, although friendships may develop among members.

Good examples of interest groups are the networks of working women that developed during the 1980s. Many of these groups began as informal social gatherings of women who wanted to meet with other women working in male-dominated organizations, but they soon developed into interest groups whose benefits went far beyond the initial social purposes. The networks became information systems for counseling, job placement, and management training. Some networks eventually were established as formal, permanent associations; some remained informal groups based more on social relationships than on any specific interest; and others were dissolved. These groups may be partly responsible for the past decade's dramatic increase in the percentage of women in managerial and administrative jobs.[12]

Although the distinction between friendship and interest groups can be hazy, the relative permanence of the association usually helps mark the difference. For example, the common interests and activities of a well-established friendship group may change over time, but the group stays together. Friendship and companionship are strong and durable ties. An interest group, though, may break up if its members' interests change.

12. "Women at Work," *Business Week,* January 28, 1985, pp. 80–85.

MANAGEMENT IN ACTION

Federal Express Uses Teams for Productivity

Being on top of the package delivery, transportation, and distribution business does not happen by accident. Federal Express did it both the old-fashioned way—by working harder—and the modern way—by using workers in participative, decision-making teams. Underlying the Federal Express approach is the principle of the company's founder, Fred Smith, that good customer relations begin with good employee relations. Other cornerstones are teamwork, participation by employees in managing the organization, adequate pay for performance, and open grievance systems. These policies have established Federal Express as one of the ten best companies to work for in the United States.

Federal Express was a pioneer in the participative management area. In 1988, the company placed some one-thousand back-office clerical workers into teams of five to ten people. These teams were trained and given the authority to manage themselves. So far, they have performed the work well and saved the company significant expense by clearing up paperwork and back-office mistakes. For example, one team discovered that in some offices, hurried package pickup and delivery personnel were not properly checking package weight, resulting in incorrect charges. Teams developed systems to check weights and contacted pickup and delivery personnel about the problem. As a result of this effort, the company saved $2.1 million in 1989 and reduced service and billing problems by 13 percent.

Federal Express continues to use teams in many innovative ways. For example, pilots, machinists, and hub employees elect coworkers to advisory boards to work with management on operations and human resources issues. If an employee has a complaint about management's handling of a problem, the employee may appeal to a peer review board of her or his choosing to listen to both sides and determine whether the employee has been fairly treated. Unions have made numerous attempts to organize employees, but their efforts have failed because workers value their role as an important part of the management team at Federal Express.

SOURCES: Brian Dumaine, "Who Needs a Boss?" *Fortune,* May 7, 1990, pp. 52–60; Tracy E. Benson, "Empowered Employees Sharpen the Edge," *Industry Week,* February 19, 1990, pp. 12–20; Therese R. Welter, "New-Collar Workers," *Industry Week,* August 15, 1988, pp. 36–39.

Reasons for Group Formation

Command groups are formed because managers expect that organizational tasks can be better completed and coordinated if people work together in work groups. On the other hand, individuals may form an informal group or join an existing one for many reasons. One of the most important purposes is affiliation with a group to satisfy a need. The sources of need satisfaction can be classified into two categories: sources inside the group (internal sources) and sources outside the group (external sources)[13] as shown in Figure 7.3

13. Shaw, *Group Dynamics,* pp. 82–98.

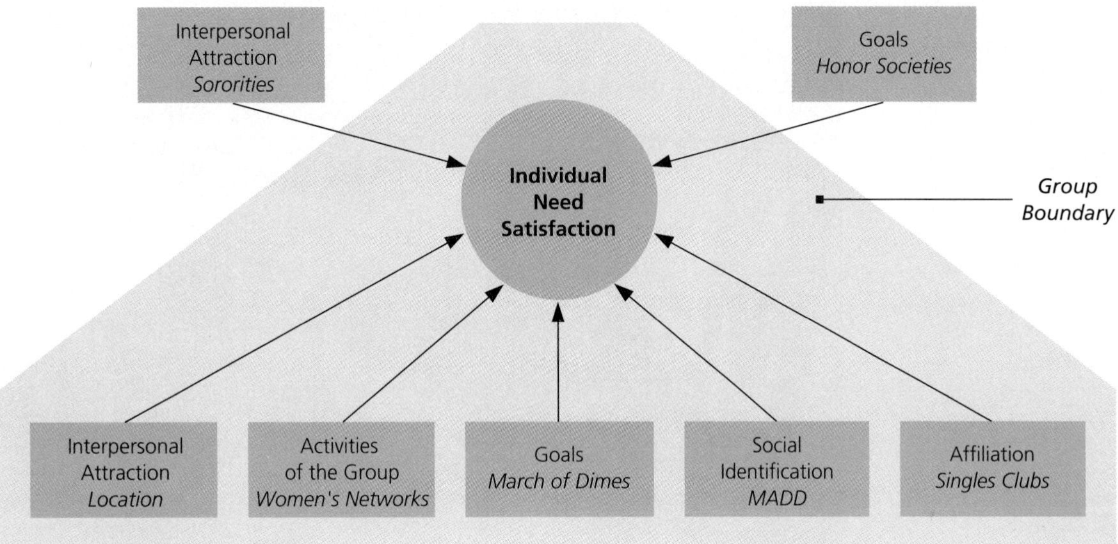

FIGURE 7.3
Sources of Need Satisfaction from Group Membership

- Internal sources of need satisfaction include interpersonal attraction, the group's activities, the group's goals, social identification, and social affiliation.

Internal Sources of Need Satisfaction

Internal sources of individual need satisfaction fall into five social categories: interpersonal attraction, the group's activities, the group's goals, identification, and social affiliation. These sources may overlap somewhat, but let us explain each and give an example.

Interpersonal Attraction *Interpersonal attraction* probably is the most obvious reason for group formation: People join or form a group because they are attracted to other people in the group. Several factors may influence interpersonal attraction, including location, physical attraction, perceived ability, and similarities in attitudes, beliefs, sex, race, and personality.

A very common factor in interpersonal attraction is location, or physical proximity. Proximity may mean nearby desks or offices or neighboring houses; it certainly is not unusual for people to form a group of coworkers or neighbors.[14] Location not only provides a setting for interpersonal attraction but also can reinforce it. Nearness increases the opportunity for interactions and, in turn, for the discovery of attractive characteristics.

When people who need to coordinate their work have offices close together, informal groups may develop, leading to more interaction and feelings of closeness. From there it is a short step to better working relationships and coordination on the job. For example, grouping offices together may improve the

14. R. Robert Huckfeldt, "Social Contexts, Social Networks, and Urban Neighborhoods: Environmental Constraints of Friendship Choice," *American Journal of Sociology.* November 1983, pp. 651–669.

Mothers Against Drunk Driving marked its tenth anniversary by displaying a "victim board" on the west steps of the U.S. Capitol. At events such as this, relatives of the victims of drunk drivers who have joined MADD bring attention to their group's cause and gain emotional support from one another.

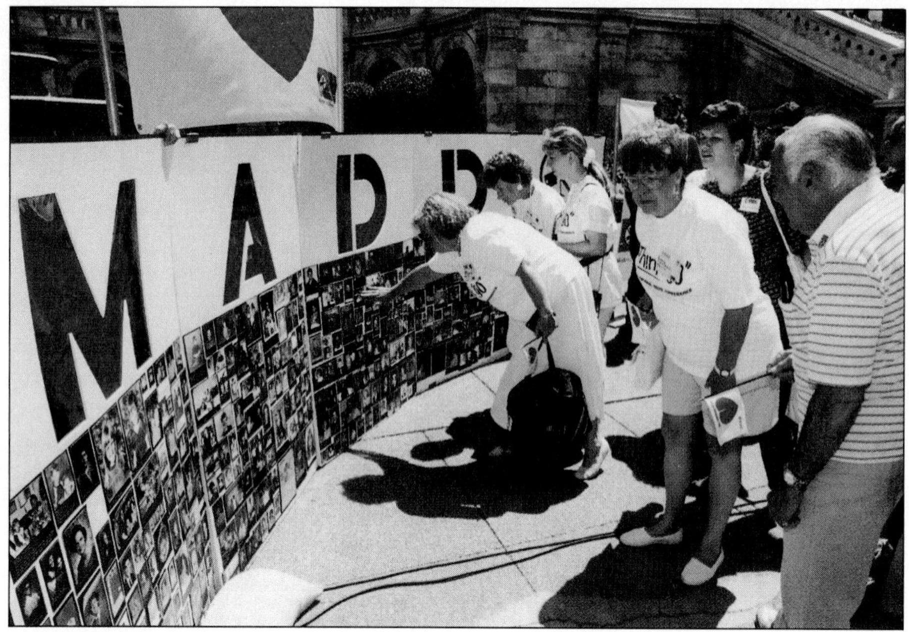

performance of executive teams.[15] With opportunities to interact in an informal group, busy executives may be better able to coordinate the operations of the organization and thus improve productivity.

The Group's Activities Group *activities* also may be a source of individual need satisfaction. The networks of working women discussed earlier were formed because the women wanted to interact with others in similar situations. Another example is a group that assembles regularly to play bridge. It may be that the people in the group enjoy playing bridge and like the competition, or perhaps they have little interest in who wins or in the intracacies of the game. Social chitchat about families, sporting events, and other subjects of mutual interest may be the group's actual basis.

The Group's Goals A third internal source of individual need satisfaction is identification with group *goals* that call for a commitment of time and effort. For example, each year thousands of volunteers throughout the United States go door to door requesting donations for the March of Dimes. The driving force behind this so-called Mothers' March is the goal of eliminating birth defects. This example also illustrates the difference between joining a group because of its activities and joining because of its goals.[16] Many individuals in the Mothers'

15. Fritz Steele, "The Ecology of Executive Teams: A New View of the Top," *Organizational Dynamics*. Spring 1983, pp. 65–78.

16. M. Sherif and C. W. Sherif, *Groups in Harmony and Tension* (New York: Harper & Row, 1953).

March may not enjoy the activity itself—canvassing neighborhoods and knocking on doors—but their commitment to the goal overrides their personal preferences. This distinction is important in the analysis of individual behavior in the group, discussed later in the chapter.

Social Identification An individual may join a group to attain a *social identity.*[17] Work, friendship, and interest groups may all offer a person a social identity. For example, when a new member is introduced to our group, we often greet the person by name and then say something about him or her, usually a group identification, to give the newcomer a social identity to the group. We may say, "Group, this is Sally, a friend who goes to my church." The individual need not engage in any behaviors to support the group's goals. Identification with the group, however, means that the individual perceives himself or herself as psychologically intertwined with the group and personally experiences the group's success or failure. For example, a person may psychologically identify with Mothers Against Drunk Driving (MADD) and even grieve when someone is killed by a drunk driver yet do nothing to further the goals of the group, such as contribute money or actively demonstrate or lobby for stricter laws against drunk driving.

Social Affiliation A final internal source of individual need satisfaction is the need for *affiliation,* or companionship[18] (a primary individual need, as noted in Chapter 5). Group membership may be the source of a good deal of personal value and emotional significance and may provide the foundation for a person's social identity.[19] The group's goals and activities may be largely irrelevant in satisfying the need for affiliation. For example, people who recently lost a spouse and join a group to replace the lost companionship may care little about the group's purpose or activities.

External Sources of Need Satisfaction

- External sources of need satisfaction include interpersonal attraction to individuals outside the group and the pursuit of goals other than those of the group.

People may also join groups for reasons that are external to the group, such as interpersonal attraction to people outside the group or the pursuit of goals other than those of the group. Although this may sound contradictory, several examples exist to support it.

Interpersonal Attraction By *interpersonal attraction* to people outside the group, we mean that a person may be able to gain access to certain people only by affiliation with a group apart from those people. Consider a female college

17. Ashforth and Mael, "Social Identity Theory and the Organization."

18. Stanley Schacter, *The Psychology of Affiliation* (Stanford, Calif.: Stanford University Press, 1959).

19. Rupert Brown and Jennifer Williams, "Group Identification: The Same Thing to All People?" *Human Relations,* July 1984, pp. 547–560.

student who wishes to meet men who are in a certain fraternity. She finds that being a member of a particular sorority might help her meet these men. Thus, she joins the sorority because of her attraction to people outside of that group.

Goals Outside the Group A person may join a group because of the status or prestige that comes with membership. For example, a college student may accept an invitation to join an honor society because membership in the society will "look good" on his or her résumé when looking for a job. The student may not identify with the goals of the society or even seek to interact with its members, because his or her reasons for joining are external to the group.

Implications of Group Formation

Understanding why a group forms is important in studying individual behavior in groups. Suppose people join a bridge group primarily for social contact. If a more competitive player substitutes one evening for a regular player, she or he joins the group (temporarily) with a different goal in mind. The substitute may be annoyed when the game slows down or stops altogether because the other players are absorbed in a discussion. The regular members, on the other hand, may be irritated when the substitute interrupts the discussion and rebukes his or her partner for faulty technique. Someone who wants to resolve the resulting conflict will need to understand the different reasons why each person joined the group. The inconsistencies in behavior probably are arising because each member seeks the satisfaction of a different need. Settling the spat may require that the regulars and the substitute be more tolerant of each other's behavior, at least for the rest of the evening. Even then, however, the substitute player may not be invited back the next time a regular member cannot attend.

Thus, understanding why people have joined a group sheds light on apparent inconsistences in behavior and the tensions likely to result from them. Such an understanding will make us better able to manage certain kinds of conflict that arise in groups in organizations. For example, the president of a community college created a task force to study and recommend changes in employee health insurance benefits. Some members of the task force volunteered to serve because they wanted to improve the benefits package. Other members were assigned to the task force by their department managers. The members who had been assigned to the task force repeatedly were late for meetings and in a hurry to adjourn because of their lack of interest in the group's goals. In effect, their goals were to complete the group's work quickly and go back to other duties rather than to realistically study alternative insurance plans. The volunteers, on the other hand, were frustrated by the assigned members' lack of cooperation. Conflict arose over many seemingly minor issues. At first, the group chairperson did not understand the source of conflict and just kept pleading for the members to cooperate. The group made little progress until the chairperson figured out the source of the bickering and asked to have the membership changed. Clearly, why people ended up in this group had a significant impact on how the group functioned.

Stages of Group Development

Groups are not static. Instead, they typically develop through a four-stage process: (1) mutual acceptance, (2) communication and decision making, (3) motivation and productivity, and (4) control and organization.[20] The stages and the activities that typify them are shown in Figure 7.4. We treat the stages as separate and distinct. However, because their activities overlap, it is difficult to pinpoint exactly when a group moves from one stage to another.

Mutual Acceptance

■ The mutual acceptance stage of group development is characterized by members sharing information about themselves *and* getting to know each other.

In the *mutual acceptance* stage of group development, members get to know one another by sharing information about themselves. They often test one another's opinions by discussing subjects that have little to do with the group, such as the weather, sports, or recent events within the organization. Some aspects of the group's task, such as its formal objectives, may also be discussed at this stage. However, such discussion probably will not be very productive because the members are unfamiliar with one another and do not know how to evaluate one another's comments. If the members do happen to know one another already, this stage may be brief; but it is unlikely to be skipped altogether because this is a new group with a new purpose. Besides, there are likely to be a few members whom the others do not know well or at all.[21]

As the members get to know one another, discussion may turn to more sensitive issues, such as the organization's politics or recent controversial decisions. In this way, the participants explore one another's reactions, knowledge, and expertise. From the discussion, members may learn one another's views on a variety of issues, how similar their beliefs and values are, and the extent to which they can trust one another. Members may discuss their expectations about the group's activities in terms of their previous group and organizational experience.[22] Eventually, the conversation will turn to the business of the group. When this discussion becomes serious, the group is moving to the next stage of development, communication and decision making.

Communication and Decision Making

■ In the communication and decision-making stage of group development, members discuss their feelings more openly and agree on group goals and individual roles in the group.

Once group members have begun to accept one another, the group progresses to the *communication and decision-making* stage. In this stage, members discuss their feelings and opinions more openly. They may show more tolerance for

20. Bernard M. Bass and Edward C. Ryterband, *Organizational Psychology*, 2nd ed. (Boston: Allyn and Bacon, 1979), pp. 252–254.

21. John P. Wanous, Arnon E. Reichers, and S. D. Malik, "Organizational Socialization and Group Development: Toward an Integrative Perspective," *Academy of Management Review*, October 1984, pp. 670–683.

22. Susan Long, "Early Integration in Groups: A Group to Join and a Group to Create," *Human Relations*, April 1984, pp. 311–332.

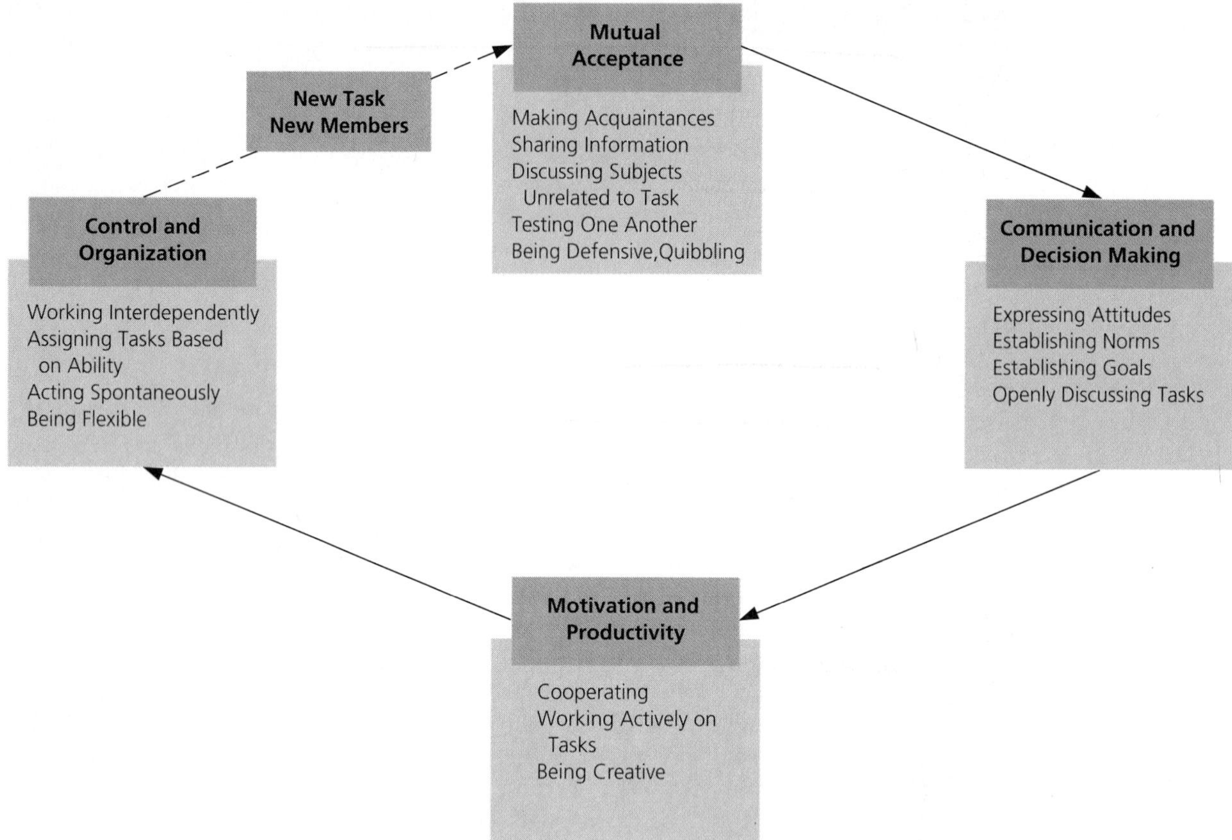

FIGURE 7.4
Stages of Group Development

opposing viewpoints and explore different ideas to bring about a reasonable solution or decision. Members discuss and eventually agree on the group's goals. Then they are assigned roles and tasks to accomplish the goals.

Motivation and Productivity

- In the motivation and productivity stage of group development, members cooperate, help each other, and work toward task accomplishment.

In the next stage, *motivation and productivity,* emphasis shifts away from personal concerns and viewpoints to activities that will benefit the group. Members cooperate and actively help others accomplish their goals. The members are highly motivated and may carry out their tasks creatively. In this stage, the group is accomplishing its work and is moving toward the final stage of development.

Control and Organization

- In the control and organization stage of group development—now a mature group—members work together and are flexible, adaptive, and self-correcting.

In the final stage, *control and organization,* the group works effectively toward accomplishing its goals. Tasks are assigned by mutual agreement and according to ability. In a mature group, the members' activities are relatively spontaneous

The Sioux shown here traveled miles on foot and horseback to mark the 100th anniversary of the massacre at Wounded Knee, South Dakota. They are part of a larger group of Native Americans who are working together to accomplish the common goal of preserving their heritage and educating their children. Thus, they clearly constitute a very important group.

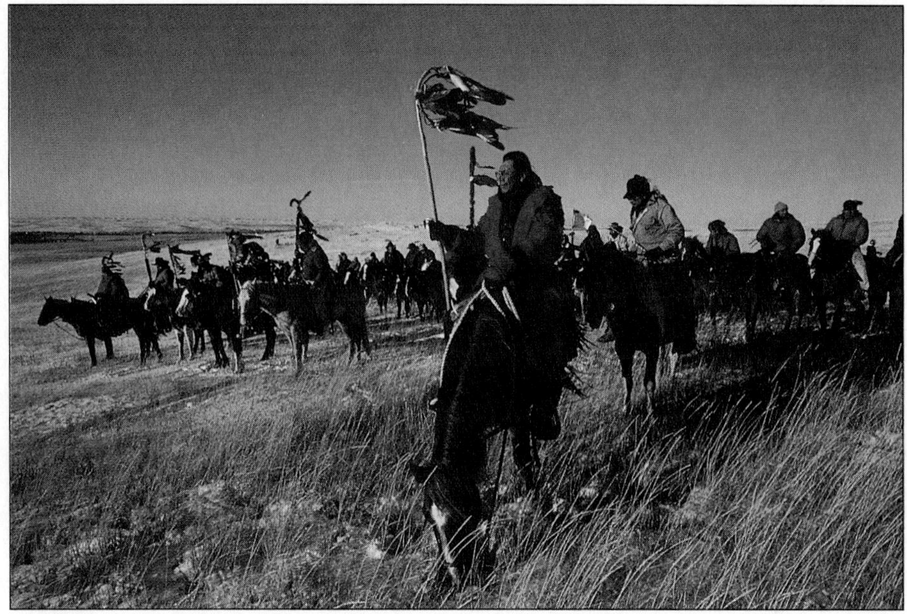

and flexible, rather than subject to rigid structural restraints. Mature groups evaluate their activities and potential outcomes and take corrective actions if necessary. The characteristics of flexibility, spontaneity, and self-correction are very important if the group is to remain productive over an extended period.

Not all groups go through all four stages. Some groups disband before reaching the final stage. Others fail to complete a stage before moving on to the next one.[23] Rather than spend the time necessary to get to know one another and build trust, for example, a group may cut short the first stage of development because of pressure from its leader, from deadlines, or from an outside threat (such as the boss). If members are forced into activities typical of a later stage while the work of an earlier stage remains incomplete, they are likely to become frustrated: the group will not develop completely and will be less productive than it could be.[24] Group productivity depends on successful development at each stage. A group that evolves fully through the four stages of development will become a mature, effective group.[25] Its members will be interdependent, coordinated, cooperative, competent at their jobs, motivated to do them, and in active communication with one another.[26]

Groups in organizations often receive the time and resources needed for development. For example, some top executive teams go on retreats periodically.

---

23. Wanous, Reichers, and Malik, "Organizational Socialization and Group Development.

24. Steven L. Obert, "Developmental Patterns of Organizational Task Groups: A Preliminary Study," *Human Relations,* January 1983, pp. 37–52.

25. Bass and Ryterband, *Organizational Psychology,* pp. 252–254.

26. Bernard M. Bass, "The Leaderless Group Discussion," *Psychological Bulletin,* September 1954, pp. 465–492.

Retreats provide a few days in an environment free from telephone calls, meetings, and other daily work pressures for the members to study information, get to know one another, and make plans for the future. A retreat may be especially useful when the membership of an executive team has changed, because it provides time for the mutual adjustment phase of the development process. By allowing the group to get away from normal day-to-day burdens and focus on itself and its tasks, the organization can improve group productivity.

Finally, as working conditions and relationships change, either through a change in membership or when a task is completed and a new task is begun, groups may need to reexperience one or more of the stages of development to maintain cohesiveness and productivity characteristic of a well-developed group. The San Francisco Forty-Niners, for example, returned from the NFL strike of 1987 to an uncomfortable and apprehension-filled period. Their coach, Bill Walsh, conducted rigorous practices but also allowed time for players to get together to air their feelings. Slowly team unity returned, and players began joking and socializing again as they prepared for the rest of the 1987 season.[27] Their redevelopment as a mature group resulted in Super Bowl victories in 1989 and 1990.

Although these stages are not separate and distinct in all groups, many groups have made fairly predictable transitions in activities at about the midpoint of the time period available for task completion.[28] *A Look at the Research* reports on a study of this phenomenon.

Group Performance Factors

- **Group performance factors**—composition, size, norms, and cohesiveness—affect the success of the group in fulfilling its goals.

The performance of any group is affected by several factors other than the reasons for its formation and the stages of its development. In a high-performing group, a group synergy often develops in which the group's performance is more than the sum of the individual contributions of its members. Several additional factors may account for this accelerated performance.[29] The four basic **group performance factors** are composition, size, norms, and cohesiveness.

Composition

- **Group composition** refers to the degree of similarity or difference in the characteristics of the members on factors important to the group's work.

The composition of a group plays an important role in determining group productivity.[30] **Group composition** is most often described in terms of the hom-

27. Jill Lieber, "Time to Heal the Wounds," *Sports Illustrated,* November 2, 1987, pp. 86–91.

28. Connie J. G. Gersick, "Marking Time: Predictable Transitions in Task Groups," *Academy of Management Journal,* vol. 32, 1989, pp. 274–309.

29. James H. Davis, *Group Performance* (Reading, Mass.: Addison-Wesley, 1964), pp. 82–86.

30. Shaw, *Group Dynamics.*

A LOOK AT THE RESEARCH

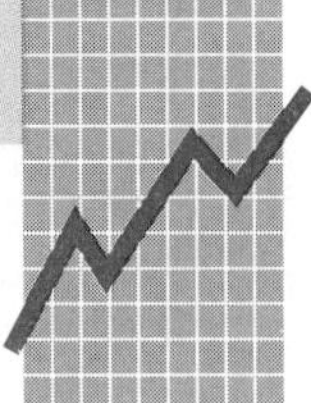

Group Development and the Midpoint Transition

Organizations often use task forces to creatively develop solutions to immediate problems. Frequently task force members are picked from different departments to provide diverse expertise and representation of relevant organizational units. Members of such a group must quickly learn how to work together to solve the problem within the prescribed time period. Professor Connie Gersick of the University of California–Los Angeles studied how groups accomplish such tasks.

Professor Gersick observed eight groups from six organizations from their projects' start, to finish. The project groups came from a bank, a hospital, a community fund-raising group, a psychiatric treatment center, and two universities. Professor Gersick analyzed transcripts of group meetings and interviewed members of four of the groups. The project groups remained in force from a few days to several months.

The analysis indicated that the developmental stages the groups went through were less separate and distinct than some models of group development suggested. However, Professor Gersick found that most of the groups went through similar phases as they formed, maintained, and changed their activities in their search for creative solutions to difficult problems.

Each group began with its own distinctive approach to the problem and maintained it until about halfway through the allotted time period. This stage essentially was one of inertia in that regardless of the approach each group took, the group stayed with it until the midpoint, when all the groups changed their approaches. The midpoint transition usually came through a burst of concentrated activity, reexamination of assumptions, dropping old patterns of activity, adopting new perspectives of the work, and making dramatic progress. During stage two, another period of inertia emerged as these new patterns of activity were maintained from the midpoint until close to the end of the prescribed time period. Still another transition occurred just before the deadline. At this transition, the groups went into the completion stage, launching a final burst of activity to finish the job.

Professor Gersick also examined the existence of this midpoint transition for problem-solving groups in more exacting laboratory situations. Her findings from that study supported the existence of the midpoint transition as a key aspect of group problem solving. Professor Gersick notes that these findings may make the common practice of shifting deadlines for task groups particularly troublesome. When the time allotted is changed significantly, severe and possibly dysfunctional effects on the group may result.

SOURCE: Connie J. G. Gersick, "Marking Time: Predictable Transitions in Task Groups," *Academy of Management Journal,* vol. 32, 1989, pp. 274–309. Reprinted by permission.

ogeneity or heterogeneity of the members. A group is *homogeneous* if the members are similar in one or several ways that are critical to the work of the group, such as age, work experience, education, technical specialty, or cultural background. In *heterogeneous* groups, the members differ in one or more ways that are critical to the work of the group. Homogeneous groups often are created in organizations when people are assigned to command groups based on a similar technical specialty. Although the people who work in such command groups may differ on some factors, such as age or work experience, they are homoge-

These men compete in the Over the Hill Hockey League in Pawtucket, Rhode Island. By keeping the group homogeneous, members are able to enjoy competition against others of similar skills and athletic prowess.

neous in terms of a critical work performance variable: technical specialty. The assignment of nurses to work groups in hospitals is an example of this.[31]

Much research has explored the relationship between a group's composition and its productivity. The group's heterogeneity in terms of age and tenure with the group have been shown to be related to turnover;[32] that is, groups with members of different ages and experiences with the group tend to experience frequent changes in membership. Table 7.2 summarizes task variables that make a homogeneous or heterogeneous group more effective than its counterpart. A homogeneous group is likely to be more productive in situations where the group task is simple, cooperation is necessary, the group tasks are sequential, or quick action is required. Teams of firefighters who put out summer forest fires are relatively homogeneous groups, usually college students majoring in forestry and working in the Forest Service for the season. Although no two fires are the same, all require swift, coordinated action to get the blaze under control.

A heterogeneous group is more likely to be productive when the task is complex, requires a collective effort (that is, each member does a different task and the sum of these efforts constitutes the group output), and demands creativity or when speed is less important than thorough deliberations. For example, a group asked to generate ideas for marketing a new product probably needs to be heterogeneous to develop as many different ideas as possible.

The link between group composition and type of task is explained by the interactions typical of homogeneous and heterogeneous groups. A homogeneous group tends to have less conflict, fewer differences of opinion, smoother communication, and more interaction. A task that requires cooperation and speed therefore makes a homogeneous group more desirable. If, however, the task requires complex analysis of information and creativity to arrive at the best

---

31. Peggy Leatt and Rodney Schneck, "Criteria for Grouping Nursing Subunits in Hospitals," *Academy of Management Journal,* March 1984, pp. 150–165.

32. Charles A. O'Reilly III, David F. Caldwell, and William P. Barnett, "Work Group Demography, Social Integration, and Turnover," *Administrative Science Quarterly,* vol. 34, March 1989, pp. 21–37.

TABLE 7.2
Task Variables and Group Composition

A homogeneous group is more useful for:	A heterogeneous group is more useful for:
Simple Tasks	Complex Tasks
Sequential Tasks	Collective Tasks
Cooperation Required	Creativity Required
Speed Required	Speed Not Important

SOURCE: Based on discussion in Bernard M. Bass and Edward C. Ryterband, *Organizational Psychology,* 2nd. ed. (Boston: Allyn and Bacon, 1979). Reprinted by permission.

possible solution, a heterogeneous group may be more appropriate because it generates a wide range of viewpoints. More discussion and more conflict are likely, both of which can enhance the group's decision making.

Group composition often becomes especially important when organizations create joint ventures with companies from other countries and form other types of international alliances. Joint ventures have become common in the automobile and electronics industries. *International Perspective* describes how managers from the United States and those from the People's Republic of China differ in their attitudes toward individual versus group goals and productivity.

Size

■ **Group size** refers to the number of members of the group and affects the number of resources available to perform the task.

A group can have as few as two members or as many members as can interact and influence one another. **Group size** can have an important effect on performance. A group with many members has more resources available and may be able to complete a large number of relatively independent tasks. Among groups established to generate ideas, those with more members tend to produce more ideas, although the *rate of increase* in the number of ideas diminishes rapidly as the group grows.[33] Beyond a certain point, the greater complexity of interactions and communication may make it more difficult for a large group to achieve agreement.

Interactions and communication are much more likely to be formalized in larger groups. Large groups tend to set agendas for meetings and to follow a protocol or parliamentary procedure to control discussion. As a result, some time that otherwise might be available for task accomplishment is taken up in administrative duties such as organizing and structuring the interactions and communications within the group. Also, the large size may inhibit participation of some people[34] and increase absenteeism[35] because so many people are trying to contribute. If repeated attempts to contribute or participate are thwarted by

33. Shaw, *Group Dynamics,* pp. 173–177.
34. Davis, *Group Performance,* p. 73.
35. Steven E. Markham, Fred Dansereau, Jr., and Joseph A. Alutto, "Group Size and Absenteeism Rates: A Longitudinal Analysis," *Academy of Management Journal,* December 1982, pp. 921–927.

INTERNATIONAL PERSPECTIVE

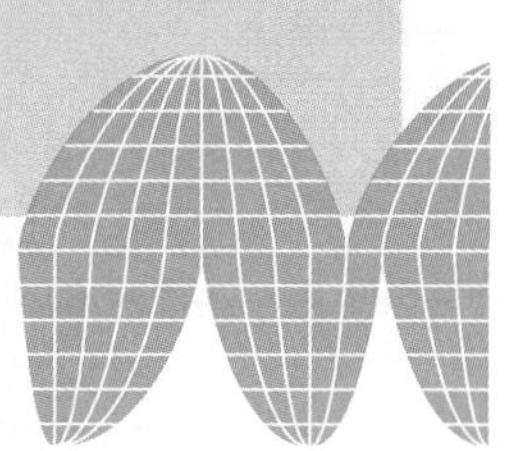

Believing in the Group: United States vs. People's Republic of China

Increasingly, organizations are operating in a global environment in which they do much more than buy from or sell to firms based in other countries. Especially complex managerial issues arise when companies form joint ventures with firms from other countries to design, make, or sell products and services—a trend that has mushroomed in the automobile, computer, and electronics industries. Increasingly, managers, engineers, sales staff, and other personnel are working with their counterparts from other countries and cultural backgrounds to make decisions and solve problems that are vital to the success of the organizations involved.

One major difference among people from different cultures is their attitudes toward individualism versus collectivism. In an individualistic culture, people are proud of their personal accomplishments and derive satisfaction from those achievements. They emphasize self-sufficiency and pursue individual goals that may or may not be consistent with group goals. Individuals from a collectivist culture, on the other hand, derive satisfaction from group accomplishment, subordinating their personal interests to the goals of the group.

These differences are clearly evident in the individualistic culture of the United States and the collectivist culture of the People's Republic of China (POR). The work ethic in the United States is based on individual accomplishment and self-interest. Chinese society, in contrast, historically has been based on social interests, collective action, and a deemphasis of personal goals and accomplishment. In a recent study, Christopher Earley observed the group task accomplishment of forty-eight managers from the United States and forty-eight similar managers from the People's Republic of China. The U.S. managers consistently exhibited individualistic behaviors, whereas those from the POR engaged in behaviors that emphasized group goals and outcomes. Earley suggested that expatriate managers with individualistic beliefs who are managing people in a collectivist culture may need to downplay management practices based on individual values in favor of group-oriented management techniques.

SOURCE: Reprinted from "Social Loafing and Collectivism: A Comparison of the United States and the People's Republic of China," by P. Christopher Earley published in *Administrative Science Quarterly*, Vol. 34 No. 4, by permission of *Administrative Science Quarterly*. © 1989 by Cornell University.

the sheer number of similar efforts by other members, some people may give up on making a meaningful contribution and may even stop coming to group meetings. Furthermore, large groups may present more opportunities for interpersonal attraction, leading to more social interactions and fewer task interactions. How much of a problem this becomes depends on the nature of the task and the characteristics of the people involved.

Figure 7.5 illustrates and summarizes the differences between large- and small-group interactions. In small groups, people can interact frequently. In large groups, however, subgroups often develop because frequent interaction among all members is impossible. Subgroups tend to take in those people who interact together most often. The effects of this subgrouping may be either beneficial or harmful for the group, depending on its mission. If the group's tasks can be subdivided into smaller tasks that the subgroups can accomplish, the formation

FIGURE 7.5
Group Size and Interpersonal Interactions

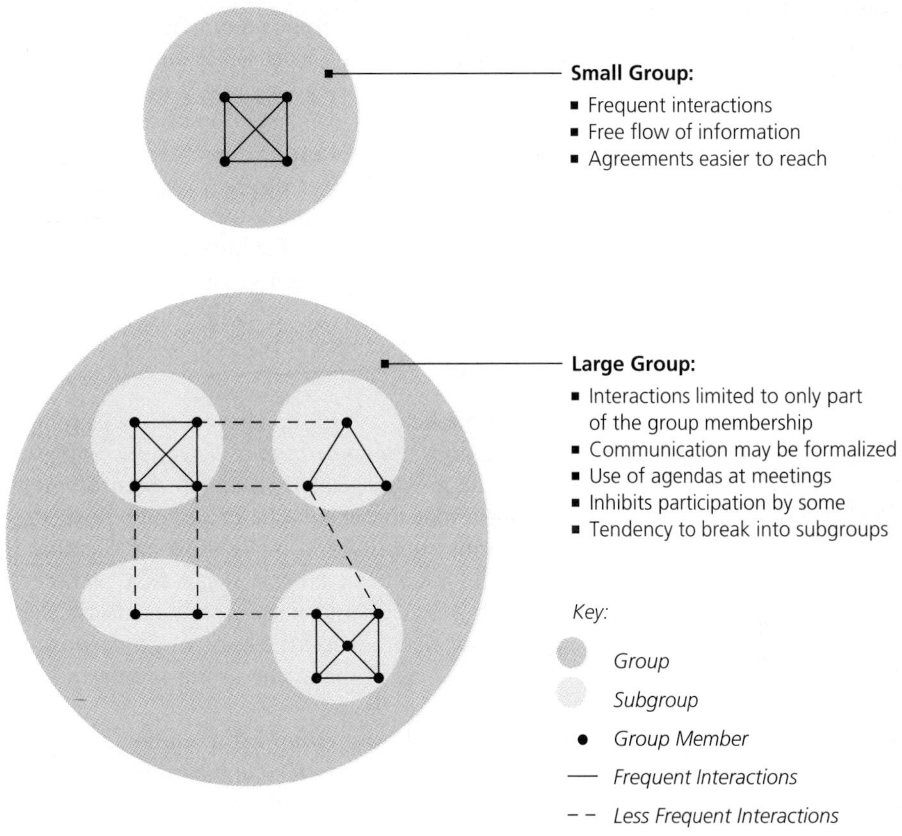

of subgroups may be advantageous. (Of course, the results eventually must be pooled into a group product.) On the other hand, if the group needs to function as a whole, the subgroups have to be integrated in performing the group's tasks.

Norms

▪ A **group norm** is a standard against which the appropriateness of a behavior is measured.

A **norm** is a standard against which the appropriateness of a behavior is judged.[36] Thus, a norm is the expected behavior or behavioral pattern in a certain situation. Group norms usually are established during the second stage of group development (communication and decision making) and carried forward into the maturity stage.[37] People often have expectations about the behavior of others. By providing a basis for predicting others' behaviors, norms enable people to formulate response behaviors. Without norms, the activities within a group would be chaotic.

36. Davis, *Group Performance,* p. 82.
37. Bass and Ryterband, *Organizational Psychology,* pp. 252–254.

Norms result from the combination of members' personality characteristics, the situation, the task, and the historical traditions of the group. Lack of conformity to group norms may result in verbal abuse, physical threats, ostracism, or ejection from the group. Group norms are enforced, however, only for actions that are important to group members.[38] For example, if the office norm is for employees to wear suits to convey a professional image to clients, a staff member who wears blue jeans and a sweatshirt violates the group norm and will hear about it quickly. But if the norm is that dress is unimportant because little contact with clients occurs in the office, someone wearing blue jeans may not even be noticed.

Norms serve four purposes:

1. Norms help the group survive. Groups tend to reject deviant behavior that does not contribute to accomplishing group goals or to the survival of the group if it is threatened. Accordingly, a successful group that is not under threat may be more tolerant of deviant behavior.
2. Norms simplify and make more predictable the behaviors expected of group members. Norms mean that members do not have to analyze each behavior and decide on a response. Members can anticipate the actions of others on the basis of group norms. When members do what is expected of them, the group is more likely to be productive and to reach its goals.
3. Norms help the group avoid embarrassing situations. Group members often want to avoid damaging other members' self-images and are likely to avoid certain subjects that might hurt a member's feelings.
4. Norms express the central values of the group and identify the group to others. Certain clothes, mannerisms, or behaviors in particular situations may be a rallying point for members and may signify to others the nature of the group.[39]

Norms usually regulate the behavior of group members rather than their thoughts or feelings.[40] Members thus may believe one thing but do another to maintain membership in a group. For example, during the Iran-Contra affair in 1985–1987, there were several meetings in which the president and aides, such as Lt. Col. Oliver North, National Security Advisor Robert McFarlane, and Central Intelligence Agency Directory William Casey discussed the sale of arms to Iran in exchange for American hostages.[41] Secretary of State George P. Schultz

38. Shaw, *Group Dynamics*, pp. 280–293.

39. Daniel C. Feldman, "The Development and Enforcement of Group Norms," *Academy of Management Review,* January 1984, pp. 47–53.

40. J. Richard Hackman, "Group Influences on Individuals," in Marvin D. Dunnette, ed., *Handbook of Industrial and Organizational Psychology* (Chicago: Rand McNally, 1976), pp. 1455–1525.

41. John Tower, Edmund Muskie, and Brent Skowcroft, *The Tower Commission Report* (New York: Joint publication of Bantam Books and Times Books, 1987); *Taking the Stand: The Testimony of Lieutenant Colonel Oliver L. North,* (New York: Pocket Books, 1987).

and Secretary of Defense Caspar W. Weinberger were known to be against the sale of arms to Iran, even indirectly through Israel. The president and others strongly favored such arms sales and were eager to achieve the release of American hostages held in Iran. Thus, Schultz and Weinberger did not attend meetings in which further arms sales were authorized.[42] Although it is not clear whether they were excluded by the members or excluded themselves by not attending, norms clearly affected the meetings and outcomes. From the group's perspective, the norms were to approve the arms transfer. Anyone who continued to argue against the transfer would not be in the group. Thus, Schultz and Weinberger knew they were in the minority and were making it uncomfortable for the president. If they wanted to maintain their valued membership in the president's cabinet as heads of two of the most powerful agencies of the executive branch, they knew they should not continue to cause trouble. Thus, the group norms regarding how presidential advisors are supposed to act may have led them to decide not to attend.

Pressures to conform to group norms can be powerful determinants of group performance. Norms affect setting goals, defining behaviors that are appropriate for members, and restricting behaviors of members.[43] Conformity to group norms may result in serious problems at work, such as unsafe work practices. For example, at a manufacturing plant strict rules were in place regarding the use of gloves in the drill press area. Company safety regulations prohibited the use of gloves for certain tasks because of the safety hazard involved if the gloves—and the worker's hands along with them—got caught in the rapidly spinning drill bit. However, the norms of the group dictated the common practice for drill press operators, which was to use gloves for several steps in the drilling process. On-the-job training, health and safety training classes, and numerous strict warnings were given to the drill press operators, but the group norms were too strong. Finally, one Monday morning an operator's glove got caught in a spinning drill bit, grabbing two of the worker's fingers, seriously twisting them, and resulting in their amputation. Obviously, this worker and the company paid a very high price for conformance to group norms.

Cohesiveness

- **Group cohesiveness** is the motivation of members to remain in the group.

Group cohesiveness results from "all forces acting on the members to remain in the group."[44] The forces that create cohesiveness are attraction to the group, resistance to leaving the group, and the motivation to remain a member of the group.[45] As shown in Figure 7.6, group cohesiveness is related to many aspects

42. Tower, Muskie, and Skowcroft, *The Tower Commission Report,* pp. 37–38.

43. Robert J. Lichtman and Irving M. Lane, "Effects of Group Norms and Goal Setting on Productivity," *Group & Organization Studies,* December 1983, pp. 406–420.

44. L. Festinger, "Informal Social Communication," *Psychological Review,* September 1950, p. 274.

45. William E. Piper, Myriam Marrache, Renee Lacroix, Astrid M. Richardson, and Barry D. Jones, "Cohesion as a Basic Bond in Groups," *Human Relations,* February 1983, pp. 93–108.

FIGURE 7.6
Factors That Affect Group Cohesiveness and Consequences of Group Cohesiveness

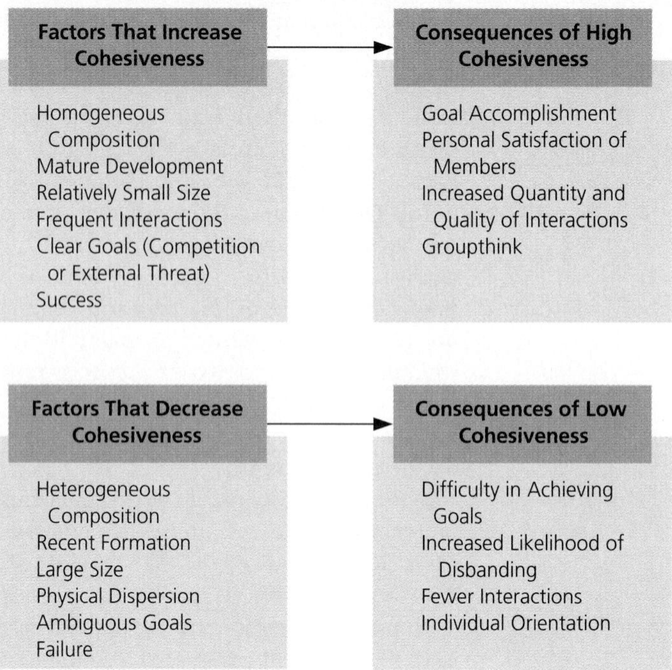

of group dynamics that we already discussed—maturity, homogeneity, and manageable size.

Factors That Increase Cohesiveness
Homogeneous Composition
Mature Development
Relatively Small Size
Frequent Interactions
Clear Goals (Competition or External Threat)
Success
Consequences of High Cohesiveness
Goal Accomplishment
Personal Satisfaction of Members
Increased Quantity and Quality of Interactions
Groupthink
Factors That Decrease Cohesiveness
Heterogeneous Composition
Recent Formation
Large Size
Physical Dispersion
Ambiguous Goals
Failure
Consequences of Low Cohesiveness
Difficulty in Achieving Goals
Increased Likelihood of Disbanding
Fewer Interactions
Individual Orientation

The figure also shows that group cohesiveness can be increased by competition or by the presence of an external threat.[46] Either factor can serve as a clearly defined goal that focuses members' attention on their task and increases their willingness to work together. The threat of NFL teams using replacement players for those on strike had the immediate effect of unifying the players against the owners. The players became more cohesive and vowed more strongly than ever to hold out.[47] Similarly, in the Iran-Contra affair, the inner group (Casey, North, McFarlane, and Vice Admiral Poindexter) became a cohesive group owing to the need for secrecy and threats of exposure by Congress and the media.[48]

Finally, successfully reaching goals often increases the cohesiveness of a group because people are proud to be identified with a winner and to be thought of as competent and successful. This may be one reason for the popular phrase "Success breeds success." A group that is successful may become more cohesive and possibly even more successful. One example is the initial success of the

46. Davis, *Group Performance,* pp. 78–81.

47. Paul Zimmerman, "When Push Came to Shove," *Sports Illustrated,* October 5, 1987, pp. 38–43.

48. Tower, Muskie, and Skowcroft, *The Tower Commission Report, Taking the Stand.*

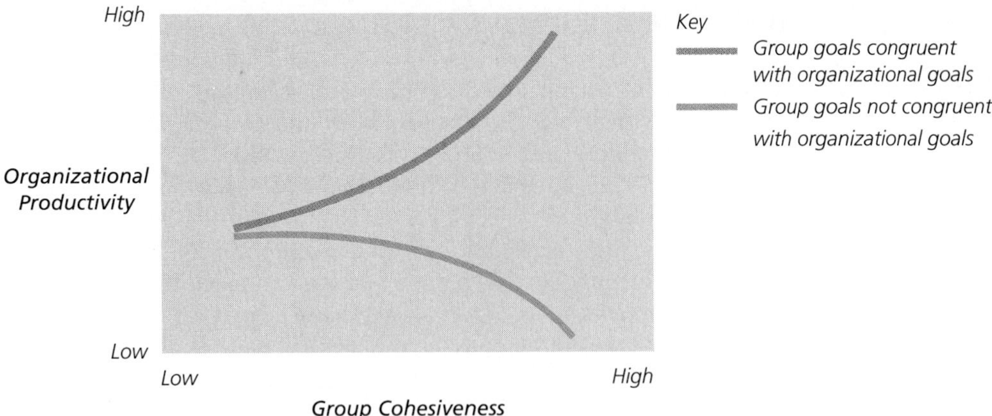

FIGURE 7.7
Group Cohesiveness, Goals, and Productivity

design group at Apple Computer in its creation of the Macintosh personal computer. The members worked and partied together and became quite cohesive. (Of course, other factors can get in the way of continued success, such as personal differences and egos and the lure of more individual success in other activities.)

Research on group performance factors has focused on the relationship between cohesiveness and group productivity. Highly cohesive groups appear to be more effective at achieving their goals than groups low in cohesiveness, especially in research and development groups in U.S. companies.[49] However, highly cohesive groups will not necessarily be more productive in an organizational sense than groups with low-cohesiveness. As Figure 7.7 illustrates, when a group's goals are compatible with the organization's, a cohesive group probably will be more productive than one that is not cohesive. In other words, if a highly cohesive group has the goal of contributing to the good of the organization, it is very likely to be productive in organizational terms. But if such a group decides on a goal that has little to do with the business of the organization, it probably will achieve its own goal, even at the expense of any organizational goal. In a recent study of group characteristics and productivity, group cohesiveness was the only factor that was consistently related to high performance for research and development engineers and technicians.[50]

Cohesiveness may also be a primary factor in the development of certain problems for some decision-making groups. An example is groupthink,[51] which occurs when a group's overriding concern is a unanimous decision rather than the critical analysis of alternatives. In Chapter 16, we go into groupthink in detail. These problems, together with the evidence regarding group cohesiveness and productivity, mean that a manager must carefully weigh the pros and cons of fostering highly cohesive groups.

49. Robert T. Keller, "Predictors of the Performance of Project Groups in R&D Organizations," *Academy of Management Journal,* December 1986, pp. 715–726.

50. Ibid.

51. Irving L. Janis, *Groupthink,* 2nd. ed. (Boston: Houghton Mifflin, 1982), p. 9.

Role Dynamics in Organizations

- A **role** is the part an individual plays in a work group.

Another useful perspective on behavior in groups is role theory. A **role** is the part an individual plays in the work group. As such, it has formal (i.e., job-related and explicit) requirements as well as informal (i.e., social and implicit) requirements. Figure 7.8 illustrates the basic role episode. This sequence suggests that people in a group expect a person in a particular role to act in certain ways. They transmit these expectations formally and informally by the way of the *sent role*. The individual perceives the role expectations with varying levels of accuracy, and then enacts his or her role. When "errors" creep into the role episode, however, either role ambiguity or role conflict can result. Role expectations can also lead to overload, which can have negative consequences.[52]

Role Ambiguity

- **Role ambiguity** occurs when a person is unsure about the exact nature of a particular job and the expectations others have of the individual are unclear.

Role ambiguity occurs when a person is uncertain as to the exact nature of a particular role. Inadequate job descriptions, vague instructions from a supervisor, or unclear cues from coworkers can all result in role ambiguity.

Role Conflict

- **Role conflict** arises when expectations about a person's role in the group contradict one another.

Another possible disruption is **role conflict**, which arises when demands of or messages about roles are essentially clear but also contradict one another somewhat. *Interrole conflict* can occur when a person experiences conflict among two or more roles. A part-time student who is told by an instructor that there will be an exam tomorrow and is also told by his boss that he has to work late tonight will experience interrole conflict.

Intrarole conflict can arise when a person gets contradictory messages from different people in the same role. Suppose one of your subordinates tells you that another subordinate is loafing and needs to be told to work harder. The second subordinate, meanwhile, expresses concern that the first is working too hard and needs to be told to ease up before she collapses from exhaustion. It will take astute investigation to find out which set of messages is more accurate.

Another example of intrarole conflict occurs in the role of the supermarket cashier. The cashier receives role expectations from three sources: management, coworkers, and customers. Role theory generally would suggest that the managers and coworkers have the dominant impact on behaviors. However, in the case of supermarket cashiers, the dominant role sender is the steady stream of customers. Furthermore, the demands of the customers often conflict with managerial or organizational rules and instructions.[53]

---

52. Daniel Katz and Robert L. Kahn, *The Social Psychology of Organizations,* 2nd ed. (New York: Wiley, 1978).

53. Anat Rafaeli, "When Cashiers Meet Customers: An Analysis of the Role of Supermarket Cashiers," *Academy of Management Journal,* vol. 32, 1989, pp. 245–273.

FIGURE 7.8
The Role Episode

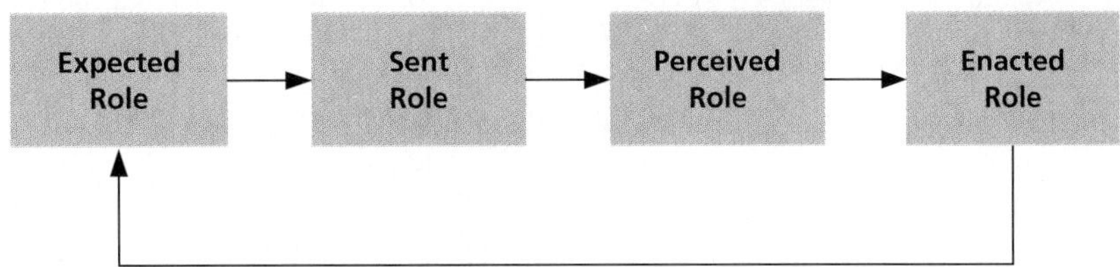

In *intrasender conflict,* the same person sends contradictory messages to the recipient. Suppose a worker tells her boss right before Christmas that she would appreciate chances to earn extra money but then refuses the first offer of overtime. The manager will be uncertain as to her true preferences.

Finally, *person-role conflict* can result if there is some basic incongruence between the person and his or her job. An active supporter of Green Peace who also works for Exxon, might have experienced person-role conflict during the follow-up to the oil spill in Prince William Sound in 1989. So too might people who are pressured to do illegal or unethical things or something distasteful like firing a favorite employee.

Thus, the way an employee perceives and acts out his or her role in the group often plays a major part in how the group functions. The role a person plays is made up of the norms that the group has for the person filling a particular role. Therefore, role interaction between the person and the group have profound impacts on cohesiveness and group performance.

Managing Groups in Organizations

Managing groups in organizations is difficult. Managers must, of course, know what types of groups—command or task, formal or informal—exist in the organization. If a certain command group is very large, there will probably be several informal subgroups to be managed. A manager might want to take advantage of existing informal groups, "formalizing" some of them into command or task groups based on a subset of the tasks to be performed. Other informal groups may need to be broken up to make task assignment easier. In assigning tasks to people and subgroups, the manager must also consider individual motivations for joining groups, as well as the composition of groups.

Quite often, a manager can help make sure a group develops into a productive unit by nurturing its activities in each stage of development. Helpful steps include encouraging open communication and trust among the members, stimulating discussion of important issues and providing task-relevant information at appropriate times, and assisting in the analysis of external factors, such as competition and external threats and opportunities. Managers might also encourage the development of norms and roles within the group to help out in development.

In managing a group, managers must consider the goals of the people in the group as well as those of the group as a whole. Developing a reward structure that lets people reach their own goals by working toward those of the group can result in a very productive group. A manager may also be able to influence some factors that affect group cohesiveness. For example, trying to stimulate competition, provoke an external threat to the group, establish a goal-setting system, or employ participative approaches might help harness the productive potential of high cohesiveness.

In summary, managers must be aware of the implications—organizational and social—of their attempts to manage people in groups in organizations. Groups affect the behavior of people and, individual efforts, when aggregated to the group level, are the source of group performance. As prevalent as groups are in our society, it is essential that managers strive to improve their understanding of people in the groups to which they belong.

Summary of Key Points

- A group is two or more people who interact so as to influence one another. It is important to study groups because groups are everywhere in our society, they can profoundly affect individual behavior, and the behavior of individuals in a group is key to the group's success or failure. The work group is the primary means by which managers coordinate individual behavior to achieve organizational goals.
- Groups may be differentiated on the bases of relative permanence and degree of formality. The two types of formal groups are command and task groups. Friendship and interest groups are the two types of informal groups. Command groups are relatively permanent work groups established by the organization and usually are specified on an organization chart. Task groups, although also established by the organization, are relatively temporary and exist only until the specific task is accomplished. In friendship groups, the affiliation among members arises from close social relationships and the enjoyment that comes from being together. The common bond in interest groups is the activity in which the members engage.
- Group formation depends on the expectation that a need will be satisfied as a result of membership. Five types of need satisfaction are internal to the group: interpersonal attraction, group activities, group goals, social identification, and the need for affiliation. Two types of need satisfaction are external to the group: interpersonal attraction to people outside the group and goals external to the group.
- Groups develop in four stages: mutual acceptance, communication and decision making, motivation and productivity, and control and organization. Although the stages are sequential, they may overlap. A group that does not fully develop within each stage will not fully mature as a group, resulting in lower group performance.

- Incomplete group development can lead to member frustration and low group productivity. A group that completes the four stages of development will become a mature, effective group whose members are interdependent, coordinated, cooperative, capable of doing their jobs, motivated to do them, and in communication with one another.
- Four additional factors affect group performance: composition, size, norms, and cohesiveness. The homogeneity of the people in the group affects the interactions that occur and the productivity of the group. The effect of increasing the size of the group depends on the nature of the tasks and the people in the group. Norms help people function and relate to one another in predictable and efficient ways. Norms serve four purposes: They facilitate group survival, simplify and make more predictable the behaviors of group members, help the group avoid embarrassing situations, and express the central values of the group and identify the group to others.
- The relationships among group cohesiveness, productivity, and other group factors are very complex. The most organizationally productive groups are highly cohesive and have goals that are compatible with the organization's. In managing groups in organizations, the manager should consider the goals of groups as well as the factors that affect group cohesiveness.
- It is important for managers to consider role dynamics. If problems arise during the role episode, role ambiguity or various forms of role conflict can arise.
- Managers must also be aware of the many factors that affect group performance and understand the people as well as the group issues.

Discussion Questions

1. Why is it useful for a manager to be familiar with the concepts of group behavior? Why is it useful for an employee to be familiar with these concepts?
2. Our definition of a group is somewhat broad. Would you classify each of the following collections of people as a group or as something else? Explain why.
   a. 70,000 people at a football game
   b. Students taking this course
   c. People in an elevator
   d. People on an escalator
   e. Employees of IBM
   f. Employees of your local college bookstore
3. List four groups to which you belong. Identify each as formal or informal.
4. For each group you listed in question 3, describe the reasons for its formation. Why did you join each group? Why might others have decided to join each group?

5. In which stage of development is each of the four groups listed in question 3? Did any group move too quickly through any of the stages? Explain.
6. Analyze the composition of two of the groups to which you belong. How are they similar in composition? How do they differ?
7. Are any of the groups to which you belong too large or too small to get its work done? If so, what can the leader or the members do to alleviate the problem?
8. List two norms of two of the groups to which you belong. How are these norms enforced?
9. Discuss the following statement: "Group cohesiveness is the good, warm feeling we get from working in groups and is something that all group leaders should strive to develop in the groups they lead."
10. List three different roles that you fill. Describe how you experience different types of role ambiguity and role conflict.

CASE 7.1

Increasing Steel Exports for Chaparral Steel

Once the backbone of U.S. industry, the steel industry faces increasing foreign competition. Foreign-made steel accounts for 20 percent of the steel used in the United States. In addition, exporting of U.S. steel to other countries has almost stopped because overseas markets are dominated by non-U.S. steel producers. Into this difficult market comes Chaparral Steel, a subsidiary of Texas Industries. In 1986, Chaparral began to ship steel to companies in Canada and Europe—up to 10,000 tons to Canada alone. Chaparral competes on the basis of quality and price. It is now one of the most efficient steel producers in the country, requiring only 1.6 human-hours per ton of production (the industry average is 1.95).

The high efficiency of this Midlothian, Texas, steel producer is due to superteams developed over the last several years. All new workers are extensively trained in the "Chaparral Process." This system encompasses the entire manufacturing process as well as the ways the company handles its finances, marketing, sales, and customer service. Thus, every worker fully understands his or her part in the total process. Workers are assigned to teams and participate in the work as well as managing it.

In the early 1980s, a team leader and three mill workers were sent to Europe, Asia, and South America to evaluate new production equipment—specifically mill stands, an integral part of the manufacturing process. The team evaluated all potential pieces of equipment, made the purchase decision, ordered the equipment, and supervised its installation—all in less than one year, whereas most companies would take several years to do the same thing. Most important, the mill stands worked on the first trial and continue to make Chaparral one of the most efficient firms in the industry. Other superteams of workers and team leaders contribute in similar ways throughout the plant.

The establishment of teams is credited with giving Chaparral the competitive advantage it needs to survive intense foreign competition.

Case Questions

1. Which type of group does the case describe?
2. What important characteristics of the members of the work team enabled them to make the equipment purchase?

SOURCES: Brian Dumaine, "Who Needs a Boss?", *Fortune,* May 7, 1990, pp. 52–60; "Making Money Making Steel in Texas," *The Wall Street Journal,* January 26, 1988. p. 37. Lisa M. Keefe, "Forward's March," *Forbes,* April 20, 1987, pp. 104–105.

CASE 7.2

A Difficult Task Force

As chairperson of a task force on in-process materials handling, Jim had scheduled an initial meeting for 10:00 A.M. A month earlier, quality assurance at the large manufacturing company where Jim works had noticed that a significant number of parts were scratched when they arrived at the assembly room. A fact-finding committee, of which Jim was a member, had determined that the problem was caused by rough handling of the parts as they were moved around the plant. The committee's solution was to transport the parts in special divider trays. Representatives of the departments involved in the processing and transportation of the parts—including process engineering, plant transportation, industrial engineering, product design, and quality assurance—had been appointed to a task force responsible for designing the trays. The members, most of whom had been with the company for a decade or more, were chosen for their expertise and familiarity with these parts and their manufacture. All had agreed to work on the project, but they had not been asked what they thought of the fact-finding committee's report.

When the task force members arrived, Jim started the meeting by reviewing the history of the problem and the activities of the fact-finding committee. He stressed that the task force was to come up with a design concept for the special divider trays. He then opened the meeting for comments and suggestions.

Bob from industrial engineering spoke first: "In my opinion, the solution to the problem is to make sure the workers are more careful in handling the parts rather than in designing some new contraption to get in the way." Mary from product design agreed. She urged the committee to recommend that new handling procedures be written and enforced. Jim interrupted the discussion: "The earlier fact-finding committee already decided, with the approval of top management, that new divider trays will be designed and used." He knew the earlier committee had considered new handling procedures with better enforcement but had rejected this solution because of the extent of the damage and the expense of the parts involved. He told the task force this and reminded them that the purpose of this committee was to design the new dividers, not to question the fact-finding committee's solution.

The task force members then began discussing the design of the dividers. But the discussion always returned to the issue of handling procedures and enforcement. Finally, George from plant transportation spoke up: "I think we ought to do what Mary suggested earlier. It makes no sense to me to design dividers when written procedures will solve the problem." The other members nodded their heads in agreement. Jim again reminded them of the task force's purpose and said a new recommendation would not be well received by top management. Nevertheless, the group insisted that Jim write a memo to the vice president of manufacturing with the recommendation. The meeting adjourned at 10:45 A.M.

Jim started to write the memo, but he knew it would anger several of his supervisors. He hoped he would not be held responsible for the actions of the task force, even though he was its chair. He wondered what had gone wrong and what he could have done to prevent it.

Case Questions

1. Which characteristics of group behavior discussed in the chapter can you identify in this case?
2. If you were in Jim's position, what would you have done differently?
3. If you were in Jim's position, what would you do now?

EXPERIENTIAL EXERCISE*

Purpose: This exercise demonstrates the benefits a group can bring to accomplishing a task.

Format: You will be asked to do the same task both individually and as part of a group.

Procedure: *Part 1*: You will need a pen or pencil and an 8½″ × 11″ sheet of paper. Working alone, do the following:

1. Write the letters of the alphabet in a vertical column down the left-hand side of the paper: *A–Z*.
2. Your instructor will randomly select a sentence from any written document and read out loud the first twenty-six letters in that sentence. Write these letters in a vertical column immediately to the right of the alphabet column. Everyone should have identical sets of twenty-six two-letter combinations.
3. Working alone, think of a famous person whose initials correspond to each pair of letters, and write the name next to the letters, for example, *MT Mark Twain*. You will have ten minutes. Only one name per set is allowed. One point is awarded for each legitimate name, so the maximum score is 26 points.
4. After time expires, exchange your paper with another member of the class and score each other's work. Disputes about the legitimacy of names will be settled by the instructor. Keep your score for use later in the exercise.

*Adapted from J. William Pfeiffer and John E. Jones, (eds.), *The 1979 Annual Handbook for Group Facilitators* (San Diego, Calif.: University Associates, 1979), pp. 19–20. Used with permission.

Part 2: Your instructor will divide the class into groups of five to ten people. All groups should have approximately the same number of members. Each group now follows the procedure given in part 1. Again write the letters of the alphabet down the left-hand side of the sheet of paper, this time in reverse order: *Z–A*. Your instructor will dictate a new set of letters for the second column. The time limit and scoring procedure are the same. The only difference is that the groups will generate the names.

Part 3: Each team identifies the group member who came up with the most names. The instructor places these "best" students into one group. Then all groups repeat part 2, but this time the letters from the reading will be in the first column and the alphabet letters will be in the second column.

Part 4: Each team calculates the average individual score of its members on part 1 and compares it with the team score from parts 2 and 3. Your instructor will put the average individual score and team scores for each group on the board.

Follow-up Questions

1. Are there differences in the average individual scores and the team scores? What are the reasons for the difference, if any?
2. Although the team scores in this exercise usually are higher than the average individual scores, under what conditions might individual averages exceed group scores?

CHAPTER OUTLINE

- Intergroup Interactions
  - *Avoidance*
  - *Accommodation*
  - *Competition*
  - *Collaboration*
  - *Compromise*
- A Model of Intergroup Dynamics
- Factors That Influence Intergroup Behavior
  - *Location*
  - *Resources*
  - *Time and Goal Interdependence*
  - *Task Uncertainty*
  - *Task Interdependence*
- Managing Intergroup Behavior in Organizations
  - *Location-Based Strategies*
  - *Resource-Based Strategies*
  - *Goal-Based Strategies*
  - *People- and Group-Based Strategies*
  - *Organization-Based Strategies*

8

INTERGROUP DYNAMICS

LEARNING OBJECTIVES

After studying this chapter, you should be able to:

Discuss the several types of group interactions that can occur in organizations and explain what makes them different from one another.

Discuss the importance of the organizational setting and specific group factors in understanding interactions among groups in organizations.

Describe several factors that influence the way groups interact.

Explain how managers can help make group interactions more productive.

"They slap you on the back and ask for cooperation with one hand and then stab you in the back with the other by violating the contract," reports a union official at a USX plant. This does not sound like a place where union-management cooperation is blossoming. Indeed, the atmosphere at USX plants had always been adversarial in this respect. As other steelmakers turned to labor-management teams as one of several means to meet the increasing quality and cost demands of foreign competition, USX maintained its stormy relationship with its workers that in 1986 culminated in a work stoppage that cost the firm $360 million. Management had never realized that quality requires a team effort between management and labor. Today, however, the labor-management relationship is improving in many USX plants.

USX's first attempt to develop cooperative teams was at its West Mifflin, Pennsylvania, plant in 1985. This initial experimental effort has blossomed into more than forty labor-management teams that meet several times a month. At the mill, one team helped reduce the customer rejection rate by more than 60 percent by developing a new process for removing speckles from finished coils of steel. Successes such as this fostered the development of similar cooperative teams at other USX plants. For example, a team of managers and steelworkers developed a more efficient way to heat metal and reduce bad batches at a mill in Lorain, Ohio.

The cooperative climate between workers and management has even extended beyond the workplace. USX recently held an outing for workers, managers, and their families at the Kennywood Amusement Park in Pittsburgh.

Not everyone agrees with the new cooperative relationship, however. Some union people still distrust USX management because of what they consider violations of the union contract. Thus, although the worker-management relationship has improved, it is far from harmonious in some areas.[1]

The changes at USX reflect the changing relationship between labor and management in many organizations. Interactions that once were characterized by conflict, hostility, and resentment are beginning to emphasize cooperation and collaboration. The improvements in the worker-management climate have contributed greatly to the success of many organizations.

---

1. "Suddenly, USX Is Playing Mr. Nice Guy," *Business Week,* June 26, 1989, p. 152; "How Roderick's Heir Apparent Earned His Hard Hat," *Business Week,* August 8, 1988, p. 75; Milton Moscowitz, Michael Katz, and Robert Levering, *Everybody's Business* (San Francisco: Harper & Row, 1980), pp. 591–599.

In the previous chapter, we noted the importance of group dynamics and performance. However, a group's contribution to an organization depends on its interaction with other groups as well as on its own productivity. Many organizations have increased their use of cross-functional teams to address more complex and increasingly important organizational issues. The result has been a heightened emphasis on teams' interactions with other groups. Groups that actively interact with other groups by asking questions, initiating joint programs, and sharing their teams' achievements usually are the most productive.[2]

There are many possible relationships among groups in organizations. Interactions may be frequent, regular, and routine, like those between waiters and cooks in a restaurant. These two groups must interact in predictable ways if hungry customers are to get their food in good time. But given the close working relationships between cooks and waiters and the demands for speed and accuracy, the potential for friction between the two groups is quite high. If conflicts arise between waiters and cooks, the result may be lower-quality service to customers and, ultimately, loss of patronage for the restaurant.

On the other hand, some groups, such as bank tellers and the personnel who design new branch banks, may interact very infrequently. In this case, the design personnel may occasionally consult with tellers for ideas on branch design, and tellers may contact the design people about rearranging office space or tearing down a wall. For the most part, however, the two groups rarely interact in the bank's daily operations.

The interactions in these situations and in the opening vignette differ in many respects. But whether the groups interact regularly (the cooks and the waiters) or infrequently (the bank tellers and the designers), the interaction between them is crucial to the organization's success and the potential for problems between them always exists. It is management's responsibility to forestall such problems and to help groups work together constructively.

■ **Intergroup behavior** is the interactions among groups of people in organizations.

In this chapter, we deal with the dynamics of **intergroup behavior,** that is, the ways groups interact with one another. The groups may be formally established work groups, task forces, departments, or even major organizational divisions. First, we discuss five basic types of interactions that occur among groups. Then we present a model of intergroup dynamics. Next, we examine the factors that influence intergroup interactions. Finally, we discuss some strategies managers can use to enhance interactions among groups.

Intergroup Interactions

Many types of interactions occur in organizations. Some interactions are everyday occurrences and may be treated quite casually by employees. Others occur infrequently but routinely and may be special occasions accompanied with great

2. Deborah Gladstein Ancona, "Outward Bound: Strategies for Team Survival in an Organization," *Academy of Management Journal,* June 1990, pp. 334–365.

fanfare. Some types of interactions are associated with antagonistic behaviors and may result in open conflict. (Conflict is a special type of interaction between people or groups and is discussed in more detail in Chapter 10.) The most common types of interactions are avoidance, accommodation, competition, collaboration, and compromise.[3]

Whenever groups interact, it is really the people in the groups who are interacting. Still, in most cases the people act as representatives of the groups to which they belong. In effect they work together, representing their group as they strive to do their part in helping the group achieve its goals. Thus, the five types of interactions we discuss here can be analyzed in terms of relationships among the goals of the interacting groups.

- Interactions among groups depend on the importance of the issues to the groups and the compatibility of the groups' goals. **Goal compatibility** is the extent to which the goals of more than one group can be achieved at the same time.

Interactions can be differentiated according to their importance to the attainment of each group's goals and the degree of compatibility among the groups' goals, as shown in Figure 8.1. The importance of the interaction to the goal attainment of each interacting group ranges from very high to very low. The degree of **goal compatibility** is the extent to which the goals of the groups can be achieved simultaneously. In other words, the goals of interacting groups are compatible if one group can accomplish its goals without preventing the other group from accomplishing its goals. The goals of interacting groups are incompatible if one group's accomplishment of its goals prohibits the other group from accomplishing its goals. The degree of goal compatibility can vary from very incompatible to very compatible. At the midpoint of each continuum, goals are neither very important nor very unimportant and neither very incompatible nor very compatible.

Avoidance

- **Avoidance** occurs when the interacting groups' goals are incompatible and the interaction is relatively unimportant to the attainment of the goals.

Avoidance occurs when an interaction is relatively unimportant to any group's goals and the groups' goals are incompatible, as in the bottom left-hand corner of Figure 8.1. Because the groups are not striving toward compatible goals and the issues in question seem unimportant, the groups simply try to avoid interacting with one another. For example, one state agency simply ignores another agency's requests for information. The requesting agency then practices its own form of avoidance by not following up on the requests.

Accommodation

- **Accommodation** occurs when the groups' goals are compatible but the interaction is relatively unimportant to their attainment.

Accommodation occurs when the groups' goals are compatible but the interactions are not considered important to overall goal attainment, as in the bottom right-hand corner of Figure 8.1. Interactions of this type may involve discussions that center on how the groups can accomplish their interdependent tasks with

3. Kenneth Thomas, "Conflict and Conflict Management," in Marvin Dunnette, ed., *Handbook of Industrial and Organizational Psychology* (Chicago: Rand McNally, 1976), pp. 889–935.

FIGURE 8.1
Five Types of Group Interactions as a Function of Goal Importance and Degree of Goal Compatibility

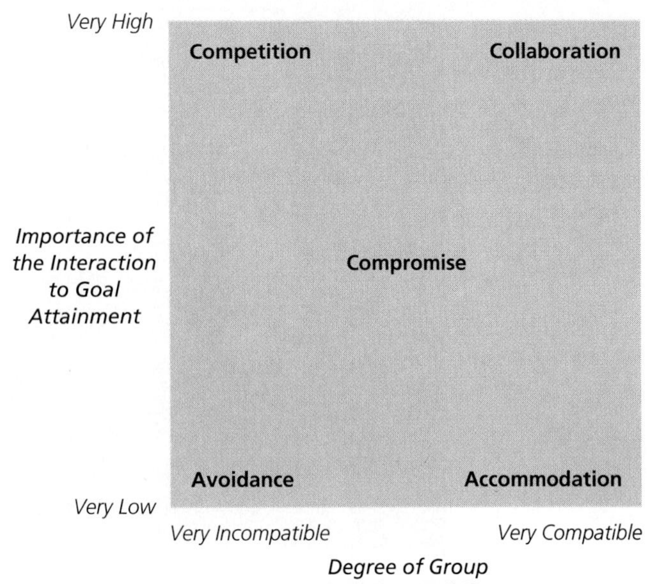

SOURCE: Adapted from Kenneth Thomas, "Conflict and Conflict Management," in Marvin Dunnette, ed., *Handbook of Industrial and Organizational Psychology* (Chicago: Rand McNally, 1976), pp. 889–935. Reprinted by permission.

the least expenditure of time and effort. This type of interaction tends to be very friendly.[4]

Departments in a manufacturing company often engage in accommodation. In one large computer manufacturing firm, the maintenance department and the production department needed to work out a procedure for reporting machine and equipment malfunctions. Production employees and supervisors believed that anyone noticing a need for repairs should be able to call the maintenance group. Maintenance, however, wanted production supervisors to investigate each situation first and place the calls personally. To the production department the issue was not extremely important, and the two groups' goals seemed compatible. It therefore accommodated the maintenance group by agreeing that supervisors would investigate and report maintenance needs.

Competition

■ **Competition** occurs when the goals of interacting groups are incompatible and the interactions are important to the attainment of each group's goals.

Competition occurs when the goals of interacting groups are incompatible and the interactions are important to the attainment of each group's goals, as in the top left-hand corner of Figure 8.1. If all groups are striving for a goal but only

4. Robert R. Blake, Herbert A. Shepard, and Jane S. Mouton, *Managing Intergroup Conflict in Industry* (Houston: Gulf, 1964).

Republic Corporation, a financial company, has been collaborating with the Community Preservation Corporation to enhance and rebuild urban housing. Representatives from the two groups are shown here reviewing work on a jointly sponsored project in Brooklyn.

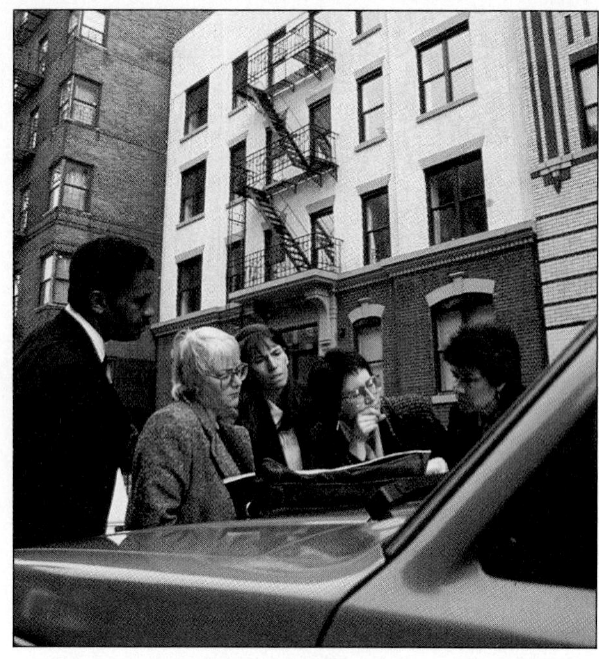

one group can reach its goal, the groups will be in competition. In one freight warehouse and storage firm, the first, second, and third shifts each sought to win the weekly productivity prize by posting the highest productivity record. Workers on the winning shift received recognition in the company newspaper. Because the issue was important to each group and the interests of the groups were incompatible, the result was competition.

The competition among the shifts encouraged each shift to produce more per week, which increased the company's output and eventually improved its overall welfare (and thus the welfare of each group). Both the company and the groups benefited from the competition because it fostered innovative and creative work methods, which further boosted productivity. Of course, competition among the groups might have led to poorer overall performance had the groups attempted to sabotage other shifts or inflate records or the competition had increased worker stress. Under these conditions, competition can actually decrease work performance.[5]

Collaboration

- **Collaboration** occurs when the interaction is very important to the groups' goal attainment and the goals of the groups are compatible.

Collaboration occurs when the interaction is very important to group goal attainment and the goals of the groups are compatible, as in the top right-hand corner of Figure 8.1. At first glance, this may seem to be a simple interaction in

5. Alfie Kohn, "How to Succeed without Even Vying," *Psychology Today,* September 1986, pp. 22–28.

which the groups participate jointly in activities to accomplish goals after agreeing on the goals and their importance. In many situations, however, it is no easy matter to agree on goals, their importance, and especially the means for achieving them. In a collaborative interaction, group goals may differ but be compatible. Groups may initially have difficulty working out the ways in which all can achieve their goals. However, because the interactions are important to goal attainment, the groups are willing to continue to work together to achieve the goals. Collaborative relationships can lead to new and innovative ideas and solutions to any differences among the groups.[6]

Collaborative relationships have become routine between suppliers and customers, or wholesalers. As the use of just-in-time inventory and production systems has expanded, the importance of dependable supplies of raw materials has increased. Customers are developing closer relationships with suppliers that result in high-volume contracts, reduce competition, and create a more predictable market for suppliers.[7] Of course, federal regulations restrict some collaborative relationships between suppliers and customers.

Compromise

- **Compromise** occurs when the interaction is moderately important to the attainment of each group's goals and the goals are neither completely compatible nor completely incompatible.

The final type of intergroup interaction, **compromise,** occurs when the interactions are moderately important to goal attainment and the goals are neither completely compatible nor completely incompatible. In a compromise situation, groups interact with other groups striving to achieve goals, but the groups may not aggressively pursue goal attainment in either a competitive or collaborative manner because the interactions are not that important to goal attainment. On the other hand, the groups may not either avoid one another or be accommodating because the interactions are somewhat important. Often each group gives up something, but because the interactions are only moderately important, members do not regret what they have given up.

Contract negotiations between union and management are an example of compromise. Each side brings numerous issues of varying importance to the bargaining table. Through rounds of offers and counteroffers, the two sides give and take on the issues. The complexity of such negotiations is increasing as negotiations spread to multiple plants in different countries. Agreements between management and labor in a plant in the United States may be unacceptable to both parties in Canada.[8] Weeks of negotiations ending in numerous compromises usually results in a contract agreement between the union and management.

To sum up, if the goals of two groups are very compatible, the groups may engage in mutually supportive interactions, that is, collaboration or accommodation. If the goals of the groups are very incompatible, each group may attempt

6. Andrew S. Grove, "How to Make Confrontation Work for You," *Fortune,* July 23, 1984, pp. 73–75.

7. "Getting Cozy with Their Customers," *Business Week,* January 8, 1990, p. 86.

8. "Ford of Canada Reaches Tentative Pact with Union Similar to Chrysler Contract," *The Wall Street Journal,* October 2, 1987, p. 5; "What's Throwing a Wrench into Britain's Assembly Lines?" *Business Week,* February 29, 1988, p. 41.

to foster its own success at the expense of the others, engaging in competition or avoidance.

A Model of Intergroup Dynamics

■ Interactions among groups are based on the organizational context within which the groups operate, the characteristics of the interacting groups, and the task and situational bases of the interactions.

As we discussed in the preceding section, interactions are the key to understanding intergroup dynamics. The orientation of the groups toward their goals takes place within a highly complex set of conditions that determine the relationship among the groups. The most important of these factors are presented in the model of intergroup dynamics in Figure 8.2. The model emphasizes three primary factors that influence intergroup interactions: group characteristics, organizational factors, and task and situational bases of interaction.

FIGURE 8.2
Factors That Influence Intergroup Interactions

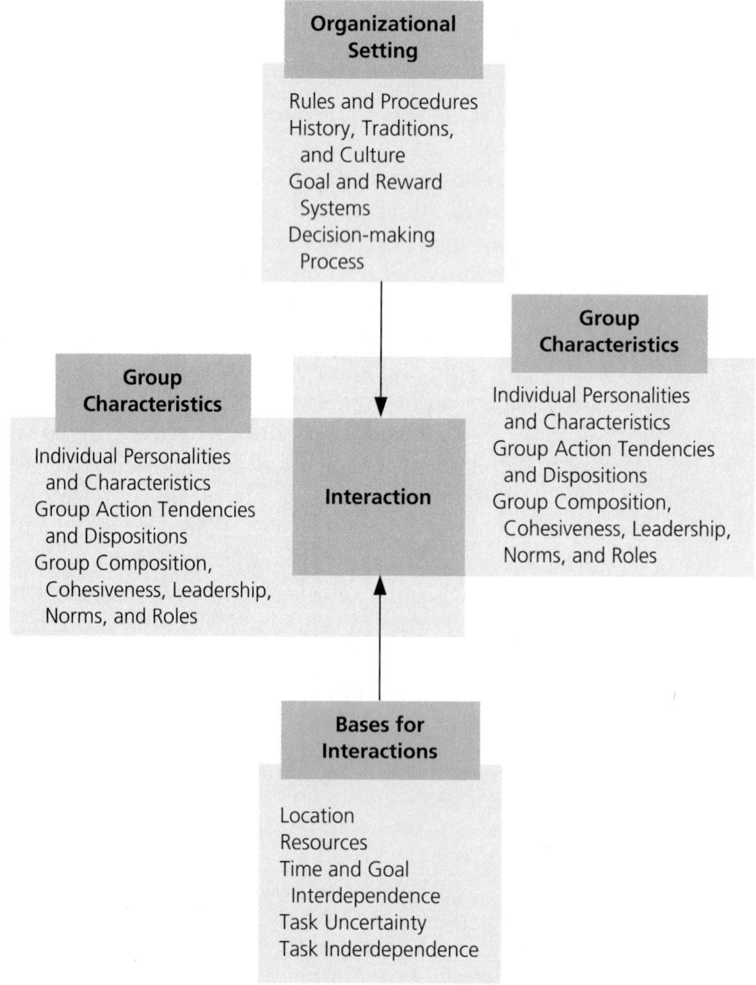

The success of the Seoul Olympics depended on the ability of many different groups to work together cooperatively. Arrangement committees, hospitality committees, housing committees, representatives of competing national sports teams, and media representatives are just a few of the many groups that participated in this complex and comprehensive set of activities.

First, we must understand the key characteristics of the interacting groups. Each group brings to the interaction its own unique features. As individuals become a part of a group, they tend to identify so strongly with the group that their views of other groups become biased, and harmonious relationships may be difficult to achieve.[9] Furthermore, because the individuals who make up each group contribute to the group processes, the groups' norms, size, composition, and cohesiveness all affect the interactions with other groups. Thus, understanding the individuals in the group and the key characteristics of the group can help managers monitor intergroup interactions.

Second, the organizational setting within which the groups interact can have a powerful influence on intergroup interactions. The organization's structure, rules and procedures, decision-making processes, and goals and reward systems all influence interactions. For example, organizations in which frequent interactions occur and strong ties among groups exist usually are characterized as low-conflict organizations.[10] *A Look at the Research* describes a recent study of interactions in organizations.

Group interactions may be prescribed by company rules and by informal practices that have evolved over many years. Certain actions may be allowed and others strictly forbidden. In addition, the reward system may be designed to

---

9. Blake E. Ashforth and Fred Mael, "Social Identity Theory and the Organization," *Academy of Management Review,* January 1989, pp. 20–39.

10. Reed E. Nelson, "The Strength of Strong Ties: Social Networks and Intergroup Conflict in Organizations," *Academy of Management Journal,* June 1989, pp. 377–401. Reprinted by permission.

A LOOK AT THE
RESEARCH

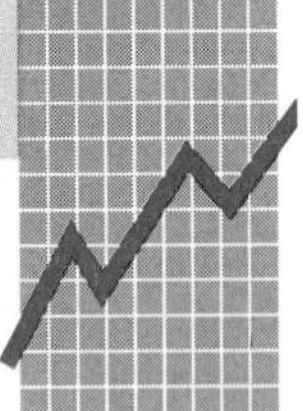

Interactions and Conflict in Organizations

The study of conflict among interacting groups typically has taken place in experimental situations or in single organizational case studies. Although organizational behavior researchers have learned a lot about interacting groups in these settings, there is much to be learned by studying interacting groups in several organizations using the same data-gathering methods and procedures. Reed Nelson, a professor at Louisiana Tech University, recently completed a study of interacting groups in twenty types of organizations. He expected to find that low-conflict organizations have groups that interact on a regular basis and high-conflict organizations have groups whose members have strong ties within the group as opposed to ties with other groups.

The twenty organizations Professor Nelson studied were from a variety of industries, including manufacturing, service, health care, electric utilities, banking, education, and public accounting. Employees who were members of interacting groups within their organizations were given a questionnaire that dealt with their relationships and interactions with other groups within the organization. Most questionnaires were distributed to the top three levels of management.

Each organization was classified as either high or low conflict based on reported occurrences of disruptive conflict. Independent raters further tested these classifications against the levels of conflict reported by managers from within each organization. Then the interacting groups and the ties among them were analyzed using a technique that clusters similar groups together and reveals the strengths of the similarities. In this case, groups with strong internal ties and weak interactions with outside groups proved to differ sharply from groups with strong ties to outside groups.

After comparing the strength of ties among groups and the level of conflict within organizations, Professor Nelson found that the high-conflict organizations had high within-group ties and low-conflict organizations had high between-group ties. That is, high-conflict organizations had groups with strong ties within their own groups and weak ties with outside groups whereas low-conflict organizations had groups with strong ties and interactions with other groups.

Professor Nelson described one hospital that was under a great deal of pressure from community groups, regulatory authorities, local universities, and professional groups. The six groups within the hospital showed very little cooperative effort, even though they all worked in the same organization. In contrast, a copper smelter that was characterized as a low-conflict organization had strong ties across groups and frequent and productive interactions among groups.

In summary, Professor Nelson's research has opened the way to examining interactions among groups in real-world organizations. By using similar network analyses that cluster like groups together, other researchers may be able to analyze interactions among groups in similar organizations. Most important, Professor Nelson has demonstrated a clear relationship between the level of conflict in organizations and the interactional patterns that occur within them.

SOURCE: Reed E. Nelson, "The Strength of Strong Ties: Social Networks and Intergroup Conflict in Organizations," *Academy of Management Journal,* June 1989, pp. 377–401. Reprinted by permission.

reward certain behaviors and ignore or punish others. All of these factors, which we discuss in more detail in Parts IV and V, may affect group interactions in organizations.

Group interactions can be especially important to the success of a new venture. Ford Motor Company attempted to build the Escort as a "world car" by creating a single design that could be produced all over the world. However, the company's design groups did not cooperate very well. The European and American versions of the car shared only one part, a water pump seal.[11] Since then, Ford has established policies that require much closer cooperation among design groups. Ford is also working with its unions to develop more cooperative relationships among departments and new work rules that provide ways for departments to interact.[12] For example, it now uses concurrent engineering in which product design, manufacturing design, and planning and quality engineering are all involved in the original concept and in product design.[13]

Third, the task and situational bases of interactions focus on the working relationships among the interacting groups and on the reasons for the interactions. We discuss these bases for interaction in the next section.

Factors That Influence Intergroup Behavior

- Five factors that determine the nature of group interactions are location, resources, time and goal interdependence, task uncertainty, and task interdependence.

As Figure 8.2 shows, there are five bases of intergroup interactions: location, resources, time and goal interdependence, task uncertainty, and task interdependence. These factors both create the interactions and determine their characteristics, such as the frequency of interaction, the volume of information exchange among groups, and the type of coordination the groups need to interact and function. For example, if two groups will heavily depend on each other to perform a task about which much uncertainty exists, they will need a great deal of information from each other to define and perform the task.

Location

The closer groups are to one another physically, the more likely it is that group members, and thus the groups themselves, will interact. Some interactions based on physical *location* may be primarily interpersonal in nature, as opposed to formal and work related.[14] They may occur initially because of physical interaction (for example, seeing members of another group in a common office area

11. "Now That It's Cruising, Can Ford Keep Its Foot to the Gas?" *Business Week,* February 11, 1985, pp. 48–52.

12. "Ford's Mr. Turnaround: 'We Have More to Do,' " *Fortune,* March 4, 1985, pp. 83–84.

13. "Ford Has a Better Idea: Let Someone Else Have the Idea," *Business Week,* April 30, 1990, pp. 116–117.

14. See Marvin E. Shaw, *Group Dynamics: The Psychology of Small Group Behavior,* 3rd ed. (New York: McGraw-Hill, 1981), pp. 83–85, for a discussion of a physical proximity and group interactions.

or in the hall), but over time they may develop into regularly occurring interactions. On the other hand, groups that are physically distant may interact infrequently, as in a decentralized sales organization with offices distributed around the country. More frequent contact with other groups will affect their interactions.

The pattern of group interactions sometimes can be changed by altering the arrangement of offices and the location of various departments. The offices of work groups can be moved nearer to one another to promote effective interactions. Conversely, it may be appropriate to separate squabbling groups to decrease the frequency of interactions among them (as long as they are not highly dependent on one another).

Resources

Organizations have material, human, financial, and information *resources,* and groups must have their proper share of these resources to accomplish their tasks. Naturally, when resources are finite but the demands on groups increase, the groups will interact over the available resources. The potential for interaction increases if the groups use the same or similar resources or if one group can affect the availability of the resources another group needs. Consider a state government office building in which only a certain amount of office space was available when two agencies each hired several new college graduates. Each agency assumed it could somehow find office space for the new workers by making small adjustments and squeezing other agencies a bit. When the new people came on board in June, however, neither agency had been able to come up with the space. Several heated discussions ensued, and interactions between the groups were extremely awkward for several months. Other typical situations in which resources cause group interactions include budget meetings, personnel assignments, and placement of office equipment.

Interactions based on resources are not always hostile. In times of a budget crunch, for instance, several government agencies may work together to help one another with paperwork processing and other activities.

Time and Goal Interdependence

Most organizations use some types of goals to give themselves direction and to serve as performance targets.[15] Usually initiated at the top level, goals filter down through an organization and are divided into subgoals that become the goals of work groups. In addition, the work of managers and work groups usually is subject to a certain time frame that involves deadlines for completing a project

15. See Richard H. Hall, *Organizations: Structure and Process,* 3rd ed. (Englewood Cliffs, N.J.: Prentice-Hall, 1982), pp. 278–294, for a more detailed discussion of goals and organizational effectiveness.

These Unisys managers worked together with a group from a Turkish equipment distributor in planning the installation of a computer system linking a Turkish bank with its 1,300 branches. Their common goal coupled with a tight time schedule caused them to work in close cooperation to get the job done. As a result, they were able to get the new system installed ahead of schedule.

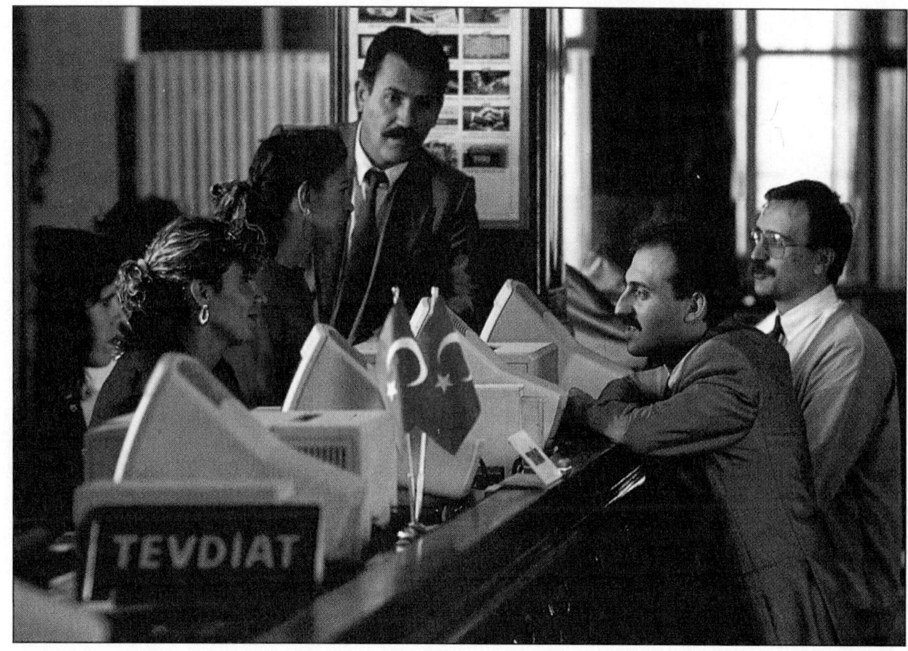

or task. Thus, *time and goal interdependence* creates interactions among groups in organizations.[16]

For example, in many companies engineers in the research department work on long-term projects whose results may not be applied to products or production processes for several months or even years. In contrast, engineers in a production department may be concerned about keeping the machines on the shop floor going to ensure that finished products are shipped on schedule. Although these different time frames are entirely appropriate to the groups' respective tasks, they can brew problems if the two groups have to work together. If the production engineers on the shop floor encounter a metallurgical problem in the machining of a piece of steel, they might call the research department for help. The production engineers expect an immediate solution to the problem so that production can resume. But the research engineers might approach the problem from a scientific point of view and spend hours, days, or even weeks analyzing it and pondering the best possible solution. Thus, while one group of engineers grows frantic for an answer, the other group comes to resent the pressure for a quick but less than ideal "fix."

In this case, the time and goal differences between the two groups are major determinants of the interactions between them. Managers responsible for coordinating diverse groups need to be sensitive to such differences and to resolve them to promote productive interactions.

16. Paul R. Lawrence and Jay W. Lorsch, *Organization and Environment* (Homewood, Ill.: Irwin, 1969), pp. 34–39.

Task Uncertainty

■ **Task uncertainty** occurs when employees or work groups lack information about what course of action to take or about future events that may affect them, the task, or the organization.

Uncertainty is a central problem in complex organizations.[17] **Task uncertainty** arises whenever employees or work groups lack information about what course of action to take or about future events that may affect them, the task, or the organization. Uncertainties may arise from changes in technology, government regulations, competition, supplier conditions, economic conditions, and other factors outside the group's control.

In many cases, work groups deal with task uncertainties in relative isolation, with little interaction from other groups. Sometimes, however, a work group seeks or is given assistance from other groups to help reduce uncertainties.

Consider an operating department that needs new employees. The task involves advertising the positions, recruiting candidates, screening and selecting applicants, and arranging for new employees to be placed on the payroll. The manager knows the duties of the jobs to be filled, but the task also requires being up to date on equal employment opportunity (EEO) and affirmative action regulations, the current labor market, salary ranges, and perhaps the requirements of the company's labor contract and the workings of the internal job-bidding system. For a busy line manager, this task clearly may involve much uncertainty.

Therefore, human resources departments often assist managers of operating departments by providing them with needed information. Without this information, a manager might make decisions that could impede the search for qualified employees. The human resources department can make a special effort to integrate its own activities with those of operating departments, such as assigning a special liaison to help department managers in recruiting, interviewing, and selecting new employees. The liaison's role is primarily to enhance communication between the groups. In this case, the human resource department absorbs some of the manager's uncertainty.[18] In such a situation, the two departments generally interact on a regular basis as long as the need to do so exists.

Task Interdependence

■ **Task interdependence** is the degree to which the activities of individual groups force the groups to depend on one another.

The most powerful basis for interaction among groups in organizations is **task interdependence,** or the degree to which the activities of various groups force them to depend on one another, thereby requiring more coordination to reach organizational goals. The three types of task interdependence—pooled, sequential, and reciprocal—require increasing levels of group interaction.[19]

■ **Pooled interdependence** exists when groups function relatively independently but their combined output contributes to the organization's profitability.

Pooled Interdependence **Pooled interdependence** exists when two or more groups function with relative independence but their aggregated, or combined,

17. James D. Thompson, *Organizations in Action* (New York: McGraw-Hill, 1967) p. 159.
18. Jay R. Galbraith, *Organization Design* (Reading, Mass.: Addison-Wesley, 1977), pp. 152–158.
19. Thompson, *Organizations in Action,* pp. 54–56.

output contributes to the output and profitability of the total organization. This relationship is shown at the top of Figure 8.3. In the automobile manufacturing process, the assembly of interior components occurs separately from the assembly of the remaining parts. It is only near the end of the process that the interior is combined with the body and engine to form the finished product. Thus, the groups that make each separate subassembly are interdependent in that their outputs are pooled.

- **Sequential interdependence** occurs when the outputs of one group become the inputs to another group.

Sequential Interdependence When departments or work groups are **sequentially interdependent,** the outputs of the first group become the inputs to the second group, as shown in the middle sequence of Figure 8.3. In automobile manufacturing, each subassembly group is a series of sequentially interdependent units. For example, the interior may start with metal parts for the frame of the seat. As the frame moves down the line, additional parts such as seat cushions, fabric, padding, and seat belts are added. Thus, outputs of one unit are part of the inputs of another.

FIGURE 8.3
Three Types of Task Interdependence

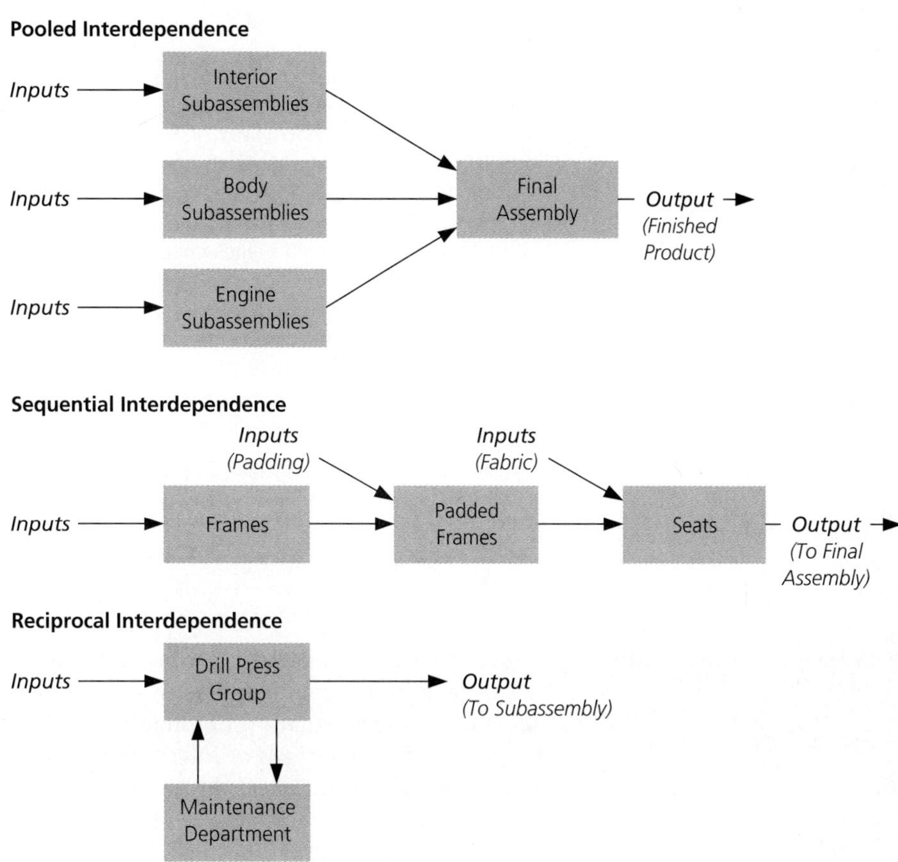

NCR Uses Parallel Engineering and Just-In-Time Inventory Systems

In traditional engineering/manufacturing companies, the typical sequence of operations goes something like this. First, product design engineers design a new product to incorporate technological advance, correct design flaws, or respond to customer needs. Then production engineers develop a production system to manufacture the new product. Next, manufacturing personnel make the product and quality assurance people inspect it to ensure that it meets specifications. Finally, marketing personnel introduce the product to consumers. This process clearly is characterized by sequential interdependence among work groups. However, worldwide competition has placed increasing demand on firms to develop products that do more, cost less, are delivered sooner, and break down less often.

One company that responded to competitive pressure to change its standard product development system was NCR Corp. NCR, formerly National Cash Register Company, makes point-of-sale terminals and transaction document printers. NCR's Atlanta plant, which makes checkout counter terminals, developed a new machine in twenty-two months, less than half the normal time. In addition, the new machine had 85 percent fewer parts and could be assembled in about two minutes. NCR did it by tearing down the walls between the various engineering and manufacturing groups. It placed people from design, purchasing, manufacturing, and field support in adjacent cubicles to allow them to communicate with one another throughout the design and manufacturing processes.

In NCR's point-of-sale terminal plant in Cambridge, Ohio, engineers from design, testing, and manufacturing worked together from the outset of the concept for a new machine. The new model reduced assembly time from thirty minutes to about five minutes and permitted assembly without special tools. The free flow of information across groups facilitated by parallel (or concurrent) engineering has enabled NCR to get better products to market much faster and therefore capitalize on changing technological and market trends.

In another move, NCR instituted a new just-in-time inventory system in its Ithaca, New York, plant. The system required that design, purchasing, and production personnel work closely together to manufacture the product efficiently. The result was greatly speeded-up delivery times.

NCR's use of parallel engineering and just-in-time inventory systems has made formerly sequentially interdependent task groups, and hence its plants, fully interdependent and integrated from design to testing.

SOURCES: "A Smarter Way to Manufacture," *Business Week,* April 30, 1990, pp. 110–117; John H. Sheridan, "An 'Edict' for Excellence," *Industry Week,* August 21, 1989, pp. 35–36; Barbara Darrow, "Engineering Tools That Really Work," *Design News,* August 22, 1988, pp. 54–55.

- **Reciprocal interdependence** exists when the outputs of one group become the inputs to another group and vice versa.

Reciprocal Interdependence **Reciprocal interdependence** occurs when the outputs of one group become inputs to another and vice versa, as in the bottom of Figure 8.3. In such situations, groups are highly interdependent. This is the most complex of the three types of interdependence and the most difficult to manage, because the groups interact constantly. Reciprocal interdependence can be illustrated by the relationships between the drill press group and maintenance groups in automobile production. Both these groups are important to the production of high-quality cars and are subject to compressed schedules created by high demand. Manufacturing provides inputs to the maintenance group in the form of machines needing preventive maintenance. The output of the maintenance group is machines for the manufacturing group to use in production. Therefore, the two groups are in reciprocal interdependence.

Many interacting groups are embedded within most large organizations. In fact, group interactions may be the foundation for an organization's structure.[20] *Management in Action* shows how one firm altered the nature of its key functional groups' interdependence to foster greater cooperation among the groups.

Managing Intergroup Behavior in Organizations

■ Managers can change the ways groups interact by altering the physical arrangements, changing the resource distribution, stressing a superordinate goal, training employees to manage group interactions more effectively, and changing the structure of the organization.

Strategies for dealing with interactions among groups must be carefully chosen, following thorough examination and analysis of the groups, their goals, their unique characteristics, and the organizational setting in which the interactions occur. Managers can use a variety of strategies to increase the efficiency of intergroup interactions. Five such choices are location-based strategies, resource-based strategies, goal-based strategies, people- and group-based strategies, and organization-based strategies. These strategies are based on the model of intergroup behavior presented in Figure 8.2. You may want to review the model before proceeding.

Location-Based Strategies

Physical location is a very simple basis of interaction among groups in organizations. Because groups located near one another tend to interact more than groups that are far apart, the most basic strategy for managing interactions is to examine and consider altering this factor. If the basis for group interaction is largely physical proximity, the interactions may decrease if the distance between the groups is increased. However, the quality of the interactions or the degree of cooperation among the groups may also change. On the other hand, if the physical location of groups is not important to their interactions, altering it may have undesirable effects on the interactions. The groups may find other ways to communicate, such as by telephone or computer hookup, that may be less efficient and more expensive.

Organizations rarely rearrange their employees' locations solely to reduce interactions among certain groups. However, they often shift groups to improve interactions and coordination. In one large manufacturing company, the quality assurance department was moved from the administration building into new

20. Clayton P. Alderfer and Ken K. Smith, "Studying Intergroup Relations Embedded in Organizations," *Administrative Science Quarterly,* March 1982, p. 35.

facilities in the center of the plant so that it would be closer to the groups with which it worked daily. As a result, the interactions and coordination of the QA efforts with production and maintenance departments increased and the department became more effective.

Resource-Based Strategies

Scarcity of resources may make group interactions more complex by requiring that groups share available resources. For example, budgetary constraints may make it impossible for each sales representative to have his or her own assistant; but it may be possible for five representatives to share an assistant. With limited resources, then, the staff members must coordinate their requests for secretarial help. Coordinating their requests may require direct personal interaction, or it may be accomplished by indirect interaction through the assistant.

Management therefore can use resources to regulate interactions. If a lack of resources causes complex interactions between groups, management may take the simple but costly step of increasing resources and, in this case, hire more assistants. Management thus may be able to reduce the complex interactions over secretarial time that cause delays in the preparation of reports and proposals. Conversely, it is possible to increase the complexity of interactions by making organizational resources more scarce (although management seldom seeks this effect deliberately).

Goal-Based Strategies

The five types of interactions discussed earlier—avoidance, accommodation, competition, collaboration, and compromise—may be viewed as goal-based strategies for managing group interactions.[21] Remember that the five types of interactions are based on the compatibility of the groups' goals and the importance of the interaction to achieving those goals.

In a situation in which a manager believes interactions could be improved, the manager should analyze the goals of the groups. For example, when two groups are not working well together, they may be experiencing goal displacement. **Goal displacement** occurs when groups overemphasize their own goals at the expense of the organization's. When two or more groups do this, their activities may interfere with one another.

- **Goal displacement** occurs when groups overemphasize their own goals at the expense of the organization's goals.
- A **superordinate goal** is an organizational goal that is more important to the well-being of the organization and its members than the more specific goals of interacting groups.

The solution to goal displacement is straightforward: The groups need to be redirected toward the overall organizational goals. A **superordinate goal** is usually a goal of the overall organization and is more important to the well-being of the organization and its members than the more specific goals of the groups. It can serve as a guide for integrating the interacting groups by redirecting their activities.

21. Blake, Shepard, and Mouton, *Managing Intergroup Conflict in Industry.*

David Robinson of the San Antonio Spurs and Tyrone Bogues of the Charlotte Hornets are two of the best known players in the NBA. They and their teammates are fierce competitors whenever the two teams take the court to play basketball. However, Robinson and Bogues recently joined forces with several other NBA stars in a program sponsored by McDonald's called the "NBA All-Star Stay in School Jam." The program is designed to keep youngsters from dropping out of school. While winning a basketball game may be important, Robinson, Bogues, and the other participants take part in this program because they also support its goal.

In most organizational situations, however, the problems of interacting groups are not obvious because of the complexity of the circumstances. Groups and their leaders may be too close to the situation, often believing that their progress toward their own goals will further the goals of the organization. In fact, as Figure 8.4 shows, groups generally do pursue organizational goals but may get sidetracked and work at cross-purposes with other groups. At this point, the manager can redirect the efforts of the groups by reminding them of a superordinate goal that all are trying to accomplish for the organization. In effect, the manager reminds the groups of the inherent compatibility of their goals and tries to foster collaborative interaction among them. The use of a superordinate goal to manage interactions can be effective when the groups' tasks are interdependent, as long as the groups really view the goal as superordinate—as important to themselves and to the organization.

In a medium-size manufacturer of computer equipment, the quality assurance group was guilty of goal displacement. Aspiring to be the best QA department in the industry, it designed unnecessarily elaborate testing equipment, established overly rigid inspection requirements, and incurred significant cost overruns. Eventually the group was reminded that the organization's goal was to make a profit by producing quality products at reasonable prices, and it had to work with manufacturing for the good of the organization, not for the glory of the QA department.

Other strategies for managing interactions may follow from an analysis of the situation. For example, if the interacting groups' goals are incompatible and affected little by the interaction, the manager may suggest that the groups avoid one another. Or, if the goals are compatible but affected little by the interaction,

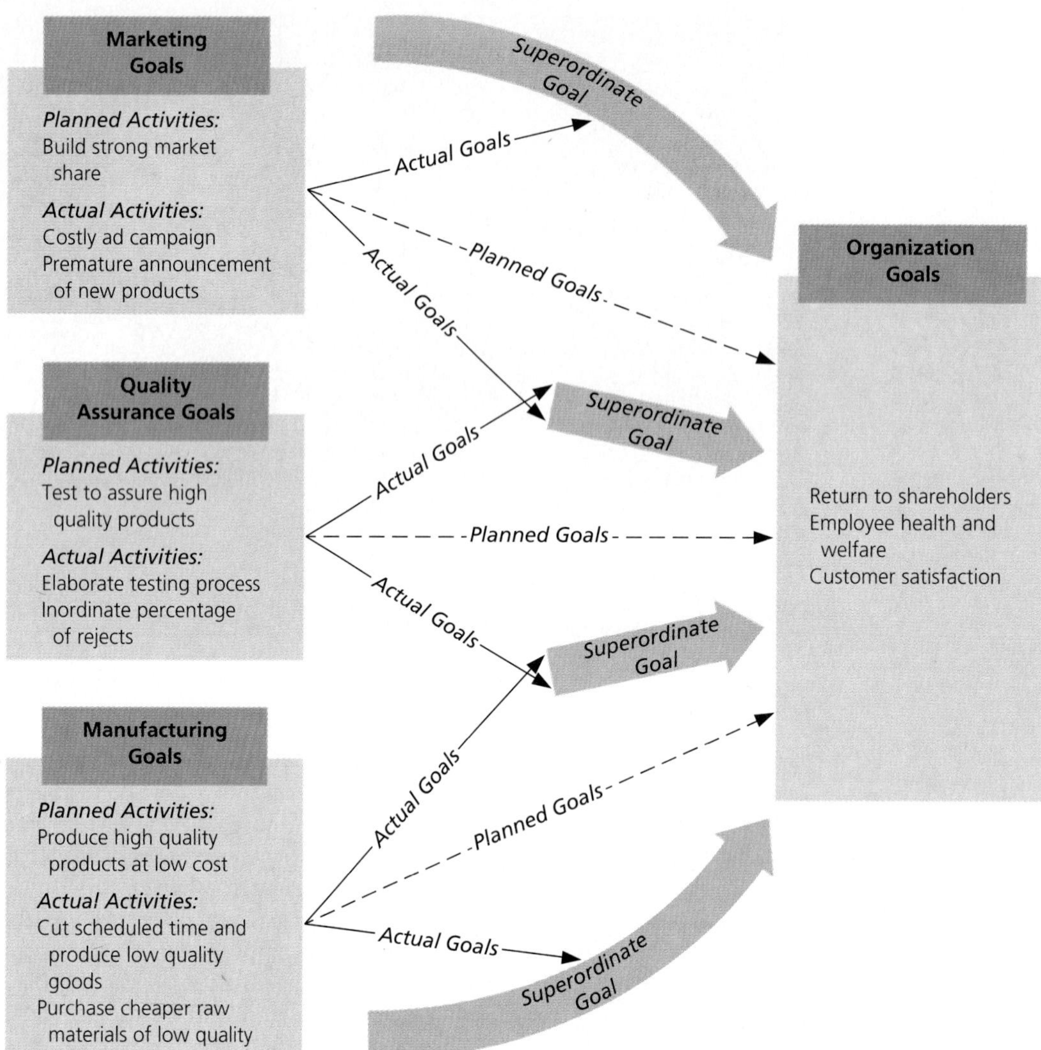

FIGURE 8.4
Goal Displacement and Superordinate Goal

the manager may suggest that one group accommodate another's wishes. Thus, the five types of interactions discussed earlier can be used to manage interactions among groups.

People- and Group-Based Strategies

Individual and group characteristics are a major influence on group interaction in our model. People-based strategies include attempts to train individuals in human relations, organizational practices, or group dynamics. The expectation is that individual behavior in the group interactions will be different after the training.[22] Organizations often hire consultants to develop a training program to teach people how to deal with group interactions. Other types of strategies include techniques intended to alter people's values and attitudes, thus affecting the ways they deal with individuals in other work groups. (Chapter 21 discusses training programs.)

In Chapter 7, we explained group performance in terms of factors such as cohesiveness, size, composition, and norms. These group characteristics, as well as the group's leadership, combine to determine how the group interacts with other groups; they can make a group very antagonistic or very congenial toward other groups. Groupthink (also discussed in Chapters 7 and 16), a mode of thinking in which striving for unanimity replaces critical evaluation of alternatives, can develop in a highly cohesive group that is insulated from expert opinions and whose leader expresses his or her preferred decision. One symptom of groupthink is a stereotypical view of other groups as stupid, slow, or evil, which naturally affects interactions with other groups.[23] Therefore, one strategy for managing a group's interactions with other groups is to effectively manage the internal dynamics of the group such that interactions with other groups become more favorable.

Organization-Based Strategies

There are five organization-based strategies for managing group interactions: linking roles, rules and procedures, task forces, member exchange, and decoupling. Figure 8.5 shows these strategies in order of complexity. The simplest strategy is to create a new position or department that serves a linking role; the most complicated mechanism is the decoupling of interdependent activities.

■ A **linking role** is a position held by a person or group that serves to coordinate the activities of two or more organizational groups.

Linking roles are established in appropriate positions in the organizational hierarchy.[24] A **linking role** is a position for a person or group that serves to coordinate the activities of two or more organizational groups. A neutral third party may serve as a bridge between interacting groups.[25] More formally established positions or groups generally are referred to as *integrating mechanisms* because they bring together groups that have become extremely specialized and hence narrow in their focus.[26] If the interactions among some groups are espe-

22. Pamela S. Shockley-Zalabak, "Current Conflict Management Training: An Examination of Practices in Ten Large American Corporations," *Group & Organizational Studies,* December 1984, pp. 491–508.

23. See Irving L. Janis, *Groupthink,* 2nd ed. (Boston: Houghton Mifflin, 1982), for more discussion of the symptoms of groupthink.

24. Rolf P. Lynton, "Linking an Innovative Subsystem into the System," *Administrative Science Quarterly,* September 1969, pp. 398–416.

25. Robert R. Blake and Jane S. Mouton, "Overcoming Group Warfare," *Harvard Business Review,* November-December 1984, pp. 98–108.

26. Lawrence and Lorsch, *Organization and Environment,* pp. 58–62.

FIGURE 8.5
Organization-Based Strategies for Managing Intergroup Interactions

High Complexity

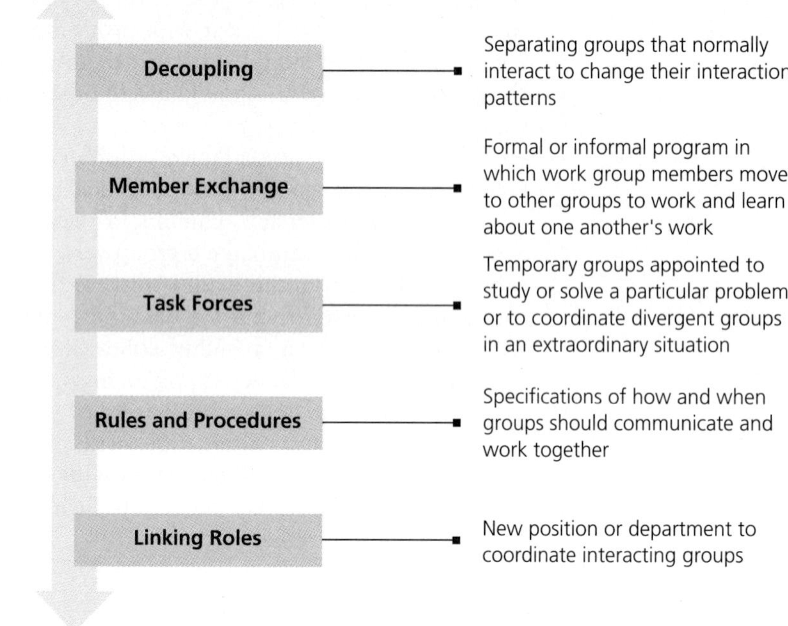
Decoupling
Separating groups that normally interact to change their interaction patterns
Member Exchange
Formal or informal program in which work group members move to other groups to work and learn about one another's work
Task Forces
Temporary groups appointed to study or solve a particular problem or to coordinate divergent groups in an extraordinary situation
Rules and Procedures
Specifications of how and when groups should communicate and work together
Linking Roles
New position or department to coordinate interacting groups

Low Complexity

cially complex or important, management may create a new position to serve as a focal point for interactions, mediating interactions, settling disputes, and resolving conflict. Figure 8.6 shows a simple linking role, the shared supervisor.

A more sophisticated device is the integrating department. Complex interactions may demand a position or department wholly devoted to managing the integration of work groups (see the bottom of Figure 8.6). This position or department may carry titles such as *project management* or *product management*. The role of this linking group is to increase information flow, coordinate the activities of several departments that relate to a product or project, provide interacting groups with better functional understanding of one another, and facilitate intergroup relations and decision making. In many multiproduct companies, a product manager's office coordinates all intergroup activities involved in the production of the company's various products. One person or a small group in the product manager's office is assigned to each product type. The responsible person or group is expected to know the details of every order for that product type and to manage the interactions among the groups in the plant that deal with that product line.

Another organizational method for managing group interactions is to establish *rules and procedures* governing how groups are to deal with one another in certain situations. Groups may be required to interact in highly specific ways; one work group may have to notify another when a certain point is reached in

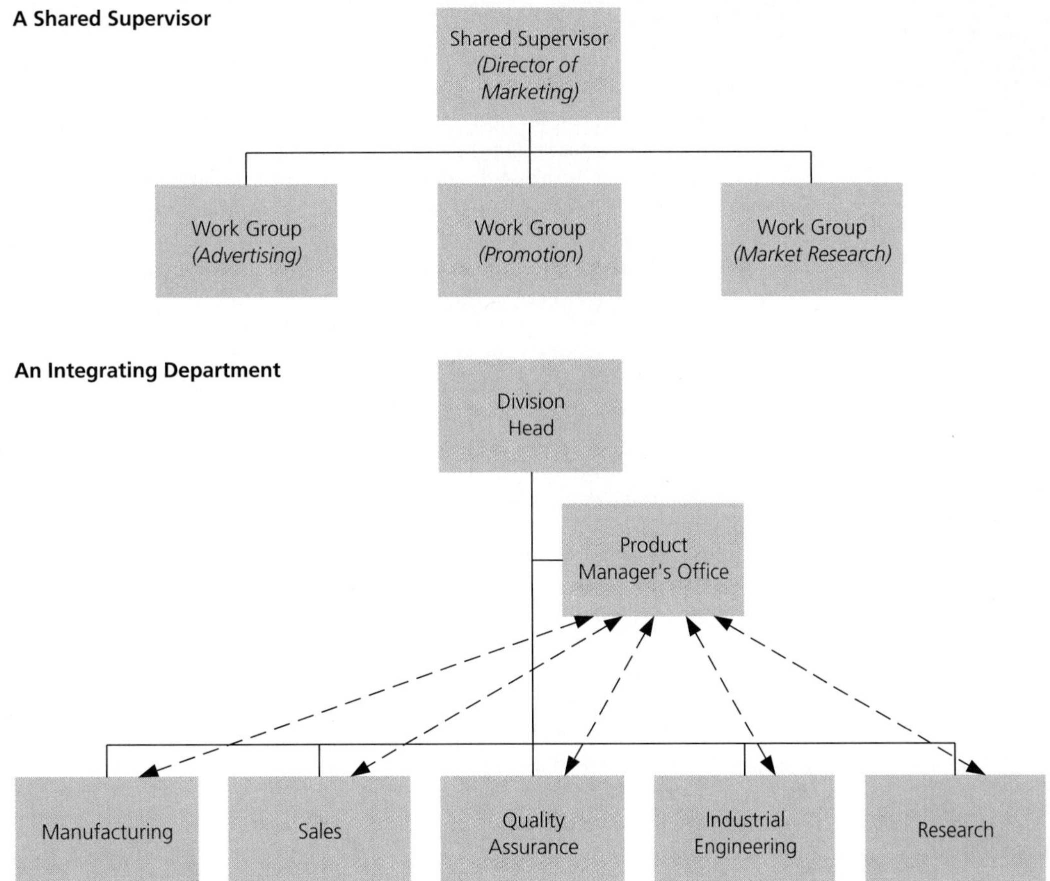

FIGURE 8.6
Organization-Based Strategies: Examples of the Linking Role

a process, or the drafting group may have to have all production drawings approved by quality assurance. Rules may force groups to interact or limit their interaction to prescribed situations. However, where interactions are very dynamic or where there is a high degree of task uncertainty, rules and procedures may be ineffective. Returning to the product manager's office, we might find that the office created a rule to cover recurring situations and solutions. For instance, for one manufacturing process that was experiencing many problems, the product manager's office authorized the quality assurance group to shut down an operation whenever it discovered a manufacturing problem that might affect the field serviceability of certain high-visibility products. The only condition was that the product manager's office had to be notified immediately. Probably the most extreme form of rules and procedures established to coordinate interacting groups is a government constitution. *International Perspective* describes interacting groups in the Soviet Union.

A less permanent way to manage intergroup interactions is to create *task forces* to handle short-term issues. A task force may be formed to study a particular situation or to act as arbitrator or coordinator of group interactions

INTERNATIONAL PERSPECTIVE

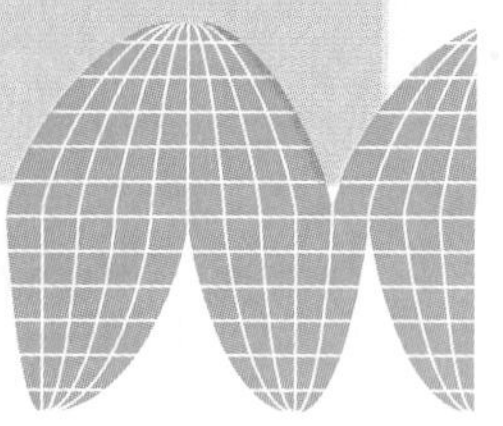

Falling Apart in the Soviet Union

Intergroup interactions do not take place only in for-profit businesses in the Western economies. Governments also must manage the interactions among the various subunits (i.e., states or republics) under their control if they are to function. Typically, there is some type of "constitution" that specifies how the subunits are to interact. Essentially this consists of a set of rules and procedures that define the relationships and interactions among the subunits. It also specifies what both the central government and the states are to do. The Union of Soviet Socialist Republics is one such federation of individual states. However, its central government is losing its hold on the states.

A new revolution is brewing in the Soviet Union. As the Eastern bloc continues to shed itself of communist control and economic reforms sweep Eastern Europe, the once solid Soviet Union appears to be coming apart at the seams. In organizational terms, the interactions among the groups are becoming increasingly hostile. As leader of the central government of the Soviet Union, Mikhail Gorbachev is similar to the president of the United States. The Soviet Union is composed of fifteen republics ranging in size from the huge Russian Republic to the tiny republics of Lithuania and Estonia. Russia is twice the size of the continental United States, covers eleven time zones, and has most of the natural resources of timber, oil, gas, gold, and diamonds. Its leader, Boris Yeltsin, is a former communist party member and an ally of Gorbachev.

The problem is that Russia and other republics, such as the Ukraine, are declaring their independence from the Soviet Union and attempting to establish their own laws, economic systems, and even banks and currency. They believe the economic reforms leading to a free-market system are essential to their survival and must proceed much faster than the central government and Gorbachev are permitting. If they do not get these reforms as quickly as they want, they plan to secede from the Soviet Union.

The situation is so volatile that business leaders around the world are hesitant to make deals with the central government for fear that the individual republics will not follow through. Also, the Soviet Union's credit rating has been downgraded and other governments, wary of a replay of defaulted loans to Latin America, are hesitant to extend credit. Some of the republics are expected to make deals of their own with foreign governments and banks.

Gorbachev has proposed a new treaty for the union that would give the republics more power. However, the independence movement may be moving faster than the new treaty talks. Meanwhile, the economy of the Soviet Union is on the brink of economic collapse and management of the interacting groups has become a hopeless prospect.

SOURCES: "Brother, Would You Lend Moscow a Dime?" *Business Week,* December 10, 1990, pp. 44–45; Paul Hofheinz, "The New Russian Revolution," *Fortune,* November 19, 1990, pp. 127–134; "Lithuania Is One Thing—but a Breakaway Ukraine Is Another," *Business Week,* November 12, 1990, p. 63.

during a particularly busy period or while a permanent solution to an intergroup problem is being studied. A task force generally is appointed by a manager who is higher up in the organizational hierarchy than the members of the interacting groups.

St. Luke's Hospital in Phoenix, Arizona, recently added a new wing of surgical suites and four hundred patient rooms onto its existing building. The expansion required blocking off the main entrance and tearing up the parking

Atlantic Richfield Company is part of the Prudhoe Bay Environmental Alliance, a collection of 20 firms that cooperate in cleaning up the oil field on the North Slope of Alaska. ARCO recently served as the lead company in carrying out this task. The firm created a task force to coordinate the joint efforts of all 20 firms. With the assistance of this linking role, the Alliance gathered over 7,000 tons of reusable scrap metal. The barges shown here are returning the scrap to the United States for recycling.

lot, thus interrupting the normal flow of traffic into and out of the hospital. To minimize disturbance of normal hospital operations, the hospital administrator appointed a task force to coordinate the necessary adjustments. The task force, headed up by the assistant administrator, was made up of one middle-level manager from each affected group in the hospital—nursing, maintenance, food services, clinic, emergency room, and others. The task force worked with the contractor and the various internal departments during each successive phase of construction to control the construction work's impact on hospital operations. Like most task forces, the group disbanded after the new wing was finished.

A more elaborate strategy is to have interacting groups exchange members. *Member exchange* can be a highly formal rotation program[27] or a temporary transfer of an employee from one group to another. An exchange program increases information flow and promotes better understanding among groups. By working in another group, employees may better appreciate the types of problems other groups face in pursuing organizational goals. Many companies have an informal exchange program in which staff project engineers move to positions in other groups. In one typical case, an engineer in the production engineering group went over to the quality assurance department. The move was a lateral one, with the engineer retaining the same title, project engineer, and getting a small raise. As a result of the transfer, coordination and communication between the two departments increased dramatically. The engineer soon understood the concerns of both departments and knew whom to contact on every issue, thus helping the two groups to interact more smoothly and productively.

27. Eric H. Nellsen, "Understanding and Managing Intergroup Conflict," in Jay W. Lorsch and Paul R. Lawrence, eds., *Managing Group and Intergroup Relations* (Homewood, Ill.: Irwin, 1972), pp. 329–343.

■ **Decoupling** occurs when two or more interacting groups are made more independent by separating them in some manner.

The final organizational mechanism for managing intergroup interactions is decoupling.[28] **Decoupling** means that two groups whose tasks require that they interact are functionally separated in some way. Decoupling may be needed when two groups have difficulty interacting positively. In one large manufacturing plant, for example, the drill press group worked on most parts immediately following the milling operation. Since the outputs of the milling group were the inputs to the drill press group, the two groups were sequentially interdependent. Late delivery of parts by the milling group disrupted the drill press group's operations. So on one occasion when the milling group experienced a rash of machine failures, its interactions with the drill press group became less than congenial. The solution to the hostile interactions was to increase the work-in-process inventory between the two groups, thus decoupling them. Future slow-downs in the milling group had little or no effect on the drill press group.

Summary of Key Points

- Five types of group interactions can occur: avoidance, accommodation, competition, collaboration, and compromise. The types of interactions are determined by the compatibility of goals and the importance of the interaction to group goal attainment.
- A model of intergroup dynamics assumes that group interactions reflect certain needs for interaction, occur within a specific organizational setting, and occur among unique groups. The five bases of intergroup interactions determine the characteristics of the interactions, including frequency, the volume of information exchanged, and the type of interaction.
- Interactions among work groups involve some of the most complex relationships in organizations. They are based on five factors: location, resources, time and goal interdependence, task uncertainty, and task interdependence. Being near one another naturally increases groups' opportunities for interactions. If groups use the same or similar resources, or if one group can affect the availability of the resources needed by another group, the potential for frequent interactions increases. The nature of the tasks groups perform further affects the interactions among them through time and goal orientation, the uncertainties of the task, and group interdependencies.
- Strategies for dealing with interactions among groups must be carefully chosen, following thorough examination and analysis of the groups, their goals, their unique characteristics, and the organizational setting in which the interactions occur. Many strategies have been developed for managing group interactions in organizations. They include location-based strategies, resource-based strategies, goal-based strategies, people- and group-based strategies, and organization-based strategies. Location-based strategies use the physical location or the arrangement of desks, offices, or departments to either reduce or promote group interactions. Resource-based strategies

28. Jeffrey Pfeffer, *Organizations and Organization Theory* (Boston: Pitman, 1982), pp. 244–245.

alter resource allocation to either reduce or force more resource sharing among groups. Goal-based strategies include those that might lead to competition, collaboration, compromise, accommodation, or avoidance. People- and group-based strategies focus on the characteristics of the people and the dynamics of the interacting groups. Organization-based strategies range from the creation of simple linking roles and groups to complex decoupling of tasks.

Discussion Questions

1. Two competing athletic teams essentially function like two interacting groups. How would you characterize the teams' interaction in terms of goal importance and goal compatibility?
2. Some researchers have asserted that people, not groups, interact and that interpersonal interactions, not group interactions, therefore should be the focus of study for group dynamics. Do you agree or disagree with this point of view? Why?
3. List four groups to which you belong that recently were involved in interactions with another group or groups. Describe the interactions in terms of the five bases of intergroup behavior discussed in the chapter.
4. If any of the interacting groups you discussed in question 3 are related by task interdependence, discuss which type of interdependence exists—pooled, sequential, or reciprocal.
5. How do the group performance factors of cohesiveness, group norms, composition, and leadership affect the interactions among groups you discussed in question 3?
6. Each group you listed in question 3 probably has different goals. Give a brief statement describing each group's goals. Compare these goals to the goals of the groups with which each interacts. Are the goals compatible? How important are the goals in terms of the interactions? Which of the five types of interactions are represented by the groups to which you belong?
7. The five strategies for managing intergroup interactions differ in the situations in which they are appropriate as well as in the amount of money, time, and effort required to implement them. How might each of these be applied in the interactions discussed in questions 3 through 6?
8. It would be a lot simpler if there were one strategy for managing intergroup interactions. Why doesn't an all-encompassing strategy exist?

CASE 8.1

A Special Type of Intergroup Relations at U-Haul

In 1945, L. S. Shoen started renting trucks and trailers to people moving from one town to another. Shoen's gray and orange U-Haul rental truck eventually came to be seen as an American symbol of do-it-yourself independence. However, recent highly publicized squabbles in the family-run organization are threatening that image.

As Shoen's rental empire grew, so did his children's involvement. After starting at the bottom doing jobs such as cleaning and painting the trucks, Shoen's twelve children worked their way up through the company. By the 1970s, Shoen had given 88% of the company stock to his children.

After decades of growth and industry dominance, economic and competitive pressures in the mid-1970s forced the company into hard times. Shoen's proposed solution was to diversify the business to include general rentals—offering everything from tools and home-care equipment to recreational equipment. Unfortunately, several members of the family did not agree with this risky venture and the family began to splinter. One group, headed by Shoen and his son Sam, supported the diversification efforts; the dissident group, headed by Shoen's son Joe, pushed for a back-to-basics strategy. As investment, maintenance, and replacement costs further eroded company profits, family tensions increased.

In 1985, angered by the dissident group's lack of support and interest in his efforts, Shoen fired seven of his children from the board of Amerco, U-Haul's holding company. But in 1986 the dissident group plotted revenge: they used their stock power to force Shoen into retirement. The board then made Sam president of U-Haul and appointed Joe chairman of the larger Amerco.

The two brothers and their respective factions soon began to squabble over differences in strategy. Sam's group insisted that U-Haul continue their father's diversification plans and, for a while, the company's financial picture supported them. Initial investment costs were behind them, interest rates were lower, rental prices were higher, earnings were up. But Joe's group continued to push for upgrading the aging fleet of trucks and focusing on the moving market. Sam was willing to compromise and paid out $410 million to upgrade the fleet. But this was not enough of a commitment for Joe, who wanted to spend $1 billion more. Sam insisted this would make the company debt too high. But Joe finally wore Sam down, and Sam quit the company in 1987.

Even with Sam out of the company, the fires of disagreement continued to rage. As profits rose, Joe and the other family members who managed the company barred Sam and his group from membership on the board of directors, arguing that open board membership would weaken the company's resolve to stay on course. Those in charge of the company believed the other siblings should be satisfied with the company's growing financial health. But Sam and his supporters began to believe it would be in the family's best financial interest to sell Amerco. Since the fall of 1988 to this writing, the factions have been waging a legal battle over company ownership and strategy.

Case Questions

1. How would you characterize the intergroup relations between the two groups at U-Haul?
2. Describe the basis for this intergroup interaction.
3. What type of management strategies for managing intergroup interactions might work for this situation?

SOURCES: "A Murder in the U-Haul Family," *Time,* August 20, 1990, p. 49; Dana Nunn, "Hired Gun Suspected in Slaying," *Grand Junction Daily Sentinel,* August 7, 1990, p. 1; "U-Haul Founder's Children Slug it Out at Meeting," *USA Today,* March 7, 1989,

p. 3b; "The Family That Hauls Together Brawls Together," *Business Week,* August 29, 1988, pp. 64–66; Brent Whiting, "U-Haul Feud Termed 'Bad Dream': Top Executive Blames Lawsuit on 'Confusion,'" *Arizona Republic,* August 9, 1988, p. B6; Brent Whiting, "Family Battles for Control of U-Haul: Founder's Faction Sues to Stop Kin from Staging 'Coup,' " *Arizona Republic,* August 4, 1988, p. C1; "A New Generation Takes the Wheel at U-Haul," *Business Week,* March 28, 1988, p. 57; "U-Haul Hits the Skids," *Newsweek,* September 14, 1987, pp. 54–55; Jan Par, "King Lear," *Forbes,* February 23, 1987, p. 84.

CASE 8.2 Seeing Where the Other Half Works

Shaun Somers was a graduate student in history at Crozet State University. Like most history graduate students at Crozet, Somers was given a teaching assistantship to help him pay his tuition. For $800 a semester, Shaun and Professor Menster's other t.a.'s attended all of Professor Menster's lectures on Mondays and Wednesdays. On Fridays, each t.a. led a discussion section. Besides preparing the topics for discussion, the t.a.'s were expected to help the students in their sections write their papers and to grade both papers and exams. So along with their $800, the teaching assistants were given offices on the third floor of the history building.

Everyone who had an office on the third floor called it "the ghetto"; three or four t.a.'s shared small offices, and the big ones were partitioned into a half-dozen small cubicles. Since the building had no elevators, everyone had to walk the three flights up, arriving at the top out of breath, to be greeted by the buckets perpetually lined up on the landing to catch leaks from the roof above.

Conversations between t.a.'s in the ghetto tended to begin with complaints about the offices and move on to how boring the professors were, how insensitive the administration was, how little anyone in the department did to make the graduate students feel welcome. The third-floor group was a tight little society whose members were happy with one another but bitter and jealous of everyone else in the building. "Us" was everyone on the third floor; "them" was anyone on the floors below. "They" all had more power, respect, pay, and space than "we" had.

At the start of his second year, Somers received a surprise in his mailbox: He had been moved down to the first floor to share an office with a new assistant professor. Complaints about the overcrowding in "the ghetto" apparently had reached the fire marshall, who had put a cap on the number of people the department could cram into the third-floor offices.

Somers's first meeting with his new officemate was awkward. He felt nervous and defensive, sure that this new professor would resent having to share an office. He was ready to say, "Yeah, I'm a graduate student, what of it?" But his officemate, Bill Peters, actually seemed glad to have Somers around. "You can show me the ropes," Peters said.

Somers did not use his new office much for the first few weeks of the semester, preferring to visit his friends on the third floor. But gradually he came to like Peters and hoped to get a new perspective on the department through talking to him. He had never realized how small assistant professors' salaries were or how much pressure they were under to do everything right—teach, publish, spend hours on committee work. Through Peters, Somers met other new assistant professors and began going out to lunch with them. Through their eyes, Somers began to see the life of a graduate student as relatively carefree. They were not making any money, but they also had relatively few responsibilities and did not have to worry about "real" jobs until they graduated.

Because of their friendship, Peters and Somers began to draw together two groups that had never paid attention to each other's existence. New junior faculty members went to graduate student parties and then returned the invitation. The groups found they had much in common, especially the feelings of being at the bottom of a rigid hierarchy and getting no respect from anyone. By the end of the year, the ghetto was still the ghetto, but it was no longer "the only place in the building a faculty member has never seen." The chair of the department was so pleased with the positive interactions between graduate students and junior faculty that he considered moving Somers into his own office the following semester to see if senior faculty too could be brought into the act.

Case Questions

1. What factors would be likely to draw graduate students and new professors together? What factors would keep them apart?
2. Would the department chair be wise to mix graduate students and junior and senior faculty members in future office assignments?
3. How might the lessons learned about graduate students and new professors be applied to the situation where a new worker joins a company and finds similar barriers to interaction? How would the location of the new person's office affect her or his assimilation into the normal work activities?

EXPERIENTIAL EXERCISE

Purpose: This exercise will help you recognize the complexities of intergroup dynamics.

Format: Your objective in this exercise is to earn as much money as possible. There will be eight decision situations, or rounds. Your group will earn positive and negative points based on your decisions in each round. Each point is worth a $100,000 profit or loss.

Procedure: The class will divide into four teams of approximately equal size. Your instructor will provide each team with a red card, a blue card, and an envelope. In each round, your team will have three minutes to choose either red or blue. Indicate your decision by placing the appropriate card in the envelope and handing it to the instructor.

When everyone is ready, the instructor will direct the teams to begin the three-minute deliberation period for the first decision. At the end of the period, the instructor will announce each team's decision and record it on the tally sheet. Points are assigned according to the payoff table, which follows. The instructor will then announce the beginning of the next three-minute deliberation period and return the cards and envelopes to the teams.

At three different times during the exercise, designated representatives of the teams will have an opportunity to meet for three minutes. The meetings should take place just outside the classroom. The representatives may discuss anything they wish at the meetings, but they may talk only among themselves. There should be no communication among teams other than during the meetings of the representatives. Note that point values are greater for rounds preceded by the meetings.

After the eight rounds, the profits and losses of each team will be totaled and displayed. Positive points are profits, and negative points are losses.

Payoff Table

In each round, the point payoffs for each team are as follows:

4 Blue, 0 Red	All four teams receive +2 points each.
3 Blue, 1 Red	Teams choosing Blue receive −4 points each, and the teams choosing Red receives + 4 points
2 Blue, 2 Red	Teams choosing Blue receive −6 points each, and teams choosing Red receive + 6 points each.
1 Blue, 3 Red	The teams choosing Blue receive +4 points, and the teams choosing Red receive −4 points each.
0 Blue, 4 Red	All four teams receive −2 points each.

Tally Sheet

	Choices				*Round Points*				*Cumulative Points*			
Round	*1*	*2*	*3*	*4*	*1*	*2*	*3*	*4*	*1*	*2*	*3*	*4*
1												
2												
3*												
4												
5												
6**												
7												
8***												

*Representatives meet for three minutes before team decisions for third round. Point values are multiplied by 2 for this round.

**Representatives meet for three minutes before teams decisions for the sixth round. All point values are multiplied by 3 for this round.

***Representatives meet for three minutes before teams decisions for the last round. All points are multiplied by 4 for this round.

Follow-up Questions

1. Did some of the teams have positive points and some negative? Did the participants figure out how all teams could have received positive points?
2. What would have happened if the teams had viewed themselves as subgroups of a larger organization with an organizational goal of maximizing the total profits for the organization?
3. What factor is most necessary for these teams to work together?

CHAPTER OUTLINE

The Nature of Leadership

A Definition of Leadership

A Framework of Leadership Perspectives

Early Approaches to Leadership

Trait Approaches to Leadership

Behavioral Approaches to Leadership

The Contingency Theory of Leadership

Basic Premises

Situational Favorableness

Scientific Evidence

The Path-Goal Theory of Leadership

Basic Premises

Scientific Evidence

The Vroom-Yetton-Jago Model of Leadership

Basic Premises

Scientific Evidence

Other Contemporary Approaches to Leadership

The Vertical-Dyad Linkage Model

The Life Cycle Theory

Leadership Substitutes

Transformational Leadership

Charismatic Leadership

Leadership as Symbolic Action

Attributional Perspectives

9

Leadership in Organizations

CHAPTER OBJECTIVES

After studying this chapter, you should be able to:

Describe the general nature of leadership.

Summarize early approaches to leadership.

Describe the contingency theory.

Explain the path-goal theory.

Describe the Vroom-Yetton-Jago model.

Identify and summarize other contemporary approaches to leadership.

It is difficult to imagine a more delicate situation than being engaged in a power struggle with the individual who founded the company, who is chair of the board of directors, and who hired you. But that is exactly what John Sculley faced in his showdown with Steve Jobs at Apple Computer. To the amazement of many, Sculley won.

The charismatic Jobs, co-founder of Apple, realized as the firm grew that he lacked the professional management skills necessary for running a big business. In 1983 he hired Sculley, an executive with PepsiCo, to serve as Apple's president. Jobs remained as chair but spent much of his time developing the Macintosh computer.

At first, everything worked fine. But gradually tension between the two men arose. The board of directors began to realize that a confrontation was inevitable. The board also realized that it was Sculley, not Jobs, who held the key to Apple's future. Accordingly, after a long and bitter battle, Jobs was forced out and Sculley took complete command.

In the intervening years, Apple has had its ups (mostly) and downs (rarely). At first, Sculley had to work hard to overcome internal resentment at Jobs's departure. But he weathered that storm and now is a respected and effective leader in one of the most turbulent and dynamic industries in the world.[1]

John Sculley is a manager. He is also a highly effective leader. This combination allows him to function successfully in the top spot of a major corporation. The mystique of leadership is one of the most widely debated, studied, and sought-after commodities of organizational life.[2] Managers talk about the characteristics that make an effective leader, and organizational scientists have extensively researched the same issue. Unfortunately, neither group has definitively answered the many questions concerning leadership.

---

1. "Computer Firm's Chief Faces Slowing Growth, Discord in the Ranks," *The Wall Street Journal,* February 15, 1990, pp. A1, A4; Brian O'Reilly, "Apple Computer's Risky Revolution," *Fortune,* May 8, 1989, pp. 75–83; Bro Uttal, "Behind the Fall of Steve Jobs," *Fortune,* August 5, 1985, pp. 20–24.

2. Bernard M. Bass, *Bass and Stogdill's Handbook of Leadership,* 3rd ed. (Riverside, N.J.: Free Press, 1990). See also James R. Meindl and Sanford B. Ehrlich, "The Romance of Leadership and the Evaluation of Organizational Performance," *Academy of Management Review,* January 1987, pp. 91–109.

In some situations, the leader has no significant effect on the organization. In others, the leader makes the difference between enormous success and overwhelming failure. Some leaders are effective in one organization but not in others. Other leaders succeed no matter where they are. Despite hundreds of studies on leadership, however, researchers cannot fully explain these inconsistencies. Why, then, should we study leadership? First, leadership is of great practical importance to organizations. Second, researchers have isolated and verified some variables that influence leadership effectiveness.[3]

We begin this chapter with a discussion of the meaning of leadership, including a definition of the concept and a framework of leadership perspectives. Then we turn to historical views of leadership, focusing on the trait and behavioral approaches. Next, we examine three leadership theories that have formed the basis for most leadership research: the contingency theory initiated by Fiedler, the path-goal theory, and the Vroom-Yetton-Jago model. We conclude by describing a number of contemporary perspectives on leadership.

The Nature of Leadership

- Management and leadership are distinct elements. Management involves formal position power, whereas leadership relies on social influence processes.

Before we define *leadership*, we need to make two key distinctions. First, management and leadership are not the same. Management relies on formal position power to influence people, whereas leadership stems from social influence processes. Thus, a person may be a manager, a leader, or both. A leader can also be formal—someone appointed to head a group—or informal—one who emerges from the ranks of the group according to a consensus of the members.

A Definition of Leadership

- **Leadership** is both a process and a property. As a process, leadership involves the use of noncoercive influence. As a property, leadership is the set of characteristics attributed to someone who is perceived to use influence successfully.

Many definitions of *leadership* have been offered, but none has won wide acceptance.[4] We will define **leadership** in terms of both process and property. As a process, leadership is the use of noncoercive influence to direct and coordinate the activities of group members toward goal accomplishment. As a property, leadership is the set of characteristics attributed to those who are perceived to use such influence successfully.[5] From an organizational viewpoint, leadership is vital because it has such a powerful influence on individual and group behavior. Moreover, because the goal toward which the group directs its efforts is the desired goal of the leader, it may or may not mesh with organizational goals.

3. Ralph M. Stogdill, *Handbook of Leadership* (New York: Free Press, 1974). See also Bass, *Bass and Stogdill's Handbook of Leadership.*

4. Ibid.

5. Arthur G. Jago, "Leadership: Perspectives in Theory and Research," *Management Science,* March 1982, pp. 315–336.

Leadership involves neither force nor coercion. A manager who relies on force to direct subordinates' behaviors is not exercising leadership.[6] Thus, as noted earlier, a manager or supervisor may or may not also be a leader. It is important to note too that the set of characteristics attributed to a leader may be characteristics that the individual really possesses, but they may also be ones that he or she is merely *perceived* to possess.

A Framework of Leadership Perspectives

Leadership theory has its base in several perspectives. Arthur Jago developed a framework for organizing the predominant leadership perspectives.[7] The framework consists of two dimensions: focus and approach.

- Some leadership approaches focus on traits, whereas others focus on behaviors.

Focus refers to the decision of whether to view leadership as a set of traits (*trait perspective*) or as a set of behaviors (*behavioral perspective*). Those working from the trait perspective see leadership primarily in terms of relatively stable and enduring individual characteristics. In other words, leaders are believed to have certain innate characteristics that are important for leader effectiveness.[8] On the other hand, supporters of the behavioral perspective focus on observable leader behaviors—the actions of the leader—rather than on inherent, unobservable traits.[9]

- Some leadership approaches take a universal perspective; others use a contingency perspective.

The second dimension of Jago's framework is *approach*. This dimension defines whether a universal or contingency perspective is adopted. The *universal perspective* assumes that there is "one best way" to lead, that effective leadership always conforms to this ideal, and that effective leadership in one situation or organization will also be effective in a different situation or organization. The *contingency perspective* assumes that the situation in which leadership is exercised is crucial. Because effective leadership depends on the situation, leadership is contingent on situational factors.

When combined, the two dimensions yield the four perspectives on leadership shown in Table 9.1. From a Type I perspective, leadership is a set of traits possessed by the effective leader in any group or organizational context. Early research on leadership, referred to as *trait theories,* took this perspective. From a Type II viewpoint, leadership is a set of behaviors displayed by the effective leader, again in any group or organizational setting. The Michigan and Ohio State studies, to be described shortly, were based on this perspective. The Type III perspective assumes that leadership traits vary with the situation. Fiedler's contingency model represents this view. Leadership from a Type IV perspective is a set of behaviors that are contingent on the situation. The path-goal theory and the Vroom-Yetton-Jago model illustrate this perspective.

---

6. Jay A. Conger, "Leadership: The Art of Empowering Others," *Academy of Management Executive,* August 1989, pp. 17–24.
7. Jago, "Leadership: Perspectives in Theory and Research."
8. Gary A. Yukl, *Leadership in Organizations,* 2nd ed. (Englewood Cliffs, N.J.: Prentice-Hall, 1989).
9. Ibid.

TABLE 9.1
A Framework of Leadership Perspectives

		Approach	
		Universal	***Contingent***
Focus	***Leader Traits***	*Type I* Trait Theories	*Type III* Fiedler's Contingency Model
	Leader Behaviors	*Type II* Michigan Studies Ohio State Studies	*Type IV* Path-Goal Theory Vroom-Yetton-Jago Model

SOURCE: Arthur G. Jago, "Leadership Perspectives in Theory and Research," *Management Science*, vol. 22, 1982, p. 316. Used by permission.

Early Approaches to Leadership

Although leaders and leadership have profoundly influenced the course of human events, it was not until the twentieth century that scientific research on leadership began. The first efforts examined traits, or personal characteristics, of leaders. This line of inquiry failed to produce consistent findings and occasionally degenerated into absurd speculation. Thus, the second phase of research turned to leader behaviors.

Trait Approaches to Leadership

■ The **trait approach** to leadership attempted to identify stable and enduring traits that differentiated effective leaders from nonleaders.

The earliest leadership researchers believed that leaders such as Lincoln, Napoleon, Hitler, and Gandhi had some unique set of qualities, or traits, that distinguished them from their peers and were presumed relatively stable and enduring. Following this **trait approach**, these researchers focused on identifying leadership traits, developing techniques for measuring them, and using the techniques to select leaders.[10]

Hundreds of studies guided by this research agenda were conducted during the first several decades of this century. The earliest writers believed that important leadership traits might include intelligence, dominance, self-confidence, energy, activity, and task-relevant knowledge. The results of ensuing studies gave rise to a long list of additional traits. Unfortunately, the list quickly became so long that its practical value was dubious. In addition, the results of many studies were inconsistent. For example, some found that effective leaders tended to be taller than ineffective leaders, whereas others came to the opposite conclusion. Some writers even suggested leadership traits based on body shape, astrological sign, or handwriting characteristics. The trait approach also had a significant theoretical problem: It could neither specify nor prove how presumed leadership

10. Bass, *Bass and Stogdill's Handbook of Leadership.*

INTERNATIONAL PERSPECTIVE

Stormin' Norman Hits a Home Run

How would you feel about placing an aging, overweight manager with a hair-trigger temper and a thin skin for criticism in charge of one of the most complex organizations ever created? Many observers were openly critical of George Bush's appointment of General H. Norman Schwarzkopf as commander-in-chief of allied military operations during the Persian Gulf war. And much of their criticism was based on the precise traits noted above.

In retrospect, however, Schwarzkopf proved to be the perfect choice for the job. He adroitly handled a military force composed of armies from dozens of different cultures. His subordinates placed their complete and total faith in his abilities and decisions. He justified their trust by plotting a truly brilliant military campaign. And the media grew to respect Schwarzkopf as a compassionate, down-to-earth, and honest leader.

After the surprisingly easy military victory in early 1991, popular opinion of many American leaders—George Bush and James Baker, for example—skyrocketed. But Schwarzkopf's star was among the brightest. In his home state of Florida a grassroots movement to draft him as a senatorial candidate was started. And many American business leaders stated that Schwarzkopf would be a marvelous CEO or director.

What qualities led to this enormous approval? One was the high quality nature of the decisions he made. Another was the fact that he genuinely was concerned about the human life that was involved—on both sides of the border. And finally, Schwarzkopf was a great communicator who presented the facts in a simple, occasionally humorous, and always direct way.

SOURCES: "Schwarzkopf for President," *Newsweek,* April 1, 1991, p. 24; "A Soldier of Conscience," *Newsweek,* March 11, 1991, p. 32–34; "General's Command Performance Has Corporate America in a Swoon," *The Wall Street Journal,* March 1, 1991, p. B1.

traits are connected to leadership per se.[11] *International Perspective* provides a good example of just how wrong trait-based predictions can be!

Behavioral Approaches to Leadership

- The **behavioral approach** to leadership tried to identify behaviors that differentiated effective leaders from nonleaders.

In the late 1940s, some researchers began to shift away from the trait approach and to look at leadership as an observable process or activity. The goal of this **behavioral approach** was to determine what behaviors are associated with effective leadership. The researchers assumed that the behaviors of effective leaders differed somehow from the behaviors of less effective leaders and that the behaviors of effective leaders would be the same across all situations. The behavioral approach to the study of leadership included the Michigan studies, the Ohio State studies, and the leadership grid.

11. See Walter Kiechel III, "Beauty and the Managerial Beast," *Fortune,* November 10, 1986, pp. 201–203, for an interesting discussion about leadership traits.

This naval officer is practicing job-centered behavior as she instructs her subordinates in exactly what they are to do and how they are to do it. Even though subsequent models of leadership point out that leader behavior is more complex than originally described by the Michigan Studies, leader behaviors similar to this job-centered approach are still commonly described in new models of leadership.

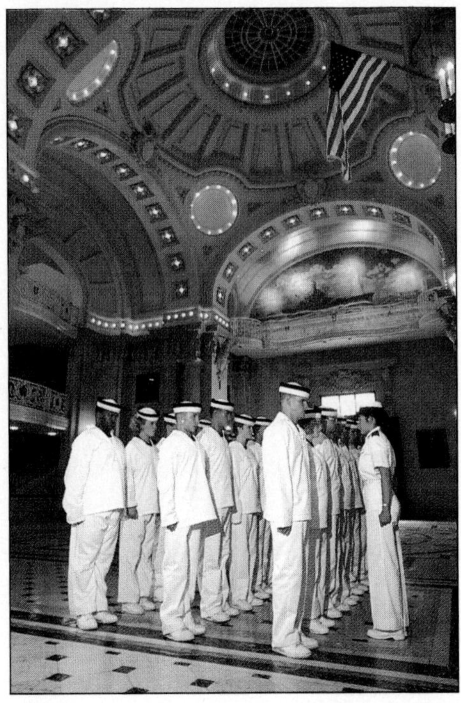

- The **Michigan leadership studies** defined job-centered and employee-centered leadership as opposite ends of a single leadership dimension.

The Michigan Studies The **Michigan leadership studies** were a program of research on leadership behavior conducted at the University of Michigan under the direction of Rensis Likert.[12] The goal was to determine the pattern of leadership behavior that results in effective group performance. From interviews with supervisors and subordinates of high- and low-productivity groups in several organizations, the researchers collected and analyzed descriptions of supervisory behavior to determine how effective supervisors differed from ineffective ones. Two basic forms of leader behavior were identified—job-centered and employee-centered—as shown in the top portion of Figure 9.1.

The leader who exhibits *job-centered leader behavior* pays close attention to the work of subordinates, explains work procedures, and is interested mainly in performance. The leader's main concern is efficient completion of the task. The leader who engages in *employee-centered leader behavior* attempts to develop a cohesive work group to ensure that employees are basically satisfied with their jobs. The leader's main concern is the well-being of subordinates. These two styles of leader behavior were presumed to be at opposite ends of a single dimension. Thus, a leader was thought to exhibit either job-centered or employee-centered leader behavior, but not both.

12. Rensis Likert, *New Patterns of Management* (New York: McGraw-Hill, 1961).

FIGURE 9.1
Early Behavioral Approaches to Leadership

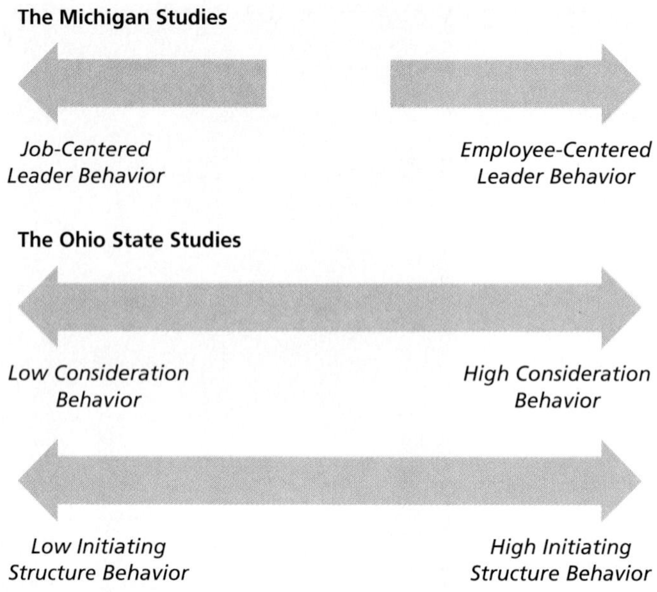

■ The **Ohio State leadership studies** defined leader consideration and initiating structure behaviors as independent dimensions of leadership.

The Ohio State Studies The **Ohio State leadership studies** were conducted about the same time as the Michigan studies (in the late 1940s and early 1950s).[13] Researchers at Ohio State University developed a questionnaire, which they administered in both military and industrial settings, to assess subordinates' perceptions of their leaders' behavior. The Ohio State studies also identified two major forms of leadership behavior: consideration and initiating structure.

When engaging in *consideration behavior*, the leader is concerned with the subordinates' feelings and respects subordinates' ideas. The leader-subordinate relationship is characterized by mutual trust, respect, and two-way communication. When using *initiating-structure behavior*, on the other hand, the leader clearly defines the leader-subordinate roles so that subordinates know what is expected of them. The leader also establishes channels of communication and determines the methods for accomplishing the group's task.

Unlike the employee-centered and job-centered leader behaviors, consideration and initiating structure were not thought to be located on the same behavioral dimension. Instead, as shown in the bottom portion of Figure 9.1, they were seen as independent dimensions. As a result, a leader could exhibit high initiating structure and low consideration or low initiating structure and high consideration. A leader could also exhibit high or low levels of each behavior simultaneously. For example, a leader may clearly define subordinate's roles and expectations but exhibit little concern for their feelings. Alternatively, she or he may be concerned about subordinate's feelings but fail to define roles and expectations clearly. Finally, the leader may do both or neither.

13. Edwin Fleishman, E. F. Harris, and H. E. Burtt, *Leadership and Supervision in Industry* (Columbus, Ohio: Bureau of Educational Research, Ohio State University, 1955).

The Ohio State researchers also investigated the stability of leader behaviors over time. They found that a given individual's leadership pattern appeared to change little as long as the situation remained fairly constant.[14] They also looked at the combinations of initiating-structure and consideration behaviors that were related to effectiveness. At first, they believed that leaders who exhibit high levels of both behaviors would be most effective. An early study at International Harvester (now Navistar), however, found that employees of supervisors who ranked high on initiating structure were higher performers but also expressed lower levels of satisfaction. Conversely, employees of supervisors who ranked high on consideration had lower performance ratings but also had fewer absences from work.[15] Later research, however, showed that these conclusions were misleading because the studies did not consider all the important variables. In other words, contingency variables limit the extent to which consistent and uniform relationships exist between leader behaviors and subordinate responses.

- The **Leadership Grid**® evaluates leader behavior along two dimensions, concern for production and concern for people. It suggests that effective leadership styles include high levels of both behaviors.

The Leadership Grid The **Leadership Grid**® was developed by Robert R. Blake and Jane Srygley Mouton as a framework for examining types of leadership.[16] As Figure 9.2 shows, the grid consists of two dimensions. The first dimension is *concern for production*. A manager's concern for production is rated along a nine-point scale, where 9 represents high concern and 1 indicates low concern. A manager who has high concern for production is task oriented and focuses on getting results, or accomplishing the mission. The second dimension is *concern for people*, also rated on a nine-point scale with 9 for high and 1 for low. As might be expected, a manager who has a high concern for people avoids conflict and strives for friendly relations with subordinates.

The two dimensions are integrated to form the grid. This grid, in turn, identifies an array of possible leader behaviors. Blake and Mouton suggested that the 9,9 position (in the upper right-hand corner of the grid) is the most effective leadership style; that is, a manager who has a high concern for both people and production simultaneously will be the most effective leader.

These behavioral models and theories attracted considerable attention from researchers, but unfortunately further research revealed significant weaknesses.[17] The behavioral approaches were valuable for identifying important leader behaviors and freeing leadership research from the traditional trait theory approach. However, in trying to specify a set of leader behaviors effective in all situations, the studies overlooked the enormous complexities of individual behavior in organizational settings. In the end, they all failed to identify universal

---

14. See Edwin A. Fleishman, "Twenty Years of Consideration and Structure," in Edwin A. Fleishman and James G. Hunt, eds., *Current Developments in the Study of Leadership* (Carbondale, Ill.: Southern Illinois University Press, 1973), pp. 1–40.

15. Fleishman, Harris, and Burtt, *Leadership and Supervision in Industry.*

16. See Robert R. Blake and Anne Adams McCanse, *Leadership Dilemmas—Grid Solutions* (Houston: Gulf, 1991); Robert R. Blake and Jane S. Mouton, *The Managerial Grid* (Houston: Gulf, 1964).

17. See Yukl, *Leadership in Organizations.*

FIGURE 9.2
The Leadership Grid®

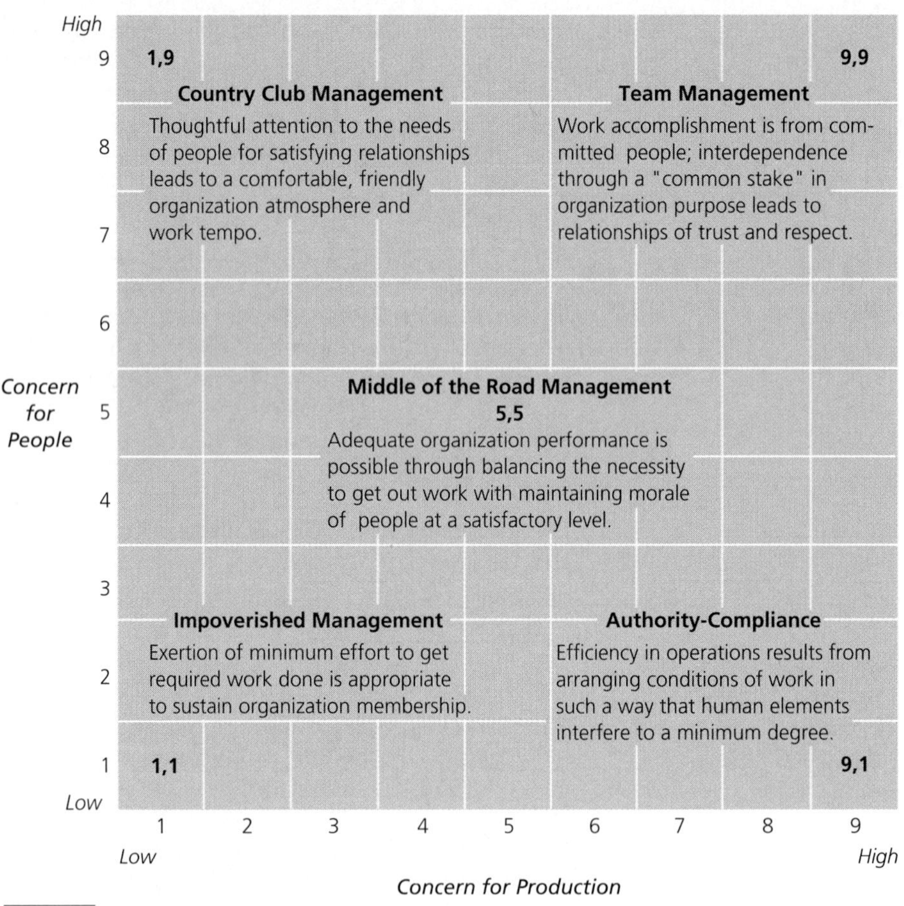

SOURCE: The Leadership Grid® Figure from *Leadership Dilemmas—Grid Solutions* by Robert R. Blake and Anne Adams McCanse. Houston: Gulf Publishing Company, p. 29. Copyright © 1991 by Scientific Methods, Inc. Reproduced by permission of the owners.

leader-behavior/follower-response relationships. A different approach was needed to accommodate the complexities of leadership, and the contingency theory was advanced for just this purpose.

The Contingency Theory of Leadership

■ The **contingency theory of leadership** suggests that a leader's effectiveness depends on the situation.

The **contingency theory of leadership** was developed by Fred Fiedler to do justice to both the leader's personality and the complexities of the situation.[18] The

18. See Fred E. Fiedler, *A Theory of Leadership Effectiveness* (New York: McGraw-Hill, 1967).

theory contends that a leader's effectiveness depends on the situation and, as a result, some leaders may be effective in one situation or organization but not in another. The theory also explains why this discrepancy may occur and identifies leader-situation matches that should result in effective performance.

Basic Premises

■ Fiedler identified two forms of leader behavior thought to reflect the leader's personality: task motivation and relationship motivation.

Fiedler and his associates maintained that leadership effectiveness depends on the match between the leader's personality and the situation. Fiedler devised a special term to describe the leader's basic personality trait: *task* versus *relationship* motivation. He described the situation in terms of its favorableness for the leader, ranging from highly favorable to highly unfavorable.

Task Versus Relationship Motivation In some respects, task versus relationship motivation resembles the concepts identified in the behavioral approaches. *Task motivation* parallels job-centered and initiating-structure leader behavior, and *relationship motivation* is similar to employee-centered and consideration leader behavior. A major difference is that Fiedler viewed task versus relationship motivation as a trait that is basically constant for any given person.

■ In Fiedler's theory, leader behavior is measured with an instrument called the *least preferred coworker scale,* or *LPC.*

The degree of task or relationship motivation is measured by the *least preferred coworker scale (LPC).* The LPC instructions ask respondents (leaders) to think of all the persons with whom they have ever worked and to select their least preferred coworker. Respondents then describe their least preferred coworker by marking a series of sixteen scales anchored at each end by a positive or negative quality. For example, three of the items Fiedler uses in the LPC are:[19]

Pleasant	___ 8	___ 7	___ 6	___ 5	___ 4	___ 3	___ 2	___ 1	Unpleasant
Inefficient	___ 1	___ 2	___ 3	___ 4	___ 5	___ 6	___ 7	___ 8	Efficient
Unfriendly	___ 1	___ 2	___ 3	___ 4	___ 5	___ 6	___ 7	___ 8	Friendly

The higher numbers on the scales are associated with a positive evaluation of the least preferred coworker. (Note that the higher scale numbers are associated with the more favorable term and that some items reverse both the terms and the scale values. The latter feature forces the respondent to read the scales more carefully and to provide more valid answers.) Respondents who describe their least preferred coworker in consistently positive terms receive a high LPC score, whereas those who use consistently negative terms receive a low LPC score.

19. From Fred E. Fielder, *A Theory of Leadership Effectiveness* (New York: McGraw-Hill, 1967). Reprinted by permission of the author.

Fiedler assumed that a respondent's descriptions say more about the respondent than about the least preferred coworker. He believed, for example, that everyone's least preferred coworker is about equally "unpleasant" and that differences in descriptions actually reflect differences in a personality trait among the respondents. Fiedler contended that high-LPC leaders are basically more concerned with interpersonal relations, whereas low-LPC leaders are more concerned with task-relevant problems.

Controversy has always surrounded the LPC scale. Researchers have offered several interpretations of the LPC score, arguing that it may be an index of behavior, personality, or some other unknown factor.[20] Indeed, the LPC measure—and its interpretation—has been one of the most debated and argued aspects of the contingency theory.

Situational Favorableness

Fiedler identified three factors that determine the favorableness of the situation. In decreasing order of influence, these are leader-member relations, task structure, and leader position power.

Leader-member relations refers to the personal relationship between the leader and subordinates. It includes the degree to which subordinates trust, respect, and have confidence in the leader, and vice versa. A high degree, obviously, signals good relations, and a low degree indicates poor relations.

Task structure has four components. *Goal-path multiplicity* is the number of ways the job can be performed. *Decision verifiability* refers to how well the job provides feedback on results. *Decision specificity* is the degree to which a task has an optimal solution or outcome. *Goal clarity* refers to how clearly the requirements of the job are stated.

Tasks that have low multiplicity and high verifiability, specificity, and clarity are considered structured. Jobs of this type are routine, easily understood, and unambiguous. As a result, contingency theory presumes structured tasks to be more favorable because the leader need not be closely involved in defining activities and can devote time to other matters. On the other hand, tasks that have high multiplicity and low verifiability, specificity, and clarity are unstructured—nonroutine, ambiguous, complex, and presumed to be more unfavorable, because the leader must play a major role in guiding and directing the activities of subordinates.

Leader position power is the power inherent in the leader's role itself. If the leader has the power to assign work, reward and punish employees, and recommend them for promotion, position power is high and favorable. If, however, the leader must have job assignments approved by someone else, does not give

20. See Chester A. Schriesheim, B. D. Bannister, and W. H. Money, "Psychometric Properties of the LPC Scale: An Extension of Rice's Review," *Academy of Management Review,* April 1979, pp. 287–294.

TABLE 9.2
Fiedler's Contingency Theory of Leadership

Leader Member Relations	Good				Poor			
Task Structure	Structured		Unstructured		Structured		Unstructured	
Position Power	High	Low	High	Low	High	Low	High	Low
Situational Favorableness	Very Favorable				Moderately Favorable		Very Unfavorable	
Recommended Leader Behavior	Task-Oriented Behavior				Person-Oriented Behavior		Task-Oriented Behavior	

rewards and punishment, and has no voice in promotions, position power is low and unfavorable; that is, many decisions are beyond the leader's control.

- In Fiedler's theory situational favorableness is determined by leader-member relations, task structure, and leader position power.

Leader Motivation and Situational Favorableness Fiedler and his associates conducted several studies examining the relationships among leader motivation, situational favorableness, and group performance. Table 9.2 summarizes the results of these studies.

Before we interpret the results, let's examine the situational favorableness dimensions shown in the table. The various combinations of these three dimensions result in eight different situations. These situations, in turn, define a continuum ranging from very favorable to very unfavorable situations from the leaders' perspective. The table also identifies the leadership approach that is supposed to achieve high group performance in each of the eight situations. A task-oriented leader is appropriate for very favorable as well as very unfavorable situations. For example, the model predicts that if leader-member relations are poor, the task is unstructured, and leader position power is low, a task-oriented leader will be effective. It also predicts that a task-oriented leader will be effective if leader-member relations are good, the task is structured, and leader position power is high. Finally, for situations of intermediate favorability, the theory suggests that a person-oriented leader will be most likely to get high group performance.

- According to Fiedler, a task-oriented leader is appropriate for a very favorable or a very unfavorable situation. Relationship-oriented behavior is predicted to work best when the situation is moderately favorable or unfavorable.

Leader-Situation Match What happens if a person-oriented leader faces a very favorable or very unfavorable situation or a task-oriented leader faces a situation of intermediate favorability? Fiedler refers to these leader-situation combinations as *mismatches*. A basic premise of his theory is that leadership behavior is a personality trait. Thus, the mismatched leader cannot adapt to the situation and achieve effectiveness. Fiedler contends that when a leader's style and the situation do not match, the only available course of action is to change the situation through "job engineering."[21]

21. See Fred E. Fiedler, "Engineering the Job to Fit the Manager," *Harvard Business Review,* September-October 1965, pp. 115–122.

Leader-member relations and leader position power are two important situational characteristics included in Fiedler's contingency theory of leadership. Gloria Molina, the first woman ever voted to the Los Angeles County board of supervisors, clearly has both. Her supporters swept her to a convincing victory over the incumbent, who outspent her during the campaign by a 2 to 1 margin. She hopes to use her new position to improve conditions for the city's large Hispanic community.

Fiedler suggests that if a person-oriented leader ends up in a situation that is very unfavorable, the manager should attempt to improve matters by spending more time with subordinates to improve leader-member relations and by laying down rules and procedures to provide more task structure. Fiedler has developed a training program for supervisors on how to assess situational favorability and change the situation to achieve a better match.[22]

Scientific Evidence

The validity of Fiedler's contingency model has been heatedly debated due to the inconsistency of the research results. Apparent shortcomings of the contingency theory are that the LPC measure lacks validity, the theory is not always supported by research, and Fiedler's assumptions about the inflexibility of leader behavior are unrealistic.[23] The theory itself, however, is an advance over previous

22. See Fred E. Fiedler, Martin M. Chemers, and Linda Mahar, *Improving Leadership Effectiveness: The Leader Match Concept* (New York: Wiley, 1976).

23. See Schriesheim, Bannister, and Moncy, "Psychometric Properties of the LPC Scale"; George Graen, K. M. Alvares, J. B. Orris, and J. A. Martella, "Contingency Model of Leadership Effectiveness: Antecedent and Evidential Results," *Psychological Bulletin,* October 1970, pp. 285–296; J. Timothy McMahon, "The Contingency Theory: Logic and Method Revisited," *Personnel Psychology,* Winter 1972, pp. 697–711. See also Lawrence H. Peters, Darrell D. Hartke, and John T. Pohlmann, "Fiedler's Contingency Theory of Leadership: An Application of the Meta-Analysis Procedures of Schmidt and Hunter," *Psychological Bulletin,* April 1985, pp. 274–285.

MANAGEMENT IN ACTION

New Leadership Styles at EDS

Electronic Data Systems (EDS) is one of the largest computer services firms in the world. It was founded by H. Ross Perot, famous for his entrepreneurship and inspirational abilities. Perot managed EDS with an iron hand. Indeed, there were always two ways of doing things: Perot's way and the wrong way.

In 1984, Perot sold EDS to General Motors. In addition to financial considerations, Perot was granted a seat on GM's board of directors and remained at the helm of EDS. Soon, however, his combative style and criticisms of GM management grew intolerable to EDS's new parent firm. Accordingly, Perot eventually was paid $742.8 million in cash to resign from his seat on the GM board and surrender his remaining EDS stock.

Nevertheless, EDS has continued to prosper. Indeed, in many ways the firm is doing better than ever. Much of the credit goes to Perot's successor, Les Alberthal. Over the years, Alberthal had had an opportunity to observe Perot at work and to see firsthand the results of Perot's behaviors and decisions. While he acknowledged that Perot had made enormous contributions to EDS, he also recognized that it might be time for a new approach.

Accordingly, when he was named CEO, Alberthal went to great lengths to alter his own behavior to be as different from Perot as possible. He loosened dress requirements and starting delegating more work. He opened up channels of communication and encouraged greater participation. At least partly as a result, revenues at EDS have skyrocketed. Sales have increased 25 percent and profits have soared by 66 percent since Perot's departure.

SOURCES: "Now in Hands of Delegator, Firm Hits Stride," *USA Today,* September 24, 1990, pp. B1, B2; "Perot War With EDS Pits Former Friends in High-Stakes Affair," *The Wall Street Journal,* October 6, 1988, pp. A1, A2; Thomas Moore, "Make-or-Break Time for General Motors," *Fortune,* February 15, 1988, pp. 32–42.

leadership approaches because it gives explicit consideration to the organizational situation and its role in effective leadership.

The Path-Goal Theory of Leadership

Another important contingency approach to leadership is the path-goal theory. Developed in the 1970s by Martin Evans and Robert House,[24] the path-goal theory focuses on the situation and leader behaviors rather than on fixed traits of the leader. The path-goal theory thus allows for the possibility of adapting leadership to the situation. *Management in Action* describes how one leader changed his behavior to accommodate new circumstances.

24. See Martin G. Evans, "The Effects of Supervisory Behavior on the Path-Goal Relationship," *Organizational Behavior and Human Performance,* May 1970, pp. 277–298; Robert J. House, "A Path-Goal Theory of Leadership Effectiveness," *Administrative Science Quarterly,* September 1971, pp. 321–339; Robert J. House and Terence R. Mitchell, "Path-Goal Theory of Leadership," *Journal of Contemporary Business,* Autumn 1974, pp. 81–98.

FIGURE 9.3
The Path-Goal Theory of Leadership

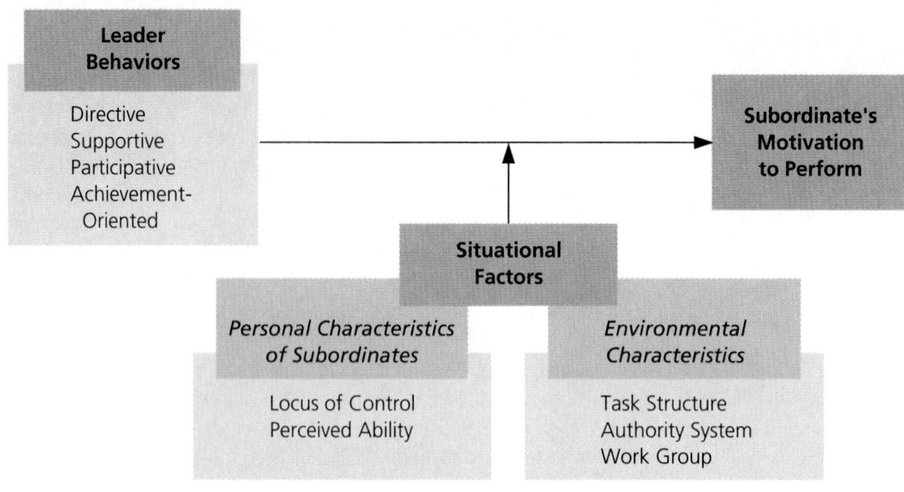

Basic Premises

The path-goal theory has its roots in the expectancy theory of motivation discussed in Chapter 6. Recall that expectancy theory says that a person's attitudes and behaviors can be predicted from two interrelated factors: the degree to which the person believes job performance will lead to various outcomes (expectancy) and the value of those outcomes (valences) to the individual. The **path-goal theory of leadership** argues that subordinates are motivated by the leader to the extent that leader behavior influences their expectancies. In other words, the leader affects subordinates' performance by clarifying the behaviors (paths) that will lead to desired rewards (goals). Ideally, of course, getting the rewards depends on effective performance. Path-goal theory also suggests that a leader may behave in different ways in different situations.

- The **path-goal theory of leadership** suggests that effective leaders clarify the paths (behaviors) that will lead to desired rewards (goals).

Leader Behaviors As Figure 9.3 shows, path-goal theory identifies four kinds of leader behavior: directive, supportive, participative, and achievement oriented. With *directive* leadership, the leader lets subordinates know what is expected of them, gives specific guidance as to how to accomplish tasks, schedules work to be done, and maintains definitive standards of performance for subordinates. The *supportive* leader is friendly and shows concern for subordinates' status, well-being, and needs. With *participative leadership*, the leader consults with subordinates about issues and takes their suggestions into account before making a decision. The *achievement-oriented* leader sets challenging goals, expects subordinates to perform at their highest level, and shows strong confidence that subordinates will put forth effort and accomplish the goals.[25] Unlike Fiedler's

- The path-goal theory proposes four kinds of leader behavior: directive, supportive, participative, and achievement oriented.

25. See House and Mitchell, "Path-Goal Theory of Leadership."

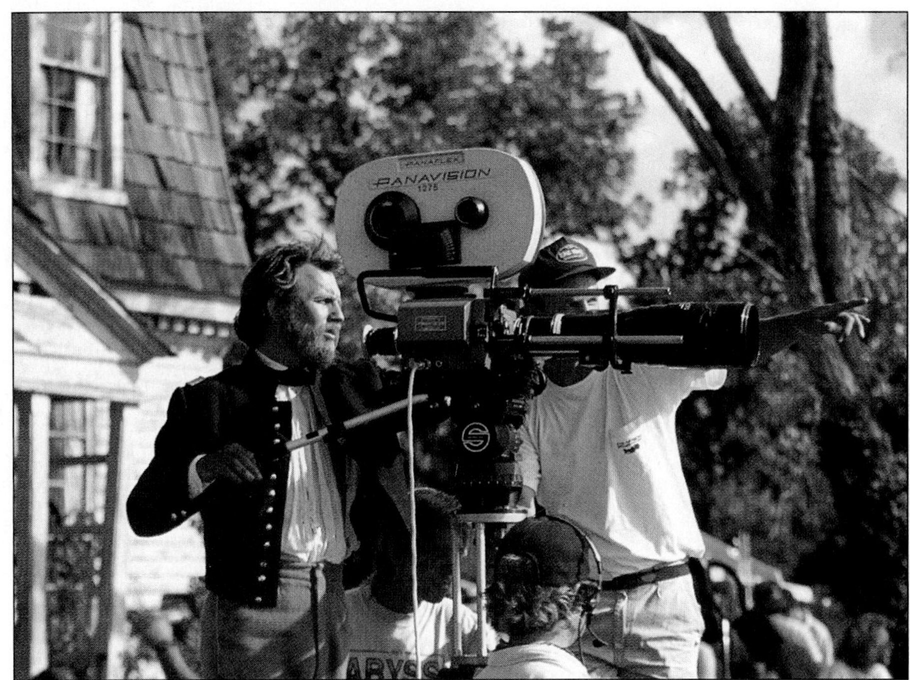

Kevin Costner has to adjust his behavior to fit his situation. When he directs a movie, such as the Oscar-winning "Dances With Wolves," he is in complete charge. He sets the schedule, positions his actors, and determines the camera angles with authoritative precision. When someone else is directing him, however, as in 1991's runaway hit "Robin Hood: Prince of Thieves," he must adjust his behavior to be more accommodating.

contingency theory, path-goal theory assumes the same leader may display any or all of these leadership styles depending on the situation.

- The path-goal theory suggests that appropriate leader behavior depends on several personal characteristics of subordinates and characteristics of the environment.
- Important environmental characteristics included in path-goal theory are task structure, the formal authority system, and the primary work group.
- Important personal characteristics included in path-goal theory are locus of control and perceived ability.

Situational Factors The path-goal theory proposes two types of situational factors that influence how leader behavior relates to subordinate satisfaction: the personal characteristics of the subordinates and the characteristics of the environment (see Figure 9.3).

Two important personal characteristics of subordinates are locus of control and perceived ability. *Locus of control*, discussed in Chapter 4, refers to the extent to which individuals believe that what happens to them results from their own behavior or from external causes. Research indicates that individuals who attribute outcomes to their own behavior may be more satisfied with a participative leader, whereas individuals who attribute outcomes to external causes may respond more favorably to a directive leader.[26] *Perceived ability* refers to how people view their ability with respect to the task. Employees who rate their own ability relatively high are less likely to accept directive leadership.

Important environmental characteristics are *task structure*, the *formal authority system*, and the *primary work group*. The path-goal theory proposes that

26. See Terence R. Mitchell, "Motivation and Participation: An Integration," *Academy of Management Journal*, June 1973, pp. 160–179.

leader behavior will motivate subordinates if it helps them cope with environmental uncertainty created by those factors. In some cases, however, certain forms of leadership will be redundant, decreasing subordinate satisfaction. For example, when task structure is high, directive leadership is less necessary and therefore less effective; similarly, if the work group gives the individual plenty of social support, a supportive leader will not be especially attractive. Thus, the extent to which leader behavior matches the people and environment in the situation is presumed to influence subordinates' motivation to perform.

Scientific Evidence

The path-goal theory was designed to provide a general framework for understanding how leader behavior and situational factors influence subordinate attitudes and behaviors. But the intention of the path-goal theorists was to stimulate research on the theory's major propositions, not to offer definitive answers. Researchers hoped that a more fully developed, formal theory of leadership would emerge from continued study. Further work actually has supported the theory's major predictions, but it has not validated the entire model.[27]

The Vroom-Yetton-Jago Model of Leadership

- The **Vroom-Yetton-Jago** model of leadership attempts to prescribe how much participation subordinates should be allowed in making decisions.

The third major contemporary theory of leadership is the **Vroom-Yetton-Jago model**, first proposed by Victor Vroom and Philip Yetton in 1973 and recently expanded by Vroom and Arthur Jago.[28] Like the path-goal theory, the model attempts to prescribe a leadership style appropriate to a given situation. It also assumes the same leader may display different leadership styles. But the Vroom-Yetton-Jago model concerns itself with only a single aspect of leader behavior: subordinate participation in decision making. The goals of the model are to protect the quality of the decision while ensuring acceptance of the decision by subordinates.

Basic Premises

- In the Vroom-Yetton-Jago model, the leader assesses critical problem attributes and then adopts one of five basic levels of participation.

The Vroom-Yetton-Jago model assumes that the degree to which subordinates should be encouraged to participate in decision making depends on the characteristics of the situation. In other words, no one decision-making process is best for all situations. After evaluating each of the *problem attributes* (characteristics

27. See Yukl, *Leadership in Organizations.*

28. See Victor H. Vroom and Philip H. Yetton, *Leadership and Decision Making* (Pittsburgh: University of Pittsburgh Press, 1973); Victor H. Vroom and Arthur G. Jago, *The New Leadership* (Englewood Cliffs, N.J.: Prentice-Hall, 1988).

of the problem or decision), the leader determines an appropriate decision style that specifies the amount of subordinate participation.

Vroom and Jago's expansion of the original model requires the use of a decision tree.[29] The manager assesses his or her situation in terms of several variables and, based on those variables, follows the paths through the tree to a recommended course of action. There are actually four trees: two for group-level decisions and two for individual-level decisions. One of each is for use when time is important and the other for when time is less important and the manager wants to develop the subordinate's decision-making abilities.

The decision tree for time-driven group problems is shown in Figure 9.4. The problem attributes (situational variables) are arranged along the top of the decision tree and are expressed as questions. To use the model, the decision maker starts at the left-hand side of the diagram and asks the first question. For instance, the manager first decides whether or not the problem involves a quality requirement, that is, are there quality differences in the alternatives, and do they matter? The answer determines the path to the second node on the decision tree, where the question pertaining to that attribute is asked. This process continues until a terminal node is reached. In this way, the manager identifies an effective decision-making style for the situation.

The various decision styles reflected at the ends of the tree branches represent different levels of subordinate participation for which the manager should strive in a given situation. The five styles are defined as follows:

AI: The manager makes the decision alone.

AII: The manager asks for information from subordinates but makes the decision alone. Subordinates may or may not be informed about the situation.

CI: The manager shares the situation with individual subordinates and asks for information and evaluation. Subordinates do not meet as a group, and the manager alone makes the decision.

CII: The manager and subordinates meet as a group to discuss the situation, but the manager makes the decision.

GII: The manager and subordinates meet as a group to discuss the situation, and the group makes the decision.*

The complete Vroom-Yetton-Jago model today is even more complex than Vroom and Yetton's earlier version. The other three trees, for example, include still different situational attributes and decision styles. Moreover, several of the questions now allow more than a simple *yes* or *no* answer. To compensate for this difficulty, Vroom and Jago have developed computer software to help managers assess a particular situation accurately and quickly and then make an

29. Vroom and Jago, *The New Leadership.*

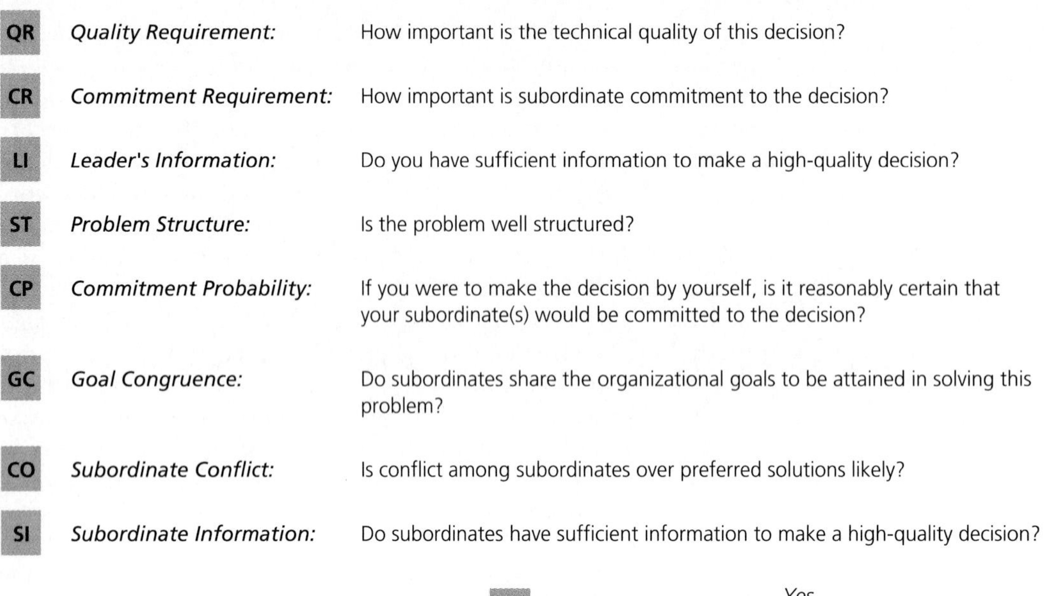

QR Quality Requirement: How important is the technical quality of this decision?
CR Commitment Requirement: How important is subordinate commitment to the decision?
LI Leader's Information: Do you have sufficient information to make a high-quality decision?
ST Problem Structure: Is the problem well structured?
CP Commitment Probability: If you were to make the decision by yourself, is it reasonably certain that your subordinate(s) would be committed to the decision?
GC Goal Congruence: Do subordinates share the organizational goals to be attained in solving this problem?
CO Subordinate Conflict: Is conflict among subordinates over preferred solutions likely?
SI Subordinate Information: Do subordinates have sufficient information to make a high-quality decision?

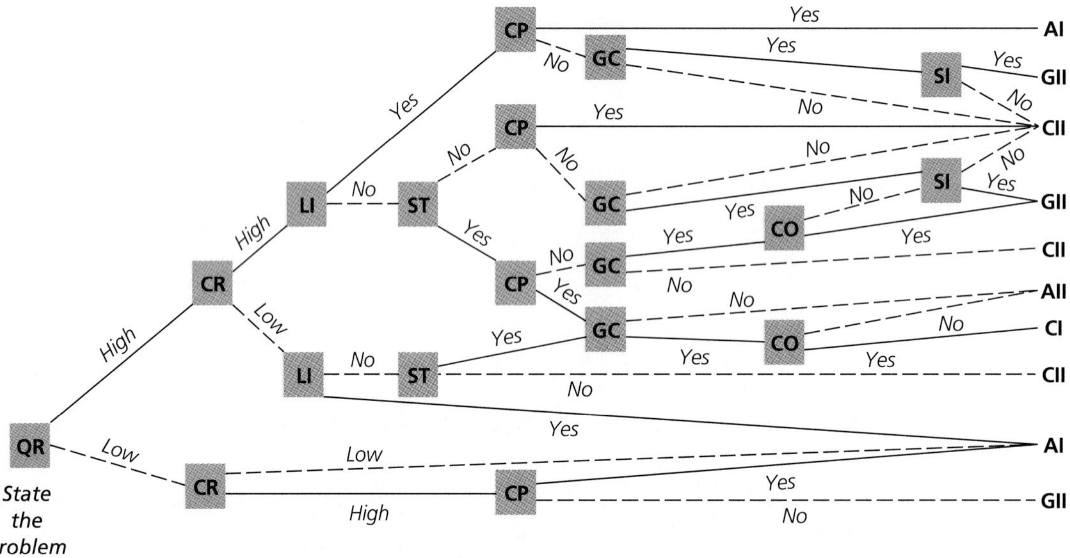

SOURCE: Reprinted from *The New Leadership: Managing Participation in Organizations* by Victor H. Vroom and Arthur G. Jago, 1988, Englewood Cliffs, NJ: Prentice-Hall. Copyright 1987 by V. H. Vroom and A. G. Jago. Used with permission of the authors.

FIGURE 9.4
The Vroom-Yetton-Jago Model (Time-Driven Group Problems)

Applying the Vroom-Yetton-Jago Model

You are the southwestern United States branch manager of an international manufacturing and sales organization. The firm's management is looking for ways to increase efficiency. As one part of this effort, the company recently installed an integrated computer network linking sales representatives, customer service employees, and other sales support staff. Sales were supposed to increase and sales expenses to drop as a result.

However, exactly the opposite has occurred: Sales have dropped a bit, and expenses are up. You have personally inspected the new system and believe the hardware is fine. However, you believe the software linking the various computers is less than ideal.

The subordinates you have quizzed about the system, on the other hand, think the entire system is fine. They attribute the problems to a number of factors, including inadequate training in how to use the system, a lack of incentives for using it, and generally poor morale. Whatever the reasons given, each subordinate queried exhibited strong feelings about the issue.

Your boss has just called you and expressed concern about the problems. He has indicated that he has confidence in your ability to solve the problem and will leave it in your hands. However, he wants a report on how you plan to proceed within one week.

Think of how much participation you normally would expect to allow your subordinates in making this decision. Then apply the Vroom-Yetton-Jago model to the problem and see what it suggests. Compare your usual approach to the recommended solution.

---

appropriate decision regarding employee participation.[30] *Developing Management Skills* provides some practice in using the Vroom-Yetton-Jago model.

Scientific Evidence

Because the expanded Vroom-Yetton-Jago model is relatively new, it has not been fully scientifically tested. The original model attracted a great deal of attention, however, and generally was supported by research.[31] For example, there is some support for the idea that individuals who make decisions consistent with the predictions of the model are more effective than those who make decisions inconsistent with it. The model therefore appears to be a tool that managers can apply with some confidence in deciding how much subordinates should participate in the decision-making process.

---

30. Ibid.

31. See Madeline E. Heilman, Harvey A. Hornstein, Jack H. Cage, and Judith K. Herschlag, "Reactions to Prescribed Leader Behavior as a Function of Role Perspective: The Case of the Vroom-Yetton Model," *Journal of Applied Psychology*, February 1984, pp. 50–60; R. H. George Field, "A Test of the Vroom-Yetton Normative Model of Leadership," *Journal of Applied Psychology*, February 1982, pp. 523–532.

TABLE 9.3
Contemporary Leadership Perspectives

Perspective	Basic Principle
Vertical-Dyad Linkage Model	Stresses the importance of individual relationships between leaders and each of their subordinates
Life Cycle Theory	Suggests that the appropriate leader behavior depends on the maturity of the leader's followers
Leadership Substitutes	Identifies factors that may substitute for leader behavior
Transformational Leadership	Focuses on the distinction between leading for change and leading for stability
Charismatic Leadership	Identifies charisma as a form of interpersonal attraction that inspires support and acceptance
Leadership as Symbolic Action	Suggests that the power of leadership lies in its symbolic nature
Attributional Perspectives	Relates attribution theory to leadership

Other Contemporary Approaches to Leadership

Because leadership is such an important area, managers and researchers continue to study it. As a result new ideas, theories, and perspectives are continuously being developed. Table 9.3 summarizes several of the newer perspectives, which we discuss in the sections that follow.

The Vertical-Dyad Linkage Model

- The **vertical-dyad linkage model** of leadership stresses the fact that leaders develop unique working relationships with each of their subordinates.

The **vertical-dyad linkage model** of leadership, conceived by George Graen and Fred Dansereau, stresses the importance of variable relationships between supervisors and each of their subordinates.[32] Each superior-subordinate pair is referred to as a *vertical dyad.* The model differs dramatically from earlier approaches in that it does not assume a supervisor behaves in the same way toward each subordinate. Figure 9.5 shows the basic concepts of the vertical-dyad linkage model.

32. George Graen and J. F. Cashman, "A Role Making Model of Leadership in Formal Organizations: A Developmental Approach," in J. G. Hunt and L. L. Larson, eds., *Leadership Frontiers* (Kent, Ohio: Kent State University Press, 1975), pp. 143–165; Fred Dansereau, George Graen, and W. J. Haga, "A Vertical Dyad Linkage Approach to Leadership within Formal Organizations: A Longitudinal Investigation of the Role-Making Process," *Organizational Behavior and Human Performance,* vol. 15, 1975, pp. 46–78.

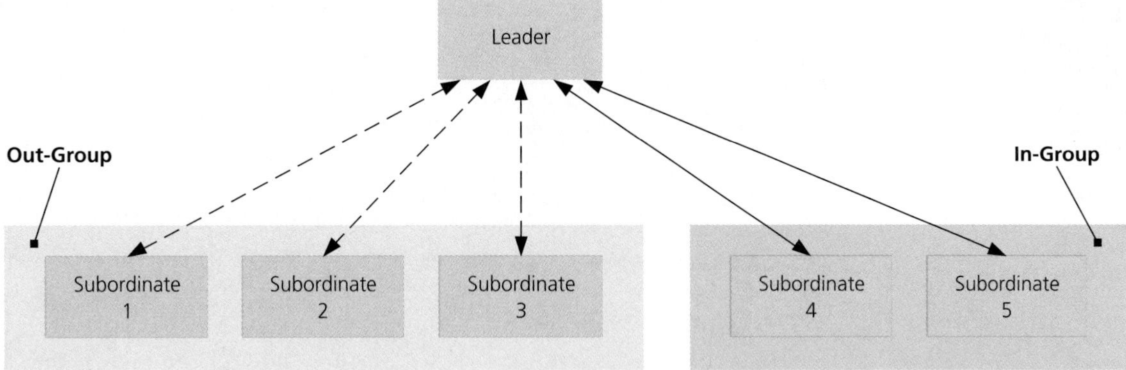

FIGURE 9.5
The Vertical-Dyad Linkage Model of Leadership

The model suggests that supervisors establish a special relationship with a small number of trusted subordinates referred to as the *in-group*. The in-group usually receives special duties requiring responsibility and autonomy and may also receive special privileges. Subordinates who are not a part of this group are called the *out-group*, and they receive less of the supervisor's time and attention. Note in the figure that the leader has a dyadic, or one-to-one, relationship with each of the five subordinates.

Early in his or her interaction with a given subordinate, the supervisor initiates either an in-group or out-group relationship. It is not clear how a leader selects members of the in-group, but the decision may be based on personal compatibility and subordinates' competence. Research has confirmed the existence of in-groups and out-groups. In addition, studies generally have found the in-group members to have a higher level of performance and satisfaction than out-group members.[33]

The Life Cycle Theory

- The **life cycle theory** of leadership identifies different combinations of leadership presumed to work best with different levels of organizational maturity on the part of followers.

Another popular perspective among practicing managers is the **life cycle theory**. This theory is based on the notion that appropriate leader behavior depends on the maturity of the leader's followers.[34] In this instance, *maturity* refers to the subordinate's degree of motivation, competence, experience, and interest in accepting responsibility.

Figure 9.6 shows the basic life cycle model. As follower maturity increases from low to high, the leader needs to move gradually from high task-oriented

33. See Robert P. Vecchio and Bruce C. Gobdel, "The Vertical-Dyad Linkage Model of Leadership: Problems and Prospects," *Organizational Behavior and Human Performance,* vol. 34, 1984, pp. 5–20. See also Dennis Duchon, Stephen G. Green, and Thomas D. Taber, "Vertical Dyad Linkage: A Longitudinal Assessment of Antecedents, Measures, and Consequences," *Journal of Applied Psychology,* vol. 71, 1986, pp. 56–60.

34. Paul Hersey and Kenneth H. Blanchard, *Management of Organizational Behavior: Utilizing Human Resources,* 3rd ed. (Englewood Cliffs, N.J.: Prentice-Hall, 1977).

FIGURE 9.6
The Life Cycle Theory of Leadership

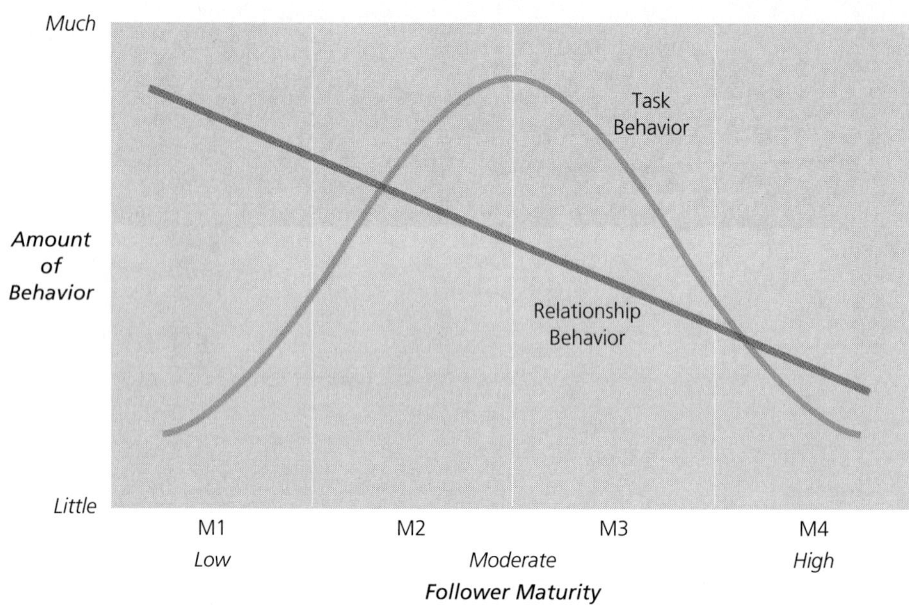

SOURCE: Hersey and Blanchard, *Management of Organizational Behavior: Utilizing Human Resources* 3/e. © 1979, p. 165. Adapted by permission of Prentice-Hall, Inc., Englewood Cliffs, N.J.

behavior to low task-oriented behavior. At the same time, person-oriented behavior (labeled *relationship behavior* in the figure) should start low, rise at a moderate rate, and then decline again.

The life cycle theory has much appeal for managers. However, it has not been thoroughly tested by scientific researchers. Hence, while it may shed some interesting light on the leadership process, managers should be cautious about adopting it too mechanistically.

Leadership Substitutes

- **Leadership substitutes** are individual, task, and organizational characteristics that can substitute for formal leadership.

Leadership substitutes are individual, task, and organizational characteristics that tend to outweigh the leader's ability to affect subordinates' satisfaction and performance.[35] In other words, if certain factors are present, the employee will perform his or her job capably without the direction of the leader. In contrast to traditional theories, which assume that hierarchical leadership is always im-

35. See Steven Kerr and John M. Jermier, "Substitutes for Leadership: Their Meaning and Measurement," *Organizational Behavior and Human Performance,* vol. 22, 1978, pp. 375–403. See also Charles C. Manz and Henry P. Sims, Jr., "Leading Workers to Lead Themselves: The External Leadership of Self-Managing Work Teams," *Administrative Science Quarterly,* March 1987, pp. 106–129.

portant, the premise of the leadership substitutes perspective is that leader behaviors are irrelevant in many situations.

Individual characteristics that may neutralize leader behaviors are ability, experience, training, knowledge, need for independence, professional orientation, and indifference toward organizational rewards. For example, an employee who has the skills and abilities to perform her job and a high need for independence may not need—and may even resent—a leader who provides direction and structure.

A task characterized by routineness, a high degree of structure, frequent feedback, and intrinsic satisfaction may also render leader behavior irrelevant. Thus, if the task provides the subordinate with an adequate level of intrinsic satisfaction, she or he may not need support from a leader.

Characteristics of the organization that may substitute for leadership include explicit plans and goals, rules and procedures, cohesive work groups, a rigid reward structure, and physical distance between supervisor and subordinate. For example, if job goals are explicit and there are many rules and procedures for task performance, a leader providing directions may not be necessary.

Preliminary research has provided support for the concept of leadership substitutes, but additional research is needed to identify other potential substitutes and their impact on leadership effectiveness. [36]

Transformational Leadership

Transformational leadership, a relative newcomer to the leadership literature, focuses on the basic distinction between leading for change and leading for stability.[37] According to this viewpoint, much of what a leader does occurs in terms of normal and routine transactions—assigning work, evaluating performance, making decisions, and so forth. Occasionally, however, the leader has to initiate and manage major change, such as managing a merger, creating a work group, or defining the organization's culture. The first set of issues involves transactional leadership, whereas the second entails transformational leadership.

- **Transformational leadership** is the process of leading for change rather than for stability.

In particular, **transformational leadership** is the set of abilities that allow the leader to recognize the need for change, to create a vision to guide that change, and to execute the change effectively. For example, John Sculley transformed Apple Computer from an idiosyncratic, antiestablishment computer firm into one that is a mainstream, business-oriented company.

Some leaders are able to adopt either transformational or transactional perspectives depending on their circumstances. Others are able to be one or the

36. Jon P. Howell, David E. Bowen, Peter W. Dorfman, Steven Kerr, and Philip Podsakoff, "Substitutes for Leadership: Effective Alternatives to Ineffective Leadership," *Organizational Dynamics,* Summer 1990, pp. 20–38.

37. See James MacGregor Burns, *Leadership* (New York: Harper & Row, 1978), and Karl W. Kuhnert and Philip Lewis, "Transactional and Transformational Leadership: A Constructive/Developmental Analysis," *Academy of Management Review,* October 1987, pp. 648–657.

Transformational leadership involves leading for change. Keenen Ivory Wayans certainly fits this description, if in an unconventional manner. In assuming the roles of producer, writer, and star for the comedy show *In Living Color,* he has used his position to help transform the way television portrays blacks.

other but not both. Steve Jobs handled the transformational processes but was a poor transactional leader. Sculley, in contrast, performed both roles well.

Charismatic Leadership

■ **Charismatic leadership** relies on charisma, presumed to be an individual characteristic of the leader.

The concept of **charismatic leadership**, like trait theories, assumes that charisma is an individual characteristic of the leader. Charisma is a form of interpersonal attraction that inspires support and acceptance and is likely to make a highly charismatic supervisor more successful in influencing subordinate behavior than a supervisor who lacks charisma. Robert House proposed a theory of charismatic leadership in 1977 based on research findings from a variety of social science disciplines.[38] The following characteristics are believed to contribute to charisma:

1. The followers trust the correctness of the leader's beliefs.
2. The followers' beliefs are similar to the leader's beliefs.
3. The followers accept the leader unquestioningly.
4. The followers feel affection for the leader.
5. The followers obey the leader willingly.

38. See Robert J. House, "A 1976 Theory of Charismatic Leadership," in J. G. Hunt and L. L. Larson, eds., *Leadership: The Cutting Edge* (Carbondale, Ill.: Southern Illinois University Press, 1977), pp. 189–207. See also Jay A. Conger and Rabindra N. Kanungo, "Toward a Behavioral Theory of Charismatic Leadership in Organizational Settings," *Academy of Management Review,* October 1987, pp. 637–647.

6. The followers have an emotional involvement in the organization's mission.
7. The followers have heightened performance goals.
8. The followers believe they can contribute to the success of the group's mission.

The theory also suggests behaviors and traits of charismatic leaders. For example, charismatic leaders are likely to have a lot of self-confidence, a firm conviction in their beliefs and ideals, and a strong need to influence people. They also tend to communicate high expectations about follower performance and express confidence in followers. Donald Trump is an excellent example of a charismatic leader. Even though he has made his share of mistakes and generally is perceived as only an "average" manager, many people view him as larger than life.[39]

Charismatic leadership ideas are a synthesis of social science research, but few studies have specifically attempted to test the theory's propositions. The theory's major contribution is its ability to explain charismatic leadership in terms of a set of testable propositions. [40]

Leadership as Symbolic Action

- In some instances, the symbolic nature of leadership is as important as its substance.

Recently some writers have argued that the true meaning of *leadership* lies in its symbolic nature as opposed to its substance. In other words, the actual decisions and actions taken by leaders matter very little; more important is the symbolic aura that the leader's behavior conveys.

Suppose a manager always tries to remember to send each subordinate a birthday card. Traditional leadership theorists would consider this a part of considerate behavior and would assume it would result in employee satisfaction. The symbolic view, however, would suggest a more complex picture. If the cards are always on time and personally signed, this will symbolically indicate caring and concern. To the extent that other behaviors are consistent with this interpretation, the manager will be respected. On the other hand, suppose the cards are often late and obviously signed by a secretary. Worse still, recipients' names are often misspelled! Then the gesture will convey a lack of attention and concern by the manager and likely result in resentment or a lack of respect. Thus, it may not be the content of the decisions (the decision to send the card) but the symbolism of the act (how it is carried out) that truly matters.[41]

39. Stratford P. Sherman, "Donald Trump Just Won't Die," *Fortune,* August 13, 1990, pp. 75–79.

40. David A. Nadler and Michael L. Tushman, "Beyond the Charismatic Leader: Leadership and Organizational Change," *California Management Review,* Winter 1990, pp. 77–97.

41. Jeffrey Pfeffer, "Management as Symbolic Action: The Creation and Maintenance of Organizational Paradigms," in Larry L. Cummings and Barry M. Staw, eds., *Research in Organizational Behavior,* vol. 3 (Greenwich, Conn.: JAI Press, 1981), pp. 1–52. See also Ricky W. Griffin, Kristen Dahlen Skivington, and Gregory Moorhead, "Symbolic and Interactional Perspectives on Leadership: An Integrative Framework," *Human Relations,* vol. 40, 1987, pp. 199–218.

Attributional Perspectives

- Attributional processes can affect how a leader will choose to behave toward subordinates.

Attribution theory, introduced in Chapter 3, also recently has been applied to the study of leadership. Recall that *attribution theory* suggests that we observe the behavior of others and then attribute causes to it. Thus, if a leader attributes subordinates' poor performance to low effort or a lack of ability, responses might include a reprimand, training, or dismissal. On the other hand, if attributions are to external factors such as a poorly designed task or work overload, the leader may instead concentrate on correcting those problems rather than on giving the subordinate negative feedback. Research on this perspective is still in its infancy.[42]

To sum up, several potentially useful leadership models are beginning to emerge. As theories and research techniques become more refined, some of these new perspectives may come to dominate the area of leadership research. Eventually they may be integrated with one or more of the major models into a more complex and valid view of leadership in organizational settings.

Summary of Key Points

- Leadership is both a process and a property. Leadership as a process is the use of noncoercive influence to direct and coordinate the activities of group members toward goal accomplishment. As a property, leadership is the set of characteristics attributed to those who are perceived to use such influence successfully. Leadership theories are concerned with either leader traits or leader behaviors and approach the concept from either a universal or a contingent perspective.
- Early leadership research attempted primarily to identify important traits of leaders. The weaknesses of the trait approach prompted researchers to examine leader behaviors to identify universally applicable forms of leadership behavior. The Michigan studies defined two kinds of leader behavior: job-centered and employee-centered. These behaviors were viewed as points on a single continuum. At about the same time, studies at Ohio State University recognized consideration and initiating structure as basic leader behaviors. These behaviors were viewed as separate dimensions. The Managerial Grid® suggested that the most effective leaders are those who have a high concern for both people and production.
- The contingency theories tried to identify appropriate leadership styles on the basis of the situation. Leadership style was viewed as a trait of the leader. Fiedler's contingency theory stated that leadership effectiveness depends on

42. Mark J. Martinko and William L. Gardner, "The Leader/Member Attribution Process," *Academy of Management Review,* April 1987, pp. 235–249.

a match between the leader's style and the favorableness of the situation, determined by task structure, leader-member relations, and leader position power.

- The path-goal theory and the Vroom-Yetton-Jago model focus on appropriate leader behavior for various situations. The path-goal theory suggests that directive, supportive, participative, or achievement-oriented leader behavior may be appropriate depending on the personal characteristics of subordinates and the characteristics of the environment. Using the same perspective, the Vroom-Yetton-Jago model suggests appropriate decision-making styles based on situation characteristics. The Vroom-Yetton-Jago theory essentially is a model for deciding how much subordinates should participate in the decision-making process. The model is designed to protect the quality of the decision and ensure decision acceptance by subordinates.
- Seven recent perspectives that are not rooted in traditional leadership theories are the vertical-dyad linkage model, the life cycle theory, leadership substitutes, transformational leadership, charismatic leadership, leadership as symbolic action, and attributional perspectives. More research is needed to validate these approaches to the study of leadership.

Discussion Questions

1. Critique the text's definition of *leadership*; that is, identify aspects of the definition with which you agree and/or disagree.
2. Cite examples of managers who are not leaders and leaders who are not managers. What makes them one and not the other? Also, cite examples of both formal and informal leaders.
3. What traits do you think characterize successful leaders?
4. What other forms of leader behavior besides those cited in the chapter can you identify?
5. Critique Fiedler's contingency theory. Are there other elements of the situation that are important? Do you think Fiedler's assertion about the inflexibility of leader behavior makes sense? Why or why not?
6. Do you agree or disagree with Fiedler's assertion that leadership motivation is basically a personality trait? Why?
7. Compare and contrast the contingency and path-goal theories of leadership. What are the strengths and weaknesses of each?
8. Of the three major leadership theories—the contingency theory, the path-goal theory, and the Vroom-Yetton-Jago model—which is the most comprehensive? Which is the narrowest? Which has the most practical value?
9. How realistic do you think it is for managers to attempt to use the Vroom-Yetton-Jago model as prescribed? Explain.
10. Which of the seven contemporary and emerging perspectives on leadership do you believe holds the most promise for future research? Which holds the least promise? Why?

11. Could any of the seven contemporary perspectives be integrated with any of the three major theories of leadership? If so, how?

CASE 9.1 Donald Petersen: A Leader for All Seasons

When Donald Petersen took the reins at Ford Motor Company, the auto giant was in shambles and headed full speed toward a brick wall. By the time Petersen stepped down, he had restored the Ford luster and positioned the firm for effective management for years to come. What did he do, and why did it work? The answers illustrate perfectly the union of leadership and management excellence.

Petersen started his career at Ford right after World War II. He walked across a field from the highway to the Ford headquarters building, climbing a fence en route, and arrived for his interview somewhat rumpled but enthusiastic. Ford executives liked what they saw and offered him a job. During his ascent through the ranks, Petersen helped develop first the Thunderbird and later the Mustang.

Petersen was named president of Ford in 1980 and CEO in 1985. During the dark days of the early 1980s, all of the U.S. automakers were struggling. But in some ways, Ford was in the worst shape of all. General Motors, for example, could have survived for years on its size alone. Chrysler had the charismatic Lee Iacocca securing government-backed loans, labor concessions, and so forth. Meanwhile, Ford was posting record loses and watching its market share get eaten away by both domestic and foreign competitors. But Ford also had a new leader with a clear vision of how best to turn things around.

Petersen realized early on that if Ford was to become successful again, it had to accomplish two basic objectives. First, it had to gain a styling and design advantage over its competitors. Second, it had to boost the quality level of its products. Petersen decided that to reach these objectives, he had to change the entire culture of the firm into one that would both appreciate and nurture its people.

Indeed, *Fortune* magazine recently called Petersen Detroit's first Japanese-style executive. The hallmark of Petersen's tenure at Ford, like that of many Japanese managers, was participation. Petersen installed participative management at the top of the firm (e.g., listening to his own executive team), the bottom of the organization (giving operating employees a meaningful voice in how things were done), and every level in between.

The turnaround Petersen first engineered and then led at Ford was nothing short of stunning. In the early 1980s, the firm lost over $3 billion. By 1987, Ford had gained 3 percent in market share and posted profits equal to its earlier losses. In 1988, Ford's profits exceeded those of General Motors and Chrysler combined.

A modest and self-effacing person, however, Petersen disdained the spotlight and personal acclaim. He continuously stressed that whatever success Ford had achieved was attributable to the full team of people working together.

Today quality circles and other forms of employee involvement efforts are working throughout Ford to continue to improve quality and productivity. Ford's Taurus, Thunderbird, Probe, and Escort remain at the forefront of styling. And quality continues to inch up.

But Ford is not out of the woods yet. Indeed, Petersen shocked the business world in 1989 when he announced he was taking early retirement. Current warning signs indicate that tough times may be on the horizon. The firm has fallen behind schedule on several new-product development programs, and experts project a worldwide auto glut for the next few years.

Nevertheless, Petersen left a capable and qualified successor, a healthy cash reserve to see the firm through the projected tough times, and a company in better shape than either General Motors or Chrysler. And what of his future plans? As he retired, Petersen simply said that he wanted to do something different and find some other areas in which to make a contribution.

Case Questions

1. Was Petersen a better leader or a better manager? How much of each characteristic do you think contributed to Ford's turnaround?
2. Do you believe Petersen could be as effective at a firm such as IBM, Exxon, or Disney?
3. How is Ford doing today?

SOURCES: Alex Taylor III, "Caution: Bumps Ahead at Ford," *Fortune,* December 18, 1989, pp. 93–96; Beverly Geber, "The Resurrection of Ford," *Training,* April 1989, pp. 23–32; "Ford's Petersen to Retire Early; Poling to Succeed Him in Top Posts," *The Wall Street Journal,* April 4, 1989, pp. A1, A4; "A Humble Hero Drives Ford to the Top," *Fortune,* January 4, 1988, pp. 23–24.

CASE 9.2 Right Boss, Wrong Company

James Kesmer was continuously on top of things. In school, he had always been at the top of his class. When he went to work for his uncle's shoe business, Fancy Footwear Inc., he had been singled out as the most productive employee and the one with the best attendance. The company was so impressed with him that it sent him to get an M.B.A. to groom him for a top management position. In school again, and with three years of practical experience to draw on, Kesmer had gobbled up every idea put in front of him, relating many of them to his work at Fancy Footwear. When Kesmer graduated at the top of his class, he returned to Fancy Footwear. To no one's surprise, when the head of the company's largest division took advantage of the early retirement plan, Kesmer was given his position.

Kesmer knew the pitfalls of being suddenly catapulted to a leadership position, and he was determined to avoid them. In business school, he had read cases about family businesses that fell apart when a young family member took over with an iron fist, barking out orders, cutting personnel, and destroying morale. Kesmer knew a lot about participative management, and he was not going to be labeled an arrogant know-it-all.

Kesmer's predecessor, Max Worthy, had run the division from an office at the top of the building, far above the factory floor. Two or three times a day, Worthy would summon a messenger or a secretary from the offices on the second floor and send a memo out to one or another group of workers. But as Kesmer saw it, Worthy was mostly an absentee autocrat, making all the decisions from above and spending most of his time at extended lunches with his friends from the Elks Club.

Kesmer's first move was to change all that. He set up his office on the second floor. From his always-open doorway he could see down onto the factory floor, and as he sat behind his desk he could spot anyone walking by in the hall. He never ate lunch himself but spent the time from 11 to 2 down on the floor, walking around, talking, and organizing groups. The workers, many of whom had twenty years of seniority at the plant, seemed surprised by this new policy and reluctant to volunteer for any groups. But in fairly short order, Kesmer established a worker productivity group, a "Suggestion of the Week" committee, an environmental group, a worker award group, and a management relations group. Each group held two meetings a week, one without and one with Kesmer. He encouraged each group to set up goals in its particular focus area and develop plans for reaching those goals. He promised any support that was within his power to give.

The group work was agonizingly slow at first. But Kesmer had been well trained as a facilitator, and he soon took on that role in their meetings, writing down ideas on a big board, organizing them, and later communicating them in notices to other employees. He got everyone to call him "Jim" and set himself the task of learning all their names. By the end of the first month, Fancy Footwear was stirred up.

But as it turned out, that was the last thing most employees wanted. The truth finally hit Kesmer when the entire management relations committee resigned at the start of their fourth meeting. "I'm sorry, Mr. Kesmer," one of them said. "We're good at making shoes, but not at this management stuff. A lot of us are heading toward retirement. We don't *want* to be supervisors."

Astonished, Kesmer went to talk to the workers with whom he believed he had built good relations. Yes, they reluctantly told him all these changes did make them uneasy. They liked him, and they didn't want to complain. But given the choice, they would rather go back to the way Mr. Worthy had run things. They never saw Mr. Worthy much, but he never got in their hair. He did his work, whatever that was, and they did theirs. "After you've been in a place doing one thing for so long," one worker concluded, "the last thing you want to do is learn a new way of doing it."

Case Questions

1. What factors should have alerted Kesmer to the problems that eventually came up at Fancy Footwear?
2. Could Kesmer have instituted his changes without eliciting a negative reaction from the workers? If so, how?

EXPERIENTIAL EXERCISE

Purpose: This exercise will help you better understand the behaviors of successful and unsuccessful leaders.

Format: You will be asked to find articles and case studies of both successful and unsuccessful leaders and then to describe how these leaders differ.

Procedure:

1. In small groups, go to the library and find brief biographies, case studies, or articles about various leaders. Sources might include periodicals such as *Fortune, Business Week,* and *Forbes;* biographies of famous and infamous personalities such as Vince Lombardi, Adolf Hitler, and Abraham Lincoln; or popular-press books about contemporary leaders like Roger Smith, Donald Petersen, or Lee Iacocca.
2. Choose two leaders who most people would consider very successful and two who would be deemed unsuccessful.
3. Identify similarities and differences between the two successful leaders and between the two unsuccessful leaders.
4. Identify similarities and differences between the two successful and the two unsuccessful leaders.
5. Relate the successes and failures to at least one theory or perspective discussed in the chapter.
6. Select one group member to report your findings to the rest of the class.

Follow-up Questions

1. What role does luck play in leadership?
2. Are there factors about the leaders you researched that might have predicted their success or failure before they achieved leadership roles?
3. What are some criteria of successful leadership?

CHAPTER OUTLINE

The Nature of Power in Organizations

A Definition of Power

The Pervasiveness of Power

Types of Power

Bases of Power

Position Power Versus Person Power

The Uses of Power

Using Referent Power

Using Expert Power

Using Legitimate Power

Using Reward Power

Using Coercive Power

Politics and Political Behavior

The Pervasiveness of Political Behavior

Managing Political Behavior

Conflict in Organizations

The Nature of Conflict

Managing Conflict

10

Power, Politics, and Conflict

CHAPTER OBJECTIVES

After studying this chapter, you should be able to:

Describe the nature of power.

Identify and discuss various types of power.

Explain how to use different kinds of power.

Discuss politics and political behavior.

Describe the nature of conflict in organizations.

When most people think of Disney, they think of Mickey Mouse, Walt Disney World, and Disneyland. While these fanciful images are indeed appropriate, the Disney organization has faced some of the same battles concerning power, politics, and conflict that plague all organizations.

One notable incident occurred several years ago. Following the death of Walt Disney in 1966, the Disney organization ground to a standstill. Managers seemed content to rest on the firm's laurels and live off past successes. Walt Disney's nephew Roy, however, wanted to bring back the magical spirit of the old Disney. After several attempts to turn things around, he took a series of bold steps.

First, he resigned his seat on the firm's board of directors. This public show of displeasure raised investor eyebrows around the country. Then he enlisted the aid of a team of corporate raiders to attempt a hostile takeover of the firm. Eventually he succeeded in forcing out the company's entrenched management team and brought in Michael Eisner to head the organization. Under Eisner's direction Disney has again soared, with new theme parks, hotels, and related ventures.

But Eisner himself has not been immune to controversy. One recent example involves the competing Universal Studios theme park twelve miles from Disney World in Florida. An executive at Universal charged that Eisner got the idea for Disney's own Disney-MGM Studios Theme Park after listening to a joint venture proposal from Universal. Eisner denied that he ever heard the proposal and pointed out that Walt Disney himself first conceived of the idea of a studio tour in the 1930s.[1]

The history of the Disney organization shows the range and complexity of issues that can arise from power, political behavior, and conflict in organizations. When managers disagree about how to run the firm or when people perceive events differently, a wide array of problems can occur.

Power, political behavior, and conflict pervade practically all organizations. Thus, they are important processes that managers need to understand. We begin this chapter by characterizing the nature of power. Then we identify types of power and discuss how each should be used. Next, we explore politics and

1. "A Real Kongfrontation," *Newsweek,* June 11, 1990, pp. 66–67; "Do You Believe in Magic?" *Time,* April 25, 1988, pp. 66–73; "Disney's Magic," *Business Week,* March 9,1987, p. 62.

political behavior. Finally, we conclude this chapter with a discussion of conflict in organizations.

The Nature of Power in Organizations

The opening vignette clearly illustrates several facets of power. But what *is* power, and how pervasive is power in organizations?

A Definition of Power

■ **Power** is the potential ability of a person or group to influence another person or group.

Power has been defined dozens of ways, but there is no one generally accepted definition. Drawing from the more common meanings of the term, we will define **power** as the potential ability of a person or group to influence another person or group.[2]

One obvious aspect of our definition is that it expresses power in terms of *potential*; that is, we may be able to influence others but may choose not to exercise that ability. Nevertheless, simply having the potential may be sufficient to influence others in some settings. We should also note that power may reside in individuals (such as managers and informal leaders), in formal groups (such as departments and committees), and in informal groups (such as a clique of influential people). Finally, we should note our definition's use of the word *influence* as the mechanism for affecting others. If a person can convince another person to change his or her opinion on some issue, to engage in or refrain from some behavior, or to view circumstances in a certain way, that person has exercised influence—and used power.

The Pervasiveness of Power

Considerable differences of opinion exist about how thoroughly power pervades organizations. Some people argue that virtually all interpersonal relations are influenced by power, whereas others believe power is confined only to certain situations. Whatever the case, power undoubtedly is a pervasive part of organizational life. It affects decisions ranging from the choice of strategies to the color of the new office carpeting. It makes or breaks careers. And it enhances or limits organizational effectiveness.

---

2. For reviews of the meaning of *power,* see Henry Mintzberg, *Power in and around Organizations* (Englewood Cliffs, N.J.: Prentice-Hall, 1983); Jeffrey Pfeffer, *Power in Organizations* (Marshfield, Mass.: Pitman Publishing, 1981); John Kenneth Galbraith, *The Anatomy of Power* (Boston: Houghton Mifflin, 1983); Gary A. Yukl, *Leadership in Organizations,* 2nd ed. (Englewood Cliffs, N.J.: Prentice-Hall, 1989).

Types of Power

Within the broad framework of our definition, there obviously are many types of power. These types usually are described in terms of bases of power and position power versus personal power.

Bases of Power

■ Five general bases of power can exist in organizations.

The most widely used and recognized analysis of the bases of power is the framework developed by John R. P. French and Bertram Raven.[3] French and Raven identified five general bases of power in organizational settings: legitimate, reward, coercive, expert, and referent power.

■ **Legitimate power** is power that is granted by virtue of one's position in the organization.

Legitimate Power **Legitimate power**, which essentially is the same thing as authority, is granted by virtue of one's position in the organization. The organization itself thus provides the power. A manager has legitimate power over his or her subordinates, over their subordinates, and so on. The organization declares that it is proper, or legitimate, for the designated individual to direct the activities of others. The bounds of this legitimacy are defined partly by the formal nature of the position involved and partly by informal norms and traditions. For example, it was once commonplace for managers to expect their secretaries not only to perform work-related activities such as typing and filing but to run personal errands like picking up laundry and buying gifts.

The degree of legitimate power varies from one organization to another. In highly mechanistic and bureaucratic organizations such as the military, the legitimate power inherent in each position is closely specified, widely known, and strictly followed. In more organic organizations, such as research and development labs, the lines of legitimate power often are blurry. Employees may work for more than one boss at the same time, and subordinates and superiors may be on a nearly equal footing.

■ **Reward power** is the extent to which a person controls rewards that another person values.

Reward Power **Reward power** is the extent to which a person controls rewards that are valued by another. The most obvious examples of organizational rewards are pay, promotions, and work assignments. If a manager has almost total control over the pay his or her subordinates receive, can make recommendations about promotions, and has considerable discretion to make job assignments, that person has a high level of reward power.

Reward power can extend beyond material rewards. As we noted in our discussions of motivation theory in Chapters 5 and 6, people work for a variety of reasons that include more than just pay. For instance, some people may be

3. John R. P. French and Bertram Raven, "The Bases of Social Power," in Darwin Cartwright, ed., *Studies in Social Power* (Ann Arbor, Mich.: University of Michigan Press, 1959), pp. 150–167. See also Philip M. Podsakoff and Chester A. Schriesheim, "Field Studies of French and Raven's Bases of Power: Critique, Reanalysis, and Suggestions for Future Research," *Psychological Bulletin,* vol. 97, 1985, pp. 387–411.

motivated primarily by a desire for recognition and acceptance. To the extent that a manager's praise and acknowledgment satisfy those needs, that manager has an additional form of reward power.

■ **Coercive power** is the extent to which a person has the ability to punish or physically or psychologically harm someone else.

Coercive Power **Coercive power** exists when someone has the ability to punish or physically or psychologically harm another person. For example, some managers berate subordinates in front of everyone, belittling their efforts and generally making their lives miserable. To the degree that subordinates try to avoid such sanctions, the manager has coercive power over them.

Certain forms of coercion may be subtle. In some organizations, a particular division may be notorious as a resting place for people who have no future with the company. Threatening to transfer someone to a dead-end branch or some other undesirable location thus is a form of coercion. Physical coercion is less common in organizations than it once was, although this type of force is still occasionally practiced in settings like factories, loading docks, prisons, merchant ships, athletic teams, and the military.

Clearly, the more negative the sanctions a person can bring to bear on others, the stronger is her or his coercive power. At the same time, the use of coercive power is used at the considerable cost of employee resentment and hostility. *The Ethical Dilemma* explores a particulary volatile form of coercion.

■ **Expert power** is the extent to which a person controls information that is valuable to someone else.

Expert Power Control over expertise or, more precisely, over information is another source of power. To the extent that, say, an inventory manager has information that a salesperson needs, the inventory manager has **expert power** over the salesperson. The more important the information and the fewer the alternative sources for getting it, the greater the power.

Expert power can reside in many niches in an organization; it transcends positions and jobs.[4] Although legitimate, reward, and coercive power may not always correspond exactly to formal authority, they often do. Expert power, on the other hand, may be much less in keeping with formal authority. Upper-level managers usually decide on the organization's strategic agenda. But individuals at lower levels in the organization may have the expertise those managers need to do this task. A research scientist may have crucial information about a technical breakthrough of great importance to the organization and its strategic decisions. Or an assistant may take on so many of the boss's routine and mundane activities that the manager loses track of such details and comes to depend on the assistant to keep things running smoothly.[5] In still other situations, lower-level participants are given power as a way to take advantage of their expertise.

■ **Referent power** exists when one person wants to be like or imitates someone else.

Referent Power **Referent power** basically is power through identification. If José is respected by Adam, José has power over Adam. Like expert power, referent

4. Michael J. Prietula and Herbert A. Simon, "The Experts in Your Midst," *Harvard Business Review,* January-February 1989, pp. 120–124.

5. Walter Kiechel III, "How to Manage Your Boss," *Fortune,* September 17, 1984, pp. 207–210.

THE ETHICAL DILEMMA

Sexual Harassment in the Workplace

Consider the following three scenarios.

The first is the case of Bill Henderson and Karen Segars. Bill is Karen's immediate supervisor. For the last several months, he has tried to get her to go out with him. Each time she has politely refused. He has just hinted that if she does not go out with him, she may get a bad performance evaluation. On the other hand, if she consents to go out with him, she will likely get a glowing evaluation and possibly a promotion.

The second scenario involves Linda Casey and Paul Martin. Linda is Paul's supervisor. Linda has asked Paul out for dinner on several occasions. Like Karen Segars, Paul has politely declined each time. Linda has made no threats, and Paul believes Linda will neither punish him if he continues to decline nor reward him if he accepts. Nevertheless, he is uncomfortable with Linda's continued invitations and is more disturbed still at the thought of dating his boss.

Finally, there are Alan Lachley and Don Reed. Alan is known to be homosexual, but he keeps his social life separate from the workplace. Whenever Alan is around, Don tells jokes about homosexuals and suggests threatening action against anyone he discovers to be gay. He really means no physical harm to Alan, but he gets pleasure from Alan's obvious discomfort.

Each of these scenarios represents an insidious aspect of organizational life known as *sexual harassment.* The first incident is the most blatant, but the second and third also involve coercive activity of a sexual nature. While there are no set procedures on how to handle such harassment, some general guidelines are recommended. First, document all incidents of harassment by writing down exactly what happened, when, and how the incident was handled. Second, tell the harasser to stop and warn him or her that a failure to cease will result in the incident being reported to someone higher in the organization. Third, if the harassment persists, carry through on the threat and report the incident.

---

power does not always correlate with formal organizational authority. In some ways, referent power is similar to the concept of charisma discussed in Chapter 9. In particular, it often involves trust, similarity, acceptance, affection, willingness to follow, and emotional involvement.

Referent power usually surfaces as imitation. For example, suppose a new department manager is the youngest person in the organization to have reached that rank. Further, it is widely believed that she is being groomed for the highest levels of the company. Other people in the department may begin to imitate her, thinking that they too may be able to advance. They may begin dressing like her, working the same hours, and trying to pick up as many work-related pointers from her as possible. Thus, this person has referent power over them.

Position Power versus Personal Power

■ **Position power** resides in the position, regardless of who is filling that position.

The French and Raven analysis is only one approach to examining the origins of organizational power. Another approach categorizes power in organizations as one of two types: position power or personal power. **Position power** resides in the position, regardless of the person holding the job. Thus, legitimate, reward, and some aspects of coercive and expert power can all contribute to position power. Position power thus is similar to authority.

In creating a position, the organization simultaneously establishes a sphere of power for the person filling that position. He or she generally will have the power to direct the activities of subordinates in performing their jobs, control some of their potential rewards, and have a say in their punishment and discipline. There are, however, limits to a manager's position power. A manager cannot order or control activities that fall outside his or her sphere of power, for instance, directing a subordinate to commit crimes, perform personal services, or take on tasks that clearly are not part of the subordinate's job.

- **Personal power** resides in the person, regardless of the position being filled.

Personal power resides in the person, regardless of his or her position in the organization. Thus, the primary bases of personal power are referent and some traces of expert, coercive, and reward power. Someone usually exercises personal power through rational persuasion or by playing on followers' identification with him or her.

An individual with personal power often can inspire greater loyalty and dedication in followers than someone who has only position power. The stronger influence stems from the fact that the followers are acting more from choice than from necessity (as dictated, for example, by their organizational responsibilities) and thus will respond more readily to requests and appeals. Of course, the influence of a leader who relies only on personal power also is limited, because followers may freely decide not to accept his or her directives or orders.

In Chapter 9, we noted the distinction between formal and informal leaders. These two concepts are also related to position and personal power. A formal

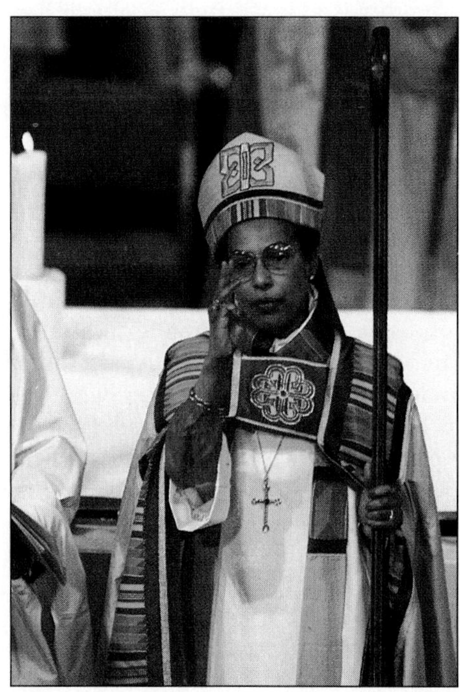

Barbara Harris was recently appointed the Episcopal church's first black woman bishop. In assuming the position of bishop, Harris now has the position power to set policy and allocate resources toward different causes.

FIGURE 10.1
Position Power and Personal Power

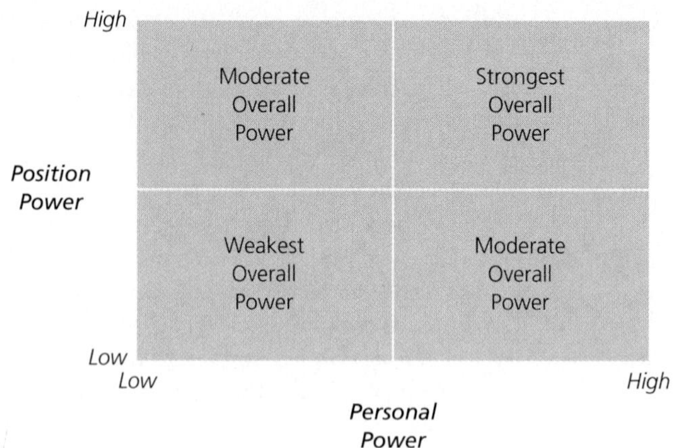

leader will have, at a minimum, position power, and an informal leader will have some measure of personal power. Just as a person may be both a formal and an informal leader, he or she can have both position and personal power simultaneously. Indeed, such a combination usually has the greatest potential influence on the actions of others.

Figure 10.1 illustrates how personal and position power may interact to determine how much overall power a person has in a particular situation. An individual with both personal and position power will have the strongest overall power. Likewise, an individual with neither personal nor position power will have the weakest overall power. Finally, when either personal or position power is high but the other is low, the individual will have a moderate level of overall power.

The Uses of Power

Power can be used in many ways. Gary Yukl has presented a useful perspective for understanding how power may be wielded.[6] His perspective has two closely related aspects. The first relates power bases, requests from individuals possessing power, and probable outcomes in the form of prescriptions for the manager, as summarized in Table 10.1. The second aspect, summarized in Table 10.2, consists of general guidelines for the exercise of power.

- Attempts to use power can result in commitment, compliance, or resistance.

Table 10.1 indicates the three outcomes that potentially result when a leader tries to exert power.[7] These outcomes depend on the leader's base of power, how that base is operationalized, and the subordinate's individual characteristics (for example, personality traits or past interactions with the leader).

6. Yukl, *Leadership in Organizations,* Chapter 3.

7. See also Thomas A. Stewart, "New Ways to Exercise Power," *Fortune,* November 6, 1989, pp. 52–64.

TABLE 10.1
The Uses and Outcomes of Power

Source of Leader Influence	Type of Outcome		
	Commitment	***Compliance***	***Resistance***
Referent Power	*Likely* If request is believed to be important to leader	*Possible* If request is perceived to be unimportant to leader	*Possible* If request is for something that will bring harm to leader
Expert Power	*Likely* If request is persuasive and subordinates share leader's task goals	*Possible* If request is persuasive but subordinates are apathetic about task goals	*Possible* If leader is arrogant and insulting, or subordinates oppose task goals
Legitimate Power	*Possible* If request is polite and very appropriate	*Likely* If request or order is seen as legitimate	*Possible* If arrogant demands are made or request does not appear proper
Reward Power	*Possible* If used in a subtle, very personal way	*Likely* If used in a mechanical, impersonal way	*Possible* If used in a manipulative, arrogant way
Coercive Power	*Very Unlikely*	*Possible* If used in a helpful, nonpunitive way	*Likely* If used in a hostile or manipulative way

SOURCE: Table adapted by Gary A. Yukl from information in John R. P. French, Jr., and Bertram Raven, "The Bases of Social Power," in *Studies in Social Power,* Dorwin P. Cartwright, ed. (Ann Arbor, Mich.: Institute for Social Research, the University of Michigan, 1959), pp. 150–167. Data used by permission of the Institute for Social Research.

Commitment probably will result from the attempt to exercise power if the subordinate accepts and identifies with the leader. Such an employee will be highly motivated by requests that seem important to the leader. For example, a leader might explain that a new piece of software will greatly benefit the organization if developed as soon as possible. A committed subordinate will work just as hard as the leader to complete the project, even if that means working overtime. Sam Walton recently asked all Wal-Mart employees to start greeting customers with a smile and an offer to help. Because Wal-Mart employees generally were motivated and loyal, most of them accepted his request.

Compliance means the subordinate is willing to carry out the leader's wishes as long as doing so will not require extra effort and energy. Thus, the subordinate may work at a reasonable pace but refuse to work overtime, insisting that the job will still be there tomorrow. Many ordinary requests from a boss and the subsequent responses of subordinates fit this description.

Resistance occurs when the subordinate fights the leader's wishes. A resistant subordinate may even deliberately neglect the project to ensure that it is not

TABLE 10.2
Guidelines for Using Power

Basis of Power	Guidelines for Use
Referent Power	Treat subordinates fairly Defend subordinates' interests Be sensitive to subordinates' needs, feelings Select subordinates similar to oneself Engage in role modeling
Expert Power	Promote image of expertise Maintain credibility Act confident and decisive Keep informed Recognize employee concerns Avoid threatening subordinates' self-esteem
Legitimate Power	Be cordial and polite Be confident Be clear and follow up to verify understanding Make sure request is appropriate Explain reasons for request Follow proper channels Exercise power regularly Enforce compliance Be sensitive to subordinates' concerns
Reward Power	Verify compliance Make feasible, reasonable requests Make only ethical, proper requests Offer rewards desired by subordinates Offer only credible rewards
Coercive Power	Inform subordinates of rules and penalties Warn before punishing Administer punishment consistently and uniformly Understand the situation before acting Maintain credibility Fit punishment to the infraction Punish in private

SOURCE: Reprinted from Gary A. Yukl, *Leadership in Organizations*, 2nd ed., © 1989, pp. 44–49. Reprinted by permission of Prentice-Hall, Inc., Englewood Cliffs, N.J.

done as the leader wants. When Frank Lorenzo ran Eastern Air Lines, some employees occasionally disobeyed his mandates as a form of protest against his leadership of the firm.

Using Referent Power

As Table 10.1 makes clear, referent power can be a great help to a leader. Table 10.2 lists Yukl's guidelines for building referent power. Note that with a somewhat mechanistic method, managers may enhance their referent power by choosing subordinates with backgrounds similar to their own. For example, they might build a referent power base by hiring several subordinates who went to the same college they did. A more subtle way to exercise referent power is through role modeling: The leader behaves as she or he wants subordinates to behave. As noted earlier, since subordinates relate to and identify with the leader with referent power, they may subsequently attempt to emulate that person's behavior.[8]

Using Expert Power

Yukl also suggested several ways managers can use expert power; these are listed in Table 10.2. Managers can promote an image of expertise by subtly making others aware of their education, experience, and accomplishments. To maintain credibility, a leader should not pretend to know things that he or she really does not know. A leader whose pretensions are exposed will rapidly lose expert power. A confident and decisive leader demonstrates a firm grasp of situations and takes charge when circumstances dictate. To enhance their expert power, managers should also keep themselves informed about developments related to tasks, valuable to the organization, relevalent to their expertise.

As Yukl described, a leader who recognizes employee concerns works to understand the underlying nature of these issues and takes appropriate steps to reassure subordinates. For example, if employees feel threatened by rumors that they will lose office space after an impending move, the leader might ask them about this concern and then find out just how much office space there will be and tell the subordinates. Finally, to avoid threatening subordinates' self-esteem, a leader with expert power should be careful not to flaunt expertise or behave like a know-it-all.

Using Legitimate Power

In general, a leader exercises legitimate power by formally requesting that subordinates do something. Once again, Yukl has provided several potentially valuable guidelines for using legitimate power. The leader should be especially careful to make requests cordially and politely if the subordinate is sensitive about his or her relationship with the leader. This might be the case, for example, if the subordinate is older or more experienced than the leader. But although the request should be polite, it should be made confidently. The leader is in charge and needs to convey his or her command of the situation. A leader who says, "I'm not sure I have the authority to do this, but . . . " is inviting lack of commitment or compliance. The request should also be clear. Thus, the leader may need to follow up to ascertain that the subordinate has understood it properly. To ensure that a request is seen as appropriate and legitimate to the situation, the leader may need to explain the reasons for it. Often subordinates do not understand the rationale behind a request and consequently are unenthusiastic about it. It is important too to follow proper channels when dealing with

8. French and Raven, "Bases of Social Power."

subordinates. Suppose a manager has asked a subordinate to spend his day finishing an important report. Later, while the manager is out of the office, her boss comes by and asks the subordinate to drop that project and work on something else. The subordinate will then be in the awkward position of having to choose which of two higher-ranking individuals to obey. Yukl also noted that exercising authority regularly will reinforce its presence and legitimacy in the eyes of subordinates.

Compliance with legitimate power should be the norm, because if employees resist a request, the leader's power base may diminish. Thus, the leader must enforce compliance, if necessary. Finally, the leader exerting legitimate power should always attempt to be responsive to subordinates' problems and concerns in the same ways we outlined for using expert power.

Using Reward Power

Reward power is, in some respects, the easiest base of power to use. By observing Yukl's guidelines, a manager can enhance its potential value. Verifying compliance simply means that the leader should find out whether subordinates have carried out his or her request before giving rewards; otherwise, subordinates may not recognize a performance-reward linkage. The request to be rewarded must be both reasonable and feasible, because even the promise of a reward will not motivate a subordinate who thinks a request should not be or cannot be carried out. The same can be said for a request that seems improper or unethical. Among other things, such a request suggests that the reward must not be perceived as a bribe or other shady offering. Finally, if the leader promises a reward that subordinates know she or he cannot actually deliver, or if they have little use for a reward the manager can deliver, they will not be motivated to carry out the request. Further, they may grow skeptical of the leader's ability to deliver rewards that are worth something to them.

Using Coercive Power

Coercion is certainly the most difficult form of power to exercise. Because coercive power is likely to cause resentment and to erode referent power, it should be used infrequently, if at all. Compliance is about all one can expect from using coercive power—and that only if the power is used in a helpful, nonpunitive way, that is, if the sanction is mild and fits the situation and if the subordinate learns from it. In most cases, resistance is the most likely outcome, especially if coercive power is used in a hostile or manipulative way.

Yukl's first guideline for using coercive power—that subordinates should be fully informed about rules and the penalties for violating them—will prevent accidental violations of a rule, which pose an unpalatable dilemma for a leader. Overlooking an infraction on the grounds of ignorance may undermine the rule or the leader's legitimate power, but carrying out the punishment probably will create resentment. As an example of providing reasonable warning before inflicting punishment, the first violation of a rule may simply be met by a warning about the consequences of another violation. Of course, a serious infraction such as theft or violence warrants immediate and severe punishment. The disciplinary action needs to be administered consistently and uniformly, because doing so will show that punishment is both impartial and clearly linked to the infraction.

Leaders should obtain complete information about what has happened before they punish, because punishing the wrong person or administering uncalled-for punishment can stir great resentment among subordinates. Credibility must be maintained, because a leader who continually makes threats but fails to carry them out will lose both respect and power. Similarly, if the leader uses threats that subordinates know are beyond his or her ability, the attempted use of power will be fruitless. Obviously, too, the severity of the punishment generally should match the seriousness of the infraction. Finally, punishing someone in front of others adds humiliation to the penalty, which reflects poorly on the leader and makes those who must watch and listen uncomfortable as well.

Politics and Political Behavior

- **Organizational politics** are activities carried out by people to acquire, enhance, and use power and other resources to obtain their desired outcomes.

A concept closely related to power in organizational settings is politics, or political behavior. Pfeffer has defined **organizational politics** as activities people perform to acquire, enhance, and use power and other resources to obtain their preferred outcomes in a situation where there is uncertainty or disagreement.[9] Thus, political behavior is the general means by which people attempt to obtain and use power. Put simply, the goal of such behavior is to get one's own way about things.

The Pervasiveness of Political Behavior

- Organizational politics are pervasive in most organizations.

A classic survey provides some interesting insights into how managers perceive political behavior in their organizations.[10] Roughly one-third of the 428 managers who responded believed political behavior influenced salary decisions in their organizations, while 28 percent felt it affected hiring decisions. As Table 10.3 shows, three-quarters of the respondents also believed political behavior is more prevalent at higher levels of the organization than at lower levels. More than half believed politics are unfair, unhealthy, and irrational but also acknowledged that successful executives must be good politicians and that it is necessary to behave politically to get ahead. The survey results suggest that managers see political behavior as an undesirable but unavoidable facet of organizational life.

Politics often are viewed as synonymous with dirty tricks or back stabbing and therefore as something distasteful and best left to others. But the results of

9. Pfeffer, *Power in Organizations.*

10. Victor Murray and Jeffrey Gandz, "Games Executives Play: Politics at Work," *Business Horizons,* December 1980, pp. 11–23. See also Jeffrey Gandz and Victor Murray, "The Experience of Workplace Politics," *Academy of Management Journal,* June 1980, pp. 237–251.

TABLE 10.3
Managerial Perceptions of Political Behavior

Statement	Mean Score[a]	Standard Deviation	Strong or Moderate Agreement %
(a) The existence of workplace politics is common to most organizations	1.59	.71	93.2
(b) Successful executives must be good politicians	1.75	.88	89.0
(c) The higher you go in organizations, the more political the climate becomes	1.99	1.10	76.2
(d) Only organizationally weak people play politics[b]	2.21	1.17	68.5
(e) Organizations free of politics are happier than those where there is a lot of politics	2.34	1.09	59.1
(f) You have to be political to get ahead in organizations	2.37	1.13	69.8
(g) Politics in organizations are detrimental to efficiency	2.57	1.14	55.1
(h) Top management should try to get rid of politics within the organization	2.67	1.23	48.6
(i) Politics help organizations function effectively[b]	2.76	1.13	42.1
(j) Powerful executives don't act politically[b]	3.87	1.15	15.7

[a]Score: 1—strongly agree; 2—slightly agree; 3—neither agree nor disagree; 4—slightly disagree; 5—strongly disagree.
[b]Reverse scoring.

SOURCE: Jeffrey Gandz and Victor Murray, "The Experience of Workplace Politics," *Academy of Management Journal,* June 1980, p. 244. Used by permission.

the survey just described demonstrate that political behavior in organizations, like power, is pervasive. Thus, rather than ignoring or trying to eliminate political behavior, managers might more fruitfully consider when and how organizational politics can be used constructively.

Gerald Cavanaugh, Dennis Moberg, and Manuel Velasquez developed a model of the ethics of organizational politics, illustrated in Figure 10.2.[11] In the model, a political behavior alternative (PBA) is a given course of action, largely political in character, in a particular situation. Cavanaugh and his associates considered political behavior ethical and appropriate under two conditions: (1) if it respects the rights of all affected parties and (2) if it adheres to the canons of justice (that is, a common-sense judgment of what is fair and equitable). Even if the political behavior does not meet these tests, it may be ethical and appropriate under certain circumstances. For example, politics may play a part in the

11. Gerald F. Cavanaugh, Dennis J. Moberg, and Manuel Velasquez, "The Ethics of Organizational Politics," *Academy of Management Review,* July 1981, pp. 363–374.

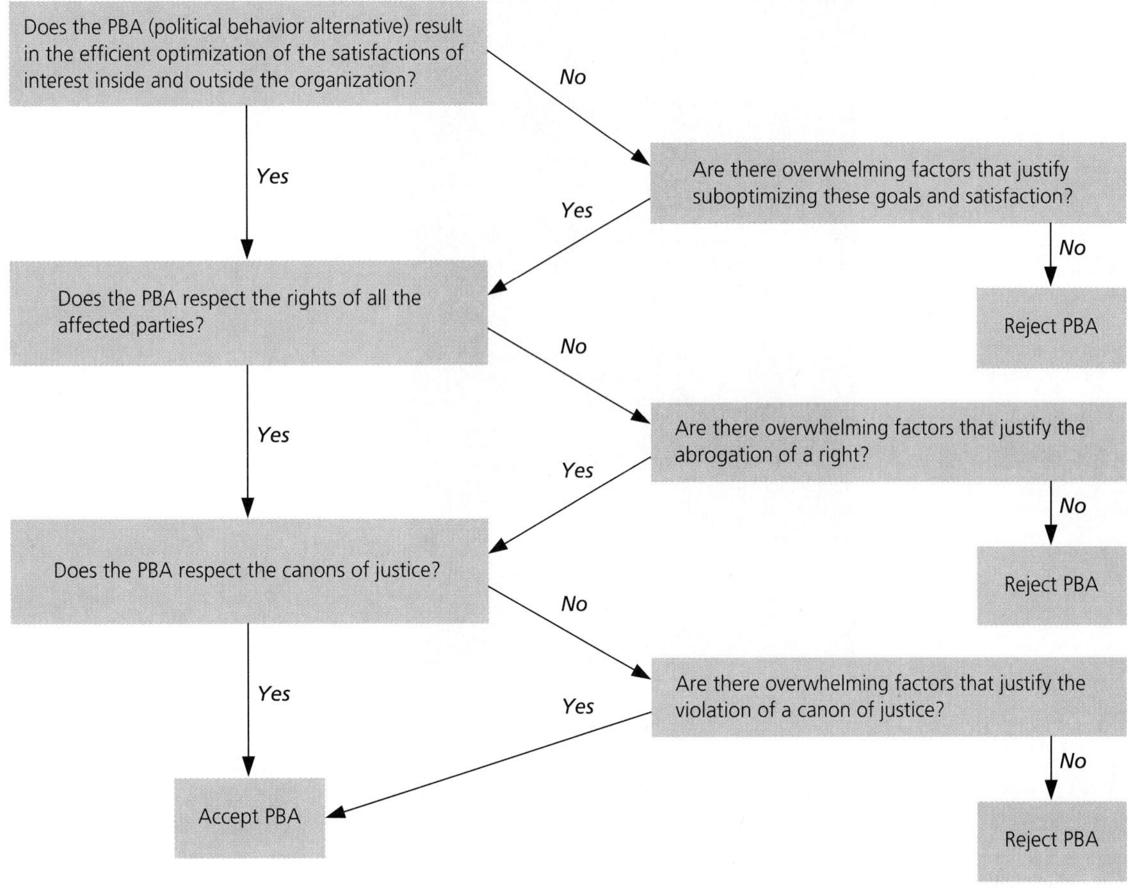

Does the PBA (political behavior alternative) result in the efficient optimization of the satisfactions of interest inside and outside the organization?
No
Yes
Are there overwhelming factors that justify suboptimizing these goals and satisfaction?
Yes
No
Reject PBA
Does the PBA respect the rights of all the affected parties?
No
Yes
Are there overwhelming factors that justify the abrogation of a right?
Yes
No
Reject PBA
Does the PBA respect the canons of justice?
No
Yes
Are there overwhelming factors that justify the violation of a canon of justice?
Yes
No
Accept PBA
Reject PBA

SOURCE: Gerald F. Cavanaugh, Dennis J. Moberg, and Manuel Velasquez, "The Ethics of Organizational Politics," *Academy of Management Review,* July 1981, p. 368. Used by permission.

FIGURE 10.2
A Model of Ethical Political Behavior

choice of employees to let go during a recessionary period of cutbacks, but they might provide the only possible basis for such decisions. In all cases where nonpolitical alternatives exist, however, the model recommends the rejection of political behavior that abrogates rights or justice.

To illustrate how the model works, consider Susan Jackson and Bill Thompson, two assistant professors of English. University regulations stipulate that only one of the assistant professors may be tenured; the other must be let go. Both Susan and Bill submit their credentials for review. By most objective criteria, such as number of publications and teaching evaluations, the two faculty members' qualifications are roughly the same. Because he fears termination, Bill begins an active political campaign to support a tenure decision favoring him. He continually reminds the tenured faculty of his intangible contributions, such as his friendship with influential campus administrators. Susan, on the other hand,

The South Florida Water Management District is controlled by these nine Governor-appointed board members. They and their counterparts around the state have considerably more policy-making authority than is the case in many states. Some observers feel their power has helped them make faster and better decisions to protect the state's natural resources. But some critics believe that each regional board puts the interests of its own region above those of the entire state water management system.

decides to say nothing and let her qualifications speak for themselves. The department ultimately votes to tenure Bill and let Susan go.

Was Bill's behavior ethical? Assuming that his comments about himself were accurate and that he said nothing to disparage Susan, his behavior did not affect her rights; that is, she had an equal opportunity to advance her own cause but chose not to do so. Bill's efforts did not directly hurt Susan but only helped himself. On the other hand, it might be argued that Bill's actions violated the canons of justice because clearly defined data on which to base the decision were available. Thus, one could argue that Bill's calculated introduction of additional information into the decision was unjust.

The model developed by Cavanaugh and his associates has not been tested empirically. Indeed, its very nature may make it impossible to test. Furthermore, as the preceding demonstrates, it often is difficult to give an unequivocal *yes* or *no* answer to the questions, even under the simplest circumstances. Thus, the model can only serve as a general framework for understanding the ethical implications of various courses of action managers might take.

How, then, should managers approach the phenomenon of political behavior? Trying to eliminate political behavior will seldom, if ever, work. In fact, such action may well increase political behavior because of the uncertainty and ambiguity it creates. At the other extreme, universal and freewheeling use of political behavior probably will lead to conflict, feuds, and turmoil.[12] In most

12. Pfeffer, *Power in Organizations.*

MANAGEMENT IN ACTION

Political Behavior at Greyhound

Most people think of Greyhound as America's bus company. In late 1990, however, the firm's days seemed numbered as its workers staged a prolonged and bitter strike. Bus travel has declined significantly in recent years as the cost of air travel has dropped and highways have improved. Thus, Greyhound has faced declining revenues for years.

The firm's CEO, Fred Currey, realized that drastic measures were necessary if Greyhound was to survive. During a labor contract negotiation meeting in early 1990, he introduced a plan that would consolidate routes and eliminate two thousand jobs. When workers got wind of what was going on, they broke off negotiations and went on strike.

At first, Currey seemed almost joyful. Some observers believe he actually sparked the strike as a way to break the union. Unfortunately, if that indeed was his intent, it backfired mightily. Picket lines sprang up like weeds, and strike-breaking workers brought in for low wages were harassed unmercifully. There were also reports of violence, including some shootings.

Currey perhaps made his biggest error when he tried to divide union members against themselves. In mid-1990, he scheduled a secret meeting with some key union officials. His apparent intent was to strike a deal with them, saving their followers' jobs but eliminating others. But again Currey had miscalculated the union's resolve and solidarity. The union faction with which he sought to align divulged the details of the meeting to both the press and other union officials, alienating workers from Currey even more.

With strike pay running out and many picketers taking other jobs, much of the union protest died down by the end of the year. But Currey was left with only a shell of a company. Tremendous debt and the unfavorable publicity during the strike had severely damaged Greyhound, perhaps irrevocably.

SOURCES: "Labor May Still Have Greyhound Collared," *Business Week,* November 26, 1990, p. 60; "Greyhound May Be Coming to the End of the Line," *Business Week,* May 21, 1990, p. 45; "Greyhound Head Holds Secret Talks with Union Groups," *The Wall Street Journal,* May 10, 1990, p. B6.

cases, a position somewhere in between is best: The manager does not attempt to eliminate political activity, recognizing its inevitability, and may try to use it effectively, perhaps following the ethical model just described. At the same time, the manager can take certain steps to minimize the potential dysfunctional consequences of abusive political behavior.

Managing Political Behavior

- Effective management of political behavior requires an understanding of the reasons it occurs, common political behavior techniques, and strategies for limiting its effects.

Managing organizational politics is no easy task. The very nature of political behavior makes it tricky to approach in a rational and systematic way. Success will require a basic understanding of three factors: the reasons for political behavior, common techniques for using political behavior, and strategies for limiting the effects of political behavior. *Management in Action* describes some political behavior that recently took place at Greyhound.

Reasons for Political Behavior Robert Miles has argued that political behavior occurs in organizations for five basic reasons: ambiguous goals, scarce resources, technology and environment, nonprogrammed decisions, and organizational change (see Figure 10.3).[13]

Most organizational goals are inherently ambiguous. Organizations frequently espouse goals such as "increasing our presence in certain new markets" or "increasing our market share." The ambiguity of such goals provides an opportunity for political behavior, because people can view a wide range of behaviors as potential contributors to goal accomplishment. In reality, of course, many of these behaviors may actually be designed for the personal gain of the individuals involved. For example, a top manager might argue that the corporation should pursue its goal of entry into a new market by buying out another firm instead of forming a new division. The manager appears to have the good of the corporation in mind. But what if he owns some of the target firm's stock and stands to make money on a merger or acquisition?

Whenever resources are scarce, some people will not get everything they think they deserve or need. Thus, they are likely to engage in political behavior as a means for inflating their share of resources. In this way, a manager seeking a larger budget might present accurate but misleading or incomplete statistics to inflate the perceived importance of her department. Because no organization has unlimited resources, incentives for this kind of political behavior are always present.

As we discuss in Chapters 18 and 19, technology and environment may influence the overall design of the organization and its activities.[14] The influence stems from the uncertainties associated with nonroutine technologies and dynamic, complex environments. These uncertainties favor the use of political behavior, because in a dynamic and complex environment, it is imperative that an organization respond to change. An organization's response generally involves a wide range of activities, from purposeful activities to uncertainty to a purely political response. In the last case, a manager might use an environmental shift as an argument for restructuring his or her department to increase his or her own power base.

Political behavior is also likely to arise whenever many nonprogrammed decisions need to be made. Nonprogrammed-decision situations involve ambiguous circumstances that allow ample opportunity for political maneuvering. The two faculty members competing for one tenured position is an example. The nature of the decision allowed political behavior, and in fact, from Bill's point of view, the nonprogrammed decision demanded political action.

---

13. Robert H. Miles, *Macro Organizational Behavior* (Glenview, Ill.: Scott, Foresman, 1980). See also Carrie R. Leana, "Power Relinquishment versus Power Sharing: Theoretical Clarification and Empirical Comparison of Delegation and Participation," *Journal of Applied Psychology,* vol. 72, 1987, pp. 228–233.

14. Joan Woodward, *Industrial Organization Theory and Practice* (London: Oxford University Press, 1965); Paul R. Lawrence and Jay W. Lorsch, *Organization and Environment* (Homewood, Ill.: Irwin, 1967).

FIGURE 10.3
Reasons for and Possible Consequences of Political Behavior

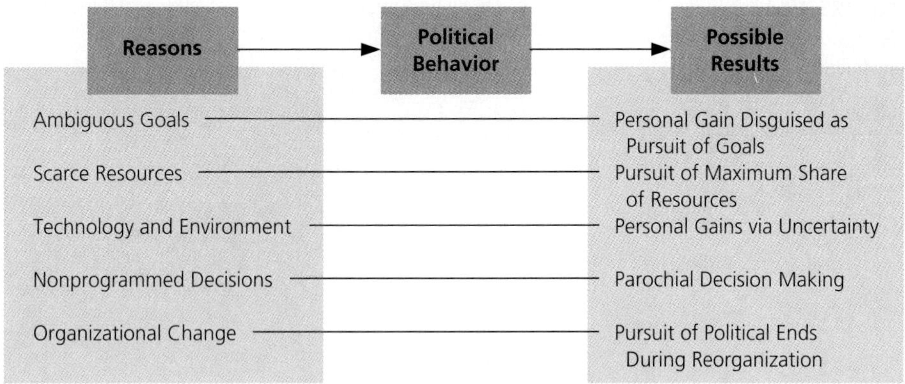

As we discuss in Chapter 21, changes in organizations occur regularly and can take many forms. Each such change introduces some uncertainty and ambiguity into the organizational system, at least until it has been completely institutionalized. This period usually affords much opportunity for political activity. For instance, a manager worried about the consequences of a reorganization may resort to politics to protect the scope of his or her authority.

The Techniques of Political Behavior Several techniques are used in practicing political behavior. Unfortunately, because these techniques have not been systematically studied, our understanding of them is based primarily on informal observation and inference.[15] To further complicate this problem, the participants themselves may not even be aware that they are using particular techniques. Figure 10.4 summarizes the most frequently used techniques.[16]

One technique of political behavior is to control as much information as possible. The more critical the information and the fewer the people who have access to it, the larger the power base and influence of those who do. For example, a top manager has a report compiled as a basis for future strategic plans. Rather than distributing the complete report to peers and subordinates, he shares only parts of it with those few managers who must have the information. Because no one but the manager has the complete picture, he has power and is engaging in politics to control decisions and activities according to his own ends.

Similarly, some people create or exploit situations to control lines of communication, particularly access to others in the organization. Secretaries frequently control access to their bosses. A secretary may put visitors in contact with the boss, send them away, delay the contact by ensuring that phone calls

15. Pfeffer, *Power in Organizations*; Mintzberg, *Power in and around Organizations.*

16. The techniques in Figure 10.4 are based on Pfeffer, *Power in Organizations;* Mintzberg, *Power in and around Organizations;* and Galbraith, *Anatomy of Power.*

FIGURE 10.4
Techniques of Political Behavior

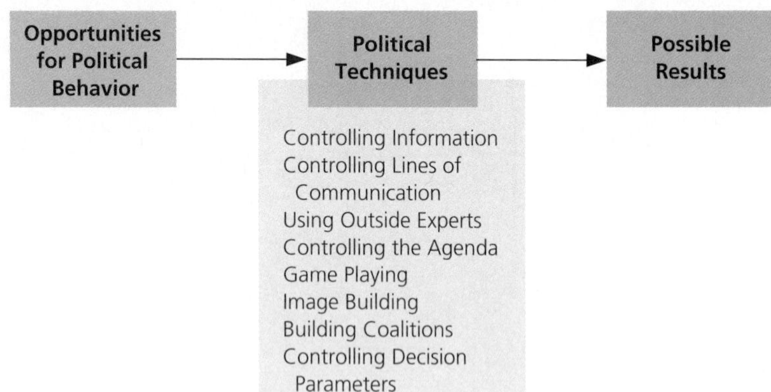

are not returned promptly, and so forth. People in these positions often find that they can use this type of political behavior quite effectively.

Using outside experts, such as consultants or advisers, can be an effective political technique. The manager who hires a consultant may select one whose views match her own. Because the consultant realizes that the manager was responsible for his selection, he feels a certain obligation to her. Although the consultant truly attempts to be objective and unbiased, he unconsciously recommends courses of action favored by the manager. Given the consultant's presumed expertise and neutrality, others in the organization accept his recommendations without challenge. By using an outside expert, the manager ultimately has gotten what she wants.

Controlling the agenda is another common political technique. Suppose a manager wants to prevent a committee from approving a certain proposal. The manager first tries to keep the decision off the agenda entirely, claiming that it is not yet ready for consideration (or attempts to have it placed last on the agenda). As other issues are decided, he sides with the same set of managers on each decision, building up a certain expectation that they are a team. When the controversial item comes up, he is able to defeat it through a combination of everyone's fatigue and wish to get the meeting over with and the support of his carefully cultivated allies. This technique, then, involves group polarization. A less sophisticated tactic is to prolong discussion of prior agenda items so that the group never reaches the controversial one. Or the manager may raise so many technicalities and new questions about the proposal that the committee decides to table it. In any of these cases, the manager will have used political behavior for his or her own ends.

Game playing is a complex technique that may take many forms. When playing games, managers simply work within the rules of the organization to increase the probability that their preferred outcomes will come about. Suppose a manager is in a position to cast the deciding vote on an upcoming issue. She does not want to alienate either side by voting on it. One game she might play is to arrange to be called out of town on a crucial business trip when the vote is to take place. Assuming no one questions the need for the trip, she will successfully maintain her position of neutrality and avoid angering either of the opposing camps.[17] Another game would involve using any of the techniques of political behavior in a purely manipulative or deceitful way. For example, a manager who will soon be making recommendations about promotions tells each subordinate, in "strictest confidence," that he or she is a leading candidate and needs only to increase his or her performance to have the inside track. Here the manager is using his control over information to play games with his subordinates.

Image building or impression management, a subtle form of political behavior, is in most cases a means of enhancing one's power base for future activity. The methods discussed earlier for enhancing expert power are effective image-building techniques. Such behavior increases an individual's power base and hence his or her opportunity for political activities. Another, more manipulative set of techniques also falls under this heading: Jockeying to be associated only with successful projects, taking credit for others' work, and exaggerating one's personal accomplishments may all lead to an enhanced image.[18]

The technique of building coalitions has as its general goal convincing others that everyone should work together to get certain things accomplished. A manager who believes she does not control enough votes to pass an upcoming agenda item may visit with other managers before the meeting to urge them to side with her. If her preferences are in the best interests of the organization, this may be a laudable strategy for her to follow. But if she herself is the principal beneficiary, the technique is not desirable from the organization's perspective.

At its extreme, coalition building, which is frequently used in political bodies, may take the form of blatant reciprocity. In return for Roberta Kline's vote on an issue that concerns him, José Montemayor agrees to vote for a measure that does not affect his group at all but is crucial to Kline's group. Depending on the circumstances, this practice may benefit or hurt the organization as a whole.

The technique of controlling decision parameters can be used only in certain situations and requires much subtlety. Instead of trying to control the actual decision, the manager backs up one step and tries to control the criteria and tests on which the decision is based. This allows the manager to take a less active role in the actual decision but still achieve his or her preferred outcome. For example, suppose a district manager wants a proposed new factory to be constructed on a site in his region. If he tries to influence the decision directly, his arguments will be seen as biased and self-serving. Instead, he may take a very active role in defining the criteria on which the decision will be based, such as target population, access to rail transportation, tax rates, distance from other facilities, and the like. If he is a skillful negotiator, he may be able to influence

17. Michael Macoby, *The Gamesman* (New York: Simon & Schuster, 1976).

18. Robert W. Allen and Lyman W. Porter, eds., *Organizational Influence Processes* (Glenview, Ill.: Scott, Foresman, 1983). See also Eric M. Eisenberg and Marsha G. Witten, "Reconsidering Openness in Organizational Communication," *Academy of Management Review*, vol. 12, 1987, pp. 418–426.

the decision parameters such that his desired location subsequently appears to be the ideal site as determined by the criteria he has helped shape. Hence, he gets just what he wants without playing a prominent role in the actual decision.

Limiting the Effects of Political Behavior Although it is virtually impossible to eliminate political activity in organizations, managers can limit its dysfunctional consequences. The techniques for checking political activity target the reasons it occurs in the first place as well as the specific techniques that people use for political gain. Figure 10.5 summarizes the primary techniques for limiting political activity.

Opening communication is one very effective technique for constraining the impact of political behavior. For instance, open communication can make the basis for allocating scarce resources known to everyone. This knowledge, in turn, will tend to reduce the propensity to engage in political behavior to acquire those resources, because people already know how decisions will be made. Open communication also limits the ability of any single person to control information or lines of communication.

A related technique is to take steps to reduce uncertainty. Several of the reasons for political behavior—ambiguous goals, nonroutine technology and an unstable environment, and organizational change—as well as most of the political techniques themselves are associated with high levels of uncertainty. Political behavior can be limited if the manager can reduce uncertainty. Consider an organization about to transfer a major division from Florida to Michigan. Many people will resist the idea of moving north and may resort to political behavior to forestall the possibility of their own transfer. However, if the manager in charge of the move announces who will stay and who will go at the same time that news of the change spreads throughout the company, political behavior related to the move may be curtailed.

The adage "forewarned is forearmed" sums up the final technique for controlling political activity: Simply being aware of the causes and techniques of political behavior can help a manager check their effects. Suppose a manager anticipates that several impending organizational changes will increase the level of political activity. As a result of this awareness, the manager quickly infers that a particular subordinate is lobbying for the use of a certain consultant only because the subordinate thinks the consultant's recommendations will be in line with his own. Attempts to control the agenda, engage in game playing, build a

FIGURE 10.5
Limiting the Effects of Political Behavior

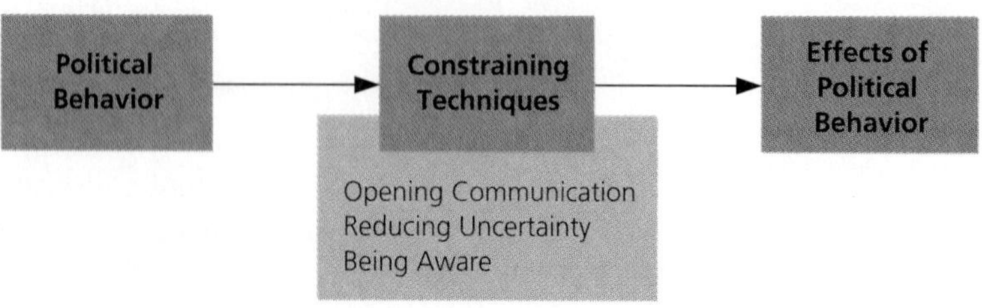

Conflict is a common outgrowth of power and politics. The northern spotted owl, an endangered species found only in the Northwest United States, is presently the subject of just this type of conflict. The Wilderness Society, a local environmental protection group, claims that 3 million acres needs to be set aside for the owls. Timber industry representatives argue that protecting the owls will cost them 100,000 jobs. The two sides are currently waging battle in the courts amid an ever-increasing context of hostility, name-calling, and threats.

certain image, and control decision parameters often are transparent to the knowledgeable observer. Recognizing such behaviors for what they are, an astute manager may be able to take appropriate steps to limit their impact.

Conflict in Organizations

■ **Conflict** is disagreement among parties. It has both positive and negative characteristics.

Related to power and politics in organizational life is conflict. In its simplest form, **conflict** is disagreement among parties. Conflict can occur among individuals or among groups. Often it is generated by political behavior. In particular, it frequently occurs when a group believes its attempts to achieve its goal are being blocked by another group. For example, conflict may arise over financial resources, the number of authorized positions in work groups, or the number of microcomputers to be purchased for departments. Conflict may also result from anticipating trouble: A group may behave antagonistically toward another group that it expects to pose obstacles to its goal achievement.[19]

While conflict often is considered harmful, and thus something to avoid, it can also have some benefits. A total absence of conflict can lead to apathy and lethargy. A moderate degree of focused conflict, on the other hand, can stimulate new ideas, promote healthy competition, and energize behavior. *A Look at the Research* summarizes some recent findings about how views of conflict vary among different kinds of organizations.

19. See Stephen P. Robbins, *Managing Organizational Conflict* (Englewood Cliffs, N.J.: Prentice-Hall, 1974), for a classic review.

A LOOK AT THE RESEARCH

The Pros and Cons of Conflict

Conventional wisdom about conflict seems pretty much cut and dried. Too little conflict breeds apathy and stagnation. Too much conflict leads to divisiveness and hostility. Moderate levels of conflict, however, can spark creativity and motivate people in a healthy and competitive way.

Recent research by Professor Charles R. Schwenk, however, suggests that the optimal level of conflict may be more complex to determine than these simple generalizations. He studied perceptions of conflict among a sample of executives. Some of the executives worked for profit-seeking organizations and others for not-for-profit organizations.

Somewhat surprisingly, Schwenk found that opinions about conflict varied systematically as a function of the type of organization. Specifically, managers in not-for-profit organizations strongly believed that conflict was beneficial to their organizations and that it promoted higher-quality decision making than might be achieved in the absence of conflict.

Managers of for-profit organizations saw a different picture. They believed that conflict generally was dysfunctional and usually led to poor-quality decision making in their organizations. Schwenk interpreted these results in terms of the criteria for effective decision making suggested by the executives. In the profit-seeking organizations, decision-making effectiveness was most often assessed in financial terms. The executives believed that consensus rather than conflict enhanced financial indicators.

In the not-for-profit organizations, decision-making effectiveness was defined from the perspective of satisfying constituents. Given the complexities and ambiguities associated with satisfying many diverse constituents, executives perceived that conflict led to more considered and acceptable decisions.

SOURCE: Reprinted by permission of Charles R. Schwenk, "Conflict in Organizational Decision Making: An Exploratory Study of Its Effects in For-Profit and Not-For-Profit Organizations," *Management Science*, Vol. 36, No. 4, April 1990. Copyright 1990, The Institute of Management Sciences.

The Nature of Conflict

Figure 10.6 illustrates the basic nature of organizational conflict. When groups strive for the same goal, hold little or no antagonism toward one another, and behave according to rules and procedures, competition is the most likely outcome. In contrast, conflict is likely when one group's goals jeopardize the others', there is open antagonism among the groups, and few rules and procedures regulate their behavior. When this happens, the goals become extremely important, the antagonism increases, and rules and procedures are violated.[20]

Managing Conflict

■ Depending on the circumstances, a manager may need to either resolve or stimulate conflict.

Given the potentially disruptive effects of conflict, managers need to be sensitive to how it can be managed. When a potentially harmful conflict situation exists,

20. Ibid.

FIGURE 10.6
Conflict-Competition Relationship

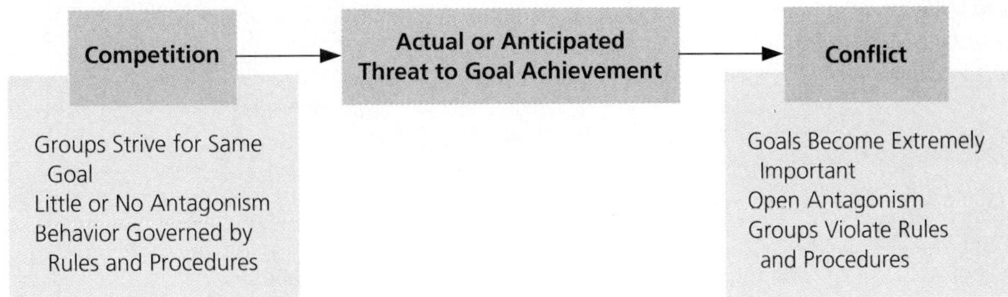

a manager needs to engage in *conflict resolution*. As Figure 10.7 shows, conflict needs to be resolved when it causes major disruptions in the organization and absorbs time and effort that could be used more productively. In addition, conflict needs to be resolved when its focus is on the group's internal goals rather than on the organizational goals.

We will describe the principal conflict-handling strategies shortly. First, remember that sometimes a manager should be concerned about the absence of conflict. An absence of conflict may indicate that the organization is stagnant and employees are content with the status quo. It may also suggest that work groups are not motivated to challenge traditional and well-accepted ideas.[21] *Conflict stimulation* is the creation and constructive use of conflict by a manager.[22] Its purpose is to bring about situations where differences of opinion are exposed for examination by all. For example, if competing organizations are making significant changes in products, markets, or technologies, it may be time for a manager to stimulate innovation and creativity by challenging the status quo. Stimulating conflict may provide employees with the motivation and opportunity to reveal differences of opinion that they previously kept to themselves. When all parties to the conflict are interested enough in an issue to be somewhat antagonistic toward other groups, they often expose their hidden doubts or opinions. This, in turn, allows the parties to get to the heart of the matter and often to develop unique solutions to the problem. Indeed, the interactions may lead the groups to recognize that a problem in fact exists. Conflict, then, can be a catalyst for creativity and change in an organization.

Several methods for stimulating conflict under controlled conditions are available.[23] These include altering the physical location of groups to stimulate more interaction, forcing more resource sharing, and implementing other changes in relationships among groups. In addition, training programs can be used to increase employee awareness of potential problems in group decision making and group interactions. Adopting the role of "devil's advocate" in discussion sessions is another method of stimulating conflict among groups. In this role, a

21. Irving Janis, *Groupthink,* 2nd ed. (Boston: Houghton Mifflin, 1982).
22. Robbins, *Managing Organizational Conflict.*
23. Ibid.

FIGURE 10.7
Conflict Management Alternatives

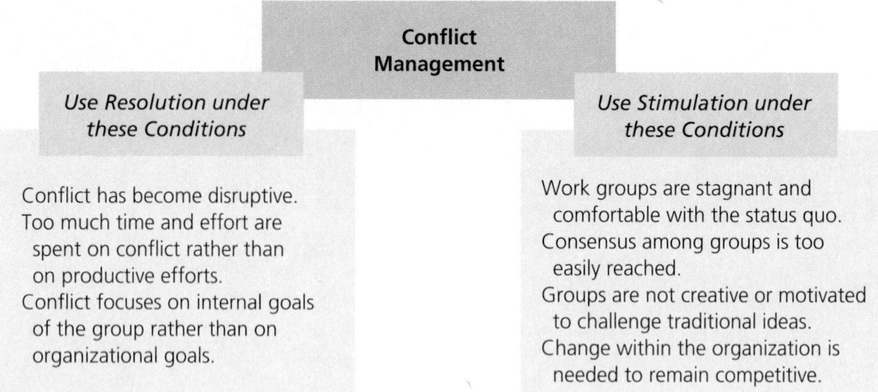

manager challenges the prevailing consensus of opinion to ensure that all alternatives have been critically appraised and analyzed. Although this role often is unpopular, it is a good way to stimulate constructive conflict.

Of course, too much conflict is also a concern. If conflict becomes excessive or destructive, the manager needs to adopt a strategy for reducing or resolving it. We described the most common strategies in Chapter 8. In particular, any of the goal-based, location-based, resource-based, or organization-based strategies, as well as people- or group-based strategies, can be used to reduce or resolve conflict among people or groups. One organization-based strategy is decoupling. If conflict has become excessive, the individuals or groups involved might be functionally separated.[24]

Thus, conflict management is the process of recognizing the proper role of conflict among groups in organizations and using resolution and stimulation techniques as needed to enhance organizational effectiveness.

Summary of Key Points

- Power is the potential ability of a person or group to influence another person or group. French and Raven identified five bases of power. Legitimate power is power granted by virtue of one's position in the organization. Reward power is the control of rewards valued by others. Coercive power is the ability to punish or harm. Expert power is control over information that is valuable to the organization. Referent power is power through personal identification.

24. See "Battling Executives Seek Out Therapists," *The Wall Street Journal,* November 7, 1988, p. B1.

- Another approach proposes two sources of power. Position power is tied to a position regardless of the individual who holds it. Personal power is power that resides in a person regardless of position.
- Attempts to use power can result in commitment, compliance, or resistance. Yukl's guidelines detail how managers can use the five bases of power to achieve commitment or compliance and to avoid resistance.
- Organizational politics are activities people perform to acquire, enhance, and use power and other resources to obtain their preferred outcomes in a situation where uncertainty or disagreement exists. Research indicates that most managers do not advocate political behavior but acknowledge it as a necessity of organizational life. Cavanaugh and his associates developed a model that attempts to specify conditions under which political behavior may or may not be ethical. Because managers cannot eliminate political activity in the organization, they must learn to cope with it.
- Understanding how to manage political behavior requires an understanding of the reasons for political behavior, the techniques of political behavior, and strategies for limiting its effects. Principal causes of political activity are ambiguous goals, scarce resources, technology and environment, nonprogrammed decisions, and organizational change. Common political techniques are controlling information, controlling lines of communication, using outside experts, controlling the agenda, game playing, image building, building coalitions, and controlling decision parameters. Ways to limit the effects of political behavior are open communication, reduction of uncertainty, and alertness to the causes and techniques of political behavior.
- Conflict is a common outgrowth of political behavior in organizations. Managers should recognize that conflict can be beneficial as well as harmful. Numerous techniques can be used to either stimulate or resolve conflict as appropriate.

Discussion Questions

1. Develop your own definition of power. Compare and contrast your definition with that in the text.
2. What might happen if two people, each with significant and equal power, attempt to influence each other?
3. Cite examples in a professor-student relationship to illustrate each of the five bases of organizational power.
4. Is there a logical sequence for the use of power bases that a manager might follow? That is, should the use of legitimate power usually precede the use of reward power, or vice versa?
5. Choose a popular political figure, and characterize his or her position and personal power. Which is stronger? Is it really possible to separate the two forms of power?

6. Cite examples in which you have been committed, compliant, and resistant as a result of efforts to influence you. Think of times when your attempts to influence others led to commitment, compliance, and resistance.
7. Do you disagree with any of the guidelines for using power cited in the chapter? What other guidelines can you suggest? Describe a situation in which you observed the successful use of one or more of these strategies.
8. Do you agree or disagree with the assertion that political behavior is inevitable in organizational settings?
9. Given its general association with governmental bodies, why do you think the term *politics* has also come to be associated with behavior in organizations as described in the chapter?
10. Recall examples of how you have either used or observed others using the techniques of political behavior identified in the chapter. What other techniques can you suggest?
11. Do you agree or disagree with the assertion that conflict can be both good and bad? Cite examples of both cases.

CASE 10.1

Power and Conflict at CBS

Most people know what *politics* means when applied to a business setting. But few get a chance to sit in on a board meeting that decides the fate of millions of dollars and thousands of jobs, careers, and reputations. In 1986, however, a top-level shakeup occurred that allowed the rest of the world to see what rarefied corporate politics is all about. The shakeup occurred at one of the nation's biggest media companies, CBS.

The showdown occurred on September 10, 1986, but the story really began in 1980, when CBS's founder and chairperson, William Paley, hired Thomas Wyman as the company's CEO. Three years later, CBS's board forced Paley out as chairperson and gave Wyman the position. Even if he didn't plan it that way, Paley got his revenge three years later.

In the meantime, CBS attracted a lot of attention both in the media and on Wall Street. In 1985, a group led by Senator Jesse Helms announced that it was going to try to buy CBS. The company's stock rose, and a number of America's financial heavyweights, including Ivan Boesky, Ted Turner, and Marvis Davis, made bids for the company. Turner wanted to divest the company of its non-broadcasting business. The latest to buy a big share of CBS was Laurence Tisch, chairman of Loew's Companies, who bought just under 25 percent of the company and was appointed to its board of directors in October 1985. CBS was not doing well, either financially or in the ratings, and everyone was waiting for something to break.

On September 10, 1986, during a nine-hour board meeting, the break came. Most of the board had met for dinner the night before, and Paley had argued, unsuccessfully, that Wyman must go. Wyman had appointed some board members, and a number of others supported him; only four or five joined Paley in opposing him. But Wyman apparently feared that Tisch intended to take over the company or that another unfriendly raider would appear with an offer that

CBS would be unable to fight off. Tisch had refused to sign a statement saying that he would not increase his holdings in CBS, although he had given the other directors his word.

After a gloomy morning meeting about the company's market and financial position, Wyman played his card: He announced that Coca-Cola Company was willing to buy CBS. He apparently anticipated that the directors would be pleased to hear of a friendly offer for CBS or that Tisch would be forced to play his hand and reveal his own interest in buying the company. In fact, the directors were stunned and appalled. After fighting to keep the company independent for two years, Wyman was asking them to sell out to a company whose leaders were, as they knew, personally friendly with Wyman. In addition, he apparently had been negotiating on his own, without telling anyone else on the board.

The move cost Wyman his credibility and, ultimately, his job. Tisch and Paley refused to consider the sale, and the other directors were even more unnerved when Wyman told them that he would need some time to get an offer on the table. He had not brought along any lawyers or investment bankers to help him make his case. Wyman left the meeting at noon, Paley and Tisch left soon after, and the remaining board members pondered the situation. Late that afternoon, two board members visited Wyman to tell him that his support among the board had disappeared. Wyman resigned, and the board asked Tisch to take over as CEO and Paley to return to his position as chairperson. Both appointments were to be temporary.

The postscript to the September 10 showdown contained many ironies. Under Tisch's leadership, CBS began selling off its record, book, and magazine publishing businesses, exactly as Ted Turner, the spurned raider, had said he himself would do. Some of the newspeople who welcomed Tisch's takeover at a party that fateful night began to have their doubts when Tisch cut the news budget and staff. And it seemed that Thomas Wyman may have been right about Laurence Tisch's motives: Two years after the shakeup, Tisch had firm control over the company—as firm as if he owned it.

Case Questions

1. What kinds of power did the various participants in the CBS shakeup wield?
2. Is it inevitable that such a boardroom battle would take on some of the aspects of a poker game?

SOURCES: "Tisch Does What CBS Feared in Turner," *The Wall Street Journal,* November 20, 1987, p. 6; "The Showdown at CBS," *Newsweek,* September 22, 1986, pp. 54–59; "How the CBS Board Decided Chief Wyman Should Leave His Job," *The Wall Street Journal,* September 12, 1986, p. 1.

CASE 10.2 The Struggle for Power at Ramsey Electronics

A vice president's position is about to open up at Ramsey Electronics, maker of components for audio and visual equipment and computers. Whoever fills the position will be one of the four most powerful people in the company and may one day become its chief executive officer. So the whole company has been watching the political skirmishes among the three leading candidates: Arnie Sander, Laura Prove, and Billy Evans.

Arnie Sander, currently head of the research and development division, worked his way up through the engineering ranks. Of the three candidates, he alone has a Ph.D. (in electrical engineering from MIT), and he is the acknowledged genius behind the company's most innovative products. One of the current vice presidents—Harley Learner, himself an engineer—has been pushing hard for Sander's case.

Laura Prove spent five years on the road, earning a reputation as an outstanding salesperson of Ramsey products before coming to company headquarters and working her way up through the sales division. She knows only enough about what she calls the "guts" of Ramsey's electronic parts to get by, but she is very good at selling them and at motivating the people who work for her. Frank Barnwood, another current vice president, has been filling the Chief's ear with Prove's praises.

Of the three candidates, Billy Evans is the youngest and has the least experience at Ramsey. Like the Chief, he has an M.B.A. from Harvard Business School and a very sharp mind for finances. The Chief has credited him with turning the company's financial situation around, although others in the company believe Sander's products or Prove's selling ability really deserves the credit. Evans has no particular champion among Ramsey's top executives, but he is the only other handball player the Chief has located in the company, and the two play every Tuesday and Thursday after work. Learner and Barnwood have noticed that the company's financial decisions often get made during the cooling-off period following a handball game.

In the month preceding the Chief's decision, the two vice presidents have been busy. Learner, head of a national engineering association, worked to have Sander win an achievement award from the association, and two weeks before the naming of the new vice president, he threw the most lavish banquet in the company's history to announce the award. When introducing Sander, Learner made a long, impassioned speech detailing Sander's accomplishments and heralding him as "the future of Ramsey Electronics."

Frank Barnwood has moved more slowly and subtly. The Chief had asked Barnwood years before to keep him updated on "all these gripes by women and minorities and such," and Barnwood did so by giving the Chief articles of particular interest. Recently he gave the Chief one from a psychology magazine about the cloning effect—the tendency of powerful executives to choose successors who are most like themselves. He also passed on to the Chief a *Fortune* article arguing that many American corporations are floundering because they are being run by financial people rather than by people who really know the company's business. He also flooded bulletin boards and the Chief's desk with news clippings about the value of having women and minorities at the top levels of a company.

Billy Evans has seemed indifferent to the promotion. He spends his days on the phone and in front of the computer screen, reporting to the Chief every other week on the company's latest financial successes—and never missing a handball game.

Case Questions

1. Who do you think the Chief will pick as the new vice president?
2. Who do you think should get the job? Why?

EXPERIENTIAL EXERCISE

Purpose: This exercise will help you appreciate some of the ambiguities involved in assessing the ethics of political activity in organizations.

Format: First, you will create scenarios that you think represent different ethical perspectives. Then your classmates will assess your interpretations and you will evaluate theirs.

Procedure: Your instructor will divide the class into an even number of small groups of three to four. Using the model of ethical political behavior presented in Figure 10.2, write several short scenarios that represent different ethical perspectives to your group. Write one scenario that follows all the "yes" branches in the model, one that follows only "no" branches, and three that follow different combinations of "yes" and "no" branches. For an example, reread the hypothetical case of the two professors up for a tenure vote.

Number your scenarios randomly from 1 to 5. Do not write down anything that might indicate which branches are to be followed. On a separate page, write a brief description of the rationale for the path your group thinks each scenario most logically follows.

Next, exchange scenarios with another group. Evaluate each of its scenarios, and determine the most logical path through the model. Then exchange "answer sheets" and compare your interpretation of each scenario with that of the other group.

The two pairs of groups will then meet to discuss their results. Discussion should center on reasons for any disagreement between the two groups.

Follow-up Questions

1. How realistic was this exercise? What did you learn from it?
2. Could you assess real-life situations relating to the ethics of political activity using the same approach?

CHAPTER OUTLINE

- Communication in Organizations
  - *Purposes of Communication in Organizations*
  - *Uncertainty and the Role of Information*
- Methods of Communication
  - *Written Communication*
  - *Oral Communication*
  - *Nonverbal Communication*
- The Basic Communication Process
  - *Source*
  - *Encoding*
  - *Transmission*
  - *Decoding*
  - *Receiver/Responder*
  - *Feedback*
  - *Noise*
- Communication Networks
  - *Small-Group Networks*
  - *Organizational Communication Networks*
- Managing Organizational Communication
  - *Improving the Communication Process*
  - *Improving Organizational Factors in Communication*
- Electronic Information Processing and Telecommunications

11

INTERPERSONAL COMMUNICATION

CHAPTER OBJECTIVES

After studying this chapter, you should be able to:

Define communication *and discuss its purposes in organizations.*

Summarize the basic methods of communication.

Describe the basic communication process.

Describe small-group and organizational communication networks.

Identify and discuss several barriers to communication in organizations and how they can be overcome.

Discuss the impact of computerized information processing and telecommunications in organizations.

The portable telephone has ushered in an entire era of communication. In 1990, there were four basic types: the mobile phone (for use in a car), the transportable phone, the bag phone, and the hand-held portable phone. One of the smallest was the 10.7 ounce MicroTAC made by Motorola.

The portable phone has become a symbol of status for professionals and nonprofessionals alike. People use portable phones on the subway or freeway commuting to and from work, in the park, and even at a Little League baseball game or youth swim meet.

Although the popularity of portable telephones probably will increase for many years to come, there are some problems associated with this communication phenomenon. Some users have complained that moving from one cell to another sometimes causes reception to fade in and out. Others dislike the requirement that each unit have a unique phone number. If a dual-income family wants one portable phone for general household use, one for the teenagers, one for the fax machine, one to hook up to the computer at the office, one for each wage earner's car, and one for each spouse's briefcase, it will need eight different phone numbers. This means that family members must memorize all eight numbers and friends and business associates several of the numbers. If each subscriber wants multiple numbers, the system may become oversubscribed quickly. In addition, the huge investment in communication equipment that such demand would require could instantly become obsolete as soon as another major breakthrough in communications technology occurs.

Obviously the portable telephone is here to stay, at least in some form. You may even have one in your book bag as you read this chapter. One hint, however: Your professors will not be pleased if your phone rings and you answer it in class. This is considered bad form and not conducive to making a good impression with the professor![1]

Portable telephones represent the latest in new technology affecting interpersonal communication. Regardless of new technology, however, the basics of interpersonal communication remain important. In this chapter, we focus on the important processes of interpersonal communication and information processing. Communication is important for all phases of organizational behavior, but it is especially crucial in decision making, performance appraisal, motivation, and

1. Andrew Kupfer, "The Go-Anywhere Phone Is at Hand," *Fortune,* November 5, 1990, pp. 143–148; Sally Solo, "The Telephone Woes of CEOs," *Fortune,* November 5, 1990, pp. 14–15; Loretta Hall, "Have Phone, Will Travel," *Home-Office Computing,* June 1990, pp. 41–43.

Communication is needed as part of the decision-making process and to achieve coordinated action. These men are part of a six-person international team making the first unmechanized crossing of Antarctica. During their mission they had to make decisions quickly and were often forced to communicate with gestures and hand signals. Clearly, effective communication was vital to the success of the expedition.

generally ensuring that the organization functions effectively. First, we discuss the importance of communication in organizations and how information is transferred and processed. We describe the methods of organizational communication and examine the basic communication process. Next, we explore the development of communication networks in organizations. Then we discuss several common problems of organizational communication and methods for managing communication. Finally, we examine the potential effects of computerized information processing and telecommunications.

Communication in Organizations

- **Communication** is the process by which two or more parties exchange information and share meaning.

Communication is the process by which two or more parties exchange information and share meaning.[2] Communication has been studied from many perspectives. In this section, we overview the complex and dynamic communication process.

Purposes of Communication in Organizations

Communication among individuals and groups is vital in all organizations. Some of the purposes of organizational communication are listed in Figure 11.1. The primary purpose is to achieve coordinated action.[3] Just as the human nervous system responds to stimuli and coordinates responses by sending messages to the various parts of the body, communication coordinates the actions of the parts

2. Charles A. O'Reilly III and Louis R. Pondy, "Organizational Communication," in Steven Kerr, ed., *Organizational Behavior* (Columbus, Ohio: Grid, 1979), p. 121.

3. Otis W. Baskin and Craig E. Aronoff, *Interpersonal Communication in Organizations* (Santa Monica, Calif.: Goodyear, 1980), p. 2.

FIGURE 11.1
Three Purposes of Organizational Communication

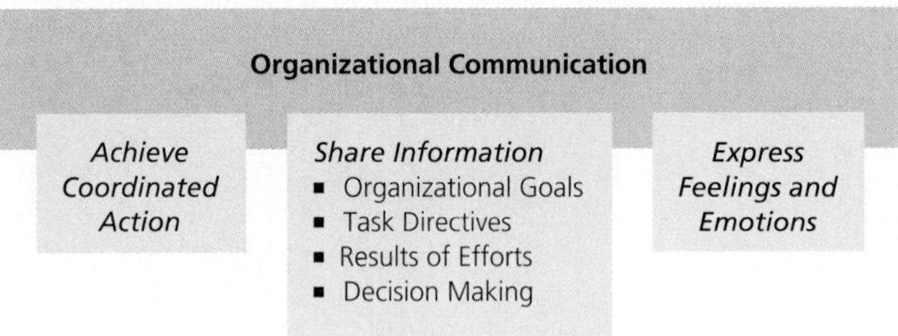

of an organization. Without communication, an organization would be merely a collection of individual workers attending to separate tasks. Organizational action would lack coordination and be oriented toward individual rather than organizational goals.

A second purpose of communication is information sharing. The most important information relates to organizational goals, which provide members with a sense of purpose and direction. Another information-sharing function of communication is the giving of specific task directions to individuals. Whereas information on organizational goals gives employees a sense of how their activities fit into the overall picture, task communication tells them what their job duties are and what they are not. Employees must also receive information on the results of their efforts, as in performance appraisals.

Communication is essential to the decision-making process as well, as we discuss in Chapter 16. Information, and thus information sharing, is needed to define problems, generate and evaluate alternatives, implement decisions, and control and evaluate results.

Finally, communication expresses feelings and emotions. Organizational communication is far from a collection of facts and figures. People in organizations, like people anywhere else, often need to communicate emotions such as happiness, anger, displeasure, confidence, and fear.

Communication is an essential element of the manager's job. Managers must communicate with people at many levels—those above, those below, and those at the same level in the hierarchy. A manager's communication with those who work for him or her may be the most important, because all aspects of the work—training, task assignment, and performance appraisal—are delivered through communication. Employees have reported higher levels of job satisfaction and work performance when they are pleased with the way their supervisor communicates and the personal feedback they get.[4] Managerial communication continues to be the focus of a great deal of research. *A Look at the Research* shows an example of recent research on communication in organizations.

Communication thus is involved in many activities of the organization. Above all, it is the process through which individual and group activities and interactions are coordinated for the improvement of organizational effectiveness.

---

4. J. David Pincus, "Communication Satisfaction, Job Satisfaction, and Job Performance," *Human Communication Research*, Spring 1986, pp. 395–419.

A LOOK AT THE **RESEARCH**

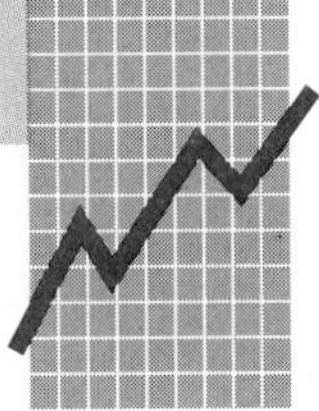

Communication Patterns in Different Organizational Structures

Communication in organizations has been viewed as something top management does to tell lower-level employees what decisions have been made regarding projects and tasks. Communication patterns have been described as top-down, bottom-up, and in terms of small-group networks (wheel, circle, chain, etc.). John A. Courtright of the University of Delaware, Gail T. Fairhurst of the University of Cincinnati, and L. Edna Rogers of the University of Utah have taken a different view. They completed a study of communication patterns between supervisors and subordinates in two different plants of a manufacturing company. Using tape-recorded discussions between managers and subordinates in each plant, they attempted to explore the extent to which communication patterns were determined by the plants' organizational structures.

The organizational structures of the two plants differed sharply. One plant was over fifty years old and was organized in the traditional hierarchical structure. The other was only about ten years old and was organized around self-managed work teams. The two plants manufactured similar products; thus, the tasks, technologies, and environmental factors were basically the same.

A total of sixty manager-subordinate pairs agreed to have their routine conversations tape recorded. Out of these, forty-five usable tape recordings were returned; nineteen were from the traditional, older plant, and twenty-six were from the newer plant. All the recorded conversations were at least thirty minutes long. Using a somewhat complex coding scheme, the researchers classified the conversations as being "top-down," "bottom-up," or "across."

Analysis of the coded conversations revealed several interesting things. First, there were significantly more top-down (manager-to-subordinate) communications at the traditional plant than at the newer, self-managed plant. Also, managers and subordinates at the traditional plant were more likely to interrupt and argue with each other. In the self-managed plant, interactions were initiated more often by questions than by top-down statements from the manager, especially at the lower levels; the opposite was true at the traditional plant.

The researchers concluded that the form of organizational structure of a firm may indeed be a primary determinant of communication and interaction patterns. Clearly, as organizations continue to experiment with new organizational structures, the impact on internal communication patterns needs to be studied and analyzed.

SOURCE: John A. Courtright, Gail T. Fairhurst, and L. Edna Rogers, "Interaction Patterns in Organic and Mechanistic Systems," *Academy of Management Journal*, December 1989, pp. 773–802. Adapted by permission.

Uncertainty and the Role of Information

- Communication can reduce the amount of uncertainty that plagues most decision making in organizations.

Decisions must be made under uncertainty when little information is available on the outcomes of alternative actions. *Uncertainty* may also be defined in a more general sense as "the difference between the amount of information required to perform the task and the information already possessed by the organization."[5] The greater the uncertainty regarding the tasks of a work group, the

5. Jay R. Galbraith, *Organization Design* (Reading, Mass.: Addison-Wesley, 1977), p. 36.

more information the group needs to operate effectively and efficiently. In other words, when task uncertainty is high, the information processing of the individual or group responsible for the task must be correspondingly high to reduce the uncertainty.[6] If the uncertainty is not reduced, task performance will suffer.

Uncertainty occurs in organizations because of size, changes in the environment, and interdependencies among departments.[7] A large organization must coordinate a substantial number of people and tasks. The complexity inevitably creates uncertainty and thus necessitates more information processing. Changing customer demands, likes, and dislikes represent increasing uncertainty, to which the organization must respond with more innovative products and services. The need for a response or for more coordinated action among interdependent units requires managers to process more information, make decisions, and communicate them to other organization members.

Methods of Communication

The three primary methods of communicating in organizations are written, oral, and nonverbal communication. Often the methods are combined. Considerations that affect the choice of method include the audience (whether it is physically present), the nature of the message (its urgency or secrecy), and the costs of transmission. Table 11.1 lists various forms each method can take.

Written Communication

Typically organizations produce a great deal of written communication of many kinds. A *letter* is a formal means of communicating with an individual, generally someone outside the organization. Probably the most common form of written communication in organizations is the *office memorandum,* or *memo*. Memos usually are addressed to a person or group inside the organization.[8] They tend to deal with a single topic and are more impersonal (as they often are destined to more than one person) but less formal than letters.

Other common forms of written communication include reports, manuals, and forms. *Reports* generally summarize the progress or results of a project and often provide information to be used in decision making. *Manuals* have various functions in organizations. Instruction manuals tell employees how to operate machines; policy and procedures manuals inform them of organizational rules;

---

6. See Joseph L. C. Cheng, "Paradigm Development and Communication in Scientific Settings: A Contingency Analysis," *Academy of Management Journal,* December 1984, pp. 870–877, for a study of task uncertainty and information processing in organizations.

7. Richard L. Daft, *Organization Theory and Design,* 2nd ed. (St. Paul, Minn.: West, 1983) pp. 306–307.

8. William J. Seiler, E. Scott Baudhuin, and L. David Shuelke, *Communication in Business and Professional Organizations* (Reading, Mass.: Addison-Wesley, 1982).

TABLE 11.1
Methods of Communication in Organizations

Written	Oral	Nonverbal
Letters	Informal conversations	*Human Elements*
Memos		Facial Expressions Body Language
Reports	Task-Related Exchanges	*Environmental Elements*
Manuals	Group Discussions	Office Design
Forms	Formal Speeches	Building Architecture

and operations manuals describe how to perform tasks and respond to work-related problems. *Forms* are standardized documents on which to report information. As such, they represent attempts to make communication more efficient and information more accessible. A performance appraisal form is an example.

Oral Communication

The most prevalent form of organizational communication is oral. Oral communication takes place everywhere—in informal conversations, in the process of doing work, in meetings of groups and task forces, and in formal speeches and presentations. This form of communication is particularly powerful because it includes not only speakers' words but also their changes in tone, pitch, speed, and volume. As listeners, people use all of these cues to understand oral messages. Moreover, receivers interpret oral messages in the context of previous communications and, perhaps, the reactions of other receivers. Quite often top management of the organization sets the tone for oral communication, as we discuss in *Management in Action.*

One particularly difficult communication situation occurs when an employee must give the boss some bad news, such as when results do not meet expectations or goals, when plans go awry, or when an unforeseen event has occurred. Most experts agree that face-to-face communication works best when giving bad news. However, it may also be useful to include some form of written documentation of facts and figures to back up the verbal message and to show some alternative ways to get out of the jam or work around the problem.[9]

Nonverbal Communication

■ Most forms of communication, including written and oral, usually are associated with some form of nonverbal communication.

Nonverbal communication includes all the elements associated with human communication that are not expressed orally or in writing. Sometimes it conveys

9. Walter Kiechel III, "Breaking the Bad News to the Boss," *Fortune,* April 9, 1990, pp. 111–112.

MANAGEMENT IN ACTION

Internal Communication at Zenith

Zenith Electronics Corp. chose to stay in the consumer electronics business, specifically television sets, when most other U.S. electronics companies sold out due to foreign competition. Although its factories are running at full capacity, Zenith's TV business has not been profitable, primarily because of what Zenith CEO Jerry Pearlman has called dumping of color television sets on the worldwide markets. Stockholders, especially those who hold large interests such as institutional investors and an entity called the Brookhurst Partners, have called for either the sale of the television division or the ouster of CEO Pearlman.

Zenith is, however, making money in its personal computer business. It is the largest IBM clone seller in the United States; its computer business showed a 1989 operating profit of about $100 million on sales of $1.7 billion. Nevertheless, Pearlman has put most of his time and effort into the television business, both traditional color sets and new developments in the high-definition television (HDTV) area. He is trying to convince the Federal Communications Commission to make Zenith's HDTV the industry standard.

Investors and other outsiders, however, believe the problem with Zenith is not in its markets and technology but in its internal management. CEO Pearlman has been known as a tough talker since his days at Harvard Business School. He often loudly berates employees in public when results are not as expected and creates embarrassing confrontations. His tough communication style, however, has failed to turn around the color television business. In fact, Pearlman may have alienated investors, employees, and retailers along the way as he sought more shelf space for his television sets and computers. One representative of an investor group described Pearlman as a "desperate man doing desperate things." His communications style may play a big role in Jerry Pearlman's ability to stay at the helm of Zenith, with or without the television business.

SOURCES: "Zenith's Jerry Pearlman Sure Is Persistent," *Business Week,* October 2, 1989, pp. 67–70; Lisa Kartus, "The Strange Folks Picking on Zenith," *Fortune,* December 19, 1988, pp. 79–84; "Changing Channels: Zenith May Shift Emphasis from TVs to PCs," *PC Week,* June 7, 1988, p. 163.

more meaning than words. Human elements include facial expressions and physical movements, both conscious and unconscious. Facial expressions have been categorized as (1) interest-excitement, (2) enjoyment-joy, (3) surprise-startle, (4) distress-anguish, (5) fear-terror, (6) shame-humiliation, (7) contempt-disgust, and (8) anger-rage.[10] The eyes are the most expressive component of the face.

Physical movements and "body language" are also highly expressive human elements. Body language includes both actual movement and body positions during communication. The handshake is a common form of body language. Other examples include making eye contact that expresses a willingness to communicate; sitting on the edge of a chair, which many indicate nervousness or anxiety; and sitting back with arms folded, which may mean an unwillingness to continue the discussion.

10. Silvan S. Tompkins and Robert McCarter, "What and Where Are the Primary Affects? Some Evidence for a Theory," *Perceptual and Motor Skills,* February 1964, pp. 119–158.

Koko, the 19-year-old "talking" gorilla, is a master at communicating nonverbally. Using an 800-word vocabulary in American Sign Language, Koko is able to make her needs and wants known. She is shown here conversing with her friend, Francine (Penny) Patterson.

Environmental elements such as buildings, office space, and furniture can also convey messages. A spacious office, expensive draperies, plush carpeting, and elegant furniture can combine to remind employees or visitors that they are in the office of the president and chief executive officer of the firm. On the other hand, the small metal desk set in the middle of the shop floor accurately communicates the organizational rank of a first-line supervisor. Thus, office arrangements convey status, power, and prestige and create an atmosphere for doing business. The physical setting can also be instrumental in the development of communication networks, because a centrally located person can more easily control the flow of task-related information.[11]

The Basic Communication Process

Communication is a social process in which information is exchanged or a common understanding is established between two or more parties. The process is social because it involves two or more people. It is a two-way process and takes place over time rather than instantaneously. The communication process illustrated in Figure 11.2 is a loop between the source and the receiver.[12] Note

11. Robert T. Keller and Winfred E. Holland, "Communicators and Innovators in Research and Development Organizations," *Academy of Management Journal,* December 1983, pp. 742–749.

12. See Everett M. Rogers and Rekha Agarwala-Rogers, *Communication in Organizations* (New York: Free Press, 1976), for a brief review of the background and development of the source-message-channel-receiver model of communication.

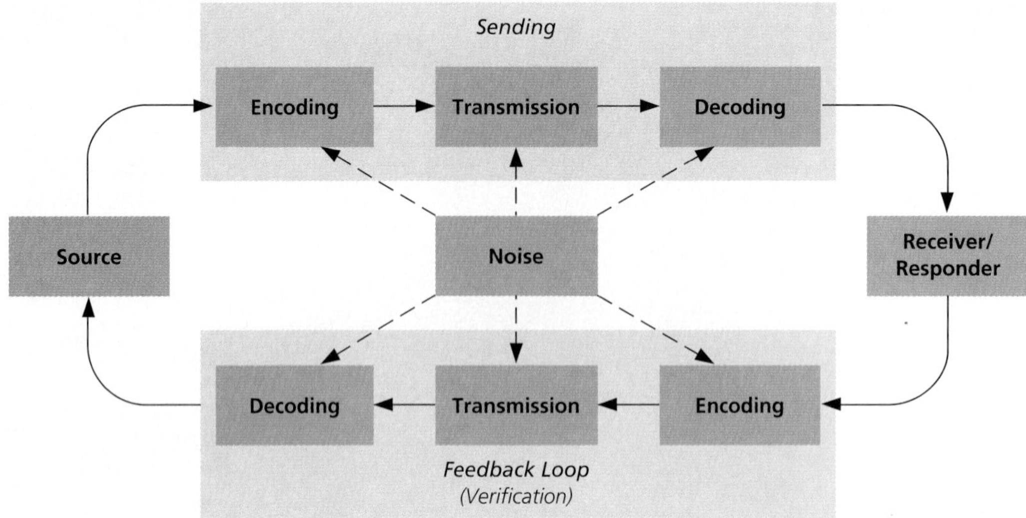

FIGURE 11.2
The Basic Communication Process

the importance of the feedback portion of the loop; upon receiving the message, the receiver responds with a message to the source to verify the communication. Each element of the basic communication process is important. If one part is faulty, the message may not be communicated as it was intended.

Source

- **The source** is the individual, group, or organization interested in communicating something to another party.

The **source** is the individual, group, or organization interested in communicating something to another party. In group or organizational communication, an individual may send the message on behalf of the organization. The source is responsible for preparing the message, encoding it, and entering it into the transmission medium. In some cases, the receiver chooses the source of information,[13] as when a decision maker seeks information from trusted and knowledgeable individuals.

Encoding

- **Encoding** is the process by which the message is translated from an idea or thought into transmittable symbols.

Encoding is the process by which the message is translated from an idea or thought into symbols that can be transmitted. The symbols may be words, numbers, pictures, sounds, or physical gestures and movements. The source must encode the message in symbols that the receiver can decode properly, that is, the source and the receiver must attach the same meaning to the symbols. When we use the symbols of a common language, we assume those symbols have the same

13. Charles A. O'Reilly III, "Variations in Decision Makers' Use of Information Sources: The Impact of Quality and Accessibility of Information," *Academy of Management Journal,* December 1982, pp. 756–771.

This billboard was created by a Hollywood artist to protest the efforts of Senator Jesse Helms to restrict and control federal grants in support of the arts. By combining words and a distinctive image, the artist has conveyed his message in a very clear and effective manner.

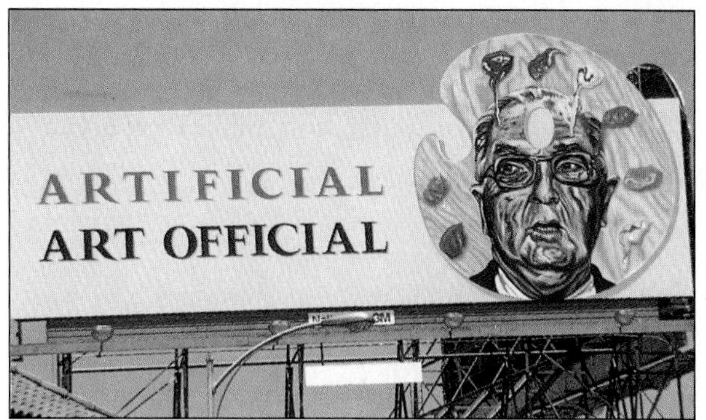

meaning to everyone who uses them. Yet the inherent ambiguity of symbol systems can lead to decoding errors. In verbal communication, for example, some words have different meanings for different people. The meaning of words used by the sender may differ depending on the nonverbal cues, such as facial expression, that the sender transmits along with them.

Transmission

- **Transmission** is the process through which the symbols that represent the message are sent to the receiver.
- The **medium** is the channel or path through which the message is transmitted.

Transmission is the process through which the symbols that carry the message are sent to the receiver. The **medium** is the channel or path of transmission. The medium for face-to-face conversation is sound waves. The same conversation conducted over the telephone involves not only sound waves but electrical impulses and the line that connects the two phones. Communications media can range from an interpersonal medium, such as talking or touching, to a mass medium, such as a newspaper, magazine, or television broadcast. Different media have different capacities for carrying information. For example, a face-to-face conversation generally has more carrying capacity than a letter, because it allows the transmission of more than just words.[14] In addition, the medium can help determine the effect the message has on the receiver. Calling a prospective client on the telephone to make a business proposal is a more personal approach than sending a letter and is likely to elicit a different response.

Decoding

- **Decoding** is the process by which the receiver of the message interprets the message's meaning.

Decoding is the process by which the receiver of the message interprets its meaning. The receiver uses knowledge and experience to interpret the symbols

14. See Richard L. Daft and Robert H. Lengel, "Information Richness: A New Approach to Managerial Behavior and Organization Design," in Barry M. Staw and L.L. Cummings, eds., *Research in Organizational Behavior,* vol. 6. (Greenwich, Conn.: JAI Press, 1984), pp. 191–233, for further discussion of media and information richness.

of the message and in some situations, may consult an authority such as a dictionary or a code book. The meaning the receiver attaches to the symbols may be the same as or different from the meaning intended by the source. If the meanings differ, of course, communication breaks down, and a misunderstanding is likely to occur.

Receiver/Responder

- The **receiver** is the individual, group, or organization that perceives the encoded symbols and may or may not decode them and try to understand the intended message.

The **receiver** of the message may be an individual, a group, an organization, or an individual acting as the representative of a group. Until the decoding step, the source has been active and the receiver passive. However, it is the receiver who decides whether to decode the message, to make an effort to understand it, and to respond. Moreover, the intended receiver may not get the message at all, whereas an unintended receiver may, depending on the medium and symbols used by the source and the attention level of potential receivers.

The expression of emotions by the sender and receiver enters into the communication process in several places. First, the emotions may be part of the message, entering into the encoding process. Second, as the message is decoded, the receiver may let his or her emotions perceive a message different than what the sender intended. Third, emotion-filled feedback from the intended receiver can cause the sender to modify her or his subsequent message.[15]

Feedback

- **Feedback** is the process in which the receiver returns a message to that sender that indicates receipt of the message.

The receiver's response to the message constitutes the feedback loop of the communication process. **Feedback** verifies the message: It tells the source whether the message has been received and understood. The feedback may be as simple as a phone call from the prospective client expressing interest in the business proposal or as complex as a written brief on a complicated point of law sent from an attorney to a judge.

Noise

- **Noise** is any disturbance in the communication process that interferes with or distorts communication.
- **Channel noise** is a disturbance in communication that is due primarily to the medium.

Noise is any disturbance in the communication process that interferes with or distorts communication. Noise can be introduced at virtually any point in the communication process. The principal type, called **channel noise,** is associated

15. Anat Rafaeli and Robert I. Sutton, "The Expression of Emotion in Organizational Life," in Larry L. Cummings and Barry M. Staw, eds., *Research in Organizational Behavior,* vol. 11 (Greenwich, Conn.: JAI Press, 1989), pp. 1–42.

with the medium.[16] Radio static and television "ghosts" are examples of channel noise. When noise interferes in the encoding and decoding processes, poor encoding and decoding can result. Emotions that interfere with an intended communication may also be considered a type of noise.

Communication Networks

Communication links individuals and groups in a social system. Initially, task-related communication links develop in an organization so that employees can get the information they need to do their jobs and coordinate their work with that of others in the system. Over a long period, these communication-relationships become a sophisticated social system composed of both small-group communication networks and a larger organizational network. These networks serve to structure both the flow and the content of communication and to support the organizational structure.[17] The pattern and content of communication also support the culture, beliefs, and value systems that enable the organization to operate.[18]

Small-Group Networks

To examine interpersonal communication in a small group, we can observe the patterns that emerge as the work of the group proceeds and information flows from some people in the group to others.[19] Four such patterns are shown in Figure 11.3. The lines identify the communication links most frequently used in the groups.

- In a **wheel network**, information flows between the person at the end of each spoke and the person in the middle.
- In a **chain network**, each member communicates with the person above and below, but not with the individuals on each end.

The **wheel network** describes a pattern in which information flows between the person at the end of each spoke and the person in the middle. Those on the ends of the spokes do not directly communicate with each other. The wheel network is a feature of the typical work group, where the primary communication occurs between the members and the group manager. In the **chain network,** each member communicates with the person above and below, except for the individuals on each end, who communicate with only one person. The chain network

16. See Jerry C. Wofford, Edwin A. Gerloff, and Robert C. Cummins, *Organizational Communication* (New York: McGraw-Hill, 1977), for a discussion of channel noise.

17. See Daniel Katz and Robert L. Kahn, *The Social Psychology of Organizations,* 2nd ed. (New York: Wiley, 1978), for more about the role of organizational communication networks.

18. Maryan S. Schall, "A Communication-Rules Approach to Organizational Culture," *Administrative Science Quarterly,* December 1983, pp. 557–586.

19. For good discussions of small-group communication networks and research on this subject, see Wofford, Gerloff, and Cummins, *Organizational Communication,* and Marvin E. Shaw, *Group Dynamics: The Psychology of Small Group Behavior,* 3rd ed. (New York: McGraw-Hill, 1981), pp. 150–161.

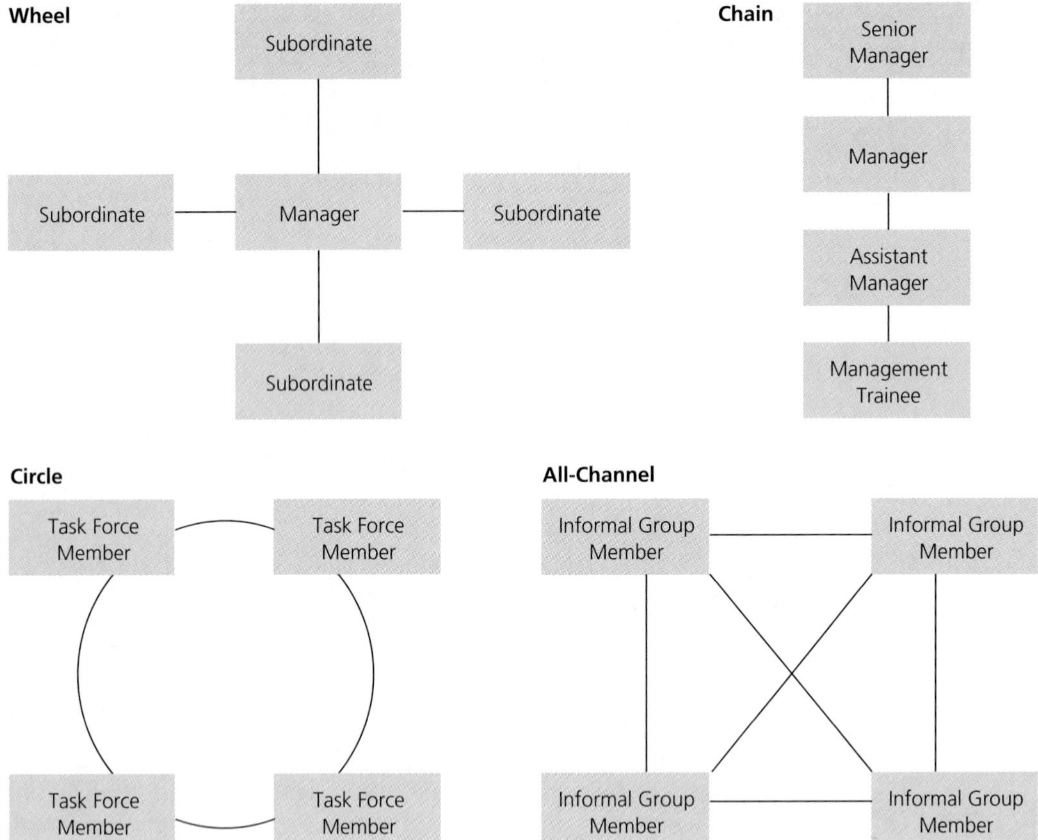

FIGURE 11.3
Small-Group Communication Networks

- In a **circle network**, each member communicates with the people on both sides but with no one else.
- In an **all-channel network**, all members communicate with all other members.

is typical of communication in a vertical hierarchy, in which most communication travels up and down the chain of command. Each person in the **circle network** communicates with the people on both sides but not with anyone else. The circle pattern often is found in task forces and committees. Finally, all the members of an **all-channel network** communicate with all the other members. The all-channel network often is found in informal groups that have no formal structure, leader, or task to accomplish.

In each of these types of small-group network, communication can be described in terms of four characteristics:

1. The *density* of the communication—the quantity of communication among members;
2. The *distance* between members—how far the message must travel through the network to reach the receiver.
3. The *relative freedom* of a member *to use different paths to communicate* with others—the ease with which members communicate with one another.

Small group networks determine how information flows among the members of the group. This group of engineers at Milacron was asked to create a prototype for a new plastics injection molding machine in an unusually short period of time. The group members made a conscious effort to create a free flow of information among every member of the team, and even moved their offices closer together. As a result, they were able to get the project completed exactly on schedule.

4. The *centrality of the positions* of members—how central or peripheral a member is to the group. Those members with central positions usually are more committed to the work of the group than those in less central positions.[20]

In a high-density situation or a situation in which communication must travel a great distance, there is a greater chance that the communication will be distorted by noise. Improvements in electronic communication technology, such as computerized mail systems, are reducing this effect.

Position in the group refers to the place of one person in the communication network relative to the others. A relatively central position provides an opportunity for the person to communicate with all of the other members. Thus, a member in a relatively central position can control the information flow and may become a leader of the group. This leadership position is separate and distinct from the formal group structure, although a central person in a group may also emerge as a formal group leader over a long period.

■ Communication networks form spontaneously and naturally as the interactions among workers continue over time.

Communication networks form spontaneously and naturally as the interactions among workers continue. They are rarely permanent, since they change as the tasks, interactions, and memberships change. The patterns and character-

20. Peter R. Monge, Jane A. Edwards, and Kenneth K. Kirste, "Determinants of Communication Network Involvement: Connectedness and Integration," *Group & Organization Studies*, March 1983, pp. 83–112.

istics of small-group communication networks are determined by the factors summarized in Table 11.2. The task is crucial in determining the pattern of the network. If the group's primary task is decision making, an all-channel network may develop to provide the information needed to evaluate all possible alternatives. If, however, the group's task mainly involves the sequential execution of individual tasks, a chain or wheel network is more likely, because communication among members may not be important to the completion of the tasks.

The environment (the type of room in which the group works or meets, the seating arrangement, the placement of chairs and tables, the geographical dispersion, and other aspects of the group's setting) can affect the frequency and types of interactions among members. For example, if most members work on the same floor of an office building, the members who work three floors down may be considered outsiders and develop weaker communication ties to the group. They may even form a separate communication network.

Personal factors also influence the development of the communication network. These include technical expertise, openness, speaking ability, and the degree to which members are acquainted with one another. For example, in a group concerned mainly with highly technical problems, the person with the most expertise may dominate the communication flow during a meeting.

The group performance factors that influence the communication network include composition, size, norms, and cohesiveness. For example, group norms in one organization may encourage open communication across different levels and functional units, whereas the norms in another organization may discourage such lateral and diagonal communication. These performance factors are discussed in Chapter 7.

Because the outcome of the group's efforts depends on the coordinated action of its members, the communication network strongly influences group effectiveness. Thus, to develop effective working relationships in the organization, managers need to make a special effort to manage the flow of information and the development of communication networks. Managers can, for example, arrange offices and work spaces to foster communication among certain employees. Managers may also attempt to involve members who typically contribute little during discussions by asking them direct questions such as "What do you think, Tom?" or "Maria, please tell us how this problem is handled in your district." Methods such as the nominal group technique, discussed in Chapter 16, can also encourage participation.

One other factor that is becoming increasingly important in the development of communication networks is the advent of electronic groups, fostered by electronic distribution lists for computer network systems.[21] Known as *electronic group mail,* this form of communication results in a network of people (or computers) who may have little or no face-to-face communication but still may be considered a group communication network.

---

21. Tom Finholt and Lee S. Sproull, "Electronic Groups at Work," *Organization Science,* vol. 1, pp. 41–64.

TABLE 11.2
Factors Influencing the Development of Small-Group Networks

Factor	Example
Task	Decision making Sequential production
Environment	Type of room, placement of chairs and tables, dispersion of members
Personal Characteristics	Expertise, openness, speaking ability, degree of familiarity among group members
Group Performance Factors	Composition, size, norms, cohesiveness

Organizational Communication Networks

■ A free flow of information to the CEO or president of the organization is essential to the organization's success.

An organization chart shows reporting relationships from the line worker up to the chief executive officer of the firm. The lines of an organization chart also represent channels of communication through which information flows; yet communication may also follow paths that cross traditional reporting lines. Information moves not only from the top down—from the chief executive officer to group members—but upward from group members to the CEO.[22] In fact, a good flow of information to the CEO is an important determinant of success for the organization.[23]

Several companies have realized that the key to their continuing success was through improved internal communication. General Motors Corp. was known for its extremely formal, top-down communication system. In the mid-1980s, however, the formality of its system came under fire from many sources: labor leaders, employees, managers, and even Ross Perot, who sold his company, Electronic Data Systems Corp., to GM in 1984 for $250 million and became a major shareholder in GM.[24] GM's response was to embark on a massive communication improvement program that included sending employees to public-speaking workshops, improving the more than 350 publications it sends out, providing videotapes of management meetings to employees, and using satellite links between headquarters and field operations to establish two-way conversations around the world.[25]

---

22. Michael J. Glauser, "Upward Information Flow in Organizations: Review and Conceptual Analysis," *Human Relations,* August 1984, pp. 613–644.

23. Irving S. Shapiro, "Managerial Communication: The View from the Inside," *California Management Review,* Fall 1984, pp. 157–172.

24. "GM Boots Perot," *Newsweek,* December 15, 1986, pp. 56–62.

25. Bruce H. Goodsite, "General Motors Attacks Its Frozen Middle," *IABC Communication World,* October 1987, pp. 20–23.

Downward communication generally provides directions, whereas upward communication provides feedback to top management. Communication that flows horizontally or crosses traditional reporting lines usually is related to task performance. It often travels faster than vertical communication, because it need not follow organizational protocols and procedures.

Organizational communication networks may diverge from reporting relationships as employees seek better information with which to do their jobs. Employees often find that the easiest way to get their jobs done or to obtain the necessary information is to go directly to employees in other departments rather than through the formal channels shown on the organization chart. Figure 11.4 shows a simple organization chart and the organization's real communication network. The communication network links the individuals who most frequently communicate with one another; the firm's CEO, for example, communicates most often with employee 5. (This does not mean that individuals not linked in the communication network never communicate but only that their communications are relatively infrequent.) Perhaps the CEO and the employee interact frequently through other means, such as church, outside organizations, or sporting events. Such interactions may lead to close friendships that carry over into business relationships. The figure also shows that the group managers do not have important roles in the communication network, contrary to common-sense expectations.

The roles that people play in organizational communication networks can be analyzed in terms of their contribution to the functioning of the network.[26] The most important roles are labeled in the bottom portion of Figure 11.4. A *gatekeeper* (employee 5) has a strategic position in the network that allows him or her to control information moving in either direction through a channel. A *liaison* (employee 15) serves as a bridge between groups, tying groups together and facilitating the communication flow needed to integrate group activities. Employee 13 performs the interesting function of *cosmopolite,* who links the organization to the external environment by, for instance, attending conventions and trade shows, keeping up with outside technological innovations, and having more frequent contact with sources outside the organization. This person may also be an *opinion leader* in the group. Finally, the *isolate* (employee 3) and the *isolated dyad* (employees 2 and 9) tend to work alone and to interact and communicate little with others.

Each of these roles and functions plays an important part in the overall functioning of the communication network and in the organization as a whole. Understanding these roles can help both managers and group members facilitate communication. For instance, the manager who wants to be sure that the CEO receives certain information is well advised to go through the gatekeeper. If the employee who has the technical knowledge necessary for a particular project is

26. See R. Wayne Pace, *Organizational Communication: Foundations for Human Resource Development* (Englewood Cliffs, N.J.: Prentice-Hall, 1983), for further discussion of the development of communication networks.

FIGURE 11.4 Comparison of an Organization Chart and the Organization's Communication Network

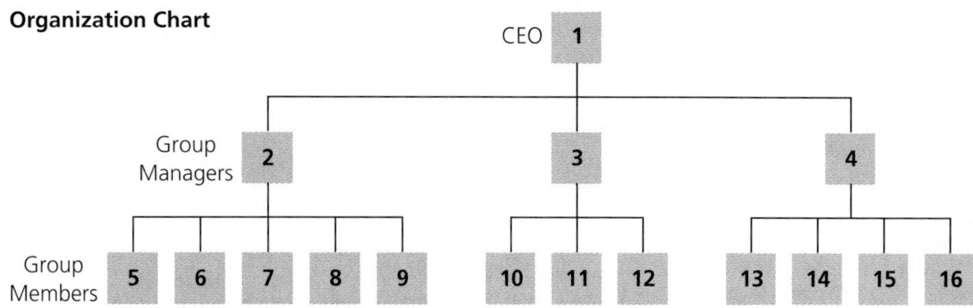

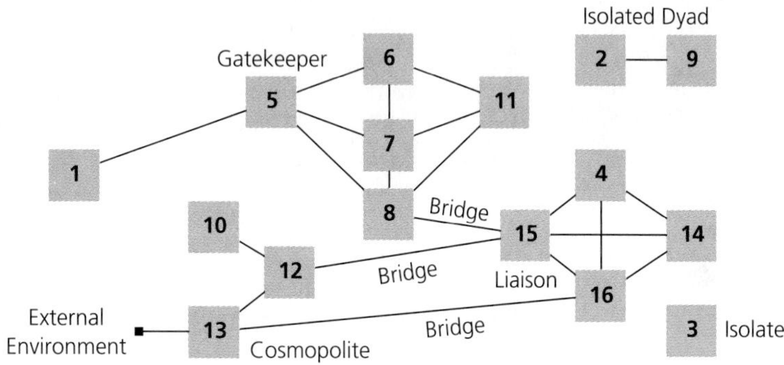

an isolate, the manager can take special steps to integrate the employee into the communication network for the duration of the project.

Recent research has indicated some possible negative impacts of communication networks. Employee turnover has been shown to occur in clusters related to employee communication networks.[27] That is, employees who communicate regularly in a network may share feelings about the organization and thus influence one another's intentions to stay or quit. Communication networks therefore may have both positive and negative consequences.

As we discuss in Chapter 17 and Chapter 19, a primary function of organizational structure is to coordinate the activities of many people doing specialized tasks. Communication networks in organizations provide this much-needed integration.[28] In fact, in some ways communication patterns influence the way an organization is structured.[29] Some companies are finding that the need for better communication forces them to create smaller divisions. The fewer mana-

27. David Krackhardt and Lyman W. Porter, "The Snowball Effect: Turnover Embedded in Communication Networks," *Journal of Applied Psychology,* February 1986, pp. 50–55.

28. Monge, Edwards and Kirste, "Determinants of Communication Network Involvement."

29. Karl E. Weick and Larry D. Browning, "Argument and Narration in Organizational Communication," *Journal of Management,* Summer 1986, pp. 243–259.

gerial levels and improved team spirit of these divisions tend to enhance communication flows.[30]

Another company that found it necessary to improve its communication is Tandem Computers. Tandem, known for its open communication and Friday afternoon parties at which its founder and president, Jimmy Treybig, gave motivational speeches to rally employees around company goals, was extremely successful. Communication was casual and friendly, but information flow usually was top down. When revenues began to fall, Treybig found that he needed to have regular business meetings with managers and department heads to get more job- and task-related information flowing from the bottom up. After some tough decisions were made during regular staff meetings the company got back on track.[31]

Large conglomerate organizations have developed very sophisticated forms of communication networks to facilitate communication among relatively autonomous operating companies. *International Perspective* describes Mitsubishi's informal communication network.

Managing Organizational Communication

■ **Communication fidelity** is the degree of correspondence between the message intended by the source and the message understood by the receiver.

As simple as the process of communication may seem, messages are not always understood. The degree of correspondence between the message intended by the source and the message understood by the receiver is called **communication fidelity.**[32] Fidelity can be diminished anywhere in the communication process, from the source to the feedback. Moreover, organizations may have characteristics that impede the flow of information. Table 11.3 summarizes the most common types of breakdowns and barriers in organizational communication.

Improving the Communication Process

An understanding of potential problems is essential to improving organizational communication. Using the basic communication process, we can identify several ways to overcome typical problems.

Source The source may intentionally withhold or filter information on the assumption that the receiver does not need it to understand the communication. Withholding information, however, may render the message meaningless or cause an erroneous interpretation. For example, during a performance appraisal interview a manager may not tell the employee all of the sources of information used

30. "Small Is Beautiful Now in Manufacturing," *Business Week,* October 22, 1984, pp. 152–156.
31. Brian O'Reilly, "How Jimmy Treybig Turned Tough," *Fortune,* May 25, 1987, pp. 102–104.
32. Pace, *Organizational Communication.*

INTERNATIONAL PERSPECTIVE

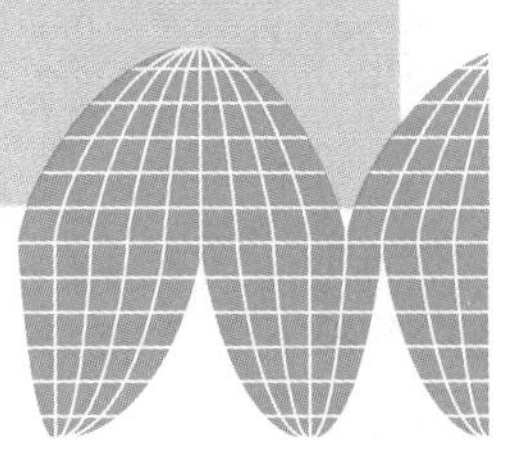

Mitsubishi May Have the Corner on Communication Networks

Management of an international corporate conglomerate made up of hundreds of companies may be one of the most difficult tasks to accomplish. Mitsubishi, however, makes it look easy—not with formal lines of reporting, authority, and responsibility but with informal ties and communication networks. At the center of the Mitsubishi group, or *keiretsu,* are Mitsubishi Corp., Mitsubishi Bank, and Mitsubishi Heavy Industries. Surrounding the *keiretsu* are hundreds of companies, some with and some without the Mitsubishi name, a significant part of whose ownership belongs to other members of the group.

Every evening, more than thirty executives of these companies gather at the Mitsubishi Club for dinner, socialization, and other activities that serve to lubricate the wheels of business. During these hours of relaxation, deals get made, ideas are shared, and trust is built. Membership is open to members of the board of directors of any Mitsubishi company, and daily attendance at these gatherings is optional.

Members of the *keiretsu* are not wholly owned subsidiaries of a typical conglomerate with centralized control. They are independent but have interlocking directorates, joint ventures, and long-term business relationships that work together for their long-term mutual benefit. Because they are independent and usually operate in different business areas, they do not conflict with traditional antitrust laws. Yet, their interdependence is their strength.

The real key to the *keiretsu's* success, however, may be the open, free, and casual communication fostered by the enduring relationships that develop after hours at the Mitsubishi Club. A pending deal depends on who can be trusted, and *keiretsu* members know they can trust one another. Experts on U.S. business have suggested that maybe U.S. industry could use a *keiretsu* or two as it attempts to deal with global market issues.

The recent rumor about a possible alliance between Daimler-Benz AG, maker of Mercedes-Benz autos and partner in the European Airbus consortium, with Mitsubishi has the global industrial world buzzing. This potential alliance would give Mitsubishi access to Europe for the critical 1992 united European markets and Daimler-Benz the opportunity to spruce up its consumer electronics business. It would also let a major European industrial power in on the climate of communication and trust of a *keiretsu.*

SOURCES: "Mighty Mitsubishi Is on the Move," *Business Week,* September 24, 1990, pp. 98–101; "Hands Across America: The Rise of Mitsubishi," *Business Week,* September 24, 1990, pp. 102–107; "Maybe the U.S. Could Use a *Keiretsu* or Two," *Business Week,* September 24, 1990, p. 162; "Courtship of Giants," *Time,* March 19, 1990, p. 53.

---

to make the evaluation, thinking that the employee does not need to know. If the employee knew, however, he or she might be able to explain certain behaviors or otherwise alter the manager's perspective of the evaluation and thereby make it more accurate. Selective filtering may cause a breakdown in communication that cannot be repaired, even with good follow-up communication.[33]

33. Losana E. Boyd, "Why 'Talking It Out' Almost Never Works Out," *Nations's Business,* November 1984, pp. 53–54.

TABLE 11.3
Communication Problems in Organizations

Root of the Problem	Type of Problem
Source	Filtering
Encoding and Decoding	Lack of Common Experience Semantics; Jargon Medium Problems
Receiver	Selective Attention Value Judgments Lack of Source Credibility Overload
Feedback	Omission
Organizational Factors	Noise Status Differences Time Pressures Overload Communication Structure

To avoid filtering, the communicator needs to understand why it occurs. Filtering can result from lack of understanding of the receiver's position, the sender's need to protect his or her own power by limiting the receiver's access to information, or doubts about what the receiver might do with the information. The sender's primary concern, however, should be the message. In essence, the sender must determine exactly what message she or he wants the receiver to understand, send the receiver enough information to understand the message but not enough to create an overload, and trust the receiver to use the information properly.

Encoding and Decoding Encoding and decoding problems occur as the message is translated into or from the symbols used in transmission. Such problems can relate to the meaning of the symbols or to the transmission itself. As Table 11.3 shows, encoding and decoding problems include lack of common experience between source and receiver, problems related to semantics and the use of jargon, and difficulties with the medium.

Clearly, the source and the receiver must share a common experience with the symbols that express the message if they are to encode and decode them in exactly the same way. People who speak different languages experience problems in this category. But even people who speak the same language can misunderstand each other.

Semantics is the study of language forms, and semantic problems occur when people attribute different meanings to the same words or language forms. For example, when discussing a problem employee, the division head may tell her assistant, "We need to get rid of this problem." The division head may have meant that the employee should be scheduled for more training or transferred to another division. However, the assistant may interpret the statement differently and fire the problem employee.

The specialized or technical language of a trade, field, profession, or social group is called *jargon*. Jargon may be a hybrid of standard language and the specialized language of a group. The use of jargon makes communication within a close group of colleagues more efficient and meaningful, but outside the group it has the opposite effect. Sometimes a source who is comfortable with jargon uses it unknowingly to communicate with receivers who do not understand it, thus causing a communication breakdown. In other cases, the source may use jargon intentionally to obscure meaning or to show outsiders that he or she belongs to the group that uses the language.

The use of jargon is acceptable if the receiver is familiar with it. Otherwise, it should be avoided. Repeating a message that contains jargon in clearer terms should help the receiver understand the message. In general, the source and the receiver should clarify the set of symbols to be used before they communicate. Also, the receiver can ask questions frequently and, if necessary, ask the source to repeat all or part of the message.

The source must send the message through a medium appropriate to the message itself and to the intended receiver. For example, a commercial run on an AM radio station will not have its intended effect if the people in the desired market segment listen only to FM radio.

- Communication problems that originate in the receiver include problems with selective attention, value judgments, source credibility, and overload.

Receiver Several communication problems originate in the receiver, including problems with selective attention, value judgments, source credibility, and overload. *Selective attention* exists when the receiver attends to only selected parts of a message—a frequent occurrence with oral communication. For example, in a college class some students may hear only part of the professor's lecture as their minds wander to other topics. To focus receivers' attention on the message, senders often engage in attention-getting behaviors such as varying the volume, repeating the message, and offering rewards.

Value judgments involve the degree to which a message reinforces or challenges the receiver's basic personal beliefs. If a message reinforces the receiver's beliefs, he or she may pay close attention and believe it completely, without examination. On the other hand, if the message challenges those beliefs, the receiver may entirely discount it. Thus, if a firm's sales manager had predicted that the demand for new baby care products will increase substantially over the next two years, he may ignore reports that the birthrate is declining.

The receiver may also judge the *credibility* of the source of the message. If the source is perceived to be an expert in the field, the listener may pay close attention to the message and believe it. Conversely, if the receiver has little respect for the source, she or he may disregard the message. The receiver considers both the message and the source in making value judgments and determining credibility. An expert in nuclear physics may be viewed as a credible source in building a nuclear power plant and yet be disregarded, perhaps rightly, on evaluating the birthrate. This is one reason that a trial lawyer asks an expert witness about his or her education and experience at the beginning of testimony: to establish credibility.

A receiver experiencing communication *overload* is receiving more information than she or he can process. In organizations, this can happen very easily; a receiver can be bombarded with computer-generated reports and messages from superiors, peers, and sources outside the organization. Unable to take in all the messages, decode them, understand them, and act on them, the receiver may use selective attention and value judgments to focus on the messages that seem most important. Although this type of selective attention is necessary for survival in an information-glutted environment, it may mean that vital information is lost or overlooked.

■ **Verification** is the feedback portion of communication in which the receiver sends a message to the source indicating receipt of the message and the degree to which he or she understood the message.

Feedback The purpose of feedback is **verification,** in which the receiver sends a message to the source indicating receipt of the message and the degree to which it was understood. The lack of feedback can cause at least two problems. First, the source may need to send another message that depends on the response to the first; if no feedback is received, the source may not send the second message or may be forced to send the original message again. Second, the receiver may act on the unverified message; if the message was misunderstood, the resulting act may be inappropriate.

Because feedback is so important, the source must actively seek it and the receiver must supply it. Often it is appropriate for the receiver to repeat the original message as an introduction to the response, although the medium or symbols used may be different. Nonverbal cues can provide instantaneous feedback. These include body language and facial expressions, such as anger and disbelief.[34]

The source needs to be concerned with the message, the symbols, the medium, and the feedback from the receiver. Of course, the receiver is concerned with these things too, but from a different point of view. In general the receiver needs to be source oriented just as the source needs to be receiver oriented. Table 11.4 gives specific suggestions for improving the communication process.

Improving Organizational Factors in Communication

Organizational factors that can create communication breakdowns or barriers include noise, status differences, time pressures, and overload. As previously stated, disturbances anywhere in the organization can distort or interrupt meaningful communication. Thus, the noise created by a rumored takeover can disrupt the orderly flow of task-related information. Status differences between source and receiver can cause some of the communication problems just discussed. For

34. Robert A. Snyder and James H. Morris, "Organizational Communication and Performance," *Journal of Applied Psychology*, August 1984, pp. 461–465.

Focus	Source		Receiver	
	Question	*Corrective Action*	*Question*	*Corrective Action*
Message	What idea or thought are you trying to get across?	Give more information. Give less information. Give entire message.	What idea or thought does the sender want you to understand?	Listen carefully to the entire message, not just part of it.
Symbols	Does the receiver use the same symbols, words, jargon?	Say it another way. Employ repetition. Use receiver's language or jargon. Before sending, clarify symbols to be used.	What symbols are being used—for example, foreign language, technical jargon?	Clarify symbols before communication begins. Ask questions. Ask sender to repeat message.
Medium	Is this a channel that the receiver monitors regularly? Sometimes? Never?	Use multiple media. Change medium. Increase volume (loudness).	What medium or media is the sender using?	Monitor several media.
Feedback	What is the receiver's reaction to your message?	Pay attention to the feedback, especially nonverbal cues. Ask questions.	Did you correctly interpret the message?	Verify receipt of message. Repeat message.

TABLE 11.4
Improving the Communication Process

example, a firm's chief executive officer may pay little attention to communications from employees far lower on the organization chart, and employees may pay little attention to communications from the CEO. Both are instances of selective attention prompted by the organization's status system.

Time pressures and communication overload are also detrimental to communication. When the receiver is not allowed enough time to understand incoming messages, or when there are too many messages, he or she may misunderstand or ignore some of them.

Effective organizational communication provides the right information to the right person at the right time and in the right form. Figure 11.5 summarizes how this goal can be achieved.

Reduce Noise Noise is a primary barrier to effective organizational communication. A common form of noise is the rumor grapevine, an informal system of communication that coexists with the formal system.[35] The grapevine usually transmits information faster than official channels do. Because the accuracy of this information often is quite low, however, the grapevine can distort organizational communication. Management can reduce the effects of the distortion by using the grapevine as an additional channel for the dissemination of information and by constantly monitoring it for accuracy.

35. Keith Davis and John W. Newstrom, *Human Behavior at Work: Organizational Behavior,* 7th ed. (New York: McGraw-Hill, 1985), pp. 314–323.

FIGURE 11.5
Improving Organizational Communication

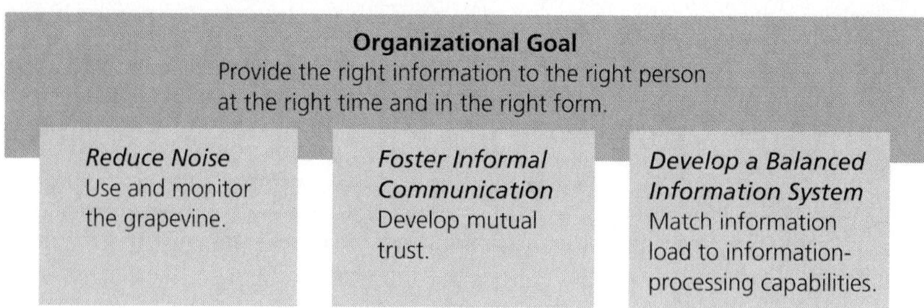

Foster Informal Communication Thomas J. Peters and Robert H. Waterman have described communication in well-run companies as "a vast network of informal, open communications."[36] Informal communication fosters mutual trust, which minimizes the effects of status differences. It also allows information to be communicated when needed rather than when the formal information system allows it to emerge. Peters and Waterman further describe communication in effective companies as chaotic and intense, supported by the reward structure and the physical arrangement of the facilities. This means that the performance appraisal and reward system, offices, meeting rooms, and work areas are designed to encourage frequent, unscheduled, and unstructured communication throughout the organization.

Develop a Balanced Information System Many large organizations have developed elaborate formal information systems to cope with the potential problems of information overload and time pressures. In many cases, however, the systems have created problems rather than solving them. Often they produce more information than managers and decision makers can comprehend and use in their jobs. They also often use only formal communication channels and ignore various informal lines of communication. Furthermore, the systems frequently provide whatever information the computer is set up to provide—information that may not apply to the most pressing problem at hand. The result of all these drawbacks is a loss of communication effectiveness.

- Organizations need to balance information load and information-processing capabilities.

Organizations need to balance information load and information-processing capabilities.[37] In other words, they must take care not to generate more information than people can handle. It is useless to produce sophisticated statistical reports that managers have no time to read. Furthermore, the new technologies that are making more information available to managers and decision makers must be unified to produce usable information.[38] Information production, stor-

36. Thomas J. Peters and Robert H. Waterman, Jr., *In Search of Excellence: Lessons from America's Best-Run Companies* (New York: Harper & Row, 1982), p. 121.

37. Charles A. O'Reilly, "Individual and Information Overload in Organizations: Is More Necessarily Better?" *Academy of Management Journal,* December 1980, pp. 684–696.

38. James L. McKenney and F. Warren McFarlan, "The Information Archipelago—Maps and Bridges," *Harvard Business Review,* September-October 1982, pp. 109–119.

age, and processing capabilities must be compatible with one another and, equally important, with the needs of the organization.

Some companies—for example, General Electric Co., McDonnell Douglas Corp., Anheuser-Busch Inc., and McDonald's Corp.—have formalized an upward communication system that uses a corporate "ombudsman."[39] This position usually is held by a highly placed executive who is available outside the formal chain of command to hear employees' complaints. The system provides an opportunity for disgruntled employees to complain without fear of losing their jobs and may help some companies achieve a balanced communication system.

Electronic Information Processing and Telecommunications

Changes in the workplace are occurring at an astonishing rate. Many innovations are based on new technologies—computerized information processing systems, new types of telecommunication systems, and combinations of these. Managers can now send and receive memos and other types of communications on their computer terminals. In addition, a whole new industry is developing in the long-distance transmission of data between computers.

The "office of the future" is here. Every office now has a facsimile (fax) machine, a copier, and personal computers, many of them linked into a single integrated system and to numerous databases and electronic mail systems. The electronic office links managers, clerical employees, professional workers, and sales personnel in a communication network that uses a combination of computerized data storage, retrieval, and transmission systems.

In fact, the computer-integrated organization is becoming commonplace. Ingersol Milling Machine Co. of Rockford, Illinois, boasts a totally computer-integrated operation in which all major functions—sales, marketing, finance, distribution, manufacturing—exchange operating information quickly and continuously via computers. For example, product designers can send specifications directly to machines on the factory floor, and accounting personnel receive on-line information about sales, purchases, and prices instantaneously. The computer system parallels and greatly speeds up the entire process.[40]

Another system is the totally computerized Human Resource Information System (HRIS) used by the Rorer Group, the world's twenty-sixth largest manufacturer of pharmaceuticals.[41] This system manages information on all of the

39. Michael Brody, "Listen to Your Whistleblower," *Fortune,* November 24, 1986, pp. 77–78.

40. Jeremy Main, "Computers of the World, Unite!" *Fortune,* September 24, 1990, pp. 115–122.

41. Tony Pompili, "Rapid Expansion Smoothed with LAN Personnel System," *PC Week,* August 25, 1987, pp. C1, C9.

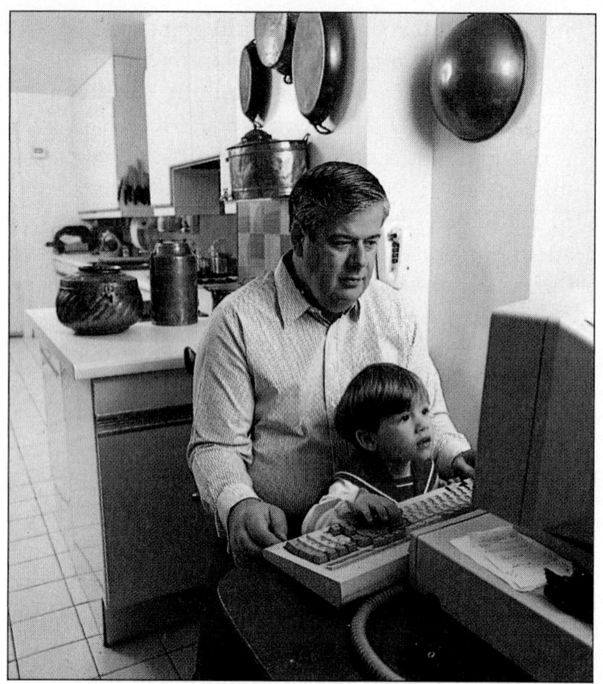

Electronic information processing has dramatically changed the way managers work. With the proper technology they can now communicate far more efficiently and quickly than ever before. Robert Dilenschneider, CEO of Hill & Knowlton, is shown here answering his E-mail at home on Easter morning. By keeping in constant touch with his office and key managers, he is able to make decisions faster while avoiding as many crisis situations as he once faced.

company's eight thousand employees, including name, position, education, employment history, and pay. Through a network of personal computers, every properly authorized office in the company can gain access to the information on the system. That means HRIS data are available any time they are needed—not only to computer experts who know the system but to authorized managers throughout the company. Such systems make information available to aid decision making on a daily basis.

The effects of automated office systems on the communication system and the management of the organization are only now being studied. Research conducted among office workers using a new electronic office system indicated that attitudes toward the system generally were favorable. The users reported improvements in "communications, information access, preparation of written material, and worker collaboration."[42] On the other hand, reduction of face-to-face meetings may depersonalize the office. Some individuals are also concerned that companies are installing electronic systems with little consideration of the social structures of the office.[43] As departments adopt computerized information sys-

42. Don Tapscott, "Investigating the Electronic Office," *Datamation,* March 1982, pp. 130–138.

43. Mary Gruhn, "Trends and Analysis in Word Processing," *Office Administration and Automation,* November 1983, pp. 100–101; Julie A. Lacity, "The Wait Is Over," *Business Credit,* January 1991, pp. 8–10.

tems, activities of work groups throughout the organization are likely to become more interdependent, which may alter power relationships among the groups.[44] Most employees quickly learn the system of power, politics, authority, and responsibility in the office. A radical change in work and personal relationships caused by new office technology may disrupt normal ways of accomplishing tasks, thereby reducing productivity. Other potential problems include information overload, loss of records in a "paperless" office, and the dehumanizing effects of electronic equipment.

- New information processing and transmission technologies have created new media, symbols, message transmission methods, and networks for organizational communication.

In effect, new information processing and transmission technologies mean new media, symbols, message transmission methods, and networks for organizational communication. These technologies must be more fully integrated with one another before their benefits can be fully realized. Clearly they will affect the daily activities of individual workers as well as the communication networks and social systems within organizations, but the extent of their effects is not yet apparent. New information processing technologies that provide more—though not necessarily better—information may place even more responsibility on the manager who must use the information properly.

Summary of Key Points

- Communication is involved in all activities of the organization. Communication is the process by which two parties exchange information and share meaning. The difference between the amount of information required to perform a task and the information the organization already possesses is known as *uncertainty*. The greater the uncertainty regarding the tasks of the organization, the more information the organization needs to operate effectively and efficiently.
- People in organizations communicate through written, oral, and nonverbal means. Written communications include letters, memos, reports, and the like. Oral communication is the type most commonly used. Personal elements, such as facial expressions and body language, and environmental elements, such as office design, are forms of nonverbal communication.
- Communication among individuals, groups, or organizations is a process in which a source sends a message and a receiver responds. The source encodes a message into symbols and transmits it through a medium to the receiver, who decodes the symbols. The receiver then responds with feedback, an attempt to verify the meaning of the original message. Noise—anything that distorts or interrupts communication—may interfere in virtually any stage of the process.

---

44. Starr R. Hiltz, "User Satisfaction with Computer-Mediated Communication Systems," *Management Science,* June 1990, pp. 739–764; Carol S. Saunders, "Management Information Systems, Communications, and Department Power: An Integrative Model," *Academy of Management Review,* July 1981, pp. 431–442.

- Communication networks are systems of information exchange within organizations. Patterns of communication emerge as information flows from person to person in a group. Typical small-group communication networks include the wheel, chain, circle, and all-channel networks. They can be described in terms of the density of communication, the distance between members, the relative freedom of a member to use different paths to communicate with others, and the positions of members.
- The organizational communication network, which describes the real communication links in an organization, usually differs from the arrangement on an organization chart. Roles people play in organizational communication networks include the gatekeeper, liaison, cosmopolite, and isolate.
- Managing communication in organizations involves understanding the numerous problems that can interfere with effective communication. Problems relate to the communication process itself and to organizational factors such as status differences.
- The fully integrated communication-information office system—the electronic office—links personnel in a communication network through a combination of computers and electronic transmission systems. The effects of such systems have not yet been fully realized.

Discussion Questions

1. How is communication in organizations an individual process as well as an organizational process?
2. In situations of high task uncertainty, why is it necessary that there be more communication?
3. Describe a situation in which you tried to carry on a conversation when no one was listening. Were any messages sent during the "conversation"?
4. The typical college classroom provides an example of attempts at communication: The professor tries to communicate the subject to the students. Describe classroom communication in terms of the basic communication process described in the chapter.
5. Is there a communication network (other than professor-to-student) in the class in which you are using this book? If so, identify any specific roles that people play in the network. If not, why has no network developed? What would be the benefits of having a communication network in this class?
6. Why might educators typically focus most communication training on the written and oral methods and pay little attention to the nonverbal methods? Do you think that more training emphasis should be placed on nonverbal communication? Why or why not?
7. Is the typical classroom form of transferring information from professor to student an effective form of communication? Where does it break down? What are the communication problems in the college classroom?
8. Whose responsibility is it to solve classroom communication problems: the students', the professor's, or the administration's?

9. Have you ever worked in an organization in which communication was a problem? If so, what were some causes of the problem?
10. What methods were used, or should have been used, to improve communication in the situation you described in question 9?
11. Would the use of advanced computer information processing or telecommunications have helped solve the communications problem you described in question 9?
12. What types of communication problems will new telecommunications methods most likely be able to solve? Why?

CASE 11.1

Exxon's Communication Problems

Exxon Corp. may have made the communication mistake of the century. When the notice of the huge oil spill in Prince William Sound off the coast of Alaska occurred in March of 1989, Exxon's problems escalated. Other disasters, such as the Christmas Eve 1989 explosion of a Louisiana refinery and the New Year's Day 1990 pipeline leak in New York, compounded the problem.

The spill in Alaska garnered the most attention as Exxon was attacked for being slow to respond to the spill, slow to own up to responsibility for it, and inadequate in its cleanup attempts. Exxon chairman Lawrence Rawl has steadfastly defended his company's actions and claims Exxon did all it possibly could. The bill for the Alaska crisis was more than $2 billion at last count, and Exxon faces a criminal trial and nearly two hundred civil lawsuits. However, some observers have suggested that the massive unexpected cash outlay may not be a problem for Exxon, whose cash flow for 1989 alone was more than $7.9 billion and net income around $5.3 billion.

Exxon's primary task was to tell the world through the media what had happened. The media discovered what Exxon did not tell and told the rest of the story. The differences between the two accounts were only part of what got Exxon in trouble. First, Rawl himself made no comment for six days after the Alaska spill but left his staff to make the first public announcements. Second, when he did comment he was unsure of the details of the cleanup. Third, an Exxon spokesperson claimed that the damage was minimal while newscasts were showing pictures of thousands of dead birds and oil-covered beaches and rocks. These errors, delays, and contradictions portrayed Exxon as arrogant, uncaring, and unaware of the world around it. Subsequently Exxon paid out $32,000 to a radio station for its costs of covering the story and $200 million to fishers for their lost income. But customers returned Exxon credit cards by the thousands and threatened a boycott. Nevertheless, in a full-page newspaper advertisement published ten days after the accident, Rawl claimed the company had acted swiftly and competently. Problems with the communication process continued to mount.

The real problems may have started for Exxon long before the oil spills. Over the past several years, chairman Rawl and his management team have been cutting costs by reducing expenditures for personnel, training, and other related factors. Exxon has reduced its staff from 180,000 to 104,000 since 1981. During this period, many employees have left the company and many more have taken early retirement; others have refused to relocate when Exxon moved its offices to a southern state. Rawl maintains that personnel from middle-management levels have been reduced, but not lower-level staff. One angry high-level manager has said, "The company is going down the poop chute." Some reports of the pipeline rupture in the Arthur Kill Waterway between Staten Island and New Jersey said that workers were told about the leak but did not act because they believed the leak detection system was faulty. Six hours after the rupture, employees finally shut the system down.

Although much of the press coverage has emphasized the difficulties Rawl has had in response to the public outcry over spills, Exxon has a serious attitude and morale problem within its ranks and equally severe image problems outside the company. Its difficulties in effectively communicating with its own employees and the public have become textbook examples of how not to manage a company.

Case Questions

1. What parts of the communication process did Exxon neglect in its handling of the Alaska oil spill?
2. Identify the "receivers" with whom Exxon was attempting to communicate. Name at least four types of receivers.
3. What barriers to communication might have hindered Exxon in its attempts to communicate?
4. What types of attitude problems might result from these failures to communicate, both externally and internally?

SOURCES: "Exxon Stops the Flow," *Time,* March 25, 1991, p. 51; Peter Nulty, "Exxon's Problem: Not What You Think," *Fortune,* April 23, 1990, pp. 202–204; Ben Yagoda, "Cleaning Up A Dirty Image," *Business Month,* April 1990, pp. 48–51; "Exxon Strikes Back," *Time,* March 26, 1990, pp. 62–63; "Exxon's Attitude Problem," *Time,* January 22, 1990, p. 51; Ellen Benoit, "The Valdez Legacy," *Financial World,* June 27, 1989, pp. 82–83.

CASE 11.2

Heading Off a Permanent Misunderstanding

Mindy Martin was no longer speaking to Al Sharp. She had been wary of him since her first day at Alton Products; he had always seemed distant and aloof. She thought at first that he resented her M.B.A. degree, her fast rise in the company, or her sense of purpose and ambition. But she was determined to get along with everyone in the office, so she had taken him out to lunch, praised his work whenever she could, and even kept track of his son's Little League feats.

But all that ended with the appointment of the new Midwest marketing director. Martin had her sights on the job and thought her chances were good. She was competing with three other managers on her level. Sharp was not in the running because he did not have a graduate degree, but his voice was thought to carry a lot of weight with the top brass. Martin had less seniority than any of her competitors, but her division had become the leader in the company, and upper management had praised her lavishly. She believed that with a good recommendation from Sharp, she would get the job.

But Walt Murdoch received the promotion and moved to Topeka. Martin was devastated. It was bad enough that she did not get the promotion, but she could not stand the fact that Murdoch had been chosen. She and Al Sharp had taken to calling Murdoch "Mr. Intolerable," because neither of them could stand his pompous arrogance. She felt that his being chosen was an insult to her; it made her rethink her entire career. When the grapevine confirmed her suspicion that Al Sharp had strongly influenced the decision, she determined to reduce her interaction with Sharp to a bare minimum.

Relations in the office were very chilly for almost a month. Sharp soon gave up trying to get back in Martin's favor, and they began communicating only in short, unsigned memos. Finally, William Attridge, their immediate boss, could tolerate the hostility no longer and called the two in for a meeting. "We're going to sit here until you two become friends again," he said, "or at least until I find out what's bugging you."

Martin resisted for a few minutes, denying that anything had changed in their relationship, but when she saw that Attridge was serious, she finally said, "Al seems more interested in dealing with Walter Murdoch." Sharp's jaw dropped; he sputtered but could not say anything. Attridge came to the rescue.

"Walter's been safely kicked upstairs, thanks in part to Al, and neither of you will have to deal with him in the future. But if you're upset about that promotion, you should know that Al had nothing but praise for you and kept pointing out how this division would suffer if we buried you in Topeka. With your bonuses, you're still making as much as Murdoch. If your work here continues to be outstanding, you'll be headed for a much better place than Topeka."

Embarrassed, Martin looked up at Sharp, who shrugged and said, "You want to go get some coffee?"

Over coffee, Martin told Sharp what she had been thinking for the past month and apologized for treating him unfairly. Sharp explained that what she saw as aloofness was actually respect and something akin to fear: He viewed her as brilliant and efficient. Consequently he was very cautious, trying not to offend her.

The next day, the office was almost back to normal. But a new ritual had been established: Martin and Sharp took a coffee break together every day at ten. Soon their teasing and friendly competition loosened up everyone with whom they worked.

Case Questions

1. What might have happened had William Attridge not intervened?
2. Are the sources of the misunderstanding between Martin and Sharp common or unusual?

EXPERIENTIAL EXERCISE

Purpose: This exercise demonstrates the importance of feedback in oral communication.

Format: You will be an observer or play the role of either a manager or an assistant manager trying to tell a coworker the location at which a package of important materials is to be picked up. The observer's role is to make sure the other two participants follow the rules and to observe and record any interesting occurrences.

Procedure: The instructor will divide the class into groups of three. (Any extra members can be roving observers.) The three people in each group will take the roles of manager, assistant manager, and observer. In the second trial, the manager and the assistant manager will switch roles.

Trial 1: The manager and the assistant manager should turn their backs to each other so that neither can see the other. Here is the situation. The manager is in another city that he or she is not familiar with but that the assistant manager knows quite well. The manager needs to find the office of a supplier to pick up drawings of a critical component of the company's main product. The supplier will be closing for the day in a few minutes; the drawings must be picked up before closing time. The manager has called the assistant manager to get directions to the office. However, the connection is faulty; the manager can hear the assistant manager but the assistant manager can hear only enough to know the manager is on the line. The manager has redialed once, but there was no improvement in the connection. Now there is no time to lose. The manager has decided to get the directions from the assistant without asking questions.

Just before the exercise begins, the instructor will give the assistant manager a detailed map of the city that shows the locations of the supplier's office and the manager. The map will include a number of turns, stops, stoplights, intersections, and shopping centers between these locations. The assistant manager can study it for no longer than a minute or two. When the instructor gives the direction to start, the assistant manager describes to the manager how to get from his or her present location to the supplier's office. As the assistant manager gives the directions, the manager draws the map on a piece of paper.

The observer makes sure that no questions are asked and records the beginning and ending times, as well as the way in which the assistant manager tries to communicate particularly difficult points (including points about which the manager obviously wants to ask questions) and any other noteworthy occurrences.

After all pairs have finished, each observer "grades" the quality of the manager's map by comparing it with the original and counting the number of obvious mistakes. The instructor will ask a few managers who believe they have drawn good maps to tell the rest of the class how to get to the supplier's office.

Trial 2: In trial 2, the manager and the assistant manager switch roles, and a second map is passed out to the new assistant managers. The situation is the same as in the first trial, except that the telephones are working properly and the manager can ask questions of the assistant manager. The observer's role is the same as in trial 1—recording the beginning and ending times, the methods of communication, and any other noteworthy occurrences.

After all pairs have finished, the observers grade the maps, just as in the first trial. The instructor will then select a few managers to tell the rest of the class how to get to the supplier's office. The subsequent class discussion should center on the experiences of the class members and the follow-up questions.

Follow-up Questions

1. Which trial resulted in more accurate maps? Why?
2. Which trial took longer? Why?
3. How did you feel when a question needed to be asked but it could not be asked in trial 1? Was your confidence in the final result affected differently in the two trials?

PART IV

Enhancing Individual and Interpersonal Processes

CONTENTS

Chapter 12 Goal Setting and Rewards

Chapter 13 Job Design and Employee Participation

Chapter 14 Performance Appraisal

Chapter 15 Managing Stress

Chapter 16 Decision Making and Creativity

CHAPTER OUTLINE

- **Goal Setting in Organizations**
  - *Motivation and Control*
  - *The Role of Goal Setting*
- **Goal Setting and Motivation**
  - *The Basic Approach*
  - *A Broader Perspective of Goals and Motivation*
  - *Research Evidence*
- **Management By Objectives**
  - *The MBO Process*
  - *MBO in Management Practice*
- **Reward Systems in Organizations**
  - *A Transaction Process*
  - *The Roles, Purposes, and Meanings of Rewards*
- **Types of Rewards**
  - *Money*
  - *Incentive Systems*
  - *Benefits*
  - *Perquisites*
  - *Awards*
- **Managing Reward Systems**
  - *Pay Secrecy*
  - *Participative Pay Systems*
  - *Flexible Reward Systems*

12

Goal Setting and Rewards

CHAPTER OBJECTIVES

After studying this chapter, you should be able to:

Discuss the role of goal setting in the workplace.

Describe goal-setting theory.

Explain management by objectives.

Discuss reward systems in organizations.

Identify several types of rewards.

Summarize issues regarding the management of reward systems.

Workers who believe leisure, family, and lifestyle are goals of life that are as important as work goals are now entering the work force. This new generation of workers is the first to follow the baby-boom generation and may look at life quite differently than its predecessor. These workers are twenty-five years old and younger, typically college educated, and willing to make employment choices that do not always mean personal sacrifice for organizational goals. Because traditional management systems are built on the assumption that employees are motivated to achieve corporate goals at the expense of personal ones, this new orientation may have far-reaching implications for organizational effectiveness. The challenge for management is to utilize the resources of this generation with new goal-oriented management solutions.[1]

The new "baby-buster" generation presents significant problems for management because of the popularity of goal-based management systems in organizations throughout the world. These traditional systems do several things for the organizations that employ them. Goal-based systems provide guidance and direction for employees, serve as motivational tools, and work with reward and compensation systems to form an integrated approach to managing the organization's human resources.

In this chapter, we focus on goals and rewards and their roles in shaping employee behavior within the organization. First, we explore the role of goals in the workplace. Next, we examine the goal-setting theory of motivation. Then we discuss management by objectives, another important approach to goal setting. Next, we turn to reward systems and their role in motivation. We identify important types of rewards and explore perspectives on managing reward systems. Finally, we look at useful managerial implications of reward systems.

Goal Setting in Organizations

■ A **goal** is a desirable objective to be achieved.

Almost everyone sets goals. A **goal** is simply a desirable objective to be achieved. Students have goals for their grades, athletes have goals for performance, politicians have goals for winning elected offices, and executives have goals for the growth of their organizations. Some organizations have set up their entire man-

1. Alan Deutschman, *Fortune,* © 1990 The Time Inc. Magazine Company. All rights reserved.

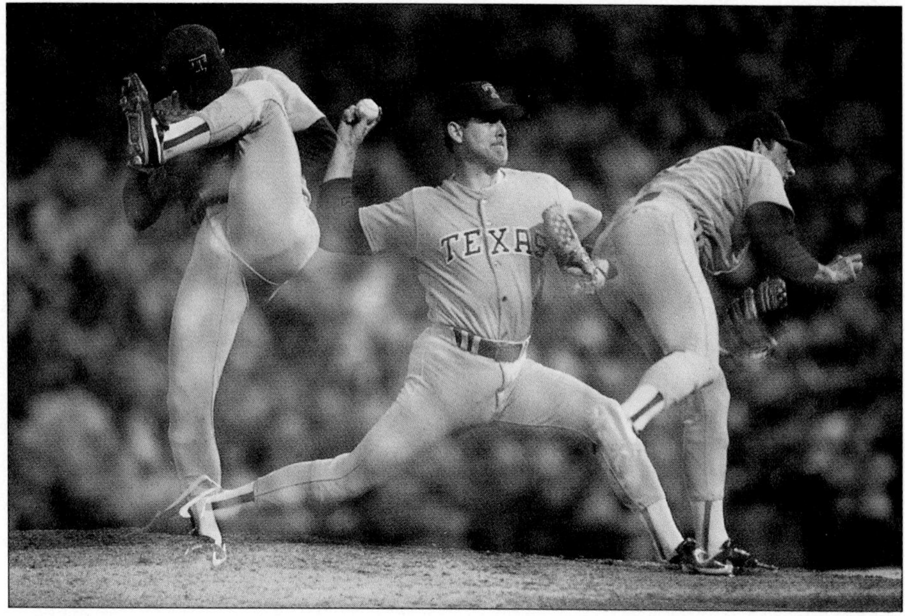

Nolan Ryan, the oldest pitcher in the major leagues, is shown recording his 300th victory in 1990, making him only the 20th player to reach that lofty level. In 1991 he threw his record seventh no-hitter. Every time Ryan goes to the mound, he has a clear and specific goal—to win the game.

agement system around goal setting. Cypress Semiconductor Corp. uses management groups to set goals each Monday morning for every employee. These goals are then entered into a computer, and each employee can check her or his progress on achieving the goals at any time. Cypress's management attributes the firm's success to this goal-based management system, because all employees know what is expected of them and managers know the exact status of every project and activity.[2] Clearly, then, goal setting is an important dimension of human behavior and management systems.

Motivation and Control

- Goals serve as both motivational tools and control devices for organizations.

In most organizational settings, goals are used for two purposes. First, they are a useful framework for managing motivation. Managers and employees can set goals for themselves and then work toward those goals. Second, goals are an effective control device.[3] *Control* is the management activity directed at monitoring how well the organization is performing. Thus, if the organization's goal is to increase sales by 10 percent, a manager can use individual goals to help attain the overall goal. Further, comparing people's short-term performances with their goals can be an effective way to monitor the organization's long-run performance.

2. Steven B. Kaufman, "The Goal System That Drives Cypress," *Business Month,* July 1987, pp. 30–32.

3. William G. Ouchi, "A Conceptual Framework for the Design of Organizational Control Systems," *Management Science,* September 1979, pp. 833–848.

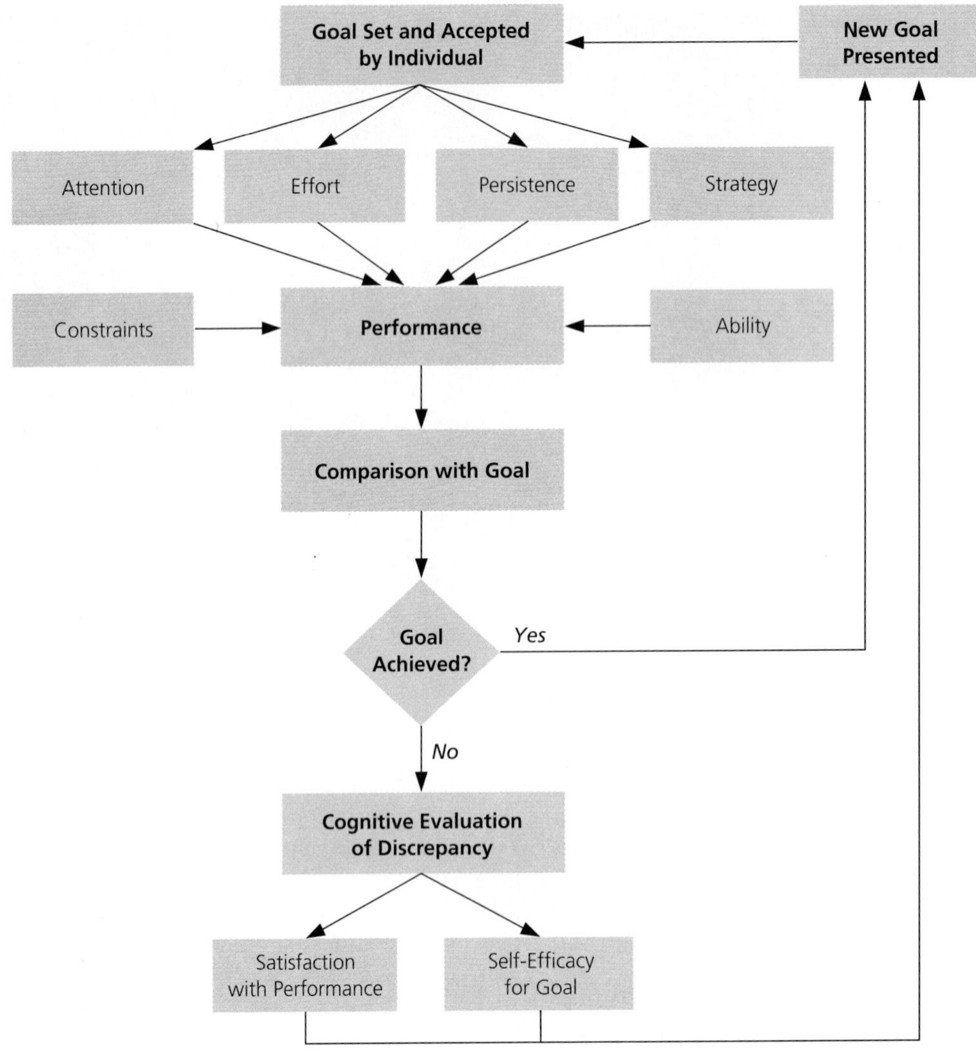

SOURCE: Adapted from Martin G. Evans, "Organizational Behavior: The Central Role of Motivation," *Journal of Management,* Summer 1986, p. 206. Reprinted by permission.

FIGURE 12.1
The Role of Goal Setting in Organizations

The Role of Goal Setting

Bandura's social learning theory perhaps best describes the role of goal setting in organizations.[4] This perspective suggests that the extent to which people achieve their goals results in feelings of pride or shame for performance. In other words, a person who achieves a goal will be proud of having done so, whereas a person who fails to achieve a goal will feel shame. The degree of pride or

4. A. Bandura, *Social Learning Theory* (Englewood Cliffs, N.J.: Prentice-Hall, 1977).

- **Self-efficacy** is the belief that one can accomplish one's goals despite previous failures.

shame a person experiences is affected by the belief that he or she can or cannot function at the desired level of performance. This belief is called **self-efficacy.** Having a sense of self-efficacy is believing that we can still accomplish our goals even if we have failed in the past.

Evans recently presented this perspective in the context of a model of motivation.[5] Figure 12.1 shows a simplified version of this approach. As a starting point, a goal is set (by either the individual or a superior) and accepted. This goal influences the individual's degree of attention, effort, and persistence, as well as the strategy the person adopts to achieve the goal. These factors, along with constraints on performance and the individual's ability, determine actual performance.

When performance has been completed, the individual compares actual performance with the original goal. If the goal has been reached, the person is ready for another goal. If the goal has not been reached, the individual cognitively evaluates the discrepancy between the goal and what has actually been achieved. This evaluation determines the person's subsequent level of satisfaction with the performance and his or her sense of self-efficacy. Finally, these attitudes also influence future goal-directed behavior.

Goal Setting and Motivation

Bandura's social learning theory and its motivational derivative are general views of human behavior. A much more specific and applied approach to goal setting is called the *goal-setting theory of motivation.* The research of Edwin Locke most decisively showed the utility of goal-setting theory in a motivational context.[6]

The Basic Approach

- The **goal-setting theory of motivation** assumes that behavior is a result of conscious goals and intentions.

The **goal-setting theory of motivation** assumes that behavior is a result of conscious goals and intentions. Therefore, by setting goals for people in the organization, a manager should be able to influence their behavior. Given this premise, the challenge is to develop a thorough understanding of the processes by which people set goals and then work to reach them. Figure 12.2 presents a model of goal setting consistent with Locke's original presentation.[7] In the model, goal difficulty and goal specificity shape performance.

5. Martin G. Evans, "Organizational Behavior: The Central Role of Motivation," *Journal of Management,* Summer 1986, pp. 203–222.

6. Edwin A. Locke, "Toward a Theory of Task Performance and Incentives," *Organizational Behavior and Human Performance,* vol. 3, 1968, pp. 157–189.

7. Locke, "Toward a Theory of Task Performance and Incentives." See also Gary Latham, "The Role of Goal Setting in Human Resources Management," in Kendrith M. Rowland and Gerald R. Ferris, eds., *Research in Personnel and Human Resource Management,* vol. 1 (Greenwich, Conn.: JAI Press, 1983), pp. 169–200.

FIGURE 12.2
The Basic Goal-Setting Approach

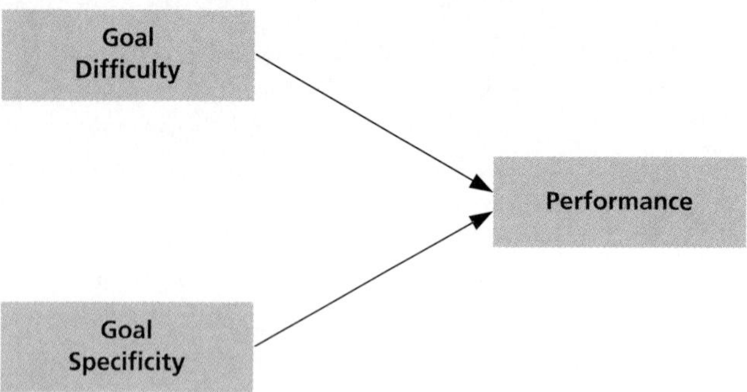

■ **Goal difficulty** is the extent to which a goal is challenging and demands effort.

Goal Difficulty Goal difficulty is the extent to which a goal is challenging and requires effort. If people work to achieve goals, it is reasonable to assume they will work harder to achieve more difficult goals. But a goal must not be so difficult that it is unattainable. If a new manager asks her sales force to increase sales by 300 percent, the group may become disillusioned. A more realistic but still difficult goal—say, a 50-percent increase—would be a better incentive. Reinforcement also fosters motivation toward difficult goals. A person who is rewarded for achieving a difficult goal will be more inclined to strive toward the next difficult goal than will someone who has received no reward after reaching the first goal.

A fairly large body of research supports the importance of goal difficulty.[8] In one study, Gary P. Latham and J. J. Baldes set difficult goals for truck drivers hauling loads of timber from cutting sites to wood yards.[9] Over a nine-month period, the drivers increased the quantity of wood they delivered by an amount that would have required $250,000 worth of new trucks at the previous per-truck average load.

■ **Goal specificity** is the definition of the target for performance.

Goal Specificity Goal specificity relates to the definition of the target for performance. *Specificity* usually means stating a goal in quantitative terms. For example, cutting costs by 10 percent and hiring twenty new minority employees are each specific goals. In areas such as employee satisfaction, however, specificity is difficult to establish.

Specificity has also been shown to be consistently related to performance.[10] The previously cited study by Latham and Baldes also examined specificity.[11]

8. Gary P. Latham and Gary Yukl, "A Review of Research on the Application of Goal Setting in Organizations," *Academy of Management Journal,* vol. 18, 1975, pp. 824–845; Mark E. Tubbs, "Goal Setting: A Meta-Analytic Examination of the Empirical Evidence," *Journal of Applied Psychology,* vol. 71, 1986, pp. 474–483.

9. Gary P. Latham and J. J. Baldes, "The Practical Significance of Locke's Theory of Goal Setting," *Journal of Applied Psychology,* vol. 60, 1975, pp. 187–191.

10. Latham and Yukl, "A Review of Research on the Application of Goal Setting in Organizations."

11. Latham and Baldes, "The Practical Significance of Locke's Theory of Goal Setting."

These people are participating in the Escape to Reality exercise at the Western Institute of Neuropsychiatry in Salt Lake City. During the exercise groups are given a set of obstacles to overcome, such as climbing a wall or crossing a log. The group members must work together as a team in order to achieve each goal. By making the goals somewhat difficult, therapists believe that the participants are more motivated to achieve them.

The initial loads the truck drivers were carrying were found to be 60 percent of the maximum weight each truck could haul. The researchers set a new goal for drivers of 94 percent. The goal thus was quite specific as well as difficult.

A Broader Perspective of Goals and Motivation

Because his theory attracted widespread interest and research support, Locke, together with Gary Latham, proposed an expanded model of the goal-setting process.[12] The expanded model, shown in Figure 12.3, attempts to capture more fully the complexities of goal setting in organizations.

- **Goal acceptance** is the extent to which an individual accepts a goal as his or her own.
- **Goal commitment** is the extent to which an individual is personally interested in reaching the goal.

Latham and Locke assume that goal-directed effort initially is a function of four goal attributes: difficulty, specificity, acceptance, and commitment. **Goal acceptance** is the extent to which a person accepts a goal as his or her own. **Goal commitment** is the extent to which he or she is personally interested in reaching the goal. The manager who vows to take whatever steps are necessary to cut costs by 10 percent has made a commitment to achieve the goal. Factors that can foster goal acceptance and commitment include participating in the

12. Gary P. Latham and Edwin Locke, "Goal Setting—A Motivational Technique That Works," *Organizational Dynamics,* Autumn 1979, pp. 68–80.

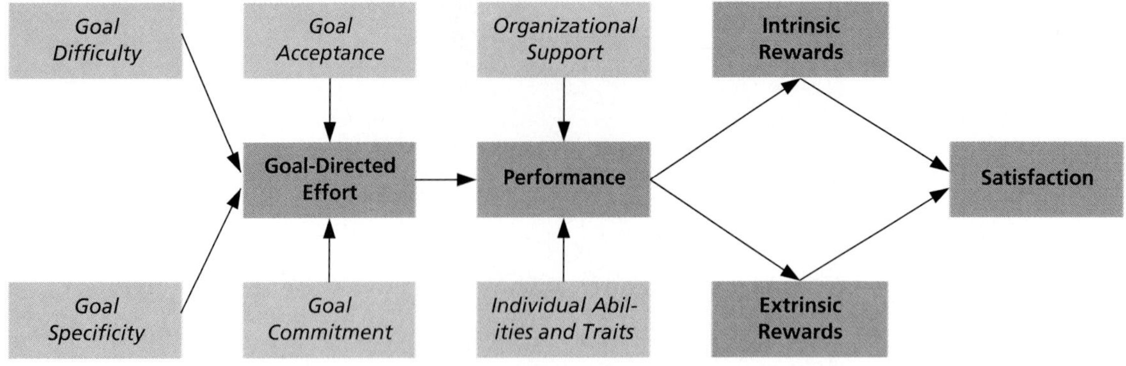

SOURCE: Reprinted, by permission of publisher, from *Organizational Dynamics,* Autumn/1979.

FIGURE 12.3
The Expanded Goal-Setting Model

goal-setting process, making goals challenging but realistic, and believing that goal achievement will lead to valued rewards.[13]

Actual performance is determined by the interaction of goal-directed effort, organizational support, and individual abilities and traits. *Organizational support* is whatever the organization does to help or hinder performance. Positive support might mean making available adequate personnel and a sufficient supply of raw materials; negative support might mean failing to fix damaged equipment. *Individual abilities and traits* are the skills and other personal characteristics necessary for doing a job. As a result of performance, a person receives various intrinsic and extrinsic rewards, which in turn influence satisfaction. Note that the latter stages of Latham and Locke's extended model are quite similar to the Porter and Lawler expectancy model discussed in Chapter 5.[14]

Research Evidence

Goal-setting theory has been widely tested in a variety of settings.[15] Research has demonstrated fairly consistently that goal difficulty and specificity are closely associated with performance. Other elements of the theory, such as acceptance

13. Gary P. Latham and Timothy P. Steele, "The Motivational Effects of Participation versus Goal Setting on Performance," *Academy of Management Journal,* September 1983, pp. 406–417.

14. Lyman W. Porter and Edward E. Lawler, *Managerial Attitudes and Performance* (Homewood, Ill.: Dorsey Press, 1968).

15. Latham and Yukl, "A Review of Research on the Application of Goal Setting Theory"; John R. Hollenback and Howard J. Klein, "Goal Commitment and the Goal Setting Process: Problems, Prospects, and Proposals for Future Research," *Journal of Applied Psychology,* vol. 72, 1987, pp. 212–220.

and commitment, have been studied less widely. A few studies have shown the importance of acceptance and commitment, but little is currently known about how people adopt acceptance and commitment.

It has been argued that goal-setting theory is not really a theory but simply an effective motivational technique. The goal-setting process may also be a narrow and unnecessarily rigid view of employee behavior. Some important aspects of behavior cannot be quantified easily, and goal setting may focus too much attention on the short run at the expense of long-term considerations. Despite these objections, however, goal setting appears to be a useful approach to motivation. In the next section, we examine a related approach through which goal setting is applied in organizational settings.

Management by Objectives

Management by objectives, or *MBO,* is a popular technique for managing the goal setting process in organizations. Figure 12.4 illustrates the basic MBO process.[16]

The MBO Process

■ **Management by objectives (MBO)** is a collaborative goal-setting process through which organizational goals systematically filter down through the organization.

Management by objectives (MBO) essentially is a collaborative goal-setting process through which organizational goals systematically cascade down through the organization. It is implemented through a series of discrete steps. The following discussion describes the steps in a general way; many organizations have adopted variations to suit their own purposes.

Starting MBO MBO must start at the top to be successful. Top management must stand behind the program and take the first step by establishing overall goals for the organization.

Establishment of Organizational Goals The initial goals are, of course, set by upper-level managers. Goals might relate to sales growth, market share growth, costs, productivity, employee absenteeism and turnover, or any other area important to the organization.

Collaborative Goal Setting Next, superiors and subordinates collaborate in setting goals. First, the organizational goals are communicated to everyone. Then each manager meets with each subordinate. During this meeting, the manager

16. See Stephen J. Carroll and Henry L. Tosi, *Management by Objectives* (New York: Macmillan, 1973).

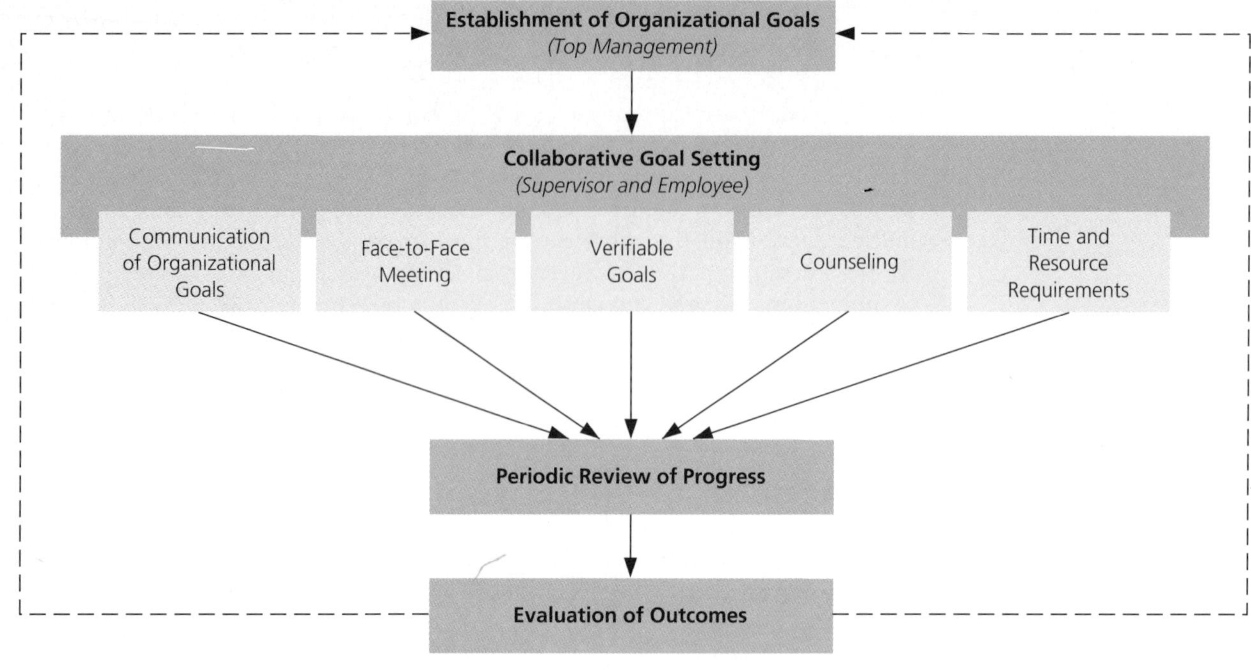

SOURCE: Adapted from Ricky W. Griffin, *Management,* 3rd ed. (Boston: Houghton Mifflin, 1990), p. 242. Adapted by permission.

FIGURE 12.4
The MBO Process

explains the unit goals to the subordinate and the two determine together how the subordinate can most effectively contribute to those goals. The manager acts as a counselor and helps ensure that the subordinate develops goals that are *verifiable.* For example, a goal of "cutting costs by 5 percent" is verifiable, whereas a goal of "doing my best" is not. Finally, manager and subordinate ensure that the subordinate has the resources needed to reach his or her goals. The entire process spirals downward as each subordinate meets with his or her own subordinates to develop their goals. Thus, as we noted earlier, the initial goals set at the top cascade down through the entire organization.

Periodic Review During the time frame set for goal attainment (usually one year), the manager periodically meets with each subordinate again to check progress. It may be necessary, for example, to modify goals in light of new information, to provide additional resources, or to take other action.

Evaluation Finally, at the end of the specified time period, managers hold a final evaluation meeting with each subordinate. At this meeting, manager and subordinate assess how well goals were met and discuss why. This meeting often serves as the annual performance review as well, determining salary adjustments and other rewards based on reaching goals. (We briefly discuss MBO as a performance evaluation technique in Chapter 14.) Finally, this meeting may also serve as the initial goal-setting meeting for the next year's cycle.

MBO in Management Practice

■ Using MBO in practice means gaining the benefits while being alert to the pitfalls.

MBO is a very popular technique. Alcoa, Tenneco, Black & Decker, General Foods, and Du Pont, for example, have used it extensively. MBO's popularity stems in part from the approach's many strengths. For one thing, MBO clearly has the potential to motivate employees because it provides unambiguous objectives for them to work toward. It also clarifies the basis for rewards, and it can spur communication. Performance appraisals are easier and more clear-cut under MBO. Further, managers can use the system for control purposes.[17]

However, there are also pitfalls in using MBO. Sometimes top managers do not really participate; that is, the goals essentially start in the middle of the organization and may not reflect the real goals of top management, and those who do participate may become cynical. That is, they interpret the lack of participation by top management as a sign that the goals are not important, and therefore view their own involvement as a waste of time. There is also a tendency to overemphasize quantitative goals to enhance verifiability. An MBO system also requires a great deal of paperwork and record keeping, since every goal must be documented. Finally, some managers do not really let subordinates participate in goal setting but, instead, assign goals and order subordinates to accept them.

On balance, MBO is often an effective and useful system for managing goal setting in organizations. Research suggests that it can actually do many of the things its advocates claim, but it must also be handled carefully. In particular, most organizations would need to tailor it to their own unique circumstances. Properly used, MBO can be an effective approach to managing an organization's reward system, the area we turn to now.[18] It requires, however, individual, one-on-one interactions between each supervisor and each individual employee. These one-on-one interactions can often be difficult situations. *Developing Management Skills* illustrates a clear, step-by-step process for holding these supervisor-employee sessions.

Reward Systems in Organizations

■ The **reward system** is composed of all organizational components involved in the allocation of compensation and benefits to employees in exchange for their contributions to the organization.

Obviously reward systems are an important tool that managers can use to channel employee motivation in desired ways. The **reward system** consists of all

17. Ibid.

18. Jack N. Kondrasuk, "Studies in MBO Effectiveness," *Academy of Management Review,* July 1981, pp. 419–430.

Developing MANAGEMENT SKILLS

Goal Setting for the Supervisor

Managing a goal-setting system can be a complex and time-consuming process. When you as a manager attempt to set goals with your employees, you may find that they are unfamiliar with goal setting and perhaps wary of any system management tells them to use. Jay Knippen and Thad Green have described a simple four-step process that can help you start goal-setting sessions with your employees.

Step 1: *Create the need* within the employee by stating the purpose and describing the events leading to the session. The events may be the creation of a new department or changes in management goals or structure.

Step 2: *Describe the goal-setting process* as it works for the whole organization and specifically how it works for that particular employee. This description should include the time frame in which things will happen and who will participate. You should also explain how the goals will be used during the year and how they will affect performance appraisals and possibly pay raises next year. The employee will also appreciate some examples of what goals should look like so that he or she will know how to write goals for her or his area.

Step 3: *Set the goals.* This should occur after the employee has had several days—ideally a week to ten days—to generate a set of goals for her or his work area. As the supervisor, you should use this time frame to set goals for each employee's work area. Remember: To be feasible, goals should be specific, measurable, and realistic.

Step 4: Develop and agree on a system of *measuring* performance in achieving the goals and on a *monitoring* process. You and the employee should agree on when performance will be measured (i.e., units sold or units produced per month) and on how units or projects will be counted.

These four steps should make the goal-setting process easier for you to implement and for your employees to follow.

SOURCE: Reprinted, by permission of publisher, from *Supervisory Management,* April/1989

organizational components—including people, processes, rules and procedures, and decision-making activities—involved in the allocation of compensation and benefits to employees in exchange for their contributions to the organization.

As we examine organizational reward systems, it is important to keep in mind their relationship to employee motivation (covered in Chapter 6). Reinforcement theory and theories of perception and learning (covered in Chapters 3 and 5) also relate to the study of organizational rewards. In short, reward systems in an organizational context cannot be studied apart from their effects on individuals.[19]

19. Edward E. Lawler, *Pay and Organization Development* (Reading, Mass.: Addison-Wesley, 1981); Edward E. Lawler, "The Design of Effective Reward Systems," in Jay W. Lorsch, ed., *Handbook of Organizational Behavior* (Englewood Cliffs, N.J.: Prentice-Hall, 1987), pp. 255–271; Jeffrey Pfeffer and Alison Davis-Blake, "Understanding Organizational Wage Structures," *Academy of Management Journal,* vol. 30, 1987, pp. 437–455.

■ **Tangible compensation** is rewards that have a definite value.

■ **Intangible compensation** is rewards whose value is not easily defined or measured.

A Transaction Process

The organizational reward system and the performance appraisal system are the key links in the exchange process between individual employees and the organization. Employees contribute many resources to the organization: time, effort, knowledge, skills, creativity, and energy. In turn, the organization rewards its employees with both tangible and intangible compensation. **Tangible compensation** consists of rewards that have a definite value, such as pay, pension plans, life and health insurance, and vacations. **Intangible compensation** refers to rewards whose value is less easily defined, such as status symbols, opportunities to be creative, and self-esteem. Figure 12.5 illustrates this transaction process.

As is typical of most areas in the field of organizational behavior, the transaction process is dynamic rather than static. If either party feels the transaction is not equitable, the parties may attempt to reach agreement on an equitable relationship or they may terminate the relationship. Nor does the transaction relationship exist in a vacuum. Both parties are at least somewhat aware of the transaction between employees and other organizations. Because an organization's reward system is the one part of the transaction process that the organization can control, the system must be properly designed and carefully managed.

The Roles, Purposes, and Meanings of Rewards

In most organizations the purpose of the reward system is to attract, retain, and motivate qualified employees.[20] Compensation philosophy centers on three issues: the concept of fairness and equality of rewards, the importance of each employee's contribution to the organization, and the status of the external labor market.

The organization's compensation structure must be equitable and consistent to ensure equality of treatment and compliance with the law. In addition, compensation should be a fair reward for the individual's contributions to the organization, although in most cases these contributions are difficult, if not impossible, to measure objectively. Given this limitation, managers should be as fair and equitable as possible. Finally, the system must be competitive in the external labor market for the organization to attract and retain competent workers in appropriate fields.

Beyond these broad considerations, an organization must develop its philosophy of compensation based on its own conditions and needs, and this philosophy must be defined and built into the actual reward system. For example,

---

20. Douglas B. Gehrman, "Beyond Today's Compensation and Performance Appraisal Systems," *Personnel Administrator,* March 1984, pp. 21–33; Jeffrey Kerr and John W. Slocum, Jr., "Managing Corporate Culture through Reward Systems," *Academy of Management Executive,* vol. 1, no. 2, May 1987, pp. 99–108.

FIGURE 12.5
The Transaction between the Organization and the Individual

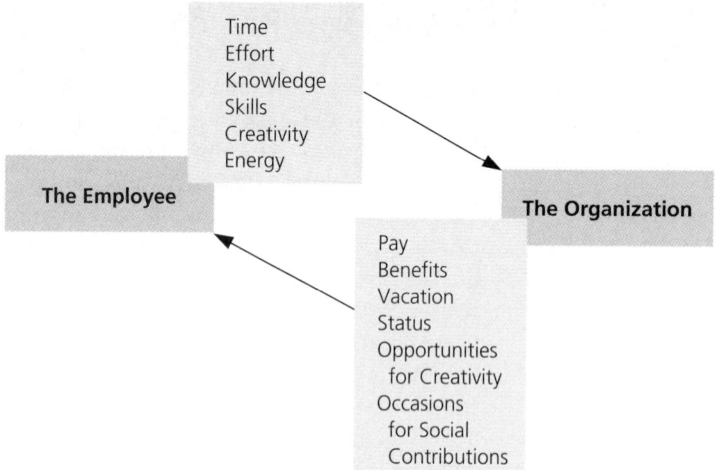

the compensation philosophy of Lincoln Electric Co. is that all employees should receive compensation in accordance with their accomplishments and should share in the profits they helped create.[21] As a result, Lincoln employees earn about twice as much as similar workers at other companies, yet labor costs per sales dollar at Lincoln are well below industry averages.

A well-developed compensation philosophy articulates the purpose of the system and provides a framework for making compensation decisions. It can serve as a point of stability in changing economic, technological, and labor market conditions. In addition, a clearly stated philosophy can give the system credibility among those most affected by it—the employees. The organization needs to decide what types of behaviors or performance it wants to encourage with a reward system, because what is rewarded tends to recur. Possible behaviors include performance, longevity, attendance, loyalty, contributions to the "bottom line," responsibility, and conformity.

Performance appraisal measures these behaviors, but the choice of which behaviors to reward is a function of the compensation system. A reward system must also take into account volatile economic issues such as inflation, market conditions, technology, labor union activities, and so forth.

- Rewards in organizations can have both surface and symbolic value.

It is also important for the organization to recognize that organizational rewards have many meanings for employees. As Figure 12.6 shows, intrinsic and extrinsic rewards carry both surface and symbolic value. The *surface value* of a reward to an employee is the meaning it has at an objective level. A salary increase of 5 percent, for example, means that an individual has 5 percent more spending power than before, whereas a promotion, on the surface, means new duties and responsibilities. Rewards also carry *symbolic value*. Consider what

21. James F. Lincoln, *A New Approach to Industrial Economics* (New York: Devin-Adair, 1961), reprinted in Arthur A. Thompson, Jr., and A. J. Strickland III, *Strategic Management: Concepts and Cases,* 3rd ed. (Plano, Tex.: Business Publications, 1984), p. 948.

FIGURE 12.6
Meanings of Rewards to Individuals

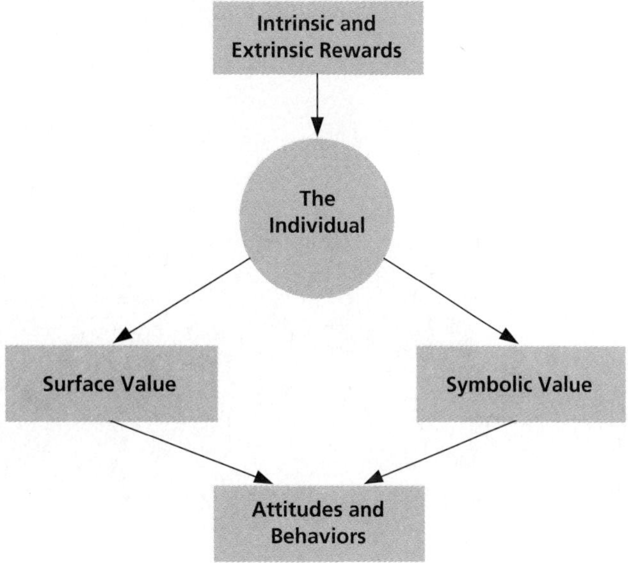

frequently happens when a pro football or basketball team signs a top college prospect for a great deal of money. The new player often feels enormous pressure to live up to the salary, and veteran players may argue that their pay should be increased to keep the salary structure in balance. Rewards convey to people how much they are valued by the organization, as well as their importance relative to others. Consider again a 5 percent salary increase. If the recipient later finds out that everyone else got 3 percent or less, he or she will feel vitally important to the organization, someone whose contributions are recognized and valued. On the other hand, if everyone else got at least 8 percent, the person probably will believe the organization places little value on his or her contributions. In short, then, managers need to tune in to the many meanings rewards can convey—not only the surface messages but the symbolic messages as well.[22]

Types of Rewards

Most organizations use several different types of rewards. The most commonly used rewards are money (wages, salary, commission), incentive systems, benefits, perquisites, and awards. The rewards are combined in a compensation package.

22. See Richard T. Mowday, "Equity Theory Predictions of Behavior in Organizations," in Richard M. Steers and Lyman W. Porter, eds., *Motivation and Work Behavior,* 4th ed. (New York: McGraw-Hill, 1987), pp. 89–110; Rabindra N. Kanungo and Jon Hartwick, "An Alternative to the Intrinsic-Extrinsic Dichotomy of Work Rewards," *Journal of Management,* vol. 13, Winter 1987, pp. 751–766.

Organizations need to rely on a variety of rewards. Jane Napoli, a New Orleans artist and gallery owner, wanted to reward kids with promising artistic skills for pursuing their interests further. She selects young artists such as the three shown and invites them to paint in her professional studio.

Money

For most people, the most important organizational reward is money. Obviously, it is important because of the things it can buy, but, as we just noted, it can also symbolize an employee's worth. A recent study by a compensation consulting firm, Hewitt Associates, found that the compensation of the chief executive officers at twenty-five major U.S. corporations increased 171 percent during the 1980s to an average of $2,670,000, including salary, bonuses, and stock options in 1989. Furthermore, the number of tax returns that reported income of more than $1 million increased from 8,408 in 1982 to 65,303 in 1988.[23] Clearly, monetary rewards play an important role in organizations.

Money is an important type of compensation for the student of organizational behavior. Employee compensation is a major cost of doing business—as much as 50 to 60 percent in many organizations. Pay is considered a major source of employee dissatisfaction.[24] As the most tangible part of the transaction relationship between the organization and the individual, it also can be used as an instrument of change within the organization. For example, salary adjustments might consciously be used to signal who is more valuable and who is less valuable to the organization and/or to clarify norms as to what is expected and what will be rewarded in the future.

23. Edmund Faltermayer, "Who Are the Rich?" *Fortune,* December 17, 1990, pp. 95–106.

24. See Lawler, *Pay and Organization Development,* for a more detailed discussion of organizational pay issues.

■ **Job analysis** is the study of tasks that make up a job conducted to establish the relative worth of that job.

The development of a pay system begins with **job analysis.** Job analysis information can be used to develop a point system in which each job is assigned a value based on its relative worth. For example, jobs can be compared on the basis of responsibility, skill, effort, and working conditions. Those jobs that require considerable responsibility, skill, and effort under harsh working conditions would be assigned a high point value and, hence, high pay. Point systems and other means of comparing jobs are used to ensure the internal fairness of pay.

To verify the competitiveness of its pay scales, an organization can also conduct a survey of pay at other companies in the same industry or use data from surveys conducted by groups such as the Bureau of Labor Statistics, the American Management Association, or the Administrative Management Society. Other issues of concern in the design of a pay system include the number of pay grades and the number of steps within each grade; the minimum, midpoint, and maximum pay levels for each grade and for the organization as a whole; the amount of overlap between grades; the way in which an employee moves from one step or grade to the next; and the effect on the pay system of changes in external conditions (for example, labor supply and demand or inflation).[25]

Incentive Systems

Incentive systems usually promise additional money for certain types of performance. Examples of incentive programs include the following:

1. *Piecework* programs that tie a worker's earnings to the number of units produced
2. *Gain-sharing* programs that grant additional earnings to employees or work groups for cost reduction efforts or ideas
3. *Commission* programs that provide sales personnel with earnings based on the number of units they sell
4. *Bonus* systems whereby management personnel receive lump sums from a special bonus pool based on the financial performance of the organization or a unit of the organization
5. *Long-term compensation* that provides management personnel with substantial additional income based on stock price performance, earnings per share, or return on equity
6. *Merit pay* plans that base raises on the employee's performance as determined by objectively measured productivity or by the results of a performance appraisal
7. *Profit-sharing* plans that distribute a percentage of the organization's profits to all employees at a predetermined rate

---

25. See Richard I. Henderson, *Performance Appraisal* (Reston, Va.: Reston, 1984), for more information on the design of pay structures.

8. *Employee stock option* plans that typically set aside a block of stock in the company for employees to purchase at a reduced rate, with the expectation that employees who own part of the company are more committed to it and work harder to increase the value of their stock

Plans oriented mainly toward individual employees may cause increased competition for the rewards and some possibly disruptive behaviors, such as sabotaging a coworker's performance, sacrificing quality for quantity, or fighting over customers. A group incentive plan, on the other hand, requires that employees trust one another and work together. Of course, incentive systems have advantages and disadvantages. Long-term compensation for executives is particularly controversial because of the large sums of money involved and the basis for the payments.[26] The successful implementation of an incentive program depends on the history and traditions of the organization; the nature of the organization's products or services; current political, economic, and legal conditions, and employee needs and perceptions about the system.

As *Management in Action* illustrates, companies that have used incentive systems in some parts of the organization are developing even more comprehensive incentive pay plans in an attempt to tie performance to pay.

Benefits

Another major component of the compensation package is the employee benefits plan. Benefits often are called *indirect compensation.* Typical benefits provided by organizations include the following:

1. *Payment for time not worked,* both on and off the job. On-the-job free time includes lunch periods, rest periods, coffee breaks, wash-up times and get-ready time. Off-the-job time not worked includes vacations, sick leaves, holidays, and personal days.
2. *Social security contributions.* The employer contributes half the money paid into the system established under the Federal Insurance Contributions Act (FICA). The employee pays the other half, making a total of approximately $3,045 per year for the average employee. The employee receives social security income when she or he retires.
3. *Unemployment compensation.* People who have lost their jobs or are temporarily laid off get a percentage of their wages from the state. Funds come from payments by companies as regulated by state laws.
4. *Disability and workers' compensation benefits.* Employers contribute funds to assist workers who are ill or injured and cannot work owing

26. Arthur M. Louis, "Business Is Bungling Long-Term Compensation," *Fortune,* July 23, 1984, pp. 64–69.

MANAGEMENT IN ACTION

Shearson Lehman Hutton Links Pay to Performance

Stockbrokers traditionally have been paid on a commission basis; that is, when they process a transaction for a client, some percentage of the cost of the stock price is charged to the customer. The fee can range from 1 to 3 percent of the transaction amount on large transactions to 20 percent on small, odd-lot purchases. The fee goes to the brokerage company, which periodically pays commissions to the brokers based on the number and value of stocks traded during the period. The broker may get about one-third to one-half of the fee. Most brokers work on a 100 percent commission basis, meaning they are paid nothing if they sell no stocks. Therefore, stockbrokers are highly motivated to sell their product.

The assumption has been that customers are paying for the broker's expertise and advice in deciding in which stock to invest their money. Some investors have been upset by what they claim are exorbitant fees. They argue that they know the market better than the brokers, do not need the investment advice, and see no reason to pay for it. The result has been the emergence of discount brokerage firms, which provide only the transaction service and no advice and thus charge lower fees for transactions.

A new form of pay for performance is developing in the stockbrokerage industry. The advice stockbrokers give clients is determined by stock market analysts who are employed by the brokerage firm to study the stock markets and provide recommendations for the brokers. Shearson Lehman Hutton Inc. recently put its analysts on a pay-for-performance system called BONUS. The acronym stands for the five levels of recommendations they provide to brokers: *b*uy, *o*utperform, *n*eutral, *u*nderperform, and *s*ell. At the end of the year, computers calculate the performance of the stocks rated on the BONUS system by each analyst, and bonuses are generated for those whose recommendations worked out the best.

The system is expected to generate better information for brokers and clients. If the broker is able to convince clients to make certain purchases, both the broker and the analyst make money. The system also keeps customers happy by making more money for them in the long run.

The idea is being tried not only at Shearson Lehman Hutton. Dean Witter Reynolds and Merrill Lynch are also using pay-for-performance systems for their analysts.

SOURCES: "Wall Street Firms Link Analysts' Pay to Performance," *The Wall Street Journal,* September 19, 1989, p. C1; "Who Cares What the Boss Picks?" *U.S. News & World Report,* June 19, 1989, p. 64; "When Shearson Calls Don't Answer," *Financial World,* December 27, 1988.

to occupational injury or ailment. These benefits are regulated by federal and state laws.

5. *Life and health insurance programs*. Most organizations offer insurance at a cost far below what individuals would pay to buy insurance by themselves.
6. *Pension plans*. Most organizations offer plans to provide supplementary income to employees after they retire. These company-paid or joint employee-and-company-paid programs are meant to supplement social security.

A company's social security, unemployment, and workers' compensation contributions are set by law. But how much to contribute for other kinds of benefits is up to each company. Some organizations contribute more to the cost of these benefits than others do. Some companies pay the entire cost; others pay a percentage of the cost of certain benefits, such as health insurance, and bear the entire cost of others. Offering benefits beyond wages became a standard component of compensation during World War II as a way of increasing employee compensation when wage controls were in effect. Since then, competition for employees and employee demands (expressed, for instance, in union bargaining) have caused companies to increase these benefits. In many organizations, benefits now account for 30 to 40 percent of payroll.

- Benefits are becoming a larger burden on organizations in the United States than on organizations in other countries.

The burden of providing employee benefits is growing heavier for firms in the United States than it is for organizations in other countries. For example, Chrysler Corp. now spends about $700 per car on health benefits for its workers, whereas foreign car manufacturers spend only about $200 per car.[27] Although these benefit costs could be reduced, employers do not know what the ramifications of cuts would be in terms of employee morale, motivation, turnover, and recruiting. Benefits therefore are a major concern for businesses, and some are trying to reduce the costs of indirect compensation. The motivational power of benefits is unknown; however, weak or poorly designed benefit packages have been shown to cause employee dissatisfaction.

Perquisites

- **Perquisites** are means of compensation in the form of special privileges associated with employees of relatively high rank in the organization.

Perquisites are an aspect of the exchange relationship that has received little theoretical consideration but much legal attention and media coverage. For years, the top executives of many organizations were allowed privileges such as unlimited use of the company airplane, motor home, vacation home, and executive dining room. Eventually, the Internal Revenue Service ruled that some "perks" constitute a form of income and thus can be taxed. The IRS decision has substantially changed the nature of these benefits, but they have not entirely disappeared, nor are they likely to. More than anything else, perquisites seem to add to the status of their recipients and thus serve to increase job satisfaction and reduce turnover.

Awards

In many companies, employees receive awards for everything from seniority to perfect attendance, from zero defects (quality work) to cost reduction sugges-

27. "Employee Benefits for a Changing Work Force," *Business Week,* November 5, 1990, pp. 31–40.

tions. Award programs can be costly in the time required to run them and in money if cash awards are given.

Award systems can improve performance under the right conditions. In one medium-size manufacturing company, careless work habits were pushing up the costs of scrap and rework (the cost of scrapping defective parts or reworking them to meet standards). Management instituted a zero-defects program to recognize employees who did perfect or near perfect work. The first month, two workers in shipping caused only one defect in over two thousand parts handled. Division management called a meeting in the lunchroom and recognized each worker with a plaque and a ribbon. The next month, the same two workers had two defects and there was no award. The following month, the two workers had zero defects and, once again top management called a meeting to give out plaques and ribbons. Elsewhere in the plant, defects, scrap, and rework decreased dramatically as workers evidently sought recognition for quality work. What worked in this particular plant may or may not work in others. The effects of award programs can be explained by reinforcement theory (Chapter 5) or the various need theories (Chapter 6).

Managing Reward Systems

Much of our discussion on reward systems has focused on general issues. As Table 12.1 shows, however, there are other issues in the development of orga-

TABLE 12.1
Issues to Consider in Developing Reward Systems

Issue	Key Examples
Pay Secrecy	▪ Open, closed, partial ▪ Link with performance appraisal ▪ Equity perceptions
Employee Participation	▪ By Human Resource Department ▪ By joint employee/management committee
Flexible System	▪ Cafeteria-style benefits ▪ Annual lump sum or monthly bonus ▪ Salary versus benefits
Ability to Pay	▪ Organization's financial performance ▪ Expected future earnings
Economic and Labor Market Factors	▪ Inflation rate ▪ Industry pay standards ▪ Unemployment rate
Impact on Organizational Performance	▪ Increase in costs ▪ Impact on performance

A LOOK AT THE **RESEARCH**

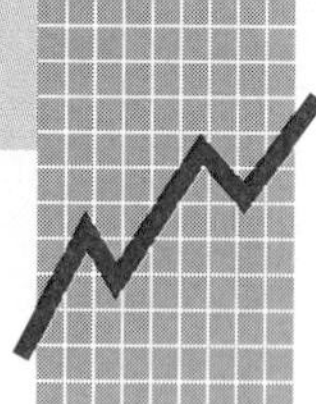

Does Pay Affect Corporate Financial Performance?

The pay most employees receive from their organizations usually consists of base pay, short-term bonuses, and long-term incentives. However, it is the combination of these elements that make the difference between organizations and the way that an employee responds. Professors Barry Gerhart and George Milkovich of Cornell University recently investigated how several organizations make the decisions to use base pay, bonuses, and long-term incentives to create the appropriate pay mix for their employees. The researchers attempted to determine how factors such as the organization's environment, industry, size, strategy, performance, and employees' personal and job characteristics affect the pay mix.

Gerhart and Milkovich used data generated by a large compensation consulting firm and collected by a survey questionnaire that covered more than three hundred companies and over twenty thousand top- and middle-level executives and managers from 1981 to 1985. The managers held a wide variety of positions, including top executive positions, marketing, finance, manufacturing, employee relations, research and development, and engineering. The researchers selected the companies based on whether the firms' pay data were complete for three of the five years covered in the study and whether at least three companies in the same industry participated. The resulting sample contained 219 organizations and about 14,000 employees.

Using the five years' worth of historical data and sophisticated computer-aided statistical analysis, Gerhart and Milkovich found several relationships. First, employee pay levels and the pay mix were affected more by organizational factors than by individual and job factors. This suggested that organizational factors such as industry membership, size, and financial performance are very influential in determining the compensation strategy. In addition, they found that the pay mix (use of base pay, bonus pay, and incentives) was related to subsequent financial performance, whereas the pay level (pay amounts) was not. In other words, different combinations of incentives and bonuses appeared to have positive effects on the firm's future financial performance.

Although research was based on five years of historical data collected in the early 1980s, the findings represent the first long-term look at relationships between pay practices and organizational performance. The results may be somewhat tentative at this time, and more research needs to be done to confirm these findings and reveal more specifics about how organizational performance can be enhanced through the use of the pay mix. Nevertheless, Gerhart and Milkovich's work appears encouraging to those who manage compensation in organizations.

SOURCE: From Barry Gerhart and George T. Milkovich, "Organizational Differences in Managerial Compensation and Financial Performance," *Academy of Management Journal,* December 1990, pp. 663–691. Adapted by permission.

nizational reward systems that the organization must address. The organization must consider its ability to pay employees at certain levels, economic and labor market conditions, and the impact of the pay system on organizational financial performance. *A Look at the Research* summarizes a recent study of some of these issues. In addition, the organization must consider the issues of pay secrecy, the degree of employee participation in the reward system, and reward system flexibility.

Pay Secrecy

- Pay secrecy is one of the most controversial topics in the area of organizational pay systems.

A policy of open salary information means that the exact salary amounts for employees are public knowledge. State governments, for instance, make public the salary of everyone on their payrolls. Complete secrecy means that no information is available to employees regarding other employees' salaries, average or percentage raises, or salary ranges. Although a few organizations have a completely public or a completely secret system, most are somewhere in the middle.

Diverse issues surround the question of secret versus open pay.[28] Some workers believe their pay is their business and no one else's; others prefer knowing exactly where they stand in relation to other employees. (The latter is a concrete example of an equity perception issue.) In an open pay system, managers must be able to defend the pay differences to those who are paid less. From a motivational point of view, an open system may clarify the relationship between pay and performance for all concerned. Moreover, research evidence suggests that in a secret system, employees tend to overestimate coworkers' pay, which can cause motivational problems.[29] In light of these considerations, many organizations have elected a compromise solution: a partially open system that lets employees know the salary range of jobs and average increases within each range.

Participative Pay Systems

- A **participative pay system** involves employees in the design and implementation of the system.

In keeping with the current trend toward worker involvement in organizational decision making, employee participation in the pay process is also increasing. A **participative pay system** may involve the employee in the system's design, administration, or both. A pay system can be designed by staff members of the organization's human resources department, a committee of managers in the organization, an outside consultant, the employees, or a combination of these sources. Organizations that have used a joint management-employee task force to design the compensation system generally have succeeded in designing and implementing a plan that managers could use and employees believed in.[30]

Employee participation in administering the pay system is a natural extension of having employees participate in its design. Examples of companies that have involved employees in the administration of the pay system include Romac Industries, where employees vote on the pay of other employees; Graphic Controls, where each manager's pay is determined by a group of peers; and the Friedman-Jacobs Co., where employees set their own wages based on their

28. See Lawler, *Pay and Organization Development,* pp. 43–50, for more discussion of the secret versus open pay system.

29. Ibid.

30. Lawler, *Pay and Organization Development,* pp. 101–111. See also Jack C. Horn, "Bigger Pay for Better Work," *Psychology Today,* July 1987, pp. 54–57.

perceptions of their performance.[31] Allowing individuals and work groups to set their own salaries may not be appropriate for all organizations, but it can be successful in organizations characterized by a climate of trust, joint problem solving, and a participative management style.

Flexible Reward Systems

■ A **flexible reward system** allows employees to choose the combination of benefits that best suits their needs.

Flexible, or cafeteria-style, reward systems are a recent and increasingly popular variation on the standard compensation system.[32] A **flexible reward system** allows employees to choose the combination of benefits that best suits their needs. For example, younger workers starting a family may prefer additional maternity or paternity benefits or a family medical plan that pays 100 percent, whereas a worker nearing retirement may want to maximize pension benefits. Organizations even get more for their benefits dollars by using the flexible approach. Flexible systems generally require more administrative time and effort to develop and maintain than the standard approach, but the benefits of the flexible approach seem to outweigh these costs. In fact, most companies save enough money to pay back the initial investment in a few years.[33]

Some organizations are starting to apply the flexible approach to pay. For example, employees sometimes have the option of taking an annual salary increase in one lump sum rather than in monthly increments. General Electric recently implemented such a system for some of its managers.[34] Although lump-sum payments necessitate special provisions for taxes and for payback if the employee quits during the year the raise was given, this alternative lets the employee lay hands on the full amount of the increase at one time, possibly resulting in a greater motivational impact. In a totally flexible reward system, employees are able to trade off salary increases for benefits increases, and vice versa.

Summary of Key Points

- Goal setting is an important dimension of human behavior in organizations. Pride or shame may follow success or failure to reach goals. Goal setting is also important to motivation and control.

---

31. See Lawler, *Pay and Organization Development,* pp. 109–110.

32. See Dale Gifford, "The Status of Flexible Compensation," *Personnel Administrator,* May 1984, pp. 19–25, for more information on flexible compensation systems.

33. Lance D. Tane and Michael E. Treacy, "Benefits That Bend with Employees' Needs," *Nation's Business,* April 1984, pp. 80–82; Henderson, *Performance Appraisal*; "Benefits Are Getting More Flexible—But Caveat Emptor," *Business Week,* September 8, 1986, pp. 64–66.

34. "How'd You Like a Big Fat Bonus—But No Raise?" *Business Week,* November 3, 1986, pp. 30–31.

- The goal-setting theory of motivation suggests that goal difficulty, specificity, acceptance, and commitment are important determinants of performance. This view generally is supported by research.
- Management by objectives is another useful approach to goal setting. It is based on collaboratively setting verifiable goals and tying rewards to goal attainment. This approach also is supported by research.
- Another major part of managing people in organizations is the reward system. The purpose of the reward system is to attract, retain, and motivate qualified employees and to maintain a pay structure that is internally equitable and externally competitive. Rewards have both surface and symbolic value.
- Rewards take the form of money, benefits, perquisites, awards, and incentives. Factors such as motivational impact, cost, and fit with the organizational system must be considered when designing or analyzing a reward system. Other issues related to reward systems are the secrecy of pay systems, employee participation in the pay system, and flexible (or cafeteria-style) reward systems.

Discussion Questions

1. Do you set goals for yourself? In what areas? How do you feel when you have been successful or unsuccessful in reaching your goals?
2. Do goals motivate you? Can you cite instances of personal goals that were difficult or specific?
3. Would you like to work in an organization that uses MBO? Why or why not?
4. Can a person set too many goals? What are the implications of this question for managers?
5. The chapter implies that goals and rewards are linked. Can you think of cases where they are not or should not be linked?
6. What are the pros and cons of participative goal setting?
7. As a student in this class, what "rewards" do you receive in exchange for your time and effort? What are the rewards for the professor who teaches this class? How do your contributions and rewards differ from those of some other student in the class?
8. Do you expect to obtain the rewards you discussed in question 7 on the basis of your intelligence, your hard work, the number of hours you spend in the library, your height, your good looks, your work experience, or some other personal factor?
9. What do Herzberg's two-factor theory and the expectancy theory of motivation (discussed in Chapters 5 and 6) tell us about rewarding employees?
10. Often institutions in the federal and state governments give the same percentage pay raise to all their employees. What do you think is the effect of this type of pay raise on employee motivation?

CASE 12.1

Apple's New Goals and Strategies Cause Lots of Other Changes

Apple Computer, Inc., revolutionized the personal computer industry by making PCs easy to use, brought the PC into schools and homes, and, in mid-1990, may have come close to dropping out of the industry. The introduction of Windows by Microsoft Corp. and intense price cutting by IBM and IBM clone competitors made the high-end Macintosh and other Apple computers too expensive for everyone but the corporate buyer. Apple's market share had dropped significantly, and several top and middle managers had left the company. Morale among employees was at an all-time low as cost cutting removed the perks that had always been a hallmark of employment with Apple. In mid-1990, experts were calling for Apple to take drastic steps to survive.

John Sculley, chief executive officer of Apple, realized the difficulties the company faced and set about to shake the company up. His first step was to set new priorities that he hoped would turn Apple around in 1991.

The first new priority is to produce a low-cost Mac that will be more affordable for consumers and more attractive to businesses. Apple's original customers, mostly schools and small businesses, have found that the Macintosh was beyond their ability to pay to upgrade. As a result, customers were either choosing not to upgrade or were switching to IBM clones. A new, low-cost Mac hopefully will encourage more people to upgrade to the new system. Also, increases in unit sales should attract software developers to write innovative software for the Mac, which in turn should make the Mac more attractive to buyers.

The second priority is to develop new laptop and notebook computers. Currently Apple offers no portable computers for travel use. The industry trend is to make computers, like telephones, smaller, faster, and completely portable so that the traveler/businessperson need never be without one.

The third priority is to increase the Mac's software capability. While the Mac is known for its distinctive software that makes it both powerful and user friendly, software such as Microsoft Windows has made IBM clones almost equally powerful and easy to use. Sculley believes Apple must not stand still and plans to revamp Apple's entire software development process.

The final priority is to develop closer relationships with other computer makers. Until now Apple has stood alone, refusing to license its products and technologies to other manufacturers. It has been quick to sue competitors believed to have copied its innovations. This stance has hindered the creation of partnerships across the industry and left Apple isolated in a relatively close-knit business.

These new priorities were first communicated to an annual meeting of three hundred top managers from around the world. These managers then spread the news to others, and the new priorities are having an impact everywhere Apple does business. The most visible changes have been in Apple's organization chart. First, Sculley named a new second-in-command, chief operating officer (COO)

Michael Spindler, a ten-year veteran at Apple who is known as "Diesel" and is well liked by employees. Second, Sculley took over the research and development department himself, thereby taking control of the product development side of the business. While this may seem like a severe and costly move, it demonstrates Sculley's emphasis on new-product development. Finally, he canceled several projects and channeled money and effort into the priorities he had established. In short, Sculley began to make his new priorities a reality by personally getting involved in making them happen.

The new priorities may be the start of a new culture at Apple. However, Spindler, the new COO, cautions that Apple must not focus on its culture when new products and strategies must have the attention of every employee in the company. By the end of 1991, the industry should have a reading on the effectiveness of the "new" Apple. Analysts predict that 1991 will be a very good year.

Case Questions

1. What aspects of MBO and goal setting did Apple use in its attempts at a turnaround in 1990?
2. On what other aspects of managing the organization did the new priorities have an impact?
3. What other changes do you think will occur at Apple because of the new priorities?

SOURCES: Brenton R. Schlender, "Yet Another Strategy for Apple," *Fortune,* October 22, 1990, pp. 81–87; "Apple: New Team, New Strategy," *Business Week,* October 15, 1990, pp. 86–96; Richard A. Shaffer, "Apple's a Buy," *Forbes,* June 11, 1990, p. 202.

CASE 12.2

No More Dawdling over Dishes

Andy Davis was proud of his restaurant, The Golden Bow. Its location was perfect, its decor tasteful, its clientele generous and distinguished. When he first took over the business a year ago, Davis had worried that the local labor shortage might make it difficult to hire good workers. But he had made some contacts at a local college and hired a group of servers who worked well with customers and with one another. The only problem he still hadn't solved was the dishwasher.

At first Davis felt lucky when he found Eddie Munz, a local high school dropout who had some experience washing dishes. Davis couldn't afford to pay a dishwasher more than $4 an hour, but Eddie didn't seem to mind that. Moreover, Eddie seemed to get the dishes clean. But he was so slow! Davis originally thought Eddie just wasn't quick about anything, but he changed his mind as he observed his behavior in the kitchen. Eddie loved to talk to the cooks, often turning his back on the dishes for minutes at a time to chitchat. He also nibbled desserts off of dirty plates and sprayed the servers with water whenever they got near him. The kitchen was always a mess, and so many dishes would pile up that often two hours after closing time, when everything else was ready for the next day, Eddie would still be scraping and squirting and talking. Davis began to wonder if there was a method to Eddie's madness: He was getting paid by the hour, so why shouldn't he dawdle? But Davis didn't like having a constantly sloppy kitchen, so he determined to have a talk with Eddie.

Davis decided that what Eddie needed was a goal. He figured out what Eddie had been making on his reasonably efficient nights—$28—and then met with Eddie and made him a proposal. First he asked Eddie how soon he thought he could finish after the last customer left. Eddie said an hour and a quarter. When Davis asked if he would be interested in getting off forty-five minutes earlier than he had been, Eddie seemed excited. And when he offered to pay Eddie the $28 for a complete job every night, regardless of when he finished, Eddie could hardly contain himself. It turned out he didn't like to work until 2:00 A.M., but he needed every dollar he could get.

The next week, a new chalkboard appeared next to the kitchen door leading out to the dining room. On top it read, "Eddie's Goal for a Record Time." By the end of the first week, Davis printed on the bottom "$1\frac{1}{4}$." Davis took to inspecting the dishes more often than usual, but he found no decrease in the quality of Eddie's work. So on Sunday, he said to Eddie, "Let's try for an hour."

A month later, the board read "42 minutes." The situation in the kitchen had changed radically. The former "Eddie the Slob" had become "Eddie the Perfectionist." His area spotless, he was often waiting when someone came from the dining room with a stack of dirty plates, and he took it as a personal affront if anyone found a spot on a plate he had washed. Instead of complaining about Eddie squirting them, the servers kidded him about what a worker he'd become, and they stacked the plates and separated the silver to help him break his record. And the first time Eddie got done at 12:42, they all went out for an hour on the town together.

Case Questions

1. What elements of goal setting did Andy Davis employ?
2. Could Davis have used a different system of rewards to get the same results from Eddie Munz?

EXPERIENTIAL EXERCISE

Purpose: The purpose of this exercise is to enable you to see the potential benefits as well as the limitations of applying goal setting and rewards to a real situation.

Format: Working alone, develop a set of goals for yourself in this class. You should develop a range of goals of varying time horizons (i.e., grade on next quiz, grade at end of course). Next, identify appropriate rewards that you would like to receive for achieving each of your goals.

Procedure: Develop a framework linking goals and rewards for the course. In one column, list your goals. In another column, list the rewards. Then connect each goal with its associated rewards.

Finally, meet with two of your classmates and compare notes. What are the similarities and differences between your goals and rewards? What are the similarities and differences in how you see goals linked to various rewards?

Follow-up Questions

1. Would a formal MBO system work in a classroom? Why or why not?
2. What are the rewards available to you in a classroom setting? How do those rewards differ in their surface and symbolic value?

CHAPTER OUTLINE

- Historical Approaches to Job Design
  - *The Evolution of Job Design*
  - *Job Specialization*
  - *Early Alternatives to Job Specialization*
  - *Job Enrichment*
- The Job Characteristics Approach
  - *Job Characteristics*
  - *Individual Differences*
  - *The Job Characteristics Theory*
  - *Evaluation and Implications*
- Designing Jobs for Groups
  - *Group Tasks*
  - *Autonomous Work Groups and Work Teams*
  - *Other Group Applications*
- Social Information and Job Design
- Emerging Perspectives on Job Design
  - *Work Schedules*
  - *Automation and Robotics*
  - *Worker Flexibility*
- Employee Participation

13

Job Design and Employee Participation

CHAPTER OBJECTIVES

After studying this chapter, you should be able to:

Summarize the historical development of job design.

Discuss the job characteristics approach to job design.

Describe how jobs can be designed for groups.

Discuss the social information processing model.

Identify other contemporary approaches to job design.

Discuss employee participation from a job design perspective.

A group of employees at First National Bank of Chicago recently participated in a major program aimed at changing how they perform their jobs. The employees work in the letter-of-credit department, preparing documents that summarize clients' financial assets and credit available through the bank.

Bank managers believed the department was not as profitable or as productive as it could be, and that the employees were not serving their customers effectively. As a starting point, department employees completed a questionnaire called the Job Diagnostic Survey, or JDS. The JDS provides measures of how people perceive their jobs and how they feel about them. The scores on the JDS indicated that most people in the department saw their jobs as boring and routine and, as a result, they were not satisfied with their work.

With the assistance of an outside consultant and the employees themselves, bank managers gradually changed all the jobs in the department. They eliminated many trivial and highly specialized jobs (for example, one job consisted of nothing more than feeding tape into a Telex machine). They gave all the employees more autonomy over how they performed their jobs. The employees themselves underwent rigorous training to help them perform more complex jobs and to become more professional in their behavior.

How successful was the program? Both customer relations and employee job satisfaction increased. So did profits and volume capacity. The time necessary to get letters prepared dropped substantially. All things considered, managers at First National evaluated the changes as a major success.[1]

The employees at First National Bank of Chicago were experiencing a situation common in American industry: unchallenging, boring, and monotonous jobs. The jobs at the bank had been structured in that fashion for logical and practical reasons, but their routineness had gone to an unnecessary extreme. As a result, whatever efficiency gains had been realized through specialization were being offset by tedium. The changes the bank undertook reflect a more contemporary approach to making jobs both efficient and motivating.

This chapter is about how people see and respond to their jobs. It also addresses how managers can deal with these perceptions and responses for the benefit of both the organization and the employees. We start with a discussion of historical approaches to job design. Then we discuss a major perspective on

1. Norm Alster, "What Flexible Workers Can Do," *Fortune,* February 13, 1989, pp. 62–66; F. K. Plous, Jr., "Redesigning Work," *Personnel Administrator,* March 1987, p. 99; Brian Dumaine, "Who Needs a Boss?" *Fortune,* May 7, 1990, pp. 52–60.

job design, the job characteristics theory (the framework used at First National Bank of Chicago). Next, we describe job design issues from the standpoint of groups and how social information affects job design. Then we identify emerging perspectives on job design. We conclude by examining how employee participation is linked to job design.

Historical Approaches to Job Design

■ Job design evolved first toward greater specialization and more recently away from extreme levels of specialization.

To understand job design, we must first trace how approaches to work have evolved. At first, the trend was toward increasing specialization and standardization of jobs. Eventually, however, this trend slowed and reversed. In this section, we examine the reasons for this developmental pattern and the dominant approaches to job design that emerged along the way.

The Evolution of Job Design

Although formal theories of job design are a fairly recent development, the actual need to design work has a long history. The construction of the pyramids in ancient Egypt, for example, was founded on job specialization: grouping jobs together by function. The ancient Romans devoted much attention to designing jobs in the production sector.[2]

Figure 13.1 traces the historical trends of job design in the United States from the mid-1800s to the present. Before the general craft stage (the initial stage in the figure), many families made and produced all the things they needed, including food. General craft jobs came about as individuals ceased or reduced their own food production, invested their labor in the production of other necessities such as clothing and furniture, and traded or bartered them for food and goods. Over time, people's work became increasingly specialized. For example, the general craft of clothing production splintered into specialized craft jobs such as weaving, tailoring, and sewing. This evolution toward specialization accelerated as the Industrial Revolution swept Europe in the 1700s and 1800s and followed in similar form in America in the later 1800s.

Eventually, the trend toward specialization became a subject of formal study. The two most influential students of specialization were Adam Smith and Charles Babbage. Smith, an eighteenth-century Scottish economist, originated the phrase *division of labor* in his classic book *An Inquiry into the Nature and Causes of the Wealth of Nations,* published in 1776.[3] The book tells the story of a group of pin makers who specialized their jobs so that they could produce many more pins per person in a day than each could have made by working alone. In Smith's time, pin making, like most other production work, was still an individual job.

2. Daniel A. Wren, *The Evolution of Management Thought,* 2nd ed. (New York: Wiley, 1979).

3. Adam Smith, *An Inquiry into the Nature and Causes of the Wealth of Nations* (New York: Modern Library, 1937). Originally published in 1776.

FIGURE 13.1
The Historical Development of Job Design in the United States

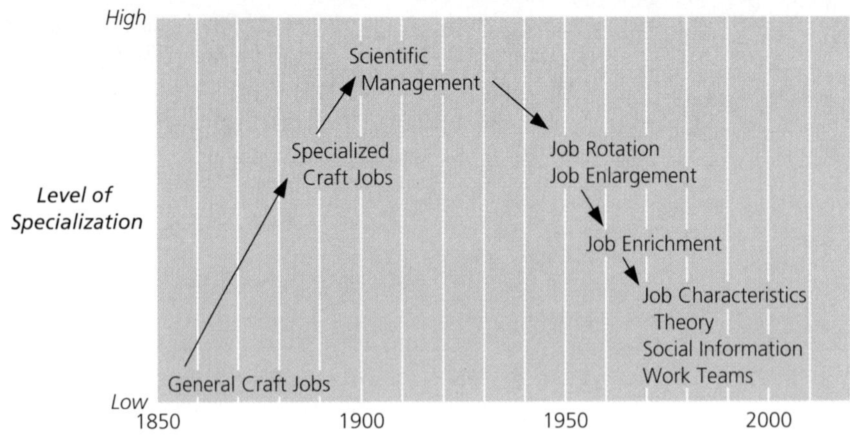

SOURCE: Adapted from *Managerial Process and Organizational Behavior,* 2nd ed. by Alan C. Filley, Robert J. House, and Steven Kerr. Copyright © 1976, 1969 by Scott, Foresman and Company. Reprinted by permission.

One person would perform all tasks: drawing out a strip of wire, clipping it to the proper length, sharpening one end, attaching a head to the other end, and polishing the finished pin. With specialization, one person did nothing but draw out wire, another did the clipping, and so on. Smith attributed the dramatic increases in output to factors such as increased dexterity owing to practice, decreased time changing from one production operation to another, and the development of specialized equipment and machinery. The basic principles described in *The Wealth of Nations* provided the foundation for the assembly line.

Charles Babbage wrote *On the Economy of Machinery and Manufactures* in 1832.[4] Extending Smith's work, Babbage cited several additional advantages of job specialization: Relatively little time was needed to learn specialized jobs, waste decreased, workers needed to make fewer tool and equipment changes, and workers' skills improved through frequent repetition of tasks.

As the Industrial Revolution spread to the United States, job specialization proliferated throughout industry. While it began in the mid-1880s, as shown in Figure 13.1, job specialization reached its peak with the development of scientific management in the early 1900s.

Job Specialization

The chief proponent of scientific management, Frederick W. Taylor, argued that jobs should be scientifically studied, broken down into their smallest component tasks, and then standardized across all workers doing the jobs.[5] (See Chapter 1

4. Charles Babbage, *On the Economy of Machinery and Manufactures* (London: Charles Knight, 1832).

5. Frederick W. Taylor, *The Principles of Scientific Management* (New York: Harper & Row, 1911).

Gerber has created several highly specialized jobs that are performed during the preparation of processed foods. This woman, for example, is washing bananas at a Gerber food processing facility in Costa Rica. More than 210 million bananas were processed by the firm in 1990 alone for products such as baby foods, beverages, and desserts.

- **Job specialization,** as advocated by scientific management, can help improve efficiency.
- Job specialization can also promote monotony and boredom.

for a full discussion of scientific management.) Taylor's view was consistent with the premises of the division of labor as discussed by Smith and Babbage. In practice, **job specialization** generally brought most, if not all, of the advantages its advocates claimed. Specialization paved the way for large-scale assembly lines and was at least partly responsible for the dramatic gains in output American industry achieved for several decades after the turn of the century.

On paper, job specialization is a rational, seemingly efficient way to organize both manufacturing and nonmanufacturing jobs. In practice, however, it can cause problems for the individuals who do the work. Foremost among the problems is the extreme monotony of highly specialized, standardized tasks. Consider the job of assembling color televisions. A person who does the entire assembly will find the job complex and challenging, but such a process is inefficient. If the job is specialized so that the worker simply inserts one circuit board into the television set as it passes along on an assembly line, the process may be efficient, but it is unlikely to interest or challenge the worker. A worker numbed by boredom and monotony may be less motivated to work hard and more inclined to be absent, to complain about the job, and to look elsewhere for more interesting employment. For these reasons, managers began to search for job design alternatives to specialization. One of the primary catalysts for this search was a famous study of jobs in the automobile industry.

In 1952, C. R. Walker and R. Guest published a study of 180 workers in a Detroit automobile assembly plant.[6] The purpose of the study was to assess how

6. C. R. Walker and R. Guest, *The Man on the Assembly Line* (Cambridge, Mass.: Harvard University Press, 1952).

satisfied the workers were with various aspects of their jobs. The workers indicated that in general they were reasonably satisfied with things such as pay, working conditions, and the quality of their supervision. However, they expressed extreme dissatisfaction with the actual work they did. During that era, automobile plants were very noisy places where the moving assembly line dictated a rigid, grueling pace and jobs were highly specialized and standardized. The workers in the study cited six facets of the work that caused dissatisfaction: mechanical pacing by an assembly line (over which they had no control), repetitiveness, low skill requirements, involvement with only a small portion of the total production cycle, limited social interaction with others in the workplace, and no control over the tools and techniques used in the job. Each of these sources of dissatisfaction were a direct or indirect consequence of the job design prescriptions of scientific management. Thus, managers began to recognize that following the strict prescriptions of scientific management might lead to efficiency but eventually—and if carried too far—extreme levels of specialization would also have a number of negative consequences.

Early Alternatives to Job Specialization

In response to Walker and Guest's findings, as well as to other reported problems with job specialization and a general desire to explore ways to create less monotonous jobs, managers formulated two alternative approaches: job rotation and job enlargement.

- **Job rotation** is the systematic movement of workers from one job to another in an attempt to minimize monotony and boredom.

Job Rotation **Job rotation** involves systematically shifting workers from one job to another to sustain their motivation and interest. Figure 13.2 contrasts job rotation and job specialization. Under specialization, each task is broken down into small parts. For example, assembling pens for distribution might involve four discrete steps: testing the ink cartridge, inserting the cartridge into the barrel of the pen, screwing the cap onto the barrel, and inserting the assembled pen into a box. Then individual workers are assigned to perform each of these four tasks.

When job rotation is introduced, the tasks themselves stay the same. However, as Figure 13.2 shows, the workers who perform them are systematically rotated across the various tasks. Jones, for example, starts out with job 1 (testing ink cartridges). On a regular basis, perhaps weekly or monthly, she is systematically rotated to job 2, to job 3, to job 4, and back to job 1. Gonzalez, who starts out on job 2 (inserting cartridges into barrels), rotates ahead of Jones to jobs 3, 4, 1, and back to 2.

Numerous firms at various times, have used job rotation including American Cyanamid, Baker International, Ford Motor Co., and Prudential Insurance Co. of America. However, job rotation, like job enlargement (discussed next), has not entirely lived up to expectations.[7] For the disappointing results, we can once

7. Ricky W. Griffin, *Task Design: An Integrative Approach* (Glenview, Ill.: Scott, Foresman, 1982).

again blame the fundamental problem of narrowly defined, routine jobs. If a rotation cycle takes workers through the same old jobs, the workers simply experience several routine and boring jobs instead of just one. Although a worker may begin each job shift with renewed enthusiasm, the effect usually is short-lived.

Rotation may also decrease efficiency. The practice clearly sacrifices the proficiency and expertise that grow from specialization. Often, however, job rotation is a very effective training technique because a worker rotated through a variety of related jobs acquires a larger set of job skills. Thus, there is increased flexibility in transferring workers to new jobs. Many American companies now use job rotation for training, but few rely on it to enhance employee motivation. We discuss a new twist on job rotation, involving flexible workers, later in the chapter.

- **Job enlargement** involves giving workers more tasks to perform.

Job Enlargement **Job enlargement,** or *horizontal job loading,* means that the worker's job is expanded to include tasks previously performed by other workers. This process is also illustrated in Figure 13.2. Before enlargement, each worker performs a narrowly defined, specialized task; afterward, he or she has a "larger" job to do. Thus, after enlargement Jones and the other workers each do "bigger" jobs than they did previously. Thus, assembling the pens has been redefined as

FIGURE 13.2
Job Specialization, Rotation, and Enlargement

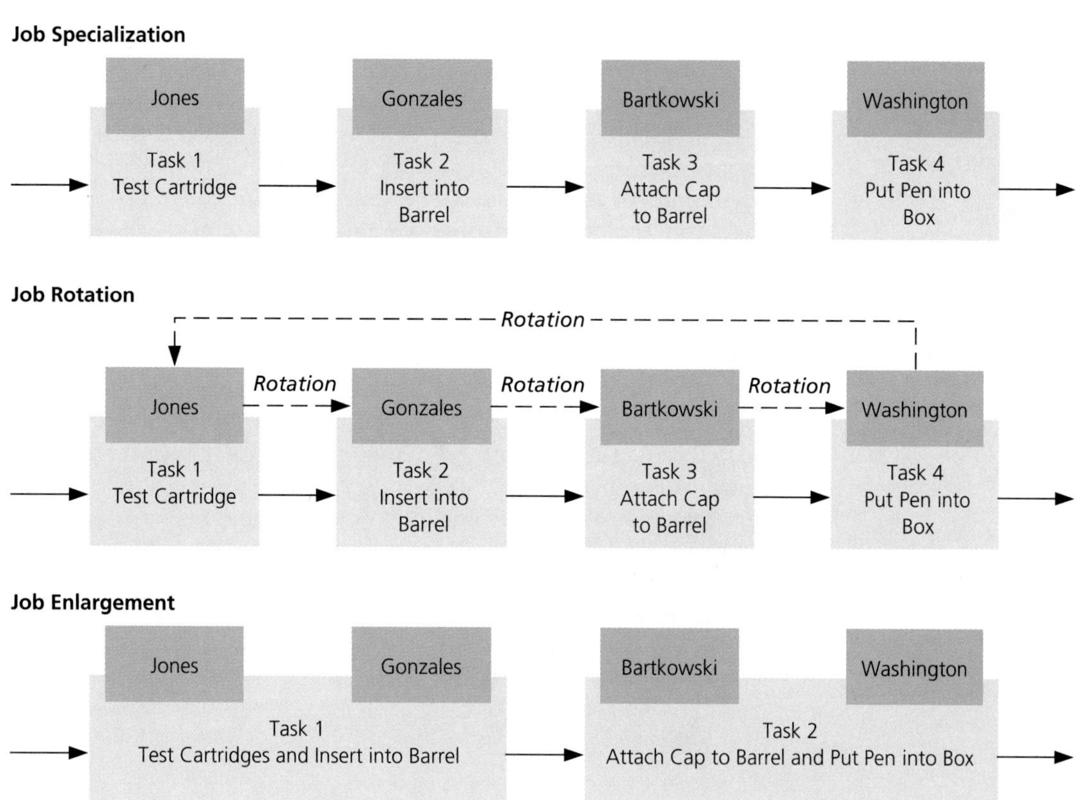

two tasks rather than four. Jones and Gonzalez do the first task, while Bartkowski and Washington do the other. The logic behind this change is that the increased number of tasks will reduce monotony and boredom.

Maytag was one of the first companies to use job enlargement.[8] In the assembly of washing machine water pumps, for example, jobs done sequentially by six workers at a conveyor belt were modified so that each worker completed an entire pump alone. Other organizations that implemented job enlargement in the 1960s included American Telephone & Telegraph Company (AT&T), the U.S. Civil Service, and Colonial Life Insurance Company.

Unfortunately, job enlargement often failed to have the desired effects. Generally, if the entire production sequence consisted of simple, easy-to-master tasks, merely doing more of them did not significantly change the worker's job. If the task of putting two bolts on a piece of machinery was "enlarged" to putting on three bolts and connecting two wires, the monotony of the original job essentially remained.

Job Enrichment

Job rotation and job enlargement seemed promising but eventually disappointed managers looking for answers to the ill effects of extreme specialization. They failed partly because they were intuitive, narrow approaches rather than fully developed, theory-driven methods. As a result, a new, more complex approach to task design—job enrichment—emerged in the late 1950s.

■ **Job enrichment** means giving workers more tasks to perform and more control over how to perform those tasks.

Job enrichment is based on Herzberg's two-factor theory of motivation (discussed in Chapter 5). Herzberg believed employees could be motivated by positive job-related experiences such as feelings of achievement, responsibility, and recognition. To this end, he advocated *vertical job loading*—not only adding more tasks to a job, as in horizontal loading, but also giving the employee more control over those tasks. Vertical job loading should enrich a job in six ways:

1. *Accountability.* Workers should be held responsible for their performance.
2. *Achievement.* Workers should believe that they are doing something worthwhile.
3. *Feedback.* Workers should receive direct and clear information about their performance.
4. *Work pace.* To the extent possible, workers should be able to set their own work pace.
5. *Control over resources.* If possible, workers should have control over the resources used in their jobs.

8. H. Conant and M. Kilbridge, "An Interdisciplinary Analysis of Job Enlargement: Technology, Cost, Behavioral Implications," *Industrial and Labor Relations Review,* Vol. 18, No. 7, 1965, pp. 377–395.

6. *Personal growth and development.* Workers should have the opportunity to learn new skills.[9]

Table 13.1 outlines how Herzberg proposed to incorporate these characteristics into a job.

Various job enrichment programs have been reported by managers. Companies with noteworthy programs have included AT&T, Texas Instruments, IBM, and General Foods. To see how job enrichment actually operates, we will describe two of these programs in some detail.

First, let's consider the experiences of AT&T. A pioneer in the use of job enrichment, AT&T conducted one experiment that involved a group of eight typists who were responsible for preparing service orders. Managers believed turnover in the group was too high and performance too low. An analysis of the situation revealed several deficiencies in the work. The typists worked in relative isolation, and any service representative could ask them to type work orders. As a result, they believed they had little client contact or responsibility, and they received scant feedback on their job performance. The job enrichment program focused on creating a typing team. Each member of the team was paired with a service representative, and the tasks were restructured: Ten discrete steps were replaced with three more complex ones. In addition, the typists began to get specific feedback on performance, and their job titles were changed to reflect their greater responsibility and status. As a result of these changes, the number of orders delivered on time increased from 27 to 90 percent, accuracy improved, and turnover dropped significantly.[10]

Texas Instruments used job enrichment to improve janitorial jobs. The company gave janitors more control over their schedules and let them sequence their own cleaning jobs and purchase their own supplies. The outcome? Turnover dropped, cleanliness improved, and the company reported estimated cost savings of approximately $103,000.[11]

At the same time, we should note that many job enrichment programs have failed. Some companies have found them cost ineffective, and others believe they simply did not produce the expected results.[12] Several programs at Prudential Insurance, for example, were abandoned because managers believed they were benefiting neither employees nor the firm. Several reasons for this pattern have been offered.

Some of the criticism is associated with Herzberg's two-factor theory of motivation, on which job enrichment is based. In Chapter 5, we reviewed the

9. Frederick Herzberg, "One More Time: How Do You Motivate Employees?" *Harvard Business Review,* January-February 1968, pp. 53–62; Frederick Herzberg, "The Wise Old Turk," *Harvard Business Review,* September-October 1974, pp. 70–80.

10. R. N. Ford, "Job Enrichment Lessons from AT&T," *Harvard Business Review,* January-February 1973, pp. 96–106.

11. E. D. Weed, "Job Enrichment 'Cleans Up' at Texas Instruments," in J. R. Maher, ed., *New Perspectives in Job Enrichment* (New York: Van Nostrand, 1971).

12. Griffin, *Task Design.*

TABLE 13.1
Herzberg's Principles of Vertical Job Loading

Principle	Motivators Involved
A. Removing some controls while retaining accountability	Responsibility and personal achievement
B. Increasing the accountability of individuals for their own work	Responsibility and recognition
C. Giving a person a complete natural unit of work (module, division, area, and so on)	Responsibility, achievement, and recognition
D. Granting additional authority to an employer in his activity; job freedom	Responsiblity, achievement, and recognition
E. Making periodic reports directly available to the worker himself rather than to the supervisor	Internal recognition
F. Introducing new and more difficult tasks not previously handled	Growth and learning
G. Assigning individuals specific or specialized tasks, enabling them to become experts	Responsibility, growth, and advancement

SOURCE: Reprinted by permission of *Harvard Business Review.* An exhibit from "One More Time: How Do You Motivate Employees?" by Frederick Herzberg (September-October 1987).

major objections: The theory confuses employee satisfaction with motivation, is fraught with methodological flaws, ignores situational factors, and is not convincingly supported by research.[13] Thus, there are still many unanswered questions about the usefulness of job enrichment. Several other specific difficulties also have been associated with job enrichment. Richard Hackman identified five major problem areas:

1. Many reports of the success of job enrichment programs have been evangelical in nature; that is, the authors of these studies overstate the potential benefits of job enrichment and minimize its pitfalls.
2. Evaluations of job enrichment programs often have been methodologically flawed. Many studies have been poorly designed, making the results subject to alternative explanation.
3. Few failures have been reported in the literature, although it is probable that some job enrichment programs have not achieved their goals. Without information about these failures, it is difficult to develop a full understanding of job enrichment.

13. Griffin, *Task Design.* See also Robert J. House and L. Wigdor, "Herzberg's Dual-Factor Theory of Job Satisfaction and Motivation: A Review of the Evidence and a Criticism," *Personnel Psychology,* vol. 20, 1967, pp. 369–389.

4. Situational factors seldom have been assessed. Some situations probably are more favorable to job enrichment efforts than others. Unfortunately, we have not developed an understanding of the factors that lead to success or failure.
5. Economic data pertaining to the effectiveness of job enrichment have been rare. Because job enrichment often is an expensive proposition, managers need a carefully developed procedure for evaluating the technique's costs and benefits. Such procedures have not been developed.[14]

Because of these and other problems, job enrichment recently has fallen into disfavor among managers. Yet some valuable aspects of the concept can be salvaged. The efforts of managers and academic theorists ultimately have led to more complex and sophisticated viewpoints. Many of these advances are evident in the job characteristics approach, which we consider next.

The Job Characteristics Approach

■ The **job characteristics approach** focuses on the motivational attributes of jobs.

The **job characteristics approach** dominated thinking about job design in the 1970s and early 1980s. It evolved from work on the motivational attributes of jobs (such as autonomy and feedback), was expanded to include explicit consideration of individual differences in employee responses to a job, and eventually was codified in the Job Characteristics Theory.[15]

Job Characteristics

The job characteristics approach began with the pioneering work of A. N. Turner and P. R. Lawrence. These researchers conducted a large-scale project to assess employee responses to different kinds of jobs.[16] Turner and Lawrence believed workers would prefer complex, challenging tasks to monotonous, boring ones. They predicted that job complexity would be associated with employee satisfaction and attendance. Tasks were described in terms of six job characteristics assumed to be desirable motivational properties of jobs: (1) variety, (2) autonomy, (3) required social interaction, (4) opportunities for social interaction, (5)

---

14. J. Richard Hackman, "On the Coming Demise of Job Enrichment," in E. L. Cass and F. G. Zimmer, eds., *Man and Work in Society* (New York: Van Nostrand, 1975).

15. J. Richard Hackman and Greg Oldham, "Motivation Through the Design of Work: Test of a Theory," *Organizational Behavior and Human Performance,* vol. 16, 1976, pp. 250–279. See also Michael A. Campion and Paul W. Thayer, "Job Design: Approaches, Outcomes, and Trade-Offs," *Organizational Dynamics,* Winter 1987, pp. 66–78.

16. A. N. Turner and P. R. Lawrence, *Industrial Jobs and the Worker* (Boston: Harvard School of Business, 1965).

knowledge and skill requirements, and (6) responsibility. Thus, a worker whose job was rated high on all six characteristics would be expected to have relatively high levels of satisfaction and attendance. If the job rated low on all attributes, the job holder would be expected to be less satisfied and more frequently absent.

These predictions were tested on 470 employees holding 47 different jobs in several manufacturing plants. Field observations and interviews were used to measure the relevant variables. Measures of the six job characteristics were combined into a single measure of task complexity, which then was compared with measures of satisfaction and attendance. The results confirmed the predicted relationship between task complexity and attendance but showed no relationship between task complexity and satisfaction.

Because of this second unexpected finding, Turner and Lawrence analyzed their data further. They found a positive relationship between task complexity and the satisfaction of workers from factories in small towns but not those in larger towns. To explain this pattern, the researchers concluded that the workers in larger communities had a variety of nonwork interests and consequently were less involved in and motivated by their work. The workers in smaller towns, on the other hand, had fewer nonwork interests and therefore were more responsive to the positive features of their jobs.

This explanation admittedly was tenuous at best, but we must consider that the original study had not been designed to assess individual differences. Recall that the implicit assumption of the study had been that everyone would respond to job conditions in the same way. An individual-difference perspective, on the other hand, would have allowed for the possibility of variations in people's reactions. Hence, the explanations were necessarily imprecise and speculative. The chief value of the unexpected findings perhaps was to call attention to the role of individual differences in the workplace.

Individual Differences

■ Individual differences may affect how workers perceive and respond to their jobs.

Among the first researchers to explore the role of individual differences among job holders were Charles Hulin and Milton Blood.[17] As a starting point, they developed a more precise explanation of Turner and Lawrence's findings, arguing that rural-urban differences actually reflected adherence to middle-class work norms such as the Protestant work ethic. They theorized that people governed by the work ethic would be highly motivated by challenging, complex jobs, whereas people who believed less strongly in the ethic would be less interested and motivated by the same kind of job. The Protestant work ethic was also assumed to influence rural workers more than urban workers. A preliminary study of this explanation provided reasonable but not total support for it.[18]

17. Charles L. Hulin and Milton R. Blood, "Job Enlargement, Individual Differences, and Worker Responses," *Psychological Bulletin,* vol. 69, 1968, pp. 41–55; Milton R. Blood and Charles L. Hulin, "Alienation, Environmental Characteristics, and Worker Responses," *Journal of Applied Psychology,* vol. 51, 1967, pp. 284–290.

18. Blood and Hulin, "Alienation, Environmental Characteristics, and Worker Responses."

In light of this mixed evidence, other researchers also tried to develop ways of understanding individual differences.[19] Foremost among these efforts was the work of J. Richard Hackman and Edward E. Lawler. These researchers suggested that psychological or motivational characteristics are what really matter in how people react to jobs.[20] Specifically, they borrowed from the need theories of motivation (discussed in Chapter 5). They reasoned that people motivated by higher-order needs, such as the needs for self-actualization and personal growth and development, would be enthused by complex, challenging jobs, whereas those with weak higher-order needs would be less motivated by such jobs. The initial test of this interpretation was promising enough to encourage the development of another formal theory of job design—the Job Characteristic Theory.[21]

The Job Characteristics Theory

- The **Job Characteristics Theory** identifies three critical psychological states: experienced meaningfulness of the work, experienced responsibility for work outcomes, and knowledge of results.

Working with Greg Oldham, Hackman used the findings from the test of the individual-differences interpretation to develop the **Job Characteristics Theory.** Figure 13.3. shows the basic features of this important theory.[22]

At the core of the theory are what Hackman and Oldham termed *critical psychological states.* These states are presumed to determine the extent to which characteristics of the job enhance employee responses to that task. The three critical psychological states are defined as follows:

1. *Experienced meaningfulness of the work:* The degree to which the individual experiences the job as generally meaningful, valuable, and worthwhile
2. *Experienced responsibility for work outcomes:* The degree to which the individual feels personally accountable and responsible for the results of his or her work
3. *Knowledge of results:* The degree to which the individual continuously understands how effectively he or she is performing the job[23]

If employees experience these states at a sufficiently high level, they are likely to feel good about themselves and to respond favorably to their jobs.

- The Job Characteristics Theory identifies five core job dimensions: skill variety, task identity, task significance, autonomy, and feedback.

Hackman and Oldham further suggest that the three critical psychological states are triggered by five characteristics of the job, or *core job dimensions:*

1. *Skill variety:* The degree to which the job requires a variety of activities that involve different skills and talents

---

19. Griffin, *Task Design.*

20. J. Richard Hackman and Edward E. Lawler, "Employee Reactions to Job Characteristics," *Journal of Applied Psychology,* vol. 55, 1971, pp. 259–286.

21. Ibid.

22. Hackman and Oldham, "Motivation Through the Design of Work"; J. Richard Hackman and Greg Oldham, *Work Redesign* (Reading, Mass.: Addison-Wesley, 1980).

23. Hackman and Oldham, "Motivation Through the Design of Work," pp. 256–257.

FIGURE 13.3
The Job Characteristics Theory

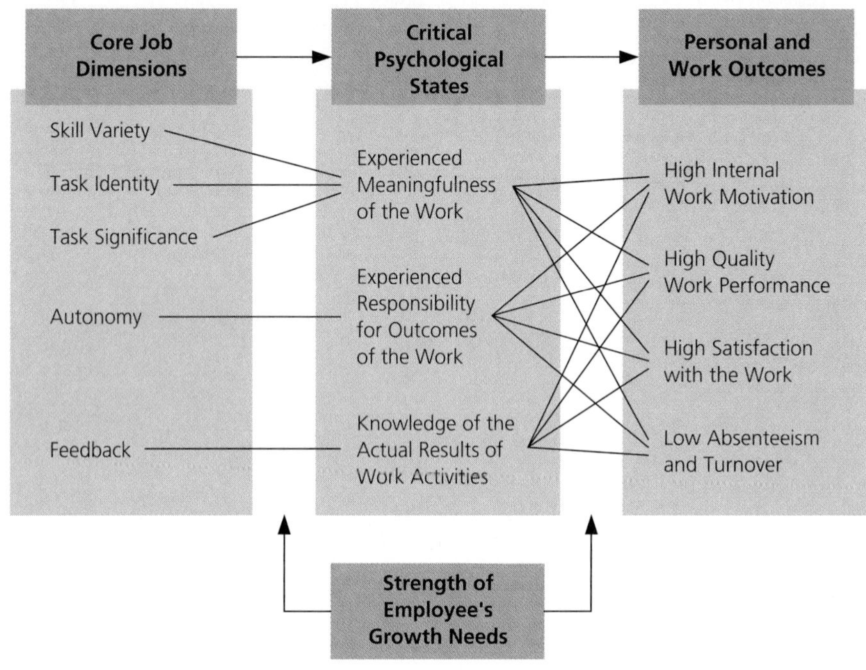

SOURCE: J. R. Hackman and G. R. Oldham, "Motivation Through the Design of Work: Test of a Theory." *Organizational Behavior and Human Performance.* Vol. 16, 1976, pp. 250–279. Used by permission.

2. *Task identity:* The degree to which the job requires completion of a "whole" and identifiable piece of work, that is, a job that has a beginning and an end with a tangible outcome
3. *Task significance:* The degree to which the job affects the lives or work of other people, both in the immediate organization and in the external environment
4. *Autonomy:* The degree to which the job allows the individual substantial freedom, independence, and discretion to schedule the work and determine the procedures for carrying it out
5. *Feedback:* The degree to which the job activities give the individual direct and clear information about the effectiveness of his or her performance[24]

Figure 13.3 shows how the core job dimensions stimulate the psychological states. Skill variety, task identity, and task significance are expected to affect the person's experienced meaningfulness of the work; autonomy is expected to influence the experienced responsibility for outcomes of the work; and feedback contributes to knowledge of the actual results of work activities. The critical

24. Ibid.

FIGURE 13.4
JDS Profile of "Good" and "Bad" Jobs

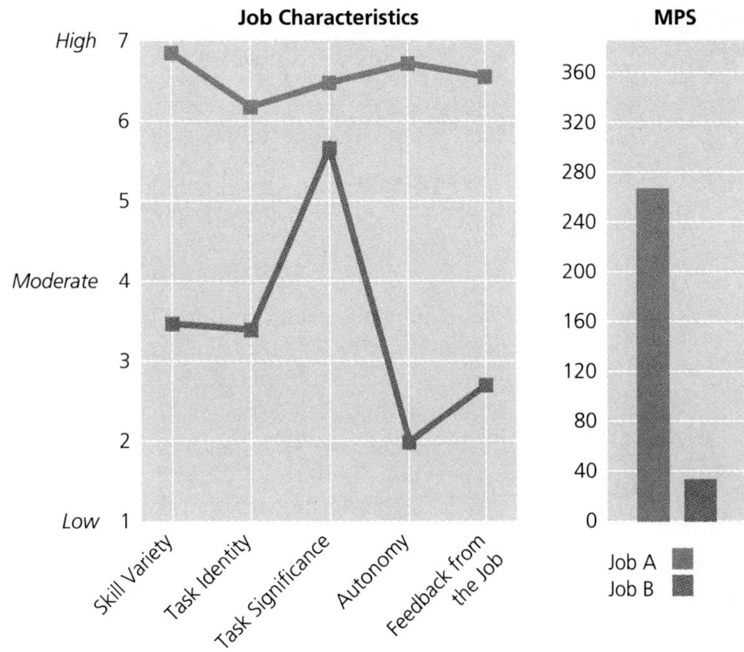

SOURCE: J. R. Hackman, "Work Design," in J. R. Hackman and J. I. Suttle (Eds.). *Improving Life at Work: Behavioral Science Approaches to Organizational Change* (Santa Monica, Calif.: Goodyear, 1977), p. 135. Used by permission.

psychological states then determine a variety of personal and work outcomes: high internal work motivation (that is, intrinsic motivation), high-quality work performance, high satisfaction with the work, and low absenteeism and turnover. Finally, the strength of the employee's growth needs is expected to influence the effects of other elements of the theory. Hackman and Lawler's earlier findings suggested that the effects would be very strong in people whose higher-order needs are strong and weaker in people whose higher-order needs are weak.[25]

- The Job Characteristics Theory is tested with the **Job Diagnostic Survey,** or **JDS.**

To test the Job Characteristics Theory, Hackman and Oldham developed the **Job Diagnostic Survey,** or **JDS.**[26] This questionnaire measures employee perceptions of job characteristics, the various psychological states, personal and work outcomes, and strength of growth needs. As described in the opening vignette, First National Bank of Chicago used the JDS in its effort to change the nature of jobs.

Figure 13.4 illustrates the use of data obtained from the JDS. The graph on the left summarizes the level of each of the five job characteristics for two hypothetical jobs. Job A clearly has higher levels of each of the five characteristics.

25. Ibid.

26. J. Richard Hackman and Greg Oldham, "Development of the Job Diagnostic Survey," *Journal of Applied Psychology,* vol. 60, 1975, pp. 159–170.

- The JDS provides a **motivating potential score,** or **MPS,** for jobs.

The chart on the right shows each job's **motivating potential score,** or **MPS,** which is calculated according to the following formula:

$$\text{MPS} = \frac{(\text{Variety} + \text{Identity} + \text{Significance})}{3} \times \text{Autonomy} \times \text{Feedback}$$

The MPS provides a summary index of a job's overall potential for motivating employees. Thus, the JDS can be used to identify jobs in the organization with high and low motivating potential. Jobs with a low MPS index are candidates for redesign to improve their potential for motivating job holders.

Hackman, with assistance from J. L. Suttle, has also developed a general set of guidelines to help managers implement the theory as set forth in Figure 13.5.[27] Managers can do things such as form natural work units (that is, group similar tasks together), combine existing tasks into more complex ones, establish direct relationships between workers and clients, increase worker autonomy through vertical job loading, and open feedback channels. Theoretically, such actions should enhance the MPS of each task. First National Bank of Chicago achieved its successful job redesign results by doing all of these things. Using these guidelines, sometimes in adapted form, several other organizations have implemented job design changes in accordance with the Job Characteristics Theory. Among them are 3M, Volvo, AT&T, Xerox, Texas Instruments, and Motorola.[28]

Evaluation and Implications

Much research has been devoted to the job characteristics view of job design.[29] This research generally has supported the Job Characteristics Theory, although performance has seldom been found to correlate with job characteristics.[30] Several apparent weaknesses in the theory also have come to light, however. First, the JDS is not always as valid and reliable as it should be. Further, the role of individual differences frequently has not been supported by scientific assessment. Finally, implementation guidelines are not specific and managers usually must modify at least part of the theory to use them.[31] Still, the Job Characteristics

27. J. Richard Hackman, "Work Design," in J. Richard Hackman and J. L. Suttle, eds., *Improving Life at Work: Behavioral Science Approaches to Organizational Change* (Santa Monica, Calif.: Goodyear, 1977).

28. Griffin, *Task Design.*

29. Griffin, *Task Design.* See also Karlene H. Roberts and William Glick, "The Job Characteristics Approach to Task Design: A Critical Review," *Journal of Applied Psychology,* vol. 66, 1981, pp. 193–217, and Ricky W. Griffin, "Toward an Integrated Theory of Task Design," in Larry L. Cummings and Barry M. Staw, eds., *Research in Organizational Behavior,* vol. 9 (Greenwich, Conn.: JAI Press, 1987), pp. 79–120.

30. Ricky W. Griffin, M. Ann Welsh, and Gregory Moorhead, "Perceived Task Characteristics and Employee Performance: A Literature Review," *Academy of Management Review,* October 1981, pp. 655–664.

31. Roberts and Glick, "The Job Characteristics Approach to Task Design."

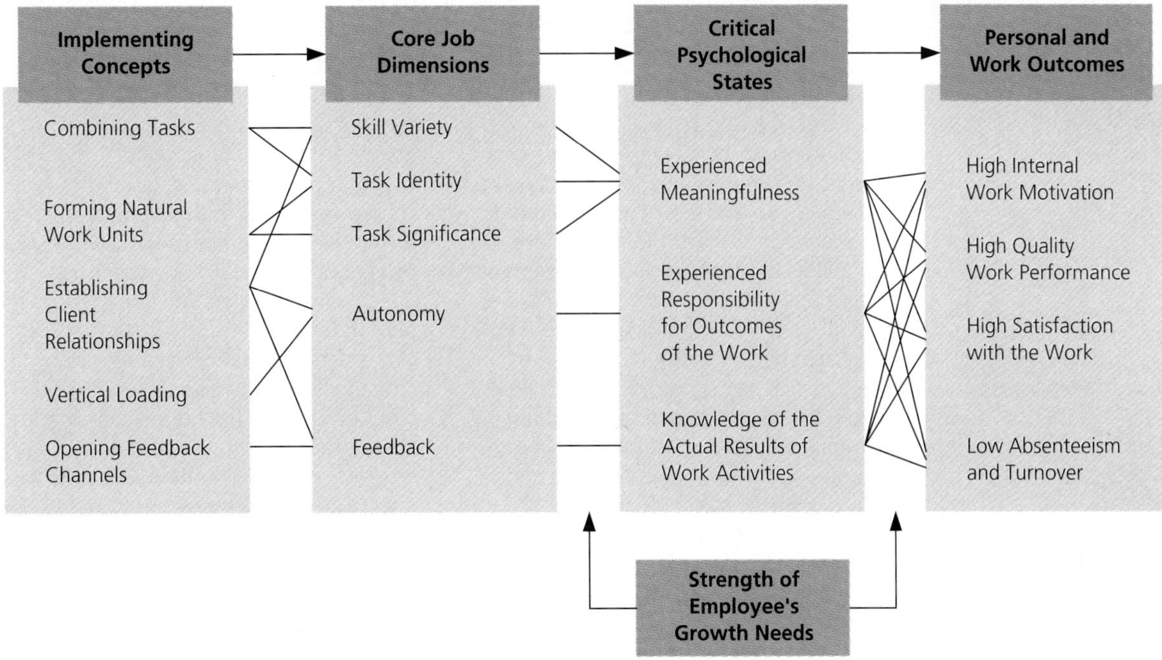

SOURCE: J. R. Hackman, G. R. Oldham, R. Janson, and K. Purdy, "A New Stage for Job Enrichment." Copyright 1975 by The Regents of the University of California. Reprinted from the *California Management Review*: Vol. 17, No. 4. By permission of The Regents.

FIGURE 13.5
Implementing the Job Characteristics Theory

Theory and its approach to job design remain a viable and popular perspective on studying and changing jobs.[32] *A Look at the Research* summarizes some additional recent empirical evidence concerning the Job Characteristics Theory itself.

Designing Jobs for Groups

■ Increasingly, many jobs are being designed for groups rather than for individuals.

The job design perspectives we have discussed to this point have focused almost exclusively on individual jobs. Many situations, however, may call for designing jobs for groups.

32. For recent examples, see Donald J. Campbell, "Task Complexity: A Review and Analysis," *Academy of Management Review,* January 1988, pp. 40–52; Donald G. Gardner, "Task Complexity Effects on Non-Task-Related Movements: A Test of Activation Theory," *Organizational Behavior and Human Decision Processes,* vol. 45, 1990, pp. 209–231; Barry M. Staw and Richard D. Boettger, "Task Revision: A Neglected Form of Work Performance," *Academy of Management Journal,* September 1990, pp. 534–559.

A LOOK AT THE **RESEARCH**

Job Design Effects Change Over Time

When an organization changes its employees' jobs, it generally expects that some positive benefits will result. But what are those benefits? And how long does it take before they start to show up?

Ricky W. Griffin recently attempted to find some answers to these questions. He studied a bank corporation that used the Job Characteristics Theory to change the jobs of its tellers. According to the theory, the tellers should actually perceive that the changes had occurred, report higher levels of satisfaction and organizational commitment, and lower levels of absenteeism and turnover intentions. In addition, performance should improve.

The bank altered the tellers' jobs with the specific intention of enhancing variety, autonomy, feedback, task identity, and task significance. The researcher measured each of the important outcome variables right before the job changes were made and again six, twenty-four, and forty-eight months later. A total of 526 tellers provided information at all time points.

Griffin's findings indicated that not all changes occurred at the same time or followed the same pattern. For example, perceptions of job dimensions increased during the first six months and remained high throughout the study. Satisfaction and organizational commitment also increased during the first six months but dropped back to the original levels after twenty-four months. Performance did not increase until the twenty-four month mark. Finally, absenteeism and turnover intentions never changed. While the study reported several methodological limitations, it nevertheless provides some interesting and useful information for organizations planning a job redesign program.

SOURCE: Ricky W. Griffin, "A Long-Term Investigation of the Effects of Work Redesign on Employee Perceptions, Attitudes, and Behaviors," *Academy of Management Journal,* June 1991, pp. 425–435. Adapted by permission.

Group Tasks

Considering a group-based approach to job design may be appropriate under either of two circumstances. First, some jobs are simply better suited to a group than to an individual. For example, it may be more efficient for British Airways to use a team to service a 747 than to assign the job to a set of individuals. Second, a group-based job design might be best when the organization wants to use groups as a mechanism for enhancing individual attitudes and behaviors, as Volvo did. One popular form of this approach is autonomous work groups and work teams.

Autonomous Work Groups and Work Teams

- Autonomous work groups and work teams are sometimes used as a basis for group job design.

In autonomous work groups and work teams, jobs are structured for groups rather than for individuals. The group or team itself is then given considerable discretion in scheduling, individual work assignments, and other matters that traditionally have been management prerogatives—even to the extent of hiring new members and determining members' pay increases.

This team of sailors is working off the coast of Hawaii. Because their tasks are highly interrelated and each member of the crew can perform several different jobs, they are using a group-based approach to job design.

Several organizations have instituted autonomous work groups and/or work teams; we discussed some of these in Chapter 7. Westinghouse, General Foods, and Volvo have enjoyed considerable success with these approaches. An autonomous work group at Volvo's Kalmar plant has its own inventory area, toilets, changing rooms, and so on. The intended effect is to make workers feel as though they work in a small machine shop rather than in a huge factory. Each group is responsible for a complete set of tasks, such as wiring or upholstery. The group itself decides who will perform each task and can control the speed at which incoming cars enter its work area. The group thus functions fairly autonomously.

More and more companies are experimenting with autonomous work groups, although technological constraints and costs can be a problem. Volvo's Kalmar plant, for instance, cost more to build and produces fewer cars than a conventional plant.[33] Work teams, in contrast, may hold more potential. Because their functions often are more service or administrative in nature, technological constraints are less significant.[34]

Other Group Applications

There are other situations in which groups are used as a basis for designing jobs. For example, committees essentially are work groups with a task to perform.

33. Griffin, *Task Design.*

34. Dumaine, "Who Needs a Boss?"

While the task may be to draft a report or make a recommendation, it nevertheless can become quite salient to the group members, and as a result they may come to see it as an important part of their job. Quality circles (discussed in Chapter 6) can also be viewed as a group-based approach to getting work done. Thus, in each instance where these or other kinds of groups are the work unit, the manager must recognize the basis for using a group task design and arrange things accordingly.[35] We discuss another aspect of group effects and task design in the next section.

Social Information and Job Design

Gerald Salancik and Jeffrey Pfeffer reviewed the theoretical and empirical literature from which the job characteristics approach to job design has grown.[36] The basic purpose of their review was to assess need theories of motivation, as we discussed in Chapter 4. In addition, however, Salancik and Pfeffer expanded their review to address job design. They question the validity of two basic assumptions of the job characteristics approach: (1) that people have basic and stable needs that can be satisfied, at least partially, by their job; and (2) that tasks have stable and objective characteristics that people perceive and respond to consistently and predictably. They claim, for example, that people probably do not think of their jobs in terms of dimensions such as variety and autonomy. Only when a questionnaire inquires about the variety and autonomy of their jobs do those dimensions come to mind. Salancik and Pfeffer also point to alleged flaws in earlier approaches to job design, such as measurement deficiencies.

Salancik and Pfeffer believe individual needs, task perceptions, and reactions are a result of socially constructed realities. In other words, social information in the workplace shapes the individual's perception of the job and responses to it. For example, if a newcomer to the organization is told, "You're really going to like it here because everybody gets along so well," he or she may begin to think that the job should be evaluated in terms of social interactions and that those interactions are satisfactory. But if the message is "You won't like it here because the boss is lousy and the pay is worse," the newcomer may think that the job's most important aspects are interactions with the boss and pay and that both areas are deficient.[37]

■ The **social information processing model** of job design suggests that individual needs, task perceptions, and reactions are socially constructed realities.

Figure 13.6 shows the complete **social information processing model.** The model obviously is quite complex. Basically, it suggests that through a variety of processes, *commitment* (discussed in Chapter 4), *rationalization* (self-interpre-

35. Griffin, *Task Design.*

36. Gerald Salancik and Jeffrey Pfeffer, "An Examination of Need-Satisfaction Models of Job Attitudes," *Administrative Science Quarterly,* vol. 22, 1977, pp. 427–456; Gerald Salancik and Jeffrey Pfeffer, "A Social Information Processing Approach to Job Attitudes and Task Design," *Administrative Science Quarterly,* vol. 23, 1978, pp. 224–253.

37. Salancik and Pfeffer, "A Social Information Processing Approach."

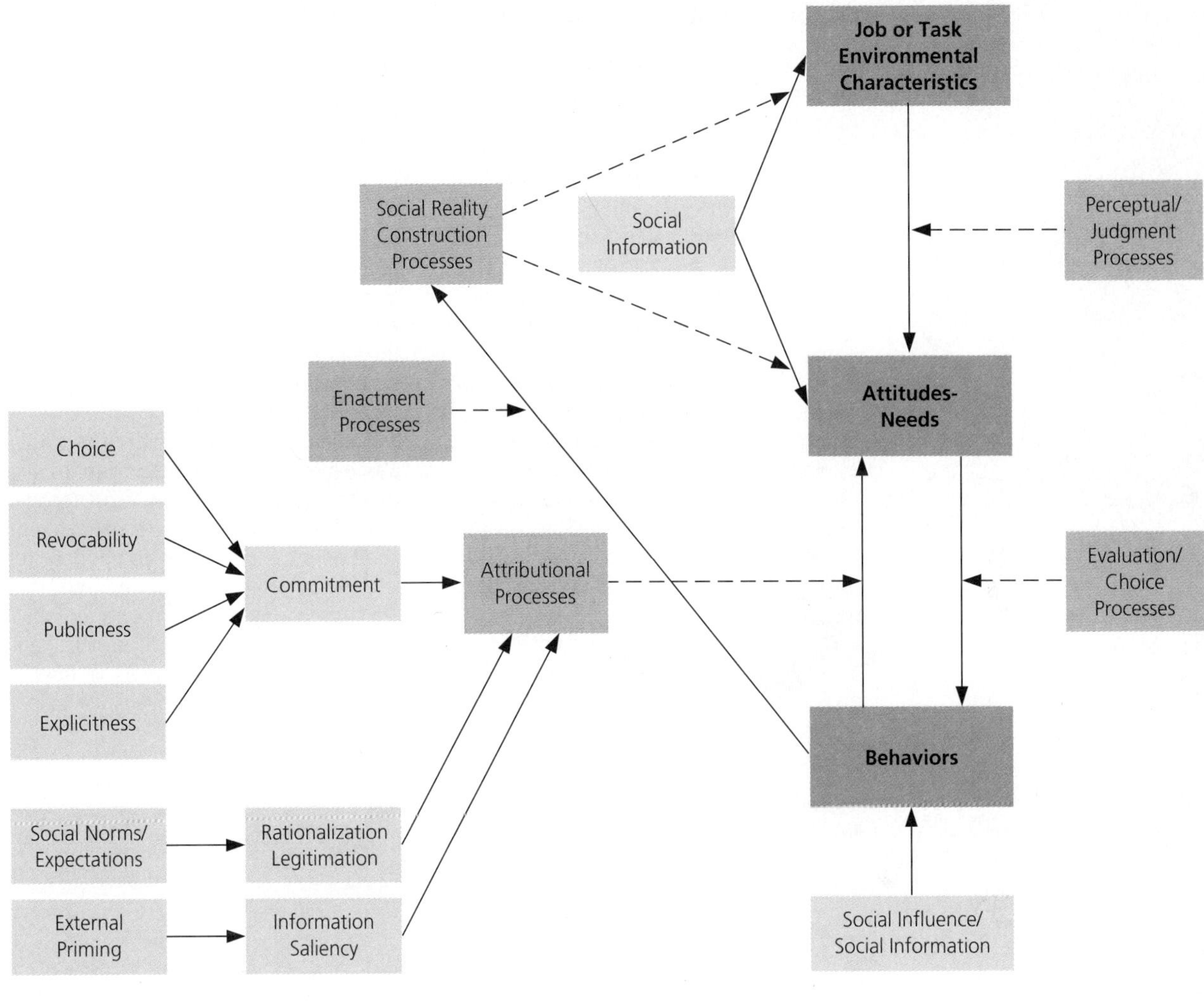

SOURCE: Reprinted from "A Social Information Processing Approach to Job Attitudes and Task Design" by Gerald M. Salancik and Jeffrey Pfeffer, published in *Administrative Science Quarterly*: Vol. 23, No. 2 (June 1978), p. 227, by permission of *Administrative Science Quarterly*. Copyright © 1978 Cornell University. All rights reserved.

FIGURE 13.6
The Social Information Processing Model of Job Design

tation of behavior), and *information saliency* (importance) are defined. These processes include the following:

1. *Choice:* The freedom to choose different behaviors
2. *Revocability:* The ability to change behaviors
3. *Publicness:* The degree of visibility to others
4. *Explicitness:* The ability to be clear and obvious

INTERNATIONAL PERSPECTIVE

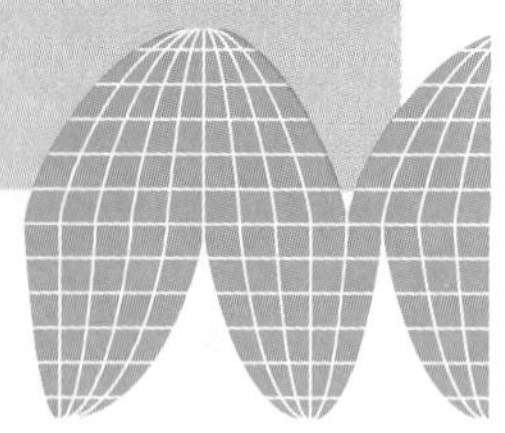

Cultural Variations in Job Definitions

Organizations in all cultures face many of the same problems and challenges. Among these are developing a better understanding of how their employees perceive and respond to their jobs. At a deeper level, the perception of what constitutes work itself varies across cultural boundaries.

Professor George England of the University of Oklahoma and Professor Itzhak Harpaz of the University of Haifa in Israel have attempted to learn more about how the meaning of work varies in different countries. They studied national samples of workers in Belgium, Germany (West Germany at the time), Israel, Japan, the Netherlands, and the United States. They found that workers in each country perceived unique aspects of what constitutes work.

For example, all workers except those in Belgium saw work as something you do for money. Both Belgium and Japanese workers also believe that work is something society expects you to do, while Germans had the fewest sentiments in this direction. Workers from the Netherlands and Japan believed most strongly that work is any activity that adds value to something, whereas workers from Germany and Israel held the weakest beliefs in this regard. The Israeli workers also believed that work is something you do from which others profit. The U.S. workers had moderately strong beliefs along the same lines, whereas workers from the other four countries saw little of this in work.

Workers from the six countries studied also expressed two basic similarities in their perceptions of work. Most recognized that work has a personal economic component and another component related to societal contribution. Thus, managers preparing to design or alter jobs in different countries need to undertake a careful analysis of what work is, how it is defined, and how employees will respond to changes in the work.

SOURCE: George W. England and Itzhak Harpaz, "How Working Is Defined: National Contexts and Demographic and Organizational Role Influences," *Journal of Organizational Behavior,* July 1990, pp. 253–266.

5. *Social norms and expectations:* The knowledge of what others expect from someone
6. *External priming:* The receiving of cues from others

Attributional and enactment processes then combine with social reality construction processes to influence perceptions, attitudes, and behaviors. *International Perspective* discusses some ways in which cultural factors may also come to influence how people in different countries perceive their jobs.

To date, the social information processing model has gotten mixed support from empirical research.[38] Laboratory experiments and field studies often have found that social information influences task perceptions and attitudes, but they

38. Joe Thomas and Ricky W. Griffin, "The Social Information Processing Model of Task Design: A Review of the Literature," *Academy of Management Review,* October 1983, pp. 672–682. See also Griffin, "Toward an Integrated Theory of Task Design."

also have shown the importance of job characteristics.[39] The findings suggest that task perceptions may be a joint function of objective task properties and social information.[40] For example, positive social information and a well-designed task may produce more favorable responses than either information or task properties alone would produce. Conversely, negative information and a poorly designed task may produce more negative reactions than either social information or job properties would by themselves. In situations where social information and task conditions do not reinforce each other, they may cancel each other out, as when negative social information may diminish the positive effects of a well-designed task. Similarly, positive information may at least partly offset the negative consequences of a poorly designed task. At present, there is considerable debate as to which of the three views—the job characteristics model, the social information processing model, or a model combining both—is correct.

Emerging Perspectives on Job Design

Three other issues pertaining to job design that are not tied to any particular theory are employee work schedules, automation and robotics, and worker flexibility.

Work Schedules

■ Alternative work schedules such as the **compressed workweek, flexible work schedules (flextime),** and **job sharing** often are used in organizations.

Employee work schedules are not related to job design in the strictest sense, but they are a direct point of contact between the employee and the job. Managers have been seeking new work scheduling methods that improve employees' work-related experiences and at the same time improve attendance, motivation, and attitudes. Three relatively new approaches to work scheduling are the compressed workweek, flexible work schedules, and job sharing.

Compressed Workweek An employee following a **compressed work week** schedule works a full forty-hour week in fewer than the traditional five days. Most typically, this schedule involves working ten hours a day for four days, leaving an extra day off. Another alternative is for employees to work slightly less than ten hours a day but to complete the forty hours by lunch time on Friday. Organizations that have used the compressed workweek include John Hancock,

---

39. Charles A. O'Reilly and D. F. Caldwell, "Informational Influence as a Determinant of Perceived Task Characteristics and Job Satisfaction," *Journal of Applied Psychology,* vol. 64, 1979, pp. 157–165; Ricky W. Griffin, "Objective and Social Sources of Information in Task Redesign: A Field Experiment," *Administrative Science Quarterly,* June 1983, pp. 184–200.

40. Griffin, "Objective and Social Sources of Information in Task Redesign." See also Griffin, "Toward an Integrated Theory of Task Design," and Donald J. Campbell, "Task Complexity: A Review and Analysis," *Academy of Management Review,* January 1988, pp. 40–52.

FIGURE 13.7
Sample Flexible Work Schedules

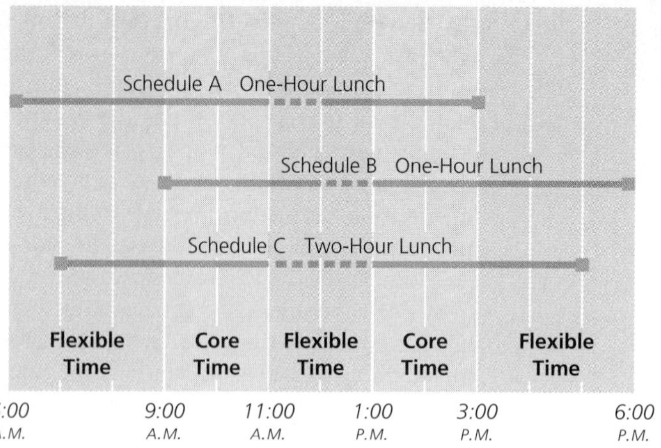

Atlantic Richfield, and R. J. Reynolds. However, research has found little evidence that a compressed workweek does anything for motivation or attendance.[41]

Flexible Work Schedules **Flexible work schedules,** or **flextime,** may be more promising. Flextime gives employees some control over their working hours and thus, from a task design point of view, contributes to employee autonomy. Research evidence suggests that flextime may be an effective motivational strategy.[42] Figure 13.7 illustrates how flextime works. The workday is broken down into two categories: flexible time and core time. All employees must be at their workstations during core time, but they can choose their own schedules during flexible time. Thus, one employee may choose to start work early in the morning and leave in midafternoon, another to start in the late morning and work until late afternoon, and still another to start early in the morning, take a long lunch break, and work until late afternoon. Organizations that have used this method include Control Data Corp., Metropolitan Life, and the federal government.

Job Sharing In **job sharing,** two part-time employees share one full-time job. One person may perform the job from 8:00 A.M. to noon and the other from 1:00 P.M. to 5:00 P.M. Job sharing may be desirable for people who want to work only part-time or when job markets are tight. For its part, the organization can accommodate the preferences of a broader range of employees and may benefit from the talents of more people. Although job sharing has not been scientifically evaluated, it appears to be a useful alternative to traditional work scheduling. Another work scheduling variation is an increasing movement toward permanent part-time, or *contingent,* workers. Organizations often do not have

41. A. R. Cohen and H. Gadon, *Alternative Work Schedules: Integrating Individual and Organizational Needs* (Reading, Mass.: Addison-Wesley, 1978).
42. Ibid.

THE ETHICAL DILEMMA

People versus Robots

Suppose you are the manager of a large manufacturing plant. You are considering replacing many of the jobs in your facility with robots. If you proceed, however, several dozen veteran employees will be put out of jobs. While they conceivably could be retrained for other jobs, many are approaching retirement age and certainly would resist your efforts.

Now consider a different example. A number of hazardous jobs must be performed in your plant. While you and your workers take all the safety precautions you can conceive of, accidents still occur. One worker recently lost a finger while working in a hazardous area. However, a new line of industrial robots that can do most of the dangerous jobs in your plant has just been introduced. Unfortunately, they are quite expensive. If you were to buy the robots, you would have to postpone some other capital improvements that your boss at headquarters has requested.

What would you do in each of these two cases? These and similar dilemmas confront many managers today. On the one hand, robots now can perform many of the tedious and routine jobs presently done by humans. Of course, the human workers in turn are displaced and put out of work. New jobs can be created and the displaced workers trained to perform them. But often the new jobs are fewer than the lost jobs, and not all employees can be retrained.

One area where both managers and workers see great potential for robots is in the performance of hazardous work. Westinghouse makes robots that can inspect and repair contaminated areas in nuclear power plants. Caterpillar is experimenting with a robot that can clean up toxic-waste deposits. And General Dynamics is planning a robot that can perform military reconnaissance. These robots are still very expensive and not yet in widespread use.

SOURCES: "How U.S. Robots Lost the Market to Japan in Factory Automation," *The Wall Street Journal,* November 16, 1990, pp. A1, A10; "It's a Dirty Job, but Something's Gotta Do It," *Business Week,* August 20, 1990, pp. 92–97; "Smart Factories: America's Turn?" *Business Week,* May 8, 1989, pp. 142–148.

to pay benefits to part-time workers and can use them to easily cut back or expand the work force as needed.

Automation and Robotics

■ Automation and robotics are changing the way many jobs are designed.

American industry's growing reliance on automation and robotics has a variety of implications for job design, some positive and others perhaps negative.[43] In general, these implications relate to the potential changes that automation and robotics may bring to existing jobs. *The Ethical Dilemma* explores some of these issues.

As *The Ethical Dilemma* describes, automation may eliminate many boring, routine, and hazardous jobs from the workplace, theoretically allowing workers

43. Hackman, "Work Design"; Griffin, *Task Design;* Hackman and Oldham, *Work Redesign.*

Some jobs are just too dangerous to assign to human beings. This police robot is able to examine and relocate a live bomb by remote control. Robots are being developed to do other hazardous jobs as well, such as handling toxic wastes and repairing high voltage power lines. These and other advances in robotics are significantly altering the design of some jobs.

to move into more interesting and challenging jobs. But automation may also dehumanize jobs. Witness the many grocery stores that are adopting optiscan technology that reads prices from printed bar codes as the check-out clerk passes products over a screen. The clerk may well be more efficient, but he or she also has much less to do. Some newer units even have audio capabilities: They call out the prices, the total bill, and the customer's change and even say, "Thank you"! Required only to pass items over the scanner, the clerk becomes merely an adjunct to the technology.

Worker Flexibility

- Worker flexibility is becoming a popular method of designing jobs. In some ways, it represents a new approach to job rotation.

Still another emerging perspective on job design is the notion of flexible workers. In some ways, this approach is a refinement of the job rotation model described earlier. Its basic idea is that organizations can enhance their effectiveness by training workers to perform a number of different jobs. Employees generally receive a pay increase when they master each new job. The organization can then transfer employees around to different jobs as needed.

Lechmere Inc.'s department stores in Florida have been very successful using flexible workers. One employee may learn to unload trucks, operate a check-out computer, and sell sporting goods. The firm benefits because it can reassign employees as needed to get different things done. Also, employees seem to like the system.[44]

44. Alster, "What Flexible Workers Can Do."

There are three basic differences between the flexible-worker approach and simple job rotation. First, people get transferred across completely different jobs rather than across narrow tasks within the same job. Second, they receive a financial incentive for becoming more flexible. Finally, the rotation itself often is spontaneous and exciting, whereas in simple job rotation the changes are mechanical and routinized. All things considered, the concept of the flexible worker is likely to become increasingly popular.[45]

Employee Participation

In Chapter 6, we discussed participative management and its role in motivation. We noted that participation can occur in many different areas and described one specific vehicle for participation—quality circles—in detail. In general, participation is on the increase in many organizations throughout the world, especially in the United States. Indeed, some experts believe that increased participation throughout the organization is the key to American competitiveness in the world economy.

■ Increased employee participation affects how the jobs of workers and supervisors should be designed.

Regardless of its area or form, participation is virtually certain to affect job design. In other words, an effort to increase participation is likely to alter jobs—and a change in jobs will likely alter participation. Thus, managers need to recognize the links between participation and job design.

As a starting point, it is possible to note many different linkages between participation and straightforward job design approaches such as the Job Characteristics Theory. For example, to increase participation, several changes will likely be made in the basic job characteristics themselves. Autonomy and feedback are the two characteristics most clearly related to participation. Thus, if a manager seeks to increase participation, a good way to start is to give employees more autonomy over how they do their jobs and more feedback about how they are performing.

But participation also is associated with more macro issues. One important consideration is that a widespread approach to increasing participation is through the use of work teams. Hence, increasing participation may require the organization to drop the individual as the basis for designing jobs and replace it with the group.

Still another aspect of participation is information. We already noted the increase in feedback that may be necessary. Organizations also find it effective to provide employees with more information about the company as a whole. Workers who are truly participating will likely need access to information about costs, quality, customer attitudes, and a variety of other issues before they can do their jobs effectively.

---

45. See John Dupuy, "Flexible Jobs: Key to Manufacturing Productivity," *The Journal of Business Strategy,* May-June 1990, pp. 28–32.

Organizations that use jobs as a vehicle for increasing participation must also be aware of two other related considerations. The first is the job of the first-line supervisor. By definition, an organization that becomes more participative will also need its supervisors to become less autocratic. Thus, if the organization changes the jobs of its operating employees and structures them into teams, it must also change supervisory jobs and make supervisors into coaches, facilitators, or information sources.

Second, the organization seeking to increase participation must be prepared to reeducate its workers. Many operating employees in the United States lack some of the basic skills necessary to interpret information they will need in the performance of their jobs. All too often, they are even deficient in basic grammatical and arithmetic skills. Organizations that want to be participative therefore must build an education component into their plans. For example, Corning Incorporated recently opened a new plant in Blacksburg, Virginia. Corning wanted the plant to be totally participative. In preparation, 25 percent of all hours worked during the plant's first year of operation were devoted to training and education. The firm now wants to increase the skill levels of all its twenty thousand employees. To do so, the firm wants 5 percent of all hours worked in 1991 to be spent in the classroom. While this obviously represents a significant expense, Corning also expects to reap big dividends.[46] (More details about Corning's use of participation are found in Case 13.1.)

Summary of Key Points

- Until about the 1950s, historical trends showed a general movement toward increasingly specialized jobs. Since then, there has been a consistent move away from extreme specialization. Two early alternatives to specialization were job rotation and job enlargement. Job enrichment stimulated considerable interest in job design.
- The Job Characteristics Theory grew from the early work on job enrichment. One basic premise of this theory is that jobs can be described in terms of a specific set of motivational characteristics. Another is that managers should work to enhance the presence of those motivational characteristics in jobs but should also take individual differences into account.
- It is sometimes appropriate to design jobs for groups rather than for individuals. Many tasks can be effectively performed by groups. Autonomous work groups and work teams also are widely used.
- Advocates of the social information processing view question some basic premises of the job characteristics approach. Social information processing theorists argue that neither employee needs nor task perceptions are stable, consistently predictable properties; rather, they are socially constructed re-

46. "Sharpening Minds for a Competitive Edge," *Business Week,* December 17, 1990, pp. 72–78.

alities. Today the emerging opinion is that employees' task perceptions and attitudes are jointly determined by objective task properties and social information.

- New issues also have emerged in the area of task design. Compressed workweeks, flexible work schedules, and job sharing are scheduling innovations. Automation and robotics also have implications for job design. Worker flexibility is still another increasingly important approach.
- Employee participation also is closely linked with job design. Changing jobs is a common vehicle for enhancing participation. Such changes affect the basic job characteristics, often result in group-based tasks, and require that additional information be made available to job holders. Organizations that want to increase participation also need to modify the jobs of first-line supervisors and provide additional training and education for their workers.

Discussion Questions

1. What are the primary advantages and disadvantages of job specialization? Were they the same in the early days of mass production?
2. When might job enlargement be especially effective and especially ineffective? How about job rotation?
3. Are there any trends today that suggest a return to job specialization?
4. What are the strengths and weaknesses of job enrichment? When might it be useful?
5. Do you agree or disagree with the idea that individual differences affect how people respond to their jobs? Explain.
6. What are the primary similarities and differences between job enrichment and the Job Characteristics Theory?
7. What alternative work schedules besides those discussed in the chapter can you think of?
8. How do automation and robotics make work easier? How do they make it more difficult?
9. What other job design alternatives can you envision emerging in the future?
10. How might it be possible to increase employee participation in the workplace without altering jobs?

CASE 13.1

Job Changes at Corning

Corning Incorporated, maker of a wide variety of glass and glass-related products from dishes to television picture tubes, was like many other large old-line American manufacturers. Labor and management were always bickering, and productivity was trailing that of the Japanese. The only sure thing seemed to be that total decline was inevitable.

Jobs were highly specialized in all Corning plants, and workers had little say over how they did their jobs. Dictatorial supervisors told them what to do, and the workers tended to rely on a rigid network of union work rules to both protect their jobs and get by with doing as little as possible. Productivity had been stagnating for years, and profit margins were getting thinner and thinner.

Fortunately, managers at Corning recognized where the firm was headed and decided to take drastic measures to change direction. Corning's CEO, James Houghton, was instrumental in setting a new course for the firm. He recognized that American business had to change the way it operated and that a real partnership with labor was the key to survival in an increasingly competitive world. He and his management team shaped a new approach to both doing business and dealing with workers.

At the foundation of Corning's efforts was a plan to change the fundamental way operating employees did their jobs. Among Corning's initial efforts to change things was a companywide employee involvement program. Such a change would take a lot of time, however, and there were many hurdles to overcome. Consequently, management then decided to take a close look at what could be done in a brand-new facility, one that had no monkey on its back.

The firm was planning a new factory in Blacksburg, Virginia, to build automobile filters. Management decided to take participation to the extreme and use state-of-the-art approaches for maximizing employee involvement. Changing the basic way jobs were to be designed was the foundation. To start with, management selected workers who were somewhat more educated than those Corning typically employed; most had at least one year of college.

To avoid repetitive and boring job assignments, Corning officials decided early on that everyone would learn a variety of jobs. Indeed, workers had to learn at least three different sets of skills within two years or lose their jobs.

Now workers have a great deal of control over how they do their jobs. They make virtually every decision and seldom have to check anything out with a supervisor. The entire plant of 150 workers functions with a single plant manager and two line managers—and even these managers are there only to advise and provide information. All the workers are organized into teams. Each team is completely responsible for all aspects of planning, executing, and monitoring its performance.

How has the plan worked? From any point of view, it seems to be a tremendous success. Workers apparently like how they are treated and their role in getting things done. Indeed, many have come to accept personal responsibility for their own job security: If they do their jobs right, their positions will become increasingly important and thus less likely to become dispensable.

Corning officials are also pleased. When the plant opened, it was projected to lose up to $2.3 million during its eight-month start-up period in the form of worker training, machinery break-in, and the like. Instead, it made $2 million in profits. Also, productivity has exceeded all expectations. Now one team of workers can retool an assembly line to produce a different filter in less than ten minutes compared to an hour in Corning's traditional plants. As a result of Corning's successes at Blacksburg, the firm has committed to introducing the same approach to getting things done in its twenty-seven other plants.

Case Questions

1. Identify aspects of the Job Characteristics Theory and the social information perspective in this case.
2. What unforeseen problems might Corning encounter when it tries to introduce its approach in Blacksburg in its other plants?
3. The union is cooperating with Corning in the firm's efforts to become more participative. Why do you think this is so?

SOURCES: "Sharpening Minds for a Competitive Edge," *Business Week,* December 17, 1990, pp. 72–78; "Labor, Management Becoming Partners for Survival," Associated Press wire story as reported in *The Bryan-College Station Eagle,* December 9, 1990, p. C1; Brian Dumaine, "Who Needs a Boss?" *Fortune,* May 7, 1990, pp. 52–60.

CASE 13.2

Enriching Jobs at Standard Decoy

Standard Decoy Co. in Witchell, Maine, has been making traditional wooden hunting decoys since 1927. Cyrus Witchell began the business by carving a couple of ducks a day by hand. Demand and competition have long since driven the company to use modern machinery and assembly line techniques, turning out two hundred ducks daily even on the slowest days.

When Stewart Alcorn, Cyrus Witchell's grandson, took over the business, he knew things needed to change. Output hadn't fallen, and the company was surviving financially despite competition from what he called "plastic ducks" from the Far East. But Alcorn noticed that productivity per worker had stayed the same for ten years, even during the period since the company bought the latest equipment. While touring the plant, he noticed many employees yawning and found himself doing the same. No one quit. No one complained. They all gave him a smile when he walked by. But no one seemed excited with the work.

Alcorn decided to take a survey. He appointed a respected worker at each step in the production process to ask each of his or her coworkers questions and to fill in the response sheets. One conclusion emerged from the survey: The "fine-tuners," as Alcorn thought of them, were the most content. That is, those who used fine tools and brushes to get the duck's heads, expressions, and feathers just right seemed to most enjoy their work. In contrast, the people who planed and cut the wood into blocks, rough-cut the body shapes, spray-painted the body color, and applied the varnish were all pretty bored.

Alcorn had heard about a technique called "job rotation," and decided to try it out. He gave all workers a taste of the "fun" jobs. He asked for volunteers to exchange jobs for one morning a week. The fine-tuners were skeptical, and the other workers were only slightly more enthusiastic. The whole program turned out a disaster. Even with guidance, the planers and spray-painters could not master the higher-precision techniques, and the fine-tuners seemed willing to give them only limited assistance. After one trial week, Alcorn gave up.

During lunch break that Friday, Alcorn was wandering around outside the plant bemoaning his failure. Then he noticed one of the rough-cutter's, Al Price, whittling at something with an ordinary pocket knife. It turned out to be a block of wood that he had cut incorrectly and normally would have thrown in the scrap heap. But as Price said, "It kind of looked like a duck, in an odd way," and he had started whittling on it in spare moments.

Alcorn liked what he saw and asked Price if he would be willing to sell him the duck when he got through with it. Price looked surprised, but he agreed. The following week, Alcorn noticed that Price had finished the whittling and was getting one of the fine-tuners to help him paint the duck in a way that made it look even odder. When it was finished, Alcorn offered it to one of his regular customers, who took a look at it, said, "You've got hand made?", and asked if he could order a gross.

By the middle of the next month, Alcorn's "Odd Ducks" program was in full swing. Workers were held responsible for producing their usual number of conventional ducks, but they were allowed to use company tools and materials any time they wanted to work on their own projects. There were no quotas or expectations for the Odd Ducks. Some employees worked on one for weeks; others collaborated and produced one or two a day. Some wouldn't sell their ducks but crafted them to practice their skills and brought them home to display on their mantles. Those who would sell kept half the selling price. That price usually did not amount to more than their regular hourly wage, but no one seemed to care about the precise amount of income.

The response to the Odd Duck program was so great that Alcorn put up a bulletin board titled "Odd Letters," where he posted appreciative notes from customers. Most of these customers, it seemed, had no interest in hunting but just liked to have the ducks around. And when Alcorn learned that some of his customers were in turn selling the ducks as "Cyrus Witchell's Olde Time Odd Ducks," he did not complain.

Case Questions

1. How did the "Odd Ducks" program enrich the jobs at Standard Decoy?
2. What motivated workers to participate in making the Odd Ducks?

EXPERIENTIAL EXERCISE

Purpose: This exercise will help you assess the processes involved in redesigning jobs.

Format: Working in small groups, you will diagnose an existing job in terms of its motivating potential, analyze its motivating potential in comparison to other jobs, suggest ways to redesign it, and then assess the effects of your redesign suggestions on other elements in the workplace.

Procedure: Your instructor will divide the class into groups of three or four. In assessing the characteristics of jobs, use a scale value of 1 ("very little") to 7 ("very high").

1. Using the scale values, assign scores on each core job dimension used in the Job Characteristics Theory (see page 397) to the following jobs:

secretary, professor, food server, auto mechanic, lawyer, short-order cook, department store clerk, construction worker, newspaper reporter.

2. Calculate the motivating potential score (MPS) (see page 400) for each job, and rank-order them from highest to lowest.
3. Your instructor will now assign your group one of the jobs from the list. Discuss how you might reasonably go about enriching the job.
4. Calculate the new MPS score for the redesigned job, and check its new position in the rank-ordering.
5. Discuss the feasibility of your redesign suggestions. In particular, look at how your recommended changes might necessitate organizational change such as changes in other jobs, the reward system, and the selection criteria used in hiring people for the job.
6. Briefly discuss your observations with the rest of the class.

Follow-up Questions

1. How might the social information processing model have explained some of your own perceptions in this exercise?
2. Are some jobs simply impossible to redesign?

CHAPTER OUTLINE

- Performance Appraisal Systems
  - *Purposes of Performance Appraisal*
- Common Questions about Performance Appraisal
  - *Who Does the Appraisal?*
  - *How Often Should Employees Be Evaluated?*
  - *How Is the Appraisal Information to Be Used?*
- Performance Appraisal Basics
  - *Commitment to Objectives*
  - *Job Analysis*
  - *Measurement of Performance*
- Performance Appraisal Techniques
  - *Individual Evaluation*
  - *Comparative Evaluation*
  - *Multiple-Rater Comparative Evaluation*

14

Performance Appraisal

CHAPTER OBJECTIVES

After studying this chapter, you should be able to:

Discuss the purposes of performance appraisal.

Identify and discuss the uses of performance appraisal information.

Describe the essential elements of performance appraisal.

Explain the strengths and weaknesses of several performance appraisal techniques.

Westinghouse Electric Corp. recently designed and implemented a new performance appraisal system to go with a new compensation system for office workers at its Pittsburgh headquarters. The project was initiated by the human resource department and used an outside consultant. A comprehensive analysis of each job description was completed and used to develop performance standards for each position. Other features included training for both the raters and the ratees, protection against the major flaws of most performance appraisal systems, provisions for one appraisal session for each employee to take place in the spring of each year, and a new form that includes the job description and performance standards for the position. In keeping with its emphasis on participative management, all of this was accomplished via a task force made up of twenty-five employees and twenty managers. The task force meetings took place in company offices and on company time. The system is now in use, and the reaction of everyone involved is quite positive. The new performance appraisal and compensation systems are intended to fit with a complete restructuring of the company that took place over the last decade.[1]

The integrated performance appraisal and compensation system at Westinghouse is intended to fit other management systems within the company and, therefore, make the system easier to use and more meaningful for managers. They hope to eliminate the typical statements that supervisors make about doing performance appraisals. "Let's be frank: Most managers hate conducting performance appraisals."[2] Managers use many different excuses to avoid formally appraising the performance of employees who work for them. The most common excuses are:

"It takes too much time."

"The form we use is bad."

"I am not qualified to judge others."

"No one does it to me."

"It is so painful."

1. Rick Teaff, "Westinghouse Recharges," *Pittsburgh Business Times and Journal,* February 12, 1990, p. 1. Adapted by permission. From David B. Cowfer and Joanne Sujansky, "Appraisal Development at Westinghouse," *Training and Development Journal,* July 1987, pp. 40–45. Reprinted from the *Training and Development Journal.* Copyright 1987, the American Society for Training and Development. Reprinted with permission. All rights reserved.

2. Walter Kiechel III, "How to Appraise Performance," *Fortune,* October 12, 1987, pp. 239–240.

To some employees, performance appraisal is an annual ordeal in which "the boss tries to explain to me why I'm not getting a raise." Other employees look forward to their performance appraisals as opportunities to examine their work and career prospects. At the management level, some line managers dread the performance appraisal system forced on them by the human resources department because of the paperwork required. Top management, in contrast, may view performance appraisal as the most important part of human resource management. What is this nearly universal organizational event that is so important to some and so loathsome to others? How can this one aspect of organizational life provoke such disparate feelings and reactions?

- **Performance appraisal** is the process by which a manager evaluates an employee's work behaviors by measurement and comparison with established standards, records the results, and communicates them to the employee.

We begin this chapter by examining the purposes of performance appraisal. Then we look at the basic questions organizations need to ask when developing an appraisal system. Next, we discuss the factors that are critical to an effective performance appraisal system. Finally, we examine basic techniques for evaluating employees both individually and in comparison to others.

- The **performance appraisal system (PAS)** consists of the organizational processes and activities involved in performance appraisals, including organizational policies, procedures, and resources that support the activity.

Performance Appraisal Systems

Performance appraisal, or *performance evaluation,* is the process by which a manager (1) evaluates an employee's work behaviors by measurement and comparison with previously established standards, (2) records the results, and (3) communicates the results to the employee. A **performance appraisal system (PAS)**

Like most other companies, America West airlines appraises the performance of each of its employees on a regular basis. The results of these appraisals are used in awarding pay increases, making promotions, and providing training. In addition, the company also pays attention to overall performance. America West employees recently attained the highest productivity rating in the airline industry. To recognize this accomplishment the firm gathered its employees together at different sites and made these group photographs.

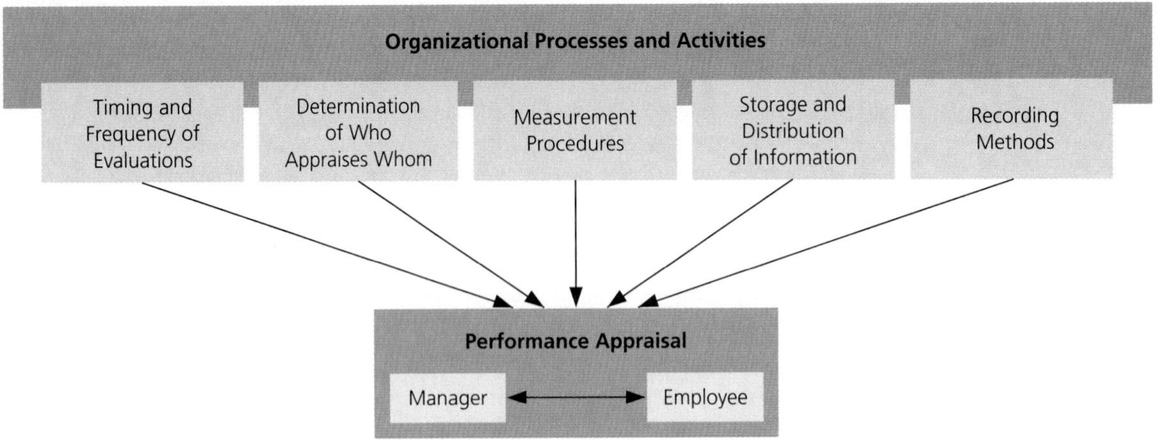

FIGURE 14.1
Performance Appraisal System

comprises the organizational processes and activities involved in performance appraisals, as shown in Figure 14.1. Performance appraisal involves a manager and an employee, whereas the PAS includes the organizational policies, procedures, and resources that support the activity. The timing and frequency of evaluations, determination of who appraises whom, measurement procedures, methods of recording the evaluations, and storage and distribution of information are all aspects of the performance appraisal system.

Although most organizations have standardized control systems for managing other types of resources and monitoring their use, the system for managing human resources typically has been neither a standardized nor a generally accepted part of organizational life. This is a residue of large-scale economic shifts. When the U.S. economy was based primarily in manufacturing, the evaluation of performance was very simple: A manager could evaluate a worker by counting the number of units produced. In a service economy, however, output is less easily measured, and the evaluation of performance is a much more subjective and less clearly defined process. Often, then, there is serious conflict not only over how evaluation should be conducted but over whether it should be conducted at all.

- Performance appraisal is one of the most powerful tools for managing people available to managers.

The modern human resource system may be divided into four parts: acquisition of human resources (recruitment and selection), training and development, motivation, and compensation. Performance appraisal is involved in all four parts and serves to tie them together by providing feedback information for all the other parts.[3] Indeed, performance appraisal has been called one of the most powerful and important tools for managing human resources in an organization.[4]

3. Gary P. Latham and Kenneth N. Wexley, *Increasing Productivity Through Performance Appraisal* (Reading, Mass.: Addison-Wesley, 1981).
4. Charles J. Fombrun and Robert L. Laud, "Strategic Issues in Performance Appraisal: Theory and Practice," *Personnel,* November-December 1983, pp. 23–31.

FIGURE 14.2
Purposes of Performance Appraisal

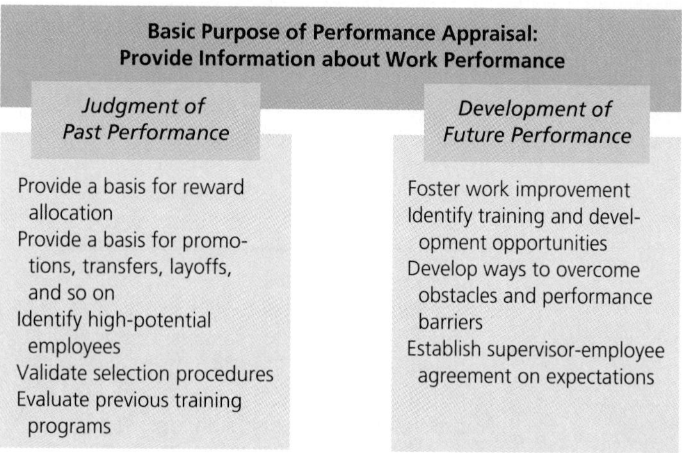

Basic Purpose of Performance Appraisal:
Provide Information about Work Performance
Judgment of Past Performance
Provide a basis for reward allocation
Provide a basis for promotions, transfers, layoffs, and so on
Identify high-potential employees
Validate selection procedures
Evaluate previous training programs
Development of Future Performance
Foster work improvement
Identify training and development opportunities
Develop ways to overcome obstacles and performance barriers
Establish supervisor-employee agreement on expectations

Purposes of Performance Appraisal

Performance appraisal may serve as many as twenty different purposes,[5] but the most basic is to provide information about work behaviors. Other purposes of performance appraisal can be grouped into two broad categories, judgmental and developmental, as shown in Figure 14.2.

Performance appraisals with a judgmental orientation focus on past performance. They are concerned mainly with the measurement and comparison of performance and also with the uses of the information generated.[6] Judgmental performance appraisals often are used in part to control employee behaviors. The organization rewards desired behaviors with wage raises, promotions, and entrance into high-potential employee development programs and punishes undesirable behaviors with transfers and layoffs, denial of wage increases, and demotions. Performance appraisal can provide the necessary documentation for the termination of employees.[7] *Developing Management Skills* describes how supervisors can do their part in due process under a union contract by properly using the performance appraisal system. Performance appraisals with a judgmental orientation also provide valuable feedback on the effectiveness of the organization's selection procedures and training programs.

Performance appraisals with a developmental orientation focus on future performance and use information resulting from evaluations for performance

5. H. John Bernardin and Richard W. Beatty, *Performance Appraisal: Assessing Human Behavior at Work* (Boston: Kent, 1984).

6. L. Cummings and Donald P. Schwab, *Performance in Organizations: Determinants and Appraisal* (Glenview, Ill.: Scott, Foresman, 1973).

7. Kenneth R. Gilberg, "Employee Terminations: Risky Business," *Personnel Administrator*, March 1987, pp. 40–46.

DEVELOPING MANAGEMENT SKILLS

How Supervisors Can Do Their Part in Due Process

Supervisors often believe that supervising employees covered by a union contract is more difficult than managing nonunion workers. One reason is that the contract makes it difficult to dismiss or punish contract-covered workers. Most union contracts are very specific about the conditions for punishment and dismissal. Some contracts now require procedural due process in performance appraisal of union employees. This type of procedural due process simply says that before disciplinary action can be taken against an employee, the company or supervisor must have followed specific procedures to inform the employee of the situation. The procedures usually include the following:

1. The employee must be notified in writing about an upcoming performance appraisal.
2. The employee must receive a copy of the appraisal results and sign a copy stating that he or she has seen and reviewed it (but not that the employee agrees with it).
3. Severe disciplinary actions such as dismissals are reviewed carefully and may be taken only when there is clear evidence that the performance appraisal indicates the employee has been notified about the poor performance and attempts to correct the situation have been made.

Under specific procedural due process provisions such as these, supervisors must take great care to ensure that performance appraisals are done regularly, accurately, and fairly. Aaron Pulhamus, an expert in the area, notes that supervisors who work in a union situation should be trained on four key principles of performance appraisal:

1. Provide feedback to employees, and give recognition to outstanding performance.
2. Raise unsatisfactory-performance issues with the employee; do not avoid them.
3. Be hard-nosed with poor performance so that it can be documented and attempts made to correct it.
4. Avoid concentrating all your efforts on the small number of employees who are poor performers. Focus more attention on developing the potential of other employees.

SOURCE: Reprinted by permission of Supervision, © 1989, The National Research Bureau, Inc., 424 North Third St., Burlington, Iowa 52601-5224.

improvement. If improved future performance is the intent of the appraisal process, the manager may focus on goals or targets for the employee, elimination of obstacles or problems that hinder performance, and future training needs.

Common Questions about Performance Appraisal

Employee appraisals are common in every type of organization. How they are done, however, differs across organizations. There are many issues to decide regarding how to conduct an appraisal. At least three general questions regarding performance appraisals always arise. The first—"Who does the appraisal?"—concerns the beginning of the process. The second—"How often should employees be evaluated?"—questions the timing of the appraisals. The third—"How is the appraisal information used?"—concerns the results.

Who Does the Appraisal?

■ In most cases, the employee's supervisor conducts the appraisal. However, other individuals often participate.

In most appraisal systems, the employee's primary evaluator is the supervisor.[8] However, many other people who observe or are affected by the employee can contribute to the process. Some of these potential raters include managers of other work units, first-level supervisors, second-level supervisors, staff personnel, peers (people at the same level within the organization, but with whom the ratee does not work), subordinates, clients or customers, coworkers (people with whom the ratee works either directly or indirectly in the organization), and other employees (people in the organization who are neither peers nor coworkers).

Appraisal problems often arise if the supervisor has less than full knowledge of the employee's performance. For example, the supervisor may have little first-hand knowledge of the performance of an employee who works alone outside the company premises, such as a salesperson who makes solo calls on clients or a maintenance person who handles equipment problems in the field. Similar problems may arise when the supervisor has a limited understanding of the technical knowledge involved in an employee's job.

One solution to these problems is a multiple-rater system that incorporates the ratings of several people who have experience with the performance of the employee being rated. Another possible solution is to use the employee as an evaluator. Although they may not actually do so, most employees can evaluate themselves in an unbiased manner.[9] Self-appraisals may be appropriate for evaluating and comparing a given employee's performance in different categories, such as performance quality, interpersonal skills, and team leadership, and they can be quite useful for development and performance improvement. However, self-appraisals have little value for comparisons of the performances of different individuals.[10]

One method of involving employees more in the appraisal process is to have the employee and the supervisor work together to do the appraisal. For some employees, this may be a good alternative. *Management in Action* describes the new system in use at Los Alamos National Laboratory that involves both the manager and the employee.

Whoever performs the evaluation must be properly trained. Training usually is designed to reduce rating errors by increasing the rater's observation and

8. Richard I. Henderson, *Performance Appraisal* (Reston, Va.: Reston, 1984).

9. P. A. Mabe and S. G. West, "Validity of Self-Evaluation of Ability: A Review and Meta Analysis," *Journal of Applied Psychology,* June 1982, pp. 280–296.

10. Clive Fletcher, "What's New in Performance Appraisal," *Personnel Management,* February 1984, pp. 20–22.

MANAGEMENT IN ACTION

Performance Appraisal at Los Alamos National Laboratory

Los Alamos National Laboratory in New Mexico is a primary supplier of nuclear material and weapons for the United States. Recently it was awarded a federal contract for a new, $210 million plutonium processing and weapons research complex. It is run primarily by engineers and scientists with Ph.D's in fields like nuclear chemistry and physics. Los Alamos is a type of organization that would seem to think very little about performance appraisal, because the work is so far-reaching and important that maximum, error-free performance should be assumed.

Such is not the case, however. Even with such a highly skilled work force, management requires the evaluation of employee performance. In 1984, the Los Alamos Laboratory introduced a new performance appraisal system that replaced a typical top-down, judgmental evaluation approach. The new system was designed to be flexible enough to apply to all employees, from clerks to scientists, and to accomplish several objectives: (1) to provide employees and supervisors with mutual understanding of job responsibilities and means of assessing performance during a specific review period; (2) to improve employee performance, satisfaction, and productivity; (3) to develop and maintain positive attitudes and communication between employees and supervisors; (4) to provide input into the salary review process; and (5) to encourage employee development.

The new system consists of eight steps:

1. Employee prepares worksheet on performance
2. Supervisor prepares worksheet on employee performance
3. Worksheet exchange and discussion
4. Supervisor prepares a draft of the written performance appraisal
5. Review of draft by higher management
6. Performance appraisal review and meeting
7. Final review and filing
8. Performance and continuing interaction

At every stage of the process, the employee and the supervisor interact and attempt to mutually agree on the content of the appraisal. In addition, the focus is on next-period goals, objectives, and tasks and how the employee can fulfill them more effectively and efficiently.

So far the impact of the new system has been quite favorable. More than 90 percent of the participants have said that they better understand their job assignments. Over 80 percent have reported that they are clear about how to do their jobs and meet performance targets. Although many employees have complained about the time involved, most believe the process took less than four hours and was worth the effort and time. Many employees reported that the employee development plans were discussed during the session.

Management has been quite pleased with how the new system is working. The experience of Los Alamos National Laboratory shows that a well-designed and managed performance appraisal system can enhance the effectiveness of an organization.

SOURCES: Peter Eichstaedt, "Bill Funds Los Alamos Plutonium Plant," *New Mexican* (Santa Fe, New Mexico), November 16, 1989; Adapted by permission. Kenneth E. Apt and David W. Watkins, "What One Laboratory Has Learned about Performance Appraisal," *Research Technology Management,* July-August 1989, pp. 22–28. Adapted by permission.

categorization skills.[11] In training sessions, raters typically are given examples of different performance levels and methods of recording observations, such as diary keeping. Employees usually perceive performance appraisals as fair if raters are trained and use some form of diary to record actual events.[12]

How Often Should Employees Be Evaluated?

Regardless of the employee's level of performance, the type of task, or the employee's need for information regarding her or his performance, the organization usually conducts performance appraisals on a regular basis, typically once a year. Annual performance appraisals make it convenient for organizational purposes such as recordkeeping and predictability. Some organizations conduct appraisals semiannually.

Recently some concern has arisen that rigidly established intervals may be inappropriate for all organizations. Three primary issues surround the timing of performance appraisals. First, the task or job cycle time may suggest more frequent performance appraisals; that is, when the employee has finished a distinct unit of work, it may be appropriate to evaluate the performance. Second, the organization may need information regarding employee performance for recordkeeping on a particular project or unit. Third, certain employees may need to have job performance information at more frequent intervals. Several systems for monitoring employee performance on an "as-needed" basis have been proposed as an alternative to the traditional annual system.[13]

How Is the Appraisal Information to Be Used?

The end product of performance appraisal is information. This information can be used as a basis for feedback, reward allocation, training and development, and personnel planning. All these uses can benefit both the employee and the organization if the appraisal system is functioning properly.

Feedback tells the employee where she or he stands in the eyes of the department managers. Appraisal results, of course, are also used to decide and justify reward allocations. Performance evaluations may be used as a starting point for discussions on training, development, and improvement. Finally, the data produced by the performance appraisal system can be used to prepare personnel needs forecasts and management succession plans and to guide human resource activities such as recruiting, training, and development programs. Performance appraisal information can indicate that an employee is ready for promotion or that he or she needs additional training to gain experience in another

---

11. Bernardin and Beatty, *Performance Appraisal.*

12. Jerald Greenberg, "Determinants of Perceived Fairness of Performance Evaluations," *Journal of Applied Psychology,* May 1986, pp. 340–342.

13. Donald B. Fedor and M. Ronald Buckley, "Issues Surrounding the Need for More Frequent Monitoring of Individual Performance in Organizations," *Public Personnel Management,* Winter 1988, pp. 435–442.

Performance appraisals are often the basis for rewarding good employees. The organization making this presentation must have some criteria for selecting who receives the award. Information provided by performance appraisals played a key role in the selection.

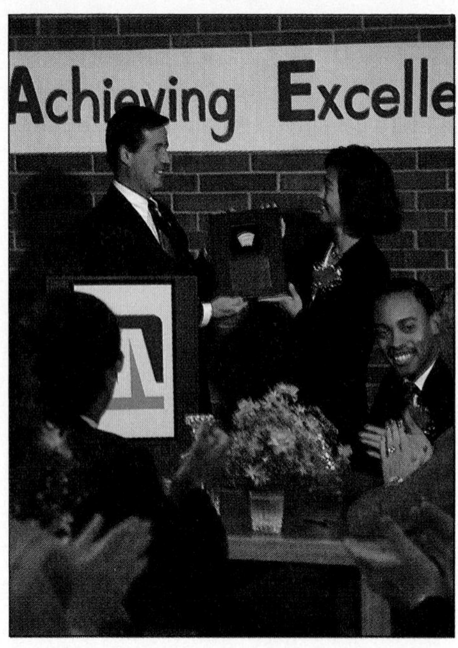

area of company operations. It may also show that an individual does not have the skills for a certain job and that another person should be recruited to fill that particular role.

■ The problem-solving style of giving feedback to employees gives manager and employee the chance to review the appraisal and discuss opportunities for improvement.

Job performance feedback is the primary use of appraisal information. Norman Maier has described three approaches to appraisal feedback: (1) tell and sell, (2) tell and listen, and (3) problem solving.[14] In the *tell-and-sell* approach, the manager gives the appraisal information and reward decision to the employee. In the *tell-and-listen* approach, the manager also listens to the employee's responses, but the comments are not used to adjust the performance appraisal or to begin a discussion of long-term concerns such as training. *Problem solving* adds to the tell-and-listen approach an opportunity for the manager and the employee to discuss differences of opinion and explore opportunities for the employee's development and improvement. At the same time, the organization can benefit from the information employees share with their managers, for instance, their future plans and career aspirations.

Performance Appraisal Basics

The performance appraisal systems organizations use vary greatly in their methods and in their effectiveness. Some are successful, and some are not; some are constantly being changed in a search for improvements. There is no one way to

14. Norman R. F. Maier, *The Appraisal Interview* (New York: Wiley, 1958).

perfect a PAS, but three factors are crucial to success: commitment to objectives, job analysis, and measurement.

Commitment to Objectives

A successful performance appraisal system is based on a strong commitment from the entire organization, especially top management. This commitment is made manifest in the objectives of the performance appraisal system. Top management must know what they want the PAS to accomplish and communicate their objectives to those responsible for developing and managing the system, as well as to all employees covered by the system. Clear objectives and strong organizational commitment give supervisors confidence that the time and effort they devote to performance evaluation is worthwhile and give employees more interest in using the evaluations to change behaviors and improve performance. Clearly stated objectives also allow managers to monitor the program, evaluate it periodically, and make any necessary adjustments.[15]

Job Analysis

■ **Job analysis** is the process of systematically collecting information about specific jobs for use in developing a performance appraisal system, in writing job or position descriptions, and in establishing equitable pay systems.

The second element of an effective PAS is a sound job analysis system that provides comprehensive and accurate descriptions of all jobs in the organization.[16] **Job analysis** is the process of systematically gathering information about specific jobs for use in developing a performance appraisal system, in writing job or position descriptions, and in developing equitable pay systems. If an employee's job performance is to be evaluated fairly, the job must be precisely and clearly defined.[17]

In undertaking job analysis, an organization must consider the factors summarized in Figure 14.3. Job analysis information may be gathered in various ways and by various people, from the job incumbent, to a specialist in the human resources department, to an outside consultant. It is of utmost importance to know the purpose of gathering the information, because particular performance evaluation methods require specific types of information from the job analysis. Therefore, the job analysis method must match the uses for the information. Some methods of job analysis can be very time consuming and expensive; others can be simple and inexpensive. The organization must be certain that the infor-

---

15. See Marshall Whitmire, "Program Evaluation of a Medical Center Performance Appraisal System" (unpublished doctoral dissertation, Arizona State University, 1985), for a discussion of the importance of setting objectives for the PAS.

16. See Henderson, *Performance Appraisal,* and Bernardin and Beatty, *Performance Appraisal,* for more detailed discussions of job analysis.

17. See Patricia S. Eyres, "Assessment: Legally Defensible Performance Appraisal Systems," *Personnel Journal,* July 1989, pp. 58–62, and Ronald G. Wells, "Guidelines for Effective and Defensible Performance Appraisal Systems," *Personnel Journal,* October 1982, pp. 776–782, for good discussions of the importance of well-defined job analysis and performance standards in performance appraisals.

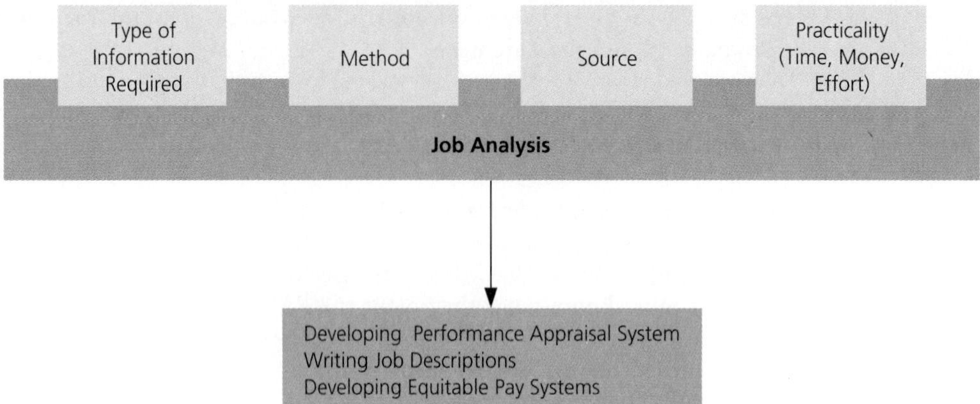

FIGURE 14.3
Job Analysis Process

mation gained from the analysis will be important enough and used often enough to justify the expense.

There are several job analysis methods, including critical incident, functional job analysis, and job inventory techniques. The best method for an organization, however, is the one that provides information appropriate for the PAS and is the most practical for the situation. Because the job analysis method used is a major determinant of the structure of the pay system that results, managers must be careful in selecting the proper job analysis techniques.

Measurement of Performance

■ Measurement of performance is the cornerstone of a sound performance appraisal system.

The cornerstone of a good performance appraisal system is the method by which performance is measured. The measurement method provides the information managers use in making decisions such as salary adjustment, promotion, transfer, and training. The courts and Equal Employment Opportunity guidelines have recommended that performance appraisal measurements be based on job-related criteria rather than on some other factor such as age, sex, religion, or national origin.[18] It is often difficult to determine exactly what is being measured with some performance appraisal systems. Some systems focus on the measurement of specific behaviors or performance outcomes, while others emphasize the measurement of personality traits, such as leadership ability, enthusiasm, or ability to work with others. *A Look at the Research* presents the results of a study that attempted to determine the relative effectiveness of two systems, one performance-based and one trait-based.

In addition, the measurement systems used in performance appraisals must be valid, reliable, and free of bias to provide useful information for the decision maker. They must not produce ratings that are consistently too lenient or too

18. Leonard Berger, "Promise of Criterion-Referenced Performance Appraisal (CRPA)," *Review of Public Personnel Administration,* vol. 3, 1983, pp. 21–32.

Gen. Colin Powell, shown here greeting tourists at the Vietnam Memorial with his Soviet counterpart, Mikhail Moiseyev, served 14 years on active duty and was then named a White House fellow in 1972. With the help of high-placed mentors, Powell has risen rapidly through the ranks, oscillating between military and political jobs, making the right contacts and learning the right skills. His efforts have not gone unnoticed by President Bush, who named him to head the Joint Chiefs in 1989.

severe or that bunch up in the middle, and they must be free of halo and timing errors.

Validity Fred Kerlinger has written that when we question the validity of a measure, we are asking whether it measures what we think it measures.[19] The **validity** of a performance evaluation method is the extent to which it reflects actual employee performance. For example, if Mary is the highest performer in a work group but performance evaluations indicate that Felipe is highest and Mary is near the bottom, we have reason to question the validity of the PAS.

- **Validity** is the extent to which a method of measurement accurately reflects the object or characteristic being measured.
- **Content validity** is the extent to which the measurement adequately assesses all important aspects of performance.

Several types of validity are relevant to performance appraisal. **Content validity** is the extent to which the measurement adequately assesses all important aspects of job performance. For example, if the method by which Mary and Felipe are evaluated measures only the performance factors in which Felipe excels and none of those in which Mary is outstanding, the system is not measuring the full content of job performance and cannot be considered valid.

- **Convergent validity** is the extent to which different measures agree in their evaluations of the same performance.
- **Discriminant validity** is the extent to which ratings of the same type of performance agree more than do ratings of different types of performance.

Convergent validity is the extent to which different measures agree in their evaluations of the same performance. Felipe may be rated higher than Mary by method 1 but lower than Mary by method 2. When ratings of performance do not agree, we must question the convergent validity of the measures.

Discriminant validity is the extent to which ratings of the same type of performance agree more than do ratings of different types of performance. For example, ratings have discriminant validity if raters 1 and 2 both rate Mary high on performance quality and low on performance quantity.

- **Reliability** is the extent to which the results of a measurement system are consistent.

Reliability A measurement system's **reliability** is the extent to which its results are consistent. (This quality is also called *stability, consistency, dependability,* and *repeatability.*) If the same performance is measured several times in the same

19. Fred N. Kerlinger, *Foundations of Behavioral Research,* 2nd ed. (New York: Holt, Rinehart and Winston, 1973).

A LOOK AT THE
RESEARCH

A Comparison of Two Performance Appraisal Systems

Traditional performance appraisal systems commonly asked managers to evaluate employees on the basis of personality traits rather than on actual performance on the job. Research found, however, that employees would rather be evaluated on how they actually perform than on a combination of personality traits such as leadership ability, enthusiasm, or ability to work with others. Managers and researchers believed employees would be more satisfied with the performance appraisal system if the performance standards were established prior to the measurement and the system was based on these standards. However, there was little research comparing the merits of the two different types of performance appraisal systems.

Professor Claudia Harris of the Philadelphia College of Textiles and Science, recently studied a county government in a large metropolitan area that was switching from a trait-based performance appraisal system to a performance standard system. Employees completed a survey before the system was changed and a follow-up survey after the county agency had used the new system for two performance review periods. The surveys asked employees to describe their understanding of the performance appraisal system, their rating of its usefulness, their satisfaction with the system, and the quality of the system.

Analysis of the resulting data indicated that employees did *not* prefer the new, performance-based system over the old, trait-based system. There was no difference in the employees' satisfaction with the system or in their perceptions of the consequences of the new system. In other words, they believed the information produced with the new system was no better than that generated under the former one. In fact, many reported that the resulting information was less helpful to them in improving their performance. Interviews with some of the employees indicated that their disappointment with the system stemmed partly from the manner in which they received feedback from their supervisors. Another problem was that the economic conditions in the area generally turned for the worse during the period of the study. Thus, the employees' outlook on their work and their future may have been somewhat dim, making them more negative generally. Furthermore, employee job descriptions had been altered just before the new system was established. Some employees were unhappy with the new job descriptions and thus may have developed unfavorable opinions about the company, their supervisors, and others in the organization.

The most important conclusion to emerge from this study is that employees do not necessarily prefer a performance-based over a trait-based system. More research is needed to evaluate this new information.

SOURCE: Claudia Harris, "A Comparison of Employee Attitudes Toward Two Performance Appraisal Systems," *Public Personnel Management,* Winter 1988, pp. 443–455. Adapted by permission.

way and the results are very similar, the measurement may be called reliable. If, on the other hand, the results are very different, we may question the reliability of the method. For example, if we use a computerized system to count the number of pieces in a box twenty times and always obtain the same result, we can call the instrument and the method reliable. But if we count the pieces manually twenty times and obtain a different number each time, we may conclude that the manual method of counting pieces is unreliable.

Another important aspect of reliability is the extent to which ratings by more than one rater agree. If two raters evaluate the same performance very differently, we can question the **interrater reliability** of the method. In the case of Mary and Felipe, suppose several people rated Felipe's performance—his peers, subordinates, and immediate supervisor. If these ratings differ, the interrater reliability is low. On the other hand, if the ratings are fairly consistent, the interrater reliability is high. Several techniques exist for establishing the interrater reliability of multiple raters.[20]

- **Interrater reliability** is the degree to which two raters of the same performance agree on the measurement of that performance.

Freedom from Bias A third condition of performance evaluation measurements is that they be free of bias. **Bias** is a personal preference or inclination that undermines impartial judgment, as in a prejudice for or against some person or group of people based on race, age, sex, seniority, or the like. In performance appraisal, a biased rater might consistently evaluate members of a certain group either higher or lower because of their membership in that group. Bias in ratings can also result from applying different criteria to different groups.[21] Bias, or even perceived bias, in ratings makes the information provided less meaningful, compromises the objectives of the appraisal system, and can result in employees' dissatisfaction with their careers.[22]

- **Bias** is a personal preference or inclination that hinders impartial judgment.

Restriction of Range Leniency, severity, and central-tendency problems in performance evaluation are special cases of the tendency of some raters to restrict the range of ratings they use. Figure 14.4 illustrates three problems that result from restriction of range. As the top portion of the figure shows, when a rater's evaluations of performance are consistently high (that is, when the standard deviation is very small and the mean is skewed toward the higher end of the scale), the rater is said to be too **lenient.** When the rater assigns all performance a moderate rating, with few, if any, high or low ratings, the restriction-of-range problem is called **central tendency;** the standard deviation is low, and the mean is centered in the middle of the scale (the middle portion of the figure). The bottom portion illustrates the problem of **severity;** here the rater assigns a low value to most or all performance, resulting in a small standard deviation and a mean that is skewed toward the low end of the scale.

- Whenever several people's ratings are bunched together rather than distributed across the available range, the measurement system may be at fault.
- **Leniency** is the tendency of the rater to evaluate performance consistently high.
- **Central tendency** is the tendency of the rater to consistently rate varying performances at about the midpoint.
- **Severity** is the rater's tendency to consistently rate varying performances at the low end of the scale.

In each of these situations, the rater is unable to distinguish between different performance levels. Recent research has indicated that the tendency to be lenient rather than accurate depends to some extent on factors such as the purpose of the appraisal, especially for self-ratings. For example, employees who are rating themselves tend to be more lenient if the rating is to be used in evaluating them

---

20. Neal Schmitt, Raymond A. Noe, and Rand Gottschalk, "Using the Lens Method to Magnify Raters' Consistency, Matching, and Shared Bias," *Academy of Management Journal,* March 1986, pp. 130–139.

21. Taylor Cox, Jr., and Stella M. Nkomo, "Differential Performance Appraisal Criteria: A Field Study of Black and White Managers," *Group & Organization Studies,* March-June 1986, pp. 101–119.

22. Jeffrey H. Greenhaus, Saroj Parasuraman, and Wayne M. Wormley, "Effects of Race on Organizational Experiences, Job Performance Evaluations, and Career Outcomes," *Academy of Management Journal,* March 1990, pp. 64–86.

FIGURE 14.4
Restriction-of-Range Problems in Performance Evaluations

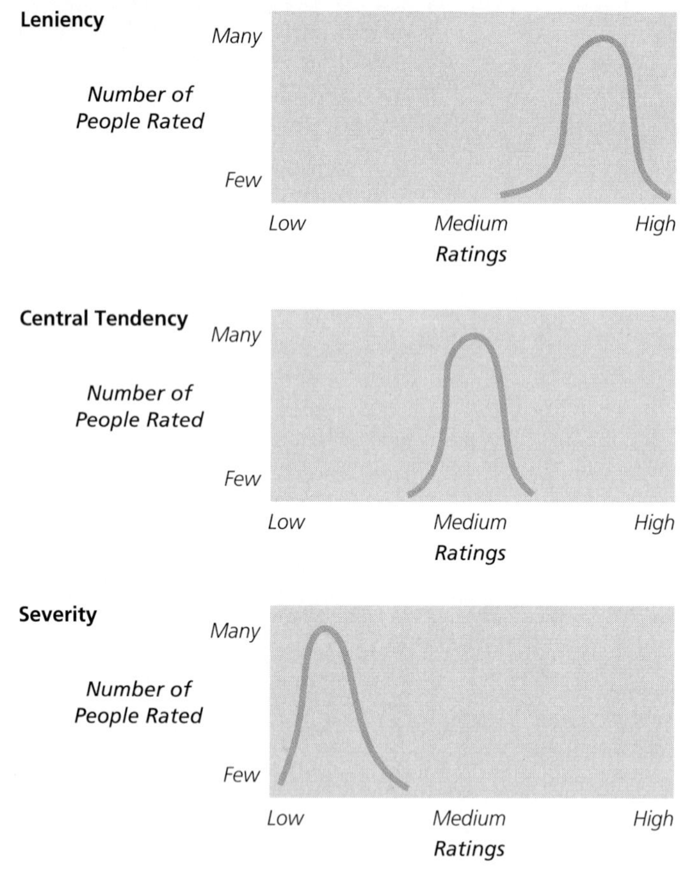

for rewards or sanctions. They tend to be more accurate, however, if they know the rating will be validated by someone else.[23]

- **Halo error** is a measurement error that occurs when a rater consistently assigns the same rating to all aspects of a person's performance, regardless of the actual performance level, because of the rater's impression of the rate.

Halo Error **Halo error** occurs when a rater consistently assigns the same rating to all aspects of a person's performance, regardless of the actual performance level, because of the rater's impression of the person. Several factors, such as personal feelings and prior expectations, can result in halo errors in ratings.[24]

For Felipe and Mary, assume the PAS requires the evaluation of several aspects of individual performance and that Felipe's and Mary's actual performance levels are those shown in the left part of Figure 14.5. If the rater evaluates their performances as shown in the right part, we have two examples of halo error. Actual performance levels differed substantially across the five factors, yet

23. Jiing-Lih Farh and James D. Werbel, "Effects of Purpose of the Appraisal and Expectations of Validation on Self-Appraisal Leniency," *Journal of Applied Psychology,* August 1986, pp. 527–529.

24. Anne S. Tsui and Bruce Barry, "Interpersonal Affect and Rating Errors," *Academy of Management Journal,* September 1986, pp. 586–599; Eileen A. Hogan, "Effects of Prior Expectations on Performance Ratings: A Longitudinal Study," *Academy of Management Journal,* June 1987, pp. 354–368.

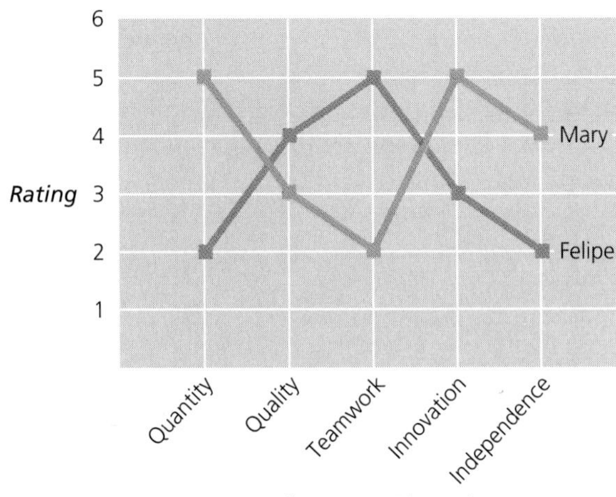

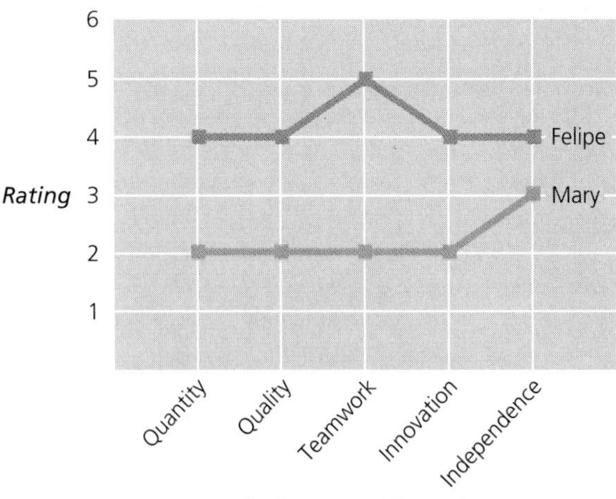

FIGURE 14.5
Examples of Halo Error in Performance Evaluation

the ratings were very similar, Mary's being consistently low and Felipe's consistently high. Halo error distorts PAS information and, like other problems of measurement, may compromise the objectives of the performance appraisal system.

- **Recency error** is a measurement error that occurs when the rater remembers only the most recent behaviors in evaluating an employee.

Timing Errors Timing can have a major impact on performance appraisal. In general, evaluations made immediately following the performance are more accurate.[25] A delay of several weeks or months between performance and rating can result in significant rating errors. A related timing problem, **recency error,** occurs when a rater remembers only the most recent behaviors in evaluating an employee. Most employees are careful to perform very well as the performance evaluation approaches. If the rater considers only this behavior in the evaluation, strong bias in the rating can result. Because accuracy is higher when the rating is based on several observations of performance over a period of time, the rater can reduce timing errors by using numerous observations and recording evaluations as soon as possible after the behavior occurs.

When the conditions of validity, reliability, or freedom from bias are not met, or when restriction of range, halo error, or timing errors are present, the effectiveness of the measurement system may be reduced. Moreover, PAS measure-

25. Kevin R. Murphy, Barbara A. Gannett, Barbara M. Herr, and Judy A. Chen, "Effects of Subsequent Performance on Evaluations of Previous Performance," *Journal of Applied Psychology,* August 1986, pp. 427–431; Kevin R. Murphy and William K. Balzer, "Systematic Distortions in Memory-Based Behavior Ratings and Performance Evaluations: Consequences for Rating Accuracy," *Journal of Applied Psychology,* February 1986, pp. 39–44; Robert L. Heneman and Kenneth N. Wexley, "The Effects of Time Delay in Rating and Amount of Information Observed on Performance Rating Accuracy," *Academy of Management Journal,* December 1983, pp. 677–686.

ment errors are likely to have a ripple effect in the organization. For example, suppose the division manager of the plant where Felipe and Mary work must promote one of them to a new staff position. He undoubtedly will consult performance appraisal records as a source of information about the two candidates. If an underlying measurement problem has consistently distorted the ratings, he may unwittingly promote the person less qualified or less appropriate for the position.

Performance Appraisal Techniques

Organizations use many different appraisal techniques, most of them derived from one or more of the methods described in this section. The techniques are grouped here according to whether they evaluate employees individually or in comparison with others.

Individual Evaluation

Individual performance appraisal methods vary greatly. Of course, each method has advantages and disadvantages. The major problems common to all methods are restriction of range and the inability to discriminate among variable levels of performance.

Graphic Rating Scales One of the simplest methods of rating individual performance is the *graphic rating scale,* illustrated in Figure 14.6. A graphic rating scale may use one global measure of performance, as shown in the top portion of the figure, or multiple measures of performance, as in the bottom portion. The rater simply checks or circles the point on the scale that best represents the employee's performance level.

■ Graphic rating scales usually are simple to use but may suffer from several measurement problems.

Graphic rating scales suffer from virtually all of the measurement problems previously discussed. For example, a scale with an odd number of points encourages the central-tendency problem. Graphic rating scales may also help produce halo error. Since the focus of the evaluation is on only one person at a time, no comparison is made between employees. Therefore, the rater may focus on one trait of the ratee, resulting in halo error. Another weakness is that graphic rating scales provide little information that can be used for employee development and performance improvement.

On the other hand, graphic rating scales are easy to use and require little time and effort to develop. They have been around for so long that they remain popular in organizations, especially for the evaluation of hourly and nonexempt personnel.[26] (Nonexempt personnel are those who, as stipulated by the Fair

26. Fombrun and Laud, "Strategic Issues in Performance Appraisal."

FIGURE 14.6
Graphic Rating Scales

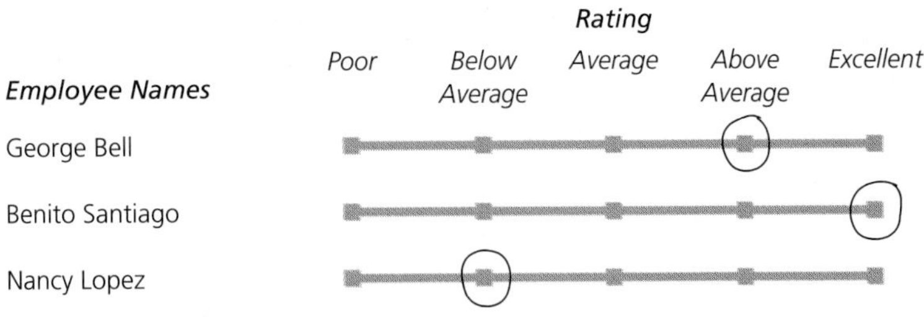

Multiple Measures of Performance

Employee Name: George Bell

Rating

Performance Dimension | *Poor* | *Below Average* | *Average* | *Above Average* | *Excellent*

1. Quantity
2. Quality
3. Teamwork
4. Creativity
5. Independence

Labor Standards Act and the Walsh-Healy Act,[27] must receive overtime pay for work over eight hours per day or over forty hours per week.) Indeed, graphic rating scales are the most widely used performance appraisal technique; a recent study showed that over 65 percent of the reporting companies used graphic rating scales for hourly personnel and over 50 percent used them for nonexempt personnel.[28]

Checklists The *checklist* rating method provides a list of work behaviors and requires the rater to check those that best describe the employee. In some cases, the items are weighted according to the importance of the behaviors. The list of behaviors and the weights assigned to them usually are generated by a group of people familiar with the job in question, such as employees, supervisors, and personnel specialists.

Unfortunately, checklists are prone to the same problems as graphic rating scales. Since both systems yield numerical ratings, however, the results are easy to use for comparisons of employees and also lend themselves to computer application.

27. Wendell L. French, *The Personnel Management Process,* 5th ed. (Boston: Houghton Mifflin, 1982), p. 420.

28. George T. Milkovich and John W. Boudreau, *Personnel/Human Management: A Diagnostic Approach,* 5th ed. (Plano, Tex.: Business Publications, 1988).

Essays A third type of individual rating method requires the rater to write narrative *essays* describing employee behaviors. These essays may be based on the rater's memory or on a diary of critical incidents that the rater keeps during the period covered by the evaluation. Essays often give a much richer picture of the employee's performance than rating scales or checklists do. They may also be more accurate, especially if based on a regularly kept diary of critical incidents. Short essays or diary notes often can be used in conjunction with quantitative methods to provide an example or justification for a numerical rating.

Essays not based on a well-kept diary, however, may be susceptible to the same halo errors as other evaluation techniques that rely on the evaluator's memory.[29] In addition, essays may not allow comparisons among employees because there may be no comparable points in narratives on different workers. Also, essays often describe an employee's personality traits rather than incidents of good or poor work behaviors. Thus, it may be necessary to train raters using this technique to focus on work behavior. Finally, the essay approach is not as easy to develop or use as quantitative methods, nor does it lend itself to numerical or computer analysis.[30]

- Behaviorally anchored rating scales (BARS) attempt to link actual behaviors to numbers on the rating scale.

Behaviorally Anchored Rating Scales *Behaviorally anchored rating scales (BARSs)* were developed in 1963 by Patricia C. Smith and Lorne M. Kendall.[31] This method combines graphic rating scales with statements of employee behaviors that characterize, or "anchor," various points on the scales. Usually, several different scales are used to evaluate an employee's performance—one for each important aspect of behavior. An example of such a scale is shown in Figure 14.7. To develop a BARS, experts (individuals familiar with the job) write behavioral statements, verify that the statements are clearly written and accurately reflect actual behaviors of employees on the job, develop scales that correlate the behavioral statements with numerical values, and verify the association between the statement and the position on the scale.

Raters find it relatively easy to use a BARS: They need only read each anchor on a particular scale and rate the employee somewhere on the continuum. Other advantages of the method include good interrater reliability, a reduction of some of the common measurement errors, such as restriction of range and halo error, a focus on job-related behaviors rather than on employee characteristics, and usefulness in training and development.

The use of BARSs also involves several potential disadvantages. Development may take a considerable amount of time, and scales may need fairly constant updating as jobs change with new technology. Therefore, the system can be very expensive to develop and maintain. In addition, raters sometimes have difficulty rating an employee's behavior when the anchors do not exactly represent the behaviors the rater has observed.

---

29. Richard I. Henderson, *Compensation Management: Rewarding Performance* (Reston, Va.: Reston, 1979).

30. Bernardin and Beatty, *Performance Appraisal.*

31. Patricia C. Smith and Lorne M. Kendall, "Retranslation of Expectations: An Approach to the Construction of Unambiguous Anchors for Rating Scales," *Journal of Applied Psychology,* vol. 47, 1963, pp. 149–155.

Rating Factors (Consider how this ratee is performing on the job.)

1. Job Capability

Not observed	Has gaps in fundamental knowledge and skills of job.	Has satisfactory knowledge and skill for the routine phases of job.	Has excellent knowledge and is well skilled on all phases of job.	Has exceptional understanding and skill on all phases of job.	Has a far-reaching grasp of entire broad job area. Authority in the field.

2. Planning Ability

Not observed	Relies on others to bring problems to attention. Often fails to see ahead.	Plans ahead just enough to get by in present job.	Is a careful effective planner. Anticipates and takes action to solve problems.	Capable of planning beyond requirements of the present job. Sees the big picture.	Capable of top level planning. A high caliber thinker and planner.

3. Executive Management

Not observed	Is a poor organizer. Does not really make effective use of material or personnel.	Maintains ordinary efficiency of operation. Control could be improved.	Gives economy of operation careful attention. Makes wise use of personnel and material.	Maintains effective economy. Carefully weighs cost against expected results.	Highly skilled in balancing cost against results to obtain optimum effectiveness.

4. Leadership

Not observed	Often weak in command situations. At times unable to exert control.	Normally develops fairly adequate control and teamwork.	Consistently a good leader. Commands respect of subordinates.	Exceptional skill in directing others to great effort.	Leadership qualities reflect potential for highest level.

SOURCE: From Mark A. McBriarty, "Performance Appraisal: Some Unintended Consequences," *Public Personnel Management,* Winter 1988, p. 423. Used by permission.

FIGURE 14.7
A Behaviorally Anchored Rating Scale (BARS)

Two other types of scales similar to the BARS have been developed: the behavioral expectation scale (BES) and the behavioral observation scale (BOS). *Behavioral expectation scales* use statements of expected behaviors as anchors. *Behavioral observation scales* use a five-point scale for each behavioral statement and require the rater to indicate how frequently the employee engages in the behavior. A behavioral observation scale is shown in Figure 14.8. Like the BARS, the BES and BOS focus on job behaviors rather than on employee characteristics. None of these methods, however, is necessarily superior to more traditional individual methods. Despite the developmental work and research that have gone

FIGURE 14.8
A Behavioral Observation Scale (BOS)

Position: Manager of an Engineering Design Group
Performance Dimension: Work Group Development

1. Manager encourages group members to attend continuing education courses to stay abreast of the latest changes in technology.

2. Manager involves members of the group in the decision-making process for development purposes.

3. Manager discusses career opportunities and development plans with each group member.

4. Manager encourages collaboration and information sharing among members on work projects.

into them, behaviorally anchored rating scales have not solved the measurement problems in performance evaluation.[32]

Forced Choice The *forced-choice* method is based on a list of behavioral statements solicited from people knowledgeable about the job. These statements are screened and grouped on the rating form so that they appear to be equally desirable. The rater must choose the one item from each group that best describes the performance of the employee. Sometimes raters are also asked to check the item that is least descriptive of the employee's behavior. This method has an unusual feature: The rater does not know the weighted values of the behavior statements when the employee is being evaluated. Following the evaluation, the values of the items chosen by the rater are summed (usually by the human resources staff) to yield an overall index of the employee's performance.

The forced-choice system is less vulnerable than other methods to halo error and central-tendency measurement problems, but the system is time consuming to develop and maintain. In addition, raters may lack confidence in the system because they do not know the values of their ratings.[33] Finally, the forced-choice system has been less useful than other methods for performance development and improvement, because the result of the evaluation is an overall index of

32. Milkovich and Boudreau, *Personnel/Human Management,* pp. 201–202.
33. Bernardin and Beatty, *Performance Appraisal.*

performance rather than a set of behavioral statements that can be reviewed with the employee.

Management by Objectives The final individual method of evaluation, *management by objectives,* or *MBO,* measures task outcomes rather than behaviors. Chapter 12 discussed MBO in detail as a goal-setting tool; this section reviews its positive and negative aspects as a performance appraisal system. If the goals set for employees are specific and measurable, the MBO system avoids the validity, reliability, and halo error problems of other appraisal methods. Moreover, an MBO system can provide useful feedback for employee development and performance improvement. Because performance goals differ for each employee, however, results cannot easily be compared. In addition, the mechanics of the MBO system—the cycle of goal setting, discussion, reporting, and review—demand a considerable amount of time and paperwork.

Comparative Evaluation

The appraisal methods discussed so far evaluate employees one at a time. Other methods require the comparative evaluation of two or more employees. In general, these methods were developed to eliminate the central-tendency problem and to provide information useful for reward allocation decisions.

Ranking *Ranking* involves arranging all employees in the same job classification in order of their performance. Most such systems use only one global criterion of performance. The rater reflects on the performance of the employees and assigns them rankings. Since most raters find it easy to identify the best and worst performers, it may be easier to rank the top and bottom performers first and then work toward the middle.

- Ranking provides information about the relative differences among employees but may make the differences seem too simple.

Ranking provides information regarding the relative performances of employees (a notable weakness of most individual methods) and by definition eliminates the central-tendency measurement problem. But ranking does have drawbacks. Rankings based on a single global performance criterion tend to reduce a very complex set of behaviors to a single number, making the method particularly vulnerable to halo error bias. Also, it is difficult to use a ranking procedure for a large number of employees.

Further, rankings cannot reveal the degrees of difference in performance levels. Assume three employees are ranked as follows: Martina first, John second, and Camilla third. From this information, we cannot determine how much better Martina is than John or how much worse Camilla is than John. Martina may be only slightly better than John, and Camilla may be totally incompetent. On the other hand, Martina may be far superior to the other two, who are about even. When human resource decisions on transfers, layoffs, or raises must be made, the decision maker must supplement rankings with additional information. Otherwise, he or she will be forced to base tough decisions on inadequate information. For similar reasons, the ranking method also provides very little information for use in performance improvement or development.

FIGURE 14.9
Examples of Forced-Distribution Ranking Systems

Five Performance Categories with Variable Distribution

Categories	*Poor*	*Below Average*	*Average*	*Above Average*	*Excellent*
Distribution	10%	20%	40%	20%	10%

Three Performance Categories with Equal Distribution

Categories	*Below Average*	*Average*	*Above Average*
Distribution	1/3	1/3	1/3

Forced Distribution The *forced-distribution* method requires the evaluator to assign employees to categories on the basis of their performance but limits the percentage of employees that can be placed in any one category. The organization determines how many categories to use and what percentage of employees to place in each category. For example, as shown in the top of Figure 14.9, the system may require that employees be placed in five categories ranging from *poor* to *excellent*. The percentages are set up to approximate a bell curve, much like the grading scales in some college classes. A second system, illustrated in the bottom part of Figure 14.9, allows only three equal categories.

The forced-distribution method involves some of the same advantages and disadvantages as the ranking method. The central-tendency problem is avoided, but halo error problems may exist. The forced-distribution system avoids at least one difficulty of the ranking method by not requiring the evaluator to assign a discrete number to each individual, even when the performance of two or more individuals is essentially the same. On the other hand, because it places all employees into only a few groups, the forced-distribution method provides even less information than the straight ranking system.

Paired Comparison The third comparative technique, the *paired-comparison* method, calls for the comparison of all employees two at a time.[34] Generally, one evaluator compares his or her ratees two at a time on one global performance criterion. By identifying the better performer in each pair, the evaluator can develop a list similar to the results of the straight ranking method. The advantage of the paired comparison method is that the evaluator is not overwhelmed and possibly confused by having to rank many employees at one time. However, if there are many employees, this method may be cumbersome to use. Halo error problems and limited feedback information are additional disadvantages.

As a whole, the comparative methods incorporate safeguards against the measurement problems of the individual rating systems, such as the restriction of

34. See Henderson, *Performance Appraisal,* for a more detailed discussion of several paired-comparison techniques.

FIGURE 14.10
Examples of Scaled Comparisons Used in the Objective Judgment Quotient (OJQ) Method

Criterion: Problem Solving

a. John Smith	*Much Better*	*Slightly Better*	*Equal*	*Slightly Better*	*Much Better*	Mary Barnes
b. Excellent	*Much Better*	*Slightly Better*	*Equal*	*Slightly Better*	*Much Better*	John Smith
c. Jerry Wood	*Much Better*	*Slightly Better*	*Equal*	*Slightly Better*	*Much Better*	Average
d. Above Average	*Much Better*	*Slightly Better*	*Equal*	*Slightly Better*	*Much Better*	Mary Barnes

range. However, they may yield even less information for decision makers than the individual methods.

Multiple-Rater Comparative Evaluation

Recent years have seen the development of new techniques that combine several evaluation methods. To avoid the problems of halo error and restriction of range as well as certain validity problems, the systems generally use more than one rater. They may also use a comparison procedure to reflect performance differences among employees. One such system is the *objective judgment quotient,* or *OJQ, method.*[35]

With this method, employees participate in the development of job-related criteria for the OJQ evaluation. Then they select several people (generally five to eight), including their supervisor, to evaluate them. The rating form contains several scaled comparison items, examples of which are shown in Figure 14.10. Each rater scores several people on numerous job criteria. The scales for each job dimension compare one person with another and also with descriptive adjectives ranging from *excellent* to *poor.* From these comparisons, a performance profile for each employee is calculated. The performance profile shows the employee how he or she stands on all performance criteria in comparison with all other rated employees.

- Techniques that use multiple raters of performance may be more accurate, but they are also relatively complex to develop and maintain.

The OJQ method provides good safeguards against most of the measurement problems discussed earlier. Because the system requires the manipulation of many rating scores, evaluating numerous employees requires a computer. The system's major problems include the expense of development and maintenance and the reluctance of employees to accept a complex procedure. In particular, supervisors

35. Mark R. Edwards, "OJQ Offers Alternative to Assessment Center," *Public Personnel Management Journal,* vol. 12, 1983, pp. 146–155.

may view the method as a threat to their power because they are no longer the sole evaluators. Finally, this and other new appraisal methods have not been extensively used or tested.

Another evaluation technique that uses multiple raters and usually compares more than one employee involves an assessment center. Many companies use assessment centers for evaluation and development. For example, British Telecom uses a "Development Center," which is similar to traditional assessment centers, to evaluate employee performance and design a unique development path for each participant.[36]

Summary of Key Points

- Performance appraisal is the process by which work behaviors are measured and compared with established standards and the results recorded and communicated. Its purposes are to evaluate employees' work performance and to provide information for organizational uses such as compensation, personnel planning, and employee training and development.
- Three primary issues of performance appraisal are who does the appraisal, how often appraisals should be done, and how the appraisal information should be used. More and more organizations are involving several people familiar with an employee's performance in the evaluation. In addition, it may be necessary to perform evaluations more frequently than the typical once-a-year cycle. Appraisal information is used in giving feedback to the employee, making decisions regarding reward allocation, planning training and development programs, and planning for future personnel needs.
- The elements of performance appraisal are commitment to objectives, job analysis, and measurement. Clear objectives and strong organizational commitment make appraisal systems meaningful to supervisors and employees. Job analysis provides job-based information to be used in developing a performance appraisal system, as well as in writing job or position descriptions. Measurement issues include validity, reliability, bias, restriction of range, halo error, and timing problems.
- Performance can be appraised through individual assessment methods (graphic rating scales, checklists, essays, behaviorally anchored rating scales, forced choice, and management by objectives); comparative techniques (ranking, forced distribution, and paired comparison); and new approaches that use multiple raters and comparative methods. Each method has advantages and disadvantages. Primary disadvantages center on measurement problems such as validity, reliability, personal bias, restriction of range, and halo and timing errors.

---

36. David Roger and Christopher Mabey, "BTs Leap Forward from Assessment Centres," *Personnel Management,* July 1987, pp. 32–35.

Discussion Questions

1. Why are employees not simply left alone to do their jobs instead of being evaluated at regular intervals?
2. In what ways is your performance as a student evaluated?
3. If you have had a performance evaluation in a full-time or part-time job, answer the following questions: (a) What performance appraisal method was used? (b) Was it an appropriate method of evaluation? If your performance in a job has never been evaluated, discuss some of the reasons why not.
4. If you were the manager of a work group, which type of performance appraisal method would you use? Why?
5. Suppose you are president of the college or school you attend. What type of performance appraisal system would you use for your employees? How would the evaluation procedure differ for the football coach, the dean of the college of business, and the head of custodial services?
6. As a middle manager, would you want your subordinates or your peers to participate in evaluating your performance? Why?
7. As a student in this class, would you want your classmates or other students in the school to evaluate your performance? Why or why not?
8. How is the performance appraisal for you in this class associated with the rewards you get? Does this differ from any organizational work experience you have? If so, how?

CASE 14.1

Performance Appraisal in the U.S. Air Force

The performance appraisal system in use in the U.S. Air Force is quite typical of many appraisal systems in other public-sector agencies in the United States. The system requires that the immediate superior of every officer below the rank of general complete a written performance report on each officer annually. The evaluation form, designed by the Military Personnel Center in San Antonio, is used for every officer regardless of rank, seniority, or duty assignment. This means that the same form is used for pilots, doctors, staff officers, and all others whether they are in the field or at headquarters. This annual performance report is the primary basis for decisions on training, retention, job assignments, and promotions.

The form is slightly modified periodically, but it usually consists of eight sections covering basic descriptive information: name; rank; job assignment; rating factors such as leadership, adaptability, job knowledge, planning, and resource management; overall evaluation of military bearing; narrative of critical facts and incidents; evaluation of promotion potential; and rater identification information. Due to the breadth of the coverage, the evaluating officer can describe any one officer's performance only in general terms. One section asks for a general assessment of the individual compared to his or her peers on a ten-point scale.

In the mid-1970s, the appraisal system was criticized for its lack of specificity in defining an officer's job assignments, which resulted in overly subjective and therefore unreliable ratings. For example, rating the leadership abilities of a staff officer to whom no one reported was required, but obviously of little use. In addition, the majority of officers were receiving top ratings in both performance and promotion potential, probably because superior officers recognized the importance of the ratings, especially their impact on an officer's career progress. Thus, rater leniency was becoming a big problem.

These criticisms brought changes that required a forced distribution of officers as "high" and "low" performers in each unit. Only 22 percent of officers could be rated in the highest of six rating categories, 28 percent could be rated in the second highest category, and the remaining 50 percent could be distributed across the last four categories. This procedure was followed as the appraisal was handed upstairs to succeeding levels of officers. Each officer was evaluated by his or her primary superior, an additional rater, and an "endorser." The endorser's ratings usually were the most important, even though the endorser might have had only very cursory knowledge about the rated individual's performance and may not even have been stationed at the same site.

The new forced-distribution aspect of the system soon became the system's most important feature, thereby rendering the other features relatively meaningless. Higher-ups soon focused only on the forced-distribution scale, because that measure made it easy to tell people apart regardless of level and job assignment. In one case, pilots were being selected for an extremely dangerous and difficult mission. Although the selected pilots were chosen because of their standing in the top 1 percent of all pilots, they had to be forced into the specified distribution. The result was that 50 percent of the best Air Force pilots were rated as average or below, whereas less qualified pilots on less dangerous and important tasks were very highly rated. Officers at every level complained. Thus, the solution to the problem of rater leniency had led to another problem.

Case Questions

1. What do you think were some of the problems created by the addition of the forced distribution to the U.S. Air Force performance appraisal system?
2. What impact do you believe the forced-distribution feature of the system would have on officer motivation? Why?
3. How do you think the rating officers reacted to the requirement to force 50 percent of all officers into the average or below categories?

SOURCE: From Mark A. McBriarty, "Performance Appraisal: Some Unintended Consequences," *Public Personnel Management,* Winter 1988, pp. 421–434. Adapted by permission.

CASE 14.2 The Principal's Dilemma

Marion Stanworth had been principal of Chester High School for less than a year. She was more than a little anxious as she sat down to do her first appraisal of the teachers working under her. The anxiety turned to outright dread when Stanworth began to look at the forms she was expected to fill out. She could not remember exactly what kinds of forms her former school had used. Then it had not mattered much, because she knew all the teachers and their supervisors, what their biases were, and how students related to them, and she felt confident that she could make a fair and accurate appraisal no matter what questions the form asked. Now, although she knew all the names and faces she was evaluating, she felt less confident about her overall judgment and had to rely more on the reports the department heads turned in and on the questions on the form—which probably had not been changed, she thought, since the school was built.

She almost gave up and went home when she saw that the first three questions all related to the teacher's appearance: Was the teacher dressed appropriately? Was the teacher neatly groomed? Did the teacher present the proper model of appearance for Chester students to emulate? Stanworth recalled her mental image of Ken Briar, the teacher in question. Was a handlebar mustache the right kind of model for students? Did the fact that he never wore a coat and tie mean that he should get a lower rating than Dick Krebbs, the biology teacher, who wore a bow tie and a white shirt that he could not keep tucked in? And what difference did it make anyway in a high school that recently had passed what she thought of as a minimalist dress code?

Mentally resolving not to let her own values be subverted by those represented in the form, she circled *excellent* for the first three questions and went on, wondering how she came to be doing a multiple-choice test in the first place. The next questions wanted to know about teaching methods, or rather "method"; Stanworth quickly noted that the form assumed all teachers lectured all the time. Did the lectures reach an appropriate conclusion before the bell rang? Did they cover as much material as those of the other teachers of the subject? How was Mr. Briar's enunciation?

Stanworth had been to some of Ken Briar's classes and had been impressed that he had elicited comments from almost every student about the Spanish-American War, but she could remember absolutely nothing about his enunciation. She remembered that students still had their hands raised when the bell rang; clearly the discussion was not finished. Was she supposed to hold that against him?

Hoping to find a question that would allow her to comment on the students' enthusiasm for Briar's class, she scanned the rest of the form. There were a number of questions on discipline: Was the noise level too loud? Did he often send unruly students to her office? When she thought she had seen all the questions about appearance, she found two more about the condition in which Briar kept his homeroom.

Finally, near the end of the form, Stanworth found a question about how the teacher related to students: Does the teacher violate the bounds between teacher and student and appear to pick favorites? After spending some time trying to decide whether *yes* or *no* was more damaging or more honest, she moved on to the last question, which asked for the department chair's rating of the teacher, on a one-to-five scale, and left a half-inch space for "principal's or department chair's comments."

Trying to calm her anger and frustration, Stanworth thought of everything that could be said in favor of the form. It was consistent; she could probably go back forty years and find how the American history teacher in those days had been rated on appearance. It was quick; she could have filled it out in five minutes had she not gotten so upset about it. And it yielded a numerical score, which was important for merit pay purposes.

Unable to face the task any longer, Stanworth threw the form into the trash and called the superintendent of schools to make an appointment to discuss instituting a new evaluation system. She was sure that whatever they came up with would take more time to fill out than the present form, but she knew that even if she spent two hours evaluating Ken Briar, she would feel better about it than if she just circled twenty-five answers and moved on.

Case Questions

1. How valid and reliable is the instrument Stanworth is trying to fill out? What are the sources of the problems?
2. What would be the basis for a better evaluation form in a high school?

EXPERIENTIAL EXERCISE

Purpose: This exercise asks you to apply the concepts of job analysis discussed in the chapter to a job with which you are familiar.

Format: You will form small groups to analyze a job. The results will be presented in class and the findings compared.

Procedure: Each group should choose a job found on or near campus. Following are typical jobs that might be interesting to analyze:

College dean	Bartender
Computer operator	Professor
Graduate teaching assistant	Secretary
Pizza delivery person	Librarian
Professional athlete	Coach
Newspaper editor	Food server

Be sure to choose a job about which you can easily gather good information. You can obtain information by interviewing job holders and others who are familiar with the job, by using a position analysis questionnaire, by observation, or by other methods. Use all available resources, and be creative in your thinking.

There are many ways to organize the information you gather. One is to categorize job activities into tasks that deal with people, data, and things, as is done in Functional Job Analysis (FJA). FJA attempts to identify exactly what the worker does in the job as well as the results of the worker's behavior—what gets done. In addition, FJA examines why the job is done and what tools, equipment, and instructions are available. Finally, it analyzes the job according to how much it involves interacting with people, being familiar with data, and manipulating things.

You can analyze the job you have chosen by answering the questions on the Functional Job Analysis Worksheet that follows. The final section on the worksheet lists activities that deal with data, people, and things. Describe the tasks of the job you have chosen by using words and numbers from each list. Within each category of worker functions, describe the task according to degree of difficulty. Information on the average amount of time the worker spends on each task may be helpful. By categorizing job activities in this way, you will be able to compare the information you have gathered with that developed by other teams. Remember: You are analyzing a job, not the person doing the job. (More information on FJA is available in the library.)

In class, groups will present their findings on the board or on charts. Each group should list the job and the activities and tasks it involves. The group may comment on the difficulty of each task and the job's overall difficulty and may compare job similarities and differences. Groups should share with the class the procedures they used to gather data and comment on the usefulness of each method in generating meaningful information.

Functional Job Analysis Worksheet

Job title
Primary job duties
Performs what action?
To whom or what?
To produce or achieve what?
Using what tools or instructions?

Worker Functions

Data	***People***	***Things***
0 Synthesize	0 Act as mentor	0 Set up
1 Coordinate	1 Negotiate	1 Perform precision work
2 Analyze	2 Instruct	2 Operate, control
3 Compile	3 Supervise	3 Drive, operate
4 Compute	4 Divert	4 Manipulate
5 Copy	5 Persuade	5 Tend
6 Compare	6 Speak-signal	6 Feed
	7 Serve	7 Handle
	8 Take instruction	

Follow-up Questions

1. Were you surprised by the level of difficulty of any of the jobs? Why or why not?
2. Did descriptions of the same job differ depending on the source of the information?
3. Which methods of gathering data seemed to yield the best results?

CHAPTER OUTLINE

- The Nature of Stress
  - *Stress Defined*
  - *Stress and the Individual*
- Common Causes of Stress
  - *Organizational Stressors*
  - *Life Stressors*
- Type A and Type B Personality Profiles
- Consequences of Stress
  - *Individual Consequences*
  - *Organizational Consequences*
  - *Burnout*
- Managing Stress in the Workplace
  - *Individual Coping Strategies*
  - *Organizational Coping Strategies*

15

MANAGING STRESS

CHAPTER OBJECTIVES

After studying this chapter, you should be able to:

Discuss the nature of work stress.

Identify and discuss several causes of stress.

Describe Type A and Type B personality profiles.

Identify and discuss several consequences of stress.

Explain ways to manage stress.

Food Lion Inc. is one of the fastest growing grocery chains in the United States. In 1989, the firm had total sales of almost $5 billion. During the 1980s, the number of Food Lion stores expanded from 106 to 663, and the company plans to open 100 or more each year during the rest of this century. In 1990, the firm had total sales of over $5 billion.

The firm has achieved this remarkable growth pattern through relentless cost control and efficiency measures. The firm's profit margins are twice the industry average. Some critics charge, however, that Food Lion employees are paying a substantial price for its growth.

Each Food Lion store manager is allocated a certain number of labor hours each week. The allocation is based on projected sales for the week and the number of items scanned at cash registers the previous week. The manager has to live within this budget. As a result, employees complain of unrelenting pressure and little slack. For example, baggers are taught to fill bags with two hands, and stockers are expected to reload shelves at the rate of fifty cases an hour.

One meat department manager recently quit because of the pressure. He noted that in his previous job with Kroger, he supervised three other meat cutters. At Food Lion, he was expected to do the same volume of work with only a single part-time assistant.

Managers also are under tremendous pressure. If they use up their labor hours, they have to pitch in themselves to get the work done. A store manager who also recently quit complained that she could never satisfy her supervisor regardless of the number of hours she worked each week. Toward the end of her time with the firm, she was averaging one hundred hours of work per week.[1]

The situation at Food Lion is perhaps a bit extreme, but it is not unusual. Organizations and the people who run them are under constant pressure to increase income while keeping costs in check. A common pitfall is to put too much pressure on people—operating employees, other managers, and oneself. The results can be higher profits and faster growth, but stress, burnout, turnover, and other unpleasant side effects also can occur.

In this chapter, we examine a number of insights into stress in the workplace. First, we explore the nature of stress. Next, we identify and discuss a number of

1. Thomas A. Stewart, "Do You Push Your People Too Hard?" *Fortune*, October 22, 1990, pp. 121–128. Gary Hoover, Alta Campbell, and Patrick J. Spain, eds., *Hoover's Handbook—Profiles of Over 500 Major Corporations* (Austin, Tex.: The Reference Press, 1990), p. 241.

Traders involved with the New York Stock Exchange experience considerable stress as they compete with one another on the floor of the exchange to buy and sell stock at the best prices. Workers involved in hazardous outdoor construction projects such as this 190-mile long high voltage transmission line in Utah also experience stress. While the jobs of these two sets of people are considerably different, stress is a common denominator.

causes of stress. Then we describe Type A and Type B personality profiles, an approach to understanding why some people are more prone to stress than others. Next, we consider the potential consequences of stress. Finally, we highlight several things people and organizations can do to effectively manage stress at work.

The Nature of Stress

Many people think they understand stress. In reality, however, stress is complex and often misunderstood. To learn how job stress truly works, we must first define it and then relate it to the individual in the workplace.

Stress Defined

Stress has been defined in many ways, but most definitions say that stress is caused by a stimulus, that the stimulus can be either physical or psychological, and that the individual responds to the stimulus in some way.[2] Here, then, we

2. See James C. Quick and Jonathan D. Quick, *Organizational Stress and Preventive Management* (New York: McGraw-Hill, 1984), for a review.

■ **Stress** is a person's adaptive response to a stimulus that places excessive psychological or physical demands on that person.

define **stress** as a person's adaptive response to a stimulus that places excessive psychological or physical demands on him or her.

Given the underlying complexities of this definition, we need to examine its components carefully. First is the notion of adaptation. As we discuss shortly, people adapt to stressful circumstances in any of several ways. Second is the role of the stimulus. This stimulus, generally called a stressor, is anything that induces stress. Third, stressors can be either psychological or physical. Finally, the demands placed on the individual by the stressor must be excessive for stress to result. Of course, what is excessive for one person may be perfectly tolerable for another. Thus, the point is simply that a person must perceive the demands as excessive or stress will not result.

Stress and the Individual

Much of what we know about stress today can be traced to the pioneering work of Dr. Hans Selye.[3] Selye identified what he called the *general adaptation syndrome* and the concepts of *eustress* and *distress*.

■ The **general adaptation syndrome (GAS)** identifies three stages of response to a stressor: alarm, resistance, and exhaustion.

General Adaptation Syndrome Figure 15.1 graphically shows the **general adaptation syndrome** (GAS). According to this view, each of us has a normal level of resistance to stressful events. Some of us can tolerate a great deal of stress and others much less, but we all have a basic threshold at which stress starts to affect us.

The GAS begins when a person first encounters a stressor. The first stage is called *alarm*. At this point, the person may feel some degree of panic, may wonder how to cope, and so forth. The individual may also have to resolve a "fight-or-flee" question. Can I deal with this, or should I run away? For example, suppose a manager is assigned a lengthy report to write overnight. Her first reaction may be "How will I ever get this done by tomorrow?"

If the stressor is too extreme, the person may simply be unable to cope with it. In most cases, however, the individual gathers his or her strength (physical or emotional) and *resists* the negative effects of the stressor. The manager with the long report to write may calm down, call home to say she is working late, roll up her sleeves, order out for dinner, and get to work. Thus, at stage 2 of the GAS, the person is resisting the effects of the stressor.

In many cases, the resistance phase ends the GAS. If our manager completes the report earlier than she expected, she may drop it in her briefcase, smile to herself, and head home tired but happy. On the other hand, prolonged exposure to a stressor without resolution may bring on phase 3 of the GAS: *exhaustion*. At this stage, the person literally gives up and can no longer fight the stressor. Our manager may fall asleep at her desk at 3 A.M. and fail to finish the report.

3. Hans Selye, *The Stress of Life* (New York: McGraw-Hill, 1976).

FIGURE 15.1
The General Adaptation Syndrome (GAS)

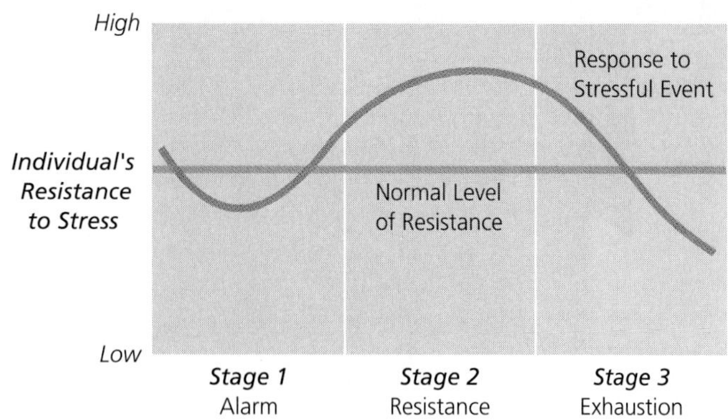

Distress and Eustress Selye also pointed out that the sources of stress need not be bad.[4] For example, receiving a bonus and then having to decide what to do with the money can be stressful. So can getting a promotion, gaining recognition, getting married, and similar "good" things. Selye called this type of stress **eustress.** As we will see later, eustress can lead to a number of positive outcomes for the individual.

- **Eustress** is the pleasurable stress that accompanies positive events.
- **Distress** is the unpleasant stress that accompanies negative events.

Of course, there is also negative stress. Called **distress,** this is what most people think of when they hear the word *stress*. Excessive pressure, unreasonable demands on our time, bad news, and so forth all fall into this category. As the term suggests, this form of stress generally results in negative consequences for the individual.

For purposes of simplicity, we will continue to use the simple term *stress*. It is important to remember throughout our discussion, however, that stress can be either good or bad. It can motivate and stimulate us, or it can lead to any number of dangerous side effects.

- Individual differences affect how people respond to stressors.

Individual Differences It is also important to note the effects of individual differences on stress. We already noted that people differ in their normal levels of resistance to stressors. The distinction between Type A and Type B personalities, discussed more fully later, is important in this regard.

Cultural differences also are important in determining how stress affects people. For example, as detailed more fully in *International Perspective*, research by Cary Cooper suggests that American executives may experience less stress than executives in many other countries, including Japan and Brazil.

Still other research suggests that women are perhaps more prone to experience the psychological effects of stress, whereas men may report more physical effects.[5] Finally, some studies suggest that people who see themselves as complex

4. Ibid.

5. Todd D. Jick and Linda F. Mitz, "Sex Differences in Work Stress," *Academy of Management Review,* October 1985, pp. 408–420; Debra L. Nelson and James C. Quick, "Professional Women: Are Distress and Disease Inevitable?", *Academy of Management Review,* April 1985, pp. 206–218.

INTERNATIONAL PERSPECTIVE

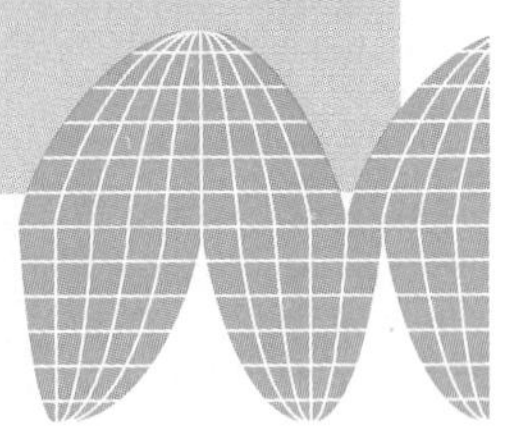

Stress Around the World

Executive stress is considered something that only afflicts U.S. managers. The stereotype of U.S. executives portrays the workaholic rushing around all day, smoking and drinking excessively, always under pressure and frequently headed toward a stress-related heart attack.

Work-related stress does cost corporations big bucks: In lost employment and decreased productivity, alcoholism costs U.S. industry $55 billion a year, according to a report of the National Institute for Occupational Safety and Health's symposium on strategy for reducing psychological disorders in the workplace.

In reality, however, the United States "comes out pretty good," when compared with other countries, said Dr. Cary L. Cooper, professor of organizational psychology at the University of Manchester's Institute of Science and Technology in Great Britain.

Based on data he collected from 1,100 senior executives in 10 countries, Cooper says executive stress has no geographical boundaries and is not limited to the Western world.

"The pressures on managers to perform in a climate of rapid sociological, technological and economic change in emerging countries such as Brazil, Nigeria, Egypt and Singapore, as well as Japan, are beginning to produce negative effects," Cooper said in the introduction to his research, "Executive Stress: A Ten-Country Comparison."

Surprisingly, the countries that emerge with good ratings for mental health and job satisfaction are Britain, West Germany and the U.S. "The country whose executives suffer the least stress is Sweden," Cooper said in a telephone interview. "They have the best mental health and are most satisfied with their lifestyles."

Cooper was surprised about the findings concerning Japanese executives and stress. "Everyone assumes the Japanese are so productive that they should be in good shape," he said. "In terms of mental health, 32 of the Japanese executives had mental ill-health scores that came close to . . . those of psychiatric outpatients."

On the other hand, the United States, West Germany and Sweden reflect overall mental health and well-being. Cooper bases his mental health percentages on the results of a questionnaire devised to measure depression, anxiety and psychosomatic tendencies.

"It's interesting to note the high levels of dissatisfaction among Japanese executives, who are internationally stereotyped as 'committed and job-satisfied,'" Cooper said. "Social institutions support executives and encourage hard work and loyalty, but many Japanese executives are beginning to experience the competitiveness of Americans and Western Europeans."

Even though U.S. executives "look good" in terms of mental health, they complain about sources of pressure at work, the study shows. U.S. executives feel considerable pressure related to business ethics, Cooper said. The United States leads the world, at 30 percent, he says, "with stress from what executives internally believe is right and just, contrasted with having to adhere to corporate expectations."

The major causes of stress among executives in the other nations reported in Cooper's survey:

- Sweden: encroachment of work on private lives.
- West Germany: time pressures and deadlines.
- Britain: keeping up with technology.
- South Africa: long hours.
- Nigeria: inadequately trained underlings.
- Brazil: time pressures and deadlines.
- Egypt: work overload and taking work home.

SOURCE: By Carol Kleiman, from *The Chicago Tribune,* March 31, 1988.

individuals are better able to handle stress than are people who view themselves as relatively simple.[6] We should add, however, that the study of individual differences in stress is still in its infancy. It therefore would be premature to draw rigid conclusions about how different types of people handle stress.

Common Causes of Stress

Many things can cause stress. Figure 15.2 shows two broad categories: organizational stressors and life stressors. It also shows three categories of stress consequences: individual consequences, organizational consequences, and burnout.

■ Basic **organizational stressors** include **task demands, physical demands, role demands,** and **interpersonal demands.**

Organizational Stressors

Organizational stressors are various factors in the workplace that can cause stress. Four general sets of organizational stressors are task demands, physical demands, role demands, and interpersonal demands.[7]

Task Demands **Task demands** are stressors associated with the specific job a person performs. Some occupations are by nature more stressful than others. The jobs of a surgeon, air traffic controller, and professional football coach obviously are more stressful than those of a general practitioner, airplane baggage loader, and football team equipment manager.

Beyond specific task-related pressures, other task demands may pose physical threats to a person's health. Such conditions exist in occupations like coal mining, toxic waste handling, and so forth. Indeed, one recent survey placed the jobs of a miner and a police officer among the ten most stressful jobs in U.S. industry.[8]

Security is another task demand that can cause stress. Someone in a relatively secure job is not likely to worry unduly about losing that position. On the other hand, if job security is threatened stress can increase dramatically. For example, stress generally increases throughout an organization during a period of layoffs or immediately following a merger with another firm. Such a phenomenon has been observed at a number of organizations, including AT&T, Safeway, and Digital Equipment.[9]

The final task demand stressor is overload. Overload occurs when a person simply has more work to do than he or she can handle. The overload can be

6. "Complex Characters Handle Stress Better," *Psychology Today,* October 1987, p. 26.

7. Selye, *Stress of Life.* See also Stephan J. Motowidlo, John S. Packard, and Michael R. Manning, "Occupational Stress: Its Causes and Consequences for Job Performance," *Journal of Applied Psychology,* vol. 71, 1986, pp. 618–629.

8. "Stress on the Job," *Newsweek,* April 25, 1988, pp. 40–45.

9. "Corporate Mergers Take a Toll on Employees in Lost Jobs and Family Strain," *The Wall Street Journal,* September 9, 1986, p. 1.

FIGURE 15.2
Causes and Consequences of Stress

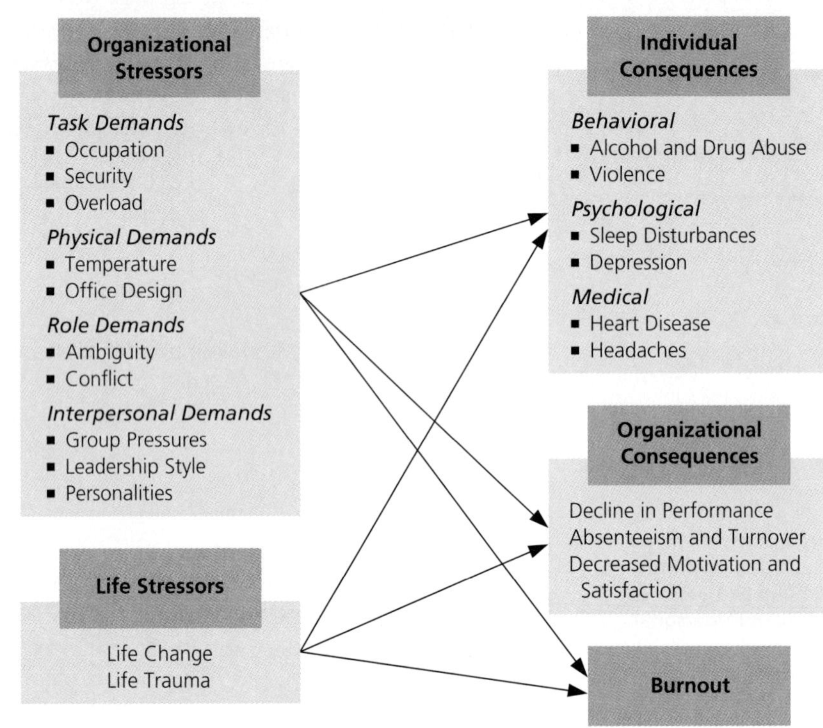

SOURCE: Adapted from James C. Quick and Jonathan D. Quick, *Organizational Stress and Preventive Management,* McGraw-Hill, 1984, pp. 19, 44, and 76. Reprinted with permission of McGraw-Hill, Inc.

either quantitative (the individual has too many tasks to perform or too little time in which to perform them) or qualitative (the person may believe she or he lacks the ability to do the job). We should also note that the opposite of overload may also be undesirable. As Figure 15.3 shows, low task demands can result in boredom and apathy just as overload can cause tension and anxiety. Thus, a moderate degree of workload-related stress is optimal, because it leads to high levels of energy and motivation.

Physical Demands **Physical demands** relate to the setting of the job. One important element is temperature. Working outdoors in extreme temperatures can result in stress, as can an improperly heated or cooled office. Strenuous labor such as loading heavy cargo or lifting packages can lead to similar results.

Office design also can be a problem. A poorly designed office can make it difficult for people to have privacy or promote too much or too little social interaction. Too much interaction may distract a person from his or her task, while too little may lead to boredom or loneliness. Likewise, poor lighting, inadequate work surfaces, and so forth can create stress.[10]

10. Robert I. Sutton and Anat Rafaeli, "Characteristics of Work Stations as Potential Occupational Stressors," *Academy of Management Journal,* June 1987, pp. 260–276.

FIGURE 15.3
Workload, Stress, and Performance

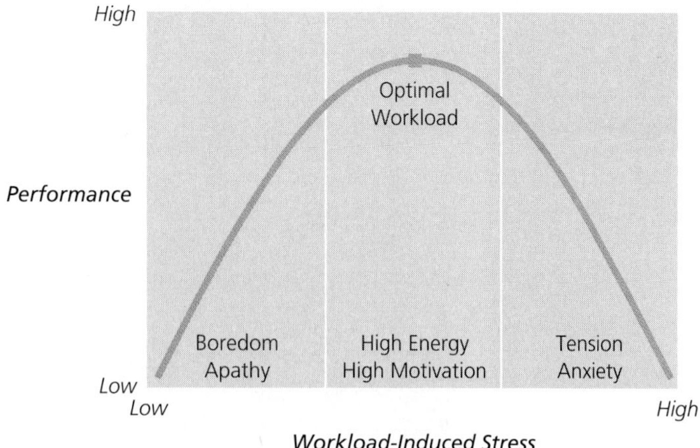

Role Demands **Role demands** also can be stressful to people in organizations. As we discussed in Chapter 7, a role is a set of expected behaviors associated with a particular position in a group or organization. A person may experience stress from either *role ambiguity* (a lack of clarity as to what is expected) or *role conflict* (incongruence among two or more roles).[11]

Interpersonal Demands A final set of organizational stressors consists of three **interpersonal demands.** Group pressures include pressure to restrict output, pressure to conform to the group's norms, and so forth. For instance, as we have noted before, it is quite common for a work group to arrive at an informal agreement about how much each member will produce. Individuals who produce much more or much less than this level may be pressured by the group to get back in line. An individual who feels a strong need to vary from the group's expectations (perhaps to get a pay raise or promotion) will experience a great deal of stress, especially if acceptance by the group also is important to him or her.

Leadership style also may cause stress. Suppose an employee needs a great deal of social support from his leader. The leader, however, is quite brusque and shows no concern or compassion for him. This employee will likely feel stressed. Similarly, assume an employee feels a strong need to participate in decision making and to be active in all aspects of management. Her boss is very autocratic and refuses to consult subordinates about anything. Once again stress is likely to result.[12]

Finally, conflicting personalities and behaviors may cause stress. Conflict can occur when two or more people must work together even though their

---

11. See Edward R. Kemery, Arthur G. Bedeian, Kevin W. Mossholder, and John Touliatos, "Outcomes of Role Stress: A Multisample Constructive Replication," *Academy of Management Journal,* June 1985, pp. 363–375, for a recent examination of the effects of role demands.

12. See Gary M. Kaufman and Terry A. Beehr, "Interactions between Job Stressors and Social Support: Some Counterintuitive Results," *Journal of Applied Psychology,* vol. 71, 1986, pp. 522–526, for an interesting study in this area.

Joe Fernandez was recently appointed chancellor of New York City's schools. The troubled school system is plagued by a budget crisis, a bureaucratic governing structure, and a poverty-ridden student body. The task demands placed on Fernandez are incredible. To help cope with the job, he is presently working twelve hour days and personally oversees many day-to-day activities previously delegated to others. He admits the stress gets to him sometimes, but he also feels he is making progress in transforming the city's school system.

personalities, attitudes, and behaviors differ. For example, a person with an internal locus of control—that is, who always wants to control how things turn out—might get frustrated working with an external person who likes to wait and just let things happen. Likewise, a smoker and a nonsmoker who are assigned adjacent offices obviously will experience stress.[13]

Life Stressors

- Common **life stressors** include **life change** and **life trauma.**

Stress in organizational settings also can be influenced by events that take place outside the organization. **Life stressors** generally are categorized in terms of life change and life trauma.[14]

Life Change Thomas Holmes and Richard Rahe first developed and popularized the notion of life change as a source of stress.[15] **Life change** is any meaningful change in a person's personal or work situation. Holmes and Rahe reasoned that major changes in a person's life can lead to stress and eventually to disease. Table 15.1 summarizes their findings on major life change events. Note that

13. David R. Frew and Nealia S. Bruning, "Perceived Organizational Characteristics and Personality Measures as Predictors of Stress/Strain in the Work Place," *Academy of Management Journal,* December 1987, pp. 633–646.

14. Quick and Quick, *Organizational Stress and Preventive Management.*

15. Thomas H. Holmes and Richard H. Rahe, "The Social Readjustment Rating Scale," *Journal of Psychosomatic Research,* vol. 11, 1967, pp. 213–218.

TABLE 15.1
Life Changes and Life Change Units

Rank	Life Event	Mean Value
1	Death of spouse	100
2	Divorce	73
3	Marital separation	65
4	Jail term	63
5	Death of close family member	63
6	Personal injury or illness	53
7	Marriage	50
8	Fired at work	47
9	Marital reconciliation	45
10	Retirement	45
11	Change in health of family member	44
12	Pregnancy	40
13	Sex difficulties	39
14	Gain of new family member	39
15	Business readjustment	39
16	Change in financial state	38
17	Death of close friend	37
18	Change to different line of work	36
19	Change in number of arguments with spouse	35
20	Mortgage over $10,000	31
21	Foreclosure of mortgage or loan	30
22	Change in responsibilities at work	29
23	Son or daughter leaving home	29
24	Trouble with in-laws	29
25	Outstanding personal achievement	28
26	Spouse beginning or stopping work	26
27	Beginning or ending school	26
28	Change in living conditions	25
29	Revision of personal habits	24
30	Trouble with boss	23
31	Change in work hours or conditions	20
32	Change in residence	20
33	Change in schools	20
34	Change in recreation	19
35	Change in church activities	19
36	Change in social activities	18
37	Mortgage or loan less than $10,000	17
38	Change in sleeping habits	16
39	Change in number of family get-togethers	15
40	Change in eating habits	15
41	Vacation	13
42	Christmas	12
43	Minor violations of the law	11

The amount of life stress that a person has experienced in a given period of time, say one year, is measured by the total number of life change units (LCUs). These units result from the addition of the values (shown in the right-hand column) associated with events that the person has experienced during the target time period.

SOURCE: Reprinted with permission from *Journal of Psychosomatic Research,* Vol. 11, pp. 213–218, Thomas H. Holmes and Richard H. Rahe, "The Social Adjustment Rating Scale," Copyright 1967, Pergamon Press plc.

several of these events relate directly (fired from work, retirement) or indirectly (change in residence) to work.

Each event's point value supposedly reflects the event's impact on the individual. At one extreme, a spouse's death, assumed to be the most traumatic event considered, is assigned a point value of 100. At the other extreme, minor violations of the law carry only 11 points. The points themselves represent life change units, or LCUs. Note also that the list includes negative events (divorce and trouble with the boss) as well as positive ones (marriage and vacations).

Holmes and Rahe argued that a person can handle a certain threshold of LCUs, but beyond that level problems can set in. In particular, they suggest that people who encounter more than 150 LCUs in a given year will experience a decline in their health the following year. A score of between 150 and 300 LCUs supposedly carries a 50 percent chance of major illness, while the chance of major illness is said to increase to 70 percent if the number of LCUs exceeds 300.

These ideas offer some insight into the potential impact of stress and underscore our limitations in coping with stressful events. However, research on Holmes and Rahe's proposals has provided only mixed support. An avenue that does seem promising, however, is based on the notion of hardiness.

The *hardiness* approach suggests that some people have what are termed *hardier* personalities than others do. People with hardy personalities have an internal locus of control, are strongly committed to the activities in their lives, and view change as an opportunity for advancement and growth. Such people are seen as less likely to suffer illness if they experience high levels of LCUs, whereas people with low hardiness may be more susceptible to the predicted effects of high LCUs.[16]

Life Trauma Approaching individual stress in terms of life trauma is similar to using the notion of life change. However, it also has a narrower, more direct, and shorter-term focus. A **life trauma** is any upheaval in an individual's life that alters his or her attitudes, emotions, or behaviors.

To illustrate, according to the life change view, a divorce adds to a person's potential for health problems in the following year. At the same time, obviously, the person will also experience emotional turmoil during the actual divorce process itself. This turmoil, the focus of the term *life trauma,* clearly will cause stress, much of which may spill over into the workplace.[17]

Major life traumas that may cause stress include marital problems, family difficulties, and health problems initially unrelated to stress. For example, sup-

---

16. Susan C. Kobasa, "Stressful Life Events, Personality, and Health: An Inquiry into Hardiness," *Journal of Personality and Social Psychology,* January 1979, pp. 1–11; Susan C. Kobasa, S. R. Maddi, and S. Kahn, "Hardiness and Health: A Prospective Study," *Journal of Personality and Social Psychology,* January 1982, pp. 168–177.

17. Evelyn J. Bromet, Mary A. Dew, David K. Parkinson, and Herbert C. Schulberg, "Predictive Effects of Occupational and Marital Stress on the Mental Health of a Male Workforce," *Journal of Organizational Behavior,* vol. 9, 1988, pp. 1–13.

pose a person learns she has developed arthritis that will limit her favorite activity, skiing. Her dismay over the news may translate into stress at work.

Type A and Type B Personality Profiles

As we noted earlier, not everyone responds to stress in the same way. In fact, virtually every aspect of stress, from what triggers it to its consequences, can vary from person to person. One line of thinking about systematic differences among people is in terms of *Type A* and *Type B* personality profiles.

The Type A and Type B profiles were first observed by two cardiologists, Meyer Friedman and Ray Rosenman.[18] The idea started when a worker repairing the upholstery on their waiting room chairs noted that many of the chairs were worn only on the front. This suggested to the two cardiologists that many heart patients were anxious and had a hard time sitting still.

Using this observation as a starting point, and based on their own clinical practice, Friedman and Rosenman concluded that their patients exhibited two very different types of behavior patterns. Their research led them to conclude that the differences were personality based. Figure 15.4 shows the basic behavioral characteristics of Type A and Type B individuals.

- **Type A** people are extremely competitive, are highly committed to work, and have a strong sense of time urgency.
- **Type B** people are less competitive, are less committed to work, and have a weaker sense of time urgency.

The **Type A** individual is extremely competitive, is very devoted to work, and has a strong sense of time urgency. Moreover, this individual is likely to be aggressive, impatient, and highly work oriented. He or she has a lot of drive and wants to accomplish as much as possible in as short a time as possible.

The **Type B** person, in contrast, is less competitive, is less devoted to work, and has a weaker sense of time urgency. This person feels less conflict with either people or time and has a more balanced, relaxed approach to life. She or he has more confidence and is able to work at a constant pace. Finally, the Type B person is not necessarily any more or less successful than the Type A individual.

Friedman and Rosenman point out that people are not purely Type A or Type B; instead, people tend toward one or the other type. This is reflected in Figure 15.4 by the overlap between the profiles. For example, an individual might exhibit marked Type A characteristics much of the time but still be able to relax once in awhile and even forget about time in a few situations.

Early research by Friedman and Rosenman on the Type A and Type B profile differences yielded some alarming findings. In particular, it was argued that Type As were much more likely to experience coronary heart disease than were Type Bs.[19] In recent years, however, follow-up research by other scientists suggests that the relationship between Type A behavior and the risk of coronary heart disease is not all that straightforward.[20]

---

18. Meyer Friedman and Ray H. Rosenman, *Type A Behavior and Your Heart* (New York: Knopf, 1974).

19. Ibid.

20. Joshua Fischman, "Type A on Trial," *Psychology Today,* February 1987, pp. 42–50.

FIGURE 15.4
Type A and Type B Personality Profiles

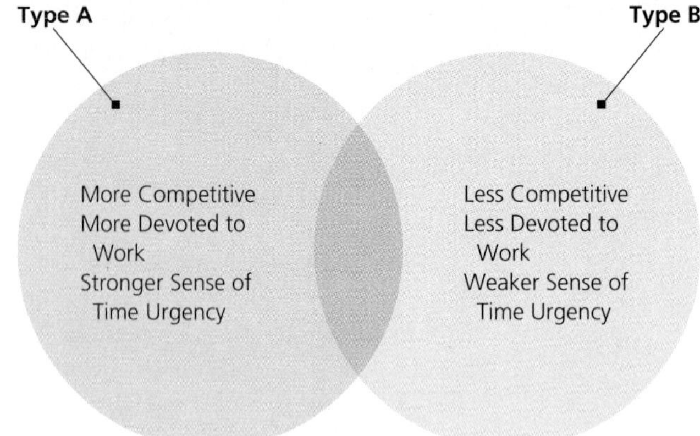

Although the reasons are unclear, recent findings suggest that Type As are much more complex than originally believed. They not only exhibit the traits noted in Figure 15.4 but are also likely to be depressed and hostile. Any one or a combination of these feelings can lead to heart problems. Moreover, different approaches to measuring Type A tendencies have yielded different results.

Finally, in one study that found Type As to actually be *less* susceptible to heart problems than Type Bs, the researchers nevertheless offered an explanation consistent with earlier thinking: Because Type As are compulsive, they seek treatment earlier and are more likely to follow their doctors' orders![21] *Developing Management Skills* will help you develop some insights into your own mix of Type A and Type B tendencies.

Consequences of Stress

A number of consequences can result from stress. As we already noted, if the stress is positive, the result may be more energy, enthusiasm, and motivation. Of more concern, of course, are the negative consequences of stress. Referring back to Figure 15.2, three sets of consequences that can result from stress are individual consequences, organizational consequences, and burnout.[22]

We should first note that many of the factors listed are obviously interrelated. For example, alcohol abuse is shown as an individual consequence. Yet alcohol abuse by an employee is also of consequence to the organization. An employee who drinks on the job may perform poorly and create a hazard for others. If the category for a consequence seems somewhat arbitrary, be aware that each consequence is categorized according to its *primary* constituent.

21. "Prognosis for the 'Type A' Personality Improves in a New Heart Disease Study," *The Wall Street Journal,* January 14, 1988, p. 27.

22. Quick and Quick, *Organizational Stress and Preventive Management.* See also John M. Ivancevich and Michael T. Matteson, *Stress and Work: A Managerial Perspective* (Glenview, Ill.: Scott, Foresman, 1980).

DEVELOPING MANAGEMENT SKILLS

Type A or Type B?

This test below will help you develop insights into your own tendencies toward Type A or Type B behavior patterns. Answer the questions honestly and accurately. Then calculate your score according to the instructions that follow the questions. Discuss your results with a classmate. Critique each other's answers and see if you can help the other person develop a strategy for reducing Type A tendencies. Choose from the following responses to answer the questions below:

a. Almost always true c. Seldom true
b. Usually true d. Never true

_____ 1. I do not like to wait for other people to complete their work before I can proceed with mine.
_____ 2. I hate to wait in most lines.
_____ 3. People tell me that I tend to get irritated too easily.
_____ 4. Whenever possible I try to make activities competitive.
_____ 5. I have a tendency to rush into work that needs to be done before knowing the procedure I will use to complete the job.
_____ 6. Even when I go on vacation, I usually take some work along.
_____ 7. When I make a mistake, it is usually due to the fact that I have rushed into the job before completely planning it through.
_____ 8. I feel guilty for taking time off from work.
_____ 9. People tell me I have a bad temper when it comes to competitive situations.
_____10. I tend to lose my temper when I am under a lot of pressure at work.
_____11. Whenever possible, I will attempt to complete two or more tasks at once.
_____12. I tend to race against the clock.
_____13. I have no patience for lateness.
_____14. I catch myself rushing when there is no need.

Score your responses according to the following key:

- *An intense sense of time urgency* is a tendency to race against the clock, even when there is little reason to. The person feels a need to hurry for hurry's sake alone, and this tendency has appropriately been called "hurry sickness." Time urgency is measured by items 1, 2, 8, 12, 13, and 14. Every A or B answer to these six questions scores one point.
- *Inappropriate aggression and hostility* reveals itself in a person who is excessively competitive and who cannot do anything for fun. This inappropriately aggressive behavior easily evolves into frequent displays of hostility, usually at the slightest provocation or frustration. Competitiveness and hostility is measured by items 3, 4, 9, and 10. Every A or B answer scores one point.
- *Polyphasic behavior* refers to the tendency to undertake two or more tasks simultaneously at inappropriate times. It usually results in wasted time due to an inability to complete the tasks. This behavior is measured by items 6 and 11. Every A or B answer scores one point.
- *Goal directedness without proper planning* refers to the tendency of an individual to rush into work without really knowing how to accomplish the desired result. This usually results in incomplete work or work with many errors, which in turn leads to wasted time, energy, and money. Lack of planning is measured by items 5 and 7. Every A or B response scores one point.

TOTAL SCORE = ____

If your score is 5 or greater, you may possess some basic components of the Type A personality.

SOURCE: Girdano/Everly/Dusek, *Controlling Stress and Tension: A Holistic Approach,* 3/e, © 1990, p. 117. Adapted by permission of Prentice-Hall, Englewood Cliffs, New Jersey.

Individual Consequences

■ Individual consequences of stress can be behavioral, psychological, or medical.

Individual consequences of stress, then, are those outcomes that mainly affect the individual. The organization also may suffer, either directly or indirectly, but it is the individual who pays the real price. Three categories of individual consequences of stress are behavioral, psychological, and medical.

Behavioral Consequences *Behavioral consequences* of stress are responses that may harm the person under stress or others. One such behavior is smoking. Research has clearly documented that people who smoke tend to smoke more when they experience stress. There is also evidence that alcohol and drug abuse are linked to stress, although this relationship is less documented.[23] Other possible behavioral consequences are accident proneness, violence, and appetite disorders.

Psychological Consequences *Psychological consequences* of stress relate to an individual's mental health and well-being. When people experience too much stress at work, they may become depressed or may find themselves sleeping too much or not enough. Stress may also lead to family problems and sexual difficulties.[24]

Medical Consequences The *medical consequences* of stress affect a person's physical well-being. Heart disease and stroke, among other illnesses, have been linked to stress. Other common medical problems resulting from too much stress include headaches, backaches, ulcers and related stomach and intestinal disorders, and skin conditions like acne and hives.[25]

Organizational Consequences

■ Organizational consequences of stress can involve performance decline, withdrawal, or unfavorable changes in attitudes.

Clearly, any of the individual consequences just discussed can also affect the organization. Still other consequences of stress have even more direct consequences for organizations. These include decline in performance, withdrawal, and negative changes in attitudes.

Performance One clear organizational consequence of too much stress is a *decline in performance*. For operating workers, such a decline can translate into poor-quality work or a drop in productivity. For managers, it can mean faulty decision making or disruptions in working relationships as people become irritable and hard to get along with.

Withdrawal *Withdrawal* behaviors also can result from stress. For the organization, the two most significant forms of withdrawal behavior are absenteeism

---

23. Quick and Quick, *Organizational Stress and Preventive Management.*

24. Ibid.

25. Ibid.

Burnout is a major consequence of stress. This phenomenon is increasingly finding its way into the clergy. Ministers are reporting that they are finding it harder and harder to cope with the stress they encounter as they counsel, preach, teach, and minister to others. Roy Oswald, a consultant to The Alban Institute, estimates that as many as 17 percent of the clergy may be suffering from burnout.

and quitting. People who are having a hard time coping with stress in their jobs are more likely to call in sick or consider leaving the organization for good. Other, more subtle forms of withdrawal also can result from stress. A manager may start missing deadlines or taking longer lunch breaks. An employee may withdraw psychologically by ceasing to care about the organization and the job.[26]

Attitudes Another direct organizational consequence of employee stress relates to *attitudes*. As we just noted, job satisfaction, morale, and organizational commitment can all suffer, along with motivation to perform at high levels. As a result, people may be more prone to complain about unimportant things, do only enough work to get by, and so forth.

Burnout

- **Burnout** is a general feeling of exhaustion that develops when an individual simultaneously experiences too much pressure and too few sources of satisfaction.

A final consequence of stress has implications for both people and organizations. **Burnout** is a general feeling of exhaustion that develops when an individual simultaneously experiences too much pressure and too few sources of satisfaction.[27]

Burnout generally develops in the following way.[28] First, people with high aspirations and strong motivation to get things done are prime candidates for

26. Quick and Quick, *Organizational Stress and Preventive Management.* See also "Stress: The Test Americans Are Failing," *Business Week,* April 18, 1988, pp. 74–76.

27. Leonard Moss, *Management Stress* (Reading, Mass.: Addison-Wesley, 1981).

28. See Susan E. Jackson, Richard L. Schwab, and Randall S. Schuler, "Toward an Understanding of the Burnout Phenomenon," *Journal of Applied Psychology,* vol. 71, 1986, pp. 630–640, and Daniel W. Russell, Elizabeth Altmaier, and Dawn Van Velzen, "Job-Related Stress, Social Support, and Burnout among Classroom Teachers," *Journal of Applied Psychology,* vol. 72, 1987, pp. 269–274.

South Korean employees have found a new way to relieve the stress of the workday. Rather than drink away their tensions in bars, many employees now go to indoor fishing pools, where for $7 they get a bamboo rod and bait and one hour to cast for bass, trout, and other fish. For another $6, the fish caught will be cleaned, sliced, and served for dinner. Employers are finding that the fishing pools help employees learn to relax.

burnout under certain conditions. They are especially vulnerable when the organization suppresses or limits their initiative while constantly demanding that they serve the organization's own ends.

In such a situation, the individual is likely to put too much of himself or herself into the job. In other words, the person may well keep trying to accomplish his or her own agenda while simultaneously trying to fulfill the organization's expectations. The most likely effects of this situation are prolonged stress, fatigue, frustration, and helplessness under the burden of overwhelming demands. The person literally exhausts his or her aspirations and motivation, much as a candle burns itself out. Loss of self-confidence and psychological withdrawal follow. Ultimately, burnout results. At this point, the individual may start dreading going to work in the morning, may put in longer hours but get less accomplished than before, and may generally display mental and physical exhaustion.

Managing Stress in the Workplace

Given that stress is widespread and so potentially disruptive in organizations, it follows that people and organizations should be concerned about how to manage it more effectively. And in fact they are. Many strategies have been developed to help manage stress in the workplace. Some are strategies for individuals, and others are geared toward organizations.[29]

Individual Coping Strategies

- Individual strategies for managing stress include exercise, relaxation, time management, role management, and support groups.

Many strategies for helping individuals manage stress have been proposed. Figure 15.5 illustrates five of the more popular strategies.

Exercise One method by which individuals can manage their stress is through exercise. People who exercise regularly are known to be less likely to have heart attacks than inactive people are. More directly, research has suggested that people who exercise regularly feel less tension and stress, are more self-confident, and show greater optimism. People who do not exercise regularly feel more stress, are more likely to be depressed, and so forth.[30] *Management in Action* summarizes how many U.S. executives are exercising as a way to help them cope with stress.

Relaxation A related method individuals can use to manage stress is relaxation. We noted at the beginning of the chapter that coping with stress requires adaptation. Proper relaxation is an effective way to adapt.

29. Quick and Quick, *Organizational Stress and Preventive Management.*

30. C. Folkins, "Effects of Physical Training on Mood," *Journal of Clinical Psychology,* April 1976, pp. 385–390.

FIGURE 15.5
Individual Mechanisms for Coping with Work Stress

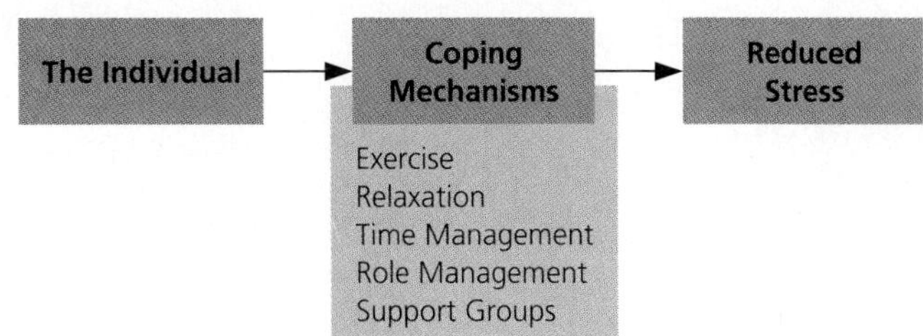

Relaxation can take many forms. One way to relax is to take regular vacations. A recent study found that people's attitudes toward a variety of workplace characteristics improved significantly following a vacation.[31] People can also relax while on the job. For example, it has been recommended that people take regular rest breaks during their normal workday. A popular way of resting is to sit quietly with closed eyes for ten minutes every afternoon. (Of course, it might also be necessary to have an alarm clock handy!)

Time Management Time management is an often recommended method for managing stress. The idea is that many daily pressures can be eased or eliminated if a person does a better job of managing time. One popular approach to time management is to make a list every morning of the things to be done that day. Then you group the items on the list into three categories: critical activities that must be performed, important activities that should be performed, and optional or trivial things that can be delegated or postponed. Then, of course, you do the things on the list in their order of importance. This strategy helps people get more of the important things done every day. It also encourages delegating less important activities to others.

Role Management Somewhat related to time management is the idea of role management, in which the individual actively works to avoid overload, ambiguity, and conflict. For example, if you do not know what is expected of you, you should not sit and worry about it. Instead, ask for clarification from your boss.

Another role management strategy is to learn to say *no*. As simple as saying *no* might sound, a lot of people create problems for themselves by always saying *yes*. Besides working in their regular jobs, they agree to serve on committees, volunteer for extra duties, and accept extra assignments. Sometimes, of course, we have no choice but to accept an extra obligation (if our boss tells us to complete a new project, we most likely will have to do it). In many cases, however, saying *no* is a viable option.[32]

31. John W. Lounsbury and Linda L. Hoopes, "A Vacation from Work: Changes in Work and Nonwork Outcomes," *Journal of Applied Psychology*, vol. 71, 1986, pp. 392–401.

32. "Eight Ways to Help You Reduce the Stress in Your Life," *Business Week Careers*, November 1986, p. 78.

MANAGEMENT IN ACTION

Executive Exercise

Executives are increasingly recognizing that exercise and physical fitness are key ingredients in the battle against stress. Lawrence Perlman, CEO of Control Data Corp., rises at 5:30 every morning and runs three to seven miles. He also lifts weights, plays squash, and cross-country skis. Why does he do it? Perlman says it makes him feel better and allows him to confront the demands of his job more effectively.

Perlman is not alone in this approach to dealing with stress. Winthrop Smith, a senior manager at Merrill Lynch, is a long-distance cyclist. Barbara Cherry, Midwest regional attorney for AT&T, is a body builder. Other managers hike, swim, row, or play basketball or racquetball. Regardless of the activity, however, virtually all say that exercise has paid dividends ranging from lower cholesterol levels to greater energy.

These executives offer some common points of advice. First, they believe the individual has to make a firm commitment to scheduling time to work out. Without making exercise a top priority, it becomes too easy to put it off and eventually drop it altogether. Second, they argue that each person has to find the activity or activities that she or he enjoys. Even though swimming is healthy, for example, if a person doesn't like to swim, he or she won't stick to an exercise program based on swimming.

While some write off exercise programs as a fad, most American executives who have made the commitment believe exercise is here to stay.

SOURCES: Fay Rice, "How Execs Get Fit," *Fortune,* October 22, 1990, pp. 144–152; Brian O'Reilly, "New Truths about Staying Healthy," *Fortune,* September 25, 1989, pp. 57–66; Marjory Roberts and T. George Harris, "Wellness at Work," *Psychology Today,* May 1989, pp. 54–56.

Support Groups A final method for managing stress is to develop and maintain support groups. A support group is simply a group of family members or friends with whom a person can spend time. Going out after work with a couple of coworkers to a basketball game, for example, can help relieve the stress that built up during the day. Supportive family and friends can help people deal with normal stress on an ongoing basis.

Support groups can be particularly useful during times of crisis. For example, suppose an employee has just learned that she did not get the promotion she has been working toward for months. It may help her tremendously if she has good friends to lean on, be it to talk to or to yell at.[33]

Organizational Coping Strategies

- Organizational strategies for helping people cope with stress include institutional programs and collateral programs.

Increasingly, organizations are realizing that they should be involved in managing their employees' stress. There are two different rationales for this view. One is that because the organization is at least partly responsible for creating the stress,

33. Daniel C. Ganster, Marcelline R. Fusilier, and Bronston T. Mayes, "Role of Social Support in the Experiences of Stress at Work," *Journal of Applied Psychology,* vol. 71, 1986, pp. 102–110.

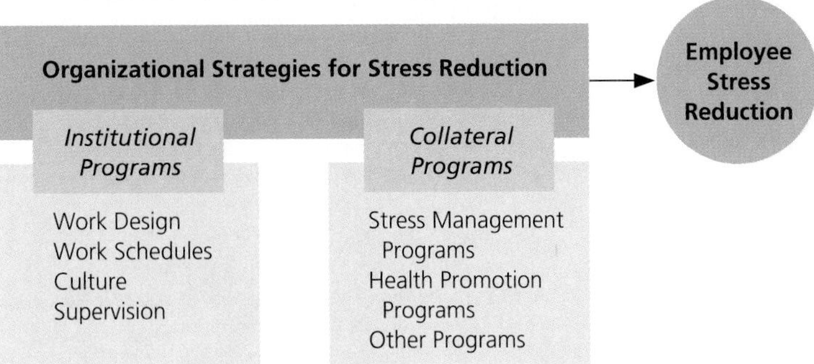

FIGURE 15.6
Organizational Strategies for Helping Employees Cope with Stress

it should help relieve it. The other is that workers experiencing lower levels of harmful stress will be able to function more effectively. Two basic organizational strategies for helping employees manage stress are institutional programs and collateral programs. Figure 15.6 shows some of the more common organizational methods in these categories.

Institutional Programs *Institutional programs* for managing stress are undertaken through established organizational mechanisms.[34] For example, properly designed jobs (discussed in Chapter 13) and work schedules can help ease stress. Shift work in particular can cause major problems for employees, as they constantly have to adjust their sleep and relaxation patterns. Thus, the design of work and work schedules should be a focus of organizational efforts to reduce stress.[35]

The organization's culture (covered in Chapter 20) also can be used to help manage stress. In some organizations, for example, there is a strong norm against taking time off or going on vacation. In the long run, such norms can cause major stress. Thus, the organization should strive to foster a culture that reinforces a healthy mix of work and nonwork activities.

Finally, supervision can play an important institutional role in managing stress. A supervisor is a potential major source of overload. If made aware of their potential for assigning stressful amounts of work, supervisors can do a better job of keeping workloads reasonable.

Collateral Programs In addition to their institutional efforts aimed at reducing stress, many organizations are turning to collateral programs. A *collateral stress program* is an organizational program specifically created to help employees deal with stress. As noted in Figure 15.6, organizations have adopted stress management programs, health promotion programs, and other kinds of programs for this purpose.

---

34. Randall S. Schuler and Susan E. Jackson, "Managing Stress through PHRM Practices: An Uncertainty Interpretation," in K. Rowland and G. Ferris, eds., *Research in Personnel and Human Resources Management,* vol. 4 (Greenwich, Conn.: JAI Press, 1986), pp. 183–224.

35. Quick and Quick, *Organizational Stress and Preventive Management.*

TABLE 15.2
Representative Approaches to Stress Management in Organizations

Examples of Stress Management Programs	Examples of Employee Fitness Programs
▪ IBM, Hewlett-Packard, and the U.S. Air Force have sponsored seminars on the value of humor in helping to minimize workplace stress. ▪ Lockheed and First Nationwide Bank have sponsored screening programs to help employees detect signs of hypertension and training programs to help cope with it. ▪ Chevron provides training sessions to educate employees about AIDS and smoking. ▪ Intel and Apple offer sabbaticals to executives to help them avoid burnout. ▪ Cambridge Research Lab in Boston offers workers a class in the Oriental art of tai to help them cope with stress.	▪ L.L. Bean maintains three different health and fitness centers for its employees. The centers are open from 6 A.M. to 6 P.M. everyday. All employees can use them for a minimal charge. ▪ Tenneco has a comprehensive health maintenance facility adjacent to its headquarters building in Houston. In addition to physical conditioning opportunities, the center sponsors numerous workshops and seminars on health maintenance. Membership is free to all employees. ▪ Saatchi & Saatchi, a New York-based advertising firm, has an elaborate gymnasium available for its employees to use. ▪ Westinghouse has started constructing employee fitness centers in all of its facilities. The centers are available at no charge to all employees and their families.

SOURCES: Faye Rice, "How Execs Get Fit," *Fortune,* October 22, 1990, pp. 144–152; Marjory Roberts and T. George Harris, "Wellness at Work," *Psychology Today,* May 1989, pp. 50–54; Brian Dumaine, "Cool Cures for Burnout," *Fortune,* June 20, 1988, pp. 78–84; "A Cure for Stress," *Newsweek,* October 12, 1987, pp. 64–65.

Table 15.2 summarizes several examples of stress management programs organizations have adopted. More and more companies are developing their own programs or adopting existing programs of this type.[36]

Table 15.2 also gives examples of firms that have employee fitness programs. These kinds of programs attack stress indirectly by encouraging employees to exercise, which in turn is presumed to reduce stress. On the negative side, this kind of effort costs considerably more than stress management programs, because the firm must invest in physical facilities. Still, more and more companies are exploring this option.[37]

Finally, organizations try to help employees cope with stress through other kinds of programs. For example, existing career development programs, like that at General Electric, are used for this purpose. Other companies use programs promoting everything from humor to massage as antidotes for stress.[38] Of course, there is little or no research to support some of the claims made by advocates of these programs. Thus, managers must take steps to ensure that any organizational effort to help employees cope with stress is at least reasonably effective.

36. Ibid.

37. Richard A. Wolfe, David O. Ulrich, and Donald F. Parker, "Employee Health Management Programs: Review, Critique, and Research Agenda," *Journal of Management,* Winter 1987, pp. 603–615.

38. "A Cure for Stress?", *Newsweek,* October 12, 1987, pp. 64–65.

Summary of Key Points

- Stress is a person's adaptive response to a stimulus that places excessive psychological or physical demands on that person. According to the general adaptation syndrome, the three stages of response to stress are alarm, resistance, and exhaustion. Two important forms of stress are eustress and distress.
- Stress can be caused by many factors. Major organizational stressors are task demands, physical demands, role demands, and interpersonal demands. Life stressors include life change and life trauma.
- Type A personalities are more competitive and time driven than Type B personalities. Initial evidence suggested that Type As are more susceptible to coronary heart disease, but recent findings provide less support.
- Stress has many consequences. Individual consequences can be behavioral, psychological, and medical problems. Organizational consequences can affect performance and attitudes or cause withdrawal. Burnout is another possibility.
- Primary individual mechanisms for managing stress are exercise, relaxation, time management, role management, and support groups. Organizations use both institutional and collateral programs for this purpose.

Discussion Questions

1. Describe one or two recent times when stress had both good and bad consequences for you.
2. Describe a time when you successfully avoided stage 3 of the GAS and another time when you got to stage 3.
3. What are the major stressors for a student?
4. Is an organizational stressor or a life stressor likely to be more powerful?
5. What consequences are students most likely to suffer as a result of too much stress?
6. Do you agree with the assertion that a certain degree of stress is necessary to induce high energy and motivation?
7. What can be done to prevent burnout? If someone you know is suffering burnout, how would you advise that person to recover from it?
8. Do you consider yourself a Type A or a Type B person? Why?
9. Can a person who is a Type A change? If so, how?
10. Do you practice any of the stress reduction methods discussed in the text? Which one(s)? Are there others that you use?

CASE 15.1

Cutback Induces Stress at Citicorp

Citicorp and its biggest operating unit, Citibank, together comprise the largest banking enterprise in the United States. The bank has over 3,300 branches in

43 states and 89 foreign countries. Over 27 million Citicorp bank credit cards—Visa and Mastercard—are in force. The firm was also a pioneer in the use of automated teller machines, opening 500 in the New York City area alone.

Citicorp lends billions of dollars annually to businesses, individuals, and governments. The firm has been a leader in innovative banking practices and generally is considered to have a strong management team. The bank was profitable every year during the 1980s except one: 1987.

Like many large organizations, Citicorp is not immune to financial problems. For example, Citicorp loans to foreign countries became a problem in the late 1980s. The firm's CEO, John Reed, boldly put $4 billion in reserve to offset possible problems with the loans. This write-off was responsible for the 1987 loss.

Despite its financial strengths and overall sound management, however, Citicorp recently has started to feel the effects of the worldwide banking crunch. As banks are failing in record numbers, even mighty Citicorp has begun to feel the effects. Three areas in particular have plagued the firm in recent years: poor performance in the trading of U.S. government bonds, difficulties with its London subsidiary, and a failure to make a big impact in the investment banking industry. A number of different strategies have failed to turn things around in these areas.

Citicorp managers recently announced plans to follow in the footsteps of many other American businesses and go through a period of cutbacks and retrenchment. Currently the firm is having no financial difficulties, but it wants to be aggressive in its efforts to avoid problems later. Management believes that cutting back now is a more manageable and logical approach than waiting until a crisis erupts.

As part of the cutbacks, the firm has decided to eliminate two thousand jobs. As might be expected, employee response has been quite unfavorable. Two employees committed suicide in 1990. Higher stress levels have led to a significant increase in work-related accidents and mistakes.

Citicorp has recognized the problems that accompany such cutbacks and is taking steps to help its employees cope with the impending uncertainties. For example, the firm is installing blood pressure monitors at several of its facilities to help employees keep better tabs on how they are handling the stress.

Another program Citicorp has implemented is a series of lunchtime programs run by stress counselors. One counselor, Dr. Art Ulene of NBC's "Today" show, recently ran a program on how to use humor to combat stress. While it is too early to assess what the final outcome will be, two things seem likely. First, no matter how hard an organization tries, cutbacks and elimination of jobs are bound to increase stress. But at the same time, Citicorp seems to be successful in minimizing the effects of its cutbacks.

Case Questions

1. What causes of stress exist at Citicorp?
2. What consequences of stress are manifesting themselves? Speculate about other consequences that also are likely to occur.
3. If you were an individual employee whose job was at risk, how would you go about coping?

SOURCES: "Fear and Stress in the Office Take Toll," *The Wall Street Journal,* November 16, 1990, pp. B1, B3; "All That Plastic Is Still Fantastic for Citibank," *Business Week,* May 28, 1990, pp. 90–92; "Citicorp Faces Tough Decisions on Loss-Plagued Units," *The Wall Street Journal,* March 9, 1990, p. A5; Gary Hoover, Alta Campbell, and Patrick J. Spain, eds., *Hoover's Handbook—Profiles of over 500 Major Corporations* (Austin, Tex.: The Reference Press, 1990), p. 170.

CASE 15.2

Stress Takes Its Toll

Larry Field had a lot of fun in high school. He was a fairly good student, especially in math, he worked harder than most of his friends, and somehow he ended up going steady with Alice Shiflette, class valedictorian. He worked summers for a local surveyor, William Loude, and when he graduated Mr. Loude offered him a job as number-three man on one of his survey crews. The pay wasn't very high, but Field already was good at the work, and he believed all he needed was a steady job to boost his confidence sufficiently to ask Alice to marry him. Once he did, the sequence of events that followed unfolded rapidly. He started work in June, he and Alice were married in October, Alice took a job as a secretary in a local company that made business forms, and a year later they had their first child.

The baby came as something of a shock to Field. He had come to enjoy the independence his own paycheck afforded him every week. Food and rent took up most of it, but he still enjoyed playing basketball a few nights a week with his high school buddies and spending Sunday afternoons on the softball field. When the baby came, however, Field's brow began to furrow a bit. He was only twenty years old, and he still wasn't making much money. He asked Mr. Loude for a raise and got it—his first.

Two months later, one of the crew chiefs quit just when Mr. Loude's crews had more work than they could handle. Mr. Loude hated to turn down work, so he made Larry Field into a crew chief, giving his crew some of the old instruments that weren't good enough for the precision work of the top crews, and assigned him the easy title surveys in town. Because it meant a jump in salary, Field had no choice but to accept the crew chief position. But it scared him. He had never been very ambitious or curious, so he'd paid little attention to the training of his former crew chief. He knew how to run the instruments—the basics, anyway—but every morning he woke up terrified that he would be sent on a job he couldn't handle.

During his first few months as a crew chief, Field began doing things that his wife thought he had outgrown. He frequently talked so fast that he would stumble over his own words, stammer, turn red in the face, and have to start all over again. He began smoking too, something he had not done since they had started dating. He told his two crew members that smoking kept his hands from shaking when he was working on an instrument. Neither of them smoked, and when Field began lighting up in the truck while they were waiting for the rain to stop, they would become resentful and complain that he had no right to ruin their lungs too.

Field found it particularly hard to adjust to being "boss," especially since one of his workers was getting an engineering degree at night school and both crew members were the same age as he. He felt sure that Alfonso Reyes, the scholar, would take over his position in no time. He kept feeling that Alfonso was looking over his shoulder and began snapping any time they worked close together.

Things were getting tense at home, too. Alice had to give up her full-time day job to take care of the baby, so she had started working nights. They hardly ever saw each other, and it seemed as though her only topic of conversation was how they should move to California or Alaska, where she had heard that surveyors were paid five times what Field made. Field knew his wife was dissatisfied with her work and believed her intelligence was being wasted, but he didn't know what he could do about it. He was disconcerted when he realized that drinking and worrying about the next day at work while sitting at home with the baby at night had become a pattern.

Case Questions

1. What signs of stress was Larry Field exhibiting?
2. How was Larry Field trying to cope with his stress? Can you suggest more effective methods?

EXPERIENTIAL EXERCISE

Purpose: This exercise is intended to help you develop a better understanding of how stress affects you.

Format: Following is a set of questions about your job. If you work, respond to the questions in terms of your job. If you do not work, respond to the questions in terms of your role as a student.

Procedure: This quiz will help you recognize your level of stress on the job. Take the test, figure your score, and then see if your stress level is normal, beginning to be a problem, or dangerous. Answer the following statements by putting a number in front of each:

1—seldom true

2—sometimes true

3—mostly true

_____ 1. Even over minor problems, I lose my temper and do embarrassing things, like yell or kick a garbage can.

_____ 2. I hear every piece of information or question as criticism of my work.

_____ 3. If someone criticizes my work, I take it as a personal attack.

_____ 4. My emotions seem flat whether I'm told good news or bad news about my performance.

_____ 5. Sunday nights are the worst time of the week.

_____ 6. To avoid going to work, I'd even call in sick when I'm feeling fine.
_____ 7. I feel powerless to lighten my work load or schedule, even though I've always got far too much to do.
_____ 8. I respond irritably to any request from co-workers.
_____ 9. On the job and off, I get highly emotional over minor accidents, like typos, spilt coffee.
_____ 10. I tell people about sports or hobbies that I'd like to do but say I never have time because of the hours I spend at work.
_____ 11. I work overtime consistently, yet never feel caught up.
_____ 12. My health is running down; I often have headaches, backaches, stomachaches.
_____ 13. If I even eat lunch, I do it at my desk while working.
_____ 14. I see time as my enemy.
_____ 15. I can't tell the difference between work and play; it all feels like one more thing to be done.
_____ 16. Everything I do feels like a drain on my energy.
_____ 17. I feel like I want to pull the covers over my head and hide.
_____ 18. I seem off-center, distracted—I do things like walk into mirrored pillars in department stores and excuse myself.
_____ 19. I blame my family—because of them, I have to stay in this job and location.
_____ 20. I have ruined my relationship with co-workers whom I feel I compete against.

Scoring: Add up the points you wrote beside the questions. Interpret your score as follows:

20–29: You have normal amounts of stress.

30–49: Stress is becoming a problem. You should try to identify its source and manage it.

50–60: Stress is at dangerous levels. Seek help or it could result in worse symptoms, such as alcoholism or illness.

SOURCE: From *USA Today,* June 16, 1987. Copyright 1987, *USA Today.* Excerpted with permission.

Follow-up Questions

1. How valid do you think your score is?
2. Is it possible to anticipate stress ahead of time and plan ways to help manage it?

CHAPTER OUTLINE

- Decision Making in Organizations
  - *Types of Decisions*
  - *Information Required for Decision Making*
- The Decision-Making Process
  - *The Rational Approach*
  - *The Behavioral Approach*
  - *The Practical Approach*
  - *The Personal Approach*
- Escalation of Commitment
- Individual versus Group Decision Making
- Decision Making in Groups
  - *Basic Factors*
  - *Group Polarization*
  - *Groupthink*
  - *Participation in Decision Making*
- Group Problem Solving
  - *Brainstorming*
  - *The Nominal Group Technique*
  - *The Delphi Technique*
- Creativity in Decision Making
  - *Preparation*
  - *Incubation*
  - *Insight*
  - *Verification*

16

Decision Making and Creativity

CHAPTER OBJECTIVES

After studying this chapter, you should be able to:

Discuss the importance of decision making in organizations.

Describe several ways of making decisions in organizations.

Discuss the differences between individual and group decision making.

Identify the most important factors that contribute to good decision making in groups.

Describe several techniques for group problem solving.

Summarize the elements of the creative process.

Imagine yourself resting comfortably in your seat on the 8:00 A.M. *flight from Chicago on your way to a busy day of meetings in New York. Suddenly the pilot announces that due to bad weather all three airports in the New York area are closed and the flight will have to be diverted. Passengers are asked to vote on whether to land at Newburgh, New York, or return to Chicago.*

This actually happened aboard American Airlines flight 492, bound for La Guardia airport in New York in November 1989. Passengers, stunned at this unexpected opportunity to participate in democracy, raised their hands for one or the other choice and were dutifully counted by the flight attendants. Newburgh won the vote, and the plane landed there safely despite severe wind and rain. Passengers claimed they had never before voted on where to land, and some were a bit upset at the idea that passengers' votes might take precedence over safety considerations. However, the pilot, crew, and Federal Aviation Administration officials agreed that there had not been a vote on where to land; rather, the vote concerned which passengers wanted ground transportation to New York and which wanted to take a return flight to Chicago.[1]

It may be hard to believe that a pilot would let passengers decide on where to land in a storm, but voting is one method groups use to make decisions. It is understandable that the pilot, crew, and FAA officials denied the passengers' claims. As in this case, however, voting often is not the best way to make decisions.

Decisions are made regarding all of the resources a company has available as it attempts to reach its goals. Such decisions determine what organizational goals will be and how they will be accomplished. Decision making thus involves all organizational activities and affects virtually all members of the organization, both as individuals and as members of groups.

Without a decision-making mechanism, an organization would collapse into a collection of individuals, each pursuing a different goal. For example, suppose a football quarterback made no decision regarding the next play but simply said to his teammates, "OK, let's run a play." The eleven players might take any position, start at any time, and run in any direction.

Now consider what actually happens on a football field. Before each play,

---

1. "Airline Denies Pilot Took Vote on Facing Storm," *Los Angeles Times,* November 23, 1989, p. A20; "Airline Pilot Allegedly Asked Riders for Advice on Flight," *The Washington Post,* November 23, 1989, p. A10; "The Goal Was Lofty, but Passenger Vote on Jet Proves a Flop," *The Arizona Republic,* November 23, 1989, pp. A1, A2.

the quarterback considers information from several sources: the game plan worked out by the coaching staff, the other team's characteristics, his own team's strengths and weaknesses, and the current situation (down, field position, and the like). He then decides which play to run and which formation and snap count to use and communicates the decision to the team members. Because of their training, the other players know what to do and when to do it. Alternatively, the decision may be made by a group; some football coaches call all offensive plays after consulting with the assistant coaches on the sidelines and in the press box.

The football example illustrates three important characteristics of decision making: (1) a decision can be made by an individual or a group, (2) even a brief decision-making process can be both logical and complex, and (3) information is an indispensable element of the decision-making process. A decision integrates the actions of individuals and makes their efforts pay off in terms of group or organizational effectiveness. Of course, success depends on the individuals' training, their willingness to perform their duties, and their motivation to work hard. But the decision initiates the action. As the starting point, it is vital to the understanding of organizational processes.

Decision Making in Organizations

- **Decision making** is the process of choosing from among several alternatives.

Decision making is choosing one alternative from several. In the football example, the quarterback can run any of perhaps a hundred plays. With the goal of scoring a touchdown always in mind, he chooses the play that seems to promise the best outcome. His choice is based on his understanding of the game situation, the likelihood of various outcomes, and his preference for each outcome.

- Managers' decisions usually are guided by a goal.

Figure 16.1 shows the basic elements of decision making. A decision maker's actions are guided by a goal. Each of several alternative courses of action is linked with various outcomes. Information is available regarding the alternatives, the likelihood that each outcome will occur, and the value of each outcome relative to the goal. On the basis of his or her evaluation of the information, the decision maker chooses one alternative.

Decisions made in organizations can be classified according to frequency and information conditions. In a decision-making context, *frequency* describes how often a particular decision recurs and *information conditions* describe how much information about the predictability of various outcomes is available.

- A **programmed decision** is a decision that recurs often enough for a decision rule to be developed.
- A **decision rule** is a statement that tells a decision maker which alternative to choose based on the characteristics of the decision situation.

Types of Decisions

The frequency of recurrence determines whether a decision is programmed or nonprogrammed. A **programmed decision** recurs often enough for a decision rule to be developed. A **decision rule** tells the decision maker which alternative to choose once he or she has information about the decision situation. Whenever the situation is encountered, the appropriate decision rule is used. Programmed

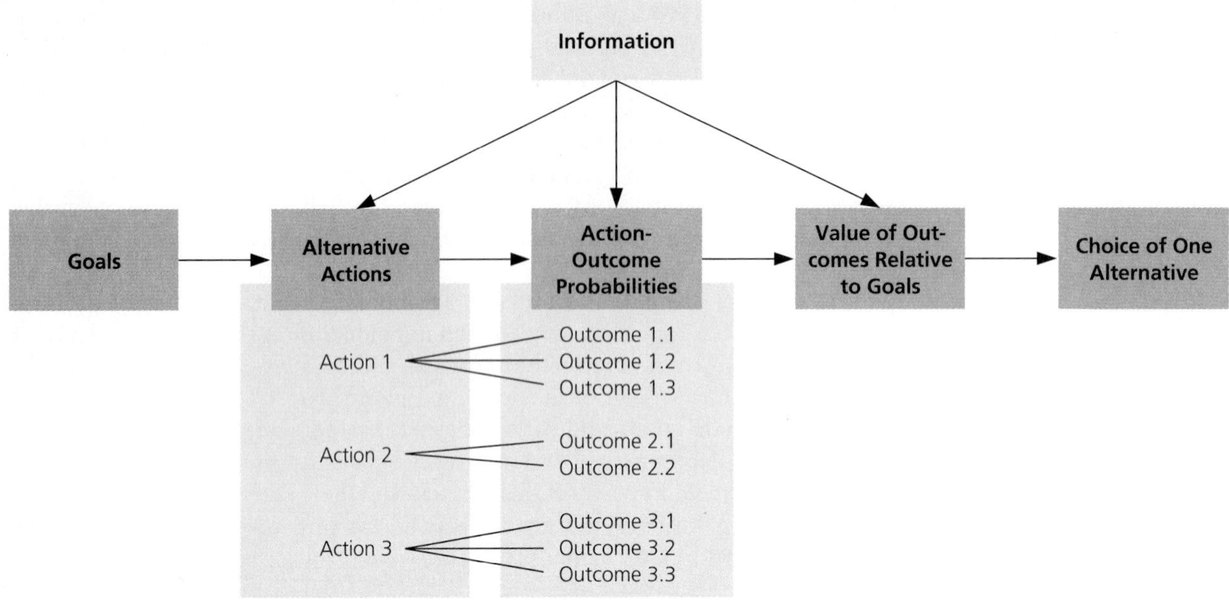

FIGURE 16.1
Elements of Decision Making

decisions usually are highly structured; that is, the goals are clear and well known, the decision-making procedure is already established, and the sources and channels of information are clearly defined.[2]

Airlines use established procedures when a piece of equipment breaks down and cannot be used on a particular flight. Passengers may not view the issue as a programmed decision, because they experience this situation relatively infrequently. But to the airlines, equipment problems that render a plane unfit for service arise regularly. This happened in March 1988 when passengers on a Southwest Airlines flight from Phoenix to Los Angeles were told that they had to deplane due to equipment problems. A few moments later, however, they watched as 150 other passengers boarded their plane, and the plane took off. A plane that had been scheduled to fly to San Diego had broken down, and because there were far more connections to Los Angeles than to San Diego, Southwest Airlines officials decided to put the San Diego passengers on the plane that originally was scheduled to fly to Los Angeles and help the Los Angeles–bound passengers find other transportation to Los Angeles. Southwest Airlines had put a programmed decision rule into effect.[3]

However, when a problem or decision situation has not been encountered before, the decision maker cannot rely on a previously established decision rule.

2. Herbert Simon, *The New Science of Management Decision* (New York: Harper & Row, 1960), p. 1.

3. "Bumped Passengers Watch 'Faulty' Jet Fly Off," *The Arizona Republic,* March 12, 1988, pp. B1, B8.

TABLE 16.1
Characteristics of Programmed and Nonprogrammed Decisions

Characteristics	Programmed Decisions	Nonprogrammed Decisions
Type of decision	Well structured	Poorly structured
Frequency	Repetitive and routine	New and unusual
Goals	Clear, specific	Vague
Information	Readily available	Not available, unclear channels
Consequences	Minor	Major
Organizational level	Lower levels	Upper levels
Time for solution	Short	Relatively long
Basis for solution	Decision rules, set procedures	Judgment and creativity

- A **nonprogrammed decision** is a decision that recurs infrequently and for which there is no previously established decision rule.
- **Problem solving** is a form of decision making in which the issue is unique and requires development and evaluation of alternatives without the aid of a programmed decision rule.

Such a decision is said to be a **nonprogrammed decision,** and it requires problem solving. **Problem solving** is a special form of decision making in which the issue is unique; it requires development and evaluation of alternatives without the aid of a programmed decision rule. Nonprogrammed decisions are poorly structured, because information is ambiguous, there is no clear procedure for making the decision, and the goals often are vague.[4]

A nonprogrammed decision was required of General Motors in 1986 when it faced a significant drop in operating income and a sagging market share. In November, GM announced plans to shut down eleven plants over an eighteen-month period, with more cuts to be announced later. It expected to reduce its salaried work force by 25 percent and cut capacity by 11 percent. The cuts would eliminate more than 29,000 jobs in four states.[5] Although the auto industry seems to face difficulty every few years, each situation is different, requiring a nonprogrammed decision or set of decisions to be made.

Table 16.1 summarizes the characteristics of programmed and nonprogrammed decisions. Note that programmed decisions are more common at the lower levels of the organization, whereas a primary responsibility of top management is to make the difficult, nonprogrammed decisions that determine the long-term effectiveness of the organization. By definition, the strategy decisions for which top management is responsible are poorly structured and nonroutine and have far-reaching consequences.

- All problems require a decision, but not all decisions require problem solving.

Programmed decisions, then, can be made according to previously tested rules and procedures. Nonprogrammed decisions generally require the decision maker to exercise judgment and creativity.[6] In other words, all problems require a decision, but not all decisions require problem solving.

4. Simon, *The New Science of Management Decision.*
5. "Reality Has Hit General Motors—Hard," *Business Week,* November 24, 1986, p. 37.
6. See Bernard M. Bass, *Organizational Decision Making* (Homewood, Ill.: Irwin, 1983), pp. 13–15, for a discussion of poorly structured and well-structured problems.

Farmland Industries, Inc., has developed several programs to assist the agriculture industry to ensure the least risk and highest yields possible. Their GROFACS® program is used by fertilizer specialists to calculate proper proportions of fertilizers and chemicals and assist fertilizer and agricultural chemical operations at local cooperatives. The information they provide is invaluable in assisting growers in the production of more high quality feed at lower costs. PIGFINDER® is a pig auctioning service for breeders and growers.

Information Required for Decision Making

Decisions are made to bring about desired outcomes, but the information about those outcomes varies. The range of available information can be represented as a continuum whose endpoints represent complete certainty, under which all alternative outcomes are known, and complete uncertainty, under which alternative outcomes are unknown. At points between the two extremes, risk is involved; the decision maker has some information about the possible outcomes and may be able to estimate the probability of their occurrence.

Different information conditions present different challenges to the decision maker.[7] For example, suppose the marketing manager of a toy company is trying to determine whether to launch an expensive promotional effort for a new video game (see Figure 16.2). For simplicity, assume there are only two alternatives: to promote the game or not to promote it. Under conditions of *certainty,* the manager knows the outcomes of each alternative. If the new game is promoted heavily, the company will realize a $1 million profit. Without a large promotional program, the company will realize only a $200,000 profit. Here the decision is simple: Promote the game.

In a *risk* situation, the decision maker cannot know with certainty what the outcome of a given action will be but has enough information to estimate the probabilities of occurrence of various outcomes. Thus, working from information gathered by the market research department, the marketing manager in our example can estimate the likelihood of each outcome in a risk situation. In this case, the alternatives are defined by the size of the market. The probability for

7. See George P. Huber, *Managerial Decision Making* (Glenview, Ill.: Scott, Foresman, 1980), pp. 90–115, for a discussion of decision making under conditions of certainty, risk, and uncertainty.

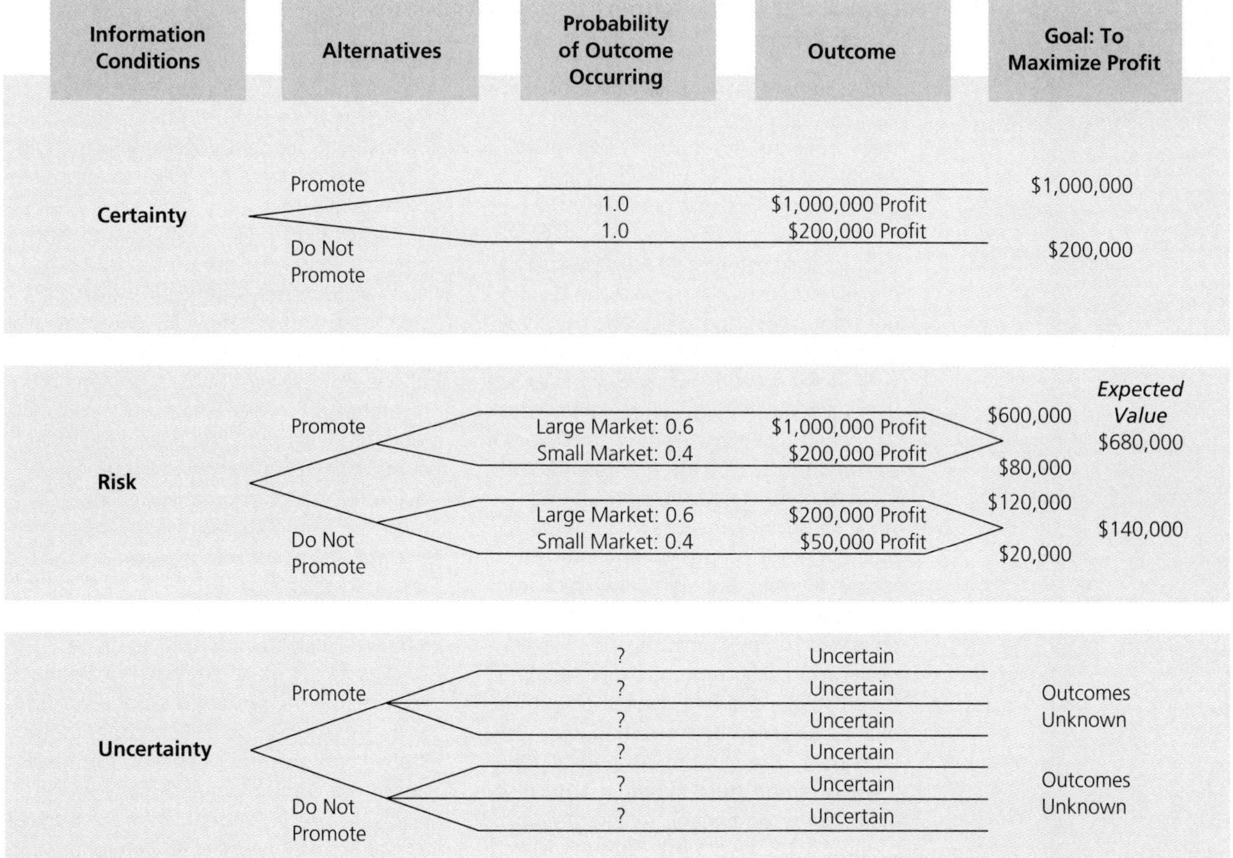

FIGURE 16.2
Alternative Outcomes under Different Information Conditions

a large video game market is 0.6, and the probability for a small market is 0.4. The manager can calculate the expected value of the promotional effort based on these probabilities and the expected profits associated with each. To find the expected value of an alternative, the manager multiplies each outcome's value by the probability of its occurrence. The sum of these calculations for all possible outcomes represents that alternative's expected value. In this case, the expected value of alternative 1—to promote the new game—is as follows:

$$\begin{array}{r} 0.6 \times \$1{,}000{,}000 = \$600{,}000 \\ +\ 0.4 \times \$\ \ 200{,}000 = \$\ \ 80{,}000 \\ \hline \text{Expected value of alternative 1} = \$680{,}000 \end{array}$$

The expected value of alternative 2 (shown in Figure 16.2) is $140,000. The marketing manager should choose the first alternative, because its expected value is higher. A caution is in order, however: Although the numbers look convincing, they are based on incomplete information and only estimates of probability.

The decision maker who lacks enough information to estimate the probability of outcomes (or perhaps even to identify the outcomes at all) faces

THE ETHICAL DILEMMA

Drexel Burnham Lambert and Its Associates Rig Stock Prices

The scandals that hit Wall Street over the past several years have sent the major stockbrokerage firms scrambling for favorable media coverage and internal programs that will rebuild trust with the investing public. After all, if you cannot trust your investment adviser, you probably will not invest. If the average person does not invest, the brokerage firms will go out of business. To many people, the Wall Street scandals were so complex that they gave up trying to understand what happened. The story of how employees of Drexel Burnham Lambert, a major investment banker, rigged the price of one stock shows how bad decisions were made in quick succession and led to the federal investigation and criminal charges.

Wickes Co., one of Drexel's clients, was obligated to pay dividends of $15 million per year on a 10 percent convertible preferred stock issue and wanted to get rid of the obligation by converting it to common stock. Conversion was possible only if the common stock closed at a price of 6⅛ or higher on twenty trading days out of any consecutive thirty. Through March 1986, the Drexel staff watched the price of Wickes common stock climb above the trigger price and then begin to wobble. At that point, Drexel suggested that Wickes make an offer to buy another company, National Gypsum, which could cause the Wickes stock price to either stabilize or go up.

Wickes bid for National Gypsum, and its price went up. Late on the thirtieth day—Wednesday, April 23—the stock was at $6 and not moving. Witnesses testified that through a complex network of phone calls, several transactions involving a total of 3.6 million shares of Wickes were made to push the price to its final close of 6⅛. Wickes called in the convertible preferred stock, converted it to common stock, and all 3.6 million shares bought at the last minute were sold off in less than thirty days.

In summary, the price of Wickes stock was artificially manipulated to allow Wickes to get rid of a dividend payment required by the preferred stock. Lawsuits and investigations will likely continue for many years as authorities seek the truth about this transaction and many others involving Drexel Burnham Lambert as well as Ivan Boesky, Michael Milken, and scores of others. With the staggering amounts of money involved, the temptation to violate the law is indeed great.

SOURCES: Carol J. Loomis, "How Drexel Rigged a Stock," *Fortune,* November 19, 1990, pp. 83–91; "Both Sides Took Their Lumps in the Milken Hearing," *Business Week,* November 19, 1990, pp. 114–115; "Milken Has Everything to Lose—and Little to Gain," *Business Week,* October 15, 1990, p. 102.

complete *uncertainty.*[8] In the toy company example, this might be the case if sales of video games had recently collapsed and it was not clear whether the precipitous drop was temporary or permanent or when information to clarify the situation would be available. Under such circumstances, the decision maker may wait for more information to reduce uncertainty or rely on judgment, experience, and intuition to make the decision. *The Ethical Dilemma* describes how Drexel Burnham Lambert and its associates in effect were reducing the uncertainty in the stock market by manipulating stock prices in the mid-1980s.

8. See Bass, *Organizational Decision Making,* pp. 83–89, for a discussion of uncertainty.

Members of the Everest Environmental Expedition load yaks with trash removed from Mount Everest, supported by a grant from Dow Chemical Company which helped fund the July 1991 expedition to clean up more than a ton of trash from the world's highest mountain. In 1989 Dow made a commitment to clean up the environment. In making decisions about how to allocate its resources it has kept that promise by funding such projects as the Mount Everest clean up and other efforts to recycle aluminum, plastic, and glass from four national parks.

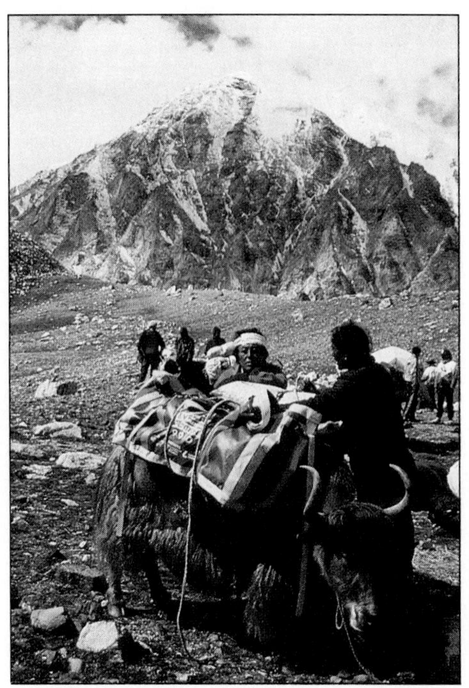

The Decision-Making Process

Several approaches to decision making offer insights into the process. The rational approach is appealing because of its logic and economy. Yet these very qualities raise questions about this approach, because actual decision making often is not a wholly rational process. The behavioral approach attempts to account for the limits on rationality in decision making. The practical approach combines features of the rational and behavioral approaches. The personal approach focuses on the decision-making processes individuals use in difficult situations.

The Rational Approach

- The **rational decision-making approach** is a systematic, step-by-step process for making decisions.

The **rational decision-making approach** outlines a systematic, step-by-step process. It assumes the organization is economically based and managed by decision makers who are entirely objective and have complete information.[9] Figure 16.3 identifies the steps of the process, starting with a statement of a goal and running neatly through the process until the best decision is made, implemented, and controlled.

9. See Bass, *Organizational Decision Making,* pp. 27–31, on the economic theory of the firm.

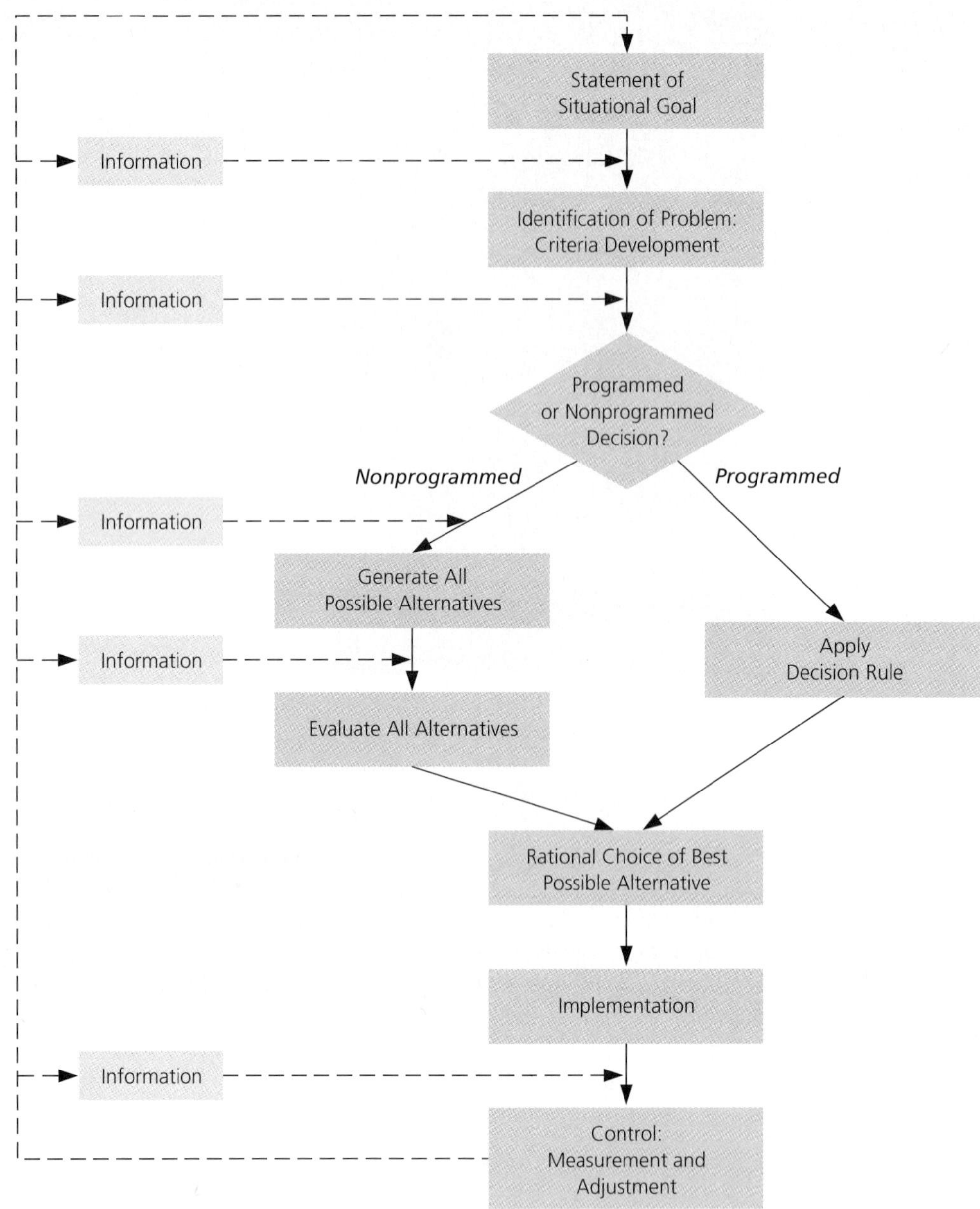

FIGURE 16.3
The Rational Decision-Making Process

Statement of Situational Goal The rational decision-making process begins with the statement of the situational goal, or desired end state. The goal of a marketing department, for example, may be to obtain a certain market share by the end of the year.

Some models of the decision-making process do not include the goal. We include it because it is the standard used to determine whether there is a decision to be made.

Identification of the Problem The purpose of problem identification is to gather information that bears on the goal. If there is a discrepancy between the goal and the actual state, action may be needed to rectify the situation. In the marketing example, the group may gather information about the company's actual market share and compare it with the desired market share. A difference between the two represents a problem that necessitates a decision. Reliable information is very important in this step. Inaccurate information can lead to an unnecessary decision or, worse, no decision when one is required. For example, if market research information indicates that market share goals have almost been reached and that sales will increase next quarter, the decision makers may see no need to change the marketing program. If the market share information is wrong, however, a future decision to change the promotional effort may come too late.

- Determination of the decision type means deciding whether a decision is to be programmed or nonprogrammed.

Determination of Decision Type Next, the decision makers must determine if the problem calls for a programmed or a nonprogrammed decision. If a programmed decision is needed, the appropriate decision rule is invoked, and the process moves on to the choice among alternatives. A programmed marketing decision may be called for if analysis reveals that competitors are outspending the company on print advertising. Because creating and buying space for print advertising is a well-established function of the marketing group, it requires only a programmed decision.

Although it may seem simple to diagnose a situation as programmed, apply a decision rule, and arrive at a solution, mistakes can occur. Choosing the wrong decision rule or assuming the problem calls for a programmed decision when a nonprogrammed decision actually is required can result in unacceptable decisions.

The same caution applies to the determination that a nonprogrammed decision is called for. If the situation is wrongly diagnosed, the decision maker wastes time and resources seeking a new solution to an old problem, or "reinventing the wheel." Nevertheless, this apparent inefficiency may occasionally be justified. It may be prudent to work through the problem-solving process if the consequences of the decision are so great that failure must be avoided at almost any cost.

Generation of Alternatives The next step in making a nonprogrammed decision is to generate alternatives. The rational process assumes decision makers will generate all possible alternative solutions to the problem. However, because even simple business problems can have scores of possible solutions, this assumption is unrealistic.

Decision makers may rely on education and experience as well as knowledge of the situation to generate alternatives.[10] In addition, they may seek information from other people such as peers, subordinates, and supervisors. Decision makers may analyze the symptoms of the problem for clues or fall back on intuition or judgment to develop alternative solutions. If the marketing department in our

10. Richard L. Daft, *Organizational Theory and Design,* 2nd ed. (St. Paul, Minn.: West, 1986).

example determines that a nonprogrammed decision is required, it will need to generate alternatives for increasing market share.

Although we treat the generation of alternatives as a stage of the decision-making process, it can have a broader application. In some models of strategic management, environmental scanning, a concept similar to generation of alternatives, plays an important role.[11] **Environmental scanning** is the process of constantly searching the business environment for new opportunities and threats to the firm. The generation of alternatives may be more realistically understood, then, as an ongoing process of environmental scanning useful in problem detection and diagnosis as well as in the alternative generation and evaluation phases of decision making.

- **Environmental scanning** is the process of continuously searching the business environment for new opportunities and threats to the organization.

Evaluation of Alternatives Evaluation involves the assessment of all possible alternatives against predetermined decision criteria. The ultimate decision criterion is "Will this alternative bring us nearer to the goal?" In each case, the decision maker must examine an alternative for evidence that it will reduce the discrepancy between the desired state and the actual state. The evaluation process usually includes (1) a complete description of the anticipated outcomes (benefits) of each alternative, (2) an evaluation of the anticipated costs of each alternative, and (3) an estimation of the uncertainties and risks associated with each alternative.[12]

In most decision situations, the decision maker does not have perfect information regarding the outcomes of all alternatives. At one extreme, as shown in Figure 16.2, outcomes may be known with certainty; at the other, the decision maker has no information whatsoever, so that the outcomes are entirely uncertain. But risk is the most common situation.

Choice of an Alternative The choice of an alternative is the crucial step in the decision-making process. Choice consists of selecting the alternative with the highest possible payoff, based on the benefits, costs, risks, and uncertainties of all alternatives. In the video game promotion example, the decision maker evaluated the two alternatives by calculating their expected values. Following the rational approach he or she would choose the one with the largest expected value.

Even in the rational approach, however, difficulties can arise in choosing an alternative. First, when two or more alternatives have equally high payoffs, the decision maker must obtain more information or use some other criterion to make the choice. Second, when no single alternative will accomplish the objective, some combination of two or three alternatives may have to be implemented. Finally, if no alternative or combination of alternatives will solve the problem,

11. John R. Montanari, "Some Tips on Clinical Policy Formulation," *Medical Group Management Journal,* vol. 23, 1976, pp. 24–27.

12. Milan Zeleny, "Descriptive Decision Making and Its Application," *Applications of Management Science,* vol. 1, 1981, pp. 327–388; Henry Mintzberg, Duru Raisinghani, and André Thoret, "The Structure of 'Unstructured' Decision Processes," *Administrative Science Quarterly,* June 1976, pp. 246–275.

the decision maker must obtain more information, generate more alternatives, or change the situational goals.[13]

- **Contingency plans** are alternative actions to take if the primary course of action is unexpectedly disrupted or rendered inappropriate.

An important part of the choice phase is the consideration of **contingency plans**—alternative actions that can be taken if the primary course of action is unexpectedly disrupted or rendered inappropriate.[14] Planning for contingencies is part of the transition between choosing the preferred alternative and implementing it. In developing contingency plans, the decision maker usually asks questions such as "What if something unexpected happens during the implementation of this alternative?"; "If the economy goes into a recession, will the choice of this alternative ruin the company?"; "How can we alter this plan if the economy suddenly rebounds and begins to grow?"

Implementation Implementation puts the decision into action. It uses the commitment and motivation of those who participated in the decision-making process (and may actually bolster individual commitment and motivation). To be successful, implementation requires the proper use of resources and good management skills. Following the decision to promote the new video game heavily, for example, the marketing manager must implement the decision by assigning the project to a work group or task force. The success of this team depends on the leadership, the reward structure, the communications system, and the group dynamics.

- Cognitive dissonance is the anxiety a person experiences when two sets of knowledge or perceptions are contradictory or incongruent.

Sometimes the decision maker begins to doubt a choice already made. This doubt is called *post-decision dissonance* or *cognitive dissonance.*[15] To reduce the tension created by the dissonance, the decision maker may seek to rationalize the decision further with new information.

Control: Measurement and Adjustment In the final stage of the rational decision-making process, the outcomes of the decision are measured and compared with the desired goal. If a discrepancy remains, the decision maker may restart the decision-making process by setting a new goal (or reiterating the existing one). The decision maker, unsatisfied with the previous decision, may modify the subsequent decision-making process to avoid another mistake. Changes can be made to any part of the process, as Figure 16.3 illustrates by the arrows leading from the control step to each of the other steps. Decision making therefore is a dynamic, self-correcting, and ongoing process in organizations.

Suppose a marketing department implements a new print advertising campaign. After implementation, it will constantly monitor market research data and compare its new market share to the desired market share. If the advertising

13. See E. Frank Harrison, *The Managerial Decision Making Process,* 2nd ed. (Boston: Houghton Mifflin, 1981), pp. 41–43, for more on choice processes.

14. Donald C. Hambrick and David Lei, "Toward an Empirical Prioritization of Contingency Variables for Business Strategy," *Academy of Management Journal,* December 1985, pp. 763–788; Ari Ginsberg and N. Ventrakaman, "Contingency Perspectives of Organizational Strategy: A Critical Review of the Empirical Research," *Academy of Management Review,* July 1985, pp. 412–434.

15. Leon Festinger, *A Theory of Cognitive Dissonance* (Palo Alto, Calif.: Stanford University Press, 1957).

has the desired effect, no changes will be made in the promotion campaign. If, however, the data indicate no change in the market share, additional decisions and implementation of a contingency plan may be necessary.

Coca-Cola Co. faced the need to change after it introduced the new Coke. The product was based on four-and-a-half years of testing and market research, but after only three months on the market, with declining market share and complaints from bottlers, Coca Cola announced the return of the old formula under the name Coca-Cola Classic.[16]

Strengths and Weaknesses of the Rational Approach The rational approach has several strengths. It forces the decision maker to consider a decision in a logical, sequential manner, and the in-depth analysis of alternatives enables the decision maker to choose on the basis of information rather than emotion or social pressure.

The rigid assumptions of this approach often are unrealistic, however.[17] The amount of information available to managers usually is limited by either time or cost constraints, and most decision makers have limited ability to process information about the alternatives. In addition, not all alternatives lend themselves to quantification in terms that will allow for easy comparison. Finally, because they cannot predict the future, it is unlikely that decision makers will know all possible outcomes of each alternative.

The Behavioral Approach

■ **Bounded rationality** is the assumption that decision makers cannot deal with all possible aspects and information about the problem and all alternatives and therefore choose to tackle some meaningful subset of it.

The crucial assumption of the behavioral approach is that decision makers operate with **bounded rationality** rather than with the perfect rationality assumed by the rational approach. The assumption rests on the argument that although individuals seek the best solution to a problem, the demands of processing all information bearing on the problem, generating all possible solutions, and choosing the single best solution are beyond the capabilities of most decision makers. Thus, individuals will accept less than ideal solutions based on a process that is neither exhaustive nor entirely rational. Decision makers operating with bounded rationality limit the inputs to the decision-making process and base decisions on judgment and personal biases as well as on logic.[18]

■ The **behavioral approach** uses rules of thumb, suboptimizing, and satisficing in making decisions.

The **behavioral approach** is characterized by (1) the use of procedures and rules of thumb, (2) suboptimizing, and (3) satisficing. Uncertainty in decision making can initially be reduced by reliance on procedures and rules of thumb. If, for example, increasing print advertising has increased a company's market share in the past, the linkage may be used by company employees as a rule of thumb in decision making. When the previous month's market share drops below

16. "How Coke's Decision to Offer 2 Colas Undid 4½ Years of Planning," *The Wall Street Journal,* July 15, 1985, pp. 1, 8.

17. See Harrison, *The Managerial Decision Making Process,* pp. 53–57, for more on the advantages and disadvantages of the rational approach.

18. See James G. March and Herbert A. Simon, *Organizations* (New York: Wiley, 1958), for more on the concept of bounded rationality.

- **Suboptimizing** is knowingly accepting less than the best possible outcome to avoid unintended negative effects on other aspects of the organization.

- **Satisficing** is examining alternatives only until a solution that meets minimal requirements is found.

- The **practical approach** to decision making combines the steps of the rational approach with the conditions in the behavioral approach to create a more realistic process for making decisions in organizations.

a certain level, the company might increase its print advertising expenditures by 25 percent during the following month.

Suboptimizing, the second feature of the behavioral approach, is knowingly accepting less than the best possible outcome. Frequently it is not feasible to optimize a particular decision in a real-world situation given organizational constraints. To avoid unintended negative effects on other departments, product lines, or decisions, the decision maker often must suboptimize.[19] An automobile manufacturer, for example, can cut costs dramatically and increase efficiency if it schedules the production of one model at a time. Thus, the production group's optimal decision is single-model scheduling. But the marketing group, seeking to optimize its sales goals by offering a wide variety of models, may demand the opposite production schedule: short runs of entirely different models. The groups in the middle, design and scheduling, may suboptimize the benefits the production and marketing groups are seeking by planning long runs of slightly different models. This is the practice of the large auto manufacturers, such as General Motors, which make several body styles in numerous models on the same production line.

The final feature of the behavioral approach is **satisficing**: examining alternatives only until a solution that meets minimal requirements is found and then ceasing to look for a better one.[20] The search for alternatives usually is a sequential process guided by procedures and rules of thumb based on previous experiences with similar problems. Often, when the first minimally acceptable choice is encountered, the search ends. The resulting choice may narrow the discrepancy between the desired and the actual states, but it is not likely to be the optimal solution. As the process is repeated, incremental improvements will slowly reduce the discrepancy between the actual and desired states.

The Practical Approach

Because of the unrealistic demands of the rational approach and the limited, short-run orientation of the behavioral approach, neither is entirely satisfactory. However, the worthwhile features of each can be combined into a practical approach to decision making, shown in Figure 16.4. The steps in this process are the same as in the rational approach; however, the conditions recognized by the behavioral approach are added to provide a more realistic process. For example, the practical approach suggests that rather than generating all alternatives, the decision maker should try to go beyond rules of thumb and satisficing limitations and generate as many alternatives as time, money, and other practicalities of the situation allow. In this synthesis of the two approaches, the rational approach provides an analytical framework for making decisions, whereas the behavioral approach provides a moderating influence.

19. Herbert A. Simon, *Administrative Behavior: A Study of Decision Making Processes in Administrative Organizations,* 3rd ed. (New York: Free Press, 1976).

20. Richard M. Cyert and James G. March, *A Behavioral Theory of the Firm* (Englewood Cliffs, N.J.: Prentice-Hall, 1963), p. 113; Simon, *Administrative Behavior.*

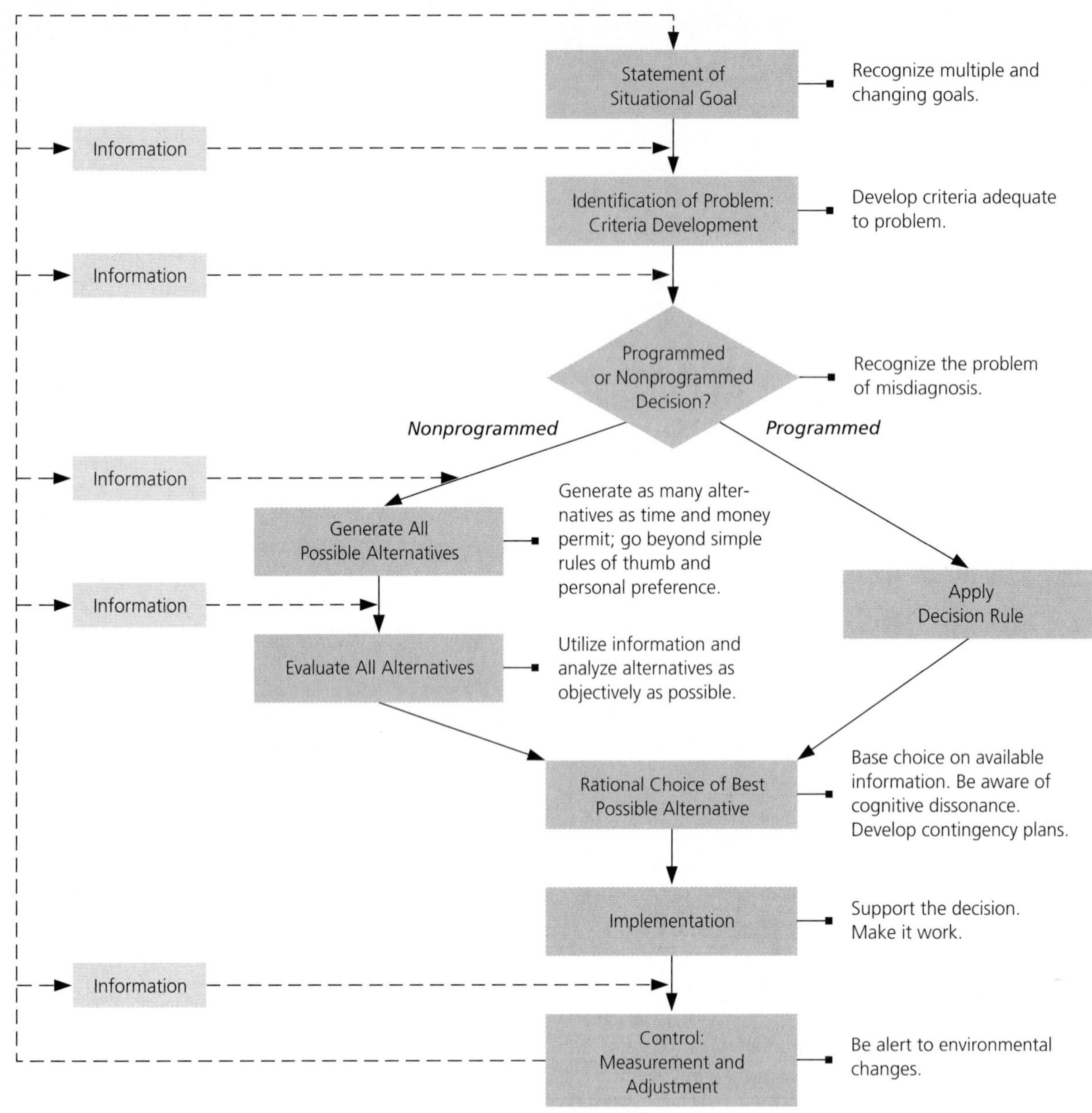

FIGURE 16.4
The Practical Approach to Decision Making with Behavioral Guidelines

In practice, decision makers use some hybrid of the rational, behavioral, and practical approaches to making the tough day-to-day decisions in running organizations. Some decision makers use a methodical process of gathering all available information, developing and evaluating alternatives, and seeking advice from knowledgeable people before making a decision. Others fly from one decision to another, making seemingly hasty decisions, and barking out orders to subordinates. The second group would seem to not use much information or a rational approach to making decisions. Recent research, however, has shown that managers who make decisions very quickly probably are using just as much, or more, information and generating and evaluating alternatives as slower, more methodical decision makers.[21]

The Personal Approach

Although the models just described have provided significant insight into decision making, they do not fully explain the processes people engage in when they are nervous, worried, and agitated over making a decision that has major implications for them, their organization, or their families. One attempt to provide a more realistic view of individual decision making is the model presented by Irving Janis and Leon Mann.[22]

- The conflict model is a very personal approach to decision making because it deals with the personal conflicts that people experience in particularly difficult decision situations.

The Janis-Mann process, called the *conflict model,* is based on research in social psychology and individual decision processes. The model makes five assumptions. First, it deals only with important life decisions—marriage, schooling, career, major organizational decisions—that commit the individual or the organization to a certain course of action following the decision. Second, the model recognizes that procrastination and rationalization are mechanisms by which people avoid making difficult decisions. They are means of coping with the stress of the choice.

Third, the model explicitly acknowledges that some decisions probably will be wrong and that the fear of making an unsound decision can be a deterrent to making any decision at all. Janis and Mann suggest that since not all decisions can be correct, the decision maker should be concerned with the overall "batting average" of good versus bad decisions.

- **Self-reactions** are comparisons of alternatives with internalized moral standards.

Fourth, the model provides for **self-reactions**—comparisons of alternatives with internalized moral standards. Internalized moral standards guide decision making as much as economic and social outcomes do. A proposed course of action may offer many economic and social rewards, but if it violates the decision maker's moral convictions, it is unlikely to be chosen.

Finally, the model recognizes that at times the decision maker is ambivalent about alternative courses of action; in such circumstances, it is very difficult to make a wholehearted commitment to a single choice. Major life decisions seldom allow compromise, however; usually they are either/or decisions that require total commitment to one course of action.

The Janis-Mann conflict model of decision making is shown in Figure 16.5. A concrete example will help explain each step. Our hypothetical individual is Richard, a thirty-year-old engineer, with a working wife and two young children. Richard has been employed at a large manufacturing company for eight years. He keeps abreast of his career situation through visits with peers at work and

21. Kathleen M. Eisenhardt, "Making Fast Strategic Decisions in High-Velocity Environments," *Academy of Management Journal,* September 1989, pp. 543–576.

22. Irving L. Janis and Leon Mann, *Decision Making: A Psychological Analysis of Conflict, Choice, and Commitment* (New York: Free Press, 1977).

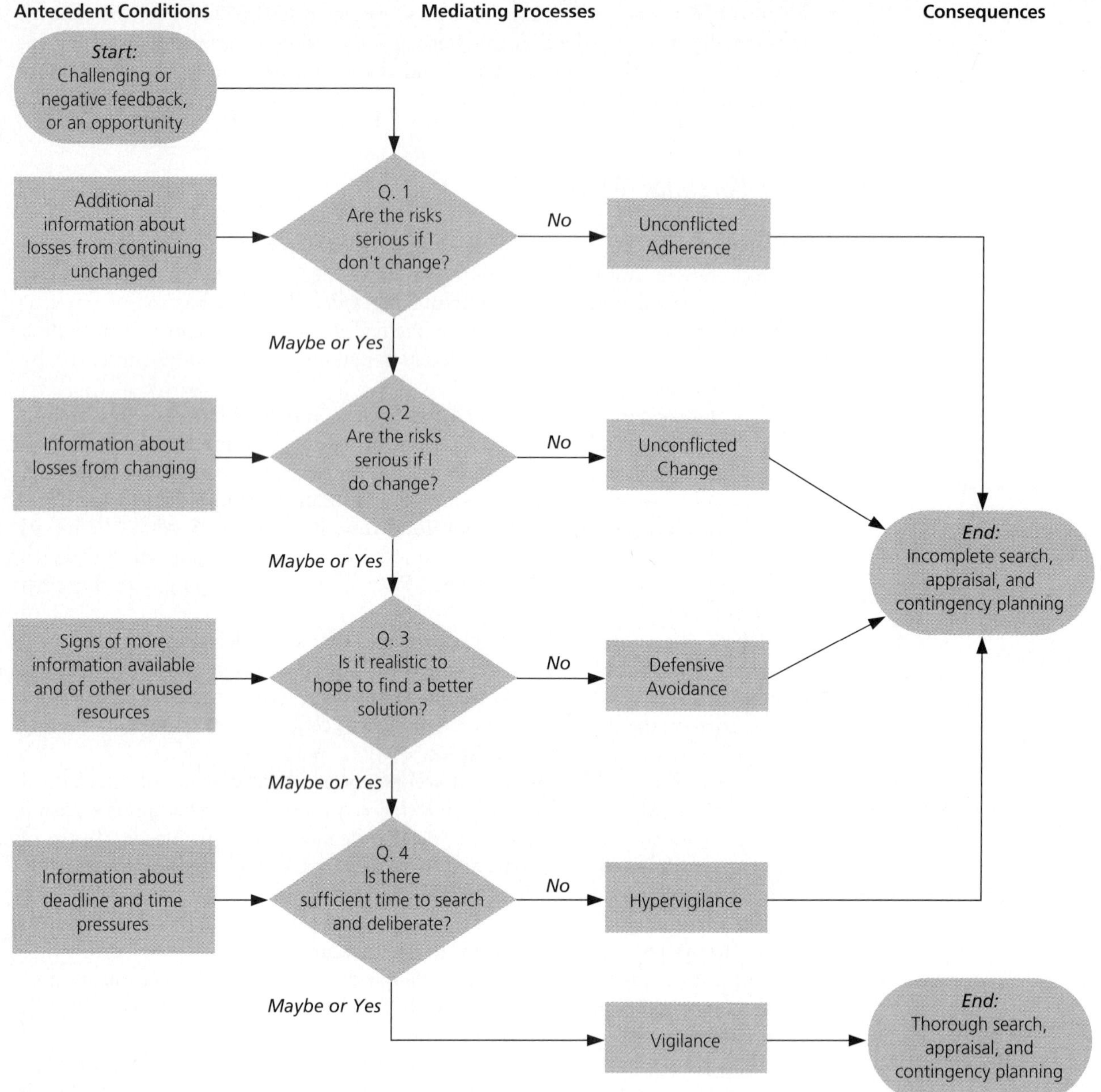

FIGURE 16.5
The Janis-Mann Conflict Model of Decision Making

SOURCE: Reprinted with permission of The Free Press, a division of Macmillan, Inc. from *Decision Making: A Psychological Analysis of Conflict, Choice, and Commitment* by Irving L. Janis and Leon Mann. Copyright © 1977 by The Free Press.

in other companies, feedback from his manager and others regarding his work and future with the firm, the alumni magazine from his university, and other sources.

At work one morning, Richard learns that he has been passed over for a promotion for the second time in a year. He investigates the information, which can be considered negative feedback, and confirms it. As a result, he seeks out other information regarding his career at the company, the prospect of changing employers and the possibility of going back to graduate school to get an MBA. At the same time, he asks himself, "Are the risks serious if I do not make a change?" If the answer is *no,* Richard will continue his present activities. In the model's terms, this option is called **unconflicted adherence.** If the answer is *yes* or *maybe,* Richard will move to the next question in the model.

- **Unconflicted adherence** means continuing with activities if doing so does not entail serious risks.

The second step asks, "Are the risks serious if I do change?" If Richard goes on to this step, he will gather information about potential losses from making a change. He may, for example, find out whether he would lose health insurance and pension benefits if he changed jobs or went back to graduate school. If he believes that changing presents no serious risks, Richard will make the change, called an **unconflicted change.** Otherwise, he will move on to the next step.

- **Unconflicted change** involves making changes in present activities if doing so presents no serious risks.

Suppose Richard has determined that the risks are serious whether or not he makes a change. Now he is in a bind. He believes he must make a change because he will not be promoted further in his present company. Yet serious risks are associated with making a change—perhaps loss of benefits, uncertain promotion opportunities in another company, lost income from going to graduate school for two years. In the third step, Richard wonders, "Is it realistic to hope to find a better solution?" He continues to look for information that can help him make the decision. If the answer to this third question is negative, Richard may give up the hope of finding anything better and opt for what Janis and Mann call **defensive avoidance;** that is, he will make no change and avoid any further contact with the issue. A positive response, however, will move Richard to the next step.

- **Defensive avoidance** means making no changes in present activities and avoiding any further contact with associated issues because there appears to be no hope of finding a better solution.

Here the decision maker, who now recognizes the serious risks involved yet expects to find a solution, asks, "Is there sufficient time to search and deliberate?" Richard now asks himself how quickly he needs to make a change. If he believes he has no time to deliberate much longer, perhaps because of his age, he will experience what Janis and Mann call **hypervigilance.** In this state, he may suffer severe psychological stress and engage in frantic, superficial pursuit of some satisficing strategy. (This might also be called *panic*!) If, on the other hand, Richard believes he has two to three years to consider various alternatives, he will undertake **vigilant information processing,** in which he will thoroughly investigate all possible alternatives, weigh their costs and benefits before making a choice, and develop contingency plans.

- **Hypervigilance** is frantic, superficial pursuit of some satisficing strategy.
- **Vigilant information processing** involves thoroughly investigating all possible alternatives, weighing their costs and benefits before making a decision, and developing contingency plans.

In the actual situation from which this example was drawn, Richard did in fact engage in vigilant information processing. He subsequently entered the MBA program at the local university and completed his degree by attending evening classes while retaining his job. Soon after graduation, he accepted a better job at another manufacturing company.

Negative answers to the questions in the conflict model lead to responses of unconflicted adherence, unconflicted change, defensive avoidance, and hypervigilance. All are coping strategies that result in incomplete search, appraisal, and contingency planning. A decision maker who gives the same answer to all the questions will always engage in the same coping strategy. However, if the answers change as the situation changes, the individual's coping strategies may change as well.

The decision maker who answers positively to each of the four questions is led to vigilant information processing, a process similar to that outlined in the rational decision-making model. The decision maker objectively analyzes the problem and all alternatives, thoroughly searches for information, carefully evaluates the consequences of all alternatives, and diligently plans for implementation and contingencies.

Escalation of Commitment

- **Escalation of commitment** is the tendency to persist in an ineffective course of action when evidence reveals that the project cannot succeed.

Sometimes people continue to try to implement a decision despite clear and convincing evidence that substantial problems exist. **Escalation of commitment** refers to the tendency to persist in an ineffective course of action when evidence indicates that the project is doomed to failure. A recent example is the decision by the government of British Columbia to hold EXPO '86 in Vancouver. Originally, the organizers expected the project to break even financially, so the province would not have to increase taxes to pay for it. As work progressed, it became clear that expenses were far greater than had been projected. But organizers considered it too late to call off the event, despite the huge losses that obviously would occur. Eventually, the province conducted a $300 million lottery to try to cover the costs.[23] Similar examples abound in stock market investments, in political and military situations, and in organizations developing any type of new project.

Barry Staw has suggested several possible reasons for escalation of commitment.[24] Some projects require much front-end investment and offer little return until the end, so the investor must stay in all the way to get any payoff. These "all or nothing" projects require unflagging commitment. Furthermore, investors or project leaders often become so ego involved with their project that their self-identities are totally wrapped up in it.[25] Failure or cancellation seems to threaten

---

23. Jerry Ross and Barry M. Staw, " 'Expo 86: An Escalation Prototype," *Administrative Science Quarterly,* June 1986, pp. 274–297.

24. Barry M. Staw, "Escalation of Commitment to a Course of Action," *Academy of Management Review,* October 1981, pp. 577–587.

25. Joel Brockner, Robert Houser, Gregg Birnbaum, Kathy Lloyd, Janet Deitcher, Sinaia Nathanson, and Jeffrey Z. Rubin, "Escalation of Commitment to an Ineffective Course of Action: The Effect of Feedback Having Negative Implications for Self-Identity," *Administrative Science Quarterly,* March 1986, pp. 109–126.

their reason for existence. Therefore, they continue to push the project as potentially successful despite strong evidence to the contrary. Other times, the social structure, group norms, and group cohesiveness support a project so strongly that cancellation is impossible. Organizational inertia also may force an organization to maintain a failing project. Thus, escalation of commitment is a phenomenon that has a strong foundation.

- "Throwing good money after bad" is the popular way of saying that even if a decision is going bad, one stays committed to it because one has invested so much in it.

How can an individual or organization recognize that a project needs to be stopped before it results in "throwing good money after bad?" Several suggestions have been made; some are easy to put to use, and others are more difficult. Having good information about a project is always a first step to prevention of the escalation problem. Usually it is possible to schedule regular sessions to discuss the project, its progress, the assumptions on which it originally was based, the current validity of these assumptions, and any problems with the project. An objective review is necessary to maintain control.

Some organizations have begun to make separate teams responsible for the development and implementation of a project to reduce ego-involvement. Often the people who initiate a project are those who know the most about it, however, and their expertise can be valuable in the implementation process. Staw suggests that a general strategy for avoiding the escalation problem is to try to create an "experimenting organization" in which every program and project is reviewed regularly and managers are evaluated on their contribution to the total organization rather than to specific projects.[26]

Although several suggestions have been made on how to prevent the escalation problem, much more research on its causes and prevention is needed.

Individual versus Group Decision Making

Both individuals and groups make decisions in organizations. Individuals and groups are subject to different types of pressures as they make decisions. Considerable research has been done to compare the decision-making success of individuals and groups in various situations.[27] When is it better to have a group make a decision than an individual? Researchers have found that the answer depends on several factors, including the type of decision, the knowledge and experience of the people involved, and the type of decision process involved.

In tasks that require an estimation, a prediction, or a judgment of accuracy—usually referred to as *judgmental tasks*—groups typically are superior to individuals, simply because more people contribute to the decision-making process.[28]

26. Barry M. Staw and Jerry Ross, "Good Money after Bad," *Psychology Today,* February 1988, pp. 30–33.

27. Marvin E. Shaw, *Group Dynamics: The Psychology of Small Group Behavior,* 3rd ed. (New York: McGraw-Hill, 1981), pp. 57–68.

28. Ibid.

INTERNATIONAL PERSPECTIVE

Big Sony Decides on Small Team to Make Big Computers

In 1986, Sony Corp. faced a big decision. Known for its dominance in consumer audio and video electronic equipment, it had had little success in the computer industry. In the 1980s, it had introduced the M15 and M35 word processing systems, which included optical disk systems to provide office systems with new capabilities. However, advances by personal computer industry leaders made these products obsolete and kept Sony on the sidelines.

Some analysts believed Sony's problem was not an inability to produce and use the technology but the firm's size. Sony was so large that developing innovative ideas into marketable products was a slow and cumbersome process. Smaller companies, in contrast, could devote 100 percent of their resources to getting personal computer innovations to the market. In 1986, Sony's manager of research and development, Toshi T. Doi, learned that it would take two years to get his newest idea for powerful desktop computing through manufacturing to the market. Doi appealed to Sony president Norio Ohga for $6 million and special permission to cut through the bureaucracy to speed up the process.

Doi created a group of eleven misfit engineers to design and produce the new system based on the latest industry standards. The team developed a very powerful workstation that was competitive with the best in the world and enabled Sony to enter the lucrative market for business workstation computers. The team members virtually lived in a small lab that became the team's home. Cots and mattresses were brought in as the team worked long hours on the workstation that they named NEWS.

Doi's team worked totally outside the normal channels at Sony in developing the technology and the software for the machine. As a result of this development effort, the NEWS workstation proved technologically equal, and in some cases superior, to models offered by Sun Microsystems and Hewlett-Packard—and at a lower price. By 1990, the NEWS workstation had become one of the three top-selling machines.

The credit for making the tough decision to break from the traditional Sony bureaucracy goes to Doi and Ohga. In this case, the decision to be innovative proved that sometimes smaller is better.

SOURCES: "How Sony Pulled Off Its Spectacular Computer Coup," January 15, 1990 issue of *Business Week* © 1990. Adapted by permission. Paula Lippin, "Sony Means Business," *Modern Office Technology*, February 1986, pp. 30–35. © 1986, Penton Publishing Co. Adapted by permission.

However, one especially capable individual may make a better judgment than a group.

In problem-solving tasks, groups generally produce more and better solutions than do individuals. But groups take far longer than individuals to develop solutions and make decisions. However, as *International Perspective* shows, small groups may be able to accomplish some things much faster than a large, bureaucratic organization.

In addition, individual decision making avoids the special problems of group decision making. If the problem to be solved is fairly straightforward, it may be

TABLE 16.2
Characteristics of Group and Individual Decision Making

Group	Individual
Slow process	Fast process
More people to contribute ideas	More appropriate for some judgmental tasks
Ability to divide complex tasks	Avoids special problems of group decision making, such as groupthink
More thorough search for alternatives	
More alternatives generated	
Greater interest stimulated	

more appropriate to have a single capable individual concentrate on its solution. On the other hand, complex problems are more appropriate for groups. Such problems can be divided into parts and the parts assigned to individuals, who bring their results back to the group for discussion and decision making.

An additional advantage to group decision making is that it often creates greater interest in the task.[29] Heightened interest may increase the time and effort given to the task, resulting in more ideas, a more thorough search for solutions, better evaluation of alternatives, and improved decision quality. Table 16.2 summarizes the characteristics of group and individual decision making.

Decision Making in Groups

This section builds on our discussion of group dynamics in Chapter 7. As we described there, people in organizations work in a variety of groups—formal and informal, permanent and temporary. Most of these groups make decisions that affect the welfare of the organization and the people in it. Here we discuss factors and behaviors that affect group decision making.

Basic Factors

The group factors discussed in Chapter 7, such as physical environment, size and composition, characteristics of members, and norms and cohesiveness, have a powerful impact on the effectiveness of group decision making. The physical environment, composition of the group, and relative status of the members are particularly important.

The physical aspects of group meetings must be conducive to open discussion, with tables, chairs, and any necessary equipment available and in working

29. Huber, *Managerial Decision Making*, pp. 140–148.

order. In an inappropriate working environment, it can be significantly more difficult for group members to cooperate in the problem-solving process.

The composition of the group must be such that the members' similarities and differences fit the demands of the problem. Recall that groups with a heterogeneous membership tend to produce a larger quantity of more diverse ideas than those whose membership is homogeneous. Heterogeneous groups are appropriate for tasks that require the generation and evaluation of many alternatives. However, it often is more difficult for a heterogeneous group to reach agreement; a homogeneous group is more appropriate when quick agreement is needed. The characteristics of individual members—personality, knowledge, expertise, and so on—also should be compatible with the problem at hand.

The third important factor is the status or power relationships inherent in the group. Individuals with more status or power may have a particularly strong influence on the group's decision. Other members may believe these higher-status individuals have superior insight; or the higher-status members may influence reward allocation or may have some coercive power they can wield in the future. Depending on how they are managed, these and other sources of individual influence can assist or impede the group decision-making process.[30]

Group Polarization

■ **Group polarization** is the tendency for a group's post-discussion attitudes to be more extreme than but in the same direction as the average pre-discussion attitudes.

Members' attitudes and opinions with respect to an issue or a solution may change during the group discussion. Some studies of this tendency have showed the change to be a fairly consistent movement toward a more risky solution, called *risky shift*.[31] Other studies and analyses have revealed that the group-induced shift is not always toward more risk; the group is just as likely to move toward a more conservative view.[32] Generally, the average of the group members' post-discussion attitudes tends to be more extreme than average pre-discussion attitudes.[33] This tendency, termed **group polarization,** is illustrated in Figure 16.6.

Several features of group discussion contribute to polarization.[34] When individuals discover in group discussion that others share their opinions, they may feel more strongly about their opinions, resulting in a more extreme view.

---

30. Shaw, *Group Dynamics.*

31. James A. F. Stoner, "Risky and Cautious Shifts in Group Decisions: The Influence of Widely Held Values," *Journal of Experimental Social Psychology,* October 1968, pp. 442–459; M. A. Wallach, N. Kogan, and D. J. Bem, "Group Influence on Individual Risk Taking," *Journal of Abnormal and Social Psychology,* August 1962, pp. 75–86.

32. Dorwin Cartwright, "Risk Taking by Individuals and Groups: An Assessment of Research Employing Choice Dilemmas," *Journal of Personality and Social Psychology,* December 1971, pp. 361–378.

33. S. Moscovici and M. Zavalloni, "The Group as a Polarizer of Attitudes," *Journal of Personality and Social Psychology,* June 1969, pp. 125–135.

34. See Shaw, *Group Dynamics,* pp. 68–76, for further discussion of group polarization.

FIGURE 16.6
Group Polarization

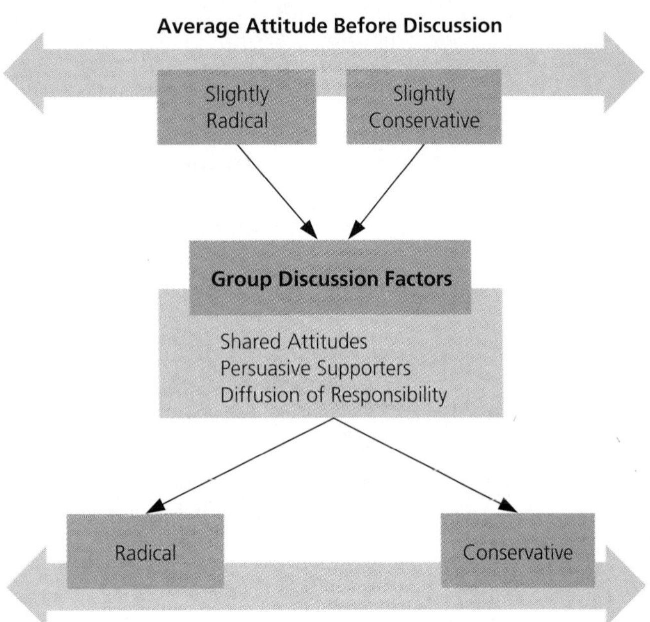

Persuasive arguments also can encourage polarization. If members who strongly support a particular position are able to express themselves cogently in the discussion, less avid supporters of the position may become convinced that it is correct. In addition, members may believe that because the group is deciding, they are not individually responsible for the decision or its outcomes. This diffusion of responsibility may enable them to accept and support a decision more radical than those they would make as individuals.

Polarization can profoundly affect group decision making. If group members are known to lean toward a particular decision before a discussion, it may be expected that their post-decision position will be even more extreme. Understanding this phenomenon may be useful for one who seeks to affect their decision.

Groupthink

- **Groupthink** is a mode of thinking that occurs when members of a group are deeply involved in a cohesive in-group and desire for unanimity offsets their motivation to appraise alternative courses of action.

Although highly cohesive groups often are very successful at accomplishing their goals, such groups have serious difficulties as well. One problem is groupthink. **Groupthink,** according to Irving L. Janis, is "a mode of thinking that people engage in when they are deeply involved in a cohesive in-group, when the members' strivings for unanimity override their motivation to realistically appraise alternative courses of action."[35] When groupthink occurs, then, the group

35. Irving L. Janis, *Groupthink,* 2nd ed. (Boston: Houghton Mifflin, 1982), p. 9.

unknowingly makes unanimity rather than the best decision its goal. Groupthink can occur in decision making within organizations, as may have been the case in the E. F. Hutton checking scandal.[36]

Symptoms of Groupthink Figure 16.7 outlines the groupthink process. The three primary conditions that foster the development of groupthink are cohesiveness, the leader's promotion of his or her preferred solution, and insulation of the group from experts' opinions. A group in which groupthink has taken hold exhibits eight well-defined symptoms:

1. An illusion of invulnerability, shared by most or all members, that creates excessive optimism and encourages extreme risk taking
2. Collective efforts to rationalize to discount warnings that might lead members to reconsider assumptions before recommitting themselves to past policy decisions
3. An unquestioned belief in the group's inherent morality, inclining members to ignore the ethical and moral consequences of their decisions
4. Stereotyped views of "enemy" leaders as too evil to warrant genuine attempts to negotiate or as too weak or stupid to counter whatever risky attempts are made to defeat their purposes
5. Direct pressure on a member who expresses strong arguments against any of the group's stereotypes, illusions, or commitments, making clear that such dissent is contrary to what is expected of loyal members
6. Self-censorship of deviations from the apparent group consensus, reflecting each member's inclination to minimize the importance of his or her doubts and counterarguments
7. A shared illusion of unanimity (resulting partly from self-censorship of deviations, augmented by the false assumption that silence means consent)
8. The emergence of self-appointed mindguards—members who protect the group from adverse information that might shatter their shared complacency about the effectiveness and morality of their decisions[37]

Janis contends that the group involved in the Watergate cover-up—Richard Nixon, H. R. Haldeman, John Ehrlichman, and John Dean—may have been a victim of groupthink. Evidence of most of the groupthink symptoms can be found in the unedited transcripts of the group's deliberations.[38]

Decision-Making Defects and Decision Quality When groupthink dominates group deliberations, the likelihood that the decision-making defects shown in

36. Daniel Goleman, "Following the Leader," *Science 85,* October 1985, p. 18; "Violation of Business Ethics or Outright Fraud?" *ASA Banking Journal,* July 1987, pp. 30–34; Harold Seneker, "Nice Timing," *Forbes,* January 27, 1986, p. 102.

37. Irving L. Janis, *Victims of Groupthink* (Boston: Houghton Mifflin, 1972), pp. 197–198.

38. Janis, *Groupthink.*

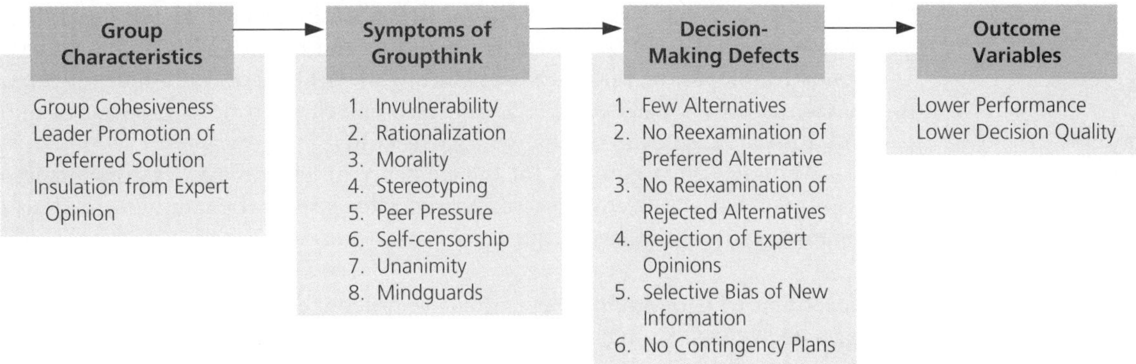

SOURCE: Adapted from Gregory Moorhead, "Groupthink: Hypothesis in Need of Testing," *Group and Organization Studies,* Vol. 7, No. 4 (December 1982), pp. 429–444. Copyright © 1982 by Sage Publications, Inc. Reprinted by permission of Sage Publications, Inc.

FIGURE 16.7
The Groupthink Process

Figure 16.7 will occur increases. The group is less likely to survey a full range of alternatives and may focus on only a few (often one or two). In discussing a preferred alternative, the group may fail to examine it for nonobvious risks and drawbacks. Even when new information is obtained, the group may not reexamine previously rejected alternatives for nonobvious gains or some means of reducing apparent costs. The group may reject expert opinions that run counter to its own views and may choose to consider only information that supports its preferred solution. The decision to launch the space shuttle Challenger in January 1986 may have been a product of groupthink, because negative information was ignored by the group that made the decision.[39] Finally, the group may not consider any potential setbacks or countermoves by competing groups and therefore may fail to develop contingency plans. It should be noted that Janis contends that these six defects may arise from other common problems as well: fatigue, prejudice, inaccurate information, information overload, and ignorance.[40]

Defects in decision making do not always lead to bad outcomes or defeats. Even if its own decision-making processes are flawed, one side can win a battle because of the poor decisions made by the other side's leaders. Nevertheless, decisions produced by defective processes have a lower probability of success.

Research Basis of Groupthink The groupthink concept emerged from research on the decision-making procedures of several U.S. military and civilian groups responsible for decisions that contributed to a notable success or fiasco. The successes were the Cuban missile crisis of 1962 and the development of the

39. Gregory Moorhead, Richard K. Ference, and Christopher P. Neck, "Group Decision Fiascoes Continue: Space Shuttle Challenger and a Revised Groupthink Framework," *Human Relations,* vol. 44, 1991, pp. 539–550.

40. Janis, *Groupthink,* pp. 193–197; Gregory Moorhead, "Groupthink: Hypothesis in Need of Testing," *Group & Organization Studies,* December 1982, pp. 429–444.

Marshall Plan after World War II. The fiascoes included the Bay of Pigs invasion in 1961, the invasion of North Korea during the Korean War, the U.S. defense against the Japanese raid on Pearl Harbor in 1941, and the military escalation in Vietnam from 1964 to 1967. The research relied on news reports, memoirs, and, in some cases, interviews with participants.

Although the arguments for the existence of groupthink are convincing, the hypothesis has not been subjected to rigorous empirical examination. Research supports parts of the model but leaves some questions unanswered.[41]

Prevention of Groupthink Several suggestions have been offered to help managers reduce the probability of groupthink in group decision making.[42] Summarized in Table 16.3, these prescriptions fall into four categories depending on whether they apply to the leader, the organization, the individual, or the process. All are designed to facilitate the critical evaluation of alternatives and discourage the single-minded pursuit of unanimity.

Participation in Decision Making

- Participation in decision making is an important part of managing motivation, leadership, organization structure, and decision-making processes.

A major issue in group decision making is the degree to which employees should participate in the process. Early management theories, such as those of the scientific management school, advocated a clear separation between the duties of managers and workers: Management was to make the decisions, and employees were to implement them.[43] Other approaches have urged that employees be allowed to participate in decisions to increase their ego involvement, motivation, and satisfaction.[44] Numerous research studies have shown that whereas employees who seek responsibility and challenge on the job may find participation in the decision-making process both motivating and enriching, other employees may regard such participation as a waste of time and a management imposition.[45]

Whether employee participation in decision making is appropriate depends on the situation. The Vroom-Yetton-Jago model of leadership (discussed in Chapter 9) is one popular approach to determining the appropriate degree of

41. Gregory Moorhead and John R. Montanari, "Empirical Analysis of the Groupthink Phenomenon," *Human Relations,* May 1986, pp. 399–410; John R. Montanari and Gregory Moorhead, "Development of the Groupthink Assessment Inventory," *Educational and Psychological Measurement,* vol. 49, Spring 1989, pp. 209–219.

42. Janis, *Groupthink.*

43. Frederick W. Taylor, *The Principles of Scientific Management* (New York: Harper & Row, 1911).

44. Rensis Likert, *New Patterns of Management* (New York: McGraw-Hill, 1961); Chris Argyris, *Personality and Organization* (New York: Harper & Row, 1957).

45. N. C. Morse and E. Reimer, "The Experimental Change of a Major Organizational Variable," *Journal of Abnormal and Social Psychology,* January 1956, pp. 120–129; Lester Coch and John R. P. French, "Overcoming Resistance to Change," *Human Relations,* vol. 1, 1948, pp. 512–532.

TABLE 16.3
Prescriptions for Prevention of Groupthink

A. Leader Prescriptions
1. Assign everyone the role of critical evaluator.
2. Be impartial; do not state preferences.
3. Assign the devil's advocate role to at least one group member.
4. Use outside experts to challenge the group.

B. Organizational Prescriptions
1. Set up several independent groups to study the same issue.
2. Train managers and group leaders in groupthink prevention techniques.

C. Individual Prescriptions
1. Be a critical thinker.
2. Discuss group deliberations with a trusted outsider; report back to the group.

D. Process Prescriptions
1. Periodically break the group into subgroups to discuss the issues.
2. Take time to study external factors.
3. Hold second-chance meetings to rethink issues before making a commitment.

employee participation.[46] The model includes decision styles that vary from autocratic (the leader alone makes the decision) to democratic (the group makes the decision, with each member having an equal say). The choice of style rests on eight considerations that concern the characteristics of the situation and the subordinates.

Participation in decision making is also related to organizational structure. For example, decentralization involves the delegation of some decision-making authority throughout the organizational hierarchy. The more decentralized the organization, then, the more its employees tend to participate in decision making. Regardless of whether one views participation in decision making as a topic of leadership, organization structure, or motivation, it remains an important aspect of organizations that continues to occupy managers and organizational scholars.[47]

Group Problem Solving

A typical interacting group may have difficulty with any of several steps in the decision-making process. One common problem arises in the alternative gener-

46. Victor H. Vroom and Arthur G. Jago, *The New Leadership* (Englewood Cliffs, N.J.: Prentice-Hall, 1988).

47. See Carrie R. Leana, Edwin A. Locke, and David M. Schweiger, "Fact and Fiction in Analyzing Research on Participative Decision Making: A Critique of Cotton, Vollrath, Froggatt, Lengnick-Hall, and Jennings," *Academy of Management Review,* January 1990, pp. 137–146, and John L. Cotton, David A. Vollrath, Mark L. Lengnick-Hall, and Mark L. Froggatt, "Fact: The Form of Participation Does Matter—A Rebuttal to Leana, Locke, and Schweiger," *Academy of Management Review,* January 1990, pp. 147–153.

ation phase: The search may be arbitrarily ended before all plausible alternatives have been identified. Several types of group interactions can have this effect. If members immediately express their reactions to the alternatives as they are first proposed, potential contributors may begin to censor their ideas to avoid embarrassing criticism from the group. Less confident group members, intimidated by members who have more experience, higher status, or more power, also may censor their ideas for fear of embarrassment or punishment. In addition, the group leader may limit idea generation by enforcing requirements concerning time, appropriateness, cost, feasibility, and the like.

To improve the alternative generation process, managers may employ any of three techniques—brainstorming, the nominal group technique, or the Delphi technique—to stimulate the group's problem-solving capabilities.

Brainstorming

- **Brainstorming** is a technique used in the alternative generation phase of decision making that assists in development of numerous alternative courses of action.

Brainstorming, a technique made popular in the 1950s, is most often used in the idea generation phase of decision making and is intended to solve problems that are new to the organization and have major consequences. For example, suppose a bank faces the broad challenges of deregulation, changing economic conditions,

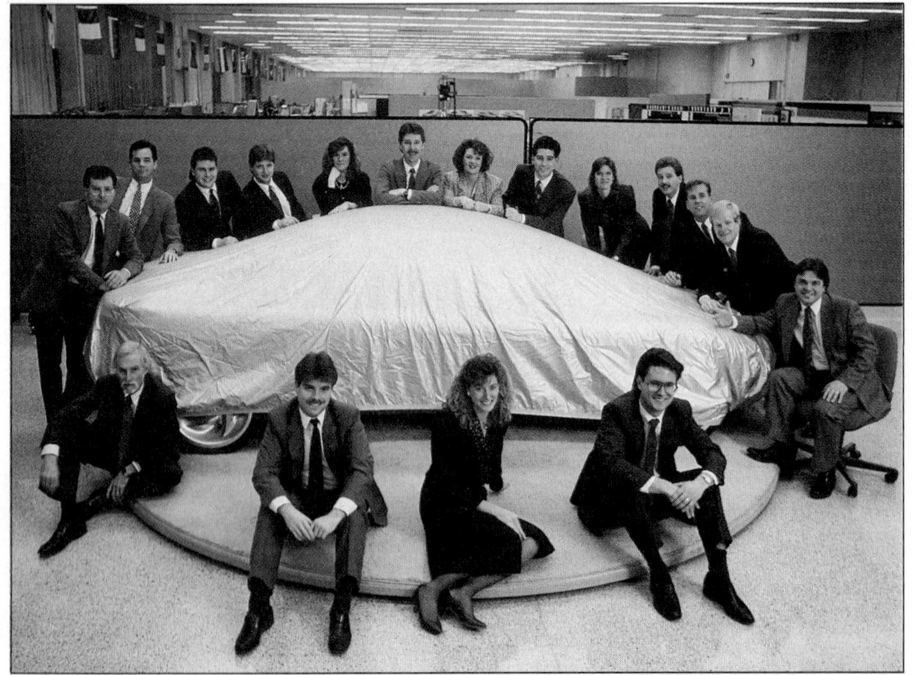

This team of young designers, planners, and engineers are part of a skunk-works team of twenty that designed and planned the 1995 Ford Mustang. From different functional areas within Ford, the team worked together under one roof to evaluate new ideas more quickly and cut costs by speeding communication and decision making.

and the possibility of interstate banking. Although currently it is the largest bank in the state, its major competitor is gaining ground. What can the bank do to stimulate deposits and respond to the challenges it faces? Bank management might use brainstorming to approach these difficult decisions.

In brainstorming, the group convenes specifically to generate alternatives. The members present ideas and clarify them with brief explanations. Each idea is recorded in full view of all members, usually on a flip chart. To avoid self-censoring, no attempts to evaluate the ideas are allowed. Group members are encouraged to offer any ideas that occur to them, even those that seem too risky or impossible to implement. (The absence of such ideas, in fact, is evidence that the group members are engaging in self-censorship.) In a subsequent session, after the ideas have been recorded and distributed to members for review, the alternatives are evaluated.

The intent of brainstorming is to produce totally new ideas and solutions by stimulating the creativity of group members and encouraging them to build on the contributions of others. Brainstorming does not provide the resolution to the problem, an evaluation scheme, or the decision itself. Instead, it should produce a list of alternatives that is more innovative and comprehensive than one developed by the typical interacting group.

The Nominal Group Technique

- With the **nominal group technique (NGT),** group members follow a generate-discussion-vote cycle until they reach an appropriate decision.

The **nominal group technique** (**NGT**) offers another means of improving group decision making. Whereas brainstorming is used primarily for alternative generation, NGT may be employed in other phases of decision making, such as identification of the problem and of appropriate criteria for evaluating alternatives. In NGT, a group of individuals convenes to address an issue. The issue is described to the group, and each individual writes a list of ideas; no discussion among the members is permitted. Following the five-to-ten-minute idea generation period, individual members take turns reporting their ideas, one at a time, to the group. The ideas are recorded on a flip chart, and members are encouraged to add to the list by building on the ideas of others. After all ideas have been presented, the members may discuss them and continue to build on them or proceed to the next phase. This part of the NGT process can also be carried out without a face-to-face meeting, for example, by mail, telephone, or computer. A meeting, however, helps members develop a group feeling and puts interpersonal pressure on the members to do their best in developing their lists.[48]

After the discussion, members privately vote on or rank the ideas or report their preferences in some other agreed-upon way. Reporting is private to reduce any feelings of intimidation. After voting, the group may discuss the results and

48. See Bass, *Organizational Decision Making,* pp. 162–163, for further discussion of the nominal group technique.

continue to generate and discuss ideas. The generation-discussion-vote cycle can continue until an appropriate decision is reached.

The nominal group technique has two principal advantages. It helps overcome the negative effects of power and status differences among group members, and it can be used in the problem exploration, alternative generation, and evaluation phases of decision making. Its primary disadvantage lies in its structured nature, which may limit creativity.

The Delphi Technique

- The **Delphi technique** is a method of systematically gathering judgments of experts for use in developing forecasts.

The **Delphi technique** originally was developed by Rand Corp. as a method of systematically gathering the judgments of experts for use in developing forecasts. It is designed for groups that do not meet face to face. For instance, the product development manager of a major toy manufacturer might use the Delphi technique to probe the views of industry experts to forecast developments in the dynamic toy market.

The manager who desires the input of a group is the central figure in the process. After recruiting participants, the manager develops a questionnaire for them to complete. The questionnaire is relatively simple in that it contains straightforward questions that deal with the issue, trends in the area, new technological developments, and other factors in which the manager is interested. The manager summarizes the responses and reports back to the experts with another questionnaire. This cycle may be repeated as many times as necessary to generate the information the manager needs.

The Delphi technique is useful when experts are physically dispersed, anonymity is desired, or the participants are known to have difficulty communicating with one another because of extreme differences of opinion.[49] This method also avoids the intimidation problems that may exist in decision-making groups. On the other hand, the technique eliminates the often fruitful results of direct interaction among group members.

Creativity in Decision Making

A goal at 3M Co. is to obtain 25 percent of sales from products that are less than five years old. To achieve this goal, 3M employees must constantly search for new ideas and breakthroughs that will keep the firm on the leading edge of its markets. Most companies consider this level of innovation impossible, but

49. See Huber, *Managerial Decision Making,* pp. 205–212, for more details on the Delphi technique.

3M frequently exceeds its goal through a combination of creativity and imagination.[50]

■ **Creativity** is the process of developing innovative views of situations.

Creativity is the process of developing original and imaginative views of situations. Creativity is an important dimension of individual behavior in organizations. Without creativity, organizations would never change, and their employees would stagnate.

Creative behaviors include all of the following:

1. Inventing a new product or service
2. Inventing a new use for an existing product or service
3. Solving a problem
4. Resolving a dispute

Unfortunately, creativity is not a mechanical process that can be turned on and off.[51] Some people are more creative than others, and no one is creative all the time. Organizations struggle with keeping their employees creative amid the daily hassles of doing their jobs. *Management in Action* illustrates how one organization has defined itself as an innovation company rather than an electronics company to keep ongoing innovation and creativity uppermost in its employees' minds.

■ Creativity is not spontaneous; it involves preparation, incubation, insight, and verification.

Despite its acknowledged importance, very little research has been done on creativity in organizational settings.[52] Nevertheless, a broad outline of the creative process, shown in Figure 16.8, has become generally accepted.[53]

Preparation

The first step in the creative process is preparation. Preparation involves more than just sitting around waiting for something to happen; it is an active process that may require strenuous effort. Many writers, for example, travel extensively, seeking new experiences and talking to a variety of people. Education and training also are necessary for much creative work. An opera singer trains under a voice coach, a scientist spends long hours in a lab, and an actor takes drama classes; all are preparing for creative activities. Creative decision makers study the issues surrounding a decision and participate extensively in group meetings where new ideas and alternative points of view abound, such as in brainstorming meetings.

---

50. Stratford P. Sherman, "Eight Big Masters of Innovation," *Fortune,* October 15, 1984, pp. 66–84.

51. Teresa M. Amabile, "The Social Psychology of Creativity: A Componential Conceptualization," *Journal of Personality and Social Psychology,* August 1983, pp. 357–376.

52. Thomas Busse and Richard Mansfield, "Theories of the Creative Process: A Review and a Perspective," *Journal of Creative Behavior,* vol. 4, 1980, pp. 91–103, 132.

53. G. Wallas, *The Art of Thought* (New York: Harcourt Brace, 1926).

MANAGEMENT IN ACTION

A Company Based on Innovation

Since its founding in 1957 by Robert Halperin and Paul Cook, Raychem Corp. has been noted for its continual emphasis on developing new electronic products that branch into the defense, aerospace, automotive, and telecommunications industries. In fact, Paul Cook describes Raychem as a company whose business is innovation, not electronics. He claims that to remain innovative, an organization must be eager to make itself obsolete as quickly as possible. Raychem was built by hiring talented people, grouping them into teams, and encouraging them to invent new products. Some analysts have called Raychem a sandbox for scientists, because scientists are free to "play" with technology until something new develops. According to Cook, Raychem's strategy has been to master a set of core technologies and develop thousands of proprietary products based on those technologies. Evidently the strategy has paid off, because Raychem has continued to be profitable for more than thirty-three years.

Things may change soon, however. Paul Cook relinquished his position as chief executive officer when he turned sixty-five in early 1990, turning things over to fifty-seven-year-old Robert Saldich, a veteran of Raychem since 1964. (Cook will stay on as chair of the board, however.) Saldich began his reign by laying off nine hundred workers and closing two major divisions. Choosing to focus on fewer operations, Saldich is betting on strong growth in the telecommunications industry in Japan and Europe and the stability of defense-related industries outside the United States. The effects of these drastic moves will be numerous. First, industry analysts say the consolidation was badly needed for the company to achieve its goals of 15 to 20 percent annual growth in the 1990s. Second, and perhaps more important, the innovators at Raychem must respond to the concerns of meeting growth targets and profitability projections. Innovation is a hard thing to develop. Once it is achieved, however, the trick is to maintain it. Can Raychem sustain its image as a hallmark of innovation?

SOURCES: Stephen Kindel, "Sand Castles: Running Raychem Like a Business May Be Robert Saldich's Toughest Challenge," *Financial World,* October 2, 1990, pp. 48–49; "Raychem Shifts Focus; Will Boost Foreign Sales," *San José Business Journal,* June 4, 1990; William Taylor, "The Business of Innovation: An Interview with Paul Cook," *Harvard Business Review,* March-April 1990, pp. 96–106; "Raychem Hopes Too Few Cooks Won't Spoil Its High-Tech Broth," *San Mateo Times and News Leader,* March 13, 1989.

Incubation

Incubation, the next step in the creative process, is a time for (often subconscious) reflection, thought, and consideration. During this stage, a person shifts direct attention away from involvement in the problem, perhaps by literally "sleeping on it," socializing with friends, or participating in some recreational activity such as hiking or mountain climbing. Meanwhile, ideas pertaining to the central issue are maturing and new ideas may be formulating in the person's mind. The desired outcome is something new: a novel idea, decision, or performance. Whatever form this burst of creativity takes, it is usually referred to as *insight.*

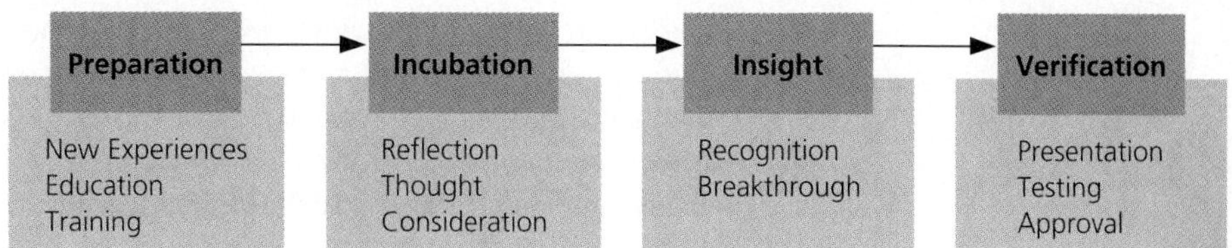

FIGURE 16.8
The Creative Process

Insight

Insight is the breakthrough achieved as a result of preparation and incubation. Suppose a manager has been told by her boss that she must fire one of two key employees because of budget cuts. The manager wants to find a way to retain both employees. She prepares by analyzing all the budget information she can find and looking over the performance record of each employee. Then she goes to a movie with a friend to think things over. At some point—perhaps during intermission, over dessert after the movie, or while driving to work the next day—she suddenly recognizes a strategy for keeping both subordinates. This recognition is insight.

Verification

The last stage of the creative process is verification: determining whether an insight is valid. The manager just described, for example, may need to present her idea to her boss. If the boss approves the idea, and thus verifies it, it can be implemented. If the idea is not accepted, however, the manager may have to continue to search for new ideas and strategies. Similarly, scientists must test their breakthroughs in the laboratory and authors must submit their work to editors for approval. Each of these checks represents a form of verification. Many verification systems have flaws, however. Kevin Costner took his script for *Dances with Wolves* to several movie studios before he found one willing to produce the film.

Summary of Key Points

- Decision making is the process of choosing one alternative from several. The basic elements of decision making include a goal; alternative courses of action; potential outcomes of the alternatives, each with its own value relative to the goal; and a choice of one alternative based on evaluation of the outcomes. Information is available regarding the alternatives, outcomes, and values.
- Programmed decisions are well-structured, recurring decisions made according to set decision rules. Nonprogrammed decisions involve nonroutine,

poorly structured situations with unclear sources of information; they cannot be made according to existing decision rules.

- Decision making may also be classified according to the information available. The classifications—certainty, risk, and uncertainty—reflect the amount of information available regarding the outcomes of alternatives.
- Decision making may be viewed as a completely rational process in which goals are established, a problem is identified, alternatives are generated and evaluated, a choice is made and implemented, and control is exercised. The behavioral model provides another view of the decision-making process. It is characterized by the use of procedures and rules of thumb, suboptimizing, and satisficing. The rational and behavioral views can be combined into a practical model. The Janis-Mann conflict model recognizes the personal anxiety individuals face when they must make highly consequential decisions.
- Escalation of commitment to an ineffective course of action occurs in many decision situations. It may be caused by psychological, social, ego, and organizational factors.
- Both individuals and groups make decisions in organizations. An individual decision maker may be preferable when time is important, when the individual is especially capable, and when it is important to avoid the pitfalls of group decision making. Groups are appropriate for most problem-solving tasks, because groups generate more ideas and more interest.
- Group decision making involves problems as well as benefits. One possible problem is group polarization, the shift of members' attitudes and opinions to a more extreme position following group discussion. Another difficulty is groupthink, a mode of thinking in which the striving for unanimity overrides the critical appraisal of alternatives. Yet another concern involves employee participation in decision making. The appropriate degree of participation depends on the characteristics of the situation.
- Brainstorming, the nominal group technique, and the Delphi technique are three methods for improving group decision making. These techniques reduce the problems of poor communication, intimidation, and premature evaluation of ideas.
- Creativity is the process of developing original and imaginative views of situations. The steps in the creative process are preparation, incubation, insight, and verification.

Discussion Questions

1. Some have argued that people, not organizations, make decisions and that the study of "organizational" decision making therefore is pointless. Do you agree with this argument? Why or why not?
2. What information did you use in deciding to enter the school you now attend?

3. When your alarm goes off each morning, you have a decision to make: whether to get up and go to school or work or stay in bed and sleep longer. Is this a programmed or nonprogrammed decision? Why?
4. Describe a situation in which you experienced escalation of commitment to an ineffective course of action. What did you do about it? Do you wish you had handled it differently? Why or why not?
5. Describe at least three points in the decision-making process at which information plays an important role.
6. How does the role of information in the rational model of decision making differ from the role of information in the behavioral model?
7. Recall a time when you were part of a group in which groupthink occurred. Describe what happened in that group. How could you have prevented groupthink from occurring?
8. How are group polarization and groupthink similar? How do they differ?
9. How do brainstorming, the nominal group technique, and the Delphi techniques differ?
10. Describe a recent decision situation in which you reached a state of hypervigilance. What could you have done to avoid this stage?

CASE 16.1 Making Tough Decisions at Burroughs Wellcome

Companies that make drugs to combat diseases are used to investing huge amounts of time and money for many years to discover new chemical compounds that work. Once they succeed, the drug must go through years of testing before the Food and Drug Administration (FDA) approves it for use. For drugs aimed at especially difficult and rare diseases, the 1983 Orphan Drug Law can provide seven years of licensing protection once the drug goes to market. The race by pharmaceutical companies to find a cure for acquired immune deficiency syndrome (AIDS) seemingly was won in 1987 by researchers at Burroughs Wellcome, a North Carolina–based subsidiary of the British company Burroughs Wellcome P.L.C.

Burroughs Wellcome is known for its efforts in researching obscure diseases and searching for antiviral compounds rather than the more common antibiotic compounds. The AIDS virus was especially difficult to deal with and became an obsession with researchers at Burroughs Wellcome in the mid-1980s. Using her knowledge of antiviral compounds and viral processes, an organic chemist, Janet Rideout, suggested that they test azidothymidine, or AZT, on the AIDS virus.

After significant early success, a crucial test was set up in 1986 in which 145 AIDS patients received AZT and 137 AIDS patients received a placebo (neutral drug). These 282 patients, their doctors, and Burroughs Wellcome officials did not know which patients received AZT; only an independent panel of doctors knew. During the summer several patients died, some got better, and some got worse. Finally, the researchers revealed that only one patient on AZT died compared to nineteen on the placebo. Based on these and further, more detailed test results, the FDA approved the drug for use.

Burroughs Wellcome then faced the task of manufacturing the drug in large quantities, getting it to market (estimated to be in the millions worldwide), and determining an appropriate price. First, it developed a complex process of converting thymidine (a biological chemical from herring sperm) into AZT. In addition to more than $50 million in early development costs, it spent millions on raw materials, plant, and equipment. Burroughs Wellcome and other pharmaceutical companies routinely spend hundreds of millions of dollars on research and development on several drugs with the expectation that one will pay off. So when one drug does, the company must charge prices that reflect the market for that drug as well as the firm's overall development costs for many drugs over many years.

AZT (sold on the market as Retrovir) originally was priced at about $1.50 per pill, which translated to more than $8,000 per year for a normal dosage. This high price caused quite an uproar among gay groups, some members of Congress, and the public at large. At this point, Burroughs Wellcome officials had expected to be hailed as heroes for finding a cure for one of the world's deadliest diseases; instead, they found themselves being crucified in the press. As subsequent research indicated that even more AIDS patients might be helped, the company reduced the price by 20 percent but still came under fire for price gouging.

The company's problem, common to all pharmaceutical companies, was how to charge for its discoveries that are essential to the health and welfare of society but are due to years of investment. In 1989, sales of AZT were estimated at approximately $200 million. This enabled the parent company, Burroughs Wellcome P.L.C., to earn $333 million on total sales of $2.4 billion and contribute $55 million to its charitable trust. Industry officials, scientists, and analysts agree that Burroughs Wellcome's strategies in developing, testing, and marketing the drug were well within the normal bounds of pharmaceutical industry standards.

Case Questions

1. Describe at least two major ethical issues Burroughs Wellcome faced in its testing, development, and marketing of AZT.
2. What factors did Burroughs Wellcome need to take into account in making its pricing decisions?
3. Do you believe Burroughs Wellcome would make the same decisions again? Why or why not?

SOURCES: Brian O'Reilly, "The Inside Story of the AIDS Drug," *Fortune,* November 5, 1990, pp. 112–129; "How Much for a Reprieve from AIDS?" *Time,* October 2, 1989, pp. 81–82; "An Advance against AIDS," *Fortune,* October 13, 1986, p. 14.

CASE 16.2 A Big Step for Peak Electronics

Lynda Murray, chief executive officer of Peak Electronics Corp., faced a difficult decision. Her company was a leader in making parts for standard cassette and reel-to-reel tape recorders. Murray had watched with some misgivings as digital technology hit the market in the form of compact disc players, and she had to decide whether to lead Peak into the digital age. Even though digital tape players were encountering legal hurdles in the American market, they were starting to take hold in Japan and Europe. Was America—and Peak—ready for them?

Murray had plenty of help in making the decision. First she met with the company's marketing division. Everyone had an opinion. Some predicted that every audio component would be digital by the turn of the century; others believed the popularity of even compact disc players was already waning. Everyone agreed that they needed time to conduct surveys, gather data, and find out what products the public really wanted and how much they would be willing to pay for them.

The people in research and development had a different approach. They were tired of making small improvements in a mature and perfected product. They had been reading technical material about digital tape, and they saw it as an exciting new technology that would give an innovative company a chance to make it big. Time was of the essence, they insisted. If Peak was to become an important supplier of parts for the new decks, it had to have the components ready. Delay would be fatal to the product.

A meeting of the vice presidents produced a scenario with which Murray was all too familiar. Years ago these executives had discovered that they could not out-argue one another in these meetings, but they had faith in their staffs' abilities to succeed where they had failed. Before Murray even walked into the room, she knew what their recommendation would be: to create a committee of representatives from each division and let them thoroughly investigate all aspects of the decision. Such an approach had worked before, but Murray was not sure it was right this time.

Desperate to make the decision and get it out of her mind, Murray mentioned it to her fifteen-year-old son, who, it turned out, knew everything about digital tape. In fact, he told her, one of his friends—the rich one—had been holding off on buying a new tape deck so that he would be on the cutting edge of digital recording. "It's gotta happen, Mom," her son said. "People want it."

Intellectually, Murray believed he was right. The past thirty years had shown that Americans had an insatiable appetite for electronic gadgets and marvels. Quadraphonic sound and videodiscs were the only exceptions she could think of to the rule that if someone invented an improved way of reproducing images or sound, someone else would want to buy it.

But intuitively, Murray was not so sure. She had a bad feeling about the new technology. She believed the record companies, which had lost the battle to tape manufacturers, might get together with compact disc makers and audio equipment manufacturers to stop the digital technology from entering the American market. So far, no American company had invested substantially in the technology, so no one had an interest in funding the legal battle to remove the barriers to the new machines.

Exhausted, Murray went to bed. She hoped that somehow her subconscious mind would sort out all the important factors and she would wake up knowing the right decision.

Case Questions

1. What sources of information and opinion about the new technology seem most reliable? Which would you ignore?
2. If you were Murray, what would your next step be?

EXPERIENTIAL EXERCISE

Purpose: This exercise will allow you to take part in a group decision and help you understand the difference between programmed and nonprogrammed decisions.

Format: You will be asked to perform a task both individually and as a member of a group.

Procedure: Following is a list of typical organizational decisions. Your task is to determine whether they are programmed or nonprogrammed. Number your paper, and write *P* for programmed or *N* for nonprogrammed next to each number.

Your instructor will divide the class into groups of four to seven. All groups should have approximately the same number of members. Your task as a group is to make the determinations outlined above. In arriving at your decisions, do not use techniques such as voting or negotiating ("OK, I'll give in on this one if you'll give in on that one.") The group should discuss the difference between programmed and nonprogrammed decisions and each decision situation until all members at least partly agree with the decision.

Decision List

1. Hiring a specialist for the research staff in a highly technical field
2. Assigning workers to daily tasks
3. Determining the size of the dividend to be paid to shareholders in the ninth consecutive year of strong earnings growth
4. Deciding whether to approve an employee's absence for medical reasons as an officially excused absence
5. Selecting the location for another branch of a 150-branch bank in a large city
6. Approving the appointment of a new law school graduate to the corporate legal staff
7. Making the annual assignment of graduate assistants to the faculty
8. Approving the request of an employee to attend a local seminar in his or her special area of expertise
9. Selecting the appropriate outlets for print advertisements for a new college textbook
10. Determining the location for a new fast-food restaurant in a small but

growing town on the major interstate highway between two very large metropolitan areas

Follow-up Questions

1. To what extent did group members disagree about which decisions were programmed and which were nonprogrammed?
2. What primary factors did the group discuss in making each decision?
3. Were there any differences between the members' individual lists and the group lists? If so, discuss the reasons for the differences.

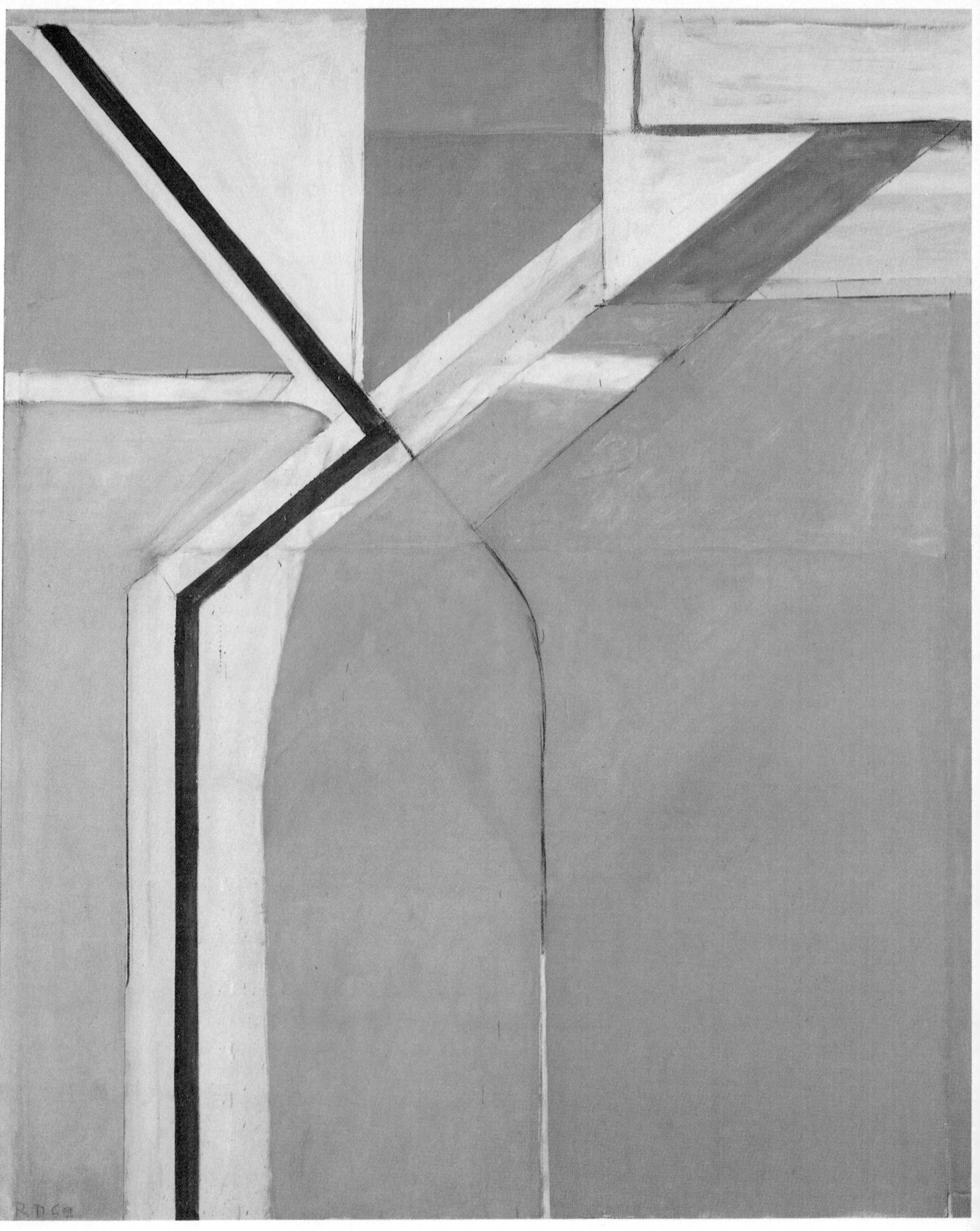

PART V

Organizational Processes and Characteristics

CONTENTS

Chapter 17 Dimensions of Organization Structure

Chapter 18 Managing Innovation and Technology in Changing Environments

Chapter 19 Organization Design

Chapter 20 Organization Culture

CHAPTER OUTLINE

Overview of Organization Structure

Organization Defined

Organization Structure

Structural Configuration

Division of Labor

Coordinating the Divided Tasks

Structure and Operations

Centralization

Formalization

Responsibility and Authority

Responsibility

Authority

An Alternative View of Authority

17

DIMENSIONS OF ORGANIZATION STRUCTURE

CHAPTER OBJECTIVES

After studying this chapter, you should be able to:

Define organization structure *and discuss its purpose.*

Describe structural configuration and summarize its four basic dimensions.

Describe two structural policies that affect operations.

Explain the dual concepts of authority and responsibility.

Most organizations have undergone restructuring by downsizing, rightsizing, and reducing their work forces. Many have then added back some laid-off workers. In addition to using these common strategies, Colgate-Palmolive changed its organization structure by eliminating the typical functional divisions, such as basic research, processing, and packaging, and put people into teams based around products such as pet food, household products, and oral hygiene products. Since the reorganization, new-product development has increased significantly and cost savings are estimated to be about $40 million.[1]

Organizations such as Colgate-Palmolive do not make major structural changes arbitrarily; rather, there must be some compelling reason. Colgate-Palmolive already was the industry leader in some of its product categories, but its managers believed reorganizing would help focus the company's efforts to serve customers better.

In this chapter, we explore how the structure of an organization can be a major factor in how successfully the organization achieves its goals. We begin with an overview of organizations and organization structure that defines each and puts organization structure in the context of organizational goals and strategy. Second, we discuss the two major perspectives of organizing, the structural configuration view and the operational view. Finally, we discuss the often confusing concepts of responsibility and authority, and present an alternative view of authority.

Overview of Organization Structure

In Parts I through IV we discuss key elements of the individual and the factors that tie the individual and the organization together. In a given organization, these factors must fit together within a common framework: the organization's structure.

---

1. Ronald Henkoff, "Cost Cutting: How to Do It Right," *Fortune,* April 9, 1990, pp. 40–50; Gary Hoover, Alta Campbell, and Patrick J. Spain, eds., *Hoover's Handbook* (Austin, Tex.: The Reference Press, 1991), p. 174.

Organization Defined

- An **organization** is a group of people working together to attain common goals.

An **organization** is a group of people working together to achieve common goals.[2] Top management determines the direction of the organization by defining its purpose, establishing the goals to meet that purpose, and formulating strategies to achieve the goals.[3]

The definition of *purpose* gives the organization reason to exist; in effect, it answers the question "What business are we in?" The establishment of goals converts the defined purpose into specific, measurable performance targets. **Organizational goals** are objectives that management seeks to achieve in pursuing the purpose of the firm. Goals motivate people to work together. Although each individual's goals are important to the organization, it is the organization's overall goals that are most important. Goals keep the organization on track by focusing the attention and actions of the members. They also provide the organization with a forward-looking orientation. They do not address past success or failure; rather, they force members to think about and plan for the future.

- **Organizational goals** are objectives that management seeks to achieve in pursuing the firm's purpose.
- Organizational goals keep the organization on track by focusing the attention and actions of its members.

Finally, *strategies* are specific action plans that enable the organization to achieve its goals and thus its purpose. They involve the development of an organization structure and the processes to do the organization's work.

Organization Structure

- **Organization structure** is a system of task, reporting, and authority relationships within which the organization does its work.

Organization structure is a system of task, reporting, and authority relationships within which the work of the organization is done. Thus, structure defines the form and function of the organization's activities. Structure also defines how the parts of an organization fit together, as in an organization chart.

The purpose of organization structure is to order and coordinate the actions of employees to achieve organizational goals. The premise of organized effort is that people can accomplish more by working together than they can separately. However, if the potential gains of collective effort are to be realized, the work must be coordinated. Suppose the thousands of employees at Ford Motor Co. worked without any kind of structure. Each person might try to build a car that he or she thought would sell. No two automobiles would be alike, and each would take months or years to build. The costs of making the cars would be so high that no one would be able to afford them. To produce automobiles that are both competitive in the marketplace and profitable for the company, Ford must have a structure in which its employees and managers work together in a coordinated manner.

---

2. See Richard Daft, *Organization Theory and Design*, 2nd ed. (St. Paul, Minn.: West, 1986), p. 9, for further discussion of the definition of *organization*.

3. John R. Montanari, Cyril P. Morgan, and Jeffrey S. Bracker, *Strategic Management* (Hinsdale, Ill.: Dryden Press, 1990), pp. 1–2.

This technician at the ARC Propulsion Division of Sequa Corporation is operating a proprietary cylindrical braider that creates three-dimensional reinforced composite materials for rockets, aircraft, and turbine engines. Tolerances on many operations on rocket engines are less than one-thousandth of an inch requiring expert training and years of experience.

The task of coordinating the activities of thousands of workers to produce cars that are not only drivable but guaranteed for 60,000 miles may seem monumental. Yet whether for mass producing cars or making soap, the requirements of organization structure are similar. First, the structure must divide the available labor according to the tasks to be performed. Even small organizations (those with fewer than one hundred employees) use division of labor.[4] Second, the structure must combine and coordinate the divided tasks to achieve a desired level of output. The more interdependent the divided tasks, the more coordination is required.[5] Every organization structure addresses these two fundamental requirements.[6] The various ways they do so are what make one organization structure different from another.

Organization structure can be analyzed in three ways. First, we can examine its configuration, or its size and shape as depicted on an organization chart. Second, we can analyze its operational aspects or characteristics, such as separation of specialized tasks, rules and procedures, and decision making. Finally, we can examine responsibility and authority within the organization. In this chapter, we look at organization structure from all three points of view.

4. A. Bryman, A. D. Beardsworth, E. T. Keil, and J. Ford, "Organizational Size and Specialization," *Organization Studies,* September 1983, pp. 271–278.

5. Joseph L. C. Cheng, "Interdependence and Coordination in Organizations: A Role System Analysis," *Academy of Management Journal,* March 1983, pp. 156–162.

6. See Henry Mintzberg, *The Structuring of Organizations* (Englewood Cliffs, N.J.: Prentice-Hall, 1979), for further discussion of the basic elements of structure.

Structural Configuration

- An **Organization Chart** is a diagram showing all people, positions, reporting relationships, and lines of formal communication in the organization.

The structure of an organization is most often described in terms of its organization chart. A complete **organization chart** shows all people, positions, reporting relationships, and lines of formal communication in the organization. (However, as we discussed in Chapter 11, communication is not limited to these formal channels.) For large organizations, several charts may be necessary to show all positions. For example, one chart may show top management, including the board of directors, the chief executive officer, the president, all vice presidents, and important headquarter staff units. Subsequent charts may show the structure of each department and staff unit. Figure 17.1 depicts two organization charts

FIGURE 17.1
Examples of Organization Charts

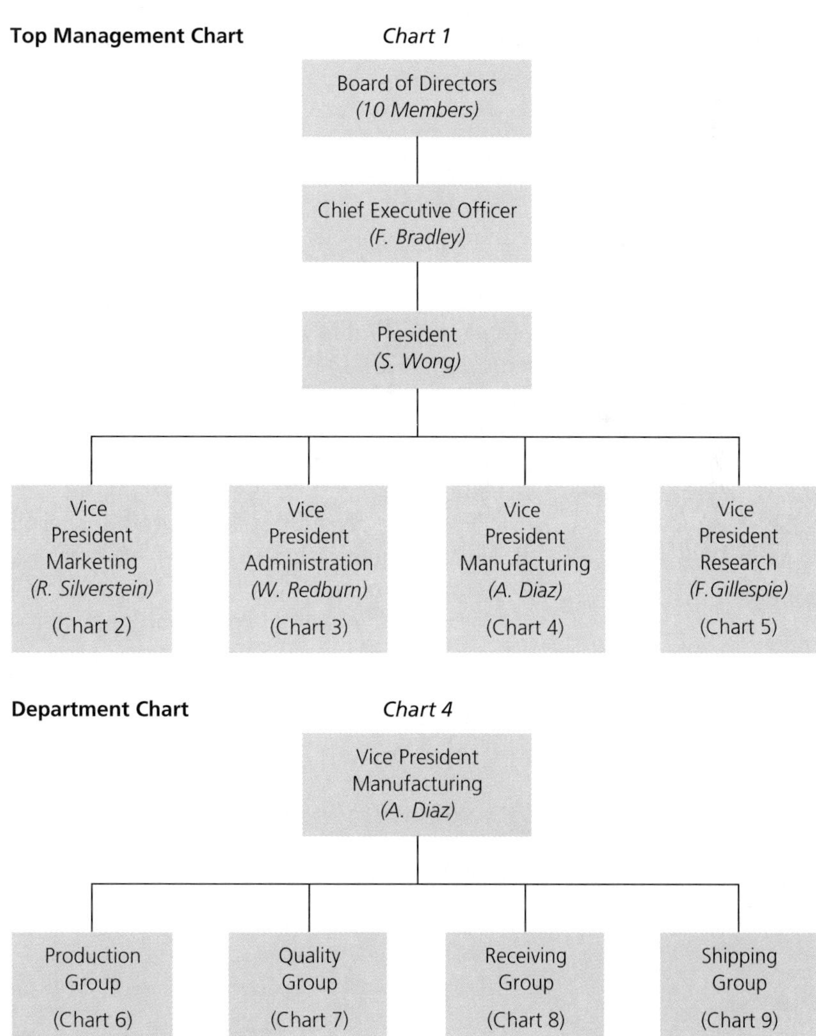

for a large firm; top management is shown in the upper portion of the figure and the manufacturing department in the lower portion. Notice that the structure of the different manufacturing groups is given in separate charts.

■ **Configuration** is the shape of the organization, made up of division of labor and the means of coordinating the divided tasks.

An organization chart depicts reporting relationships and work group memberships and shows how positions and small work groups are combined into departments, which together make up the **configuration,** or shape, of the organization. The configuration of organizations can be analyzed in terms of how the two basic requirements of structure—division of labor and coordination of the divided tasks—are fulfilled.

Division of Labor

■ **Division of labor** is the extent to which the organization's work is divided into different jobs to be done by different people.

Division of labor is the extent to which the organization's work is separated into different jobs to be done by different people. Division of labor is one of the seven primary characteristics of structuring described by Max Weber,[7] but the concept can be traced back to the eighteenth-century economist Adam Smith. As we noted in Chapter 1, Smith used a study of pin making to promote the idea of dividing production work to increase productivity.[8] Division of labor continued to increase in popularity as large organizations became more prevalent in a manufacturing society. This has continued, and most research indicates that large organizations usually have more division of labor than smaller ones.[9]

Division of labor has also been found to have both advantages and disadvantages (see Table 17.1). Modern managers and organization theorists are still struggling with the primary disadvantage: Division of labor often results in repetitive, boring jobs that undercut worker satisfaction, involvement, and commitment.[10] In addition, extreme division of labor may be incompatible with new, integrated computerized manufacturing technologies that require teams of highly skilled workers.[11]

However, division of labor need not result in boredom. Visualized in terms of a small organization such as a basketball team, it can be quite dynamic. A basketball team consists of five players, each of whom plays a different role on the team. In professional basketball the five positions typically are center, power forward, small forward, shooting guard, and point guard. The tasks of the players in each position are quite different, resulting in players of different sizes and skills being on the floor at any one time.

---

7. Max Weber, *The Theory of Social and Economic Organization,* trans. A. M. Henderson and Talcott Parsons (New York: Free Press, 1947).

8. Adam Smith, *An Inquiry into the Nature and Causes of the Wealth of Nations* (London: Dent, 1910).

9. Nancy M. Carter and Thomas L. Keon, "The Rise and Fall of the Division of Labour, the Past 25 Years," *Organization and Studies,* 1986, pp. 54–57.

10. Glenn R. Carroll, "The Specialist Strategy," *California Management Review,* Spring 1984, pp. 126–137.

11. "Management Discovers the Human Side of Automation," *Business Week,* September 29, 1986, pp. 70–75.

TABLE 17.1
Advantages and Disadvantages of Division of Labor

Advantages	Disadvantages
Efficient use of labor	Routine, repetitive jobs
Reduced training costs	Reduced job satisfaction
Increased standardization and uniformity of output	Decreased worker involvement and commitment
Increased expertise due to repetition of tasks	Increased worker alienation
	Possible incompatibility with computerized manufacturing technologies

Consider the Los Angeles Lakers. Magic Johnson is trained to play point guard. During the 1980s he was paired with the premier center Kareem Abdul-Jabbar. Abdul-Jabbar did not try to be a point guard; he played the position of center as well as it can be played. In other words, the roles of professional basketball players are very clearly specified and divided into clear-cut jobs. In some experts' opinion, there will not be another team as dominant as the Lakers have been until one team has another set of players who are superstars at the center and point guard positions, as Abdul-Jabbar and Johnson were in the 1980s. Division of labor thus is important to a basketball team; players specialize in doing specified tasks, and they learn to do them impeccably. Similarly, organizations must have specialists who are highly trained and know their specific jobs very well.

Coordinating the Divided Tasks

Three basic mechanisms are used to help coordinate the divided tasks: departmentalization, span of control, and administrative hierarchy. These mechanisms focus on grouping tasks in some meaningful manner, creating work groups of manageable size, and establishing a system of reporting relationships among supervisors and managers.

- **Departmentalization** is the manner in which divided tasks are combined and allocated to work groups.
- Divided tasks can be combined into departments by function, process, product, customer, and geography.

Departmentalization **Departmentalization** describes the manner in which divided tasks are combined and allocated to work groups. It is a consequence of the division of labor. Because employees engaged in specialized activities can lose sight of overall organizational goals, their work must be coordinated to ensure that it contributes to the welfare of the organization.

There are many possible ways to group, or departmentalize, tasks. The five most often used methods are by business function, by process, by product or service, by customer, and by geography. The first two, function and process, derive from the internal operations of the organization; the others are based on external factors. Most organizations tend to use a combination of methods, and departmentalization often changes as organizations evolve.[12]

12. See Robert H. Miles, *Macro Organizational Behavior* (Santa Monica, Calif.: Goodyear, 1980), pp. 28–34, for a discussion of departmentalization schemes.

This Soviet worker in the Republic of Uzbekistan inspects the cleanliness of raisins during the first stage of a three-stage washing process made by the Food Machinery Group of FMC Corporation. FMC participates on a worldwide basis in selected segments of five broad markets; Industrial Chemicals, Performance Chemicals, Precious Metals, Defense Systems, and Machinery and Equipment.

Departmentalization by business function is based on the traditional business functions such as marketing, manufacturing, and human resource administration (see Figure 17.2). In this configuration employees most frequently associate with those engaged in the same function, which helps in communication and cooperation. In a functional group, employees who do similar work can learn from one another by sharing ideas about opportunities and problems they encounter on the job. Unfortunately, the functional grouping lacks an automatic mechanism for coordinating the flow of work through the organization.[13] In other words, employees in a functional structure tend to associate little with those in other parts of the organization. The result can be a narrowness of focus that limits the coordination of work among functional groups, as when the engineering department fails to provide marketing with product information because it is too busy testing materials to think about sales.

Departmentalization by process is similar to functional departmentalization except that the focus is much more on specific jobs grouped according to the activity. Thus, as Figure 17.2 illustrates, the firm's manufacturing jobs are divided into certain well-defined manufacturing processes: drilling, milling, heat treating, painting, and assembly. Hospitals often use process departmentalization, grouping the professional employees, such as therapists, according to the types of treatment they provide.

13. Mintzberg, *The Structuring of Organizations,* p. 125.

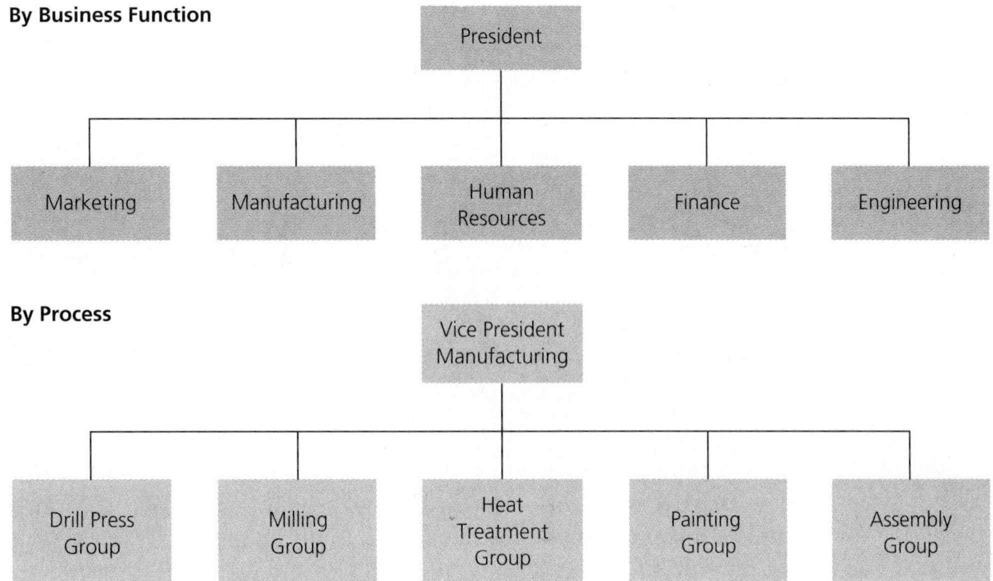

FIGURE 17.2
Departmentalization by Business Function and by Process

Process groupings encourage specialization and expertise among employees, who tend to concentrate on a single operation and share information with departmental colleagues. A process orientation may develop into an internal career path and managerial hierarchy within the department. As in functional grouping, however, narrowness of focus can be a problem in process departmentalization. Employees in a process group may become so absorbed in the requirements and execution of their operations that they disregard broader considerations such as overall product flow.[14]

Departmentalization by product or service occurs when employees who work on a particular product or service are members of the same department regardless of their business function or the process in which they are engaged. This configuration is shown in Figure 17.3. In this way, IBM reorganized its operations into five autonomous business units: personal computers, medium-size office systems, mainframes, communications equipment, and components.[15]

Garrett Turbine Engine Co., a division of Allied-Signal Aerospace Co., recently changed its organization structure to departmentalization by product. It went from a single integrated unit to two separate divisions: Garrett Engine Division and Garrett Auxiliary Power Division. Garrett Engine Division will build aircraft engines for general aviation (private airplanes) and various military applications. Garrett Auxiliary Power Division will specialize in gas turbines for ground and airborne auxiliary power applications.[16]

14. Miles, *Macro Organizational Behavior,* pp. 122–133.
15. "Big Blue Wants to Loosen Its Collar," *Fortune,* February 29, 1988, p. 8.
16. "Two New Units Created by Garrett," *The Arizona Republic,* January 12, 1988, p. 5.

FIGURE 17.3
Departmentalization by Product

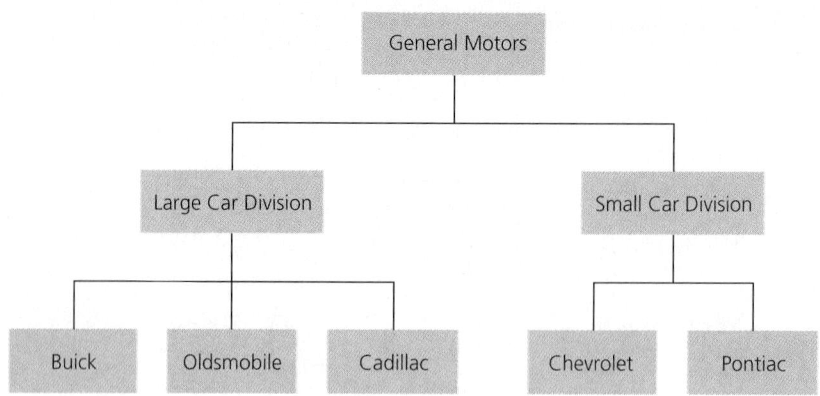

Departmentalization according to product or service obviously enhances interaction and communication among employees who produce the same product or provide the same service. Such a grouping may reduce product- or service-related coordination problems. In this type of configuration, there may be less process specialization but more specialization in the peculiarities of the specific product or service. IBM expects that the new alignment will allow all employees, from designers to manufacturing workers to marketing experts, to become specialists in a particular product line. The disadvantage is that employees may become so interested in their particular product or service that they miss technological improvements or innovations developed in other departments. Honda Motor Co. chose a product departmentalization strategy when it introduced the Acura.[17]

Departmentalization by customer often is referred to as departmentalization by market. Many lending institutions in Texas, for example, have separate departments for retail, commercial, agriculture, and petroleum loans, as shown in Figure 17.4. When significant groups of customers differ substantially from one another, organizing along customer lines may represent the most effective way to provide the best product or service possible. This is why hospital nurses often are grouped by the type of illness they handle; the various maladies demand different treatment and specialized knowledge.[18] *Management in Action* reports how Procter and Gamble made several changes in its brand manager system to establish a customer-based structure.

With customer departmentalization there usually is less process specialization, because employees must remain flexible to do whatever is necessary to enhance the relationship with customers. This configuration offers the best coordination of the work flow to the customer; however, it may isolate employees

17. "The Selling of Acura—a Honda That's Not a Honda," *Business Week,* March 17, 1986, p. 93.

18. Peggy Leatt and Rodney Schneck, "Criteria for Grouping Nursing Subunits in Hospitals," *Academy of Management Review,* March 1984, pp. 150–165.

FIGURE 17.4
Departmentalization by Customer and by Geographic Region

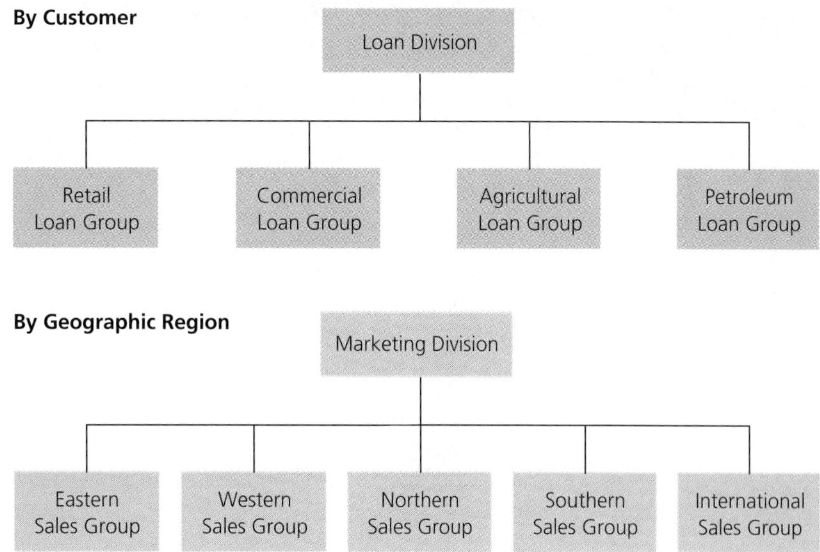

from others in their special areas of expertise. For example, if each of a company's three metallurgical specialists is assigned to a different market-based group, these individuals are unlikely to have many opportunities to discuss the latest technological advances in metallurgy.

Departmentalization by geography means that groups are organized according to a region of the country or world. Sales or marketing groups often are arranged by geographic region. As Figure 17.4 illustrates, the marketing effort of a large, multinational corporation can be divided according to major geographical divisions.

Using a geographically based configuration may result in significant cost savings and better market coverage. On the other hand, it may isolate work groups from activities in the organization's home office or in the technological community, because the focus of the work group is solely on the affairs within the region. This may foster loyalty to the work group that exceeds commitment to the larger organization. In addition, work-related communication and coordination among groups may be somewhat inefficient.

Many large organizations use a mixed departmentalization scheme. Such organizations may have separate operating divisions based on products, but within each division departments may be based on business function, process, customers, or geographic region (see Figure 17.5). Which methods work best depends on the organization's activities, communication needs, and coordination requirements. Another type of mixed structure often occurs in joint ventures, which are becoming increasingly popular. For example, Caterpillar, a long-time industry leader in heavy earth-moving equipment, faced major competition from the Japanese company Komatsu. In response, Caterpillar contracted with Daewoo Heavy Industries of South Korea to make some of its trucks. Then it formed a joint venture, Shin Caterpillar-Mitsubishi, to make excavators. The

MANAGEMENT IN ACTION

Procter & Gamble Changes Its Organization Structure

How can the company that virtually created product marketing suddenly change the structure of its consumer packaged goods business and survive? In fact, *why* would such a successful operation undertake a major structural change? The answer lies in the need to be more globally oriented. It also was a response to critics who claimed that Procter & Gamble was too arrogant, brusque, deliberate, and bureaucratic.

The need for a more global orientation became painfully clear when P&G found itself facing stiff competition from Japan's Kaio Corporation and the Anglo-Dutch Unilever N.V. In addition, P&G, the industry leader in twenty-two of its thirty-seven product categories, was active in twenty-seven countries in 1984 but operated in forty-eight countries just five years later. Former chief executive officer John G. Smale initiated the changes before stepping down to let then vice chairman Edwin L. Artzt take over. Artzt, who is dedicated to continuing the changes and making P&G much quicker to respond to change, especially on a worldwide scale, has significant international experience. He spent much of the last fifteen years in overseas assignments for P&G. His two executive vice presidents are both foreign born and have significant experience in managing in an international arena. Furthermore, the person who most believed would take the top job, John E. Pepper, Jr., was assigned to take Artzt's place in international operations to obtain international experience.

P&G's first change was to create a new position, called *category manager,* over the former relatively autonomous *product manager.* The category manager will have broad spending authority and be able to direct all the products in a single product category rather than only one product line. In effect, this has added another layer of management when most companies are reducing the number of management levels. P&G believes the new level will permit better coordination among the activities for different brands.

Second, P&G created another new position called *product supply manager.* This manager will work with representatives from manufacturing, engineering, distribution, and purchasing to cut product development time and costs.

Together the two new positions are expected to significantly change the way P&G does its marketing, distribution, and manufacturing and thus ensure that the firm is well positioned in the 1990s. This change represents a departure from a product to a customer orientation. Teams of people are assigned to major retailers such as supermarket chains so that individual customers can receive specialized attention.

The new structure eliminates the need for the brand manager to go through four layers of management to get a decision on a simple change such as package design. Now the brand manager goes to her or his category manager, who has the authority to make quick decisions. The new organization structure should enable P&G to respond more quickly to changes in the market.

SOURCES: Gary Hoover, Alta Campbell, and Patrick J. Spain, eds., *Hoover's Handbook* (Austin, Tex.: The Reference Press, 1991), p. 447; Brian Dumaine, "P&G Rewrites the Marketing Rules," *Fortune,* November 6, 1989, pp. 34–48; "P&G's Worldly New Boss Wants a More Worldly Company," *Business Week,* October 30, 1989, pp. 40–41.

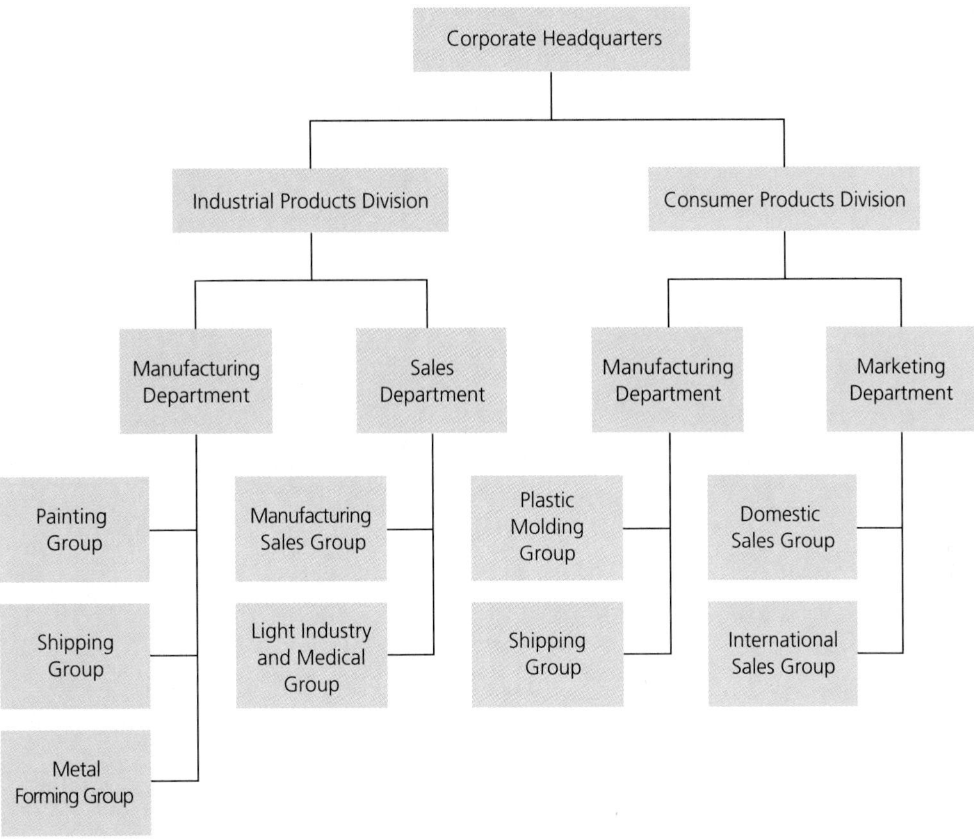

FIGURE 17.5
Mixed Departmentalization

new venture drew on Mitsubishi's expertise in designing and manufacturing quality excavators and on Caterpillar's unrivaled dealer network and manufacturing capacity.[19]

■ The **span of control** is the number of people who report to a manager.

Span of Control The second dimension of organizational configuration, **span of control,** is the number of people reporting to a manager; thus it defines the size of the organization's work groups. Span of control is also referred to as *span of management.* A manager who has a small span of control can maintain close control over the workers and stay in contact with daily operations. If the span of control is large, close control is not possible. Figure 17.6 shows examples of small and large spans of control. Supervisors in the upper portion of the figure have a span of control of 16, whereas in the lower portion their span of control is 8.

19. Tsukasa Furukawa, "Global Construction Machinery Battle Looms," *Metalworking News,* July 27, 1987, p. 5, 31; "A Weakened Komatsu Tries to Come Back Swinging," *Business Week,* February 22, 1988, p. 48.

FIGURE 17.6
Span of Control and Levels in the Administrative Hierarchy

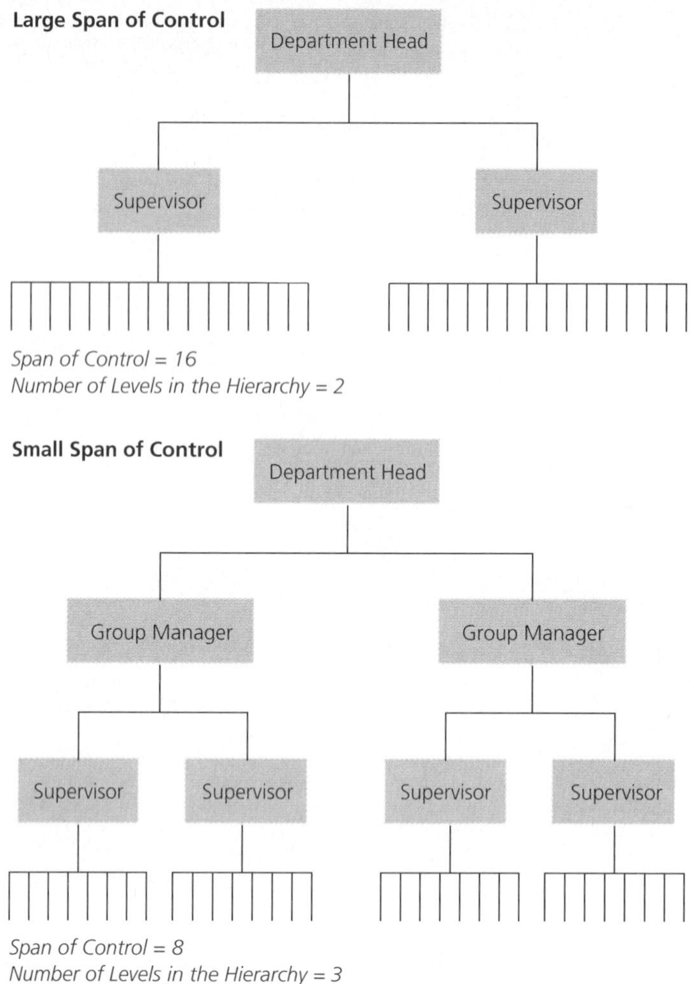

A number of formulas and rules have been offered for determining the optimal span of control in an organization,[20] but research on the topic has not conclusively identified a foolproof method.[21] Henry Mintzberg concluded that the optimal unit size depends on the coordination requirements within the unit, including factors such as the degree of job specialization in the unit, the similarity of the tasks in the unit, the type of information available or needed by unit members, differences in the members' need for autonomy, and the extent to

20. Lyndall F. Urwick, "The Manager's Span of Control," *Harvard Business Review,* May-June 1956, pp. 39–47.

21. Dan R. Dalton, William D. Tudor, Michael J. Spendolini, Gordon J. Fielding, and Lyman W. Porter, "Organization Structure and Performance: A Critical Review," *Academy of Management Review,* January 1980, pp. 49–64.

which members need direct access to the supervisor.[22] Because results so far are inconclusive, research on span of control continues.[23]

■ The **administrative hierarchy** is a system of reporting relationships in the organization from the lowest to the highest managerial levels.

Administrative Hierarchy The **administrative hierarchy** is a system of reporting relationships in the organization, from the first level up through the president or CEO. It results from the need for supervisors and managers to coordinate the activities of employees. The size of the administrative hierarchy is inversely related to the span of control: In organizations with a small span of control, there are many managers in the hierarchy; those with a large span of control have a smaller administrative hierarchy.

Using Figure 17.6 we can examine the effects of small and large spans of control on the number of hierarchical levels. The smaller span of control for the supervisors in the lower portion of the figure requires that there be four supervisors rather than two. Correspondingly, another management layer is needed to keep the department head's span of control at two. Thus, the span of control is small, the workers are under tighter supervision, and there are more administrative levels. In the upper portion of the figure, production workers are not closely supervised, and there are fewer administrative levels. As a measure of the number of management personnel, or administrators, in the organization, the administrative hierarchy sometimes is called the *administrative component, administrative intensity,* or *administrative ratio.*

The size of the administrative hierarchy also relates to the overall size of the organization. As an organization's size increases, so do its complexity and the requirements for coordination, necessitating proportionately more people to manage the business.[24] However, this conclusion defines the administrative component as including all of the administrative hierarchy, that is, all of the support staff groups, such as personnel and financial services, legal staff, and others. Defined in this way, the administrative component in a large company may seem huge when compared to the number of production workers. On the other hand, research that separates the support staff and clerical functions from the management hierarchy has found that the ratio of managers to total employees actually decreases with increases in the organization's size.[25] Still other, more recent research has shown that the size of the administrative hierarchy and the overall size of the organization are not related in a straightforward manner, especially during periods of growth and decline.[26]

---

22. Mintzberg, *The Structuring of Organizations,* pp. 133–147.

23. See David Van Fleet, "Span of Management Research and Issues," *Academy of Management Journal,* September 1983, pp. 546–552, for an example of research on span of control.

24. John B. Cullen and Douglas D. Baker, "Administration Size and Organization Size: An Examination of the Lag Structure," *Academy of Management Journal,* September 1984, pp. 644–654.

25. See Daft, *Organization Theory and Design,* pp. 181–182, for a discussion of the research on administrative hierarchy.

26. John R. Montanari and Philip J. Adelman, "The Administrative Component of Organizations and the Rachet Effect: A Critique of Cross-Sectional Studies," *Journal of Management Studies,* March 1987, pp. 113–123.

These workers are laying fiber optic cable along a 100 mile stretch of railroad right-of-way that runs north to Anchorage Alaska. Workers make day-to-day decisions involved in installing the cable within the guidelines established by management of PacifiCorp.

Structure and Operations

Some important aspects of organization structure do not appear on the organization chart and thus are quite different from the configurational aspects discussed in the previous section. In this section, we examine the structural policies that affect operations and prescribe or restrict how employees behave in their organizational activities.[27] The two primary aspects of these policies are centralization of decision making and formalization of rules and procedures.

Centralization

- **Centralization** is a structural policy wherein decision-making authority is concentrated at the top of the organizational hierarchy.

The first structural policy that affects operations is **centralization,** wherein decision-making authority is concentrated at the top of the organizational hierarchy. This structural aspect is in contrast to *decentralization,* in which decisions are made throughout the heirarchy.[28] Increasingly, centralization is being discussed in terms of participation in decision making.[29] In decentralized organizations, lower-level employees participate in making decisions. The recent changes in the organization structure at IBM have decentralized the decision making in some areas. No longer will all marketing decisions be made at the

27. Dalton et al., "Organization Structure and Performance."

28. See John Child, *Organization: A Guide to Problems and Practice,* 2nd ed. (New York: Harper & Row, 1984), pp. 145–153, for a detailed discussion of centralization.

29. Richard H. Hall, *Organization: Structure and Process,* 3rd ed. (Englewood Cliffs, N.J.: Prentice-Hall, 1982), pp. 87–96.

corporate headquarters in Armonk, New York. Each product-centered division will make marketing decisions affecting its own products.[30]

Decision making in organizations is more complex than indicated by the simple centralized/decentralized classification. In Chapter 16, we discussed organizational decision making in more depth. One of the major distinctions we made there was that some decisions are relatively routine and require only the application of a decision rule. These decisions are *programmed* decisions, whereas those that are not routine are *nonprogrammed.* The decision rules for programmed decisions are formalized for the organization. This difference between programmed and nonprogrammed decisions tends to cloud the distinction between centralization and decentralization. For even if decision making is decentralized, the decisions themselves may be programmed and tightly circumscribed.

Figure 17.7 summarizes the three possible types of centralization and decentralization in organizations. If there is little participation in decision making, the organization structure is *centralized,* regardless of the nature of the decisions being made. At the other extreme, if individuals or groups participate extensively in making nonprogrammed decisions, the structure can be described as *truly* decentralized. If individuals or groups participate extensively in decision making but mainly in programmed decisions, the structure is said to be *formalized* decentralization. Formalized decentralization is a common way to provide decision-making involvement for employees at many different levels in the organization while maintaining control and predictability.

Participative management has been described as a total management system in which people are involved in the daily decision making and management of the organization. As part of an organization's culture, it can contribute significantly to the long-run success of the organization.[31] It has been described as effective and, in fact, morally necessary in organizations.[32] Thus, for many people, participation in decision making has become more than a simple aspect of organization structure. *A Look at the Research* indicates, however, that much of the effort devoted to decentralizing decision making and encouraging participative decision making by middle-level managers may not be working quite as well as some would expect.

Formalization

■ **Formalization** is the degree to which rules and procedures shape the jobs and activities of employees.

Formalization is the degree to which rules and procedures shape employees' jobs and activities. The purpose of formalization is to predict and control how employees behave on the job.[33] Rules and procedures can be both explicit and

30. "Big Blue Wants to Loosen Its Collar."

31. Daniel R. Denison, "Bringing Corporate Culture to the Bottom Line," *Organizational Dynamics,* Autumn 1984, pp. 4–22.

32. Marshall Sashkin, "Participative Management Is an Ethical Imperative," *Organizational Dynamics,* Spring 1984, pp. 4–22.

33. Mintzberg, *The Structuring of Organizations,* pp. 83–84.

FIGURE 17.7
Participation in Decision Making and Decision Type

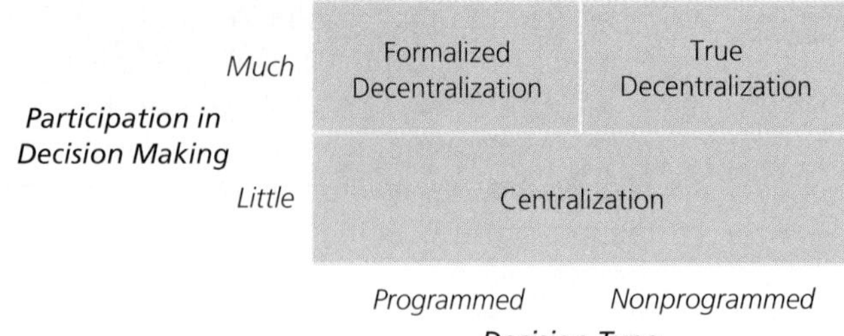

implicit. *Explicit rules* are set down in job descriptions, policy and procedures manuals, or office memos. (In one large company that continually issues directives attempting to limit employee activities, workers refer to them as "Gestapo" memos because of their prescriptive tone.) *Implicit rules* may develop as employees become accustomed to doing things a certain way over a period of time.[34] Though unwritten, these established ways of getting things done become standard operating procedures (SOPs) with the same effect on employee behavior as written rules.

We can assess formalization in organizations by looking at the proportion of jobs that are governed by rules and procedures and the extent to which those rules permit variation. More formalized organizations have a higher proportion of rule-bound jobs and less tolerance for rule violations.[35] Increasing formalization may affect the design of jobs throughout the organization[36] as well as employee motivation[37] and work group interactions.[38] The specific effects of formalization on employees are still unclear, however.[39]

Organizations tend to add more rules and procedures as the need for control of operations increases. For example, Lotus Development Corp. instituted more rules and procedures, especially in the areas of hiring and personnel, to gain control of its operations in the face of rapid growth.[40] Some organizations have become so formalized that they have rules for how to make new rules! One large state university created such rules in the form of a three-page document entitled

34. Arthur P. Brief and H. Kirk Downey, "Cognitive and Organizational Structures: A Conceptual Analysis of Implicit Organizing Theories," *Human Relations,* December 1983, pp. 1065–1090.

35. Jerald Hage, "An Axiomatic Theory of Organizations," *Administrative Science Quarterly,* December 1965, pp. 289–320.

36. Gregory Moorhead, "Organizational Analysis: An Integration of the Macro and Micro Approaches," *Journal of Management Studies,* April 1981, pp. 191–218.

37. J. Daniel Sherman and Howard L. Smith, "The Influence of Organizational Structure on Intrinsic versus Extrinsic Motivation," *Academy of Management Journal,* December 1984, pp. 877–885.

38. John A. Pearce II and Fred R. David, "A Social Network Approach to Organizational Design-Performance," *Academy of Management Review,* July 1983, pp. 436–444.

39. Eileen Fairhurst, "Organizational Rules and the Accomplishment of Nursing Work on Geriatric Wards," *Journal of Management Studies,* July 1983, pp. 315–332.

40. "Coming of Age at Lotus: Software's Child Prodigy Grows Up," *Business Week,* February 25, 1985, pp. 100–101.

A LOOK AT THE **RESEARCH**

The Growing Gap in the Middle

One of the most popular changes occurring in corporations today is the shifting of power and decision making down to lower levels within the hierarchy. This trend has resulted from the increasing complexity of the business environment, deregulation of markets, the proliferation of international firms invading U.S. markets or buying U.S. corporations to quickly capture a share of the U.S. market, the increasing speed of technological change, and competitive pressures. Leonard Johnson and Alan Frohman examined the impact of this trend toward lowering decision-making authority to middle management and found a disabling blockage in the middle-management ranks that may cause problems.

Johnson and Frohman studied three organizations: a service firm, a consumer durable products company, and a technology-oriented manufacturer of automated machinery. They used in-depth interviews with executives and managers at several levels and survey questionnaires with all managers. They expected to find different levels of involvement in decision making among the three firms.

Their findings were surprising. All three firms had similar problems. Middle-level managers in all the firms reported a great deal of difficulty with their new roles as key decision makers. They tended to have a myopic view of the issues facing the organization as a whole; they lacked understanding of the organization's strategy; communication among departments was poor; and coordination and teamwork across functions were inadequate. In other words, the people and work groups at the middle levels were not equipped to make the far-reaching, organizationwide types of decisions now required of them.

The researchers concluded that now that responsibility for many operational decisions has been delegated to those in the middle, these managers need the information with which to make decisions. It is no wonder that when the required information is not available to them, they feel frustrated and incapable of making decisions. Furthermore, when their performance will be evaluated based on their achieving results for their divisions because of their decisions, as will their raises and bonuses, the gap Johnson and Frohman describe becomes apparent.

SOURCE: Leonard W. Johnson and Alan L. Frohman, "Identifying and Closing the Gap in the Middle of Organizations," *Academy of Management Executive,* May 1989, pp. 107–114. Adapted by permission.

"Procedures for Rule Adoption" that was added to the four-inch-thick *Policy and Procedures Manual.* The new policy first defines terms such as *University, Board* and *rule* and lists ten exceptions that describe when this policy on rule adoptions does not apply. It then presents a nine-step process for adopting a new rule within the university.

Other organizations are trying to become less formalized by reducing the number of rules and procedures employees must follow. In this way, Chevron recently cut the number of its rules and procedures from over four hundred to eighteen. Highly detailed procedures for hiring were eliminated in favor of letting managers make hiring decisions based on common sense.[41]

41. "Chevron Corp. Has Big Challenge Coping with Worker Cutbacks," *The Wall Street Journal,* November 4, 1986, pp. 1, 25.

A relatively new approach to organizational formalization attempts to describe how, when, and why good managers should bend or break a rule.[42] Although rules exist in some form in almost every organization, how strictly they are enforced may vary significantly from one organization to another and even within a single organization. Some managers argue that "a rule is a rule" and all rules must be enforced to control employee behaviors and prevent chaos in the organization. Other managers act as if "all rules are made to be broken" and see rules as stumbling blocks to effective action. Neither point of view is better for the organization; rather, a more balanced attitude is recommended. The test of a good manager in a formalized organization may be the use of appropriate judgment in making exceptions to rules.

A balanced approach to making exceptions to rules should do two things. First, it should recognize that individuals are unique and that the organization can benefit from making exceptions that capitalize on exceptional capabilities. For example, an engineering design department with a rule mandating equal access to tools and equipment acquires a limited amount of specialized equipment, such as personal computers. The department manager decides to make an exception to the equal-access rule by assigning the computers to designers the manager believes will use them most and with the best results instead of making them available for use by all. Second, a balanced approach should recognize the commonalities among employees. Managers should make exceptions to rules only when there is a true and meaningful difference between individuals rather than base exceptions on features such as race, sex, appearance, or social factors.

Responsibility and Authority

Responsibility and authority are related to both configurational and operational aspects of organization structure. For example, the organization chart shows who reports to whom at all levels in the organization. From the operational perspective, the degree of centralization defines the locus of decision-making authority in the organization. However, often there is some confusion about what responsibility and authority really mean for managers and how the two terms relate to each other.

Responsibility

■ **Responsibility** is an obligation to do something with the expectation of achieving some act or output.

Responsibility is an obligation to do something with the expectation that some act or output will result. For example, a manager may expect an employee to write and present a proposal for a new program by a certain date; thus, the employee is "responsible" for preparing the proposal.

42. F. Neil Brady, "Rules for Making Exceptions to Rules," *Academy of Management Review,* July 1987, pp. 436–444.

Narasimha Rao is the new Prime Minister of India, having ascended to power following the assassination of the Congress party leader Rajiv Gandhi and recent elections. Although he has been active and a strong supporter of the Gandhi family, his calm, conciliatory style did not seem to fit the role of powerful leader of a country facing great difficulties of civil unrest and a poor economy. He now needs to use his responsibility and authority to bring together the many factions within the country to solve its many problems.

Responsibility ultimately derives from the ownership of the organization. The owners hire or appoint a group, often a board of directors, to be responsible for managing the organization, making the decisions, and reaching the goals set by the owners. A downward chain of responsibility is then established. The board hires a president to be responsible for running the organization. The president hires more people and holds them responsible for accomplishing designated tasks that enable the president to produce the results expected by the board and the owners. The chain extends throughout the organization, because each manager has an obligation to fulfill: to appropriately employ organizational resources (people, money, and equipment) to meet the owners' expectations. Although managers seemingly pass responsibility on to others to achieve results, each manager is still held responsible for the outputs of those to whom he or she delegates tasks.

A manager responsible for a work group assigns tasks to members of the group. Each group member is then responsible for doing his or her task. Yet the manager remains responsible for each task and for the work of the group as a whole. This means managers can take on the responsibility of others but cannot shed their own onto those below them in the hierarchy.

Authority

- **Authority** is power that has been legitimized within a particular social context.

Authority is power that has been legitimized within a specific social context.[43] (Power is discussed in Chapter 10.) Only when power is part of an official organizational role does it become authority. Authority includes the legitimate right to use resources to accomplish expected outcomes. As we discussed in the previous section, the authority to make decisions may be restricted to the top levels of the organization or dispersed throughout the organization.

43. See Jeffrey Pfeffer, *Power in Organizations* (Boston: Pittman, 1981), pp. 4–6, for a discussion of the relationship between power and authority.

■ Authority and responsibility are closely related in that managers must have the authority to carry out their responsibilities.

Like responsibility, authority originates in the ownership of the organization. The owners establish a group of directors who are responsible for managing the organization's affairs. The directors, in turn, authorize people in the organization to make decisions and to use organizational resources. Thus, they delegate authority, or power in a social context, to others.

Authority is linked to responsibility, because a manager responsible for accomplishing certain results must have the authority to use resources to achieve those results.[44] The relationship between responsibility and authority must be one of *parity;* that is, the authority over resources must be sufficient to enable the manager to meet the output expectations of others.

But authority and responsibility differ in significant ways. Responsibility cannot be delegated down to others, but authority can. One complaint often heard from employees is that they have too much responsibility but not enough authority to get the job done. This indicates a lack of parity between responsibility and authority. Managers usually are quite willing to hold individuals responsible for specific tasks but are reluctant to delegate sufficient authority to do the job. In effect, managers try to rid themselves of responsibility for results (which they cannot do), yet they rarely like to give away their cherished authority over resources.

The delegation of authority to make decisions to lower-level managers is common in organizations today. The important thing is to give lower-level managers authority to carry out the decisions they make. *International Perspective* illustrates how British Petroleum reorganized by delegating decision-making authority to managers lower in the organizational hierarchy.

The Iran/Contra affair of 1987–88 is a good example of the difference between authority and responsibility. Some believe the Reagan administration confused delegation of authority with abdication of responsibility.[45] President Reagan delegated a great deal of authority to subordinates but did not require that they keep him informed. The subordinates thus made no effort to keep the president informed of their activities. Hence, delegation of authority by the administration was appropriate and necessary, but failing to require progress reports to keep informed and in control of operations resulted in the administration trying to avoid responsibility. Although the president did hold his subordinates responsible for their actions, he ultimately—and rightfully—retained full responsibility.

An Alternative View of Authority

So far we have described authority as a "top-down" function in organizations; that is, authority originates at the top and is delegated downward as the managers at the top consider appropriate. In Chester Barnard's alternative perspective, authority is seen as originating in the individual, who can choose whether or

44. John B. Miner, *Theories of Organizational Structure and Process* (Hinsdale, Ill.: Dryden Press, 1982), p. 360.

45. "Management Lesson of Irangate," *The Wall Street Journal,* March 24, 1987, p. 36.

INTERNATIONAL PERSPECTIVE

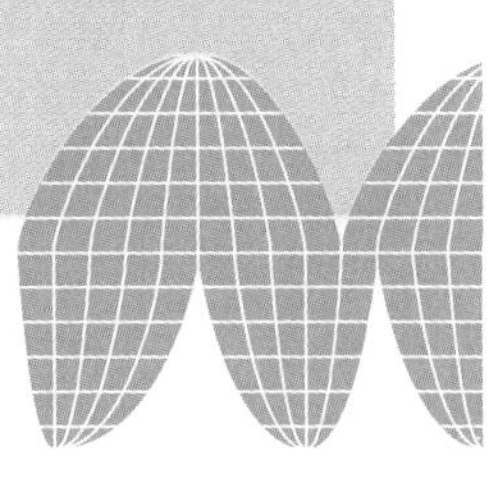

British Petroleum Breaks Up the Bureaucracy

The tendency of large bureaucracies to perpetuate themselves and create even more rules and procedures was never more evident than in the huge bureaucracy called British Petroleum (BP). Based in London with operations in seventy countries, BP is the fourth largest private oil company in the world. The bureaucracy of BP consisted of more than 119,000 employees, over 2,500 corporate staff, over 80 standing committees, and 11 layers of management between Robert Horton, chair and chief executive officer, and first-line supervisors.

After he became CEO, Horton realized that if BP was to survive the changing environment of petroleum finding, developing, and marketing into the next century, the rigid, sluggish bureaucracy had to be changed into a flexible, adaptive, fast-moving organization. Such an organization would have to move quickly to find new oil reserves and capitalize on them quickly. To implement the necessary changes, Horton appointed a task force called Project 1990, composed of seven highly respected middle managers, to study the organization and make recommendations for change.

Project 1990 is well under way and is making BP a less bureaucratic, hierarchical organization. Features of the reorganization included changing the organization structure, shifting authority and responsibility, and creating a significant cultural change. The structural changes consisted of decreasing the number of management levels from eleven to six, reducing corporate staff from twenty-five hundred to around three hundred, and combining the eleven different businesses in seventy countries into four operating divisions in three regional blocks. Another change was to more clearly define manager and staff authority and responsibility. For example, spending limits for lower- and middle-level managers were more clearly specified and increased by two-and-a-half times, and the number of authorizations required to spend larger amounts was reduced from twelve to three in most cases and to two in others.

The new vision and shared values may have as great an impact as any other change. Horton wants all employees to share his goal of making BP the most successful oil company in the 1990s and beyond. The new shared values include commitments to employees, customers, suppliers, the community, and shareholders. Horton envisions that the new culture will be based on trust, openness, and teamwork, which he knows will take several years to fully develop. He contends, however, that without the organizational and cultural changes, his vision of BP will not materialize.

SOURCES: Gary Hoover, Alta Campbell, and Patrick J. Spain, eds., *Hoover's Handbook* (Austin, Tex.: The Reference Press, 1991), p. 138; Peter Nulty, "Batman Shakes BP to Bedrock," *Fortune,* November 19, 1990, pp. 155–162; Robert B. Horton, "Planning for Surprise," *Industry Week,* August 6, 1990, p. 27.

not to follow a directive from above. The choice of whether to comply with a directive is based on the degree to which the individual understands it, feels able to carry it out, and believes it to be in the best interests of the organization and consistent with personal values.[46] This perspective has been called the **acceptance theory of authority** because it means that the manager's authority depends on

■ The **acceptance theory of authority** is the perspective that the authority of a manager depends on the subordinate's acceptance of the manager's right to give and expect compliance with the directive.

46. Chester Barnard, *The Functions of the Executive* (Cambridge, Mass.: Harvard University Press, 1938), pp. 161–184.

the subordinate's acceptance of the manager's right to give the directive and expect compliance.

For example, suppose you are a sales analyst. Your company has a painting crew, but for some reason your manager has told you to repaint your own office over the weekend. You probably would question your manager's authority to make you do this work. In fact, you would likely refuse to do it. A similar request to work over the weekend to finish a report would more likely be accepted and carried out. Thus, workers can either accept or reject the directives of a supervisor and thus limit supervisory authority.[47] In most organizational situations, employees accept a manager's right to expect compliance on normal, reasonable directives because of the manager's legitimate position in the organizational hierarchy or in the social context of the organization. When they do not accept the manager's right, they may choose to disobey the directive and must accept the consequences.

Summary of Key Points

- The structure of an organization is a system of task, reporting, and authority relationships within which the work of the organization is done. The purpose of organization structure is to order and coordinate the actions of employees to achieve organizational goals. Every organization structure addresses two fundamental issues: the division of available labor according to the tasks to be performed and the combination and coordination of divided tasks to ensure task accomplishment.
- An organization chart shows reporting relationships, work group memberships, departments, and formal lines of communication. In a broader sense, an organization chart shows the configuration, or shape, of the organization. Configuration has four dimensions: division of labor, departmentalization, span of control, and the administrative hierarchy. Division of labor is the extent to which the work is separated into different jobs to be done by different people. Departmentalization is the manner in which the divided tasks are combined and allocated to work groups for coordination. Tasks can be combined into departments on the basis of business function, process, product, customer, and geographic region. Span of control is the number of people reporting to a manager; it also defines the size of work groups and is inversely related to the number of hierarchical levels in the organization. The administrative hierarchy is the system of reporting relationships in the organization.
- Structural policies that affect operations prescribe how employees should behave in their organizational activities. Such policies include formalization of rules and procedures and centralization of decision making. Formalization is the degree to which rules and procedures shape employees' jobs and activities. The purpose of formalization is to predict and control how em-

47. Pfeffer, *Power in Organizations,* pp. 366–367.

ployees behave on the job. Explicit rules are set down in job descriptions, policy and procedures manuals, and office memos. Implicit rules develop over time as employees become accustomed to doing things a certain way.

- Centralization concentrates decision-making authority at the top of the organizational hierarchy; under decentralization, decisions are made throughout the hierarchy.
- A final aspect of organization structure is the dual concepts of authority and responsibility. Responsibility is an obligation to do something. Authority is power that has been legitimized within a specific social context. Authority includes the legitimate right to use resources to accomplish expected outcomes. The relationship between responsibility and authority needs to be one of parity; that is, authority over resources must be adequate to enable the employee to meet the expectations of others.

Discussion Questions

1. Define *organization structure* and explain how it fits into the process of managing the organization.
2. What is the purpose of organization structure? What would an organization be like without a structure?
3. In what ways are aspects of the organization structure similar to the structural parts of the human body?
4. How is labor divided in your college or university? In what other ways could your college or university be departmentalized?
5. What types of organizations could benefit from a small span of control? What types might benefit from a large span of control?
6. Discuss how increasing formalization might affect the role conflict and role ambiguity of employees. How might the impact of formalization differ for research scientists, machine operators, and bank tellers?
7. How might centralization or decentralization affect the job characteristics specified in job design?
8. When a group makes a decision, how is the responsibility for the decision apportioned among the members?
9. Why do employees typically want more authority and less responsibility?
10. Considering the job you now hold or one that you have held in the past, does your boss have the authority to direct your work? Why does he or she have this authority?

CASE 17.1

The Big Dilemma at Goodyear

Goodyear Tire & Rubber Co., headquartered in Akron, Ohio, is the last remaining independent tire company in the United States. The rest have been bought by non-U.S. companies. Japanese Bridgestone bought Firestone, Italian Pirelli bought Armstrong, Japanese Sumitomo Rubber Industries bought Dunlop,

West German Continental bought General Tire, Yokohama Rubber bought Mohawk, and French Michelin bought Uniroyal Goodrich—all between December 1986 and mid-1990. Goodyear is left with its U.S. roots, a slumping tire industry, and increased competitive pressure from the new owners, who seem to have deeper pockets for research, advertising, and marketing promotions.

Goodyear remains the leader in U.S. tire sales, but in 1990 its production capacity was greater than market demand. In 1988–89, Goodyear raised wholesale prices because the industry was at full capacity and it appeared to be an optimal time to make the increase. However, the strategy backfired. Wholesalers, unable to sell the Goodyear tires, started selling other brands. Thus, Goodyear had to roll back prices. In addition, it pushed its low-priced brand, Kelly-Springfield Tires, to boost overall volume. But profits remained down. Goodyear continues to spend heavily on research in an effort to stay ahead of the pack. But with revenue and earnings down, maintaining the research budget may be tough.

In 1983, Goodyear made an unusual move, presumably to avoid being an attractive takeover target and to spread out the effects of the roller coaster tire business, by paying $825 million for Celeron, a Louisiana gas pipeline company with oil and gas interests. Later that year a decision was made to build a crude-oil pipeline from California to Texas to offset the high costs and the potential effects of tanker spills and tank problems in the process of getting crude to the refineries in Texas. However, by the time the pipeline was built and ready to operate and because oil and gasoline prices remained low in early 1991, the new pipeline was operating at only 30 percent of capacity and was generating little contribution to earnings.

Goodyear management now faces an extremely competitive tire industry and low earnings from its oil group. Company executives recognize the financial difficulties and are making adjustments. The adjustments probably will include a reorganization of Goodyear's U.S. operations and European sales staff. In addition, they expect to trim about three thousand employees and shut down part or all of three tire plants. The changes also include plans to push decision-making authority down into the lower ranks of management.

No specific changes have been announced regarding the future of Goodyear's oil and gas pipeline business. It continues to be a drain on cash; construction costs of the California-to-Texas pipeline were estimated at $1.2 billion in 1989. CEO Tom Barrett, a thirty-five-year Goodyear veteran who took over in April 1989, says the decentralization is necessary to make the company responsive to worldwide competition. After decision making is shifted downward into operation divisions, each division can be held accountable for producing operating results.

Part of Goodyear's problems began when French corporate raider Sir James Goldsmith started buying Goodyear shares—up to 11.5 percent—and threatened to break up the company. Goodyear borrowed $3.2 billion to buy back 47 percent of its own shares and fend off the takeover attempt. At the same time, it started selling off assets such as its Motor Wheel Corp., Goodyear Aerospace, and Celeron, all at lower prices. The pipeline has been offered for sale, but no takers have surfaced. It continues to divert cash and management's attention away from Goodyear's basic tire business. Barrett hopes the reorganization will refocus attention where he thinks it ought to be—on tires—and put the company back on track. Only time will tell whether it will work.

Case Questions

1. What are the features of organization structure that Goodyear expects to change with its reorganization?
2. How do you think the reorganization will affect organizational performance?
3. How did events in the environment contribute to Goodyear's need to reorganize?

SOURCES: "Investors Cheer Goodyear's CEO," *USA Today,* June 6, 1991, p. 3B; "How Well Can Goodyear Take the Bumps Up Ahead?" *Business Week,* October 15, 1990, pp. 31–32; "After a Year of Spinning Its Wheels, Goodyear Gets a Retread," *Business Week,* March 26, 1990, pp. 56–58; Suzanne Loeffelholz, "Goodyear's Albatross," *Financial World,* October 31, 1989, pp. 30–31.

CASE 17.2

Changing the Rules At Cosmo Plastics

When Alice Thornton took over as chief executive officer at Cosmo Plastics, the company was in trouble. Cosmo had started out as an innovative company, known for creating a new product just as the popularity of one of the industry's old stand-bys was fading. In two decades, it had become an established maker of plastics for the toy industry. Cosmo had grown from a dozen employees to four hundred, and its rules had grown haphazardly with it. Thornton's predecessor, Willard P. Blatz, had found the company's procedures chaotic and had instituted a uniform set of rules for all employees. Since then, both research output and manufacturing productivity had steadily declined. When the company's board of directors hired Thornton, they emphasized the need to evaluate and revise the company's formal procedures in an attempt to reverse the trends.

First, Thornton studied the rules Blatz had implemented. She was impressed to find that the entire procedures manual was only twenty pages long. It began with the reasonable sentence "All employees of Cosmo Plastics shall be governed by the following. . . ." Thornton had expected to find evidence that Blatz had been a tyrant who ran the company with an iron fist. But as she read through the manual, she found nothing to indicate this. In fact, some of the rules were rather flexible. Employees could punch in anytime between 8:00 and 10:00 A.M. and leave nine hours later, between 5:00 and 7:00 P.M. Managers were expected to keep monthly notes on the people working for them and make yearly recommendations to the human resources committee about raises, bonuses, promotions, and firings. Except for their one-hour lunch break, which they could take at any time, employees were expected to be in the building at all times.

Puzzled, Thornton went down to the lounge where the research and development people gathered. She was surprised to find a time clock on the wall. Curious, she fed a time card into it and was even more flabbergasted when the maching chattered noisily, then spit it out. Apparently R&D was none too pleased with the time clock and had found a way to rig it. When Thornton looked up in astonishment, only two of the twelve employees who had been in the room were still there. They said the others had "punched back in" when they saw the boss coming.

Thornton asked the remaining pair to tell her what was wrong with company rules, and she got an earful. The researchers, mostly chemists and engineers with advanced graduate degrees, resented punching a time clock and having their work evaluated once a month, when they could not reasonably be expected to come up with something new and worth writing about more than twice a year. Before the implementation of the new rules, they often had gotten inspirations from going down to the local dimestore and picking up $5 worth of cheap toys, but now they felt they could make such trips only on their own time. And when a researcher came up with an innovative idea, it often took months for the proposal to work its way up the company hierarchy to the attention of someone who could put it into production. In short, all these sharp minds felt shackled.

Concluding that maybe she had overlooked the rigidity of the rules, Thornton walked over to the manufacturing building to talk to the production supervisors. They responded to her questions with one word: *anarchy.* With employees drifting in between 8:00 and 10:00 and then starting to drift out again by 11:00 for lunch, the supervisors never knew if they had enough people to run a particular operation. Employee turnover was high, but not high enough in some cases; supervisors believed the rules prevented them from firing all but the most incompetent workers before the end of the yearly evaluation period. The rules were so "humane" that discipline was impossible to enforce.

By the time Alice Thornton got back to her office, she had a plan. The following week, she called in all the department managers and asked them to draft formal rules and procedures for their individual areas. She told them she did not intend to lose control of the company, but she wanted to see if they could improve productivity and morale by creating formal procedures for their individual departments.

Case Questions

1. Do you think Alice Thornton's proposal to decentralize the rules and procedures of Cosmo Plastics will work?
2. What risks will the company face if it establishes different procedures for different areas?

EXPERIENTIAL EXERCISE

Purpose: This exercise will help you understand the configurational and operational aspects of organization structure.

Format: You will interview employees of a small- to medium-size organization and analyze its structure. (You may want to coordinate this exercise with the exercise in Chapter 19.)

Procedure: Your first task is to find a local organization with fifty to five hundred employees. (It should not be part of your college or university.) The organization should have more than two hierarchical levels, but it should not be too complex to understand in a short period of study. You may want to check with your professor before contacting the company. Your initial contact should be with the highest-ranking manager, if possible. Be sure that top management is aware of your project and gives their approval.

Using the material in this chapter, interview employees to obtain the following information on the structure of the organization:

1. The type of departmentalization (business function, process, product, customer, geographic region)
2. The typical span of control at each level in the organization
3. The number of levels in the hierarchy
4. The administrative ratio (number of managers to total employees and number of managers to production employees)
5. The degree of formalization (to what extent are rules and procedures written down in job descriptions, policy and procedures manuals, and memos?)
6. The degree of decentralization (to what extent are employees at all levels involved in making decisions?)

Interview at least three employees of the company at different levels and in different departments. One should hold a top-level position. Be sure to ask the questions in a way that is clear to the respondents; they may not be familiar with the terminology used in this chapter.

The result of the exercise should be a report with a paragraph on each configurational and operational aspect of structure listed in this exercise, an organization chart of the company, a discussion of differences in responses from the employees you interviewed, and a discussion of any unusual structural features (for example, a situation in which employees report to more than one person or to no one). You may want to send a copy of your report to the company's top management.

Follow-up Questions

1. Which aspects of structure were the hardest to obtain information about? Why?
2. If there were differences in the responses of the employees you interviewed, how do you account for them?
3. If you were president of the organization you analyzed, would you structure it in the same way? Why or why not? If not, how would you structure it differently?

CHAPTER OUTLINE

- Innovation in Organizations
  - *Innovation*
  - *New Ventures*
  - *Corporate Research*
- Technology in Organizations
  - *Five Perspectives on Technology*
  - *Technology in Practice*
- Organizational Environments
  - *Environmental Components*
  - *Environmental Uncertainty*
- Organizational Responses
  - *Structural Contingency Perspective*
  - *Resource Dependence Perspective*
  - *Population Ecology Perspective*

18

Managing Innovation and Technology in Changing Environments

CHAPTER OBJECTIVES

After studying this chapter, you should be able to:

Describe three aspects of managing innovation and technology in organizations.

Identify and discuss five perspectives of organizational technology.

Define organizational environment *and discuss its importance to organizations.*

Describe several components of the organizational environment and explain their contribution to environmental uncertainty.

Growing brain cells in test tubes from immature cells into mature, normal ones is now possible. The next step is to modify some cells and then experiment with transplanting them into diseased brains as a potential treatment. Researchers at Oregon Health Science Center are experimenting with solutions that enable cancer-fighting drugs to penetrate the blood-brain barrier that prevents most compounds from entering the brain. Scientists believe this breakthrough may make possible the treatment of diseases such as Alzheimer's, Parkinson's, stroke, epilepsy, and AIDS-induced dementia.

At last, new imaging techniques are creating windows into the brain that enable researchers to "see" brain activity. For example, positron emission tomography, or PET, allows researchers to actually trace thoughts occurring within the brain. This type information may lead to the development of treatments for anxiety, depression, eating disorders, Alzheimer's disease, and migraine headaches.

The potential is so great that new ventures have raised over $250 million in start-up capital and the big pharmaceutical firms have more than doubled their spending on neuroscience research to over $800 million per year. One installation of the PET imaging technique costs over $5 million.

How does all of this affect managing organizations? No one knows. That is precisely what makes it so difficult to manage organizations.[1]

Management traditionally has been concerned with opportunities presented by the environment and demands from new technologies, suppliers, customers, government regulations, and economic conditions. Managers have had to determine ways to manage the organization so as to satisfy these demands and hence to survive. In other words, pressures from many different sources necessitate adjustments on the part of the organization. But how do organizations adjust and respond? How can an organization and its management make sense out of an environment fraught with continuously changing demands?

In this chapter, we explore the complexities of managing innovation and technological change in the face of changing environmental conditions. First, we discuss the process of innovation in organizations. Next, we explore several

1. Gene Bylinsky, "The Inside Story of the Brain," *Fortune,* December 3, 1990; Shannon Brownlee, "Blitzing the Defense," *US News & World Report,* October 15, 1990, pp. 90–92; David Churbuck, "Breaking the Barrier," *Forbes,* August 6, 1990, p. 106.

Filippo Petrignani enters data into a computer assisting in the restoration of Creation's fourth day portion of the frescos by Michelangelo in the Sistene Chapel. The computer mapping is based on a photogrammetric survey that details even small surface variations. The cleaning project has taken nine years and wiped out centuries of dust, oils, and candle tallow. It took Michelangelo only about four years to paint it originally.

perspectives on managing technology in organizations. Then we examine the environments within which organizations operate. Finally, we discuss the various ways organizations respond to changing environments.

Innovation in Organizations

- **Innovation** is the process of creating and doing new things that are introduced into the marketplace as new products, processes, or services.

Innovation is the process of creating and doing new things that are introduced into the marketplace as new products, processes, or services. In organizations, innovation involves every aspect of managing technology, from research through development, manufacturing, and marketing. One of the organization's biggest challenges is to bring creative technology to the needs of the marketplace in the most cost-effective manner possible.[2]

Many risks are associated with being an innovative company. The most basic is the risk that the new technology or innovation will not work. As research proceeds and engineers and scientists continue to develop new ideas or solutions to problems, there is always the possibility that the innovation will fail to perform. For this reason, organizations commit considerable resources to testing new innovations.

2. Watts S. Humphrey, *Managing for Innovation: Leading Technical People* (Englewood Cliffs, N.J.: Prentice-Hall, 1987), p. 92.

INTERNATIONAL PERSPECTIVE

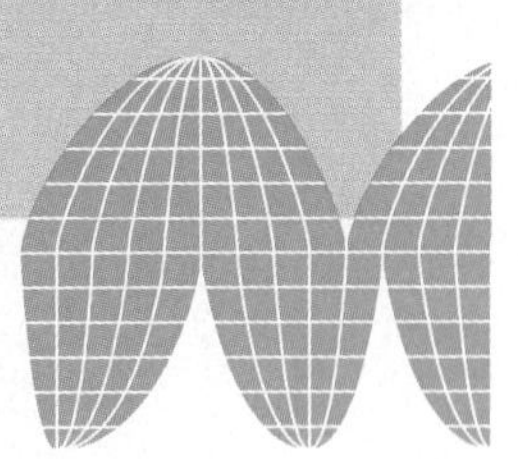

GE's New Technology Makes the Firm Go International

General Electric Co. was established in 1892. In 1989, GE had sales of more than $53 billion following an extensive restructuring of its assets during the 1980s. The restructuring was aimed at retaining only those businesses that had the potential to become first or second in world markets. One of those businesses was what had been the heart of GE's appliance business for many years—refrigerators. Little did GE know, however, that Japanese expertise at innovation was about to attack the core of its refrigerator business.

In the early 1980s, Matsushita and Necchi introduced new, high-quality compressors that were cheaper than anything GE could manufacture. GE management realized that even the refrigerator business was at the mercy of Japanese technological advances in the design and manufacture of refrigerator compressors. GE managers refused to buy from foreign manufacturers. Because meeting the challenge head on was the GE way, GE's appliance group went to work to develop a radical new compressor design and a new factory to produce it. In 1986, GE introduced a line of refrigerators that incorporated the new compressor design.

Sales of the new refrigerator went quite well at first. But in 1989, GE had to replace 1.1 million new compressors with foreign-made compressors, and hundreds of thousands were still waiting to be replaced. GE executives, many of whom now work for other companies (often outside of the appliance business), blame the failure of the new compressor on several factors. Some say the new compressor had been rushed through design at the expense of adequate testing. Others believe communication was the real problem. When things began to go sour, lower-level employees were unable to get the bad news to top-level executives, who continued to believe that design, testing, and manufacturing were going along smoothly.

The Japanese design and manufacturing methods were far superior to those used by GE. Sophisticated machining processes are only one example of how the Japanese were making a better product cheaper. These pressures from Japanese competition forced the normally well-managed GE to bypass the lessons of good product innovation and rush the new refrigerator to market. Now GE is paying the price for forcing innovation beyond its limits.

SOURCES: Gary Hoover, Alta Campbell, and Patrick J. Spain, eds., *Hoover's Handbook: Profiles of over 500 Major Corporations* (Austin, Tex.: The Reference Press, 1991), p. 253; "GE Refrigerator Woes Illustrate the Hazards in Changing a Product," *The Wall Street Journal,* May 7, 1990, p. 1; Ira C. Magaziner and Mark Patinkin, "Cold Competition: GE Wages the Refrigerator War," *Harvard Business Review,* March–April 1989, pp. 114–124.

A second risk is the possibility that a competitor will get a new innovation to the market first. This has been the case with many developments in the past decade (see *International Perspective*). The marketplace has become a breeding ground for continuous innovation. Motorola, for example, is striving to build a company in which customer needs shape new-product development without crippling the firm's technological leadership in its basic products.[3]

3. Bernard Avishai and William Taylor, "Customers Drive a Technology-Driven Company: An Interview with George Fisher," *Harvard Business Review,* November-December 1989, pp. 107–114.

TABLE 18.1
Types of Innovation in Organizations

Type	Example
Radical	Xerography Internal combustion engine
Systems	Integrating engine with carriage technology
Incremental	Continuous improvements in copying machines and cars

Innovation

■ Innovation can be radical, systems, or incremental.

As Table 18.1 shows, innovation can be either radical, systems, or incremental.[4]

Radical innovation represents a major breakthrough that changes or creates whole industries. Examples include xerography (which was invented by Chester Carlson in 1935 and became the hallmark of Xerox Corp.), steam engines, and the internal combustion engine (which paved the way for today's automobile industry).

Systems innovation creates a new functionality by assembling parts in new ways. For example, the gasoline engine began as a radical innovation and became a systems innovation when it was combined with bicycle and carriage technology to create automobiles.

Incremental innovation continues the technical improvement and extends the applications of radical and systems innovations. There are many more incremental innovations than there are radical and systems innovations. In fact, several incremental innovations often are necessary to make radical and systems innovations work properly. Incremental innovations force organizations to continuously improve their products and keep abreast or ahead of the competition.

New Ventures

New ventures based on innovations require *entrepreneurship,* or good leadership, to make the new idea a technological reality and a marketing success. The profile of the entrepreneur typically includes the need for achievement, a desire to assume responsibility, a willingness to take risks, and a focus on concrete results.[5] Others view entrepreneurship as a series of activities and behaviors that make up the role in which the entrepreneur engages. One researcher suggests that from an organizational point of view, the organizational system can encourage entrepreneurship by fostering behaviors such as fanaticism, commitment, and acceptance of chaos, as well as low start-up costs, incentives and rewards, and a lack of detailed controls.[6]

---

4. Frederick Betz, *Managing Technology* (Englewood Cliffs, N.J.: Prentice-Hall, 1987), pp. 7–8.
5. Karl H. Vesper, *New Venture Strategies* (Englewood Cliffs, N.J.: Prentice-Hall, 1980), p. 9.
6. James B. Quinn, "Managing Innovation: Controlled Chaos," *Harvard Business Review,* May-June 1985, pp. 73–84.

Entrepreneurship can occur inside or outside large organizations. Outside entrepreneurship requires all of the complex aspects of the innovation process. Inside entrepreneurship also requires entrepreneurial activity within a system that usually discourages chaotic activity. Large organizations typically do not accept entrepreneurial types of activities. Thus, for a large organization to continue to be innovative and develop new ventures, it must encourage entrepreneurial activity within the organization. This form of activity, often called **intrapreneurship,** usually is most effective when it is a part of everyday life in the organization and occurs throughout the organization rather than in the research and development department alone.

- **Intrapreneurship** is entrepreneurial activity within the organization.

Corporate Research

- Managing innovation means encouraging activities that involve innovation, new ventures, and corporate research.

The most common aspect of developing innovation in the traditional organization takes the form of *corporate research,* or research and development. Corporate research usually is set up to support existing businesses, provide incremental innovations in the organization's businesses, and explore potential new technology bases. Often it is established in a laboratory either on the site of the main corporate facility or some distance away from normal operations.

Corporate researchers are responsible for keeping the company's products and processes technologically advanced. Product life cycles vary a great deal depending on the rate at which a product becomes obsolete and whether substitutes for the product are developed. Obviously, if a product becomes either obsolete or substitutable, the profits from its sales will decrease. The job of corporate research is to prevent this from happening by keeping the company's products current.

Technology in Organizations

- **Technology** consists of the mechanical and intellectual processes that transform inputs into outputs.

The management of technology continues to be a source of concern for managers of organizations. In systems theory, **technology** refers to the mechanical and intellectual processes that transform inputs into outputs. For example, the primary technology employed by Mobil Corp. transforms crude oil (input) into gasoline, motor oil, heating oil, and other petroleum-based products (outputs). Prudential Insurance Co. uses actuarial tables and information processing technologies to produce its insurance services. Of course, most organizations use multiple technologies. Mobil Oil uses research and information processing technologies in its laboratories where new petroleum products and processes are generated.

Five Perspectives on Technology

Although there is general agreement with the systems view of technology, the means by which this technology has been evaluated and measured have varied

TABLE 18.2
Summary of Several Approaches to Technology

Approach	Classification of Technology
Woodward (1958 and 1965)	Unit or small-batch Large-batch or mass production Continuous process
Burns and Stalker (1961)	Rate of technological change
Perrow (1967)	Routine Nonroutine
Thompson (1967)	Long-linked Mediating Intensive
Aston Studies: Hickson, Pugh, and Pheysey (1969)	Work flow integration; operations, materials, and knowledge technologies

widely. Five approaches to examining the technology of the organization are shown in Table 18.2. For convenience, we have classified these approaches according to the names of their proponents.

Woodward In an early study of the relationship between technology and organization structure, Joan Woodward categorized manufacturing technologies by their complexity. Her research was based on the practices of one hundred British manufacturing companies, primarily electronics, chemical, and engineering firms.

Woodward identified the simplest technological classification as unit, or small-batch, production. This type of production is used, for example, in the manufacture of custom products, in which customized parts are made one at a time or in small batches. Large-batch, or mass, production, as used in automobile assembly lines, is more complicated and involves manufacturing standardized parts in very large batches. The most complex technologies are those of continuous-process production, in which a continuous stream of material is run through a process, such as through pipes and heating, cooling, and separation tanks. Chemical plants and petroleum refineries use continuous-process production.

Woodward found that the span of control and the number of levels in the administrative hierarchy were very similar for the successful firms within a technological classification. Supervisory span of control decreased and executive span of control and number of levels of management increased as technological complexity increased from unit to large-batch to continuous-process.[7]

Although Woodward developed her classification scheme in the late 1950s, her categories are still useful for analyzing manufacturing organizations. Some critics have argued that her classifications are simplistic and may represent

7. Joan Woodward, *Management and Technology: Problems of Progress in Industry,* no. 3 (London: Her Majesty's Stationery Office, 1958); Joan Woodward, *Industrial Organizations: Theory and Practice* (London: Oxford University Press, 1965).

This lineworker in a National Bicycle Industrial Company bicycle plant, a subsidiary of Matsushita, in Japan is taking one of its mass-produced bikes for a spin on a simulated bumpy road. This plant uses flexible manufacturing that is a combination of small batch and mass production processes to create essentially custom-fitted unique bikes on an assembly line, using computers, robots, and people.

smoothness of the production system rather than technological complexity.[8] Nevertheless, Woodward's work has made a significant contribution toward better understanding of organizations and technology.

Burns and Stalker At about the same time that Woodward was publishing her work, several other researchers were considering the fit between technology and structure. Tom Burns and George Stalker examined twenty manufacturing firms in England and Scotland—fifteen electronics firms, four research organizations, and a major manufacturing organization.[9] Based on their study, they proposed that the rate of change in the technology determines the best method of structuring the organization. For example, if the rate of change is slow, the most effective design is bureaucratic or, to use Burns and Stalker's term, *mechanistic.* But if the technology is changing rapidly, the organization needs a structure that allows more flexibility and quicker decision making so that it can react quickly to change. This design is called *organic.* We discuss these organization designs in more detail in Chapter 19.

Perrow Another view of the technology-structure fit was developed by Charles Perrow.[10] On the basis of his research with juvenile correction facilities, hospitals, and numerous manufacturing firms, Perrow developed a technological continuum, with routine technologies at one end and nonroutine technologies at the other. Whereas Woodward and Burns and Stalker dealt primarily with manufac-

8. Arthur G. Bedeian, *Organizations: Theory and Analysis,* 2nd ed. (Hinsdale, Ill.: Dryden Press, 1984).

9. Tom Burns and George M. Stalker, *The Management of Innovation* (London: Tavistock, 1961).

10. Charles B. Perrow, "A Framework for the Comparative Analysis of Organizations," *American Sociological Review,* April 1967, pp. 194–208.

turing firms, Perrow claimed that all organizations could be classified on his routine-to-nonroutine continuum.

The degree of routineness of a technology is defined by the number of exceptions to routine encountered in the work and the type of search processes used in deciding on a response to the exceptions. Where there are few exceptions and the search processes are based on logical, rational analysis, the technology is routine. A manufacturer of standardized products, such as Procter & Gamble and General Foods Corp., is likely to use routine technology, as well as organizational features such as low interdependence among groups, coordination by planning, and a highly formalized and centralized structure.

Where many exceptions are encountered and no well-established ways to solve the problems exist, the technology is nonroutine. High-tech research and development firms such as Hewlett-Packard Co. and Tandem Computers Inc. tend to use nonroutine technology and to have high interdependence among groups, coordination through feedback and mutual adjustment, and a flexible structure.[11]

Thompson Another approach to the technology of organizations was proposed by James Thompson.[12] His technological categories, which he argued could be used to classify all organizations, are long-linked, mediating, and intensive.

Long-linked technologies are serially linked operations whose relationships are much like the sequential interdependence discussed in Chapter 8. Operation A feeds to operation B, which feeds to operation C, and so on through the entire process. The assembly line is the best example of long-linked technology.

Mediating technology links otherwise independent units of the organization or different types of customers. Examples include banks, employment agencies, schools, and telephone companies. In banks, for example, some customers are depositors of money and some are borrowers. The bank serves the role of bringing these types of customers together. Each customer's needs are first categorized according to type; then the transaction is handled in a standard manner. Thus, the technology consists of linking units' uniform operating practices, rules, and controls.

Intensive technologies use skills, crafts, or services in an appropriate and often unique way to accomplish a task. A typical user of intensive technology is the general hospital. Despite increasing standardization in hospitals, each patient must be handled individually. Skills and resources are applied to each case in a unique combination that depends on the patient's condition and response to treatment.

Thompson suggested that organizations arrange themselves to protect the dominant technology, smooth out problems, and minimize coordination costs. Structural components such as inventory, warehousing, and shipping help buffer the technological transformation subsystem from environmental disturbances. For example, inventories and warehousing help manufacturing systems function as if the environment accepted output at a steady rate. In fact, however, demand

11. Charles B. Perrow, *Organizational Analysis: A Sociological View* (London: Tavistock, 1970).

12. James D. Thompson, *Organizations in Action* (New York: McGraw-Hill, 1967).

for products usually is cyclical or seasonal and is subject to many disturbances. The warehouse inventory makes it possible to produce at a constant rate, maximizing technological efficiency and thus the organization's ability to respond to the fluctuating demands of the market.

The Aston Studies A group of English researchers at the University of Aston, including David J. Hickson, Derek S. Pugh, and Diana C. Pheysey, examined the relationship between technology and structure for fifty-two firms near Birmingham, England.[13] They focused their attention on the transformation of inputs into outputs and the flow of work (work flow integration). These researchers broke technology down into three categories: operations, materials, and knowledge. Operations technology includes the techniques used in the transformation process. Materials technology deals with the specific characteristics of the materials, for example, hardness, availability, ease of machining, and ease of transportation. Knowledge technology refers to the level of technological sophistication and the complexity and specificity of knowledge required to do the job.

The Aston studies continued over several years as the researchers examined many aspects of organization structure, size, and type and compared their results with those of Woodward and others. They concluded that operations technology is associated with organization structure in those areas of the organization affected by the work flow. They also showed that when technology differs from one part of the organization to another, the organization structure of the parts differs as well.

- Technology usually means some type of adaptability to change in the way the organization does its work.

These perspectives on technology are somewhat similar in that all (except the Aston typology) reflect the adaptability of the technological system to change, as shown in Figure 18.1. Large-batch or mass production, routine, and long-linked technologies are not very adaptable to change. At the opposite end of the continuum, continuous-process, nonroutine, and intensive technologies are readily adaptable to change.

Technology in Practice

- Three myths about organizational technology exist: It affects only the production function; that simple technologies are old, boring, and of no value in modern organizations; and large expenditures on new technology are necessary to reduce payroll costs.

Several myths concerning the impact of technology on the organization exist. First, this impact often is assumed to be limited to the production function. In fact, the effects of technology are much more far-reaching. One such example is the organizational impact of international innovation on GE's refrigerator business described in *International Perspective.* New office technologies also are being examined for their impact on the structure of the office.[14]

13. David J. Hickson, Derek S. Pugh, and Diana C. Pheysey, "Operations Technology and Organization Structure: An Empirical Reappraisal," *Administrative Science Quarterly,* September 1969, pp. 378–397.

14. John Storey, "The Management of New Office Technology: Choice, Control, and Social Structure in the Insurance Industry," *Journal of Management Studies,* January 1987, pp. 43–62.

FIGURE 18.1
Adaptability of Technology to Change

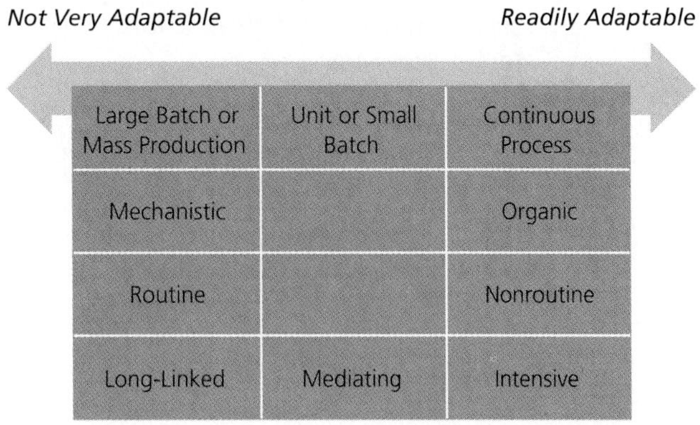

Not Very Adaptable — *Readily Adaptable*

Large Batch or Mass Production	Unit or Small Batch	Continuous Process
Mechanistic		Organic
Routine		Nonroutine
Long-Linked	Mediating	Intensive

SOURCE: Figure adapted from *Organizations: Theory and Analysis,* Second Edition by Arthur G. Bedeian, copyright © 1984 by The Dryden Press, reprinted by permission of the publisher.

A second myth is the assumption that relatively simple technologies are old, boring, and therefore incapable of being useful in the modern age of high technology. There are numerous examples of unit or small-batch production systems that can benefit from advances in manufacturing technology. Computer-integrated manufacturing has proven valuable in the aerospace industry and to many makers of custom-made products, for example.[15] In these situations, a new technology producing a computerized flow of information about the production process is added to the basic unit or small-batch technology.

A third myth is the assumption that large expenditures on new technology will allow an organization to reduce the skill level of employees and thus reduce overall payroll and training costs. This "deskilling" does occur in some situations, such as when complex procedures and decision parameters can be programmed into a computer routine. However, more training often is required for employees to be able to run more complex machinery, monitor automatic equipment, and install or repair sophisticated systems. The difficult task for management is to determine the requirements of the new technology.[16] Managers must identify the level of skills required, the number of personnel needed, and the points in the process where the need for people will be either larger or smaller. Westinghouse has had difficulty integrating and managing the technology involved in making robots, as discussed in *Management in Action.*

Organization structure bears the major impact of technology. The relationship between an organization and its technologies turns out to be much more complex than anyone, including Joan Woodward, first assumed in the 1950s. In the next chapter, we address the relationship of the organization and technology in more detail.

15. Cynthia A. Lengnick-Hall, "Technology Advances in Batch Production and Improved Competitive Position," *Journal of Management,* Spring 1986, pp. 75–90.

16. Paul Adler, "New Technologies, New Skills," *California Management Review,* Fall 1986, pp. 9–27.

MANAGEMENT IN ACTION

Westinghouse and Unimation: A Lesson in How *Not* to Do Business

The idea was to buy Unimation and capitalize on its leadership in the robotics industry to launch a billion-dollar industry in factory automation. Thus, in 1963 Westinghouse outbid General Electric and bought Unimation, Inc., joining IBM, GE, Cincinnati Milacron, and United Technologies in the rapidly expanding robotics business. By 1987, most had left the business and the Japanese dominated the market. The story of how Westinghouse managed to misuse the technology of Unimation is a lesson in how not to manage technology and innovation.

Westinghouse originally was a start-up company capitalizing on the new technology of electricity. George Westinghouse founded Westinghouse Electric Co. in 1886 and entered the fledgling electric industry by inventing a system of transmitting electric current over long distances. He bought the rights to AC electric patents and installed the first AC power system in Telluride, Colorado, in 1891.

From its early days as an entrepreneurial start-up based on new technology, Westinghouse expanded into major appliances, building nuclear generating reactors, and operating radio stations. By the 1970s it had become a huge conglomerate, operating businesses in such diverse industries as soft-drink bottling, watches, and low-income housing. Currently it has six operating groups: broadcasting, commercial, electronics systems, energy and utility systems, financial services, and industries.

When Westinghouse bought Unimation, most U.S. firms viewed robotics as a novelty rather than a serious solution to manufacturing problems, as the Japanese did. Westinghouse took the movement seriously, however. It had great expectations for the future of robots, especially in the automobile industry. However, it relied solely on the hydraulic system of the original Unimation machine instead of continuing to invest in the development of innovative ideas in what had become a very dynamic industry. At one point, the company landed a $5 million contract with Ford Motor Co. that included $160,000 for drip pans to catch the oil that leaked out of the robots. Rather than developing a robot that did not leak—perhaps by using electric robot technology—Westinghouse chose to stick with the early technology and try to make the initial investment pay off.

Instead of keeping the robotics group separate and letting it concentrate on its specialty and the rapid changes in the area, Westinghouse attempted to integrate the group into its factory automation group. Soon thereafter, the former Unimation software group defected and formed its own company. By 1985, sales of Unimation products had dropped and losses amounted to between $15 million and $20 million a year. With declining sales and mounting losses, Westinghouse dismantled Unimation and sold what remained to a company in Switzerland. In 1990, Westinghouse announced a new partnership with Carnegie-Mellon University and RedZone Robotics, Inc., to develop robot technology for use in the nuclear service and nuclear waste markets. One can only wonder if Westinghouse learned anything.

SOURCES: "Westinghouse Electric Corp.," *The Wall Street Journal,* May 17, 1990, p. B4; Gary Hoover, Alta Campbell, and Patrick J. Spain, eds., *Hoover's Handbook: Profiles of over 500 Major Corporations* (Austin, Tex.: The Reference Press, 1991), p. 586; "How U.S. Robots Lost the Market to Japan in Factory Automation," *The Wall Street Journal,* November, 1, 1990, pp. A1, A9.

Organizational Environments

■ The **organizational environment** consists of all elements—people, other organizations, economic factors, objects, and events—that exist outside the organization's boundaries.

The **organizational environment** includes all elements—people, other organizations, economic factors, objects, and events—that lie outside the boundaries of the organization. People in the organizational environment include customers, donors, regulators, inspectors, and shareholders. Among the other organizations are competitors, legislatures, and regulatory agencies. Economic factors include interest rates, the trade deficit, and the growth rate of the gross national product. Objects include things such as buildings, vehicles, and trees. Events that may affect organizations involve occurrences of weather, elections, or war.

It is necessary to determine the boundaries of the organization to understand where the environment begins. These boundaries may be somewhat elusive, or at least changeable, and thus difficult to define. But for the most part we can say that certain people, groups, or buildings are either in the organization or in the environment. For example, a college student shopping for a personal computer is part of the environment of Apple, Compaq, IBM, and other computer manufacturers. However, if the student works for one of these computer manufacturers, he or she is not part of that company's environment but is within the boundaries of the organization.

This definition emphasizes the expanse of the general environment within which the organization operates. It may indeed give managers the false impression that the environment is outside their control and interest. But because the environment completely encloses the organization, managers must be constantly concerned about it. As Jeffrey Pfeffer and Gerald Salancik have said, "Organizations are inescapably bound up with the conditions of their environment."[17]

The manager, then, faces an enormous, only vaguely specified environment that somehow affects the organization. Managing the organization within such an environment may seem an overwhelming task. The alternatives for the manager are to (1) ignore the environment because of its complexity and focus on managing the internal operations of the company; (2) exert maximum energy in gathering information on every part of the environment and trying to react to every environmental factor; and (3) pay attention to specific aspects of the environment, responding only to those that most clearly affect the organization.

To ignore environmental factors entirely and focus on internal operations leaves the company in danger of missing major environmental shifts, such as changes in customer preferences, technological breakthroughs, and new regulations. To expend inordinate amounts of energy, time, and money exploring each and every facet of the environment may take more out of the organization than it returns.

The third alternative—to carefully analyze those segments of the environment that most affect the organization and to respond accordingly—represents the most prudent course of action. The issue, then, is to determine which parts of the environment are appropriate for the manager's attention. In the remainder

17. Jeffrey Pfeffer and Gerald R. Salancik, *The External Control of Organizations: A Resource Dependence Perspective* (New York: Harper & Row, 1978), p. 1.

of this section, we examine two perspectives on the organizational environment: the analysis of environmental components and environmental uncertainty.

Environmental Components

The first task is to identify the environmental components that are important to the organization. As Figure 18.2 shows, the general environment can be divided into nine components: human resources, competitors, shareholders, the economy, the market, physical resources, sociocultural factors, government, and financial resources.

Human Resources The human resources component is made up of the general labor market, including the people who work or look for work (potential employees) and the suppliers of talent, such as employment agencies, colleges and universities, and trade schools. Note that although employees are part of the internal operations of the organization, the general labor market is external and thus is part of the environment. The human resources component also includes the labor unions that serve as the dominant suppliers and representatives of labor for the organization.

Competitors Competitors include all the people and organizations that compete in the same market with the same or similar products or services or for the same customers. The competitive environment can change a great deal over time. For example, for years the major U.S. automobile manufacturers understood that

FIGURE 18.2
Components of the Organization's Environment

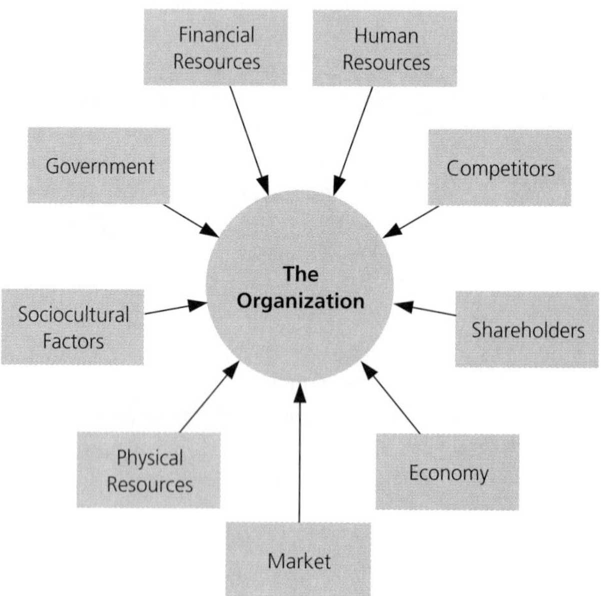

John Filipowski is holding fluorescent light bulbs that are not connected to an electrical socket but are being lighted up by the 345-kilovolt power lines overhead. John and his neighbors believe that radiation from power lines on their land is powerful enough to endanger their health. After paying for the land and building the power lines the New York Power Authority was faced with a law suit from Mr. Filipowski and 139 other property owners.

they were competing only with one another for the U.S. car buyer. In the 1950s and 1960s, they found they were also in competition with Sears, Roebuck, other automobile repair facilities, and auto parts manufacturers because customers had a choice between fixing their old cars and buying new ones. Japanese manufacturers became a major competitive force in the 1970s. Today Honda Motor Co., Ltd., the Japanese manufacturer, is building cars in Ohio so rapidly that it is closing in on Chrysler Corp. as the third largest U.S. automaker.[18]

Shareholders Shareholders are flexing new muscle, partly because pension fund managers and corporate raiders have convinced even small investors that they have the right to make demands of the company's management.[19] There may be some confusion regarding whether shareholders are internal or external to the organization. In some organizations, the majority of shareholders are employees, directors, and managers of the company. In the majority of cases, the shareholders are part of the company and not part of the environment. But in many organizations, shareholders are not employees, managers, officers, or directors but large pension funds and other institutional investors.

Economy The economic component of the environment includes the basic factors of the national and global economy that reflect buying and spending patterns,

---

18. "The Americanization of Honda," *Business Week,* April 25, 1988, pp. 90–96.
19. "The Battle for Corporate Control," *Business Week,* May 18, 1987, pp. 102–109.

such as interest rates, trade deficits, housing starts, new factory orders, unemployment rates, and economic growth. The unemployment rate obviously is related to the general labor market, included earlier under *Human Resources,* but it is also considered an indicator of economic conditions.

Market The market component of the environment includes customers, clients, and all potential consumers of the organization's product or service. Customers indicate whether the product or service is acceptable by their willingness to pay for it. Changes in customers' preferences directly affect the company, its sales performance, its manufacturing schedules, and its inventories. Peters and Waterman have emphasized that one characteristic of an excellent company is staying close to the customer.[20]

Physical Resources Physical resources include all of the physical raw materials used as inputs into the organization's transformation process. Examples are parts such as plastic, steel, and windows as well as buildings, warehouses, tools, and equipment. Shortages in raw materials caused by supplier problems such as strikes can create serious difficulties for the organization.

Sociocultural Factors The sociocultural component includes all of the personal and social factors that affect people in and around the organization: the work force, customers, suppliers, and competitors. Such factors have many effects on management decisions. Cultural factors, for example, may determine which holidays are paid for as part of the company benefit plan. It may be necessary to make adjustments for differences in values among employees in different parts of the world or even in different groups within the U.S. population. Motivational and disciplinary programs, the design of jobs, the use of autonomous work groups, and the degree to which work groups participate in decision making may need to be built around the sociocultural features of specific population segments.

Government All organizations must comply with laws and regulations of local, state, and federal governments. Typical regulations deal with environmental impact, hiring, taxes, competitive practices, and labor relations and collective bargaining. The impact of government regulations can be great. When Honda established its Marysville, Ohio, plant, it hired employees from a limited area to build local community relations. By doing so, it excluded the minority population forty miles away in Columbus. It settled with the Equal Employment Opportunity Commission by paying $6 million and promising to boost minority hiring.[21] *The Ethical Dilemma* shows how government regulations can change.

---

20. Thomas J. Peters and Robert H. Waterman, Jr., *In Search of Excellence: Lessons from America's Best-Run Companies* (New York: Harper & Row, 1982).

21. "The Americanization of Honda."

THE ETHICAL DILEMMA

Uranium Radiation and Protection of Employees

New technology for uranium extraction was available but was never introduced into the mines. First, it cost too much. Second, miners were accustomed to the hazards of working in the mines. Now, however, around forty years later, these miners are experiencing more health problems than anyone thought possible. Prostate and bladder cancer, lung cancer, headaches, and sleep disorders are only a few of the ailments former uranium miners are experiencing.

At the time of the rush to extract more ore and develop nuclear capability, the United States was in the middle of a nuclear arms race with the Soviet Union. Anyone who dared suggest that mining methods were hazardous was in danger of being accused of consorting with the enemy. The Atomic Energy Commission was charged with the task of improving U.S. nuclear capability and knew about the dangers inherent in mining uranium and testing nuclear devices in the open air. In fact, open-air testing took place only on days when the wind was blowing away from highly populated Las Vegas. Some have declared that miners and people in the path of nuclear radiation were actually guinea pigs for the federal government.

Congress has established a $100 million trust fund to pay $100,000 each to disabled uranium miners or their families. In most cases, the money will go to paying for part of the medical bills that have piled up over the years. Lawsuits over the issue so far have failed to make any progress in the court system. In a recent twist in the legal arena, a group of former employees of NL Industries, Inc., filed a $1.9 billion suit for medical charges and punitive damages resulting from years of exposure to hazardous materials in weapons. The suit was brought by several unions representing employees who had worked at the plant.

Technology is useful only if it is used. Evidence indicates that the AEC knew the potential hazards in uranium mining and had the ability to prevent the damage. It appears that it chose not to do so because of other considerations. At the time, the environment surrounding uranium mining seemed to the AEC to indicate the proper course of action. Years later, it appears the AEC's decision was less than prudent.

SOURCES: "'These People Were Used as Guinea Pigs,'" *Business Week,* October 15, 1990, p. 98; "Keeping a Deadly Secret," *Newsweek,* June 18, 1990, p. 20; "Unit Sued for $1.9 Billion in Hazardous Material Issue," *The Wall Street Journal,* January 31, 1990, p. A12.

Financial Resources Financial resources include all sources of money available to the organization. For publicly held corporations, these include stocks and bonds as well as money borrowed from a variety of sources. Privately held organizations may seek funds from lenders and sometimes from venture capitalists. For not-for-profit organizations, funding sources may include charitable contributions, legislative acts, and fee-for-service arrangements. Without an adequate source of capital, most organizations cannot survive.

In summary, these nine components cover the major environmental factors that affect organizations. In most situations, only a subset of these components affect an organization significantly.

This boy holds a ninja turtle doll, the most recent fad in the toy industry. Toy companies must move very fast to take advantage of demand created by popular movie and television characters. Manufacturers of these ninja turtles, Playmates Toys, is trying to avoid the boom-to-bankruptcy fate experienced by makers of Cabbage Patch dolls and Teddy Ruxpin.

Environmental Uncertainty

- The **task environment** is the particular set of environmental forces that affect the organization's operations.
- **Environmental uncertainty** exists when managers have little information about environmental events and their effects on the organization.
- **Environmental complexity** is the number of environmental components that bear on organization decision making.
- **Environmental dynamism** is the degree to which the environmental components change.
- All organizations have many components in their environment; it is the number that are important to them and the rate at which they change that makes the difference.

Another view of the environment focuses on the uncertainty of the environment and the impact of various environments on different organizations. Not all forces in the general environment affect all organizations in the same way. Hospital Corp. of America, for example, is very much influenced by government regulations and medical and scientific developments. McDonald's Corp., on the other hand, is affected by quite different environmental forces: consumer demand, disposable income, cost of meat and bread, and gasoline prices. Thus, the **task environment**—the specific set of environmental forces that affect the operations of an organization—varies among organizations.

The environmental characteristic that appears to have the most influence on the structure of the organization is uncertainty. **Environmental uncertainty** exists when managers have little information about environmental events and their impact on the organization.[22] Uncertainty has been described as resulting from complexity and dynamism in the environment. **Environmental complexity** is the number of environmental components that impinge on organizational decision making. **Environmental dynamism** is the degree to which these components change.[23] With these two dimensions, we can determine the degree of environmental uncertainty as illustrated in Figure 18.3.

In cell 1, a low-uncertainty environment, there are few important components, and they change infrequently. A company in the cardboard container industry might have a highly certain environment when demand is steady, man-

22. Richard L. Daft, *Organization Theory and Design,* 2nd ed. (St. Paul, Minn.: West, 1986), p. 55.
23. Robert B. Duncan, "Characteristics of Organizational Environments and Perceived Uncertainty," *Administrative Science Quarterly,* September 1972, pp. 313–327.

Rate of Environmental Change	Simple	Complex
Static	**Cell 1: Low Perceived Uncertainty** 1. Small number of factors and components in the environment 2. Factors and components are somewhat similar to one another 3. Factors and components remain basically the same *Example: Cardboard Container Industry*	**Cell 2: Moderately Low Perceived Uncertainty** 1. Large number of factors and components in the environment 2. Factors and components are not similar to one another 3. Factors and components remain basically the same *Example: State Universities*
Dynamic	**Cell 3: Moderately High Perceived Uncertainty** 1. Small number of factors and components in the environment 2. Factors and components are somewhat similar to one another 3. Factors and components of the environment continually change *Example: Fashion Industry*	**Cell 4: High Perceived Uncertainty** 1. Large number of factors and components in the environment 2. Factors and components are not similar to one another 3. Factors and components of environment continually change *Example: Banking Industry*

Environmental Complexity

SOURCE: Reprinted from "Characteristics of Organizational Environments and Perceived Uncertainty" by Robert B. Duncan, published in *Administrative Science Quarterly,* Vol. 17, No. 3 (Sept. 1972) p. 320, by permission of *Administrative Science Quarterly.*

FIGURE 18.3
Classification of Environmental Uncertainty

ufacturing processes are stable, and government regulations have remained largely unchanged.

In cell 4, in contrast, many important components are involved in decision making, and they change often. Thus, cell 4 represents a high-uncertainty environment. The banking environment is now highly uncertain. With deregulation and the advent of interstate operations, banks today must compete with insurance companies, brokerage firms, real estate firms, and even department stores. The toy industry also is in a highly uncertain environment. As they develop new toys, toy companies must stay in tune with movies, television shows, and cartoons as well as with public sentiment. In the 1983–1988 period, the Saturday morning cartoons were little more than animated stories about children's toys. Recently, however, due to disappointing sales of many toys presented in cartoons designed to promote them, most toy companies have left the toy-based cartoon business.[24]

Environmental characteristics and uncertainty have been important factors in explaining organization structure, strategy, and performance. For example,

24. "Toy Makers Lose Interest in Tie-Ins with Cartoons," *The Wall Street Journal,* April 28, 1988, p. 29.

FIGURE 18.4
Three Perspectives on the Environment-Organization Relationship

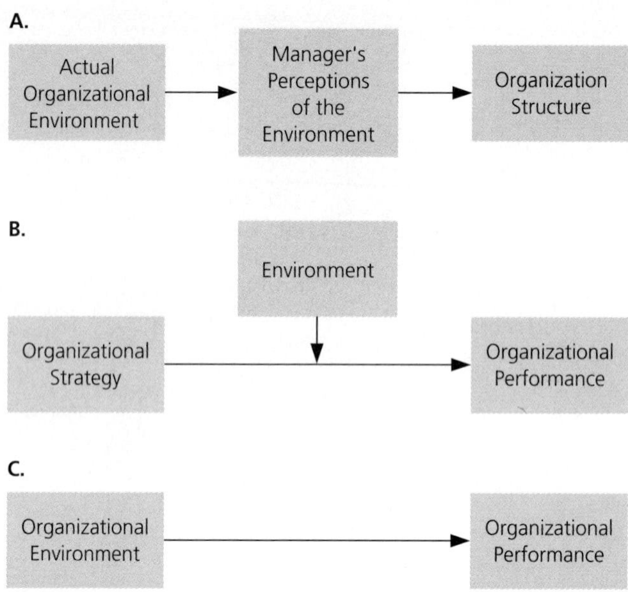

the characteristics of the environment affect how managers perceive the environment, which in turn affects how they adapt the structure of the organization to meet environmental demands.[25] This relationship is shown in part A of Figure 18.4. The environment has also been shown to affect the degree to which a firm's strategy enhances its performance (part B);[26] that is, a certain strategy will enhance organizational performance to the extent that it is appropriate for the environment in which the organization operates. Finally, the environment is directly related to organizational performance, as shown in part C.[27] The environment and the organization's response to it are crucial to success.

Organizational Responses

An organization's response to its environment can take many forms. In this section, we describe three particular ways that this response or adaptation can take place: through the structural contingency, resource dependence, or population ecology perspectives.

25. Masoud Yasai-Ardekani, "Structural Adaptations to Environments," *Academy of Management Review,* January 1986, pp. 9–21.

26. John E. Prescott, "Environments as Moderators of the Relationship between Strategy and Performance," *Academy of Management Journal,* June 1986, pp. 329–346.

27. Timothy M. Stearns, Alan N. Hoffman, and Jan B. Heide, "Performance of Commercial Television Stations as an Outcome of Interorganizational Linkages and Environmental Conditions," *Academy of Management Journal,* March 1987, pp. 71–90.

Structural Contingency Perspective

■ The **structural contingency perspective** suggests that the most appropriate structure for an organization depends on the environment.

One of the most popular approaches to the study of the organization and its environment is the **structural contingency perspective,** which suggests that the best structure for an organization is dependent, or contingent, on the environment in which it operates. We will discuss this approach in more detail in Chapter 19; here we briefly examine the concept to emphasize the importance of the environment's effect on organizations.

One of the earliest structural contingency approaches is the framework presented by Paul Lawrence and Jay Lorsch, who examined companies in three different industries and their environments.[28] They categorized the environment of the plastics industry as diverse, dynamic, and uncertain; the environment of the container industry as stable and certain; and the environment of the food industry as midway between the other two.

The effective firms in the plastics industry were found to be highly *differentiated* and have similar features that enabled them to prosper in the uncertain environment characteristic of that industry. Tasks were divided among departments, and employees' primary orientation was toward the goals of their departments. When departments were highly differentiated, Lawrence and Lorsch found a high potential for conflict among the functional specialists because of their vastly different orientations. Yet the uncertain environment demanded that the groups collaborate for the overall benefit of the organization. The authors used the term *integration* to refer to the process of collaboration to resolve conflict. In plastics firms, they found, integration often was accomplished by individuals, groups, or departments whose primary role was to resolve conflict.

The container companies, in contrast, were in a more certain environment and were less differentiated in structure and orientation, experienced less conflict, and thus had less need for formal integration of groups or individuals. Most conflicts were resolved by a person in a top management position.

Environmental uncertainty was a major factor in understanding why firms in these two industries were either successful or unsuccessful. The successful firms' structures were appropriate for meeting the demands of the environment. As we noted, the next chapter gives more detail on organization structure.

Resource Dependence Perspective

■ The **resource dependence perspective** of organization-environment relationships emphasizes the importance of resources—human, financial, and physical—and proposes that organizations seek to accomplish resource exchange with relevant environments through interorganizational linkages and changing the environment.

Another view of the relationship between the organization and the environment emphasizes the importance of resources. Recall from Figure 18.2 that three of the environmental components are resources: human, financial, and physical. Organizations need resources to operate. For example, a bank could not function without the money customers deposit and other customers withdraw in the form

28. Paul R. Lawrence and Jay W. Lorsch, *Organizations and Environment: Managing Differentiation and Integration* (Homewood, Ill.: Irwin, 1969; first published by the Division of Research, Graduate School of Business Administration, Harvard University, 1967).

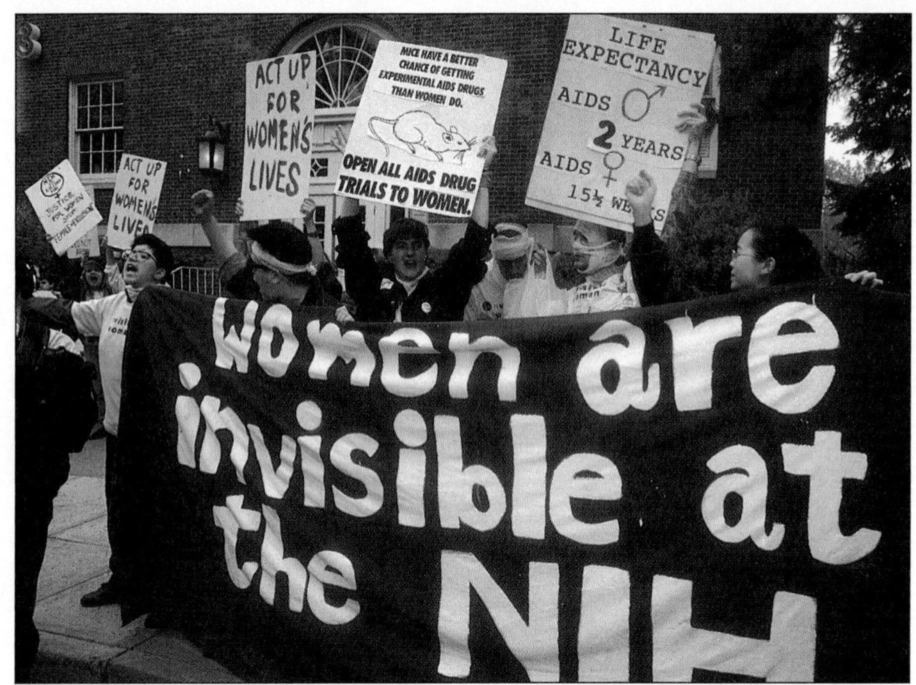

Members of the AIDS activist group, ACT UP, lobby and demonstrate at the National Institute of Health in an effort to obtain more research funding for women with AIDS. These women seek increased recognition for AIDS symptoms typically experienced by women which would lead to more money for research. Thus, in order to get the resources, they must change the environmental definitions of symptoms.

of loans. The bank must also have people to be tellers, loan officers, customer service personnel, and managers.

The more important and scarce the resource, the more the organization depends on the environment—specifically, on the environmental component that provides the resource. Naturally, the organization is vulnerable to problems if the supply of the scarce input is threatened, reduced or cut off. For example, if the supply of an essential raw material is stopped, as with a strike by a supplier's employees, the company may have to shut down its operation. Prior to the development of a nonstrike agreement between the labor unions and the steel companies in the 1970s, as labor contract renewal time neared for workers in the steel industry, automobile companies would stockpile steel for months in the event of a strike by steelworkers. The steel companies, in turn, considered the car companies valuable to their existence, because a strike by auto workers could affect the demand for steel.

Organizations must maintain *resource exchanges* with their environments to survive.[29] They can accomplish such exchanges in two primary ways: by developing interorganizational linkages and by changing the environment[30] as

29. Ephraim Yuchtman and Stanley Seashore, "A System Resource Approach to Organizational Effectiveness," *American Sociological Review*, December 1967, pp. 891–903.

30. Daft, *Organizational Theory and Design*, pp. 70–76.

shown in Figure 18.5. Developing interorganizational linkages involves identifying organizations that control vital resources and then developing relationships with those organizations to ensure a constant flow of raw materials. Interorganizational linkages can take the form of (1) joint ventures, (2) contractual relationships, (3) mergers, (4) acquisitions, or (5) cooptation of outsiders, such as the appointment of leaders of other organizations to the company's board of directors.

Sometimes it may be easier to change the environment to make the organization's current structure appropriate than to make major structural adjustments. To change the environment, the organization can do several things: (1) change the organization to operate in a different set of environmental conditions, as the tobacco companies did during the last decade by buying companies in recreation, leisure, clothing, and food industries to reduce their dependence on tobacco products; (2) join trade associations to further the cause of the entire industry; (3) engage in political activities such as lobbying in an attempt to alter regulations affecting the organization; and (4) engage in behaviors—perhaps even illegal activities—to affect other organizations in the environment. An example of the last type is the insider stock trading schemes in which individuals engage in illegal practices by twisting the rules to create a more favorable environment for trading.

The more the organization depends on other organizations for scarce resources, the more likely the organization will be to either develop interorganizational relationships or seek to change the environment. If, on the other hand,

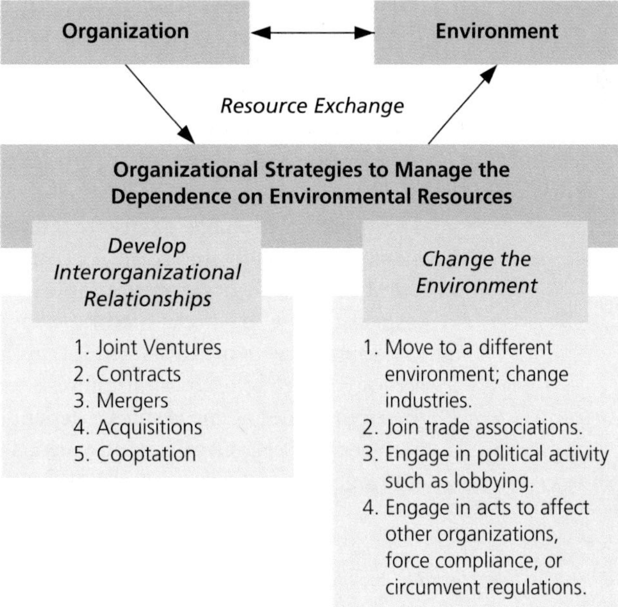

FIGURE 18.5
The Resource Dependence Perspective

the organization depends very little on other organizations for its resources, it may remain free to do as it pleases with few threats from the environment. However, such freedom is rare in today's complex business environment.

Population Ecology Perspective

- The **population ecology perspective** proposes that organizations survive on the basis of fit between their structural attributes and environmental characteristics.

The population ecology perspective of organizations proposes that organizations survive on the basis of fit between their structural attributes and environmental characteristics.[31] It is similar to the biological theory of natural selection in its emphasis on survival of the fittest. When there is an overabundance of a species—more than the environment can support—survival of the fittest determines which individuals last and which die. Environments and organizations function in much the same way. When the environment cannot support all the organizations that exist, those that maintain the best fit with the environment will survive.

The personal computer market may be experiencing this phenomenon. Soon after Apple showed that a market existed for these machines, personal computer manufacturers seemed to spring up overnight. However, after several years of technological development and expansion of products and related services, the number of companies in the industry began to decrease. We no longer hear of Osborne Computer Corp. or Victor Technologies Inc., for example. The primary players in the personal computer market are IBM, Apple, Compaq, Tandy/Radio Shack, and a few others who specialize in certain applications, such as networking. It can be argued that these companies have survived through a process of natural selection.

The population approach provides a fascinating means for comparing industries over the years. It can help explain what happens as entire industries change. However, it has several limitations.[32] It is not specific in many areas. For example, although it stresses the total capacity of the environment to support a certain number of organizations, it has done little as yet to help explain why some organizations survive and others do not. Therefore, it cannot provide prescriptions for managers to use to adapt a specific organization for survival.

The three approaches to organizational response, or adaptation, to the environment described in this section provide somewhat different views of the relationship between an organization and its environment. Although they differ in some respects, there are areas of congruence as well. These similarities and differences are summarized in Table 18.3. The structural contingency and the population ecology approaches assume there is an optimal fit between the organization and the environment. The resource dependence view focuses on the resource exchange between the organization and various environmental components. The structural contingency and resource dependence approaches assume managers can make

---

31. Howard E. Aldrich and Jeffrey Pfeffer, "Environments of Organizations," *Annual Review of Sociology,* 1976, pp. 80–83.

32. Bedeian, *Organizations: Theory and Analysis.*

TABLE 18.3
Comparison of Three Approaches to Environmental-Organizational Response

Feature	Approach: Structural Contingency	Resource Dependence	Population Ecology
Optimal fit	Yes	No	Yes
Resources	No	Yes	No
Managerial prescriptions	Yes	Yes	No

decisions to adapt the organization to its environment. The population ecology perspective does not deal with managerial involvement in determining the optimal fit.[33] Nevertheless, all three perspectives emphasize the importance of the environment-organization relationship.

Summary of Key Points

- Managing innovation in organizations involves managing the processes of innovation, new ventures, and corporate research. Innovation can be radical, systems, or incremental.
- The organization's technology includes all the processes an organization uses to transform inputs into outputs. The impact of technology on organizations has been extensively studied. Woodward classified technologies as unit or small-batch, large-batch or mass production, and continuous-process. Burns and Stalker described the impact of technology on organizations in terms of the rate of technological change. Perrow focused on the routine or nonroutine nature of the work. Thompson described technology as long-linked, mediating, or intensive. Finally, the Aston studies described work flow integration and the operations, materials, and knowledge technologies.
- Environment and technology summarize the major sets of pressures or demands on the organization. The environment includes all elements outside the organization's boundaries. It can be viewed in terms of its components, its causal nature, and its uncertainty. The components include human resources, competitors, shareholders, the economy, the market, physical resources, sociocultural factors, government, and financial resources.
- Environmental uncertainty exists when managers have little information about environmental events and their impact on the organization. Two factors contribute to environmental uncertainty: complexity and dynamism. A complex and dynamic environment is the most uncertain.
- Three approaches to organizational response, or adaptation, to the environ-

33. Aldrich and Pfeffer, "Environments of Organizations."

ment are the structural contingency, resource dependence, and population ecology perspectives. The structural contingency perspective suggests that the structure of the organization depends on the environment in which the firm operates. The resource dependence perspective focuses on the exchanges between the organization and the various environmental components. As the organization seeks to manage its relationships with environmental components, it may either develop interorganizational relationships or try to change the environment. According to the population ecology perspective, organizations survive on the basis of the fit between their structural attributes and environmental characteristics.

Discussion Questions

1. Define *organizational environment* and *organizational technology.* In what ways do these concepts overlap?
2. Describe the environment of your college or university by giving examples of each of the nine environmental components and discussing the complexity and dynamism of the environment.
3. Under what conditions would it be possible for a person to be part of an organization and part of the organization's environment?
4. Are you, or is anyone you know, a shareholder in a company? In what ways is a shareholder part of the environment as well as part of the organization? Discuss what conflicts could arise from a shareholder's being part of both the environment and the organization.
5. In the early 1980s, Chrysler Corp. was on the verge of bankruptcy. Discuss how the near failure of Chrysler could have been a result of its failure to maintain a proper resource exchange with its environment and how its recovery could have been due to its ability to reestablish an appropriate resource exchange.
6. According to the population ecology perspective, what is the most important factor in determining organizational success? What can managers do to help their organizations survive? What is the role of chance in organizational success?
7. How would you describe the technology of management? Does managing people in organizations use a technology similar to those described by Thompson and Perrow or to those described by Woodward and the Aston studies? Explain.
8. Is the technology of management different for lower-level managers (supervisors) than for upper-level managers (CEO and vice presidents)?
9. How would you describe the technology of the college or university you attend? To what extent does this technology affect the way the organization operates (structure, decision making, and so on)?
10. If someone asked you why you are studying environment and technology in a course on organizational behavior, how would you respond?
11. How do innovation and creativity differ? How are they similar?

CASE 18.1

Environmental Protection: Problems or Opportunities?

The environmental protection movement has had a checkered past. During the 1970s, the issue was forced on the public by activist groups that managed to get regulations passed by legislators. In the 1980s, companies resisted the regulations and often implemented minimalist strategies, doing only enough to just meet government requirements at the least expense. Some companies that were caught in flagrant violations of environmental protection regulations paid huge fines. Hundreds of other companies, however, were able to escape prosecution with skillful lobbying, by begging for leniency due to the high cost of compliance, or by covering up the evidence.

The 1990s may be an entirely different story. On April 22, 1990, hundreds of millions of people worldwide celebrated the twentieth anniversary of Earth Day. After Earth Day 1990, however, numerous environment-oriented issues went down to defeat at the ballot box and in legislative halls as the general populace and legislators faced mind-boggling decisions. Even the environmentalists have been unable to agree on how to proceed in many areas of environmental cleanup and thus have failed to put forth a cohesive program. Often the choice has been between a sound economy and a healthy environment.

Probably the biggest single issue is global warming. Some have warned that intense global warming will bring catastrophic flooding of coastal lowlands in the twenty-first century. Computer models have predicted that the mean global temperature will increase from 1.8 to 10 degrees Fahrenheit during the next fifty to one hundred years. A 2-degree rise in the next century might be manageable, but a 10-degree rise in the next fifty years will likely be disastrous. Experts cannot even agree on the causes of global warming, much less how to correct the situation. Part of the problem appears to be the amount of carbon dioxide in the atmosphere, which traps heat within and causes the overall temperature to rise. Burning of fossil fuels has put more CO_2 into the atmosphere. Trees and other vegetation take in CO_2 to make new cells for growth and put oxygen back into the air. Some complain that the deforestation of the rain forests of Brazil must be stopped. Others are promoting the planting of more trees to use up more CO_2. One of the more creative efforts to save the Amazon forests has been the use of Brazil nuts in the Rain Forest Crunch flavor of ice cream at Ben & Jerry's Homemade, Inc., in Vermont. Ben and Jerry's figures that creating more demand for Brazil nuts might save a few trees from destruction.

Several large, multinational corporations have backed up their interest in environmental issues. H. J. Heinz and other major tuna canners stopped buying fish from fleets that use the dangerous drift net methods. As a result, Japan, Taiwan, and South Korea agreed to stop using these methods. McDonald's stopped using polystyrene wrappings for its fast food. Conoco will use only double-hulled tankers to avoid the risk of tanker spills. Du Pont has vowed to reduce emissions by 60 percent by 1993 and toxic wastes by 35 percent by 2000. Kodak is spending $100 million to replace or upgrade one thousand chemical storage tanks and solvent-carrying pipes. Monsanto expects to reduce toxic-air emissions by 90 percent by 1992 and to spend $600 million on environmental projects in the early 1990s.

Evidently these companies believe a small number of dollars expended now can prevent the expenditure of large dollars later on. This has been experienced in Eastern Europe, where no concern for the environment was exhibited for decades. The region's polluted air and water are costing government and industry in that area hundreds of millions to clean up. In addition, it has been estimated that the market for pollution control and cleanup equipment is over $100 billion, a growth rate of more than 10 percent per year.

The result is that companies are spending money and effort to clean up the environment. Internally, these expenditures affect decision making in marketing, packaging, research and development, manufacturing, and even public relations. One indication of this trend is that the people responsible for environmental issues are climbing the corporate ladder. At Union Carbide, the top environmental position is the vice president for environmental affairs. Texaco and Chevron each have a top corporate environmental officer who reports directly to the CEO. Companies seem to be doing everything possible to clean up their act and the environment as well.

Case Questions

1. Why do corporations feel responsible for cleaning up the environment?
2. Describe several things companies can do to contribute to the cleanup effort.
3. How does the need to be environmentally safe translate into changes in how the organization does business?

SOURCES: "Is the Planet on the Back Burner?" *Time,* December 24, 1990, pp. 48–51; Kevin O'Farrell, "The Case for 'Clean and Green' in the Workplace," *Canadian Business Review,* Winter 1990, pp. 26–29; "The Greening of Corporate America," *Business Week,* April 23, 1990, pp. 96–103; Peter Nulty, "Global Warming: What We Know," *Fortune,* April 9, 1990, pp. 101–105.

CASE 18.2 Technological Shakeup at Smith, Burns, & Graulik

The law firm of Smith, Burns, & Graulik handled most of the legal work for a small midwestern town. The firm employed three secretaries: Pam Henry, Melvin Tarn, and Judi Maylocks. The three got along well. In fact, the office was known as the best place in town to work—until the technology in the office began to change.

When Pam Henry, the oldest of the secretaries, joined the firm in 1955, her workday consisted of responding to the call "Take a letter please, Mrs. Henry," hurrying into one of the big offices, scribbling shorthand on a pad while the boss dictated, then typing out the letter and submitting it for the boss's approval. Quick and accurate at each step in the process, she became the most important person in the office.

In the 1970s, the firm hired Tarn and Maylocks and introduced a new machine into the office: the dictaphone. The three secretaries spent most of their days hooked up to an earphone, typing out the dictation that one of the lawyers had recorded the day before. Tarn, who could not imagine himself jotting squiggles on a yellow pad, liked the system. Maylocks, who had been an English major, complained about the lawyers' grammar and the long pauses on the tape. Henry hated the whole system. Her tape player never seemed to be functioning right, the volume was always too loud or too soft, and the contraption made her so nervous that her formerly perfect typing began to suffer. She still ran the office and made more money than the others, but she felt like a bumbling newcomer.

Then, in 1984, the company purchased a personal computer. Henry would not go near it. Tarn tolerated it and learned how to type his letters on it. Judi Maylocks, in contrast, was fascinated by it. She created stock paragraphs—the kinds of paragraphs she had typed so often she knew them by heart—and saved them on disks so that she could construct certain kinds of letters or court documents almost instantly. She took the computer manuals home to read and learned to use the accounting software that came with the machine.

Gradually the office became a very tense place. The three secretaries had always worked as a pool, each taking the next piece of work when she or he got done with the last one. Now the lawyers began asking Maylocks to do specific documents, because they knew she could turn them out in half the time it took the other two. They began to realize the value of all the material she had stored on disk, and they consulted her often, asking for copies of documents they had sent out months ago. They also began to appreciate the value of having all their accounts on the computer, available at any time, and of being able to save money by having their accountant check the books less often.

All of this attention was not lost on Melvin Tarn and Pam Henry, who began to resent Judi Maylocks and her machine. Henry began to spend more of her time in the waiting room, drinking coffee and smoking cigarettes, and Tarn sabotaged Maylocks' work on a couple of occasions so she would not seem so perky and efficient. Maylocks saw what was happening, and she tried to familiarize the other two with the machine so she could spread the work out. But they perceived her efforts as attempts to impress them with her superiority, and they did not respond.

Finally, the lawyers caught on to the problem and had a meeting with the three secretaries. During the meeting, all the animosity came out. One of the older lawyers, who was new to the firm, was surprised and delighted to hear that Henry preferred old-fashioned dictation and asked her if she would mind dusting off her shorthand notebook. That suggestion led to a reorganization of the entire office to be more consistent with each person's skills and preferences. Judi Maylocks took official charge of the work she already was doing, and because that work amounted to minor legal research and accounting, she was given a raise and the title of administrative assistant. Melvin Tarn and Pam Henry divided up the other office responsibilities; there were still plenty of letters that had to be dictated and enough filing and other jobs to keep everyone busy.

At first Judi Maylocks feared her coworkers would resent her title and raise, but in fact both agreed she deserved them. They just had not liked the feeling that she, as an equal, was making them look bad, and they had worried that they should be matching her efforts. But once they all had more clearly defined responsibilities and were doing work they felt comfortable with, the office was a much more pleasant place.

Case Questions

1. Could the lawyers have made the office more efficient if they had insisted that all three secretaries learn all the functions of the computer?
2. In what ways did technology sharpen or blur the distinctions among jobs in the law firm?

EXPERIENTIAL EXERCISE

Purpose: This exercise will help you develop better understanding of the environmental components that affect several types of organizations.

Format: Working in small groups in class, you will analyze the environment of an organization in terms of its components, the relative importance of the environmental components to the organization, and the uncertainty of the environment.

Procedure: Your instructor will place you in groups of four to six. Each group will analyze the environment of an organization by answering the following questions. The instructor may provide each group with an organization to analyze or may supply a list of organizations from which each group can select. Although you may not have all the information you need to do a complete analysis, your knowledge of the general environment should be enough to illustrate its importance to the organization.

1. What are the environmental components of the organization that your group is to study?
2. Which components are most important to the organization? Which are least important?
3. How would you characterize the uncertainty of the environmental components? (Are there many important components? At what rate do they change?)
4. What types of organizational responses or adaptations has the organization implemented in the recent past?
5. What types of organizational responses or adaptations do you think the organization will need to implement in the near future?

Each group should make notes of the answers to the questions and be prepared to discuss them in class. You will be able to compare your analysis with those done by other groups.

Variations: The instructor may use several variations in this exercise. As noted, each group may be assigned an organization, or a list may be provided from which each group may choose an organization. One interesting possibility is to assign all groups the same organization and compare their different points of view. Or one organization may be assigned to half of the groups and a very different organization to the other half and the two organizations compared in class discussion.

Follow-up Questions

1. What kinds of differences did you observe in the environmental analyses of the different organizations and groups?
2. Which part of the analysis was the most difficult to do? Was it difficult for most groups? Why was that part difficult for your group?
3. Were the groups' recommendations for future organizational response, or adaptation, similar or very different? What accounts for the similarities or differences?

CHAPTER OUTLINE

- Universal Approaches to Organization Design
  - *The Ideal Bureaucracy*
  - *The Classic Principles of Organizing*
  - *The Human Organization*
- Contingency Approaches to Organization Design
  - *Sociotechnical Systems Theory*
  - *Structural Imperatives*
  - *Strategy and Strategic Choice*
- The Mintzberg Framework
  - *Simple Structure*
  - *Machine Bureaucracy*
  - *Professional Bureaucracy*
  - *Divisionalized Form*
  - *Adhocracy*
- Matrix Organization Design
- Contemporary Organization Design

19

ORGANIZATION DESIGN

CHAPTER OBJECTIVES

After studying this chapter, you should be able to:

Summarize and discuss three major universal organization design approaches.

Describe three contingency approaches to organization design.

Summarize Mintzberg's classification of the five structural forms.

Define matrix organization design and summarize its advantages and disadvantages.

Discuss contemporary approaches to organization design.

Illinois Tool Works (ITW) is making progress in factory efficiency the old-fashioned way—by earning it. It is meeting the challenge of expiring patents and low-cost foreign competition through constant innovation on the factory floor. The results have been impressive. Its 1989 revenues were reported at $2.2 billion, with profits of $164 million—not bad for a relatively little-known old-style manufacturer.

ITW manufactures screws, valves, capacitors, adhesives, and the tools that apply them. It is also the world's largest supplier of plastic bucklers, a leading supplier of fasteners to General Motors, and the inventor of the plastic loops that hold six-packs together.

ITW has ninety divisions that operate autonomously. Each division head controls manufacturing, marketing, and research and development for that division. The largest division (with revenues of $420 million) has a headquarters staff of three: the division president, a controller, and a shared secretary. With a corporate staff of fewer than one hundred, administrative overhead is also low. The idea is to let each division run its own show. Top management does not even know the exact number of products the company makes and sells.[1]

ITW is renewing its success by decentralizing its organization structure so that each division is run like a small company. Why is it that when some companies' products mature and low-cost foreign competition enters the market, the companies die but other firms adjust and become stronger than ever? One key reason is the organization's design. Within the organization, design coordinates the efforts of the people, work groups, and departments. Designing a system of task, reporting, and authority relationships that leads to the efficient accomplishment of organizational goals is a challenge managers must be prepared to face. In Chapters 17 and 18, we discussed the tools with which managers design a system that will enable the organization to be effective. In this chapter, we integrate these basic elements of structure, environment, and technology by presenting several perspectives on organization design.

Organization designs vary from rigid bureaucracies to flexible matrix systems. Most theories of organization design represent either a universal or a contingency approach. A **universal approach** is one whose prescriptions or propositions are designed to work in any situation. Thus, a universal design prescribes the "one best way" to structure the jobs, authority, and reporting relationships

■ With the **universal approach** to organization design, prescriptions or propositions are designed to work in any circumstances.

1. Ronald Henkoff, "The Ultimate Nuts and Bolts Co.," *Fortune,* November 16, 1990, pp. 69–75.

■ With the **contingency approach** to organization design, the desired outcomes for the organization can be achieved in several ways.

of the organization, regardless of factors such as the organization's external environment, the industry, and the type of work to be done. A **contingency approach,** on the other hand, suggests that the desired outcome of organizational efficiency can be achieved in several ways. In a contingency design, specific conditions such as the environment, technology, and the organization's work force determine the structure. Figure 19.1 shows the distinction between the universal and contingency approaches. This distinction is similar to that between universal and contingency approaches to motivation (Chapter 6), job design (Chapter 13), and leadership (Chapter 9). Although no one particular form of

FIGURE 19.1
Universal and Contingency Approaches to Organization Design

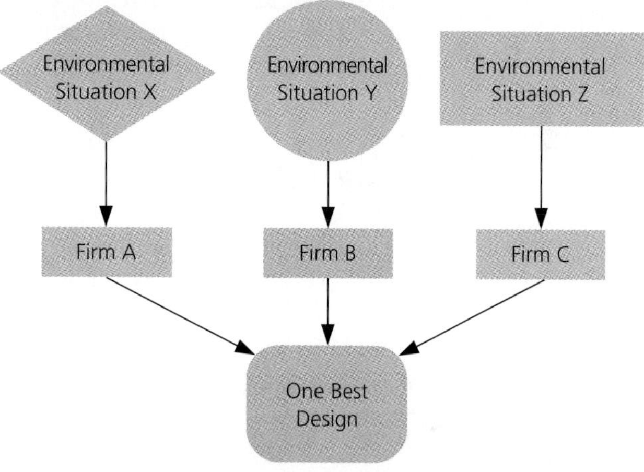

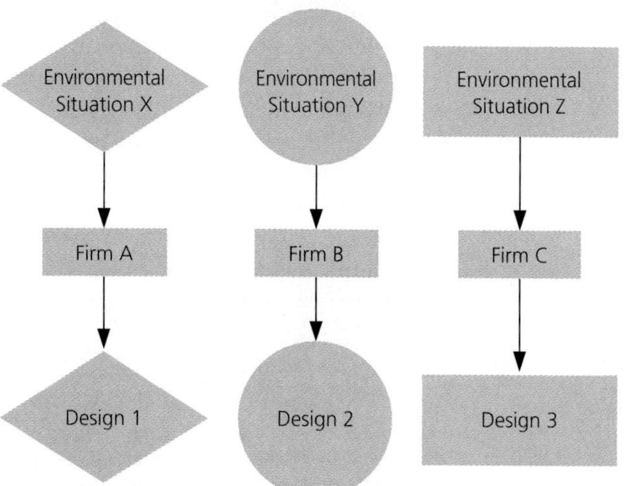

organization is generally accepted, the contingency approach to organization design most closely represents current thinking.

We begin this chapter by discussing organization designs based on the universal and contingency approaches. Next, we examine the Mintzberg framework for classifying organization structures. We conclude with an examination of the matrix design and contemporary organization design.

Universal Approaches to Organization Design

Three of the most popular and influential universal approaches to organization design are the ideal bureaucracy of Max Weber, the classic principles of Henri Fayol, and the human organization of Rensis Likert. Although all are universal approaches, their concerns and structural prescriptions differ significantly.

The Ideal Bureaucracy

- A **bureaucracy** is a type of organization structure conceived by Max Weber as a powerful and efficient form of administration (rather than one characterized by red tape, inefficiency, and "passing the buck," as traditionally believed).
- Weber's **ideal bureaucracy** is characterized by a hierarchy of authority and a system of rules and procedures designed to create an optimally effective system for large organizations.

The term **bureaucracy** has come to be associated with rigid rules and procedures, red tape, passing the buck, sluggishness, and inefficiency. However, the first theorist of bureaucracy, Max Weber, writing at the turn of the century, conceived of a bureaucracy as a powerful and efficient form of administration. Weber's **ideal bureaucracy** is an organizational system characterized by a hierarchy of authority and a system of rules and procedures that, if followed, will create a maximally effective system for large organizations.

Weber was trained in Germany as a lawyer and had wide-ranging intellectual interests. He published books and articles on history, law, political science, and religion, but he is best known for his contributions to sociology and particularly for his theory of bureaucracy.[2] Weber claimed the bureaucratic form of administration is superior to other forms of management with respect to stability, control, and predictability of outcomes.[3]

Weber's ideal bureaucracy has seven essential characteristics. We already discussed three of these characteristics—division of labor, hierarchy of authority, and rules and procedures—as key aspects of organization structure.

1. *Rules and procedures.* A system of rules and procedures defines the duties of employees and is strictly enforced so that the actions of all members of the organization are controlled and predictable.

2. John B. Miner, *Theories of Organizational Structure and Process* (Hinsdale, Ill.: Dryden Press, 1982), p. 386.

3. Max Weber, *The Theory of Social and Economic Organization,* trans. A. M. Henderson and Talcott Parsons (New York: Oxford University Press, 1947).

Shipping of goods around the world remains one of the most basic industries contributing to a global economy. Without a strong and efficient shipping industry the various economies of the world would remain isolated. Sailors working on a ship are required to adhere to a strict chain of command in order to properly coordinate all of the shipboard activities.

2. *Division of labor.* Tasks are clearly divided among employees who have the competence and authority to carry them out.
3. *Hierarchy of authority.* Each position reports to a position one level higher in the hierarchy. This creates a chain of command (which later was called a *scalar chain*) in which each member of the organization is supervised by a single higher-ranking individual except the top position, which usually reports to a board of directors or the owners.
4. *Technical competence.* The selection and promotion of organization members are based on technical competence and training. This dictum ensures that individuals are qualified to do their jobs and enhances predictability and control. Favoritism, nepotism, and friendship are specifically excluded from the process of selection and promotion.
5. *Separation of ownership.* Employees, especially managers, should not share in the ownership of the organization. This ensures that employees will make decisions in the best interests of the organization rather than for their own interests.
6. *Rights and property of the position.* The rights and control over property associated with an office or position belong to the organization, not to the person who holds the office. This also prevents the use of a position for personal ends.
7. *Documentation.* All administrative decisions, rules, and actions are detailed in writing to provide a continuous record of the organization's activities.[4]

Weber intended these characteristics to ensure order and predictability in relationships among people and jobs in the bureaucracy. But it is easy to see how these same features can lead to sluggishness, inefficiency, and red tape. If any of the characteristics are carried to an extreme or are violated, the administrative system can easily break down. For example, if never-ending rules and procedures bog down employees with finding the precise rule to follow every time they do something, responses to routine client or customer requests may slow to a crawl. Moreover, subsequent theorists have said Weber's view of authority is too rigid and have suggested that the bureaucratic organization may impede creativity and innovation and result in a lack of compassion for the individual in the organization.[5] In other words, the impersonality that is supposed to foster objectivity in a bureaucracy may result in serious difficulties for both employees and the organization. However, some organizations retain some characteristics of a bureaucratic structure while remaining innovative and productive. For more on the new bureaucracy and how TRW plans to be focused and flexible, see *Management in Action.*

---

4. This summary of the elements of bureaucracy is based on the Henderson and Parsons translation of Weber's *Theory of Social and Economic Organization* and on the discussion of bureaucracy in Arthur G. Bedeian, *Organizations Theory and Analysis,* 2nd ed. (Hinsdale, Ill.: Dryden Press, 1984), and in Richard I. Daft, *Organization Theory and Design,* 2nd ed. (St. Paul, Minn.: West, 1986).

5. For more discussion of these alternative views, see Miner, *Theories of Organizational Structure and Process.*

MANAGEMENT IN ACTION

TRW Reorganizes under Joe Gorman

When Joe Gorman took over the reins at TRW, he found a company deeply immersed in advanced technology. In fact, TRW's scientists and engineers may have been working too far afield for the company's good. Now Gorman is trying to bring the company back into order—and is doing it his way.

TRW started as Cleveland Cap Screw Co. in 1901. It went through several name and product changes as it capitalized on inventions and alliances with other companies. In 1958 the Thompson Co. merged with Ramo-Wooldridge Corp. and became what is now TRW. New innovations and expanding technology have been the hallmark of TRW throughout all stages of its evolution. During its extensive acquisition activity in the 1960s and 1970s, however, the firm may have gone beyond its ability to manage the technological diversity.

Joe Gorman has reshuffled management and reorganized major business units. For example, the auto business group was reorganized into three groups—steering systems, engine components, and air bags—all reporting directly to Gorman. During the shakeup, executives quit or were fired, 1,600 jobs were eliminated at the space and defense plant in Los Angeles, and entire divisions were sold. One notable move was TRW's sale of its customer service division to Phoenix Technologies Inc. in 1990. Gorman expects the new TRW to be focused and flexible in its operations and more profitable in its bottom line.

SOURCES: Gary Hoover, Alta Campbell, and Patrick J. Spain, eds., *Hoover's Handbook* (Austin, Tex.: The Reference Press, 1990), p. 544; Ronald Henkoff, "How to Plan for 1995," *Fortune,* December 31, 1990, pp. 70–77; "TRW Cuts 1,600 Jobs," *The New York Times,* November 14, 1990, p. D16; "Just Don't Get in Joe Gorman's Way," *Business Week,* November 12, 1990, pp. 88–90; "TRW Agrees to Sell Division," *The Wall Street Journal,* October 30, 1990, p. C12.

The Classic Principles of Organizing

- The **management functions** set forth by Henri Fayol include planning, organizing, command, coordination, and control.

A second universal design was presented at the turn of the century by Henri Fayol, a French engineer and chief executive officer of a mining company. Drawing on his experience as a manager, Fayol was the first to classify the essential elements of management—now usually called **management functions**—as planning, organizing, command, coordination, and control.[6] In addition, he presented fourteen principles of organizing that he considered an indispensable code for managers. These principles are shown in Table 19.1.

Fayol's principles have proved extraordinarily influential; they have served as the basis for the development of generally accepted means of organizing. For example, Fayol's unity of command means that employees should receive directions from only one person, and unity of direction means that tasks with the

6. This summary of the classic principles of organizing is based on Henri Fayol, *General and Industrial Management,* trans. Constance Storrs (London: Pittman, 1949), and the discussions in Bedeian, *Organizations: Theory and Analysis,* pp. 58–59 and Miner, *Theories of Organizational Structure and Process,* pp. 358–381.

TABLE 19.1
Fayol's Classic Principles of Organizing

Principle	Fayol's Comments
1. Division of work	Individuals and managers work on the same part or task
2. Authority and responsibility	Authority—right to give orders; power to exact obedience; goes with responsibility for reward and punishment
3. Discipline	Obedience, application, energy, behavior Agreement between firm and individual
4. Unity of command	Employee receives orders from one superior
5. Unity of direction	One head and one plan for activities with the same objective
6. Subordination of individual interest to general interest	Objectives of the organization come before objectives of the individual
7. Remuneration of personnel	Pay should be fair to the organization and the individual; discussed various forms
8. Centralization	Proportion of discretion held by the manager compared to that allowed to subordinates
9. Scalar chain	Line of authority from lowest to top
10. Order	A place for everyone and everyone in their place
11. Equity	Combination of kindness and justice; Equality of treatment
12. Stability of tenure of personnel	Stability of managerial personnel; time to get used to work
13. Initiative	Power of thinking out and executing a plan
14. Esprit de corps	Harmony and union among personnel is strength

SOURCE: From *General and Industrial Management* by Henri Fayol. Copyright © Lake Publishing 1984, Belmont, CA 94002. Used by permission.

same objective should have a common supervisor. Combining these two principles with division of labor and authority and responsibility results in a system of tasks and reporting and authority relationships that is the very essence of organizing. Fayol's principles thus provide the framework for the organization chart and the coordination of work.

The classic principles have been criticized on several counts. First, they ignore factors such as individual motivation, leadership, and informal groups—the human element in organizations. This line of criticism asserts that the classic principles result in a mechanical organization into which people must fit, regardless of their interests, abilities, or motivations. The principles also have been criticized for their lack of operational specificity in that Fayol described the principles as universal truths but did not specify the means of applying many of them. Finally, Fayol's classic principles have been discounted because they were not supported by scientific evidence; Fayol presented them as universal principles, backed by no evidence other than his experience.[7]

7. Miner, *Theories of Organizational Structure and Process,* pp. 358–381.

The Human Organization

- Rensis Likert's **human organization** approach to organization design is based on supportive relationships, participation, and overlapping work groups.
- In **supportive relationships,** people are treated in a manner that fosters feelings of support, self-worth, and importance.
- **Participation** means that work groups are involved in decisions that concern them.
- In **overlapping work groups,** managers serve as linking pins between groups.

Rensis Likert called his approach to organization design the **human organization.**[8] Because Likert and others had criticized Fayol's classic principles for overlooking human factors, it is not surprising that his approach centered on the principles of supportive relationships, employee participation, and overlapping work groups.

The term **supportive relationships** suggests that in all organizational activities, individuals should be treated in such a way that they experience feelings of support, self-worth, and importance. **Participation** means that the work group needs to be involved in decisions that affect it, thereby enhancing the sense of supportiveness and self-worth. The principle of **overlapping work groups** means that work groups are linked as shown in Figure 19.2, with managers serving as linking pins between groups. Each manager (except the highest ranking) is a member of two groups: a work group that he or she supervises and a management group composed of the manager's peers and their supervisor. Coordination and communication grow stronger when the managers perform the linking function by sharing problems, decisions, and information both upward and downward in the groups to which they belong. The human organization concept rests on the assumption that people work best in highly cohesive groups oriented toward organizational goals. Management's function is to make sure the work groups are linked for effective coordination and communication.

Likert described four systems of organizing, whose characteristics are summarized in Table 19.2. System 1 is called Exploitive Authoritative and can be characterized as the classic bureaucracy. System 4, the Participative Group, is the organization design Likert favored. System 2, the Benevolent Authoritative system, and System 3, the Consultative system, are less extreme than either System 1 or System 4.

Likert described all four systems in terms of eight organizational variables: leadership processes, motivational forces, communication processes, interaction-influence processes, decision-making processes, goal-setting processes, control processes, and performance goals and training. Let us run through the characteristics of System 4:

1. Leaders show complete trust and confidence in employees. Employees feel free to discuss their jobs with their supervisor, who solicits and uses their ideas and opinions.
2. The organization recognizes and uses the full range of employee motives; attitudes are favorable to and supportive of organizational goals.
3. Communication flows freely and in all directions (upward, downward, and horizontally), is initiated at all levels, and promotes a closeness between subordinate and supervisor.

8. See Rensis Likert, *New Patterns of Management* (New York: McGraw-Hill, 1961), and Rensis Likert, *The Human Organization: Its Management and Value* (New York: McGraw-Hill, 1967), for a complete discussion of the human organization.

FIGURE 19.2
Likert's Overlapping Work Groups (The Linking-Pin Organization)

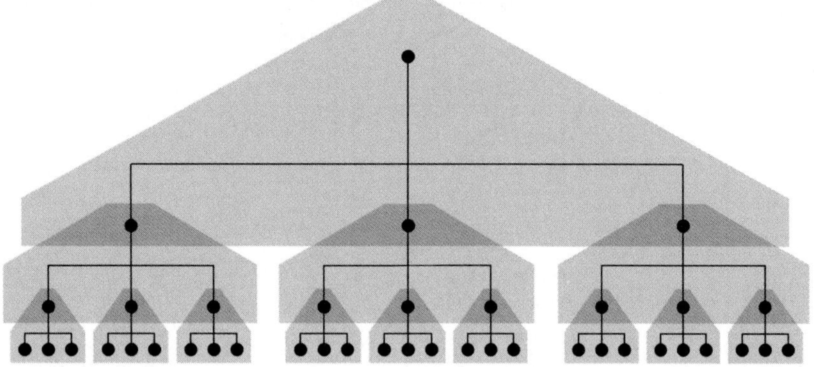

SOURCE: Rensis Likert, *New Patterns of Management* (New York: McGraw-Hill, 1961), p. 105. Reprinted by permission.

4. Interaction-influence processes between employees are extensive and friendly, with much confidence, trust, and teamwork. Employees can influence the goals, methods, and activities in their work groups.
5. Decisions are made throughout the organization at the level at which the information is most adequate. Decision making is integrated by the system of overlapping groups.
6. Goal setting is a group activity; the goals are fully accepted by all involved.
7. Control processes are the concern of people throughout the organization; there are strong pressures to obtain complete and accurate information for self-guidance and coordinated problem solving.
8. Top management sets high performance goals for the organization, and employees receive a great deal of management training.[9]

Likert believed that work groups should be able to overlap horizontally as well as vertically where necessary to accomplish tasks. This feature is directly contrary to the classic principle that advocates unity of command. In addition, Likert favored the linking-pin concept of overlapping work groups for making decisions and resolving conflicts over the hierarchical chain of command.

- Some of the features of Likert's human organization are still popular today, particularly the ideas of overlapping work groups and participation.

Research support for Likert's human organization emanates primarily from Likert and his associates' work at the Institute for Social Research at the University of Michigan. Although their research has upheld the basic propositions of the approach, it is not entirely convincing. One review of the evidence has suggested that although research has shown characteristics of System 4 to be associated with positive worker attitudes and, in some cases, increased productivity, it is not clear that the characteristics of the human organization "caused"

9. Adapted from Likert, *Human Organization,* pp. 197–211.

TABLE 19.2
Characteristics of Likert's Four Management Systems

Characteristic	System 1: Exploitive Authoritative	System 2: Benevolent Authoritative	System 3: Consultative	System 4: Participative Group
Leadership				
▪ Trust in subordinates	None	None	Substantial	Complete
▪ Subordinates' ideas	Seldom used	Sometimes used	Usually used	Always used
Motivational forces				
▪ Motives tapped	Security, status	Economic, ego	Economic, ego, and others	All motives
▪ Level of satisfaction	Overall dissatisfaction	Some moderate satisfaction	Moderate satisfaction	High satisfaction
Communication				
▪ Amount	Very little	Little	Moderate	Much
▪ Direction	Downward	Mostly downward	Down, up	Down, up, lateral
Interaction-influence				
▪ Amount	Very little	Little	Moderate	Much
▪ Cooperative teamwork	None	Virtually none	Moderate	Substantial
Decision making				
▪ Locus	Top	Policy decided at top	Broad policy decided at top	All levels
▪ Subordinates involved	Not at all	Sometimes consulted	Usually consulted	Fully involved
Goal setting				
▪ Manner	Orders	Orders with comments	Set after discussion	Group participation
▪ Acceptance	Covertly resisted	Frequently resisted	Sometimes resisted	Fully accepted
Control processes				
▪ Level	Top	All levels	Some below top	All levels
▪ Information	Incomplete, inaccurate	Often incomplete, inaccurate	Moderately complete, accurate	Complete accurate
Performance	Mediocre	Fair to good	Good	Excellent

SOURCE: Adapted from Rensis Likert, *New Patterns of Management* (New York: McGraw-Hill, 1961), pp. 223–233, and Rensis Likert, *The Human Organization* (New York: McGraw-Hill, 1967), pp. 197, 198, 201, 203, 210, and 211. Reprinted by permission of McGraw-Hill, Inc.

the positive results.[10] It may have been that positive attitudes and high productivity allowed the organization structure to be participative and provided the atmosphere for the development of supportive relationships. Likert's design has also been criticized for focusing almost exclusively on individuals and groups and not dealing extensively with structural issues.[11] Overall, the most compelling support for this approach is at the individual and work group levels. Support for System 4 as a universally applicable organizational system is not strong.

Contingency Approaches to Organization Design

Weber, Fayol, and Likert each proposed an organization design that is independent of the nature of the organization and its environment. Although each of these approaches contributed to an understanding of the organizing process and the practice of management, none has proved universally applicable. In this section we turn to several contingency designs, which attempt to specify the conditions, or contingency factors, under which they are likely to be most effective. The contingency approach to organization structure has been criticized as being unrealistic in that managers are expected to observe a change in one of the contingency factors and to make a rational structural alteration. On the other hand, Donaldson has argued that it is reasonable to expect that organizations respond to lower organizational performance that may result from a lack of response to some significant change in one or several contingency factors.[12]

Sociotechnical Systems Theory

■ The **sociotechnical systems approach** to organization design sought to integrate the technical and social subsystems into a single management system.

The foundation of the sociotechnical systems approach to organizing is systems theory, discussed in Chapter 1. There we defined a *system* as an interrelated set of elements that function as a whole. A system has numerous subsystems, each of which, like the overall system, includes inputs, transformation processes, outputs, and feedback. We also defined an *open system* as one that interacts with its environment. Figure 19.3 shows how the environment and subsystems interact in a system. Note that a complex system is made up of numerous subsystems in which the outputs of some are the inputs to others. The **sociotechnical systems approach** views the organization as an open system structured to integrate the two important subsystems: the technical (task) subsystem and the social subsystem.

10. Miner, *Theories of Organizational Structure and Process,* pp. 17–53.

11. Daniel Katz and Robert L. Kahn, *The Special Psychology of Organizations,* 2nd ed. (New York: Wiley, 1978), pp. 278–282.

12. Lex Donaldson, "Strategy and Structural Adjustment to Regain Fit and Performance: In Defense of Contingency Theory," *Journal of Management Studies,* January 1987, pp. 1–24.

FIGURE 19.3
Interaction of the Environment and Subsystems

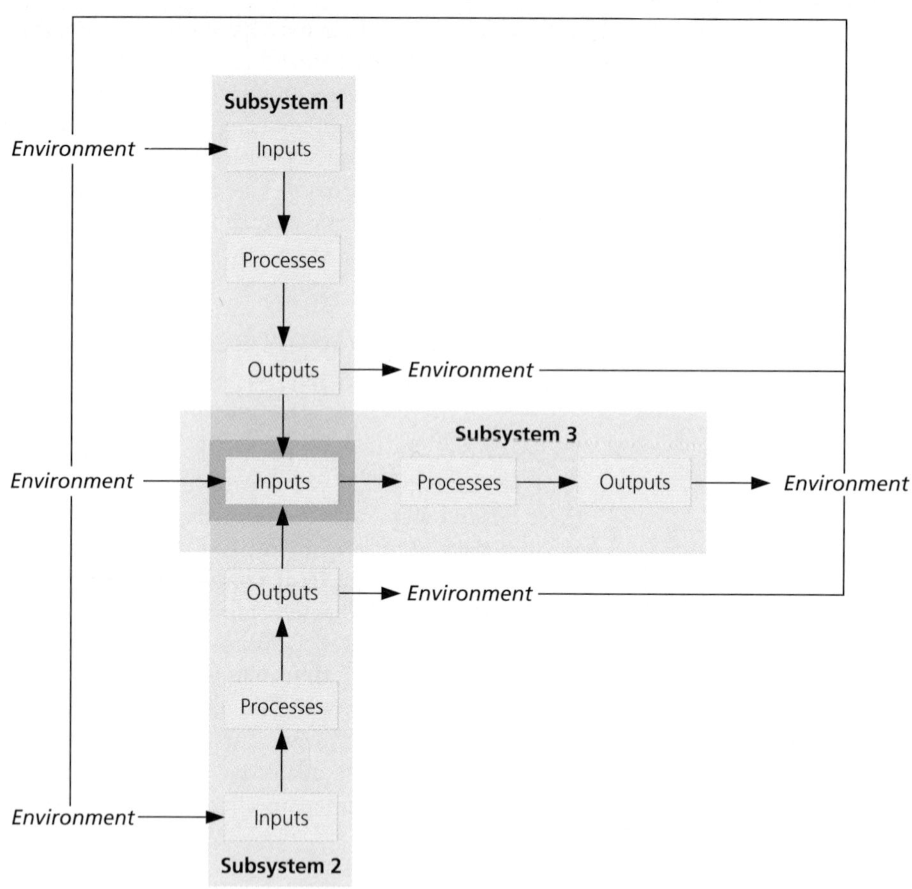

The *technical (task) subsystem* is the means by which inputs are transformed into outputs. The transformation processes may be the way steel is formed, cut, drilled, chemically treated, and painted or the ways information is processed in an insurance company or financial institution. Often significant scientific and engineering expertise is applied to these transformation processes to get the highest productivity at the lowest cost. For example, Fireplace Manufacturers Inc. of Santa Ana, California, a manufacturer of prefabricated metal fireplaces, implemented new *just-in-time (JIT)* manufacturing and inventory systems to improve the productivity of its plant.[13] JIT is a system in which component parts arrive just in time to be used in the manufacturing process, thereby reducing the costs of storing them in a warehouse until they are needed. In effect, it redesigns the transformation process, from the introduction of raw materials to the shipping of the finished product. In three years, Fireplace Manufacturers' inventory costs dropped from $1.1 million to $750,000, while sales doubled over the same

13. "Small Manufacturers Shifting to 'Just-In-Time' Techniques," *The Wall Street Journal,* December 21, 1987, p. 25.

period. The transformation process usually is regarded as technologically and economically driven; that is, whatever process is most productive and costs the least generally is the most desirable.

The *social subsystem* includes the interpersonal relationships that develop among people in organizations. Employees learn one another's work habits, strengths, weaknesses, and preferences while developing a sense of mutual trust. The social relationships may be manifested in personal friendships and interest groups. Communication, about both work and employees' common interests, may be enhanced by friendship or hampered by antagonistic relationships. The Hawthorne studies (discussed in Chapter 1) were the first serious studies of the social subsystems in organizations.[14]

The sociotechnical systems approach was developed by members of the Tavistock Institute in England as an outgrowth of a study of coal mining. The study concerned new mining techniques that were introduced to increase productivity but failed because they entailed splitting up well-established work groups.[15] The Tavistock researchers concluded that the social subsystem had been sacrificed to the technical subsystem. Thus, improvements in the technical subsystem were not realized because of problems in the social subsystem. Recently a company that implemented JIT systems, Lifeline Systems, Inc., a manufacturer of electronic medical equipment, recognized the potential problems of employee acceptance and emphasized the role of management in getting employees to go along with the changes.[16]

The Tavistock group proposed that an organization's technical and social subsystems could be integrated through autonomous work groups. *Autonomous work groups* are related to task design, particularly job enrichment, but also bring in concepts of group interaction, supervision, and other characteristics of organization design. The aim of autonomous work groups is to make technical and social subsystems work together for the benefit of the larger system. Accordingly, to structure the task, authority, and reporting relationships around work groups, organizations should delegate decisions regarding job assignments, training, inspection, rewards, and punishments to the work groups. Management has the responsibility of coordinating the groups according to the demands of the work and task environment. Figure 19.4 shows how the relationships among the environment and the technical and social subsystems should be integrated according to the sociotechnical systems approach.

Organizations in turbulent environments tend to rely less on hierarchy and more on the coordination of work among autonomous work groups. Sociotechnical systems theory asserts that the role of management is twofold: to monitor the environmental factors that impinge on the internal operations of the organization and to coordinate the social and technical subsystems.

---

14. Elton Mayo, *The Human Problems of an Industrial Civilization* (New York: Macmillan, 1933); F. J. Roethlisberger and W. J. Dickson, *Management and the Worker* (Cambridge, Mass.: Harvard University Press, 1939).

15. Eric L. Trist and K. W. Bamforth, "Some Social and Psychological Consequences of the Longwall Method of Coal-Getting," *Human Relations,* February 1951, pp. 3–38.

16. "Small Manufacturers Shifting to 'Just-In-Time' Techniques."

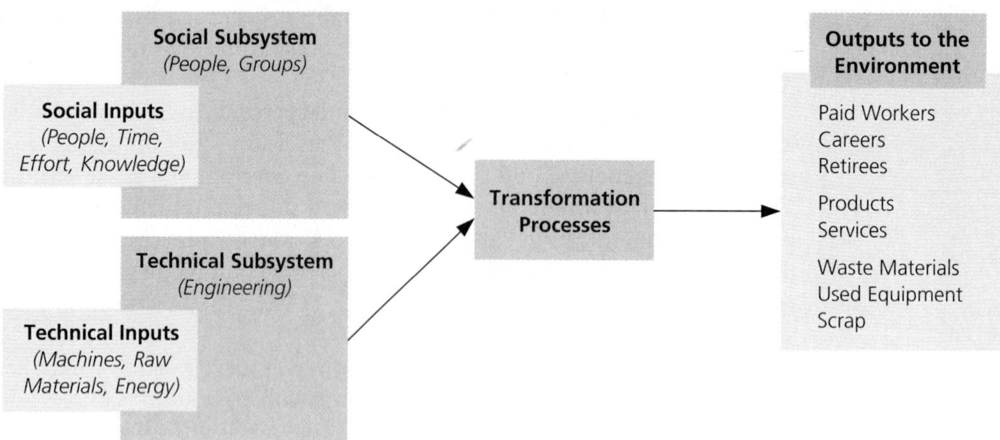

FIGURE 19.4
Sociotechnical Systems: Integration of Social and Technical Subsystems

Two major criticisms have been leveled against the sociotechnical systems approach. First, little research has been done on how the environment affects the characteristics of the work groups. Second, the approach fails to clearly predict how individual differences might affect participation in work groups.[17]

Although the sociotechnical systems approach has not been thoroughly tested, it has been tried with some success in the General Foods plant in Topeka, Kansas, the Saab-Scania project in Sweden, and the Volvo plant in Kalmar, Sweden[18] (the last discussed in Chapter 13). The development of the sociotechnical systems approach is significant in its departure from the universal approaches to organization design and in its emphasis on jointly harnessing the technical and human subsystems. It is also notable for its classification of the environment into four types, each with distinct characteristics that affect organizational functioning.

Structural Imperatives

The structural imperatives approach to organization design probably has been the most discussed and researched contingency approach of the last thirty years. The perspective was not formulated by a single theorist or researcher, and it has not evolved from a systematic and cohesive research effort; rather, it gradually emerged from a vast number of studies that sought to address the question "What are the compelling factors that determine how the organization must be structured to be effective?" As Figure 19.5 shows, the three factors that have been identified as **structural imperatives** are environment, technology, and size.

- **Structural imperatives**—environment, technology, and size—are the three primary determinants of organization structure.

17. Miner, *Theories of Organizational Structure and Process,* pp. 85–116.

18. Richard E. Walton, "How to Counter Alienation in the Plant," *Harvard Business Review,* November-December 1972, pp. 70–81; Richard E. Walton, "Work Innovations at Topeka: After Six Years," *Journal of Applied Behavioral Science,* July-August-September 1977, pp. 422–433; Pehr G. Gyllenhammar, "How Volvo Adapts Work to People," *Harvard Business Review,* July-August 1977, pp. 102–113.

FIGURE 19.5
The Structural Imperatives Approach

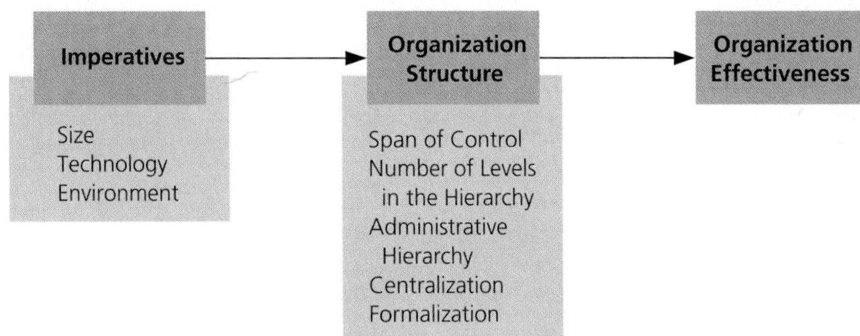

We discussed environment and technology in Chapter 18 in terms of the many ways they are classified and studied. In this section, we add size to environment and technology as an important factor to consider in designing organizations.

The Size Imperative The size of an organization can be gauged in many ways. Usually it is measured in terms of total number of employees, value of the organization's assets, total sales in the previous year (or the number of clients served), or physical capacity. The method of measurement is a very important consideration, although the different measures usually are correlated.[19]

Generally, it is assumed that larger organizations have a more complex structure than smaller ones. Research on the relationship between size and structure supports that view. Peter Blau and his associates concluded that large size is associated with greater specialization of labor, a larger span of control, more hierarchical levels, and greater formalization.[20] These multiple effects are shown in Figure 19.6. Increasing size leads to more specialization of labor within a work unit, which increases the amount of differentiation among work units and the number of levels in the hierarchy and, consequently the need for more intergroup formalization. With greater specialization within the unit, there is less need for coordination among groups; thus, the span of control can be larger. Larger spans of control mean fewer first-line managers, but the need for more intergroup coordination may require more second- and third-line managers and staff personnel to coordinate them. Large organizations therefore may be more efficient because of their large spans of control and reduced administrative overhead; however, the greater differentiation among units makes the system more complex. Studies by researchers associated with the University of Aston in Birmingham, England, and others have shown similar results.[21]

---

19. John R. Kimberly, "Organizational Size and the Structuralist Perspective: A Review, Critique, and Proposal," *Administrative Science Quarterly,* December 1976, pp. 571–597.

20. Peter M. Blau and Richard A. Schoenherr, *The Structure of Organizations* (New York: Basic Books, 1971).

21. The results of these studies are thoroughly summarized in Richard H. Hall, *Organizations: Structure and Process,* 3rd. ed. (Englewood Cliffs, N.J.: Prentice-Hall, 1982), pp. 89–94. For a recent study in this area, see John H. Cullen and Kenneth S. Anderson, "Blau's Theory of Structural Differentiation Revisited: A Theory of Structural Change or Scale?" *Academy of Management Journal,* June 1986, pp. 203–229.

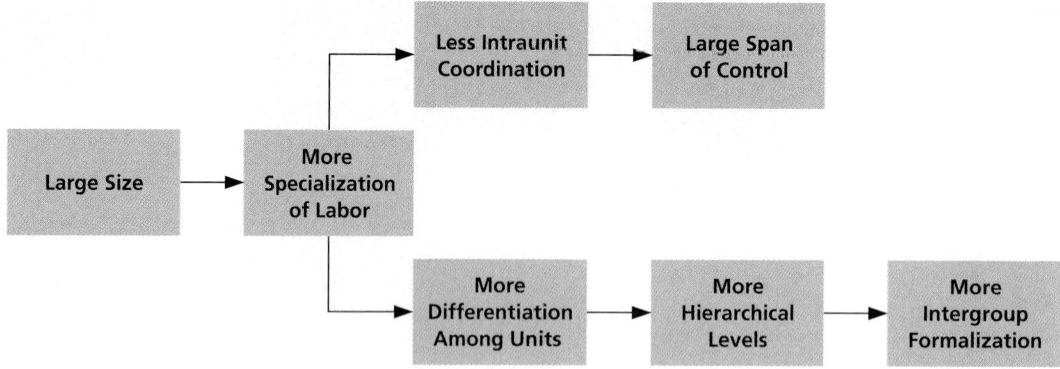

FIGURE 19.6
Impact of Large Size on Organization Structure

Economies of scale are another advantage of large organizations. In a large operation, fixed costs—for example, plant and equipment—can be spread over more units of output, thereby reducing the cost per unit. In addition, some administrative activities, such as purchasing, clerical work, and marketing, can be accomplished for a large number of units at the same cost as for a small number. Their cost then can be spread over the larger number of units, again reducing unit cost.

Recently, however, companies such as AT&T Technologies, General Electric's Aircraft Engine Products Group, and S. C. Johnson & Son, Inc., have gone against the conventional wisdom that larger is always better in manufacturing plants. They cite the smaller investment required for smaller plants, the reduced need to produce a variety of products, and the desire to decrease organizational complexity (that is, reduce the number of hierarchical levels and shorten lines of communication) as the main reasons. In a number of instances, the smaller-sized plant has resulted in increased team spirit, improved productivity, and higher profits.[22]

Traditionally, as organizations have grown, several layers of advisory staff have been added to help coordinate the complexities inherent in any large organization. In contrast, a current trend is to cut staff throughout the organization. Known as *organizational downsizing,* this popular trend is aimed primarily at reducing the size of corporate staff. Companies such as Mobil, AT&T, and Burlington Northern recently cut back headquarters and corporate staff significantly.[23] The results have been mixed, with some observers noting that indiscriminate across-the-board cuts may leave the organization weak in certain key areas. However, positive results often include quicker decision making because fewer layers of management must approve every decision. One recent review of research on organizational downsizing found both psychological and sociological impacts of downsizing. This study suggested that the relationship

22. "Small Is Beautiful Now in Manufacturing," *Business Week,* October 22, 1984, pp. 152–156.

23. Thomas Moore "Goodbye, Corporate Staff," *Fortune,* December 21, 1987, pp. 65–76.

Members of the North Dakota State Legislature discuss a bill under review. Computer workstations allow legislators to review and edit bills, track bills in progress, and communicate with each other faster and more efficiently. Their work and their relationships are being altered as computer technology replaces traditional bill books.

between size in a downsizing environment affects organization design in very complex ways.[24]

Other studies have found that the relationship between size and structural complexity is less clear than the Blau results indicated. Instead, these studies suggest that size must be examined in relation to the technology of the organization.[25]

The Technology Imperative As we discussed in Chapter 18, the technology an organization uses to transform inputs into outputs is a major factor to consider in designing its structure. In that chapter, we reviewed the approaches to technology of Woodward, Burns and Stalker, Perrow, Thompson, and the researchers at the University of Aston.[26] Burns and Stalker also categorized organization structures as either mechanistic or organic. As summarized in Table 19.3, a **mechanistic structure** is primarily hierarchical in nature, interactions and communications are mostly vertical, instructions come from the boss, knowledge is

- A **mechanistic structure** is primarily hierarchical; interactions and communications typically are vertical, instructions come from the boss, knowledge is concentrated at the top, and loyalty and obedience are required to sustain membership.

24. Robert I. Sutton and Thomas D'Anno, "Decreasing Organizational Size: Untangling the Effects of Money and People," *Academy of Management Review,* May 1989, pp. 194–212.

25. Richard H. Hall, J. Eugene Haas, and Norman Johnson, "Organizational Size, Complexity, and Formalization," *American Sociological Review,* December 1967, pp. 903–912.

26. Joan Woodward, *Industrial Organizations: Theory and Practice* (London: Oxford University Press, 1965); Joan Woodward, *Management and Technology: Problems of Progress in Industry,* no. 3 (London: Her Majesty's Stationery Office, 1958); Tom Burns and G. M. Stalker, *The Management of Innovation* (London: Tavistock Publications, 1961); Charles B. Perrow, "A Framework for the Comparative Analysis of Organizations," *American Sociological Review,* April 1967, pp. 194–208; Charles B. Perrow, *Organizational Analysis: A Sociological View* (Belmont, Calif.: Brooks/Cole; London: Tavistock Publications, 1970); James D. Thompson, *Organizations in Action* (New York: McGraw-Hill, 1967); David J. Hickson, Derek S. Pugh, and Diana C. Pheysey, "Operations Technology and Organization Structure: An Empirical Reappraisal," *Administrative Science Quarterly,* September 1969, pp. 378–397.

TABLE 19.3
Mechanistic and Organic Structures

Characteristic	Mechanistic	Organic
Structure	Hierarchical	Network based on interests
Interactions, communication	Primarily vertical	Lateral throughout
Work directions, instructions	From supervisor	Through advice, information
Knowledge, information	Concentrated at top	Throughout
Membership, relationship with organization	Requires loyalty, obedience	Commitment to task, progress, expansion

- An **organic structure** is set up like a network; interactions and communications are lateral and horizontal, knowledge resides wherever it is most useful to the organization, and membership requires a commitment to the organization's tasks.
- When technology is changing rapidly, the organization needs a structure which provides flexibility and quick decision making.

concentrated at the top, and continued membership requires loyalty and obedience. In contrast, the **organic structure** is structured like a network, interactions and communications are more lateral and horizontal, knowledge resides wherever it is most useful to the organization, and membership requires a commitment to the tasks of the organization. Burns and Stalker noted that if the rate of technological change is slow, the more effective design is a mechanistic structure. But if the technology is changing rapidly, the organization will need a structure that provides more flexibility and quicker decision making to be able to react quickly to change; that is, an organic structure.

One of the major contributions of the study of organizational technology is the revelation that organizations have more than one important "technology" that enables them to accomplish their tasks. Recall that the Aston studies noted that organizations have operations, materials, and knowledge technology. Instead of examining technology in isolation, the Aston group also recognized that size and technology are related in determining organization structure.[27] They also found that in smaller organizations, technology had more direct effects on the structure. In large organizations, however, they found, like Blau, that structure depended less on the operations technology and more on size considerations such as the number of employees. In other words, in small organizations the structure depended primarily on the technology, whereas in large organizations the need to coordinate complicated activities was the most important factor. Thus, both organizational size and technology are important considerations in organization design.

Environmental Considerations In Chapter 18, we discussed several perspectives on the organizational environment: the concept of environmental uncertainty, the resource dependence view, and the population perspective. These varying viewpoints provide the organization designer with different frameworks for understanding how environmental factors influence the organization.

27. Hickson, Pugh, and Pheysey, "Operations Technology and Organization Structure."

An organization attempts to continue as a viable entity in a dynamic environment. The environment completely encloses the organization, and managers must be constantly concerned about it. The organization as a whole, as well as departments and divisions within it, is created to deal with different challenges, problems, and uncertainties. James Thompson suggested that organizations design a structure to protect the dominant technology of the organization, smooth out any problems, and keep down coordination costs.[28] Thus, organization structures are designed to coordinate relevant technologies and protect them from outside disturbances. Structural components such as inventory, warehousing, and shipping help buffer the technology used to transform inputs into outputs. For instance, demand for products usually is cyclical or seasonal and is subject to many disturbances, but the warehouse inventory helps the manufacturing system function as if the environment accepted output at a steady rate, maximizing technological efficiency and helping the organization respond to fluctuating demands of the market. The relationship between environmental factors and organization structure often differs according to the availability of resources to the organization.[29]

Strategy and Strategic Choice

The final contingency approach to organization design we consider here is based on the strategic orientation of the organization. *Strategy* is defined in Chapter 17 as the plans and actions necessary to achieve organizational goals.[30] Kellogg, for example, has pursued a strategy that combines product differentiation and market segmentation in attempting to be the leader in the ready-to-eat cereal industry. Over the years Kellogg has successfully introduced new cereals from different grains in different shapes, sizes, colors, and flavors to provide any type of cereal the consumer might want.[31]

After studying the history of seventy companies, Alfred Chandler drew certain conclusions about the relationship between an organization's structure and its business strategy.[32] Chandler observed that a growth strategy to expand into a new product line usually is matched with some type of decentralization, a decentralized structure being necessary to deal with the problems of the new product line.

---

28. Thompson, *Organizations in Action,* pp. 51–82.

29. Masoud Yasai-Ardekani, "Effects of Environmental Scarcity and Munificence on the Relationship of Context to Organizational Structure," *Academy of Management Journal,* March 1989, pp. 131–156.

30. John R. Montanari, Cyril P. Morgan, and Jeffrey Bracke, *Strategic Management* (Hinsdale, Ill.: Dryden Press, 1990), p. 114.

31. See Arthur A. Thompson, Jr., and A. J. Strickland III, *Strategic Management,* 3rd ed. (Plano, Tex.: Business Publications, 1984), pp. 19–27.

32. Alfred D. Chandler, *Strategy and Structure: Chapters in the History of the American Industrial Enterprise* (Cambridge, Mass.: MIT Press, 1962).

These boxes of supplies are sitting in the desert of Saudi Arabia awaiting shipment to further distribution points. They exemplify good planning in that they are ready in advance of being needed and are readily accessible when needed. The capabilities of the forces to do their job was dependent on their having the supplies necessary to do their jobs.

Chandler's "structure follows strategy" concept seems to appeal to common sense. Yet it is contradicted by the structural imperatives approach, which recommends that design decisions be based on size, technology, and environment, not on strategy. This apparent clash has been resolved by refining the strategy concept to include the role of the top management decision maker in determining the organization's structure.[33] In effect, this view inserts the manager–decision maker between the structural imperatives and the structural features of the organization. This distinction can be understood by comparing Figure 19.7 with Figure 19.5.

Figure 19.7 shows the structural imperatives as contextual factors within which the organization must operate and that affect the purposes and goals of the organization. The manager's choices for organization structure are affected by the organization's purposes and goals, the imperatives, and the manager's personality, value system, and experience.[34] Organizational effectiveness depends on the fit among the imperatives, the strategies, and the structure.

Another perspective on strategy-structure linkage is that the relationship may be a reciprocal one; that is, structure may be set up to implement the strategy, but it may also affect the strategic decision-making process via the centralization or decentralization of decision making and formalization of rules and procedures.[35] Thus, strategy determines structure, which in turn affects

33. For more information on managerial choice, see John R. Montanari, "Managerial Discretion: An Expanded Model of Organizational Choice," *Academy of Management Review,* April 1978, pp. 231–241, and John Child, "Organizational Structure, Environment, and Performance: The Role of Strategic Choice," *Sociology,* vol. 6, 1972, pp. 1–22.

34. H. Randolph Bobbitt and Jeffrey D. Ford, "Decision Maker Choice as a Determinant of Organizational Structure," *Academy of Management Review,* January 1980, pp. 13–23.

35. James W. Fredrickson, "The Strategic Decision Process and Organization Structure," *Academy of Management Review,* April 1986, pp. 280–297.

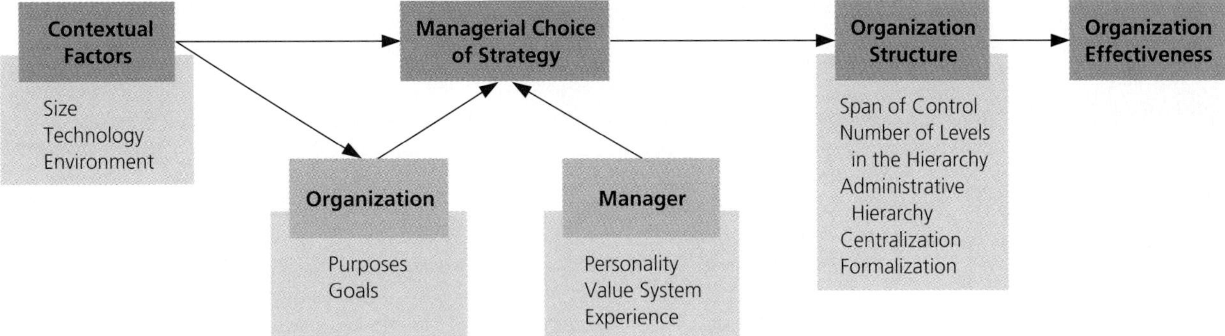

FIGURE 19.7
The Strategic Choice Approach to Organization Design

strategic decision making. However, a more complex view, suggested by Herman Boschken, is that strategy is a determinant of structure and long-term performance when the subunits doing the planning have distinctive competence in how to do planning.[36]

The role of strategic choice in determining organization structure actually goes a step beyond the view that structure follows strategy. However, it has received less research attention than have structural imperatives. And of course, some might simply view strategy as another imperative along with size, technology, and environment. Strategy does, though, seem to differ from the imperatives because it is a product of the analysis of the imperatives and an articulation of the organization's direction, purpose, and plans for the future.

One way strategy differs from the imperatives is that the strategy may form new organizational entities to facilitate management of the organizational-environmental interface. For example, organizations create new organizations through mergers and acquisitions, joint ventures, and other contractual alliances. Hybrid alliances have received very little attention in the literature.[37] *International Perspective* examines how Mazda is developing many different types of strategic alliances.

The Mintzberg Framework

We have examined universal and contingency approaches to organization design but have not yet considered specific designs. In the remainder of this chapter, we describe concrete organization designs. The universe of possible designs is large, but fortunately it is possible to identify a few basic forms that designs take.

36. Herman L. Boschken, "Strategy and Structure: Reconceiving the Relationship," *Journal of Management,* March 1990, pp. 135–150.

37. Bryan Borys and David B. Jemison, "Hybrid Arrangements as Strategic Alliances: Theoretical Issues in Organizational Combinations," *Academy of Management Review,* May 1989, pp. 234–249.

INTERNATIONAL PERSPECTIVE

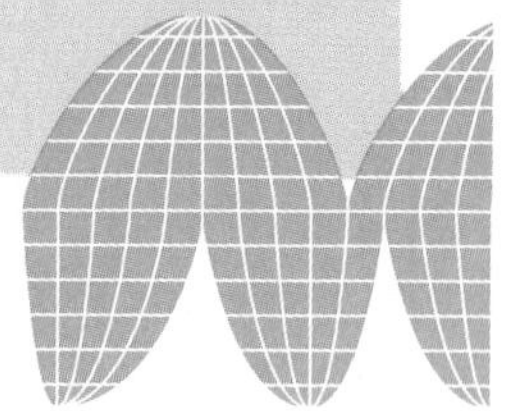

Mazda's Alliance Strategy

Norimasa Furuta, president of Mazda Motor Corp., argues that the future of the worldwide auto industry lies in well-targeted alliances rather than in cutthroat competition. This is quite a radical viewpoint for the auto industry, which is known for its worldwide competitive practices. It is especially extreme for a relatively small company like Mazda, which runs a distant fourth place in Japanese car sales behind Toyota, Nissan, and Honda. Mazda's 1989 sales were about $15 billion compared to Toyota's $60 billion. Some have suggested that only five or six auto companies can survive into the next century. Furuta disagrees; he argues that for any of them to survive, they must put together alliances among themselves and other companies in related industries. He projects that buyers will increasingly demand cars tailored to their specific wants and that smaller companies working together will be best able to satisfy such needs.

The list of alliances Mazda has put together is impressive. Mazda has production, sales, and import agreements with Ford Motor Co., which owns 24 percent of Mazda. Mazda has also developed storefront Autorama showrooms that display and sell Mazdas, Fords, and other makes such as Citroen (French) and Fiat (Italian). It has a joint venture with a Swiss engineering firm to make superchargers for diesel engines, Hertz to lease cars in Japan, and Sanyo and Ford to make car radios in Malaysia. Mazda recently made arrangements to build service stations in Poland, Yugoslavia, and former East Germany. In addition, it will increase its sales and maintenance outlets in Czechoslovakia, Bulgaria, and Romania.

Furuta claims his company already has reaped benefits from its many alliances. For example, from Ford it has learned better marketing and cost control. Furuta says that Ford has profited in turn by learning more about how to build small cars. He continues to assert that such alliances are necessary for dealing with the increasingly complex automobile industry environment.

SOURCES: Reuters, "Mazda Expansion in Eastern Europe," *The New York Times,* December 28, 1990, p. D3. Adapted by permission. Carla Rapoport, "Mazda's Bold New Global Strategy," *Fortune,* December 17, 1990, pp. 109–113,

- Rather than focus on structural imperatives, people, or rules, Mintzberg's description of structure emphasizes the ways activities are coordinated.

Henry Mintzberg proposed a range of coordinating mechanisms that are found in operating organizations.[38] In his view, organization structure corresponds to the way tasks are first divided and then coordinated. Mintzberg described five major ways in which tasks are coordinated: by mutual adjustment, by direct supervision, and by standardization of worker (or input) skills, work processes, or outputs (see Figure 19.8). These five methods can exist side by side within an organization.

Coordination by mutual adjustment simply means that workers use informal communication to coordinate with one another, whereas *coordination by direct supervision* means that a manager or supervisor coordinates the actions of workers. As noted, *standardization* may be used as a coordination mechanism in three different ways: We can standardize the *worker skills* that are inputs to the work

38. Henry Mintzberg, *The Structuring of Organizations: A Synthesis of the Research* (Englewood Cliffs, N.J.: Prentice-Hall, 1979).

FIGURE 19.8
Mintzberg's Five Coordinating Mechanisms

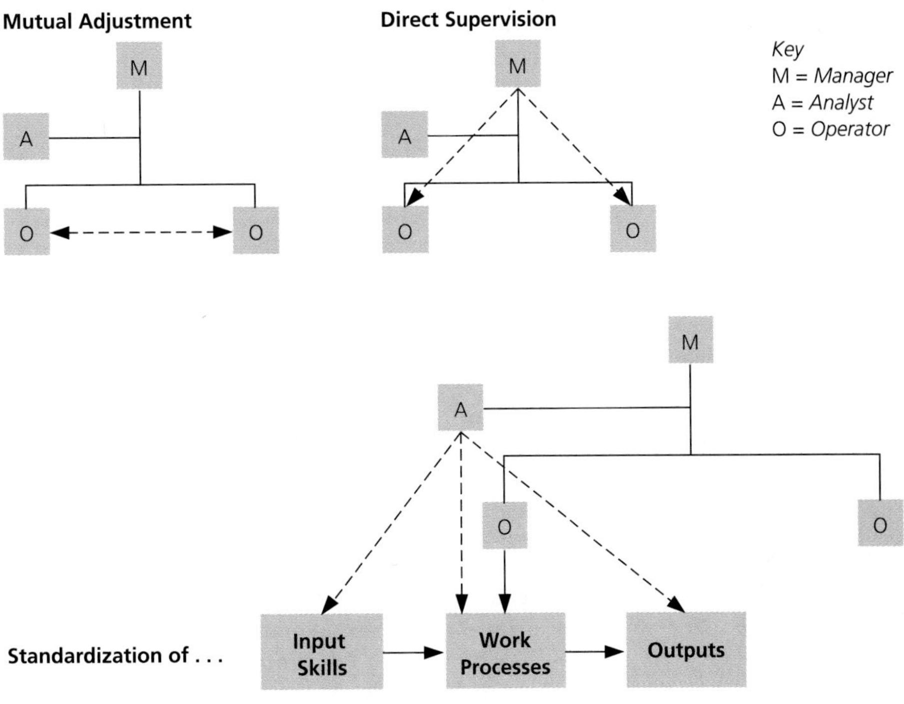

SOURCE: Henry Mintzberg, *The Structuring of Organizations: A Synthesis of the Research.* © 1979, p. 4. Reprinted by permission of Prentice-Hall, Inc., Englewood Cliffs, N.J.

process; the *processes* themselves, that is, the methods workers use to transform inputs into outputs; or the *outputs,* meaning the products or services or the performance levels expected of workers. Standardization usually is developed by staff analysts and enforced by management such that skills, processes, and output meet predetermined standards.

Mintzberg further suggested that the five coordinating mechanisms roughly correspond to stages of organizational development and complexity. In the very small organization, individuals working together communicate informally, achieving coordination by mutual adjustment. As more people join the organization, coordination needs become more complex, and direct supervision is added. For example, two or three people working in a small fast-food business can coordinate the work simply by talking to each other about the incoming orders for hamburgers, fries, and drinks. However, in a larger restaurant with more complex cooking and warming equipment and several shifts of workers, direct supervision becomes necessary.

In large organizations, standardization is added to mutual adjustment and direct supervision to coordinate the work. What type of standardization depends on the nature of the work situation, that is, the organization's technology and environment. When the organization's tasks are fairly routine, standardization of work processes may achieve the necessary coordination. Thus, the larger fast-food outlet may standardize the making of hamburger patties: The meat is weighed, put into a hamburger press, and compressed into a patty. McDonald's is well known for this type of standardized process.

In other complex situations, standardization of the output may allow employees to do the work in any appropriate manner as long as the output meets specifications. Thus, the cook may not care how the hamburger is pressed, only that the right amount of meat is used and the patty is the correct diameter and thickness. In other words, the worker may use any process as long as the output is a standard burger.

A third possibility, most often adopted in situations where processes and outputs are difficult to standardize, is to coordinate work by standardizing worker skills. In a hospital, for example, each patient must be treated as a special situation; the hospital process and output therefore cannot be standardized. Similar diagnostic and treatment procedures may be used with more than one patient, but the skills of the physicians and nurses, which are standardized through their professional training, are relied on to coordinate the work. In the most complex work situations, however, organizations may have to depend on workers' mutual adjustment to coordinate their own actions; here the salient elements of coordination are the workers' professional training and communication skills. In effect, mutual adjustment can be an appropriate coordinating mechanism in both the simplest and most complex situations.

Mintzberg pointed out that the five methods of coordination can be combined with the basic components of structure to develop five structural forms: the simple structure, the machine bureaucracy, the professional bureaucracy, the divisionalized form, and the adhocracy. Mintzberg called these structures *pure* or *ideal* types of designs.

Simple Structure

■ The **simple structure,** typical for relatively small or new organizations, has little specialization and formalization, and power and decision making are concentrated in the chief executive.

The **simple structure** characterizes relatively small, usually young organizations in a simple, dynamic environment. The organization has little specialization and formalization, and its overall structure is organic. Power and decision making are concentrated in the chief executive, often the owner-manager, and the flow of authority is from the top down. Direct supervision is the primary coordinating mechanism. Given its dynamic and often hostile environment, the organization must adapt quickly to survive. Most small businesses—a car dealership, a locally owned retail clothing store, or a candy manufacturer with only regional distribution—have a simple structure.

Machine Bureaucracy

■ In a **machine bureaucracy,** which typifies large, well-established organizations, work is highly specialized and formalized and decision making usually is concentrated at the top.

The **machine bureaucracy** is typical of a large, well-established company in a simple and stable environment. Work is highly specialized and formalized, and decision making usually is concentrated at the top. Standardization of work processes is the primary coordinating mechanism. Because the environment is both simple and stable, this highly bureaucratic structure does not have to adapt quickly to changes. Examples include large mass-production firms, such as Container Corp. of America, some automobile companies, and providers of services to mass markets, such as insurance companies.

Professional Bureaucracy

- A **professional bureaucracy** is characterized by horizontal specialization by professional area of expertise, little formalization, and decentralized decision making.

Usually found in a complex and stable environment, the **professional bureaucracy** relies on standardization of skills as the primary means of coordination. There is much horizontal specialization by professional area of expertise but little formalization. Decision making is decentralized and takes place where the expertise is. The only means of coordination available to the organization is standardization of skills—the professionally trained employees. Although it lacks centralization, the professional bureaucracy stabilizes and controls its tasks with rules and procedures developed in the relevant profession. Hospitals, universities, and consulting firms are examples.

Divisionalized Form

- The **divisionalized form,** typical of old, very large organizations, is divided according to the different markets served, horizontal and vertical specialization exist between divisions and headquarters, with decision making divided between headquarters and divisions, and outputs are standardized.

The **divisionalized form** characterizes old and very large firms operating in a relatively simple, stable environment with several diverse markets. It resembles the machine bureaucracy except that it is divided according to the various markets it serves. There is some horizontal and vertical specialization between the divisions (each defined by a market) and headquarters. Decision making is clearly split between headquarters and the divisions, and standardization of outputs is the primary means of coordination. The mechanism of control required by headquarters encourages the development of machine bureaucracies in the divisions.

The classic example of the divisionalized form is General Motors, which, in a reorganization in the 1920s, adopted a design that created divisions for each major car model.[39] Although the divisions have been reorganized and the cars changed several times, the concept of the divisionalized organization is still very evident at GM.[40] General Electric uses a two-tiered divisionalized structure, dividing its numerous businesses into strategic business units, which are further divided into sectors.[41]

---

39. See Harold C. Livesay, *American Made: Men Who Shaped the American Economy* (Boston: Little, Brown, 1979), pp. 215–239, for a discussion of Alfred Sloan and the development of the divisionalized structure at General Motors.

40. Anne B. Fisher, "GM Is Tougher Than You Think," *Fortune,* November 10, 1986, pp. 56–64.

41. Thompson and Strickland, *Strategic Management,* p. 212.

Adhocracy

- In an **adhocracy,** typically found in young organizations in highly technical fields, decision making is spread throughout the organization, power resides with the experts, horizontal and vertical specialization exist, and there is little formalization.

The **adhocracy** typically is found in young organizations engaged in highly technical fields where the environment is complex and dynamic. Decision making is spread throughout the organization, and power is in the hands of experts. There is horizontal and vertical specialization but little formalization, resulting in a very organic structure. Coordination is by mutual adjustment through frequent personal communication and liaison devices. Specialists are not grouped together in functional units but are deployed into specialized market-oriented project teams.

The typical adhocracy usually is established to foster innovation, something to which the other four types of structures are not particularly well suited. Numerous U.S. organizations—Johnson & Johnson, Procter & Gamble, Monsanto, and 3M, for example—are known for their innovation and constant stream of new products.[42] These organizations are either structured totally as an adhocracy or have large divisions set up as an adhocracy. Johnson & Johnson established a new-products division over thirty years ago to encourage continued innovation, creativity, and risk taking. The division continues to succeed; more than two hundred new products have been introduced by Johnson & Johnson in the United States in the past several years.

Mintzberg believed that the most important consideration in designing an organization is the fit among parts. Not only must there be a fit among the structure, the structural imperatives (technology, size, and environment), and organizational strategy; the components of structure (rules and procedures, decision making, specialization) also must fit together and be appropriate for the situation. Mintzberg suggested that when these characteristics are not put together properly, an organization will not function effectively.[43]

Matrix Organization Design

One other organizational form deserves attention here: the matrix organization design. Matrix design is consistent with the contingency approach, because it is useful only in certain situations. One of the earliest implementations of the matrix design was at TRW Systems Group in 1959.[44] Following TRW's lead, other firms in aerospace and high-technology fields created similar matrix structures.

- The **matrix design** combines two different designs to gain the benefits of each; typically combined are a product or project departmentalization scheme and a functional structure.

The **matrix design** attempts to combine two different designs to gain the benefits of each. The most common matrix form superimposes product or project departmentalization on a functional structure (see Figure 19.9). Each department

42. Kenneth Labich, "The Innovators," *Fortune,* June 6, 1988, pp. 51–64.

43. Henry Mintzberg, "Organization Design: Fashion or Fit," *Harvard Business Review,* January-February 1981, pp. 103–116.

44. Harvey F. Kolodny, "Managing in a Matrix," *Business Horizons,* March-April 1981, pp. 17–24.

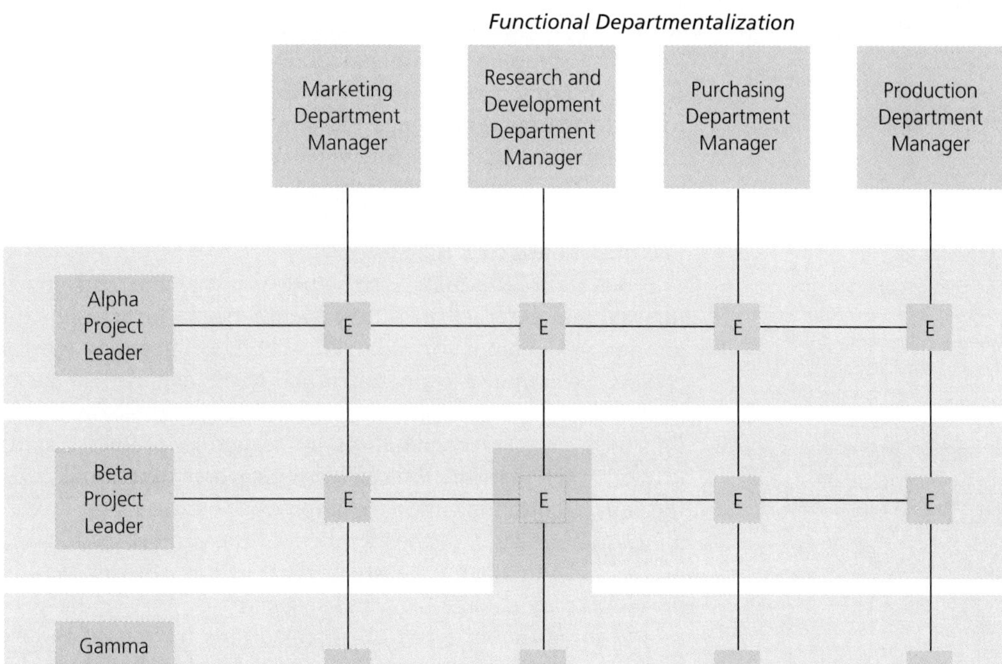

FIGURE 19.9
A Matrix Design

and project has a manager; each employee, however, is a member of both a functional department and a project team. The dual role means that the employee has two supervisors, the department manager and the project leader.

A matrix structure is appropriate when three conditions exist:

1. There is external pressure for a dual focus, meaning that factors in the environment require the organization to focus its efforts equally on responding to multiple external factors and emphasizing internal operations.
2. There are pressures for a high information processing capacity.
3. There are pressures for shared resources.[45]

In the aerospace industry in the early 1960s, all these conditions were present. Private companies had a dual focus: their customers, primarily the federal government, and the complex engineering and technical fields in which they were

45. Stanley M. Davis and Paul R. Lawrence, *Matrix* (Reading, Mass.: Addison-Wesley, 1977), pp. 11–36.

engaged. Moreover, the environments of these companies were changing very rapidly. Technological sophistication and competition were on the increase, resulting in growing environmental uncertainty and, consequently, an added need for information processing. The final condition stemmed from the pressure on the companies to excel in a very competitive environment despite limited resources. The companies concluded that it was inefficient to assign their highly professional—and highly compensated—scientific and engineering personnel to just one project at a time.

- The matrix structure attempts to build into the organization structure the ability to be flexible and provide coordinated responses to both internal and external pressures.

Built into the matrix structure is a flexible and coordinated response to internal and external pressures. Members can be reassigned from one project to another as demands for their skills change. They may work for a month on one project, be assigned to the functional home department for two weeks, and then be reassigned to another project for the next six months. The matrix form improves project coordination by assigning project responsibility to a single leader rather than dividing it among several functional department heads. Furthermore, communication is improved because employees can communicate about the project with the members of the project team as well as with members of the functional unit to which they belong. In this way, solutions to project problems may emerge from either group.

Many different types of organizations have used the matrix form of organization, notably large-project manufacturing firms, banks, and hospitals. *A Look at the Research* illustrates the use of the matrix form in hospitals.

The matrix organizational form thus provides several benefits for the organization. It is not, however, trouble free. Typical problems include the following:

1. The dual reporting system may cause role conflict among employees.
2. Power struggles may occur over who has authority on which issues.
3. Matrix organization often is misinterpreted to mean that all decisions must be made by a group; as a result, group decision-making techniques may be used when they are not appropriate.
4. If the design involves several matrices, each laid on top of another, there may be no way to trace accountability and authority.[46]

Only under the three conditions listed earlier is the matrix design likely to work. In any case, it is a complex organizational system that must be carefully coordinated and managed to be effective.

Contemporary Organization Design

The current proliferation of design theories and alternative forms of organization provide the practicing manager with a dizzying array of choices. The task of the organization manager–designer is to examine the firm within its situation and

46. Ibid., pp. 129–154.

A LOOK AT THE RESEARCH

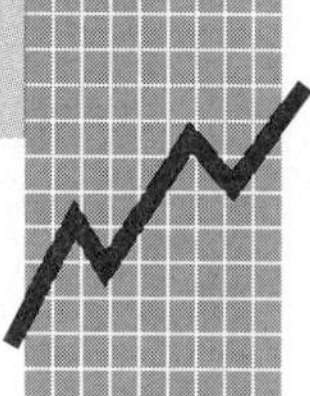

Matrix Management in Hospitals

Matrix management has been described as a useful form of organization for many years. To date, however, most of the research on matrix management has been in the form of cases, anecdotes, and organizational histories rather than rigorous research testing the efficacy of its propositions. Professor Lawton R. Burns of the University of Arizona attempted to provide more information on matrix management by studying 163 hospitals that used matrix management between 1972 and 1978.

Survey questionnaires were sent to the administrative director and head nurse of these hospitals. The questions concerned the director of each hospital unit, the relationships among administrative levels and types (administrator and head nurse), the hierarchy, and decision- and policy-making influence. Follow-up interviews were conducted with the administrators and head nurses where their questionnaire responses differed.

The results of the study reveal several significant things. First, matrix management was a relatively stable form of management in hospitals. Over 80 percent of the matrix programs operating in 1972 were still functioning in 1978. Although much of the literature on matrix organizations suggests that the matrix approach was a transitional form in that it rarely remained in place for a long time, these results indicate that in the hospitals surveyed, the matrix organization program remained relatively stable with consistent levels of organizational complexity over the five-year period.

However, the results also showed that the level of complexity differed among the hospitals studied. In other words, the matrix form usually was put in place in a manner based on local personal and historical considerations and then remained more or less in that form during the period of the study. It did not continue to change and evolve into a relatively complex form over time.

The researcher concluded that the matrix was a stable and effective form of organization for those hospitals that used it. It appeared to be effective for hospitals to decentralize some functions to the specialty areas while maintaining centralized functions for personnel and other hospitalwide activities.

SOURCE: Reprinted from "Matrix Management in Hospitals: Testing Theories of Matrix Structure and Development," by Lawton R. Burns published in *Administrative Science Quarterly,* Vol 34, No. 3 September 1989, adaptation of the Survey Methodology pp. 355–358 by permission of *Administrative Science Quarterly.*

to design a form of organization that meets its needs. The three dominant themes of current design strategies are the effects of technological (or environmental) change, the importance of people, and the necessity of staying in touch with the customer.

Technological change is most evident in the information processing revolutionized by microelectronics.[47] The effects on organizational communication have been significant, as we discussed in Chapter 11. Because modern information processing is so fast, enhances coordination among work groups, and provides almost instantaneous feedback on performance, allowing better control of operations, its impact is felt in the structural form itself. Contemporary structural designs must be capable of handling this type of information technology.

47. John Child, *Organizations: A Guide to Problems and Practice* (New York: Harper & Row, 1984), p. 246.

Federal Express reorganized 1,000 clerks into superteams of five to ten people. These superteams were trained to manage themselves and utilize authority to make decisions. This team saved Federal Express $2.1 million dollars by developing a way to eliminate billing errors.

Current design strategies also reflect a strong concern for people. In their best-selling book on effective companies, *In Search of Excellence,* Thomas Peters and Robert Waterman, Jr., stress the theme of productivity through people.[48] Well-run organizations treat their employees as adults who need to be developed and nurtured as valued resources. The organization structure and processes are the primary vehicles for accomplishing that task. The performance appraisal, reward, and communication systems must be integrated into the overall structure of the organization to provide relevant information regarding the firm and the employees' roles in it and appropriate feedback on the results of employees' efforts. The structure must provide people with jobs that are appropriate for their skills, coordinated with other jobs consistent with the purpose of the organization, and capable of providing a sense of belongingness and contribution to the organization.

The final design factor has an external focus: staying in touch with the customer, client, or constituent. Thomas Peters and Nancy Austin have followed up on the Peters-Waterman theme by stressing the importance of an external orientation.[49] They emphasize paying attention to the end users of the firm's product or service. Organization designers need to develop systems for encouraging and rewarding employee behaviors that keep them in touch with such

48. Thomas J. Peters and Robert H. Waterman, Jr., *In Search of Excellence: Lessons from America's Best-Run Companies* (New York: Harper & Row, 1982), pp. 235–278.

49. Thomas J. Peters and Nancy K. Austin, "A Passion for Excellence," *Fortune,* May 13, 1985, pp. 20–32.

groups. The systems must also allow employees to act on what they learn, correcting deficiencies, making adjustments to current offerings, and developing new products or services to meet new demands.

■ There is no "one best way" to design an organization.

These three dominant factors argue for a contingency design perspective. Unfortunately, there is no "one best way." The designer must consider the impact of multiple factors—sociotechnical systems factors, the structural imperatives, strategy, changing information technology, people, and a concern for end users—on his or her particular organization.

Summary of Key Points

- A universal approach to organization design suggests that its prescriptions will work in any situation or circumstance. A contingency approach, on the other hand, suggests that there are several ways to achieve an outcome; the best way depends on several factors.
- Weber's ideal bureaucracy, Fayol's classic principles of organizing, and Likert's human organization are important universal design approaches. Weber's bureaucratic form of administration was intended to ensure stability, control, and predictable outcomes. The ideal bureaucracy is characterized by rules and procedures, division of labor, hierarchy of authority, technical competence, separation of ownership, rights and property differentiation, and documentation.
- Fayol presented a fourteen-point code for managers. His classic principles, which included departmentalization, unity of command, and unity of direction, became generally accepted means of organizing. Taken together, the fourteen principles provided the basis for the modern organization chart and the coordination of work.
- Likert's human organization was based on the principles of supportive relationships, employee participation, and overlapping work groups. Likert described the human organization in terms of eight variables based on the assumption that people work best in highly supportive and cohesive work groups oriented toward organization goals.
- Important contingency approaches to organization design center on sociotechnical systems, structural imperatives, and organizational strategy. The sociotechnical systems approach viewed the organization as an open system structured to integrate two important subsystems: the technical (task) subsystem and the social subsystem. According to this approach, organizations should structure the task, authority, and reporting relationships around the work group by delegating to it decisions regarding job assignments, training, inspection, rewards, and punishments. The task of management is to monitor the environment and coordinate the structures, rules, and procedures.
- The structural imperatives are size, technology, and environment. In general, large organizations have more complex structures and usually more than one technology. The structure of small organizations, on the other hand, may be dominated by one core operations technology. The structure of the

organization is also established to fit with the environmental demands and buffer the core operating technology from environmental changes and uncertainties.

- Initially, strategy was seen as the determinant of structure: The structure of the organization was designed to implement its purpose, goals, and strategies. The concept of managerial choice in determining organization structure represents a modification of this view. The manager designs the structure to accomplish organizational goals, guided by an analysis of the contextual factors, the strategies of the organization, and personal preferences.
- Mintzberg's ideal types of organization design were derived from a framework of coordinating mechanisms. The five types are simple structure, machine bureaucracy, professional bureaucracy, divisionalized form, and adhocracy. Most organizations have some characteristics of each type, but one is likely to predominate. Mintzberg believed the most important consideration in designing an organization is the fit among parts of the organization.
- The matrix design combines two types of structure (usually functional and project departmentalization) to gain the benefits of each. It usually results in a multiple command and authority system. Benefits of matrix form are increased flexibility, cooperation, communication, and use of skilled personnel. Its problems typically are associated with the dual reporting system and the complex management system needed to coordinate work.
- Contemporary organization design is contingency oriented. Three factors influencing design decisions are the changing information and technological environment, concern for people as a valued resource, and the need to keep in touch with customers.

Discussion Questions

1. Why is it important to distinguish between organization structure and organization design?
2. Explain why the "ideal" bureaucracy is no longer considered ideal.
3. Why do bureaucracies tend to be characterized by slow decision making?
4. Discuss how the federal government continues to observe the bureaucratic principles of separation of ownership and of rights and property in making appointments to high-level government positions.
5. Do you believe the classic principles of organizing and the human organization are opposites? Why or why not?
6. What might be the advantages and disadvantages of structuring the faculty members at your college or university as an autonomous work group?
7. What do you think are the purpose, goals, and strategies of your college or university? How are they reflected in its structure?
8. Which of Mintzberg's pure forms is best illustrated by a major national political party (Democratic or Republican)? Religious organizations? A football team? The U.S. Olympic Committee?

9. In a matrix organization would you rather be a project leader, a functional department head, or a highly trained technical specialist? Why?
10. Discuss what you think the important design considerations will be for organization designers in the year 2000.

CASE 19.1

A Wolfpack at Cincinnati Milacron

Cincinnati Milacron is a leading machine tool maker that has been run by a member of the founding Geier family since 1884. As chair of the board James A. D. Geier neared retirement age in April 1990, Daniel J. Meyer was named CEO. Meyer had joined Cincinnati Milacron in 1969 and worked in financial operations for most of his career until he became president in 1987. After his appointment as CEO, Meyer announced that no major changes would take place and that he expected the company to focus on improving its worldwide competitive position in its core businesses.

In reality, however, major changes had been in the works for the previous two years. There was reorganization aimed at positioning the company to deal with foreign competition by improving quality and productivity throughout its plants. The changing environment had caused Cincinnati Milacron to reevaluate the way it did business and develop a new organization design to help it survive increasing foreign and domestic competition. Cincinnati's sales had dropped to $850 million, with net profit reported at $17.5 million in 1989. The reorganization had yet to produce the desired numbers, but significant improvements were under way and expectations were high.

One example of doing things differently was the redesigning of one of Cincinnati's major products, a plastics injection molding machine. The machine had been losing market share to foreign made models, particularly to machine tool companies in Japan. After analyzing market conditions, a regional sales manager and a product manager at Cincinatti sketched out a "dream machine" that would be competitive in the now foreign-dominated market. They took their idea to corporate headquarters and received approval. Their objective was to produce and market the machine, reducing costs by 40 percent and cutting the normal two-year development time in half. If they could not do both, the machine could not be built.

With neither manager certain that both goals could be attained, they began to formulate a strategy to make it happen. They received permission to approach the task in any manner they believed would work. They put together a hand-picked team of engineers, marketers, designers, production personnel, and even someone from accounting to keep track of costs. This group broke all standard operating procedures in its efforts to design, build, and sell the new plastic injection molding machine. At one point near the end of the project, it looked as if costs savings would be only around 35 percent instead of the required 40 percent. The project was in danger of being put on hold. But the team got together and found the extra 5 percent in cost savings to keep the program alive. The machine is now on the market, and sales have skyrocketed. Once again the company is a major force in plastic injection molding machines.

Although Meyer promised no major changes in the direction of the company, he did make substantial changes in the way the company pursues its direction. In August 1990, with the success of the plastic injection molding machine under his belt, Meyer initiated a new strategy that he compares to a "wolfpack." He claims wolves are survivors, work in teams, and go for the kill and wants Cincinnati Milacron to do the same. Meyer believes almost all of Cincinnati's products and manufacturing processes need to undergo the same type of process as the plastic injection molding machine to survive foreign competition.

Meyer expects the wolfpack concept to stimulate employees and managers to focus on what they do best and find ways to become more competitive in those areas. The back-to-basics approach will feature small, focused factories in which decision making for the plant will be decentralized to the plant manager level. Plant managers will no longer have to constantly look over their shoulders for advice or directions from headquarters. The wolfpack idea is intended to bring out the entrepreneurial spirit among all employees, most of whom have become accustomed to the stricter bureaucratic style. Every activity area has become a profit center—including the company cafeteria, which now is available to be rented out to private parties and wedding receptions. Local personnel have become responsible for innovating and contributing to the small business of which they are a part and to the company as a whole. Meyer has even developed a logo incorporating the wolfpack concept to continuously remind employees to pursue their work like wolves.

Case Questions

1. How would you characterize the forces that prompted Cincinnati Milacron to make significant organizational changes?
2. What specific aspects of organization structure did Cincinnati Milacron change to meet the demands of its changing environment?
3. How does the image of the wolfpack contribute to or hinder the changes Daniel Meyer has in mind?

SOURCES: "Milacron Wolfpack Goes in for the Kill," *The Wall Street Journal,* August 14, 1990, p. A11; Peter Nulty, "The Soul of an Old Machine," *Fortune,* May 21, 1990, pp. 67–72; "President Named Chief at Cincinnati Milacron," *The New York Times,* April 25, 1990, p. D5.

CASE 19.2 A Structural Straitjacket at Wild Wear

Wild Wear, Inc., makes clothing, raingear, and sleeping bags for hikers and other outdoor enthusiasts. The company began when Myrtle Kelly began sewing pile jackets that her husband Ray sold on college campuses. It now employs almost five hundred people organized into traditional divisions such as marketing, manufacturing, and research and development.

Recently it became apparent that although Wild Wear's balance sheet appeared healthy, the company was stagnant. Everyone seemed to work hard, and the company's products seldom flopped. Yet Wild Wear seemed to have developed a "me too" posture, bringing new products to market a season or a full year after competitors.

The Kellys, who still run the company, pored over performance appraisals looking for the weak points that might be holding the company back. But it seemed the human resources department had been doing its work. R&D was coming up with a respectable number of new products, the manufacturing facility was modern and efficient, and the marketing tactics often won praise from customers.

Baffled, the Kellys called a meeting of middle-level managers, hoping they could provide some answers they had missed. They were shocked when they noticed that the managers were introducing themselves as they came in and sat down. People who had been working in the same company for years had never even met! The meeting began with this observation, and for ninety minutes the Kellys sat back and listened to the problems their managers raised.

It became clear that in the attempt to grow from a family operation into a larger company, the Kellys had assumed the two needed to be very different. When they started out, the two of them handled all aspects of the business. Ray would hear from a customer that backpackers really needed a certain product, would pass the idea on to Myrtle and order the materials she needed, and within a few weeks would offer the product to the same—now delighted—customer. As the company grew, the Kellys began to worry about their lack of formal business training and hired professionals to run each division and set up appropriate rules and procedures.

What they had created, the middle managers informed them, was a number of very efficient, productive divisions that might as well have been separate companies. The R&D people might come up with a new breathable fabric for raingear only to find that production had just begun making a new rainwear line out of the old fabric and that marketing was turning all its attention to selling the big inventory of sleeping bags. Each division did the best it could with the information it had, but that information was very incomplete. Products progressed linearly from one division to the next, but it always seemed as though an idea that had been ahead of its time did not yield a product until the time had passed.

To remedy the problem, the Kellys decided to call in a management consultant to create more of a matrix structure for Wild Wear. While they were waiting for the consultant's solutions, they began holding weekly "Horizon" meetings. The group of middle managers would get together every Monday and discuss what they saw on their horizon. After less than a month of such meetings, the excitement generated promised better things for Wild Wear as the managers stretched to expand their own horizons and to help others bring their ideas to light.

Case Questions

1. What would be the ideal organizational design for a company like Wild Wear?
2. What does Wild Wear's experience say about the need for periodic corporate restructuring?

EXPERIENTIAL EXERCISE

Purpose: This exercise will help you understand the factors that determine the design of organizations.

Format: You will interview employees of a small- to medium-size organization and analyze the reasons for its design. (You may want to coordinate this exercise with that in Chapter 17.)

Procedure: Your first task is to find a local organization with between fifty and five hundred employees. (It should not be part of your college or university.) If you did the exercise for Chapter 17, you can use the same company for this exercise. The organization should have more than two hierarchical levels, but it should not be too complex to understand in a short period of study. You may want to check with your professor before contacting the company. Your initial contact should be with the highest-ranking manager you can reach. Make sure that top management is aware of your project and gives its approval.

Using the material in this chapter, you will interview employees to obtain the following information on the structure of the organization:

1. What is the organization in business to do? What are its goals and its strategies for achieving them?
2. How large is the company? What is the total number of employees? How many work full time? How many work part time?
3. What are the most important components of the organization's environment?
4. Is the number of important environmental components large or small?
5. How quickly or slowly do these components change?
6. Would you characterize the organization's environment as certain, uncertain, or somewhere in between? If in between, describe in detail approximately how certain or uncertain.
7. What is the organization's dominant technology, that is, how does it transform inputs into outputs?
8. How rigid is the company in its application of rules and procedures? Is it flexible enough to respond to environmental changes?
9. How involved are employees in the daily decision making related to their jobs?
10. What methods are used to ensure control over the actions of employees?

Interview at least three employees of the company at different levels and in different departments. One should hold a top-level position. Be sure to ask the questions in a way the employees will understand; they may not be familiar with some of the terminology used in this chapter.

The result of the exercise should be a report describing the technology, environment, and structure of the company. You should discuss the extent to which the structure is appropriate for the organization's strategy, size, technology, and environment. If it does not seem appropriate, you should explain the reasons. If you also used this company for the exercise in Chapter 17, you can comment further on the organization chart and its appropriateness for the company. You may want to send a copy of your report to the cooperating company.

Follow-up Questions

1. Which aspects of strategy, size, environment, and technology were the most difficult to obtain information about? Why?
2. If there were differences in the responses of the employees you interviewed, how do you account for them?
3. If you were the president of the organization you analyzed, would you structure it in the same way? Why or why not? If not, how would you structure it differently?
4. How did your answers to questions 2 and 3 differ from those in the exercise in Chapter 17?

CHAPTER OUTLINE

The Nature of Organization Culture

What Is Organization Culture?

Historical Foundations

Three Basic Approaches to Describing Organization Culture

The Parsons AGIL Model

The Ouchi Framework

The Peters and Waterman Approach

Managing Organization Culture

Taking Advantage of the Existing Culture

Teaching the Organization Culture: Socialization

Changing the Organization Culture

20

ORGANIZATION CULTURE

CHAPTER OBJECTIVES

After studying this chapter, you should be able to:

Define organization culture and explain how it affects employee behavior.

Summarize the historical development of organization culture.

Describe three views of culture in organizations.

Discuss the key elements of managing the organization culture.

When Walter A. Haas, Jr., bought the Oakland Athletics (A's) for $12.5 million in 1980, the A's were in the worst shape in the American League. Attendance averaged 3,788 per game, the anemic front office staff had 6 employees, the minor league system of 4 teams was in disarray, and a shoe box of index cards recorded the 75 season ticket holders. The Haas family was concerned about the losses that would mount over the next few years as well as the embarrassment of a losing team. However, in less than ten years the franchise became one of the most powerful in professional baseball, capturing the American League pennant three years in a row and winning the World Series in 1989.

The turnaround of the A's did not happen overnight; it followed a steady upward trend created by new management. The management team consisted of Haas's son-in-law Roy Eisenhardt, a former lawyer, as general manager and CEO; his son Wally, a former manager at Levi Strauss, as executive vice president; a young lawyer named Sandy Alderson to help with contract negotiations; and a former Madison Square Garden employee to head up business operations.

This small band of nonbaseball people created a work- and preparation-oriented culture in the A's organization. Player trades and other deals were based on a strategic plan for the organization. Some trades were made during the winter and were based on moving the ballclub in a winning direction. Others were made during the season to replace regular position players lost due to injuries or other developments on the club.

Today some people compare the A's to the great baseball dynasties such as the New York Yankees. Their influence is so pervasive that some stock market experts predict market trends based on their winning or losing the World Series.[1]

Many organizations attribute their success to a strong and firmly entrenched culture. The culture that Roy Eisenhardt instilled in the Oakland A's organization transformed the A's from a listless, losing ballclub into one of the most successful franchises in professional baseball. What is organization culture, and how does an organization develop one?

We begin this chapter by exploring the nature and historical foundations of organization culture. Then we examine three basic approaches to defining the

1. Brenton R. Schlender, "Take Me Out to the Gold Mine," *Fortune,* August 13, 1990, pp. 93–100; Alvin P. Sanoff, "Baseball Meets Harvard Law," *US News & World Report,* July 31, 1989, pp. 48–49; Thomas Jaffe, "Some Good News, Sort of," *Forbes,* November 12, 1990, p. 368.

characteristics of organization culture. Finally, we discuss how organization culture can be managed to enhance the organization's effectiveness.

The Nature of Organization Culture

In the early 1980s, organization culture became a central concern in the study of organizational behavior. Hundreds of researchers began to work in this area. Numerous books were published, important academic journals dedicated entire issues to the discussion of culture, and—almost overnight—organizational behavior textbooks that omitted culture as a topic of study became obsolete.

Interest in organization culture was not limited to the ivory towers of academia. Businesses expressed an interest in culture that was far more intense than their concern with other aspects of organizational behavior. *Business Week, Fortune,* and other business periodicals published articles that touted culture as the key to an organization's success and suggested that managers who could manage through their organization's culture almost certainly would rise to the top.[2]

Although the enthusiasm of the early 1980s has waned somewhat, the study of organization culture remains important. Many researchers have begun to weave the important aspects of organization culture into their research in the more traditional topics. Now there are relatively few headline stories in the popular business press about culture and culture management, but organization culture has become a common topic in the study of management. The enormous amount of research on culture completed in the early 1980s has fundamentally shifted the way both academics and managers look at organizations. Some of the concepts developed in the analysis of organization culture have become basic parts of the business vocabulary, and the analysis of organization culture is one of the most important specialties in the field of organizational behavior.

What Is Organization Culture?

A surprising aspect of the recent rise in interest in organization culture is that the concept, unlike virtually any other concept in the field of organizational behavior, has no single widely accepted definition. Indeed, it often appears that authors feel compelled to develop their own definitions, which range from very broad to highly specific. For example, Deal and Kennedy define a firm's culture as "the way we do things around here."[3] This very broad definition presumably

2. See "Corporate Culture: The Hard to Change Values That Spell Success or Failure," *Business Week,* October 27, 1980, pp. 148–160, and Charles G. Burck, "Working Smarter," *Fortune,* June 15, 1981, pp. 68–73.

3. T. E. Deal and A. A. Kennedy, *Corporate Cultures: The Rites and Rituals of Corporate Life* (Reading, Mass.: Addison-Wesley, 1982), p. 4.

These three British men indicate how pervasive the little things are in getting along in business in various cultures. Although they are not purposefully in costume, they obviously know how to dress in order to be accepted in certain business circles in England. U.S. companies such as Pacific Telesis Group, hoping to capitalize on new opportunities in Europe and the Pacific Rim, must know how to do business in these far reaching cultures.

could include the way a firm manufactures its products, pays its bills, treats its employees, and performs any other organizational operation. More specific definitions include those of Schein, "the pattern of basic assumptions that a given group has invented, discovered, or developed in learning to cope with its problems of external adaptation and internal integration,"[4] and Peters and Waterman, "a dominant and coherent set of shared values conveyed by such symbolic means as stories, myths, legends, slogans, anecdotes, and fairy tales."[5] Table 20.1 lists these and other important definitions of organization culture.

- Most definitions of organization culture include values, symbols, and other factors that communicate the culture to employees.

Despite the apparent diversity of these definitions, a few common attributes emerge. First, all the definitions refer to some set of values held by individuals in a firm. These values define what is good or acceptable behavior and what is bad or unacceptable behavior. In other some organizations, for example, it is unacceptable to blame customers when problems arise. Here the value "the customer is always right" tells managers what actions are acceptable (not blaming the customer) and what actions are not acceptable (blaming the customer). In other organizations, the dominant values might support blaming customers for problems, penalizing employees who make mistakes, or treating employees as the firm's most valuable assets. In each case, values help members of an organization understand how they should act in that organization.

A second attribute common to many of the definitions in Table 20.1 is that the values that make up an organization's culture often are taken for granted; that is, rather than being written in a book or made explicit in a training program, they are basic assumptions made by the firm's employees. It may be as difficult for an organization to articulate these basic assumptions as it is for people to

4. E. H. Schein, "The Role of the Founder in Creating Organizational Culture," *Organizational Dynamics,* Summer 1983, p. 14.

5. Thomas J. Peters and Robert H. Waterman, *In Search of Excellence: Lessons from America's Best-Run Companies* (New York: Harper & Row, 1982), p. 103.

TABLE 20.1
Definitions of Organization Culture

Definition	Source
"A belief system shared by an organization's members"	J. C. Spender, "Myths, Recipes, and Knowledge-Bases in Organizational Analysis" (Unpublished manuscript, Graduate School of Management, University of California at Los Angeles, 1983), p. 2.
"Strong, widely-shared core values"	C. O'Reilly, "Corporations, Cults, and Organizational Culture: Lessons from Silicon Valley Firms" (Paper presented at the Annual Meeting of the Academy of Management, Dallas, Texas, 1983), p. 1.
"The way we do things around here"	T. E. Deal and A. A. Kennedy, *Corporate Cultures: The Rites and Rituals of Corporate Life* (Reading, Mass. Addison-Wesley, 1982), p. 4.
"The collective programming of the mind"	G. Hofstede, *Culture's Consequences: International Differences in Work-related Values* (Beverly Hills, Calif.: Sage, 1980), p. 25.
"Collective understandings"	J. Van Maanen and S. R. Barley, "Cultural Organization: Fragments of a Theory" (Paper presented at the Annual Meeting of the Academy of Management, Dallas, Texas, 1983), p. 7.
"A set of shared, enduring beliefs communicated through a variety of symbolic media, creating meaning in people's work lives"	J. M. Kouzes, D. F. Caldwell, and B. Z. Posner, "Organizational Culture: How It Is Created, Maintained, and Changed" (Presentation at OD Network National Conference, Los Angeles, October 9, 1983).
"A set of symbols, ceremonies, and myths that communicate the underlying values and beliefs of that organization to its employees"	W. G. Ouchi, *Theory Z: How American Business Can Meet the Japanese Challenge* (Reading, Mass.: Addison-Wesley, 1981), p. 41.
"A dominant and coherent set of shared values conveyed by such symbolic means as stories, myths, legends, slogans, anecdotes, and fairy tales"	T. J. Peters and R. H. Waterman, In *Search of Excellence: Lessons from America's Best-Run Companies* (New York: Harper & Row, 1982), p. 103.
"The pattern of basic assumptions that a given group has invented, discovered, or developed in learning to cope with its problems of external adaptation and internal integration"	E. H. Schein, "The Role of the Founder in Creating Organizational Culture," *Organizational Dynamics*, Summer 1985, p. 14.

express their personal beliefs and values. Several authors have argued that organization culture is a powerful influence on individuals in firms precisely because it is not explicit but becomes an implicit part of employees' values and beliefs.[6]

Some organizations have been able to articulate the key values in their cultures. Some have even written down these values and made them part of

6. See M. Polanyi, *Personal Knowledge* (Chicago: University of Chicago Press, 1958); E. Goffman, *The Presentation of Self in Every Day Life* (New York: Doubleday, 1959); and P. L. Berger and T. Luckman, *The Social Construction of Reality* (Garden City, N.Y.: Anchor, 1967).

FIGURE 20.1
Statement of an Organization's Values

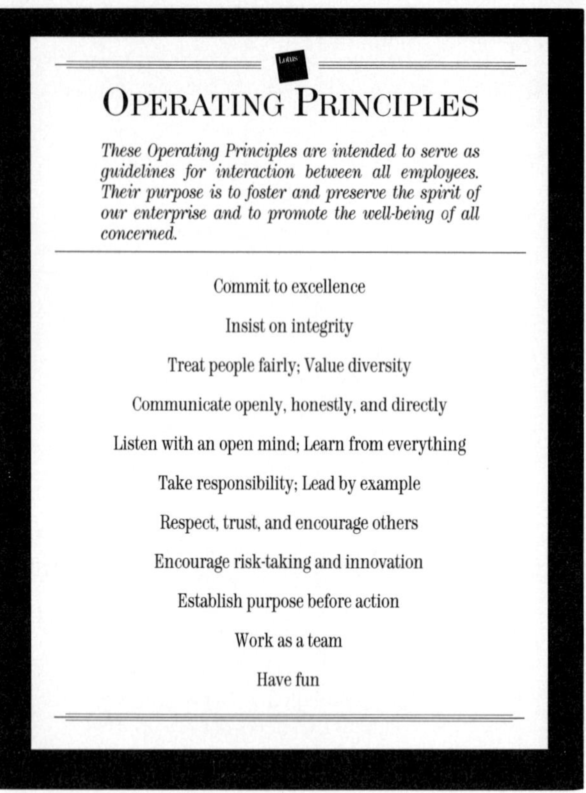
OPERATING PRINCIPLES

These Operating Principles are intended to serve as guidelines for interaction between all employees. Their purpose is to foster and preserve the spirit of our enterprise and to promote the well-being of all concerned.

Commit to excellence

Insist on integrity

Treat people fairly; Value diversity

Communicate openly, honestly, and directly

Listen with an open mind; Learn from everything

Take responsibility; Lead by example

Respect, trust, and encourage others

Encourage risk-taking and innovation

Establish purpose before action

Work as a team

Have fun

SOURCE: Courtesy of Lotus Development Corp.

formal training procedures. For example, Lotus has written "Operating Principles" to guide interaction between employees (see Figure 20.1). At Hewlett-Packard a brief summary of "The HP Way" is given to all new employees. This pamphlet describes the basic values of the culture at Hewlett-Packard.[7] NCR recently began a national advertising campaign featuring its statement of organizational values.[8] Levi Strauss & Co. has embarked on an intense effort to communicate its values through the development of an "Aspirations Statement."[9] *Management in Action,* presents more details about this organization's culture.

Even when firms are able to articulate and describe the basic values that make up their cultures, however, the values most strongly affect actions when people in the organization take them for granted. An organization's culture is not likely to powerfully influence behavior when employees must constantly refer

7. W. G. Ouchi, *Theory Z: How American Business Can Meet the Japanese Challenge* (Reading, Mass.: Addison-Wesley, 1981).

8. See the NCR advertisement in *Fortune,* February 29, 1988, pp. 62–63.

9. Robert Howard, "Values Make the Company: An Interview with Robert Haas," *Harvard Business Review,* September-October 1990, pp. 133–144.

Levi Strauss & Co. Emphasizes Values and Culture

From its earliest beginnings as a maker of blue jeans for miners in California, Levi Strauss & Co. has been focused on important values and traditions. After going public in 1971 and diversifying its product line into sportswear as well as blue jeans, the owners believed the company had lost some of its values. In 1985, they regained control through a leveraged buyout to go private again. The firm's 1990 worldwide sales were $4.2 billion, making it the largest apparel manufacturer in the world. Robert Haas, chairman and CEO and the great-great-grandnephew of company founder Levi Strauss, an immigrant from Bavaria, continues to guide the company through its commitment to social responsibility and to its work force.

Haas contends that management of the "soft stuff," exemplified by Levi Strauss's genuine concern for its employees, is an integral part of the firm's competitive success. He believes that values drive the business. For this reason, his management philosophy is to listen to employees, suppliers, and customers and develop managerial strategies around what he hears.

Valuing the work force is one of Haas's recurring themes. The company no longer assumes that what happens to an employee outside of the workday is not important to the company. For example, child care problems may create chronic tardiness or otherwise affect an employee's performance. Haas believes that if the company can do something to help out, it should—not just for humanitarian reasons but for the benefit of the company as well.

The company's values are expressed in an "Aspirations Statement," which has influenced Levi Strauss's business strategies. The Aspirations Statement describes the company's belief in diversity, recognition for contributions to the firm's success, ethical management practices, communications, and empowerment of employees. Haas contends that the company's most fundamental value is honesty in its dealings with employees, customers, and suppliers. Levi Strauss reinforces these principles in the development of new processes, products, and marketing strategies.

Many experts believe that these basic values and the organization culture have helped the company survive the leveraged buyout—and, in fact, be seven years ahead of schedule in repaying the $1.5 billion the family had to borrow to finance the buyout. Evidently, company values can be as important to the bottom line as to employees.

SOURCES: Gary Hoover, Alta Campbell, and Patrick J. Spain, eds., *Hoover's Handbook: Profiles of over 500 Major Corporations* (Austin, Tex.: The Reference Press, 1990), p. 333; Robert Howard, "Values Make the Company: An Interview with Robert Haas," *Harvard Business Review,* September-October 1990, pp. 133–144; Brenton R. Schlender, "How Levi Strauss Did an LBO Right," *Fortune,* May 7, 1990, pp. 105–107.

to a handbook to remember what the culture is. When the culture becomes part of them—when they can ignore what is written in the book because they already have embraced the values it describes—the culture can have an important impact on their actions.

The final attribute shared by many of the definitions in Table 20.1 is an emphasis on the symbolic means through which the values in an organization's culture are communicated. Although, as we noted, companies sometimes can directly describe these values, their meaning perhaps is best communicated to employees through the use of stories, examples, and even what some authors call "myths" or "fairy tales." Stories typically symbolize important implications of values in a firm's culture. Often they develop a life of their own. As they are told and retold, shaped and reshaped, their relationship to what actually occurred becomes increasingly tenuous. Yet such stories communicate the meaning of organizational values much more powerfully than does a listing of values in a booklet.

Some organization stories have become famous. Two examples from Hewlett-Packard demonstrate how stories help communicate and reinforce important organizational values. One of the key values listed in "The HP Way" is that Hewlett-Packard avoids bank debt. A story is told of a senior manager in the finance area who was given free rein to develop a financing plan for a new investment. As she applied the best of finance theory, it became clear to her that part of the financial package should include bank debt. When her proposal reached Mr. Hewlett and Mr. Packard, however, it was rejected—not because the financial reasoning was unsound but because at Hewlett-Packard "we avoid bank debt."[10] This story shows that avoiding bank debt is more than a slogan at Hewlett-Packard; it is a fact.

Another value at Hewlett-Packard is that "employees are our most important asset." A story that helps communicate the reality of this value tells what happened when the company was struggling through some difficult financial times. While virtually all other firms in the industry were laying people off, HP asked all its employees to take one day of unpaid vacation every two weeks. By working nine days and then taking one day off, the firm was able to avoid layoffs. All employees were hurt because all received a reduction in pay, but none had to bear the total cost of the firm's reduced performance.[11] The message communicated by this story is that Hewlett-Packard will go to great lengths to avoid layoffs to keep its employment team intact.

- **Organization culture** is the set of values that helps the organization's employees understand which actions are considered acceptable and which unacceptable.

We can use the three common attributes of definitions of culture just discussed to develop a definition with which most authors probably could agree: **Organization culture** is the set of values, often taken for granted, that help people in an organization understand which actions are considered acceptable and which are considered unacceptable. Often these values are communicated through stories and other symbolic means.[12]

Historical Foundations

- Our basic understanding of organization culture includes research in anthropology, sociology, social psychology, and economics.

Although research on organization culture exploded onto the scene in the early 1980s, the antecedents of this research can be traced to the origins of social science. Understanding the contributions of other social science disciplines is particularly important in the case of organization culture, for many of the

10. A. Wilkins, "Organizational Stories as Symbols Which Control the Organization," in Louis R. Pondy, Peter J. Frost, Gareth Morgan, and Thomas C. Dandridge, eds., *Organizational Symbolism* (Greenwich, Conn.: JAI Press, 1983), pp. 81–82.

11. Ibid.

12. This definition is very similar to the definition of culture proposed in M. R. Lewis, "Culture Yes, Organization No" (Paper presented at the Annual Meeting of the Academy of Management, Dallas, Texas, 1983).

dilemmas and debates that continue in this area reflect differences in historical research traditions. Table 20.2 summarizes the disciplinary approaches.

Anthropologic Contributions Of all the social science disciplines, anthropology is most closely related to the study of culture and cultural phenomena. Indeed, anthropology can be defined as the study of human cultures.[13] Anthropologists seek to understand how the values and beliefs that make up a society's culture affect the structure and functioning of that society. Many anthropologists believe that to understand the relationship between culture and society, it is necessary to look at a culture from the viewpoint of the people in a society—from the "native's point of view."[14] To reach this level of understanding, anthropologists immerse themselves in the values, symbols, and stories that people in a society use to bring order and meaning to their lives.

Whether the culture is that of a large, modern corporation or a primitive tribe in New Guinea or the Philippines, the questions asked are the same: How do people in this culture know what kinds of behavior are acceptable and what kinds are unacceptable? How is this knowledge understood? How is this knowledge communicated to new members?

- **Thick description research methods** attempt to describe the totality of daily life through in-depth questioning and observation.

Practitioners of this anthropological approach usually use **thick description research methods**, which involve attempting to describe the totality of day-to-day life through in-depth questioning and observation.[15] Such methods are quite different from those used in other areas of organizational behavior research—experiments and questionnaire-based surveys, for example. Through this intense descriptive effort, the values and beliefs that underlie actions in an organization become clear. However, these values can be fully understood only in the context of the organization in which they developed. In other words, a description of the values and beliefs of one organization is not transferable to those of other organizations.

Sociological Contributions Sociologists also have had a long-term interest in studying the causes and consequences of culture. Many sociological methods and theories have found expression in the analysis of organization cultures.

In studying culture, sociologists most often have focused on informal social structure. Émile Durkheim, an important early sociologist, argued that the study of myth and ritual is an essential complement to the study of structure and rational behavior in societies.[16] By studying rituals, Durkheim argued, we can understand the most basic values and beliefs of a group of people. The same argument was developed by another sociologist, Max Weber, in his now famous description of the relationship between the Protestant ethic and the development

---

13. A. L. Kroeber and C. Kluckhohn, "Culture: A Critical Review of Concepts and Definitions," in *Papers of the Peabody Museum of American Archaeology and Ethnology,* vol. 47, No. 1 (Cambridge, Mass.: Harvard University Press, 1952).

14. C. Geertz, *The Interpretation of Cultures* (New York: Basic Books, 1973).

15. Ibid. pp. 5–6.

16. E. Durkheim, *The Elementary Forms of Religious Life,* trans. J. Swain (New York: Collier, 1961), p. 220.

TABLE 20.2
Social Science Contributions to Organization Culture Analysis

Contributor	Areas of Study	Methods of Study
Anthropology	▪ Human cultures ▪ Values and beliefs of society	▪ Thick description ▪ Interviews and observations
Sociology	▪ Categorization of social system structures	▪ Systematic interviews ▪ Questionnaires ▪ Statistics
Social psychology	▪ Creation and manipulation of symbols ▪ Use of stories	▪ Surveys ▪ Observations ▪ Statistics
Economics	▪ Economic conditions of a company in a society	▪ Statistics ▪ Mathematical modeling

of capitalism in Western Europe.[17] Weber argued that the religious values and beliefs of individuals in Western Europe supported the accumulation of material goods. The effort to accumulate material goods, in turn, was an important prerequisite for the development of capitalist economies.

This sociological approach to the study of culture perhaps is most evident in the methods used to study organization culture. Sociologists use systematic interviews, questionnaires, and other quantitative research methods rather than the thick description methods of anthropologists. Whereas anthropologists usually produce a book-length description of values, attitudes, and beliefs that underlie the behaviors of people in one or two organizations,[18] practitioners using the sociological approach generally produce a fairly simple typology of cultural attributes and then show how the cultures of a relatively large number of firms can be analyzed with this typology.[19]

Although both the anthropological and sociological approaches to studying organization culture are important, the recent emergence of organization culture as a major field of research primarily reflects work done in the sociological tradition. The major pieces of research on organization culture that later spawned widespread business interest—including Ouchi's *Theory Z,* Deal and Kennedy's *Corporate Cultures,* and Peters and Waterman's *In Search of Excellence*[20]—used sociological methods. Later in this chapter, we will review some of this work in more detail.

Social Psychology Contributions Most research on organization culture has used anthropological or sociological methods and theories. However, some has borrowed heavily from social psychology. Social psychological theory, with its em-

17. H. H. Gerth and C. Wright Mills, *From Max Weber* (New York: Oxford University Press, 1976), pp. 267–362.

18. See, for example, B. Clark, *The Distinctive College* (Chicago: Adline, 1970).

19. See Ouchi, *Theory Z,* and Peters and Waterman, *In Search of Excellence.*

20. See Ouchi, *Theory Z,* Deal and Kennedy, *Corporate Cultures,* and Peters and Waterman, *In Search of Excellence.*

phasis on the creation and manipulation of symbols, provides a natural setting within which to analyze organization culture.

For example, research in social psychology suggests that people tend to use stories or information about a single event more than they use multiple observations to make judgments.[21] Thus, the fact that your neighbor had trouble with a certain brand of automobile means that you probably will conclude that the brand is bad even though the car company can generate reams of statistical data to prove your neighbor's car was a rarity.

The impact of stories on decision making suggests an important reason why organization culture has such a powerful influence on the people in an organization. Unlike other organizational phenomena, culture is best communicated through stories and examples, and these become the basis on which individuals in the organization make judgments. If a story says that blaming customers is a bad thing to do, then blaming customers *is* a bad thing to do. This value is communicated much more effectively through the cultural story than through some statistical analysis of customer satisfaction.[22]

Economics Contributions The influence of economics on the study of organization culture, although it has been less significant than the influence of anthropology and sociology, is substantial enough to warrant attention. Economic analysis treats organization culture as one of a variety of tools that managers can use to give some economic advantage to the organization.

When sociological and anthropological research on culture moves beyond simply describing the cultures of companies, it usually focuses on linking the cultural attributes of firms with their performance. In *Theory Z,* for example, Ouchi does not just say that Type Z companies differ from other kinds of companies; rather, he asserts that Type Z firms will outperform other firms.[23] When Peters and Waterman say they are in search of excellence, they define *excellence,* in part, as consistently high financial performance.[24] These authors are seeking cultural explanations of financial success.

Researchers disagree about the extent to which culture affects organization performance. The conditions under which organization culture is linked with superior financial performance have been investigated by several authors.[25] This research suggests that under some relatively narrow conditions, this culture-performance link may exist. However, simply because a firm has a culture does

---

21. E. Borgida and R. E. Nisbett, "The Differential Impact of Abstract vs. Concrete Information on Decisions," *Journal of Applied Social Psychology,* July-September 1977, pp. 258–271.

22. J. Martin and M. Power, "Truth or Corporate Propaganda: The Value of a Good War Story," in Louis R. Pondy, Peter J. Frost, Gareth Morgan, and Thomas C. Dandridge, eds., *Organizational Symbolism* (Greenwich, Conn.: JAI Press, 1983), pp. 93–108.

23. A. Wilkins and W. G. Ouchi, "Efficient Cultures: Exploring the Relationship between Culture and Organizational Performance," *Administrative Science Quarterly,* September 1983, pp. 468–481; W. G. Ouchi, "Markets, Bureaucracies, and Clans," *Administrative Science Quarterly,* March 1980, pp. 129–141.

24. Peters and Waterman, *In Search of Excellence.*

25. J. B. Barney, "Organizational Culture: Can It Be a Source of Sustained Competitive Advantage?" *Academy of Management Review,* July 1986, pp. 656–665.

not mean that it will perform well. A variety of cultural traits can actually hurt performance.

Consider, for example, a firm whose culture includes values like "customers are too ignorant to be of much help," "employees cannot be trusted," "innovation is not important," and "quality is too expensive." This firm has a strong culture, but its financial success is far from assured. Clearly, the relationship between culture and performance depends, to some extent at least, on the content of the values that exist in the organization's culture.

Three Basic Approaches to Describing Organization Culture

No single framework for describing the values in organization cultures has emerged; however, several frameworks have been suggested. Taken together, these models provide insights into the dimensions along which organization cultures vary.

The Parsons AGIL Model

One framework for analyzing the content of cultural values comes from the American sociologist Talcott Parsons.[26] Parsons was a general sociological theorist whose work was dominant from the 1940s through the 1960s but came to be seen as too abstract and obscure to inform more recent sociological work. Interest in Parsons began to wane during the late 1960s, and today his work usually is studied only in classes on the history of sociological thought.[27]

- Parsons' **AGIL model** attempts to specify certain functions that all social systems must meet to survive and prosper.

Yet embedded in Parsons' work is perhaps the first attempt to develop a framework for understanding the content of values in cultural systems, including organization culture systems. Parsons developed the **AGIL model** to specify certain functions that any social system—whether a society, an economy, or an organization—must meet to survive and prosper. These functions are represented by the letters *AGIL: A* for adaptation, *G* for goal attainment, *I* for integration, and *L* for legitimacy. To survive and prosper, a social system must be able to adapt, attain its goals, integrate its parts, and be considered legitimate to people and other organizations external to itself. Table 20.3 describes these functions further.

- For successful **adaptation,** an organization must be aware of its environment, understand how it is changing, and make the necessary adjustments.
- To realize **goal attainment,** an organization must have processes that specify goals and specific strategies for reaching them.

Adaptation and **goal attainment** are relatively clear concepts. To adapt successfully, a social system must be aware of its environment, understand how that environment is changing, and make the appropriate adjustments. To attain

26. T. Parsons, *The Structure of Social Action* (New York: McGraw-Hill, 1937); T. Parsons and E. Shills, eds., *Toward a General Theory of Action* (Cambridge, Mass.: Harvard University Press, 1951).

27. See, for example, W. Buckley, *Sociology and Modern Systems* (Englewood Cliffs, N.J.: Prentice-Hall, 1967).

TABLE 20.3
Parsons' AGIL Model

Adaptation	the ability to adapt to changing circumstances
Goal Attainment	the ability to articulate and reach system objectives
Integration	the ability to integrate different parts of a system
Legitimacy	the right to survive and be accepted

its goals, a social system must have processes that specify those goals, as well as specific strategies for reaching them.

- **Integration** refers to the organization's need to keep its constituent parts together.
- **Legitimacy** is the organization's need to be granted the right to survive by elements in its environment.

Parsons' concepts of integration and legitimacy are perhaps somewhat less clear. **Integration** refers to the need that every social system has to keep its constituent parts together. The parts of a social system must be brought in contact with one another, interdependencies understood and organized, and the need for coordinated action resolved. **Legitimacy** refers to the need of every social system to be granted the right to survive by elements in its environment. A social system is said to be legitimate, in this sense, when society as a whole agrees that it is appropriate for that system to continue.

Clearly, Parsons' AGIL model is abstract. How does it help describe the dimensions along which values in an organization culture may vary? The answer to this question is found in the recognition that an organization's cultural values are some of the most important tools it can use to accomplish the AGIL functions. Thus, Parsons would expect to see that some of an organization's cultural values have to do with how it adapts to changes in its environment. Other cultural values should address how the firm defines and reaches its goals. Still others should affect how the firm integrates and unites its parts to make a coherent whole. Finally, some of the organization's cultural values should help maintain its legitimacy in the environment. The abstract nature of the model reflects an attempt to develop a general framework for analysis, one that can be applied in the analysis of any organization culture.

We can find examples of values that fulfill all these functions in real organizations. When a company's managers say they value technological change (as is asserted at 3M), they are stating a value that has to do with adaptation.[28] When a firm enshrines the value of "adding economic wealth to shareholders" at the center of its culture (as Hewlett-Packard does), it is partly meeting criteria for goal attainment.[29] When a firm says that its most important assets are its people (as many firms, including Westinghouse, do), it is addressing the need to integrate the diverse parts of its organization.[30] Finally, when a company says that its goal is to meet the needs of all its external constituent groups, including society at large (as NCR has suggested), it is addressing the question of legitimacy.[31]

---

28. Peters and Waterman, *In Search of Excellence.*
29. Ibid.
30. J. Main, "Westinghouse's Cultural Revolution," *Fortune,* June 15, 1981, p. 74.
31. See the NCR advertisement in *Fortune,* February 29, 1988, pp. 62–63.

The Ouchi Framework

In contrast to Parsons' very general framework, a number of authors have attempted to develop models for analyzing the cultural systems of specific groups of organizations. One of the first researchers to focus explicitly on analyzing the cultures of a limited group of firms was William G. Ouchi. Ouchi analyzed the organization cultures of three groups of firms, which he characterized as typical U.S. firms, typical Japanese firms, and **Type Z** U.S. firms.[32]

- The **Type Z** firm is committed to retaining employees, evaluates workers' performance based on both qualitative and quantitative information, emphasizes broad career paths, exercises control through informal, implicit mechanisms, requires that decision making occur in groups and be based on full information sharing and consensus, expects individuals to take responsibility for decisions, and emphasizes concern for people.

Through his analysis, Ouchi developed a list of seven points on which these three types of firms can be compared. Ouchi argued that the cultures of typical Japanese firms and U.S. Type Z firms are very different from those of typical U.S. firms and that these differences explain the success of many Japanese firms and U.S. Type Z firms at the expense of the latter. The seven points of comparison developed by Ouchi are presented in Table 20.4.

Commitment to Employees According to Ouchi, typical Japanese and Type Z U.S. firms share the cultural value of trying to keep employees. Thus, both types of firms lay off employees only as a last resort. In Japan, the value of "keeping employees on" often takes the form of lifetime employment. A person who begins working at some Japanese firms has a virtual guarantee that she or he will never be fired. In U.S. Type Z companies, this cultural value is manifested in a commitment to what Ouchi called "long-term employment." Under Japanese lifetime employment, employees usually cannot be fired. Under U.S. long-term employment, workers and managers can be fired, but only if they are not performing acceptably.

Ouchi suggested that typical U.S. firms do not have the same cultural commitment to employees as Japanese firms and U.S. Type Z firms. For this reason, typical U.S. firms have an expectation of short-term employment for their workers and managers. In reality, U.S. workers and managers spend their entire careers in a relatively small number of companies. Still, the cultural expectation exists that if there were a serious downturn in a firm's fortunes, workers and maybe even managers would be let go.[33]

Evaluation Ouchi observed that in Japanese and U.S. Type Z companies, appropriate evaluation of workers and managers is thought to take a very long time—up to ten years—and requires the use of qualitative, as well as quantitative, information about performance. For this reason, promotion in these firms is relatively slow, and promotion decisions are made only after interviews with many people who have had contact with the person being evaluated.

In typical U.S. firms, on the other hand, the cultural value concerning evaluation suggests that evaluation can and should be done rapidly and should emphasize quantitative measures of performance. This value tends to encourage short-term thinking among workers and managers.

---

32. Ouchi, *Theory Z.*

33. "The Next Act at Chrysler," *Business Week,* November 3, 1986, pp. 66–69.

TABLE 20.4
The Ouchi Framework

Cultural Value	Expression in Japanese Companies	Expression in Type Z American Companies	Expression in Typical U.S. Companies
Commitment to employees	Lifetime employment	Long-term employment	Short-term employment
Evaluation	Slow and qualitative	Slow and qualitative	Fast and quantitative
Careers	Very broad	Moderately broad	Narrow
Control	Implicit and informal	Implicit and informal	Explicit and formal
Decision making	Group and consensus	Group and consensus	Individual
Responsibility	Group	Individual	Individual
Concern for people	Wholistic	Wholistic	Narrow

Careers Ouchi next observed that the careers most valued in Japanese and Type Z U.S. firms span multiple functions. In Japan this value has led to very broad career paths, which may lead to experience in six or seven distinct business functions. The career paths in Type Z U.S. firms are somewhat narrower.

However, the career path valued in typical U.S. firms is considerably narrower. Ouchi's research indicated that most U.S. managers perform only one or two different business functions in their careers. This narrow career path reflects, according to Ouchi, the value of specialization that is part of so many U.S. firms.

Control All organizations must exert some level of control. (In terms of Parsons' model, they must integrate their parts.) Without control, it is impossible to achieve coordinated action. Thus, it is not surprising that firms in the United States and Japan have developed cultural values related to organizational control and how to manage it.

Most Japanese and Type Z U.S. firms assume control will be exercised through informal, implicit mechanisms. One of the most powerful of these mechanisms is the organization's culture. Managers expect to obtain guidance in what actions to take from the cultures of their firms. Stories, for example, communicate important information about what upper-level managers expect lower-level managers to do.

In contrast, typical U.S. firms expect that guidance will come not from informal and implicit cultural values but through explicit directions in the form of job descriptions, delineation of authority, and various rules and procedures. Stories about control may exist in these firms, but they typically communicate the message that to stay out of trouble it is best to follow explicit, written guidelines.

Decision Making Japanese and Type Z U.S. firms hold the strong cultural expectation that decision making will occur in groups and be based on principles of full information sharing and consensus. In most typical U.S. firms, individual decision making is considered appropriate. Managers and workers given the responsibility of making decisions are not expected—and certainly not required—to obtain information or suggestions from others in the firm.

Responsibility Closely linked with Ouchi's discussion of group versus individual decision making is his discussion of responsibility. Here, however, the parallels between Japanese firms and Type Z U.S. firms break down. Ouchi showed that in Japan, strong cultural norms support collective responsibility; that is, the group as a whole, rather than a single person, is held responsible for decisions made by the group. In both Type Z U.S. firms and typical U.S. firms, individuals expect to take responsibility for decisions.

Linking individual responsibility with individual decision making, as typical U.S. firms do, seems logically consistent. After all, if individuals are expected to make decisions, it makes sense that they should be held responsible for the decisions they make. Similarly, group decision making and group responsibility, the situation in Japanese firms, seem to go together. But how do Type Z U.S. firms combine the cultural values of group decision making and individual responsibility?

Ouchi suggested that the answer to this question depends on a cultural value we already discussed: slow and qualitative evaluation. The first time a manager uses a group to make a decision, it is not possible to tell whether the outcomes associated with that decision resulted from the manager's influence or the quality of the group. However, if a manager works with many groups over time, and if these groups consistently generate positive results for the organization, it is likely that the manager is skilled at getting the most out of groups. This manager can be held responsible for the outcomes of group decision-making processes. Similarly, managers who consistently fail to work effectively with the groups assigned

This committee at Corning, Inc. is discussing diversity and minority issues at the $3 billion company. All managers and salaried workers attend seminars to build sensitivity and support for women and black coworkers. Workforce diversity has become part of the culture at Corning, partly due to the personal emphasis of its CEO, James R. Houghton, and two high-level teams that have focussed on the complex issues of diversity.

TABLE 20.5
The Peters and Waterman Framework

Attributes of an Excellent Firm	
1. Bias for action	5. Hands-on management
2. Stay close to the customer	6. Stick to the knitting
3. Encourage autonomy and entrepreneurship	7. Simple form, lean staff
4. Encourage productivity through people	8. Simultaneously loosely and tightly organized

to them can be held responsible for the lack of results from the group decision-making process.

Ouchi suggested that the value of individual responsibility in U.S. Type Z firms reflects very strong cultural norms of individuality and individual responsibility in American society as a whole. As suggested by Parsons' notion of legitimacy, organization cultures do not exist in isolation from broader cultural influences. Societal expectations and values can strongly influence the values in an organization's culture.

Concern for People The last cultural value examined by Ouchi deals with a concern for people. Not surprisingly, in Japanese firms and Type Z firms, the cultural value that dominates is a wholistic concern for workers and managers. Wholistic concern extends beyond concern for a person simply as a worker or manager to concern with that person's home life, hobbies, personal beliefs, hopes, fears, and aspirations. In typical U.S. firms, the concern for people is a narrow one that focuses on the workplace.

Theory Z and Performance Ouchi argued that the cultures of Japanese and Type Z firms help them outperform typical U.S. firms. Toyota is now trying to import the management style and culture that have succeeded in Japan into its new manufacturing facilities in North America. The reasons for Toyota's success often have been attributed to the ability of Japanese and Type Z firms to systematically invest in their employees and in their operations over long periods of time and thus to obtain steady and significant improvements in long-term performance.

The Peters and Waterman Approach

Tom Peters and Robert Waterman, in their best seller *In Search of Excellence,* focused even more explicitly than Ouchi on the relationship between organization culture and performance. Peters and Waterman chose a sample of highly successful U.S. firms and sought to describe the management practices that led to their success.[34] Their analysis rapidly turned to the cultural values that led to successful management practices. These "excellent" values are listed in Table 20.5.

34. Peters and Waterman, *In Search of Excellence.*

Employees at USAA, a major insurance and investment company, are part of the company's efforts to provide better customer service. Teams of USAA employees made up of sales, telephone, and office personnel are charged with the responsibility of meeting each customer's needs.

Bias for Action According to Peters and Waterman, successful firms have a bias for action. Managers in these firms are expected to make decisions even if all the facts are not "in." Peters and Waterman argued that for many important decisions, all the facts will never "be in." Delaying decision making in these situations is the same as never making a decision. Meanwhile, other firms probably will have captured whatever business initiative existed. On average, according to Peters and Waterman, organizations with cultural values that include a bias for action outperform firms without such values.

Stay Close to the Customer Peters and Waterman believe that firms whose organization cultures value customers over everything else will out-perform firms without this value. According to these authors, the customer provides a source of information about current products, a source of ideas about future products, the ultimate source of a firm's current financial performance, and the source of future performance. Focusing on the customer, meeting the customer's needs, pampering the customer when necessary are all actions that lead to superior performance. *International Perspective* describes how Scandanavian Airlines System has focused its culture on customer service.

Peters and Waterman also suggest that firms that adhere to keeping close to the customer do so not because the sales manager or the marketing handbook says it is a good idea. For true customer-satisfying companies, customer satisfaction lies at the core of the organization culture.

Autonomy and Entrepreneurship Peters and Waterman maintained that successful firms fight the lack of innovation and the bureaucracy usually associated

INTERNATIONAL PERSPECTIVE

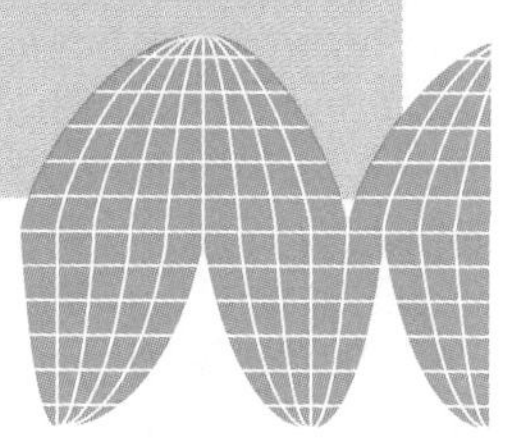

SAS Changes Its Culture

Sweden-based Scandinavian Airlines System had been losing money for years. Jointly owned by the governments of Sweden, Denmark, and Norway, SAS had lost money in 1978 and 1979 when Jan Carlzon took over as president in 1980. Carlzon decided to reposition SAS as the airline for business travelers who are less sensitive to price but demand excellent service. The new SAS business-class service, called EuroClass, provided larger, leather-covered seats, more leg room, and other in-flight amenities.

Carlzon's most difficult task was to persuade every SAS employee that customer service was the top priority. He wanted to develop intense brand loyalty in customers by providing the best service in the industry at every point of contact with the customer: at check-in, boarding, in-flight, and on the ground. He expected that employees would be able to handle any and all problems at the point of customer contact and not have to seek upper management approval to provide something customers would appreciate. The process of preaching the new way of doing things to employees took several months.

Eventually, Carlzon's efforts paid off. SAS reported revenues of $4.6 billion and operating income of $193 million in 1989, a year in which TWA, Pan Am, and Alitalia lost money and Eastern stopped flying due to bankruptcy. Furthermore, in 1988 SAS had increased its ownership of troubled Continental Airlines to 16.8 percent and forced the departure of its tyrannical leader, Frank Lorenzo. Continental already had declared bankruptcy once and, due to losses reaching $522.8 million in the first nine months of 1989, was well on the way to doing it again. In October 1990, Continental overspent its fuel budget by $70 million, due largely to the Persian Gulf crisis.

Carlzon's current challenge is to turn Continental around and install the new culture he created at SAS. He has created an intensive two-day training program for all Continental employees at their home base in Houston. Thousands of Continental employees have gone through the "attitude adjustment" program, and enthusiasm seems to be on the increase. It will be interesting to see if the special class of service for which SAS has become known will show up on Continental's mostly domestic flights.

SOURCES: Kenneth Labich, "An Airline That Soars on Service," *Fortune,* December 31, 1990, pp. 94–96; "Why Did Lorenzo Bail Out?" *Forbes,* September 3, 1990, pp. 14–15; "Gone But Not Forgotten," *Time,* August 20, 1990, p. 48.

with large size. They do this by breaking the company into small, more manageable pieces and then encouraging independent, creative, even risk-taking activity within these smaller business segments. Stories often exist in these organizations about the junior engineer who, by taking a risk, is able to influence major product decisions or of the junior manager, dissatisfied with the slow pace of a product's development, who implements a new and highly successful marketing plan. These kinds of actions are not merely encouraged; they are the "stuff of organizational legends."

Productivity through People Like Ouchi, Peters and Waterman believe successful firms recognize that their most important assets are their people—both workers and managers—and that the organization's purpose is to let its people flourish. Again, this commitment to people is not simply written on plaques or announced in company magazines. Rather, it is a basic value of the organization culture—a belief that treating people with respect and dignity is not only appropriate but essential to success.

Hands-on Management Peters and Waterman noted the tendency in many large companies for senior managers to lose touch with the basic businesses they are in. For example, presidents of large electronics firms end up knowing less about electronics than they do about office politics, and presidents of large automobile companies inevitably learn less about cars than about finance.

Peters and Waterman noted that to counter this tendency, the firms they studied insisted that their senior managers stay in touch with the firms' essential business. It is an expectation, reflecting a deeply embedded cultural norm, that managers should manage not from behind the closed doors of their offices but by "wandering around" the plant, the design facility, the research and development department, and so on.

- "Stick to the knitting" is a popular management practice in which management chooses not to diversify into many unrelated businesses.

Stick to the Knitting Another cultural value characteristic of excellent firms is their reluctance to engage in business outside their expertise. These firms reject the concept of diversification, the practice of buying and operating businesses in unrelated industries. If managers in such a company suggest that the firm begin operations in an unrelated business, the response to their efforts is not likely to be "where are the figures that justify this business move?" Rather, others in the firm are likely to simply shake their heads and say, "That's not they way we do business around here."

Simple Form, Lean Staff According to Peters and Waterman, successful firms tend to have few administrative layers and relatively small corporate staff groups. In many organizations, managers measure their status, prestige, and importance by the number of people who report to them. In excellently managed companies, however, importance is measured not by the number of people who report to a manager but by the manager's impact on the organization's performance. The cultural values in these firms tell managers that their staffs' performance rather than their size is important.

Simultaneously Loosely and Tightly Organized The final attribute of organization culture identified by Peters and Waterman appears contradictory. How can a firm be simultaneously loosely organized and tightly organized? The resolution of this apparent paradox is found in the firms' values. The firms are tightly organized because all their members understand and believe in the firms' values. This common cultural bond makes a strong glue that holds the firms together. At the same time, however, the firms are loosely organized because they tend to have less administrative overhead, fewer staff members, and fewer rules and regulations. All this, Peters and Waterman believe, encourages innovation and risk taking.

This loose structure is possible only because of the common values held by people in the firm. When these people must make decisions, they can evaluate their options in terms of the organization's underlying values—whether the options are consistent with a bias for action, service to the customer, and so on. By referring to commonly held values, individuals often can make their own decisions about what actions to take. In this sense, the tight structure of common cultural values makes the loose structure of fewer administrative controls possible.

Managing Organization Culture

The work of Ouchi, Peters and Waterman, and many others demonstrates two important facts. First, organization cultures differ among firms; second, these different organization cultures can affect a firm's performance. Based on these observations, managers in the early 1980s began to be concerned about how to best manage the cultures of their organizations. Three elements of managing organization culture—taking advantage of the existing culture, teaching organization culture, and changing organization culture—are shown in Figure 20.2.

Taking Advantage of the Existing Culture

Most managers are not in a position to create an organization culture; rather, they work in an organization that already has cultural values. For these managers, the central issue in managing culture is how best to use the cultural system that already exists.

To take full advantage of an existing cultural system, managers must first be fully aware of what values the culture includes and what behaviors or actions those values support. Becoming fully aware of an organization's values usually

FIGURE 20.2
Three Elements of Managing Organization Culture

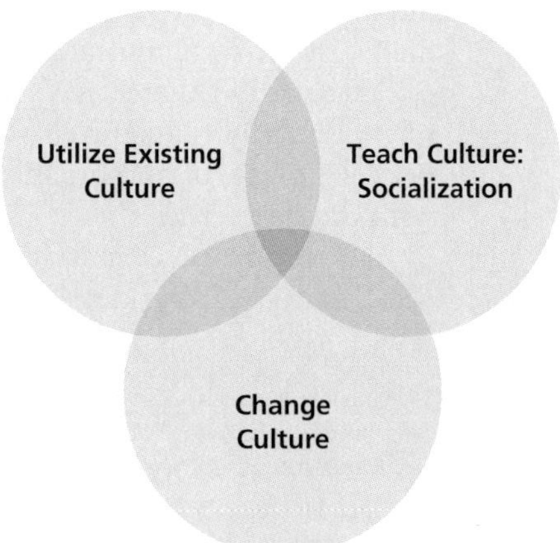

is not easy, however. It involves more than reading a pamphlet about what the company believes in. It requires that managers develop a deep understanding of how organizational values operate in the firm—an understanding that usually comes only through experience.

Understanding, once achieved, can be used to evaluate the performances of others in the firm. Articulating organizational values can be useful in managing others' behavior. For example, suppose a subordinate in a firm with a strong cultural value of "sticking to its knitting" develops a business strategy that involves moving into a new industry. Rather than attempting to argue that this business strategy is economically flawed or conceptually weak, the manager who understands the corporate culture can point to this organizational value: "In this firm, we believe in sticking to our knitting."

Senior managers who understand their organization's culture can communicate that understanding to lower-level individuals. Over time, as these lower-level managers begin to understand and accept the firm's culture, they will require less direct supervision. Their understanding of corporate values will guide their decision making.

Teaching the Organization Culture: Socialization

Socialization is the process through which individuals become social beings.[35] As studied by psychologists, it is the process through which children learn to be adults in a society—the way they learn what is acceptable and polite behavior and what is not, the way they learn to communicate, the way they learn to interact with others, and so on. In complex societies, the socialization process may take many years.

■ **Organizational socialization** is the process through which employees learn about the firm's culture and pass their knowledge and understanding on to others.

Organizational socialization is the process through which employees learn about their firm's culture and pass their knowledge and understanding on to others. Just as people are socialized into societies, so are they socialized into organizations; that is, they come to know over time what is acceptable in the organization and what is not, how to communicate their feelings, and how to interact with others. They learn through observation and through efforts by managers to communicate this information to them. Research into the process of socialization indicates that for many employees, socialization programs do not necessarily change their values but make them more aware of the differences between personal and organization values and help them develop ways to cope with the differences.[36]

A variety of organizational mechanisms have been shown to affect the socialization of workers in organizations.[37] Most important are the examples

35. Socialization also has been defined as "the process by which culture is transmitted from one generation to the next." See J. W. M. Whiting, "Socialization: Anthropological Aspects," in D. Sils, ed., *International Encyclopedia of the Social Sciences,* vol. 14 (New York: Free Press, 1968), p. 545.

36. J. E. Hebden. "Adopting an Organization's Culture: The Socialization of Graduate Trainees," *Organizational Dynamics,* Summer 1986, pp. 54–72.

37. Barney, "Organizational Culture."

that people new to a firm see in the behavior of experienced people. Through example, new employees develop a repertoire of stories they can use to guide their actions. When a decision needs to be made, new employees can ask, "What would my boss do in this situation?" This is not to suggest that formal training, corporate pamphlets, and corporate statements about organization culture are unimportant in the socialization process. However, these factors tend to support the socialization process based on people closely observing the actions of others.

In some organizations, the culture written down in pamphlets and presented in formal training sessions conflicts with the values of the organization as they are expressed in the actions of its people. For example, a firm may say that employees are its most important asset but may treat employees badly. In this setting, new employees quickly learn that the rhetoric of the pamphlets and formal training sessions has little to do with the reality of the organization culture. Employees who are socialized into this system usually come to accept the actual cultural values rather than those formally espoused.

The stories of how Teresa Fischette, a ticket agent for Continental Airlines who fought a company policy, will be told for years as a story of how one woman took on the company and won. Fischette was fired on May 3, 1991 for not wearing makeup—a violation of the company's new appearance code—and was reinstated on May 15 after national attention was focused on her dismissal.

Changing the Organization Culture

Much of our discussion to this point has assumed that an organization's culture enhances its performance. When this is the case, learning what an organization's cultural values are and using those values to help socialize new workers and managers is very important, for such actions help the organization succeed. However, as Ouchi's and Peters and Waterman's research indicates, not all firms have cultural values that are consistent with high performance. Ouchi found that Japanese firms and U.S. Type Z companies have performance-enhancing values, whereas typical U.S. firms have performance-reducing values. Peters and Waterman identified performance-enhancing values associated with successful companies. By implication, some firms not included in Peters and Waterman's study must have had performance-reducing values. What should a manager who works in a company with performance-reducing values do?

The answer to this question is, of course, that top managers in such firms should try to change their organizations' cultures. However, this is a difficult thing to do.[38] For all the reasons that culture is a powerful influence on behavior—the fact that it embodies the basic values in the firm, is often taken for granted, and typically is communicated most effectively through stories or other symbols—it resists change. When managers attempt to change a culture, they are attempting to change people's basic assumptions about what is and what is not appropriate behavior in the organization. *The Ethical Dilemma* describes how Corning Inc. is having some success in changing its values and culture.

Despite these difficulties, some organizations have changed their cultures from performance-reducing to performance-enhancing.[39] This change process

38. Ibid.

39. Main, "Westinghouse's Cultural Revolution"; and "Corporate Culture: The Hard to Change Values That Spell Success or Failure."

THE ETHICAL DILEMMA

Corning Changes Its Culture on Job Bias

For years, Corning Inc. hired women and blacks in large numbers as mandated by the federal government and advocacy groups. A world leader in specialty-glass manufacturing, clinical and environmental testing, and life science research, Corning noted that after several years minority recruits were no longer around to be promoted into middle and upper management ranks. As late as 1987, out of the 150 top managers there were only 4 white women and 1 black man. Across the United States, fewer than 1 percent of top executive positions were held by women or minority members.

Since 1987, however, things have changed at Corning. Under CEO James R. Houghton, the company is making a concerted effort to integrate minorities and women in all aspects of the company, from initial hiring to climbing the corporate ladder—and making it all the way to the top. Corning is now in the midst of an ambitious commitment to "cultural engineering" through intensive training programs, hiring and mentoring programs, and evaluating, promoting, and rewarding all employees on the basis of their commitment and involvement in furthering the careers of blacks and women. Specifically, raises and bonuses for executives, mostly white males, depend on recruiting blacks and women and on their success in training and promoting them. The training programs include two-day courses in sexism and racism and are required for thousands of managers and professional employees.

Houghton contends that companies of the future will be unable to prosper in a diverse, multicultural world unless they reflect that diversity. He is committing Corning to building a multicultural work force and using the different talents and abilities of its employees to position the company for future success.

So far, Houghton's approach appears promising. Of the salaried employees Corning hired from 1987 to 1990, 52 percent were women and 16 percent were blacks. The top 150 positions now include 7 women and 5 blacks. Of the 5,365 salaried personnel, 33.6 percent are women and 5.5 percent are blacks. However, the CEO and succeeding seven positions are still held by white males.

A special problem concerns whether the women and minorities are receiving raises, promotions, and privileged treatment because of their special classification at the expense of equally qualified white males. Are approximately three thousand white males getting passed over for advancement because of their race or sex? Is there anything this group can do to avoid paying for the discriminatory practices of previous generations?

SOURCES: Gary Hoover, Alta Campbell, and Patrick J. Spain, eds., *Hoover's Handbook: Profiles of over 500 Major Corporations* (Austin, Tex.: The Reference Press, 1990), p. 189; "A Company Recasts Itself to Erase Years of Job Bias," *The New York Times,* October 4, 1990, pp. A1, C21; Kenneth Labich, "Employees Must Reflect the Diverse World," *Fortune,* March 26, 1990, p. 56.

will be described in more detail in Chapter 21. Here we will briefly summarize several elements of the cultural change process.

Managing Symbols Research suggests that organization culture is understood and communicated through the use of stories and other symbolic media. If this is correct, managers interested in changing cultures should attempt to substitute stories and myths that support new cultural values for those that support old ones. They can do so by creating situations that give rise to new stories.

Suppose an organization traditionally has held the value "employee opinions are not important." When management meets in this company, the ideas and opinions of lower-level people—when discussed at all—normally are rejected as foolish and irrelevant. The stories that support this cultural value tell about managers who tried to make a constructive point only to have that point lost in personal attacks from superiors.

An upper-level manager interested in creating a new story, one that shows lower-level managers that their ideas are important and valuable, might ask a subordinate to prepare to lead a discussion in a meeting and follow through by asking the subordinate to take the lead when the topic arises. The subordinate's success in the meeting will become a new story, one that may displace some of the many stories suggesting that the opinions of lower-level managers do not matter.

The Difficulty of Change Changing a firm's culture is a long and difficult process. A primary problem is that upper-level managers, no matter how dedicated they are to implementing some new cultural value, may sometimes inadvertently revert to old patterns of behavior. This happens, for example, when a manager dedicated to implementing the value that lower-level employees' ideas are important vehemently attacks a subordinate's ideas.

This mistake generates a story that supports old values and beliefs. After such an incident, lower-level managers believe that the boss may say she or he wants their input and ideas, but nothing could be further from the truth. No matter what the boss says or how consistent his or her behavior, some credibility has been lost, and cultural change has been made more difficult.

The Stability of Change The process of changing a firm's culture starts with a need for change and moves through a transition period wherein efforts are made to adopt new values and beliefs. In the long run, a firm that successfully changes its culture will find that the new values and beliefs are just as stable and influential as the old ones. Value systems tend to be self-reinforcing. Once they are in place, changing them requires an enormous amount of effort.[40] Thus, if a firm can change its culture from performance reducing to performance enhancing, it is likely that new values will remain in place for a long time.

Summary of Key Points

- Organization culture has become one of the most discussed subjects in the field of organizational behavior. It burst on the scene in the 1980s with books by Ouchi, Peters and Waterman, and others. Interest has not been restricted to academics, however. Practicing managers also are interested in organization culture, especially as it relates to performance.

40. Barney, "Organizational Culture."

- There is relatively little agreement about how to define organization culture. A comparison of several important definitions suggests that most have three things in common: They define culture in terms of the values that individuals in organizations use to prescribe appropriate behavior; they assume these values are usually taken for granted; and they emphasize the stories and other symbolic means through which the values typically are communicated.
- Current research on organization culture reflects various research traditions. The most important contributions have come from anthropology and sociology. Anthropologists have tended to focus on the organization cultures of one or two firms and have used thick description to help outsiders understand organization culture from the "natives' point of view." Sociologists typically have used survey methods to study the organization cultures of larger numbers of firms. Two other influences on current work in organization culture are social psychology, with its emphasis on the manipulation of symbols in organizations, and economics. The economics approach sees culture both as a tool used to manage and as a determinant of performance.
- Although no single framework for describing organization culture has emerged, several have been suggested. One of the earliest, and most abstract, is Parsons' AGIL model. More recent efforts in this area have been Ouchi's comparison of U.S. and Japanese firms and Peters and Waterman's description of successful firms in the United States. Ouchi and Peters and Waterman suggested several important dimensions along which organizational values vary, including treatment of employees, definitions of appropriate means for decision making, and assignment of responsibility for the results of decision making.
- Managing the organization culture requires attention to three factors. First, managers can take advantage of cultural values that already exist and use their knowledge to help subordinates understand them. Second, employees need to be properly socialized, or trained, in the cultural values of the organization, either through formal training or by experiencing and observing actions of higher-level managers. Third, managers can change the culture of the organization through managing the symbols, dealing with the extreme difficulties of such a change, and relying on the permanence of the new organization culture once the change has been implemented.

Discussion Questions

1. A sociologist or anthropologist might suggest that the culture in U.S. firms simply reflects the dominant culture in the society as a whole. Therefore, to change the organization culture of a company, one must first deal with the inherent values and beliefs of the society. How would you respond to this claim?
2. Psychology has been defined as the study of individual behavior. More specifically, organizational psychology is the study of individual behavior in organizations. Many of the theories described in the early chapters of this book are based in organizational psychology. Why was this field not iden-

tified as a contributor to the study of organization culture along with anthropology, sociology, social psychology, and economics?

3. Describe the culture of an organization with which you are familiar. It might be one in which you currently work, one in which you have worked, or one in which a friend or family member works. What values, beliefs, stories, and symbols are significant to employees of the organization?
4. Discuss the similarities and differences among the organization culture approaches of Parsons, Ouchi, and Peters and Waterman.
5. Describe how symbols and stories are used in organizations to communicate values and beliefs. Give some examples of how symbols and stories have been used in organizations with which you are familiar.
6. What is the role of leadership (discussed in Chapter 9) in developing, maintaining, and changing organization culture?
7. Review the characteristics of organization structure described in earlier chapters, and compare them with the elements of culture described by Ouchi and Peters and Waterman. Describe the similarities and differences, and explain how some characteristics of one may be related to characteristics of the other.
8. Discuss the role of organization rewards in developing, maintaining, and changing the organization culture.

CASE 20.1

Tandem's Most Successful Export: Its Culture

California-based Tandem Computers Inc. is a favorite of both Wall Street investors and management experts. Chief executive officer Jimmy Treybig founded the company in 1974 after realizing that his former employer, Hewlett-Packard Co., was unresponsive to customer demand for a computer that would not break down. Tandem made its reputation by building NonStop computer systems, which contain identical processors working in parallel so that if one breaks down, another will take over its functions. Tandem claims that none of its machines have ever been returned, and its computers handle some of the busiest, most important data processing jobs in the world. The NonStop system that links the New York and American stock exchanges, for instance, handles up to 450 million transactions a day, and even during the stock market crash of October 1987 it remained in operation. Based on such successes, Tandem's recent financial growth has been impressive: 1987 was its first billion-dollar year, with net income two-thirds higher than in 1986.

Equally famous is Tandem's organization culture, which has been described as "Californiaesque." In the company's early years, Treybig avoided making organizational charts and holding committee meetings. The company had no punch clocks, and Treybig tried to maintain a personal relationship with all his employees. Tandem's Friday afternoon beer blasts became legendary. However, a major slump in the mid-1980s forced some changes in the company's culture. Treybig had to become, in his words, a manager, not a cheerleader. Yet Tandem has preserved most of what was unique and effective about its organization culture, and it has been exporting that culture far from Silicon Valley.

Europe is now the fastest-growing computer market, and overseas customers are increasingly demanding that computer companies provide worldwide support and manufacturing. Tandem now gets over 40 percent of its revenues from abroad, and some industry analysts are surprised to find that its employees elsewhere in the world develop the same loyalty to the company as their American counterparts do.

In part to introduce Tandem's overseas employees to its organization culture, the company produced an employee handbook known simply as "The Book," noting in the preface that putting the Tandem culture into print "fills most of us with horror." The culture outlined in "The Book," including the beer blasts, seems as popular in London as in Cupertino. Perhaps more important, the philosophy the Friday parties are designed to encourage—open communication across all boundaries of rank—continues to be crucial to Tandem's operations.

At home, Treybig makes his appointment calendar available to all employees. Around the world, virtually all Tandem workers have electronic mail terminals that give them instant access to anyone in the company. A secretary who is upset about pay increases can send an angry message directly to Treybig, as happened in 1985 when the company was in financial trouble. The company also uses the electronic mail system to conduct employee opinion surveys every six months. Company branches use satellite dishes to pick up televised material broadcast from Tandem's own facilities, and teleconferencing brings company leaders virtually face to face with employees in Europe. This emphasis on open communication has allowed the company to integrate its worldwide operations to a remarkable degree.

Tandem also allows employees six consecutive weeks of paid time off for every four years of continuous service. Public service tasks earn employees extra days off. These sabbaticals allow employees the opportunity to do whatever they wish, from hiking in the Himalayas to participating in an international development project in Africa. Sabbaticals help prevent the job stress buildup, or burnout, that can result from the pressure-packed, fast-paced computer business. Employees have reported feeling refreshed and ready to tackle their work. Further, training their replacements helps employees realize that they are never indispensable and gain an appreciation of the importance of each team member to a team. Rather than protect his or her job, employees turn their attention to the good of the company.

A sense that the boss is listening, even though he is thousands of miles away, combined with an employee stock ownership plan and constant after-hours gatherings and volunteer work, creates unusually high employee morale. Even in the company's bad years, employee turnover was lower than the industry average, and in good years it was close to half that average. Tandem's story demonstrates that a company really can live up to the employee-centered goals to which many businesses give lip service.

Case Questions

1. How do you think Peters and Waterman would assess the organization culture at Tandem?

2. What are the disadvantages of having such open organization communication?

SOURCES: Dee DiPietro, "Fresh Ways to Make Jobs Richer," *Design News,* June 5, 1989, pp. 140–144; Jagannath Dubashi, "Instant Gratification," *Financial World,* January 26, 1988, pp. 42–43; Leigh Bruce, "Exporting Tandem's Californiaesque Corporate Culture," *International Management,* July-August 1987, p. 35; Anne Ferguson, "Tandem on Target," *Management Today,* June 1987, p. 81; Brian O'Reilly, "How Jimmy Treybig Turned Tough," *Fortune,* May 25, 1987, p. 102–104.

CASE 20.2

Surviving Plant World's Hard Times

In ten years, Plant World had grown from a one-person venture to the largest nursery and landscaping business in its area. Its founder, Myta Ong, combined a lifelong interest in plants with a botany degree to provide a unique customer service. Ong had managed the company's growth so that even with twenty full-time employees working in six to eight crews, the organization culture was still as open, friendly, and personal as it had been when her only "employees" were friends who would volunteer to help her move a heavy tree.

To maintain that atmosphere, Ong increasingly involved herself with people and less with plants as the company grew. With hundreds of customers and scores of jobs at any one time, she could no longer say without hesitation whether she had a dozen arborvitae bushes in stock or when Mrs. Carnack's estate would need a new load of bark mulch. But she knew when Rose had been up all night with her baby, when Gary was likely to be late because he had driven to see his sick father over the weekend, and how to deal with Ellen when she was depressed because of her boyfriend's behavior. She kept track of the birthdays of every employee and even those of their children. She was up every morning by 5:30, arranging schedules so that John could get his son out of day care at 4:00 or Martina could be back in town for her afternoon equivalency classes.

All this attention to employees may have led Ong to make a single bad business decision that almost destroyed the company. She provided extensive landscaping to a new mall on credit, and when the mall never opened and its owners went bankrupt, Plant World found itself in deep trouble. The company had virtually no cash and had to pay off the bills for the mall plants, most of which were not even salvageable.

One Friday, Ong called a meeting with her employees and leveled with them: Either they would not get paid for a month or Plant World would fold. The news hit the employees hard. Many counted on the Friday paycheck to buy groceries for the week. The local unemployment rate was low, however, and they knew they could find other jobs.

But as they looked around, they wondered whether they could ever find this kind of job. Sure, the pay was not the greatest, but the tears in the eyes of some were not because of pay or personal hardship; they were for Ong, her dream, and her difficulties. They never thought of her as the boss or called her anything but "Myta." And leaving the group would not be just a matter of saying goodbye to fellow employees. If Bernice left, the company softball team would lose its best pitcher, and the Sunday game was the height of everyone's week. Where else would they find people who spent much of the weekend working on the best puns with which to assail one another on Monday morning? At how many offices would everyone show up twenty minutes before starting time just to catch up with friends on other crews? What other boss would really understand when you simply said, "I don't have a doctor's appointment, I just need the afternoon off"?

Ong gave her employees the weekend to think over their decision: whether to take their pay and look for another job or to dig into their savings and go on working. Knowing it would be hard for them to quit, she told them they did not have to face her on Monday; if they did not show up, she would send them their checks. But when she arrived at 7:40 Monday morning, she found the entire group already there, ready to work even harder to pull the company through. They were even trying to top one another with puns about being "mall-contents."

Case Questions

1. How would you describe the organization culture at Plant World?
2. How large can such a company get before it needs to change its culture and structure?

EXPERIENTIAL EXERCISE

Purpose: This exercise will help you appreciate the fascination as well as the difficulty of examining culture in organizations.

Format: The class will divide into groups of four to six. Each group will analyze the organization culture of a college class. Students in most classes that use this book will have taken many courses at the college they attend and therefore should have several classes in common.

Procedure: The class is divided into groups of four to six on the basis of classes the students have had in common.

1. Each group should first decide which class it will analyze. Each person in the group must have attended the class.
2. Each group should list the cultural factors to be discussed. Items to be covered should include
   a. Stories about the professor
   b. Stories about the exams
   c. Stories about the grading
   d. Stories about other students
   e. The use of symbols that indicate the values of the students
   f. The use of symbols that indicate the values of the instructor
   g. Other characteristics of the class as suggested by the frameworks of Ouchi and Peters and Waterman.

3. Students should carefully analyze the stories and symbols to discover their underlying meanings. They should seek stories from other members of the group to ensure that all aspects of the class culture are covered. Students should take notes as these items are discussed.
4. After twenty to thirty minutes of work in groups, the instructor will reconvene the entire class and ask each group to share its analysis with the rest of the class.

Follow-up Questions

1. What was the most difficult part of this exercise? Did other groups experience the same difficulty?
2. How did your group overcome this difficulty? How did other groups overcome it?
3. Do you believe your group's analysis accurately describes the culture of the class you selected? Could other students who analyzed the culture of the same class come up with a very different result? How could that happen?
4. If the instructor wanted to try to change the culture in the class you analyzed, what steps would you recommend that he or she take?

PART VI

Integrating Individuals, Groups, and Organizations

CONTENTS

Chapter 21 Organization Change and Development

Chapter 22 International Aspects of Organizations

Chapter 23 Career Dynamics

CHAPTER OUTLINE

Forces for Change

People

Technology

Information Processing and Communication

Competition

Resistance to Change

Organizational Sources of Resistance

Individual Sources of Resistance

Managing Resistance

Processes for Planned Organization Change

Process Models

Transition Management

Integrated Process of Organization Change

Organization Development

Definition of Organization Development

Systemwide Organization Development

Task-Technological Change

Group and Individual Change

Managing Organization Development

Major Problems in Organization Development Efforts

Keys to Successful Organization Development

21

Organization Change and Development

Chapter Objectives

After studying this chapter, you should be able to:

Summarize the dominant forces for change in organizations.

Explain resistance to change.

Describe the process of planned organization change.

Discuss several approaches to organization development.

Identify five keys to successful organization development.

Aluminum Co. of America (Alcoa) is making a dramatic turnaround by pushing safety and sticking to its basic business: aluminum. But how is this a major turnaround when Alcoa has been the number one name in aluminum for more than one hundred years? The significance is that in 1983, under its previous CEO, Charles W. Parry, Alcoa embarked on a substantial effort to diversify into businesses other than aluminum. Parry's goal was for 50 percent of Alcoa's revenues to come from nonaluminum businesses by 1995. His efforts did not succeed, and, after a boardroom coup in 1988, Paul. H. O'Neill became CEO.

Rather than buy other companies in aerospace, trucking, or heavy-equipment manufacturing, O'Neill focused the company on its core aluminum businesses by stressing safety and teamwork. Alcoa had always had the best safety record in the industry, but O'Neill told his safety director that the only acceptable goal was zero on-the-job injuries. Instead of pushing cost-cutting and efficiency measures to squeeze more out of less, O'Neill introduced a host of workplace improvements. These measures translated into improvements in quality and productivity that, coupled with modernization efforts, increased capacity by 50 percent. The company reported combined 1988 and 1989 profits that were more than double the combined total for the previous years. Back to basics obviously was a major change for Alcoa.[1]

Companies such as Alcoa are constantly faced with pressures to make changes. Forecasts of changing economic conditions, consumer purchasing patterns, technological and scientific factors, and foreign competition force top management to evaluate their organization and consider significant changes. Alcoa decided to diversify its interests in 1983 and then switched its focus back to aluminum in 1988.

This chapter presents a view of change in organizations by first examining the forces for change and then discussing the resistance to change that usually occurs. Next, we present our approach to planned organization change. Then we discuss the important topic of organization development and the management of organization development efforts in organizations.

1. Thomas A. Stewart, "A New Way to Wake Up a Giant," *Fortune,* October 22, 1990, pp. 90–103; "Has Alcoa Found a Way to Foil the Aluminum Cycle?" *Business Week,* January 8, 1990, p. 36; Lad Kuzela, "Here Comes the Automated Manager," *Industry Week,* November 20, 1989, p. 45; "The Quiet Coup at Alcoa," *Business Week,* June 27, 1988, pp. 53–65.

TABLE 21.1
Pressures for Organization Change

Category	Examples
People	Baby boomers Senior citizens Coming generations
Technology	Manufacturing in space Robotics
Information Processing and Communication	Artificial intelligence Computer, satellite communications Videoconferencing
Competition	Worldwide markets Emerging nations

Forces for Change

- The complexity of events and the rapidity of change make it difficult to predict future sources of pressure for change.

An organization is subject to many pressures for change from a variety of sources—far too many to discuss here. Moreover, because the complexity of events and the rapidity of change are increasing, it is difficult to predict what type of pressure for change will be most significant in the next decade. It is possible, however—and important—to discuss the broad categories of pressures that probably will have major effects on organizations. The four areas in which the pressures for change appear most powerful involve people, technology, information processing and communication, and competition. Table 21.1 gives examples of each of these categories.

People

Approximately 56 million people were born between 1945 and 1960. These baby boomers differ significantly from previous generations with respect to education, expectations, and value systems.[2] As this group has aged, the median age of the U.S. population has gradually increased; recently it passed thirty-two for the first time.[3] The special characteristics of baby boomers show up in distinct purchasing patterns that affect product and service innovation, technological change, and marketing and promotional activities.[4] Employment practices, compensation systems, promotion and managerial succession systems, and the entire concept of human resource management are also affected.

Other population-related pressures for change involve the generations that

2. "Baby Boomers Push for Power," *Business Week,* July 2, 1984, pp. 52–56.
3. "Americans' Median Age Passes 32," *The Arizona Republic,* April 6, 1988, pp. A1, A5.
4. Geoffrey Colvin, "What the Baby Boomers Will Buy Next," *Fortune,* October 15, 1984, pp. 28–34.

sandwich the baby boomers: the increasing numbers of senior citizens and those born after 1960. The parents of the baby boomers are living longer, healthier lives than previous generations, and today they expect to live the "good life" that they missed when they were raising their children. The impact of the large number of senior citizens is already evident in part-time employment practices, in the marketing of everything from hamburgers to packaged tours of Asia, and in the service areas such as health care, recreation, and financial services.[5] The post-1960 generations that will be entering the job market over the next ten to fifteen years will differ from the baby boomers. But how? Will they be more or less liberal? More or less job or career oriented? More or less materialistic? More or less internationally aware? The answers to these and other questions will need to be asked—and answered—as these generations make their presence felt in organizations.

Technology

Not only is technology changing; the rate of technological change is itself increasing. In 1970, for example, all engineering students owned slide rules and used them in almost every class. By 1976, slide rules had given way to portable electronic calculators. In the mid-1980s, some universities began issuing microcomputers to entering students or assuming students already owned them. In the 1990s, a student cannot make it through the university without owning or at least having ready access to a personal computer.

Interestingly, change as it affects organizations is self-perpetuating. Advances in information technology have meant that more information is generated within organizations and it circulates more quickly. Consequently, employees are able to respond more quickly to problems, which enables the organization to respond more quickly to demands from other organizations, customers, and competitors.[6] New technology will affect organizations in ways we cannot yet predict. Artificial intelligence—computers and software programs that think and learn in much the same way as human beings do—already is assisting in geological exploration.[7] Several companies are developing systems to manufacture chemicals and exotic electronic components in space. Robotics is developing so rapidly that annual U.S. sales of robots are expected to exceed $7 billion by 1990.[8] Robot sales in other countries, most notably Japan, are expected to increase even faster. Thus, as organizations respond more quickly to changes, change occurs more rapidly, which in turn necessitates more rapid response.

---

5. "The New Old," *The Wall Street Journal,* May 11, 1987, pp. 1, 15.

6. Peter Nulty, "How Personal Computers Change Managers' Lives," *Fortune,* September 3, 1984, pp. 38–48.

7. "Artificial Language Is Here," *Business Week,* July 9, 1984, pp. 54–62.

8. Robert U. Ayres and Steven M. Miller, *Robotics: Applications and Social Implications* (Cambridge, Mass.: Ballinger, 1983).

Blockbuster Entertainment Corporation, head of more than 700 Blockbuster Video stores, estimates that by 1995 90 percent of U.S. homes will have VCRs to play rental videos. Blockbuster faces many different types of competitors: other video rental stores, network television, cable television, pay-per-view movies on cable, new technology such as laser disk video systems.

Information Processing and Communication

Advances in information processing and communication have paralleled each other. A new generation of computers, which will mark another major increase in processing power, is being designed. Satellite systems for data transmission already are in use. Today people can carry telephones in their briefcases along with their portable computers and pocket-size televisions.

In the future, people may not need offices as they work with computers and communicate through new data transmission devices. Workstations, both in and outside of offices, will be more electronic than paper and pencil. Videoconferencing now is available at competitive prices.[9]

Competition

Although competition is not a new force for change, competition today has some significant new twists. First, most markets will soon be international because of decreasing transportation and communication costs and the increasing export orientation of business. In the future, competition from the industrialized countries such as Japan and Germany will take a back seat to competition from the booming industries of developing nations. An example close to home is the maturing economy of Mexico. Developing nations may soon offer different, newer, cheaper, or higher-quality products while enjoying the benefits of low labor costs, abundant supplies of raw materials, expertise in certain areas of production, and financial protection from their governments that may not be available in the older industrialized states. Organizations that are not ready for these new sources of competition in the next decade may not exist by the year 2000.

---

9. "Videoconferencing: No Longer Just a Sideshow," *Business Week,* November 12, 1984, pp. 116–120.

MANAGEMENT IN ACTION

Wang Creates a Turnaround Team

"Another family start-up in the computer industry bites the dust," or so the typical story went during the computer industry shakeout in the mid-1980s. Wang Laboratories was founded in Boston by An Wang in 1951 based on the patent of a magnetic pulse device that led to the development of memory cores. Through the years, the company's products progressed through custom digital devices, business calculators, word processors, and computers. During the computer industry shakeout, several companies were driven out of the market by IBM, Digital Equipment, Intel, Apple, and others. It appeared that the demise of Wang Laboratories would coincide with the retirement of founder An Wang and the ascension to the top of his son Fred, who became president in 1985.

Fred Wang's style of management was exactly the opposite of his father's chaotic and confrontational style and did not fit with the first tier of management that An had built. As other companies developed new products to meet the changing environment, Wang Laboratories was stuck in the middle of a family quarrel. Three years after Fred took over, An returned from cancer surgery, removed his son, and took the reins once again. At this time, the company was losing money rapidly ($962 million in operating losses in 1989) and going downhill. An Wang installed Richard Miller as president in 1989 and tried to supervise Miller's early days. After An died in 1990, Miller was finally able to make changes and try to turn the company around.

One of Miller's first moves was to create a turnaround team of seventy middle managers from all areas of the company. The team's first directive was to find ways to raise cash, mostly by selling off assets. Miller's only rules were not to sell anything that would weaken the firm's long-run future and not to cut research and development, which Miller considered vital to the firm's survival. Miller was determined not to cut the company up by running off its highest potential managers. Therefore he made the middle management contingent the backbone of his turnaround team. He assigned middle managers projects to research and make recommendations on lines of business and strategies for their management; then he let them lead the turnaround. Although the turnaround was just getting started in late 1990, the future for Wang Laboratories appeared brighter than it had been since the family feud began. The turnaround team will play a major role in determining how far around it comes.

SOURCES: Gary Hoover, Alta Campbell, and Patrick J. Spain, eds., *Hoover's Handbook: Profiles of over 500 Major Corporations,* (Austin,Tex.: The Reference Press, 1990), p. 580; Brian Dumaine, "The New Turnaround Champs," *Fortune,* July 16, 1990, pp. 35–44; Ellen Wojahn, "Fathers and Sons," *INC.,* April 1990, pp. 81–84; Daniel Cohen, "The Fall of the House of Wang," *Business Month,* February 1990, pp. 23–31.

Resistance to Change

- Resistance to change within the organization can come from sources that are either external or internal to the organization.

Just as change is inevitable, so is resistance to change. Paradoxically, organizations both promote and resist change. As an agent for change, the organization asks prospective customers or clients to change their current purchasing habits by switching to the company's product or service and asks current customers to change by increasing their purchases. At the same time, the organization resists change in that its structure and control systems protect the daily tasks of producing a product or service from uncertainties in the environment. Because an organization is constantly buffeted by the forces of change, it must have some elements of permanence to avoid mirroring the instability of the environment. Yet it also must react to external shifts with internal change to maintain currency and relevance in the marketplace. *Management in Action* illustrates how a long-needed turnaround became possible only when a drastic change in the organization's leadership occurred at Wang Laboratories.

A commonly held view is that all resistance to change needs to be overcome, but that is not always the case. Resistance to change can be compared to the property of materials that restricts the passage of electrical current and causes the material to give off heat, a property also known as *resistance*. The heating coils in a toaster, waffle iron, and hair dryer all use this principle. If the resistance is complete, however, no current flows and thus no heat is given off. Thus, resistance to the passage of current is useful as long as some current can flow through the material.

Similarly, organizational resistance to change need not be eliminated entirely but can be used and controlled for the benefit of the organization. By revealing a legitimate concern that a proposed change may not be good for the organization, resistance may alert the organization to investigate and reexamine the change.[10] For example, an organization may be considering the acquisition of a company in a completely different industry. Resistance to such a proposal may cause the organization to examine the advantages and disadvantages of the move more carefully. Without resistance, the decision might be made before the pros and cons have been sufficiently explored.

Resistance may come from the organization, the individual, or both. It is often difficult to determine the ultimate source, however, because organizations are composed of individuals. Table 21.2 summarizes various types of organizational and individual sources of resistance.

Organizational Sources of Resistance

Daniel Katz and Robert Kahn have identified six major organizational sources of resistance: overdetermination, narrow focus of change, group inertia, threatened expertise, threatened power, and changes in resource allocation.[11] Of course, not every organization or every change situation displays all six sources.

■ **Overdetermination** occurs because numerous organizational systems are in place to ensure that behavior of employees and systems is as expected to maintain stability.

Overdetermination Organizations have several systems designed to maintain stability. For example, consider how organizations control employees' performance. To ensure that as employees they will do the job the organization desires, job candidates must meet specific requirements to be hired. As soon as a person

10. Paul R. Lawrence, "How to Deal with Resistance to Change," *Harvard Business Review,* May-June, 1954, reprinted in Gene W. Dalton, Paul R. Lawrence, and Larry E. Greiner, eds., *Organizational Change and Development* (Homewood, Ill.: Irwin, 1970), pp. 181–197.

11. Daniel Katz and Robert L. Kahn, *The Social Psychology of Organizations,* 2nd ed. (New York: Wiley, 1978), pp. 36–68.

TABLE 21.2
Organizational and Individual Sources of Resistance

Organizational Sources	Examples
Overdetermination	Employment system, job descriptions, evaluation and reward system
Narrow Focus of Change	Structure changed with no concern given to other issues, e.g., jobs, people
Group Inertia	Group norms
Threatened Expertise	People move out of area of expertise
Threatened Power	Decentralized decision making
Resource Allocation	Increased use of part-time help
Individual Sources	**Examples**
Habit	Altered tasks
Security	Altered tasks or reporting relationships
Economic Factors	Changed pay and benefits
Fear of the Unknown	New job, new boss
Lack of Awareness	Isolated groups not heeding notices
Social Factors	Group norms

is hired, he or she is given a job description, and the supervisor trains, coaches, and counsels the employee in job tasks. The new employee usually serves some type of probationary period that culminates in a performance review; thereafter, the employee's performance is regularly evaluated. Finally, rewards, punishment, and discipline are administered depending on the level of performance. Such a system is said to be characterized by **overdetermination,** or *structural inertia,*[12] in that the same effect on employee performance probably could be achieved with fewer procedures and safeguards. In other words, the structure of the organization provides resistance to change because it was designed to maintain stability.

Narrow Focus of Change Many efforts to create change in organizations adopt too narrow a focus. Any effort to force change in the tasks of individuals or groups must take into account the interdependencies among organizational elements such as people, structure, tasks, and the information system. For example, some attempts at redesigning jobs are unsuccessful because the organization structure within which jobs must function is inappropriate for the redesigned jobs.[13]

12. See Michael T. Hannah and John Freeman, "Structural Inertia and Organizational Change," *American Sociological Review,* April 1984, pp. 149–164, for an in-depth discussion of structural inertia.

13. Gregory Moorhead, "Organizational Analysis: An Integration of the Macro and Micro Approaches," *Journal of Management Studies,* April 1981, pp. 191–218.

Group Inertia When an employee attempts to change his or her work behavior, the group may resist by refusing to change other behaviors that are necessary complements to the individual's changed behavior. In other words, group norms may act as a brake on individual attempts at behavior change.

Threatened Expertise A change in the organization may threaten the specialized expertise that individuals and groups have developed over the years. A job redesign or a structural change may transfer the responsibility for a specialized task from the current expert to someone else, thus threatening the specialist's expertise and building his or her resistance to the change.

Threatened Power Any redistribution of decision-making authority may threaten an individual's power relationships with others. If an organization is decentralizing its decision making, managers who wielded their decision-making powers in return for special favors from others may resist the change because they do not want to lose their power base.

Resource Allocation Groups that are satisfied with current resource allocation methods may resist any change they believe will threaten their future allocations. Resources in this context can mean anything from monetary rewards and equipment to additional seasonal help to more computer time.

These six sources explain most types of organization-based resistance to change. All except the second (narrow focus of change) are based on people and social

Bernadette Locke is assistant head coach of the men's basketball team at the University of Kentucky—the first woman in such a position at a Division I university. Although Title IX legislated equal opportunity for women in college athletics in 1972 and women's and men's programs have merged in many universities, only 47 percent of women's teams and 1 percent of men's teams are coached by women. Experts suggest that the disparity is due to strong resistance to change from the "old boy network" and the fact that men tend to recommend men for coaching and athletic administrative positions.

relationships. Furthermore, many of these sources of resistance can be traced to groups or individuals afraid of losing something—resources, power, or comfort in a routine.

Individual Sources of Resistance

Individual sources of resistance to change are rooted in basic human characteristics such as needs and perceptions. Researchers have identified six reasons for individual resistance to change: habit, security, economic factors, fear of the unknown, lack of awareness, and social factors (see Table 21.2).[14]

Habit It is easier to do a job the same way every day. If the steps in the job are repeated over and over, the job becomes increasingly easier. But learning an entirely new set of steps makes the job more difficult. For the same amount of return (pay), most people prefer to do easier rather than harder work.

Security Some employees like the comfort and security of doing things the same old way. They gain a feeling of constancy and safety in knowing that some things stay the same despite all the change going on around them. Thus, people who believe their security is threatened by a change are likely to resist the change. For instance, the many changes that occurred in jobs, departments, and divisions at General Motors when the company reorganized several years ago evoked some resistance because they threatened employees' security.[15]

Economic Factors Change may also threaten employees' steady paychecks. Workers may fear that change will make their jobs obsolete.

Fear of the Unknown Some people fear anything unfamiliar. Changes in reporting relationships and job duties create anxiety for such employees. Employees become familiar with their boss, their job, and relationships with others within the organization, such as contact people for certain situations. These relationships and contacts help facilitate their work. Any disruption of familiar patterns may create fear because it can cause delays and the belief that nothing is getting accomplished. The previously mentioned changes at GM created a situation described as "quicksand": There were so many transfers of people among divisions that it became difficult to find phone numbers for coworkers.[16]

Lack of Awareness Because of perceptual limitations, such as lack of attention or selective attention, a person may not recognize a change in a rule or procedure

---

14. David A. Nadler, "Concepts for the Management of Organizational Change," in J. Richard Hackman, Edward E. Lawler III, and Lyman W. Porter, eds., *Perspectives on Behavior in Organizations,* 2nd ed. (New York: McGraw-Hill, 1983), pp. 551–561; G. Zaltman and R. Duncan, *Strategies for Planned Change* (New York: Wiley, 1977).

15. "GM's Smith Presses for Sweeping Changes but Questions Arise," *The Wall Street Journal,* March 14, 1985, pp. 1, 18.

16. Ibid.

and thus may not alter behavior. People may pay attention only to those things that support their point of view. As an example, employees in an isolated regional sales office may not notice—or may ignore—directives from headquarters regarding a change in reporting procedures for expense accounts. They therefore may continue the current practice as long as possible.

Social Factors People may resist change for fear of what others will think. As we have mentioned before, the group can be a powerful motivator of behavior. Employees may believe change will hurt their image, result in ostracism from the group, or simply make them "different." For example, an employee who agrees to conform to work rules established by management may be ridiculed by others who openly disobey the rules. The Japanese may be facing a similar resistance to change by not recognizing their role in the international marketplace.[17]

Managing Resistance

- Managing resistance to change means working with the sources of resistance rather than trying to overpower or overcome resistance.

Managing resistance to change is much like managing organizational conflict, a topic discussed in Chapter 10. Rather than think of resistance as something to be avoided or overcome, managers should recognize it as a cue to reexamine the merits of a proposed change. Resistance can be constructive if it prompts managers to communicate more with employees, reevaluate the decision to make a change, and perhaps search for new ways to reach the desired goals. A new method may be better than the one originally proposed. It may, for example, accomplish the desired goals with less resistance and thus less expense. Moreover, reevaluating the proposed change in response to employee resistance may be a symbolic act that tells employees management listens to and cares about them.[18] Table 21.3 lists six methods for dealing with resistance to change.[19]

Education and Communication If resistance is based on inaccurate or inadequate information, a program of communication about the change may be appropriate. Communication can help dissipate some fears of unknown elements, such as a new job or a supervisor change. Such an effort is likely to work best when it is undertaken before the change is implemented, the reasons for the change are fully explained, and communication is two-way.

Participation and Involvement Resistance may be reduced when those affected by the change are involved in designing it. This strategy is especially useful when

---

17. "Japan Just Can't Believe It's a Superstar," *Business Week,* July 13, 1987, p. 64; Frank Gibney, *Japan: The Fragile Super Power* (New York: Norton, 1979); G. Packard, "Japan: A Valued U.S. Partner Peers at the Future," *Context,* vol. 13, no. 2, 1984, pp. 1–7.

18. Jeffrey Pfeffer, "Management as Symbolic Action: The Creation and Maintenance of Organizational Paradigms," in Larry L. Cummings and Barry M. Staw, eds., *Research in Organizational Behavior,* vol. 3 (Greenwich, Conn.: JAI Press, 1981), pp. 1–52.

19. John P. Kotter and Leonard S. Schlesinger, "Choosing Strategies for Change," *Harvard Business Review,* March-April 1979, pp. 106–114.

TABLE 21.3
Methods for Managing Resistance to Change

Method	Examples
Education and Communication	Open communication Training program to increase awareness
Participation and Involvement	Collaborative design of changes
Facilitation and Support	Emotional support and attentiveness Specific problem-related training
Negotiation and Agreement	Labor contract Mutual goal-setting sessions
Manipulation and Cooptation	Appointment of a member of an opposing group, such as a member of the union, to board of directors
Coercion	Threats of punishment or dismissal for noncompliance

employee commitment is essential to successful implementation. It is important to note, however, that involving employees in the change can be quite time consuming and must be managed properly. This approach can be useful in overcoming resistance caused by a narrow focus of change and lack of awareness.

Facilitation and Support Facilitation and support are effective in combating problems arising from desires for security and fear of the unknown. When employees are having difficulty in adjusting to new arrangements and new ways of doing things, a manager may need to arrange for additional training or provide extra emotional support while employees become accustomed to the new system. Such facilitation may take time and effort. When employees are struggling with a new machine or technique, it is easy for a supervisor to stop by their work area and encourage them to work harder, but it takes more time to sit down with them over a cup of coffee and listen to their problems. Although a discussion over coffee may not solve these problems, it leaves a message that the supervisor (and maybe top management) cares, which may encourage the employees to work harder to solve the problem.

Negotiation and Agreement If people or groups are losing something significant in the change and if they have enough power to resist strongly (as a union might), a manager may use a negotiation strategy. Negotiation before implementation can make the change go much more smoothly. Should problems arise later, the conflicting parties can be referred to the negotiated agreement. This is a useful technique when resistance is due to threatened power relationships and group factors.

Manipulation and Cooptation In situations where other methods are not working or are not available, a manager may resort to manipulating information, resources, and favors to overcome resistance. Cooptation may involve including representatives of groups likely to offer resistance in the design and implementation of the change whether or not the manager is really interested in their ideas. The manager hopes that inclusion in a planning group will cause the resisters to support the change when it is introduced into the organization. When

Chrysler was in difficulty, it tried to forestall labor union resistance to change by electing the union president to the corporate board of directors. The technique often is used when resistance is due to resource allocation changes, economic factors, habit, and group factors.

Coercion Managers may resort to coercion to overcome resistance if all other methods fail or for some reason are inappropriate. Compliance can be coerced by threats of pay reduction, loss of job, or demotion or transfer. Although force may be a quick method of overcoming resistance, it can seriously affect employee attitudes and have adverse consequences in the long run.

Processes for Planned Organization Change

External elements may force change on an organization. Ideally, however, the organization will not only respond to change but anticipate it, prepare for it through planning, and incorporate it in the organization strategy.

Process Models

Planned organization change requires a systematic process of moving from one condition to another. Three approaches to change that emphasize the change process are Lewin's three-step change process, an expanded process model, and action research.

- Lewin's three-stage model of planned organization change suggests that change is a systematic process of moving from one stage to another.
- **Unfreezing** is the process by which people become aware of the need for change.

Lewin's Three-Step Change Process Kurt Lewin suggested that efforts to bring about planned change in organizations should approach change as a multistage process.[20] His model of planned change is made up of three steps—unfreezing, change, and refreezing—as shown in Figure 21.1

Unfreezing is the process by which people become aware of the need for change. Satisfaction with current practices and procedures may result in little or no interest in making changes. The key factor in unfreezing is making employees knowledgeable about the importance of a change and how their jobs will be affected by it. The employees who will be most affected by the change must be made aware of the need for it, in effect making them dissatisfied enough with current operations to be motivated toward change.

Change is the movement from an old stage to a new one. Change may mean the installation of new equipment, the restructuring of the organization, the implementation of a new performance appraisal system—anything that alters existing relationships or activities.

- **Refreezing** is the process of making new behaviors become relatively permanent and resistant to further change.

Refreezing makes new behaviors relatively permanent and resistant to further change. Examples of refreezing include repeating newly learned skills in a training session and role playing to teach how the new skill can be used in a

20. Kurt Lewin, *Field Theory in Social Science* (New York: Harper & Row, 1951).

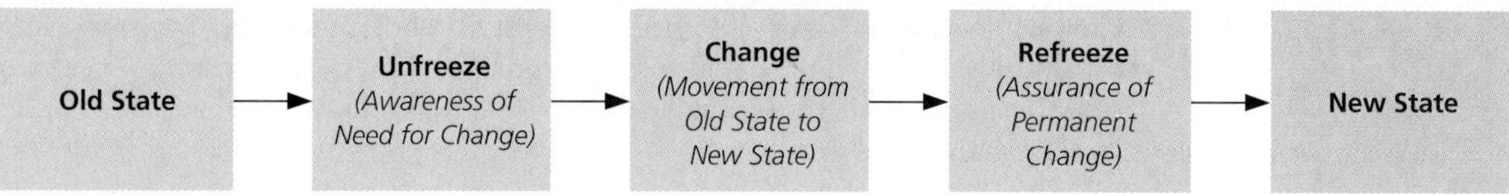

FIGURE 21.1
Lewin's Process of Organization Change

real-life work situation. Refreezing is necessary because without it, the old ways of doing things might soon reassert themselves while the new ways were forgotten. For example, many employees who attend special training sessions apply themselves diligently and resolve to change things in their organizations. But when they return to the workplace, they find it easier to conform to the old ways than to make waves. There usually are few, if any, rewards for trying to change the organizational status quo. In fact, the personal sanctions against doing so may be difficult to tolerate. Learning theory and reinforcement theory (Chapter 5) can play important roles in the refreezing phase.

- The expanded process model combines the Lewin three-stage model of organization change and integrates the standard decision-making/problem-solving approaches.

The Expanded Process Model Perhaps because Lewin's model is very simple and straightforward, virtually all models of organization change use his approach. However, it does not deal with several important issues. A more complex, and more helpful, approach is illustrated in Figure 21.2. This approach looks at planned change from the perspective of top management. The model incorporates Lewin's concept into the implementation phase.

In this approach, top management perceives that certain forces or trends call for change, and the issue is subjected to the organization's usual problem-solving and decision-making processes (see Chapter 16). Usually, top management defines its goals in terms of what the organization or certain processes or outputs will be like after the change. Alternatives for change are generated and evaluated, and an acceptable one is selected.

- The **change agent** is the person responsible for managing the change effort.

Early in the process, the organization may seek the assistance of a **change agent**—a person who will be responsible for managing the change effort. The change agent may also help management recognize and define the problem or the need for the change and may be involved in generating and evaluating potential plans of action. The change agent may be a member of the organization or an outsider such as a consultant or even someone from headquarters whom employees view as an outsider (see *International Perspective*). An internal change agent is likely to know the organization's people, tasks, and political situations, which may be helpful in interpreting data and understanding the system; but an insider may also be too close to the situation to view it objectively. (In addition, a regular employee would have to be removed from his or her regular duties to concentrate on the transition.) An outsider, then, often is received better by all parties because of her or his assumed impartiality.

Unless the change agent is a member of top management, his or her power to bring about change must emanate from some source other than hierarchical position and legitimate authority within the organization. Although the support

FIGURE 21.2
An Expanded Model of the Organization Change Process

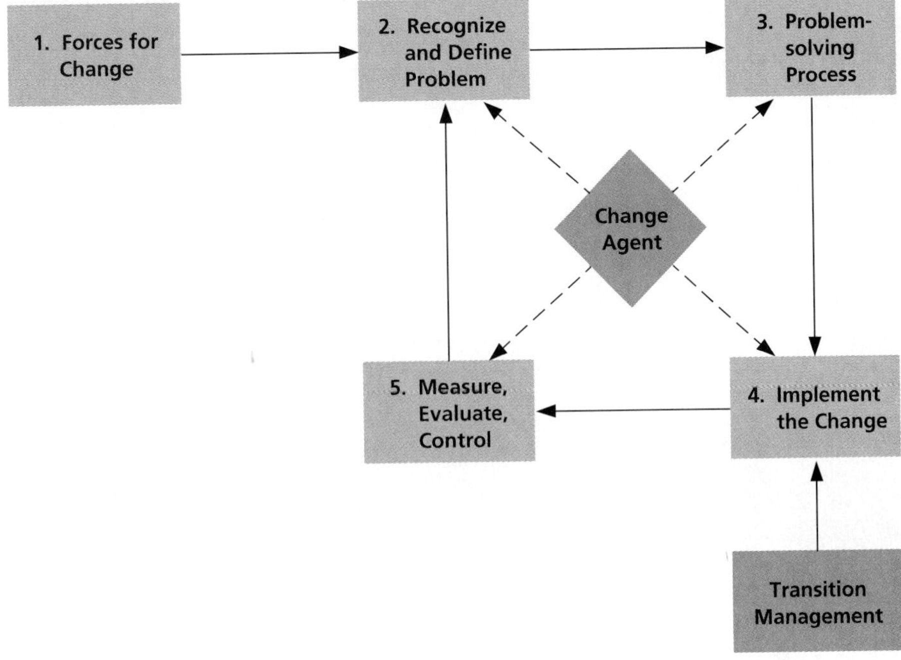

of top management is essential, it is not enough. Michael Beer describes five sources of power for the change agent:

1. High status given by members of the client organization, based on their perception that the change agent is similar to them in behaviors, language, values, and even dress
2. Trust in the change agent based on his or her consistent handling of information and maintaining a proper role in the organization
3. Expertise in the practice of organization change
4. Established credibility based on experiences with previous clients or previous projects with the client organization
5. Dissatisfied constituencies inside the organization who see the change agent as the best opportunity to change the organization to meet their needs[21]

Under the direction and management of the change agent, the organization implements the change through Lewin's unfreeze, change, and refreeze process.

In the final step, evaluation and control, the change agent and the top management group assess the degree to which the change is having the desired

21. Michael Beer, *Organization Change and Development: A Systems View* (Santa Monica, Calif.: Goodyear, 1980), p. 78.

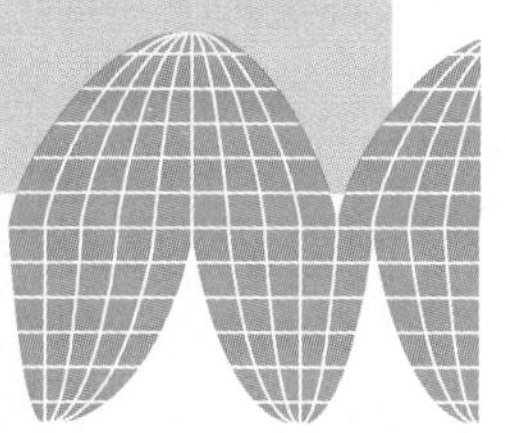

INTERNATIONAL PERSPECTIVE

Motorola Goes South to Make a Major Change

From car radios in 1928 to the latest in cellular telephones and integrated circuits and microprocessors, Motorola has always led the rapidly advancing field of electronics. It now employs more than one hundred thousand people worldwide, and in 1989 it reported net income of $498 million on sales of $9.7 billion. The third generation of the Galvin family is now in the three-person "office of the chief executive" and trying to lead the company through its most complex times.

As has been typical of many companies, especially those in electronics, Motorola has shifted much of its production to other countries to take advantage of low labor costs. Mexico has been particularly appealing for its cheap labor and its proximity to the United Sates, making marketing and transportation efficiencies possible. Its Guadalajara plant, however, recently experienced some difficulties due to superinflation of the Mexican economy and low morale among employees. Motorola management knew that traditional means of improving quality and productivity would not work because of the unique characteristics of the Mexican labor market.

The head of human resources for the semiconductor products sector, of which the Mexican plant was a part, met with top management of the Guadalajara plant and initiated steps to use a change model for organization effectiveness that had been developed by his headquarters staff in Phoenix, Arizona. The seven-step change model began with ensuring that all employees knew of Motorola's vision to be a world-class manufacturer of semiconductors. Other steps included the development of strategies consistent with the vision, changing organization structures to fit with the strategies, matching staff to the organization's needs, training workers in essential skills, using a participative style, and developing systems to manage the company on a daily basis.

The most essential element of the process was recognizing the importance of teamwork and pride in accomplishment, two key values in the Mexican culture. It became clear that the focus on competitiveness that worked so well in North America would not be appropriate in the Guadalajara plant. In Mexico, the priorities are family, religion, and work, in that order. The organization change model thus was adapted to appeal to the culture of Mexico.

The program appears to have succeeded. Productivity has increased 30 to 40 percent plantwide, on-time deliveries are nearly 100 percent, cycle times have been cut in half, and employee morale is high.

SOURCES: Kent Banning and Dick Wintermantel, "Motorola Turns Vision to Profits," *Personnel Journal,* February 1991, pp. 51–55; Norm Alster, "A Third Generation Galvin Moves Up," *Forbes,* April 30, 1990, pp. 57–59; Gary Hoover, Alta Campbell, and Patrick J. Spain, eds., *Hoover's Handbook: Profiles of over 500 Major Corporations,* (Austin, Tex.: The Reference Press, 1990), p. 389.

effect; that is, they measure progress toward the goals of the change and make appropriate changes if necessary.

The more closely the change agent is involved in the change process, the less distinct the steps become. As the change agent becomes immersed in defining and solving the problem with members of the organization, she or he becomes a "collaborator" or "helper" to the organization. When this happens, the change agent may be working with many individuals, groups, and departments within the organization on different phases of the change process. Because of the total involvement of the change agent in every phase of the project, it may not be readily observable when the change process is moving along from one stage to another. Throughout the process, however, the change agent brings in new ideas and viewpoints that help members look at old problems in new ways. Change often comes from the conflict that results when the change agent challenges the organization's assumptions and generally accepted patterns of operation.

- **Action research** is an organization change process that is based on a research model, specifically one that contributes toward the betterment of the sponsoring organization and to advancement of knowledge of organizations in general.

Action Research Another view of the organization change process is **action research,** an organization change process that is based on a research model, specifically one that contributes toward the betterment of the sponsoring organization and to advancement of knowledge of organizations in general.[22] In action research, the researcher, or change agent, usually is an outside person who is involved in the total change process from diagnosis to evaluation. This person usually contracts with the sponsoring organization to engage in organizational research, whereas the typical change agent is called in to make a specific change.

The research process generally is composed of in-depth searching, asking questions, interviewing employees, and evaluating records, all of which lead to analysis and synthesis of information. The researcher's questioning of employees and searching leads to the development of suggested actions for the organization. The action researcher works with employees to develop action plans that will best meet the needs of all concerned.

The researcher uses the initial data gathered in the early stages as points of comparison for data collected during and after any subsequent change made in the organization. In this manner, the researcher can evaluate the effects of the change on the organization. The evaluation of the organization and any changes taken to improve it over a period of change can provide valuable information to both the organization and the researcher.

Transition Management

Organization change does not happen overnight. It takes time for employees to absorb even simple changes. For example, suppose a change involves the creation of a new position: a coordinator between two departments. It will take some time for employees in the departments to become accustomed to going through the coordinator with certain types of requests and seeking a decision or approval from that person. Much more time and effort may be required for employees to adapt to complex changes. Such changes need to be managed, not merely implemented. The results of major changes within organizations may take years to fully realize. For example, K Mart has been changing its stores and expanding into new areas since 1985.[23]

---

22. Peter A. Clark, *Action Research and Organizational Change* (New York: Harper & Row, 1972).

23. "K Mart Boss Wants Chain to Become Most Respected in U.S.," *The Arizona Republic,* October 4, 1987, pp. E1, E9; "Attention, K Mart Shoppers!" *Direct Marketing,* May 1987, p. 8; "K Mart to Santa: Ho, Ho, Ho-Hum," *Business Week,* December 7, 1987, pp. 60–61.

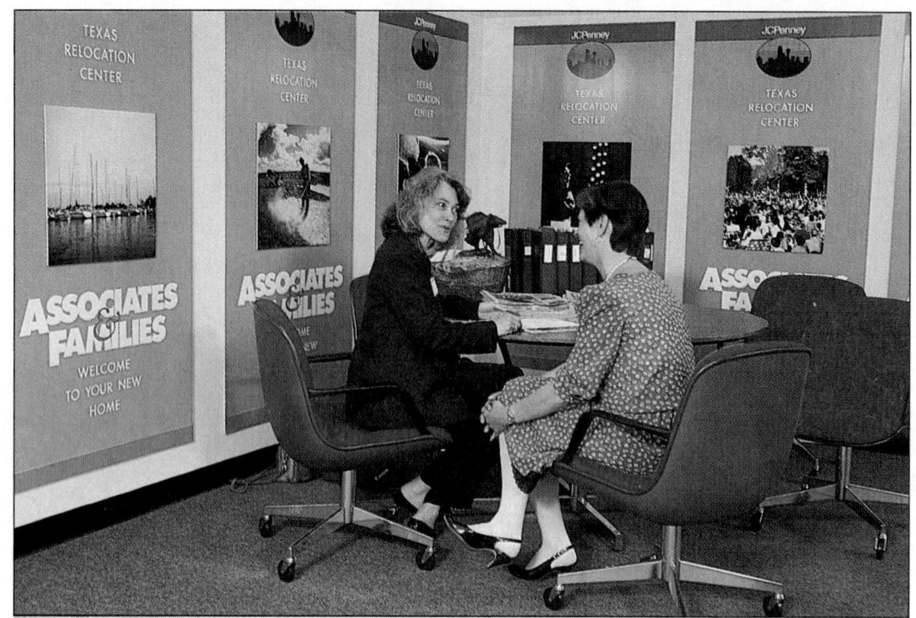

J.C. Penney is making one of the most drastic of organizational transitions—moving its corporate headquarters from New York to Dallas. Preparations for the relocation have included providing employees with information about Dallas through special booths near the company cafeteria and company-paid week-end trips to Dallas to tour the area. Although the move will be very expensive for the company, J.C. Penney expects to save $60 million per year by being in Dallas.

■ **Transition management** is the process of systematically planning, organizing, and implementing change.

Transition management is the process of systematically planning, organizing, and implementing change, from the disassembly of the current state to the realization of a fully functional future state within an organization.[24] Once change begins, the organization is in neither the old state nor the new state; yet business must continue. Transition management ensures that business continues while the change is occurring, and thus it must begin before the change occurs. The members of the regular management team must take on the role of transition managers and coordinate organizational activities with the change agent. An interim management structure or interim positions may be created to ensure continuity and control of the business during the transition. Communication of the changes to all involved, from employees to customers and suppliers, plays a key role in transition management.[25]

Integrated Process of Organization Change

Successful organization change projects integrate all or most of the elements of change discussed so far in this chapter. The integrative framework, illustrated in Figure 21.3, shows how the organization is relatively stable at phase 1; unfreezes, changes and refreezes in phase 2; and becomes a new, stable system in phase 3.

24. Linda S. Ackerman, "Transition Management: An In-Depth Look at Managing Complex Change," *Organizational Dynamics,* Summer 1982, pp. 46–66; David A. Nadler, "Managing Transitions to Uncertain Future States," *Organizational Dynamics,* Summer 1982, pp. 37–45.

25. Noel M. Tichy and David O. Ulrich, "The Leadership Challenge—A Call for the Transformational Leader," *Sloan Management Review,* Fall 1984, pp. 59–68.

FIGURE 21.3
Integrated Process of Organization Change

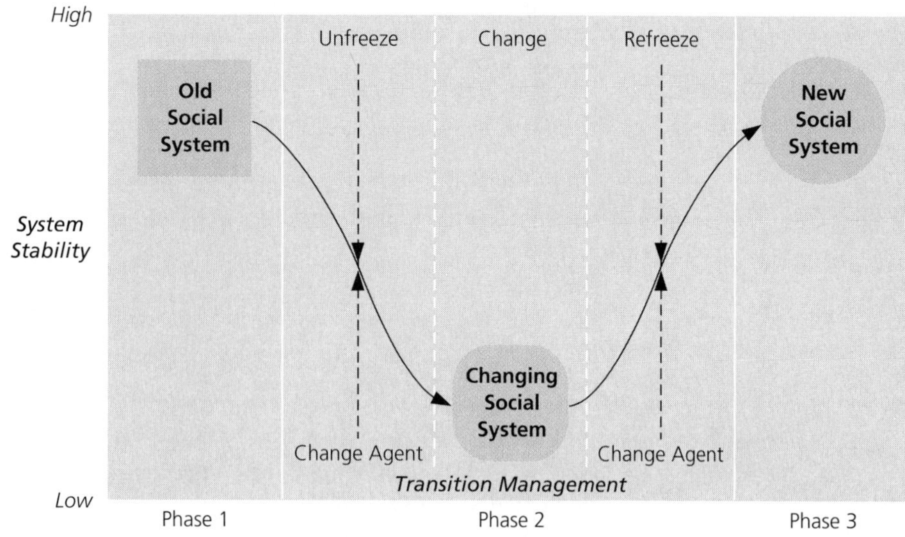

Throughout the process, transition management keeps the organization functioning.

Changes at Keithley Instruments, Inc. (KII), illustrate the management of a major change.[26] In 1979 KII, a manufacturer of industrial and scientific equipment, suffered from a cluttered shop floor, unpredictable inventory, frequent production errors, and worker discontent. The company had grown very quickly from a relatively small, well-organized operation based on engineering expertise to a large, poorly structured one in which production bottlenecks occurred regularly. As one person put it, the organization was limiting the people.

Hired as director of human resources, Mark Frohman acted as an internal change agent. In fact, however, because he had been with the company only a short time, he was an outsider in many ways. Before holding meetings with employees throughout the organization, Frohman convinced top management to write down the company's purpose and goals, which he used as guidelines for change. The change strategy included training, redesign of jobs and work flow, and development of better communications. The key element of the change was the establishment of production teams, the first of which was formed in October 1979. Top manufacturing managers held one- and two-day meetings to plan the change and makeup of the production teams. Supervisors received training that included case studies, lectures, discussion, and role playing on participative team management. Team members attended one-day meetings on the company itself, its products, and basic economics.

Although the first team initially was uncertain about its role, it was a success. Other teams were formed, and by the end of 1982 all production in the company

26. Perry Pascarella, "Change Champion Builds Teamwork." Reprinted with permission of *Industry Week,* March 19, 1984. Copyright Penton Publishing Inc., Cleveland, Ohio.

was being accomplished by twelve production teams. Each group meets twice a month to review performance, discuss problems, and set goals for the next period. The ratio of raw materials to finished goods has decreased, the rate of in-warranty repairs has decreased, and the labor relations atmosphere has improved. KII reported that in the five-year period ending in 1983, sales nearly doubled to $35 million and profits increased to $2 million despite a recessionary economy. As the change agent, Frohman was involved in the entire process, from problem diagnosis to implementation. He used an integrated change process to effect major changes in the organization.

Organization Development

On one level, organization development is simply the way organizations change and evolve. Organization change can involve personnel, technology, competition, and other areas. Employee learning and formal training, transfers, promotions, terminations, and retirements are all examples of personnel-related changes. Thus, in the broadest sense, *organization development* means organization change.[27] However, the term as used here means something more specific. Over the past twenty years, organization development (OD) has emerged as a distinct field of study and practice. There is now substantial agreement as to what OD is in general, although arguments about details continue.[28] Our definition of organization development is an attempt to describe a very complex process in a simple manner. It is also an attempt to capture the best points of several definitions offered by writers in the field.

Definition of Organization Development

■ **Organization development (OD)** is the process of planned change and improvement of the organization through the application of knowledge of the behavioral sciences.

Organization development (OD) is the process of planned change and improvement of organizations through the application of knowledge of the behavioral sciences. Three points in this definition make it simple to remember and use. First, OD involves attempts to plan organization changes, thus excluding spontaneous, haphazard initiatives. Second, the specific intention of OD is to improve organizations. This point excludes changes that merely imitate those of another organization, are forced on the organization by external pressures, or are undertaken merely for the sake of changing. Third, the planned improvement must be based on knowledge of the behavioral sciences, such as psychology, sociology, cultural anthropology, and related fields of study, rather than on financial or technological considerations. Under our definition, the replacement of manual personnel records with a computerized system would not be considered an instance of organization development. Although such a change has behavioral

27. W. Warner Burke, *Organization Development: Principles and Practices* (Boston: Little, Brown, 1982).

28. Burke, *Organization Development;* Beer, *Organization Change and Development.*

effects, it is a technology-driven reform rather than a behavioral one. Likewise, alterations in recordkeeping necessary to support new government-mandated reporting requirements are not a part of organization development, because the change is obligatory and the result of an external force.

Although many experts accept a basic definition similar to ours, they vary in the emphasis they place on its elements. Michael Beer has stressed the process of OD by adding that organization improvement comes about through systemwide data collection, diagnosis, action planning, implementation, and evaluation.[29] Wendell French and Cecil Bell have accented changing the organization culture in their approach to OD.[30] They say the aim of OD is to improve the collaborative management of the organization's culture, that is, the joint management by employees and managers of the organization's prevailing patterns of activities, interactions, norms, feelings, beliefs, attitudes, and values. The importance of culture has also been underscored by W. Warner Burke, who has suggested that a change cannot be considered organization development unless it modifies the culture of the organization.[31] These viewpoints are valuable supplements to our definition.

Change can be introduced into the organization in any number of places. Viewing the organization as a social system of interrelated parts, however, emphasizes that a change in any one element has impacts throughout the organization. Suppose an organization wishes to change its performance appraisal system (discussed in Chapter 14). A new performance appraisal system can affect supervisor-subordinate relationships, the reward system, peer relationships, and many other systems. If the new system significantly changes how highly valued behaviors and activities are measured or observed, employee relationships may be drastically altered, both socially and professionally. The changed relationships may in turn affect attitudes, commitment to the organization, willingness to work, and productivity.

With this clarification of our definition of OD, we are ready to examine some popular organization development techniques. The three most basic types of techniques are systemwide, task-technological, and group and individual.

Systemwide Organization Development

The most comprehensive type of organization change involves a major reorganization, usually referred to as a *structural change*—a systemwide rearrangement of task division and authority and reporting relationships. A structural change affects performance appraisal and rewards, decision making, and communication and information processing systems.

An organization may change the way it divides tasks into jobs, groups jobs into departments and divisions, and arranges authority and reporting relation-

---

29. Beer, *Organization Change and Development.*

30. Wendell L. French and Cecil H. Bell, *Organization Development: Behavioral Science Interventions for Organization Improvement,* 2nd ed. (Englewood Cliffs, N.J.: Prentice-Hall, 1978).

31. Burke, *Organization Development.*

ships among positions. It may move from functional departmentalization to a system based, for example, on products or geography or from a conventional linear design to a matrix design. Other changes may include dividing large groups into smaller ones or merging small groups into larger ones. In addition, the degree to which rules and procedures are written down and enforced, as well as the locus of decision-making authority, may be altered. If all these changes are made, the organization will have transformed both the configurational and operational aspects of its structure.

No systemwide structural change is simple.[32] A company president cannot just issue a memo notifying company personnel that on a certain date they will report to a different supervisor and be responsible for new tasks. Employees have months, years, and sometimes decades of experience in dealing with people and tasks in certain ways. When these patterns are disrupted, employees need time to learn the new tasks and to settle into the new relationships. Moreover, the change may be resisted for any or all of the reasons discussed earlier. Therefore, organizations must manage the change process.

- Systemwide organization development can be a major restructuring of the organization or programs such as quality of work life.
- **Quality of work life** is the extent to which workers are able to satisfy important personal needs through their experiences in the organization.

Another systemwide change is the introduction of quality-of-work-life (QWL) programs. J. Lloyd Suttle has defined **quality of work life** as the "degree to which members of a work organization are able to satisfy important personal needs through their experiences in the organization."[33] QWL programs focus strongly on providing a work environment conducive to the satisfaction of individual needs. The emphasis on improving life at work developed during the 1970s, a period of increasing inflation and deepening recession. The development was rather surprising, because an expanding economy and substantially increased resources are the conditions that usually induce top management to begin people-oriented programs. Improving life at work evidently was viewed by top management as a means of improving productivity.

Any movement with broad and ambiguous goals tends to spawn diverse programs, each claiming to be based on the movement's goals, and QWL is no exception. QWL programs differ substantially, although most espouse a goal of "humanizing the workplace." Richard Walton has divided QWL programs into the eight categories shown in Figure 21.4.[34] Obviously, many types of programs can be accommodated by the categories, from changing the pay system to establishing an employee bill of rights that guarantees workers the rights to privacy, free speech, due process, and fair and equitable treatment.

A ten-year effort at General Motors is one of the most comprehensive QWL programs yet instituted. Shop floor employees have been involved in making improvements in jobs, work procedures, production and product design, and

32. Danny Miller and Peter H. Friesen, "Structural Change and Performance: Quantum versus Piecemeal-Incremental Approaches," *Academy of Management Journal,* December 1982, pp. 867–892.

33. J. Lloyd Suttle, "Improving Life at Work—Problems and Prospects," in J. Richard Hackman and J. Lloyd Suttle, eds., *Improving Life at Work: Behavioral Science Approaches to Organizational Change* (Santa Monica, Calif.: Goodyear, 1977), p. 4.

34. Richard E. Walton, "Quality of Work Life: What Is It?" *Sloan Management Review,* Fall 1983, pp. 11–21.

FIGURE 21.4
Walton's Categorization of Quality-of-Work-Life (QWL) Programs

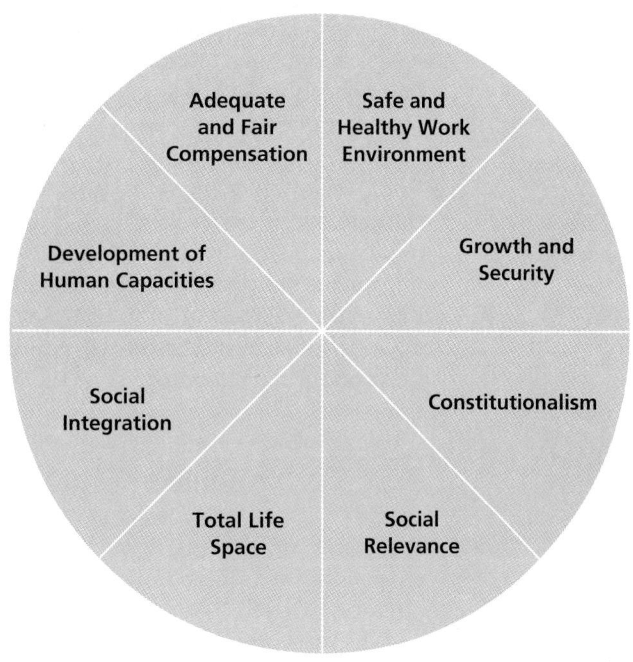

SOURCE: Reprinted (adapted) from Richard E. Walton, "Quality of Work Life: What Is It?" *Sloan Management Review,* Fall 1973, pp. 11–21, by permission of the publisher.

quality control.[35] QWL programs have also been successful at Xerox, IBM, and numerous smaller organizations. The benefits gained from the programs differ substantially, but generally they are of three types. A more positive attitude toward the work and the organization, or increased job satisfaction, perhaps is the most direct benefit.[36] Another is increased productivity, although it often is difficult to measure and separate the effects of the QWL program from the effects of other organizational factors. A third benefit is increased effectiveness of the organization as measured by its profitability, goal accomplishment, shareholder wealth, or resource exchange. The third gain follows directly from the first two: If employees have more positive attitudes about the organization and their productivity increases, everything else being equal, the organization should be more effective.

As useful as QWL programs can be, they present several potential pitfalls.[37] First, management and labor must cooperate in the design and implementation

35. Burke, *Organization Development,* pp. 322–323.

36. Daniel A. Ondrack and Martin G. Evans, "Job Enrichment and Job Satisfaction in Greenfield and Redesign QWL Sites," *Group & Organization Studies,* March 1987, pp. 5–22.

37. Suttle, "Improving Life at Work," pp. 14–20.

of the program. Otherwise, each side may view the program as an opportunity to get something out of the other. Worker-management committees on work improvement can function effectively to increase cooperation. Second, the action plans developed must be followed through to completion. Plans can easily be lost and forgotten amidst the problems of the shop floor or office. Everyone, from top management to production employees, must remember to follow through on the plans. The third pitfall is the failure to support the often forgotten middle manager, who is pressured by both top management and line workers to implement the program.[38] Finally, the focus of QWL programs must be kept on the joint objectives of increasing the quality of work life and maintaining organization efficiency. There is no inherent incompatibility between the interests of the worker and the interests of the organization.[39]

Task-Technological Change

Another way to bring about systemwide organization development is through changes in the task and/or the technology involved in doing the work. The direct alteration of jobs usually is called *task redesign.* Changing the way inputs are transformed into outputs is called *technological change* and also usually results in task changes. Strictly speaking, changing the technology typically is not part of organization development, whereas task redesign usually is.

The structural changes discussed in the preceding section are explicitly systemwide in scope. Those we examine in this section are more narrowly focused and may not seem to have the same far-reaching consequences. It is important to remember, however, that their impact is felt throughout the organization. The discussion of task design in Chapter 13 focused on job definition and motivation and gave little attention to implementing changes in jobs. Here we discuss task redesign as a mode of organization change.

Several approaches to introducing job changes in organizations have been proposed. One is by a coauthor of this book, Ricky W. Griffin. Griffin's approach is an integrative framework of nine steps that reflect the complexities of the interfaces between individual jobs and the total organization.[40] The process, shown in Table 21.4, includes the steps usually associated with change, such as recognition of the need for a change, selection of the appropriate intervention, and evaluation of the change. But Griffin's approach inserts four additional steps into the standard sequence: diagnosis of the overall work system and context, including examination of the jobs, technology, organization design, leadership, and group dynamics; evaluation of the costs and benefits of the change; formulation of a redesign strategy; and implementation of supplemental changes.

38. Leonard A. Schlesinger and Barry Oshry, "Quality of Work Life and the Manager: Muddle in the Middle," *Organizational Dynamics,* Summer 1984, pp. 4–19.

39. David A. Nadler and Edward E. Lawler III, "Quality of Work Life: Perspectives and Directions," *Organizational Dynamics,* Winter 1983, pp. 20–30.

40. Ricky W. Griffin, *Task Design: An Integrative Framework* (Glenview, Ill.: Scott, Foresman, 1982).

TABLE 21.4
Integrative Framework for Implementation of Task Redesign in Organizations

Step 1: Recognition of a need for a change
Step 2: Selection of task redesign as a potential intervention
Step 3: Diagnosis of the work system and context
  a. Diagnosis of existing jobs
  b. Diagnosis of existing work force
  c. Diagnosis of technology
  d. Diagnosis of organization design
  e. Diagnosis of leader behaviors
  f. Diagnosis of group and social processes
Step 4: Cost/benefit analysis of proposed changes
Step 5: Go/no-go decision
Step 6: Formulation of the strategy for redesign
Step 7: Implementation of the task changes
Step 8: Implementation of any supplemental changes
Step 9: Evaluation of the task redesign effort

SOURCE: Ricky W. Griffin, *Task Design: An Integrative Framework* (Glenview, Ill.: Scott, Foresman, 1982), p. 208. Used by permission.

Diagnosis includes analysis of the total work environment within which the jobs exist. When job changes are being considered, it is important to evaluate the organization structure, especially the work rules and decision-making authority within a department.[41] For example, if jobs are to be redesigned to give employees more freedom in choosing work methods or scheduling work activities, diagnosis of the present system must determine whether the rules will allow that to happen. Diagnosis must also include evaluation of the work group and intragroup dynamics (discussed in Chapter 7). Furthermore, it must determine whether workers have or can easily obtain the new skills to perform the redesigned task.

It is extremely important to recognize the full range of potential costs and benefits associated with a job redesign effort. Some are direct and quantifiable; others are indirect and nonquantifiable. Redesign may involve unexpected costs or benefits; although these cannot be predicted with certainty, they can be weighed as possibilities. Factors such as short-term role ambiguity, role conflict, and role overload can be major stumbling blocks to a job redesign effort.

Implementing a redesign scheme takes careful planning, and developing a strategy for the intervention is the final planning step. Strategy formulation is a four-part process. First, the organization must decide who will design the changes. Depending on the circumstances, the planning team may consist of only upper-level management or may include line workers and supervisors. Next, the team undertakes the actual design of the changes based on job design theory and the needs, goals, and circumstances of the organization. Third, the team decides the timing of the implementation, which may require a formal transition period during which equipment is purchased and installed, job training takes place, new

41. Gregory Moorhead, "Organizational Analysis: An Integration of the Macro and Micro Approaches," *Journal of Management Studies*, April 1981, pp. 191–218.

physical layouts are arranged, and the "bugs" in the new system are worked out. Fourth, strategy planners must consider whether the job changes require adjustments and supplemental changes in other organizational components, such as reporting relationships and the compensation system.

Implementation of Supplemental Changes As we mentioned earlier, a major job redesign effort may dictate planned adjustments in other parts of the organization. For example, work rules established to support the previous arrangement of tasks may not be appropriate for the new jobs. The performance appraisal system usually should be changed to reflect the changes in task division and responsibility. The reward system, recruiting and selection criteria, physical layout, reporting relationships, and in-house training programs also may have to be adapted. Although it may be necessary to make some adjustments after the job changes have been implemented, careful advance planning can minimize potential problems.

Group and Individual Change

There are a vast number of ways to involve groups and individuals in organization change. The retraining of a single employee can be considered an organization change if the training affects the way the employee does her or his job. Familiarizing managers with the Blake-Mouton grid or the Vroom-Yetton-Jago decision tree (Chapter 9) is an attempt at change. In the first case, the goal is to balance management concerns for production and people; in the second, it is to increase the participation of rank-and-file employees in the organization's decision making. In this section, we present an overview of four popular types of people-oriented change techniques: training, management development programs, team building, and survey-feedback.

Training Training generally is designed to improve employees' job skills. Employees may be trained to run certain machines, taught new mathematical skills, or exposed to personal growth and development methods. Stress management

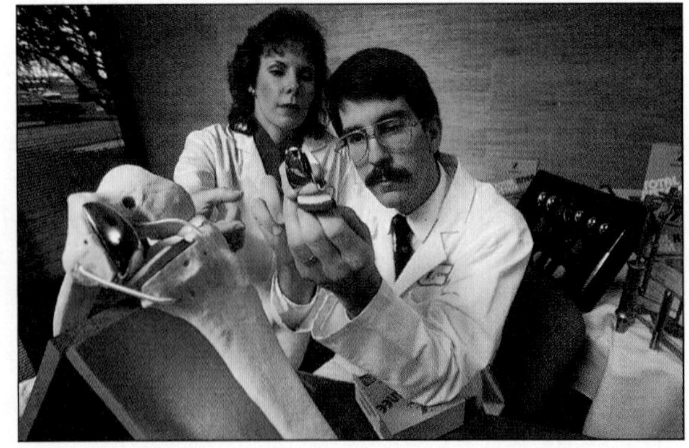

The Miller/Gallant Unicompartmental Knee System is one new system being marketed by Zimmer, a division of Bristol-Myers Company. One very important type of training that must go on is the training of health care teams in the use of such highly technical medical devices as this new knee system.

Developing Management Skills

Getting Ready to Do Business with the Japanese

Instead of shaking hands and saying the name of the person you meet, when you greet someone in Japan you need to bow deeply from the waist and present your business card with two hands. You accept the business card of your new acquaintance with two hands. Saying the person's name means saying their last name followed by "san," as in Moorhead-san. In addition, you will probably take off your shoes when you enter a traditional Japanese home, sit on the floor to eat, and offer a gift to your host, again with two hands while bowing. Be sure to offer the gift several times, because it may be turned down more than once. If you are offered a gift, you should turn it down at least once before accepting. Never chew gum or yawn in public.

When doing business with the Japanese, several things are more important than just learning the language. Lisa Gianotti teaches courses in Scottsdale, Arizona, in beginning Japanese that go far beyond the language. She outlines five steps that are essential to doing business with the Japanese:

1. Always use the person's position and title, followed by the person's last name. Never address Japanese businesspeople by their first names; doing so is considered rude.
2. Always exchange business cards when meeting Japanese people. It is a casual ritual similar to the shaking of hands in other cultures.
3. Volunteer and pitch in. The Japanese consider failure to volunteer a sign of disrespect.
4. Think collectively rather than individually as in Western cultures.
5. Always stay at work well after the normal quitting time. The Japanese assume that leaving work at the exact quitting time is a sign of losing interest in the job.

Whether negotiating a big business deal with Japanese companies or simply taking care of Japanese customers, Gianotti suggests that these five principles will make the process much smoother.

SOURCE: "Class Gives Broad Look at Japan," *The Arizona Republic,* March 6, 1991, p. 9; Rober E. Axtell, ed., *Do's and Taboos around the World,* (New York: Wiley, 1990); *Culturgram for the '90s,* (Provo, Ut.: Brigham Young University, David M. Kennedy Center for International Studies, 1990).

programs are becoming popular for helping employees, particularly executives, understand organizational stress and develop ways to cope with it.[42] Training may also be used in conjunction with other, more comprehensive organization changes. For instance, if an organization is implementing an MBO program, training in establishing goals and reviewing goal-oriented performance likely is needed.

One important type of training that is becoming increasingly common is training people to work in other countries. *Developing Management Skills* describes one training program for employees who work with the Japanese.

Among the many training methods, the most common are lecture, discussion, a lecture-discussion combination, experiential methods, case studies, and

42. James C. Quick and Jonathan D. Quick, *Organizational Stress and Preventive Management* (New York: McGraw-Hill, 1984).

films or videotapes. Training can take place in a standard classroom, either on company property or in a hotel, at a resort, or at a conference center. On-the-job training provides a different type of experience, in which the trainee learns from an experienced worker. Most training programs use a combination of methods determined by the topic, the trainees, the trainer, and the organization.

A major problem of training programs is transferring employee learning to the workplace. Often an employee learns a new skill or a manager learns a new management technique but, upon returning to the normal work situation, finds it easier to go back to the old way of doing things. As we discussed earlier, the process of refreezing is a vital part of the change process, and some way must be found to make the accomplishments of the training program permanent.

- Management development programs attempt to develop managers' skills, abilities, and perspectives.

Management Development Programs Management development programs, like employee training programs, attempt to foster certain skills, abilities, and perspectives. Often, when a highly qualified technical person is promoted to manager of a work group, he or she lacks training in how to manage or deal with people. In such cases, management development programs can be important to organizations, both for the new manager and for his or her subordinates.

Typically, management development programs use the lecture-discussion method to some extent but rely most heavily on participative methods, such as case studies and role playing. Participative and experiential methods allow the manager to experience the problems of being a manager as well as the feelings of frustration, doubt, and success that are part of the job. The subject matter of this type of training program is problematic, however, in that management skills, including communication, problem diagnosis, problem solving, and performance appraisal, are not as easy to identify or to transfer from a classroom to the workplace as the skills required to run a machine. In addition, rapid changes in the external environment can make certain managerial skills obsolete in a very short time. As a result, some companies are approaching the development of their management team as an ongoing, career-long process and are requiring their managers to attend refresher courses periodically.

One training approach involves managers in an intense exercise that simulates the daily operation of a real company. Such simulations emphasize problem-solving behavior rather than competitive tactics and usually involve extensive debriefing, in which a manager's style is openly discussed and criticized by trained observers as the first step to improvement. IBM and AT&T have commissioned experts to create a simulation specifically for their managers. Although the cost of custom simulations is high, it is reportedly repaid in benefits from individual development.[43]

As corporate America invests hundreds of millions of dollars in management development, certain guiding principles are evolving: (1) Management development is a multifaceted, complex, and long-term process for which there is no quick or simple solution; (2) organizations should pay close attention to the systematic identification of their unique developmental needs and evaluate their programs accordingly; (3) management development objectives must be com-

43. Peter Petre, "Games That Teach You to Manage," *Fortune,* October 29, 1984, pp. 65–72.

patible with organizational objectives; and (4) the utility and value of management development remains more an article of faith than a proven fact.[44]

Team Building When interaction among group members is critical to group success and effectiveness, team development, or team building, may be useful. The term *team building* emphasizes the importance of members' working together in a spirit of cooperation.

Team-building efforts generally have one or more of the following goals:

1. To set team goals and/or priorities
2. To analyze or allocate the way work is performed
3. To examine the way a group is working—that is, to examine processes such as norms, decision making, and communications
4. To examine relationships among the people doing the work[45]

One of these goals usually dominates the development effort. If no goal is dominant, considerable time and energy are wasted, because each member tends to engage in behaviors that will accomplish what he or she perceives to be the goal.[46] In a case where the goals of the team-building effort are not clear, the process must start with the examination of the reasons for team building. The team-building effort then proceeds in much the same way as other change processes: identification of the problem, data gathering, diagnosis, planning, implementation, and evaluation,[47] as shown in Figure 21.5. Its distinctive feature is group participation at all points. In this process, the group is simultaneously the object of and a participant in the process. A change agent usually is needed at first but becomes increasingly less necessary as the group develops into a team. Occasionally—especially if the work situation or membership has changed—the mature, well-functioning team may need a consultant to observe and provide insight into its operation.[48]

Participation is especially important in the data-gathering and evaluation phases of team development. In data gathering, the members share information on the functioning of the group. The opinions of the group thus form the foundation of the development process. In the evaluation phase, the members are the source of information about the effectiveness of the development effort.[49]

---

44. Kenneth N. Wexley and Timothy T. Baldwin, "Management Development," *1986 Yearly Review of Management of the Journal of Management,* pp. 277–294.

45. Richard Beckhard, "Optimizing Team-Building Efforts," *Journal of Contemporary Business,* Summer 1972, pp. 23–27, 30–32.

46. Ibid.

47. William G. Dyer, "Basic Programs and Plans," in *Team Building: Issues and Alternatives* (Reading, Mass.: Addison-Wesley, 1977), pp. 41–50.

48. Dianne McKinney Kellogg, "Contrasting Successful and Unsuccessful OD Consulting Relationships," *Group & Organization Studies,* June 1984, pp. 151–176.

49. William M. Vicars and Darrel D. Hartke, "Evaluating OD Evaluations: A Status Report," *Group & Organization Studies,* June 1984, pp. 177–188; Bernard M. Bass, "Issues Involved in Relations between Methodological Rigor and Reported Outcomes in Evaluations of Organizational Development," *Journal of Applied Psychology,* February 1983, pp. 197–201.

FIGURE 21.5
The Team-Building Process

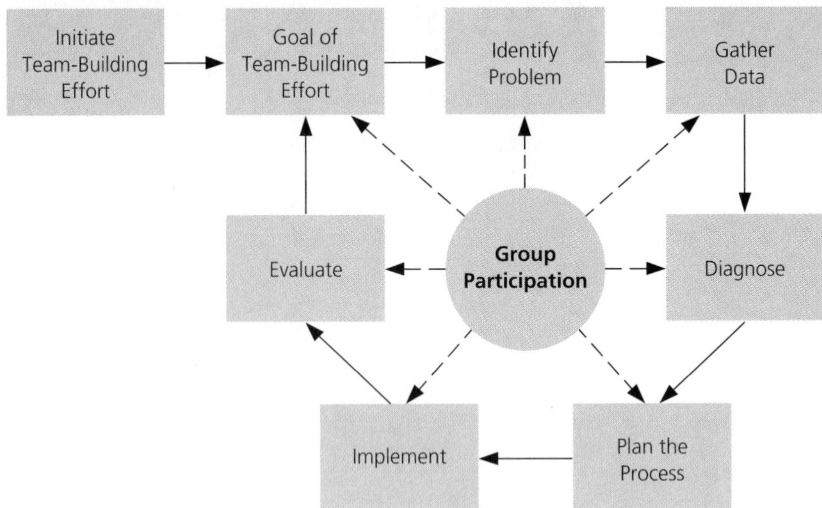

Team building should not be thought of as a one-time experience, perhaps something undertaken on a retreat from the workplace; rather, it is a continuing process. It may take weeks, months, or years for a group to pull together and function as a team. Team development can be a way to train the group to solve its own problems in the future. Research on the effectiveness of team building as an OD intervention tool thus far is mixed and inconclusive.

Survey-Feedback Survey-feedback techniques can form the basis for a change process in which data are gathered, analyzed, summarized, and returned to those who participated in its generation for identification, discussion, and solution of problems. A survey-feedback process often is set in motion by either the organization's top management or a consultant to management. By providing information about employees' beliefs and attitudes, a survey can help management diagnose and solve an organization's problems. A consultant or change agent usually coordinates the process and is responsible for data gathering, analysis, and summary. The three-stage process is shown in Figure 21.6.[50]

The use of survey-feedback techniques in an organization development process differs from their use in traditional attitude surveys. In an organization development process, data are (1) returned to employee groups at all levels in the organization and (2) used as the basis for problem identification and solution by all employees working together in their normal work groups. In traditional attitude surveys, top management reviews the data and may or may not initiate a new program to solve problems the survey has identified.

In the data-gathering stage, the change agent interviews selected personnel from appropriate levels to determine the key issues to be examined. In a small study, these interviews may provide sufficient information to proceed to the next

50. Beer, *Organization Change and Development.*

FIGURE 21.6
The Survey-Feedback Process

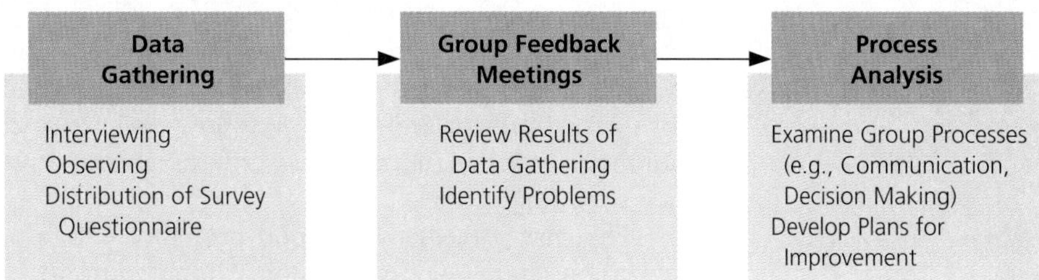

step. However, in more comprehensive studies in large organizations, the interviews serve as the basis for a survey questionnaire to be distributed to a large sample of employees.

The questionnaire may be a standardized instrument, an instrument developed specifically for the organization, or a combination of the two. Standardized instruments are readily available, psychometrically sound, and thoroughly pretested; they may also offer comparison data from other organizations. Sometimes, however, they are not relevant to the organization under study and may confuse the situation more than help it.

The questionnaire data are analyzed and aggregated by group or department to ensure anonymity of individual respondents.[51] Then the change agent prepares a summary of the results for the group feedback sessions. From this point on, the consultant is involved in the process as a resource person and expert.

The feedback meetings generally involve only two or three levels of management. These family groups, as they are called, are kept small to facilitate individual discussion and interaction. Meetings usually are held serially, beginning with a meeting of the top management group, which is followed by meetings of employees throughout the organization. Sessions typically are led by the group manager rather than the change agent to transfer "ownership" of the data from the change agent to the work group. The change agent helps the manager prepare for the meeting by reviewing the data and suggesting ways to stimulate discussion, problem identification, and problem solving. The feedback consists primarily of profiles of the groups' attitudes toward the organization, the work, the leadership, and other topics on the questionnaire. During the feedback sessions, participants discuss reasons for the scores and the problems that the data reveal.

In the process analysis stage, the group examines its process for making decisions, communicating, and accomplishing work, usually with the help of the consultant. Unfortunately, groups often overlook this stage as they become absorbed in the survey data and the problems revealed during the feedback sessions. Occasionally, group managers simply fail to hold feedback and process analysis sessions. Change agents should ensure that managers hold these sessions and that they are rewarded for doing so. The process analysis stage is important because its purpose is to develop action plans for making improvements. Several sessions may be required to discuss the process issues fully and settle on a strategy

51. Jerome L. Franklin, "Improving the Effectiveness of Survey Feedback," *Personnel,* May-June 1978, pp. 11–17.

for improvements. Groups often find it useful to document the plans as they are discussed and to appoint a member to follow up on implementation. Generally, the follow-up concerns whether communication and communication processes have actually been improved. A follow-up survey can be administered several months to a year later to assess how much these processes have changed since they were first reported.

The survey-feedback method probably is one of the most widely used organization change and development interventions. If any of its stages are compromised or omitted, however, the technique becomes less useful. A primary responsibility of the consultant or change agent, then, is to ensure that the method is fully and faithfully carried through.

Managing Organization Development

The management of change in organizations is one of the most difficult tasks of the modern manager. Earlier in this chapter, we emphasized that change is inevitable and that, for the well-being of the organization, it must be planned for and managed. Yet most organization change and development efforts—including those that are well planned—encounter problems, some significant enough to threaten the entire change program. Typically, change efforts take longer and incur higher costs than expected, and they may be only partially successful.[52]

Given the difficulty of realizing organization change, it is useful to discuss some criteria by which to judge the effectiveness of change efforts. A change effort can be considered effectively managed if

1. The organization is moved from the current state to the planned future state.
2. The functioning of the organization in the future state meets expectations.
3. The transition is accomplished without undue cost to the organization and its individual members.[53]

In short, the desired system must be successfully established and must provide the expected benefits at minimal cost to the organization and its members. If the intended change is a new performance appraisal system, for instance, the change may be deemed a success when the new system is being used by managers to evaluate their employees' performance, is providing the correct types of information in the right form to the right people at the appropriate time, and has been implemented without unreasonable cost to individual employees or to the

52. See John P. Kotter and Leonard A. Schlesinger, "Choosing Strategies for Change," *Harvard Business Review,* March-April 1979, pp. 106–114.

53. David A. Nadler, "Concepts for the Management of Organizational Change," in J. Richard Hackman, Edward E. Lawler III, and Lyman W. Porter, eds., *Perspectives on Organizational Behavior,* 2nd. ed. (New York: McGraw-Hill, 1983), pp. 551–561.

FIGURE 21.7
Four Major Problems in Change Management

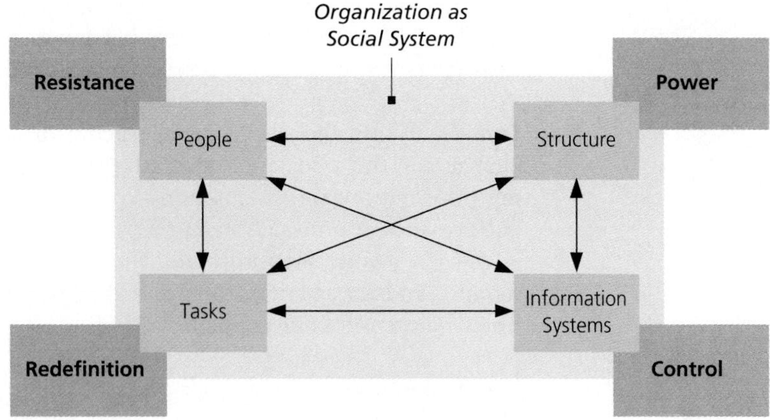

organization as a whole. In practice, a manager or change agent would have to define the criteria for evaluating a change project more specifically. However, these broad criteria suggest the standards that a particular change ought to meet.

Major Problems in Organization Development Efforts

■ The major problems of managing change can be organized into four categories: resistance, power, control, and task redefinition.

David Nadler has argued that the major problems of managing change can be organized into four categories: resistance, power, control, and task redefinition.[54] Figure 21.7 pairs these four problem categories with the four basic elements of the social system of the organization: people, structure, information system, and tasks. Note that the four basic elements of the social system are related to one another such that what happens to one part affects all the others. Assuming the current state has been properly diagnosed and the change to be implemented is appropriate, these four factors represent the major hurdles to effective organization change.

Resistance We already noted that resistance from employees is a key factor in any organization change effort. A primary factor contributing to resistance is the organization culture, which usually is the result of many years of doing things in a certain way.

Power Power can become an important issue in the transition from the current state to the future state, especially when the change has a substantial impact on organization structure and the people or groups that have the most power. The transition stage, during which the old structure is torn down and the new one is established, is fraught with uncertainty. People are naturally concerned about their place in the new order, and they may exercise power or engage in political activity to influence their future position. Typically, employees attempt to ensure

54. Ibid.

that they will be in a better position in the new social order as they perceive it will be after the transition. These behaviors may or may not be appropriate for their current position or for the change as planned by management.

Control While the old system is being dismantled and the new one shaped, change and the associated uncertainties can make the existing means of processing information and maintaining control—such as the communication system, performance appraisal system, reward structures, and other organizational processes—irrelevant, inappropriate, and ineffective. Thus, it may be difficult to monitor and reward performance and take corrective action during the transition. The result is a loss of control.

Task Redefinition Because all parts of the system interact, individual jobs are affected by any change, even one intended to affect another part of the organization (for example, the performance appraisal system). Rather than let new tasks evolve in response to changes in other areas, the organization should specify what the employees' tasks are and how they relate to other new jobs. If attention is not given to redefining jobs, the change may not have its intended effects throughout the organization.

Keys to Successful Organization Development

In conclusion, we offer five keys to managing OD. They relate directly to the problems identified earlier and to our view of the organization as a social system. Each can influence the elements of the social system and may help the organization avoid some of the major problems in managing the change. Table 21.5 lists the points and their potential impacts.

Take a Holistic View Managers must take a holistic view of the organization and the OD project. Because the subsystems of the organization are interdependent, a limited view can endanger the change effort. A holistic view encompasses

TABLE 21.5
Keys to Successful Organization Development Management

Key	Impacts
Take a holistic view of the organization	Anticipate effects on social system and culture
Secure top management support	Get dominant coalition on the side of change; safeguard structural change; head off problems of power and control
Encourage participation by those affected by the change	Minimize transition problem of control, resistance, and task redefinition
Foster open communication	Minimize transition problems of resistance and information and control systems
Reward those who contribute to change	Minimize transition problems of resistance and control systems

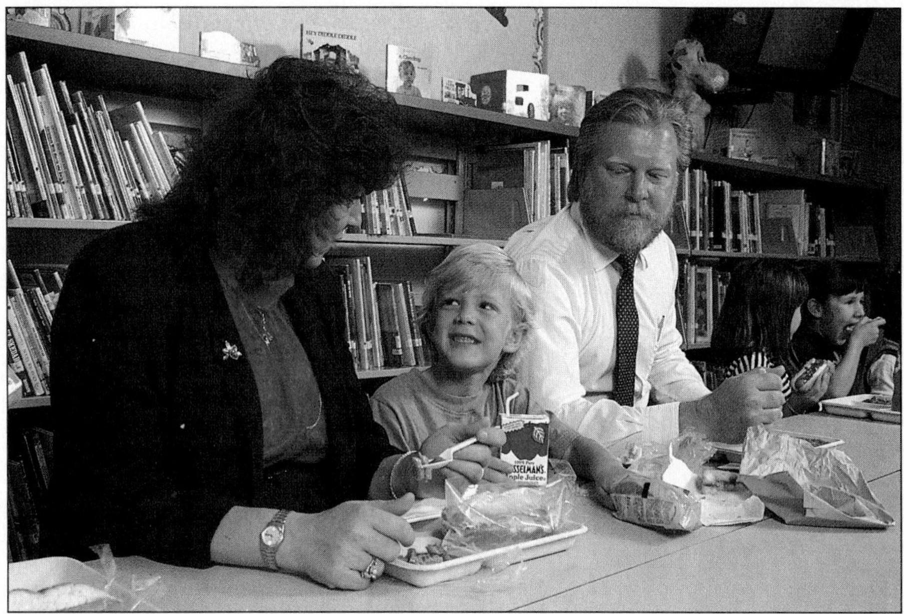

The provision of company-sponsored day care for employee dependents is a common practice among progressive companies. The American Bankers Insurance Group has gone one step further and taken a holistic approach to this issue by providing a company-owned school and day care center on property adjacent to the company headquarters. Mr. and Mrs. Jones can have lunch with their son, Richie, or visit the school at any time.

the culture and dominant coalition as well as the people, tasks, structure, and information subsystems.

Secure Top Management Support The support of top management is essential to the success of any OD effort. As the organization's probable dominant coalition, it is a powerful element of the social system, and its support is necessary for dealing with control and power problems. For example, a manager who plans a change in the way tasks are assigned and responsibility is delegated in his or her department must notify top management and gain its support. Complications may arise if disgruntled employees complain to high-level managers who have not been notified of the change or do not support it. The employees' complaints may jeopardize the manager's plan—and perhaps her or his job.

Encourage Participation Problems related to resistance, control, and power can be overcome by broad participation in planning for OD. Giving people a voice in designing the change may give them a sense of power and control over their own destinies, which may help to win their support during implementation.

Foster Open Communication Open communication is an important factor in managing resistance to change and overcoming information and control problems during transition. Employees typically recognize the uncertainties and ambiguities that arise during a transition and seek information on the change and their place in the new system. In the absence of information, the gap may be filled with inappropriate or false information, which may endanger the change process. Rumors tend to spread through the grapevine faster than accurate information can be disseminated through official channels. A manager should always be sensitive to the effects of uncertainty on employees, especially in a period of change; any news, even bad news, seems better than no news.

Reward Contributors Although this last point is simple, it can easily be neglected. Employees who contribute to the change in any way need to be rewarded. Too often the only people who are acknowledged after a change effort are those who tried to stop it. Those who quickly grasp new work assignments, work harder to cover what otherwise might not get done in the transition, or help others adjust to changes deserve special credit—perhaps a mention in a news release or the internal company newspaper, special consideration in performance appraisal, a merit raise, or a promotion. From a behavioral perspective, individuals need to benefit in some way if they are to willingly help change something that eliminates the old, comfortable way of doing the job.

In the current dynamic environment, managers must anticipate the need for change and satisfy it with more responsive and competitive organization systems. Because organizations must change or face elimination, these five keys to managing organization change may also serve as general guidelines for managing organizational behavior.

Summary of Key Points

- Change may be forced on an organization, or an organization may change in response to the environment or an internal need. The forces for change are interdependent and influence organizations in many ways. Currently, the areas in which the pressures for change seem most powerful involve people, technology, information and communication, competition, and social trends.
- Resistance to change may arise from several individual and organizational sources. Resistance may indicate a legitimate concern that the change is not good for the organization and may warrant a reexamination of plans. Resistance to change can be managed through communicating and educating employees more effectively and involving employees in the change as much as possible.
- Planned organization change involves anticipating change and preparing for it. Lewin described organization change in terms of unfreezing, change, and refreezing. In the expanded model of planned change, top management recognizes forces that call for change, engages in a problem-solving process to design the change, and implements and evaluates the change.
- Organization development is the process of planned change and improvement of organizations through the application of knowledge of the behavioral sciences. OD uses a systematic change process and focuses on managing the culture of the organization. The most comprehensive change involves altering the structure of the organization through a reorganization of departments, reporting relationships, or authority systems.
- Quality-of-work-life programs focus on providing a work environment in which employees can satisfy individual needs. Task-technological changes

alter the way the organization accomplishes its primary tasks. Task redesign includes, along with the steps usually associated with change, diagnosis, cost/benefit analysis, formulation of a redesign strategy, and implementation of supplemental changes.

- Frequently used group and individual approaches to organization change are training and management development programs, team building, and survey-feedback techniques. Training programs usually are designed to improve employees' job skills; help employees adapt to other organization changes, such as an MBO program; or develop employees' awareness and understanding of problems such as workplace safety or stress. Management development programs attempt to foster in current or future managers the skills, abilities, and perspectives important to good management. Team-building programs are designed to help a work team or group develop into a mature, well-functioning team by helping it define its goals or priorities, analyze its tasks and the way they are performed, and examine relationships among the people doing the work. As used in the OD process, survey-feedback techniques involve gathering data, analyzing and summarizing them, and returning them to employees and groups for discussion and for identification and solution of problems.
- The management of change in organizations requires careful diagnosis, planning, implementation, and control. Even then change is likely to be slower than desired, more costly than expected, and less successful than planned. A change effort has been effectively managed if the desired change has taken place and expectations are being met without undue cost to the organization.
- Major problems in achieving changes in organizations are resistance, power, control, and task redefinition. These problems are directly linked to the elements of the organization's social system. Five keys to successful management of change are taking a holistic view of the organization, obtaining the support of top management, encouraging participation in the design of change by all those affected by it, openly communicating throughout the process, and rewarding those who contribute to the change.

Discussion Questions

1. Is most organization change forced on the organization by external factors or created from within? Explain.
2. What broad category of pressures for organization change other than the five discussed in the chapter can you think of? Briefly describe it.
3. Which sources of resistance to change present the most problems for an internal change agent? For an external change agent?
4. Which stage of the Lewin model of change do you think is the most often overlooked? Why?
5. What are the advantages and disadvantages of having an internal change agent rather than an external change agent?
6. How does organization development differ from organization change?

7. How and why would OD differ if the elements of the social system were not interdependent?
8. Do quality-of-work-life programs rely more on individual or organizational aspects of organizational behavior? Why?
9. Describe how the job of your professor could be redesigned. Include a discussion of other subsystems that would need to be changed.
10. How can a manager determine whether an OD effort has met the three criteria of effectiveness discussed in this chapter?

CASE 21.1

Burger King Pulls One Out with Vacuum Management

While under the ownership of Pillsbury, Burger King languished under rigid, unimaginative management. Then Pillsbury was bought by an even bigger conglomerate, Britain's Grand Metropolitan PLC. In 1988, Burger King was at a crossroads. The market for fast foods was glutted, its primary source of labor, teenagers, was drying up, the competition was discounting heavily, and its principal customers, baby boomers, were becoming increasingly nutrition conscious. The environment was changing rapidly, and Burger King's more than six thousand outlets were not keeping pace. Profits had plunged 59 percent to about $48.2 million in the previous two years because per-store sales had remained relatively flat at about $1 million per year.

Then Barry J. Gibbons was brought in from Grand Met's restaurant division in Britain to turn things around. In the spring of 1988, Gibbons cut 550 management jobs, consolidated marketing, financial, and personnel functions in the field into headquarters, and eliminated layers of middle management. Then, in 1990, he eliminated the chief operating officer position and created two presidents to report directly to him: one for franchise operations and one for company-owned operations. With these tactics, as well as pushing more store decisions down to the store level rather than middle management, he gave each store more responsibility for its own operations. As long as company-owned stores stay within budget, store managers now can make expenditure decisions of up to $25,000.

Gibbons created the concept of "vacuum management" by stepping in when these changes took place. He believed that when a major change occurs, a "vacuum" is created that can be filled either by the people with bad information or by individuals with positive ideas. He therefore traveled the country to spread the good word to the more than 35,000 Burger King workers. His message was that Burger King was healthy with its 6,252 outlets, new management, and aggressive new ideas for products and services. He created an 800-number customer service hotline so that customers could call headquarters directly with complaints. Secret shoppers visited stores monthly and reported their findings to headquarters.

New products began hitting the stores almost immediately. Burger King's new broiled chicken sandwich finally caught on and now sells at the rate of almost 1 million per day. The company switched to 100 percent vegetable oil for frying, and its popular prepackaged salads with Paul Newman dressing have replaced its low-performing salad bars. By mid-1990, more than a dozen new products were launched. At last new ideas had a chance. A Burger King on wheels was test marketed, as was individual-size Domino's pizza ("Burger King pizza" just didn't sound right). Not all ideas were received positively by customers, but employees from top to bottom were convinced that management was committed to turning Burger King around.

In addition to offering new products and services, Burger King is experimenting with new electronic and software systems and more automated food preparation to compensate for the declining teenage labor pool. People are believing in Gibbons by watching his results. Last-quarter earnings in 1989 rose 25 percent, and per-store sales growth rebounded in early 1990. Obviously, Gibbons has made a strong initial impact on the former fast-food king. Whether or not it is strong enough for its parent company remains to be seen.

Case Questions

1. What forces for change were occurring at Burger King?
2. What types of organization change techniques did Barry Gibbons use to turn Burger King around?
3. Which of Gibbons' actions would you classify as organization development? Why?

SOURCES: "Can Barry Gibbons Put the Sizzle Back in Burger King?" *Business Week,* October 22, 1990, pp. 60–61; Brian Dumaine, "The New Turnaround Champs," *Fortune,* July 16, 1990, pp. 35–44; "Can a New CEO Pull Burger King Out of the Fire?" *Business Week,* May 22, 1989, p. 40.

CASE 21.2 Spooked by Computers

The New England Arts Project had its headquarters above an Italian restaurant in Portsmouth, New Hampshire. The project had five full-time employees, and during busy times of the year, particularly the month before Christmas, it hired as many as six part-time workers to type, address envelopes, and send out mailings. Although each of the five full-timers had a title and a formal job description, an observer would have had trouble telling their positions apart. Suzanne Clammer, for instance, was the executive director—the head of the office—but she could be found typing or licking envelopes just as often as Martin Welk, who had been working for less than a year as office coordinator, the lowest position in the project's hierarchy.

Despite a constant sense of being a month behind, the office ran relatively smoothly. No outsider would have had a prayer of finding a mailing list or a budget in the office, but project employees knew where almost everything was, and after a quiet fall they did not mind having their small space packed with workers in November. But a number of the federal funding agencies on which the project relied began to grumble about the cost of the part-time workers, the amount of time the project spent on handling routine paperwork, and the chaotic condition of its financial records. The pressure to make a radical change was on. Finally Martin Welk said it: "Maybe we should get a computer."

To Welk, fresh out of college, where he had written his papers on a word processor, computers were just another tool to make a job easier. But his belief was not shared by the others in the office, the youngest of whom had fifteen years' more seniority than he. A computer would eat the project's mailing list, they said, destroying any chance of raising funds for the year. It would send the wrong things to the wrong people, insulting them and convincing them that the project had become another faceless organization that did not care. They swapped horror stories about computers that had charged them thousands of dollars for purchases they had never made or had assigned the same airplane seat to five people.

"We'll lose all control," Suzanne Clammer complained. She saw some kind of office automation as inevitable, yet she kept thinking she would probably quit before it came about. She liked hand-addressing mailings to arts patrons whom she had met, and she felt sure that the recipients contributed more because they recognized her neat blue printing. She remembered the agonies of typing class in high school and believed she was too old to take on something new and bound to be much more confusing. Two other employees, with whom she had worked for a decade, called her after work to ask if the prospect of a computer in the office meant they should be looking for other jobs. "I have enough trouble with English grammar," one of them wailed. "I'll never be able to learn Pascal or Lotus or whatever these new languages are."

One morning Clammer called Martin Welk into her office, shut the door, and asked him if he could recommend any computer consultants. She had read an article that explained how a company could waste thousands of dollars by adopting integrated office automation in the wrong way, and she figured the project would have to hire somebody for at least six months to get the new machines working and to teach the staff how to use them. Welk was pleased because Clammer evidently had accepted the idea of a computer in the office. But he also realized that as the resident authority on computers, he had a lot of work to do before they went shopping for machines.

Case Questions

1. Is organization development appropriate in this situation? Why or why not?
2. What kinds of resistance to change have the employees of the project displayed?
3. What can Martin Welk do to overcome the resistance?

EXPERIENTIAL EXERCISE

Purpose: This exercise will help you understand the complexities of change in organizations.

Format: Your task is to plan the implementation of a major change in an organization.

Procedure: *Part 1.* The class will divide into five groups of approximately equal size. Your instructor will assign each group one of the following changes:

1. A change from the semester system to the quarter system (or the opposite, depending on the school's current system)
2. A requirement that all work—homework, examinations, term papers, problem sets—be done on computer
3. A requirement that all students live on campus
4. A requirement that all students have reading, writing, and speaking fluency in at least three languages, including English and Japanese, to graduate
5. A requirement that all students room with someone in the same major

First, decide what individuals and groups must be involved in the change process. Then decide how the change will be implemented using Lewin's process of organization change (Figure 21.1) as a framework. Consider how to deal with resistance to change, using Tables 21.2 and 21.3 as guides. Decide whether a change agent (internal or external) should be used. Develop a realistic timetable for full implementation of the change. Is transition management appropriate?

After all groups have developed plans, they will present them to the class.

Part 2. Using the same groups as in part 1, your next task is to describe the techniques you would use to implement the change described in part 1. You may use structural changes, task-technology methods, group and individual programs, or any combination of these. You may need to go to the library to gather more information on some techniques.

You should also discuss how you will deal with the common OD problems: resistance, power, control, and task redefinition. The five keys to successful change management discussed at the end of the chapter should play important roles in your plan.

Your instructor may make this exercise an in-class project, but it is also a good semester-ending project for groups to work on outside class. Either way, the exercise is most beneficial when the groups report their implementation programs to the entire class. Each group should report on which OD techniques are to be used, why they were selected, how they will be implemented, and how the typical OD problems will be avoided.

Follow-up Questions

Part 1:

1. How similar were the implementation steps for each change?
2. Were the plans for managing resistance to change realistic?
3. Do you think any of the changes could be successfully implemented at your school? Why or why not?

Part 2:

1. Did various groups use the same technique in different ways or to accomplish different goals?
2. If you did outside research on OD techniques for your project, did you find any OD techniques that seemed more applicable than those in this chapter? If so, describe one of them.

CHAPTER OUTLINE

- The Emergence Of International Management
  - *The Growth of International Business*
  - *Trends in International Business*
  - *Cross-Cultural Differences and Similarities*
- Individual Behavior in an International Context
  - *Individual Differences across Cultures*
  - *Managerial Behavior across Cultures*
  - *Motivation across Cultures*
- Interpersonal Processes in an International Context
  - *Group Dynamics across Cultures*
  - *Leadership across Cultures*
  - *Power and Conflict across Cultures*
  - *Communication across Cultures*
- Enhancing Individual and Interpersonal Processes
  - *Rewards across Cultures*
  - *Job Design across Cultures*
  - *Performance Evaluation across Cultures*
  - *Stress across Cultures*
  - *Decision Making across Cultures*
- Organization Characteristics in an International Context
  - *Environment and Technology across Cultures*
  - *Organization Structure and Design across Cultures*
- Integrating Individuals, Groups, and Organizations
  - *Organization Change in an International Context*
  - *Careers across Cultures*

22

INTERNATIONAL ASPECTS OF ORGANIZATIONS

CHAPTER OBJECTIVES

After studying this chapter, you should be able to:

Describe the emergence of international management.

Describe individual behavior in an international context.

Discuss interpersonal processes in an international context.

Discuss organization characteristics in an international context.

Describe organization processes in an international context.

Summarize organization change in an international context.

For decades, Lionel Train Co. made toy electric trains at its factory in Michigan. Lionel trains once were a fixture under many Christmas trees. To some people, Lionel *has even become a generic term referring to any electric train. Over the past several years, however, demand for traditional toys like electric trains has dropped in favor of more contemporary toys like Nintendo, G.I. Joe, and so forth.*

As a result of falling demand and increasing costs, managers at Lionel have had to search for ways to maintain acceptable profit margins. They believed they were on the right track in moving their operations to Tijuana, Mexico; after all, wages were only 55 cents an hour, so how could they lose? Thus, they closed their plant in Michigan, gave all the workers termination notices, packed up, and moved.

Unfortunately, things did not work out as planned. First, the company forced just-fired workers to load their trucks; as a result, the packing was done poorly. Next, the trucks were stalled at the border because of communications problems with customs agents. Then the company found it could not hire managerial talent locally and therefore had to send down more U.S. managers than originally planned. Finally, the workers who were available were not motivated enough to do a high-quality job. The company saw its market share drop by 10 percent and annoyed customers by failing to fill orders.

So Lionel packed up again and moved back home. It leased the plant it had sold earlier and rehired many of its former workers. Things are almost the same as before, but not quite—many of the rehired workers are still angry at the company for moving in the first place.[1]

Lionel Train's experiences provide many insights into international business and its relationship to organizational behavior. The company moved its operations to take advantage of cheaper labor. But communications problems disrupted the move, as did a lack of managerial talent. Local labor conditions led to motivational problems. Finally, even though Lionel's U.S. workers have been rehired, they still hold negative attitudes toward the company and no doubt have a low level of organizational commitment.

This chapter is about organizational behavior in an international context. First, we trace the emergence of international management. In subsequent discussions, we parallel the overall organization of the book by relating international

1. "Some Firms Resume Manufacturing in U.S. after Foreign Fiascoes," *The Wall Street Journal,* October 14, 1986, pp. 1, 27. Reprinted by permission of *The Wall Street Journal,* © 1986 Dow Jones & Company, Inc. All Rights Reserved Worldwide.

The Hewlett-Packard News Network allows dealers in 12 countries to get immediate access to news and information about the company's products and their availability for shipment. Advances in communication such as this one have played a significant role in the enormous growth in international business during the last decade.

issues to individual behavior, the individual-organization interface, organization characteristics, organization processes, and organization change and development.

The Emergence of International Management

■ The rapid growth in international business makes an understanding of organizational behavior all the more important for contemporary managers.

In many ways, international management is nothing new. Centuries ago, the Roman army was forced to develop a management system to deal with its widespread empire.[2] Likewise, the Olympic games, the Red Cross, and many similar organizations have international roots. From a business standpoint, however, international management is relatively new, at least to the United States.

The Growth of International Business

In 1990, the volume of international trade in current dollars was almost thirty times greater than that amount in 1960, and the figures are projected to continue escalating during the remainder of this decade. What has led to this dramatic increase? As Figure 22.1 shows, four major factors account for much of the momentum.

First, communication and transportation have advanced dramatically over the past few decades. Telephone service has improved, communication networks span the globe and can interact via satellite, and access to remote areas has been vastly facilitated. Facsimile machines allow managers to send documents around the world in seconds as opposed to days just a few years ago. In short, it is simply easier to conduct international business today.

2. M. J. Gent, "Theory X in Antiquity, or the Bureaucratization of the Roman Army," *Business Horizons,* January-February 1984, pp. 53–54.

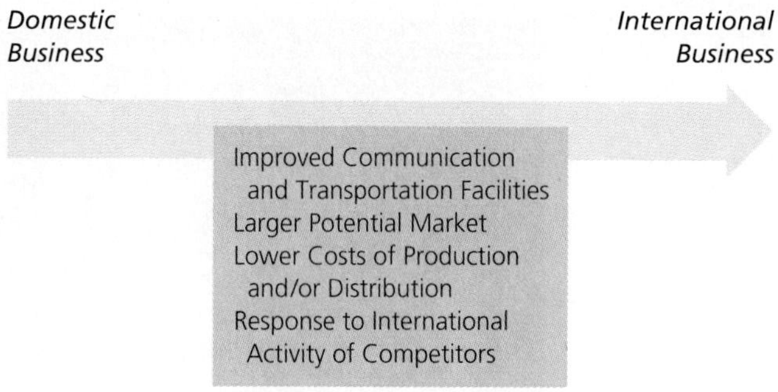

FIGURE 22.1
Forces That Have Increased International Business

Second, businesses have expanded internationally to increase their markets. Companies in smaller countries, such as Nestlé Co., Inc., in Switzerland, recognized long ago that their domestic markets were too small to sustain much growth and therefore moved into international activities. Many U.S. firms, on the other hand, had all the business they could handle until recently; hence, they are just beginning to consider international opportunities.

Third, more and more firms are moving into the international realm to control costs. The opening vignette noted that Lionel moved to lower its labor costs. Things did not work out as planned, but many other firms are successfully using inexpensive labor in the Far East and Mexico.[3]

Finally, many organizations have become international in response to competition. If an organization starts gaining strength in international markets, its competitors often must follow suit to avoid falling too far behind in sales, profitability, and so forth. Mobile, Texaco, and Exxon realized they had to increase their international market share to keep pace with foreign competitors such as British Petroleum and Royal Dutch Shell.

Trends in International Business

The most striking trend in international business is obvious: growth. More and more businesses are entering the international marketplace, including many smaller firms. We read a great deal about the threat of foreign companies. For example, successful Japanese automobile firms like Toyota and Nissan produce higher-quality cars for lower prices than do U.S. firms. What we often overlook, however, is the success of U.S. firms abroad. Ford, for example, has long had a successful business in Europe and today employs less than half its total work force on U.S. soil. And U.S. firms make dozens of products better than anyone else in the world.[4]

Business transactions are also becoming increasingly blurred across national boundaries. Ford owns 25 percent of Mazda, General Motors and Toyota have

---

3. Henry W. Lane and Joseph J. DiStefano, *International Management Behavior* (Ontario: Nelson, 1988).

4. Christopher Knowlton, "What America Makes Best," *Fortune,* March 28, 1988, pp. 40–54.

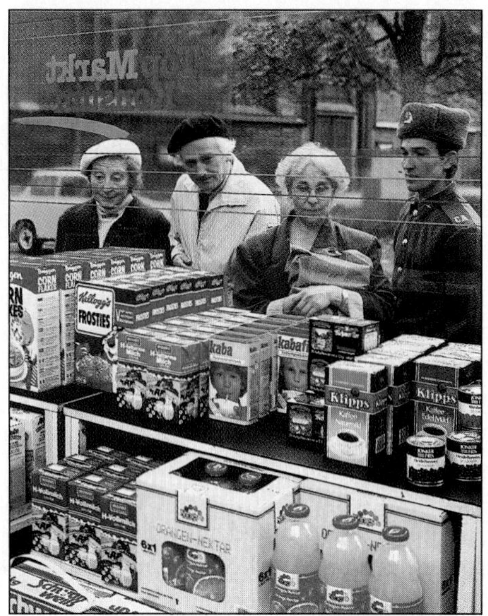

Since the reunification of Germany, shoppers in what was East Germany have an increasingly wide variety of products to choose from. Tandem Computers, who is the supplier of this grocery chain's computer systems, helped the chain move quickly into the newly opened market by providing a computer system that handles the distribution of its goods. American consumer-products companies like Kellogg have also benefited from this sudden expansion of their established German market.

a joint venture in California, Ford and Volkswagen have one in Argentina, and Honda and British Sterling have one worldwide. Indeed, some experts have started predicting that some multinational firms will soon start to lose their national identity altogether and become truly global corporations.

International involvement has also increased across nonbusiness organizational forms. Universities offer study programs abroad, health care and research programs span national boundaries, international postal systems are working more closely together, and athletics programs are increasingly being transplanted to different cultures.

Recent events in other parts of the world also will have a major effect on business. The fall of the Berlin Wall and the movement of the Eastern bloc toward a free-market economy will provide many new opportunities and challenges to business in the years to come.[5]

In many ways, then, we are becoming a truly global economy. No longer will a firm be able to insulate itself from foreign competitors or opportunities. Thus, it is imperative that every manager develop and maintain at least a rudimentary understanding of the dynamics of international management.[6]

Cross-Cultural Differences and Similarities

Since the primary concern of this discussion is human behavior in organizational settings, we will focus on differences and similarities in behavior across cultures.

5. Peter Nulty, "The Era of Possibilities," *Fortune,* January 15, 1990, pp. 42–54.

6. Richard M. Steers and Edwin L. Miller, "Management in the 1990s: The International Challenge," *Academy of Management Executive,* February 1988, pp. 21–22.

Unfortunately, research in this area is still in its infancy.[7] Thus, many of the research findings we can draw on are preliminary at best.

Nevertheless, we can note a few ideas about differences and similarities at a general level. First, cultures and national boundaries do not necessarily coincide. Some areas of Switzerland are very much like Italy, other parts like France, and still other parts like Germany. Similarly, within the United States there are profound cultural differences among southern California, Texas, and the East Coast.[8]

■ Behavior in organizational settings varies across culures.

Given this basic assumption, one recent review of the literature on international management reached five basic conclusions.[9] First, behavior in organizational settings indeed varies across cultures. Thus, employees in companies based in Japan, the United States, and Germany are likely to have different attitudes and patterns of behavior. The behavior patterns are likely to be widespread and pervasive within an organization.

■ Culture is a major cause of behavioral variation.

Second, culture itself is one major cause of this variation. Thus, while the behavioral differences just noted may be caused in part by different standards of living, different geographical conditions, and so forth, culture itself is a major factor apart from other considerations.

■ Behavior across cultures remains diverse, but organizations themselves are becoming more similar.

Third, although behavior within organizational settings (e.g., motivation and attitudes) remains quite diverse across cultures, organizations themselves (e.g., organization design and technology) appear to be increasingly similar. Hence, managerial practices at a general level may be more and more alike, but the people who work within organizations still differ markedly.

■ The same manager behaves differently in different cultures.

Fourth, the same manager behaves differently in different cultural settings. A manager may adopt one set of behaviors when working in one culture but change those behaviors when moved to a different culture. For example, Japanese executives who come to work in the United States slowly begin to act more like U.S. managers and less like Japanese managers. This often is a source of concern for them when they are transferred back to Japan.[10]

■ Cultural diversity can be an important ingredient in achieving synergy.

Finally, cultural diversity can be an important source of synergy in enhancing organizational effectiveness. More and more organizations are coming to appreciate the virtues of cultural diversity, but they still know surprisingly little about how to manage it.[11] Organizations that adopt a multinational strategy can—with effort—become more than a sum of their parts. Operations in each culture can benefit from operations in other cultures through an enhanced understanding of how the world works.[12]

---

7. David A. Ricks, Brian Toyne, and Zaida Martinez, "Recent Developments in International Management Research," *Journal of Management,* June 1990, pp. 219–254.

8. Simcha Ronen and Oded Shenkar, "Clustering Countries on Attitudinal Dimensions: A Review and Synthesis," *Academy of Management Review,* July 1985, pp. 435–454.

9. Nancy J. Adler, Robert Doktor, and Gordon Redding, "From the Atlantic to the Pacific Century," *Journal of Management,* Summer 1986, pp. 295–318.

10. Brian O'Reilly, "Japan's Uneasy U.S. Managers," *Fortune,* April 25, 1988, pp. 245–264.

11. "Learning to Accept Cultural Diversity," *The Wall Street Journal,* September 12, 1990, pp. B1, B9.

12. Tamotsu Yamaguchi, "The Challenge of Internationalization," *Academy of Management Executive,* February 1988, pp. 33–36.

FIGURE 22.2
Differences in Individual Behaviors among Cultures

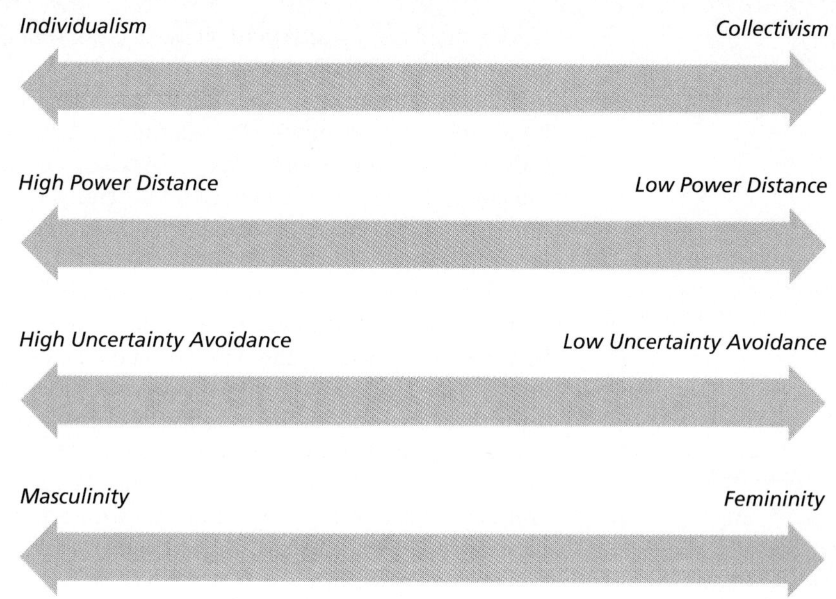

Individual Behavior in an International Context

The first two conclusions we just noted clearly suggest that individual behavior varies across cultures. These variations can be viewed in terms of individual differences, managerial behavior, motivation, and rewards across cultures.

Individual Differences across Cultures

Figure 22.2 highlights some of the more important dimensions along which behavior varies. These dimensions were identified in a large-scale study of 160,000 people working in 60 countries.[13]

- **Individualism** and **collectivism** reflect whether individuals place primary value on themselves or on the good of the group or society.

Individualism/Collectivism **Individualism** is a state of mind in which people view themselves first as individuals and believe their own interests and values take priority. **Collectivism,** on the other hand, is a feeling that the good of the group or society should come first.

People in a culture characterized by individualism tend to put their careers before their organizations and usually assess situations in terms of how decisions and alternative courses of action will affect them personally. People in a culture dominated by collectivism, in contrast, often put the needs of the organization

13. Geert Hofstede, *Culture's Consequences: International Differences in Work Related Values* (Beverly Hills, Calif.: Sage, 1980).

before their own needs and view decisions and alternatives in terms of their impact on the organization.

The United States, Australia, Great Britain, the Netherlands, Canada, and New Zealand are among the most individualistic cultures. Colombia, Pakistan, Taiwan, Peru, Singapore, Japan, Mexico, Greece, and Hong Kong are among the countries in which collectivism is stronger.

- **Power distance** is the extent to which people accept the right of organizations to grant power.

Power Distance **Power distance** reflects the extent to which employees accept the idea that people in an organization rightfully have different levels of power. In a high-power-distance culture, for example, a boss makes decisions simply because he or she is the boss; others do not question it but merely follow instructions. In a low-power-distance culture, employees recognize few power differences and follow the boss's lead only when they believe the boss is right or when they feel explicitly threatened.

The United States, Israel, Austria, Denmark, Ireland, Norway, Germany, and New Zealand represent cultures with a low power distance. Spain, France, Japan, Singapore, Mexico, Brazil, and Indonesia are examples of cultures with a high power distance.

- **Uncertainty avoidance** reflects how much certainty or uncertainty people will accept.

Uncertainty Avoidance **Uncertainty avoidance** is the extent to which people accept or avoid feelings of uncertainty. Some people, for example, thrive on the excitement and stimulation they experience from the prospect of new opportunities and challenges. Other people want predictable and certain futures.

Employees in Denmark, the United States, Canada, Norway, Singapore, Hong Kong, and Australia are among those who can tolerate high levels of uncertainty. Workers in Israel, Austria, Japan, Italy, Argentina, Peru, France, and Belgium are more highly motivated to avoid uncertainty in their work lives.

- Masculinity and femininity are indicators of what a culture values.

Masculinity/Femininity The degree of masculinity or femininity is seen as the extent to which cultures value qualities like assertiveness and materialism on the one hand and people and the quality of life on the other. Masculine societies define male-female roles more rigidly than do feminine societies. Japan and Austria are highly masculine, the United States slightly masculine, and Norway, Sweden, Denmark, and Finland highly feminine.

Managerial Behavior across Cultures

Individual differences across cultures obviously can shape managerial as well as employee behavior. Beyond those differences are others specific to managerial behavior.[14]

In general, these differences relate to managerial beliefs about the role of authority and power in the organization. For example, managers in Indonesia,

14. André Laurent, "The Cultural Diversity of Western Conceptions of Management," *International Studies of Management and Organization,* Spring-Summer 1983, pp. 75–96.

Italy, and Japan tend to believe that the purpose of an organization structure is to let everyone know who his or her boss is. Managers in the United States, Germany, and Great Britain, in contrast, believe the organization structure is intended to coordinate group behavior and effort. On another dimension, Italian and German managers believe it is acceptable to bypass one's boss to get things done, whereas managers in Sweden and Great Britain hold the strongest prohibitions against bypassing one's superior.

Figure 22.3 illustrates findings on another interesting point. Managers in Japan strongly believe that a manager should be able to answer any question he or she is asked. Thus, they place a premium on expertise and experience. In contrast, Swedish managers have the lowest concern for knowing all the answers. They view themselves as problem solvers and facilitators who make no claim to omnipotence.

Some recent evidence also suggests that managerial behavior is rapidly changing, at least among European managers. In general, these managers are

FIGURE 22.3
Differences across Cultures in Managers' Beliefs about Answering Questions from Subordinates

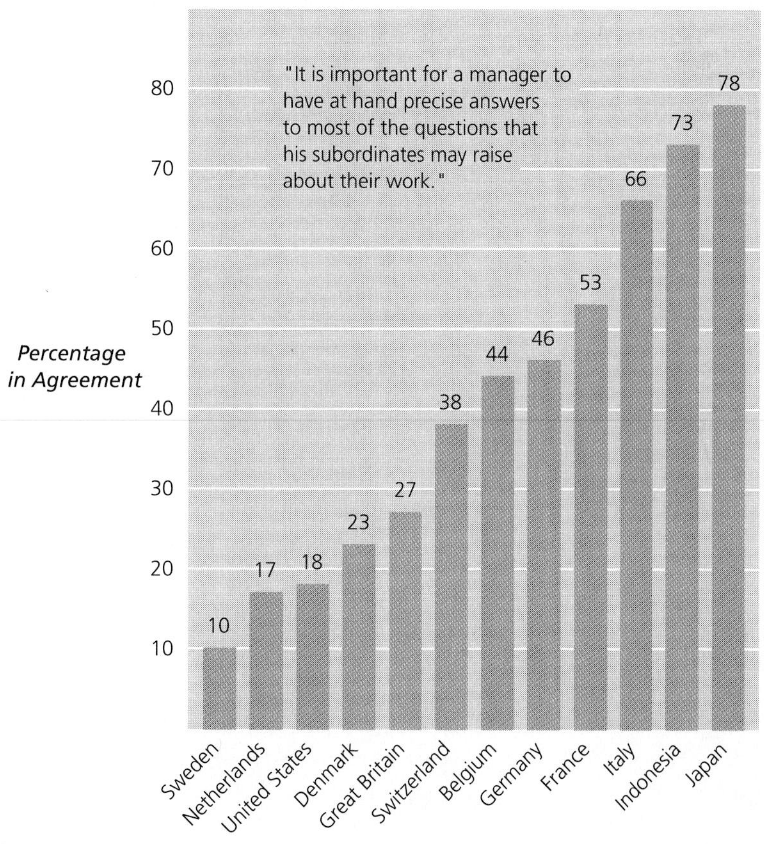

SOURCE: Reprinted from *International Studies of Management and Organization,* Vol. XIII, No. 1–2, Spring-Summer 1983, by permission of M. E. Sharpe, Inc., Armonk, N.Y. 10504.

THE ETHICAL DILEMMA

The Highest Form of Apology

In 1985 when a Japan Air Lines jet crashed, its president, Yasumoto Takagi, made arrangements for burying the dead, called victims' families to apologize, and then promptly resigned. So did the president of Kikkoman Corporation after his corporation was hit by a scandal about tainted wine. And in 1987, when a subsidiary of Toshiba sold sensitive military technology to the Soviet Union, both CEO Sugiichiro Watari and Chairman Shoichi Saba also gave up their posts.

These executive actions, which Toshiba calls "the highest form of apology," may seem bizarre to U.S. managers. No one at Boeing resigned after the JAL crash, which may have been caused by a faulty Boeing repair. No Union Carbide executive quit after the company's plant in Bhopal, India was the site of this era's worst industrial accident. "Golden parachutes" that ease executives out of their positions are more common in America than public apologies.

The difference between the two business cultures centers around different definitions of delegation. While U.S. executives give both responsibility and authority to their employees, Japanese executives delegate only authority—the responsibility is still theirs. Although Toshiba made it clear that the subsidiary that had sold the sensitive technology to the Soviets had its own management, the Toshiba top executives said they "must take personal responsibility for not creating an atmosphere throughout the Toshiba group that would make such activity unthinkable, even in an independently run subsidiary."

Such acceptance of community responsibility is not unique to businesses in Japan. School principals in Japan have resigned when their students committed major crimes after school hours. Even if they do not quit, Japanese executives will often accept primary responsibility in other ways, such as taking the first pay cut when a company gets into financial trouble. Such personal sacrifices, even if they are largely symbolic, help to create the sense of community and employee loyalty that is crucial to the Japanese way of doing business.

Harvard Business School professor George Lodge calls the ritual acceptance of blame "almost a feudal way of purging the community of dishonor," and to some in the United States, such resignations look cowardly. However, in an era in which both business and governmental leaders seem particularly adept at passing the buck, many U.S. managers would probably welcome an infusion of the Japanese sense of responsibility. If, for instance, U.S. automobile company executives offered to reduce their own salaries before they asked their workers to take pay cuts, negotiations would probably take on a very different character.

SOURCE: Christopher J. Chipello, "Matter of Honor: Japanese Top Managers Quick to Resign When Trouble Hits Firm," *The Wall Street Journal,* July 10, 1987, p. 19. Reprinted by permission of *The Wall Street Journal.*

becoming more career oriented, better educated, more willing to work cooperatively with labor, more willing to delegate, and more cosmopolitan.[15] *The Ethical Dilemma* describes another area in which significant cultural differences influence managerial behavior.

---

15. Richard I. Kirkland, Jr., "Europe's New Managers," *Fortune,* September 29, 1986, pp. 56–60.

Motivation across Cultures

Some specific implications can also be drawn regarding motivation across cultures. Maslow's hierarchy of needs, for example, has been shown to vary across some cultures and remain stable across others. In some countries, such as Japan and Greece, security needs are most important, whereas social needs tend to dominate in Sweden and Norway.[16] On the other hand, the hierarchy seems to be fairly stable in Peru, India, Mexico, the Middle East, and parts of Canada.[17]

Research has also found that the need for achievement, Herzberg's two-factor theory, and the expectancy theory of motivation all vary across cultures. For example, many U.S. managers have a high expectancy that their hard work will lead to high performance. In contrast, Moslem managers believe their success is determined solely by God.[18]

Interpersonal Processes in an International Context

■ Interpersonal processes vary across cultures, especially in terms of group dynamics, leadership, power and conflict, and communication.

Just as individual behavior varies from culture to culture, so do interpersonal processes. As Figure 22.4 illustrates, four key areas of variation are group dynamics, leadership, power and conflict, and communication.

Group Dynamics across Cultures

As we already noted, cultures differ in the importance they place on group membership. Attention also has been focused on how to deal with groups made up of people from different cultures.[19]

In general, a manager in charge of a culturally diverse group can expect several things. First, there is a high probability that distrust will exist among group members. Stereotyping also will present a problem. Finally, communication problems almost certainly will arise. Thus, the manager needs to recognize that such groups will seldom function smoothly, at least at first. Therefore, he or she may need to spend additional time helping the group through the rough spots as it matures and should allow a longer than normal time before expecting it to carry out its assigned task.

16. Adler, Doktor, and Redding, "From the Atlantic to the Pacific Century."

17. Nancy J. Adler, *International Dimensions of Organizational Behavior,* 2nd ed. (Boston: Kent, 1991).

18. Ibid.

19. Ibid.

FIGURE 22.4
Differences in Interpersonal Processes across Cultures

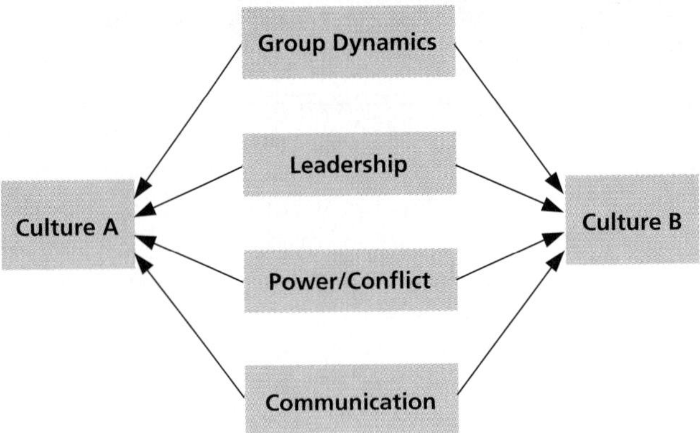

Leadership across Cultures

We already noted variations in managerial behavior across cultures. Leadership is another important dimension. In many ways, the issue of leadership in an international context parallels our discussions of leadership as a situational process in Chapter 9. Specifically, cultural factors comprise another important set of situational elements that dictate appropriate leadership style.

One highly important situational factor we already discussed is power distance. In a culture with a high power distance, employees routinely expect the leader to make decisions, solve problems, and assign tasks. Thus, when a leader in such a culture tries to promote participation, his or her efforts will likely be rebuked. Under conditions of low power distance, on the other hand, employees expect a greater say in how they do their jobs. Too much directive behavior and too few opportunities to participate may create problems.[20]

Finally, we should note the different roles leaders play in various cultures. Only recently have managers in Europe, for example, recognized that their jobs extend beyond the formal boundaries of managerial roles. In China, leaders are expected to remain formal and behave only within the clear confines of their legitimate power. In Japan, leaders serve more to facilitate group performance than as a control or supervisory mechanism.

Power and Conflict across Cultures

In the United States, power and conflict are a normal part of work life. When we see people striving to increase their power or two people arguing about something, we think nothing of it. In general, we accept the fact that these situations, as long as they do not become too dysfunctional, are just a part of doing business.

20. See James B. Shaw, "A Cognitive Categorization Model for the Study of Intercultural Management," *Academy of Management Review,* October 1990, pp. 626–645.

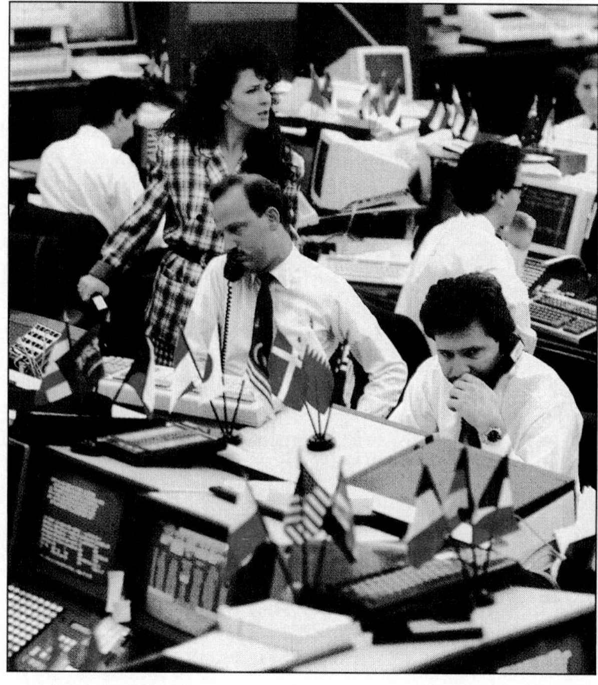

These managers are working in the foreign exchange office at Republic National Bank of New York. They spend much of their time interacting with traders in other countries. They must recognize that their counterparts in these other countries may have very different styles of doing business. Without this understanding, excessive conflict is likely.

In some other countries, however, power and conflict are even more pronounced. Great Britain, for example, is more prone to conflict in the workplace. This stems in part from the generally hostile nature of labor-management relations in that country. Bitter strikes make conflict commonplace.

The Japanese are at the other extreme. Attempts to increase one's power are frowned on, and instigating or promoting conflict is considered unseemly. Instead, the norms focus more on group harmony, mutual acceptance, and the like.

Communication across Cultures

Communication is an aspect of interpersonal relations that obviously is affected by the international environment, partly because of language issues and partly due to coordination issues.

Language Differences in languages are compounded by the fact that the same word can mean different things in different cultures. For example, Table 22.1 shows that Chevrolet's Nova did not fare well in Italy until managers there changed its name; in Italian, *no va* means "doesn't go." The table lists other interesting examples of communication foibles across cultures.

Note in the table that elements of nonverbal communication also vary across cultures. For example, colors and body language can convey quite a different message in one culture than in another. Thus, managers should be forewarned

TABLE 22.1
Examples of International Communication Problems

Source of Problem	Examples
Language	One firm, trying to find a name for a new soap powder, tested the chosen name in fifty languages. In English, it meant *dainty*. Translations into other languages meant *song* (Gaelic), *aloof* (Flemish), *horse* (African), *hazy* or *dim-witted* (Persian), *crazy* (Korean). The name was obscene in several Slavic languages. The Chevy Nova was *no va* in Italian, which means "doesn't go." *Coca-Cola* in Chinese meant "Bite the head of a dead tadpole." Idioms cannot be translated literally: "to murder the King's English" becomes "to speak French like a Spanish cow" in French.
Nonverbal Signs	Shaking your head up and down in Greece means *no*, and swinging it from side to side means *yes*. In most European countries, it is considered impolite not to have both hands on the table. The American sign for *OK* is an obscenity in Spain.
Colors	Green: Popular in Moslem countries Suggests disease in jungle-covered countries Suggests cosmetics in France, Sweden, Netherlands Red: Blasphemous in African countries Stands for wealth and masculinity in Great Britain
Product	Campbell Soup Co. was unsuccessful in Britain until the firm added water to its condensed soup so the cans would be the same size as the cans of soup the British were used to purchasing. Long-life packaging, which is commonly used for milk in Europe, allows milk to be stored for months at room temperature if it is unopened. Americans are still wary of it. Coca-Cola had to alter the taste of its soft drink in China when the Chinese described it as "tasting like medicine."

SOURCES: Adapted from David A. Ricks, *Big Business Blunders: Mistakes in Multinational Marketing* (Homewood, Ill.: Dow Jones–Irwin, 1983); Nancy Bragganti and Elizabeth Devine, *The Traveler's Guide to European Customs and Manners* (St. Paul, Minn.: Meadowbrook Books, 1984); several *Wall Street Journal* articles.

that they can take nothing for granted in dealing with people from another culture. They must take the time necessary to become as fully acquainted as possible with the verbal and nonverbal languages of that culture. *Management in Action* summarizes some of the steps organizations are having to take regarding communication and language barriers.

Coordination International communication is closely related to issues of coordination. For example, an American manager who wants to talk with his or her counterpart in Hong Kong or Singapore must contend not only with differences in language but with a time difference of several hours. When the American manager needs to talk on the telephone, the Hong Kong executive may be home asleep. Organizations are having to find increasingly innovative methods for

MANAGEMENT IN ACTION

Cultural Communication Barriers

Along with the advantages of cultural diversity come some fundamental problems that organizations must address. One very basic—and very important—problem involves communication.

In 1985, immigrants made up 7 percent of the American work force; the figure is projected to be 22 percent by the year 2000. Along with the diversity comes some interesting questions. For example, should an organization hire someone with limited skills in the English language? If so, should that employee be allowed to speak in his or her native tongue while at work? From a different perspective, should bilingual workers be paid a premium if their native language is an asset to the organization?

Firms across the country are taking a wide variety of positions regarding these questions. Motorola is spending $30 million for language training for many of its Polish, Greek, and Hispanic employees. Pace Foods in San Antonio faces a different problem. Because 35 percent of its workers are Hispanic, all staff meetings and company literature (handbooks, policy manuals, etc.) must be translated into Spanish.

Not all organizations respond in such a positive way. In California, a Filipino nurse is suing her former employer on the grounds that she was fired for using her native language at work. At Contel Corp., an Atlanta-based telephone company, bilingual workers charge that they are often pulled off their regular jobs to translate language for customers. They believe their language thus constitutes an additional skill, one for which they should be compensated.

While many questions about the various practices remain to be answered, the Equal Employment Opportunity Commission recently ruled that the required use of English-only in the workplace is appropriate only when it is necessary for business-related purposes. Thus, the burden of proof has shifted to employers that seek to enforce a common language requirement for all employees.

SOURCES: Nancy J. Adler, *International Dimensions of Organizational Behavior,* 2nd ed. (Boston: Kent, 1991); "Learning to Accept Cultural Diversity," *The Wall Street Journal,* September 12, 1990, pp. B1, B9; "Firms Grapple with Language," *The Wall Street Journal,* November 7, 1989, pp. B1, B10.

coordinating their activities in scattered parts of the globe. Merrill Lynch, for example, has developed its own satellite-based telephone network to monitor and participate in the worldwide money and financial markets.[21]

Enhancing Individual and Interpersonal Processes

- Approaches to enhancing individual and interpersonal processes vary across cultures, especially in terms of rewards, job design, performance evaluation, stress, and decision making.

In Part IV, we described several ways organizations can enhance individual and interpersonal processes. In this section, we consider a few of the international extensions and implications that parallel those topics.

21. "How Merrill Lynch Moves Its Stock Deals All Around the World," *The Wall Street Journal,* November 9, 1987, pp. 1, 8.

Rewards across Cultures

To date no one has systematically studied reward systems across cultures. However, given that motivational processes vary across cultures, it follows that the rewards people want also vary. For example, job security clearly is more valued in some cultures than in others. Similarly, employees in some cultures, like the United States, put greater emphasis on individual rewards such as recognition, promotion, and merit salary increases. In other cultures, such as Japan, employees place a higher value on group rewards and recognition.

Whatever the situation, the manager must be prepared to thoroughly assess what employees want before presuming to know. Adler provides two examples wherein U.S. managers overgeneralized from their own experiences and failed to anticipate problems. In one, salaries were increased for a group of Mexican workers. Unexpectedly, they started working fewer hours. Why? Because their higher salaries allowed them a better lifestyle, and they wanted to enjoy it. In the other case, a Japanese employee was promoted by an American manager as a reward for high performance. This made him feel less a part of the group and led to a performance decline.[22]

Job Design across Cultures

Job design clearly varies across cultures.[23] We noted many such differences in Chapter 13 and will summarize them here. Scandinavian companies, especially Volvo in Sweden, pioneered the use of work teams as a basis for job design. Workers in Germany, especially what was formerly West Germany, also have enjoyed innovative and progressive approaches to the design of their jobs. And in many ways, the participative management systems and quality circle programs so widespread in Japan represent aspects of job design. Beyond simple case analyses, however, job design has not been systematically studied across cultural boundaries.

Performance Evaluation across Cultures

Cross-cultural variation in performance evaluation includes two points of particular interest: what constitutes performance and how people respond to evaluation.

Measures of Performance Unfortunately, little has been written about what constitutes performance in various cultures. Some insights, however, can be inferred from our earlier discussion of motivation. Recall the Mexican workers

22. Adler, *International Dimensions of Organizational Behavior,* pp. 132–133.
23. Ricky W. Griffin, *Task Design* (Glenview, Ill.: Scott, Foresman, 1982).

who worked fewer hours after getting pay increases. Perhaps they saw their performance in terms of how much time they gave to the organization. Workers in a highly group-focused culture such as Japan's might shy away from performance measures that assess the individual's contributions. Instead, they may see their performance in terms of what they contribute to the group.

Reactions to Evaluation Similar differences characterize responses to actual evaluations of performance. People in some cultures accept critical evaluation, and negative feedback about performance may be appreciated and may result in improved performance. In other cultures, people take criticism much more seriously. Indeed, a recipient of criticism may be embarrassed enough to withdraw from the organization. The manager dealing with a new culture should develop a clear understanding of the role of performance feedback and its likely effects before undertaking any form of performance evaluation.

Stress across Cultures

In Chapter 15, we described many of the individual and organizational consequences of excessive stress. Given the variations across cultures in the role of work in people's lives, their motivation, and other factors, it is logical to conclude that both the causes and consequences of stress can vary across cultures. So too can individual coping levels, tolerance for stressors, and so forth.

For example, review International Perspective on page 456 of Chapter 15. It summarizes how different executives from various countries report very different levels of experienced stress. We still know little about stress among operating employees in other countries, but future research no doubt will yield some insights soon.

Decision Making across Cultures

Chapter 16 describes the steps involved in making decisions. Nancy Adler recently explained how these steps, in a slightly modified form, can vary across cultures.[24] Table 22.2 shows the steps she identified and the range of variation.

First, managers in different cultures are likely to recognize problems and decision situations differently. Managers in the United States, for example, see problems as situations that require change. In contrast, managers in cultures like Indonesia and Thailand argue that one should accept the situation as it is instead of trying to change it.

Second, managers in some cultures see information as fact and make decisions accordingly. Others see information in terms of its possibilities and use it as a means of generating alternatives. For example, managers in some countries might see the citizens of an underdeveloped nation as being too poor to buy the

---

24. Adler, *International Dimensions of Organizational Behavior.*

TABLE 22.2
Cultural Variations in Decision Making

Steps in Decision Making	Cultural Variations	
1. Problem Recognition	*Problem Solving*	*Situation Accepting*
	Situation should be changed	Some situations should be accepted, not changed
2. Information Search	*Gather "facts"*	*Gather ideas and possibilites*
3. Constructing Alternatives	*New, future-oriented alternatives*	*Focus includes past, present, and future alternatives*
	People can learn and change	Adults cannot change substantially
4. Choice	*Individuals make decisions*	*Groups make decisions*
	Decision-making responsibility delegated	Only senior management makes decisions
	Decisions made quickly	Decisions made slowly
	Decision rule: Is it true or false?	Decision rule: Is it good or bad?
5. Implementation	*Fast*	*Slow*
	Managed from the top	Involves the participation of all levels
	Responsibility of one person	Responsibility of the group

SOURCE: Nancy J. Adler, *International Dimensions of Organizational Behavior,* 2nd ed. (PWS-Kent Publishing Company, 1991), p. 163.

products their companies make and therefore choose not to introduce the products there. Other managers might see the same reality but figure out how to lower the products' cost to make them more affordable.

Third, people in different cultures see different alternative solutions to problems. For example, managers in the United States tend to see future-oriented alternatives, whereas managers in Great Britain focus more on the past. Thus, U.S. managers may be more inclined to figure out a new technology for doing something, whereas the British may concentrate on modifying an existing technology to do the same thing.

Next, there are variations in people's perceptions about making choices. The notion of power distance we discussed earlier has clear implications as to who is expected to make the choices. Time urgency also varies. For example, U.S. managers make decisions very rapidly, whereas managers in some other cultures, as in the Middle East, are more deliberate and dislike having to make snap decisions.

Finally, cultures differ in how chosen alternatives are implemented. In the United States, managers tend to believe the implementation of decisions should be managed from the top and be the responsibility of one person. In contrast, Japanese managers believe participation is needed at all levels and responsibility should be shared.

Organization Characteristics in an International Context

- Organization characteristics vary across cultures, particularly in terms of cultural influences on environment, technology, organization structure, and organization design.

At a still higher level of analysis, we now examine cultural influences on environment, technology, organization structure, and organization design.

Environment and Technology across Cultures

Variation in environment across cultures can be assessed at several levels. As we described in Chapter 18, environments can be viewed in terms of their complexity and their dynamism. Figure 22.5 shows that organizations with international operations must contend with additional levels of complexity and dynamism, both within and across cultures.

Environmental Complexity and Dynamism Many cultures have relatively stable environments. For example, the economies of Sweden, Japan, and the United States are fairly stable. Although competitive forces within them vary, they generally remain strong, free-market economies. In contrast, the environments of other countries are much more dynamic. For example, France's policies on socialism versus private enterprise tend to change dramatically with each election. At present, far-reaching changes in the economic and management philosophies of most Western European countries make their environments far more dynamic.

Environments also vary widely in terms of their complexity. The Japanese culture, which is fairly stable, is also quite complex. Japanese managers are subject to an array of cultural norms and values that are far more encompassing and resistant to change than those U.S. managers face. India too has an extremely complex environment, which remains influenced by its old caste system.

FIGURE 22.5
Environmental Complexity and Dynamism within and across Cultures

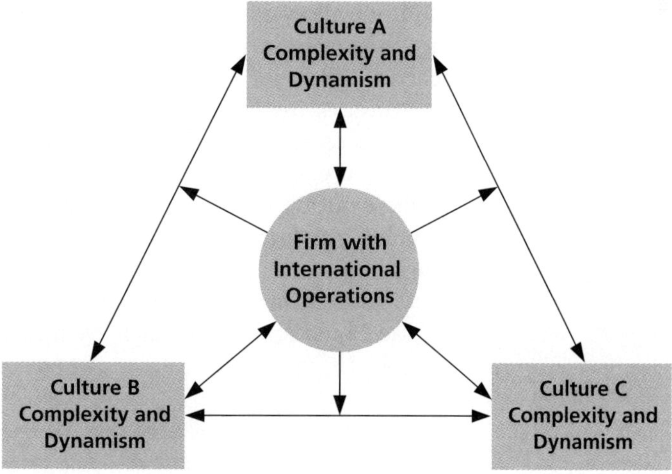

These two men are participating in a camel trading fair in the state of Rajasthan in India. His yellow turban indicates that the man on the right is from the Brahmin caste, while the man with the red turban belongs to the soldier caste. The manner in which each turban is tied also indicates each man's home village. Such subtle indicators of rank and hierarchy must be understood when dealing with organizational characteristics in an international context.

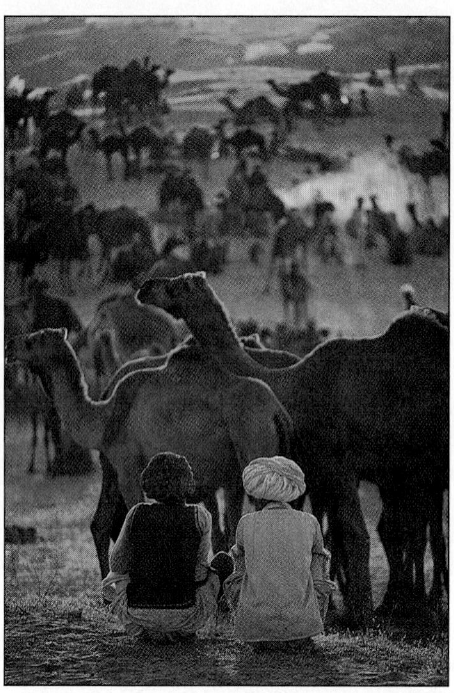

Technology Technological variations come in two forms: variations in available technology and variations in attitudes toward technology. Available technology affects how organizations can do business. Many underdeveloped countries, for example, lack electric power sources, telephones, and trucking equipment, not to mention computers and robots. A manager working in such a country must be prepared to deal with many frustrations. A few years ago, some Brazilian officials convinced a U.S. company to build a high-tech plant in their country. Midway through construction, however, the government of Brazil decided it would not allow the company to import some accurate measuring instruments it needed to produce its products. The new plant was abandoned before it ever opened.[25]

Attitudes toward technology also vary across cultures. Surprisingly, Japan has only recently begun to support basic research. For many years, the Japanese government encouraged its companies to take basic research findings discovered elsewhere (often in the United States) and figure out how to apply them to consumer products (applied research). Now, however, the government has changed its stance and has started to encourage basic research as well.[26] Most of the Western nations have a generally favorable attitude toward technology, whereas China and other Asian countries (with the exception of Japan) do not.

25. Andrew Kupfer, "How to Be a Global Manager," *Fortune,* March 14, 1988, pp. 52–58.

26. "Going Crazy in Japan—In a Break from Tradition, Tokyo Begins Funding a Program for Basic Research," *The Wall Street Journal,* November 10, 1986, p. 20D.

Organization Structure and Design across Cultures

Cross-cultural considerations related to organization structure and design include not only similarities and differences among firms in different cultures but structural features of multinational organizations.

Between-Culture Issues By *between-culture issues,* we mean comparisons of the organization structure and design of companies operating in different cultures. As might be expected, there are both differences and similarities. For example, one recent study compared the structures of fifty-five U.S. and fifty-one Japanese manufacturing plants. Results suggested that the Japanese plants had less specialization, more "formal" centralization (but less "real" centralization), and taller hierarchies than their U.S. counterparts. The Japanese structures were also less affected by their technology than were the U.S. plants.[27]

Many cultures still take a traditional view of organization structure not unlike the approaches used in this country during the days of classical organization theory. For example, Tom Peters, a leading U.S. management consultant and coauthor of *In Search of Excellence,* recently spent some time lecturing to managers in China. They were not interested in his ideas about decentralization and worker participation, however. Instead, the question most often asked involved how a manager determined the optimal span of control.[28]

In contrast, many European companies are increasingly patterning themselves after successful U.S. firms. This stems in part from corporate raiders in Europe emulating their U.S. counterparts and partly from a better educated managerial work force. Taken together, these two forces have caused many European firms to become more decentralized and to adopt divisional structures by moving from functional to product departmentalization.[29]

Multinational Organization More and more firms have entered the international arena and have found it necessary to adapt their designs to better cope with different cultures.[30] For example, after a company has achieved a moderate level of international activity, it often establishes an international division, such as that shown in Figure 22.6. Levi Strauss uses this organization design. One division, Levi Strauss International, is responsible for the company's business activities in Europe, Canada, Latin America, and Asia.

For an organization that has become more deeply involved in its international activities, a logical form of organization design is the international matrix, illustrated in Figure 22.7. This type of matrix arrays product managers across the top. Project teams headed by foreign market managers cut across the product

---

27. James R. Lincoln, Mitsuyo Hanada, and Kerry McBride, "Organizational Structures in Japanese and U.S. Manufacturing," *Administrative Science Quarterly,* September 1986, pp. 338–364.

28. "The Inscrutable West," *Newsweek,* April 18, 1988, p. 52.

29. Kirkland, "Europe's New Managers"; Shawn Tully, "Europe's Takeover Kings," *Fortune,* July 20, 1987, pp. 95–98.

30. Lane and DiStefano, *International Management Behavior.*

FIGURE 22.6
International Division Approach to Organization Design

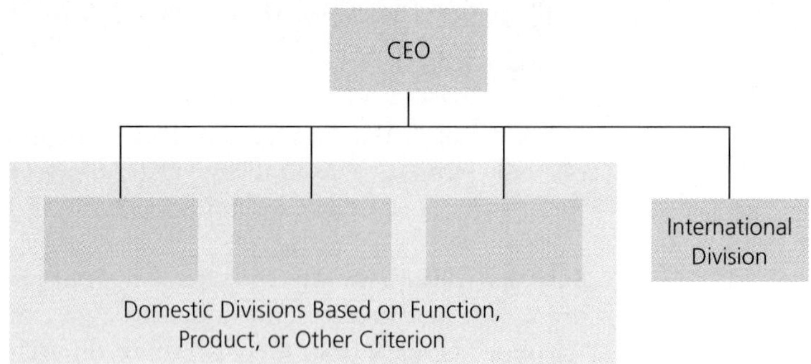

departments. A company with three basic product lines, for example, might establish three product departments (of course, it contains domestic advertising, finance, and operations departments as well). Foreign market managers can be designated for, say, Canada, Japan, Europe, Latin America, and Australia. Each foreign market manager is then responsible for all three of the company's products in his or her market.[31]

Finally, at the most advanced level of multinational activity, a firm might become an international conglomerate. Nestlé and Unilever N.V. fit this typology. Each has an international headquarters (Nestlé in Vevey, Switzerland, and Unilever in Rotterdam, Netherlands) that coordinates the activities of businesses scattered around the globe. Nestlé has factories in fifty countries and markets its products in virtually every country in the world. Over 96 percent of its business is done outside of Switzerland, and only about 7,000 of its 160,000 employees reside in its home country. *A Look at the Research* summarizes some recent findings regarding multinational organization structure and design.

Integrating Individuals, Groups, and Organizations

- Managing organization change and managerial careers also varies significantly across cultures.

Two final aspects of international organizational behavior that warrant discussion are organization change and careers.

Organization Change in an International Context

Organization change and development were the topic of Chapter 21, so our discussion at this point will be brief. One factor to consider is how international environments dictate organization change. As we already noted, the environment can be a significant factor in bringing about organization change. Given the

31. William H. Davison and Philippe Haspeslagh, "Shaping a Global Product Organization," *Harvard Business Review,* July-August 1982, pp. 125–132.

FIGURE 22.7
An International Matrix

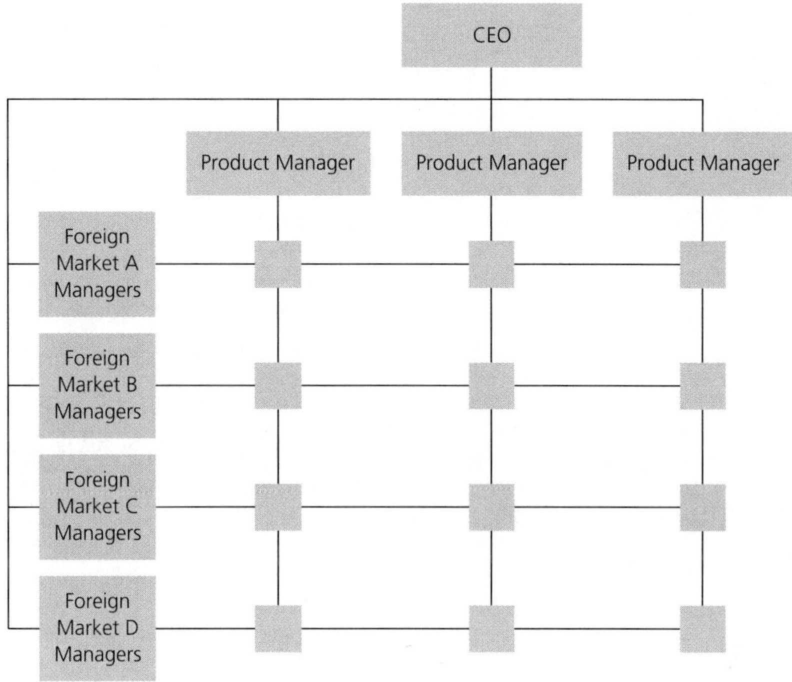

additional environmental complexities multinational organizations face, it follows that organization change may be even more critical to them than to purely domestic organizations.

A second point to remember is that acceptance of change varies widely around the globe. In some cultures, as we noted earlier, change is a normal and accepted part of organization life. In other cultures, change causes many more problems. The manager should remember that techniques for managing change that have worked routinely back home may not work at all and may even trigger negative responses if used indiscriminately in other cultures.[32]

Careers across Cultures

An understanding of careers, which we discuss in Chapter 23, is also becoming increasingly important for managers. It should come as no surprise that there are international implications to be drawn from career-related concerns. Some of these center on career paths in different cultures; others involve career concerns for managers in international businesses.

Cultural Variations in Careers Perhaps the most important career-related issue for the manager to understand is that different cultures have different norms and

32. Alfred M. Jaeger, "Organization Development and National Culture: Where's the Fit?" *Academy of Management Review,* January 1986, pp. 178–190.

A LOOK AT THE RESEARCH

International Forms of Organization Design

As part of the growing movement toward globalization, organizations are becoming increasingly concerned with how to structure themselves most effectively. A firm with headquarters in New York, manufacturing plants in Kansas City and Houston, and regional sales offices in Dallas, Portland, Chicago, and Baltimore has specific coordination needs and concerns. But if the plants are in Taiwan and Mexico and the sales offices are in London, Tokyo, Vancouver, and India, the coordination needs and concerns are magnified.

As a result, several research initiatives recently have been undertaken to determine the key organization design issues multinational firms need to consider. Professors Richard N. Osborn and C. Christopher Baughn of Wayne State University have studied how multinational alliances might be most effectively structured. Their findings recently were published in the *Academy of Management Journal.*

Osborn and Baughn focused their study on two basic forms of structure: joint ventures wherein a new corporate entity is created with equity ownership by the two partners and simpler contractual agreements such as licensing, technical assistance, and marketing agreements. Their preliminary findings suggest that variables such as the intent to conduct research and development, the technological intensity of the alliance's products, and the relative size of the two parent organizations are all important factors to consider.

In another recent article published in the *Academy of Management Review,* Professor Sumantra Ghoshal of INSEAD (a French university) and Professor Christopher A. Bartlett of Harvard developed a new model of the multinational corporation. They argue that a multinational corporation is best seen as an interorganizational network. Such a network is conceptualized as being embedded in an external network of all elements of the firm's task environment. Thus, the basic model represents an effort to extend organization-environment linkages that exist within a single culture to one that functions in several cultures simultaneously.

SOURCES: Sumantra Ghoshal and Christopher A. Bartlett, "The Multinational Corporation as an Interorganizational Network," *Academy of Management Review,* October 1990, pp. 603–625; Richard N. Osborn and C. Christopher Baughn, "Forms of Interorganizational Governance for Multinational Alliances," *Academy of Management Journal,* September 1990, pp. 503–519. Adapted by permission.

standards relevant to career paths. The U.S. culture, for example, generally supports people who are ambitious, want to succeed, and strive for advancement. In other cultures, personal ambition is less acceptable. The Japanese, for example, are expected to put organizational concerns and priorities above personal ones. Working to better one's own position in the organization is considered unseemly.

Widespread sex discrimination exists in many parts of the world. In Japan and Finland, women are quite restricted in their opportunities for advancement. Japanese women are expected to become wives and mothers. Even those who graduate from college usually take jobs as clerks and seldom move up the corporate ladder. (This is beginning to change somewhat, although the changes are still indiscernible in most organizations.[33]) In Finland, women have a strong

33. "Look Whose Sun Is Rising Now: Career Women," *Business Week,* August 25, 1986, p. 50.

When Disney announced plans to build a theme park on the outskirts of Paris, not everyone greeted the news with enthusiasm. Some protestors, for example, resisted what they saw as an intrusive cultural change likened to the domination of Native Americans in the United States. These young communists are carrying a banner that says "We Don't Want to be Indians of Eurodisney."

heritage of working outside the home but still lag behind men in both income and opportunities for advancement.[34]

International Career Paths As businesses become increasingly international, they must devote more attention to how this change affects their managers' careers. For example, a manager who is transferred from New York to Dallas to Seattle obviously experiences a certain amount of trauma and stress. But this pales by comparison to what happens to the manager transferred from New York to Tokyo to Bangkok. Thus, the firm must carefully consider both the advantages and disadvantages of international assignments.[35]

Summary of Key Points

- International business has rapidly become an important part of almost every manager's life and is likely to become even more so in the future. Thus, managers need to recognize that both similarities and differences exist across cultures.
- One important concern is individual behavior. Managers must recognize that patterns of individual differences, managerial behavior, motivation, and rewards vary across cultures.

34. Kaisa Kauppinen-Toropainen, Irja Kandolin, and Elina Haavio-Mannila, "Sex Segregation of Work in Finland and the Quality of Women's Work," *Journal of Organizational Behavior,* vol. 9, 1988, pp. 15–27.

35. Mark Mendenhall and Gary Oddou, "The Dimensions of Expatriate Acculturation: A Review," *Academy of Management Review,* January 1985, pp. 39–47.

- Interpersonal processes also vary across cultures. Particularly important are concerns related to group dynamics, leadership, power and conflict, and communication.
- Similarly, just as domestic managers work to enhance individual and interpersonal processes, the international manager confronts the same opportunities and challenges. Concerns regarding rewards, job design, performance evaluation, stress, and decision making are as significant in an international context as in a domestic one.
- International management also involves an understanding of how organization characteristics vary in an international context. Environment, technology, and organization structure and design are especially important characteristics to understand.
- Forces for and techniques of organization change also vary systematically across cultures. Career-related issues are another special consideration for managers receiving international assignments.

Discussion Questions

1. Identify ways in which international business affects businesses in your community.
2. All things considered, do you think people from diverse cultures are more alike or more different? Why?
3. What stereotypes exist about the motivational patterns of workers from other cultures?
4. What can U.S. managers learn about individual behavior from other cultures? What can managers in other cultures learn about individual behavior from U.S. managers?
5. Which dimension of the individual-organization interface is most likely to vary across cultures? Which is least likely to vary?
6. If you had just been appointed leader of a group of employees from another culture, what would you do first to be more effective?
7. At present, the United States limits the importation of many products into this country. Do you agree or disagree with this policy? Why?
8. If you were offered a temporary assignment abroad, would you be inclined to take it? Why or why not?
9. Suppose you work for a firm that recently transferred in a manager from another country. The transfer represents this manager's first international exposure. What might you do to help the manager adjust?
10. What are the advantages and disadvantages of transferring managers across a variety of locations scattered around the world?

CASE 22.1

British Airways Bounces Back

British Airways has made one of the most stunning turnarounds of any business in history. Much of the credit for that turnaround goes to people—the individuals who manage the firm and operating employees who carry out mundane jobs ranging from handling baggage to preparing meals in flight.

When Margaret Thatcher became prime minister of Great Britain in 1979, many of the country's largest businesses were owned and operated by the government. One of her first agenda items was to privatize (sell to private owners and investors) most of these businesses.

But no one wanted British Airways. The firm had a huge, unproductive work force, suffered from lax management, and was incurring annual losses approaching $1 billion. Service had slipped badly; many joked that the acronym BA stood for "Bloody Awful!"

Thatcher asked John King, a leading British industrialist, to step in and restore British Airways' image, competitiveness, and effectiveness. One of King's first major decisions was to cut the work force. Within a few months of taking over, he cut the payroll from 59,000 to 36,000 employees. To help ease the pain of such a cutback, he offered a generous severance package to all employees who left voluntarily.

Then King made major changes on the firm's board of directors. Membership on the board had been largely symbolic, and directors really knew little about running a business. King convinced most of the current directors to leave and replaced them with experienced executives. He also changed advertising agencies and even moved the firm's insurance coverage to a different carrier.

King also recognized that he needed to direct a lot of attention to the remaining British Airways employees, many of whom felt bitter and insecure. Some of the changes in this area also were largely symbolic. For example, King bought all employees new uniforms (some uniforms had not been changed in over twenty years), adopted a new corporate slogan, and repainted all British Airways aircraft.

King had known all along that his job was not to run the "new" airline. Instead, his charge was to manage its transformation. Thus, while all these changes were going on, he was also looking for a new CEO to take over when the transformation and privatization were complete. Colin Marshall was selected to take over in early 1983 and received immediate opportunities to make his own assessments of the changes taking place.

Marshall recognized that employees needed more than just new uniforms, so he initiated a series of training seminars for them. The seminars were designed to change their attitudes about the company and to motivate them to provide better customer service. These seminars were a big success, and a whole new culture began to emerge.

British Airways was privatized in February 1987. A key part of the initial stock packages was to allow employees to participate in ownership. Around 74 percent of them took advantage of this opportunity. Many noted that as owners they would be even more dedicated to improving service and profits.

Since then, the foundation laid by King and Marshall has paid enormous dividends. British Airways has become the largest airline in the world and also one of the most profitable. And customers rate its service as the best in the industry. The current state of affairs is a far cry from the days of "Bloody Awful," and much of the credit goes to a large group of people working together for a common cause.

Case Questions

1. Identify as many behavioral concepts and processes in this case as you can.
2. Do you think King and Marshall made any serious mistakes?
3. What perils or threats does British Airways face in the future?

SOURCES: "How British Airways Butters Up the Passenger," *Business Week,* March 12, 1990, p. 94; "From 'Bloody Awful' to Bloody Awesome," *Business Week,* October 9, 1989, p. 97; Kenneth Labich, "The Big Comeback at British Airways," *Fortune,* December 5, 1988, pp. 163–174; Patricia Sellers, "How to Handle Customers' Gripes," *Fortune,* October 24, 1988, pp. 88–100.

CASE 22.2 Culture Shock

Warren Oats was a highly successful executive for American Auto Suppliers, a Chicago-based company that makes original-equipment specialty parts for Ford, GM, and Chrysler. Rather than retreat before the onslaught of Japanese automakers, AAS decided to counterattack and use its reputation for quality and dependability to win over customers in Japan. Oats had started in the company as an engineer and worked his way up to become one of a handful of senior managers who had a shot at the next open vice presidential position. He knew he needed to distinguish himself somehow, so when he was given a chance to lead the AAS attack on the Japanese market, he jumped at it.

Oats knew he did not have time to learn Japanese, but he had heard that many Japanese executives speak English, and the company would hire a translator anyway. The toughest part about leaving the United States was persuading his wife, Carol, to take an eighteen-month leave from her career as an attorney with a prestigious Chicago law firm. Carol finally persuaded herself that she did not want to miss an opportunity to learn a new culture. So, armed with all the information they could gather about Japan from their local library, the Oats headed for Tokyo.

Known as an energetic, aggressive salesperson back home, Warren Oats wasted little time getting started. As soon as his office had a telephone—and well before all his files had arrived from the States—Oats made an appointment to meet with executives of one of Japan's leading automakers. Oats reasoned that if he was going to overcome the famous Japanese resistance to foreign companies, he should get started as soon as possible.

Oats felt very uncomfortable at that first meeting. He got the feeling that the Japanese executives were waiting for something. It seemed that everyone but he was in slow motion. The Japanese did not speak English well and appeared grateful for the presence of the interpreter, but even the interpreter seemed to take her time in translating each phrase. Frustrated by this seeming lethargy and beginning to doubt the much-touted Japanese efficiency, Oats got right to the point. He made an oral presentation of his proposal, waiting patiently for the translation of each sentence. Then he handed the leader of the Japanese delegation a packet containing the specifics of his proposal, got up, and left. The translator trailed behind him as if wanting to drag out the process even further.

By the end of their first week, both Oats and his wife were frustrated. Oats' office phone had not rung once, which did not make him optimistic about his meeting with another top company the following week. Carol could scarcely contain her irritation with what she had perceived of the Japanese way of life. She had been sure that a well-respected U.S. lawyer would have little trouble securing a job with a Japanese multinational corporation, but the executives she had met with seemed insulted that she was asking them for a job. And the way they treated their secretaries! After only a week in Japan, both Carol and Warren Oats were ready to go home.

A month later, their perspective had changed radically, and both looked back on those first meetings with embarrassment. Within that month, they had learned a lot about the Japanese sense of protocol and attitudes toward women. Warren Oats believed he was beginning to get the knack of doing business with the Japanese in their manner: establishing a relationship slowly, almost ritualistically, waiting through a number of meetings before bringing up the real business at hand, and then doing so circumspectly. It was difficult for Oats to slow his pace, and it made him nervous to be so indirect, but he was beginning to see some value in the sometimes humbling learning process he was going through. Perhaps, he thought, he and Carol could become consultants for other executives who needed to learn the lessons he was beginning to understand.

Case Questions

1. What specific errors did Warren and Carol Oats make during their first week in Japan?
2. If you were talking to a non-U.S. businessperson making a first contact with an American company, what advice would you give?

EXPERIENTIAL EXERCISE

Purpose: This exercise will help you develop a better understanding of the complexities involved in international management.

Format: The instructor will divide the class into small groups of three to four. Assume you are a task force for a medium-size manufacturing company. Top management has just decided to open a new facility in an overseas location. Your instructor will specify the location for your group.

Procedure: Your assignment is to learn as much about the culture of your location as possible and report back to top management about the advantages and disadvantages of the location. Try to identify three major advantages and three major concerns that need to be addressed. Report your findings to the class.

Follow-up Questions

1. In a situation like this, can you ever learn all you need to know about a different culture and how it will affect a business?
2. How easy or difficult is it to learn about other cultures?

CHAPTER OUTLINE

- Individual and Organizational Perspectives on Careers
- Career Choices
  - *Choice of Occupation*
  - *Choice of Organization*
  - *Changing Careers*
- Career Stages
  - *Entry*
  - *Socialization*
  - *Advancement*
  - *Maintenance*
  - *Withdrawal*
  - *Mentoring*
- Organizational Career Planning
  - *Purposes of Career Planning*
  - *Types of Career Programs*
  - *Career Management*
  - *Results of Career Planning*

23

Career Dynamics

CHAPTER OBJECTIVES

After studying this chapter, you should be able to:

Describe individual and organizational perspectives on careers.

Identify three elements of career choices.

Identify the typical career stages and discuss their importance to individuals and organizations.

Discuss organizational career planning and career management.

Keith Beck, forty-five years old, already has had an impressive career. Following graduation from college, Beck was an English teacher in Micronesia with the Peace Corps, a management trainee at J.C. Penney, and a life insurance salesperson. In 1972 he joined Mervyn's, where he worked his way up through the ranks of management. In 1980 he joined the senior corporate staff as manager of executive placement and development. Then he was passed over for promotion to director of store personnel services and was put in charge of layoffs. After laying off hundreds of people in the mid-1980s, many of whom were his friends and coworkers, Beck "mentally resigned" from the company and finally quit in 1987. Now Beck is running a small start-up company and does not miss his former life as an executive.[1]

■ Almost one-fourth of U.S. workers are dissatisfied with their occupations.

Keith Beck is not the only middle- or executive-level manager to become disillusioned with his job and resign. Many managers have quit their jobs for a variety of personal and professional reasons. Some finally discover that they are in the wrong occupation. After a long career in corporate finance with numerous companies, Douglas Flaherty admitted that if he had it all to do over again, he would have gone to medical school.[2] In a recent study initiated by Robert Half International, vice presidents and human resources directors from one hundred of the nation's top one thousand corporations estimated that 24.3 percent of employees (that is, almost one out of four workers) are unhappy and/or unsuccessful because they are in the wrong occupation or profession.[3] This means that nearly thirty million people are unhappy in their jobs. The impact on organizational productivity is immense. Clearly, if this problem is to be solved, both individuals and organizations need to know more about careers, career choices, and career management.

Why are so many people dissatisfied with their jobs and careers? How can organizations help employees pursue the careers that offer the greatest benefit to both employees and the organization? Why do many people change not only their jobs but the type of work they do several times during their work lives? How can organizations ensure that when employees leave the company, by either quitting or retiring, they will be quickly and efficiently replaced by highly qual-

1. Source: Kenneth Labich, "Breaking Away to Go on Your Own," *Fortune,* December 17, 1990.

2. "Stars of 1962: How the Top Students at Harvard Business School Fare 20 Years Later," *The Wall Street Journal,* December 20, 1982, pp. 1, 12.

3. *Banker's Digest,* June 22, 1987, p. 8.

The career of James DePreist, music director of the Oregon Symphony, has been part proper preparation and part serendipity—a home full of music, undergraduate training in economics, graduate studies in film, and study in musical composition at the Philadelphia Conservatory. On an Asian tour with the U.S. Department of State he had a chance to conduct an orchestra and knew immediately that he wanted to make conducting his life's work. Additional planning involved getting good opportunities to conduct and study with top conductors.

ified people? The issues reflected in these questions have led organizations to invest large amounts of money, time, and effort in developing career management programs. In addition, researchers have begun to systematically study careers.

In this chapter, we examine individual and organizational perspectives on careers. We describe several aspects of career choices. Then we explore the career stages and conclude by discussing organizational career planning.

Individual and Organizational Perspectives on Careers

■ A **career** is a perceived sequence of attitudes and behaviors associated with work-related experiences and activities over the person's life span.

People often use the word *career* to refer to professional occupations of others and not to their own work or job. Indeed, many people do not even expect to have careers, they expect to have jobs.[4] A **career** is a "perceived sequence of attitudes and behaviors associated with work-related experiences and activities over the span of the person's life."[5] Whereas a job is what a person does at work to bring home a paycheck, a career means being engaged in a satisfying and productive activity.[6] Thus, a career involves a long-term view of a series of jobs and work experiences.

Individuals may have personal interests in careers, specifically their own. As people evaluate job opportunities, those with a career perspective usually are concerned with factors such as those listed in Table 23.1. Note how these concerns have a long-term perspective: concerns for the future of technological change, economic conditions, and personal advancement. Many individuals see

4. M. W. McCall and E. E. Lawler III, "High School Students' Perceptions of Work," *Academy of Management Journal,* March 1976, pp. 17–24.

5. D. T. Hall, *Careers in Organizations* (Santa Monica, Calif.: Goodyear, 1976), p. 4.

6. M. Breidenbach, *Career Development: Taking Charge of Your Career* (Englewood Cliffs, N.J.: Prentice-Hall, 1988).

TABLE 23.1
Individual Career Issues

Career Issues	Examples
Opportunity for advancement slowing	More people entering popular careers
Technical obsolescence accelerating	Rapidly changing automation, computerization
Rate of economic growth declining	Economy not expanding, fewer jobs created
New entrants into the labor market receiving more favorable treatment	Higher starting salaries and prerequisites for new hires
Companies reorganizing	Downsizing, reducing layers of middle management
Aging	Career options narrow, fewer opportunities

SOURCE: Adapted from C. Hymowitz, "Stable Cycles of Executive Careers Shattered by Upheaval in Business," *The Wall Street Journal*, May 26, 1987, p. 31. Reprinted by permission of *The Wall Street Journal,* © 1987 Dow Jones & Company, Inc. All rights Reserved Worldwide.

opportunities for advancement slowing as more people enter popular career fields. They see the rate of technical obsolescence accelerating with the advent of new and better computers and automated manufacturing processes. Individuals trying to establish their careers may have serious concerns when the rate of economic growth is declining. Individuals also perceive that new entrants are treated better than people already in the labor market—getting higher starting salaries, better opportunities, and the like. Furthermore, companies are reorganizing and down sizing, which is increasing uncertainty and decreasing opportunities for advancement. Finally, aging is a concern; as people get older, their career options frequently narrow and their opportunities shrink.[7]

Organizations have a different perspective on careers.[8] They want to ensure that managerial succession is orderly and efficient so that when managers need to be replaced because of promotion, retirement, accident or illness, termination, or resignation, they can be replaced quickly and easily by highly qualified people. Organizations also want their employees to pursue careers in which they are interested and for which they have been properly trained. If individuals are unhappy with their career choices and opportunities, they may not perform well or may choose to leave the organization. Thus, organizations have an investment in ensuring people-career matches will achieve high levels of performance and lower levels of turnover.

Clearly, although their perspectives are not identical, individual employees and organizations can benefit from working together to improve career management. Career choices, however, remain in the hands of individuals.

7. "Stable Cycles of Executive Careers Shattered by Upheaval in Business," *The Wall Street Journal*, May 26, 1987, p. 31.

8. D. B. Miller, *Careers '79* (Saratoga, Calif.: Vitality Associates, 1979).

Career Choices

Career choices arise more than once during a lifetime, because both people and career opportunities change. People need not be "locked in" to a particular career choice. Knowing that a change can be made should help individuals avoid becoming poor performers in their jobs as a result of career frustration.

Career choices are not something to take lightly, however; they are important in their own right and form the basis for future career decisions. As Figure 23.1 indicates, making a career choice involves six steps. First, an individual must become aware that a career choice is needed. This awareness may come about in a variety of ways. A recent high-school graduate may recognize the need to make a choice after being urged to find a job or declare a college major. A person already pursuing a career may consider choosing a new one after receiving a negative performance evaluation, being turned down for a big promotion, or being fired or laid off.

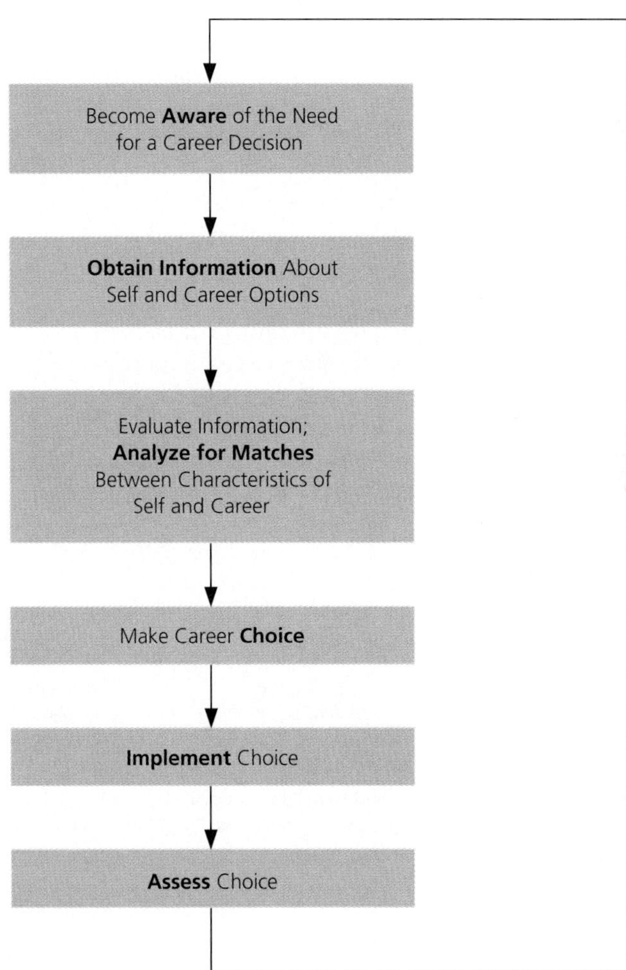

FIGURE 23.1
A Simplified Model of Individual Career Choice

Second, the individual must obtain information about himself or herself and about available career options. Personal interests, skills, abilities, and desires can be identified by self-reflection as well as by formal and informal consultation with others. In addition, information about the demands and rewards of various careers is available from numerous sources, including career counselors, placement officers, friends, and family.

- Career advisers and counselors can help people find and analyze career information, but the ultimate career decision must be made by the individual.

The third step in the career choice process involves evaluating the information and looking for matches between the wants and needs of the individual and the characteristics of potential careers. This can be a frustrating and confusing time as the person finds there are advantages as well as disadvantages to every career. Although the help of a competent adviser or counselor is valuable, the next step—the career decision—rests with the individual. In the fourth step, the individual must make a commitment to a career or a set of highly similar careers. Commitment means making the decision and initiating the next step, implementation.

Implementing the decision involves actively pursuing the career; preparing through training, education, or internships; obtaining a position; and, finally, working. After a time, the individual must assess the choice. As long as the result of the assessment is satisfactory, the individual continues to pursue the career. If the conclusion is not satisfactory, the individual becomes aware of the need for another career choice, and the process begins again.

In making career decisions, people are subjected to a number of pressures. As indicated in Figure 23.2, these pressures may be personal, social, or work related. An individual's personality and goals may be better suited to certain careers than to others, and a lack of agreement between the types of careers that suit the person's personality and those appropriate to his or her personal goals can create internal conflicts. Social factors that create career pressure include urging from family or friends to quit a job or to take one job rather than another. Religious dictates can impose powerful career-related pressures on some individuals.

Work-related factors can also create career-related pressures. A person's current position in an organization may open certain career options; other options may simply be unavailable to one in that position. This is true of some

FIGURE 23.2
Pressures on Individual Career Choice

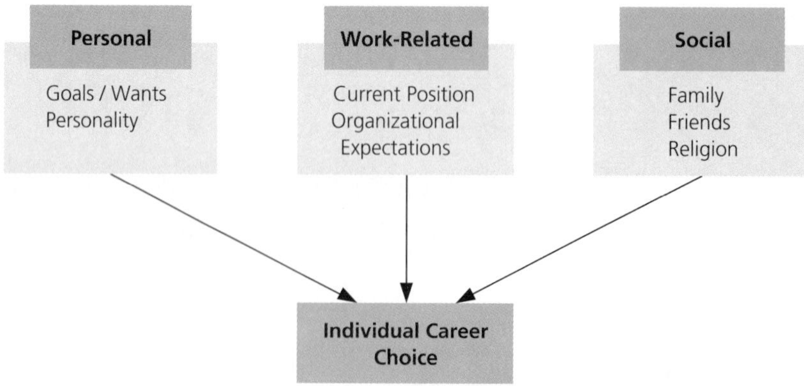

William H. Moore is an ocean engineer who specializes in failures of structures in and on the ocean. His specialty is much in demand as oil spills from tankers and offshore drilling rigs gain increasing attention around the world. He chose this field because of his love for scuba diving and his ability to solve complex engineering problems.

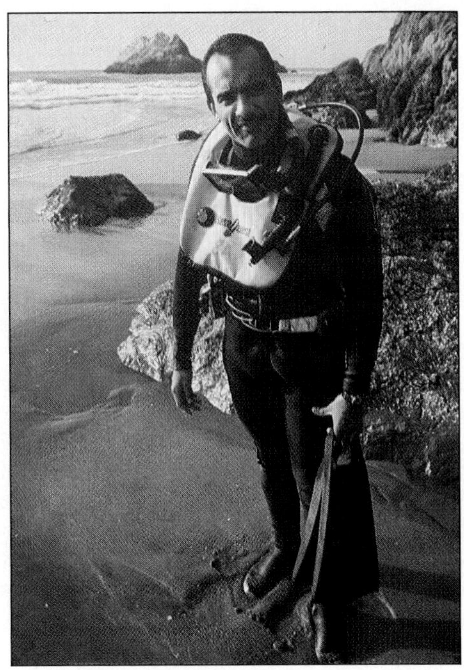

state government jobs; if one wants to run for political office, one must resign any other government job first. In addition to formal requirements, informal expectations are associated with most positions in organizations. Certain job and career-related behaviors may be expected from a person in a particular position, which usually will put pressure on the job holder to do the things expected. For example, coworkers may expect a colleague to seek managerial jobs to advance in the organization, whereas the person may enjoy her or his current position and not wish to move into management.

Choice of Occupation

- An **occupation** is a group of jobs that are similar with respect to the type of tasks and training involved.

One major career choice confronting individuals is the choice of occupation. An **occupation,** or *occupational field,* is a group of jobs that are similar in terms of the type of tasks and training involved. Occupations usually are found in many different organizations, whereas jobs are organization specific. The United States Bureau of the Census identifies hundreds of occupations, including such diverse ones as accountant, auctioneer, baker, carpenter, cashier, dancer, embalmer, farmer, furrier, huckster, loom fixer, railroad conductor, receptionist, stockhandler, waiter, weaver, and weigher.[9] Of course, these occupations are not equally appealing to people.

9. U.S. Bureau of the Census, *1980 Census of the Population: Alphabetical Index of Industries and Occupations* (Washington, D.C.: U.S. Government Printing Office, 1981).

Developing Management Skills

Tips for Managing Your Career

Most managers are good at managing their subordinates, whether the latter are engineers, accountants, or welders. When it comes to managing their own careers, however, managers' track records may fall short. Many managers simply do the job they have until they lose it and then start looking for a new one. In their job search, most managers simply send out résumés and answer employment ads. Experts in the career field, however, suggest that managers can manage their careers much better than most currently do. One overall aspect of managing your career as a manager is to look at it as a constant process of change and development. In addition, career experts suggest that you can do at least four things to enhance your job prospects specifically and your career in general:

1. Use networks
2. Use friends and family members
3. Build on your experience
4. Find a job that you love

Networks can be extremely useful when it is time to find a new job. For example, acquaintances from professional associations can be good sources of information on jobs, as can friends and family members. Letters to such individuals should be brief and emphasize that you seek information on jobs in your area of expertise.

The second tip is to build on your experience. Rather than apologize for your age (whether "too old" or "too young"), your letters of inquiry should emphasize your experience in the field and note your outstanding accomplishments.

The final tip is to figure out what you really like to do and then look for jobs in that area. A high-paying job doing something you do not like will bring you little satisfaction and probably will not last long. Once you are in the field, you should learn as much as you can about other jobs in it and build your skills in that area. Long, successful careers are built by people doing what they love and excelling at what they do.

SOURCES: "Networking Opens More Doors to Jobs," *USA Today,* November 19, 1990, p. 7B; "Seek a Job with a Little Help from Your Friends," *USA Today,* November 19, 1990, p. 7B; "Older Workers: Focus on Experience," *USA Today,* November 19, 1990, p. 7B; "Find the Career You Love and Grow in It," *USA Today,* November 19, 1990, p. 7B.

Rankings of the desirability of occupations have shown a general stability. For instance, professions dominate the upper end of such evaluations. Physicians are nearly always among the occupations with the highest prestige, as are college and university professors, judges, and lawyers. The lowest-prestige occupations are more mixed. Bellhops, bootblacks, cleaners and janitorial workers, teamsters, and ushers are among those consistently low in prestige. *Developing Management Skills* provides several practical tips on how to find an occupation that fits you.

Theories that explain how people choose among the many occupations available to them emphasize either content or process.[10] Content theories deal with factors—prestige, pay, and working conditions, for example—that influence career decisions. Process theories, on the other hand, deal with how people make these decisions.

10. D. C. Feldman, *Managing Careers in Organizations* (Glenview, Ill.: Scott, Foresman, 1988), pp. 189–192.

Content theories focus on six major factors that influence the occupations people choose:

1. Values and attitudes of the individual's family, especially parents[11]
2. Interests and needs[12]
3. Skills and abilities[13]
4. Education
5. General economic conditions
6. Political and social conditions

Process theories suggest that people make occupational choices in stages over time, seeking a match between their needs and their occupational demands. According to this approach, although people begin considering occupations when they are very young, their thinking evolves and becomes more specific over time.[14]

One process model of occupational choice has been proposed by J. L. Holland. According to Holland, there are six basic personality types—realistic, investigative, artistic, social, enterprising, and conventional—each of which is characterized by a set of preferences, interests, and values. Occupations can also be grouped: working with things, working with observations and data, working with people, working in very ordered ways, exercising power, and using self-expression.[15] As people evaluate occupations over time, they attempt to match their occupational activities to their personality types. Table 23.2 shows Holland's proposed matching between personality types and various occupational activities.

Another process model is similar to the expectancy model of motivation introduced in Chapter 6. This framework assumes that people base their occupational choices on their probability of success.[16] Thus, in an expectancy approach, a person uses information on the anticipated outcomes of being employed in a given occupation and the probability of obtaining those outcomes to try to assess the attractiveness of the occupation.

This process may be used in comparing two occupations. For example, some people face a new occupational choice after several years in their chosen field.

---

11. P. M. Blau, J. W. Gustad, R. Jesson, H. S. Parnes, and R. C. Wilcox, "Occupational Choices: A Conceptual Framework," *Industrial and Labor Relations Review,* July 1956, pp. 531–543.

12. Hall, *Careers in Organizations;* J. L. Holland, *Making Vocational Choices* (Englewood Cliffs, N.J.: Prentice-Hall, 1973).

13. D. C. Feldman and H. J. Arnold, "Personality Types and Career Patterns: Some Empirical Evidence on Holland's Model," *Canadian Journal of Administrative Science,* June 1985, pp. 192–210.

14. E. Ginzberg, S. W. Ginzberg, W. Axelrod, and J. L. Herna, *Occupational Choice: An Approach to a General Theory* (New York: Columbia University, 1951); Hall, *Careers in Organizations.*

15. Holland, *Making Vocational Choices.*

16. T. R. Mitchell and B. W. Knudsen, "Instrumentality Theory Predictions of Students' Attitudes toward Business and Their Choice of Business as an Occupation," *Academy of Management Journal,* March 1973, pp. 41–52; S. L. Rynes and J. Lawler, "A Policy-Capturing Investigation of the Role of Expectancies in Decisions to Pursue Job Alternatives," *Journal of Applied Psychology,* November 1983, pp. 620–631.

TABLE 23.2
Holland Typology of Personality and Sample Occupations

I. Realistic	
Personal Characteristics:	Shy, genuine, materialistic, persistent, stable.
Sample Occupations:	Mechanical engineer, drill press operator, aircraft mechanic, dry cleaner, waitress.
II. Investigative	
Personal Characteristics:	Analytical, cautious, curious, independent, introverted.
Sample Occupations:	Economist, physicist, actuary, surgeon, electrical engineer.
III. Artistic	
Personal Characteristics:	Disorderly, emotional, idealistic, imaginative, impulsive.
Sample Occupations:	Journalist, drama teacher, advertising manager, interior decorator, architect.
IV. Social	
Personal Characteristics:	Cooperative, generous, helpful, sociable, understanding.
Sample Occupations:	Interviewer, history teacher, counselor, social worker, clergyman.
V. Enterprising	
Personal Characteristics:	Adventurous, ambitious, energetic, domineering, self-confident.
Sample Occupations:	Purchasing agent, real estate salesperson, market analyst, attorney, personnel manager.
VI. Conventional	
Personal Characteristics:	Efficient, obedient, practical, calm, conscientious.
Sample Occupations:	File clerk, CPA, typist, keypunch operator, teller.

SOURCE: Table from *Career Management* by Jeffrey H. Greenhaus, copyright © 1987 by The Dryden Press, reprinted by permission of the publisher. Adapted from J. L. Holland, *Making Vocational Choices: A Theory of Careers,* Englewood Cliffs, N.J.: Prentice-Hall, 1973. Used with permission of the author.

From an expectation point of view, the person may attempt to compare the costs and benefits of remaining in his or her current field against the advantages and disadvantages of a new occupation. The costs may be the loss of things such as seniority, pension benefits, and earning power if extensive retraining is involved. Benefits may include higher long-term earnings, different lifestyles, and daily activities that seem inherently more enjoyable.

Choice of Organization

People must choose not only an occupation but an organization in which to pursue that occupation. This is an important choice because, for example, being

Cynthia Buzzetta recently made a significant change in her career. After many years at Digital Equipment Corporation, several as a high ranking executive in human resources, she felt overmanaged and generally mistreated. She found herself in constant pain with chronic backaches and other stress-related woes, and finally quit her job in search of a better way. Her better way did not come easily but led to her new life as a consultant in human resources to other organizations.

an engineer for a municipal government may be far different from being an engineer for a private aerospace corporation. Indeed, some organizational differences—profit versus not-for-profit, large versus small, private versus governmental, and military versus nonmilitary, for instance—may be very important for the individual's ability to reach his or her goals and have a satisfying career.

Research suggests that in choosing an organization, individuals generally seek companies that can provide some minimally acceptable level of economic return—a sort of "base pay." Beyond that, the most frequently sought-after features of an organization involve the opportunity it offers the individual to engage in interesting, challenging, or novel activities.[17] The type and size of the organization, its reputation, and its geographic location do not seem as important to people making career choices as the level of economic return and the nature of the activities in which they can expect to engage.[18] *International Perspective* describes what you might expect if you choose to work for a Japanese firm.

Changing Careers

As people change, grow older, and mature, they may need to reevaluate their careers and make new choices. Someone who dropped out of school early in life, for example, may decide the career options that resulted from that choice are no longer acceptable and may return to school to open up new career opportu-

17. P. A. Renwick, E. E. Lawler III, and staff, "What You Really Want From Your Job," *Psychology Today,* May 1978, pp. 53–65.

18. D. C. Feldman and H. J. Arnold, "Position Choice: Comparing the Importance of Job and Organizational Factors," *Journal of Applied Psychology,* December 1978, pp. 706–710.

INTERNATIONAL PERSPECTIVE

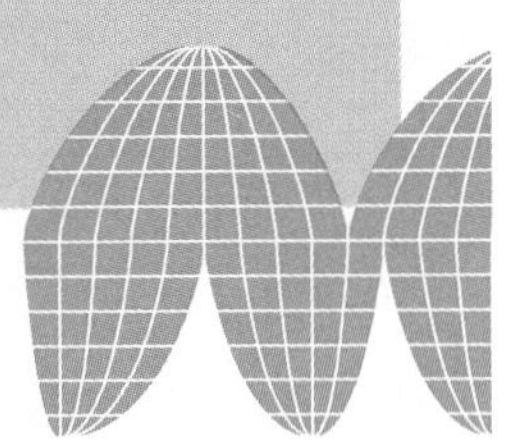

Fujitsu and Others Become the Bosses

International management of organizational behavior doesn't always mean learning how to do business and manage people in other countries. It also means learning how to work for—and be managed by—managers from other countries. During the ongoing shakeout in the computer industry, the Japanese computer giants are swooping in on weak computer manufacturers, buying them, and bringing in Japanese managers to run them. For example, the powerful Japanese company Fujitsu agreed to buy 80 percent of the British computer maker International Computers Ltd. and is aiming at the number one international position in mainframe computers. In other industries, such as automobiles, Japanese companies are either buying firms or bringing their own management and setting up shop, employing host country workers, and taking the profits back to Japan. In companies started or bought in the United States, only 31 percent of the senior managers are reported to be from this country.

People who have worked for the Japanese have many interesting stories to tell about how the Japanese manage workers, organize production lines, and stress teamwork. Some U.S. managers have succeeded and been promoted to very high positions. Michael Schulhof, for example, worked for Sony for 16 years and rose to become president of Sony USA and one of two nonJapanese members of the board of the parent company.

Others, however, have not prospered. For example, three former employees of Fujitsu were fired and have filed suit for $79 million, contending that they were treated very badly by Japanese managers and discriminated against on the basis of national origin and age. As of early 1991, Fujitsu had made no comment and evidently was preparing for the trial. Obviously, working for the Japanese can have its pitfalls.

Experts have suggested several guidelines for working for Japanese firms:

1. Do not assume that all Japanese companies are alike.
2. Do not expect to be a star.
3. Do not expect a lot of "pats on the back."
4. Do not expect your pay to always reflect your performance.
5. Do not expect to one day head the company's global operations.
6. Be ready to deal with a great deal of ambiguity.

Another major problem is that Japanese managers have not yet learned how to deal with young, aggressive, highly educated (usually M.B.A.'s) female workers. Often the job description for a responsible position specifies a "man," even when a woman is available for the job.

The Japanese system is based on a deep sense of trust among all groups in the organization and a belief in collectivism over individualism. When the Japanese system owns the business, that system will prevail and employees will need to learn to function in it. It may take several years and much concerted effort before working for a manager from another country becomes universally comfortable.

SOURCES: "Culture Shock at Home: Working for a Foreign Boss," *Business Week,* December 17, 1990, pp. 80–84; Susan Moffat, "Should You Work for the Japanese?" *Fortune,* December 3, 1990, pp. 107–120; "In Computers, a Shakeout of Seismic Proportions," *Business Week,* October 15, 1990, pp. 34–36.

nities. Life experiences may broaden a person's skills so that new career options become available. One increasingly popular career change option is to take one or more part-time jobs. Some research suggests that the part-time option may benefit the employee as well as the organization.[19]

Sometimes people find that as they have changed, their careers have changed. Although these people may not need to move from one occupation to another, some adaptation may be in order. Career adaptation may involve retraining to perform better on the job or to move to another job within the same career field. Adaptation may also mean changing organizations while pursuing the same career.

Career Stages

- **Career stages** are the periods in which the person's work life is characterized by specific needs, concerns, tasks, and activities.

The gradual changes that occur over time in careers are called **career stages,** which are periods in which the individual's work life is characterized by distinctive needs, concerns, tasks, and activities. Career stages are closely associated with but not identical to the adult life stages identified by Erikson: adolescence, young adulthood, adulthood, and senescence.[20] As shown in Figure 23.3, there are five general career stages: entry, socialization, advancement, maintenance, and withdrawal.

Entry

The *entry* stage is also known as the *exploration* stage. *Exploration* may be the more accurate label for the early part of the stage, in which self-examination, role tryouts, and occupational exploration occur. Individuals in this stage are usually, but not necessarily, young. This is the stage during which education and training are most commonly pursued. During the latter part of the stage, the individual enters a career, albeit tentatively, by trying out jobs associated with the career. This trial period may involve many different jobs as the individual explores a variety of organizations, occupations, and careers. Performance during this stage is represented in Figure 23.3 as a dashed line to indicate unpredictability.[21]

Socialization

The *socialization* stage has also been called the *establishment* stage. It usually begins with a trial period (shown in the figure by a dashed line) during which

19. Ellen F. Jackofsky and Lawrence H. Peters, "Part-Time Versus Full-Time Employment Status Differences: A Replication and Extension," *Journal of Occupational Behaviour,* 8, 1987, 1–9.

20. E. H. Erikson, *Childhood and Society* (New York: Norton, 1963).

21. Hall, *Careers in Organizations.*

FIGURE 23.3
A Model of Career Stages

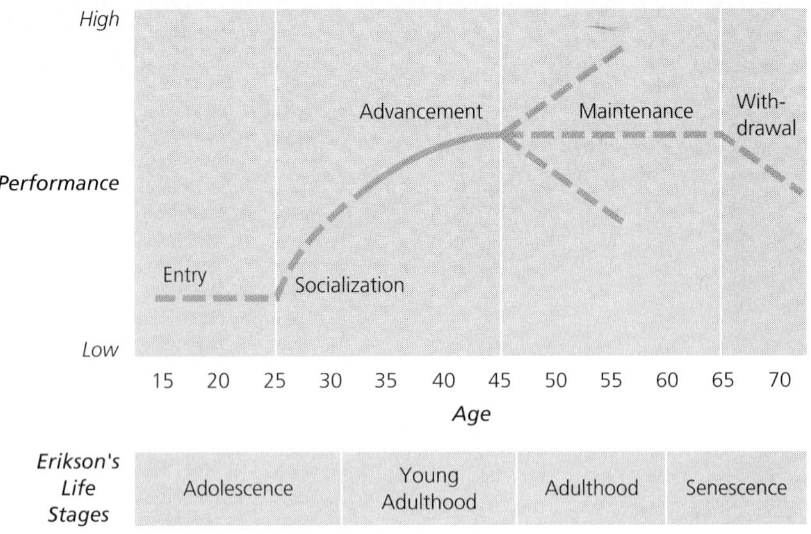

the individual continues to explore jobs, but much more narrowly than before. Then, as the individual becomes focused on a specific job, performance begins to improve. The individual is becoming established in the career. The sequence of getting established has been found to consist of three phases: *getting in* (entry), *breaking in* (trial period), and *settling in* (establishment).[22]

During the socialization stage, people begin to form attachments and make commitments, both to others (new friends and coworkers) and to their employing organizations. Employees begin to learn the organization's goals, norms, values and preferred ways of doing things; in other words, they learn the culture of the organization (see Chapter 20). In particular, they learn an appropriate set of role behaviors and develop work skills and abilities particular to their jobs and organizations. They begin to demonstrate that, at least to some degree, they are learning to accept the values and norms of the organization.[23]

During the socialization stage, individuals must make many adjustments. They must learn to accept the fact that the organization and its people may be quite different from what they had anticipated. When they learn, for example, that other people do not appreciate their ideas, they must learn to deal with such resistances to change. Employees must also be prepared to face dilemmas that involve making on-the-job decisions. Dilemmas may pit loyalties to the job, to

22. D. C. Feldman, "A Socialization Process That Helps New Recruits Succeed," *Personnel,* March-April 1980, pp. 11–23.

23. D. C. Feldman, "The Multiple Socialization of Organization Members," *Academy of Management Review,* April 1981, pp. 309–318.

Dr. Dee Soder is a "corporate coach" who helps executives advance in their careers by identifying the personality flaws that can cost them key promotions. Coaches are often called industrial consultants, personnel specialists, and career counsellors, but they usually have some background in psychology as well as business experience. Their most important asset is the ability to spot career problems and help managers overcome them.

good performance, to the boss, and to the organization against one another. Career dilemmas may also involve ethical considerations.[24]

An organization can take actions to ensure that the socialization stage is successful.[25] It can provide a relaxed orientation program for new personnel. It can see to it that the first job is challenging and that relevant training is provided. It can ensure that timely and reliable feedback is provided to people in this early stage of their careers. Finally, it can place new personnel in groups with high standards to encourage modeling of acceptable norms.

Advancement

The *advancement* stage, also known as the *settling-down* stage, evolves as the individual is recognized for the improved performance that comes with development and growth. The individual is learning his or her career and performing well in it. Soon he or she becomes less dependent on others.

As in the socialization stage, adjustments often are necessary within the advancement stage. Some individuals, of course, are less likely to make adjustments and learn than others. Those who are unsuccessful may change careers or adapt in another way—by job hopping. **Job hopping** occurs when individuals make fewer adjustments within organizations and instead move to different organizations to advance their careers. This practice is becoming more characteristic of the advancement stage. It has gained acceptance and increased in

■ **Job hopping** occurs when an individual makes fewer adjustments within the organization and moves to different organizations to advance his or her career.

24. E. Schein, *Career Dynamics: Matching Individual and Organizational Needs* (Reading, Mass.: Addison-Wesley, 1978); R. A. Webber, "Career Problems of Young Managers," *California Management Review,* Summer 1976, pp. 19–33.

25. D. C. Feldman, "A Practical Program for Employee Socialization," *Organizational Dynamics,* Autumn 1976, pp. 64–80.

recent years as more organizations have used outsiders to replace key managers to improve organization performance.[26]

Vertical and horizontal, or lateral, movement also occurs frequently in the advancement stage. Vertical movement involves promotions, whereas lateral movement involves transfers. These kinds of movements teach people about various jobs in the organization, a broadening experience that can benefit both the individuals and the organization. Organizations meet their staffing needs through such movement, and individuals satisfy their needs for achievement and recognition.

Job moves, whether to a new organization or within the same organization, can cause problems, however. Invariably, higher-level jobs bring increased demands for performance, and frequently there is less preparation for managers moving into these jobs. They usually are expected to step right into top executive positions and perform well, with little time for socialization into a new system. Furthermore, moves often necessitate relocation to other parts of the country, placing stress on not only the job holder but also his or her family.

Organizations can take steps to manage promotions and transfers to reduce problems. Longer-term, careful career planning may reduce the need to relocate, since much of the broadening may be accomplished at one location. The timing and spacing of moves can be coordinated with, or at least adjusted to, the individual's family situation. More important, better training can be provided to enable the individual to make the move more readily and with substantially less stress.

Maintenance

In the *maintenance* stage, individuals develop a stronger attachment to their organizations and, hence, lose some career flexibility. Performance varies considerably in this stage. It may continue to grow, level off, or decline. If performance continues to grow, this stage progresses as a direct extension of the advancement stage. If performance levels or drops, career changes may result.

If leveling off occurs, the individual is said to have reached a *plateau* in her or his career. Responses to plateauing can be effective or ineffective for the individual and the organization. Those who respond effectively to plateaus have been termed *solid citizens;* they have little chance for further advancement but continue to make valuable contributions to the organization. Those whose responses are ineffective are referred to as *deadwood;* they too have little chance for promotion, but they also contribute little to the organization.[27]

Solid citizens become interested in establishing and guiding the next generation of organization members. As a result, they frequently begin to act as mentors for younger people in the organization (we discuss mentoring later). As

26. "Should Companies Groom New Leaders or Buy Them?" *Business Week,* September 22, 1986, pp. 94–96.

27. T. P. Ference, J. A. F. Stoner, and E. K. Warren, "Managing the Career Plateau," *Academy of Management Review,* October 1977, pp. 602–612.

Frederic S. Bogart is sitting in a vault with piles of gold ingots. Mr. Bogart started as trainee with Republic National Bank in 1967 and has become one of the world's foremost authorities on gold. He has built the precious metals department into a significant profit center for the bank and has worked his way up to executive vice president of precious metals trading.

mentors, they show younger members the "ins and outs" of organization politics and help them learn the values and norms of the organization. These individuals also begin to reexamine their goals in life and rethink their long-term career plans. In some cases, this leads to new values (or the reemergence of older ones) that cause the individuals to quit their jobs or pass up chances for promotions.[28] In other cases, individuals achieve new insights and begin to move upward again; such individuals are known as *late bloomers*.[29]

■ As people move into the maintenance and withdrawal stages of their careers, there are still many contributions they can make to the organization.

Individuals who have become deadwood are more difficult to deal with. However, their knowledge, loyalty, and understanding of plateauing represent value to the organization and could make them salvageable. Perhaps rewards other than advancement would keep these persons productive. Their jobs may be redesigned (see Chapters 13 and 21) to facilitate performance, or they may be reassigned within the organization. And, of course, career counseling programs (discussed later in this chapter) could help them reach a better understanding of their situations and opportunities.[30]

If performance declines, the individual may be experiencing some type of midlife crisis, which is associated with effects such as awareness of physical aging and the nearness of death, a reduction in career performance, the recognition that life goals may not be met, and changes in family and work relationships. Individuals handle midlife crises differently. Some develop new patterns for

28. D. LaBier, "Madness Stalks the Ladder Climbers," *Fortune,* September 1, 1986, pp. 79–84.
29. F. Rice, "Lessons from Late Bloomers," *Fortune,* August 31, 1987, pp. 87–91.
30. R. C. Payne, "Mid-Career Block," *Personnel Journal,* April 1984, pp. 38–48.

coping with the pressures of careers. They may change careers or modify the way they are handling their current careers. Others have a more difficult time and may need professional assistance.

Changing jobs has become fairly common during the maintenance stage. Many such moves have proven highly beneficial to the person. Several "executive dropouts," for example, have become successful entrepreneurs, such as James L. Patterson, who left IBM to cofound Quantum Corp.[31] Of course, not all job changes at this stage lead to success. Some job changers find, much to their dismay, that the grass is not greener in the new job, and they experience just as much frustration and disappointment as they did in the old job.[32]

Withdrawal

The final stage—the *withdrawal,* or *decline,* stage—frequently involves the end of full-time employment as the individual faces retirement and other end-of-career options. Some individuals begin new careers at this stage and others level off, but the general pattern is one of decreasing performance. Again, individual adaptation may be positive—beginning a new career, helping others, or learning to accept retirement—or negative—becoming indifferent, giving up, or developing abnormally high dependence on family and friends.

Although legislation may restrict an organization's power to force retirement at age sixty-five, many individuals nevertheless quit full-time employment at about that age, and a number of organizations encourage even earlier retirement for many of their members. Problems may arise for people who are not prepared for the changes retirement brings. An individual who is not ready to retire or feels forced to do so may have an especially difficult time adapting to those changes. To help employees adjust, many organizations are initiating preretirement programs that include information on health, housing, financial planning, legal issues, time management, and social programs for maintaining involvement in the community.

Hall and Hall have argued that the use of the career growth cycle can help organizations manage careers, especially at this crucial stage.[33] The career growth cycle is shown in Figure 23.4. Initially, the organization ensures that jobs offer challenging goals and supports employees' efforts to achieve those goals. If feedback is positive, the employees experience psychological success, which enhances their self-esteem and leads to greater involvement. Less positive feedback, however—which people often receive in the withdrawal stage—has the opposite effect. In this instance,the organization provides counseling to help the individual adapt to the changing circumstances.

---

31. J. Main, "Breaking Out of the Company," *Fortune,* May 25, 1987, pp. 81–88.

32. "Crushed Hopes: When a New Job Proves to Be Something Different," *The Wall Street Journal,* June 10, 1987, p. 27.

33. D. T. Hall and F. S. Hall, "What's New in Career Management," *Organizational Dynamics,* Summer 1976, pp. 17–33.

FIGURE 23.4
The Career Growth Cycle

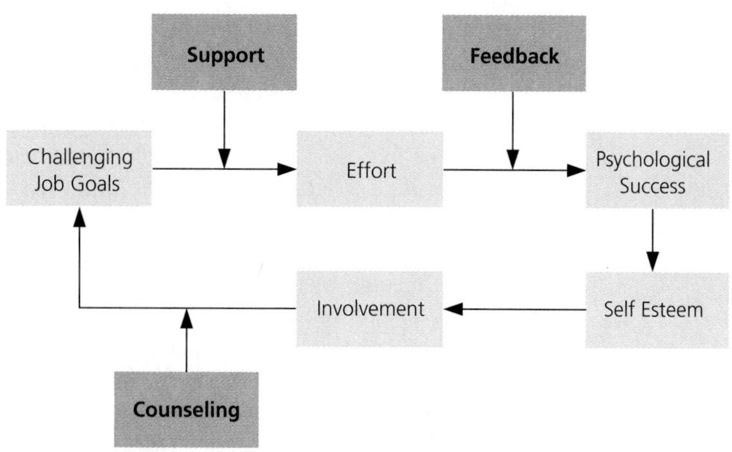

SOURCE: Reprinted by permission of the publisher from "What's New in Career Management," by D. T. Hall and F. S. Hall, *Organizational Dynamics,* Summer 1976, p. 31.

Mentoring

- **Mentoring** occurs when an older, more experienced person helps a younger employee grow and advance by providing advice, support, and encouragement.

Mentoring programs can be an excellent way for an organization to help manage the career stages of its employees. **Mentoring** occurs when an older, more experienced person helps a younger individual grow and advance by providing advice, support, and encouragement. Despite some criticisms of formal mentoring programs, many organizations recently have implemented formal mentoring programs, and many others rely on more traditional informal networks. These companies believe that creating a bond between a senior and a junior employee helps both individuals and benefits the company as well. The mentor often gets in touch with the feelings and attitudes of a younger generation and can learn about new research and techniques from the protégé. The younger colleague can pick up practical skills from the mentor and also gain insights into the organization culture and philosophy that otherwise might take years to discover. A strong, secure bond between the two can lead one or both to do more innovative, important work than they might do on their own.[34]

For the company, this kind of bond can pay off in a number of ways. As the baby-boom generation ages, businesses have to try harder to find and keep good employees. An employee who feels secure in the company because of a good mentoring relationship is less likely to think about looking for another job. Mentors can be especially important for employees who might have trouble fitting into the organization. To move up in a company dominated by an "old-boy" network, for instance, women and minority employees often need contacts of their own in the company's higher ranks. Similarly, multinational corporations

34. Dan Hurley, "The Mentor Mystique," *Psychology Today,* May 1988, pp. 39–43.

may find mentors useful in helping managers from other countries fit into the culture of the corporation. Mentors can also help executives of merged companies adjust to the philosophies and expectations of their new employers.[35]

To get the most out of mentoring programs, experts say, companies must do more than just put two people together and hope for the best.[36] They need to determine what the goals of the program are: to teach specific skills, help new people get along with other employees, or introduce employees to corporate philosophies. Clarifying these goals should help the organization decide who will make the best mentors. Middle managers may be best at helping new people develop specific skills, whereas senior managers may be more effective at passing on the company's vision. In any case, a key element in any mentoring program is matching the two individuals, for the protégé needs to believe that he or she is gaining a friend rather than another boss.

Research into the career stages of people in organizations continues. A recent phenomenon among managers is the occurrence of gaps in career development. These may occur because of changing lifestyles, taking time off for childbearing and child rearing, and for a variety of other reasons. A recent study, however, showed that such career gaps seem to have more negative effects on the careers of men than on those of women.[37]

Organizational Career Planning

- In **career planning,** individuals evaluate their abilities and interests, consider alternative career opportunities, establish career goals, and plan practical development activities.

Career planning is the process of planning one's life work and involves evaluating abilities and interests, considering alternative career opportunities, establishing career goals, and planning practical development activities.[38] Organizations have a vested interest in the careers of their members, and career planning and development programs help them enhance employees' job performance and thus the overall effectiveness of the organization.

Purposes of Career Planning

- Organizational career planning is a complex process involving many conflicting concerns that involve employees, the organization, and social issues.

Organizational career planning programs can help companies identify qualified personnel and future managers, improve job satisfaction and other attitudes, increase involvement of key employees, and improve the vital match between individual and organizational wants and needs.[39] The purposes of career plan-

35. Michael G. Zey, "A Mentor for All Reasons," *Personnel Journal,* January 1988, pp. 47–51.

36. "Guidelines for Successful Mentoring," *Training,* December 1984, p. 125.

37. Joy A. Schneer and Frieda Reitman, "Effects of Employment Gaps on the Careers of M.B.A.'s: More Damaging for Men Than for Women," *Academy of Management Journal,* June 1990, pp. 391–406.

38. J. Walker, "Does Career Planning Rock the Boat?" *Human Resource Management,* Spring 1978, pp. 2–7.

39. C. S. Granrose and J. D. Portwood, "Matching Individual Career Plans and Organizational Career Management," *Academy of Management Journal,* December 1987, pp. 699–720.

FIGURE 23.5
Organizational Career Planning Concerns

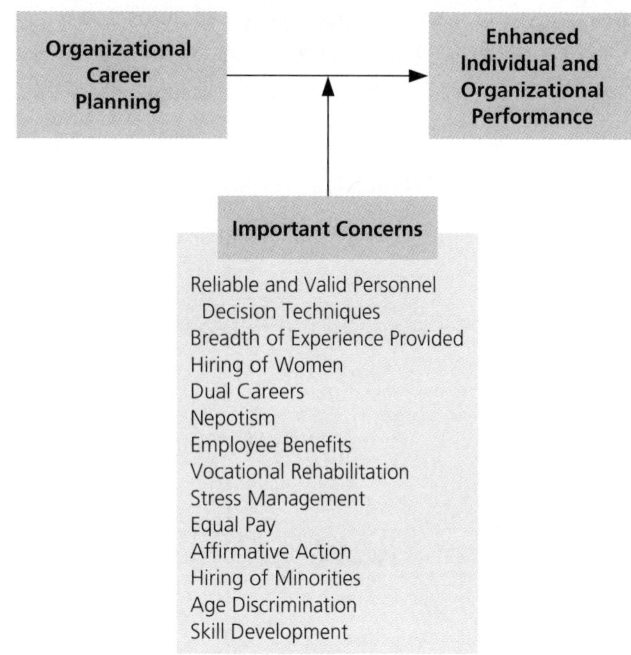

ning, then, involve ensuring that such enhanced individual and organizational performance occurs.

Organizational career planning is a complex process involving many conflicting concerns, some of which are listed in Figure 23.5. Reliable and valid personnel decision techniques must be used in organizations to ensure that career planning achieves its purposes. Careers should provide a breadth of experience for organizational members to foster skill development. The organization must act to ensure that women and minorities are hired, especially in managerial positions, and that these individuals are compensated fairly. These concerns also include issues such as nepotism, dual careers, and age discrimination. Career planning may also involve establishing a functional stress management program (see Chapter 15).

Types of Career Programs

Research suggests that organizational career planning programs fit into seven general categories: career pathing, career counseling, human resource planning, career information systems, management development, training, and special programs.[40]

40. M. A. Morgan, D. T. Hall, and A. Martier, "Career Development Strategies in Industry—Where Are We and Where Should We Be?" *Personnel,* March-April 1979, pp. 13–30.

FIGURE 23.6
Two Examples of Possible Career Paths

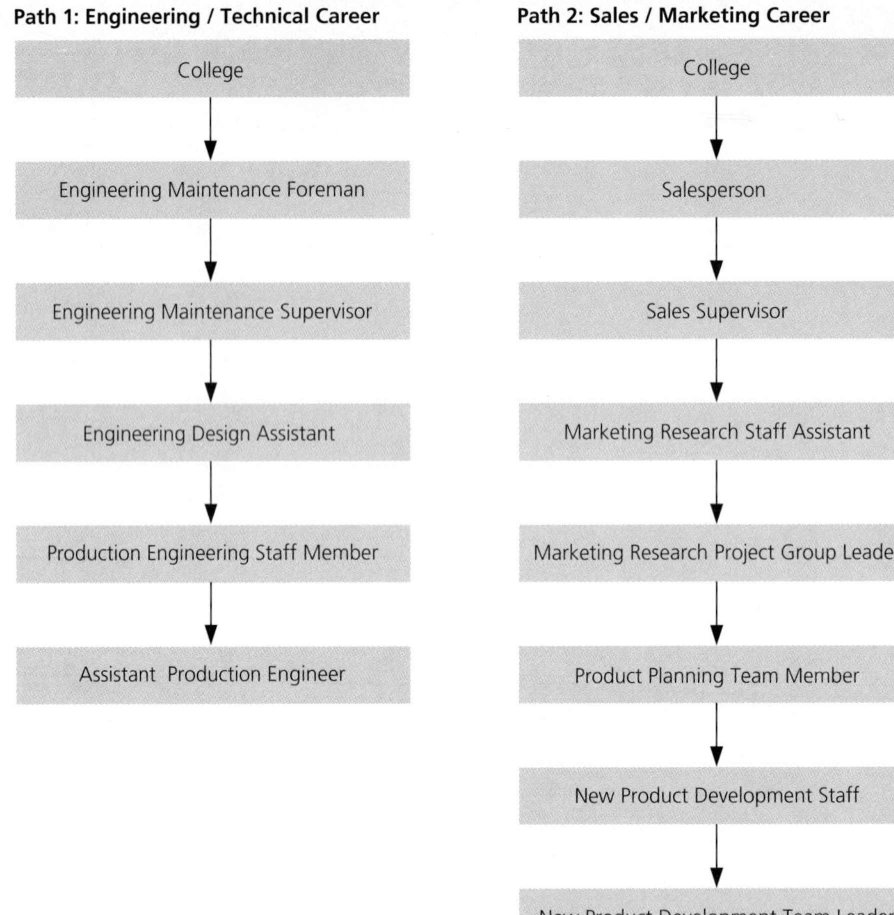

Career Pathing *Career pathing* is the identification of career tracks, or sequences of jobs, that represent a coherent progression vertically and laterally through the organization. Figure 23.6 illustrates two such paths for college graduates, one for an engineering/technical career and one for a sales/marketing career. Paths like these may be clearly specified in some organizations, whereas other organizations may allow far more flexibility. Most organizations do not adhere too strictly to specific career paths, because doing so might limit the full utilization of individual potential, and there are always many exceptions to specified paths.[41] Such organizations provide opportunities for both horizontal and vertical movement to enable individuals to develop their skills and breadth of experience. Some career paths include assignments overseas to help prospective top managers

41. T. A. DiPrete, "Horizontal and Vertical Mobility in Organizations," *Administrative Science Quarterly,* December 1987, pp. 422–444.

gain an understanding of the organization's international operations. Career paths usually have a time frame (frequently five to ten years), may be updated periodically, and may be developed to ensure that the work experiences are relevant to a particular target (that is, higher-level) position in the organization.

Career Counseling Organizations use both informal and formal approaches to career counseling.[42] Counseling occurs informally as part of the day-to-day supervisor-subordinate relationship and often during employment interviews and performance evaluation sessions as well (see Chapter 14). More formally, career counseling often is provided by the human resources department and is available to all personnel, especially those who are being moved up, down, or out of the organization.[43]

Human Resource Planning Human resource planning involves forecasting the organization's human resource needs, developing replacement charts (charts showing planned succession of personnel) for all levels of the organization, and preparing inventories of the skills and abilities individuals need to move within the organization. As Figure 23.7 shows, human resource planning and development systems can be quite complex and involve both individual and organizational activities. Basically, however, such systems involve developing plans, matching organizations and individuals, assessing needs, and implementing the plans. It is the specific applications that lead to the complexity of the system.

Career Information Systems When internal job markets are combined with formal career counseling to establish a career information center for organization members, the result is a career information system. Internal job markets exist when job openings within the organization are announced first to organization members. News about openings may appear on bulletin boards, in newsletters, and in memoranda. A career information center keeps up-to-date information about such openings, as well as information about employees who are seeking other jobs or careers within the organization. Career information systems, then, can serve not only to develop the organization's resources but to provide information that may increase the motivation of organization members to perform.

Management Development Management development programs vary considerably. They may consist simply of policies that hold managers directly responsible for the development of their successors, or they may set out elaborate formal educational programs. Management development is receiving increasing attention in all types of organizations. On average, managers are participating

---

42. N. C. Hill, "Career Counseling: What Employees Should Do—and Expect," *Personnel,* August 1985, pp. 41–46.

43. W. Kiechel III, "Passed Over," *Fortune,* October 13, 1986, pp. 189–191; J. C. Latack and J. B. Dozier, "After the Ax Falls: Job Loss as a Career Transition," *Academy of Management Review,* April 1986, pp. 375–392.

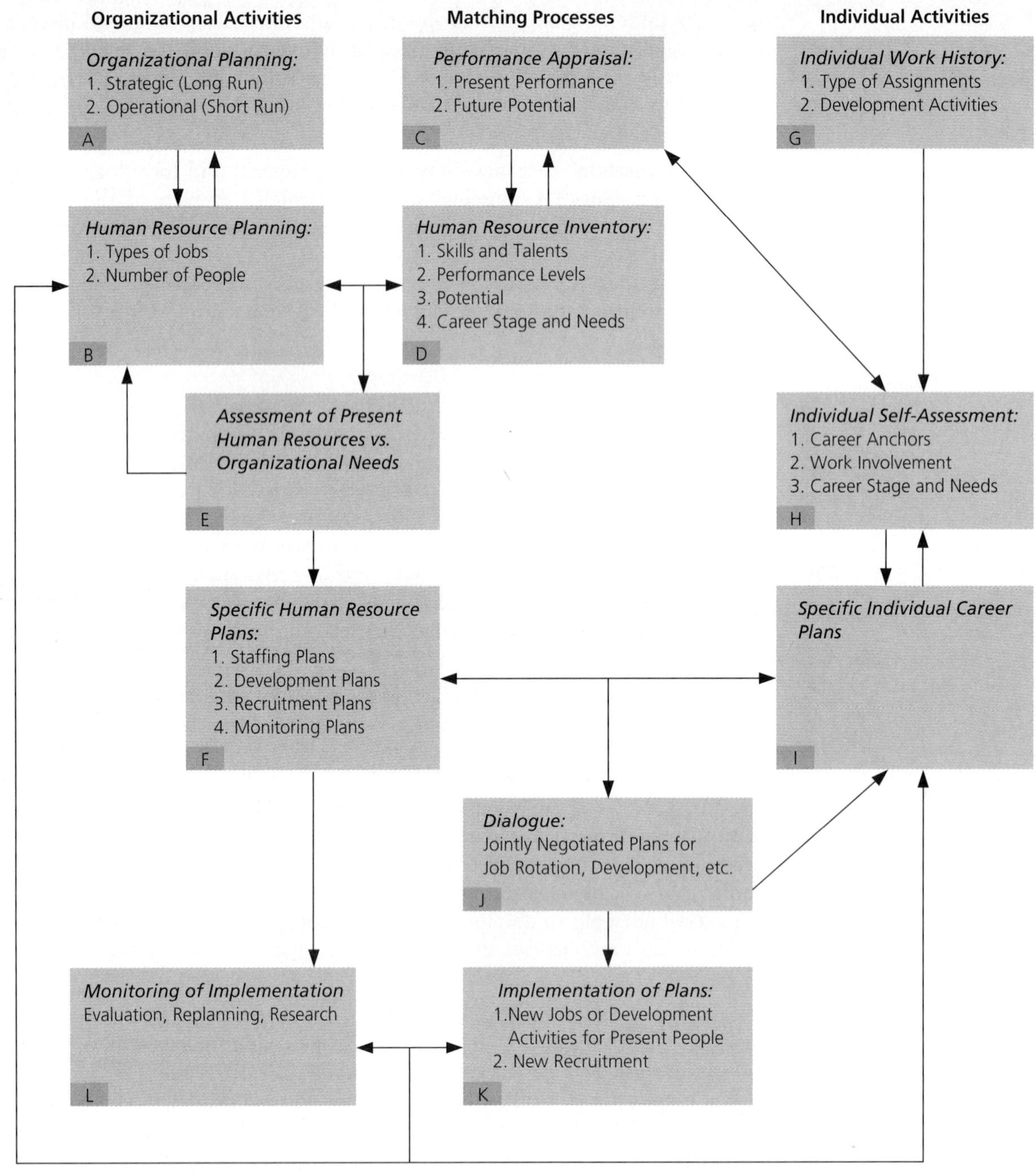

SOURCE: Edgar H. Schein, *Career Dynamics: Matching Individual and Organizational Needs,* p. 4, Figure 1.2. © 1978, Addison-Wesley Publishing Company Inc. Reprinted with permission of the publisher.

FIGURE 23.7
A Human Resource Planning and Development System

in from twenty to forty hours per year of education and development activities[44] dealing with topics such as time management, problem solving and decision making, strategic planning, and leadership. Developmental programs in smaller organizations (those with fewer than one thousand employees) tend to focus on management and supervisory skills, communication, and behavioral skills. In larger organizations, development activities typically concentrate on executive development, new management techniques, and computer literacy.[45] Management development is discussed in more detail in Chapter 21.

Training More specialized efforts to improve skills usually are termed *training*. These activities include on-the-job training, formalized job rotation programs, in-house training sessions for the development of specific technical job skills, programs on legal and political changes that affect specific jobs, tuition reimbursement programs, and student intern programs. The emphasis usually is on specific job skills, with immediate performance being of greater concern than long-term career development. Of course, continued improvement in job performance carries implications for evolving career opportunities.

Special programs Training and development programs may be designed for and offered to special groups within the organization. Preretirement programs offer one example, as do programs designed to help organization members cope with midlife career crises. Many organizations now offer outplacement counseling—programs designed to help employees who are leaving the organization, either voluntarily or involuntarily.[46] Outplacement programs help people preserve their dignity and self-worth when they are fired and can reduce negative feelings toward the organization. Other special programs have been developed for women, minorities, and handicapped personnel to help them solve their special career problems.[47] Some organizations also have special programs to assist personnel in the career move from technical to managerial positions. Still other organizations have begun programs to deal with smokers, because it has become clear that they pose health risks not only to themselves but to others.[48]

---

44. E. H. Burack, *Creative Human Resource Planning and Applications: A Strategic Approach* (Englewood Cliffs, N.J.: Prentice-Hall, 1988).

45. Ibid.

46. T. M. Camden, "Using Outplacement as a Career Development Tool," *Personnel Administrator,* January 1982, pp. 35–44.

47. See, for example, D. D. Bowen and R. D. Hisrich, "The Female Entrepreneur: A Career Development Perspective," *Academy of Management Review,* April 1986, pp. 393–407; "Male vs. Female: What a Difference It Makes in Business Careers," *The Wall Street Journal,* December 9, 1986, p. 1; "In Dad's Footsteps: More Women Find a Niche in the Family Business," *The Wall Street Journal,* May 28, 1987, p. 29; D. D. Van Fleet and J. Saurage, "Recent Research on Women in Leadership and Management," *Akron Business and Economic Review,* Summer 1984, pp. 15–24; E. M. Van Fleet and D. D. Van Fleet, "Entrepreneurship and Black Capitalism," *American Journal of Small Business,* Fall 1985, pp. 31–40.

48. "Cigarette Smoking Is Growing Hazardous to Careers in Business," *The Wall Street Journal,* April 23, 1987, pp. 1, 19.

TABLE 23.3
Key Ingredients for Career Management

Coordination with other human resource activities	Equal access and open enrollment
Involvement of supervisors	Focus on psychological success rather than advancement
Use of human resource managers as consultants	Flexibility for individual needs
Periodic skill assessment	Climate setting for career development
Realistic feedback about career progress	Small pilot programs
Top management support	Periodic program assessment

SOURCE: From *Managing Careers in Organizations* by Daniel C. Feldman. Copyright © by Scott, Foresman and Company. Reprinted by permission of HarperCollins Publishers.

Career Management

■ **Career management** is the process of implementing organizational career planning.

Career management is the process by which organizational career planning is implemented. As Table 23.3 shows, top management support is needed to establish a climate that fosters career development. All human resource activities within the organization must be coordinated, and human resource managers from various areas should be involved at least as consultants. The career planning programs must be open to all members of the organization and thus must be flexible to accommodate the variety of individual differences that will be encountered. Realistic feedback should be provided to participants with the focus on psychological success rather than simply advancement. Implementation of new programs should begin with small pilot programs that emphasize periodic assessment of employee skills and experiences of the program itself.[49] *A Look at the Research* describes the career development programs that are used in many companies.

■ Each supervisor and manager in the organization plays a key role in making the organization's career planning program work to the benefit of the organization and its employees.

It is extremely important that supervisors be involved and that they are trained carefully lest they neglect or mishandle their role and negate the positive effects of career planning programs. The role of supervisors includes communicating information about careers; counseling to help subordinates identify their skills and to understand their options; evaluating subordinates' performance, strengths, and weaknesses; coaching or teaching skills and behaviors to those who need support; advising about the realities of the organization; serving as a mentor or role model for subordinates; brokering, or bringing together subordinates and those who might have positions better suited to them; and informing subordinates about opportunities.[50]

49. Adapted from Feldman, *Managing Careers in Organizations,* pp. 189–192. See also K. B. McRae, "Career-Management Planning: A Boon to Managers and Employees," *Personnel,* May 1985, pp. 56–61.

50. Z. B. Leibowitz and N. K. Schlossberg, "Training Managers for Their Role in a Career Development System" *Training and Development Journal,* July 1981, pp. 72–79.

A LOOK AT THE
RESEARCH

Career Development Programs in Fortune 500 Companies

Many organizations have career development programs as part of their human resources development programs. Only recently, however, have researchers evaluated these career development programs. One study of existing programs was done by Jack Keller and Chris Piotrowski of the University of West Florida. Published in *Psychological Reports,* the study covered career development programs in Fortune 500 firms.

Professors Keller and Piotrowski found that most career development programs in organizations are conducted by in-house professionals and are intended for employees at all levels. Most of the programs they surveyed were sponsored or initiated by a top administrator, chief executive officer, or top person within the human resources department. Over 80 percent of the existing programs ran one day or longer. Overall, the participants rated the programs as at least "somewhat helpful" or very "helpful."

The results of this study indicate that career development programs are widely used in organizations and represent substantial expenditures of company resources. Such programs have top management support and appear to be well received by the middle-level managers who participate. The researchers suggest that more research is needed to further our understanding of career development programs in organizations.

SOURCE: Keller, J., & Piotrowski, C., "Career Development Programs in Fortune 500 Firms," *Psychological Reports,* December 1987, 61, 920–922.

Results of Career Planning

Organizational career planning has many important results.[51] Employees develop more realistic expectations of what is expected of them on the job and what their future with the organization will entail. Supervisory roles in career counseling are clarified, personal career planning ability is increased through knowledge and education, and human resource systems within the organization are more effectively utilized. All of these effects serve to strengthen career commitment as individuals develop plans to take charge of their careers. Ultimately, then, the organization is able to better use the talent of its members, turnover is reduced, and individual and corporate performance is increased.

These benefits are not, however, guaranteed. If the existence of an organizational career planning program raises individuals' expectations unrealistically, dysfunctional consequences may result. Anxiety may increase, supervisors may spend too much time counseling their subordinates, and human resource systems may become overloaded. These effects lead to frustration, disappointment, and reduced commitment. In the end, talent is inadequately used, turnover increases, and individual and organizational performances suffer. The key to keeping employee expectations realistic is for all supervisors and managers to be trained to

51. Walker, "Does Career Planning Rock the Boat?"

provide only factual information about jobs and the true prospects for an employee. Clearly, organizations must use career planning programs carefully to ensure positive results.

Summary of Key Points

- Individuals' concerns about careers are related to their perceived opportunities for success. Organizations, on the other hand, want to ensure smooth managerial succession and high levels of individual and organizational performance. These two perspectives are compatible, because individuals who are achieving their career goals are likely to be high performers. Thus, organizations can achieve their objectives by helping individuals accomplish theirs.
- Career choice occurs whenever an individual makes a conscious decision about beginning or continuing a career. It involves six steps: becoming aware of the need for a career choice, getting information about oneself and career options, evaluating the information, making a career choice, implementing the choice, and assessing the choice.
- In addition to a basic career choice, people make two associated types of decisions: a choice of occupation and a choice of organization. Content and process theories of occupational choice recognize both the complexity of the process by which such choices are made and the variety of forces that influence the choices. Organizational choice generally involves selecting an organization that will provide some minimally acceptable level of economic benefit as well as the opportunity to engage in interesting, challenging, or novel activities.
- Research suggests that careers evolve through a series of general stages. Although career stages are closely associated with adult life stages, they are not the same. The career stages are entry, socialization, advancement, maintenance, and withdrawal.
- Organizations engage in career planning to achieve a variety of purposes of value to both them and their members. Seven general categories of career planning programs are career pathing, career counseling, human resource planning, career information systems, management development, training, and special programs.
- Career management is the process by which organizational career planning is implemented. It requires top management support, widespread use of human resource personnel, and a favorable climate for utilizing the organization's human resources to the fullest. Especially important is the involvement and cooperation of supervisors.
- The results of organizational career planning may be beneficial or dysfunctional. Careful monitoring of the program should ensure that benefits are obtained. Such benefits include the development of realistic expectations on the parts of all involved, with a resulting full utilization of human resources to increase both individual and organizational performance.

Discussion Questions

1. Have you known anyone who seemed to be in the wrong occupation? What evidence made it appear that way?
2. Are individual and organizational perspectives on careers always compatible? Why or why not?
3. What career choices might exist for someone with an undergraduate business degree? A graduate business degree?
4. Differentiate the terms *jobs, occupations,* and *careers.*
5. Discuss the five career stages and the possible options for an individual who changes careers during one of the latter stages.
6. What happens when a relatively young worker—someone in his or her mid-forties—moves into the career stage of maintenance or withdrawal? Is this positive for the organization or the individual? What can the organization do about it?
7. Briefly discuss each of the seven general categories of career planning programs. How might each category apply to people at different career stages?
8. What is meant by the statement that careers are managed? Who actually manages careers?
9. Is the concept of organizational career planning realistic in the rapidly changing environment of today's business? Why or why not?
10. Changing occupations in mid-career can be traumatic. What is the role of the organization in helping employees to change jobs in the middle of their careers?

CASE 23.1

Careers Are Changing as Fast as the Times

Years ago, a person joined a company for life. Through both good and bad times, the traditional worker was a "company man." But times have changed, and today a career may consist of a variety of work experiences, job categories, and, of course, organizations. The scenario of a worker retiring after forty years with the same company may be a thing of the past.

Two major problem areas seem to be surfacing in the 1990s. The first concerns women who hit the "glass ceiling" on their way up the corporate ladder. By the year 2000, women will comprise about one-half of the work force, but very few will be at the top. In 1990, fewer than one-half of 1 percent of the top-paying jobs in the largest U.S. corporations were held by women—specifically, 19 out of 4,012 officers and directors. Women have been graduating from colleges and universities in record numbers for more than twenty years, many from the top business schools. Yet, unlike their male baby-boomer classmates, they are not moving into the executive suites. About two-thirds of the work force at Continental Corp., a property and casualty company, consists of women, but 90 percent of the senior executives are men. Price Waterhouse, a management consulting firm, recently was ordered to make a woman a partner and pay her $370,000 in back wages because it had excluded her in partnership decisions in 1982.

Businesses have made many excuses for the continuing problem, from the socialization processes of young children to the subtle networking that goes on during social outings. One factor is the experience of many women who have tried to balance the child-rearing process and their career tracks. Few companies offer equal maternal and paternal benefits, and even fewer provide child care on the work site. When children need attention, are sick, or have school problems, the mother more often than not interrupts her workday to attend to them. Such interruptions can only delay progress toward the top.

Some women have chosen to remain childless to pursue their careers. Others have tried to combine child rearing and work and experienced burnout and stress from the burden of two full-time jobs. In addition, many women who chose to forego a career in favor of raising a family have had trouble getting a satisfying job when they entered the work force after their children were grown.

The second area of emerging concern regarding careers is the tendency of middle managers and professionals in large companies to leave their firms to go somewhere else. Many managers have gotten their feet in the door to the executive suite only to reject the opportunity for the next promotion and quit. It appears they have peeked over the fence to see what is on the other side and chosen not to jump over. A national marketing director of United Parcel Service who had been with the company for twenty years abruptly quit to start his own company despite a family, the usual financial responsibilities, and no job prospects. Evidently he had grown tired of the rigid bureaucracy of big business and wanted something different.

Similarly, a female fast-track manager on Wall Street suddenly quit her job to "get her brains back." She subsequently moved to the West Coast and started her own business. Another example is a woman who had been born in Malaysia, raised in Hong Kong, and became an accountant for The Gap, Inc., an apparel retailer, after college. Within three years she had been promoted several times, increased her salary by 50 percent, and become the manager of an accounting group. She quit because of the stress from her sixty-hour workweeks and the uncertainty of her future. She now works forty hours a week as an accountant in another firm and enjoys several leisure-time hobbies.

Several factors may be contributing to the flight of middle managers from their organizations. The current trend toward downsizing is putting many middle managers out of work and scaring off those who remain but fear an impending job cut. Many middle managers in large organizations believe their futures are at the mercy of the current management team. A significant number of these managers are choosing to leave the large conglomerates in favor of smaller operations over which they expect to wield more control.

Case Questions

1. Which career stage do you believe will be most applicable to each of these two areas of concern?
2. What types of career development programs could corporations implement to address these areas?

SOURCES: Kenneth Labich, "Breaking Away to Go on Your Own," *Fortune,* December 17, 1990, pp. 40–56; Alan Deutschman, "What 25-Year-Olds Want," *Fortune,* August

27, 1990, pp. 42–50; Jaclyn Fierman, "Why Women Still Don't Hit the Top," *Fortune,* July 30, 1990, pp. 40–62.

CASE 23.2 Tom Wayland's Choice

Tom Wayland was a superb engineer. Rather than graduate with a mechanical engineering degree and go right to work, he spent an extra three semesters in college to finish a second major in electrical engineering. he took a job at Precision Products and soon distinguished himself, coming up with a new design for a temperature-sensitive switch that the company sold to all three American automakers to use in air-conditioning systems. By age thirty-three, Wayland had been promoted to chief of engineering at Precision, a position that had always been held by people with doctorates. But after enjoying two years at the top of his area, Wayland wondered, "What next?"

Wayland had always strived to keep all his options open; yet as he evaluated his situation and tried to plan for the future, he found the number of possibilities overwhelming. In college, his goal had been to reach something like the position he now held. Precision paid him well, and company engineers and executives uniformly respected him. His wife Jenny was working her way up in the management of a nearby computer company, and their two children were in elementary school and did not demand as much of their parents' time as they used to. Most people who had reached his position, Wayland thought, would breathe a sigh of relief, relax, and enjoy family life and a stable job.

But the prospect of spending the rest of his career in the same position depressed Wayland. Although his rise at Precision had been fast, the company president had made it clear that technical expertise alone would not get Wayland out of engineering and into an executive suite. Wayland had considered going back to school and getting an M.B.A., but the time he would have to take off from the job would mean lost income for his family. Besides, he was not sure he wanted to deal with finances, marketing, and personnel; he liked being an engineer and saw executive positions as stressful and uncreative.

Sometimes Wayland thought his growing dissatisfaction was a sign that he missed the challenge of proving himself to people who were not yet convinced of his abilities. He was sure he could land a job at a larger company and work his way up to a position with more pay, power, and prestige. But a skeptical voice in his head told him that to be chief of engineering anywhere else he would need a Ph.D., and he doubted that a larger corporation would have the same friendly atmosphere as Precision.

A number of Wayland's colleagues at Precision had gone out on their own, and their success encouraged Wayland to consider that option. The life of a consultant would give him a lot of freedom and could lead to some interesting challenges, although Wayland feared that he would miss working with others. He also considered starting his own business, building something he could call his own, perhaps making a fortune or creating a product that would make him famous. But that was a big, risky step, and Wayland was not sure he had the drive to be an entrepreneur.

Finally, Wayland thought about teaching. He had enjoyed college immensely, and he liked working with younger engineers. He was confident that with a Ph.D. he could get a college teaching job, but he would be forty before he could complete the degree, and he knew he would never make a salary that equaled what Precision was paying him. Teaching math or science in a local high school would be intriguing, he thought, but he feared he would go stale after a short time.

Jenny discussed all the options with her husband and said she would support whatever decision he made. He appreciated her confidence in him, but it did not make the decision any easier. So, after months of debating with himself, Wayland decided to get some advice from his mentor, Rudolph Bailey, who had been chief of engineering when Wayland joined the company and was now vice president for research and development. Bailey had watched a lot of engineers move up and out of the company, and Wayland hoped the older man could at least help him narrow his choices.

Case Questions

1. What seems to be Wayland's best choice? Why?
2. Besides talking to his wife and his mentor, what might Wayland do to help him make his important career decision?

EXPERIENTIAL EXERCISE

What career are you planning to pursue? Why? Have you carefully assessed the match between your skills, abilities, and wants and those appropriate for success in that career?

Purpose: This exercise will give you an opportunity to evaluate your career plans and the career options open to you.

Format: Working alone, you will complete a worksheet that will help you analyze your thoughts and plans about your career. After you have filled out the worksheet as best as you can, you and another member of the class will review each other's worksheets.

Procedure: Use the worksheet in Figure 23.8 to analyze your chosen career. Some of you may already have begun your careers and therefore have a good idea of how to answer the questions. Others may be unclear about what career you want to pursue after you leave school. If this is the case, choose the career you think you want and do your best to answer the questions.

In column 1, list four to six major tasks or activities required in the job you wish to hold three to five years from now. In column 2, list the skills you will need to do each of those tasks. In column 3, evaluate the degree to which your present qualities fulfill the skill requirements listed in column 2.

The questions in columns 4 to 6 refer to the tasks and activities described in column 1. In column 4, indicate the extent to which the task or activity will change in the next five years. In column 5, indicate the importance of the task

Chosen Career : ______________________

Column 1	Column 2	Column 3			Column 4	Column 5	Column 6
Task or Activity	Skill Required	Education	Experience	Personal Characteristics	Change in the Task in 5 Years	Importance of the Task in 5 Years	Your Preparation for this Task in 5 Years
		Very Little *Very Much*	*Very Little* *Very Much*	*Bad Fit* *Good Fit*	*Very Little* *Very Much*	*Not Important* *Very Important*	*Not Ready* *Very Ready*
		1 2 3 4 5	*1 2 3 4 5*	*1 2 3 4 5*	*1 2 3 4 5*	*1 2 3 4 5*	*1 2 3 4 5*
1.							
2.							
3.							
4.							
5.							
6.							

FIGURE 23.8 Career Assessment Worksheet

to the overall job five years from now. In column 6, describe the things you are doing to become better qualified for the job five years from now.

Finally, pair up with a classmate and compare worksheets. Working together, make suggestions for improving each other's worksheets by filling in blank spots on both worksheets, making more accurate estimates of future tasks, and explaining the rationale for your answers on the worksheet.

Follow-up Questions

1. As a result of this exercise, do you have a better picture of what your career might be? Explain.
2. Do you now know some specific steps you can take to be ready for possible career changes in the next five years? What are some of those steps?

APPENDIX: RESEARCH METHODS IN ORGANIZATIONAL BEHAVIOR

Throughout this book, we referred to theories and research findings as a basis for our discussion. In this appendix, we further examine how theories and research findings are developed. First, we highlight the role of theory and research. Then we identify the purposes of research and describe the steps in the research process, types of research designs, and methods for gathering data. We conclude with a brief discussion of some related issues.

The Role of Theory and Research

Some managers—and many students—fail to see the need for research. They seem confused by what appears to be an endless litany of theories and by sets of contradictory research findings. They often ask, "Why bother?"

Indeed, few absolute truths have emerged from studies of organizational behavior. Management in general and organizational behavior in particular, however, are in many ways fields of study still in their infancy. Thus, it stands to reason that researchers in these fields have few theories that always work and that their research cannot always be generalized to settings other than those in which it was originally conducted.

Still, theory and research play valuable roles.[1] Theories help investigators organize what they do know. They provide a framework that managers can use to diagnose problems and implement changes. They also serve as road signs that help managers solve many problems involving people. Research too plays an

1. Jeffrey Pfeffer, "The Theory-Practice Gap: Myth or Reality?" *Academy of Management Executive*, February 1987, pp. 31–33.

important role. Each study conducted and published adds a little more to the storehouse of knowledge available to practicing managers. Questions are posed and answers developed. Over time, researchers can become increasingly confident in findings as they are applied across different settings.[2]

Purposes of Research

- **Scientific research** is the systematic investigation of hypothesized propositions about the relationships among natural phenomena.
- **Basic research** involves discovering new knowledge rather than solving specific problems.
- **Applied research** is conducted to solve particular problems or answer specific questions.

As much as possible, researchers try to approach problems and questions of organizational behavior scientifically. **Scientific research** is the systematic investigation of hypothesized propositions about the relationships among natural phenomena. The aims of science are to describe, explain, and predict phenomena.[3]

Research can be classified as basic or applied. **Basic research** is concerned with discovering new knowledge rather than solving particular problems. The knowledge made available through basic research may not have much direct application to organizations, at least when it is first discovered.[4] Research scientists and university professors are the people who most often conduct basic research in organizational behavior.

Applied research, on the other hand, is conducted to solve particular problems or answer specific questions. The findings of applied research are, by definition, immediately applicable to managers. Consultants, university professors, and managers themselves conduct much of the applied research performed in organizations.

The Research Process

To result in valid findings, research should be conducted according to the scientific process shown in Figure A.1. The starting point is a question or problem.[5] For example, a manager wants to design a new reward system to enhance employee motivation but is unsure about what types of rewards to offer or how to tie them to performance. This manager's questions therefore are "What kinds of rewards will motivate my employees?" and "How should those rewards be tied to performance?"

---

2. Eugene Stone, *Research Methods in Organizational Behavior* (Santa Monica, Calif.: Goodyear, 1978).

3. Fred N. Kerlinger, *Foundations of Behavioral Research,* 3rd ed. (New York: Holt, Rinehart and Winston, 1987).

4. Richard L. Daft, Ricky W. Griffin, and Valerie Yates, "Retrospective Accounts of Research Factors Associated with Significant and Not-So-Significant Research Outcomes," *Academy of Management Journal,* December 1987, pp. 763–785.

5. Richard L. Daft, "Learning the Craft of Organizational Research," *Academy of Management Review,* October 1983, pp. 539–546.

FIGURE A.1
The Research Process

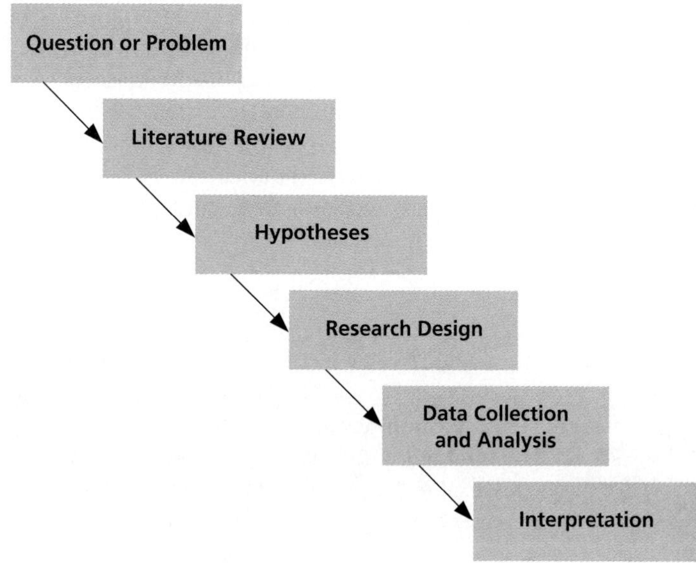

The next step is to review the literature to determine what is already known about the phenomenon. It is quite likely that something has been written about most problems or questions today's managers face. Thus, the goal of the literature review is to avoid "reinventing the wheel" by finding out what others have already learned. Basic research generally is available in journals such as the *Academy of Management Journal, Academy of Management Review, Administrative Science Quarterly, Journal of Applied Psychology, Organizational Behavior and Human Decision Processes,* and *Journal of Management.* Applied research findings are more likely to be found in sources such as the *Harvard Business Review, Academy of Management Executive, Organizational Dynamics, HRMagazine,* and *Personnel Psychology.*

Based on the original question and the review of the literature, the researcher formulates hypotheses—statements of what he or she expects to find. The hypothesis is an important guide for the researcher's design of the study, because it provides a very clear and precise statement of what the researcher wants to test. That means the study can be specifically designed to test the hypothesis.

The research design is the plan for doing the research. (We discuss the more common research designs later.) As part of the research design, the researcher must determine how variables will be measured. Thus, if satisfaction is one factor being considered, the researcher must decide how to measure it.

After data have been collected, they must be analyzed. (We also discuss common methods for gathering data later.) Depending on the study design and hypotheses, data analysis may be relatively simple and straightforward or require elaborate statistical procedures. Methods for analyzing data are beyond the scope of this discussion.

Finally, the results of the study are interpreted; that is, the researcher figures out what they mean. They may provide support for the hypothesis, may fail to support the hypothesis, or may suggest a relationship other than that proposed in the hypothesis. An important part of the interpretation process is recognizing the limitations imposed on the findings by weaknesses in the research design.

Some researchers go a step further and try to publish their findings. Several potential sources for publication are the journals mentioned in the discussion of literature review. Publication is important, because it helps educate other researchers and managers and also provides additional information for future literature reviews.[6]

Types of Research Designs

■ A **research design** is the set of procedures used to test the predicted relationships among natural phenomena.

A **research design** is the set of procedures used to test the predicted relationships among natural phenomena. The design addresses such issues as how the relevant variables are to be defined, measured, and related to one another. Managers and researchers can draw on a variety of research designs, each with its own strengths and weaknesses. Four general types of research designs often are used in the study of organizational behavior (see Table A.1); each type has several variations.[7]

Case Study

■ A **case study** is an in-depth analysis of one setting.

A **case study** is an in-depth analysis of a single setting. This design frequently is used when little is known about the phenomena being studied and the researcher wants to look at relevant concepts intensively and thoroughly. A variety of methods are used to gather information, including interviews, questionnaires, and personal observation.[8]

The case study research design offers several advantages. First, it allows the researcher to probe one situation in detail, yielding a wealth of descriptive and explanatory information. The case study also facilitates the discovery of unexpected relationships. Because the researcher observes virtually everything that happens in a given situation, she or he may learn about issues beyond those originally chosen for study.

The case study design also has several disadvantages. The data it provides cannot be readily generalized to other situations, because the information is so closely tied to the situation studied. In addition, case study information may be biased by the researcher's closeness to the situation. Case study research also tends to be very time consuming.

6. Larry L. Cummings and Peter Frost, *Publishing in Organizational Sciences* (Homewood, Ill.: Irwin, 1985).

7. D. T. Campbell and J. C. Stanley, *Experimental and Quasi-Experimental Designs for Research* (Chicago: Rand McNally, 1963).

8. R. Yin and K. Heald, "Using the Case Study Method to Analyze Policy Studies," *Administrative Science Quarterly,* June 1975, pp. 371–381.

TABLE A.1
Types of Research Designs

Type	Dominant Characteristic
Case Study	Useful for thorough exploration of unknown phenomena
Field Survey	Provides easily quantifiable data
Laboratory Experiment	Allows researcher high control of variables
Field Experiment	Takes place in realistic setting

Nevertheless, the case study can be an effective and useful research design as long as the researcher understands its limitations and takes them into account when formulating conclusions.

Field Survey

- A **field survey** typically relies on a questionnaire distributed to a sample of people selected from a larger population.

A **field survey** usually relies on a questionnaire distributed to a sample of people chosen from a larger population. If a manager is conducting the study, the sample often is drawn from a group or department within her or his organization. If a researcher is conducting the study, the sample typically is negotiated with a host organization interested in the questions being addressed. The questionnaire generally is mailed or delivered by hand to participants at home or at work and may be returned by mail or picked up by the researcher. The respondents answer the questions and return the questionnaire as directed. The researcher analyzes the responses and tries to make inferences about the larger population from the representative sample.[9]

Field surveys can focus on a variety of topics relevant to organizational behavior, including employees' attitudes toward other people (such as leaders and coworkers), attitudes toward their jobs (such as satisfaction with the job and commitment to the organization), and perceptions of organizational characteristics (such as the challenge inherent in the job and the degree of decentralization in the organization).[10]

Field surveys provide information about a much larger segment of the population than do case studies. They also provide an abundance of data in easily quantifiable form, which facilitates statistical analysis and the compilation of normative data for comparative purposes.

Field surveys also have several disadvantages. First, survey information may reveal only superficial feelings and reactions to situations rather than deeply held feelings, attitudes, or emotions. Second, the design and development of field surveys require a great deal of expertise and can be very time consuming. Furthermore, relationships among variables tend to be accentuated in responses to questionnaires because of what is called *common method variance*. This means

9. Kerlinger, *Foundations of Behavioral Research.*

10. Ramon J. Aldag and Timothy M. Stearns, "Issues in Research Methodology," *Journal of Management,* June 1988, pp. 253–276.

that people tend to answer all the questions in the same way, creating a misleading impression. Finally—and very important—field surveys give the researcher little or no control. The researcher may lack control over who completes the questionnaire, when it is filled out, the mental or physical state of the respondent, and many other important conditions. Thus, the typical field survey has many inherent sources of potential error.

Nonetheless, surveys can be a very useful means of gathering large quantities of data and assessing general patterns of relationships among variables.

Laboratory Experiment

■ A **laboratory experiment** involves creating an artificial setting similar to a real work situation to allow control over almost every possible factor in that setting.

The **laboratory experiment** gives the researcher the most control. By creating an artificial setting similar to a real work situation, the researcher can control almost every possible factor in that setting. He or she can manipulate the variables in the study and examine their effects on other variables.[11]

As an example of how laboratory experiments work, consider the relationship between how goals are developed for subordinates and the subordinates' subsequent level of satisfaction. To explore this relationship, the researcher structures a situation in which some subjects (usually students but occasionally people hired or recruited from the community) are assigned goals while others determine their own goals. Both groups then work on a hypothetical task relevant to the goals, and afterward all subjects fill out a questionnaire designed to measure satisfaction. Differences in satisfaction could be attributed to the method used for goal setting.

Laboratory experiments prevent some of the problems of other types of research. Advantages include a high degree of control over variables and precise measurement of variables. A major disadvantage is the lack of realism; rarely does the laboratory setting exactly duplicate the real-life situation. A related problem is the difficulty in generalizing the findings to organizational settings. Finally, some organizational situations, such as plant closings or employee firings, cannot be simulated in a laboratory.

Field Experiment

■ A **field experiment** is similar to a laboratory experiment but is conducted in a real organization.

A **field experiment** is similar to a laboratory experiment except that it is conducted in a real organization. In a field experiment, the researcher attempts to control certain variables and manipulate others to assess the effects of the manipulated variables on outcome variables. For example, a manager interested in the effects of flexible working hours on absenteeism and turnover might design a field experiment in which one plant adopts a flexible work schedule program and another plant, as similar as possible to the first, serves as a control site.

11. Cynthia D. Fisher, "Laboratory Experiments," in Thomas S. Bateman and Gerald R. Ferris, eds., *Method and Analysis in Organizational Research* (Reston, Va.: Reston, 1984); Edwin Locke, ed., *Generalizing from Laboratory to Field Settings* (Lexington, Mass.: Lexington Books, 1986).

Attendance and turnover are monitored at both plants. If attendance increases and turnover decreases in the experimental plant and there are no changes at the control site, the manager probably will conclude that the flexible work schedule program was successful.

The field experiment has certain advantages over the laboratory experiment. The organizational setting provides greater realism, making generalization to other organizational situations more valid. Disadvantages include the lack of control over other events that might occur in the organizational setting (such as additional changes the firm introduces), contamination of the results if the various groups discover their respective roles in the experiment and behave differently because of that knowledge, greater expense, and the risk that the experimental manipulations will contribute to problems within the company.

Methods of Gathering Data

- Data-gathering methods may be grouped into four categories: questionnaires, interviews, observation, and nonreactive measures.

The method of gathering data is a critical concern of the research design. Data-gathering methods may be grouped into four categories: questionnaires, interviews, observation, and nonreactive measures.[12]

Questionnaires

A *questionnaire* is a collection of written questions about the respondents' attitudes, opinions, perceptions, and/or demographic characteristics. Usually the respondent fills out the questionnaire and returns it to the researcher. To facilitate scoring, the researcher typically uses multiple-choice questions. Some questionnaires have a few open-ended questions that allow respondents to elaborate on their answers. Designing a questionnaire that will provide the information the researcher desires is a very complex task and one that has received considerable attention.

Interviews

An *interview* resembles a questionnaire, but the questions are presented to the respondent orally by an interviewer. The respondent usually is allowed to answer questions spontaneously rather than asked to choose among alternatives defined by the researcher. Interviews generally take much more time to administer than questionnaires, and they are more difficult to score. The benefit of interviews is the opportunity for the respondent to speak at length on a topic, thereby providing a richness and depth of information not normally yielded by questionnaires.

12. Stone, *Research Methods in Organizational Behavior.*

Observation

Observation, in its simplest form, is watching events and recording what is observed. Researchers use several types of observation. In structured observation, the observer is trained to look for and record certain activities or types of events. In participant observation, the trained observer actually participates in the organizational events as a member of the work team and records impressions and observations in a diary or daily log. In hidden observation, the trained observer is not visible to the subjects. A hidden camera or a specially designed observation room may be used.

Nonreactive Measures

When a situation is changed because of data gathering, we say the activity has caused a reaction in the situation. *Nonreactive,* or unobtrusive, *measures* have been developed for gathering data without disturbing the situation being studied. Nonreactive measures include examination of physical traces, use of archives, and simple observation. When questionnaires, interviews, and obtrusive observations may cause problems in the research situation, the use of nonreactive measures may be an appropriate substitute. At some universities, for example, sidewalks are not laid down around a new building until it has been in use for some time. Rather than ask students and faculty about their traffic patterns or try to anticipate them, the designers observe the building in use, see where the grass is most heavily worn, and put sidewalks there.

Related Issues in Research

- Three other issues important to research are causality, reliability and validity, and ethical concerns.

Three other issues are of particular interest to researchers: causality, reliability and validity, and ethical concerns.[13]

Causality

Scientific research attempts to describe, explain, and predict phenomena. In many cases, the purpose of the research is to reveal causality; that is, researchers attempt to describe, explain, and predict the cause of a certain event. In everyday life, people commonly observe a series of events and infer causality about the relationship among them. For example, you might observe that a good friend is skipping one of her classes regularly. You also know she is failing that class. You might infer that she is failing the class because of her poor attendance. But

13. Philip M. Podsakoff and Dan R. Dalton, "Research Methodology in Organizational Studies," *Journal of Management,* Summer 1987, pp. 419–441.

the causal relationship may be just the reverse: Your friend may have had a good attendance record until her poor performance on the first test destroyed her motivation and led her to stop attending class. Given the complexities associated with human behavior in organizational settings, the issues of causality, causal inference, and causal relations are of considerable interest to managers and researchers alike.

In the behavioral sciences, causality is difficult to determine because of the interrelationships among variables in a social system. Causality cannot always be empirically proven, but it may be possible to infer causality in certain circumstances. In general, two conditions must be met for causality to be attributed to an observed relationship among variables. The first is temporal order: If x causes y, then x must occur before y. Many studies, especially field surveys, describe the degree of association among variables with highly sophisticated mathematical techniques, but inferring a causal relationship is difficult because the variables are measured at the same point in time. On the basis of such evidence, we cannot say whether one variable or event caused the other, whether they were both caused by another variable, or whether they are totally independent of each other.

The second condition is the elimination of spuriousness. If we want to infer that x caused y, we must eliminate all other possible causes of y. Often a seemingly causal relationship between two variables may be due to their joint association with a third variable, z. To be able to say the relationship between x and y is causal, we must rule out z as a possible cause of y. In the behavioral sciences, so many variables may influence one another that tracing causal relationships is like walking in an endless maze. Yet despite the difficulties of the task, we must continue trying to describe, explain, and predict social phenomena in organizational settings if we are to advance our understanding of organizational behavior.[14]

Reliability and Validity

- The **reliability** of a measure is the extent to which it is consistent over time.

The **reliability** of a measure is the extent to which it is consistent over time. Suppose a researcher measures a group's job satisfaction today with a questionnaire and then measures the same thing in two months. Assuming nothing has changed, individual responses should be very similar. If they are, the measure can be assessed as having a high level of reliability. Likewise, if question 2 and question 10 ask about the same thing, responses to these questions should be consistent. If measures lack reliability, little confidence can be placed in the results they provide.

- **Validity** is the extent to which a measure actually reflects what it was intended to measure.

Validity describes the extent to which research measures what it was intended to measure. Suppose a researcher is interested in employees' satisfaction with their jobs. To determine this, he asks them a series of questions about their pay, supervisors, and working conditions. He then averages their answers and

14. Stone, *Research Methods in Organizational Behavior.*

uses the average to represent job satisfaction. We might argue that this is not a valid measure. Pay, supervision, and working conditions, for example, may be unrelated to the job itself. Thus, the researcher has obtained data that do not mean what he thinks they mean—they are not valid. The researcher, then, must use measures that are valid as well as reliable.[15]

Ethical Concerns

Last, but certainly not least, the researcher must contend with ethical concerns. Two concerns are particularly important.[16] First, the researcher must provide adequate protection for participants in the study and not violate their privacy without their permission. For example, suppose a researcher is studying the behavior of a group of operating employees. A good way to increase people's willingness to participate is to promise that their identities will not be revealed. Having made such a guarantee, the researcher is obligated to keep it.

Likewise, participation should be voluntary. All prospective subjects should have the right to not participate or to withdraw their participation after the study has begun. The researchers should explain all procedures in advance to participants and should not subject them to any experimental conditions that could harm them either physically or psychologically. Many government agencies, universities, and professional associations have developed guidelines for researchers to use to guarantee protection of human subjects.

The other issue involves how the researcher reports the results. In particular, it is important that research procedures and methods be reported faithfully and candidly. This enables readers to assess for themselves the validity of the results reported. It also allows others to do a better job of replicating (repeating) the study, perhaps with a different sample, to learn more about how its findings generalize.

---

15. Kerlinger, *Foundations of Behavioral Research.*

16. Mary Ann Von Glinow, "Ethical Issues in Organizational Behavior," *Academy of Management Newsletter,* March 1985, pp. 1–3.

Glossary

Absenteeism Failure to report to work. (6)

acceptance theory of authority Suggests that the authority of the manager depends on the subordinate's acceptance of the manager's right to give the directive and expect compliance. (17)

accommodation A type of intergroup interaction that occurs when the goals are compatible but not considered to be very important to goal attainment. (8)

action research The process used by a change agent consisting of (a) directing the organizational change and (b) documenting it to contribute to the empirical body of knowledge about organizations. (21)

adaptation In a social system, fitting into the environment by being aware of the environment, understanding how that environment is changing, and making the appropriate adjustments. (20)

adhocracy A form of organization design that has horizontal and vertical specialization but little formalization, resulting in a very organic structure. Decision making is spread throughout the organization. It is one of Mintzberg's structural forms and is typically found in young organizations engaged in highly technical fields where the environment is complex and dynamic. (19)

administrative hierarchy A system of reporting relationships in the organization, from the first level up through the president or CEO. (17)

AGIL model Developed by Parsons, this model specified certain functions that any social system must meet to survive and prosper: adaptation, goal attainment, integration, and legitimacy. (20)

all-channel network A small-group network in which all members communicate with all the other members. (11)

applied research Research conducted to solve particular problems or answer specific questions. (App.)

attribution theory Suggests that we observe the behavior of others and then attribute causes to it. The theory is associated with Heider and Kelley. (3)

authoritarianism The extent to which a person believes that there should be power and status differences within a social system such as an organization. The stronger the belief, the more the individual is said to be authoritarian. (4)

authority Power that has been legitimized within a specific social context. (17)

autonomous work groups An innovation in task design whereby jobs are structured for groups rather than for individuals. The group itself is given considerable discretion in scheduling, individual work assignments, and other matters that have traditionally been management prerogatives. (13)

avoidance (negative reinforcement) A concept of reinforcement theory that occurs when the individual is engaging in desired behavior in order to avoid an unpleasant, or aversive, consequence. The effect of avoidance is to increase the frequency of a desired behavior. (3)

avoidance A type of intergroup interaction that occurs when the interaction is not considered to be important to any group's goal attainment and the goals are considered to be incompatible. (8)

Note: The number in parentheses after each entry refers to the chapter in which the term is discussed.

Basic research Research concerned with discovering new knowledge rather than solving particular problems. (App.)

behavior modification (OB Mod.) The application of reinforcement theory principles to individuals in organizational settings. It is usually aimed at increasing desired behaviors by employees through the use of positive reinforcement. (12)

behavioral approach (to leadership) Approach designed to determine the behaviors associated with effective leadership. These approaches to the study of leadership began in the late 1940s. (9)

behavioral approach to decision making A decision-making model characterized by the use of procedures and rules of thumb, suboptimizing, and satisficing. (16)

behaviorally anchored rating scale (BARS) Essentially graphic rating scales with statements of employee behaviors that characterize, or "anchor," various points on the scale. It is a performance evaluation method developed by Smith and Kendall in 1963. (19)

belongingness needs Primarily social in nature, including, for example, the need for love and affection and the need to be accepted by peers. (5)

bias A personal preference or inclination that undermines impartial judgment. (14)

bounded rationality A decision-making process whereby the decision maker limits the inputs to the decision-making process and makes decisions based on judgment and personal biases as well as logic. (16)

brainstorming A technique for stimulating imaginative and novel ideas. Participants in brainstorming are encouraged to suggest as many innovative and extreme ideas as possible as solutions to the identified problem. Participants are forbidden to discourage the ideas of others and are encouraged to build on the ideas of others. (16)

bureaucracy A type of organizational structure proposed by Max Weber. The ideal bureaucracy is characterized by Weber as having a hierarchy of authority, a system of rules and procedures, and division of labor. (19)

burnout The overall feeling of exhaustion a person feels when simultaneously experiencing too much pressure and too few sources of satisfaction. (15)

Career A perceived sequence of attitudes and behaviors associated with work-related experiences and activities over the span of the person's life. (23)

career management The process by which organizational career planning is implemented. (23)

career planning The process of planning one's life work; involves evaluating abilities and interests, considering alternative career opportunities, establishing career goals, and planning practical development. (23)

career stages The gradual changes that occur over time in careers. (23)

case study An in-depth analysis of one setting. This design is frequently used when little is known about the phenomena in question and the researcher wants to look at relevant concepts intensively and thoroughly. (App.)

causality The attempt by researchers to describe, explain, and predict the cause of a certain event. The purpose of scientific research is to reveal causality. (App.)

centralization Decision-making authority is concentrated at the top of the organizational hierarchy. (17)

central tendency In performance evaluation, the tendency of a rater to evaluate performance moderately, with few if any high or low ratings. (14)

chain network A small group network in which each member communicates with the person above and below, except the individuals on each end, who communicate with only one person. (11)

change agent A person who is responsible for managing the change effort in the organization. The change agent may be a member of the organization or an outsider. (21)

channel noise The principal type of noise in the communication process. (11)

charismatic leadership An approach to leadership that assumes charisma is an individual characteristic of the leader. Charisma is a form of interpersonal attraction that inspires support and acceptance. It is presumed that a supervisor who is very charismatic may be more successful in influencing subordinate behavior than one lacking charisma. (9)

circle network A small group network in which each person communicates with the people on both sides but no one else. (11)

classic principles of organizing Fourteen principles that provide the framework for the organization chart and the coordination of work. These principles were identified by Fayol and have been criticized for ignoring the human element in organizations. (19)

classical conditioning An approach to learning stating that if a conditioned stimulus is repeatedly paired with an unconditioned stimulus, the conditioned stimulus will eventually become associated in the mind of the learner with the same response that is elicited by the unconditioned stimulus. This approach is associated with Pavlov and his experiments with dogs. (3)

classical organization theory A branch of management that was concerned with structuring organizations effectively. (1)

coercive power A base of power identified by French and Raven that exists when someone has the ability to punish or to inflict physical or psychological harm on someone else. (10)

cognitive dissonance The anxiety a person experiences when two sets of knowledge or perceptions are contradictory or incongruent. It also occurs when a person behaves in a way inconsistent with her or his attitudes. (4)

cognitive process A process that assumes people are conscious, active participants in how they learn. People draw on their experiences and use past learning as a basis for present behavior. People make choices about their behavior and then recognize the consequences of their choices. Finally, people evaluate those consequences and add them to prior learning, affecting future choices. (3)

cohesiveness See **group cohesiveness.**

collaboration A type of intergroup interaction that occurs when the interaction is important to goal attainment and the groups' goals are compatible. (8)

collectivism A feeling that the good of the group or society should come first. (22)

command group A type of formal group that is relatively permanent. A command group is also referred to as a functional group. (7)

commitment Individual's feelings of identification with and attachment to the organization. (4)

communication A process in which information is exchanged or a common understanding is established between two or more parties. (11)

communication fidelity The degree of correspondence between the message intended by the source and the message understood by the receiver. (11)

communication network Links that develop so that employees can obtain the necessary information to do their jobs and coordinate their work with others in the system. It serves to structure both the flow and the content of communication and support the organization structure. (11)

competition A type of intergroup interaction that occurs when the goals of the groups are incompatible and interactions are important to goal attainment of each group. (8)

compressed workweek A work schedule in which an employee works a full forty-hour week in less than the traditional five days. Typically, an employee may work ten hours a day for four days, with an extra day off. (13)

compromise A type of intergroup interaction that occurs when the interactions are of moderate importance to goal attainment and goals are neither completely compatible nor incompatible. (8)

configuration The size and shape of an organization as depicted on an organization chart. (17)

conflict A form of group interaction that occurs whenever one group perceives that its attempts to accomplish its goals have been frustrated by another group. (10)

conflict model The Janis-Mann process of decision making based on research in social psychology and individual decision processes. The model makes five assumptions. (16)

content-process distinction A differentiation of the need (content) and process theories of motivation. (6)

content validity In performance appraisal, the extent to which the measurement adequately assesses all important aspects of job performance. (14)

contingency approach to organization design The structure determined by specific conditions such as the environment, technology, and the organization's work force. (19)

contingency perspective A theory that suggests that in most organizations situations and outcomes are contingent on, or influenced by, other variables. (1)

contingency plans Alternative actions that can be taken if the primary course of action is unexpectedly disrupted or rendered inappropriate. (16)

contingency theory of leadership A theory that contends that a leader's effectiveness depends upon a match between the leader's style and the favorableness of the situation. Situational favorability is determined by task structure, leader-member relations, and leader position power. The theory was advanced by Fiedler in 1967. (9)

continuous reinforcement The rewarding of behavior every time it occurs. (3)

controlling The process of monitoring and correcting the actions of the organization and people and activities within it so as to keep them headed toward their goal. (2)

convergent validity In performance appraisal, the extent to which different measures agree in the evaluations of the same performance. (14)

creativity The process of developing original and imaginative perspectives on situations. (16)

critical incident technique Involves interviewing individuals who are familiar with the target job; each person is asked to describe specific incidents of effective and ineffective behaviors in the job. (14)

Decision making The process of choosing one alternative from several alternatives. (16)

decision rule A statement that tells the decision maker which alternative to choose once she or he has information about the decision situation. (16)

decision-making roles One of Mintzberg's three general categories of managerial roles including the entrepreneur, the disturbance handler, the resource allocator, and the negotiator roles. These roles closely relate to decision making. (1)

decoding The process by which the receiver of the message interprets its meaning. (11)

decoupling The functional separation in some way of two groups whose tasks require that they interact. (8)

defensive avoidance In the conflict model of decision making, making no changes in present activities and avoiding any further contact with issues affecting the activities because there seems to be no hope of finding a better solution. (16)

deficiency needs The three sets of needs at the bottom of the hierarchy which must be satisfied for the individual to be fundamentally comfortable. (5)

Delphi technique A method of improving group decision making that involves systematically gathering the judgments of experts and developing forecasts. When using the Delphi technique, groups do not meet face to face. (16)

departmentalization The manner in which divided tasks are combined into work groups for coordination. The most common methods are by business function, process, product or service, customer, and geography. (17)

discipline An attempt to punish that is structured, official, and organizationally sanctioned. (3)

discriminant validity In performance appraisal, the extent to which ratings of the same type of performance agree more than do ratings of different types of performance. (14)

dispositional view of attitudes A view that suggests that people respond in predictable ways depending on their affect, cognitions, and intentions. (2)

disseminator role The manager who transmits the information gathered by the monitor to others. (2)

dissonance reduction An attempt by an individual to reduce the tension and discomfort that attitudes and behaviors not consistent with each other cause. Generally, the person tries to change the attitude, change the behavior, or perceptually distort the circumstances. (4)

distress A negative form of stress that can lead to dangerous side effects. (15)

disturbance handler role The manager who helps settle disputes between various parties, such as other managers and their subordinates. (2)

division of labor The extent to which the work of the organization is separated into different jobs to be done by different people. (17)

divisionalized form An organization design that resembles the machine bureaucracy except that it is divided according to the different markets it serves. Standardization of outputs is the primary means of coordination. It is one of Mintzberg's structural forms that characterizes old, very large firms operating in a relatively simple, stable environment with several diverse markets. (19)

Effort-to-performance expectancy The perceived probability that effort will lead to performance. The probability may range between 0 and 1.0. It is a major concept of expectancy theory. (6)

encoding The process by which the message is translated from an idea or thought into symbols that can be transmitted. (11)

entrepreneur role The manager who voluntarily initiates change, such as innovations or new strategies. (2)

environmental complexity The number of environmental components that affect organizational decision making. (18)

environmental dynamism The degree to which environmental components change. (18)

environmental scanning The process of constantly searching the business environment for new opportunities and threats to the organization. (16)

environmental uncertainty A condition that exists when managers have little information about environmental events and their impact on the organization. It results from environmental complexity and environmental dynamism. (18)

equity theory A theory based on the premise that people want to be treated fairly and that they compare their own input-to-outcome ratio in the organization to the ratio of a comparison-other. If they feel that, in a relative sense, they are being treated inequitably, they take steps to reduce the inequity. The theory was articulated by Adams. (6)

ERG theory A theory that suggests that people may be motivated by more than one kind of need at the same time. The theory also includes a frustration-regression component and a satisfaction-progression component. Associated with Alderfer, this theory is an extension and refinement of Maslow's needs hierarchy. It identifies three basic need categories: existence, relatedness, and growth. (5)

escalation of commitment The tendency to persist in an ineffective course of action when evidence indicates the project is doomed to failure. (16)

esteem needs Encompasses two slightly different kinds of needs: the need for a positive self-image and self-respect and the need to be respected by others. (5)

ethics Personal beliefs about what is right and wrong or good and bad. (2)

eustress A positive form of stress that can motivate, stimulate, and, often, reward a person. (15)

existence needs Needs perceived as necessary for basic human existence. (5)

expectancies The probabilities linking effort and performance and performance and rewards in the expectancy model. (6)

expectancy theory Assumes that motivation depends on how much we want something and how likely we think we are to get it. (6)

expert power A base of power identified by French and Raven that relates to control over expertise or, more precisely, over information. (10)

extinction A concept of reinforcement theory that decreases the frequency of undesired behavior, especially behavior that was previously rewarded. Extinction occurs when rewards are removed from behaviors that were previously reinforced. (3)

Feedback Verification of a message sent from the receiver to the source. (11)

field experiment A type of research design similar to a laboratory experiment, but it is conducted in a real organization. The researcher is able to control certain variables and manipulate others in order to assess the effects of the manipulated variables on outcome variables. (App.)

field survey A type of research design that usually relies on a questionnaire distributed to a sample of people chosen from a larger population. The researcher analyzes the responses to the questionnaire and tries to make inferences about the larger population the sample was chosen to represent. (App.)

figurehead role A role sometimes taken by the manager wherein he or she serves as a symbol of the organization. (2)

fixed interval reinforcement Reinforcement provided on a predetermined, constant schedule. (3)

fixed ratio reinforcement Reinforcement where the number of behaviors needed to obtain reinforcement is constant. (3)

flexible reward system A compensation system that lets employees choose the combination of benefits that best suits their needs. (12)

flexible work schedules (flextime) A work schedule in which the work day is broken down into two categories: flexible time and core time. All employees must be at their work stations during core time, but they can choose their own schedules during flexible time. Flexible time enables employees to have some control over their working hours. (13)

flextime (flexible work schedules) See **flexible work schedules.**

forced choice method (in performance appraisal system) A method of evaluating individual performance whereby the rater must choose one item from among a group of behavioral statements which is most descriptive of the performance of the employee. (14)

forced distribution method (in performance appraisal system) A method of evaluating individual performance that forces the evaluator to assign employees to categories on the basis of their performance but limits the percentage of employees that can be placed in any one category. (14)

formal groups Groups established by the organization to do its work and usually identifiable on an organization chart. Include the command (functional) group, which is relatively permanent, and task (special projects) group, which is relatively temporary. (7)

formalization The degree to which the jobs and activities of employees are codified by rules and procedures. (17)

friendship group A type of informal group that is relatively permanent. The association among the members is due to friendly relationships and the pleasure that comes from being together. (7)

functional group See **command group.**

functional job analysis technique Identifies the specific tasks that make up a job and examines how much each task involves data, people, and things. Each task's complexity in each respect is rated from 1 to 10. (14)

General adaptation syndrome (GAS) Begins when a person first encounters a stressor. The basic threshold at which stress starts to affect individuals. The three stages of response to stress are alarm, resistance, and exhaustion. (15)

goal A desirable objective individuals or organizations want to achieve. (12)

goal acceptance The extent to which an individual accepts a goal as his or her own. (12)

goal attainment The reaching of goals in a social system. The system must have processes that specify those goals and specific strategies for reaching the goals. (20)

goal commitment The extent to which an individual is personally interested in reaching a goal. (12)

goal compatibility The extent to which the goals of more than one group can be achieved at the same time. (8)

goal difficulty The extent to which a goal is challenging and demands effort. (12)

goal displacement A process that occurs when groups overemphasize their own goals at the expense of the organization's goals. (8)

goal setting theory of motivation This theory, developed by Locke, assumes that behavior is a result of conscious goals and intentions. Goal difficulty and goal specificity shape performance. (12)

goal specificity Setting a goal in quantitative terms. It is consistently related to performance. (12)

graphic rating scale One of the simplest methods of rating individual performance whereby the rater checks or circles the point on the scale that best represents the performance level of the employee. (14)

group Two or more persons interacting with one another in such a manner that each person influences and is influenced by each other person. (7)

group cohesiveness How strongly members of a group feel about remaining in the group. Attraction to the group, resistance to leaving the group, and motivation to remain a member of the group are the forces that create cohesiveness. Group cohesiveness may be increased by competition or the presence of an external threat. (7)

group composition The makeup of a group. It is often described in terms of the homogeneity or heterogeneity of the members. (7)

group development The stages and activities groups progress through in order to become mature, effective groups. The four general stages are: mutual acceptance, communication and decision making, motivation and productivity, and control and organization. (7)

group performance factors Factors that influence the formation and development of the group. They describe the way group members do their jobs and relate to each other. Primary factors are composition, size, norms, and cohesiveness. (7)

group polarization The shift of member attitudes and opinions to a more extreme position following group discussion. It arises due to the expression of shared attitudes in the discussion, persuasive arguments by supporters of the extreme position, and the feeling that responsibility is diffused by the group process. (16)

group size The number of members of a group. The size of a group can vary from two members to as many members as can interact and influence each other. (7)

groupthink A mode of thinking that people engage in when they are deeply involved in a cohesive ingroup, when the members' strivings for unanimity override their motivation to realistically appraise alternative courses of action. (16)

growth needs The top two sets of needs, focusing on personal growth and development. (5)

Halo error In performance appraisal, occurs when a rater consistently assigns the same rating to all aspects of a person's performance, regardless of the actual performance level, because of an overall favorable or unfavorable impression of the person. (14)

Hawthorne studies A series of experiments that played a major role in developing the foundations of the field of organizational behavior. The studies were conducted at the Hawthorne Plant of Western Electric near Chicago between 1927 and 1932. The overall conclusion of the studies was that individual and social processes are too important to ignore. (1)

hedonism A concept that dominated the earliest views on human motivation. Hedonism argues that people seek pleasure and comfort and try to avoid pain and discomfort. (5)

hierarchy of needs Maslow theory that assumes human needs are arranged in a hierarchy of importance. (5)

high tech/high touch Refers to Naisbitt's contention that the more new technology is forced on people, the more need there is for the human touch. (21)

human organization A system that centers on the principles of supportive relationships, employee participation, and overlapping work groups. The human organization is an approach to organization design presented by Likert. (19)

human relations movement A movement that played a major role in developing the foundations of the field of organizational behavior. The basic premise of the movement was that people respond primarily to their social environment. McGregor's Theory X and Theory Y and Maslow's hierarchy of needs were predominant theories of this period. (1)

hygiene factors Extrinsic to the work itself, including factors such as pay and job security. (5)

hypervigilance In the conflict model of decision making, frantic and superficial pursuit of some satisficing strategy. (16)

Ideal bureaucracy An organizational system characterized by a hierarchy of authority and a system of rules and procedures designed to create an optimally effective system for large organizations. (19)

individual characteristics One of five basic categories of organizational behavior concepts. Among such characteristics are learning, perception, attitudes, personalities, employee motivation, goal setting, rewards, and stress. (1)

individual differences A set of factors that includes the ways we think, the ways we interpret our environment, and the ways we respond to that environment. (4)

individualism A state in which people view themselves first as individuals and believe their own interest and values take priority. (22)

individual-organization interface One of the five basic categories of organizational behavior concepts. It includes job design, role dynamics, group and intergroup dynamics, leadership, power, politics, and conflict. (1)

informal groups Groups formed by members of an organization. They include the relatively permanent friendship group and the interest group, which may be less long-lived. (7)

informational roles One of Mintzberg's three general categories of managerial roles including the monitor, the disseminator, and the spokesperson roles. These roles involve some aspect of information processing. (1)

innovation The process of creating and doing new things that are introduced into the marketplace as new products, processes, or services. (18)

inputs An individual's contribution to the organization, such as experience, effort, and loyalty. (6)

intangible compensation Rewards whose value is not easily defined or measured. (12)

integration The need every social system has to keep its constituent parts together. The parts of the system must be brought in contact with one another, interdependences understood and organized, and the need for coordinated action resolved. (20)

interactionalism A perspective that attempts to explain how people select, interpret, and change various situations. The individual and the situation are presumed to interact continuously; this interaction determines the individual's behavior. (1)

interest group A type of informal group that is relatively temporary. An interest group is organized around a common interest of the members. (7)

intergroup behavior The ways groups interact with each other. (8)

interpersonal demands The demands from other people or groups confronting those in organizational settings, such as group pressures, leadership style, and personalities and behavior. (15)

interpersonal roles One of Mintzberg's three general categories of managerial roles including figurehead, leader, and liaison roles. These roles are primarily social in nature. (1)

interrater reliability The extent to which ratings by more than one rater agree. (14)

interview A method of gathering data whereby questions are presented to the respondent by an interviewer. The respondent is usually allowed to answer questions spontaneously rather than asked to choose among alternatives defined by the researcher. (App.)

intrapreneurship Entrepreneurial activity within the organization. (18)

involvement A person's willingness to go beyond the standard demands of his or her job as an organizational "citizen." (4)

Jargon The specialized or technical language of a trade, field, profession, or social group. (11)

job analysis The process of systematically gathering information about specific jobs for use in developing a performance appraisal system and in writing job descriptions. (12)

job characteristics approach Began with the work of Turner and Lawrence, who believed that workers would prefer complex, challenging tasks to monotonous, boring ones, and who predicted that job complexity would be associated with employee satisfaction and attendance. (13)

Job Characteristics Theory A model of job enrichment that defines job enrichment as increasing the amounts of certain core dimensions—skill variety, task identity, task significance, autonomy, and feedback. The core dimensions lead to three psychological states that result in positive personal and work-related outcomes. (13)

job design The specification of an employee's task-related activities, including both structural and interpersonal aspects of the job, as determined by both the organization's and the individual's needs and requirements. (13)

Job Diagnostic Survey A questionnaire that measures employee perceptions of job characteristics, the various psychological states, personal and work outcomes, and strength of growth needs. (13)

job enlargement Expansion of a worker's job to include tasks previously performed by other workers. Also called horizontal job loading, it is one alternative to job specialization. (13)

job enrichment A technique based on Herzberg's two-factor theory of motivation. Employees could be motivated by positive job-related experiences through job loading (giving employees more control over those tasks added by horizontal loading). (13)

job hopping Moving to different organizations rather than making adjustments within the present organization. (23)

job rotation Systematically shifting workers from one job to another, with the goal of sustaining worker motivation and interest. It is one alternative to job specialization. (13)

job satisfaction or dissatisfaction An individual's attitude toward his or her job. It is one of the most widely studied variables in the entire field of organizational behavior. (4)

job sharing An approach to work schedules whereby two part-time employees share one full-time job. For example, one person may perform the job from 8:00 A.M. until noon, and the other from 1:00 P.M. until 5:00 P.M. (13)

job specialization An historical approach to the design of jobs whereby jobs are scientifically studied, broken down into their smallest component parts, and then standardized across all workers doing those jobs. It is a rational, seemingly efficient way to organize jobs, but it can also cause problems due to the monotony of highly specialized, standardized tasks. (13)

Laboratory experiment A type of research design whereby the researcher creates an artificial setting similar to a real work situation. The experimenter has a great deal of control and can manipulate the variables in the study and examine their effects on the other variables in the experiment. (App.)

leader role A role sometimes served by the manager during which he or she works to hire, train, and motivate employees. (2)

leadership Both a process and a property. As a process, leadership is the use of noncoercive influence to direct and coordinate the activities of group members toward goal accomplishment. As a property, leadership is the set of characteristics attributed to those who are perceived to employ such influence successfully. (9)

leadership grid A framework for examining types of supervision developed by Blake and Mouton. Two dimensions are identified: concern for production and concern for people. It is suggested that a manager who has a high concern for people and production will be very effective. (9)

leadership substitutes Individual, task, and organizational characteristics that tend to negate the leader's ability to affect subordinate satisfaction and performance. (9)

leadership traits Unique set of qualities or traits that early research leaders thought distinguished leaders from their peers. The traits were presumed to be relatively stable and enduring. (9)

leading The process of getting members of the organization to work together in a fashion consistent with the goals of the organization. (2)

learning A relatively permanent change in behavior or potential behavior that results from direct or indirect experience. (3)

legitimacy The need every social system has to be granted the right to survive by elements in its environment. (20)

legitimate power A base of power identified by French and Raven that is granted by virtue of one's position in the organization. (10)

lenient In performance evaluation, the tendency of a rater to evaluate performance consistently high. (14)

liaison role A role sometimes played by the manager that consists of relating to others outside the group or organization. (2)

life change Any meaningful change in a person's personal or work situation. (15)

life cycle theory According to this theory, appropriate leader behavior depends on the maturity of the leader's followers. The maturity is how motivated, competent, experienced, and interested in accepting responsibility the subordinates are. (9)

life stressors Events taking place outside the organization that cause stress in organizational settings, generally categorized in terms of life change and life trauma. (15)

life trauma Any single upheaval in an individual's life that disrupts his or her attitudes, emotions, or behaviors. (15)

linking role A position for a person or a group that serves to coordinate the activities of two or more organizational groups. It is an organization-based strategy for managing intergroup interactions. (8)

locus of control The extent to which a person believes that his or her behavior has a direct impact on the consequences of that behavior. Individuals with an internal locus of control believe that if they work hard, they will be successful. People who have an external locus of control tend to think that what happens to them is a function of fate or luck. (4)

Machiavellianism A person's motivation to gain power and control the behavior of others. (4)

machine bureaucracy An organization design in which work is highly specialized and formalized, and decision making is usually concentrated at the top. It is one of Mintzberg's structural forms and is typical of a large, well-established company in a simple and stable environment. (19)

management by objectives (MBO) A process in which managers and employees collaborate to set verifiable employee goals. Progress is periodically reviewed, and at the end of the process, employee performance is evaluated. (12)

management development Attempts to foster certain skills, abilities, and perspectives important to good management. (21)

manifest needs theory An abstract theory presented by Murray in 1938 and translated into a more concrete, operational framework by Atkinson. The theory assumes that people have a set of multiple needs that motivates behavior simultaneously rather than in a preset order. Each need has two components: direction and intensity. (5)

Maslow's hierarchy of needs According to Maslow's theory, human needs are arranged in a five-tiered hierarchy of importance, from physiological needs at the bottom, to security needs, belongingness needs, esteem needs, and, at the top, self-actualization needs. (5)

matrix design An attempt to combine two different designs to gain the benefits of each. In the most common form, product or project departmentalization is superimposed on a functional structure. (19)

mechanistic structure A type of organization design that is primarily hierarchical in nature, interactions and communications are primarily vertical, instructions come from the boss, knowledge is concentrated at the top, and continued membership requires loyalty and obedience. Burns and Stalker state that this type of structure is appropriate if the rate of change in technology is slow. (19)

medium The channel or path by which the encoded message travels from the source to the receiver. (11)

mentoring Occurs when an older, more experienced person helps a younger employee grow and advance by providing advice, support, and encouragement. (23)

Michigan leadership studies A program of research on leadership behavior conducted at the University of Michigan. Two basic forms of leader behavior were identified: job-centered and employee-centered leader behaviors. These styles are presumed to be at opposite ends of a single dimension. (9)

modeling Learning through the experience of others. It is also referred to as vicarious learning. (3)

monitor role An informational role that consists of actively seeking information that might be of value to the organization in general or to specific managers. (2)

motivating potential score (MPS) A measurement included in the *Job Diagnostic Survey* that provides a summary index of a job's overall potential for motivating employees. (13)

motivation The set of factors that cause people to behave in certain ways. (5)

motivation factors Intrinsic to the work itself and including factors such as achievement and recognition. (5)

Need for achievement Reflects an individual's desire to accomplish a goal or task more effectively than in the past. High need achievers tend to set moderately difficult goals, assume personal responsibility for getting things done, want immediate feedback, and are preoccupied with the task. It is associated with the work of McClelland. (5)

need for affiliation The need for human companionship. People with a high need for affiliation tend to want reassurance and approval from others, have a genuine concern for the feelings of others, and are likely to conform to the wishes of others, especially those with whom they strongly identify. (5)

need for power The desire to control one's environment, including financial resources, material resources, information, and other people. (5)

need A deficiency experienced by an individual. (5)

negative reinforcement (avoidance) A concept of reinforcement theory that occurs when the individual is engaging in desired behavior in order to avoid an unpleasant, or aversive, consequence. The effect of negative reinforcement is to increase the frequency of a desired behavior. (3)

negotiator role The manager who represents the organization in reaching agreements with other organizations, such as contracts between management and labor unions. (2)

noise Any disturbance in the communication process that interferes with or distorts the intended communication. (11)

nominal group technique (NGT) A method of improving group decision making whereby group members follow a generate-discussion-vote cycle until they reach an appropriate decision. (16)

nonprogrammed decision A problem or decision situation that has not been encountered before such that the decision maker cannot rely on a previously established decision rule. A nonprogrammed decision is poorly structured because goals are vague, information is ambiguous, and there is no clear procedure for making the decision. (16)

norm The expected behavior or behavioral pattern in a certain situation. A norm is usually associated with a group and is established during the group development process. (7)

Objective judgment quotient (OJQ) method A multiple-rater comparative system of evaluating employee performance differences. (14)

observation A method of gathering data that may include observing and recording events, structured observations, participant observation, and hidden observation. (App.)

occupation A group of jobs similar as to the type of tasks and training involved. (23)

Ohio State leadership studies A series of studies conducted by researchers at Ohio State University designed to assess subordinates' perceptions of their leaders' actual behavior. The studies identified two dimensions of leadership behavior: consideration and initiating structure. The two dimensions were presumed to be independent. (9)

operant conditioning (reinforcement theory) Suggests that behavior is a function of its consequences. It is generally associated with the work of Skinner. (3)

oral communication A form of communication in organizations whereby the message is encoded into audible sounds. It is the most prevalent form of organizational communication. (11)

organic structure A type of organization design that is structured like a network, interactions are more lateral and horizontal, knowledge resides wherever it is most useful to the organization, and membership requires a commitment to the tasks of the organization. Burns and Stalker state that this type of structure is appropriate if the rate of change in technology is high. (19)

organization A group of people working together to attain common goals. (17)

organization (and perception) The human tendency to view things in ordered, logical, and consistent systems of meaning. (4)

organization change and development One of the five basic categories of organizational behavior concepts. (1)

organization chart Shows all people, positions, reporting relationships, and lines of formal communication in the organization. (17)

organization development The process of planned change and improvement of organizations through the application of knowledge of the behavioral sciences, such as psychology, sociology, cultural anthropology, and other related fields of study. (21)

organization structure A system of task, reporting, and authority relationships within which the organization's work is done. (17)

organizational behavior (OB) The study of human behavior in organizational settings, the interface between human behavior and the organizational context, and the organization itself. (1)

organizational behavior modification (OB Mod) The application of reinforcement principles and concepts to people in organizational settings to achieve motivational improvements. (6)

organizational characteristics One of the five basic categories of organizational behavior concepts. Among such characteristics are organization structure, environment, technology, organization design, and organizational culture. (1)

organizational culture That set of values that help people in an organization understand which actions are considered acceptable and which are considered unacceptable. (20)

organizational environment The people, other organizations, economic factors, and objects that are outside the boundaries of the organization. (18)

organizational goals Objectives management seeks to achieve in pursuing the firm's purpose. (17)

organizational politics Activities carried out by people to acquire, enhance, and use power and other resources to obtain their preferred outcomes in a situation where there is uncertainty or disagreement. (10)

organizational processes One of the five basic categories of organizational behavior concepts. Includes decision making, creativity, communication, information processing, performance appraisal, careers, and international aspects of organizational behavior. (1)

organizational socialization The process through which employees learn about a firm's culture and pass their knowledge and understanding on to others. (20)

organizational stressors Factors in the workplace that can cause stress: task demands, physical demands, role demands, and interpersonal demands. (15)

organizing The process of designing jobs, grouping jobs into manageable units, and establishing patterns of authority among jobs and groups of jobs. (2)

outcomes Anything an individual receives from the organization as a result of performance such as pay, recognition, and intrinsic rewards, or anything that might possibly result from performance. (6)

overdetermination Also called structural inertia: The structure of the organization provides resistance to change because it was designed to maintain stability. (21)

overlapping work groups Situation where managers serve as linking pins between groups. (19)

overload More information than the receiver can process. (11)

Paired comparison method A method of evaluating individual performance that calls for the comparison of all employees two at a time. Generally, there is one evaluator who compares all employees two at a time on one global performance criterion. (14)

participative management A way of thinking about the human resources of an organization. Employees are viewed as valued human resources capable of making substantive and valuable contributions to organizational effectiveness. Employees are allowed the opportunity to participate in decisions. (6)

participative pay system The participation of employees in either the design of the compensation system or the administration of it, or both. (12)

path-goal theory of leadership A theory that focuses on appropriate leader behavior for various situations. The path-goal theory suggests that directive, supportive, participative, or achievement-oriented leader behavior may be appropriate, depending on the characteristics of the person and the environment. It was developed in the 1970s by Evans and House and is based on the expectancy theory of motivation. (9)

perception The set of processes by which the individual receives and interprets information about the environment. (3)

performance The total set of job-related behaviors engaged in by employees. (6)

performance appraisal (performance evaluation) The process of evaluating work behaviors by measurement and comparison to previously established standards, recording the results, and communicating them back to the employee. It is an activity between a manager and an employee. (14)

performance appraisal system (PAS) The organizational processes and activities involved in performance appraisals. It includes organizational policies, procedures, and resources that support the performance appraisal activity. (14)

performance-to-outcome expectancy A person's perception of the probability that performance will lead to certain outcomes. The probability may range between 0 and 1.0. It is a major concept of expectancy theory. (6)

perquisites Means of compensation in the form of special privileges associated with employees of relatively high rank in the organization. (12)

personal power Power that resides in the person, regardless of his or her position in the organization. (10)

personality The set of distinctive traits and characteristics that can be used to compare and contrast individuals. (4)

physical demands Demands relating to the setting of the job, such as temperature, office design, and poor lighting. (15)

physiological needs The most basic needs in the hierarchy, including food, sex, and air. (5)

planning The process of determining the organization's desired future position and the best means to get there. (2)

pooled interdependence A situation that exists when two or more groups function with relative independence, but their aggregated, or combined, output contributes to the output and profitability of the total organization. (8)

population ecology perspective Proposes that organizations survive on the basis of fit between their structural attributes and environmental characteristics. (18)

Porter-Lawler model This model suggests that performance may lead to various intrinsic and extrinsic rewards. When an individual perceives the rewards as equitable, the rewards lead to satisfaction. (6)

position power Power that resides in the position, regardless of the person involved. (10)

positive reinforcement A concept of reinforcement theory in which positive reinforcement is a reward that follows desirable behavior. Its effect is to maintain or increase the frequency of a desired behavior. (3)

power The potential ability of a person or group to influence another person or group. (10)

power distance The extent to which employees accept the idea that people in an organization rightfully have different levels of power. (22)

problem solving A special kind of decision making in which the issue is unique. It requires development and evaluation of alternatives without the aid of a programmed decision rule. (16)

productivity How many goods and services an organization creates from its resources. (2)

professional bureaucracy An organization design in which standardization of skills is the primary means of coordination. Specialization is horizontal, and decision making is decentralized. It is one of Mintzberg's structural forms and is usually found in a complex, stable environment. It is a special type of bureaucracy. (19)

programmed decision A decision that recurs often enough for decision rules to be developed. A decision rule is a statement that tells the decision maker which alternative to choose once she or he has information about the decision situation, such as outcomes, action-outcome probabilities, and values of outcomes. (16)

projection Occurs when we see ourselves in others. (3)

punishment The presentation of unpleasant, or aversive, consequences as a result of undesirable behaviors. It is a concept of reinforcement theory that decreases the frequency of undesired behaviors. (3)

Quality The total set of features and characteristics of a product or service that determines its ability to satisfy stated or implied needs. (2)

quality circles (QCs) Small groups of volunteers who meet regularly to identify, analyze, and solve quality and related problems that pertain to their work. (6)

quality of work life The degree to which members of a work organization are able to satisfy important personal needs through their experiences in the organization. (21)

questionnaire A collection of written questions about the respondents' attitudes, opinions, perceptions, and/or demographic characteristics. (App.)

Rational decision-making model A systematic, step-by-step process that assumes objectivity and complete information. The steps are: statement of goal, identification of the problem, determination of decision type, generation of alternatives, evaluation and choice of alternatives, implementation, and control. (16)

receiver An individual, a group, or an individual acting as the representative of a group that is the receiver of the message. (11)

recency error In performance evaluation, the rater remembers only the most recent behaviors in evaluating an employee. (14)

reciprocal interdependence A situation that exists when the outputs of one group become the inputs to another group and vice versa. (8)

referent power A base of power identified by French and Raven that is basically power through identification. It usually manifests itself through emulation and imitation. (10)

refreezing The process of making new behaviors relatively permanent and resistant to further change. It is the third step of Lewin's model of planned change. (21)

reinforcement The consequences of behavior. The four basic kinds of reinforcement are positive, negative (avoidance), extinction, and punishment. (3)

reinforcement theory (operant conditioning) A theory that suggests that behavior is a function of its consequences. It is generally associated with the work of Skinner. (3)

relatedness needs Those involving the need to relate to others. (5)

reliability The extent to which a measurement system's results are consistent. (14, App.)

research design The set of procedures used to test the predicted relationships among natural phenomena. (App.)

resource allocator role The manager who decides how resources in the organization will be distributed among various individuals and groups. (2)

resource dependence perspective The organization-environment relationships that emphasize the importance of resources—human, financial, and physical. Proposes that organizations seek to accomplish resource exchange with relevant environments through interorganizational linkages and changing the environment. (18)

responsibility The obligation to do something under the expectation that some act will be done or certain outputs achieved. (17)

restriction of range The tendency of some raters in performance evaluation to restrict the range of ratings that they assign to performance. The three types are leniency, severity, and central tendency problems. (14)

reward power A base of power identified by French and Raven that is the extent to which one person controls rewards that are valued by another. (10)

reward system All parts of the organization that are involved in the allocation of compensation and benefits to employees in exchange for their contributions to the organization. (12)

role The part an individual plays in the work group. (7)

role ambiguity A situation that occurs when it is unclear or uncertain what behavior is expected of a role occupant. (7)

role conflict A situation that arises when demands of or messages about roles are essentially clear but also contradict each other somewhat. The four types of role conflict are interrole, intrarole, intrasender, and person-role. (7)

role demands The demands of the expected set of behaviors (role) associated with a particular position in a group or organization. (15)

Satisficing A situation that occurs in decision making when the decision maker examines alternatives only until a solution that meets minimal requirements is found and then ceases to look for a better one. (16)

schedules of reinforcement The various ways in which a manager may attempt to reinforce desired or undesired behavior. The five types of schedules include continuous reinforcement, fixed interval, variable interval, fixed ratio, and variable ratio. (3)

scientific management An approach to designing jobs emphasizing efficiency. It served as the foundation for job specialization and mass production. Employees performed a small part of a complete task and were paid on a piece-rate system. Primarily associated with the work of Taylor, it was one of the first approaches to the study of management. (1)

scientific research The systematic investigation of hypothesized propositions about the relationships among natural phenomena. (App.)

security needs Things that offer safety and security, such as adequate housing and clothing and freedom from worry and anxiety. (5)

selection (and perception) The process by which we pay attention to objects we are comfortable with and filter out those that cause us discomfort. (3)

selective attention The receiver attends to only selected parts of a message. (11)

self-actualization needs Needs that involve the realization of our full potential and becoming all that we can be. (5)

self-efficacy An individual's belief that she or he can still accomplish goals, even if that person has failed in the past. (12)

self-monitoring The extent to which people emulate the behavior of others. A high self-monitor tends to pay close attention to the behaviors of others and to model his or her own behavior after that of the individuals observed. A low self-monitor tends to react to situations without looking to others for behavioral cues. (4)

self-reactions In the conflict model of decision making, comparisons of alternatives with internalized moral standards. (16)

semantics The study of meaning in language forms. (11)

sequential interdependence A situation that exists when the outputs of one group become the inputs to another group. (8)

severity In performance evaluation, the tendency of a rater to assign a low value to most or all performances. (14)

simple structure An organization design that has little specialization and formalization, and its overall structure is organic. It is one of Mintzberg's structural forms and characterizes a relatively small, usually young organization in a simple, dynamic environment. (19)

situational view of attitudes A view that argues that attitudes evolve from socially constructed realities. (4)

social information processing model A perspective presented by Salancik and Pfeffer. The model suggests that through various processes, commitment, rationalization, and information saliency are defined. These attributional and enactment processes then combine with social reality construction processes to influence perceptions, attitudes, and behaviors. (13)

social learning A specific type of vicarious learning. It is assumed that people learn behaviors and attitudes partly in response to what others expect of them. (3)

social responsibility The organization's obligation to protect and/or contribute to the social environment in which it functions. (2)

sociotechnical systems approach An approach that views the organization as an open system structured to integrate the two important subsystems: the technical (task) subsystem and the social subsystem. The approach is based on systems theory. (19)

source The individual, group, or organization interested in communicating something to another party. (11)

source credibility The receiver considers both the message and the source in making value judgments and determining credibility. (11)

span of control The number of people reporting to a manager. It defines the size of the organization's work groups. (17)

specialization The number of distinct occupational titles or activities accomplished within the organization. (17)

spokesperson role The manager who speaks for the organization to outsiders. (2)

stereotyping The process of categorizing people into groups on the basis of certain characteristics or traits. (3)

stimulus discrimination The ability of the individual to recognize differences between stimuli. (3)

stimulus generalization The process by which people recognize the same or similar stimuli in different settings (3)

strategic choice An approach to organization design whereby the manager is viewed as the decision maker. The manager's choices of how to structure the organization are affected by the purposes and goals, the imperatives, and her or his personality, value system, and experience. (19)

stress A person's adaptive response to a stimulus that places excessive psychological or physical demands on that person. (15)

structural change A type of organizational change that consists of a system-wide rearrangement of task division and authority and reporting relationships. (21)

structural contingency perspective A popular approach to the study of the organization and its environment. It suggests that the most appropriate structure for an organization is dependent, or contingent, on the environment it operates in. (18)

structural imperatives Factors that determine how the organization must be structured in order to be effective. The three factors that have been identified as structural imperatives are size, technology, and environment. (19)

suboptimizing Occurs in decision making when decision makers trade off the gains of some outcomes to avoid the potential negative aspects of those outcomes. Occurs when the less than best possible outcome is accepted. (16)

superordinate goal A solution to goal displacement, it is usually a goal of the overall organization and is more important than the more specific goals of interacting groups. (8)

supportive relationships Relationships where people are treated in a manner that fosters feelings of support, self-worth, and importance. (19)

survey-feedback A process of gathering, analyzing, and summarizing data and returning it to employees and groups for discussion, and identification and solution of problems. (21)

system An interrelated set of elements functioning as a whole. (1)

systems theory A theory popularized in the physical sciences and extended to the area of management. An organizational system receives various inputs from its environment, transforms these inputs into products or services, and creates various outputs of the system. The system receives feedback from the environment regarding those outputs. (1)

Tangible compensation Rewards that have a definite value. (12)

task demands Stressors associated with the specific job a person is performing, such as the job surgeons and coaches, for example, face. (15)

task environment The particular environmental forces that affect an organization's operations. (18)

task group A type of formal group that is relatively temporary. (7)

task interdependence The degree to which the activities of separate groups force them to depend on each other, thereby requiring more coordination to realize organizational goals. The three types of task interdependence are pooled, sequential, and reciprocal. (8)

task uncertainty A situation that arises whenever employees or work groups lack information about what course of action to take or about future events that may affect them, the task, or the organization. (8)

team building Programs designed to assist a work team (group) in developing into a mature, well-functioning team by helping it define its goals or priorities, analyze its tasks and the way they are performed, and examine relationships among people doing the work. (21)

technology The mechanical and intellectual processes that transform inputs into outputs. (18)

thick description methods Attempts to describe the totality of day-to-day life through in-depth questioning and observation. (20)

training Specialized efforts to improve specific employee job skills. Such activities include on-the-job training, formalized job rotation programs, and student intern programs. (21)

trait approaches Attempts to identify stable and enduring traits that differentiate effective leaders from nonleaders. (9)

transformational leadership The process of leading for change rather than for stability. (9)

transition management The process of systematically planning, organizing, and implementing change, from the disassembly of the current state to the realization of a fully functional future state within an organization. (21)

transmission The process through which the symbols that carry the message are sent to the receiver. (11)

turnover The permanent cessation of working for the organization. (6)

two-factor theory A theory that suggests that job satisfaction is a two-dimensional construct. One dimension ranges from satisfaction to no satisfaction and is affected by motivation factors. The other dimension ranges from dissatisfaction to no dissatisfaction and is affected by hygiene factors. It was developed by Herzberg in the late 1950s and early 1960s. (5)

Type A person A person who is extremely competitive, highly committed to work, has a strong sense of time urgency, is aggressive, impatient, and very work oriented, has much drive, and wants to accomplish as much as possible as quickly as possibe. (15)

Type B person A person who, in comparison with the Type A person, is less competitive, is less committed to work, has a weaker sense of time urgency, feels less conflict with people or time, has a more balanced and relaxed approach to life, has more confidence, and is able to work at a constant pace. (15)

Type Z (American firms) One of the three types of firms analyzed by Ouchi. As compared to typical American and Japanese firms, Type Z American firms have a wholistic concern for workers and managers. The firms have a long-term employment commitment, evaluate employees slowly through both qualitative and quantitative information about performance, emphasize somewhat broad career paths, exercise control through informal, implicit mechanisms, have a strong cultural expectation that decision making will occur in groups and will be based on full information sharing and consensus, and expect individuals to take responsibility for decisions. (20)

Uncertainty avoidance The extent to which people in a culture accept or avoid feelings of uncertainty. (22)

unconflicted adherence In the conflict model of decision making, continuing with activities if doing so does not entail serious risks. (16)

unconflicted change In the conflict model of decision making, making changes in present activities if doing so entails no serious risks. (16)

unfreezing The process by which people become aware of the need for change. It is the first step of Lewin's model of planned change. (21)

universal approach An approach whose prescriptions or propositions are designed to work in any situation or circumstance. This is the "one best way" to structure the jobs, authority, and reporting relationships of any organization's external environment, the industry, and the type of work to be done. (19)

Valences The attractiveness or unattractiveness of any given outcome to any given person. It is a concept of expectancy theory. (6)

validity The extent to which research measures what it is intended to measure. (App.) The extent to which a performance evaluation method reflects actual employee performance. (14)

value judgments The degree to which a message reinforces or challenges the receiver's basic personal beliefs. (11)

variable interval reinforcement Using time as the basis for applying reinforcement, but varying the interval between reinforcements. (3)

variable ratio reinforcement Reinforcement where the number of behaviors between reinforcement varies. (3)

verification The receiver indicates to the source that the receiver received the message and the degree to which it was understood. (11)

vertical-dyad linkage model A model that stresses the importance of variable relationships between supervisors and each of their subordinates. Each superior-subordinate pair is referred to as a vertical dyad. Early in the history of the dyadic interaction, the supervisor initiates either an in-group or out-group relationship. The model was developed by Graen and Dansereau. (9)

vicarious learning Learning through the experiences of others. It is also referred to as modeling. (3)

vigilant information processing In the conflict model of decision making, thoroughly investigating all possible alternatives, weighing their costs and benefits before making a decision, and developing contingency plans. (16)

Vroom-Yetton-Jago model First developed by Vroom and Yetton in 1973 and recently expanded by Vroom and Jago. Prescribes a leadership style appropriate to a given situation and presumes that one leader may display various leadership styles. The model is concerned with only one aspect of leader behavior: subordinate participation in decision making. The goals of the model are to protect the quality of the decision and ensure decision acceptance by subordinates. (9)

Wheel network A small group network pattern in which information flows between the person at the end of each spoke and the person in the middle. (11)

written communication A form of communication in organizations. Common forms of written communication include letters, memos, reports, manuals, and forms. (11)

PHOTO CREDITS *continued from page ii*

p. 42 Courtesy of Knight-Ridder, Inc. p. 47 Courtesy of Dow Chemical Company. p. 53 © David Klutho. **CHAPTER 3:** p. 64 © 1989 James Sugar/Black Star. p. 74 © David Hiser Photographers/Aspen. p. 77 © 1991 Taro Yamasaki. p. 79 Charles William Bush/ Shooting Star. **CHAPTER 4:** p. 97 © Reisig/Ringier Dokumentationszentrum. p. 102 © R. Wallis/Sipa Press. p. 107 © Howard Simmons. p. 116 Photo by Joseph Rodriguez. **CHAPTER 5:** p. 129 © Gary Hannabarger. p. 131 © Will and Deni McIntyre. p. 132 © David Hiser, Photographers/Aspen. p. 143 © T. Westenberger/SYGMA. **CHAPTER 6:** p. 157 © Nina Barnett. p. 162 © Christopher Morris/Black Star. p. 166 © Robin Moyer/TIME Magazine. p. 170 Ford Motor Company. p. 174 Courtesy Northeast Utilities. **CHAPTER 7:** p. 189 © Allsport USA/Ken Levine, 1990. p. 194 The Bettman Archive. p. 199 © Springer/Gamma Liason. p. 202 Courtesy Bristol-Myers Squibb Co. **CHAPTER 8:** p. 224 © William Taufic 1990/with permission by Republic N.Y. Corp. p. 227 © Allsport USA/Pascal Rondeau. p. 231 Unisys Corporation. p. 237 © Nathaniel Butler/NBA Photos 1991. p. 243 with permission of the Alaska Support Industry Alliance. **CHAPTER 9:** p. 257 U.S. Naval Academy photo by Ken Mierzejewski. p. 264 © Mark Richards/SIPA. p. 267 © Ben Glass/Orion Pictures Corp 1990. p. 276 © Harry Benson. **CHAPTER 10:** p. 291 © 1989 Rick Friedman/Black Star. p. 300 © Kevin Fleming 1989. p. 307 © David Leversee/The Wilderness Society. **CHAPTER 11:** p. 319 © 1989 Will Steger/Black Star. p. 325 Ronald H. Cohn/The Gorilla Foundation. p. 327 © 1990 Michael Grecco/Outline Press. p. 331 © Rob Kinmonth. p. 344 © Rob Kinmonth. **CHAPTER 12:** p. 357 Bill Smith/John Biever/Sports Illustrated. p. 361 Courtesy National Medical Enterprises, Inc. p. 370 © Robert Maas/Photoreporters. **CHAPTER 13:** p. 389 © R. Hirneisen 1990. p. 403 © Sharon Green/Adventure Photo. p. 410 © Spencer Grant/The Picture Cube. **CHAPTER 14:** p. 421 Courtesy of America West. p. 428 With permission by Jostens. p. 431 © Linda L. Creighton/USN&WR. **CHAPTER 15:** p. 453 (left) © David Ball/The Picture Cube. p. 453 (right) © 1990 Ovak Arslanian/Courtesy Pacifcorp. p. 460 © Joanna B. Pinneo/USN&WR. p. 467 © Michael J. Howell/The Picture Cube. p. 468 © Paul Chesley, Photographers/Aspen. **CHAPTER 16:** p. 484 © Dan White 1991. p. 487 Courtesy of the Dow Chemical Company/Tui de Roy, 1990. p. 508 © 1991 Louis Psihoyos/Matrix. **CHAPTER 17:** p. 526 Photo by John Earle/Courtesy of Sequa Corporation. p. 530 Photo courtesy of FMC Corporation. p. 538 Alascom photo by Sean Reid. p. 543 © Baldev/SYGMA. **CHAPTER 18:** p. 555 © Nippon Television Network Corporation Tokyo, Japan 1991. p. 560 © 1991 Louis Psihoyos/Matrix. p. 567 © Andy Freeburg. p. 570 © Joanna B. Pinneo/USN&WR. p. 574 © Pam Price/The Picture Group. **CHAPTER 19:** p. 589 © Dallas & John Heaton/Tony Stone Worldwide. p. 601 Courtesy IBM Corporation/photo by Chris Maynard. p. 604 © Christopher Morris 1990/Black Star. p. 614 © 1990 C. Archambault. **CHAPTER 20:** p. 626 © Magnum Photos, Inc. p. 638 © Greenlar/The Image Works, Inc. p. 640 © 1991 Louis Psihoyos/Matrix. p. 645 AP/WIDE WORLD. **CHAPTER 21:** p. 661 © Ken Kerbs 1991. p. 665 © Mark Tucker. p. 674 With permission JC Penny Inc. p. 682 Bristol-Myers Squibb Company. p. 691 © Gerald Davis. **CHAPTER 22:** p. 701 Photo courtesy of Hewlette Packard Company. p. 703 © George Fry/courtesy Tandem Corp. p. 711 © 1991 William Taufic/The Image Bank. p. 718 © Stephen Saks/The Picture Cube. p. 723 © Thomas Craig/The Picture. **CHAPTER 23:** p. 731 © C. Bruce Forster. p. 735 © Liane Enkelis. p. 739 © 1990 Bob Sacha. p. 743 © 1990 by George Lange. p. 745 © 1991 William Taufic/with permission Republic N.Y. Corporation.

Name Index

Abdul-Jabbar, Kareem, 529
Ackerman, Linda S., 674n
Adams, J. Stacey, 155–157
Adelman, Philip J., 537n
Adler, Nancy J., 101n, 704n, 709n, 713n, 714, 715
Adler, Paul, 563n
Administrative Management Society, 371
Adorno, T. W., 106n
Agarwala-Rogers, Rekha, 325n
Akins, Gib, 63n
Alberthal, Les, 265
Aldag, Ramon J., 767n
Alderfer, C. P., 137–138, 145, 235n
Alderson, Sandy, 624
Aldrich, Howard E., 576n, 577n
Allen, Robert W., 305n
Allied-Signal Aerospace Company, 531
Allport, Gordon W., 102–103, 108n
Alster, Norm, 386n, 410n, 672n
Altmaier, Elizabeth, 467n
Aluminum Company of America (Alcoa), 365, 658
Alutto, Joseph A., 203n
Alvares, K. M., 264n
Amabile, Teresa M., 511n
Amerco, 246
American Airlines, 49, 96, 480
American Cyanamid, 390
American Express Corporation, 154
American League, 624
American Management Association, 371
American Telephone & Telegraph Company (AT&T), 126, 392, 393, 400, 457, 600, 684
Ancona, Deborah Gladstein, 221n
Anderson, Craig A., 172n
Anderson, Jerry W., Jr., 47n
Anderson, Kenneth S., 599n
Anheuser-Busch, Inc., 343
A. O. Smith Corporation, 177–179
A&P, 126
Apple Computer, Inc., 42, 126, 143, 209, 252, 275, 380–381, 565, 576, 662
Apt, Kenneth E., 426n
Argyris, Chris, 103–104
Aristotle, 9
Armstrong tires, 547
Arnold, H. J., 737n, 739n
Aronoff, Craig E., 319n
Artzt, Edwin L., 534
Arvey, Richard, 75n, 76n
Asch, S., 85n
Ashforth, Blake E., 187n, 195n, 227n
Atari, 143
Atkinson, J. W., 42, 135
Atkinson, Richard C., 129n
Atlantic Richfield, 408
Atomic Energy Commission, 569
Austin, Nancy K., 614
Avishai, Bernard, 556n
Axelrod, W., 737n
Axtell, Robert E., 683n
Ayres, Robert U., 660n

Babbage, Charles, 387, 388
Baker, Douglas D., 537n
Baker International, 390
Baldes, J. J., 360n
Baldwin, Timothy T., 685n
Balzer, William, 435n
Bamforth, K. W., 597n
Bandura, Albert, 66n, 74n, 358
Banning, Kent, 672n
Bannister, Brendan D., 87n, 262n, 264n
Barnard, Chester, 544–545
Barnett, William P., 202n
Barney, J. B., 633n, 644n, 645n, 647n
Barrett, Gerald V., 66n
Barrett, Tom, 548–549
Barry, Bruce, 434n
Bartlett, Christopher A., 722
Baskin, Otis W., 319n
Bass, Bernard M., 197n, 199n, 205n, 252n, 255n, 483n, 486n, 487n, 509n, 685n
Bateman, Thomas S., 112n, 114n, 115n, 118n, 768n
Baudhuin, E. Scott, 322n
Baughn, C. Christopher, 722
Bazerman, Max H., 66n
Beardsworth, A. D., 526n
Beatty, Richard W., 423n, 427n, 429n, 438n, 440n
Beck, Keith, 730
Becker, Wendy, 127n
Beckhard, Richard, 685n
Bedeian, Arthur, 459n, 560n, 576n, 589n
Beech-Nut, 47
Beehr, Terry, 459n
Beer, Michael, 671, 677, 686n
Bell, Cecil H., 677
Bem, D. J., 502n
Ben Franklin, 54
Benoit, Ellen, 348n
Benson, Tracy E., 192n
Berger, Leonard, 430n
Berger, P. L., 627n
Bernardin, H. John, 423n, 427n, 429n, 438n, 440n
Bethlehem Steel Company, 11
Betz, Frederick, 557n
B. F. Goodrich, 169
Bhide, Amar, 84n
Binker, K. A., 85n
Birnbaum, Gregg, 498n
Black & Decker, 365
Blake, Robert R., 223n, 236n, 239n, 259
Blanchard, Kenneth H., 273n
Blau, Peter M., 599, 737n
Blood, Milton R., 396
Bobbitt, H. Randolph, 604n
Boeing, 48, 708
Boesky, Ivan, 163, 312, 486
Boettger, Richard D., 401n
Bois, Clay, 148
Bookman, Valerie M., 141n
Borgida, E., 633n
Borys, Bryan, 605n
Boschken, Herman L., 605
Boudreau, John, 437n, 440n
Bowen, David E., 275n
Bowen, D. D., 753n
Boyd, Losana E., 337n
Bracke, Jeffrey, 603n
Bracker, Jeffrey S., 525n
Brady, F. Neil, 108n, 542n
Brannick, Michael T., 163n
Brehm, Jack W., 127n
Breidenbach, M., 731n
Bridgestone, 547
Bridwell, Lawrence G., 135n
Brief, Arthur P., 540n
British Airways, 724–726
British Petroleum, 545, 702
British Sterling, 703
Brockner, Joel, 498n
Brody, Michael, 343n
Bromet, Evelyn, 462n
Brookhurst Partners, 324
Brown, Rupert, 195n
Browning, Larry D., 335n
Brownlee, Shannon, 554n
Bruce, Leigh, 651n
Bruning, Nealia, 460n
Bryman, A., 526n
Buckley, M. Ronald, 427n
Buckley, W., 634n
Buick, 45
Burack, E. H., 753n
Burck, Charles G., 625n
Bureau of the Census, 735
Bureau of Labor Statistics, 371
Burger King, 694–695
Burke, W. Warner, 676n, 677, 679n
Burlington Northern, 600
Burnham, David H., 145n
Burns, James MacGregor, 275n
Burns, Lawton R., 613
Burns, Tom, 560, 601–602
Burroughs Wellcome, 515–516
Burtt, H. E., 258n, 259
Bush, George, 256
Bushnell, Nolan, 143
Busse, Thomas, 511n
Bylinsky, Gene, 554n

Cage, Jack H., 271n
Calder, Bobby J., 109n
Caldwell, David F., 202n, 407n
Calonius, Erik, 34n
Camden, T. M., 753n

Campbell, Alta, 452n, 524n, 534n, 545n, 556n, 564n, 590n, 629n, 646n, 662n, 672n
Campbell, D. T., 766n
Campbell, Donald J., 401n, 407n
Campbell, John P., 141n, 142n, 155n, 164n
Campion, Michael A., 395n
Cantor, Nancy, 106n
Carey, Alex, 15n
Carlson, Chester, 557
Carlzon, Jan, 641
Carnation, 48
Carnegie-Mellon University, 564
Carroll, Glenn R., 528n
Carroll, John S., 66n
Carroll, Stephen J., 9n, 363n, 365n
Carson, Robert C., 98n
Carsrud, Alan L, 143n
Carter, Nancy M., 528n
Cartwright, Darwin, 288n, 502n
Casey, James E., 148–149
Casey, William, 206, 208
Cashman, J. F., 272n
Cass, E. L., 395n
Castro, Janice, 62n
Caterpillar, 49, 533, 535
Cattell, Raymond, 102, 103
Cavender, Jerry, 117n
Cavanaugh, Gerald F., 298
CBS, 126, 312–313
Celeron, 548
Cellar, Douglas F., 66n
Chandler, Alfred D., 603–604
Chao, Georgia T., 80n
Chaparral Steel, 214–215
Chemers, Martin M., 264n
Chen, Judy, 435n
Cheng, Joseph L. C., 322n, 526n
Cherry, Barbara, 470
Chevron, 541, 580
Chew, W. Bruce, 173n
Child, John, 538n, 604n, 613n
Chipello, Christopher J., 708n
Chrysler Corporation, 34, 45, 126, 178, 280, 281, 374, 567
Churbuck, David, 554n
Cincinnati Milicron, 564, 617–618
Citicorp, 473–475
Citroen, 606
Clark, Alfred W., 189n
Clark, Peter A., 673n
Cleveland Cap Screw Company, 590
Coca-Cola Company, 48, 81, 313, 492
Coch, Lester, 506n
Cohen, A. R., 408n
Cohen, Daniel, 662n
Cohen, S. L., 85n
Colgate-Palmolive, 524
Collins, Paul D., 46n
Colonial Life Insurance Company, 392
Colvin, Geoffrey, 104n, 659n
Compaq Computer, 565, 576
Conant, H., 392n
Conger, Jay A., 254n, 276n
Conoco, 579
Container Corporation of America, 609
Contel Corporation, 713
Continental, 548
Continental Airlines, 120, 121, 641
Continental Corporation, 757
Control Data Corporation, 408
Cook, Paul, 512
Cooper, Cary L., 78n, 112n, 172n, 456
Corning Incorporated, 412, 413–415, 646
Cosier, Richard A., 159n
Costello, Timothy W., 80n
Costner, Kevin, 513
Cotton, John L., 507n
Courtright, John A., 321
Cowfer, David B., 420n
Cox, Taylor, 433n
Crandall, Robert, 96, 97
Cronshaw, Steven F., 80n, 85n
Crystal, Graef S., 49n, 62n
Cullen, John B., 537n
Cullen, John H., 599n
Cummings, Larry L., 7n, 25n, 66n, 80n, 109n, 110n, 118n, 127n, 175n, 277n, 327n, 328n, 400n, 423n, 667n, 766n
Cummins, Robert C., 329n
Currey, Fred, 301
Cyert, Richard M., 493n
Cypress Semiconductor Corporation, 357

Daewoo Heavy Industries, 533
Daft, Richard L., 322n, 327n, 489n, 525n, 537n, 570n, 574n, 764n
Daimler-Benz, 337
Dalton, Dan R., 159n, 536n, 538n, 770n
Dalton, Gene W., 663n
Dandridge, Thomas C., 630n, 633n
D'Anno, Thomas, 601n
Dansereau, Fred, Jr., 203n, 272
Darrow, Barbara, 234n
David, Fred R., 540n
Davis, James H., 200n, 203n, 205n, 208n
Davis, Keith, 341n
Davis, Marvin, 312
Davis, Stanley M., 611n, 612n
Davis-Blake, Alison, 366n
Davison, William H., 720n
Deal, T. E., 625, 632
Dean, John, 504
Dean Witter Reynolds, 47, 373
Dearborn, DeWitt C., 83
Deci, E. L., 173
Deese, J., 63n, 66n
Deitcher, Janet, 498n
Denison, Daniel R., 539n
De Pree, D. J., 28–29
Deutschman, Alan, 42, 126n, 137n, 356n, 758n
Dew, Mary, 462n
Dickinson, William J., 14
Dickson, W. J., 597n
Digital Equipment, 457, 662
DiPietro, Dee, 651n
DiPrete, T. A., 750n
Disney, 62, 286
Disney, Roy, 286
Disney, Walt, 286
DiStefano, Joseph J., 702n, 719n
Doi, Toshi T., 500
Doktor, Robert H., 49n, 704n, 709n
Donaldson, Lex, 595
Dorfman, Peter W., 275n
Downey, H. Kirk, 540n
Dozier, J. B., 751n
Drexel Burnham Lambert Inc., 47, 163, 486
Dreyfuss, Joel, 45n
Dubinsky, Alan J., 189n
Duchon, Dennis, 273n
Dumaine, Brian, 29n, 192n, 215n, 386n, 403n, 415n, 662n, 695n
Duncan, R., 666n
Duncan, Robert B., 570n
Dunlop, 547
Dunnette, Marvin D., Jr., 112n, 141n, 142n, 155n, 164n, 206n, 222n
Du Pont, 172, 365, 579
Dupuy, John, 411n
Durkheim, Émile, 631
Dyer, William G., 685n

Earley, P. Christopher, 204
Eastern Air Lines, 120–121, 294
Eastman Kodak, 26, 48, 171, 579
Edwards, Jane A., 331n, 335n
Edwards, Mark, 443n
E. F. Hutton, 504
Egeth, H., 63n, 66n
Ehrlich, Sanford B., 252n
Ehrlichman, John, 504
Eichstaedt, Peter, 426n
Eisenberg, Eric M., 305n
Eisenhardt, Kathleen M., 495n
Eisenhardt, Roy, 624
Eisenhardt, Wally, 624
Eisner, Michael, 62, 286
Electrolux, 84
Electronic Data Systems Corporation (EDS), 265, 333
Ellis, Rebecca A., 107n
Emerson, Harrington, 10
Emery Air Freight, 169
England, George W., 406
Equal Employment Opportunity Commission, 713
Erikson, Erik H., 101–102, 741
European Airbus, 337
Evans, Martin G., 265, 359, 679n
EXPO '86, 498
Exxon Corporation, 19, 40, 347–348, 702
Eyres, Patricia S., 429n

Fairhurst, Eileen, 540n
Fairhurst, Gail T., 321
Faltermayer, Edmund, 370n
Farh, Jiing-Lih, 434n
Fayol, Henri, 12, 590–591
Federal Aviation Administration, 480
Federal Express, 76, 149, 192
Fedor, Donald B., 427n
Feldman, Daniel C., 206n, 736n, 737n, 739n, 742n, 743n, 754n
Ference, Richard K., 505n
Ference, T. P., 744n
Ferguson, Anne, 651n
Ferris, Gerald R., 188n, 359n, 471n, 768n
Festinger, Leon, 110n, 207n, 491n
Fiat, 606
Fiedler, Fred E., 260, 260–265
Field, R. H. George, 271n
Fielding, Gordon J., 536n
Fierman, Jaclyn, 126n, 759n
Finholt, Tom, 332n
Fireplace Manufacturers Inc., 596–597
Firestone, 547
First National Bank of Chicago, 386, 400
Fischman, Joshua, 463n
Fisher, Anne B., 609n
Fisher, Cynthia, 117n, 768n
Flaherty, Douglas, 730
Fleishman, Edwin A., 258n, 259n

Fletcher, Clive, 425n
Folkins, C., 468n
Follett, Mary Parker, 14
Fombrun, Charles J., 422n, 436n
Food and Drug Administration (FDA), 515
Food Lion Inc., 452
Ford, J., 526n
Ford, Jeffrey D., 85n, 604n
Ford, R. N., 393n
Ford Motor Company, 45, 46, 48, 49, 63, 126, 178, 229, 280–281, 390, 564, 606, 702, 703
Forest Service, 202
Franklin, Jerome L., 687n
Fredrickson, James W., 604n
Freeman, John, 664n
French, John R. P., 288, 295n, 506n
French, Wendell, 437n, 677
Frenkel-Brunswick, E., 106n
Freud, Sigmund, 101
Frew, David, 460n
Friedman, Meyer, 463
Friedman-Jacobs Company, 377–378
Friesen, Peter H., 678n
Froggatt, Mark L., 507n
Frohman, Alan L., 541
Frohman, Mark, 675
Frontier Airlines, 120
Frost, Peter J., 630n, 633n, 766n
Fuji Bank, 133
Fujisawa, T., 49
Fujita, Den, 25
Fujitsu, 740
Furukawa, Tsukasa, 535n
Furuta, Norimasa, 606
Fusilier, Marcelline R., 470n

Gadon, H., 408n
Galbraith, Jay R., 232n, 321n
Galbraith, John Kenneth, 287n, 303n
Gale, Tom, 34
Gandz, Jeffrey, 297n
Gannett, Barbara, 435n
Ganster, Daniel C., 470n
Gantt, Henry, 10
Gap, Inc., The, 758
Gardner, Donald G., 401n
Gardner, William L., 85n, 278n
Garrett, Thomas M., 47n
Garrett Turbine Engine Company, 531
Geber, Beverly, 29n, 281n
Geertz, C., 631n
Gehrman, Douglas B., 367n
Geier, James A. D., 617
General Electric Company, 6, 14, 343, 378, 472, 556, 564, 600, 609
General Foods Corporation, 186, 365, 393, 403, 561, 598
General Motors Corporation, 21, 126, 178, 190, 265, 280, 281, 333, 483, 493, 609, 666, 678–679, 702, 711
General Tire, 548
Gent, M. J., 701n
Gerhart, Barry, 108n, 376
Gerloff, Edwin A., 329n
Gersick, Connie J. G., 200n, 201
Gerth, H. H., 632
Ghoshal, Sumantra, 722
Gianotti, Lisa, 683
Gibbons, Barry J., 694
Gibney, Frank, 667n
Gifford, Dale, 378n
Gilberg, Kenneth R., 423n
Gilbreth, Frank, 10
Gilbreth, Lillian, 10
Gillen, Dennis A., 9n
Ginsberg, Ari, 491n
Ginzberg, S. W., 737n
Ginzberg, E., 737n
Gioia, Dennis A., 74n, 87n
Gist, Marilyn E., 104n
Glauser, Michael J., 333n
Glick, William, 400n
Gobdel, Bruce C., 273n
Godfather's Pizza, 38
Goffman, E., 627n
Goldsmith, James, 548
Goleman, Daniel, 504n
Goodman, Paul S., 155n, 158n
Goodsite, Bruce H., 333n
Goodyear Aerospace, 548
Goodyear Tire & Rubber Company, 547–549
Gorbachev, Mikhail, 242
Gorman, Joe, 590
Gottschalk, Rand, 433n
Graen, G., 264n, 272
Grand Metropolitan P.L.C., 694
Granrose, C. S., 748n
Graphic Controls, 377
Gray, Harry, 104
Green, Stephen G., 273n
Green, Thad B., 366n
Greenberg, Jerald, 156n, 159n, 427n
Greenhaus, Jeffrey, 433n
Greiner, Larry E., 663n
Greyhound, 301
Griffin, Ricky W., 110n, 112n, 115n, 171n, 172n, 277n, 390n, 393n, 394n, 397n, 400n, 402, 403n, 404n, 406n, 407n, 409n, 680, 714n, 764n
Grove, Andrew S., 77, 225n
Gruhn, Mary, 344n
Guest, R., 389
Gustad, J. W., 737n
Gutfreund, John, 62
Gyllenhammar, Pehr G., 598n

Haas, J. Eugene, 601n
Haas, Robert, 629
Haas, Walter A., Jr., 91, 624
Haavio-Mannila, Elina, 723n
Hackman, J. Richard, 165n, 206n, 394–395, 397, 398n, 399, 400, 409n, 666n, 678n, 688n
Haga, W. J., 272n
Hage, Jerald, 46n, 540n
Hakel, Milton, 141n, 142n
Haldeman, H. R., 504
Hall, D. T., 731n, 737n, 741n, 746, 749n
Hall, F. S., 746
Hall, Loretta, 318n
Hall, Richard H., 230n, 538n, 599n, 601n
Halperin, Robert, 512
Hambrick, Donald C., 491n
Hamner, Ellen P., 169n
Hamner, W. Clay, 169n
Hanada, Mitsuyo, 719n
Hannah, Michael T., 664n
Hara, Akiko, 133
Harker, Phillip, 107n
Harpaz, Itzhak, 406
Harrell, Adrian M., 161n
Harris, Claudia, 432
Harris, E. F., 258n, 259n
Harris, T. George, 470n, 472n
Harrison, E. Frank, 491n, 492n
Hartke, Darrell D., 264n, 685n
Hartwick, Jon, 369n
Haspeslagh, Philippe, 720n
Hass, Marsha E., 179n
Hatfield, John D., 155n, 159
Heald, K., 766n
Hebden, J. E., 644n
Heide, Jan B., 572n
Heider, Fritz, 86
Heilman, Madeline E., 271n
Heller, Agnes, 108n
Helmreich, Robert L., 143n
Helms, Jesse, 312
Henderson, A. M., 12n, 378n, 442n, 588n, 589n
Henderson, Richard I., 371n, 425n, 429n, 438n
Heneman, Robert, 435n
Henkoff, Robert, 590n
Henkoff, Ronald, 137n, 524n, 586n
Herman Miller, Inc., 28–29, 76
Herna, J. L., 737n
Herr, Barbara, 435n
Herschlag, Judith K., 271n
Hersey, Paul, 273n
Hertz, 606
Herzberg, Frederick, 139–142, 145, 146, 392–393
Hewitt Associates, 370
Hewlett-Packard Company, 81, 171, 500, 561, 628, 630, 635, 649
Hickson, David J., 562, 601n, 602n
Hilgard, Ernest R., 129n
Hill, N. C., 751n
Hiltz, Starr R., 345n
Hisrich, R. D., 753n
H. J. Heinz, 579
Hoffman, Alan N., 572n
Hofheinz, Paul, 242n
Hofstede, Geert, 705n
Hogan, Eileen, 434n
Holland, J. L., 737
Holland, Winfred E., 325n
Hollenback, John R., 362n
Holmes, Thomas H., 460
Honda Motor Company, Ltd., 45, 49, 76, 78, 532, 567, 568, 606, 703
Hoopes, Linda L., 469n
Hoover, Gary, 452n, 524n, 534n, 545n, 556n, 564n, 590n, 629n, 646n, 662n, 672n
Horn, Jack C., 377n
Hornstein, Harvey A., 271n
Horton, Robert B., 545
Houghton, James R., 414, 646
House, R. J., 142n, 265, 266n, 276, 394n
Houser, Robert, 498n
Howard, Robert, 628n, 629n
Howell, Jon P., 275n
Huber, George P., 484n, 501n, 510n
Huckfeldt, R. Robert, 193n
Huey, John, 55n
Hulin, Charles L., 141n, 396
Hull, Frank M., 46n
Hulse, S. H., 63n, 66n
Hummel, Ralph P., 179n
Humphrey, Watts S., 555n
Hunt, James G., 259n, 272n, 276n

Hurley, Dan, 747n
Huseman, Richard C., 155n, 159

Iacocca, Lee, 26, 280
IBM, 26, 48, 81, 126, 380, 393, 531, 532, 538, 564, 565, 576, 662, 679, 684
Illinois Tool Works (ITW), 586
Ingersol Milling Machine Company, 343
Inhelder, B., 102n
Intel Corporation, 77, 662
Internal Revenue Service, 374
International Computers Ltd., 740
International Harvester, 259
Ivancevich, John M., 75n, 76n, 464n

Jackofsky, Ellen F., 741n
Jackson, Susan, 467n, 471n
Jaeger, Alfred M., 721n
Jaffe, Thomas, 624n
Jago, Arthur G., 253n, 254, 268, 269, 271n
James, William, 129–130
Janis, Irving L., 209n, 239n, 309n, 495, 503, 504n, 505n, 506n
Japan Air Lines (JAL), 49, 708
Jemison, David B., 605n
Jerdee, T. H., 85n
Jermier, John M., 274n
Jesson, R., 737n
Jet Capital, 120
Jick, Todd, 455n
Jobs, Steven, 143, 252, 276
John Hancock, 407
Johnson, Leonard W., 541
Johnson, Magic, 529
Johnson, Norman, 601n
Johnson, Ross, 45n
Johnson & Johnson, 47, 610
Johnsonville Foods, 76
Jones, Barry D., 207n
Jordan, Paul C., 173n

Kahn, Robert L., 210n, 329n, 595n, 663
Kahn, S., 462n
Kaio Corporation, 534
Kandolin, Irja, 723n
Kanter, Rosabeth Moss, 35n
Kanungo, Rabindra N., 276n, 369n
Kartus, Lisa, 324n
Kast, Fremont, 22n, 23n
Katz, Daniel, 210n, 329n, 595n, 663
Katz, Michael, 220n
Kaufman, Gary, 459n
Kaufman, Steven B., 357n
Kauppinen-Toropainen, Kaisa, 723n
Keefe, Lisa M., 215n
Keil, E. T., 526n
Kelleher, Herb, 96, 97
Keller, Jack, 755
Keller, Robert T., 209n, 325n
Kelley, H. H., 86, 172n
Kellogg, 603
Kellogg, Dianne McKinney, 685n
Kemery, Edward, 459n
Kendall, Lorne, 438
Kendrick, John W., 44n
Kennedy, A. A., 625, 632
Keon, Thomas L., 161n, 164, 528n
Kerlinger, Fred, 431, 764n, 767n, 772n
Kerr, Jeffrey, 367n
Kerr, Steven, 274n, 275n, 319n
Kiechel, Walter, III, 76n, 137n, 256n, 289n, 323n, 420n, 751n
Kiethley Instruments, Inc. (KII), 675–676
Kikkoman Corporation, 708
Kilbridge, M., 392n
Kimberly, John R., 599n
Kindel, Stephen, 512n
King, John, 725
King, Nathan, 142n
King, Pamela, 186n
Kirkland, Richard I., Jr., 708n, 719n
Kirste, Kenneth K., 331n, 335n
Kleiman, Carol, 456n
Klein, Howard J., 362n
Klonoski, Richard J., 47n
Kluckhohn, C., 631n
K Mart, 54, 573
Knippen, Jay T., 366n
Knowlton, Christopher, 702n
Knudsen, B. W., 737n
Kobasa, Susan, 462n
Kogan, N., 502n
Kohn, Alfie, 224n
Kolodny, Harvey F., 610n
Komatsu, 49, 533
Kondrasuk, Jack N., 365n
Konovsky, Mary A., 118n
Kotter, John P., 667n, 688n
Kozlowski, Steve W. J., 80n
Kraar, Louis, 78n
Krackhardt, David, 335n
Kreitner, Robert, 67n, 69n, 70n, 76n, 77n, 166n, 168n
Kroeber, A. L., 631n
Kroger Company, 452
Kuhnert, Karl W., 275n
Kupfer, Andrew, 318n, 718n
Kuzela, Lad, 658n

Labich, Kenneth, 29n, 96n, 149n, 610n, 641n, 646n, 726n, 730n, 758n
LaBier, D., 745n
Lacity, Julie A., 344n
Lacroix, Renee, 207n
Landy, Frank J., 127n
Lane, Henry W., 702n, 719n
Lane, Irving M., 207n
Larson, L. L., 272n, 276n
Lasorda, Tommy, 90–91
Latack, Janina C., 161n, 164, 751n
Latham, Gary P., 78n, 359n, 360, 361, 362n, 422n
Laud, Robert L., 422n, 436n
Laurent, André, 706n
Lawler, Edward E., III, 155n, 163, 165, 362, 366n, 370n, 377n, 378n, 397, 666n, 680n, 688n, 689n, 731n, 739n
Lawler, J., 737n
Lawrence, Paul R., 15n, 231n, 239n, 243n, 302n, 395, 573, 611n, 612n, 663n
Leana, Carrie R., 302n, 507n
Leatt, Peggy, 202n, 532n
Lechmere Inc., 410
Lei, David, 491n
Leibowitz, Z. B., 754n
Lengel, Robert H., 327n
Lengnick-Hall, Cynthia A., 563n
Lengnick-Hall, Mark L., 507n
Levering, Robert, 220n
Levine, Dennis, 163
Levine, M. W., 80n, 81n
Levinson, D. J., 106n
Levi Strauss & Company, 48, 628, 629, 719
Lewin, Kurt, 160, 669–670
Lewis, M. R., 630n
Lewis, Philip, 275n
Lichtman, Robert J., 207n
Lieber, Jill, 189n, 200n
Lifeline Systems, Inc., 597
Lincoln, James F., 368n
Lincoln, James R., 49n, 719n
Lincoln Electric Company, 368
Lionel Train Company, 700, 702
Lippin, Paula, 500n
Livesay, Harold C., 609n
Lloyd, Kathy, 498n
Locke, Edwin A., 12n, 112n, 169n, 359, 361, 507n, 768n
Lodge, George, 708
Loeffelholz, Suzanne, 549n
Long, Susan, 197n
Loomis, Carol J., 486n
Lord, Robert G., 80n, 85n
Lorenzo, Frank, 120–121, 294, 641
Lorsch, Jay W., 15n, 17n, 231n, 239n, 243n, 302n, 366n, 573
Los Alamos National laboratory, 426
Los Angeles Dodgers, 91
Los Angeles Lakers, 529
Lotus Development Corporation, 540–541, 628
Louis, Arthur M., 372n
Lounsbury, John W., 469n
Luckman, T., 627n
Luthans, Fred, 67n, 69n, 70n, 76n, 77n, 166n, 168n
Lutz, Robert, 34
Lynton, Rolf P., 239n

Mabe, P. A., 425n
Mabey, Christopher, 444n
McBride, Kerry, 719n
McCall, M. W., 731n
McCanse, Anne Adams, 259
McDonald's Corporation, 25, 42, 48, 81, 343, 570, 579
McFarlan, F. Warren, 342n
McFarlane, Robert, 206, 208
McGee, Gail, 117n
McGregor, Douglas, 15
McGuire, Joseph W., 18n
Machiavelli, Niccolò, 106
McKenney, James L., 342n
McMahon, Timothy, 264n
Macoby, Michael, 305n
McRae, K. B., 754n
Maddi, S. R., 462n
Mael, Fred, 187n, 195n, 227n
Magaziner, Ira C., 556n
Mahar, Linda, 264n
Maher, J. R., 393n
Maier, Norman R. F., 428
Main, Jeremy, 343n, 635n, 645n, 746n
Malik, S. D., 100n, 197n, 199n
Mann, Leon, 495
Manning, Michael R., 457n
Mansfield, Richard, 511n
Manz, Charles C., 274n
March, James G., 492n, 493n
March of Dimes, 194–195
Markham, Steven E., 203n

Marrache, Myriam, 207n
Marshall, Colin, 725
Martella, J. A., 264n
Martier, A., 749n
Martin, J., 633n
Martinez, Zaida, 704n
Martinko, M. J., 85n, 278n
Maslow, Abraham H., 15, 16, 131, 132–135
Matsushita, 556
Matsushita Electric Industrial Company, 46
Matteson, Michael, 464n
Mausner, Bernard, 139n, 140n
Mayes, Bronston T., 470n
Mayo, Elton, 14, 597n
Mayo Clinic, 40
Maytag, 392
Mazda Motor Corporation, 606, 702
Meer, Jeff, 188n
Meindl, James R., 252n
Mendenhall, Mark, 723n
Merrill Lynch, 373
Mervyn's, 730
Metropolitan Life, 408
Meyer, Daniel J., 617–618
Michelin, 548
Michigan Bell, 169
Microsoft Corporation, 380
Midvale Steel Company, 10–11
Miles, Edward W., 155n, 159
Miles, Raymond E., 170n
Miles, Robert H., 302, 529n, 531n
Milgram, Stanley, 101, 106
Milken, Michael, 163, 486
Milkovich, George, 376, 437n, 440n
Miller, Danny, 678n
Miller, D. B., 732n
Miller, Edwin L., 703n
Miller, Herman, 28
Miller, Richard, 662
Miller, Steven M., 660n
Mills, C. Wright, 632n
Miner, John B., 544n, 588n, 589n, 590n, 591n, 595n, 598n
Mintzberg, Henry, 37, 39, 287n, 303n, 490n, 526n, 530n, 536–537, 539n, 606, 610
Mischel, Walter, 98n, 99n, 102n
Mitchell, Terence R., 84n, 164n, 265n, 266n, 267n, 737n
Mitsubishi Bank, 337
Mitsubishi Corporation, 337, 535
Mitsubishi Heavy Industries, 337
Mitz, Linda, 455n
Moberg, Dennis J., 298
Mobil Corporation, 558, 600, 702
Moffat, Susan, 46n, 740n
Mohawk, 548
Money, W. H., 262n, 264n
Monge, Peter R., 331n, 335n
Monsanto, 579, 610
Montanari, John R., 490n, 506n, 525n, 537n, 603n, 604n
Moore, Thomas, 265n, 600n
Moorhead, Gregory, 277n, 400n, 505n, 506n, 664n, 681n
Morgan, Cyril P., 525n, 603n
Morgan, Gareth, 630n, 633n
Morgan, M. A., 749n
Morris, James H., 340n
Morse, N. C., 506n
Moscovici, S., 502n
Moscowitz, Milton, 220n
Moss, Leonard, 467n
Mossholder, Kevin, 459n
Motorola, 318, 400, 672, 713
Motor Wheel Corporation, 548
Motowidlo, Stephan, 457n
Mouton, Jane S., 223n, 236n, 239n
Mowday, Richard, 116n, 155n, 175, 369n
Mulligan, John W., 10n
Munchus, G., 171n
Munsterberg, Hugo, 13, 14
Murphy, Kevin, 435n
Murray, H. A., 135–136
Murray, Victor, 297n
Muskie, Edmund, 206n, 207n, 208n
Myers, Bettye, 188n

Nader, Ralph, 21
Nadler, David A., 165, 277n, 666n, 674n, 680n, 688n, 689
Nathanson, Sinaia, 498n
National Cash Register Company, 234
National Football League (NFL), 189, 200, 208
National Gypsum, 486
National League, 91
Navistar, 259
NCR Corporation, 234, 635
Necchi, 556
Neck, Christopher P., 505n
Nellsen, Eric H., 243n
Nelson, Debra, 455n
Nelson, Reed E., 227n, 228
Nelson-Horchler, Joani, 62n
Nestlé Company, Inc., 48, 702, 720
Newstrom, John W., 341n
Nisbett, R. E., 633n
Nissan, 78, 133, 178, 606, 702
Nixon, Richard, 504
Nkomo, Stella, 433n
NL Industries, Inc., 569
Noe, Raymond A., 433n
Nord, W. R., 72n
North, Oliver, 206, 208
Nulty, Peter, 121n, 348n, 545n, 580n, 618n, 660n, 703n
Nunn, Dana, 246n

Oakland Athletics, 91, 624
Obert, Steven L., 199n
Oddou, Gary, 723n
O'Farrell, Kevin, 580n
Ohio State University, 258
Oldham, Greg, 395n, 397, 398n, 399, 399n, 409n
Olympic games, 701
Ondrack, Daniel A., 679n
O'Neill, Paul H., 658
Oregon Health Science Center, 554
O'Reilly, Brian, 154n, 252n, 336n, 470n, 516n, 651n, 704n
O'Reilly, Charles A., III, 202n, 319n, 326n, 342n, 407n
Organ, Dennis W., 114n, 118
Ornstein, Suzyn, 156n
Orris, J. B., 264n
Osborn, Richard N., 722
Osborne Computer Corporation, 576
Oshry, Barry, 680n
Ouchi, William G., 357n, 628n, 632, 633, 636–639, 645
Owen, Robert, 13, 14
Pace, R. Wayne, 334n
Pace Foods, 713
Packard, G., 667n
Packard, John, 457n
Paley, William, 312, 313
Panasonic, 48
Par, Jan, 247n
Parasuraman, Saroj, 433n
Parker, Donald F., 472n
Parkinson, David, 462n
Parnes, H. S., 737n
Parry, Charles W., 658
Parsons, T., 12n, 588n, 589n, 634–635
Pascarella, Perry, 675n
Patinkin, Mark, 556n
Patterson, James L., 746
Pavlov, Ivan P., 64–65
Payne, R. C., 745n
Pearce, John A., II, 540n
Pearlman, Jerry, 324
People Express, 120
Perlman, Lawrence, 470
Perot, H. Ross, 265, 333
Perroni, Amedeo G., 12n, 130n
Pervin, Lawrence A., 98n
Peters, Lawrence H., 264n, 741n
Peters, Thomas J., 342, 568, 614, 626, 632, 633, 635n, 639–643, 645, 719
Petersen, Donald, 280–281
Petre, Peter, 684n
Petty, M. M., 117n
Pfeffer, Jeffrey, 18n, 110, 132n, 146, 244n, 277n, 287n, 297, 300, 303n, 366n, 404, 543n, 546n, 565, 576n, 577n, 667n, 763n
Phatak, Arvind, 48n
Pheysey, Diana C., 562, 601n, 602n
Philbrick, Jane Hass, 179n
Phillips Petroleum Company, 81
Phoenix Technologies Inc., 590
Piaget, Jean, 101, 102
Pillsbury, 38, 694
Pincus, J. David, 320n
Pinder, Craig, 129n, 131n, 141n, 142, 145n, 146, 158n, 164
Piotrowski, Chris, 755
Piper, William E., 207n
Pirelli, 547
Plato, 9
Plous, F. K., Jr., 386n
Podsakoff, Philip M., 275n, 288n, 770n
Pohlmann, John T., 264n
Polanyi, M., 627n
Polaroid, 9
Pompili, Tony, 343n
Pondy, Louis R., 319n, 630n, 633n
Porter, Lyman W., 16n, 98n, 116n, 127n, 132n, 155n, 163, 165n, 305n, 335n, 362, 369n, 536n, 666n, 688n, 689n
Portwood, J. D., 748n
Powell, Robert J., 189n
Power, M., 633n
Prescott, John E., 572n
Price Waterhouse, 757
Prietula, Michael J., 289n
Pritchard, Robert D., 164n
Procter & Gamble, 171, 532, 534, 561, 610
Prudential Insurance Company of America, 390, 393, 558
Pryor, Robert G. L., 99n
Pugh, Derek S., 562, 601n, 602n
Pulakos, Elaine D., 89n
Pulhamus, Aaron, 424

Quantum Corporation, 746
Quick, James, 453n, 455n, 460n, 467n, 468n, 471n, 472n, 683n
Quick, Jonathan D., 453n, 460n, 467n, 468n, 471n, 472n, 683n
Quinn, James B., 557n

Rafaeli, Anat, 210n, 328n, 458n
Rahe, Richard, 460
Raisinghani, Duru, 490n
Ramo-Wooldridge Corporation, 590
Rand Corporation, 510
Rapoport, Carla, 606n
Raven, Bertram, 288, 295n
Rawl, Lawrence, 347–348
Raychem Corp., 512
Reagan, Ronald, 82
Recruit, 47
Red Cross, 701
Redding, Gordon, 704n
RedZone Robotics, Inc., 564
Reed, John, 474
Regina Company, 84
Reichers, Arnon E., 25n, 100n, 197n, 199n
Reimer, E., 506n
Reitman, Frieda, 748n
Renwick, P. A., 739n
Reserve Officers Training Corps (ROTC), 111
Rhodes, Susan R., 174
Rice, Fay, 470n, 745n
Richardson, Astrid M., 207n
Richman, Louis S., 137n
Ricks, David A., 704n
Rideout, Janet, 515
R. J. Reynolds, 408
Robbins, Stephen P., 307n, 308n, 309n
Roberts, Karlene H., 400n
Roberts, Marjory, 470n
Robertson, Ivan T., 78n, 112n, 172n
Roethlisberger, Fritz J., 14, 597n
Roger, David, 444n
Rogers, Everett M., 325n
Rogers, L. Edna, 321
Romac Industries, 377
Romzek, Barbara, 116n
Ronen, Simcha, 704n
Rorer Group, 343
Rose, Frank, 6n, 35n
Rosen, B., 85n
Rosenman, Ray, 463
Rosenzweig, James, 22n, 23n
Rosenzweig, Mark R., 98n, 127n
Ross, Jerry, 498n, 499n
Rotter, J. B., 104n, 105n
Rowland, Kendrith M., 188n, 359n, 471n
Royal Dutch Shell, 702
Russell, Daniel W., 467n
Rynes, S. L., 737n
Ryterband, Edward C., 197n, 199n, 205n

Saab-Scania, 598
Saba, Shoichi, 708
Safeway, 126, 457
Salancik, Gerald R., 110, 132n, 146, 155n, 404, 565
Saldich, Robert, 512
Salomon Brothers, 62
Salpukas, Agis, 121n
Sanford, R. N., 106n
San Francisco Forty-Niners, 200
Sanoff, Alvin P., 624n
Sanyo, 606
Saporito, Bill, 55n, 189n
Sashkin, Marshall, 539n
Saunders, Carol S., 345n
Saurage, J., 753n
Sawin, Linda L., 143n
Scandinavian Airlines System (SAS), 121, 641
Schachter, Stanley, 144n, 195n
Schall, Maryan S., 329n
Schein, E. H., 626, 743n
Schlender, Brenton R., 92n, 381n, 624n, 629n
Schlesinger, Leonard A., 680n, 688n
Schlesinger, Leonard S., 667n
Schlossberg, N. K., 754n
Schmitt, Neal, 433n
Schneck, Rodney, 202n, 532n
Schneer, Joy A., 748n
Schneider, Benjamin, 25n, 127n
Schoenherr, Richard A., 599n
Schriesheim, Chester A., 262n, 264n, 288n
Schulberg, Herbert, 462n
Schuler, Randall S., 467n, 471n
Schulhof, Michael, 740
Schultz, George P., 206–207
Schurr, Paul H., 109n
Schwab, Donald P., 423n
Schwab, Richard L., 467n
Schwartz, Howard S., 135n
Schwarzkopf, H. Norman, 256
Schweiger, David M., 507n
Schwenk, Charles R., 308
S. C. Johnson & Son, Inc., 600
Scott, William G., 84n
Scowcroft, Brent, 206n, 207n, 208n
Sculley, John, 252, 275, 276, 380
Sears, Roebuck, 37, 81, 567
Seashore, Stanley, 574n
Seiler, William J., 322n
Self, Elizabeth A., 127n
Sellers, Patricia, 726n
Selye, Hans, 454, 455, 457n
Seneker, Harold, 504n
Shaffer, Richard A., 381n
Shapiro, Irving S., 333n
Shaw, James B., 710n
Shaw, Marvin E., 188, 192n, 200n, 203n, 206n, 229n, 329n, 499n, 502n
Shearson Lehman Hutton Inc., 373
Sheelen, Don, 84
Shefner, J. M., 80n, 81n
Sheldon, William H., 100n
Shell Oil Company, 22–23, 48
Shenkar, Oded, 704n
Shepard, Herbert A., 223n, 236n
Sheridan, John H., 234n
Sherif, C. W., 194n
Sherif, M., 194n
Sherman, J. Daniel, 540n
Sherman, Stratford P., 6n, 277n, 511n
Shills, E., 634n
Shin Caterpillar-Mitsubishi, 533, 535
Shockley-Zalabak, Pamela S., 239n
Shoen, Joe, 246
Shoen, L. S., 245–247
Shoen, Sam, 246
Shuelke, L. David, 322n
Sils, D., 644n
Simon, Herbert A., 83, 289n, 482n, 483n, 492n, 493n
Simonds Rolling Machine Company, 11
Sims, Henry P., Jr., 74n, 87n, 274n
Skinner, B. F., 67
Skivington, Kristen Dahlen, 277n
Sloan, Alfred, 609n
Slocum, John W., Jr., 367n
Smale, John G., 534
Smith, Adam, 387–388, 528
Smith, Carlla S., 163n
Smith, Howard L., 540n
Smith, Ken K., 235n
Smith, Patricia C., 141n, 438
Smith, Winthrop, 470
Smithsonian Institution, 40
Snyder, Mark, 106n
Snyder, Robert A., 340n
Snyderman, Barbara, 139n, 140n
Solo, Sally, 318n
Sony Corporation, 500
Sorrels, J. Paul, 188n
Southwest Airlines, 96, 482
Spain, Patrick J., 452n, 524n, 534n, 545n, 556n, 564n, 590n, 629n, 646n, 662n, 672n
Spector, Paul, 104n
Spendolini, Michael J., 536n
Spindler, Michael, 381
Sproull, Lee S., 332n
St. Luke's Hospital (Phoenix), 242–243
Stahl, Michael J., 143n, 161n
Stalker, George M., 560, 601–602
Standard Oil of Ohio, 169
Stanley, J. C., 766n
Staw, Barry M., 7n, 25n, 66n, 80n, 109n, 110n, 111, 118n, 127n, 155n, 175n, 277n, 327n, 328n, 400n, 401n, 498, 499n, 667n
Stearns, Timothy M., 572n, 767n
Stedt, Bonnie, 154
Steele, Fritz, 194n
Steele, Timothy P., 362n
Steers, Richard, 116, 116n, 127n, 132n, 155n, 174, 175, 369n, 703n
Stevenson, Howard H., 84n
Stewart, Thomas A., 154n, 292n, 452n, 658n
Stogdill, Ralph M., 253n
Stoka, Ann Marie, 12n
Stone, Eugene, 764n, 769n, 771n
Stoner, James A. F., 502n, 744n
Storey, John, 562n
Storrs, Constance, 590n
Strickland, A. J., III, 368n, 603n, 609n
Sujansky, Joanne, 420n
Sumitomo Rubber Industries, 547
Sun Microsystems, 500
Suttle, J. L., 400, 678, 679n
Sutton, Robert I., 328n, 458n, 601n

Taber, Thomas D., 273n
Takagi, Yasumoto, 708
Tandem Computers Inc., 24, 336, 561, 649–651
Tandy/Radio Shack, 576
Tane, Lance D., 378n
Tanner, J. M., 102n
Tapscott, Don, 344n
Tavistock Institute, 597
Taylor, Alex, III, 34n, 78n, 281n
Taylor, Frederick W., 10–12, 130n, 388, 389, 506n
Taylor, M. Susan, 107n
Taylor, William, 512n, 556n
Teaff, Rick, 420n
Teamsters Union, 149
Tenneco, 365

Terborg, James, 25n, 99n
Texaco, 126, 580, 702
Texas Air, 120, 121
Texas Industries, 214
Texas Instruments, 126, 171, 393, 400
Texas International, 120
Tharenou, Phyllis, 107n
Thatcher, Margaret, 725
Thayer, Paul W., 395n
Thomas, Joe, 406n
Thomas, Kenneth, 18n, 222n
Thompson, Arthur A., Jr., 368n, 603, 609n
Thompson Company, 590
Thoret, André, 490n
3M Company, 400, 510–511, 610, 635
Tichy, Noel M., 674n
Tisch, Laurence, 312–313
Tolman, Edward C., 160
Tompkins, Silvan S., 324n
Toshiba, 49, 708
Tosi, Henry L., 363n, 365n
Touliatos, John, 459n
Tower, John, 206n, 207n, 208n
Toyne, Brian, 704n
Toyota, 45, 78, 133, 178, 606, 639, 702–703
Treacy, Michael E., 378n
Treybig, Jerry, 336
Treybig, Jim, 24, 649
Trist, Eric L., 597n
Trump, Donald, 26, 277
TRW Systems Group, 590, 610
Tsui, Anne, 434n
Tubbs, Mark E., 360n
Tudor, William D., 536n
Tully, Shawn, 190n
Turner, A. N., 395–396
Turner, Ted, 312, 313
Tushman, Michael L., 277n
Tymon, Walter G., 18n

U-Haul, 245–247
Ulene, Art, 474
Ulrich, David O., 472n, 674n
Unilever N.V., 534, 720
Unimation, 564
Union Carbide, 580, 708
Uniroyal Goodrich, 548
United Parcel Service, 148–149
U. S. Air Force, 445–446
U. S. Civil Service, 392
U. S. Postal Service, 172
United Technologies Corporation, 104, 564
Universal Studios, 286
University of Michigan, 257
Urwick, Lyndall F., 12, 536n
Uttal, Bro, 252n

Van Fleet, David D., 172n, 537n, 753n
Van Fleet, E. M., 753n
Van Velzen, Dawn, 467n
Vecchio, Robert P., 273n
Velasques, Manuel, 298
Ventrakaman, N., 491n
Vesper, Karl H., 557n
Vicars, William M., 685n
Victor Technologies Inc., 576
Volkswagen, 703
Vollrath, David A., 507n
Volvo, 400, 403, 598
Von Glinow, Mary Ann, 772n
Vroom, Victor H., 127n, 160, 268, 269, 271n

Wahba, Mahmond A., 135n
Walker, C. R., 389
Walker, J., 748n, 755n
Wallach, M. A., 502n
Wallas, G., 511n
Wal-Mart, 54–55, 293
Walsh, Bill, 200
Walsh, James P., 83n
Walton, Richard E., 598n, 678
Walton, Sam, 54–55, 293
Wang, An, 662
Wang, Fred, 662
Wang Laboratories, 662
Wanous, John P., 100n, 161n, 164, 197n, 199n
Warren, E. K., 744n
Watari, Sugiichiro, 708
Waterman, Robert H., Jr., 342, 568, 614, 626, 632, 633, 635n, 639–643, 645
Watkins, David W., 426n
Webber, R. A., 743n
Weber, Max, 12, 528, 588–589, 631–632
Weed, E. D., 393n
Weick, Karl E., 155n, 335n
Weiss, H. M., 73n
Welch, Jack, 6
Wells, Ronald G., 429n
Wells Fargo & Company, 9, 10
Welsh, M. Ann, 400n
Welter, Therese, 192n
Werbel, James, 434n
West, S. G., 425n
Western Electric, 14
Westinghouse, George, 564
Westinghouse Electric Company, 40, 76, 171, 403, 420, 564, 635
Wexley, Kenneth N., 77n, 89n, 422n, 435n, 685n
Weyerhauser, 169
Whistler Corporation, 45
Whitely, William, 39n
Whiting, Brent, 247n
Whiting, J. W. M., 644n
Whitmire, Marshall, 429n
Whitsett, David A., 15
Wickes Company, 486
Wigdor, L., 142n, 394n
Wilcox, R. C., 737n
Wilkins, A., 630n, 633n
Williams, Jennifer, 195n
Winchell, William O., 45n
Wintermantel, Dick, 672n
Witten, Marsha G., 305n
Wofford, Jerry C., 329n
Wojahn, Ellen, 662n
Wolfe, Richard A., 472n
Wood, Robert, 66n
Woods, Wilton, 96n
Wormley, Wayne, 433n
Worthy, Ford S., 34n
Wrege, Charles D., 12n, 130n
Wren, Daniel A., 9n, 12n, 15, 131n, 169n, 387n
Wyman, Thomas, 312–313

Xerox Corporation, 400, 557, 679

Yagoda, Ben, 348n
Yamaguchi, Tamotsu, 704n
Yammarino, Francis J., 189n
Yasai-Ardekani, Masoud, 572n, 603n
Yates, Valerie, 764n
Yeltsin, Boris, 242
Yetton, Philip H., 268
Yin, R., 766n
Yokohama Rubber, 548
Yorks, Lyle, 15n
Yuchtman, Ephraim, 574n
Yukl, Gary A., 254n, 259n, 268n, 287n, 292–297, 360n, 362n

Zalkind, Sheldon S., 80n
Zaltman, G., 666n
Zavalloni, M., 502n
Zeleny, M., 490n
Zenith Electronics Corporation, 324
Zey, Michael G., 748n
Zimmer, F. G., 395n
Zimmerman, Paul, 208n

Subject Index

Absenteeism, 51
job dissatisfaction and, 114
motivation and, 174
Acceptance
of goals, 361
mutual acceptance stage of group development and, 197
Acceptance theory of authority, 545–546
Accommodation, intergroup, 222–223
Accountability, job enrichment and, 392
Achievement, job enrichment and, 392
Achievement need, 142–144, 146
characteristics of high need achievers and, 142–143
consequences of, 143
economic development and, 144
learning, 143
Achievement-oriented leader, 266
Action, bias for, organization culture and, 640
Action research, 673
Adaptation, organization culture and, 634–635
Adherence, unconflicted, 497
Adhocracy, 610
Administrative hierarchy, 537
ideal bureaucracy and, 589
power and decision making shifted downward in, 541
technology and, 559
Advancement stage of career, 743–744
Affect, attitudes and, 109
Affiliation
group formation and, 195
need for, 144–145
Age
changing worker needs and, 137
midlife crisis and, career and, 745–746
organization change and, 659
of work force, 42
Agenda, control of, political behavior and, 304
AGIL model, 634–635
Agreement, overcoming resistance to change and, 668
Alarm stage of general adaptation syndrome, 454
All-channel network, 330
Allocator role, of manager, 38–39
Anthropology
influence on field of organizational behavior, 17
organization culture and, 631
Applied research, 764
Approach, leadership perspectives and, 254
Artificial intelligence, as force for organization change, 660
Aspirations, job satisfaction and, 113–114
Attention, selective, 83
communication process and, 339
Attitudes, 107–117
behaviors and, 117
changing, 112
cognitive dissonance and, 110–112
dispositional view of, 108–109
individual, organizational effectiveness and, 51
job-related, 112–116
perception and, 82
situational view of, 110
stress and, 467
Attitude surveys, 114
Attraction, interpersonal, group formation and, 193–194, 195–196
Attribution, 85–89
hiring and, 88
leadership and, 278
motivation and, 88, 172–173
performance evaluation and, 88–89
Attribution theory, 172–173
Authoritarianism, 106
Authority, 543–544. *See also* Administrative hierarchy
acceptance theory of, 545–546
delegation of, 544
formal authority system and, 267–268
ideal bureaucracy and, 589
responsibility and, 544
Automated office systems, communication and, 344–345
Automation, 46, 409–410, 660, 661
Autonomous work groups, 597
Autonomy
as core job dimension, 398
employee participation and, 411
organization culture and, 640–641
Avoidance, 69
defensive, 497
intergroup, 222
Awards, as rewards, 374–375
Awareness, lack of, resistance to change and, 666–667

Baby boomers
changing worker needs and, 137
as force for organization change, 659
BARSs (behaviorally anchored rating scales), for performance appraisal, 438–440
Baseline performance, organizational behavior modification and, 168
Basic research, 764
Behavior
attitudes and, 117
consideration, of leaders, 258
employee-centered, of leaders, 257
individual, organizational effectiveness and, 50–51
initiating-structure, of leaders, 258
intergroup, *see* Intergroup behavior
job-centered, of leaders, 257
learning and, 63
managerial, across cultures, 706–708
organizational, *see* Organizational behavior
performance-related, organizational behavior modification and, 166–168
political, 297–307
relationship, life cycle theory of leadership and, 274
stress and, 466
Behavioral approaches to leadership, 254, 256–260
leadership grid and, 259–260
Michigan leadership studies and, 257
Ohio State leadership studies and, 258–259
Behavioral contingencies, organizational behavior modification and, 168
Behavioral decision-making approach, 492–493
Behavioral expectation scale (BES), 439–440
Behaviorally anchored rating scales (BARSs), for performance appraisal, 438–440
Behavioral observation scale (BOS), 439–440
Behavior modification, organizational, 77, 166–169
results of, 169
Belongingness needs, 133, 134, 145
Benefits
flexible reward systems and, 378
as rewards, 372–374
Benevolents, 159
BES (behavioral expectation scale), 439–440
Between-culture issues, organization structure and design and, 719
Bias
job, 646
performance appraisals and, 433
Biological factors, personality and, 99–100
"Body language," 324
Bonus systems, 371
BOS (behavioral observation scale), 439–440
Bounded rationality, 492
Brainstorming, 508–509
Breaking-in phase of career, 742
Bureaucracy, 12–13, 588
ideal, 588–589
machine, 608–609
professional, 609
Burnout, stress and, 467–468
Business function, departmentalization by, 530

Cafeteria-style reward systems, 378
Career(s), 729–756
changing, 739, 741
across cultures, 721–723
individual and organization perspectives on, 731–732
midlife crisis and, 745–746
organization culture and, 637
stages of, 741–748
Career choices, 733–741
changing careers and, 739, 741
choice of occupation and, 735–738
choice of organization and, 738–739

Career counseling, 751
Career development programs, 755
stress management and, 472
Career information systems, 751
Career management, 736, 754
Career pathing, 750–751
Career planning, 748–756
career management and, 736, 754
purposes of, 748–749
results of, 755–756
types of programs for, 749–753
Case study, 766–767
Causality, research and, 770–771
Centralization, 538–539
Central tendency, performance appraisals and, 433
Certainty, decision making under, 484
Chain network, 329–330
Change. *See also* Organization change
in attitudes, 112
difficulty of, 647
group and individual, 682–688
inequity reduction and, 157–158
learning and, 63
life change and, 460–462
management development programs and, 684–685
of organizational culture, 645–647
of organizational structure, 534, 545
of organization design, 590
stability of, 647
structural, 677–680
survey-feedback and, 686–688
task-technological, 680–682
team building and, 685–686
technological, 613, 680
training and, 682–688
unconflicted, 497
in workers' needs, 133, 137
Change agent, 670–673
Charismatic leadership, 276–277
Checklists, for performance appraisal, 437
China
group performance and, 204
organization structure and design in, 719
Choice, social information processing model and, 405
Circle network, 330
Classical conditioning, 64–65
Classical organization theory, 12–13
Coalition building, political behavior and, 305
Coercion, overcoming resistance to change and, 669
Coercive power, 289
using, 296–297
Cognition, attitudes and, 109
Cognitive dissonance, 110–112
decision making and, 491
Cognitive process, learning as, 65–66
Collaboration, intergroup, 224–225
Collateral programs, stress management and, 471–472
Collectivism, culture and, 705–706
Command (functional) groups, 189–190
Commission programs, 371
Commitment, 116
to employees, organization culture and, 636
escalation of, 498–499
to goals, 361–362
to performance appraisal system, 429
power and, 293
social information processing model and, 404
Common method variance, 767–768
Communication, 317–346
"across," 321
"bottom-up," 321
characteristics of, 330–331
control of, political behavior and, 303–304
across cultures, 711–713
downward, 334
electronic information processing and telecommunications and, 343–345
as force for organization change, 661
group size and, 203–204
growth of international business and, 701
improving organizational factors in, 340–343
informal, fostering, 342
managing, 336–343
networks and, *see* Communication networks
nonverbal, 323–325
opening, limiting political behavior and, 306
oral, 323
organizational structure and, 321
organization development and, 691–692
overcoming resistance to change and, 667–668
process of, 325–329
purposes of, 319–320
"top-down," 321
uncertainty and, 321–322
upward, 334
written, 322–323
Communication and decision-making stage of group development, 197–198
Communication fidelity, 336
Communication networks, 329–336
all-channel, 329
chain, 328–329
circle, 329
culture and, 337
keiretsu and, 337
negative impact of, 335
organizational, 333–336
patterns and characteristics of, 331–332
small-group, 321, 329–332
wheel, 328
Communication process, 325–329
decoding in, 327–328, 338–339
encoding in, 326–327, 338–339
feedback in, 328, 340
improving, 336–340
noise in, 328–329
receiver/responder in, 328, 339–340
source in, 326, 336–338
transmission in, 327
Comparison, social, *see* Equity theory of motivation
Compensation. *See also* Reward(s); Reward systems
corporate financial performance and, 376
indirect, 372–374
long-term, 371
performance-linked, 373
tangible and intangible, 367
for top management, 62
Competition
as force for organization change, 661
growth of international business and, 702
intergroup, 223–224
in organizational environment, 45, 566–567
Compliance, power and, 293
Compressed workweek, 407–408
Compromise, intergroup, 225–226
Computer(s), as force for organization change, 661
Computer-assisted manufacturing, 46
Conditioning
classical, 64–65
operant, *see* Reinforcement theory
Conflict, 307–310
across cultures, 710–711
excessive, 310
intergroup, 228
interrole, 210–211
intrarole, 210–211
intrasender, 211
managing, 308–310
nature of, 308
person-role, 211
pros and cons of, 307, 308
among roles, stress and, 459
stress and, 459–460
Conflict model of decision making, 495
Conflict resolution, 309
Conflict stimulation, 309–310
Conglomerate, international, 720
Consensus, attribution and, 86
Consideration behavior, of leaders, 258
Consistency, attribution and, 86
Consultants, political behavior and, 304
Content theories of occupational choice, 736, 737
Content validity, 431
Contingencies, behavioral, organizational behavior modification and, 166–168
Contingency perspective, 23–24
on organization design, 587, 595–605
Contingency plans, 491
Contingency theory of leadership, 254, 260–265
basic premises of, 261–262
scientific evidence for, 264–265
situational favorableness and, 262–264
Continuous-process production, 559, 562
Continuous reinforcement, 70
Contract negotiations, intergroup compromise and, 225
Contrast, perception and, 80
Control
of agenda, political behavior and, 304
of communication, political behavior and, 303–304
of decision parameters, political behavior and, 305–306
goal setting and, 357
of information, political behavior and, 303
locus of, 267
organization culture and, 637
organization development and, 690
of resources, job enrichment and, 392
span of, 535–537, 559
Control and organization stage of group development, 198–200
Controlling, as managerial function, 37
Convergent validity, 431
Cooptation, overcoming resistance to change and, 668–669
Coordinating mechanisms, 606–608
Coordination, communication across cultures and, 712–713
Coping strategies
individual, 468–470
organizational, 470–472

Core job dimensions, Job Characteristics Theory and, 397–399
Cosmopolite role, in communication networks, 334
Costs, growth of international business and, 702
Coworkers
job satisfaction and, 113
least preferred coworker scale and, 261–262
Creativity in decision making, 510–513
incubation and, 512
insight and, 513
preparation and, 511
verification and, 513
Credibility, of source of communication, 339–340
Critical psychological states, Job Characteristics Theory and, 397
Cultural diversity, managing, 49–50
Culture. *See also* International business; International perspective
careers and, 721–723
communication and, 711–713
cross-cultural differences and similarities and, 703–704
decision making and, 715–716
environment and technology and, 717–718
group dynamics and, 709
individual differences and, 705–706
job design and, 714
leadership and, 710
managerial behavior and, 706–708
motivation and, 709
organization, *see* Organization culture
organization change and, 720–721
organization structure and design and, 719–720
performance evaluation and, 714–715
personality and, 101
power and conflict and, 710–711
reward and, 714
stress and, 455, 715
Customer
departmentalization by, 532–533
organization culture and, 640

Data analysis, 765
Data gathering, 769–770
interviews and, 769
nonreactive measures and, 770
observation and, 770
questionnaires and, 769
surveys and, 114, 686–688, 767–768
Deadwood, 744, 745
Decentralization, 538–539
formalized, 539
Decision(s)
nonprogrammed, 302, 483, 489, 539
programmed, 481–482, 489, 539
Decision making, 481–513
behavioral approach to, 492–493
centralization and, 539
communication and, 320
communication and decision-making stage of group development and, 197–198
creativity in, 510–513
across cultures, 715–716
employee participation in, 506–507
escalation of commitment and, 498–499
frequency and, 481
group problem solving and, 507–510
in groups, 499–507
individual versus group, 499–501
information conditions and, 481
information required for, 484–486
organization culture and, 637–638
personal approach to, 495–498
practical approach to, 493–495
rational approach to, 487–492
shifting downward in hierarchy, 541
types of decisions and, 481–483, 489
Decision-making roles, of manager, 38–39
Decision parameters, control of, political behavior and, 305–306
Decision rule, 481, 482–483
Decision specificity, task structure and, 262
Decision tree, Vroom-Yetton-Jago model of leadership and, 267
Decision verifiability, task structure and, 262
Decline stage of career, 746
Decoding, in communication process, 327–328, 338–339
Decoupling, management of intergroup behavior and, 244
Defensive avoidance, 497
Deficiency needs, 133
Delphi technique, 510
Demographics. *See also* Age
as force for organization change, 659–660
of workplace, 41–43
Density, of communication, 330
Departmentalization, 529–535
by business function, 530
by customer, 532–533
by geography, 533
mixed departmentalization scheme and, 533, 535
by process, 530–531
by product or service, 531–532
Description, as goal of organizational behavior, 18
Differentiation, structural contingency perspective and, 573
Direction, manifest needs and, 135
Directive leadership, 266
Disability benefits, 372–373
Discipline, 75
Dispositions
attitudes and, 108–109
perception and, 82
Dissonance reduction, 111
Distance, communication and, 330
Distinctiveness, attribution and, 86–87
Distress, 455
Disturbance handler role, of manager, 38
Divergent validity, 431
Divisionalized form, 609
Division of labor. *See also* Specialization
ideal bureaucracy and, 589
Documentation, ideal bureaucracy and, 589

Eastern bloc, globalization and, 48
Economic development, achievement and, 144
Economic factors
in organizational environment, 565, 567–568, 569
resistance to change and, 666
Economics (field of)
influence on field of organizational behavior, 18
organization culture and, 633–634
Economies of scale, 600
Education. *See also* Training
overcoming resistance to change and, 667
Effort-to-performance expectancy, 161
Electronic group mail, 332
Electronic information processing, 343–345
Employee(s). *See also* Coworkers; Human resource(s); Individual(s); People
absenteeism of, 51, 114, 174
age of, 42, 137, 659
changing needs of, 133, 137
commitment to, organization culture and, 636
compensation of, *see* Compensation; Incentives; Incentive systems; Reward(s); Reward systems
job satisfaction of, *see* Job satisfaction/dissatisfaction
nonexempt, 436–437
performance appraisal and, *see* Performance appraisal
privacy of, 43
rights of, 43
selection of, perception and attribution and, 88
training of, *see* Training
turnover of, 51, 114, 174–175, 335
Employee-centered leader behavior, 257
Employee fitness programs, stress management and, 472
Employee participation, 592
organization development and, 691
Employee participation, 411–412. *See also* Participative management
in decision making, 506–507
Employee stock option plans, 372
Encoding, in communication process, 326–327, 338–339
Engineering, influence on field of organizational behavior, 18
Entitleds, 159
Entrepreneur role, of manager, 38
Entrepreneurship
need for achievement and, 143
new ventures and, 537–538
within organization, 558
organization culture and, 640–641
outside, 558
Entry stage of career, 741
Environment
organizational, *see* Organizational environment
task, 570
Environmental complexity, 570
Environmental dynamism, 570
Environmental scanning, 490
Environmental uncertainty, 570–572
Equity, defined, 155
Equity sensitivities, 159
Equity theory of motivation, 155–160
equity sensitivity construct and, 159
evaluation of, 158–159
formation of equity perceptions and, 155–156
managerial implications of, 159–160
responses to perceptions of equity/inequity and, 157–158
ERG theory of motivation, 137–138, 145, 146
Escalation of commitment, 498–499
Essays, for performance appraisal, 438
Establishment stage of career, 741–743

Esteem needs, 133, 134
Ethics, 47
 Exxon *Valdez* oil spill and, 19
 as individual differences, 108
 job bias and, 646
 personality and, 107
 research and, 772
 robotics and, 409
 securities industry and, 163, 486
 sexual harassment and, 290
 uranium exposure and, 569
Ethnic composition, of work force, 43
Eustress, 455
Evaluation, organization culture and, 636
Exchanges
 of members, management of intergroup behavior and, 243
 of resources, 574–575
Exercise, stress management and, 468, 470, 472
Exhaustion stage of general adaptation syndrome, 454
Existence needs, 137
Expanded process model of organization change, 670–673
Expectancy theory of motivation, 160–165
 basic expectancy model and, 160–163
 effort-to-performance expectancy and, 161
 evaluation of, 164–165
 managerial implications of, 165
 outcomes and valences and, 162–163
 performance-to-outcome expectancy and, 161–162
 Porter-Lawler extension of, 163–164
Expectations, social, social information processing model and, 406
Experience, learning and, 63–64
Experiment
 field, 768–769
 laboratory, 768
Expertise, threatened, resistance to change and, 665
Expert power, 289
 using, 295
Explicitness, social information processing model and, 405
Explicit rules, 540
Exploration stage of career, 741
External locus of control, personality and, 104
External priming, social information processing model and, 406
Extinction, 69
Extrinsic rewards, 164
Extroversion, 107

Facilitation, overcoming resistance to change and, 668
Fair Labor Standards Act, 436–437
Fear, resistance to change and, 666
Feedback
 in communication process, 328, 340
 as core job dimension, 398
 employee participation and, 411
 job enrichment and, 392
 need for achievement and, 143
 providing, 428
 as purpose of performance appraisal, 428
 verification and, 340
Field experiment, 768–769
Field survey, 767–768
"Fight-or-flee" question, 454
Figurehead role, of manager, 37–38
Financial performance, employee pay and, 376
Financial resources, in organizational environment, 569
Fixed-interval reinforcement, 70
Fixed-ratio reinforcement, 71
Flexible reward systems, 378
Flexible-worker approach, 410–411
Flexible work schedules, 408
Flextime, 408
Focus, leadership perspectives and, 254
Forced-choice method, for performance appraisal, 440–441
Forced-distribution method, for performance appraisal, 442
Form(s), 323
Formal authority system, path-goal theory of leadership and, 267–268
Formal groups, 189–190
Formalization, 539–542
Formalized decentralization, 539
Formal leader, position power and, 291–292
Frequency, decision making and, 481
Friendship groups, 191
Frustration-regression process, in Alderfer's ERG theory, 138
Functional (command) groups, 189–190

Gain-sharing programs, 371
Game playing, political behavior and, 304–305
GAS (general adaptation syndrome), 454
Gatekeeper role, in communication networks, 334
Gender. *See also* Sexual harassment
 masculinity/femininity and, culture and, 706
 sex discrimination and, 722–723
 stress and, 455, 457
 of work force, 42–43
General adaptation syndrome (GAS), 454
Geography, departmentalization by, 533
Getting-in phase of career, 742
Globalization, 48–49, 702–703
Goal(s)
 ambiguity of, political behavior and, 302
 defined, 356
 of group, 188, 194–195
 outside group, group formation and, 196
 organizational, 525
 superordinate, 236
 time and goal interdependence and, intergroup behavior and, 230–231
 verifiability of, 364
Goal acceptance, 361
Goal attainment, organization culture and, 634–635
Goal-based strategies for management of intergroup behavior, 236–238
Goal clarity, task structure and, 262
Goal commitment, 361–362
Goal compatibility, intergroup, 222
Goal difficulty, motivation and, 360
Goal displacement, management of intergroup behavior and, 236
Goal-path multiplicity, task structure and, 262
Goal setting, 356–365
 control and, 357
 management by objectives and, 363–365
 motivation and, 357, 359–363
 role of, 358–359
 for supervisors, 366
Goal-setting theory of motivation, 359–361
 goal difficulty and, 360
 goal specificity and, 360–361
Goal specificity, motivation and, 360–361
Good citizen syndrome, 118
Government, in organizational environment, 568
Graphic rating scales, for performance appraisal, 436–437
Great Britain, conflict in, 711
Group(s), 185–213
 activities of, group formation and, 194
 characteristics of, intergroup dynamics and, 227
 cohesiveness of, 207–209
 command (functional), 189–190
 communication networks and, 329–336
 composition of, 200–203, 502
 conflict among, 228
 cultural attitudes and, 204
 defined, 187–188
 development of, 197–200, 201
 effectiveness of, communication networks and, 332
 electronic, 332
 formal, 189–190
 formation of, reasons for, 192–196
 friendship, 191
 goals of, group formation and, 194–195
 heterogeneous, 201, 202
 homogeneous, 201–202
 importance of studying, 188–189
 informal, 191
 interest, 191
 job design for, 401–404
 managing in organizations, 211–212
 midpoint transition and, 201
 norms of, 205–207
 organizational effectiveness and, 52
 role dynamics in organizations and, 210–211
 size of, 188, 203–205
 support, stress management and, 470
 task (special-project), 190
 task and, 202–203
 work, 402–403, 592–593
Group-based strategies for management of intergroup behavior, 239
Group cohesiveness, 207–209
 groupthink and, 209
 productivity and, 209
Group composition, 200–203
 decision making and, 502
 task and, 202–203
Group decision making, 500–507
 basic factors in, 501–502
 group polarization and, 502–503
 groupthink and, 503–506
 individual decision making versus, 499–501
 participation in decision making and, 506–507
Group dynamics, across cultures, 709
Group incentive plans, 372
Group inertia, resistance to change and, 665
Group performance, communication networks and, 332
Group performance factors, 200–209
 cohesiveness as, 207–209
 composition as, 200–203
 norms as, 205–207
 size as, 203–205
Group polarization, decision making and, 502–503

Group pressures, stress and, 459
Group problem solving, 507–510
brainstorming and, 508–509
Delphi technique and, 510
nominal group technique and, 509–510
Group size, 203–205
rate of increase of, 203
Group tasks, 402
group composition and, 202–203
Groupthink, 209, 503–506
decision-making defects and decision quality and, 504–505
prevention of, 506
research basis of, 505–506
symptoms of, 504
Growth needs
in Alderfer's ERG theory, 137, 145, 146
in Maslow's hierarchy, 133
Growth strategy, organization design and, 603

Habit, resistance to change and, 666
Halo effect, perception and, 85
Halo error, performance appraisals and, 434–435
Hands-on management, organization culture and, 642
Hardiness approach, life change and, 462
Hawthorne studies, 14–15, 131
Health, stress and, 466
Health insurance benefits, 373
Hidden observation, 770
Hiring, perception and attribution and, 88
Horizontal job loading, 391–392
HRIS (Human Resources Information System), 343–344
Human organization, 592–595
Human relations approach, to motivation, 131
Human relations movement, 15–16
Human resource(s). *See also* Employee(s); Individual(s); People
in organizational environment, 566
performance appraisal and, 422. *See also* Performance appraisal
Human resource planning, 751
Human Resources Information System (HRIS), 343–344
Hygiene factors, in Herzberg's two-factor theory, 140–141, 145
Hypervigilance, 497
Hypotheses, 765

Ideal bureaucracy, 588–589
Ideal (pure) organization design, 608
Identification, social, group formation and, 195
Image building, political behavior and, 305
Immaturity-maturity model of personality, 103–104
Implicit rules, 540
Impression management, political behavior and, 305
Incentives. *See also* Motivation; Reward(s); Reward systems
goal difficulty and, 360
Incentive systems, 371–372
individual versus group orientations for, 372
piecework, 14
Incremental innovation, 557
Incubation, insight, 512
Indirect compensation, 372–374

Individual(s). *See also* Employee(s); Human resource(s); People
abilities and traits of, goals and, 362
attitudes of, organizational effectiveness and, 51
coping strategies of, 468–470
decision making by, group decision making versus, 499–501
international business and, 705–709, 713–716
organization development and, 682–688
perspectives on careers, 731–732
sources of resistance in, 666–667
stress and, 454–457
Individual behaviors, organizational effectiveness and, 50–51
Individual differences, 95–119. *See also* Attitudes; Personality
across cultures, 705–706
ethics as, 108
job characteristics approach to job design and, 396–397
managerial implications of, 117–118
situations and, 98
stress and, 455, 457
uniqueness of people and, 97
values as, 108
Individualism, culture and, 705–706
Individual-level outcomes, management and, 50–51
Inequity
defined, 155
reduction of, 157–158
Inertia
group, resistance to change and, 665
structural, resistance to change and, 663–664
Informal communication, fostering, 342
Informal groups, 191
Informal leader, personal power and, 292
Information
control of, political behavior and, 303
for decision making, 484–486
employee participation and, 411
filtering, 336–338
saliency of, social information processing model and, 405–406
uncertainty and, 321–322
Informational roles, of manager, 38
Information conditions, decision making and, 481
Information processing
electronic, 343–345
as force for organization change, 661
social information processing model and, 404–407
vigilant, 497
Information system, balanced, 342–343
Information technology, as force for organization change, 660
In-group, vertical-dyad linkage model of leadership and, 273
Initiating-structure behavior, of leaders, 258
Innovation, 555–558
corporate research and, 558
incremental, 557
new ventures and, 557–558
radical, 557
systems, 557
Inputs, in equity theory of motivation, 156, 157, 158
Insight, creativity and, 511

Institutional programs, stress management and, 471
Intangible compensation, 367
Integrating department, management of intergroup behavior and, 240
Integrating mechanisms, management of intergroup behavior and, 239–240
Integration
communication networks and, 335–336
organization culture and, 635
structural contingency perspective and, 573
Intensity
manifest needs and, 135
perception and, 80
Intensive technologies, 561, 562
Intention, attitudes and, 109
Interaction, 188
group size and, 203–205
intergroup, *see* Intergroup behavior
Interactionalism, 24–25
Interdependence
pooled, 232–233
reciprocal, 234–235
sequential, 233
time and goal, intergroup behavior and, 230–231
Interest groups, 191
Intergroup behavior, 219–245
accommodation and, 222–223
avoidance and, 222
collaboration and, 224–225
competition and, 223–224
compromise and, 225–226
goal-based strategies for management of, 236–238
within governments, 242
location and, 229–230
location-based strategies for management of, 235–236
management of, 235–244
model of intergroup dynamics and, 226–229
organization-based strategies for management of, 239–244
people- and group-based strategies for management of, 238–239
resource-based strategies for management of, 236
resources and, 230
task interdependence and, 232–235
task uncertainty and, 232
time and goal interdependence and, 230–231
Internal locus of control, personality and, 104
International business, 699–724
careers and, 721–723
cross-cultural differences and similarities and, 703–704
enhancing individual and group processes and, 713–716
growth of, 701–702
individual behavior and, 705–709
interpersonal processes and, 709–713
organization change and, 720–721
organization characteristics and, 717–720
organization design and, 722
trends in, 702–703
International conglomerate, 720
International division, 719
International matrix, 719
International perspective
communication networks and, 337
cultural variations in job definitions and, 406
decision making and, 500

International perspective (*cont.*)
executive stress and, 456
globalization and, 48
groups and, 204
intergroup behavior within governments and, 242
leadership and, 256
McDonald's foreign franchises and, 25
on management styles, 49
managing cultural diversity and, 49–50
needs of Japanese workers and, 133
training approaches and, 78
International perspective. *See also* Culture; International business
Interpersonal attraction, group formation and, 193–194, 195–196
Interpersonal demands, as organizational stressors, 459–460
Interpersonal roles, of manager, 37–38
Interrater reliability, 433
Interrole conflict, 210
Intervention strategy, organizational behavior modification and, 168
Interviews, 769
Intrapreneurship, 558
Intrarole conflict, 210
Intrasender conflict, 211
Intrinsic rewards, 164
Introversion, 107
Inventory, just-in-time inventory systems and, 234, 596–597
Involvement, 116
Isolated dyad role, in communication networks, 334
Isolate role, in communication networks, 334

Japan
careers in, 722
communication networks in, 337
competition from, quality improvement and, 45
doing business in, 683
environmental complexity in, 717
globalization and, 48
job security in, 43
McDonald's franchise in, 25
management style in, 49
managerial responsibility in, 708
organizational culture in typical firms in, 636–639
organization structure and design in, 719
power and conflict in, 711
quality circles in, 171
robotics in, 660
training approach of, 78
worker needs in, changing, 133
Jargon, 339
JDS (Job Diagnostic Survey), 386, 399–400
Job(s), attitudes toward, 112–116
Job analysis
pay systems and, 371
performance appraisal and, 429–430
Job-centered leader behavior, 257
Job characteristics approach to job design, 395–401
evaluation and implications of, 400–401
individual differences and, 396–397
job characteristics and, 395–396
Job Characteristics Theory and, 397–400
Job definitions, cultural variations in, 406
Job design, 387–411
automation and robotics and, 409–410
changes effected by, 402
across cultures, 714
early alternatives to job specialization and, 390–392
evolution of, 387–388
for groups, 401–404
job characteristics approach to, 395–401
job enrichment and, 392–395
job specialization and, 388–390
social information and, 404–407
stress management and, 471
worker flexibility and, 410–411
work schedules and, 407–409
Job Diagnostic Survey (JDS), 386, 399–400
Job enlargement, 391–392
Job enrichment, 141, 392–395
effects of, 392–393
problem areas in, 394–395
Job hopping, 743–744
Job rotation, 390–391
flexible-worker approach versus, 411
Job satisfaction/dissatisfaction, 112–114
causes of, 113–114
consequences of, 114
good citizen syndrome and, 118
Herzberg's two-factor theory of, 139–141
measuring, 114
Job security, in Japan, 43
Job sharing, 408–409
Job specialization, 388–390
early alternatives to, 390–392
Joint ventures, mixed structures in, 533, 535
Judgmental tasks, 499–500
Just-in-time (JIT) manufacturing and inventory systems, 234, 596–597

Keiretsu, 337
Knowledge technology, 562

Laboratory experiment, 768
Language, communication across cultures and, 711–712
Large-batch production, 559, 562
Late bloomers, 745
LCUs (life change units), 462
Leader(s)
formal and informal, 291–292
leader-situation match and, 263–264
motivation of, situational favorableness and, 263
position power of, 262–263
Leader-member relations, contingency theory of leadership and, 262–264
Leader role, of manager, 38
Leadership, 251–279. *See also* Management; Top management
achievement-oriented, 266
attributional perspective on, 278
behavioral approaches to, 254, 256–260
charismatic, 276–277
contingency theory of, 254, 260–265
across cultures, 710
defined, 253–254
directive, 266
framework of perspectives on, 254
leadership substitutes and, 274–275
life cycle theory of, 273–274
management differentiated from, 253
nature of, 253–254
new ventures and, 537–538
participative, *see* Employee participation; Participative management
path-goal theory of, 265–268
style of, stress and, 459
supportive, 266
as symbolic action, 277
trait approaches to, 254, 255–256
transformational, 275–276
vertical-dyad linkage model of, 272–273
Vroom-Yetton-Jago model of, 268–271
Leadership grid, 259–260
Leadership substitutes, 274–275
Leading, as managerial function, 37
Learning, 63–79
of achievement, 143
classical conditioning and, 64–65
as cognitive process, 65–66
defined, 63–64
motivation and, 77
in organizations, 66
performance evaluation and rewards and, 78
positive reinforcement and, 78
punishment and, 75–76
reinforcement theory and, 67–72
social, 74–75
stimulus discrimination and, 72–73
stimulus generalization and, 72
training and, 77
vicarious, 64, 73–75
Least preferred coworker (LPC) scale, 261–262
Legitimacy, organization culture and, 635
Legitimate power, 288
using, 295–296
Letter (correspondence), 322
Lewin's three-step change process, 669–670
Liaison role
in communication networks, 334
of manager, 38
Life change, 460–462
Life change units (LCUs), 462
Life cycles, of products, research and development and, 558
Life cycle theory of leadership, 273–274
Life insurance benefits, 373
Life stressors, 460–463
life change as, 460–462
life trauma as, 462–463
Life trauma, 462–463
Linking role, management of intergroup behavior and, 239–240
Literature review, research and, 765
Location, intergroup behavior and, 229–230
Location-based strategies for management of intergroup behavior, 235–236
Locus of control
internal and external, 104, 105
path-goal theory of leadership and, 267
personality and, 104, 105
Long-linked technologies, 561, 562
Long-term compensation, 371
LPC (least preferred coworker) scale, 261–262

Machiavellianism, 106
Machine bureaucracy, 608–609
Maintenance stage of career, 744–746

Management, 33–53. *See also* Leadership; Supervisor(s); Top management
of conflict, 308–310
cultural diversity and, 49–50
for effectiveness, 50–53
equity theory of motivation and, 159–160
ethics and social responsibility and, 47
expectancy theory's implications for, 165
functions of, 36–37, 590–591
in global environment, 48–49
group-level outcomes and, 52
of groups, 211–212
hands-on, organization culture and, 642
of high need achievers, 144
human context of, 39–41
individual differences and, 117–118
individual-level outcomes and, 50–51
of intergroup behavior, 235–244
leadership differentiated from, 253
of organizational environment, 565
of organization change, 673–674
of organization culture, 643–647
of organization development, 688–692
organization-level outcomes and, 52–53
participative, *see* Participative management
perspective on organizational behavior, 35–36
of political behavior, 301–307
productivity enhancement and, 44–45
of products, 240
of projects, 240
punishment and, 75–76
quality improvement and, 45–46
of resistance to change, 667–669
of reward systems, 375–378
scientific, 10–12, 130–131
span of, 535–537, 559
technology management and, 46
Theory X, 15
Theory Y, 15
Theory Z, 633
worker needs and, 137
work force demographics and, 41–43, 659–660
workplace issues and challenges and, 43–44
Management by objectives (MBO), 363–365
organization development and, 683
performance appraisal and, 441
pitfalls in, 365
in practice, 365
process of, 363–365
Management development, 751, 753
organization development and, 684–685
Manager(s). *See also* Supervisor(s)
activities of, 35, 39
behavior of, across cultures, 706–708
communication and, 320
functions of, 36–37, 590–591
job satisfaction and, 113
roles of, 37–39
Manifest needs, 135–136
Manipulation, overcoming resistance to change and, 668–669
Manuals, 322–323
Markets
growth of international business and, 702
in organizational environment, 568
Masculinity/femininity, culture and, 706
Mass production, 559, 562
Materials technology, 562
Matrix organization design, 610–612, 613
international, 719
Maturity, life cycle theory of leadership and, 273–274
MBO, *see* Management by objectives
Mechanistic structure, 560, 601–602
Mediating technology, 561
Medical consequences of stress, 466
Medicine, influence on field of organizational behavior, 18
Medium, in communication process, 327
Member exchange, management of intergroup behavior and, 243
Memo, 322
Mentoring, 747–748
Merit pay plans, 371
Michigan leadership studies, 257
Midlife crisis, career and, 745–746
Mintzberg framework, 605–610
adhocracy and, 610
divisionalized form and, 609
machine bureaucracy and, 608–609
professional bureaucracy and, 609
simple structure and, 608
Mixed departmentalization scheme, 533, 535
Modeling, 64, 73–75
Money, as reward, 370–371
Monitor role, of manager, 38
Mood tendencies, 107
Motivating potential score (MPS), 400
Motivation, 16, 125–147, 153–177. *See also* Need(s)
absenteeism and turnover and, 174–175
Alderfer's ERG theory of, 137–138
attribution theory and, 172–173
across cultures, 709
early views of, 129–130
equity theory of, 155–160
expectancy theory of, 160–165
framework of, 127–128
goal setting and, 357, 359–363
of group members, 188
Herzberg's two-factor theory of, 139–142
human relations approach to, 131
importance of, 127
integration of need perspectives on, 145–146
of leader, situational favorableness and, 263
learning and, 77
Maslow's hierarchy of needs and, 132–135
Murray's manifest needs theory of, 135–136
need for achievement and, 142–144, 146
need for affiliation and, 144
need for power and, 145
organizational behavior modification and, 166–169
participative management and, 169–172
perception and attribution and, 88
performance and productivity and, 173–174
scientific management approach to, 130–131
task versus relationship, contingency theory of leadership and, 261–262
Motivation factors, in Herzberg's two-factor theory, 139–140, 145
Motivation and productivity stage of group development, 198
Movement
communication and, 324
perception and, 81
MPS (motivating potential score), 400
Multinational organizations, organization structure and design and, 719–720
Multiple-rater comparative evaluation, 425, 443–444
Mutual acceptance stage of group development, 197
Mutual adjustment, coordination by, 606

Need(s)
for achievement, 142–144, 146
for affiliation, 144–145
Alderfer's ERG theory and, 137–138
of American workers, changing, 137
belongingness, 133, 134, 145
deficiency, 133
esteem, 133, 134
existence, 137
external sources of satisfaction of, 195–196
growth, 133, 137, 146
internal sources of satisfaction of, 193–195
of Japanese workers, changing, 133
job satisfaction and, 113–114
manifest needs theory and, 135–136
Maslow's hierarchy of, 132–135, 145
nature of, 128
physiological, 133, 134
for power, 145, 146
relatedness, 137, 145
security, 133–134
self-actualization, 133, 134–135, 146
Negative reinforcement, 69
Negotiation, overcoming resistance to change and, 668
Networks. *See also* Communication networks
of working women, 191
New ventures, 537–538
NGT (nominal group technique), 509–510
Noise
in communication process, 328–329, 341
reducing, 341
Nominal group technique (NGT), 509–510
Nonexempt personnel, 436–437
Nonprogrammed decisions, 483, 489
centralization and, 539
political behavior and, 302
Nonreactive measures, 770
Nonverbal communication, 323–325
Norms, 205–207
pressures to conform to, 207
purposes served by, 206
social information processing model and, 406
Novelty, perception and, 81

OB, *see* Organizational behavior
Object, characteristics of, perception and, 80–81
Objective(s). *See* also Management by objectives
of performance appraisal system, commitment to, 429
Objective judgment quotient (OJQ) method, 443
OB Mod., *see* Organizational behavior modification
Observation, 770
hidden, 770
participant, 770
structured, 770
OCB (organizational citizen behavior), 118
Occupation, choice of, 735–738
OD, *see* Organization development

Office design, stress and, 458
Office memorandum, 322
Ohio State leadership studies, 258–259
OJQ (objective judgment quotient) method, 443
Open pay system, 377
Open system, defined, 595
Operant conditioning, *see* Reinforcement theory
Operations technology, 562
Opinion leader role, in communication networks, 334
Opinion surveys, 114
Oral communication, 323
Organic structure, 560, 602
Organization (process)
control and organization stage of group development and, 198–200
perception and, 83
Organization(s)
choice of, career choice and, 738–739
communication networks in, 333–336
defined, 525
group-level outcome variables and, 52
human, 592–595
individual-level outcome variables and, 50–51
intergroup dynamics and, 227
learning in, 66
multinational, organization structure and design and, 719–720
in organizational environment, 565, 566–567
organization-level outcome variables and, 52–53
people as, 39–40
perspectives on careers, 732
purpose of, 525
sources of resistance in, 663–666
Organizational behavior (OB)
basic concepts of, 19–21
characteristics of field of, 17–18
classical organization theory and, 12–13
contemporary, 17–22
contingency perspective on, 23–24
defined, 7–9
descriptive nature of, 18
emergence as field of study, 16–17
Hawthorne studies and, 14–15
historical roots of, 9–13
human relations movement and, 15–16
importance of, 21–22
interactionalism view of, 24–25
interdisciplinary nature of, 17–18
managerial perspective on, 35–36
popular-press perspectives on, 26
precursors of, 13–14
scientific management and, 10–12
systems approach to, 22–23
Organizational behavior modification (OB Mod.), 77, 166–169
results of, 169
Organizational citizen behavior (OCB), 118
Organizational downsizing, 600–601
Organizational environment, 565–572
boundaries of, 565
communication and, 325
communication networks and, 332
complexity and dynamism of, 717
components of, 566–569
across cultures, 717
organization design and, 614–615
structural imperatives and, 602–603
uncertainty and, 570–572
Organizational goals, 525
Organizational politics, 297–307
managing political behavior and, 301–307
pervasiveness of, 297–301
Organizational responses, 572–577
population ecology perspective on, 576
resource dependence perspective on, 573–576
structural contingency perspective on, 573
Organizational socialization, 644–645
Organizational stressors, 457–460
interpersonal demands as, 459–460
physical demands as, 458
role demands as, 459
task demands as, 457–458
Organizational structure, 523–547
administrative hierarchy and, 537
authority and, 543–546
centralization and, 538–539
changing, 534, 545
communication patterns and, 321
across cultures, 719–720
defined, 525
departmentalization and, 529–535
division of labor and, 528–529
formalization and, 539–542
mechanistic, 560, 601–602
operations and, 538–542
organic, 560, 602
organization defined and, 525
responsibility and, 542–543
simple, 608
size and, 599
span of control and, 535–537
strategy and, 603–605
structural configuration and, 527–537
Organizational support, goals and, 362
Organization-based strategies for management of intergroup behavior, 239–244
Organization change, 657–676
competition as force for, 661
across cultures, 720–721
information processing and communication as forces for, 661
integrated process of, 674–676
narrow focus of, resistance to change and, 664
people as force for, 659–660
process models of, 669–673
resistance to, 662–669
supplemental, 682
technology as force for, 660
transition management and, 673–674
Organization chart, 527
Organization culture, 623–648
changing, 645–647
common attributes of, 626–630
defined, 625–630
existing, taking advantage of, 643–644
historical foundations of, 630–634
managing, 643–647
Ouchi framework and, 636–639
Parsons' AGIL model of, 634–635
Peters and Waterman approach to, 639–643
stress management and, 471
teaching, 644–645
Organization design, 585–616
change of, 590
classic organizing principles and, 590–591
contemporary, 612–615
contingency approaches to, 587, 595–605
culture and, 722
across cultures, 719–720
human organization and, 592–595
ideal bureaucracy and, 588–589
matrix, 610–612, 613, 719
Mintzberg framework and, 605–610
pure (ideal), 608
sociotechnical systems theory and, 595–598
strategy and strategic choice and, 603–605
structural imperatives and, 598–603
universal approaches to, 586–587, 588–595
Organization development (OD), 676–692
defined, 676–677
group and individual change and, 682–688
management of, 688–692
problems in, 689–690
successful, keys to, 690–692
systemwide, 677–680
task-technological change and, 680–682
Organizing, as managerial function, 37
Outcomes
in equity theory of motivation, 156, 157, 158
in expectancy theory of motivation, 162–163
Out-group, vertical-dyad linkage model of leadership and, 273
Outplacement counseling, 753
Outputs, standardization of, 607, 608
Overdetermination, resistance to change and, 663–664
Overlapping work groups, 592
Overload
communication networks and, 340
stress and, 457–458
Ownership, ideal bureaucracy and, 589

Paired-comparison method, for performance appraisal, 442–443
Parallel engineering, 234
Parity, 544
Participant observation, 770
Participative leadership, 266. *See also* Employee participation; Participative management
Vroom-Yetton-Jago model of leadership and, 267
Participative management, 192. *See also* Employee participation
areas of participation and, 170–171
decentralization and, 539
historical perspectives on, 169–170
motivation and, 169–171
quality circles and, 171, 172
Participative pay systems, 377–378
PAS (performance appraisal system), 421–424
trait-based versus performance standard system, 432
Path-goal theory of leadership, 265–268
basic premises of, 266–268
scientific evidence for, 268
Pay secrecy, 377
Pay systems, *see* Compensation; Reward systems
PBA (political behavior alternative), 298
Pension plans, 373
People. *See also* Employee(s); Human resource(s); Individual(s)
concern for, 259, 639

as force for organization change, 659–660
in organizational environment, 565, 566
organization culture and, 639, 641–642
organization design and, 614
as organizations, 39–40
as people, 40
productivity through, organization culture and, 641–642
as resources, 40
uniqueness of, 97. *See also* Attitudes; Individual differences; Personality
People-based strategies for management of intergroup behavior, 238–239
People's Republic of China (POR)
group performance and, 204
organization structure and design in, 719
Perception, 79–85
of ability, leadership and, 267
defined, 79–80
of equity and inequity, *see* Equity theory of motivation
hiring and, 88
motivation and, 88
object characteristics and, 80–81
in organizations, 80–85
performance evaluation and, 88–89
person characteristics and, 81–83
reality versus, 84
situational processes and, 83–85
Performance, 51
baseline, organizational behavior modification and, 168
effort-to-performance expectancy and, 161
of groups, 200–209, 332
motivation and, 173–174
organization culture and, 639
pay linked to, 373
performance-to-outcome expectancy and, 161–162
rewards for, 164
stress and, 466
Performance appraisal, 419–444
commitment to objectives and, 429
comparative, 441–444
across cultures, 714–715
developmental orientation and, 423–424
frequency of, 427
individual, 436–441
job analysis and, 429–430
judgmental orientation and, 423
learning and, 78
multiple-rater, 425, 443–444
perception and attribution and, 88–89
performance appraisal systems and, 421–424
performance measurement and, 430–436, 714–715
persons performing, 425, 427
purposes of, 423–424
self-appraisals and, 425
supervisors' roles in, 424, 425
uses of appraisal information, 427–428
Performance appraisal system (PAS), 421–424
trait-based versus performance standard system, 432
Performance measurement, 430–436
culture and, 714–715
freedom from bias in, 433
halo error in, 434–435
job-related criteria for, 430
reliability of, 431–433
restriction of range in, 433–434
timing errors in, 435
validity of, 431
Performance-related behavioral events, organizational behavior modification and, 166–168
Performance standard system, trait-based performance appraisal system versus, 432
Performance-to-outcome expectancy, 161–162
Perquisites, as rewards, 374
Person. *See also* Employee(s); Human resource(s); Individual(s); People
characteristics of, perception and, 81–83
Personal decision-making approach, 495–498
Personal dispositions, 103
Personal factors, communication networks and, 332
Personal growth and development, job enrichment and, 393
Personality, 98–107
authoritarianism and, 106
conflicts between, stress and, 459–460
determinants of, 99–100
development of, stages in, 101–102
good citizen syndrome and, 118
immaturity-maturity model of, 103–104
locus of control and, 104, 105
Machiavellianism and, 106
nature of, 99
perception and, 82–83
self-esteem and, 107
self-monitoring and, 106
trait approaches to, 102–103
Type A and Type B, 107, 455, 463–464, 465
Personal power, 291–292
position power versus, 291–292
Person-role conflict, 211
Persuasive arguments, group polarization and, 503
Peters and Waterman approach to organization culture, 639–643
Physical demands, as organizational stressors, 458
Physical resources, in organizational environment, 568
Physiological needs, 133, 134
Piecework incentive systems, 14, 371
Planning
careers and, *see* Career planning
as managerial function, 37
Plateau, in career, 744
Political behavior, 297–307
limiting effects of, 306–307
managing, 301–307
pervasiveness of, 297–301
reasons for, 302–303
recognizing, limiting political behavior and, 306–307
techniques of, 303–306
Political behavior alternative (PBA), 298
Political science, influence on field of organizational behavior, 17–18
Popular press, influence on organizational behavior, 26
Population ecology perspective, 576
POR (People's Republic of China), *see* People's Republic of China
Portable telephones, 318
Porter-Lawler extension, 163–164
Position, rights and property of, ideal bureaucracy and, 589
Position power, 290–292
of leaders, 262–263
personal power versus, 291–292
Positive reinforcement, 68–69
learning and, 68–69, 78
Post-decision dissonance, 491
Power, 287–297
bases of, 288–290
of change agent, 670–671
coercive, 289, 296–297
across cultures, 710–711
defined, 287
expert, 289, 295
group decision making and, 502
legitimate, 288, 295–296
need for, 145
organization development and, 689–690
personal, 291–292
pervasiveness of, 287
position, 290–292
of leaders, 262–263
referent, 289–290, 294–295
reward, 288–289, 296
shifting downward in hierarchy, 541
threatened, resistance to change and, 665
uses of, 292–297
Power distance, culture and, 706
Practical decision-making approach, 493–495
Preoccupation, with work, need for achievement and, 143
Preparation, creativity and, 511
Preretirement programs, 753
Primary work group, path-goal theory of leadership and, 267–268
Priming, external, social information processing model and, 406
Privacy, of employees, 43
Problem attributes, Vroom-Yetton-Jago model of leadership and, 267
Problem solving, 483
in groups, 507–510
Problem solving approach to performance appraisal feedback, 428
Process, departmentalization by, 530–531
Process models of organization change, 669–676
Process theories of occupational choice, 736, 737–738
Product, departmentalization by, 531–532
Production. *See also* Technology
concern for, leadership and, 259
just-in-time manufacturing and inventory systems and, 234, 596–597
Production processes, 559, 561, 562
standardization of, 607, 608–609
Productivity, 50
enhancing, 44–45
group cohesiveness and, 209
Hawthorne studies and, 14–15
motivation and, 173
motivation and productivity stage of group development and, 198
organization culture and, 641–642
quality and, 45
teams and, 192
Product life cycles, research and development and, 558
Product management, 240
Professional bureaucracy, 609
Profit-sharing plans, 371

Programmed decisions, 481–482, 489
centralization and, 539
Projection, perception and, 85
Project management, 240
Psychological consequences of stress, 466
Psychology
influence on field of organizational behavior, 17
organization culture and, 632–633
Publicness, social information processing model and, 405
Punishment, 69–70
in organizations, 75–76
Pure (ideal) organization design, 608

QCs (quality circles), 171, 172, 404
Quality, 45
improving, 45–46
productivity and, 45
Quality circles (QCs), 171, 172, 404
Quality-of-work-life (QWL) programs, 678–680
Questionnaires, 769

Radical innovation, 557
Ranking, for performance appraisal, 441
Rational decision-making approach, 487–492
choice of alternative and, 490–491
determination of decision type and, 489
evaluation of alternatives and, 490
generation of alternatives and, 489–490
implementation and, 491
measurement and adjustment in, 491–492
problem identification and, 489
statement of situational goal and, 488
strengths and weaknesses of, 492
Rationality, bounded, 492
Rationalization, social information processing model and, 404–405
Receiver, in communication process, 328, 339–340
Referent power, 289–290
using, 294–295
Refreezing, 669–670
Reinforcement theory, 66, 67–62
avoidance and, 69
extinction and, 69
positive reinforcement and, 68–69
punishment and, 69–70
reinforcement schedules and, 70–72
Relatedness needs, 137, 145
Relationship behavior, life cycle theory of leadership and, 274
Relationship motivation, contingency theory of leadership and, 261–262
Relaxation, stress management and, 468–469
Reliability, 431–433, 771
interrater, 433
Repetition, perception and, 81
Reports, 322
Research, 763–772
action, 673
applied, 764
basic, 764
causality and, 770–771
corporate, 558
data gathering for, 769–770
on equity sensitivity construct, 159
ethical concerns in, 772
good citizen syndrome and, 118
group development and midpoint transition and, 201
intergroup conflict and, 228
interpretation of results and, 765–766
managerial activities and, 39
process of, 764–766
purposes of, 764
reliability and validity and, 771–772
role of theory and research and, 763–764
scientific, 764
Research and development, 558
Research design, 765, 766–769
case study, 766–767
field experiment, 768–769
field survey, 767–768
laboratory experiment, 768
Resistance
to organization development, 689
to power, 293–294
Resistance to change, 662–669
individual sources of, 666–667
managing, 667–669
organizational sources of, 663–666
Resistance stage of general adaptation syndrome, 454
Resource(s)
allocation of, resistance to change and, 665–666
control over, job enrichment and, 392
intergroup behavior and, 230
in organizational environment, 568
people as, 40
scarce, political behavior and, 302
Resource-based strategies for management of intergroup behavior, 236
Resource dependence perspective, 573–576
Resource exchanges, 574–575
Responsibility, 542–543
authority and, 544
managerial, in Japan, 708
need for achievement and, 143
organization culture and, 638–639
Retirement, 746
Revocability, social information processing model and, 405
Reward(s). *See also* Compensation; Incentives; Incentive systems
awards as, 374–375
benefits as, 372–374
across cultures, 714
incentive systems and, 371–372
intrinsic and extrinsic, 164
money, 370–371
organization development and, 692
perquisites as, 374
Reward power, 288–289
using, 296
Reward systems, 365–378. *See also* Compensation; Incentives; Incentive systems
flexible, 378
intergroup dynamics and, 227, 229
managing, 375–378
participative, 377–378
pay secrecy and, 377
roles, purposes, and meanings of rewards and, 367–369
as transaction process, 367
types of rewards and, 369–375
Rights, of employees, 43
Risks
decision making and, 484–485
innovation and, 555–556
need for achievement and, 142
willingness to take, 107
Risky shift, 502
Robotics, 46, 409–410
ethics and, 409
as force for organization change, 660
Role(s), 210–211
in communication networks, 334
linking, management of intergroup behavior and, 239–240
managerial, 37–39
of rewards, 367–368
sent, 210
Role ambiguity, 210
stress and, 459
Role conflict, 210–211
stress and, 459
Role demands, as organizational stressors, 459
Role management, stress management and, 469
Routineness, of technology, 561
Rules and procedures
exceptions to, 542
ideal bureaucracy and, 588
implicit and explicit rules and, 540
intergroup dynamics and, 227, 229
management of intergroup behavior and, 240–241
standard operating procedures and, 540

Salience
of information, social information processing model and, 405–406
perception and, 81
Satisfaction, 112–115
with job, 112–114, 118, 139–141
of needs, group formation and, 193–196
Satisfaction-progression process, in Alderfer's ERG theory, 138
Satisficing, 493
Scalar chain, *see* Administrative hierarchy
Scale economies, 600
Schedules of reinforcement, 70–72
Scientific management, 10–12
motivation and, 130–131
Scientific research, 764. *See also* Research
Security
job, in Japan, 43
resistance to change and, 666
stress and, 457
Security needs, 133–134
Selective attention
communication process and, 339
perception and, 83
Self-actualization needs, 133, 134–135, 146
Self-appraisals, 425
Self-concept, perception and, 82
Self-esteem, personality and, 107
Self-monitoring, 106
Self-reactions, decision making and, 495
Semantics, communication process and, 338–339
Sent role, 210
Service, departmentalization by, 531–532
Settling-down stage of career, 743–744
Settling-in phase of career, 742
Severity, performance appraisals and, 433
Sex discrimination, culture and, 722–723
Sexual harassment, in workplace, 290
Shareholders, in organizational environment, 567

Simple structure, 608
Situation(s)
attitudes and, 110
favorableness of, contingency theory of leadership and, 262–264
individual differences and, 98
leader-situation match and, 263–264
path-goal theory of leadership and, 267–268
perception and, 83–85
personality and, 101
Size imperative, 599–601
Skill variety, as core job dimension, 397
Small-batch production, 559
Social affiliation, group formation and, 195
Social comparison, *see* Equity theory of motivation
Social expectations, social information processing model and, 406
Social factors
personality and, 100
resistance to change and, 667
Social identification, group formation and, 195
Social information processing model, job design and, 404–407
Socialization, organizational, 644–645
Socialization stage of career, 741–743
Social learning, 74–75
Social norms, social information processing model and, 406
Social psychology, organization culture and, 632–633
Social responsibility, 47
Social security contributions, 372
Social subsystem, 597
Sociocultural factors, in organizational environment, 568
Sociology
influence on field of organizational behavior, 17
organization culture and, 631–632
Sociotechnical systems theory, 595–598
Soldiering, 10
Solid citizens, 744–745
SOPs (standard operating procedures), 540
Source
in communication process, 326, 336–338, 339–340
credibility of, 339–340
Span of control, 535–537
technology and, 559
Specialization, 388–390, 528–529
early alternatives to, 390–392
Special-project (task) groups, 190
Spuriousness, causality and, 771
Standardization
as coordination mechanism, 606–608
of work processes, 608–609
Standard operating procedures (SOPs), 540
Status, group decision making and, 502
Stereotyping, perception and, 84–85
Stimulus discrimination, 72–73
Stimulus generalization, 72
Strategies, 525
coping, 468–472
for management of intergroup behavior, 235–244
organizational behavior modification and, 168
organization design and, 603–605
Stress, 451–473
causes of, 457–463
consequences of, 464–468
across cultures, 715
defined, 453–454
individual and, 454–457
international differences in, 456
organizational effectiveness and, 51
Type A and Type B personality profiles and, 463–464
Stress management, 468–472
individual coping strategies and, 468–470
organizational coping strategies and, 470–472
organization development and, 682–683
Stressors
life, 460–463
organizational, 457–460
Structural change, 677–680
Structural contingency perspective, 573
Structural imperatives, 598–603
environment and, 602–603
size and, 599–601
technology and, 601–602
Structural inertia, resistance to change and, 663–664
Structured observation, 770
Suboptimizing, 493
Superordinate goals, management of intergroup behavior and, 236
Supervision
direct, coordination by, 606
stress management and, 471
Supervisor(s)
employee participation and, 412
goal setting for, 366
job satisfaction and, 113
performance appraisal and, 424, 425
Support
organizational, goals and, 362
overcoming resistance to change and, 668
Support groups, stress management and, 470
Supportive leader, 266
Supportive relationships, 592
Surface value, of rewards, 368
Survey(s)
of attitudes and opinions, 114
field, 767–768
Survey-feedback techniques, organization development and, 686–688
Symbol(s), managing, 646–647
Symbolic action, leadership as, 277
Symbolic value, of rewards, 368–369
System
defined, 22, 595
open, 595
Systems innovation, 557
Systems theory, 22–23

Tangible compensation, 367
Task(s)
group, 202–203, 402
judgmental, 499–500
Task demands, as organizational stressors, 457–458
Task environment, 570
Task forces, management of intergroup behavior and, 241–243
Task (special-project) groups, 190
Task identity, as core job dimension, 398
Task interdependence
intergroup behavior and, 232–235
pooled, 232–233
reciprocal, 234–235
sequential, 233
Task motivation, contingency theory of leadership and, 261–262
Task redefinition, organization development and, 690
Task redesign, 680
Task significance, as core job dimension, 398
Task structure
contingency theory of leadership and, 262
path-goal theory of leadership and, 267–268
Task-technological change, 680–682
Task uncertainty, intergroup behavior and, 232
Team building, organization development and, 685–686
Teams, 192. *See also* Work groups
autonomous, 402–403
employee participation and, 411
Technical competence, ideal bureaucracy and, 589
Technical (task) subsystem, 596–597
Technological change, 680
Technology, 46, 558–564. *See also* Production
Ashton studies of, 562
Burns and Stalker's perspective on, 560
culture and, 718
across cultures, 718
as force for organization change, 660
intensive, 561, 562
knowledge, 562
long-linked, 561
managing, 46
materials, 562
mediating, 561
myths about impact on organizations, 562–563
nonroutine, 561, 562
operations, 562
organization design and, 613
Perrow's perspective on, 560–561
in practice, 562–563
routine, 561, 562
Thompson's perspective on, 561–562
Woodward's categorization of, 559–560
Technology imperative, 601–602
Telecommunications, 343–345
Telephones, portable, 318
Tell-and-listen approach to performance appraisal feedback, 428
Tell-and-sell approach to performance appraisal feedback, 428
Temperature, stress and, 458
Temporal order, causality and, 771
Theory, role of, 763–764
Theory X, 15
Theory Y, 15
Theory Z, 633
Thick description research methods, 631
Three-step change process, 669–670
Time and goal interdependence, intergroup behavior and, 230–231
Time management, stress management and, 469
Timing errors, performance appraisals and, 435
Top management
compensation for, 62
need for achievement and, 143
organization development and, 691
stress and, 456, 470

Training
career planning and, 753
employee participation and, 412
Japanese and American approaches to, 78
learning and, 77
need for achievement and, 143
organization development and, 682–684
for performance appraisal, 425, 427
Trait approaches
to leadership, 254, 255–256
to personality, 102–103
Trait-based performance appraisal system, performance standard system versus, 432
Transformational leadership, 275–276
Transition management, 673–674
Transmission, in communication process, 327
Transportation, growth of international business and, 701
Trauma, life, 462–463
Turnover, 51
communication networks and, 335
job dissatisfaction and, 114
motivation and, 174–175
Two-factor theory of motivation, 139–142
evaluation of, 141–142, 145
Type A personality, 107
stress and, 455, 463–464, 465
Type B personality, 107
stress and, 455, 463–464, 465
Type Z firms, 636–639

Uncertainty
decision making under, 486
environmental, 570–572
information and, 321–322
reducing, limiting political behavior and, 306
Uncertainty avoidance, culture and, 706
Unconflicted adherence, 497
Unconflicted change, 497
Unemployment compensation benefits, 372
Unfreezing, 669
Unionization, 43–44
United States
globalization and, 48
group performance and, 204
management style in, 49
organizational culture in typical firms in, 636–639
organization structure and design in, 719
quality circles in, 171, 172
training approach of, 78
Unit production, 559
Universal approach, 13
to leadership, 254
to organization design, 586–587, 588–595
shift to contingency perspective from, 24

Valences, in expectancy theory of motivation, 161, 162–163
Validity, 431, 771–772
content, 431
convergent, 431
discriminant, 431
Value(s). *See also* Organization culture
as individual differences, 108
personality and, 107
surface, of rewards, 368
symbolic, of rewards, 368–369
Value judgments, communication process and, 339
Variable-interval reinforcement, 70
Variable-ratio reinforcement, 71
Verification
creativity in decision making and, 513
feedback and, 340
insight, creativity in decision making and, 513
Vertical-dyad linkage model of leadership, 272–273
Vertical job loading, *see* Job enrichment
Vicarious learning, 64, 73–75
Vigilant information processing, 497
Vroom-Yetton-Jago model of leadership, 268–271
application of, 271
basic premises of, 268–271
scientific evidence for, 271

Walsh-Healy Act, 437
Wheel network, 329
Withdrawal, stress and, 466–467
Withdrawal stage of career, 746
Worker flexibility, 410–411
Workers' compensation benefits, 372–373
Worker skills, standardization of, 606–607, 608
Work flow integration, 562
Work groups. *See also* Work teams
autonomous, 402–403
overlapping, 592–593
Path-goal theory of leadership and, 267–268
Work pace, job enrichment and, 392
Workplace
attitudes toward, 112–115
demographics of, 41–43
sexual harassment in, 290
Work schedules, 407–409
compressed workweek and, 407–408
flexible, 408
job sharing and, 408–409
Work teams. *See also* Work groups
autonomous, 402–403
employee participation and, 411
Workweek, compressed, 407–408
Written communication, 322–323

Zero-defects program, 375